TINDER BOX

HBO's Ruthless Pursuit of New Frontiers

James Andrew Miller

HENRY HOLT AND COMPANY

NEW YORK

Henry Holt and Company
Publishers since 1866
120 Broadway
New York, NY 10271
www.henryholt.com

Henry Holt® and Ⓗ● are registered trademarks of
Macmillan Publishing Group, LLC.

Library of Congress Cataloging-in-Publication Data is available.

ISBN: 9781250624017

Our books may be purchased in bulk for promotional, educational, or business
use. Please contact your local bookseller or the Macmillan Corporate and
Premium Sales Department at (800) 221-7945, extension 5442, or by e-mail at
MacmillanSpecialMarkets@macmillan.com.

First Edition 2021

Designed by Meryl Sussman Levavi

Printed in the United States of America

1 3 5 7 9 10 8 6 4 2

for my mother, Leatrice Weiss-Miller,
with love, gratitude, and
the promise to always remember

"HBO was what is was because of its outward grace,
in spite of its inward turmoil.

Like any great actor."

—FORMER HBO EXECUTIVE

Contents

Prologue

Although Chris Albrecht owned a beautiful Mediterranean-style house in the Brentwood section of Los Angeles, for his East Coast sojourns HBO rented its CEO a showpiece apartment in Midtown Manhattan's Museum Towers, not far from Radio City Music Hall. In the late spring of 2003, Albrecht played host there to more than a dozen invited friends and associates for an urgent meeting, one that concerned the pay network's most important show, and one of the most celebrated dramas ever—*The Sopranos*. Then in its fourth season, *The Sopranos* was proving immensely popular with audiences and was in the process of becoming as much a watershed for television as *Citizen Kane* had been for motion pictures.

And yet the show that had come shockingly close to never existing in the first place was, at that moment, on the cusp of collapse.

David Chase, auteur of the series, had originally written the pilot script for the Fox television network, but after a short flirtation Fox executives passed on the project, condemning it to turnaround, that limbo from which many a series or film has failed to return. HBO came on board shortly thereafter, however, and produced a pilot. After it was shot and edited, the pilot was test-marketed in several cities, to a tepid response. Most broadcast networks confronting such a meager reaction would likely have passed on the pilot then and there. At HBO, where things were done differently, Albrecht and colleague Carolyn Strauss—fully supported by HBO CEO Jeff Bewkes—decided to go with their guts rather than succumb to the research. *The Sopranos* was ordered to series.

At this point, the show's leading man, James Gandolfini, was a little-known character actor who tended to disappear artfully into his roles—some of them, appropriate to his size, "heavies." Whether he was playing a ruthless mob henchman in *True Romance* or a bearded Southern stuntman in *Get Shorty*, his work had not been wildly auspicious or lavishly praised by critics. Nevertheless, Chase—who had earlier considered actor Michael Rispoli and musician Steven Van Zandt for the lead role (both men would end up in the series—as Jackie Aprile and Silvio Dante, respectively)—personally picked Gandolfini as his guy because he passed the "real world" test. Simply put, he looked the part. Casting Gandolfini turned out to be a stroke of brilliance. When, on January 10, 1999, *The Sopranos* premiered with Gandolfini, then thirty-eight, in the plum role of Tony, the Soprano paterfamilias, the actor would soon find himself aglow in the brightest spotlight of his career. The series didn't start with that big a bang commercially, but then, in episode five of that first season—when Tony strangled and sent an old nemesis to hell while touring potential colleges with his teenage daughter, Meadow—something on the show clicked confidently into place. Gandolfini's life would never be the same and, arguably, neither would television.

The Sopranos—for anyone who was in a coma or visiting other planets at the time—is a drama about the double life of Anthony "Tony" Soprano, husband and father to an upper-middle-class family in suburban New Jersey and, simultaneously, *capo di tutti i capi* to another sort of family, organized-crime division. For both Tonys, the times they were a-changin'; a series of panic attacks rattles his world, compelling him to secretly consult a psychiatrist, brilliantly played by Lorraine Bracco. They have lots to talk about, including the fact that Tony's Machiavellian mother and his sinister uncle Junior figure prominently in the crime family's operations. Real-life realities would impose themselves on the narrative; Nancy Marchand, the veteran character actress cast as Tony's mother, who served as one of the show's most essential arteries, became very, very sick, and ultimately died, at the end of season two. But by that time Chase, who ran the show tirelessly, had been hard at work creating countless new dimensions to his magnum opus, expanding it to a much larger scale than previously envisioned. The *New York Times* would call *The Sopranos* "the greatest work of American popular culture of the last quarter century." As a result, even more weight was placed on Tony's, and Gandolfini's, shoulders.

To say that Gandolfini rose to the occasion would be putting it mildly. His complex, nuanced, and inspired performance demonstrated remarkable range, not just over the course of the series, or any one episode, but often within a scene, a confrontation, even a single moment, that seemed to transcend mere "acting." No matter how despicable Tony's behavior appeared on the surface, Gandolfini was so persuasive and affecting—whether conveying Tony's rage, passion, or some fleeting flash of guilt—that the audience never turned its back on him. In a troubling age of antiheroes, Tony Soprano was royalty. His eyes told a million tales, and his performance elevated him to the upper echelon of American actors. He adapted handily to the series' widened scope, its growth from intimate portrait to rich, blood-splattered tapestry, and he was enormously instrumental in making *The Sopranos* an epochal cultural event—unofficially the start of what some would call television's "second golden age." Whether that's true or not, it *was* a golden age of Gandolfini.

"Jimmy," to his friends, wasn't just the lead actor in a cast of character actors—adroit professionals all—but was also the leader of the surrogate family that evolved off-screen. Gandolfini set the tone, not by asserting star clout on the set, but because his fellow actors shared great respect and admiration for him as both artist and friend. He returned their affection with a sincerity that embraced deeds as well as words, typically declining interview requests from the press until reassured that another cast member would be included to share the limelight. Gandolfini was so patient with clamoring fans that he didn't even balk when one of them asked to shake his hand as he stood at a men's room urinal.

Gandolfini's worldview soon exceeded the boundaries of show business. He became, for instance, deeply involved in the plight of battle-scarred veterans from Iraq and Afghanistan, even to the point of later producing a documentary about their struggles, conducting many of the interviews himself. When playing Tony, though, Gandolfini underwent an awe-inspiring facial and bodily transformation; the lovable pussycat turned into a ruthless and philandering gangster. Somehow it seemed beyond acting, beyond even intuitive skills; Jimmy *became* Tony, an actor of unimpeachable credibility.

There's no way of knowing if *The Sopranos* would have been the sensation it became if some other actor had been cast in the role that Gandolfini made so irrevocably his, but chances are that magical alchemy would not have happened. He elevated his fellow actors, as well as every script, and was incalculably instrumental in making *The Sopranos* an international phenomenon. People didn't just admire Gandolfini; they were drawn to him, and the character he played, passionately.

For all his brilliance in the central role, however, the road to glory for Gandolfini and *The Sopranos* would be cratered with potholes. There were, for instance, fitful bouts of disruptive incredulousness as he reacted to certain scripts he was handed. Gandolfini, who once remarked that after a day of shooting, he often had to take a shower because he felt "dirty" playing the role, would sometimes balk at a particular scene and instead of asking Chase, "Do I have to do this?" he would wonder out loud, "What the fuck *is* this?" and then declare flatly, "I'm not doing it."

Gandolfini's longest and strongest tantrum erupted over a script that called for Tony to dash into a gas-station bathroom and masturbate during a period when Tony was having an affair with feisty realtor Julianna Skiff, played forcefully by Julianna Margulies. But even that time, despite his earlier protests, Gandolfini relented and played the scene as written. As it turned out, the gas-station sequence was shot but then edited out of the finished episode. To his credit, Gandolfini never complained to Chase that the difficult scene ended up on the cutting room floor.

Gandolfini and his team would prove much more formidable when it came to business. They understood how indispensable he was to the series. They knew no one could replace him. So Gandolfini, at the urging of his representatives, staged a notorious holdout during particularly prickly contract negotiations. Gandolfini's contract wasn't even up, but HBO had agreed to open up discussions in 2003 to give him a new deal, a concession it didn't legally have to make. What began as a stubborn standoff between star and network grew increasingly nasty, so much so that at one point during negotiations, an angered Albrecht called Gandolfini a "fat slob," an outburst that he later regretted, especially since he'd been one of Gandolfini's most devout champions from the beginning. Indeed, the show and its star would never have made it through the HBO chain of command if not for Albrecht's essential and passionate advocacy. As for the big blowup over contract terms, the two sides found a way through the impasse after three months, and Gandolfini was back in action.

A long-running television series can be hard on everybody involved. Cast, crew, and network executives get tossed together in a pressure cooker for years on end, and it's rare that some don't suffer accordingly. The very success that many dream about can become a gilded cage; confinement on a show—even one like *The Sopranos*, with its long, built-in hiatuses between seasons—can't necessarily exorcise agitated personal demons.

It wasn't just a matter of coming up with quality scripts and continuing to make talked-about episodes, although that's hardly child's play, by any means. Even with new contract terms in place, Gandolfini and the show weren't out of the woods. One of the reasons Gandolfini had been able to hold such a tough line during contract negotiations is that a part of him had realized a horrible secret: Tony Soprano's struggles on-screen not only often mirrored his own but at times amplified them. So there was a part of Gandolfini that wanted to leave the show because he understood, as he told a friend, that in order to "become" Tony, he had to connect with his darkest side. In essence, the cost of him playing Tony went beyond just being an actor. He lamented several times, "You don't understand what this is doing to me."

The more audiences watched and praised Gandolfini as Tony, the more his personal journey became problematic. Jimmy had suffered from alcohol and drug abuse—those twin consoling companions of both success and failure—for years, and the stress of occupying the lead role in a smash hit was formidable. Of his substance abuse, Gandolfini said: "When I was twenty or eighteen, it started . . . and it progressed through the years." In 1997, he was arrested for DUI and adopted antics befitting a living legend, which at the time he had yet to become.

Fame rarely, if ever, makes past struggles disappear. Since *The Sopranos'* premiere, dark murmurs had circulated regarding Gandolfini's behavior, tales that admittedly started out more amusing than alarming—such as when, at a glittery Golden Globes affair, upon hearing Time Warner chairman Jeff Bewkes griping that "this wine is shitty," Gandolfini grandly reached under HBO's table and produced three bottles of Brunello that he'd just happened to bring along. It was hardly scandalous comportment, but it did qualify as quixotic and thus in character—not Jimmy being Tony but just Jimmy being Jimmy.

Many more, and considerably worse, stories were to come.

There followed a spate of awkward MIA situations—Gandolfini arriving late for a shoot or failing to show up altogether. One day filming was halted while a search party looked high and low for their star, eventually locating him in a Brooklyn nail salon. In the wake of such episodes, Gandolfini appeared at times embarrassed to be around those who knew of his "issues," and, ever the good soul, would express his contrition by spreading gifts among all those affected.

Nevertheless, Gandolfini misdemeanors mounted. There were several more disruptive disappearances that resulted in halted production, costing HBO several million dollars. Executives at HBO and Time Warner, HBO's corporate parent, initially believed the best policy was that, no matter what, the Great Gandolfini was not to be issued ultimatums or otherwise threatened. As one executive noted, the object was always to be "helpful, not punitive." Accordingly, the errant actor was gently reminded that he was a member of the great HBO "family" and that his ongoing issues would be dealt with in that spirit.

The approach failed. Gandolfini had been announced as a star presenter for the Golden Globes telecast in 2005 but was missing when the curtain was about to go up. Word circulated among the tightly knit group that Jimmy was MIA again. Minutes later, Gandolfini was located lying on the ground outside the Los Angeles Hilton where the ceremony took place, making snow angels on the lawn, so inebriated that he didn't seem to notice the absence of snow. Clearly, a Golden Globes plan B needed to be hurled into action. Michael Imperioli, who co-starred in *The Sopranos* as headstrong Christopher Moltisanti, was quietly approached to take over presenting chores for Gandolfini, but he was hesitant to attempt filling the big guy's shoes. Besides, a worldwide audience was expecting Gandolfini. When it became clear there was no practical alternative, Imperioli relented and executed his role deftly, later telling Gandolfini that he thought he, Michael, deserved the $25,000 "goody bag" of gifts that presenters received from the sponsoring Hollywood Foreign Press Association. Gandolfini was more than glad to hand it over.

It was the type of situation close friends, family, and key individuals involved in *The Sopranos* had hoped to avoid when they gathered in Albrecht's elegant Manhattan apartment that night in May 2003. Most shared the belief that the intervention they were about to attempt was not just advisable but a matter of life and death—Gandolfini's, and that of the entire series.

When Gandolfini entered Museum Towers, he was still under the impression that he and Albrecht were having a casual get-together, little suspecting he'd be confronted by an intervention committee of about a dozen—among them, David Chase and several friends and family members. Nor did Jimmy know that a private plane was standing by to take him directly to rehab. There had even been two days of intervention "rehearsals" testing myriad scenarios and trying to anticipate Gandolfini's possible maneuvers.

As it turned out, none of that preparation proved helpful. The entire intervention lasted ten seconds. Gandolfini walked into the apartment, saw everyone, sized up the situation in a snap, and immediately barked, "Oh, fuck this. Fuck all of you." Glowering at Albrecht, Gandolfini dared him with "Fire me," then stormed out. While the others sat stunned, one of Gandolfini's sisters chased her brother down the hall and begged him to come back.

But Jimmy was having none of that.

Introduction

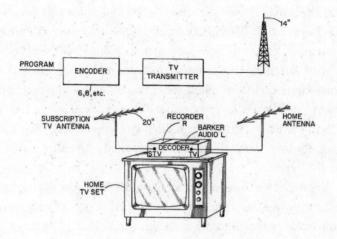

HBO transmogrified television.

Claims like that are usually hype, right? But by any measure, television has not been the same since the meteoric arrival of Home Box Office.

And HBO's impact surpassed the world of media, having a powerful effect on American life.

The supporting evidence begins with HBO's Original Programming, a bill of fare that rocketed across screens with series, movies, specials, and documentaries, many of which were so vital, so novel, and often so electrifying that they changed the way stories are told. Audiences had never encountered anything like them on television. HBO built a reputation for high-quality shows beginning with the breakthrough prison drama *Oz*, and the wickedly hilarious comedy *The Larry Sanders Show*, followed by HBO's now-legendary *The Sopranos*.

These game changers highlighted the fact that HBO was able to broadcast language, violence, and nudity that the networks couldn't (or wouldn't) touch. Exceptional writing and production values began to obscure, or erase altogether, the line between TV and motion pictures. A-list actors, along with top-notch writers, producers, and directors (many making their

TV debuts), flocked to the fiesta. HBO was the first "outsider" to begin to compete with the broadcast networks at the Emmy Awards; soon enough, it was blowing the competition away, year after year, when the trophies were trotted out.

And HBO didn't produce programming exclusively for its own use. It also became the first cable entity to create shows for other networks—including *Everybody Loves Raymond* on CBS and *Martin* on Fox.

HBO's impact on the world of comedy alone was unprecedented, elevating the art of stand-up to new prominence. Comedy "concerts"—usually replete with language and subject matter previously unthinkable for television—came early and often. HBO made comics into celebrities, elevating them to rock star levels of fame. Robert Klein, George Carlin, Steve Martin, Eddie Murphy, Chris Rock, Ellen DeGeneres, Jerry Seinfeld, Sarah Silverman, Rodney Dangerfield, and others made signature career appearances on the network.

HBO created a business, an art form, and a format with stand-up comedy events; they were hot tickets, whether for audiences attending in person (thus conveniently serving both as laugh tracks and as props in reaction shots) or for those watching at home. Proof of HBO's tremendous influence: nationwide there were only ten major comedy clubs when the network launched in 1972; by the end of the next decade that number had grown to four hundred.

Long-standing restrictions that had dulled the potentially sharp edges of broadcast comedy—including many an outdated holdover from the sponsor-controlled, three-network era and, earlier, the radio generation—exploded upon HBO's arrival. The obstructive Hays Code had long banned words like "damn" and "shit" from the screen (in perhaps the most notorious case, even eliminating the wholesome word "pregnant" from the 1950s megahit *I Love Lucy*); HBO simply ignored old "standards and practices" and fought back, not just with naughty words and risqué subject matter, but by attacking the institution of censorship itself. This breakthrough—a liberation of ideas as well as mere words—was a significant move in the evolution of movies *and* television; indeed, perhaps culture itself.

A pivotal moment occurred when HBO aired comic George Carlin's now immortal routine "Seven Words You Cannot Say on Television." Not only did Carlin *say* all seven words, and plenty of others, on HBO, but his performance generated a ripple effect for the network. Soon, long-forbidden words and phrases, in both drama and comedy programming, were commonplace. HBO fueled the collapse of the language barrier on television.

Standards changed to such a degree that HBO started to encourage producers to include "adult" language in scripts "so that viewers know it's HBO." The network's programmers insisted that what appeared on the channel be far removed from the tame, timid fare folks were used to seeing on ABC, CBS, and NBC. Much of what had been forbidden—violence, nudity, "vulgar" language—soon became unexceptional.

Major changes were due in the world of the documentary as well. "We go low, but we also go high" would have been an apt motto. While there was sex and titillation aplenty in some HBO docs (*Real Sex*, *Taxicab Confessions*, and *Cathouse*, for example), other documentary films produced by the network took on controversial, emotional, and even incendiary subjects—such hot topics as abortion, race, and sexuality. HBO's programs won Peabodys, Emmys, and other upstanding awards; they made headlines and reinvigorated old narrative structures and, in the process, reached record numbers of viewers.

Remember TV boxing before HBO Sports? It was a dying format, at least until HBO came along to make it competitive again. "Friday Night Fights" had long since faded from the three-network landscape, victim of various demographic vagaries, but HBO dusted off the sport and made it classy, fueling the careers of larger-than-life superstars. Boxing wasn't just for the TV down at the corner bar anymore. Its locus moved to—where else?— the home. HBO Sports also brought investigative sports journalism to new heights via *Real Sports with Bryant Gumbel*.

In movies, HBO's exclusive theatrical film franchise was the bedrock of the service's value proposition to the consumer, even before there was enough notable original programming to make a difference. For many years, film programming constituted the majority of total programming hours on HBO (and 100 percent of Cinemax). HBO became the first location on the "dial" to showcase the majority of theatrically released films in their original uncut, uncensored versions. In fact, many of those films might never have been released through large swaths of the country, due to limited screens or local censorship. HBO could also boast the majority of major studio releases in its repository and the best library of classic films, too. Blockbuster titles were always among the highest-rated programs in their premieres, not to mention in repeatability, and HBO paid dearly for them. If it didn't build a network on top of those exclusives, somebody else would.

Later on, as its swagger and sway increased, HBO was no longer at the mercy of Hollywood studios to supply movies. The company rewrote rules, determining which movies would end up on pay TV and when. Then HBO began heading Hollywood studios off at the pass, dealing directly with film-makers, buying pay-TV and home video rights to some titles in advance (sometimes based only on the script), a sea change that delivered an important lifeline to the nascent independent film business.

Finally, in its zeal to further diminish the controlling power of the studios, HBO went into the movie business for itself, ensuring a reliable stream of high-quality content for its ever-increasing viewing audience. With this brilliant expansion of its turf, HBO created a safeguard against erratic movie droughts and found yet another way to lure in subscribers and win coveted awards, both of which mattered (if not always equally) to HBO management.

HBO was also the first network to show viewers what a commercial-free viewing universe might look like: a veritable paradise, compared to what had come before. Since TV's beginning, commercials had been virtually inescapable, disrupting the viewing experience and shattering narrative continuity. Even "noncommercial" public TV subjected viewers to advertising of some sort—sponsorships by "underwriters" whose initially tasteful entreaties would later turn into unabashed hard sells.

For much of its history, HBO continued to innovate. It was a satellite pioneer—*before* the Turner networks and ESPN—and among the first television companies to expand overseas, with programming beamed to Asia and South America. One senior HBO executive described HBO as a "programming company that floated on a sea of technology." And HBO's introduction of multiplexing—providing numerous HBO and Cinemax channels to consumers—fundamentally altered the nature of *all* cable TV.

All this would appear to be enough to ensure HBO's place in entertainment history. But to understand fully its nothing-if-not-meteoric rise, one must understand how and why HBO became the first successful television subscription service, proving that people would pay for content and thus enabling pay TV to evolve from a pipe dream to a high-concept, high-revenue horn of plenty. There had been many attempts before; a plethora of failures dotted pay TV's version of Boot Hill.

On January 1, 1951, approximately three hundred fortunate families in the city of Chicago had the opportunity to witness a wonder called "Phone-vision," which, despite its clunky name, emerged as the leader in a new generation of pay-TV systems. Unlike some others of the era (and there'd be many), this gizmo employed a set-top converter box and marked the biggest step forward, so far, in the borderline-wacky experiment then known generally as "subscription" television, the precursor to pay TV. Offerings, typically, were movies. Phonevision's creator, Zenith Electronics, tellingly billed it as a "home box office" for the delectation of the Great American Family.

Zenith CEO Eugene McDonald Jr. tried to frame Phonevision not as problem but as, *voilà!,* solution. "The American family, put on the road by Henry Ford," could be encouraged back onto the living-room couch (like the Simpsons would be at the start of each episode) by the Phonevision "miracle." Or so they claimed.

In the spring of 1954, the Federal Communications Commission (FCC) granted Zenith approval for expanded test-marketing of Phonevision, this time on the big stage—New York City. Simultaneously, test runs of the system were also approved in Australia and New Zealand. Other entrepreneurs couldn't help noticing, and patent applications exploded from 1955 through 1957. Inventors Isaac Blonder and Ben Tongue filed for their own pay-TV patent, consisting of twin signals, one scrambled and the other clear; the former could be unscrambled by the simple payment of a fee.

Zenith sought to reassure the movie studios that they could all co-exist harmoniously in the new communications paradise. This was a wise move, considering the studios had originally sought to block even the tiniest blip of their massive output from appearing on television screens.

But some movie industry veterans were smart enough to perceive the inexorable and to tactfully adjust. The great producer-director Cecil B. DeMille, who'd literally been present at the birth of Hollywood, put it well: "What the movies did to the theater and vaudeville, television is doing to the movies. *You can't stop progress.*"

On December 12, 1968, the FCC—despite dogged and noisy opposition from movie theater owners—gave its approval for the development of pay-TV systems across the country. Ever the surly churls and sore losers, theater managers blacked out marquees in mourning for one day of protest—and sponsored as many "Ban Pay-TV" rallies as possible.

The futility of it all was just short of tragicomic.

Three years later, in 1972, Home Box Office was born, and despite several ensuing near-death experiences it managed to survive a painful infancy.

Since then, many an attack has been launched, from a range of enemies, and there's been no shortage of gladiatorial struggles within. The battles ended with more victories than defeats for HBO, and the company prevailed to become one of the most venerated brands in entertainment history.

Despite what movie traditions and clichés often suggest, the notion of living "happily ever after" is pretty much out of the question—for HBO anyway.

Today, HBO's future is more tipsily unstable than it has been in more than four decades. Those three iconic letters that form the company's name are embroiled in a fight for their lives. HBO survived its infancy on the wings of new technology—specifically the communications satellite—and, along the way, was able to twist ancillary technological advancements to its benefit. But that began to change after 2010, as new competitors rose up against the once-indomitable King of Content. As a result, HBO now faces the most competitive climate in its history. It is a scary time to be HBO.

This, then, is the story of a half century's long, helter-skelter, topsy-turvy roller-coaster ride—replete with bruises, woes, and joys from sets of shows and movies, a look behind closed-door meetings and inside musty corporate boardrooms. Power struggles, creative battles, flagrant jealousy, toxic personalities, cutthroat rivalries, and sheer ambition all play starring roles. Indeed, the company's saga is stocked with enough Sturm und Drang to fill years of comedy and drama programming—though even HBO, who proved willing to air almost anything, may consider some or much of it unfit for public consumption.

Enjoy . . .

1

Time Immemorial

NOVEMBER 3, 1971–JUNE 30, 1974

HBO's birth was a quiet affair.

Gestation began in 1971 when a hush-hush memo revealing a big, bold idea from salesman-turned-entrepreneur Charles "Chuck" Dolan made its way into the executive offices of Time Inc., at that point one of the country's most venerated journalistic institutions.

CHUCK DOLAN, Entrepreneur:

I got a check for $150,000 from Time Inc. as an investment in our Sterling Communications company on a Friday, back in the mid-1960s. I was so proud of it that I displayed it on our mantle for a day, then brought it into the den. Monday morning, one of the kids was gathering up a bunch of Valentine's Day cards his mother had gotten for him to give to classmates and accidentally took the envelope with the check in it. I was on the train headed to a bank downtown when I realized I didn't have it, so I got off the train, took another train back home, my wife drove me to the school, we looked through their things, found the check, and I went back into the city.

Time Inc. became a partner in our new cable start-up in the southern half of Manhattan in the mid- to late 1960s. We were little guys, and they were a well-known powerful corporation in a big building up in Midtown. It was a thrill to have them with us.

Before we delve into nearly half a century of programming that would change the culture and refashion the medium; before we assess actions and motives of stars, writers, and directors caught up in the allure of this new playground; before we explore maneuvers of executives brimming with gumption, ego, and paranoia, making business decisions that ran the gamut from the seemingly shrewd to the debatably preposterous; and before we consider other arcane intricacies of HBO's growth, we first need to understand how HBO survived its troubled infancy. That is key to all that followed.

A determining fact to remember regarding its genesis—and the decades to come—is that HBO has never been "on its own."

Nobody has ever traded a stock called "HBO."

HBO was always, and remains to this day, attached to some larger entity. That would prove to be both boon and bane throughout its life, and in terms of origins, nothing would be more critical. Chuck Dolan would come up with the idea that became HBO, but the network would never have seen the light of day if Dolan's partner hadn't been that player of players Time Inc.

Founded in 1922 by two twenty-three-year-olds, Henry Luce and Briton Hadden, Time Inc.'s pedigree was solidly Establishment, run by a coven of white businessmen who were nearly all proud products of the country's top schools. Through the decades, Time Inc. would become a media superpower, home to a prestigious weekly magazine bearing its name as well as to more than a hundred other household titles including **Fortune**, **Sports Illustrated**, **Life**, *and* **People**, *all of them gigantic brands in their own right.*

In addition to traditional print, the company expanded into the world of movies, acquiring a minority investment in one of the most iconic of Hollywood hit factories, MGM, while Time-Life Books was busily mutating into Time-Life Films. By the late 1960s, a new video-strategy contingent was making its own waves inside Time Inc., operating outside the sphere of the mighty publication divisions and with designs on the wider media landscape.

Such diversification is what fueled Time Inc.'s investment in Dolan's operation— Sterling Communications—which was awarded the franchise to wire all of Lower Manhattan for cable TV. This was thought to be a gift for Manhattanites who had long suffered poor reception due to skyscrapers; but wiring Lower Manhattan for cable turned into a project to rival the building of the pyramids. For much of the country, wiring for cable meant relatively easy installation on civic telephone poles; there was no such option in New York City. There, it was a costly subterranean affair, besieged by bureaucracy and unions, and requiring cables to reach up into high-rise apartment *buildings, then wend their ways into individual units. From 1962 to 1967, Dolan managed to complete wiring for only thirty-four blocks, and it had cost a cool $2 million to connect just four hundred subscribers.*

By 1970, Dolan and Sterling Cable TV were both facing financial collapse. A large loan from Chase Bank to the company—one guaranteed by none other than Time Inc.—was nearing default. Already, the other two major investors in Sterling—William Lear and Elroy McCaw—had backed out, each unloading his involvement on a less-than-eager Time Inc. The situation, as one Time Inc. executive recalled, was: "Most unappetizing."

After completing a stellar trifecta at Andover, Princeton, and Harvard Business School, Nick Nicholas joined Time Inc. in 1964 and moved nimbly up the ranks, establishing a reputation for astute financial analysis and serious-minded decision-making.

NICK NICHOLAS, Executive, Time Inc.:

When Time Inc. initially invested in Sterling Communications, it had one asset, a cable operation in the southern half of Manhattan, and we initially owned 20 percent of the company. Wiring Lower Manhattan was a struggle for them. It was proving to be very expensive, and it was attracting little interest. Urban cable hadn't been successful anywhere in the United States, because all cable back then was a master antenna system. If you got the networks from rabbit ears or had a roof antenna, you didn't need cable because cable wasn't offering any original programming. This was the late 1960s, and the idea for HBO had not been launched. It wasn't anywhere on our radar.

Sterling was bleeding cash and had a negative cash flow. In 1970, Jim Shepley, who was president of Time Inc. at the time, said to me, "Nick, how do we fix this?" So I in effect became in charge of the cable company's operations for Time and served on the board of Sterling along with a guy named Barry Zorthian.

The banks wouldn't lend Sterling any more money, so we advanced funds to the company—not out of great pleasure, by the way. At first, we took shares of Sterling stock based on the market price. Later on, we took converts [convertible debentures] because they were less risky and gave us more equity.

Apart from innumerable mechanical challenges facing Sterling as it made Herculean attempts to wire Lower Manhattan, there were local politicians and other fiefdoms to deal with as well.

CHUCK DOLAN:

The unions were pretty tough. We had some difficult times with them, including sidewalk brawls. John Tatta handled them well, but I don't remember anything unlawful. John was just a great facilitator. He could accomplish anything.

John Tatta was a key Dolan operative in the project, and an appropriately take-charge man. At one point, Tatta hired a tugboat from which workers proceeded to staple cable wire along the seawall in the East River—without bothering to get anyone's permission. That wiring might have gone undiscovered had a little boy not toppled off a boat into the East River one afternoon, prompting one of the New York tabloids to run a picture with the sea wall and its illicitly attached wires visible in the background. When authorities saw the photo, they were livid. But the agile Tatta proved masterful at dispensing with that crisis, along with numerous others.

Tatta's approach to doing business, however, didn't exactly mesh with the starchy corporate ways of Time Inc. Its executives were, not surprisingly, aghast at Tatta's ends-justify-means philosophy, particularly when urged to join union reps on visits to "shooting clubs," or when told to pony up cash donations to union coffers.

NICK NICHOLAS:

This was my first big operational job, and it was not easy. There were tons of issues. Apart from huge costs, we were dealing with city unions like Local 3, and those guys were tough. There were stories written about how they would lock down LaGuardia Airport if they had problems receiving their payments. They would drive their trucks onto the ramps at LaGuardia, turn their motors off, then just walk away. It would paralyze the whole airport. They were famous for things like that, and I had to deal with them every day. John Tatta had great relationships with these guys, but I was new and couldn't operate the way John did. I had to figure out how to survive. I wound up befriending a key union shop steward working on the project and letting him know what was at stake, meaning, we were in danger of shutting this thing down. Once they understood this wasn't about cash in an envelope but whether or not the operation would survive, they realized their jobs were in jeopardy. That was a whole different thing. So together we figured out a way to get things done without putting the company in danger.

In the summer of 1971, Dolan, then a forty-five-year-old communications entrepreneur, took his family on a cruise from New York to Le Havre, France, aboard the **Queen Elizabeth 2**. *Perhaps it was the luxurious surroundings of the ship, or the contemplation offered by bobbing up and down on the Atlantic Ocean, but by the time the* QE2 *reached France, Dolan had a big idea in his head.*

CHUCK DOLAN:

I grew up on radio, and radio was free. Then television arrived and it was free, too. The only reason anybody paid for cable was that their reception was bad. They lived either behind a mountain or behind tall buildings, so they needed a wire service in order to get reception for their television.

I had been at a cable convention in 1971 in California where I saw a new device, a twelve-channel box that would receive cable television signals by wire. It involved customers getting a box and connecting it to a cable. I thought we could reserve one of those channels to use for a pay-TV operation and offer programming you couldn't get elsewhere.

We came along with the idea that regardless of how their reception was, people would pay for content they couldn't get elsewhere. This was fundamentally new at the time, and it was a big bet.

While his wife and children frolicked at the château they had rented for a family vacation, Dolan put pen to paper and created a proposal for a new type of TV service. The memo, submitted on July 29, 1971, to the Sterling board of directors, discussed the feasibility of a "Coded Channel Network," a pay television network where Sterling would charge a subscription to consumers.

"The basic needs of the coded network are A) Programming B) a means of transmission, and C) affiliation contracts." Dolan wrote that he believed affiliation to be "the critical" element but that programming was an immediate priority. "In programming, our primary interest is in live, professional sports, particularly the regional games of the National Basketball Association and the National Hockey League. From discussions with team owners, we believe it is now possible to write contracts with enough NBA and NHL teams to create the sports programming source that would be required by the network."

CHUCK DOLAN:

I sent the memo weeks before we returned from our vacation, and I could hardly wait to find out what they thought of it. But I was shocked when I got home. They hadn't read it yet.

Soon after Dolan returned, the memo was read, and on November 3, 1971, the Sterling board of directors—including Time Inc. representatives Nicholas and Zorthian—approved the idea for the "Coded Channel."

It was one of those fateful decisions that can rewrite history. And did.

Two other actions of note took place at the meeting. The name "Coded Channel" was replaced by "The Green Channel" and Time Inc. made a further investment with Dolan of $300,000.

The idea for the new endeavor was far from a slam dunk. Subscription-only services had been tried before. There had been coin boxes back in the 1950s and prepaid ticket schemes, for example, but they had all failed. Beyond programming, marketing, and technological challenges, the big three networks (ABC, CBS, and NBC) regularly fought hard against any encroachment on their turfs; the Federal Communications Commission (FCC) was equally unreceptive to change; and movie theater owners campaigned vigorously and self-protectively against any subscription-pay model that offered films at home.

Perhaps equally significant was concern from several key Time Inc. executives that "old" movies and "second-rate sports" would not be enough to attract paying customers. One Time Inc. executive scoffed at the prospect of obtaining significant sports programming, writing: "I suggest that pay-TV entrepreneurs examine introductory offers from sports promoters as cautiously as if they were come-ons from Mephistopheles or a heroin dealer."

Nevertheless, the Green Channel moved forward with plans to launch, perhaps as early as late 1972. Subscribers would pay $6 per month; movies, along with sports, would be central to the programming strategy. Sterling would rent uncut versions of films from the Hollywood studios, thereby distinguishing them from airings on the broadcast networks. And of course, because this was pay television, there would be no commercials, nor any of the pressures traditionally associated with pleasing advertisers.

CHUCK DOLAN:

Around this time, Jack Diller, a friend and associate of ours, was working at Madison Square Garden, and he introduced me to a young attorney who had just returned from an assignment in the Middle East. His name was Jerry Levin. Jerry was smart and loved movies, so we engaged him right away to run programming for our new network. We put Jerry in a small office that had a television, and he sat there all day watching movies.

JERRY LEVIN, Executive:

I had two careers before I joined Time Inc., but I had no real knowledge of who I was before I arrived there.

Gerald M. "Jerry" Levin was born the son of a piano-teaching mother and a father who ran a local store in Philadelphia. At school, Jerry was a stand-out student; at his local synagogue, he knew enough Hebrew by the age of ten to substitute on occasion for the congregation's cantor. After attending Haverford College, he destroyed his own college papers *in an effort, he said later, to avoid the pitfalls of ego, at least as defined by the Roman poet Virgil. He received his law degree from the University of Pennsylvania in 1963.*

Levin began his working life as an antitrust lawyer at Simpson, Thacher & Bartlett in Manhattan; in 1967, he joined an international consulting firm called the Development & Resources Corporation and, in late 1970, spent almost a year working for them on a dam construction project in Iran.

JERRY LEVIN:

When I began to work for Chuck, there was no Home Box Office, there was just a memo Chuck had written, which at the time was tied to Sterling Manhattan Cable. So we just started dreaming about it. A lot of the time, there were only four people in the room: me, Chuck Dolan, Frank Randolph, an attorney, and Tony Thompson, who came from Time's magazine division and was a marketing type. That's all. Reva Melniker helped me with business plans, which Time Inc. appreciated, but we were faced with a lot of decisions right away, like what do we put on the screen? What do we do between programs? Play music? What do we want the consumer to feel? It was all primitive. This was the first time these questions were ever being asked, because there had never been a subscription service like this before.

We thought a lot of the answers didn't matter as long as people would subscribe, but then we asked ourselves, "Well, *why do* they subscribe?"

Members of the Green Channel's "brain trust" realized they needed a snappier name, one that signaled to potential customers that here, finally, was a place where movies came to you, not the other way around. The new moniker was created right before a printing deadline for a research brochure and was meant to be a placeholder only.

JERRY LEVIN:

We were at a pivot point in our door-to-door research, and it became very clear that people didn't know what the Green Channel was and where it was. There were a few of us sitting around a table. Chuck wasn't there. We were like troops who were going to overthrow the name. It was time to start selling it as something else. Seeing the name Sterling Cable Network attached wasn't helping at all.

The term "box office" came up because if it's a box office, you can justify getting paid for it—it's more like being in a movie theater or a sports stadium. People feel like they are getting value for their money at a box office.

I'll take credit for inserting the word "home" in front of "box office," and the reason I take credit for it is because my whole instinctual base concerns the home. I wanted people to experience the word "home" like in *The Wizard of Oz*: "Oh Auntie Em, there's no place like home." Everybody wants to go home. There's something about home, and the word "home," that I believed would put people in the right frame of mind, especially since it was being delivered into the home.

Home is a place that indicates who people are, and what they select on Home Box Office gives them a sense of who they are. I'm on dialysis now, but I'm not doing it at some big clinic where they don't give a shit about you. I'm doing it from my home, and that makes all the difference in the world. I'm in an environment where I feel good about it, and I wanted people to have a good feeling back then about HBO. I know it may sound strange to connect all these things, but my sister had autism. We didn't know that's what it was at the time, but she was very violent, never spoke, and they put her in an institution outside of Philadelphia. She left our home. That continues to haunt my soul.

So it's all very simple. I lived in Tehran, worked in Vietnam, and I'd come home—literally, figuratively, and metaphorically to Home Box Office. It's not just another network. I had a life before HBO. It was fascinating, but my real life began *with* HBO. It was my first kiss. It was my first and greatest love.

CHUCK DOLAN:

There was a franchise provision that prevented us from doing pay TV in Manhattan, so we started looking for a location where we could launch. John Walson worked at a place called Service Electric out in Wilkes-Barre, Pennsylvania, a giant cable system. The TV reception was very bad there, so they had put a transmitter up on the mountain to reach customers. But the transmitter was limited, and when we came along with our box, John was very supportive and enthusiastic.

In addition to the franchise provision prohibiting pay TV in the city, there was another problem: security. Sterling had yet to figure out a way that would prevent nonsubscribers from stealing the service outright.

In suburban and rural areas, in order for a customer to be connected to HBO, an installer would need to come to their property, climb the pole in front of their house, and put in what was called a "trap," an electronic device that was attached to the cable wire and would allow the HBO signal to enter the home. Later, cable company technicians would use binoculars to see if there was a trap at the home, and thus whether the service was being stolen or not. But in a city full of apartment buildings, there was a vertical wire in each building going up a conduit from the basement to the top—and if a trap had been installed on that wire, all the apartments would have access to HBO if they paid for it or not.

This was 1972, a big year in the worlds of film and television, with the top-grossing theatrical films headed up by classics-to-be **The Godfather,** **The Poseidon Adventure,** **What's Up, Doc?,** *and* **Last Tango in Paris.** *More notoriously,* **Deep Throat** *made a splash in the adult film world.*

*Prime-time television was dominated by genius producer Norman Lear, who masterminded three of the four top hits—***All in the Family, Sanford and Son,** *and* **Maude** *(***Hawaii Five-0** *was the fourth show)—and they were having an incalculable effect on the mores and manners of the American people.*

This would also be the first year of a new cultural touchstone, **Dick Clark's New Year's Rockin' Eve.** *At the other extreme, ABC's 1972 Olympic coverage from Munich was shattered when Palestinian terrorists took nine Israeli athletes hostage and eventually viciously murdered them. ABC's Olympic sportscasters were suddenly thrust into a new spotlight, becoming breaking-news reporters for one of the most tragic stories in sports television history.*

HBO's premiere came just twenty-four hours after Richard Nixon defeated George McGovern in one of the nation's most decisive presidential victories.

CHUCK DOLAN:

HBO's official premiere was November 8, 1972. That evening, because of the box, we took the audience to a higher level for sports and movies. We launched with 365 homes in Wilkes-Barre, Pennsylvania.

We were down on Twenty-third Street at our new studio. There was a lot of anxiety about whether everything would work. We had never done this before. A lot was tentative.

For all the planning, no one imagined weather would be a factor in the first transmissions of HBO.

HBO's signal was transmitted by microwave from New York via towers to a microwave dish on the top of Bear Creek Mountain in Wilkes-Barre, and then on into John Walson's cables and subscribers' homes—all 365 of them. But extremely heavy winds blew the receiving dish sideways.

DICK MUNRO, Executive, Time Inc.:

There was a huge rainstorm in the city; Tony Thompson and I got stuck on the West Side Highway. We wound up having to get out of our car, which was trapped in traffic, and walk up the highway so we could get a taxi back into the city. We never made it to opening night.

DOM SERIO, Producer:

There was no press, no photographers. The only way we commemorated the official start of HBO was when Jerry put his hand over mine, and together we connected the video patch cord from the output of the studio to the line of the microwave system that was on the roof of our studio, which then sent the signal to Wilkes-Barre.

JERRY LEVIN:

It wasn't pleasant when the dish blew down, but we got it repositioned. We went on at seven p.m. and I was the first image on camera from our small studio operation down on Twenty-third Street. We had set up a sofa, a lamp, and a TV to simulate what a living area would look like, and I was enthralled with it. I wore a suit and a tie, and I looked into the camera and said something to the effect of, "Welcome to your box office in the home, which will be here for eternity. It's never going to stop." But you won't be able to watch my opening because given the austere financial constraints of our operation back then, we only had so many two-inch tapes. I said, "Let's use them for what's really important," and we erased our beginning to rerecord on that tape.

After my introduction, we wanted to start with a live event to demonstrate who we are, and we went right to Marty Glickman at Madison Square Garden for our hockey game, the New York Rangers against the Vancouver Canucks.

NICK NICHOLAS:

If the Knicks or the Rangers hadn't been available, we may not have had a business. Chuck did that, and he was in the process of negotiating a Lakers deal at the time, too, as a way of strengthening program offerings on the West Coast. It was remarkable. And don't forget, Chuck was smart enough to have hired Marty Glickman, HBO's first play-by-play announcer—a man with one of those great ballsy broadcaster voices that audiences found unforgettable.

Martin Irving Glickman played a key role in the infancy and growth of Home Box Office. His ties to Madison Square Garden (MSG), one of America's—if not the world's—most iconic sports venues, would help HBO acquire a wide variety of attractions. Well known and highly regarded, Glickman had for some time been calling games from MSG for Manhattan Cable, and, more significantly, had served as the fabled voice of the New York Knicks. He also called Jets and Giants games.

These were minor matters compared to events that occurred decades earlier in his life during the ominous pause between two world wars, when Glickman and Jewish teammate Sam Stoller would play roles that were more conspicuous in the annals of sports history than deciding who did play-by-play.

During a drama that played out in the global political arena at the 1936 Olympic Games in Berlin, Glickman (then eighteen) and Stoller were set to run in the Men's 4x100 meter relay until the details surrounding the event were mysteriously altered. With the starting gun just hours from being fired, as dreams of gold medals jingled in the athletes' imaginations, word came suddenly that the two Jewish runners had been summarily yanked from the lineup—obviously, it was felt, in deference to Adolf Hitler's notorious anti-Semitism. Glickman and Stoller, the only Jews on the team, were replaced by Ralph Metcalfe and none other than Jesse Owens, the illustrious Black superstar, who had just run the 200-meter dash, in which Mack Robinson, Jackie Robinson's older brother, had beaten the Olympic record. Unfortunately for Robinson, his time was 0.4 seconds behind Owens's.

Ironically, Owens would have preferred to sit the relay out and let the two Jewish athletes have their moments in the sun. "I've won my three gold medals," Owens told team coach Dean Cromwell. "I'm tired, I've had it. Let Marty and Sam run; they deserve it." Cromwell, however, was less than sympathetic. "You'll do as you're told," he said to Owens, thereby ending the discussion. Glickman and Stoller were banished to the stands where they watched Owens and the US team win the gold. Glickman would later call it the "most humiliating episode" of his life.

CHUCK DOLAN:

If you want to give anybody credit for HBO getting underway, give it to Jerry. He was the backbone of HBO's beginning. He didn't start with an official title; he was master of everything. Another key person at the time was Lou Wasserman over at Universal. Nobody would give us their new movies because they didn't want to offend the theaters, but I met with Wasserman and he said, "Okay." He gave us our start.

After the Rangers won the game, 5–2, HBO's premiere night continued with Universal's movie **Sometimes a Great Notion**, directed by and starring Paul Newman—and co-starring Henry Fonda and Lee Remick—which had been nominated for two Academy Awards but failed at the box office. It wouldn't air on commercial television until five years later; by then, it had been renamed, somewhat illiterately, **Never Give a Inch**.

JERRY LEVIN:

That first night I said, "This is an experience." I go by experiences, and if the experience is something that is fundamental to human psychology, that's more important than any analytics that ask what's the market, how fast is it growing, or who's the competition?

When we began, we only had enough programming for two months. In retrospect, that sounds hairy, but we just had to figure out how often we were going to repeat things, and what else we could do to gain subscribers.

Two months after the Rangers had bested the Canucks, the new channel aired its first boxing match, signaling the start of a storied partnership between the sport and HBO. And it wasn't just any old fight.

In the ring on the night of January 22, 1973, in the National Stadium in Kingston, Jamaica, stood thirty-one-year-old legend Joe Frazier and the pre-grilling upstart, twenty-four-year-old George Foreman. Frazier had defeated Muhammad Ali in "the Fight of the Century" two years earlier in Jamaica. Not surprisingly, few gave Foreman much hope against the undisputed heavyweight champion of the world. This was supposed to be a cakewalk for Frazier.

Don Dunphy began his fight commentary with the simple detail that the two men were wearing "8-ounce gloves." Then blink and you missed it—the fight was over at 1:35 of the second round. But it wasn't Frazier celebrating; Foreman had battered his opponent, knocking him down six times before the ref, Arthur Mercante Sr., stopped the fight. Howard Cosell, commentating on the ABC broadcast of the fight, famously chanted, "Down goes Frazier! Down goes Frazier! Down goes Frazier!"

JERRY LEVIN:

When boxing started on HBO, I would go to every match. There was a bout at Madison Square Garden where one of the fighters was Jewish and the other fighter was Irish. In the end, the Jewish fighter won, and the Irish fans were furious and started to throw things at the ring. We had been sitting ringside, and I didn't know what to do, until Don Dunphy said, "We better get under the ring, it'll be the only safe place." So there I was next to Floyd Patterson under the ring, and I hear Don say, "And this is Don Dunphy for HBO Boxing, signing off under the ring at Madison Square Garden."

With Levin running programming for Dolan, and Nicholas overseeing the operation for Time Inc., the two men began to take stock of each other. Each knew from the start that they were different creatures; they had little in common and didn't socialize with each other.

From his vantage point at Sterling, Levin began to press his nose up against the glass at Nicholas's envied Time Inc. spot. Nicholas had no reason to believe their paths would cross in the future. In his mind, there was nothing coming from Levin's manage-ment of Sterling that would suggest a future career at Time Inc.

NICK NICHOLAS:

By early 1973, no one had a firm grasp on what HBO's future would be, but my area of responsibility—and concern—centered on the financial health of Sterling. It wasn't well-run. Don't forget, we, Time Inc., were the guys at this point putting all the money into what was then still called Sterling, HBO's parent company. We only wanted to maintain our 25 percent share, but Chuck was now out of money. Chase was refusing to lend him any additional funds, and he was struggling to maintain control and influence. Meetings were going on and on. Chuck was just a pain in the ass in a very polite way. Ask anybody who's negotiated with Chuck, anyone, whether they love him or not. He looks and sounds like he's being truthful but it's what he *doesn't* tell you that usually turns out to be important. It was almost as if we had to translate information from hieroglyphics. As a result, we were never comfortable doing business on a handshake with Chuck.

JERRY LEVIN:

Time Inc. was uncomfortable with Chuck from the start, and with the whole setup. He wrote the memo that became HBO, it was very forward-looking, but he wasn't the Time Inc. type. Frankly, neither was I, but with Chuck it was more apparent.

Chuck hadn't grown up in the Time Inc. system, and hired friends and family, many from Long Island. Let's just say they weren't exactly Time's type. And the way Chuck ran a meeting, the way information was exchanged, the way the driving force of HBO was articulated, was all over the place and problematic for Time Inc. Chuck's cable aspirations, as brilliant as they may have been, didn't have the gravitas or stability required by a place like Time Inc. But the employees who were all hired by Chuck were the ones who gave me a crash course in how you make television. I couldn't have been luckier.

NICK NICHOLAS:

Jim Shepley and I decided that from a business perspective we needed to have better and quicker meetings with more transparency. And we started to realize Jerry wanted to take Chuck out because he didn't want anybody in his way.

JERRY LEVIN:

I wasn't looking to overthrow Chuck—I didn't have any problem working around him. Someone had told me that Andrew Heiskell [Time Inc.
chairman and CEO] had asked about me, saying, "Who is this brilliant kid?
He's very articulate." It was also a lesson for me as to what business is all
about. It's not about loyalty. It's about who's got what and how you're going
to advance your career.

I never planned for Chuck to have a falling-out with Nick, but I could
see it coming.

I couldn't think of two more opposite personalities than Nick Nicholas and Chuck Dolan. They're both very smart—Chuck was smarter than
any of my colleagues—but he showed it in untraditional ways. Nick was
finance-smart, Time Inc. political–smart, and he was after only one thing:
to one day get recognized as the number one person in Time Inc. I didn't
have that ambition back then, but I got it after a while.

*As power dynamics continued to heat up between the troika of Dolan, Levin, and Nich-
olas, HBO was increasingly desperate for programming. On March 23, 1973, viewers
who happened to be in the shaded center of an imaginary Venn diagram—one that
paired "fans of polka music" with "one of the fourteen thousand homes in America
that had a subscription to the fledgling Home Box Office"—were probably watching
HBO's coverage of—hold on to your lederhosen—the Pennsylvania Polka Festival.*

*"In cooperation with the Service Electric Company" and televised live for no less
than three bouncy hours from the Allentown Fairgrounds in eastern Pennsylvania, the
festival would go down in history as HBO's first live (non-sport) event, though it went
largely unnoticed at the time—at least by everyone who was not a member of Pennsylvania's polka community. In terms of powerhouse entertainment offerings, HBO had
nowhere to go but up.*

NICK NICHOLAS:

Along comes a guy named Russell Karp representing Twentieth Century
Fox who said, "We want to buy thirty-seven and a half percent of HBO
stock from Sterling and will pay you three quarters of a million." I was asked
to put together a plan to respond. This Fox offer was a key development
because it gave us, for the first time, an arm's-length independent value for
HBO.

Before that offer, even though we didn't know what HBO was worth,
we did know we didn't want to sell it. In fact, we knew we wanted to buy
the whole goddamn thing. From day one, HBO appealed very much to

the Time Inc. experience with magazine subscriptions: you get something every month and you pay us—it wasn't that big a price, and there were no commercials.

But instead of deciding to buy just HBO, we decided we wanted to buy the remaining 30 percent of Sterling, its parent company, as well. As a result, Chuck Dolan became our adversary—not personally, but he made it clear that he didn't want us to buy out his minority interest in Sterling, and he wanted to stay in HBO as an equity holder. That wasn't going to happen. If Chuck had been financially stable, there was no way we would have gotten HBO from him.

In late spring of 1973, Time Inc. acquired Sterling's assets and assumed its liabilities, which included public debt that was redeemed for $3.1 million. Shareholders received $2.625 per share, and Sterling was dissolved.

JERRY LEVIN:

I was the one who told Chuck Dolan that he was out. It was awkward for me because I was still pretty young. I think he already knew, actually, and it became a meeting confirming that he was getting the tremendously valuable cable franchises out in Long Island. It wasn't clear then that HBO was going to dominate the world at all. Chuck was really a cable man and saw HBO as a way to increase his cable penetration rather than seeing it as a phenomenal new business that would one day take on a meaning of its own.

CHUCK DOLAN:

I don't think we worried that much about Time Inc. walking away with HBO. We weren't that emotionally involved at that point. Yes, we were leaving equity ownership in HBO, but we weren't totally leaving HBO. We were continuing our relationship with HBO in a different form as part of our cable system. When I hear about having sold HBO, I hardly remember it.

NICK NICHOLAS:

We didn't want Long Island Cable, so Chuck said he would buy it. We assumed Chuck didn't have the funds, but Frank Randolph, who we trusted absolutely, told us that Chuck had just secured private financing from a fellow in Chicago who excelled at tax shelter financing.

The Long Island cable systems at that time had fewer than one hundred subscribers. In the early 1970s, suburban cable was not viewed as a sustainable business. Why would anyone pay $7 for cable when rabbit ears or a good roof antenna would bring you decent service for the three networks which had 90+ percent audience shares at the time. Chuck saw the future in ways that others, including us at Time Inc., did not—once again, people buying cable for original programming that did not exist. It was a brilliant play on the future.

Dolan's nonchalance at being driven out of HBO—which had been his idea—and only roughly six months after it made its debut—may appear quixotic, but it's honest. There's no question that Dolan fought hard to keep his equity piece of HBO, but the problem was, he had no leverage. It was one of the great paradoxes of HBO's early life, and of Dolan's career at that point, that the financial weakness of Dolan's company prevented him from maintaining his large chunk of HBO but would then lead to his establishing Long Island and Cablevision as his beachheads. His early bet, even when HBO was founded, was on franchises, and that was a strategy that would eventually garner him enormous success and wealth.

Just how much of Dolan's HBO blood is on Levin's hands? Dolan gave Levin his first job in the television business, even putting him in charge of programming, though Levin had no background in it whatsoever. That fueled gratitude on Levin's part, and, for a while, his loyalty. Yet Levin, who was becoming smarter and smarter at executive chess, saw the disconnect growing between Dolan and Time Inc., and, instead of moving to thwart it, he let it unfold. A key example of this was related to presentations. Early on there had been wide criticism of Dolan's presentations to Time Inc. management. They were judged too informal and lacked critical analysis, and they believed Dolan wasn't polished enough to make it all work. Levin heard this, but his solution was not to work with Dolan to improve but rather to tell Dolan it would be better if he, Levin, made the presentations. Dolan was all too willing to hand over that chore. It wound up marginalizing Dolan and giving Levin great airtime in front of Time Inc., particularly Dick Munro, who had become head of the company's video strategy group.

DICK MUNRO:

I was a print guy. I had been the general manager at *Sports Illustrated* when Time Inc. bought a string of newspapers in Chicago and they said, "Let's send Munro out there." So they send me to Chicago, and about five minutes later the guy who ran *Sports Illustrated*, Garry Valk, got promoted to publisher of *Life* magazine. I'd been in training ten years for that job and was the heir apparent, but chairman Heiskell said, "Well, shit, we can't bring Munro back. We just sent him out there, we'll look like damn fools." And thank God Garry wasn't in the men's room at that time because he said, "Bullshit. I've been training Munro for this job for years. We gotta bring him back," which they did. If they hadn't brought me back to *Sports Illustrated*, it would have been a whole different life.

When they put me in charge of the video group, I have to admit that I didn't know much about it. HBO was a bit of a tough sell to the board, and I had very little to do with the operation of the company. I was trying to defend this little something, despite its early troubles and doubters. Then one day, probably late '73 or '74, we had a senior management presentation for Wall Street types at the Harvard Club. I recall vividly that everybody in the audience wanted to know about HBO and my fellow executives kept looking down the table at me. Before that day, they didn't think that HBO was going to amount to a row of beans, and suddenly a lightbulb went off saying we may well be on to something here. I think people in the audience that day were more excited about HBO than Time Inc.'s board of directors. Jim Shepley was a supporter, however, and that was significant.

When Chuck left, HBO was 100 percent part of Time Inc. I guess you could say it was my call, as head of the video strategy group, who we would have run HBO. People were pretty impressed with the job Jerry had done. He was smart as hell. There weren't a lot of options, not a lot of people competing for the job at the time. We weren't sure if he could do the job, but it made sense to give it to him and find out.

NICK NICHOLAS:

Every time we had a budget meeting at Time Inc. where Sterling and HBO's losses were shown, it was clear few had an appetite to continue. Our chairman, Andrew Heiskell, would say, "Why do we want to put another $1 million into that?" A million bucks was a lot of money back then.

We were fortunate, however, with another transaction at the time. In addition to Long Island, we decided we also didn't want Manhattan Cable, so we went to Amos Hostetter of Continental, and Monte Rifkin of ATC. Continental got interested and did some due diligence, but they got scared and said no. Steve Ross offered us one million, and we were good with that. But when Jim Shepley and I went over and visited Steve, he said he wasn't going to pay more than eight hundred grand—and we said no. It turned out there were no other buyers, we wound up keeping it, and I wound up running it against my will. By the way, it's worth $5 billion today.

JIM HEYWORTH, Executive:

I haven't thought about all this stuff for quite some time, although I must confess, I do sometimes dream about it.

I had grown up in Libertyville, Illinois, went to Yale for college, then the University of Chicago B-School, where I got my MBA. I was interested in media, and in 1967 I went to *Time* magazine. Shortly after arriving there, my army reserve unit was activated following the Tet Offensive in Vietnam, so I was back in the army for eighteen months. I got a job in Time Inc's Broadcast and Cable Television division at the end of 1969. I was basically the financial person overseeing the company's cable properties scattered around the country—the biggest of which was Manhattan Cable, owned by Sterling Communications.

When Chuck left HBO, Jerry, who had been the programming vice president, became HBO president, and I was the treasurer. It was fun and it was fascinating. There were very few of us trying to create and program this new business. We had to make it up as we went along.

In the beginning, it was a challenge to find a way to deliver HBO programming to these cable systems. The cost of a T1 Telco transmission line was more than the revenue coming back, and the programming was not overwhelming, so there was a lot of churn. Once we got into a cable system, some would buy the service to try it, and then figure it wasn't worth the $7 a month that they were paying and cancel. The marketing was done by the cable operators. We would provide them with ideas and materials, but it was up to them to sell it to their subscribers.

Our lineup of movies was limited. The programming was movies and sports and the sports were primarily Madison Square Garden events. MSG was very important to the beginnings of HBO. The Knicks were in their heyday: Dave DeBusschere, Willis Reed, Bill Bradley, Earl the Pearl, and so on.

In May 1973, Time Inc. announced the sale of its other cable properties to American Television and Communications Corporation. The eight operating systems from five different states were jettisoned along with three franchises (two in California, and the other in North Carolina). With the sale, Time got around a 9 percent interest in ATC, and Time Inc. president Jim Shepley joined its board—he commented that Time Inc. was evolving from "cable operator to cable investor and programmer."

By June 1973, HBO had acquired 12,500 subscribers, but that would prove to be its high-water mark for the near future. As the summer came, fewer people were home to worry about what was on TV; local operators didn't market the service well enough to attract new customers; and the lackluster content was hardly causing people to gather round proverbial water coolers to discuss HBO's latest triumph. By the end of 1973, the number of HBO households had dwindled to just over 8,600 subscribers, *contributing to an annual loss of $1,013,281. Time Inc.'s total investment in HBO was $3.6 million.*

Not surprisingly, Dick Munro was called before the board in January 1974 to report on the status of its video business. His memorandum that day highlighted three critical elements.

First, though HBO's accomplishments in its initial year were considerable—it proved the validity of central organization, network and system interconnection, availability of programming and the marketing of that programming, and even ended the year on budget—it failed to achieve its goals in terms of affiliates and subscribers: "Whereas, HBO's first set of projections provided for a positive cash flow three years out, it now looks like five years."

Second, "And whereas, it was always assumed that Time Inc. would be sharing these losses with others, it turned out that there is no partner, tax-loss or otherwise, to offset a substantial part," adding, "And that's where we are at the moment in terms of financing. Beginning to seek, with the help of Salomon Brothers, a major partner for HBO."

Finally, and perhaps most ominously, "Despite considerable progress and some very major achievements we aren't yet convinced that HBO will meet its projections and thereby be a viable business by 1977. In December we examined the options available to us and decided that instead of terminating at year end 1973, we would invest an additional $500,000 to carry HBO through the first half of 1974 when we'll be in a considerably stronger position to evaluate the venture."

Following that meeting, Jim Shepley rang in the New Year by all but tattooing the figure "20,000" on the palms of Jerry Levin's hands. That was the number of subscribers HBO needed by June 30, he told Levin. If this benchmark is not met, "we will recommend termination."

Levin described the stakes to his team in a memo highlighted by the phrase "no ifs, ands or buts." This was HBO's first lesson in the delicate art of survival. Levin had finally arrived on the big stage with his move from Sterling to Time Inc. and immediately determined that he wouldn't fail, no matter what it took.

JERRY LEVIN:

Jim Shepley was bare knuckles, as opposed to the very nice Dick Munro. It was embarrassing to be in Wilkes-Barre or Allentown or wherever the fuck we were, as opposed to a major market, like Los Angeles. Some people inside Time Inc. saw the promise of HBO but many more clearly didn't. There was a dissonance and I felt it.

So every time I got called to Shepley's office, I had to put a bulletproof jacket on, because that was his style. I had to promise him we were going to make twenty thousand by July. I knew he would close us down if we didn't.

I sat there looking at the numbers realizing everybody who was working their asses off was in danger of not having a job by the summer, including me. I knew the numbers would eventually get better, but they probably wouldn't improve enough to get us to twenty thousand before Shepley's deadline. So I deployed a dual strategy. First, we began to give away a lot of free turkeys to new subscribers. As many as we could. Nothing wrong with that. Second, we had a company that was doing door-to-door numbers for us, and let's just say they were incentivized to slow down their reporting of disconnects. I didn't view it as a shady, underhanded thing—it was just about adjusting the timing of those disconnects. If we had reported the real rates, we would never hit twenty thousand, and HBO would have died a quiet death that summer.

JIM HEYWORTH:

We just squeaked by that twenty thousand number.

*HBO had survived its infancy, but barely. It had escaped termination thanks to an unlikely collusion between fake numbers and free turkeys. In late '73, **The Poseidon Adventure**, a hit movie, aired on HBO and was one of the channel's first perceived victories with subscribers. Yet from a Time Inc. perspective, HBO had, in less than two years, quickly devolved into an outlier—a relatively conspicuous loss leader in a prestigious portfolio otherwise bursting with triumphs. There were still calls for HBO to be exiled to the purgatory of corporate write-offs, but a handful of men—President Jim Shepley chief among them—operating from the top of Time Inc.'s pinnacle, decided to keep the idea going. In doing so, they challenged themselves and their underlings to make the newborn thrive.*

From the start, HBO had been prominently splayed atop Time Inc.'s ever-ready guillotine. Now there was enough of a foundation to at least pull its neck away from the blade. But the coming year would not be one for taking deep sighs of relief and kicking back confidently on all that had been accomplished. Indeed, the stakes would balloon even higher as to whether or not the fledgling company stood a chance at survival.

2

Opposable Thumbs

JULY 1, 1974–DECEMBER 10, 1984

JIM LAMPLEY, Sportscaster:

Muhammad Ali was the premier sociopolitical figure in the history of American sports, and you could not draw a more logical HBO subject than Ali. Various worlds coalesced around Ali—politics, societal change, race, and the preeminence of the great athlete who surpasses everyone around him. HBO was extremely interested in all of these, and they became natural HBO topics. "Rumble in the Jungle" and, more significantly, "The Thrilla in Manila" were major passages for Ali, and they were equally meaningful for HBO.

HBO had survived a treacherous birth. Barely. But the fresh-faced upstart was hardly in the clear. A multitude of challenges, serious ones, faced the ailing firm: major financial and legal hurdles to jump, a conspicuous shortage of key operating principles, and growing resentment from HBO's uneasy partners at the movie studios.

There was limited time to figure it all out and fix it all up. The corporate parent would not endure significant losses for an indeterminate period, and the next several years were likely to be the most critical in HBO history.

HBO had yet to take what might be called a Great Leap Forward on the programming front, and for good reason: few dollars were available for content acquisitions, and the idea of original production, with the exception of live sports coverage, seemed like a fantasy from the future.

So what was left? Basically, something between mishmash and hodgepodge.

HBO started to experiment with rotating in-studio on-camera hosts like Carol Channing, Henry Fonda, Greer Garson, Angela Lansbury, Leonard Nimoy, Tony Randall, Diana Ross, and others to introduce movies and add a certain starry panache to the proceedings.

Primeval "specials" in HBO's early years included **Antiques**, an off-Broadway flop starring Jane Curtin (pre-SNL); a Woody Herman concert; and a Bob (Elliott) and Ray (Goulding) comedy show. In these early years, HBO also introduced its first original children's entertainment series—**Martha's Attic**, which ran for 104 episodes.

Subscribers who picked up their trusty little HBO program guides on a July evening in 1973—to cite an example—would see a prime-time offering at eight that was less than tantalizing: Connie Smith and Tom T. Hall in a not-quite-all-star Country & Western Music Show from Nashville's Grand Ole Opry, followed by a demolition derby crashing and bashing its way into viewers' brains from the Allentown (Pennsylvania) State Fair. Soon thereafter, a quieter HBO evening would begin with the series **Colonial Crafts**, one of its juicy episodes devoted to "Basket-making in Williamsburg." This was immediately followed by an entry from the "Artist at Work" anthology; that night's episode, "A Bowl of Fruit." Seriously.

Executives at other networks weren't exactly trembling in their Gucci loafers.

At least there were sports to mitigate the fare. Marty Glickman, HBO's sports director, made impressive hires: Dick Stockton, Ray Scott, Phil Rizzuto, Don Dunphy, Floyd Patterson, Red Auerbach, Len Berman, Steve Albert, and Spencer Ross. That talent, along with the channel's early and abiding commitment to boxing (as many as two or three bouts a week), gave the corporate higher-ups a glimmer of hope. HBO offered harness racing from Yonkers, New York; wrestling from "Parts Unknown"; roller derbies; rodeos, dog shows, and the semifinals and finals of the Atlantic City Tennis Classic; plus a smattering of matches from "World Team Tennis."

Amazingly, there were playoffs involving the NBA, NHL, along with the ABA, college basketball, and a number of actual regular season games from MLB, North American League Soccer, and the Canadian Football League. There was a weekly sports highlight show hosted by future great Dick Stockton, plus "previews" of upcoming football, baseball, basketball, and hockey seasons. At this stage, however, HBO could only sample a few varieties of gridiron greatness—games from the mercifully short-lived World Football League.

And on June 10, 1973, in Winston-Salem, HBO had begun its pro-bowling coverage, with Stockton, Glickman, Spencer Ross, and the colorfully named Skee Foremsky as commentators. Two years later, no less notable a star than Pat Summerall would call *one of the twenty-one finals HBO showed from 1973 to 1975. By late July 1974, the bowling had rolled on over to Houston, Hartford, and Buffalo.*

But then came Africa.

"Ali bomaye" went the cry—"Ali, kill him!" It was Wednesday, October 30, 1974, in Kinshasha (then Zaire), and the great Muhammad Ali was set to meet the also-great George Foreman for the heavyweight championship of the world. The legendary fight, which was the debut of Ali's risky but brilliant rope-a-dope strategy, would forever be known as the "Rumble in the Jungle."

Handicappers didn't give Ali, then thirty-two, much of a chance. He had lost to Joe Frazier in 1971 and Ken Norton in 1973, and though he had bested Frazier in January 1974 to earn a shot at Foreman, word was that his legs were gone. Foreman, twenty-five, had already shown what he could do by brutally beating Joe Frazier in an upset, then pummeling Norton just a couple of months later.

JERRY LEVIN:

I had read the announcement of the fight in the trade press and called Bob Arum's company to ask if we could air the fight. I told them we were available on such a limited basis that it wasn't going to affect their pay-per-view receipts and that we could help them by being another form of promotion.

LARRY MERCHANT, Sportscaster:

I was on the plane to Africa with Ali, and after we were up in the air, he commandeered the loudspeaker system and was having fun with the fact that there were two Zairean pilots and musing about whether they could find Zaire or even land the plane. Then he sat down next to me. He told me the one flaw in George Foreman that had been exposed was his stamina because he came out so hard in the beginning. Ali said, "If I can carry him into the late rounds, that's going to be my best chance to win." Then he said to me, and I'll never forget it, "If he doesn't get me in seven, his parachute won't open."

Ali came out in the first round and realized Foreman was even quicker than he thought. I believe he went back into the ropes in an experimental way, to figure out whether he could take all of Foreman's punches and tire him out. Bundini Brown, his sidekick and court jester, was yelling from the ring, "Champ, Champ, get off the ropes, get off the ropes!"

JERRY LEVIN:

"Rumble in the Jungle" was the first time we ran an HBO program in one of the Time Inc. screening rooms. Before that fight, we weren't fully accepted within Time Inc., but it was a great fight, and people in the company noticed.

Subscriptions didn't necessarily increase after that—we couldn't deliver a duplicate of that fight every month—but it definitely helped HBO's standing internally. Despite that, there was still a lot of pressure on us to grow nationally.

In 1975, HBO made it to the hallowed grass courts of the All England Lawn Tennis Club, Wimbledon. While NBC had a lock on the semifinals and finals, you could have watched many of the matches over the fortnight leading up to the final weekend if you'd had a subscription to HBO, marking the first time Wimbledon tennis could be seen on TV in the United States on a weekday. That year, Arthur Ashe (for the first time) and Billie Jean King (for the sixth) won the singles championships. Both would become popular members of the HBO Sports family.

Coverage wasn't live, but to get tapes of the action back to the States as quickly as possible, HBO used the gorgeous supersonic Concorde as its carrier pigeon.

JERRY LEVIN:

Wimbledon was the pinnacle—London, grass courts, the Queen and other VIPs making appearances, and terrific athletes. Rarely in cable were you able to get your hands on that top-notch programming, but it was our sports director Marty Glickman's idea to do midweek coverage, and he was able to work out the deal. It was a brilliant stroke.

With roots now planted in boxing and tennis, HBO soon managed to find a way to match brands with the daddy of all daddies, the National Football League.

In September of 1977, the network launched **Inside the NFL,** *a weekly look at the previous week's games, with footage—and important audio—supplied by NFL films. The show received a lot of attention in the sports television world. Once ESPN got started a few years later, HBO's* **Inside the NFL** *would be one of the first shows they would attempt to mimic. This weekly magazine show would go on to be both the longest-running series on HBO (three decades plus) and the longest-running series in cable history. Hall of Famers Len Dawson and Nick Buoniconti were the longest-serving hosts, and the show established the post-game careers of Cris Collinsworth, Dan Marino, and Cris Carter.*

Soon, baseball programming came aboard as well, with **Race for the Pennant,** *featuring clips from games, and Len Berman's* **Follow the Bouncing Ball** *awards show. Joining Berman for the first shows was Hall of Fame pitcher Bob Gibson; subsequent on-air talent would include Tim McCarver, Barry Tompkins, and Maury Wills.*

By the end of 1973, Time Inc.'s investment in HBO totaled $3.6 million, a substantial sum for the company at the time. Requirements for 1974 included another $3.6 million, and it was projected that an additional $4.7 million was needed to make the company cash-positive by 1977.

Among numerous daunting challenges: insufficient subscriber growth, the questionable quality of movies made available by the studios, an inadequate number of cable systems signing up to be affiliates, and, perhaps most troublingly, the untenable cost of microwave transmission—the only viable vehicle for the company at the time.

JERRY LEVIN:

In 1973, I went to a cable convention in Anaheim, and what struck me the most was when Congressman Carl Albert gave remarks via a satellite hookup. I had been sitting there trying to think of what to do with HBO, which wasn't going the way I wanted it to, and here was Carl Albert on a screen with phenomenal picture quality. I called up my friend Bob Button at Teleprompter, and he said, "We figured out how to get the signal all the way from DC to the state of California! Isn't it thrilling?"

I spent time with Teleprompter engineers and spoke briefly to Scientific Atlantic about their work with satellites; then I talked to RCA.

HBO's move to satellite received a big assist from then treasurer Jim Heyworth, who turned a vacation into a pivotal coalition-building effort.

JIM HEYWORTH:

The challenge was how do we expand further? One answer was, we've got Madison Square Garden sports. A lot of people down in Florida are former New Yorkers. Maybe we can expand there.

We were well aware of this new satellite technology. In another part of Time Inc. there were conversations going on with Hughes Aircraft about satellite-distributed program services, but we thought using a satellite for HBO was beyond our reach.

I went on a working vacation with my heroic wife and one-year-old son to Florida and worked intermittently, calling on cable systems up and down the two coasts. There was a microwave system in the state that could be used for transmission, and I would walk into these cable guys' offices, introduce myself, describe the concept, and ask if they would be interested. They all said yes. Based on that, I went back to New York, reported on my trip to Levin, did the numbers on Florida, and we concluded Florida could help pay for a satellite transponder.

JERRY LEVIN:

Advocating for HBO to be on the satellite was one of the most important decisions of my entire career.

The only way you get ahead is if you see something that no one else sees and it's a little crazy. Satellite at that time was kind of a dreamy thing, but the idea of making HBO into a national network rather than relying on a lot of little cable networks was a pretty big idea.

Now I had to get Time Inc. to put up more than $7 million to pay for us to be on a satellite. Some people inside Time Inc. saw the promise of HBO and others clearly didn't. The latter thought about Time Inc.'s pedigree, about *Time* magazine, *Sports Illustrated*, many others, and their millions of subscribers. I was about to get up and talk about 350 subscribers in Wilkes-Barre, Pennsylvania. They didn't even know where Wilkes-Barre was. And I was asking for a lot of money.

There were cultural differences as well. I wasn't a Time Inc. type. Time had few Jewish people. I didn't dress the way they dressed. I didn't talk about closing advertising deals on a golf course in Connecticut. I wasn't getting shit-faced on martinis at lunch. When I told my father I was there, he said, "Why are you doing that?"

I started my presentation saying, "You may think HBO's a little thing in Pennsylvania, but we're going to put it on a satellite, and it's going to become a national service." Then I said, "It doesn't matter that no one's tried it yet. There's nothing to be concerned about. It's easily doable."

It turned out, Andrew Heiskell, the chairman, was behind what I was doing. Jim Shepley, our president, who was known to be a rough customer, told me, "You better be right."

JOHN MALONE, Executive, Tele-Communications, Inc.:

Satellite was a huge differentiator for HBO. Time Inc. were the only guys with the juice and the scale to do it at that time. It gave them an enormous head start, and it made HBO distribution available to every cable system instead of just the biggest ones. Technology gave them a big tailwind.

ROBBIN AHROLD, Executive:

I was the quote unquote communications guy at HBO at the time. We were a small but tight group, all in the same suite of offices in the northeast corner of the Time-Life Building. Most of us were putting in sixteen-, eighteen-hour days, doing everything we could to make this thing succeed.

I worked with people at RCA and Jerry to draft the press release announcing the satellite. From that point on, everything changed dramatically.

JIM HEYWORTH:

Jerry and I did the deal to lease two transponders from RCA at their New Jersey offices, and months later the signal went up. We went from having a difficult terrestrial distribution system for parts of the Northeast to national distribution overnight.

In the years ahead, Showtime, The Movie Channel, Ted Turner's Superstation, and Pat Robertson's CBN would all come aboard Satcom 1. Ironically, in 1978, ESPN was able to secure a transponder on Satcom 1 that provided 24/7 service. No other entity had wanted that, and it turned out the price for that transponder was less per hour than the one HBO had been paying for.

JOHN BILLOCK, Executive:

Now we had to get big receiver dishes deployed, but not many cable systems had them, or the capital to buy them. So HBO instituted a volume scale lease program where we would lease dishes back to cable operators at discounted prices. This lowered their risk and was a head of steam for us. I came on board in 1978 as a marketing manager, and we were pounding out new HBO launches all over America.

DOM SERIO:

A lot of viewers didn't understand what satellites were. We did an LA Lakers game that went into overtime, but we had a movie scheduled for ten o'clock and had to stay on schedule so we didn't cover the rest of the game. The announcers made an excuse that we were losing the satellite because it was going behind mountains, which was false.

Adoption of the epoch-making satellite technology enabled HBO to score the landmark boxing match "Thrilla in Manila" in 1975 between Muhammad Ali and Joe Frazier that dwarfed even the success of "Rumble in the Jungle" and began HBO's march to dominance of the sport.

To understand why HBO was able to step in and take over the boxing space, it's instructive to back up and consider the communications history of the sport. In the 1920s and 1930s, radio programs amplified fighters' stories, helping to make boxing one of America's most avidly followed sports, alongside horse racing and baseball. Then, as early television arrived in the '40s and '50s, boxing made the transition from radio to TV, occupying as many as six prime-time slots per week. NBC aired "Friday Night Fights" from Madison Square Garden until 1960, when it dropped boxing, partly because of the rising number of criminal accusations associated with it. *ABC picked it up for four more years, before integrating fight coverage into its* **Wide World of Sports.** *CBS also had an early hand in boxing with something called* **Pabst Blue Ribbon Bouts** *as of 1948.*

Boxing's fan base grew from die-hard followers to include casual viewers who happened upon the matches while channel surfing. However, things were shaken up when promoters discovered they could make more of a profit offering matches live via closed-circuit or theater television, especially when the regular networks, nervous over decreased ratings, and over the violence central to the sport, stopped putting fights into prime-time spots. With this switch, fans would pay to watch major fights in a limited number of theaters.

Pay-per-view soon transitioned out of theaters and into homes. The 1960 rematch between Floyd Patterson and Ingemar Johansson was the first such broadcast accessible from the comfort of a viewer's own couch. Subscribers mailed $2 to access the match. HBO had shattered the PPV record with "Rumble in the Jungle," but that record crumbled with "Thrilla in Manila."

Jerry Levin secured "Thrilla" by once again making a selling point out of HBO's modest subscriber base. It was a visionary move. HBO carried the Ali–Frazier fight live on October 1, 1975, scooping the competition by inaugurating its continual satellite feed. (Regular TV stations had to wait for videotapes of the fight to arrive from the Philippines, which took days.)

The world had gotten smaller, and instant delivery would soon be engraved in the psyches of HBO Sports fans.

BOB ARUM, Promoter:

I co-promoted that fight with King and was in Manila. HBO at that point basically had no subscribers; we didn't have to worry about them cannibalizing our pay-per-view. The deal was just extra cash.

JERRY LEVIN:

The negotiation tactic was, "I don't know how many satellite dishes are going to be up by the fight, but it won't be a lot and I'm going to give you money anyway." I believe it was about $100,000. We threw a big party at Fort Pierce Beach, and one of the thrills of a lifetime was standing near the satellite receiver dish when the signal was being tested from Manila. It was an extraordinary feeling.

STU CHUZMIR, Executive:

It was a big deal. We did photo opportunities by the dish, and when the signal came in, there was a lot of cheering. But we needed a continuous signal from the Philippines, and it was a long fight, so there were a lot of nervous technicians and executives.

JERRY LEVIN:

The picture quality was perfect, the fight was spectacular, and there were no technical issues. Our audience wasn't huge, but it was a meaningful number for us at that time, and we got a lot of press attention. I invested a lot of my energy into our adopting satellite transmission during a scary time for the company. After "Thrilla in Manila," I wasn't the crazy idea guy anymore.

BOB ARUM:

It was one of the great fights of all time. We walked out of the dark, dingy Coliseum into the bright Manila sunlight. It was an unreal experience for us, and for HBO.

STU CHUZMIR:

Up until that time, getting a signal to a sorely needed new affiliate required a "leg analysis," which involved plotting out various microwave paths to see whether the prospect was economical. The satellite made it possible to hit a dish anywhere in the country, was a godsend, and put us on the map.

DICK MUNRO:

"Thrilla in Manila" was a big night for us, but a lot of people inside the company were still leery. We still didn't know if HBO would survive. We didn't have a lot of affiliates. We needed more cable systems and more subscribers.

BRIAN ROBERTS, Executive, Comcast:

My first job was as a Comcast trainee in New Kensington, Pennsylvania. I was a door-to-door salesman. When you knocked on the door, you asked: "How would you like better reception?" And, "How would you like this new service called cable? It has HBO, and what is HBO? It's pay television. You won't have any commercials, and you'll get movies and sports." Then I would hand them the HBO marketing brochure. We were very proud of the product. We were the de facto exclusive distributor. The only way to get HBO there was if you said yes to our offer. If you saw a Comcast truck, you would see HBO on the side. We helped build that brand.

MATT BLANK, Executive:

I came to HBO in '76 as an affiliate marketing manager and spent most of the next couple years going to nearly forty states marketing HBO. The business was really primitive. Cable systems were built on delivering TV to those who would never get a good television signal without cable, and they were selling a half dozen broadcast stations for $5 to $8 per month.

Our pitch to cable operators was that for the first time they could build a second revenue stream from programming. HBO's basic economic model was to charge about half of the $8 or so they would get from their customers for HBO.

But cultural challenges sometimes got in the way. In certain parts of the country, people weren't happy about R-rated movies and other HBO content coming into their homes. Some cable operators worried that when they went to the local municipality to renew their franchise, they'd hear, "You're the people bringing that filth into our town."

When we would do weekend promotions, where we'd be showing up for free on everyone's TV, we tried to be really careful. We didn't want to be showing an R-rated movie when somebody didn't invite us into their home. One cable operator in Mississippi said, "No worries, it won't be a problem," and insisted on taking the regular HBO satellite feed, which was playing *The Exorcist* and had a fairly graphic masturbation scene. He got a lot of complaints, but the real surprise was they weren't about the explicit scenes. This was the Bible Belt. People weren't happy about a movie that had the devil showing up unannounced in their living rooms. That would not have occurred to someone from Queens like me.

DOM SERIO:

There were sensitivities even on non-free weekends. I was in the master control room in December 1975 when we were playing the movie *Groove Tube*, and after one particular sexy part, Jerry called and said, "Pull it off the air." I said, "But we're in the middle of the movie," and he told me, "I don't care. Put a slide up." I took it off, and we put up a note that said the program was being interrupted.

ROBBIN AHROLD:

There were cable systems down in Texas where they called us "The Dirty Movie Channel."

I would speak at city council hearings where a vote was coming up for approval, and there was a lot of opposition. Cable system offices were getting picketed. Newspapers and local television stations covered them. The protests were of course ironic: they were a godsend for HBO because they brought free publicity. I don't think our opposition ever understood that. We talked to all the media outlets, priming the pump all the time. I can't remember a time we ever lost even a single vote.

Still, it wasn't enough. Even though HBO finished 1975 with nearly 300,000 subscribers and would add 600,000 in the next twelve months, a shocking 320,000 subscribers implicitly concluded that they could live satisfying lives without HBO. Churn, which is shorthand for the subscriber cancellation rate, would only be a problem at HBO . . . forever. Add significant costs for satellite distribution, and the combination turned 1976 into the most difficult year in HBO's financial history, with nearly $6 million in losses. It was a catastrophe that in another company might have cost Levin his job. Dick Munro, vice president of Time's video group, however, wasn't that type of guy.

NICK NICHOLAS:

In 1976, Dick Munro, who was my boss, came to see me at my office on Twenty-third Street. I was running Manhattan Cable for Time Inc. He said, "Nick, we are going to be shutting HBO down unless there's a big change. We want you to take over HBO." I told him, "I will do anything the company asks me to do short of committing suicide, but I'm not going to go work alongside Levin. I just can't do it. The guy's smart as hell and one of the most articulate people I've ever met, but he operates in a different way than I do. I'm sorry." So Dick goes back, talks to his boss, Jim Shepley, and comes back several months later. He tells me, "Nick, you've got to do this, and we will meet your condition." I quickly learned he wasn't going to fire Jerry, but rather create camouflage and actually promote him. They were going to make him "chairman." I couldn't believe it. Then I said, "Dick, I won't take the job if I have to report to Levin. I will only report to you." Munro said to me, "Okay. I'll tell him."

I needed to make sure Levin understood my arrangement with Munro, so we met for lunch, which was room service in a Time Inc. suite at the late Dorset Hotel. I told him, "You will be invited to any meeting you want, and I will always show respect to you, but Dick will be my boss. I will report only to him. What do you think, Jerry, can this work?" He appeared to be very thoughtful, and said, "Okay."

JERRY LEVIN:

Nick was inserted as a well-respected Time Inc.'er who was driven to achieve good financial results. But I don't think Nick was brought in under me solely for him to do HBO—and I didn't think I was going to be doing my job forever.

This was a moment to be remembered: Levin is named chairman of HBO and Nicholas becomes the second president in HBO history.

Now the what-ifs: If Munro, after closely examining the dire state, and straits, in which HBO was mired, had simply fired Levin outright, then the next twenty-five years of HBO, Time Inc., Time Warner, and AOL Time Warner would have been vastly different. It could, in fact, be easy to contend that there might never have been an AOL Time Warner at all.

Similarly, if someone other than Nicholas had been brought in to "save" HBO, there's no guarantee he or she would have prevailed; might the network have crumbled?

Though it may have seemed conclusive at the time, what was then transpiring between Levin and Nicholas would hardly turn out to be the last chapter in their saga. Over the next sixteen years, the relationship would turn out to be veritably Shakespearean.

JERRY LEVIN:

When Nick became the head of HBO, I was concerned he was going to run HBO the way he ran the cable company, primarily as a stepping-stone for his future. Even though I was senior to him, I was running against the tide. Nick was well liked in the Time Inc. family.

NICK NICHOLAS:

HBO was a fucking mess. When I showed up, there was no office, just a desk and phone. On the affiliate side of the business, there was no clarity on pricing, or a single playbook for handling cable operators. They had just been making things up.

I said, "I want a rate card. I want real contracts. We need better channel location on the dial. We will give favored nations treatment, which is if we make a better deal with anybody else of a similar size to your cable business, we will call you up and give you that better deal."

We readjusted our programming schedule for when people were actually at home watching, and we found a potential late-night audience, which astonished us.

ROBBIN AHROLD:

We had many challenges and were blessed to have somebody with Nick's expertise come on board. We needed somebody who knew finance and who could communicate properly with the board.

NICK NICHOLAS:

As CEO, I brought Time Inc. standards to HBO. My first week on the job, all the women who were not paid the equivalent of their male counterparts got immediate raises. Time had a history of doing that.

DICK MUNRO:

I gave Nick an awful lot of leeway because he was very competent. And since he was doing so well, I let him run the show. I wish I could remember exactly what Jerry was doing at that stage, but my recollection is he was more interested in the larger video group.

NICK NICHOLAS:

Austin Furst was my first hire. What Austin did was to make much more sense of how we paid for programming and how we scheduled it. One of his early hires was a research guy named Lee deBoer. We didn't know anything about what time we should play something, what should come on either side, or how to maximize our audience in general.

AUSTIN FURST, Executive:

Home Box Office was on a death march. It was losing so much money, we were worried it wouldn't last another year.

The way the industry was structured at that time was that there was a six-month window during which a studio would release a film theatrically and then there was a six-month window that was known as the pay window, short for pay television, which was ours. Following that six-month window was the beginning of the television window, which ran for as short as twelve months and as long as ten years. That meant we had to milk whatever value we could from a movie in a period of six months. Timing was very important.

But the negotiating process was awful. It was complex and emotional. A lot of people I negotiated against were experienced theatrical negotiators; they were used to setting rules and being king of the mountain.

And the competitive climate was more complicated than you might think. In addition to our primary competitor, Showtime, the studios had developed direct relationships with a number of cable operators who were licensing directly to them. That was antithetical to the whole concept of a network. We needed to be negotiating with the studios, not competing. I had to have a subservient role emotionally to calm them and not rock the boat, but I also had to lower my costs compared to my competitors'. Then I needed to fund all of our programming that was not theatrical out of those savings.

My first big challenge was to stop paying the studios per subscriber fee, which is what I inherited. I converted as many of those deals to flat fees as possible. Eventually, Showtime saw the wisdom in doing that.

We developed a strategy that won the early war called Odd Man Out, the concept being that we could live without any one studio at any one point in time. We would go into a negotiation and apologize for it rather than threaten with it. That proved highly effective.

NICK NICHOLAS:

You know how I got Michael? Neal Pilson, who was at William Morris at the time, used the same train station, and I got to know him on the train. At one point I said, "You've got to join HBO as our programming guy." Neal said, "Let me think about it." He talked to his wife and a couple of days later said, "Nick, I got a mortgage and two kids. I can't do something so risky, but I got this guy who works with me at William Morris named Michael Fuchs. He doesn't have a mortgage or a wife."

MICHAEL FUCHS, Executive:

You get to William Morris and they lie to you. They tell you you're coming in to eventually be the president. You should never take a job waiting for old Jews to die.

Neal came into the office one day and said, "I've got two offers: Business Affairs at CBS Sports and a programming job at HBO." I asked, "Which are you taking?" He said, "CBS. There's too much programming at HBO." To me that was like someone saying, "There's too much hot fudge on this vanilla ice cream." He gave me Austin Furst's name, and I immediately called him. I said, "I hear you're looking for talent. Why don't I save you some time?" And he said, "I love that." Then I said to myself, "Listen, you haven't done any of this shit before. Don't go over there until you've had a couple of days to put something together." Just as I was instructing myself, he says, "How would you like to come over now?" I said, "Sure."

AUSTIN FURST:

Michael was a little cocky, but he had an intuitive knowledge of how the pieces fit together in terms of talent, producers, and financing, and we got along very well. I interviewed several other people, but Michael was clearly the most capable.

He quickly proved he could sit down with anybody. He had strong self-confidence to make decisions and was a good communicator so he could get to the heart of a seller's idea, then explain internally why something was worth buying. He would meet talent, develop a relationship with them, and understand their needs. Michael was a born buyer.

MICHAEL FUCHS:

My grandfather came over around 1900 from Lithuania. When things got too dirty for the Nazis, they would give it to the Lithuanians. I lived in the Bronx several blocks from Yankee Stadium until I was five and we moved to Mount Vernon. My father owned the Concourse Plaza Hotel. We're talking upper middle class.

I went from law school to the reserves to beat the draft. Mount Vernon was a ferocious fucking draft board. It's a miracle we didn't get called up. After the army, I got a job on the night shift at CBS News as a copy boy for Richard C. Hottelet, one of the CBS reporters who had covered World War II. The only order they gave me was to stay away from the Cronkite desk. It was like a shrine. Right. It's three a.m. Of course, I'm going to sit at Cronkite's desk and "do" the news.

I practiced law before William Morris and thought if I can't find an entertainment job in New York, I'll go to LA. I was thirty when I got to HBO.

JERRY LEVIN:

Fuchs was a big personality, much different than who I was, but we were close for a long time. He had that X factor that would drive some people crazy, but drive others to realize their God-given talents. I knew from the day he arrived, he wanted to be me or have my job.

MICHAEL FUCHS:

Entertainment is one of the more democratic industries. Diller didn't go to college. Geffen didn't go to college. If you have it, you have it. I had been reading *Variety* since I was a kid, and I had watched every television program. I looked at what the networks were doing, and it was easy for me to figure out where HBO could fit in. I wanted to be a counter-puncher. I was chockablock with ideas. I got hired on a Friday. By the time the weekend was over, I had a book of about fifty shows I thought HBO should do.

IRIS DUGOW, Executive:

A headhunter arranged for me to meet Michael at the Dorsett Hotel. I walked in, sat down, and the first thing he said to me was, "I've already hired somebody for this job." I said, "Okay." Then the waiter came over and I said, "I'll have an iced tea," and Michael says, "You drink iced tea in the morning?" I said, "I've never had a cup of coffee in my life." He said, "I've never had a cup of coffee in my life. I drink iced tea."

I don't know how it came up, but I said, "I was ranked number seven in California as a junior tennis player." He asked, "Does that mean you would be my doubles partner?" I later found out Michael loved tennis and was very competitive. He said, "This is great. We can take on everybody." He called the guy he had hired and said, "I'm sorry, I have to take back the offer. I've hired somebody else."

I was basically in charge of creating programming where none existed. I would call people and say, "Hi, this is Iris Dugow, I'm with Home Box Office." And they'd say, "Home who, box what?"

Comedy, like boxing and tennis, would prove essential to HBO's growing profile—it was cheap to produce, but more importantly, the channel could boast of being "uncensored"—not only to the audience, but to talent who had been under the thumbs of network censors. Over time, getting your own HBO special would replace late-night berths as the game changer of a comedy career. And it all started on New Year's Eve 1975 with the great Robert Klein.

ROBERT KLEIN, Comedian:

When I would appear on *The Tonight Show*, *Merv Griffin*, *Mike Douglas*, or Della Reese's *Reese*, I had only five minutes and every word was parsed. The network wanted to hear everything in advance. I had some big arguments in the halls of NBC about my wanting to say bad things about Spiro Agnew. When I heard HBO wanted to do a full concert of mine that would be uncensored, I was thrilled.

Back in 1967, I had seen Joan Rivers recording the material she was doing onstage at the Improv, and I thought, "What a great idea." Ahead of the concert, I worked with my recordings on a good hour and a half of material. That night, I put on a colorful sweater and saddle shoes, and we were off and running.

MARTY CALLNER, Director:

I directed HBO's first ever stand-up comedy show, called *An Evening with Robert Klein*. We did it at Haverford College because that's where Jerry Levin went to college.

ROBERT KLEIN:

I told Callner I patrolled the stage like a cat. I didn't stand still or sit down on a stool. He was so terrified about not having enough close-ups that he decided to do a preamble of me backstage where we weren't trying to be too funny. It was great.

MARTY CALLNER:

For the opening, I decided to go verité and take the audience behind the scenes. We put a camera on our cameraman's shoulder and shot Robert before the show started. Now it's routine, but it had never been done before.

The next day John O'Connor, in the *New York Times*, wrote four columns about Robert Klein, how well the program worked, and my innovative concepts.

ROBERT KLEIN:

There would be no HBO without me.

MARTY CALLNER:

I was a star based on that one review and was quickly given *On Location*, *Young Comedians*, even *Standing Room Only*. I always took the tack that the minute I fucked one up, I would be out. I did everything I could to make each as unique as possible. In the beginning, the backbone of HBO was its specials.

"The show you are about to see is an exact record of what happened live, onstage, at the Cleveland Music Hall. . . . No laugh tracks or applause tracks have been added. Nothing has been overdubbed or altered in any way. This is the way it was."

With those genre-defining words, HBO introduced **The Bette Midler Show** *on June 19, 1976, simultaneously broadening its offerings and establishing itself as television's premier outlet for full-length, "way-they-were," almost-live music concerts. Just as with the Klein comedy special, the channel had the space to air complete shows, and with the hugely entertaining Bette Midler—whose concert lasted a full 134 minutes.*

The adored pop diva began the special sitting up in a hospital bed under a sheet, singing the verse to her trademark number "Friends": "And I am all alone / There is no one here beside me . . ." and then romped through her many signature songs—"Boogie-Woogie Bugle Boy," "In the Mood," "Lullaby of Broadway," interspersed with Midler's cheerfully racy, adult comedy. The special, part of her facetiously titled "Depression Tour" and specially produced for HBO, wound up a ginormous hit, enticing a monumental tune-in.

BETTE MIDLER, Singer:

My manager at the time, rotund gadfly Aaron Russo, called me and said, "There's this new thing called HBO, and you can swear and do things you've never said or done on television before. It's very racy."

JERRY LEVIN:

Shepley says, "Bette Midler? I've never heard of her." I thought, What the fuck? but still believed she was the ideal candidate to break open our music special business because she had pay television sauciness. It was a terrific show and won us our first ACE award.

BETTE MIDLER:

People started saying, "I saw you on HBO." I don't even think I had HBO. I'm very modest. I don't say I put them on the map, but I was gratified to play a role helping them become the premier cable network.

*"Well excuuuuuuse me." Taped at the legendary Troubadour in Los Angeles on Halloween night, 1976, Steve Martin's HBO special boosted both his career and HBO's own reputation. Though he'd hosted **Saturday Night Live** one week before the special, Martin's uncut one-man show included neo-vaudeville moments supplied by mimes, banjo playing, crazy-legged dancing, jugglers, magicians, and even the arduous assembly of balloon animals.*

MICHAEL FUCHS:

Our Steve Martin show caused a fucking sensation across the country, and it helped his career. He ran his concert tour on our markets, and the crowd was standing up doing his show with him. From the beginning, I believed the keys to our success were quality control and, whenever possible, being controversial.

*Enter George Carlin, who had been hosting HBO's **On Location**, where he mainly introduced acts. But it was his own special, recorded in the summer of 1977 at the University of Southern California, that would bring HBO the attention it craved. Carlin* *did his now iconic "Seven Dirty Words" riff, which had evolved from pioneer shock comic Lenny Bruce's multiple arrests for profanity in the 1960s and would change television for, one might say, all time to come.*

Carlin's "dirty words" had first joined his repertoire in 1972, resulting in his arrest on obscenity charges. While radio stations had played excerpts from Carlin albums that featured the notorious list of words, his act had never aired uncut on TV. The propriety of airing the words would eventually reach the US Supreme Court, where a 1978 lawsuit brought by the FCC against radio station WBAI in New York would attempt to establish limits on how much the federal government could regulate TV and radio content. HBO, mainly on its own, had to fight the FCC for the right to air the segment on cable. Prior to the special, HBO displayed this message on screen:

"THE FINAL SEGMENT OF MR. CARLIN'S PERFORMANCE CONTAINS ESPE-CIALLY CONTROVERSIAL LANGUAGE. PLEASE CONSIDER WHETHER YOU WISH TO CONTINUE VIEWING."

MARTY CALLNER:

George did the seven words you couldn't say on television—shit, piss, fuck, cunt, cocksucker, motherfucker, and tits.

MICHAEL FUCHS:

Our scheduling guys made a little mistake and put it out on Good Friday, but what the hell. My feeling was you don't have to watch pay TV. Let the Supreme Court come after us. I wanted to show we had balls.

MARTY CALLNER:

That special turned out to be the best and worst day I had at HBO. Worst because we got a directive from Time Inc. that said we had to put a disclaimer up before that the language was going to be offensive, and we could mention the words only a certain number of times. Why could I use it ten times but not thirty times? It was censorship that I didn't bargain for. One of the things I had loved about HBO was that it was not censored. We fought it with everything we had but lost. But that night was also my best at HBO because we got to break down those walls.

IRIS DUGOW:

Every month Michael and I would fly to LA and go to Mitzi's Comedy Store to find talent for our young comedians show. Agents knew to get their clients onstage then. It was a big deal. We booked Robin Williams, Chevy Chase, and many others. We were moving fast.

MICHAEL FUCHS:

We had two shows a month and they were quite popular. One was *Standing Room Only*, which was girly shows from Paris. Trust me, no one else was going to Paris and shooting naked women. The other was *On Location*, featuring top comedians.

RICHARD LEWIS, Comedian and Actor:

HBO's young comic special was hosted by the Smothers Brothers from the Roxy. It was my first time on HBO, and I killed on it. I had already done some *Tonight Show*s with Johnny but being on that special was really important to me. HBO was the rocket booster for my career.

MIKE BINDER, Comedian and Actor:

I came from Detroit in '77 and was at the Comedy Store for probably ten years. Marty Callner and Michael Fuchs were the two guys who could make it happen for you, and I was lucky because those guys liked me. Mitzi loved Marty, and he retrofitted the main room of the Comedy Store with great lighting. I believe he shot seven, maybe eight specials for HBO with Seinfeld, Howie Mandel, Dice, Kinison, Jim Carrey, Jimmie Walker, everybody. I did a special there with Victor Borge as the host. It was me, Robert Wuhl, and Paul Reubens, who did his early version of Pee-wee Herman.

BILLY CRYSTAL, Comedian and Director:

HBO was my lifeblood. It was so important to me. It was always my home, a safe haven. Their belief in what I could do was tremendous, and it started at a time when I wasn't sure which way my career was going. After *Soap*, I had a series briefly at NBC, and a variety show that didn't get a chance to develop. Then this life raft appears in the ocean and it says "HBO" on it. I did a special for them in early '84, which led me to *SNL* and turned my career around.

Twenty-two-year-old Eddie Murphy, the youngest performing member of **Saturday Night Live,** *was ready to face the world on his own star-spangled night, August 17, 1983—performing his very first HBO stand-up concert at stately Constitution Hall, a mere two blocks from the White House.*

Murphy's seventy-minute special would be one of the transformative events in stand-up comedy. From the start, when he walked onstage in his wild-man red suit, the comic let it be known this would be unlike anything anyone had seen before. No, profanity wasn't new, but saying "fuck" 230 times; "shit" 171 times; and saying the word "faggot" at all (for which he issued an apology in 1996) was unheard of.

When the special was released as an album, **Eddie Murphy: Comedian,** *it won a Grammy. Eddie Murphy had helped save SNL when it was on the ropes, and now he'd helped give HBO a crucial boost as well.*

CHRIS ROCK, Comedian and Actor:

I watched all the HBO specials. Eddie Murphy's *Delirious* is the best. There were so many great HBO specials, but nothing, nothing, had the cultural impact of *Delirious.*

That was the gold standard. Eddie had such a command of the stage. It's not just a material thing. I mean it's funny as hell. A lot of it would be inappropriate today, but damn, it's good, man. I did one of my specials at Constitution Hall in a maroon suit as an homage to *Delirious.*

"My goodness, you look terrific!" Diana Ross told hundreds of adoring fans at Caesars Palace during her now-legendary 1980 HBO concert, **Standing Room Only: Diana Ross.** *Fresh from breaking away from the stern control of Motown, the show broke new ground for production and direction in music specials. During the concert, Ross approached Marvin Gaye, who was in the audience, and the two sang a harmony so sublime that it would be resurrected in memorial clips after Gaye was violently murdered less than five years later.*

MARTY CALLNER:

Diana Ross at Caesars Palace was the most important music show HBO ever did. Michael wanted to kill me because I went so far over budget, but I said, "Trust me, this is important." The engineer had said she can't wear white. The cameras can't handle it. I said, "I want everything white." I put her in white, the mic stand was in white, the mic cord's white, the floor's white, the set's white, the band in white, and I used contrast filters to give it a glow. That show announced that HBO was for real in the music world, and it sold in syndication for the most money of any television show at that time in history.

No sooner had Lorne Michaels, inventive executive producer of **Saturday Night Live,** *walked away (on May 24, 1980) from the show that he created than he came bouncing back to television, this time with* **The Concert in Central Park,** *a definitive piece of event TV that united Michaels's longtime friend Paul Simon with Simon's longtime collaborator Art Garfunkel. The result,* **Simon and Garfunkel: The Concert in**

Central Park, *marked another giant career step for the artful duo. For the Canadian-born Michaels, who had brought live TV back to the city where it started with* **SNL,** *it was the chance to be a New York hero once again.*

The duo took center stage amid rousing audience applause, then exchanged hand-shakes, and began the concert with the 1968 superhit "Mrs. Robinson," the virtual theme song for another zeitgeist blockbuster **The Graduate.** *Simon later said, "I didn't get what had happened, how big it was, until I went home, turned on the television, and saw it on all the news."*

LORNE MICHAELS, Executive Producer:

It was my first time working with HBO, and Michael Fuchs couldn't have been more supportive. There were discussions beforehand, but once we were doing it, they left us alone. And you remember that.

We were outside and had three different lighting conditions—late afternoon, twilight, and night. So Eugene [Lee] designed a New York rooftop with a water tower as a set. And then it was about getting enough different looks, because you're basically shooting two people and a crowd. But there was so much warmth in the crowd. Everybody was so excited that this was actually happening.

The stunning thing about that show was, despite there being between a half million and seven hundred thousand people in the park, there was nothing in any way disruptive.

IRIS DUGOW:

We did a great special with Stevie Nicks that we filmed on the last night of her solo tour, and then I wanted to do Lionel Richie. Michael told me, "Iris, this guy is going nowhere, he isn't big enough for HBO." I got such joy walking into Michael's office after Lionel hit so big and saying, "Is he big enough yet?"

Dick Cavett once said, "All I wanted to do was get famous and meet famous people. That's a pitiful goal." But scan even a partial list of guests who appeared on Cavett's legendary ABC talk show (1968–75) and you'll see why he's remembered by many as television's preeminent "intellectual" interviewer.

In 1979, with its eyes on an upscale demographic that commercial TV largely ignored, HBO hit upon a winning formula when it gave Cavett an apt new outlet: **Time Was,** *a seven-part documentary that proved as popular as it was bizarre, each episode detailing one decade of twentieth-century history.*

Time Was *combined the inventive use of green-screen video technology (which* *helped bring the decades alive) with the affection that serious TV fans still had for Cavett's smarts and quick-wittedness. The technology permitted Cavett to be realistically and almost seamlessly inserted into newsreel and documentary footage from the past so that he appeared to interact with such historical figures as Irving Berlin.*

One moment, Cavett was larking about New York of the 1920s in an antique Ford, and the next he was lounging shirtless on a beach in America of the 1960s—and at yet another juncture storming a wartime beach alongside five-star general Douglas MacArthur.

Cavett's show was the first time his close friend Woody Allen saw the capabilities of "green-screen." A few years later, Allen wrote and directed **Zelig**, *a "mockumentary" entirely built around the technology.*

DICK CAVETT, Host:

I couldn't imagine how this technology was going to work. You feel kind of silly taking steps into one pail of water after another and hoping to make it splash. They used that camera technique to capture my wading ashore with MacArthur. It was done so brilliantly. When I watched it, I was convinced I was in that picture. People loved those shows. It was the happiest thing I've done outside of my own show, and we were able to do follow-ups.

In 1977, a US court of appeals overturned the FCC regulation colloquially known as the "three-to-ten-year rule," which banned pay-TV screenings of any film within three to ten years of its original release.

Since its birth, HBO had been constrained to showing films within a narrow window of their release. A further appeal would be brought to the Supreme Court, but on October 3, 1977, the decision was upheld. The FCC could no longer restrict access to certain films. It became known as the Home Box Office decision.

NICK NICHOLAS:

If that law hadn't been struck down, it would have been a problem. The movies on average would have been older, post-theatrical releases. The decision made our inventory more current for subscribers.

In 1976, when I arrived, HBO lost $6 million. I was told, "You have less than twelve months to turn this around." In August of '77, we had our first profitable month. And they never stopped after that. In 1978, we made about $40 million in profits.

For the first six years of its life, from 1972 to 1978, the cumulative loss of HBO was $14 million, before it finally broke even.

NICK NICHOLAS:

Looking back, it almost looks magical, but it didn't feel that way at the time. It was nonstop. We were attentive about everything. We started putting more and more emphasis on making our partners happy. They stopped yelling and screaming at us. Austin was improving the presentation of the product. On-air promotion got better. We did a zillion little improvements. And our content had vastly improved.

STEVE SCHEFFER, Executive:

I started in 1977 at Time-Life Films and moved over to HBO in 1980. Early on, uncut, unedited theatrical movies were why people were coming to HBO, and they made up the bulk of our marketing efforts.

The studios were licensing the same movies to all of the pay-TV services at the same time. This meant that every home with HBO, Showtime, or any other pay-TV service had to compete for viewers, and since all of the services would schedule new hit titles at the beginning of the month, by the middle of the month some customers would say, "There's nothing to watch." This reached a peak when several services unwittingly played *Heaven Can Wait* at the same time.

DAVE BALDWIN, Executive:

We were inventing research for premium television. We weren't big enough yet to be getting Nielsen's. We couldn't afford it anyway. So, we sent out a monthly survey to about twenty-five hundred of our subscribers, and they would tell us what they watched and how much they liked it on a four-point scale. Excellent, good, fair, poor. From that, we created "total subscriber satisfaction." I manipulated numbers and got really good at lies and statistics. I could prove anything. But the bosses said they didn't want that. "Just tell us the truth, Dave."

There was one movie early on that we couldn't play enough, *Two Mules for Sister Sara* with Clint Eastwood, because it attracted male and female viewers. That was when lightbulbs went off that some movies were different than others.

As the company grew, so did its need for additional management. In 1978, Fuchs hired Frank Biondi away from the Children's Television Workshop. Fuchs told Furst and Nicholas, "Frank knows cable, we need that." Biondi's title, head of co-productions, was a made-up one designed simply to get Biondi through the door as quickly as possible

NICK NICHOLAS:

Michael brought Frank in. They were good friends. Michael had introduced Frank to his wife, Carol, and was godfather to at least one of the daughters by then.

MICHAEL FUCHS:

I was a little rough around the edges. I wasn't the corporate type, and I wasn't married, which some people felt was a sign of immaturity. Frank had worked on Wall Street. He knew the business world.

JIM HEYWORTH:

In a test market in Orlando, we launched alongside HBO a new channel called Take 2. It was intended to address consumer complaints that HBO was too expensive and had too much "adult" programming. We called Take 2 a "mini-pay" channel. Fewer movies, lower price, no R-rated movies. The problem was it didn't work. Almost all the households of Take 2 were also HBO subscribers. The subscribers who complained about pay TV just didn't want pay TV. So much for market research.

Despite the failure of Take 2, HBO was determined to get its next channel launch, Cinemax, right. Cinemax wasn't trying to attract a cheaper version of the HBO fan. Instead, the channel was positioned as a service for an additional set of movie lovers not already served by HBO. And that's all Cinemax was in the beginning: movies, movies, movies—unbroken by ads. Cinemax's raison d'être was to take aim at the then popular Movie Channel. Cinemax would distinguish itself from HBO in one other important way—at least in the short term: in January 1981, Cinemax became a twenty-four-hour service, a landmark that HBO itself wouldn't hit for more than a year.

MATT BLANK:

Cinemax was designed to be a "flanker brand" and push Showtime to third position in the home. That would mean they would have fewer subscribers, have less money to invest in programming, and be less of a competitive threat. It was an absolutely brilliant strategy that benefited HBO for more than a decade.

DAVE BALDWIN:

When we launched Cinemax, we had the wrongheaded notion that it shouldn't duplicate anything on HBO. So, HBO had all the good stuff, leaving

Cinemax with all the crap. But I had a genius working for me in research, Tim Daly, and he figured out a new way for us to optimize our movie plays.

We called it multi bursting. It greatly expanded the number of movie titles available each month, playing our entire inventory three or four times per window so new subscribers could enjoy movies we'd had and preexisting subscribers could see the new titles. That changed everything. Once we saw that it worked for Cinemax, we began bursting titles back and forth between HBO and Cinemax.

HBO didn't have deep pockets for sports rights like the broadcast networks, and leagues were fearful about taking their product behind a paywall. But Fuchs, a big sports fan, was convinced there were plenty of opportunities, nevertheless. His first step was to build his own broadcast Sports team.

ROSS GREENBURG, Executive:

When I first got to HBO in February 1978, there were only two people in the sports department, me and Tim Braine. They didn't have an office for me, so they said, "Just use that one." I went in there every day, and this guy in the next office keeps saying hi to me. We'd chat a little bit coming and going, and after a month or so, I found out it was Jerry Levin. I was a production assistant, and this guy was running the place. That's how small HBO was. He couldn't have been nicer. Love that guy.

SETH ABRAHAM, Executive:

I wanted to be a professional baseball player and was very good but had two professional tryouts and did really badly. So I got an undergraduate and master's degree in journalism, worked for the *New York Times* in Boston, then for the commissioner of baseball with a guy named David Meister. David got hired by Michael Fuchs to build the sports department, contacted me to come over, but I turned him down.

David called back and said, "I get it, you don't want to leave baseball, but would you just meet my boss?" So I agreed to go to the HBO offices on the fifteenth floor of the Time-Life Building. I walk into Michael's office, shake hands with him, haven't sat down yet, and he says, "I don't understand why the fuck you want to waste my time." And I said, "Excuse me." He said, "You must be a schmuck. There are a hundred and fifty guys who want this job. If you're not interested, I'm not interested in you." I'm standing at his desk. This is the first twenty seconds. So I said, "Michael, I don't want to waste your time," and walked out.

About eight thirty, this is a Friday night, David calls and says, "Michael loved you." I said, "David, if Michael loved me, you're working in a looney bin." He says, "Michael wants you to fly in the Time Inc. helicopter out to East Hampton tomorrow and have lunch with him." I said, "David, you're crazy." He calls me back at eleven o'clock. "Seth, Michael won't take no for an answer." The next morning, my wife and I flew out to East Hampton, took a cab, and went to Michael's house that he was renting. It was bizarre. He started up again being very aggressive about "I'm obviously not smart enough to work at HBO if I'm being so difficult." Then he calmed down, and we started talking. I knew nothing about HBO, didn't have HBO, but told him what sports I watch. He was a rabid Yankee fan, and I was born around the corner from Ebbets Field in Brooklyn. For the next two hours we were two fans talking about baseball. HBO made me an offer on Monday.

ROSS GREENBURG:

I had worked briefly at ABC Sports, and Roone Arledge was, for me, the most impressive sports leader of my lifetime, and because of him, from the beginning, I wanted HBO Sports to have the best production team and do the best storytelling. Wimbledon and boxing were our foundations.

SETH ABRAHAM:

In 1979 I read in the *New York Post* that Don King was at loggerheads with ABC Sports over a Larry Holmes/Mike Weaver World Heavyweight title fight at Madison Square Garden. I called up Don, introduced myself, and told him, "Maybe HBO can give you an alternative?" He said, "Would you put it on in prime time?" I said, "Yes, prime time and live." He said, "ABC is refusing to put it in prime time. They want to put it on Saturday at three o'clock because they don't think much of Mike Weaver, which gives me the opportunity to shop it to somebody else. How much are you talking about?" I went on this whole spiel that HBO is going to break the bank, people are going to have to eat peanut butter and jelly, and he says, "Get to the point." I said, "More than we ever paid—$125,000." Don starts laughing and says, "ABC is offering me seven hundred fifty thousand for the afternoon." I said, "Don, I'm serious. A hundred and twenty-five is all I've got and more than we've ever paid for a prizefight. We'll put it on live prime time." He says, "Go back and find me some more money."

I went to Michael who was willing to give me more money, but I said, "If we give Don more now, it will make future negotiations very difficult." Michael said, "It's your decision." I called Don up and said, "My piggy bank has only a hundred and twenty-five." He's laughing and says, "You've got a deal." Don didn't want to put the heavyweight champion of the world on in the afternoon. So HBO puts the fight on live from Madison Square Garden, and for the first time in his career Larry Holmes gets knocked down. He came back, knocked out Weaver in the twelfth, and the next day in the *New York Times*, the great Red Smith wrote a column on "The Big One That Got Away" about ABC losing the fight to us. I can almost repeat it like the Gettysburg Address, and because it was Red Smith, a lot of media executives reading it in New Canaan or Greenwich said, "Wow, maybe they really have something there."

BOB ARUM:

I got a call from Seth Abraham, who told me Michael Fuchs had authorized him to buy three Marvin Hagler fights, all of which would take place in prime time, with a rights fee approximately two and a half to three times what I was getting from the network for an afternoon fight. I signed the deal, and everything exploded. HBO was doing a great job getting movies after they had played in theaters, but when they started showing Hagler fights, the number of subscribers increased beyond their wildest dreams, particularly in New England.

SETH ABRAHAM:

Bob Arum understood what HBO could be for his business, and we understood that promoters would make more money if their fights were at night. People had things to do during weekend daytime, but at night, they were looking to be entertained. HBO offered him prime time for all his big fighters, and that completely changed his business model because now he could go into arenas at night with higher attendance and higher ticket prices. He began migrating his stars off ABC, and other promoters quickly saw that and followed suit.

In the tradition of "Rumble in the Jungle" and "Thrilla in Manila," HBO continued to grow subscribers by showing marquee boxing. In 1981, HBO aired one of the greatest-ever fights in the history of boxing: "The Showdown," Thomas Hearns versus Ray Leonard, Hit Man versus Sugar Ray, September 16, 1981, Caesars Palace.

HBO had bought the re-air rights for three quarters of a million dollars, beating out all other networks who'd submitted bids.

ROSS GREENBURG:

Michael Fuchs walked into the truck the night of the fight, folded his arms, and said, "Gentlemen, we have arrived." I'm getting chills right now because that was the night we all realized holy shit, we had ascended to the number one position. Even ABC had the delay after us.

LARRY MERCHANT:

If you're asking me about the biggest events in HBO Boxing history, it's a long list, but in my mind, certainly one of the first big ones was Leonard/ Hearns. Ray Leonard was a huge star, and the fight itself was phenomenal.

ROSS GREENBURG:

During that fight, we pioneered having mics in the corner live between rounds. Remember, we didn't have commercials; we didn't have to break away like the networks. We stayed with the story, and we wound up with the first historic miked moment in boxing history. Angelo Dundee said to Ray Leonard before the thirteenth round with Hearns, "You're blowing it son, you're blowing it. You gotta be quicker. You've got to take it away from him. Speed!" And as Dundee was saying those words, our director Marc Payton zoomed into Ray's left eye from a corner camera, and you could see how swollen it was. Ray went out, floored Hearns in the thirteenth, and TKO'd him in the fourteenth.

BARRY TOMPKINS, Sportscaster:

The best fight I've ever done was Pryor versus Argüello in Miami in '82. There was a civil war in Nicaragua and Argüello had given a whole bunch of money to, I believe it was the Contras, and South Florida was largely Hispanic. Pryor himself wasn't a bad guy, but the people around him were not exactly folks you would want to have over for Thanksgiving. There were all kinds of threats going back and forth to the point where they decided it was too dangerous to play the national anthem of either country.

The Orange Bowl was pretty much sold out. There must have been forty-five thousand or fifty thousand people. Then they turned off all the lights in the stadium, except for the lights on me and Larry Merchant. I was saying to myself, I hope no one thinks I'm a Sandinista supporter, because I'm an easy target.

ROSS GREENBURG:

Pryor's trainer, Panama Lewis, is trying to keep him superhumanly active in the fight. We go back to the corner early in the fight when Pryor returns to the stool and one of the seconds hands Panama a bottle to give to Pryor and Panama says, "Give me the other bottle. The one that I mixed." For the rest of the fight whenever Pryor returned to his corner there was that bottle, and there was Panama Lewis getting Pryor to chug it.

BARRY TOMPKINS:

It was one of the greatest fights maybe ever, a once-in-a-lifetime event. Ross Greenburg boosted the audio in the corner so the audience got to hear what turned into a huge controversy at the time about what was in that bottle. It was a turning point for HBO Boxing.

ROSS GREENBURG:

Those sound bites changed our coverage of boxing forever.

LINDA JACKSON, Executive:

I traveled to Panama to shoot a feature on Roberto Duran as he trained to go up against Wilfred Benitez. It was not too long after the "No Mas" fight. He'd isolated himself on a nearly deserted island off Panama so as not to be tempted by food, drink, women, or any other distractions that might take away his focus on training. The island is called Coiba and the only inhabitants on this island surrounded by shark-infested waters were convicted rapists and murderers—the worst felons in all of Panama. We took off from Panama City headed for Coiba on the tiniest of army planes—basically a van with wings—flown by members of the military. We arrived and went to work shooting surroundings and getting ready for interviews. All of the inmates roamed freely about—there were no bars or fences anywhere because there was no escape for these guys; they were surrounded by sharks. It was a bit of a stir for them to see a woman walking around. My colleague Tim told me that several guys asked if they could kiss me since they hadn't seen a woman in years. His response? "I don't know, you can ask her." Thanks, Tim!

After a long day of shooting, we boarded our "van" to leave. After takeoff, I dozed off and when I opened my eyes, we were flying through a storm and this tiny plane didn't have the instruments to travel through it and there was zero visibility. Back to Coiba. We had no choice but to bunk there for the night. I had to notify our office in New York as to our unexpected detour. Somewhere there is a picture of two inmates holding together phone cable while I spoke through an army field phone. I think it was the first and perhaps only international phone call made from that island. We dined on prison food and Roberto Duran graciously gave up his bed for me, and that's how I found myself sleeping in the bed belonging to the Hands of Stone.

MICHAEL FUCHS:

I loved boxing, but there was nothing better than Wimbledon, even though NBC still really controlled it. We were picking up a BBC feed and satelliting it back to America. We didn't have our own newscasters at the beginning, but the fact that we were televising it, and people were able to see weekday matches they couldn't see on NBC, was a big deal for us. And there were great players like Borg, Connors, McEnroe, Chris Evert, and Martina.

JOHN McENROE, Sportscaster:

I was lucky to be a professional athlete, but early in my career I noticed that once the cat's out of the bag, man, you're screwed. If you see a three-hour match and then they replay this thirty-second or minute clip over and over of me yelling, "You cannot be serious!" it definitely can give people the wrong idea. I didn't think, "Oh my God, how could HBO do that," but it did exacerbate what was already a bad situation. It was bizarre and surreal, and exploded to the point where I thought, "If I can just get out of here alive, I'll be happy to never come back." That was the worst thing, after that moment I wasn't enjoying the experience of playing at Wimbledon.

I certainly didn't think forty years later people would come up to me and encourage me to say, "You cannot be serious!" or that I would use that as a title of my book. During my fifteen-year career, I said it that one time, but over twenty years playing on the champions tour, if I didn't say it at least once a match they'd be disappointed. I suppose at the end of the day it's better to be remembered for something than not be remembered at all.

HBO was about to enter a new era of intense competition. When it went on the satellite, some of its smaller competitors couldn't compete with HBO's sports, special events, and ease-of-offering pay TV. But some big players decided they still wanted in.

JIM HEYWORTH:

One day I received a call from Bob Wright—later vice-chairman of GE who was running Cox Cable at the time. He called to tell me that Cox, Times Mirror, TCI, and a couple other cable providers had agreed to form and fund a pay-TV network they were calling "Spotlight." They would be replacing HBO with Spotlight in some of their systems and launching Spotlight alongside HBO in others. This was a serious threat. We were able to solve the problem by introducing a "volume discount" in our financial deal with cable companies. TCI was our biggest affiliate; they got the best discount. Getting a much better HBO deal, TCI's John Malone chose to abandon the Spotlight venture, and without TCI it fell apart.

The studios had been painfully slow to understand the power HBO had amassed, until Austin Furst began his ingenious and devilish Odd Man Out game of musical chairs, and friendly negotiations became outright wars. Fox tried to retaliate in 1979 when it sold rights to the engaging coming-of-age comedy **Breaking Away** *to NBC without carving out a pay-TV window. HBO retaliated by refusing to execute any deals for a Fox movie over the next twelve months.*

The studios began to realize HBO was making a significant amount of revenue with the studios' product. And because HBO could negotiate with each of the six major studios individually, it could play them off one another.

So the majors began talking with one another to figure things out. How do we stop or slow down HBO?

First, they went to Showtime and said, essentially, "We want to control this market and fight against HBO. We're going to work out an exclusive deal with you." But Showtime, fearing antitrust backlash, said, "Thanks but no thanks."

Then the studios teamed up with a guy named Stuart Evey, a key executive with Getty Oil who, thanks to his close relationship with John Paul Getty's son, had enormous control over Getty's non-oil money, of which there was plenty. Evey happened to be coming off a major investment in ESPN that would enable that spunky new cable sports start-up to survive. Soon, with Evey's backing, the four leading movie companies—Paramount, Twentieth Century Fox, Columbia, and Universal—came together to form a new cable network and called it Premiere.

HBO and Showtime quickly provided lengthy memos to the Department of Justice claiming Premiere was an abomination and violated antitrust laws. They filed a preliminary injunction to stop the launch just before Premiere was about to lift off.

The case would be the most critical legal decision in the history of HBO.

MICHAEL FUCHS:

Premiere was a big scare for us. The studios tried to put us out of business. We went to the government to stop them. Columbia had a very attractive female lawyer, who I was very friendly with, and we decided to go to the newly opened Mauna Kea on the Big Island. The whole industry was watching for one of us to steal documents from the other. That was hardly what we had in mind.

NICK NICHOLAS:

If we had been forced to compete against a clone of HBO, with the movie companies giving themselves favorable deals, we would have been up shit's creek. To have people who have better than 50 percent market share get together to control pricing and availability was outrageous. I was very concerned. Winning this case was crucial.

On December 31, 1980, the US District Court for the Southern District of New York handed down a decision regarding Premiere that would be crucial to the continued existence of HBO and all other pay-TV networks.

The court held that "the implementation of the Premiere venture has a high potential for the ultimate raising of prices . . . for use of their motion pictures" and was "also likely to have the indirect effect of driving up the prices for those major motion pictures not controlled by the defendants. These higher prices will be passed on to the consumers." Premiere was D.O.A. HBO and Showtime, as well as The Movie Channel, had dodged a cannonball.

MICHAEL FUCHS:

Gene Jankowski at CBS approached me about running Ovation, their new cultural channel, and as I was leaving the CBS building, going down Sixth Avenue, the idea of a CBS/Time news channel popped into my head. Cable was desperate for programming, and why shouldn't Time want a piece of this new business? CBS was considered the finest electronic news organization and Time was considered the finest print company. The industry would have an orgasm if those two brands got together.

I brought it right to Frank. He and I were a great team. He liked it. We called a friend who had been a designer at CBS, Tony Lover, and he did a great logo. Then we brought it to Nick, Jerry, and Austin. They turned it down in five seconds.

*Columbia Pictures went to HBO directly at the end of 1981 and hammered out an exclusive deal to offer HBO its movies in exchange for some funding on the front end, with the licensing fees tied to Columbia films' box-office performance. The deal was creative and original, right up HBO's wheelhouse. Frank Biondi was a major advocate of the deal, and under his advice and the advice of his boss, Jerry Levin, HBO gladly accepted. And yet HBO had neglected to insist on a cap on the licensing fees. (This would come to haunt HBO when the movie **Ghostbusters** became a jolly juggernaut in 1984.)*

JON DOLGEN, Executive, Columbia Pictures:

I have an old view of negotiations and I still believe it. If I can get you to sit down and talk to me, we will make a deal.

I don't think I'm the smartest guy in the world, but I don't think I'm a dope either. HBO had all these MBA types in New York who dealt with us on the studio side as if we were a bunch of yahoos. We did very well in those types of circumstances.

In 1983, CBS joined HBO and Columbia to create TriStar (known initially as Nova), a new and potentially major film studio.

Still, HBO remained, to a large degree, dependent on which movies it could acquire, or lock down exclusively, from the major studios. With that in mind, in June 1983, HBO tried to add to its exclusive offerings by developing its own production company. Naturally, any movie HBO developed for movie theaters would, once released to TV, be unavailable to its main competitors, Showtime and The Movie Channel.

The initial response was spectacular: Silver Screen Partners raised $83 million via thirteen thousand investors by the fall of 1985. Trouble was, the seven HBO movies financed by the first iteration of Silver Screen Partners were all pretty terrible, making Silver Screen a place of last refuge for unproduced scripts. The challenge proved too much for HBO, and it pulled out. Later iterations of Silver Screen Partners—there were three—raised significant funds and were hugely successful for Disney.

STEVE SCHEFFER:

In the wake of the Justice Department's decision regarding Premiere, HBO and Columbia concluded the first major studio "output deal." Up to that point, the studios would license their movies from the previous year (a slate deal) or individual titles in a horse trade with HBO holding most of the cards (the money). The strong titles would sometimes be cherry-picked and the weaker titles would be rejected or heavily discounted. Because of the great disparity in the size of the pay-TV services, there wasn't much of an alternative for a studio. The output deal provided for all of the year's releases to be licensed at a price mostly based on a formula relating to box-office performance.

In what was likely a negotiating ploy, in 1982 there was speculation that Columbia, Fox, and ABC were planning to buy Showtime. Whether a ploy or not, the possibility was enough to cause Jerry Levin to convince Fay Vincent, chairman of Columbia, to form a venture with HBO and CBS that included the creation of TriStar Pictures. As part of the agreement, HBO concluded the first major studio exclusive output deals with both Columbia and TriStar.

JERRY LEVIN:

Columbia became one of HBO's best partners.

Unfortunately, as with Silver Screen Partners, the movies TriStar green-lit mostly didn't work, and within two years CBS had sold its shares in the start-up to Columbia, and Time had sold half its interest to Columbia, too.

Meanwhile, HBO took another big step into the world of original series in 1983.

BRIDGET POTTER, Executive:

I had worked on the Dick Cavett and Mike Douglas shows, and then developed *Three's Company* at ABC. In 1982, I was hired at HBO to be the vice president of Original Programming, reporting directly to Michael. In my last conversation with him before I was offered the job, I had this dilemma, because I really wanted the job, but I was pregnant. Even though it wasn't visible, I didn't want to start off without coming clean. I had a daughter who was a little over two years old, and even though I was not a single parent at the time, the nature of my marriage was not so liberated.

So Michael hired me pregnant for a very important job. Is he a sexist on that metric? No. My problem would become less about being pregnant, and more that I wasn't a tennis player and not part of the boys' club.

At that point HBO was small. I had one person on the West Coast and three people in New York. There was a production wing, too, because comedy specials were produced in-house.

I had some very, very rough times. Once I had a problem with my childcare person who I relied on so deeply. She went back to Jamaica, and they didn't let her back in the country. So I didn't have my childcare and had to patch coverage together. It was tough. Before I left on vacation, Michael said to me, "I don't know what's going on with your life, but you've got to get it together. If you can't, this is not going to work out." I took the vacation and got it together.

In succession, new programming for 1983 included the premieres of **Not Necessarily the News**, *a new topical sketch show; Jim Henson's* **Fraggle Rock**, *an irreverent kids' series from the creator of* **The Muppets**; *and a horror anthology,* **The Hitchhiker**, *which would debut in November.*

Not Necessarily the News *was based on BBC2's* **Not the Nine O'Clock News**. *The show, which employed comic neologisms called sniglets and used doctored videotape to create comic juxtapositions, ran first as a special on HBO in September 1982, and then premiered as a series on January 3, 1983.*

PAT TOURK LEE, Executive Producer:

John Moffitt was in London and saw *Not the Nine O'Clock News*, and we agreed he should buy the rights. When we pitched it to Michael, we said we were going to make it more political, which Michael loved.

Michael never said, "We have to be fair. We have to do both sides." Every time we nailed Reagan, he was thrilled. The only problem was they never scheduled the show regularly. We'd have one slot, then it would be somewhere else. I would invariably run into people and they'd say, "Oh, I love that show, but I can never find it."

STUART PANKIN, Actor:

I was working on a show called *No Soap Radio* and ran into Ron Richards who used to be one of our writers. He said, "I'm doing a show called *Not Necessarily the News*. Do you want to do it?" I said, "Sure, what is it?" He said, "Cable." I said, "What's cable?"

It started out rough. Our first dressing room was in the bathroom of the men's room at a Shell station. I actually used to buy gas from there so we could keep using their bathroom. The girls would have to open their car doors and dress behind them. Nancy Severinsen, Doc Severinsen's daughter, was our location manager, and sometimes she got permits, and sometimes she didn't. We would have to sneak in like guerrilla theater, shoot what we needed, and then get out before somebody would come and stop us.

There's probably not a sketch you could mention that I wouldn't have a positive feeling for. Gandhi loves Tootsie, Nadia Comaneci, which, as an older out of shape person, was one of my favorite sketches. I played Don King, Mr. T, and Alfred Hitchcock. Slowly but surely, the show picked up momentum and became very popular.

Fraggles, Doozers, Gorgs, and Silly Creatures: these were the inhabitants of a world that would become a benchmark for children's TV, the much-beloved and still much-missed **Fraggle Rock.**

The series debuted in 1983 to almost universal acclaim, so HBO found itself in the children's TV business, at least for then. A Jim Henson creation, **Fraggle Rock** *used the best parts of the Muppets concept—silliness, music, and overt kindness.*

MICHAEL FUCHS:

Bernie Brillstein, a good friend of mine and Jim Henson's long-standing manager, brought Jim in to see me with three pages of *Fraggle Rock*. After fifteen minutes, I bought thirty-six episodes. The next day I thought, Shit, you don't even have children, maybe something like this is already on. So, I gave it to Frank Biondi, saying, "Take it to the girls (his two daughters, the younger, Janie, being my goddaughter). Let me know if they like it." And they did. It's amazing how many grown-ups still refer to *Fraggle Rock*.

Fraggle Rock's place in HBO's programming slate was a topic of debate among the programmers—who finally settled on the thought that parents will want their kids to watch the show when they didn't have a babysitter.

In 1983, HBO also went after horror-loving viewers with **The Hitchhiker,** *an anthology series co-produced with French and Canadian interests. Running for four seasons on HBO, each show saw the mysterious "hitchhiker" introduce various accounts of mystery, the paranormal, and the eminently horrible.*

BRIDGET POTTER:

Our joke about it was, "It's called 'Fuck a stranger, and die.'" It was embarrassing, absurd, just an excuse for sexual material, but Michael really liked it. Lewis Chesler, the creator, did get some interesting people to write episodes once in a while.

GEORGE R. R. MARTIN, Writer and Executive Producer:

My first material on HBO was not *Game of Thrones*—they adapted one of my short stories for *The Hitchhiker*. It was a story called "Remembering Melody." That was a kick. I wrote a lot of short stories and early novels; I've had a lot of movie and film options over the years. Most of them pay you a little money, nothing happens, and you get it back every few years. I always had warm feelings toward HBO for making my *Hitchhiker* episode.

By 1983, Biondi, the man who Sherry Lansing had described as "always calm . . . he handled everything with such dignity [and] proved that nice guys can finish first," did indeed come first: Biondi was elevated to the position of HBO's CEO in February 1983, leapfrogging over his boss, Michael Fuchs, who had brought him into his company.

MICHAEL FUCHS:

There was a point when Jerry Levin was video group head, Jim Heyworth was CEO reporting to him, and Frank, Tony Cox, and I were underneath him. Then Frank and I met with Levin and he said to us, "Jim is going to be leaving. Let's meet on Monday and talk about a new arrangement."

When I got to the office on Monday, Jerry had already decided on Frank as CEO, which was a little awkward for me. It was clear Jerry had told Frank over the weekend without telling me. I wasn't surprised that Frank was given the job. It was Time Inc. He was more of a corporate type. So I said to myself, As long as you have programming, you should be fine. I didn't go out and get drunk, probably because I didn't drink.

NICK NICHOLAS:

Frank was a much broader-experienced executive than Michael was, and Michael hadn't actually run a business with a P&L. Frank had.

Concurrent with Biondi's announcement, Fuchs was named president of HBO Entertainment Group.

MICHAEL FUCHS:

When I got promoted to president of the entertainment group, it wasn't a surprise to anyone. I had become a very good executive. I was told by different corporate people that I had a terrific management approach, a word I hardly knew when I started. But it didn't take long for me to feel less cavalier about not having the CEO job. Whether I was the traditional fit or not, I knew what to do with HBO.

Then Frank and Nick weren't getting along. They were both financial guys and competitive, speaking a language I hardly knew. Someone asked me about their arguing, and I said, "I don't know what they're talking about, but it's not good for Frank."

NICK NICHOLAS:

Frank and Michael had this deadly rivalry. Remember, Michael brought Frank to HBO, and they had had a close relationship. But they were so competitive with each other. There was a lot of gotcha stuff going on. I didn't live at HBO at the time, I had been promoted to this higher-up position, so I lived on the thirty-fourth floor at Time Inc. I didn't see the day-to-day stuff, but we all knew there were huge amounts of tension inside the company.

The summer of 1983 proved to be a whopper for HBO. On Sunday, June 12, the cover of the **New York Times Magazine,** *one of the most visible and influential publications, carried the headline, "Home Box Office Moves into Hollywood," with the initials HBO replacing the Hollywood sign.*

The article, written by Los Angeles bureau chief Robert Lindsey, detailed HBO's emergence as a filmmaking power player.

In the article, Lindsey outlined the factors behind HBO's rise, and suggested moguls were not pleased with HBO and the company's increasing power. Gulf and Western's Barry Diller was quoted saying, "At issue was the influx of money HBO had thrown at the movie industry." It was true. Due to what Biondi referred to as an "annuity" (that monthly fee subscribers paid whether HBO proffered gems or bombs), HBO was indeed throwing more and more money into the fires of Hollywood.

According to the piece, HBO had disturbed studio dominance. "Plainly stated," Lindsey wrote, "Hollywood simply did not recognize the importance of a fundamental shift in the way many Americans are going to the movies nowadays—in their homes instead of a theater. Now that Hollywood has awakened with a start, it may be too late."

At the quiet center sat HBO's Steve Scheffer. Scheffer, who attracted "neither glances of recognition nor the kind of fawning that men of power customarily attract at Hollywood parties," had long flown under the radar. Lindsey noted that at one such post-Oscar bash, Scheffer sat all but unnoticed, though Lindsey conceded that "Scheffer was in many ways more powerful than any mogul in the room."

Up until this point, a **Times** story on the "Thrilla in Manila" had been the company's biggest coup. Neither HBO nor its big brass was flying under the radar anymore.

STEVE SCHEFFER:

HBO was the first opportunity viewers had to see a movie in their home. In the early 1980s, approximately 80 percent of HBO's programming was theatrical movies.

When we negotiated with the studios, we'd look at all of the studios' line-ups for the year and we'd look at when each movie was going to be made available. The strongest titles would determine which studios we wanted to negotiate with first. One problem for them was that if they had a huge hit, they'd expect a lot of money for it, and we'd say, it did a lot at the box office, but it's the wrong demographics for us. So it was a very tough negotiation for them. In the early 1980s, the movie studios were hurting. The HBO money was very important to them. It went straight to the bottom line. It didn't cost them anything, they didn't have to advertise, all they had to do was give us access to the duplicating materials. It was money from heaven. That dynamic started the hostility between the studios and HBO. They had become dependent on the money but HBO had so much leverage.

By the early 1980s HBO had become an important part of independent movie financing with an aggressive strategy of "pre-buying" exclusive pay-TV rights from independent producers. Producers were similarly able to license broadcast network rights, TV syndication rights, and later home video rights, which added to subsidies, tax shelters, etc., that enabled them to finance their movies. Titles like *The Terminator* and *Rambo* were owned exclusively by HBO and provided fresh programming for HBO later in the month. In 1981, HBO had pre-bought most of Universal's summer releases, including *On Golden Pond*, which would have been Universal's leading titles in negotiating with HBO. Universal and other studios soon refused to distribute independently produced movies to theaters if they didn't also have the pay-TV rights.

MICHAEL FUCHS:

Pre-buys were our answer to not getting every studio movie shoved down our throats and having to settle for subpar titles regarded as clunkers incapable of generating significant viewership. Now, pre-buys were overrated. They weren't blockbusters. If you wanted *Jaws*, you had to take crap with it. Pre-buying did, however, make the studios crazy. It was ego. This is our territory!

BRIDGET POTTER:

Michael's concept of a good deal was one where everybody other than him felt like they had been fucked. He would say that—"We fucked 'em, we fucked 'em!" HBO had a horrible reputation in California.

HENRY McGEE, Executive:

That *New York Times* cover story, in which the paper of record put Hollywood on notice that this company from New York was about to change everything they knew about television and the movie business in Hollywood, was catalytic. Certainly it gave new weight to HBO. It was a big motivator within the company, giving dimension and life to our ambitions.

An **Esquire** *article several months later was more singular, branding Michael Fuchs as "The Man Who Ate Hollywood" and describing him as "accountable to no man," "cable's first mogul," "notable for his cockiness," and "the most potent, feared, and hated man in Hollywood."*

Fuchs could afford to shrug off those opinions. By 1982, HBO's revenues had soared to $440 million, $100 million of which was profit—a cool ten times more than any other pay-cable option, including Showtime. **Esquire** *noted that HBO had become "the single most powerful entity in the entertainment business," given that its money could be the difference between a movie getting made or not.*

And the power came down to Fuchs's notoriously confrontational relationships with the studios. **Esquire** *recounted the legend that Fuchs—in an act of "brinkmanship," and because he was pissed off at Fox for a botched previous deal to buy* **Breaking Away,** *a big hit in 1979—delayed buying the rights to Fox's* **Star Wars** *in 1982* *until the last possible moment (he'd even originally passed). The article also recounted the tale of a Frank Sinatra special that Fuchs desperately wanted and placed a $1 million bid on. Fuchs was reportedly off on vacation when Paramount accepted an offer from a consortium offering 50 percent more. Afterward, Fuchs refused to buy another piece of original programming from Paramount.*

MICHAEL FUCHS:

"The Man Who Ate Hollywood"? Everyone likes to make up fucking titles like that. We weren't going to eat Hollywood. I was in a summerhouse with a bunch of close friends, and everyone read it and made a lot of fun of me.

JEFF BEWKES, Executive:

Michael created all the genres of HBO Original Programming. Early on, he was the one with relationships. He started with comedy specials, with big name comics coming through HBO, then music with equally big names. Michael was personally involved in figuring out what to do and how to shape it all.

JERRY LEVIN:

Executive Producer Michael Fuchs. It's a metaphor for Michael that he put his credentials on programs. Does that make you happy? Does that give you more a sense of self? Okay. As long as you're taking HBO to new levels at the same time.

MICHAEL FUCHS:

I don't think that Jerry enjoyed the press I was getting.

*When the Columbia Pictures film **Ghostbusters** became a huge national sensation in 1984, HBO discovered that they had some lessons to learn on the hard road toward maturity. Its 1981 licensing deal with Columbia Pictures had brought in a box-office hit, but because HBO had neglected to put a cap on those fees, a breakaway hit meant a financial disaster for HBO.*

STEVE SCHEFFER:

The deal failed to provide a cap on the license fee of an individual movie, which led to the infamous payment of some $40 million for *Ghostbusters*. While this didn't sink the ship, the lesson learned was that the value to HBO of any one movie was finite. Thereafter, license fees were capped.

NICK NICHOLAS:

It was an outrageously favorable deal for Columbia. But you can't blame them. Jon Dolgen, Victor Kaufman, and Fay Vincent made an excellent deal for their studio, and it was done with Frank and Jerry's approval. When we at Time Inc. understood how serious an economic problem it was for HBO, that was the end of Levin for Munro. But once more, he didn't fire him. He moved Levin to another job and asked me to take over for him. Again. I became vice president for video.

JERRY LEVIN:

Fuchs was railing about what a lousy deal it had been, but it turned out to be not that bad at all.

NICK NICHOLAS:

Fay Vincent said at the time, if I remember it correctly, "Columbia now has a direct hookup to the Time Inc. treasury."

JON DOLGEN:

In what was an extremely long negotiation, we made our overall deal with HBO, which we were very pleased with. There was a lot of bloodletting over there.

JERRY LEVIN:

We had what I'll call the ability to live with that deal, and it was never going to put HBO under. There was a lot of browbeating. My whole life has been about taking responsibility when no one else would stand up, and by the way, I was doing a lot more at the time than the Columbia Pictures deal.

JEFF BEWKES:

Ghostbusters took the income of HBO, which at the time was somewhere between $110 million to $130 million, and practically wiped it out, because it was such a huge percent of the box office. We ended up inventing a new accounting treatment for film expense, which was called the first window and the second window.

That accounting change saved tens of millions to our balance sheet.

On January 17, 1984, the US Supreme Court handed down a ruling that bolstered HBO's appeal to customers—a ruling known as the Betamax Case.

STEVE SCHEFFER:

The Betamax decision came down in the early 1980s, which permitted recording in the home, and enabled people to record movies off HBO. You could now build your own library, a compelling proposition. That really helped HBO. Our maximum leverage was in the early 1980s. It was a tough time for the studios and pay-TV revenue could represent as much as 25 to 50 percent of the cost of a movie.

In 1983 we launched our first original series, *Not Necessarily the News*, an irreverent newscast satire. That same year, I suggested that we should get into the made-for-HBO movie business. Our first movie was *The Terry Fox Story*.

The Terry Fox Story was a biopic of Canadian hero Terry Fox, who, in 1980 having lost a leg to cancer, attempted to run across his country raising money. Fox, then twenty-two, made it 3,339 miles before chest pains and breathlessness forced him to stop (his cancer would kill him less than a year later). The film, favorably received, starred Eric Fryer (himself an amputee) and Robert Duvall. Fuchs was low-key as ever about HBO producing its own movies, telling the **New York Times,** *"It may not rival the discovery of the proscenium arch, but I'm sure it will have the biggest impact on the entertainment industry since the advent of television itself."*

JANE DEKNATEL, Executive:

I was in the NBC movie of the week department working for Deanne Barkley, who was considered the grandmother of movies of the week. We made something like forty hours a year of miniseries: *Shogun*; *Rich Man, Poor Man*; and others that went on to become very well known. I had breakfast or a glass of wine a few times with Michael Fuchs.

I left NBC and went to work with David Susskind, and about a year later, Michael called me and said, "I want to hire you. HBO is finally at the stage where we are going to do movies of the week."

I hired Ilene. We raised a lot of capital and started making movies. I had been told you can't use television actors, you've got to use film actors, but back then, nobody of any standing did television.

ILENE KAHN POWER, Executive:

The business did not take us very seriously, but we figured we could cast movie stars with name value—Elizabeth Taylor, Carol Burnett, Jimmy Stewart, Bette Davis, people on the other side of the apex of their careers—and they would draw attention.

JANE DEKNATEL:

Elizabeth Taylor was in the first movie we did for our new banner, "HBO Premiere Films." It was called *Between Friends*, and Carol Burnett was her co-star. It was about a friendship between a woman who was getting divorced and a woman who wasn't married, and their sex lives. This was the early 1980s, a time of possibilities for women in a way that didn't exist before. We were very excited to make it, and it did really well.

RICHARD LICATA, Executive:

We were in Toronto shooting, and Elizabeth Taylor was blackmailing the producer, saying, "I won't come on the set unless you give me a present." She would name what present she wanted, he would get it for her, and then she would go out on the set. She was a very privileged, spoiled character.

I was put in charge of promoting all of those movies and went up there with a reporter from *TV Guide* who had flown in from New York because Elizabeth Taylor agreed to do an interview with him. My main challenge was to keep everything that was going on behind the scenes a secret, but when we got to her trailer, she wouldn't come out. We waited for fifteen minutes, and then Carol Burnett came up to me and asked, "What's wrong?" I told her, and she said, "Wait here." She went into the trailer and was in there for quite a while. Then she came out and said, "Give her five minutes, and then you can go in and do the interview."

ILENE KAHN POWER:

Michael was very gutsy. We were making movies that broadcast movies couldn't do. I did two HBO movies with Bette Davis in '83 and '86.

In the first, *Right of Way*, she co-starred with Jimmy Stewart. It was about a husband and wife—one of whom is diagnosed with terminal cancer and the other one says, I don't want to live without you, so they decided to kill themselves. It was a provocative subject at the time.

Three years later, Bette Davis was in her late seventies when she did our movie *As Summers Die*. She'd had a stroke, her mouth was twisted but she was still Bette Davis, the former top star of Hollywood. The first day, Bette arrives and she's wearing her little Chanel suit, weighing probably a hundred pounds. I had to call her Ms. Davis—no one could call her Bette.

She didn't want any female drivers, only males—young, handsome guys, preferably cowboys with cowboy hats.

Jerry Schatzberg, our original director, gets fired early on, and we bring in Sue Mengers's husband, Jean-Claude Tramont. He winds up bringing a wad of Parmesan cheese and Louis Vuitton luggage to this dumpy place down in Valdosta, Georgia. Jean-Claude never had the right coverage. He hadn't directed in a long time. The movie is set in the 1950s, and there's a pivotal scene where Jamie Lee Curtis is wearing a sweet dress and a necklace given to her by Aunt Hannah, who is played by Bette Davis. Jamie Lee walks in, twirls around, and says, "Hi," and Aunt Hannah is supposed to say, "Why Whitsey, you remind me of me." That's the line. So Bette Davis goes, "Why Whitsey, you look good enough to eat." Everybody's convulsed on the floor, thinking this has become a lesbian love scene when it's supposed to be a sweet moment between niece and aunt.

Bette says the line that way every time they do a take, and Jean-Claude doesn't correct her. We all thought, this movie is going to put us all out of business. We clearly needed to loop the line, but no one had the courage to talk to Bette Davis. So I got elected to make the phone call. Bette is now sitting in her apartment in West Hollywood, and I call her: "Ms. Davis." "Hi." "My name is Ilene Kahn, remember we met." "Yes." So I said, "Ms. Davis, we need to rework one line, and we'll be happy to send someone over to record it." "Why? Why do I need that?" I said, "Well, Ms. Davis, we just need it to be the way it was in the script. We need to finish out the scene."

"I still don't understand, and I don't want to do it." "Well, Ms. Davis," I said, "It's such a sweet Southern drama, but it has caused some unnecessary laughter." "What?" And I said, "Well, it had lesbian overtones." Then there's complete silence on the phone. And she said, "Lesbian? Call my agent." And she hangs up on me.

I call Marion Rosenberg, who was her agent at the time, and explain it to her. We wound up getting the best-looking sound guy, sent him to her apartment, and he got the correct line.

In 1984, HBO Premiere Films began to show signs of life. **Sakharov,** *written by David Rintels and starring Jason Robards and Glenda Jackson as the Russian dissident and his wife, was rushed into release to coincide with the physicist's hunger strike (he was starving to force authorities to allow his wife, Dr. Yelena Bonner, to go to the United States for an operation).* **Sakharov** *won best movie/miniseries at the next year's CableACE awards (cable's equivalent to the Emmys before they became eligible for such).*

MICHAEL FUCHS:

Sakharov wound up on the front page of the *New York Times,* before we could even get into the TV listings. I thought there was no reason we couldn't do intelligent, entertaining, relevant programming.

BRIDGET POTTER:

I inherited a staff person on the West Coast called Iris Dugow who was Michael's closest staff person. She'd been in New York, she'd had the job that I had, then wanted to move to LA, so he moved her to LA.

The big problem was she had the same attitude to dealmaking as Michael. She was hostile and rude in meetings.

IRIS DUGOW:

As HBO got bigger, it became more political and that wasn't good. When I moved out to the West Coast, Bridget Potter was left on the East Coast and that was a difficult relationship.

I was very close to Michael. We were like brother and sister, and she resented that.

MICHAEL FUCHS:

I picked up the value of retreats from Time Inc. They were a big deal at Time, and I started to have HBO retreats so everyone could be together, and hear the same thing, and so we could use the retreats as a reward, and have them be fun.

DAVE BALDWIN:

We had an offsite down in Puerto Rico at a golf and tennis resort. Bob Becker, our comptroller at the time, and I were going to find a colleague, and he looks at this lineup of golf carts and says, "Let's take one of these." I said, "Okay, but don't they belong to someone?" Bob says, "You're new to this whole corporate side. They just leave them at resorts like this. You borrow them and then you put them back when you're finished." I was dumb enough to believe him. So he gets down on his belly and starts unchaining the fucking cart from the front axle, "Bob, if they're free to take, why did someone chain it up?"

This was a big four-seater gas cart. I mean, it flew. We went up and down the resort and then he said, "She's probably on the beach." So we went down to the beach. I said, "Bob it's getting late, we have a nine a.m. call, we gotta go back." Instead of doing a nice U-turn on the hard sand, Bob does a K-turn, backs into the soft sand, guns it, and the wheels go all the way down to the axles. "All right, Dave, get out. Give me a push." So he rocks it. I'm now covered with seawater and sand. And I finally said, "Bob, no mas. Let's just leave it. I can't do this anymore." So we leave it and start walking up the beach and the hotel house dicks come out and start screaming at us. "Are you guys crazy? Where's the golf cart?" It was dark, you couldn't see it against the ocean. We said, "We did have a golf cart a while ago, but we put it back." I looked over at Bob and said, "Come on, we can outrun these guys." He was a downhill skier in Colorado. I was still in good shape. He said, "You don't understand. He has a gun in my back."

We get up to the hill, and the head of film acquisition, Bob Kreek, comes out, goes into the office with them, and doesn't even negotiate. He just laid down his Amex card and said, "Whatever the damages, this should cover it." He signed a voucher and walked out. Next morning we're all having breakfast on a deck overlooking the beach and all you can see is the pink and white Surrey top of a golf cart floating in the ocean. Everybody was laughing, but Fuchs reamed us out. We were scheduled to have a big affiliate's gathering there for the Super Bowl in the next few weeks, and they threatened to cancel the contract. Biondi then comes over to me and says, "As soon as we get back to New York, I want to see you in my office." I'm thinking, "I've been here for three years and my career's over. I am fucked."

That next night was our talent show. I was part of this band, and we persuaded Michael to let us close the show. Well, we tore up the place; people were on chairs flicking BICs. I go back to New York, and Biondi says, "I never ever want to see you with Bob Becker again. He is not good for your career. And if I ever hear about you two together, there's not going to be a happy ending." I think that show saved my career. I went to Becks and said, "Hey, I still got a job. Let's go down to the bar."

MICHAEL FUCHS:

We wanted to come away from these trips and not have them just be bonding, but when we made a decision where everyone sat, and heard and participated, it lent credibility.

One of the key philosophies was to do what other people didn't do. We decided on a trip to Scottsdale, Arizona, to capture the documentary business, which had become neglected.

IRIS DUGOW:

My greatest achievement was, after much effort, I hired Sheila Nevins away from Don Hewitt.

Sheila Nevins was born on April 6, 1939, and grew up on the Lower East Side of Manhattan. Her father was a Russian immigrant bookie and her mother suffered from a severe case of Raynaud's disease, a usually benign condition in which one displays poor circulation, but which in Nevins's mother's case led to the loss of her left arm below the elbow. Nevins recounts in her memoir, **You Don't Look Your Age . . . and Other Fairy Tales,** *how she once failed to stick up for her mother in a coffee shop when another customer obnoxiously complained that the amputation was spoiling her meal. Nevins's "failure" led to her lifelong effort to "champion stories about those less fortunate . . . anonymous victims of unfairness, deprivation, and poverty."*

SHEILA NEVINS, Executive:

I went to Barnard College, majored in English, then went to the Yale School of Drama and majored in directing. I wanted to be in the theater and direct, but there were no jobs, so I got a job at Children's Television Workshop. From there I went to *The Reasoner Report* at ABC, then moved to CBS and a celebrity show called *Who's Who?* The first piece I went out on alone was Diane von Furstenberg's wrap dress.

MICHAEL FUCHS:

I had a fixed philosophy. We weren't going to do what the networks were doing unless we could do it better. It was a religion with me. So, I thought one area that had become neglected by the networks was documentaries. They used to do white papers and they were pretty good, but they had disappeared.

Our first deal was coincidentally with a company from Mount Vernon, New York, where I grew up. *Consumer Reports.* We did a show on hair dyes. Then I thought, every documentary maker at some point in time needs $60,000. We almost had the field to ourselves.

LEE GRANT, Documentarian and Actor:

Around *Shampoo* or *Voyage of the Damned*, I was aging out. Around that time, the American Film Institute asked if I wanted to take a director's workshop, and it turned my life around. I found the same passion for directing that I had for acting. It was like a new love in my life.

Sheila gave my husband and me our first assignment, *Women Who Kill*, which was about a women's prison, and I cannot be more grateful. It took us to upstate New York and to LA to see the Manson girls.

In 1982, just as she was starting to hit her stride, Sheila Nevins decided to leave HBO. In the years to follow, Nevins would continue to produce hit documentary work for HBO. But for now, at least, she would do so from the outside, as an independent producer. And why? Because she refused to tolerate co-worker Bridget Potter any longer.

MICHAEL FUCHS:

Bridget and Sheila hated each other.

BRIDGET POTTER:

When I went to work at HBO, Sheila was working for me and I had an idea that there were all these great stories that were being done as movies of the week, and we should do the documentary version. So we called it *America Undercover* and it became a documentary series of films about true crime mostly. Sheila hated the idea and left. She resigned and went to produce her own children's programming.

SHEILA NEVINS:

I quit because I couldn't work with Bridget anymore. She was driving me crazy. She was not evil, she just had a very unusual relationship with women. I didn't care as long as I could do my work, but one day she said, "I want to be in the editing room with you when you do your films." Editing was my holy space, I lived for that room. And I said, "I don't think that will work, Bridget." She wanted the sex shows to be only about the burgeoning AIDS epidemic. I wanted them to be fun too. I couldn't win with her. It was impossible.

In 1983, I set up my own company in a dentist office on Eighty-ninth Street and began producing for HBO. I made six *Eros America*s and six *Braingames* and one show with Elliott Erwitt. So that was twelve, thirteen shows. *Braingames* was based on a place mat in a restaurant that I'd seen. *Eros* was a book that I'd found. I was doing a kid's show, and a sex show, and I was able to be with my young son. He had Tourette's and he needed me. I thought it was my fault. It was a time when women felt guilt if there was something wrong with their kid.

BRIDGET POTTER:

Braingames was a very clever show. There were very few episodes in 1983–85, and there were maybe six episodes each time, but they were very good and my kids really loved them. But I don't think that they got a lot of attention.

CIS WILSON, Executive:

Sheila Nevins is one of the smartest people alive. She is so savvy, and she is a survivor. I had worked with Sheila as an outside producer on a comedy series for HBO, and when she left HBO, she said to Michael Fuchs, "You should hire Cis Wilson." There was an opening in the documentaries because Jean Abounader was elevated to Sheila's position. "You should hire

Cis Wilson." We used to laugh about it, I think it was her way to get back at Bridget Potter, because I was outspoken, nonconformist, and not somebody easily controlled by hierarchy.

On Saturday, November 19, 1983, at ten p.m., Sheila Nevins's career as godmother to a new era of documentaries and documentarians—one in which she reveled in the various vagaries of human sexuality—officially began, even though she was working on **Eros** *as a freelance producer.*

Eros America *was a magazine show filled with short segments on how regular people and professionals exposed and indulged their various sexual proclivities. The first episode typified Nevins's eclectic approach—profiling a Florida housewife and mother who moonlit as a stripper in her spare time; another career woman who worked as a prostitute and likened it to babysitting (noting that she never left home without a whip and some talcum powder—useful for either job); and an opening-night finale devoted to a fireman who, playing off the image of the job as fitfully erotic, stripped for extra money.*

In between each story came vignettes about sex manuals, cartoon depictions of famous people chatting about sex (including a quote from Henry Kissinger—Mister "Power Is the Ultimate Aphrodisiac" himself), and even an illustrated claim that the first diaphragm was created by Cleopatra.

The show struck a resounding chord with the audience and became a huge hit, even traveling far overseas in the process. One **Eros** *piece titled "69 Positions in 60 Seconds" somehow found its way to New Zealand, airing (without warning) on a news program there.*

HBO had shown R-rated movies aplenty, their soundtracks liberally peppered with racy language not to be found, at least then, on any commercial network. But the raw sexuality of **Eros America** *magnified even HBO's unashamedly "adult" image—as evidenced a few years later, when HBO aired* **It's Not Easy Bein' Me,** *a comedy special hosted by Rodney Dangerfield with stand-up performances by Rodney himself, Roseanne Barr, Jerry Seinfeld, and easily the most sexually audacious of the group, the great, late Sam Kinison, comic extraordinaire.*

During his little-more-than-ten-minute set, Kinison reflected on men's tireless attempts to satisfy women sexually. "We don't get sex education, come on; men don't get a lot of information in this country. Nobody helps us. The first time we have, like, intimate sex—oh, this is HBO—" (correcting himself): "The first time we were licking pussy . . ." The line sent many at HBO into spins of delight.

SHEILA NEVINS:

We put *Braingames* on HBO, but *Eros* was too racy for HBO, so it went to Cinemax. I couldn't show pubic hair; I couldn't show dicks. God knows we graduated from that, but back then it was carefully cleansed by the legal department. It was fun. Sex was still a secret in America.

HAL AKSELRAD, Executive:

We filed an amicus brief in the Supreme Court to try to support some of the edgy comedies we were taking on. HBO's content was under attack statutorily. I brought challenges to stop the city of Miami, or the city of Denver, or the State of Colorado from regulating our content based on Southern decency.

CIS WILSON:

When I went to HBO Documentaries, Michael said to us, "We are in a position to speak out, and that's what your job is. Speak out." Social issue documentaries were one of Michael's priorities in programming.

BILL COUTURIÉ, Documentarian:

I was a kid, California surfer type, USC cinema, and we had done a film on ABC *Who Are the DeBolts? And Where Did They Get Nineteen Kids?* which won an Oscar. I got a call from Iris Dugow saying, "I want you to come out and talk about doing a sequel to that," which was strange. Sequels to documentaries weren't done in those days. But I was doing animation for *Sesame Street*, so I was in New York often, and came by to meet with Iris. She was literally the only person in the programming department.

So we're sitting there talking in her office and suddenly the door bursts open and some guy says, "We fucked them. We fucked them. We really fucked them." It was Michael Fuchs. He had just gotten a good deal on a package of films from Fox.

But he can't see me, and Iris is looking aghast. She points to me and Michael turns around, sees me, and says, "Oh, hi. You here for the doc?" I said, "Yeah." He said, "We don't have money to make feature films. We don't have money to make sitcoms, but we can make a documentary. Do you think you can win us awards?" I said, "Yeah, sure." And he said, "Okay." That was my intro to Michael, whom I love.

He put me under his wing and allowed me to make films that were, in those days, unimaginable. We had a guy come to us with an idea for a film about what happened to football players after the NFL. I loved it and thought it would be appropriate for HBO. So I took it to Jean Abounader who had taken Sheila's job, and I pitched it to her. All I can remember her saying is, "Who's going to watch a film about football?" Apparently she tossed my treatment in the wastepaper basket after I left, but Cis picked it out, read it, and loved it. Cis gave it to Michael and he said, "This is exactly the kind of docs HBO should be doing."

In what would become a trademark of HBO's documentary department, the early to mid-1980s were a time of both high- and lowbrow creations. In 1985, decades before the National Football League was plunged into scrutiny for the long-lasting consequences of repeated head impacts—a degenerative brain disease called chronic traumatic encephalopathy (CTE)—HBO took viewers inside the suffering of two former NFL linemen who faced physical and mental anguish following their days on the field with **Disposable Heroes: The Other Side of Football.**

CIS WILSON:

Disposable Heroes was a film so ahead of its time. These guys got beaten up every Sunday on the field, and no one was talking about it.

BILL COUTURIÉ:

I'm not sure that being way ahead of your time is good or bad. If you look at it now, we focused on physical damage, and didn't get into brain damage, but we featured Jim Otto, a very famous player who went to Al Davis and told him he wanted the league to give us some footage. As a result, we got the footage and shot some of a Super Bowl. That would never happen today.

CIS WILSON:

HBO Sports was covering NFL football and there might've been blowback, but Michael said to us, "Just tell the truth. This is an important issue. Make this film."

Since its founding, HBO had been headquartered in Manhattan's Time-Life Building, often occupying whatever offices Time wasn't using. HBO's growth—in terms of both personnel and revenues—demanded that change, so in 1984, HBO moved ten blocks south to Sixth Avenue and Forty-second Street, across from Bryant Park.

In the 1980s, Bryant Park was, as the **New York Times** *put it, "best known for its trash, graffiti and drug pushers."*

SHELLEY FISCHEL, Executive:

The move meant we had our own separate existence from Time, which was important and very good for the company. We wanted to make the move a positive experience, so we had our own cafeteria, fitness center, and medical center. Years down the road, every time we looked at reducing costs, those were among the things nobody would agree to cut.

By late 1984, HBO had hit an earnings and subscriber plateau. Third-quarter earnings were $1.6 million below the same period in 1983, and within the Time Inc. corridors, there was a consensus that HBO had stalled. On Wall Street, one analyst commented, "Time Inc. is having a fantastic year. And everybody liked HBO because of its growth. But now it is grinding to a halt."

Years later, in an interview with the Cable Center, Biondi shared his thoughts on what had been going on. "There were essentially two reasons [why we stopped growing] in hindsight. First of all, cable deregulation hadn't happened, so all the cable operators were holding back their construction. And something called the VCR had started to happen. It was still small, but it was the two combined that began to slow HBO's growth."

At the time, Nick Nicholas was in charge of video strategy at Time Inc., and had a weekly meeting with Biondi, Tony Cox, and Michael Fuchs. The four men would spend forty-five minutes together, and it became apparent in those meetings that Biondi and Fuchs were in a bad way. Prior to working together at HBO, they had been very close, but each was now openly competitive. Quarrels broke out regularly, which led Nicholas to do some digging behind the scenes. It turned out that Biondi wasn't getting along with anyone.

HAL AKSELRAD:

The staff was very unsettled. There were also rumors about financial distress and layoffs. Nick called an HBO staff meeting at Roseland Ballroom where he apprised the staff that Frank would remain CEO.

KEN SCHICK, Executive:

At Roseland, Frank got up in front of the whole company and said, "As long as I am in charge, there will be no layoffs. Go back to the office and get some work done."

HAL AKSELRAD:

Tony Cox, Michael Fuchs, and Frank Biondi had adjacent offices on the seventh floor of the Time Inc. building. The tension between them was enormous; their relationships had become hostile and were dysfunctional for the company.

NICK NICHOLAS:

Biondi and Fuchs came to my office, and I asked them, "Did your parents ever fight?" Yes. "Did they ever fight in front of you kids?" Yes. "Do you remember how you felt?" Yes. "Well, that's exactly how the staff with HBO feels, with you guys trying to one-up each other every damn day. It's got to stop. And if it doesn't, something's going to change."

JEFF BEWKES:

Nicholas called a meeting and brought his boss, Dick Munro, along. I can see it now. Michael and Frank at one end of the table, and Joe Collins and Trygve Myhren, the two guys running ATC, our second-largest affiliate, at the other end. I was there as the note taker, after being drafted up to the video group with Nick.

It was a shitshow, a huge fight. Frank and Michael were furious. They felt the cable operators were criminally negligent by failing to market HBO sufficiently. The cable guys didn't want us to succeed too much because then we could raise the price on them. Frank and Michael had been fighting with other cable companies. Now they were fighting with the cable system that Time Inc. owned 85 percent of. They were fighting with our own cable company.

Frank and Michael were yelling. Munro's head was moving back and forth like at a tennis match. Trygve was firing back, and Joe was getting quieter and redder.

JOE COLLINS, Executive:

Not a way to treat your biggest customers. I think Frank used to go to bed at night dreaming that suddenly K-band satellites were going to allow him to go direct-to-consumer and completely eliminate HBO having to go through the cable operators.

JEFF BEWKES:

Afterward, Michael calls me into his office and says, "Well, we kicked their butts." I said, "What the fuck were you thinking? You can't beat up our second-largest affiliate in front of Nick and Munro—which, by the way, we happen to own so you may want to consider you shouldn't be so happy fucking over one of our sister companies."

Frank was a good executive, and he was better able to run HBO than Mikey, but Frank had gotten too belligerent and way too aggressive.

MICHAEL FUCHS:

Nick was telling Frank that things were so fucked-up at HBO, top levels at Time were talking about it. Frank would defend everything. They would have these financial analysis battles. It was all wrapped in numbers. It turned out that Nick was right.

Nicholas had had enough. In his mind, Biondi left him with no choice. Nicholas fired Biondi on October 10, 1984.

NICK NICHOLAS:

Ultimately for me, the deciding factor was Frank's behavior as CEO. He wasn't acting as a leader. He was acting as a competitor.

Some thought Frank had been fired because of the Columbia deal, and that didn't help, but because Levin, Frank's boss, approved it all along the way, I couldn't hold Frank fully accountable.

For years Biondi made it clear to anyone who would listen that Nicholas had been wrong to let him go. Eventually, in 1996, Nicholas reached out to make peace and a lunch was set up. On arrival at Viacom, Nicholas was asked to wait in Biondi's office while he finished a meeting elsewhere. Fifteen minutes later, Biondi appeared and told Nicholas he had just been fired by Sumner Redstone.

MICHAEL FUCHS:

I knew that Nick was going to fire Frank and replace him with me, but I didn't go running to Frank to tell him. His wife, Carol, who I knew longer than Frank did, probably never forgave me.

CURT VIEBRANZ, Executive:

Frank's departure in 1984 surprised everybody—and in time-honored corporate fashion, the way that it became known to the rank and file at HBO was that we were in the process of moving from 1271 Avenue of the Americas to Forty-second Street, and the maintenance guys who were going to do the move were told, "Forget Frank Biondi. He's not moving." That piece of information rippled through the building.

On October 22, 1984, two weeks after he was named CEO to replace Biondi, Michael Fuchs was also named chairman of HBO. It would be his seventh promotion since he arrived at the company in 1976.

Extremely competitive, loved or hated, Fuchs, never one to be plagued by anything even vaguely resembling self-doubt, was ready for (virtually) anything. And just what would a Fuchs Era be like? Insiders and outsiders alike agreed on one item: it wouldn't be dull.

MICHAEL FUCHS:

My father still didn't understand what I did. He said, "I know you're doing something good because they keep trying to give me résumés for you at the club."

JEFF BEWKES:

When Nick and Dick made Michael CEO, Michael had to accept Joe Collins reporting to him as president. They thought Michael needed someone to run the business while he focused on programming.

A former naval officer and Harvard Business School graduate from Troy, New York, Joseph J. Collins had been with American Television and Communications (ATC), a subsidiary of Time Inc., since 1972. And now that Collins was no longer on the other side of the table, Fuchs decided to keep past tensions in the past.

JOE COLLINS:

Nick, who was the head of the video group at that point, basically said, "We have big trouble at HBO. We want you to come to New York and do what you can to help." I went home, talked to my wife, and we said, "We'll do it." It turned out to be a very interesting part of my career.

JEFF BEWKES:

Joe never wanted to run HBO, he was just waiting for Trygve to move on so he could go back and run the cable company. Nick had said to him, "Do a couple years with Mike and then you can go run ATC (Time Warner Cable)," which is exactly what happened.

JOHN MALONE:

Joe Collins is 100 percent cable. Everything he did was from a cable perspective. So we were very parallel in our thinking.

Michael was Hollywood. Content. He didn't care much about what the distribution technology was. He was more into what I would call high-quality addictive programming.

MICHAEL FUCHS:

I wasn't what you'd call a financial guy, but I always made sure to have a good CFO, and they educated me. Nick put Joe Collins under me to send a comforting signal to the cable industry and encourage the industry to buy into the KU satellite, which was an upgrade over the C-band that the industry was using.

JOE COLLINS:

I didn't realize how big the problems were until I got there. We were in a period where there was an enormous amount of new cable construction, basically the late 1970s and early 1980s. The cable industry was spending billions and billions of dollars to pull cables up and down the streets of America and lots of new franchises were granted all over the country. Customers were literally falling out of the trees. In the cable industry, we used to call these customers truck chasers, because literally as the lineman would go down the street, bringing cable to the city, the people would run alongside their trucks, bang on his side, and say, "When can we have it? When is HBO coming?" So selling that first 25 percent of those homes for HBO was easy. When you opened your doors, they were there to sign up.

What nobody realized was that it was all going to eventually come to an end. You were going to run out of new territories and make the other 75 percent want to buy HBO. The company hadn't figured that out yet.

But HBO did have a big marketing department with a lot of very smart, capable people, and they hired good agencies who were coming up with the most entertaining ads you'd ever seen. So the awareness levels were good. If you went out and tested people, asking, "Have you heard of HBO?" the answer was, "Oh yeah, that's great," but nobody could go to the store and buy it. You had to have the cable operator take the order, then have somebody from a cable company run a nice little piece of RG 59 into your house to hook you up, and then send you a bill every month. HBO needed cooperation.

When I got to HBO, I realized we had cable operators who owed us millions and millions of dollars, and then we'd send somebody to knock on their door, and they'd say, "Get lost." It was pretty amazing. There was that huge chunk of the business that literally nobody was managing.

MICHAEL FUCHS:

On my first day as CEO in 1984, we had to make layoffs. Curt Viebranz was my financial translator at that time and told me we had to cut the budget. We tried to limit the number as best as possible.

SHELLEY FISCHEL:

Michael asked me to run HR, which I was very reluctant to do because I didn't want to be an HR person, but my then boss, the general counsel, made it clear that these were tough times for HBO and I had to be a good team player, so I took the job. The VCR had just been introduced, and some thought HBO could be toast. We were ordered to do layoffs because Time Inc. was concerned about the future of pay TV and wanted us to control our costs.

Michael Fuchs, Curt Viebranz, and I spent weeks trying to figure who was going to go and who was going to stay. By this time, HBO was such a player in the media industry that even though we were laying off slightly more than a hundred people, it was on the first page of the *New York Times*.

MICHAEL FUCHS:

A lot of companies say, "Okay, let's take 20 percent of the people out," like people are the real expense, but I went to everyone running a budget and said, "I want 20 percent from you, but you better not take out too many people." So we did that without a lot of pain. Corporations always have a little extra flab hanging around.

SHELLEY FISCHEL:

At one point I told Michael that the layoffs would have no integrity unless he fired a specific person who was known to be a friend of his but didn't do a decent job at anything. Curt was trying to say the same thing. Finally, I just said, "I'm sorry, Michael, no one's going to have any respect for you if you don't do this." He stood over me, pointed a finger at me, and said, "Shelley, I take all this fucking shit from you, but even I have limits where you're concerned." But he did it.

You would think layoffs meant employees no longer trusted the company, but largely the staff understood why it was necessary. Obviously for people who got terminated, it was horrible. Afterward, we were very conscious of the fact that we needed to make the company feel whole again, build morale, and we worked at that.

JOE COLLINS:

For some reason, the management of HBO had decided that they needed pomp, so they decided all the senior executives should have company cars. The company is headquartered on Sixth Avenue in New York City, and all of the senior executives wind up with cars, like Mercedes, Jaguars, and other nifty cars. Dick Munro used to tell the story about having a party in his house in New Canaan, and he had to borrow his neighbor's driveway to park all these fancy HBO cars in their driveway, so other management people of Time Inc. didn't see them.

I'm telling you this was amazing stuff. Time Inc. itself had a policy about entertainment expenses. Basically, if you were an HBO executive in the old days, and you and another person, same department, were having a conversation about some business thing, you could go to the 21 Club for lunch and charge it to the company expense account. They didn't require a customer in order to write it off.

We tightened all that stuff down, including the cars. People had to buy them from the company if they wanted to keep them. And we said, "Look, we got a brand-new building here on Sixth Avenue. It has a wonderful cafeteria, and we'll subsidize it. If you want to take a colleague to lunch, go to the cafeteria."

MATT BLANK:

Michael taking over as CEO was the first real stake in the ground in terms of HBO saying, "We're a content company." Michael was a tough businessman, but fundamentally he was more a guy who wanted to make great content. That was his mission, and HBO was his life.

SETH ABRAHAM:

I once watched a president of ABC Sports ask somebody to take his coat. Michael would never do that. He'd hang up his fucking coat himself.

MATT BLANK:

There was a certain arrogance at HBO then, a "how dare anybody compete with us" attitude. "We created this business, it's our inalienable right to own the business. If there is money to take out of the home, how dare somebody else think they could take that money? How can you even consider bringing in Showtime? It's a crappy network." That was our pitch. It was the beginning of an impenetrable, "we are the kings of the world" culture that would continue for decades. Some of it was the personalities of the people who were there, and some was the personality of the company as a whole. We were a great cult to be part of. Say what you want, it worked.

MICHAEL FUCHS:

I had a vision for HBO from the first day. I thought HBO matched up with my personality, or maybe I had already imposed my personality on HBO.

Edgy, irreverent, funny, unconventional, contentious, risk oriented, etc. And soon after getting the top job, HBO passed me in most of these categories.

MATT BLANK:

Michael Fuchs's Tuesday morning staff meetings were full of smart young executives waiting their turn for the future opportunities. I was very close to Tony Cox and Frank Biondi—both had been mentors of mine at HBO—and both had gone on to work for Redstone, who had just gotten control of Viacom after a nasty fight. Tony was the CEO of Showtime and was operating under a noncompete and nonsolicit agreement. He had left Time Inc. to go directly to Showtime a few months earlier, so he couldn't be the one to bring me over. But Frank, who had been pushed out of HBO before that, had no such issues, and he asked me to come to Showtime on Tony's behalf.

Tony had said to me, "You might be CEO of HBO someday, but it's going to be fifteen years from now. If you come to Showtime and help us grow it, you could be CEO in a few years." I was thirty-seven years old and decided to take a shot. Fortunately, that's what happened.

Someone once accused HBO of suffering from a Copernicus complex. HBO was the center of the universe and everything else revolved around it. I saw this firsthand when I resigned. I couldn't believe how many people told me Showtime had no future, including Jerry Levin and Nick Nicholas. No one had ever left voluntarily to go to the competition before me. Up until then, there were never employment contracts at HBO. Within a week of my leaving, many execs at HBO found an employment contract on their desks.

When I resigned, I told Michael Fuchs that I wanted to have an opportunity to step up more quickly and be in charge of programming in the near future. He replied, "Matty, just know that you'll never buy a show that I haven't dumped on first." He was right, but that motivated me to make sure that wouldn't be true for long.

CURT VIEBRANZ:

In the early days, we could go into a room, scream and shout at each other about ideas, then leave the room and everything was okay. That healthy irreverence and constructive conflict was a hallmark of Michael's. He set the culture.

ILENE KAHN POWER:

There were strong personalities. We were all young. There were no elders in the company. The HBO culture was difficult to penetrate. It was very collegial, and even with all the rivalries that occurred there was unbelievable esprit de corps.

The programming people came from very different backgrounds. Michael wanted to hire really smart people, people who were well educated, but we didn't all have cookie-cutter backgrounds. We all loved hanging out together, drinking together, and playing together. We had very good expense accounts. It was a magical time.

There were a lot of relationships. Tremendous amount. Michael was always very good to the women he was involved with. I was a married woman, I was never involved with Michael, but there were a lot of women who were involved with him. He was quite good to them, and he's still friends with some of them today.

STEVE SCHEFFER:

Michael was the perfect storm, the right guy at the right time. He was smart. He was charismatic. He was a great leader. He was the face of HBO. He wanted the best people and gave them free rein. We had a company of a bunch of young Turks. A lot of them were single. At the end of the day, a lot of people from various departments would get together at the US Steakhouse, which was located in the lobby of the Time-Life Building, for cocktails, then go on to dinner. The workday never ended so everybody knew what was going on and were working toward the same goals.

QUENTIN SCHAFFER, Executive:

One time after Henry Schleiff had a bunch of us laughing, I made the mistake of telling Michael I thought Henry was the funniest person at the company. Michael glared at me and said, "Quentin, *I'm* the funniest person at the company."

NICK NICHOLAS:

Michael was the guy with a shitload of talent and a shitload of demons.

3

Richness & Improbability

DECEMBER 11, 1984–JANUARY 10, 1990

CHRIS ALBRECHT, Executive:

I didn't know my dad. Whatever his story was with my mom, they got divorced by the time I was a year old. She was twenty-one, a single mom, and never got the chance to go to college.

When I was in high school, my mother was in a group called the Association for Research and Enlightenment, so I got introduced to reincarnation and many things metaphysical. After that, I bounced around with a couple of majors in college and took some drama lit classes at Hofstra. There was this great professor who took us from the Greeks to Albee and made everything come alive. He would give us these tough fucking quizzes, but one of the results of being in his classes was having the awareness that there are only twelve stories that are part of the human journey, and they each get told in different ways by different cultures. I was greatly influenced by all of it.

Fast-forward to nothing. In my twenties, I was a comedian—my only claim to fame was that I was getting on before Larry David—then I owned a nightclub, became a comedian manager, and moved to LA. By this time, I'm a dad. I was having a hard time finding my place. Drinking was never my thing, but I did wind up in AA, and then tried to go back to meditating. Once again, there's my mother. She asked me, "Have you seen what Bill Moyers did on PBS with Joseph Campbell? You must watch it." Well, I started watching it, and Campbell kept mentioning Carl Jung. Jung, Jung, Jung. He also did this edition called *The Portable Jung*, and I became obsessed with it, eventually joining the Jung Institute. My wife was pregnant with our second child, and at one point I had thought of retiring from show business to become a Jungian analyst.

When I was twenty-eight, I went to ICM and became an agent. I signed all my former friends and colleagues from the Improv—Keenan Wayans, Joe Piscopo, Dana Carvey, Jim Carrey, eventually Billy Crystal, Whoopi Goldberg, Paul Rodriguez, and others.

Bridget Potter offered me a job around '83 to come to New York and be HBO's specials guy, but I wasn't interested. Then ICM fell apart. Jeff Berg was nobody's idea of a friendly boss, and Lee Gabler and a bunch of good people left. At HBO, things weren't great between New York and LA. Michael had pitted Iris Dugow and Bridget Potter against each other, and after Iris left, Bridget called me again. This was the beginning of June '85.

BRIDGET POTTER:

Chris consulted for me as a scout when I was at ABC, to look at potential performers for sitcoms in the comedy world. He would put together these evenings at the Improv, I would take notes, then select my top six or seven for West Coast execs to see when they came out for pilot season. We had a good working relationship and had some long conversations about why he wasn't happy at ICM.

CHRIS ALBRECHT:

I got hired by Bridget as vice president of original programming, West Coast. Here's my first day at HBO: I meet her in Vegas at the cable show along with the two guys who were going to report to me, Bill Sanders and Jeff Bricmont. I said to Bridget, "Wait a minute, Jeff and Bill are vice presidents and I'm a vice president. How's anybody going to know that they report to me?" She said, "We'll just tell people, and they'll learn." I asked her, "What was Iris?" And she said, "She was a senior vice president of original programming." I said, "Why aren't I an SVP? It's the job of running the West Coast, I'm not asking for more money, and it's better for you if you've got a senior vice president reporting to you." She goes into a phone booth, calls Michael, comes out a minute later, and says, "Okay, you're a senior vice president." I hadn't even started work yet and I got promoted. That was the cool thing about HBO in those days. It was still a small company.

When I got to HBO, there was a belief that cable operators didn't care about original programming. They thought viewers could get lots of programs from broadcast networks, and only wanted HBO for movies and sports. That was the strategic mandate for how we should be spending our money. Our programming budget then was only $50 million to $60 million a year. Movies and specials were big priorities.

MICHAEL FUCHS:

Our Whoopi special got a lot of attention. Mike Nichols had directed her show on Broadway, and when we bought the rights, he wanted to direct it for television. We knew live television entertainment better than anyone, but Sam Cohn, Mike's agent, said, "Mike gets final cut." I told him, "There's no such thing as final cut in television." And that was the end of that. I'm probably one of the few people who ever turned down Mike Nichols.

WHOOPI GOLDBERG, Actor and Comedian:

I was so happy HBO allowed me to do my special for them. It wasn't like there was anyone to compare myself to; they were taking a big chance on me, doing me a solid, and it turned out to be a really important night for my career. Chris Albrecht helped out a lot.

BRIDGET POTTER:

Chris injected a high level of energy into the Hollywood community on behalf of HBO, which was terrific.

When famine ravaged Ethiopia in 1983, pop stars Bob Geldof of the Boomtown Rats and Midge Ure of Ultravox founded the Irish-British supergroup Band Aid, whose first single, "Do They Know It's Christmas?," would raise millions for relief and be succeeded the following summer by **Live Aid**, *a concertus magnum opus featuring pickups from around the world. The satellite spectacular was anchored by a major show from London's Wembley Stadium, which featured a legendary performance by Freddie Mercury and Queen. American musicians, led by reigning superstar Michael Jackson, released the immodestly titled single, "We Are the World," to keep donations pouring in.*

*It wasn't only the music world that organized: the comedy community did its part, too. In the UK, Comic Relief was cofounded by Richard Curtis (***Four Weddings and a Funeral, Notting Hill***) and comedian Lenny Henry.*

HBO then created **Comic Relief USA**, *which was televised on March 29, 1986, a*

four-hour epic with Robin Williams, Billy Crystal, and Whoopi Goldberg as co-hosts,
backed by Gilda Radner, Martin Short, Michael J. Fox, George Carlin, and many others.

HBO gave permission for the shows to be simulcast on basic cable, and basic cable
operators agreed to help raise money, on the condition that, for the first hour of the
show, the hosts watch their language. This was, after all, free family television. Gold-
berg, though, was not feeling accommodating; the very first line of her show was, "Long
time no see. Shit."

CHRIS ALBRECHT:

It happened pretty quickly. Our first Comic Relief was just nine months
after I came to HBO. I had this conversation after Live Aid with my old
comedy partner and longtime friend Bob Zmuda over dinner with my
wife, Annie. He said, "We should do Live Aid, but instead of musicians,
we should use comics." Then Annie said, "I think people are getting a little
overdone with, 'Let's help the refugees.' Why don't you guys do something
for people in America?"

I pitched the idea to Bridget and Michael, then we brought on Pat Tourk
Lee and John Moffitt to produce. We formed an advisory board of managers, and HBO lawyers got involved to figure out how to collect and distribute the money.

We needed to find hosts and wanted to make sure there was a woman
and diversity in there. We had done the special with Whoopi and got lucky
because Whoopi had just come out in *The Color Purple* and been nominated for an Academy Award. The whole month before Comic Relief,
everybody wanted to talk to Whoopi, and every time she did an interview
for the awards, she talked about Comic Relief.

BILLY CRYSTAL:

The homeless problem was becoming a national disgrace. So many people
were falling through the cracks and ending up on the streets. They brought
Whoopi, Robin, and me in for a meeting and said, "We want to unite the
comedy world, like Live Aid, and get every stand-up we can." It was an audacious idea. They asked, "Would you guys be interested in doing it together?"
And without looking at each other, we all said yes at the same time.

WHOOPI GOLDBERG:

I'd known Robin, I didn't know Billy. After I got done fanning out on him, I
was like, "We can do this and know that we tried to do something to help."
They had us go to different shelters and we started to see the severity of the

problem. Then they had us go down to Washington and talk with important figures in politics. It was an amazing awakening for the three of us. This problem was much bigger than anybody thought, and we wanted to bring some dignity back to folks.

BILLY CRYSTAL:

The three of us wrote the opening, which was six minutes long, and when we came offstage, Pat Lee met us and said, "The phones are ringing." Robin, Whoopi, and I started crying.

WHOOPI GOLDBERG:

There were the wonderful dick jokes and me having to play Vanna White and say, "Yes, yes, yes, all of that is true and funny as hell, but can you give us some money?" I watched masters at work. I got better at what I did.

DAVID STEINBERG, Manager:

Comic Relief was massive. Robin was into it from the start. He played the bad boy on Comic Relief. If you look at what he did with Whoopi and Billy, Robin got himself into and out of trouble and it was hilarious.

JUDD APATOW, Writer and Executive Producer:

The first job I had in show business was working for Comic Relief. I was in college at USC and saw the press conference where they announced it. I instantly called the office and said, "I will work for free. I will do anything." They couldn't have seemed less interested. Then three months later, out of the blue, they called and asked me to come in. I worked there for the next four or five years. They would do the show for HBO, and I would produce satellite shows at comedy clubs and small theaters around the country raising money for the homeless locally.

CHRIS ALBRECHT:

It was the first time I'd ever done live television. We filled the Universal Amphitheatre and were amazed by the response and the money we raised. Fuchs was so happy. That was a giant star on my homework with him.

BILLY CRYSTAL:

When the money came in, Robin, Whoopi, and I traveled around the country delivering checks in person. Michael always provided the HBO plane because he wanted us to get everywhere as easy as possible and feel taken care of. HBO paid all the bills. Whatever came in, the charities got. That was pretty extraordinary. That was HBO. That was Michael and Chris and the heart of who they were.

PAT TOURK LEE:

HBO let the show run on forever, so comics took as much time as they wanted. After several years they decided it's going to be no more than three hours, so we told everyone they only had five minutes.

Now it's the night of the show and I don't even remember who the comic was, but I'm standing in the wings with Robin and we're watching this guy who's not really scoring but doing okay. His time was up, but he's going on and on and I said, "Dammit, why doesn't he get off. We're showing him the red light." Robin looks at me and says, "Pat, he hasn't come. When you're out there, it's like sex, and if you don't get the response you want, you do it and do it until you come."

PHIL SAVENICK, Producer:

Local Channel 9 in New York said they would cover Comic Relief to see if they could raise money, and the time just so happened to coincide with Whoopi's set. Whoopi wanted to talk about how white men can't give good head, or won't. Obviously that wasn't going to fly on free TV, so they asked if she could change it a little bit, which didn't go over well. She came out and just started saying it. Channel 9 cut us right off.

BILLY CRYSTAL:

We raised around $75 million over the years we did Comic Relief.

WHOOPI GOLDBERG:

We were so naive as to think that we would do it, raise enough money, and wouldn't have to do it again. That clearly didn't turn out to be the case. Now I'm quite sad because we stopped and no one else has picked up the job. I thought the younger comics would, but I haven't seen it.

HBO wanted to own big-event television and to treat talent like members of its family. Many comics and musical performers were royally and repeatedly welcomed.

The network loved Robin Williams, and he loved them. (When Albrecht had told his friend Williams that he called his Sicilian grandparents his nana and his nanu, Williams couldn't stop laughing, and **Mork and Mindy's** *"Nanu-Nanu!" was born.)*

Set to a background of Mozart's **Marriage of Figaro**, *HBO's next big entertainment* *extravaganza, on October 11, 1986, began with scenes of Manhattan shot from a town car window and ended at the world-famous Metropolitan Opera House. Dissolve to the turning pages of a fake classical program reading, "Home Box Office presents . . . Robin Williams, An Evening at the Met." A voice-over by Williams himself intoned, "The part of Robin Williams will be played by the Temptations," and suddenly there he was, America's hirsute clown prince, bounding onstage as only he could, amped up. His then recently achieved sobriety (he quit cocaine after the fatal overdose of pal John Belushi in 1982) didn't inhibit Williams's manic antics one kilowatt. The evening was one of the level jumps in Williams's career, and a huge coup for HBO.*

BILLY CRYSTAL:

One day Michael calls me and says, "What do you think about performing in the Soviet Union? No one's done stand-up in this period of Glasnost with Gorbachev." We made a scouting trip to see if it was possible, and took the midnight train from Leningrad to Moscow, hence the title of the show, *Midnight Train to Moscow.*

CHRIS ALBRECHT:

We were in this old Soviet fucking sleeper car with the furnace at one end and a samovar sitting on top so we could have tea.

BILLY CRYSTAL:

While we were there, we found out I had a lot of family there that I didn't know existed, and that became a big part of the show. Michael came with me and my wife, Janice, to a dinner with my newfound cousins. I wanted to include him because he made it all possible.

I didn't know these people, but I'm getting emotional thinking about them now. They looked like my relatives. They had that familiar joy and sadness on their face at the same time. When the wall went up, they couldn't get out like my grandparents did. If that didn't happen, if I had been raised there, who am I? Who would I be?

On a deep level, I had started out as a kid making my parents and my family laugh. They were my first audience. And now, here I was, thousands of miles away in Moscow with new family.

When we first got there, we were asked to go to the US embassy and meet the ambassador. He made a sign to me like, don't talk here, then led me to another office where we were basically hiding behind a plant. He told me, "There are bugs throughout this place," then said, "What are you planning on saying? Please don't go too far." I assured him it would be okay, but there was concern about it, and soldiers were in the audience. We were always followed by a KGB guy when we were out shooting stuff on the streets. So for the beginning, we had a life-size cutout of Gorbachev with a movable arm. I come out, and we shook hands. That melted them right away. Then I did a ten-minute opening in Russian. I wrote the material and had a Russian translator write it out phonetically for me.

Soon after, I came to Michael with a show I had written called *Sessions*, which turned out to be one of the best things I've ever done without being in it.

It starred Michael McKean and Elliott Gould, and it was about a man in therapy going through a midlife crisis. It was very funny and very perceptive. We got phenomenal reviews. The audience wasn't big, but that didn't matter. Michael was awesome, gave it a chance to grow. And then *City Slickers* happened and suddenly there were more movies, and not enough time to do the shows the way I wanted to. Michael had ordered like forty-four shows. We did six and I couldn't fill the order because I couldn't trust anyone else to write it the way I wanted to write it. But he was brave enough to put that show on. And this is before *Analyze This* and *The Sopranos*.

George Carlin, another HBO favorite, did fourteen specials for HBO and was one of the most important comedians in the network's history. And vice versa. Throughout this career, Carlin, a part-time social scientist, was on an unrelenting journey to engineer societal change and disruption through his comedy. It was a perfect marriage, considering HBO's persistent desire to seek out controversy and break barriers whenever possible.

ROCCO URBISCI, Director:

I was driving down Wilshire Boulevard and saw "George Carlin" atop the Wadsworth theater marquee. I bought a ticket, saw the show, and went backstage. I hadn't seen him in years, but when he saw me, he said, "Hey man, good to see you." And then just like that, "Do you want to do my next HBO special?" I said, "Yes, I'd love to do that." It was called *Playin' with Your Head*, and we made what was then the most expensive opening for any HBO special.

The conceit was there were three demons in George's life: his diet, his drinking, and his drugs. I got my DP Bruce Logan to find 35-millimeter black-and-white film, which was almost nonexistent, and we used Panavision cameras. We shot it like a motion picture.

Artistic freedom was incredibly important to George. One day we were in the car talking about it, and he took a deep breath and said, "Thank God for HBO."

George Carlin: Jammin' in New York focused on the environment and included this amazing piece he did about Mother Nature. George said many times this was his favorite special. He thought he had turned a new corner on material, and it was a big breakthrough not only with his acting discipline, but his writing.

If you watch the construction of the Mother Earth section, there was a part in the show where somebody booed because they thought he was making fun of trying to save the planet. If that guy would've listened for just a couple fucking seconds more, the reason he was laying all that out was to drop the bomb on us when he said, "The planet isn't going anywhere, we are. We're going away. Pack your shit, folks."

RICHARD LEWIS:
George Carlin was the king of specials.

One night, a special of mine was on TV, we were in the same hotel, and he slipped a note under my door telling me he loved it. That made me feel like a million bucks. For his specials, he choreographed every word. He wanted to make it like a play and worked harder than anyone.

We became really close, and I called him once when he was preparing for his God knows three thousandth special for HBO, and asked, "Pastor, how's the new special coming?" He said, "All I have is a minute and twelve seconds left to write."

I started to hole up in hotels in every city trying to memorize thousands of new pieces of material, but I still had little idea of what I was going to say when I went onstage and was ad-libbing at least half of my shows. So I stopped doing those specials because the directors wanted to know everything in advance.

SUSIE ESSMAN, Actor and Comedian:
I did a *One Night Stand* for HBO that we shot in Miami Beach. They were doing a whole bunch of them and had two comics a night. It was me and Gilbert Gottfried on our night, and it was at a gay nightclub that they had taken over. These things are very hard because they need high ceilings for lighting, but high ceilings are death for stand-up. Comedy clubs always have low ceilings because laughs hover under a low ceiling and then they roll through the room. And laughter is contagious.

An HBO special was a big deal to get. I had been in the business about eight years at that point, but I had to figure out how to put this special together because it wasn't naturally the way that I worked. It's one of the reasons why I never did spots on *Letterman* and those other shows. A four-minute set just isn't my style. I always worked spontaneously on stage, but when you're doing a special, you can't do that, and that was completely against my grain.

Carlin, Jerry Seinfeld, they're a different type of comic than Richard Lewis and I are. Lewis and I like to go up on stage and just go off. And you can't do that on a special. You have to have it checked.

RICHARD LEWIS:

If you were going to be a successful comedian, you had to have your own HBO special. It was akin to wanting to get on Carson in the old days. And when you did a special on HBO, you could really be yourself, not worry about language, and be as provocative as you wanted.

I was a recovering addict. I got sober in '94. It wasn't as if I was drunk when I did most of my shows, but I wanted to do another HBO special completely sober. In 1990, I was still in recovery.

I loved my special. I was in a phone booth in Venice calling people like Marv Albert, Mickey Mantle, and Howard Stern, asking them for the name of a shrink, and at the end there was a group therapy scene, with a shrink, me, Dudley Moore, and O. J. Simpson.

I had a couple of breaks in my life that were huge. Johnny Carson, then David Letterman, then Jamie Lee Curtis wanted me to be her love interest. I was the first Jew with bad posture to make love to Jamie Lee Curtis on a television series. HBO is definitely up on that list.

MIKE BINDER:

I made a special in Detroit called *The Detroit Comedy Jam* with myself, Howie Mandel, Dave Coulier, and Paul Rodriguez. George Carlin's company sold it to HBO and were executive producers. It actually got me banned from the Comedy Store. Mitzi [Shore] had produced all these specials at the Comedy Store that I'd been part of, and HBO was very important to her. When she found out she wasn't attached as a producer, she was furious. "Why do you have Carlin doing this?" I said, "Mitzi, he is my childhood idol."

So I'm in Detroit working on the special and I get a call from a friend who ran the door at the Comedy Store. He says, "I was told if you come here to have you thrown out." That was like my home. Mitzi took my name and pictures off the wall *and* my neon sign. In retrospect, I probably should've gotten her a credit. She'd been so good to me, but I wasn't sophisticated enough then to know you can get people credits.

ROSEANNE BARR, Actor and Comedian:

I was told Rodney Dangerfield wanted to meet me, and I was thrilled. All the comedians wanted to meet Rodney, and he was my dad's favorite. They brought me into his dressing room after his show, he was wearing a robe, and of course his balls were hanging out, like all the comics always talk about.

He asked me to do my "suck my dick" joke and he thought it was so funny. Then he says, "I want you to play my wife in my special. I've never had anyone play my wife, but you're going to be my wife." And I said, "Oh my God. Okay." I was so excited, I called my dad and said, "Rodney wants me for his wife." Doing that special with him was a thrill of a lifetime, and I got to say the line to him, "You're going to take shit from me, and take shit from my mother, too."

He wrote all those lines for me. He loved me, and I loved him. When he died, he left me his medical marijuana and his pipe.

ANDREW DICE CLAY, Comedian and Actor:

He was Rodney Dangerfield. I wasn't a big name. I never bothered big stars when they came to the Comedy Store, but he was hanging out after my set, so I asked him, "What'd you think?" He goes, "Man, you are crazy." I went for it, and said, "I'd love to be part of your next special." He said "It's going to be on HBO, and the answer is yes."

I prepared for that special like nothing else. I wasn't going to fuck around. I had three months. I trained physically and worked nonstop on my material.

Then it was about getting the right things to wear. I still have the giant belt buckle and jacket. I wanted to present to America the ultimate rock and roll comedian, to give them an image of Elvis as a comic. I knew if I did it right, I would go through the roof.

We did it for two nights. After the first, I walked over to my dad and I go, "It's done. I'm the biggest comic the world's ever seen." Everybody in that room knew it, including Rodney. He was so happy with me.

Sandy Gallin saw it and told me, "I'm going to sign you. We're going to do great things together." I said, "Wait a minute. If you want to sign me, I want a one-hour HBO special." He said to me, "I don't audition for clients." I sat there and looked at him, smoking a cigarette. He was a great guy. He looked at me and smiled, then yelled to his assistant, "Sheila, can you get me

Chris Albrecht on the phone?" He puts him on speaker. "Chris, I'm sitting here with Andrew Dice Clay, and I'm wondering if we could have a one-hour special for Mr. Clay. Would that be possible?" Then he takes Chris off speaker, talks to him for a minute, then hangs up and says, "You'll have your answer tomorrow, and I'll have the papers ready."

The next day he calls and tells me I got the special. I said, "Great, and I want it to air at midnight, New Year's Eve '88 going into '89." He asks, "Why's that?" And I go, "Because many people have house parties. It'll be great to know a couple million people are gathering and watching this one hour." He liked that idea and got it for me. It was amazing.

While Potter and Albrecht had creative latitude at HBO that their peers at broadcast networks often envied but seldom enjoyed, HBO was still very much "The Fuchs Broadcasting Company." Michael Fuchs had very specific likes and dislikes that would occasionally gum up the works, as was the case when comedian Howie Mandel and his manager, Terry Danuser, met Albrecht for lunch. According to an internal CAA memo, Albrecht made a commitment to Mandel that HBO would air a comedy special featuring the manic Mandel before the year was out.

PHIL KENT, Agent:

After Chris made the deal with me, Fuchs put a stop to it, leaving me in a horrible position where I had to tell Howie that the agreement I told him about was no longer in existence. You never want to be in that position with a client.

MICHAEL FUCHS:

There were certain artists who I didn't believe were special enough for HBO. Like I had said, "No one better come to me with Liberace." *Howie from Maui* stirred me. Probably a bottom ten all-time show. I had put Mandel on the "No HBO" list. When Chris committed to another one, I told him to kill it.

CHRIS ALBRECHT:

When Michael canceled the special, it was embarrassing.

After months of back-and-forth finger pointing and deflections, Bill Haber, one of CAA's co-founders, went nuclear. "We will withdraw CAA's client participation in any projects involving HBO on any level," he wrote to Fuchs. "I respect your decision to do whatever you wish as regards the Howie Mandel commitment. Nevertheless, you must also respect my obligation to this Company and its clients to guarantee we are in business with honorable and trustworthy contractors."

PHIL KENT:

Bill wanted to show that we would not be fucked with.

MICHAEL FUCHS:

Bill Haber writes me, "If you don't do the Howie Mandel show, the agency will boycott you on all other talent. No one has ever reneged on us and we don't renege on anyone. Ever." It took me fifteen seconds to remind him that Kirk Douglas, who I had a personal relationship with, had pulled out of an HBO project, but we hadn't pulled a Haber.

PHIL KENT:

We were suddenly out of business with each other, and Bridget Potter called me screaming, "What have you done? We're at thermonuclear war now over Howie Mandel? Are you serious?"

Then I get a call from [Michael] Ovitz, who's on a yacht somewhere in the Mediterranean, and he, too, is screaming at me. "How could you fucking let Bill Haber get into a whose dick is bigger contest with Michael Fuchs?" I said, "Michael, he's my boss. Was I supposed to throw myself across his assistant's typewriter and stop the letter?"

He flew into his Master of the Universe mode, yelling, "Now I've got to go patch this up."

MICHAEL FUCHS:

Haber actually apologized. Later I got a call from Ovitz. He said, "Do me a favor. Throw out that shit that Haber wrote you."

PHIL KENT:

We sold the Howie Mandel special to Showtime. Howie ended up leaving the agency; I had to fly to New York, humiliate myself, and apologize in Michael Fuchs's office with the sunken floor; and Bill and Michael became great friends.

Despite wanting to be controversial and provocative and having shown the gumption to take on social issues like abortion, guns, and civil rights, HBO had made an effort to stay on the sidelines when it came to party politics. Yet such was the power and promise of a live Barbra Streisand performance—her first in more than six years—that Fuchs bought the rights to telecast Streisand's **One Voice** *concert without hesitation. The show was recorded at her Malibu home for an audience of five hundred celebs on September 6, 1986, as a fundraiser for various liberal causes* *with Streisand's own foundation and California senator Alan Cranston's campaign, among them.*

Attended by such stars as Jane Fonda, Whitney Houston, Bette Midler, Sally Field, Bruce Willis, Sydney Pollack, Burt Bacharach, and others, **One Voice** *featured a white-bedecked Streisand who wasn't just in "good voice," she was in great voice, and when that happens, there are arguably none greater.*

BARBRA STREISAND, Singer:

When Chernobyl happened, it was a jolt. If we needed any reminder that we were living in dangerous times, this showed us that nuclear facilities were like ticking bombs. It was a wake-up call. The election was approaching, and I was a member of the Hollywood Women's Political Committee. We decided we wanted to be a force in electing a Democratic majority in the Senate that would hopefully stop nuclear proliferation. It was my friend and fellow member Marilyn Bergman who said, "We could raise a lot of money if we put on a fundraiser where you would sing." I was reluctant. The last time I did a concert was in 1967, when I gave a free concert in Central Park and forgot the words to a song, which really spooked me. I didn't want to do concerts anymore. But then I realized that I was more frightened of a nuclear accident than singing in public again.

I decided to have the concert in my own backyard (and avoid overhead costs, like renting an arena) because I wanted all the money to go to the candidates. So we cleared a space at the ranch and built a small stage to hold eight musicians, and a half circle of tiered seating that could hold five hundred people. That meant two hundred and fifty couples.

MICHAEL FUCHS:

Between the Hollywood Women's Political Committee and us, we got her to sing at her house. Barbra had not performed in public for a long time. I went for a tech rehearsal, and she had this sort of Greek theater in her woods, and before you could see the stage, I heard her voice come out from the trees. It was something special.

BARBRA STREISAND:

The committee wanted to charge $5,000 per couple, and I thought, "Who the hell is ever going to pay that?" Well, everyone they invited said yes and we raised an unprecedented amount of money with *One Voice*, the largest ever by a one-night live performance in the history of California. Reagan had a competing fundraiser with three times the number of guests, but as the *New York Times* printed, we raised more and the best part was we were able to change the Senate back to being Democratic, because five of our six candidates won! That was a terrific feeling of accomplishment.

By then they had developed teleprompters that could stand on the ground like huge speakers, so I had some confidence that if I forgot the words I could see them there. The night before, we taped a dress rehearsal, and thank God we did that. I didn't realize people would stand when I sang "America, the Beautiful," and when they did, they blocked my teleprompters. I couldn't see the words so we wound up having to use the dress rehearsal for that song on the actual show.

The evening went well. Robin Williams opened with a hilarious monologue and I felt very supported because so many of the Hollywood community turned out, including Quincy Jones, who brought Whitney Houston, Barry Diller, Jack Nicholson, who came with Anjelica Huston, Whoopi Goldberg, Sally Field, Bette Midler, Henry Winkler, and Norman Lear, among many others.

In addition to the candidates we were supporting, like Alan Cranston and Tim Wirth, it was wonderful to have representative Barbara Jordan there in her wheelchair, Mayor Tom Bradley, Senator George Mitchell, Senator Howard Metzenbaum, and Representative Henry Waxman.

MICHAEL FUCHS:

We needed the event to be somewhat nonpolitical. We couldn't make an ad for the Democratic Party. I ended up talking with Barbra on the phone, going over songs and things she would say in between. It's not that we would've gotten in trouble, but being overtly political wasn't a smart thing for us to do.

BARBRA STREISAND:

I edited the concert for HBO and left out some of the more overtly political material. I made those choices myself, to reflect the fact that this was a concert, not a paid political broadcast.

Adding Streisand to HBO's already impressive list of associated musicians was no small feat, and a testament to the network's unparalleled ability to land the biggest names.

STU SMILEY, Executive:

Bridget sent me to London to track *Max Headroom*, which was an English show developed by producer/executive Peter Wagg, with an inspired performance by Matt Frewer as a computer-generated TV host. It was playing on Channel 4 and was a sensation over there and Bridget made a deal to bring *Max Headroom* to the States. It was a media rocket when it landed here, with the cover of *Newsweek*, and was regarded as the next new thing. ABC had contracted to make a version of the English show as a one-hour drama, so *Max Headroom* was everywhere. *The Max Headroom Talk Show* that we produced aired on Cinemax. Robert Morton, who was a segment producer at *Letterman*, took a leave to produce our show, and Larry David was on the writing staff [this was prior to *Seinfeld*].

I had worked at Showtime, which was much smaller and didn't have the financial capabilities HBO had. At HBO you felt no limitations, financial or otherwise. Michael referred to it as "the big store" compared to Showtime, and HBO did feel like a much bigger canvas.

HBO's **1st & Ten,** *a drama-comedy series chronicling the exploits of a fictitious NFL team called the California Bulls, debuted in December 1984. At first glance—and at second—the show was little more than an opportunity for HBO to feature nudity and spicy language. Those qualities, plus the presence of Delta Burke as team owner, were more than enough to guarantee a second season, when O. J. Simpson joined the cast. His wasn't the only bold-faced name to appear before the show expired after seven seasons. Along the way came soft-core star Shannon Tweed, Lawrence Taylor, A. C. Cowlings (later O.J.'s driver in the infamous Bronco motorcade), and running back Marcus Allen, who also knew Simpson's ex-wife Nicole Brown Simpson.*

CHRIS ALBRECHT:

The pilot for *1st & Ten* was done before I got there. It wasn't a good show and had no connection to reality, but Michael was friends with the producers, and I wasn't about to start off by getting rid of things.

GARY H. MILLER, Writer and Producer:

I sometimes had to do casting, and part of my job this one day was to pick out two women for that week's episode who would appear topless. I was sitting in my trailer with my assistant where forty women were scheduled to come in, strip for me down to their waist, at which point she would take a Polaroid of each of them. So I've got a naked woman in my trailer, and there's a knock on the door, and it's my wife, Karen, and my two little kids. I go to the door, open it a crack, and say, "Uh, honey, go to the set. You can't come in here now." She goes, "Why not?" "I'm casting for topless women." My wife gets this look on her face and says, "Let's go, children. Your father is busy." Then my little son Max said, "I want to stay here with Dad." He got the gist of it.

BRIDGET POTTER:

I inherited *1st & Ten*, which Iris Dugow had supervised and Michael loved. I had my issues with it, but it wasn't terrible. When we picked the show up for a second season, we had a press event, and O.J. was there, just so handsome and so charming. At the end, Peter Locke whispered in my ear, "Do not go anywhere or ever be alone with O.J." I asked, "What are you talking about?" He said, "Trust me."

GARY H. MILLER:

We were all on a plane and hit unbelievable turbulence, then we dropped altitude very quickly. It was frightening. All these giant linemen were really, really scared and barfing in bags. I turned around and O.J. was sitting there with a smile on his face, like he was in a car. I'll never forget how eerie that was. Then there was a time we needed to shoot a sequence on the field and needed O.J. for the scene, but he was in his trailer with one of the women who played a cheerleader.

We had nudity throughout the show, and I tried to work against it. They'd say, "Let's have a party scene so waitresses can walk around topless," and I'd say, "What parties have you been to?" But other producers would say, "This is what people want to see."

I tried to change the show around as best I could. I said, "Let's inject some story lines into the show that actually happen in football." I developed a steroid arc, about an aging lineman who resorted to steroids to keep up with the younger guys coming into the league. We hired John Matuszak for a three-episode arc, who said, "This is exactly how I feel. This is what a football player on steroids goes through. I want to play this part so badly. I am this guy."

When it was time to shoot the scene where he dies on the field, it was in August, and about 110 degrees. I got players in pads, and the second AD comes over me and says, "John Matuszak refuses to come out of his trailer. Please go talk to him."

I said, "John, this is the big scene. This is what we've been working toward over three episodes." He says, "I don't want to die. I want to stay on the show." I said, "You can't stay on with the show. Your character is supposed to die. That's the deal. That's the arc. It's going to be very dramatic."

He said, "I'm not doing it." Now if you've ever seen John Matuszak, you know you don't argue with him. He's huge and looks like he's crazy. I said, "John, do me a favor, please, just die on the field today, and I'll bring you back next season as a different character." His eyes went wide, and he starts coming toward me and says, "I'm a six-foot-nine, two-hundred-seventy-pound white man. They're going to know the new character is me." I finally convinced him to go out there. The irony of it all is in real life John Matuszak died from a drug overdose.

Sports—whether scripted or live events—continued to be a cornerstone of successful HBO programming during this period, as the network maintained its male-oriented focus.

Throughout the 1980s—arguably one of the best decades in boxing history—boxing and HBO went together like cornermen and Vaseline, and the majority of the most memorable fights were on HBO, either live or on delayed broadcast.

SETH ABRAHAM:

We had had the end of Ali, the beginning of Larry Holmes, and a lot to work with in between, including Sugar Ray Leonard, Marvin Hagler, Tommy Hearns, Roberto Duran, and ultimately Mike Tyson. This was a fantastic time. Our goal was to own and milk the biggest boxing events.

ROSS GREENBURG:

HBO looked at sporting events as mini movies with swirling subplots. Fighters have stories before they ever enter the ring—previous injuries, relationships with their trainers, and personal challenges. We wanted to cover all of it.

SETH ABRAHAM:

We would do elaborate profiles on each boxer for air prior to fights. The networks generally didn't do that, but because we didn't have commercial time, we had time to give the audience far more background.

ROSS GREENBURG:

After fights, we didn't have to cut away, and we would go directly into the ring with the fighters, then to Merchant and Lampley to bring viewers different perspectives. We'd wrap up the fight in a bow in terms of what it meant that night and for the future.

We always wanted to challenge ourselves to come up with new innovations that would change the way people watch the sport. I had seen a photo of Ali taken from overhead where Cleveland Williams was flat on his back and Ali was standing over him. I thought, wouldn't it be great if we could do that for a live fight, and started sending cameramen up into the rafters in arenas before we had remote cameras so we could create overhead shots. They added a lot of drama, not only in slow motion replay, but were a beautiful ending to knockouts.

SETH ABRAHAM:

Ross had flights of genius. He was inventive and shared my view about broadcasters as journalists. I went to Tim Braine, the executive producer who I inherited, and said, "Tim, I'm going to find you a different job at HBO that will not be a demotion, so I can give Ross your job." Tim said, "As long as you're doing that, get me a really good job, one that I like." I put Tim in charge of all on-air promotion that aired between the shows, what HBO called "interstitials," and he was pleased. Ross took over and did a great job.

MARGARET GROSSI, Executive Producer:

Ross's temper could flare at times. As a joke, we'd made a little "Ross-O-Meter" to gauge his temper, and we'd move the needle around. We usually left it pegging on high. There were times, if we weren't rolling back a highlight fast enough, when he'd come running around the corner from the control room to yell at us, oftentimes with his headset on, but the cord was too short to reach the tape room and his head would get yanked back. It was all we could do to not laugh. Other times he would lay into people unnecessarily, like one year, he picked on a guy who worked in graphics. It was relentless. It became ridiculous. Ross felt badly afterward. At the wrap party, he gave the guy an award and apologized to him in front of everybody. Ross was fine but, yeah, he could get hot. I'm sure he felt the pressure of trying to turn around a lot of stuff quickly.

One of the greatest fights in the annals of boxing aired originally on closed circuit April 15, 1985, and then a week later on HBO: a middleweight bout between Marvelous (his legal name) Marvin Hagler and Thomas Hearns. Fights don't have to be long to be memorable; after perhaps the most action-packed first round in boxing history, HBO's Barry Tompkins exulted, "And this is just the first round!"

HENRY SCHLEIFF, Executive:

Hagler, Hearns. People say there was more leather thrown in those three rounds than any other fight in the history of boxing.

All of us HBO execs were sitting fifth row center; we had a pool going on who was going to win and what round. Hearns approaches the ring with an entourage behind him. He's under a hoodie and everybody's in a conga line with their arms on the person's shoulders in front of them.

Hagler knocks Hearns out in the third round. They scrape him off the floor and now the conga line starts going out with Hearns in front and three people behind him. And in the true tradition of HBO where you always have to be doing something that's a little off the charts, I duck into the conga line as it starts to move out of the arena. I have my hands on the shoulder in front of the guy in front of me, and Michael is laughing hysterically.

I hold on as we go through the bowels of Caesars Palace and into his dressing room. The door closes, and I say to myself, I have way overplayed this hand.

Tommy is stretched out, his brother and another guy are crying, and they all of a sudden notice me, and are like, who the fuck are you? I come up with, "No crying, no crying. You're still a champion," and with that, there's a knock on the door. It's the Nevada health examiner. Even when you lose a fight, they test you. The guy says, "I need everybody out of here. Tommy, you need to give me some urine." Nobody moves. Then I think, here's my get out of jail card, and say, "Did you hear the commissioner? Everybody out of here now!"

Boxing had become fragmented. At the time, three ruling bodies each had its own anointed champion: the International Boxing Federation, the World Boxing Association, and the World Boxing Council. Three entities, three different champions, three belts. HBO saw an opening. Why not put all those belts together in one tournament and anoint a true heavyweight champion? The previous undisputed, unified champion that HBO stabled was Marvin Hagler.

SETH ABRAHAM:

I was frustrated with all these boxing organizations. Each one had a different title holder, and it minimized the expression "heavyweight champion of the world" because you had three and a half organizations with three and a half champions. The half was a newly sprung organization called the WBO, the World Boxing Organization.

Our daughter was born on the sixteenth of October in 1985. Five or six days later, Don [King] came over to see her, watch the World Series, and he stayed for dinner. I said, "Don, you talk about yourself as the best promoter in the history of boxing. Let's try to do something historical." He controlled two of the three champions, and Butch Lewis, a rival of Don's, controlled Michael Spinks. Don and I kept going back and forth, back and forth, and we finally sketched out this idea of seven fights to unify the three belts. He left at three a.m.

On January 17, 1986, HBO, along with Don King, announced plans to finance this new seven-fight tournament with the goal being to produce one unified champion, leaving other promoters, lawyers, and managers both complaining and scrambling to get involved.

"HBO is acting as a promoter without a license," Dennis Rappaport, a manager for Gerry Cooney, complained. There were concerns from left and right that by trying to unify the title, HBO was meddling in the sport.

The Heavyweight Unification Series wouldn't be the only shiny new thing about to come HBO's way. As the decade reached its midway point, and familiar names grew old, HBO envisioned a dream scenario from which a heroic new name would emerge: a spectacular talent to electrify existing boxing fans, whose exceptional prowess and personality might create a new and larger audience for the sport. In 1966, Brownsville, Brooklyn, gave birth to such a man—Michael Gerard Tyson.

Boxing had never seen anything quite like Mike Tyson—a combination of talent and rage fronted by a surprisingly sweet voice and, even early on, equipped with enough backstories to keep writers churning out one fanciful fable after another. Tyson became a magnificent obsession for HBO, particularly Fuchs.

MICHAEL FUCHS:

I used to have a list that had special assignments I gave myself every month. I'll never forget looking at it once and seeing only one item: "Get Tyson." I had seen Tyson on an afternoon fight on ABC.

ROSS GREENBURG:

Back in 1984, I got a three-quarter-inch cassette from Jim Jacobs, a manager, with a note, "Ross, here's a new young heavyweight I'd like you take a look at." I watch the tape, and it's this guy's first fourteen fights, and there are fourteen knockouts. Forget what he was doing in the ring, which was impressive as hell. You could also feel the electricity he generated. Then Jacobs says, "Why don't you come up to New York. I want you to see this guy for yourself." I went into the office the next day and walked into Seth's office and said, "I just saw something incredible. We have to get this kid." I'm not taking credit for being the only one, but within a week or so, we had a three-fight deal with Tyson.

Tyson's first fight on HBO was on May 20, 1986, against Mitch "Blood" Green, a one-sided thrashing that Tyson won via near-unanimous decision. (His first-ever televised professional fight had aired on ABC three months earlier against Jesse "The Boogie-man" Ferguson, lasting six rounds. Mike was nineteen years old.) In his July 1986 bout against Lorenzo Boyd, Tyson broke Boyd's nose in the first round and then knocked him out just 1:43 into the second. No one could believe the speed, force, and power of Mike Tyson.

SETH ABRAHAM:

After Tyson finished his three-fight deal with us, I was negotiating with his managers Jim Jacobs and Bill Cayton for a new one. Don King was not involved yet, just on the periphery as an adviser to Mike. We worked out a deal: ten fights for $62 million.

I had a presentation scheduled for Michael to approve it with Ross and several others, but he wasn't coming in until later that day and told me, "We don't need a meeting. Let's do this by phone." I said, "Michael, it's over sixty million dollars. I want your attention on this." He says, "Okay, I'm coming in around two. No charts, no graphs, just you and me." Now I have to disinvite everybody who had done a lot of work on this and go into Michael's office that afternoon. He's sitting at his desk reading something, and I ask, "You want me to wait?" He said, "No, go ahead." I start the presentation about the deal, but he never looked up. He could have been booking his date for that night for all I knew. I said, "Michael, why don't I come back." Now he looks up, puts his glasses on his head, and says, "I assume that since you're in my office, you've thought this all the way through, but if you haven't and you're in my office, then clearly, you're the wrong guy for this job and I need to fire you." I asked him, "Did you hear anything I said?" And now he's looking down again, and says, "Yeah, I did. Okay." I said, "Okay what?" And he said, "You got sixty-two million, go sign him." I said, "Michael, are you sure?" He said, "Get the fuck out of my office." The whole thing took forty-five seconds.

RICK BERNSTEIN, Executive:

Most of the stories I shot with Mike took place in the Catskills where he trained, and there were at least a couple of occasions when I would drive Mike up there for our shoot. There was one conversation when he was telling me that he was at some bar in Scranton, Pennsylvania, and there was a room above the bar and the entire evening they were bringing one woman after the next up to be with Mike, and he was having sex with each of them.

Mike told me it was as many as twenty different women he had had sex with on that given night. I said, "I don't know how you could perform that many times." And he laughed and said, "They called me the stallion."

He turned to me and said, "Rick, how many different women have you had sex with in one day?" I said, "Mike, only nineteen less than you," and then he laughed.

JOE COLLINS:

From a marketing standpoint, the tournament worked terrifically. We fell upon an incredible cast of characters. Leon Spinks sparked the imagination of the public, and you couldn't have invented Tyson. He was like a cartoon character, exactly perfect for the role he played.

MICHAEL FUCHS:

I said, "Guys, I have a feeling this kid Tyson is going to be able to come in and kick the shit out of the champion."

ROSS GREENBURG:

There was only one problem. Halfway through, Michael Spinks decided to bolt because he didn't want to fight Tyson in the finals for what was going to be meager dollars compared to what they would do on pay-per-view. So Butch Lewis yanked Michael Spinks out of the series.

SETH ABRAHAM:

I don't know if Spinks got the heebie-jeebies, but we sued, and Spinks won. Here's how: Spinks voluntarily gave up his IBF belt and the judge ruled that since he was no longer a heavyweight champion, he was not bound by the contract.

ROSS GREENBURG:

All hell broke loose. It took an extra eighteen months to finish the series. Tyson ended up having all three belts wrapped around him, but you still had the lineal champion, Michael Spinks, out there. They ended up fighting closed circuit, which we did, then Tyson was anointed.

MICHAEL FUCHS:

As a result of the tournament, Tyson became the youngest heavyweight champion in history, and one of the highest-rated fixtures on HBO. Tyson fights got unbelievable numbers.

DAVE HARMON, Producer:

That heavyweight tournament set the Mike Tyson era off and running.

SETH ABRAHAM:

We had one executive, Lou DiBella, who used to go to boxing clubs at night. He went to gyms. First executive I ever saw with an earring, Harvard undergraduate, Harvard Law School.

LOU DiBELLA, Executive:

I applied to be general counsel of the Yankees. It was down to three or four of us. I was on my way to the interview when I got a call from Steinbrenner's office. The secretary said, "The boss saw on your résumé that you're only 29 years old, and he thinks you are too young for the job." I was bummed out. She said, "I don't know if this helps you, but the guy I think he's offering the job to was also interviewing for the job as the general counsel of HBO Sports."

My two favorite sports from the time I learned to walk were baseball and boxing. As soon as she said, "HBO," I thought to myself, Seth Abraham, HBO, the biggest fights, and literally my suit was on, my résumé already in my pocket. And back then in 1989, there wasn't big security in buildings. I literally just walked past the security desk in the HBO building and found my way to the general counsel of HBO's office.

SETH ABRAHAM:

Lou would come into work at 2:30, and people would say to me, "How do you allow that?" I said, "I don't care. He does his job, he does it extremely well." He was out with managers and fighters and would sometimes not get to sleep until 3 o'clock in the morning.

Lou and I went to Madison Square Garden to see a Showtime fight. It may have been the only time I ever did this. The headliner was the Canadian fighter Donovan "Razor" Ruddock. We were negotiating with Don to have Tyson fight Ruddock, and I had never seen him fight. We go early to see the undercard fights. Our seats were in the front row, professional courtesy. Lou goes off to schmooze, and I head to our seats. All of a sudden, this big hand came out and said, "You're Seth Abraham, aren't you?" I looked, and it was John Gotti. He said, "My God, I'm such a fan of yours. I won't go out on a Saturday night with the guys until the HBO fights are over. I'm such a fan of what you guys do." Meanwhile, this big hand is out there. I'm thinking if I shake this guy's hand and a photographer takes my picture, that can literally be a career ender. I'm perspiring, trying to figure out how not to shake his hand, but I don't want to show a lack of respect. I'm trying to figure out what to do when suddenly the boxing manager Lou Duva comes over and bear hugs Gotti. I ran to the other side of the ring.

The next significant step for HBO Sports was to add to its efforts to strengthen the pedigree of its on-air talent.

JIM LAMPLEY:

I was finishing a master's degree program at the University of North Carolina in Chapel Hill, when in 1974, ABC Sports launched a gimmick one-time-only idea to put a college-age announcer on the sidelines of the college football telecast. They interviewed more than four hundred people. I was eventually one of two people who were chosen to be the guinea pigs.

That led to three seasons on the sidelines, and for whatever reason Roone Arledge, the leader of ABC Sports, had me also doing a whole bunch of stuff on *Wide World of Sports* and other things, including the Olympics as a feature reporter. I wound up spending thirteen years at ABC.

I left under not terribly favorable circumstances, forced out by a new executive, Dennis Swanson, who didn't like me. My agent asked me, "What do you want to do?" I said, "I want to work at HBO, because if I say something controversial on a Saturday night, no executive is going to get a call from an advertiser on Monday morning, complaining. I want that freedom."

My longtime good friend and golfing buddy, Jack Nicholson, used to sort of look at me admiringly and pat me on the back and say, "Lamp, you're just like me, you don't sell soap."

SETH ABRAHAM:

We read in the papers that Jim Lampley was disappointed ABC Sports had not given him a bigger role, starting with the Olympics, and we met with him about coming to HBO. For many men and women at that time, the idea of going from network broadcast television to HBO cable was a trade down. It sometimes would take a lot of proselytizing to convince broadcasters and production people to join us. I told Jim, "You're going to be the Babe Ruth of HBO broadcasting."

BILLIE JEAN KING, Sportscaster:

What was different at HBO from everywhere else was how Seth and Ross put things in motion. Their leadership equaled their philosophy. I've been in a lot of production meetings elsewhere and they tell you what to do. "We're going to do this; we want it slick; we want it this way." Seth and Ross were just the opposite. They said, "We don't want it slick. We want you to talk from your heart and minds." They asked talent and everyone involved for their opinions and went deeper from there.

JIM LAMPLEY:

Working on Wimbledon telecasts for HBO, I sat every day shoulder to shoulder with Billie Jean King, Arthur Ashe, Martina Navratilova, and I can go on and on. These are figures not just of athletic significance, but of great societal significance. That wasn't an objective in commercial network television, but it was an objective at HBO. You couldn't do many things that were more exciting than what I was doing at Wimbledon for HBO.

When talent sets the bar for themselves higher than anyone else, it makes the job of producing them far easier.

RICK BERNSTEIN:

Jim Lampley is probably the most underappreciated broadcaster I've ever worked with. I don't think viewers and television executives realize how talented this man is. A riot once broke out at a boxing event we were covering at Madison Square Garden. Jim immediately transitioned from sports announcer to news reporter. Chairs were flying in the air and brawls were spreading like wildfire throughout the arena, yet Jim somehow managed to make his way to our elevated camera platform and cover the mayhem without missing a beat. For thirty minutes, if not more, Jim single-handedly reported on something that none of us had ever experienced in our decades of producing boxing. And mind you, Jim did so knowing that his young daughter was seated somewhere near ringside. Few sports broadcasters could have handled that level of pandemonium.

When we would rehearse Jim's opening remarks, every single take he would recite his opening comments word for word, then two hours later, when we were live, he would repeat it verbatim, the same exact way. All without a teleprompter of course. If you told Jim you needed one minute, with or without a producer's count in his ear, he would always hit the one-minute mark.

BILLIE JEAN KING:

Lampley was a really quick learner. Oh my God. He's so smart. He's very observant. Encyclopedic. He's ridiculous, doesn't need a script or a teleprompter.

He just goes. He's amazing. He always wrote in his book. He wrote in three things every day, to reflect on the summary of the day.

SETH ABRAHAM:

We were at Wimbledon during one of these interminable rain delays in the pre-roofs era, and I took Billie Jean to breakfast. I said, "Billie, your boss now is the HBO viewer. You owe it to them to be honest. If a player is playing like shit, you've got to say it, even if it's your best friend. You're no longer a free agent. You're a responsible journalist, broadcasting to millions of HBO viewers." That took quite some time for Billie to put into her mind, but she worked at it. She saw the people who were surrounding her, Arthur Ashe, Jim Lampley, and Frank Deford, who was a roving journalist at Wimbledon, and Billie, who is as competitive as they come, I think her pride kicked in and she wanted to be as good. It took a couple of seasons, but she turned herself into a first-rate broadcaster.

BILLIE JEAN KING:

I love the players and I care about them. When I called matches from the booth at Wimbledon, I always tried to make my commentary fair. You don't have a choice. You've got an audience; you owe them the truth. I told the players, "I'm in a very different role now. I'm now a broadcaster, I'm not a tennis player anymore. And when you retire, you get older and you want to be in broadcasting, you'll see what I mean. It's really hard. I do try to take a beat before I say anything, but if I have an opinion, I have to say it for the audience."

As HBO Sports beefed up its broadcasting team, another department looked to fortify its creative ranks. The year is 1984, and a prodigal daughter is about to return to HBO's documentary department.

SHEILA NEVINS:

When *Braingames* won the Peabody, I was told that award meant a lot to Jerry Levin. Then Michael called and said, "I heard you're going to get a Peabody. Don't you want to come back?" In the four years that I was away from HBO, I had been extremely successful, but I couldn't make any money. Let's say the budget of a show was $250K and it needed another $15K to make it better. HBO would refuse to give it to me, so I would put my own money into the show. That was not a good arrangement for me.

This call from Michael was something I had been praying for, and I had even rehearsed a response with my girlfriends. I didn't have the balls to tell him I refused to report to Bridget; all I said was, "I'd love to come back, but I'll need to report to you." He didn't say, "This is terrific news," he just went, "Yeah, yeah, yeah." And that was it.

I came back more determined than ever. I reminded the group that we weren't broadcasting to ourselves, we were broadcasting to an audience that was paying. I grew up in the theater and thought of it as us wanting people to buy tickets because that's really what pay TV was. And why should you pay for television when you can get it for free? I'll tell you why. Because we're going to give your kids shows that make them smart, not cartoons, and we're going to give you hot stuff at night. In between, we're going to tell you things you don't know about, plus things you're curious about. And we're not going to rub your nose in liberal-only thinking.

The mid-1980s showcased not only the reflective but the predictive power of HBO's documentary film division.

1985's **What Sex Am I?** *chronicled the personal and professional struggles of transgender individuals making their way in the United States at a time when even support for gay marriage was still a minority view.*

Another HBO effort, the Academy Award–winning documentary **Down and Out in America** *(1986), showcased the effects of a recession on rural and city-going Americans alike, foreshadowing the explosion of income inequality that has gripped the United States since the 1980s. Telling especially human stories became something of a specialty for HBO, stories that audiences at home didn't know they wanted—or needed—to hear.*

LEE GRANT:

I was so disturbed after doing *When Women Kill* because I was leaving all these women in prison, and I needed some fun. With documentaries, the door opens and you go into a brand-new world. And of course that was *What Sex Am I?*, which I think was a very important voyage for us.

CIS WILSON:

What Sex Am I? was way before its time. Sheila really supported it. She's a futurist and she wanted to do something on gender confusion. Lee Grant brought us this proposal on transgender people, and Sheila jumped on.

LEE GRANT:

I was acting to support us along the way, and I was acting in the former Yugoslavia, playing Mrs. Mussolini. George Scott was Mussolini. My husband asked me, "When are you going to be home? Because HBO is interested in giving this project to somebody else." I'd been on my knees, begging them for it, and I managed to get back just in time.

CIS WILSON:

Down and Out was the first HBO documentary to win an Academy Award for best documentary and Lee Grant and her husband Joe Feury directed and produced it. It was a very significant film.

I had no screen credit. I don't even think Sheila got screen credits at that time. Now it's standard that there's credits for HBO people who worked on the documentaries.

LEE GRANT:

There were many outlier moments in *Down and Out in America*, like that last line from the mom and the dad who were staying at the hotel with their kids, "Where'd the sweetness go?" That was pretty haunting.

HBO's 1987 documentary **Dear America: Letters Home from Vietnam** *painted a raw and authentic portrait of the sacrifice that marked that war by using real letters that American soldiers had written to loved ones. Their words, honest and often wrenching, were used as narration and served as poignant touchstones of the strong antiwar sentiment prevalent at the time.*

CIS WILSON:

Michael and I talked about the Vietnam War. I was an antiwar protester. Michael did not go, and we thought it was very important for us to give voice to the men and women who served in Vietnam. At the time, there was a theater company called the Veterans Ensemble Theatre Company in New York. Tom Bird, who was a Vietnam vet, headed that company, and he got the producer credit on the film. Tom and I were boyfriend and girlfriend at the time. I learned a lot about Vietnam through Tom, and through my brother who served there.

BILL COUTURIÉ:

Michael was on the board of the New York Vietnam Veterans. He said, "Vets got screwed on this deal. Why don't we do a film about Vietnam heroes, and show them as good guys?"

I said, "That's totally appropriate. They were certainly heroes in Vietnam." But I didn't think that was the right way to remember them. He'd have

Cis call me once a month, and say, "Michael wants to do the movie." I said, "I don't feel comfortable about doing a movie about heroes." It was around the time of *Rambo,* and I thought, what he really wants is a documentary *Rambo*. I don't want to make that movie.

CIS WILSON:

Because I had worked with Bill on *Disposable Heroes*, I was impressed with his ability as a filmmaker and his ability to empathize. I said, "Let's develop something and see if we can make it happen."

BILL COUTURIÉ:

Then one day I was at a bookstore and there was this book called *Dear America: Letters Home from Vietnam.* I picked it up and started flipping through it and said, "Oh my God, this is the movie." I got all excited and said, "Michael, I found the movie, it's going to be great." I wrote it up, sent it in, and they said, "What the fuck is this?" I said, "I'll have actors read the letters and we'll have actual footage. It'll be the real Vietnam. It'll be wall-to-wall rock and roll, and it'll show that these soldiers were innocent kids who got pulled into this rat's nest and Vietnam wasn't their fault. It was our fault."

Michael gave us the money to write a screenplay using the letters, and I said, "Michael, it's going to work. Just trust me." He said, "Okay, let's do it. What's the budget?"

I did the budget and it was $1 million, which was unheard of in those days. Michael said, "This is crazy. I can't do this." He said, "What can you do for half a million?" I said, "I can do a rough cut. I can get the letters recorded. I can get the footage, I can get music. I just can't license it at all." He said, "Okay, I'll give you half a million bucks, then we'll decide whether we want to finish it."

There was a big screening for the programming department. I brought it in and I was very proud of it. Michael was not there. This was just Bridget, Sheila, and Cis, a couple of other folks. We watched the film. Bridget looked at me and said, "This is a piece of shit. It's the worst film that HBO has ever done. It's unbroadcastable." I'd been working really hard and was emotional. I burst into tears and left. Cis came running after me. She's like, "Bill, Bill, no, no, no. That's not how you do it. You can't burst into tears. Be a big boy." But they were adamant. They hated it. Then Cis did something that most people wouldn't do. Because she loved the film, and by that time we were close friends, she showed it to Michael behind their backs. And Michael said, "This is the best thing HBO has ever done."

Dear America *would garner attention from far beyond the world of cable. Director and co-writer Couturié (with Richard Dewhurst) won two Emmys, the first in HBO history. The success of* **Letters Home from Vietnam** *was yet another reminder that a lot of guesswork still went into HBO programming and that there's never a guarantee of success. HBO didn't have stacks of research to suggest what its audience wanted, and apart from projects featuring big stars, much of their strategy involved just taking gambles on ideas—sometimes because a trusted element was involved.*

When Lorne Michaels was growing up in Canada, his grandparents owned a movie theater, and Michaels often found himself surrounded by aunts, uncles, and other family members whose favorite topic of conversation was, inevitably, the movies. Later, once Michaels had made his way south to the United States, it was the small-screen medium that enticed him, though movies would also eventually enter the picture. Regardless, Michaels retained strong connections to his homeland, hiring such fellow Canadians as Dan Aykroyd, Martin Short, Phil Hartman, Norm Macdonald, and Mike Myers for **Saturday Night Live,** *the revolution in television comedy that Michaels had invented in 1975.*

On one of Michaels's periodic trips home to Toronto, he caught a performance by The Kids in the Hall, a local comedy troupe with original slants on topics of the time and a cast of bright young men who wrote and performed sketches about them: Dave Foley, Kevin McDonald, Bruce McCulloch, Mark McKinney, and Scott Thompson, who played virtually all the characters in the sketches.

Michaels would produce five seasons of **Kids** *shows for HBO from 1988 to 1995, even when CBS brought the series to late night. McKinney would himself join SNL as a cast member in 1995 and '96, though otherwise there was very little crossover between the shows; each developed its own style of satirical lampooning—* **Kids in the Hall'**s *being arguably gentler and more subtle than that of the big extravaganza out of Rockefeller Center.*

LORNE MICHAELS:

I saw them a bunch of times when I would go up to Toronto, and I thought they were brilliant. When it came time to do a series, Ivan Fecan, who was running the CBC, called and said, "We'll do it with you if you'll do the pilot, you'll come up, and we'll need an American outlet." Fuchs was really helpful. It was a hit in Canada.

STU SMILEY:

Sandy Warner called us up and said, "You guys should come see this group." Chris and I went to see them in Toronto and they were very unique. Afterward Chris said, "There hasn't been something like that since *Monty Python*. This could really be something different."

BRIDGET POTTER:

When we picked it up, we were co-financers, and when we worked on it, they weren't incredibly receptive to anything, so there was very little for us to do to help them, except get them on the air. We still loved them.

There was one moment where I was really having a hard time with some things they were doing and then I got Lorne Michaels involved and he helped me. He wasn't hands-on, but I love Lorne.

LORNE MICHAELS:

Originally, I thought I would take one or two of them and do something else, but I'd had this experience with Second City when I went up there and saw John Candy and all the people who were in that, and I thought you can't break up a group. There's something where the whole thing falls apart after, you know what I mean? It's never the same.

On February 15, 1988, HBO would do something it would repeat often during its ambitious early years: take the ordinary, jiggle it like gin, flip it over, and voilà—get something extra. What plopped out this time, all a-fizz, was **Tanner '88,** *a studied yet sardonic breakthrough in political docudrama that mixed real names with invented characters (à la* **Ragtime***) and sent critics into sonnets of superlatives, partly because the credits were bursting with prestigious pedigrees.*

*Among the auspicious contributors were thinking person's cartoonist Garry Trudeau, who wrote the script, and Robert (**Nashville***) Altman directing. The result was a sort of ersatz, semi-surrealistic series that followed the fate of a wannabe presidential candidate played by Michael Murphy—a lowly Democratic representative who almost has greatness thrust upon him, along with a twenty-two-year-old Cynthia Nixon (ten years before* **Sex and the City***) as his daughter. The sharp-tongued tale featured Trudeau's satirical dialogue jumbling with Altman's partly improvisational ensembles.*

Along the way, real-life politicians such as Bob Dole, Jesse Jackson, and Gary Hart, as well as cultural pop stars including Studs Terkel and Gloria Steinem, wandered into and out of the story, lending their cameo creds to the ten much-discussed thirty-minute episodes that followed the one-hour pilot. The show would last only one season, though its reputation has grown with each passing year.

GARRY TRUDEAU, Writer and Executive Producer:

HBO was experimenting a bit and they apparently gave Bridget quite a lot of license. She called me in the fall of '87 and said, "We'd like to run a candidate, a fictional candidate for president." Period. That was the extent of her idea. And she said, "Would you be interested in writing on it?" I had a full-time job and three small children and the last thing I needed was another project at the time. I tossed out a proviso I was almost a hundred percent sure she couldn't meet. I said, "I'll do it if you can get Robert Altman to do it." I barely knew Altman, but greatly admired and had fallen in love with his work going back to *M*A*S*H* when I was a college student.

She called back a few days later and said, "He'll do it if you do it." So now we found ourselves in late November, early December, with a show where there had been no development, no script, and no characters.

BRIDGET POTTER:

Over the objection of my boss, my ass on the line, I approved that show without a script, without anything, because we had to get it done really quickly.

GARRY TRUDEAU:

We had this vague idea of following a campaign in real time before "real" was in the language. It got a little scary, especially when Bob started hiring actors for whom there were no characters. So this room full of anxious actors were all looking at me, and I'll never forget Danny Jenkins who played Stringer—he was a hot young Broadway actor, and he asked me, "Tell me about Stringer." And I looked at him; he's quite tall. And I said, "Well, he's really tall." That's all I could think of.

But Bob looked comfortable with this. He was so suited for any kind of guerrilla theatrical. He had made his bones on television in the 1950s, and those guys had to do a lot with a little. He didn't look the slightest bit perturbed that I hadn't written a word. He was sure it was all going to work out.

In December, early January, I started writing in earnest, and we came up with this idea of the focus group in New Hampshire and the really bad bio of Tanner for them to react to. Bob went to New Hampshire and worked his magic with his usual mix of real people and actors.

I had written the scene in Elaine's that was ten pages. It went on and on, I don't know what I was thinking. We had one day to shoot it. It had all the different characters and all the cross talk that Bob's so good at, but I didn't give him any time to do it. I get to the set and it's in full motion and everybody's improvising. Bob had decided he's going to end up where he needs to end up, but how he gets there is his business, because I've put him in an impossible position.

At the end of the day, I'm sitting at a table, and he can tell I'm a little depressed by this. He sits down, and he says, "Trudeau, you know why you write?" And I said, "No, and on days like this it's not abundantly clear to me why I bother." And he said, "You write so the characters know who they are." And what he meant by that is if I wrote carefully enough, with enough specificity and enough nuance, then the actors would be so secure in the truth of that character that he could then lead them off in any direction he chose, and they would act appropriately. That was his working method. If you talked to any writers who worked with him, they'll have a similar story of the script being just a road map on some days. On other days, it's word perfect. The actors didn't have any quarrel with the dialogue I was writing for them. His view is that the writer's job was to give them their bearings.

MICHAEL FUCHS:

Howard Rosenberg from the *LA Times* said, "You don't have to do anything else ever again. *Tanner*'s enough for me." *Tanner* didn't get an audience. That didn't bother me.

It was a very cool show. It was Garry Trudeau mixing politics and real people. We out-Dukakis'ed Dukakis. It was brilliant. I loved that show.

BRIDGET POTTER:

Michael hated the show, hated it. I was lucky to keep my job. But this is what my instinct told me: even if it was bad, the press would like it, and not only that, people in the industry who I wanted to come and do shows for HBO would watch it, and that's exactly what happened. Everybody who saw it wrote about it. Maybe only fifty people saw it, and maybe all of them were journalists, but it wasn't just on the TV pages—it was everywhere.

SASHA EMERSON, Executive:

When *Tanner '88* aired, it signaled to a lot of people how imaginative and how artist-friendly HBO was. I would call it a creative loss leader. It made the phone ring with filmmakers and agents asking, "Can I work with you guys? I need to be there." That was part of the genius of doing weird, innovative shows that not a lot of people watched; filmmakers watched them, and it elevated the status of all of us as creative stalwarts of the network.

GARRY TRUDEAU:

My only exposure to HBO was Bridget. She was a doll. I went in to visit her once in the middle of this, because she had just okayed another project, *The Trial of the Chicago 8*, around the same time. And so I'm thinking, God, who is this? She looks like a regular executive and dresses professionally and has this sort of calm demeanor, but why is she interested in projects like ours and *Chicago 8*?

I started asking her about herself and said, "Bridget, why the *Chicago 8*?" She said, "Well, do you remember when the Yippies threw the money on the Wall Street Stock Exchange floor?" If you're of a certain age, that's an iconic moment from the 1960s. All the stockbrokers reaching up for these fluttering bills while they were being filmed by the media that had been called. It was one of the Yippies' better stunts. And I said, "Sure, I remember that." And she said, "You know how much money it was?" And I said, "No, Bridget, how much money?" She said, "It was $138 in one-dollar bills. And the reason I know that is it was a week's salary of mine. I was the only one in the group with a job."

And that little girl grew up to run original programs. That explained so much to me.

AARON SORKIN, Creator:

I'm a *Tanner* zealot and Garry Trudeau has been a big influence on me. Just the way he buries a punch line is worthy of a doctoral dissertation. *Tanner '88* was probably the first series I watched on HBO and it very much made its way into the blood supply of *The West Wing* and *The Newsroom*.

MICHAEL FUCHS:

Bob Altman had a reputation in the film business of turning on you and boy did he lay into us, so we finally canceled the show.

JANE DEKNATEL:

I went to Canada to see a movie we were shooting there, and Michael said to me, "Come to New York on your way back from Canada. Let's talk." I went back to New York, and he said to me, "Whenever I walk into a restaurant with you, people look at you and not me." I laughed and said, "Michael, I'm a woman, I'm a foot taller than you and better looking." But he wouldn't let up. He told me he had been asked by the HBO board to go to the Midwest and take over a Time Life company that was in trouble, not an entertainment company, and turn it around. Michael said, "I can't go because there's no one to run HBO." And they said, "We thought we'd put Jane in charge of HBO." Michael said to me, "You are not going to run HBO. I am not going to be replaced by some girl I hired."

MICHAEL FUCHS:

Look at my career. I didn't fire a lot of people at HBO. She was always in Europe doing American projects and flying people in for interviews. It's nice to work for a corporation, but you can't be a pig about it. She was, and wasn't so great. She came in there and she began to act like she had invented the place.

I thought Jane's behavior was counter to what our culture was. She was living bigger than anyone else in the company, and there was no reason for that.

SHELLEY FISCHEL:

There was a bit of a frat house feeling inside HBO in the very early days. At times it could be a messed-up place. A secretary complained to me that her boss used to ask her to come into the office by saying, "Get your tits and ass in here." But it didn't stay that way for long. It grew up and so did the staff. It was clear there was an increasingly big media spotlight on us always.

ILENE KAHN POWER:

I produced four movies at HBO. The first one was *Murderers Among Us: The Simon Wiesenthal Story*, which was very close to Michael's heart. We filmed while Simon was still alive, and he came to the set and talked with Ben Kingsley, who was playing him. Ben had lost a lot of weight to play this skinny guy in the barracks. It was a solemn and very emotional time. Everyone was in tears.

We all went out to dinner and Simon was really engaged. The next day we started shooting and the scene was when Nazis were shooting Jews by a pit. The director was the late Brian Gibson, who also did our Josephine Baker movie. Everyone was very emotional, we're carrying the gravitas of what we were filming, then all of a sudden you hear this voice boom, "Cut, cut." And it wasn't Brian, it was Simon. Everybody turns around, and he says, "Women and men did not get shot together in the pit. They separated them out. This is not accurate."

Simon was there for about a week. He drove us crazy because he was such a stickler for detail, but then we realized his attention to detail was how he became Simon Wiesenthal. He was brilliant. That movie was seminal for us.

Wiesenthal was once asked why he lived in Austria, where he felt unwelcome, and his answer was remarkable: "When you fight malaria, you go where the mosquitoes are."

He knew all too well that Austrian bookstores and newspapers didn't display his work or write positively about him and was delighted that the film, in effect, eliminated the middleman and allowed people to see and understand his work directly. Wiesenthal wrote personal letters of gratitude to both Fuchs and Cooper, telling Fuchs: "I feel that the movie has influenced public opinion in my favor."

MICHAEL FUCHS:

I put Andrei Sakharov and Wiesenthal together. This was Paul Newman and Robert Redford to me. I didn't know Sakharov that well. I particularly was close to Wiesenthal. Leonard Lauder was holding a humanities dinner at his house. We went to that dinner and I introduced them to each other. They spent about four or five minutes looking for a language that they could both speak. Polish, Russian, German. The fact that I did not get a picture with those two has driven me crazy since then.

Yelena Bonner was Sakharov's wife. She came to America when he was in internal exile. We had a little dinner up at HBO. From the HBO dining room, you can see the Empire State Building. I asked this stupid question, "This is your first trip to America. What do you like most about America? Is it the Empire State Building? Is it democracy?" She said, "The washing machines are fabulous."

BOB COOPER, Executive:

I was in Budapest producing the Simon Wiesenthal film when Michael offered me a job at HBO. I always believed in betting on myself, so I said, "Yes." My wife was concerned about me going to work for Michael. She said, "He's very opinionated, and so are you, but he's the boss." I understood. Michael was a macho guy, and I am not. It could have been a chemically bad relationship, but that didn't wind up being the case.

People said I was tough and fearless. Why? Because I had a guy behind me, Fuchs, who said, "I don't care how much blood is on the floor. We need to create a brand." He was extraordinary.

One of the first movies we were doing, we realized the director wasn't working out properly. We had to stop it. And I couldn't sleep at night because I realized we lost $600,000. Michael Fuchs just laughed.

Bob Cooper was given charge of HBO's film production unit, the name HBO Premiere Films giving way to the simpler HBO Pictures. Meanwhile, in 1987, HBO baptized a new East Coast, indie-oriented production house, HBO Showcase, under the leadership of a new hire, Colin Callender.

MICHAEL FUCHS:

I hired Colin. I had run into him in England and we had a lot of fun together. He was a good kid. He did *Nicholas Nickleby*, and I thought he was really talented.

COLIN CALLENDER, Executive:

Before HBO, I had run one of the first independent production companies in the UK, won an Emmy for *The Life and Adventures of Nicholas Nickleby*, which I produced for Channel 4, and been the UK co-producer of choice for HBO.

One of the early HBO films we made was the Alan Bates, Julie Christie drama *Separate Tables*. So I had a relationship with them. When I joined, HBO Showcase was Michael Fuchs's attempt to create a *Playhouse 90* within HBO.

Michael had this notion that HBO was simply the best, and it was indeed the log line for the network, but at that time, it wasn't the case. There was great programming being made elsewhere, but there was something absolutely aspirational about what we wanted to achieve.

CHRIS ALBRECHT:

Colin had a really difficult job. He reported to Bridget, and there were difficulties there. He had to distinguish his work from HBO Pictures and do so with less money. But he had really good taste and found really interesting material. In his heart, and his creative instincts, Colin became very much an HBO guy. He just had an English accent and got tainted by difficulties with Bridget.

COLIN CALLENDER:

At some point, in 1986 or '87, there was a BBC adaptation of one of Dickens's novels on PBS, and there was a review in the *New York Times* about the importance of Dickens as a novelist, and his role as a social commentator. Michael circulated a photocopy of the review with a handwritten note scribbled on it, "HBO should be the Dickens of American television." That was a brilliant notion.

Dickens had shed light on corners of British society that the average reader would never have encountered firsthand. He created characters from all different layers of British life, making them accessible and compelling to audiences. He dealt head-on with the social issues of the day, but he did so in the form of a great storyteller, in a way that actually engaged and enthralled the reader. And what I understood from Michael was that we could do the same thing with our programming. We could tell stories that nobody else was telling. We could pull back the veil on lives that would not normally be seen on mainstream television.

Dickens notwithstanding, the breadth of HBO offerings continued to be wide. There was no HBO sweet spot, except for the constant essential element: doing things networks wouldn't or couldn't.

The original comic-book incarnation of the horror anthology **Tales from the Crypt** *had already brought controversy to its publisher, EC Comics (an offshoot of DC Comics). That dated back to the relative innocence and Commie-crazy hubbub of mid-1950s America—a time when Congress had held subcommittee hearings about the supposedly deleterious effects that comic books might be having on America's innocent, vulnerable youth. Horror made up a third of all comic-book publishing by then, and the daring William Gaines, EC's majordomo at the time, was forced to cancel the series that he and Al Feldstein had created, amid protests from politicians and panicked parents.*

Half a century later, comic-book controversies now a dim memory, **Tales from the Crypt***, with its puppet-like "Crypt-Keeper" as on-screen host and guide, was resuscitated for HBO by Steven Dodd—on a much larger scale and with far greater impact than any ink-and-paper comic book could have hoped to achieve.*

HBO constituted the perfect outlet for the blood-soaked anthology concept, although the **Los Angeles Times** *did manage to tsk-tsk in its first review of* **Crypt***: "When a hateful spouse lands not one but two sharp objects in her husband's forehead . . . we get to hear the resulting thud, plus subsequent squishing sounds when she twists said objects around. Oh, and let's not forget the nudity and sailor-style language. Isn't cable great?"*

Whatever objections there may have been from the nation's far-flung pulpits and peevish parsons, the series' liberal mix of gore and nudity seemed to delight HBO's subscriber base. **Tales from the Crypt** *ran for nearly a decade starting in June 1989, and in its long and oddly chic history, the anthology managed to provide first-time director credits for several of the industry's top TV-to-movie stars.*

JOEL SILVER, Producer:

When I was a kid, I went to a Jewish sleepaway camp in Rhinebeck, New York. It was a very intellectual, artistic crowd and kids would always come to camp with trunks of comic books. Those comic books were the litmus test for being cool, and if you had a *Tales from the Crypt* comic book in your pile, that was gold.

They were banned, there were no new ones, and years later, I found a big compendium of all the stories. I started reading through them and said to my colleague Walter Hill, "We should do this."

I tried everywhere and nobody wanted it. We met this young agent at CAA, Phil Kent, who said, "I can set this up for you." A few weeks later, we met with Bridget Potter, and she said, "Okay, let's do it."

BRIDGET POTTER:

Joel was the definition of a big-time Hollywood producer and brought us great people to work with. It was a very good arrangement.

JOEL SILVER:

Bridget changed the fucking narrative. I can talk to you about Michael Fuchs, Steve Scheffer, and others at HBO, but she was the creative brains. If anybody is an unheralded voice from the beginning of the new world of the cable industry, it was her. She's the one that saw what non-network, no commercial–type creative activity could be.

BRIDGET POTTER:

The thing about *Tales from the Crypt* was, we didn't have money. We couldn't finance anything 100 percent. Sometimes we financed things 50 percent or less. Joel is a controversial figure, but I just adored him. This was a guy who did not know how to *not* get something done. And putting together the deal for that show was all Joel.

JOEL SILVER:

When I directed my episode, I had a scene where these two crazy girls with lingerie and chain saws cut Joe Pesci in half. They put the chain saw right between his legs and they start cutting through his balls. There's blood going everywhere. I knew the MPAA would never have approved that in a million years, but there were no standards and practices per se at HBO. There was nobody looking at what I was doing and saying, "You can't do that."

We had to find ways to get stars, so we had the idea to give actors their first directing job. They'd get to direct an episode, we'd help them, and they could get their friends to be in the show. Who's going to say no to Schwarzenegger or Tom Hanks? Tom did the first one, then Arnold did one and Michael J. Fox did one. Whoopi starred in one, then I got Demi Moore to do one. Elizabeth Taylor called me and said, "I want to do a *Tales from the Crypt*." I kept sending her ideas but she never liked any. As the show got successful, more people wanted to be part of it.

TOM HANKS, Actor and Executive Producer:

Oh, man. I learned how hard directing is. Great cast and crew, charitable to a first timer.

BRIDGET POTTER:

Joel got Bob Zemeckis, and all these sorts of bad boys who were obsessed by the *Crypt* people. I had more fun with Joel on that show than anyone in the TV world.

*Fuchs remained focused on programming but also kept one eye toward empire build-ing, usually in the form of an acquisition. In the mid-1980s he became enamored of CNN, the twenty-four-hour news service that had been founded by Ted Turner in 1980. Just how it would be connected to HBO wasn't clear, but Fuchs thought it would be natural for the company that had **Time** magazine as its flagship.*

Fuchs and Curt Viebranz made their pitch to corporate. The deal was thwarted by economic analyses that had failed to impress Nick Nicholas and his boss Dick Munro.

MICHAEL FUCHS:

I was always peeking over at CNN. Nick had just become president and I told him, "There's only one of these things. I don't care what the numbers say. I've never seen a pro forma that made any sense a week later. Once you get into a company, pro formas are full of shit. This is a rare commodity, and we are a part publishing information company. There's an incredible synergy here."

It was in our DNA. We were a journalistic company and I thought that Time Inc. should be deeper in cable than just HBO.

CURT VIEBRANZ:

I was working for Nick Nicholas at the video group, and Nick sent Tony Cox and I down to Ted Turner in Atlanta to try to buy CNN.

We offered them $225 million for 50 percent of CNN. Ted had done the MGM deal and was in trouble. Ted had this gigantic office in the old Turner mansion with America's Cup memorabilia, and shots of him with all these famous people. We were sitting there listening to Ted tell us what a valuable asset CNN was, and he started looking for a piece of paper with ratings date. His desk is absolutely clean, and he reaches down underneath it and pulls out an in-box with a foot and a half pile of paper, and says, "I just had the Pepsi guys in here about the Goodwill Games. I didn't want them to think I was disorganized."

We got close to pulling off the deal, but ultimately there was no agreement. I was disappointed we couldn't get that one through.

JERRY LEVIN:

CBS was my target. Steeped in history. The network where the news division and the programming were not the lowest common denominator, that appealed to me. That's why I think Time and CBS should be together. We looked at it in the early 1980s. When we started TriStar, I looked at it, but it was just too much.

In 1986, Time Inc. CEO Dick Munro announced his plans to retire by 1990, bringing to a head one of the most competitive and psychologically complicated "bake-offs" in modern media history. The race to name a successor pitted two prominent HBO veterans who had been climbing the ladder at Time Inc. for quite some time against one another: Jerry Levin, who'd been first to hold the title of HBO president, versus Nick Nicholas, who had helped rescue the once-sinking HBO ship. The suspense was ended when, as part of his retirement announcement, Munro had named Nicholas as president and COO of Time Inc. Munro offered Levin the opportunity to stay inside the company, tossing a bone to him in the form of a "chief strategist" title, despite the fact that Levin would be getting kicked off the Time Inc. board.

In the space of less than fifteen years, the careers of Nicholas and Levin had played out like a gigantic and dramatic game of Chutes and Ladders, with the advantage now going to Nicholas. This Nicholas victory would appear to be game, set, and match; many expected Levin, who was clearly upset at not being chosen, to carve out a future for himself elsewhere. And if that wasn't the case, they expected Nicholas to show him the door. Amazingly, neither happened.

DICK MUNRO:

Nick and Jerry were my right arm and my left arm. We were a trio for a number of years. They were both a lot brighter than I was, a lot better trained than I was. I was really dependent upon those two guys. We had mandatory retirement at sixty, and I was turning sixty.

When I had to decide who was going to succeed me, it was obviously going to be either Jerry or Nick, and I chose Nick. When I shared that decision with Jerry, he said, "Well, I'm out of here." But he slept on that and decided to swallow hard and stay. That wasn't easy for Jerry. He was a lot more ambitious than Nick or me. I think Nick really appreciated that Jerry was a great asset to the company, and we probably shouldn't lose him.

JERRY LEVIN:

When Nick had gotten the nod—and I didn't—he got what he wanted. Dick Munro and the Time Inc. board worked in accordance with history and style picking him. They couldn't take a chance on me. I had no choice then but to accept that and ride it out for a while. In the meantime, I wanted to be the best person Nick could have picked to work under him. And for a while that was true.

That same year, HBO named a new CFO: Jeff Bewkes.

JERRY LEVIN:

You wanted somebody who grew up in the company. Someone who didn't come from the outside. So Bewkes grew up with the culture, but just the opposite in temperament to Michael. He had the financial skills, he had the intellectual skills, he had the graciousness to deal with the talent, with Wall Street, with Time management. Seemed an easy choice.

Time Inc.'s experience with HBO, now nearing two decades, had only made the company more eager to play a bigger role in the world of media. For Munro, who was approaching retirement, and Nicholas, who was about to start his new job as leader of the company, the idea of a merger or takeover was a welcome opportunity.

No matter how successful HBO became, the network never got to set out on its own. From day one, HBO had been both an obstreperous yet remarkable child to parent Time Inc.—with little shared DNA. Time Inc. was a last bastion of upper-income Republicanism, old-money families, and Connecticut golf-club memberships, while HBO was progressive-minded, populated with many first-generation success stories, and characteristic of Jewish sensibilities more aligned with those found in Hollywood.

Time Inc. had numerous divisions and companies, of course, but none were as sensitive about "the folks" at the top as was HBO, whose employees were on average younger and tended to look on "Mom and Pop" more as "Granny and Gramps." Even when HBO moved into its own building at Forty-second Street and Sixth Avenue, the bratty "kids" were living a short eight blocks from their parents at Fiftieth and Sixth. Not far enough. (When Dick Munro once came "downtown" for a visit, he and his lieutenants were "taken aback" to detect the smell of marijuana on their tour.)

The idea that HBO's parent company would someday be merging—"marrying"—outside the family was repugnant to HBO management, and when word circulated that the prospective spouse might be Warner Communications, it was immediately seen as consummate bad news. Of all the prickly relationships that HBO had with film studios, none had been pricklier than the one with Warner Bros., aka "Warners." And if that studio were to become a sister biz, this was likely to be a deeply dysfunctional family. Many at HBO prayed it would never happen, and those in the programming department feared what it might mean for their jobs.

NICK NICHOLAS:

I had been named president of Time Inc. in '86 and announced as the next CEO after Dick Munro would step down. Jim Shepley, when he had been president, had been driving a major transformation of Time Inc. away from print. And rightfully so. We had a quarter of the print industry, and it was dying. Then we asked, "Where are the targets of opportunity?"

Levin was head of strategy, reporting to me, and he had spent months with a group trying to answer this question. But he came back with a report advocating for us to merge with Gannet, a print company, and to buy several local television stations. That didn't solve the problem and lacked vision.

JEFF BEWKES:

There had been a series of big write-offs on Jerry's watch over the years: TV Cable Week, Full-Service network, the ATC capital budget, and there were people saying he had been failing upward when he took over the strategy group.

NICK NICHOLAS:

I put together my own group and challenged a bunch of pretty smart people like Dick Stolley, Lenny Jones, Stan Thomas, and others to think strategically on behalf of the company.

They decided we should use our common shares to acquire or merge with a company that had assets that went on screens—movies, television, education. I agreed, believing we needed those skills, including production capabilities and distribution.

We prepared a ten-page summary for the board, with a list of potential targets or partners in rank order. We asked for authority to move ahead with discussions, and most approved. Andrew Heiskell thought the film business was beneath us.

We started focusing on Warner. Stewardship of the studio by Warner Bros. co-CEOs Terry Semel and Bob Daly had been amazing. They were the most consistent leadership team in Hollywood, had creative judgment and rigorous analytical skills. I put in a call to Warner chairman Steve Ross.

ED BLEIER, Executive, Warner Bros.:

Steve said to me, "Shouldn't I be dealing with Dick Munro?" I told him, "Munro is effectively retired. You want to deal with Nick Nicholas." Steve said, "Okay, set up a date, make it for my apartment." That was Steve saying he would show Nick what money could buy. He had a palatial apartment at 740 Park.

NICK NICHOLAS:

I went to Steve's apartment several times. It was just the two of us at the start, and our conversations were cordial and productive. I told Steve, "We've got similar market caps, $12 billion, $13 billion, and we both have AA credits. Let's take two decent balance sheets, merge them, and build a very strong one." He liked the idea.

JEFF BEWKES:

There had been discussions about merging our cable company with Warner Amex cable, so they sent Jerry over to talk. Next thing we all knew, it morphed into we're merging the whole company with Warner Communications. I had heard from a banker friend who was working for Steve Ross that Steve had come out of a meeting with Jerry and a couple of our other guys and said, "We can take the whole company!"

NICK NICHOLAS:

Dealmaking is tedious, lawyerlike, covering every goddamn detail. Both Levin and [Ed] Aboodi from the Warner side had temperaments and personalities that facilitated that kind of a process. So I asked Munro, "What do you think about Jerry carrying the water on this deal?"

Jerry would do his best to negotiate what we wanted, and our team would meet every other day to make decisions on behalf of Time Inc. What then happened is Jerry insinuated himself into the Warner camp, and Aboodi and Levin became very, very close, to the point where they could communicate by winking, body language, smoke signals, you name it. Several years later, I realized I should have been suspicious at that point, which was my fault, but it's my character to trust colleagues.

And even though Steve was a true gentleman to work with, behind the scenes there was incessant pushing, pushing. Ultimately, Steve wanted to do this cockamamie deal, merging part of us but leaving part of us unmerged. We were too uncomfortable with that, and said, "We can't do it that way."

Steve was crestfallen. He wanted Time Warner to happen. That's when it leaked to the papers, and two things happened.

First, Michael Fuchs and I had dinner with Lew Wasserman and Sid Sheinberg from Universal Studios over room service at the Plaza Athénée. It was a failure of dramatic proportions. Lew said something like, "We read in the paper about you meeting with Steve Ross, and we'd like to be part of it, not as a three-way deal, rather for you to consider MCA." I believe Sid then said, "What are we, chopped liver? What's your problem with MCA?" And I said, "You're the problem, Sid. You have a way of dealing with people and issues that's anathema to us." I don't remember a lot of what followed, but it wasn't pleasant.

Second, Warren Buffett called me. We first met when I was running HBO, and he started taking me to lunch maybe once every two years. Why? Because he was trying to figure out whether HBO was a sustainable business asset or a flash in the pan. Warren said, "Don't do business with Steve Ross. Come do business with Tom Murphy [CEO of Capital Cities]." Buffett was pretty comfortable with the future of HBO. It wouldn't surprise me if you gave him a truth serum that he would have said HBO was the crown jewel.

Dick and I did not know Murphy and his number two, Dan Burke, well at all; they were broadcast; we were cable guys. We had a five-person meeting where Warren suggested the terms of the deal: even-steven, merger of equals. Then he said, "I know you guys really well, and I think you all get along." Murphy then said, "I'm retiring. It's already been announced. Dick, you're not going to be in the job much longer, right? So it's going to be Dan Burke and Nick Nicholas. I think those two should go off and talk about how they would run it and whether they want to work with each other."

On the first date, Dan says to me, without asking, "Murphy and I have gotten along well for years, but we're not getting along well recently. He promised me a run at CEO of Cap Cities but he never cleared way for it, so don't be so sure Murphy and I are together on all the governance issues because we really haven't discussed them." Dan and I then spent a lot of private time together talking about whether it was a good idea to put the two companies together, and I came to admire and trust him. When we talked over our roles, I said, "I'll tell you what, Dan. You're ten or fifteen years older than me, and have more experience, so I'm happy to report to you, and I would like to be your successor as CEO. You don't have to make a commitment as part of the deal, I would just like it verbally." He appreciated that and we met several more times.

A week or so after our last meeting, Dick comes rushing in, out of breath, like he'd just run a hundred miles. He said, "Murphy just called, and they don't want this to be a merger of equals. They want to take the directors down to fifteen and they would have eight and we would have seven. So basically, they're taking us over, but they don't want to pay for our shares that a takeover would call for." This was stunning to me.

DICK MUNRO:

There was no way we were going to proceed with Cap Cities under those terms—we told them as such—but they stood by their position.

NICK NICHOLAS:

There had been no blowup, nobody getting angry. It was just over.

Then Mike Dingman, a director of Time Inc., went to see Steve Ross at the behest of Dick and explained why we couldn't do the deal he had wanted but that we should continue talking.

On March 4, 1989, Time Inc. and Warner Communications Inc. announced a marriage that caused many an industry jaw to drop.

The array of entities under each brass plate was significant: Time brought to the table significant magazine titles, including **Life, Fortune, People, Money,** *and* **Sports Illustrated;** *it controlled American Television and Communications, the country's number two cable system; hit channels HBO and Cinemax; the Book-of-the-Month Club, Time-Life Books, and Little, Brown publishing. Warner, for its part, had Warner Bros. Studios, then the world's most successful; the recently acquired Lorimar Telepictures, who'd created* **Dallas** *and* **Falcon Crest,** *among others; a raft of record labels, including Atlantic, Elektra, and Asylum; and various publishing concerns, including DC Comics, Warner Books—the then dominant force in the burgeoning world of mass-market paperbacks.*

But then, an even bigger surprise: Gulf and Western's (Paramount's parent company) chairman and CEO Martin S. Davis went on the offensive that same summer, saying the projected merger with Warner meant that Time had put itself "in play. It's an open market now—anyone can come in with a bid."

Paramount made several efforts to block the transaction. The first was a $10.7 billion offer for Time Inc. made by Paramount on June 7, 1989. Time and Warner responded to Paramount's hostile bid by rejiggering the deal so that Time would effectively be buying Warner for cash and stock totaling $14 billion. Paramount took the companies to court in Delaware over the deal, but the merger prevailed.

At the time of the merger, Time Inc. had boasted revenues of $4.5 billion, yielding profits of just under $300 million; Warner's spreadsheet showed revenues of $4.21 billion and profits of $423 million.

The driving forces behind the merger were disparate: fears of a takeover from Time Inc.'s side; the looming power of the European Union (just three years away); and a recognition that large media conglomerates were the wave of the future, and to do business effectively you had to be able to scale on the huge side. Already, Bertelsmann in Germany (with $6 billion in revenues), Hachette in France (roughly $4.25 billion), and Rupert Murdoch's News Corp ($7 billion) were better positioned to dominate as conglomerates across broadcast and cable, publishing, movie and TV studios, and music, before the emergence of Time Warner.

The perspective of the networks would be summed up by George F. Schweitzer, senior vice president for communications at CBS, who told the New York Times that it was "another example of how all our competitors can build very powerful communications complexes, while the networks are held back by twenty-year-old regulations"—rules that, Schweitzer charged, had become "increasingly unfair and outmoded."

CHRIS ALBRECHT:

Time and Warner were going to merge and then Paramount came in with a hostile offer to buy Time. So our stock went up and I had a lot of stock at that point, and everyone was like, wow, we should sell our stock. And then the word came down: if you sell your stock, you're being disloyal.

CURT VIEBRANZ:

I'm getting married in 1989, and Bridget Potter offered to throw this party for us at her apartment near Central Park West. The party's going on and Nick, Jerry, Michael, and Jeff are all there. We found out the next day that Paramount had launched their hostile bid, causing these guys to basically say, "We've got to reconfigure the deal and take on all this debt to acquire Warner communications."

JEFF BEWKES:

The original idea for the merger was basically a share-for-share exchange. That got interrupted because Marty came in and offered $180 a share, and we figured he would go up to $200 if we negotiated.

NICK NICHOLAS:

We had a deal and Gulf and Western attacked, but Martin Davis was a nonstarter for us. Character matters.

MICHAEL FUCHS:

Nobody liked Martin Davis and he let the word out that the first two people he was going to fire if the deal went through were me and Nick.

JERRY LEVIN:

Marty Davis had been told, with great urgency, by people at Simpson Thacher that unless you do this deal, you're going to be a second-class citizen. He thought they made a compelling case and jumped in. But Martin Davis was not a good manager, and Paramount was in no position to effectively manage such a combination. That was not who should have had control of those assets. Period.

During the Paramount tender offer for Time, I set up a 24/7 fortress to fend off the assault. I became the point of contact; if any decision needed to be made, I made it. I'm telling you, I organized those battle stations with every trick known to humankind to defeat Paramount.

At that moment, I didn't care about ethics. If we came up with something dirty on those guys, we needed to use it. And don't forget, I knew Simpson Thacher. That was not alien territory. It was clear to me that the future of the company was at stake.

JEFF BEWKES:

We said no to Marty. Now we had to buy Warner for cash.

BOB DALY, Executive, Warner Bros.:

Time bought us. Paid us cash. If you were at Warner Bros. and had stock options, it was Christmas. I received a check on January 10, and it was staggering because they had to buy out all of our options, and they then had to replace those options with new options in the new company.

So from our standpoint, meaning the Warner side, it was heaven. And, to top it all off, who's going to be the CEO of the company? Steve Ross. The scenario could not have been better for us. But for the people at Time, like Michael Fuchs, it was Good Friday. This was horrible. I mean, horrible. You now have a new CEO who's with the company that you're buying, and you're making no money on your stock.

MICHAEL FUCHS:

I was pissed. We got taken as usual. I was not in a good mood.

Everyone over there loved Steve. He knew how to buy their affection.

He was very generous. If they weren't already rich, they got richer from the Time Warner deal.

ED BLEIER:

Just before the deal was about to close, Aboodi said, "I think I can push and get a few more dollars." Steve said, "Don't. We're rich enough. These guys have made a very bad deal for themselves and the company. Don't increase the debt." It was the most selfless corporate gesture I've ever seen. Steve never thought Nick and Jerry did a good job negotiating for Time on that deal.

JOHN MALONE:

I was a big fan of Steve Ross. I had almost gone to work for him in 1972. He tried to hire me to build him a cable business. It wasn't clear to me what that merger was really all about. Perhaps the Paramount merger would have been more profitable for Time, but Steve Ross with his charismatic nature was able to convince Time Inc. that they could acquire Warner Bros. and it would be very synergistic, and that Time Inc. could stay effectively in control—which of course is not what turned out.

JEFF BEWKES:

Do you think Steve Ross shorted himself in that deal, knowing we were desperate to avoid being taken over by Paramount?

Let's say he got full value. That means in the original share exchange deal of .465 of a Time share for a Warner share, which now we're buying for seventy bucks each, we were trading or selling Time Inc. for $150 a share. If you're holding Time shares, which do you want, $180 to $200 cash from Paramount? Or the chance to trade your Time share for a hundred and fifty bucks into the new Time Warner combination?

Bruce Wasserstein at First Boston gave projections to the board saying Time shares would end up worth $300 in five years if we merged with Warner, so don't take the Paramount offer. Everybody wanted to avoid a shareholder vote for fear that the people who actually owned the stock would take the bird in the hand Paramount was offering, so the whole thing ended up in Delaware court, which decided under the business judgment rule that the board could decide on its own, without consulting shareholders. The board decided it was better for the shareholders to take the Warner deal. That's how the court case went.

Our stock didn't move much over the next five years; history would say we should have taken the Paramount money. If you were working on the Time side, you got fucked.

ED BLEIER:

We looked rich and they looked poor. I understood why the Time guys were bitter. And there was so much debt.

MICHAEL FUCHS:

I thought Jerry almost colluded with Warner on the deal, but Nick shouldn't have handed him all of that responsibility. Then there was a rumor that Bob Pittman, who was Steve Ross's latest flavor at that time, was going to take over HBO. I was furious. It was like the whole fucking Warner deal was going to eat us alive.

According to terms in the Time Inc. and Warner Communications deal, Dick Munro and Steve Ross would act as co-chairmen and co–chief executive officers. Nick Nicholas, the then president of Time, became president of the combined company and was slated to replace his soon-to-be-retiring boss Munro within two years, and Ross within five. Jerry Levin, who served as vice-chairman at Time, became vice-chairman of the new company. Michael Fuchs remained chairman of HBO.

ED BLEIER:

Long before the Time Inc. negotiations started, one of Steve's and the board's goals was a transaction that could produce a CEO, even though we all thought his surgery had removed the cancer. Bob Daly didn't want to move to New York to run the corporation, and nobody else inside had the magnitude and talent, like Steve, to be his successor. Steve easily accepted Time's terms that he and Nick would be co-CEOs, and at a certain point, Nick would take over.

NICK NICHOLAS:

Steve was dying from cancer. He knew it, but he didn't know we knew it. We had commissioned a gumshoe who found out, and we had other investigators who got reports that he had seen doctors down in Baltimore. We told them what we had, and we even gave Steve a copy of the report. Steve still wanted a five-year contract, which we agreed to in the deal, along with committing to putting something like $20 million into a private equity fund that he would run after he left. Then I was designated to be sole CEO. I had never had a contract in my life.

Jerry runs all the staff, finance law, et cetera, et cetera. I run all the Time Inc. stuff. Steve runs the old Warner operations. Steve and I collaborate, share information. And in five years I take over the whole shebang. That's the agreement.

JERRY LEVIN:

Steve Ross was the farthest thing from a Time Inc., financially driven, ambitious as hell person. He was a visionary, and he was very good financially, but not to the point where it swallowed his character. At the end of the day, say whatever you want to say about Steve, he had character. It's just not Time Inc. character and not crazy games character. He had a natural affinity for programming and distribution. The only other person I've met like that is myself.

At the board meeting where we approved the merger with Warner Bros., I played a number of Warner Bros. clips from history and coming attractions. I started crying.

Time Inc.'s acquisition of Warner Communications first came together almost too easily, then hit serious roadblocks, and finally managed to cross the finish line with only members of team Warner cheering. It would garner few benefits, particularly those considered to fall under the all-too-often-mentioned "synergy" banner. The merger would prove hardly as financially attractive as the Paramount offer had been and, ironically, would likely make things even more difficult between HBO and the Warner studio.

As a final insult, the merger created a serious and bitter cultural gulf between Time Inc. and Warner executives over the huge disparity in financial rewards that Warner's employees enjoyed that would last for years. It would also wreak havoc on the executive ranks at Time Inc., fueling familial dissent and ultimately ending the career of one of its finest employees. Time Warner stock would be in intensive care for the next five years.

All in all, the Time Warner merger was a disaster, and even more bloodshed was yet to come.

JERRY LEVIN:

There was always tension between HBO and Warner Bros., always, well before the deal was transacted. It was more than a personality clash between HBO and the studio. They were too much on a parallel track to work together.

CHRIS ALBRECHT:

We had spent our firepower to make the Warners guys wealthy, while we at Time Inc. were now considered inferior. It was a really challenging time.

There was also a huge difference in cultures. The Warners people thought they were in show business and we weren't. There was a lot of resentment.

NICK NICHOLAS:

Monday morning quarterbacking, the most preferable deal was the one that was a straight merger of equals. That was what the two boards initially approved. Then Marty Davis launched his grenade, and we switched our deal from a merger to an acquisition. That was not a smart move. In retrospect, it was the wrong move. Now, none of us admired the way Martin Davis ran that company, Paramount wasn't running as well as Warner's studio, and they didn't have the million cable subscribers that we wanted. So Warner's was a preferable deal from a strategic view. But looking back from the hindsight of today, we should have done ABC or Paramount.

It is my single biggest professional regret that we didn't figure out a better way through that minefield.

4

Showman

Television ameliorated the documentary form, which dated back to the invention of motion pictures and led to films that are still widely considered masterpieces of the genre, including Robert Flaherty's trailblazing 1921 silent feature **Nanook of the North**, a film that raised the first questions in an enduring debate over how much "reality" there was in reality TV. Pare Lorentz furthered the form once the sound era arrived with two especially influential films: **The Plow That Broke the Plains** (1936) and **The River** (1938), both of which affirmed that documentaries could be made as artfully and creatively as any fiction film. When television networks started showing documentaries, it wasn't always through the kindness of broadcasters' hearts. The federal government through the FCC required stations to devote a certain amount of airtime to worthwhile "public service"—implicitly nonfiction—programming in return for receiving a broadcast license, the key to the kingdom.

Among the inarguable classics that made history and ennobled the medium were Edward R. Murrow's **See It Now** series, especially its 1954 two-part challenge to hysterical right-wing senator Joe McCarthy (R-WI), during the iciest days of the Cold War. Six years later, via **CBS Reports**, Murrow's **Harvest of Shame**, which alerted the nation to the hardships facing migrant workers, became a touchstone in long-form journalism and one of the most critical achievements in network history.

NBC News also got in on the documentary action, airing a series of doc-style reports called **NBC White Paper**, in addition to occasional prime-time specials.

In the 1960s, revolutionary new production technology allowed documentary film-makers to shoot video and audio on separate devices, synchronizing the two elements later in the editing process. This made it possible to leave behind the clunky, immobile equipment of studio sets, instead employing handheld cameras and bringing the audience closer to the action. This documentary style, originally known by the French term "cinema verité" and later dubbed "direct cinema," was popularized by directors including D. A. Pennebaker, Robert Drew, and sibling team Albert and David Maysles, among others.

It was on the night of September 24, 1968, that a true game changer in nonfiction network television was christened. The program **60 Minutes** wasn't a huge hit at first, but the innovative "weekly newsmagazine of the air" went on to become, obviously, an American institution, especially when moved from its initial weeknight berth to a firm place on Sunday evening.

CBS Reports continued to air important documentaries, like **The Selling of the Pentagon** (1971), an exposé about the way the US military was using tax money to fund publicity campaigns for the Armed Forces. The Peabody Award winner was so explosive that CBS and its president, Dr. Frank Stanton, were nearly cited for contempt of Congress. When Congress, shall we say, backed down, the power of media was made dramatically more evident, for good or ill. Television had won that battle, though the war would go on, and on, and on.

Few institutions, however, would have the impact on the documentary landscape that HBO has had. Michael Fuchs gave docu chief Nevins miles of creative runway and plenty of autonomy. When you added in her protean interests and unbridled ambition, HBO's documentary unit quickly established itself as the premier destination for the form. Though she wasn't always right.

BILL COUTURIÉ:

I was in the room when Michael said, "I can't do films, I can't do sitcoms, but I can do fucking docs and I want you to win awards." He's the one who had that vision.

The AIDS quilt, formally known as the "NAMES Project Aids Memorial Quilt," began in 1985 to bring both awareness and funds to the AIDS epidemic, which was then escalating. At the time, many funeral homes and cemeteries were so afraid of the disease that they didn't let victims inside. For many relatives, the opportunity to donate a panel in their loved one's name (panels were three feet by six feet—the average size of a grave) was an essential solace.

ROB EPSTEIN, Writer and Director:

People would send in a panel for the quilt with a letter about the person it was in honor of, and we had the idea to do a film focusing on those letters to create a whole other layer of what the quilt represented.

HOWARD ROSENMAN, Executive Producer:

The quilt was the size of two football fields. They were taking it on a tour around the country and the first stop was Los Angeles. I was there with panels of my four best friends and flying right above me was one of my boyfriends who had died. I was a mess. At the end, I lay down in a fetal position on the quilt, crying. Hugh Hudson came over, cradled me in his arms, and said, "You've got to put all this anger and grief into a movie. Why don't you make a documentary about this?" It was like the Liberty Bell fell on my head.

I called up the only documentary filmmaker I knew, Bill Couturié, who had done *Dear America: Letters Home from Vietnam*, for which he won an Emmy, and told him, "I want to make a movie about the quilt." He says to me, "I'm talking already to Rob Epstein and Jeff Friedman about the same idea. Why don't we all get together?" I raised a lot of money for the film, and then we went to see Cis Wilson at HBO.

JEFFREY FRIEDMAN, Writer and Director:

Cis was on board with the idea, but Sheila was doubtful the HBO audience would care about what was then thought of as a San Francisco gay story.

CIS WILSON:

I believed we should be doing something on the AIDS epidemic. These were the Reagan years; we needed to speak out.

BILL COUTURIÉ:

After *Dear America* won HBO's first two Emmys, Michael came to LA and threw this big dinner party at the Four Seasons. We were drinking champagne and patting ourselves on the back. My fee for that film as I recall was $35,000, so he gave me a bonus and said, "I'm going to let you do whatever you want for your next movie. You pick it, I'll do it."

My wife went to see the AIDS quilt at the Moscone Center and told me, "I've seen your next film." The more I heard, I realized she was right. I told Michael, "I want to do a story about the AIDS quilt and tell the story of AIDS." He said, "You can't do that." I said, "Michael, you made me a promise."

He said, "I assumed you'd make a movie about something people will want to watch. No one is going to want to watch a film about the fucking AIDS quilt." At this point, Cis saves me, tells Michael the quilt is coming to New York, and they should see it. He goes, but he's a busy guy and doesn't want to stick around. He's taking a final glance around, then looks down at his feet, and he is literally standing on a panel for another guy named Michael Fuchs. True story. Luck is better than skill. I can't make this shit up.

SHEILA NEVINS:

We were doing *AIDS: Everything You and Your Family Need to Know . . . But Were Afraid to Ask*. People were terrified about what AIDS was. Someone asked, "Is it safe to have a gay secretary?" I believed it was better to assuage the fear than to celebrate the dying. I wasn't sure the dying had earned America's sympathy yet.

Then they told me Dustin Hoffman was going to narrate; I thought that was hokey because he wasn't gay. More importantly, I wasn't interested in isolated groups, I wanted America.

CIS WILSON:

Sheila was completely transparent. She always stated her opinions. If she didn't like something, you would know. We rarely agreed, but she gave me the space to fight for things, and that's one of the reasons why I have so much respect for her. Even though she didn't like this idea, she let us run with it and was always there when we needed her.

JEFFREY FRIEDMAN:

Doing the interviews was very intense, profound, and intimate. We knew we had strong material to work with, but I'm not sure we really knew we had a film until we were well into it. We had a rough-cut screening for twenty or so filmmaker friends and got a sense that it was going to be very devastating for an audience to watch.

ROB EPSTEIN:

It far exceeded our expectations. We got handwritten letters from people about what the film meant to them. One of the most profound was from a young woman who told us her father had stopped talking to her brother because he was gay, and she had watched the film with her father. After it ended, he got up, picked up the phone, and called his son. We also got a lovely note from Sheila.

JEFFREY FRIEDMAN:

She wrote, "You were right. I was wrong. You made a beautiful film. Thank you."

SHEILA NEVINS:

I remember saying to one of my many psychiatrists, "I made a mistake," and he asked, "Are you right more than you're wrong?" I said, "Oh, by far." He said, "That's all that matters. Everybody makes mistakes." I've always held on to that. The volume of ideas that came into us was extraordinary. At that time, it was PBS or us. There were a lot of things I didn't do because I didn't see the juice in them. I made a lot of mistakes.

In 1990, **Common Threads: Stories from the Quilt** *won the Academy Award for Best Documentary Feature. One of the other entries it defeated was* **Crack USA: County Under Siege***, another HBO documentary.*

JEFFREY FRIEDMAN:

HBO organized a great premiere in Washington, DC, and invited members of Congress and policy people. That was a powerful moment for all of us. I believe there were people inside HBO who were getting infected, so this was also a personal time for them.

HAL AKSELRAD:

In 1989, I learned one of our prized business affairs vice presidents, Sam Newman, had contracted AIDS and, to my alarm, had not signed up for the company's health insurance. That was now a big problem because he needed to be in the hospital. I went to Michael and said, "He's deeply ill. We have to protect him." Without hesitation, Michael said, "Okay." I don't know how many other CEOs would have said that.

In 1990, seven years after its debut on Cinemax, Sheila Nevins changed the name of her flourishing late-night **Eros America** *series to* **Real Sex** *and moved it from Cinemax to HBO, where it would reign for nearly twenty years. Thirty-three episodes were made that ran the erotic gamut: there were stories about sex stores, sex toys, sex clubs, and sex dolls; about sloshing (sexy food) and mud play; about erotic objects made from latex and Pyrex; about a masturbation club and the Sex Maniacs Ball. Some episodes were oddly tedious, even asexual, but for those years before access to the Internet became ubiquitous and easy,* **Real Sex** *was where HBO subscribers went to discover not only what they liked but what they liked to look at. Repeatedly.*

PATTI KAPLAN, Producer:

Sheila created this fabulous network of people who did a lot of different things for her and to whom she was marvelously loyal. If she liked you and respected your work, she would keep using you. We called ourselves permalancers.

My first career was academic, I was teaching art at the City University. Sheila got me involved in a Children's Television Workshop project, and after a year, I was doing better with her than most because others were incredibly frustrated when she would change her mind every day.

SHEILA NEVINS:

I picked Patti for *Real Sex* because she had a PhD in art. I wasn't going to use a guy with a cigar, know what I mean? We had a ball making *Real Sex*. Patti was great. And ruthless.

PATTI KAPLAN:

At first, I thought Sheila was talking to someone behind me because her office was always like Grand Central Station with people popping in and out all the time. She said, "What about sex?" I looked at her, my face screwed up, and I said, "What about it?" It suited me, not the sex part, but Sheila and I share an affection for the absurdity of things people do. I started to research and knew some pretty funky characters who were really enlightened. I came up with a bunch of ideas and they turned out to be segments rather than a single hour show. We shot it on film so it would have less of a hard, pornographic edge. There was huge resistance at HBO to this show, but Michael was Sheila's protector.

MICHAEL FUCHS:

We knew sex worked through *Eros America*, which was on Cinemax. We wanted to get nudity and sex on HBO; the trick became: How could we put sex on without it looking dirty? We were very concerned about our reputation. This was AIDS time, and we decided the thesis of the program was anything that involved safe sex was okay. That gave us cover. I came up with the title *Real Sex*.

PATTI KAPLAN:

We drew the line at children, no unwilling participants, and someone being hurt—unless they wanted to be. It was no different than D. H. Lawrence or Henry Miller. It was sexy. I grew up on those novels. I mean, what are we hiding from? Literature? In *Real Sex*, there really wasn't sex. There were strip clubs, but that's not sex. There were workshops on how to give a good blow job, which was beyond amusing.

SHEILA NEVINS:

We could now show penises so we would do Chippendales and things like that, show it wagging in the wind, but we couldn't show it upright. No erect ones. I mean come on. We couldn't show penetration, and in the beginning, we could show tits and vaginas, but you couldn't be touching a vagina. The very first piece was "Sex for One" with Betty Dodson, who taught classes on the West Side about masturbation. We filmed eight or nine women and we got releases from them. I thought their husbands were going to call to complain after, but we put it on and nothing happened.

MICHAEL FUCHS:

John Redpath, the lawyer for HBO, comes to me with a scene from *Real Sex* with a guy in a hot tub. John pauses the tape, says, "I think he's erect. We can't have that." The lawyers may have had that rule in their head because there was concern over the Supreme Court's incomplete effort to define obscenity. I'm looking at this and saying, "Are you crazy? Who can see this? What are we, on dick patrol now?"

JOE BERLINGER, Documentarian:

I got a job working for the Maysles brothers doing marketing and publicity to get them more film and TV commercial work and used that as my film school, which is how I met Sheila. I confided in her that I wanted to become a filmmaker myself; out of that grew her invitation for me to do man-on-the-street interviews for the *Real Sex* pilot, asking people about their sexual habits. I had to take a deep breath and muster up the courage and had mixed feelings about doing it. I didn't want to go into documentary work to do salacious material, but it did give me the opportunity to start my career as a director.

QUENTIN SCHAFFER:

We were very careful. At that time, we used to send out VHS cassettes to critics for reviews, but we would do sex shows only upon request. Let's face it. These shows got huge ratings without any press. Subscribers knew how to find them. There were critics who found them to be filthy and would lash out.

SHEILA NEVINS:

Real Sex was the birth of the R-rated documentary. It was the highest-rated show on HBO bar none. It didn't matter how profound my other documentaries were, that's what they were watching, and they knew when it was on. It blew away the rest of the week.

JULIE ANDERSON, Documentarian:

The ratings for *Real Sex* gave Sheila a lot of power. Nobody saw my credit on any of the other shows I worked on except *Real Sex*. Everybody was watching it. There was nothing else on TV like that.

SHEILA NEVINS:

Men were often embarrassed about themselves in front of me, because in a sense, I was like a man when it came to sex. I showed it like it was. Everybody thought I did the sex shows so I could make serious docs, like Peter to pay Paul, but that wasn't true at all. I liked them as much as I liked the serious docs. The people in them lived a life I couldn't live.

Comic Relief *and* **Tanner '88** *were two strong examples of original HBO programming; despite their success and numerous specials in the 1980s, both Potter and Albrecht still had their noses pressed against the window into series television. That was the big ticket for both, the field of endeavor that they both believed would carry HBO to new heights, but early opportunities were killed off, much to Albrecht's frustration.*

ROSEANNE BARR:

I was pretty happy to get an HBO special, to be the woman who broke all the rules and broke down all the doors. I was pretty proud of myself, and very excited to have America see me. It was the very beginning; It was very exciting.

I had a lot of restrictions from most of the media I did back then. I couldn't just go out there and drop bombs. I had to be nuanced. But HBO didn't censor me at all, and it gave me a chance to do a full presentation of my comedy, and for people to see that my writing was far more intellectual and radical than what often appeared. Doing that special was so great. My HBO special pretty much served as a pilot to my TV show.

ROCCO URBISCI:

Chris called me up and said, "Roseanne Barr's performing in Pasadena. Can you go see her and tell me if there's an HBO special for her?" I drove to the

Ice House, saw the show, then went backstage and talked to her. I came back and told Chris, "I think she has forty-five great minutes. Maybe what we should do is create a short ten-to-fifteen-minute sitcom within the special, and we can spin a sitcom off of it."

The conceit was she got a call from HBO and had to drive across the country in an Airstream trailer to do her first HBO show from the Mayfair Theatre. Chris loved it. I shot her real family, her real kids in the kitchen of the house she was living in on Genesee Avenue in Los Angeles, and the opening was an Airstream trailer driving across country with time-lapse photography. Then they'd park the Airstream in the alley so she could go do her stand-up special.

When I was casting her husband, I looked at a videotape of a guy named Tom Arnold, and said to Roseanne, "I think I found the guy to play your husband." She said, "I love Tom Arnold, hire him." So I hired Tom Arnold to play her fake husband in her special; he later became her husband in real life.

We did two shows that night at the Mayfair, and between the first and second, she changed wardrobe. I said, "What are you doing?" She says, "I nailed the first show." I said, "No, no, HBO paid for two shows, not one. We're going to tape both shows so we can make the best special. Put the dress you had been wearing back on." She got real belligerent, went off on me, and said, "I nailed the first show, but I'll do it."

Then she came to the stage wearing a necklace she didn't have on in the first show. I told the stage manager, "Whisper in Roseanne's ear the following: Rocco says if you don't take that necklace off right now, he's going to walk onstage." When I screened the special for her, she was so happy and thought it was great. Then I told her more than 60 percent was from her second show. She couldn't believe it.

CHRIS ALBRECHT:

We do the special, and now Roseanne wants to do a series. Rocco, who is one of the great variety show producers, and worked with Carlin, Pryor, Tomlin, and others, says, "Let's do this." I said the same thing.

ROCCO URBISCI:

Go watch the opening of that special. That is the Roseanne show.

CHRIS ALBRECHT:

Rocco felt he could deliver her to HBO. She wanted to do it, we just needed to step up to at least a series. There might've been an ABC conflict, but she loved the experience of working with us, and she knew she'd have more freedom and control. Plus she loved Rocco.

But Michael would not let us do Roseanne as a series. That was the first time I heard his "we can't compete with the broadcast networks" speech. He said, "We can't do sitcoms, we can't compete there, and how do we know they're going to be successful?" I said, "Are you kidding me? We just say they're successful. There are no ratings on HBO. No one fucking even knows how many people watch us. We'll keep them on the air for five years, then sell them to syndication." Michael didn't believe in it. Roseanne went off and did her show on ABC and it made billions.

ROSEANNE BARR:

I always wanted to work with Chris at HBO. I would've gone much deeper with my show. Way more working-class subject matter, and way more about my real life and real-life controversies. It would have been great, and a lot of fun.

HBO treated me so well, and they were so supportive; they made it easy for me. I hope Chris and others know how grateful I am for the amazing opportunity they gave me. They changed my life and made everything possible for me.

CHRIS ALBRECHT:

It was a turbulent time. The other one we could have had was Tim Allen. Peter Locke said, "I've got this relationship with Tim Allen. Let's do a show based on his act." Michael shot that down, too.

SASHA EMERSON:

Seinfeld and Roseanne were examples of where we gave people a very big opportunity to burnish their brand and develop their character and style through great HBO specials, but then they would go off to NBC or ABC and become famous sitcom stars. We thought, "If we're the place of quality and creativity, why aren't we holding on to these people?"

MICHAEL FUCHS:

We weren't ready for it. We didn't have the money. I didn't want to go to corporate and ask for money to do what wasn't in our mainstream. We were starting to do great stuff. Our movies were receiving a lot of attention. We had to grow our own business. That was more important than having Roseanne in a series.

CHRIS ALBRECHT:

Keenen Wayans came to me after he had sold *In Living Color* to Fox and wanted us to become the production company. It would have only been a $50,000 deficit per episode, but Michael said no again. I had to tell Keenen, "You're my buddy, you're my former client, but there is total unwillingness to do this. I'm sorry."

MICHAEL FUCHS:

I kept us out of *In Living Color* because once again I was nervous about the deficits. I kept telling people, "We don't need a show in September. We're not even listed in the newspaper TV sections. We have to make our own publicity and do certain kinds of programming to get that." We needed to be a network with a personality, one that was controversial.

We weren't worried about filling up space. We didn't have to make twenty shows. We didn't have a schedule. We didn't really have ratings, because we had no advertising, so we made up our rating system. I knew what was a hit and what wasn't. We made up our mind to stress quality.

Networks make tons of pilots trying to do their shows; it deletes creativity and dilutes your attention. HBO was a very smart company.

CHRIS ALBRECHT:

After Michael said no to *In Living Color*, it was a moment of clarity for me. It all became too frustrating, and I told him I was leaving because he was saying no to everything. I was going to go to CAA. They had already made me an offer.

CARMI ZLOTNIK, Executive:

Then Chris said to them, "If you won't let me make shows for HBO, let me be entrepreneurial for HBO and develop and produce shows for other networks."

SASHA EMERSON:

Chris and I wrote up a proposal to develop a number of projects, thinking we'd be lucky to produce two to three a year for the networks. We asked for $1 million to option writers' ideas, make holding deals for talent, and put together a small slate of development for shows that wouldn't be on HBO. They would be shows that carried our aesthetic and "brand" into new worlds. We named it HBO Independent Productions or HIP. Michael approved of the idea and assigned Jeff Bewkes to oversee the new mini division. I went to New York and met with Tibor Kalman, a brilliant and celebrated graphic designer, and he and his team at M and Co. did all our branding.

CHRIS ALBRECHT:

We started HIP, but Michael wound up screwing me in the sense that he didn't live up to a lot of what he promised.

SASHA EMERSON:

It was like working for the television equivalent of the hippest little movie studio in town. I believed the number one responsibility of my job was to help artists make cool television, to give them opportunity and voice and transform their careers.

Within a very short period of time, we ended up having *Roc, Down the Shore*, and *The Ben Stiller Show* on the air along with producing a Michael O'Donoghue pilot. The next wave of shows included *Martin*.

JUDD APATOW:

When I created *The Ben Stiller Show* in 1991, we pitched it to Chris Albrecht and he liked it, so we thought it was going to be on HBO. Then they called us and said, "We just sold it to Fox." They were now going to be the producers of it as HIP. I'm twenty-four years old, never worked on a TV series in any capacity, only produced a couple of variety specials, and now I'm co-running the show with zero experience.

We were doing cutting-edge filmic sketch comedy before people were interested in that. We didn't last long. We shot thirteen episodes, twelve of which aired, and then six months later we won the Emmy for best writing of a variety show. We had a very positive end to a nightmarish reception.

CHRIS ALBRECHT:

Part of our deal on some comedy specials was that we gave them money for a holding deal or for a pilot. So we were able to take these stand-up comics and pitch them, which is where *Martin* came from.

When we gave Ray Romano a *One Night Stand*, Stu Smiley—who by that time was a producer with us at HIP—reached out to Robert Morton who was running Letterman's company, Worldwide Pants. They had a deal with CBS. By that time HIP had made a distribution deal with CBS, where they were taking the rights of anything that we did at HIP and selling it in syndication. So we got Ray's show in development and then they decided to make the pilot for *Everybody Loves Raymond*.

CBS had a third, Worldwide Pants had a third, and HBO had a third. It was hundreds and hundreds of millions. Stu walked away with a little, and I had a piece of HBO's piece. It was good divorce money. My ex-wife still gets checks.

CARMI ZLOTNIK:

Chris was one of those people who implicitly understood that while something may not be funny to you, that's not the same as it not being funny. He was willing to trust his sensibilities about what was funny in order to make smart decisions and give notes that pushed boundaries and fostered creativity without squelching it.

CHRIS ALBRECHT:

For almost no money, I had built a TV business with the broadcast networks. Now we had something that Warners had—not anywhere near the level of success that they had, but we were doing it with literally smoke and mirrors.

I did so well that when Peter Chernin was being moved from running Fox Broadcasting Company to running the movie studio, Peter introduced me to Rupert Murdoch and they offered me the job to run FBC. But Michael wouldn't let me out of my contract. Then later when Warner started the WB, Jamie Kellner wanted to hire me to run that, but Michael's words, I think, literally were, "What's in it for me?" I didn't know it was about him. I thought I was wasting my time.

By the start of the 1990s, HBO's subscriber base was running around 17 million per year, up from just under 10 million a decade earlier, and the company boasted revenues of $1 billion annually (its profits ranged anywhere from 9 percent to 13 percent). Despite those billion bucks, the general consensus was that cable was slumping, hurt by a doubling in the price of basic cable during the 1980s (from around $8 to $16; if you wanted to add a pay-TV channel like HBO, it would cost you another ten bucks on top of that). In addition, what was once a niche purchase—the VCR—had now become a standard household item; they sat under TV sets in around 70 percent of homes by the start of the decade.

In an internal programming memo dated February 26, 1992, Fuchs listed several concerns, including the need to improve late night; produce "super documentaries," i.e., **History of Comedy;** *rejuvenate the "mature sex" franchise and discuss the VCR threat; and instill "creative freedom" by attracting the "best Hollywood talent."*

MICHAEL FUCHS:

HBO was somewhat male oriented, because commercial TV is female oriented. But I did want something for everyone in the family. That's the reason it took me only ten minutes to buy *Fraggle Rock* from Jim Henson. Boxing was enough for most of our subscribers to cover the subscription. They knew what it costs to go to a boxing event and we did fantastic boxing coverage. Sex was something everyone liked. Movies began to generate publicity. We did more Central Park concerts than anyone.

BILL NELSON, Executive:

Michael was a very capable guy, and he had a lot of leeway. I'm not saying he had an open purse, but the latitudes were there because a lot of people at Time Inc. had come up through the magazine business and didn't understand what the HBO business really was about. Michael took that and ran with it.

HBO created the Comedy Channel for cable on November 15, 1989. Less than two years later it merged with a Viacom comedy effort called Ha! and the new entity was shortly named Comedy Central.

STU SMILEY:

Art Bell, who worked for Larry Carlson, contacted me and said, "We're thinking of doing a comedy channel." We sat down, we talked, and I was all up for it. We shot a pilot. The premise was that we were going to have hosts like MTV and show comedy clips from movies that Steve Scheffer's department was going to clear with studios. We would do comedy bits in between and build a channel much like MTV. We created this prototype, showed it to Michael in a big conference room, and Michael said, "Let's do this."

I was a young man and took it all very seriously. I was so scared that we were gonna fuck up.

My mandate was to get the studio set up, hire writers, the cast, and get a logo for the Comedy Channel. So I brought in the people who did the MTV logo and they unveiled this cartoon of a dog. At the end of the meeting, Michael said, "First of all, I'm not going to have a business card with a dog on it. Second, of however many years I've been at HBO, this is the worst meeting I've ever had."

MICHAEL FUCHS:

I liked the idea for the Comedy Channel because I thought we could build a comedy assembly line, starting with stand-up in cable, Warners for TV, and then HBO for features.

I was actually thinking, my God, of synergy, and helping the corporation. It became a success. Most of it was ours, in terms of the good ideas and what survived. I was the lead HBO person, and Tom Freston was the leading Viacom person. Tom quite honestly was probably more of a music guy, not so much a comedy guy, so I made some of the big decisions. I brought in *Absolutely Fabulous* after they turned it down. At the same time, I brought in *Mr. Bean*, but I decided to take it to HBO. A lot of that was very natural for me.

NANCY GELLER, Executive:

I was hired in 1991 to run HBO's Comedy Channel. It didn't last long. Naturally I was devastated when they decided to merge with Showtime's comedy network, Ha!, so I suggested to Michael Fuchs that we create a production company and produce all the shows on our comedy channel for Comedy Central. He really liked the idea and said, "What would we call it?" I said, "Well, we are downtown on Twenty-third Street, how about HBO Downtown Productions?" He said, "Okay!"

After joining HBO original programming in 1986, Sasha Emerson moved to HBO Independent Productions in 1990. Emerson—who had a graduate degree from Yale School of Drama and a bachelor's from Brown—had an extramarital relationship with her boss Chris Albrecht, who was also married.

Their affair was no secret around the office; one executive recalls riding in an elevator with the two of them after lunch and Emerson noticing Albrecht had a seed stuck between his teeth, then using one of her fingernails to dislodge it.

Emerson continued to work for Albrecht after the relationship ended until they had a loud screaming match one day—a spat that could be heard in other offices on the floor. Emerson was physically attacked. She then faced the choice of calling the police or reporting the incident to HBO and chose the latter, though she would subsequently tell friends that had been a huge mistake. Albrecht offered to resign, but Fuchs told him, "You're not resigning. We're going to handle this." HR chief Shelley Fischel brought a mediation team—husband and wife, lawyer and psychologist. After both parties met with the mediators, a recommendation was made to the company that included a payout to Emerson that reportedly was between $800,000 and $1.4 million. In a public divorce filing, Emerson's husband noted that she was going to receive a "personal injury settlement award from HBO as a result of a petitioner's claim against HBO."

HBO's payment to Emerson was deemed tax-free because it was classified as a tort under California state law and because it involved the term "discrimination."

MICHAEL FUCHS:

This was the first wild incident on my guard. I only say this because it's been repeated to me a million times by people from the company that HBO was the greatest place to work. I told them, "If you win, you'll get paid better than everyone else, and we'll have a great fucking time." And we did. It was a place where people got married. When we had bad male-female stuff going on, we dealt with it immediately.

It was an open secret within HBO that Michael Fuchs had relationships with colleagues. Sure, he "saw" people outside the walls of HBO as well, but he wasn't above "dating where he ate," either. While hardly unique to Fuchs—these were prelapsarian and pre–Me Too days—at times the prevailing atmosphere seemed to be that a lot of HBO employees were sleeping with a lot of other HBO employees.

Even though the landmark Anita Hill–Clarence Thomas hearings were held in 1992, it was not until the late 1990s that HBO came up with an actual policy forbidding sexual relationships with underlings. Change was right around the corner, but what a big corner it turned out to be.

SHELLEY FISCHEL:

We started doing sexual harassment training in the early 1990s, around the time of the Anita Hill hearings. We looked at programs that were being done on the outside, but a lot of them were canned and just awful. I figured I could do it better and faster if I did it myself. So for years, I went through the entire company training groups of thirty people at a time. I tried to use examples that were real to them, so they got the message.

We encouraged people if they had a sexual harassment problem to report them, and people did. One of the things I learned early on was finding out the facts was always very tough, because everybody's got a different perspective. There's her story, there's his story. Then there's the truth, which frankly, I learned, was more likely to be the victim's story than not. I handled all of those investigations for many years, and there was only one time that a woman lied to me and made a story up. More often than not, the men would confess to me at some point. I used to run bets with my outside lawyer about how long it was going to take for the guy to admit what he did. The real key was listening and responding to make sure it didn't ever happen again. I think in the course of my thirty-plus-year tenure I had one sexual harassment litigation and it was withdrawn with prejudice. We had no lawsuits, which is quite an extraordinary statistic.

MICHAEL FUCHS:

Women are more task oriented; they like to work. Guys are measuring ceiling tiles to make sure their office is as big as the guy next door. I have to say that in twenty years, I don't think a woman ever walked into my office to complain about salary.

SUSIE FITZGERALD, Executive:

There was this idea that broadcast networks catered to a female audience and HBO was showing Hollywood movies and had boxing so we attracted a male audience, therefore we should draft off of that audience and do more male programming. The research we heard said that men controlled the remote control at home and women were willing to co-view. It was a compelling point of view, but seemed to miss the point that half the subscribers were women and they might want some premium programs. After *Thelma and Louise* came out and was a big hit, I tried to make the case that there was an eager audience for female-led adult stories.

I kept trying to do female programming, and once, someone said to me, "But then the lead would have to take her top off and no actress that we want is going to do that." I asked that person, "Why did she have to take her top off?"

HAL AKSELRAD:

We did a film called *By Dawn's Early Light* with Rebecca De Mornay, and there was a scene where she's nude, and there was tape across her bottom that said, "You're not getting this shot." That became a refrain for many female actors who weren't willing to take their clothes off on HBO. They might do it on a theatrical movie, but in those days, HBO was regarded as just television; that didn't feel right to some of them. Eventually we got credibility by showing we were doing quality, tasteful stuff, and that resistance went away.

HBO had come to realize that although movies had always been its lifeblood, it was TV series—repeatable, rerunnable franchises that ideally HBO would own—that could attract long-term, devoted audiences, bringing back subscribers season upon season.

In 1990, the programming team was able to finally convince Fuchs to take a step into the land of sitcoms with **Dream On**, *an oddball comedy created by Marta*

Kauffman and David Crane, the duo who would go on to create **Friends** *for NBC.*
Dream On *ran for six seasons on HBO, between 1990 and 1996, with its ribald tales*
of the tangled family, professional, and romantic life of a New York book editor, Martin
Tupper. Brian Benben played Martin, and the show's central conceit was that his head
was filled with snippets of television and movie clips, all of which happened to come
from the Universal library.

Despite the gimmickry, reviews for the series were largely positive. Most critics
focused on the R-rated language and full or partial nudity, as though it was the first
time HBO had ever indulged in either or both.

DAVID CRANE, Creator:

We were still living in New York and would come out to LA every few months
to do our little dog and pony show, trying to sell things. We were in LA for
meetings and about to get on a plane when Nancy Josephson called us and
said, "I've got one more meeting for you." It was at Universal. Some executives showed us ten minutes of black-and-white 1950s and 1960s television
footage that Universal owned and asked, "What would you do with this?"
Apparently, we were the absolute last people they had gone to with this.

MARTA KAUFFMAN, Creator:

We were these musical theater writers, and they were scraping the bottom
of the barrel.

DAVID CRANE:

We got on the plane, started talking, and thought we could do a sitcom and
the clips are this guy's thoughts. We land in New York, call them, and basically pitched them the four-line version. They said, "Get back on the plane,"
which we did, then pitched it to John Landis.

SUSIE FITZGERALD:

Dream On was made at a time when HBO did not have money to own their
own series and was looking for shows from studios that were inexpensive.

Universal owned a library of TV movies that were made before the SAG
rule about residuals. Jordan Davis, an executive there, found Marta Kauffman and David Crane, who went on to create *Friends*. They came up with
the character, Martin Tupper, who had been raised on TV and had these
flights of fancy which were the old movie clips. Very clever.

And even more clever was that he was divorced and was out dating
women so there was sexuality and nudity which HBO could show because

it was a subscription service. But the endearing part was while he was out dating, he was still trying to win his wife back.

MARTA KAUFFMAN:

We had a history of pitching and nothing happens, pitching and nothing happens, pitching and nothing happens.

DAVID CRANE:

There was an executive at CBS who we had pitched to over the years who almost fell asleep during one of our pitches.

MARTA KAUFFMAN:

It was post lunch. He literally held his eye open.

DAVID CRANE:

We were convinced nothing was ever going to come of anything, so we went back to New York and they sent us thirty or forty hours of black-and-white TV to use as a guide. We wrote the pilot, inserting all the clips where we thought they should go, then John read it and came to New York for a meeting.

MARTA KAUFFMAN:

I remember so clearly his note: "Make it funnier."

While rewriting the show, Kauffman and Crane moved to LA and signed a two-year development deal with Norman Lear's Act III television company.

DAVID CRANE:

We were working for Norman Lear and got a call telling us HBO was going to shoot the pilot, and we said, "What do you mean?" because we had never had anything we'd written be shot. It was stunning. Weeks later John called and told us, "HBO wants to go to series and offered six episodes so I told them I was insisting on thirteen and if not, they could go fuck themselves." And Marta and I were like, "No, no, no. No one fuck themselves. No fucking of selves."

MARTA KAUFFMAN:

They ended up giving us thirteen, and we looked at each other. We had only been in LA for six months and had never worked on a show, let alone run a show. We were definitely flying by the seat of our pants, but we worked very hard to try to figure out how to do this. Having studied theater didn't hurt. I've got to say, in many ways we were spoiled by that experience. We had table reads but very rarely got big, troubling notes. Everybody seemed to be on the same page.

DAVID CRANE:

I would also say that because we hadn't done it before, that in many ways worked to our advantage. We didn't know enough to give HBO familiar TV. We were terrified, but we didn't have a formula for the work that we produced. For their part, HBO was incredibly hands-off.

MARTA KAUFFMAN:

And they were very supportive. We had wonderful writers we worked with, and our only marching orders were in every episode there should be something that could never be on network television. The story of Martin teaching his son how to use a condom is not something you would have seen on network television.

DAVID CRANE:

And when he says to his son, "If you have any questions about sex, just ask me," and the first thing his son asks is, "What's cunnilingus?" Obviously that led to some funny "Oh my God" clips. But our feeling was the clips were the icing. Any one of these stories would work if you took the clips out.

MARTA KAUFFMAN:

I do remember they did not pay us very well.

DAVID CRANE:

Not a complaint.

MARTA KAUFFMAN:

We never complained.

DAVID CRANE:

And I will say, for whatever it's worth, our deal was up after three seasons and had they thrown in a teeny bit more, we would have stayed with the show all the way to the end, because we were loving the show. From a business standpoint, Universal-slash-HBO still thought of us as these two musical theater writers, which is fair enough, but there were other places that did want to make deals with us.

CHRIS ALBRECHT:

The biggest irony about *Dream On* was that we wanted to continue working with David and Marta, and they wanted to stay with the show, but I couldn't afford them because Universal wasn't going to let them stay with the show. By that time, they were looking for an overall deal, and I called Les [Moonves], an old friend who was running Warner Bros. television, and said, "You should get them." I said, "I'll put up $1 million toward their overall if you'll let them do our show while they are developing for you." He called me back and said they could only consult on our show; he wanted them in first position. They wound up making their deal at Warners, because he was going to let them continue to be associated with *Dream On*, which was what they really wanted to do.

DAVID CRANE:

Ultimately, we ended up going to Warner Bros. Had HBO stepped up and made even a fraction of the deal Warner Bros. offered, we probably would have stayed on because we didn't want to leave *Dream On*.

CHRIS ALBRECHT:

And that's why Warners had *Friends*.

By 1989, fully one-fifth of all HBO viewers cited Mike Tyson as the key reason for their subscription to HBO, and therein, most likely, lies the reason Michael Fuchs had paid Tyson some $26.5 million over the previous two years to appear exclusively on the network. By the time Tyson had eviscerated Carl "The Truth" Williams on July 21 of that year, an extension to the contract was in the offing.

The Tyson-Williams fight was simply no contest. Tyson, then only twenty-three years old, came into the bout as the prohibitive favorite. It didn't take long—with 1:43 left in just the first round—for "Iron Mike" to connect with an extraordinary left hook that sent Williams to the mat, flat on his ass.

Tyson was seemingly unstoppable; his record now stood at 37–0, and he was headed to Tokyo, where he would face Buster Douglas on February 11, 1990. Everyone, including Jim Lampley and Larry Merchant on the HBO telecast, expected another quick victory for Tyson (ninety seconds was the expectation). Douglas was widely seen as a journeyman opponent and not a contender. This was merely a setup bout for an upcoming huge Tyson-Holyfield pay-per-view mega-event. HBO's marketing machine had already spent significant money on promotional materials ready to be sent out at the closing bell.

DAVE HARMON:

Two days before the fight, we were shooting Buster while he was sparring, and he looked so bad. His team didn't want our cameras recording. So they stopped and made Buster go home. The next day we went to shoot Buster doing road work. Well, Buster probably only ran about half a mile just for me and my camera, and when we said we were done, he was done. I'm glad I didn't bet on fights, because I thought this guy was going to get killed.

ROSS GREENBURG:

Tyson-Douglas was insane. Tyson was king of the world. Godzilla. The day before the fight, we had our fighter meeting where we'd go with our announcers, sit down with the fighters, and check on their state of the mind. Now Merchant at that point was persona non grata with Tyson. They had just had too many wars after fights. And Don King was stoking it, too. So Tyson says, "I'll only see Ross and Sugar Ray Leonard." So Ray Leonard and I go up to his room at the hotel, and Tyson goes, "Guys, come back here, check this out." And he's watching a real death video—people lying there dead, people being taken up from the river after car crashes, dead, dead, dead. Ray and I are looking at each other thinking, "Wow, guess he's ready for this fight. He's gonna kill Douglas."

A couple hours later we go to see Douglas. It's me, Ray, Lampley, and Merchant. We walk in, and Douglas has the worst cold of any human being I've ever seen in my life. He was so stuffed up; it was as if there were cobwebs in his head. He could barely talk. We walked out of there and thought, this is going to be horrible. There's going to be a murder. No wonder the odds were 42 to 1.

Thirty seconds into the fight, Douglas is moving around the ring, sticking a jab, Tyson's head is flying back, and I'm thinking, "Oh my God." It was the most stunning moment I've ever witnessed in sports.

It was, indeed, one of the biggest upsets in sporting history, let alone in boxing—a talented if inconsistent boxer had finally put Iron Mike Tyson on the canvas, and there went all his titles. Holyfield was crushed as well by Tyson's defeat—his much-anticipated "Fight of the Century" instantly vaporized.

JIM LAMPLEY:

The very first live prizefight I ever attended was February 25, 1964. I was fourteen, had saved lawn mowing and car washing money for months to buy a ticket, and my mother took me from our crappy track house community in Southwest Miami over to Miami Beach and dropped me off outside the convention center. I watched that night my idol, the twenty-one-year-old Cassius Clay, beat Sonny Liston to become the heavyweight champion of the world, and the youngest heavyweight champion ever. An indelible memory that sticks with me forever. Now it's the morning of February 11, in Tokyo in 1990, and somewhere in the middle rounds, it suddenly strikes me: the very first live fight I ever attended was the fight that was called the biggest upset in the history of boxing, and now I'm calling a fight that will succeed it as the biggest upset in the history of boxing. It was almost too cool and coincidental to be real.

LARRY MERCHANT:

My favorite moment as an interviewer was with Buster Douglas after he beat Tyson. He was so wound up about what he had just accomplished. His mother had died two or three weeks before the fight. After trying basketball and football, he then tried to make some money in boxing and got the Tyson fight. In the interview, he was so emotional that he couldn't speak. I held the mic out to him, and he moved back. I said to myself, "Larry, maybe this time it's just show and tell. Just stand here and let him act it out." He walked away for twenty to thirty seconds, which is a year in television time without anything being said. Then his handlers wanted to take him back to the dressing room. But he pulled away from them and came back to me because he wanted to tell his story. Inevitably, when you're on television, you're part of the show.

DAVE HARMON:

The fight ends, Douglas wins, and Larry and I get into the ring. What I'm about to say, you can't see in the video, because I was too smart. Buster's people are jumping up and down celebrating, and they know me from the past couple days of shooting, so they bring me into their jumping-up-and-down circle. And I say, "Hey, I can't be seen celebrating with you guys," and quickly back out before any of the cameras could see it. I did that for impartiality reasons, and I'm glad I did. In the aftermath of that fight, Don King tried to overturn the decision, and if they had seen me doing that, they'd be saying someone from HBO was celebrating the upset. When we finished, Larry gave me a "Well done, kid."

Though Tyson would win two more heavyweight titles, his career was already starting to spiral downward. Less than a year later, Tyson's contract with HBO would be up for renewal.

SETH ABRAHAM:

Our last deal with Tyson ended in 1990, Don is now the promoter, and we hammered out a ten-fight deal for about $85 million. It was very complicated and took about sixteen months. Maybe three or four times during this period, Don makes reference to the fact that he and Mike do not like Larry Merchant doing Tyson's fights. They thought Larry was too tough and asked nasty questions. Don hangs it out there that in this new deal, Larry would not be a broadcaster on the Tyson fights, or alternatively, somebody else would ask questions of Mike before and after the fight. I would just brush it aside, and we never had a serious conversation about Larry.

JIM LAMPLEY:

Larry Merchant is one of the instrumental pioneers of lifting the veil and injecting social realism into sports reporting. He demonstrated to the public that truth is more interesting than fantasy. I was a big admirer.

LARRY MERCHANT:

Tyson was becoming one of those personalities who was on the front pages of the papers as well as the back pages—stories that come with quick stardom and wealth that happen to young men and women.

They become performers, and my role is as a critic. King and Tyson felt that because they had a contract with HBO, we should be their cheerleaders.

SETH ABRAHAM:

We get this ten-fight deal done and the next day my secretary says, "Don and Mike are on the line." I get on and the conversation is celebratory. Mike's approved the deal, now we're going to get the lawyers to get contracts out for signature. Then Mike says, "And Seth, thank God I won't have to deal with Larry Merchant anymore." And I said, "Excuse me?" He says, "Don told me, Larry's not going to do my fights. That makes me as happy as the money." I said, "Mike, wait a second. I never agreed to that. Don brought it up, but I brushed it aside. We can't have you dictating who our announcers are." Now all hell breaks loose. They're screaming at me. Two days later, Don sends me a letter accusing me of bad faith, et cetera, and since we didn't have a signed deal at that point, he's going to pull out of the deal.

LARRY MERCHANT:

Normally when a network gets involved with a major star and everybody is making money, a commentator is expendable. But HBO hired me because they wanted someone like me who could speak truth to power.

SETH ABRAHAM:

Next day, Michael says, "It's not such a big deal. Let's keep Tyson. Get something else for Larry," and he used an example. "You know Seth, in Hollywood, Eddie Murphy dictates who the director is. This is no different." I said, "It's totally different. That's fantasy, this is real life. It's journalism. We want journalists reporting on HBO Sports." He and I went at it. I mean really went at it. Finally, he said, "Enough. I've got other things to do. You know I disagree with you. But I'm never going to step in and overrule you." I refused to give in on the point. And Tyson and King went to Showtime.

LARRY MERCHANT:

Seth Abraham once said to me, and I'm paraphrasing, "You make my job harder, but keep doing what you do."

ROSS GREENBURG:

Tyson's fights were some of the highest ratings we ever had. And then the big blow: Tyson's deal with Showtime. That was tough.

MICHAEL FUCHS:

Larry Merchant was controversial but had never bothered anyone before. Don made that an issue, but it was a bullshit issue. Don also made up this bullshit about HBO being a Jewish network. But the reason King wanted to go to Showtime was because he wanted pay-per-view and it made it easier for him to manipulate Mike. Because you could tell Mike, it takes a long time for the pay-per-view money to come in. With HBO you get a check.

ROSS GREENBURG:

King was set up at Showtime and Viacom to get a multiyear, huge deal for pay-per-view which included stock for himself. He knew that there was a big pay-per-view deal there and that the HBO deal had a ceiling because it was just a live HBO deal.

JIM LAMPLEY:

The most empowered I ever felt on the air was the night of our last Mike Tyson exposure at HBO. It was the Alex Stewart fight in Atlantic City. He was going from there onto his Showtime contract. Seth Abraham called me to his hotel suite before the fight and said, "Look, we've never done this before, but for the sake of being straight with the public and covering our own base here, I want to give you the details of this contract negotiation so if Mike says something that is patently false, you can correct him on the air."

ROSS GREENBURG:

It was pretty much a given that Larry Merchant could not conduct the interview. Ironically, because Don King refused to let us use Larry to interview Tyson after the fight, Jim Lampley did the interview.

JIM LAMPLEY:

They bring Tyson to ringside for me to do the post-fight interview, and I said, "Okay, this is our last exposure with you and you're going to Showtime. What's that about?" Instantly Mike said something to the effect that, "Well, they offered me a better deal." And I said, "Really? That's interesting because their offer is ten fights for $85 million, and ours is eight fights for $120 million. And another big difference, by the way, is that Don King shares in 50 percent of the pay-per-view revenue in your contract with Showtime." Mike didn't have anything to say in response to that because I had been armed with the truth. It was a fascinating moment.

SETH ABRAHAM:

Did it sting losing Tyson? Absolutely. But it also presented the challenge of asking: Now what should HBO Boxing look like?

MATT BLANK:

Showtime was in boxing before I got there on a small level. Both Tony Cox, my boss, and I believed strongly in boxing. HBO couldn't afford to buy every fighter, though they certainly tried. Don King felt marginalized by HBO and navigated the move to Showtime. We had Holyfield and a few others and now we had managed to steal Tyson away. We thought we were in the driver's seat. Then Tyson goes to prison, and all bets were off. While

Mike was away King had grown more alienated from HBO, but we still had to compete with HBO and others to sign him again when he was released a few years later. We did sign him, and that really gave us half a dozen years of controversial, sometimes disappointing fights; but Tyson always drew a crowd so the deal was a massive success in terms of exposure for the [Showtime] brand, especially the ear bite fight.

DAVE HARMON:

There had been so many worries throughout HBO's years in boxing. Who's going to be the next Muhammad Ali? Well, Larry Holmes tried. Boxing survived. Then we had Hagler, Hearns, Sugar Ray Leonard, Duran, and as those guys faded out we heard, "Oh my God, who's going to replace them?" It was Mike Tyson. And after Tyson, there was more handwringing, but we knew there were others coming like Floyd Mayweather, Manny Pacquiao, and Lennox Lewis.

In 1991, HBO's boxing coverage expanded to add pay-per-view with a new venture: TVKO, as it was called, was introduced as a monthly boxing series—not only mega-fights under the bright light city of Las Vegas, but smaller events from Davenport to Sacramento as well. Its tagline: Month After Month, Round After Round, the Hardest Punches Land Here. For many, this was the beginning of the end of an era—fights that would have once been on network or HBO were now costing extra dollars per month. (Hence, a mass return to bars to see them.)

ROSS GREENBURG:

In the 1980s we had huge numbers of significant fights on network, and in those days it was a lot tougher to break into closed circuits. You needed Super Bowl matchups like Hagler, Leonard, Hearns, Duran, super fights to get on closed circuits, because there wasn't pay-per-view until 1990.

I think a lot of the reasons why TVKO and pay-per-view were formed at HBO was in reaction to the loss of Tyson to Showtime.

MARK TAFFET, Executive:

I was a specialist on the financial and strategic planning side of the company, and Seth said to me, "Tyson's deal is ending. I'd love you to do a study of the boxing marketplace and give me recommendations about how you think we should go forward."

I found out that in six cities across America, there were microwave dish antennas on top of people's rooftops, and some savvy entrepreneurs were buying the rights to some boxing matches and selling them on a per transaction basis and generating as much revenue in six cities as we were paying for national rights for Tyson's fights. I concluded that if we didn't get into the pay-per-view business, we could be out of the boxing business at HBO. I proposed that HBO get into the pay-per-view business to generate substantial revenues, and create an engine that would have promoters and fighters wanting to be with HBO. The plan went to Michael Fuchs, then to folks at Time Warner, and it was approved. Seth asked me if I wanted to come over and run the pay-per-view business, which we called TVKO.

SETH ABRAHAM:

We realized what was coming because we saw it with Vince McMahon and *World Wide Wrestling*—all of his shows were on pay-per-view and they all did spectacularly well. We didn't have to be hit over the head to see that we had to be in the pay-per-view business.

EVANDER HOLYFIELD, Boxer:

Tyson was champ, and Tyson was at Showtime. I was pretty much just after belts. I wanted to fight whoever had a belt. I wasn't going to get caught up on which television stations wanted me. I was happy boxing, and if I had to fight for another network, that's just part of life.

SETH ABRAHAM:

We opened TVKO with George Foreman against Evander Holyfield. Mark Taffet deserves a lot of credit for the marketing and distribution of it. We had an enormous budget and rollout.

MARK TAFFET:

TVKO defined and established HBO as the place to watch boxing in America, and it wouldn't have happened without Fuchs and Abraham. No one had a revenue-generating capability like we did. As a result, the promoters knew they would maximize their revenue working with me.

One day I'm in my office and the phone rings and it's Don King. And I hear, "Mark Taffet?" "Yeah?" "Calling to say goodbye." "Calling to say goodbye? Where are you?" "I'm on the plane." And in the background, I heard what sounded like a dozen people screaming, hysterically, uncontrollably. And Don said, "We're going down. We're going down. I couldn't go down without saying goodbye to my friend Mark Taffet." And he said, "Hold on a minute," then yelled out, "Quick, bring me some of them chicken wings. If I'm going down, I'm having chicken wings."

Needless to say, the plane somehow landed safely.

On April 19, 1991, the aptly monikered "Battle for the Ages" between HBO's Evander Holyfield and the aging George Foreman ushered in a new age of HBO Boxing: the network's first, homegrown, major pay-per-view event. Holyfield-Foreman was the replacement fight to Tyson-Holyfield that was KO'd by Tyson's loss in Tokyo. At the time, only around 17 million homes could even get PPV events (these days the number is well in excess of 100 million). And while closed-circuit events had been the principal vehicle for top-line fights, this first PPV fight between Holyfield and Foreman brought in an unheard-of 1.4 million buys. It shattered records, and changed the game for HBO Boxing, as pay-per-view quickly became the home of the network's biggest fights.

So while fighters like Holyfield and Foreman were right-hooking and uppercutting and power-punching each other on the big stage, a lot was happening just outside the ring, to keep the boxing train chugging along with the business stuff, the legal stuff, the silent fight that would help build boxing and HBO into an empire.

EVANDER HOLYFIELD:

I became the heavyweight champion of the world once I beat Buster Douglas. My first fight as champion was fighting George Foreman, even though I really didn't want to fight George. I wanted to fight Tyson. My manager, Shelly Finkel, was telling me they would pay more money for me to fight Mike Tyson. I said, "Shelly, why would I want to go $20 million when I can get $30?" But Shelly Finkel said, "Look, if you play George first, you beat George, then they'll give you $30 for Mike. If you fight Tyson first, they ain't gonna give you no $20 to fight George Foreman. And you should get $50." So that's the decision that it took to fight George Foreman.

LINDA JACKSON:

I was the senior vice president in charge of production for TVKO, and when we were announcing Holyfield-Foreman, we went to do a photo op, and they put me next to George Foreman.

George says, "I'm not standing next to a woman in this picture." I waited for the chuckle to come, but it was no joke, he was dead serious. He did not want to stand next to me, to a woman. It was the first time I encountered anything like that.

When the fight came, there was a lot of animosity from my counterparts in HBO—really one counterpart—who felt like the job I had should be his. So the teamwork that I had experienced for thirteen years at HBO, and HBO Sports, was out the window. It was very difficult and painful.

ROSS GREENBURG:

Seth had split production in half and there was now a full TVKO production crew.

I really like Linda. We're still close friends, my frustration had nothing to do with her. Seth thought she would be up to the job. That wasn't the issue. It was more that he wanted to make sure that he could keep me in check as much as anything. He wanted to establish another sports division separate from anything that involved me.

LINDA JACKSON:

So right before a fight, it's very natural that all the announcers and producers go and visit with the boxers in their dressing room before the event, the day before. Our announcers get color information, things that they can talk about while they're on the air, "Holyfield is feeling like he's going to work the body," or whatever little tips that we could get out of them—nursing a cold, whatever we can see. And George Foreman tried to bar me from coming into his locker room, which I've done a hundred times in my life.

But I got in—my announcers and I said, "No, I'm coming in." And in particular, Len Berman, one of my announcers, was adamant. He went toe to toe with George Foreman, so to speak. And we just went and did our job and left, but it was such a bizarre thing. Then the cooperation between the two trucks wasn't what it usually is. My name was cursed, somebody out loud on the headset said "'F' Linda Jackson." I didn't hear it, but my staff hears it and they were very upset. So it was a bit untenable. That was a very bad experience.

ROSS GREENBURG:

The predominant part of TVKO was obviously pay-per-view boxing and it launched with Holyfield-Foreman, which was fantastic. And did 1.4 million buys at a time when pay-per-view was in its infancy and made a lot of money. HBO would get a percentage fee from on demand for each pay-per-view buy. It wasn't a lot of money, but it was at least a business. And then what happened is Seth started giving out guarantees.

Seth and Taffet worked hand in hand, but neither of them would take ownership of that idea, because there were a couple of big fights that really tanked. The one that was a total wreck was a $3 million guarantee for a Holmes fight. He wasn't the champion anymore. I can't remember who it was against, but it was a monumental flop. It went from 1.4 million buys to less than 100,000 for a series of pay-per-view events. It was really not a good situation.

SETH ABRAHAM:

Lou DiBella, Mark Taffet, Ross Greenburg, and I were in Ross's office. We got into an argument about an advertising and marketing campaign for the boxer Naseem Hamed of Sheffield, England. It got hot. Then it got hotter. Then Ross and Lou began to yell at one another. Ross's secretary/assistant Florence Savarese knocked on the door, came in, and said, "Fellas, you are frightening everyone out here. The pictures are shaking. Can't you just all behave?" We resolved the issue, of course. Later that week in my weekly with Michael I retold the story. Michael said, "Let me tell you what I would have done. What you should have done. Fire two of them and scare the shit out of the third."

I remember vividly my response to my boss. "Michael," I said, "these guys on any given day are terrific. Not every day, but on frequent occasions, and for those gifts, I will put up with their egos and narcissism. It's on me and I can live with it and manage it. But thanks for your sage advice."

DAVE HARMON:

At that time, Lou and Ross were having their big showdown, and Ross came into my office one day and said, "I have to know, are you with me, or are you with Lou?" I had never had any bumps with Ross, he had given me *Inside the NFL* and Wimbledon, and that moment was a big one. What I managed to do was give Ross my support without saying, "Fuck that other guy." That day also reflected all the drama that was going on inside HBO Sports at the time. You had three guys, Greenburg, DiBella, and Taffet, all of them, wanted Seth's job. A lot of us were in difficult positions.

Nearly two years after Tyson's upset loss to Buster Douglas derailed the much-anticipated Tyson-Holyfield "Fight of the Century," HBO managed to get the legendary fighters lined up once more for a fight. On November 8, 1991, Caesars Palace was slated to feature the first meeting of Tyson and the now undisputed heavyweight champion Evander Holy-field. Fate, yet again, had other plans. Tyson had been indicted that September for the rape of a contestant in an Indianapolis beauty pageant two months before but had been released on $30,000 bail ahead of his trial the following year. Yet just weeks before the *bout, the fight was called off. Tyson had suffered a "noncontact cartilage injury to his left rib cage" in early October, then reinjured the same area one week later.*

The following January, Tyson was sentenced to ten years in prison in his rape trial. At his sentencing hearing, Judge Patricia Gifford effectively shortened that sentence to six years.

ROSS GREENBURG:

We didn't miss Tyson as much as we thought. He lost to Douglas, went off to jail, and suddenly Bowe, Holyfield, and Lennox Lewis emerged as really strong heavyweights in his absence.

EVANDER HOLYFIELD:

It was sad because everybody wanted to see me fight Tyson. He was the guy that everybody felt I had to beat to prove who I was. He broke his rib doing a sit-up. You can't break your rib doing a sit-up. Something's really wrong with you if you can break your rib doing a sit-up. But nobody said nothing. And then all of a sudden, he got in trouble, which prolonged the fight for years.

The sad thing is that people act like I did something wrong. I'm like, I don't know why you are all so upset, like I did something wrong, when he's the one that said he broke his rib. I didn't say whether he did or not, but it just doesn't sound logical to break your rib doing a sit-up. But that was his excuse, then he went to jail with the incident that happened, and he came back. He was ranked number one, I don't know how you go to jail for two years and come back ranked number one, come back with more money than everybody, but he did. And people were excited about him coming back. And, of course, then we fought.

Tyson's sentence was ultimately commuted to roughly three years for "good behavior," leading to a March 1995 release. Tyson-Holyfield finally happened in November 1996 at the MGM Grand in Las Vegas. Holyfield bested him with a TKO in the eleventh round.

In 1985, HBO had produced the documentary special The Not-So-Great-Moments in Sports. The special itself was nothing to write home about, but it did two things: it did incredibly well in the aftermarket of VHS for HBO and, more important, it begat HBO Sports' documentary production unit. There had been a short documentary history prior to this. Two commissioned series, Greatest Sports Rivalries and Sports Dynasties, appeared in 1981 and 1982, not HBO produced. In 1983, HBO aired the documentary History of Pro Football, a co-production with NFL Films.

Then in 1984, with **NSG Moments,** *HBO was fully producing its own docu clip show, improving production values and establishing the HBO host role.*

TIM BRAINE, Executive:

I had co-written a book with a friend of mine called *The Not-So-Great Moments in Sports*, which was basically funny takes on screwups in the history of sports, and I said, "Why not let me do this as a TV show." Fuchs or Seth said, "Let's try and get John Madden to be the host," because John Madden had a sense of humor. I went out and met with John Madden and he wanted nothing to do with it. It was one of those meetings where I went, "Oh man, I wish I hadn't come all the way out here to meet with you." He didn't want to make fun of people's mistakes. Which I totally respected. So we got Tim McCarver to do it.

Seven years later, in one of HBO's most ambitious feats to date, HBO Sports collected home movies taken by both the baseball players and fans from 1934 to 1957 and created **When It Was a Game,** *warmly documenting America's favorite pastime. With an exciting collection of readings, baseball-themed music, and interviews with former players, this film established HBO as doing something "different" in the sports world.*

Gone was the high-profile host of past historical specials. Gone were the predictable on-camera talking head testimonial interviews. This one broke the mold. It had celebrities reading baseball prose, music scored to the picture, and a strong sense of sentimentality. **When It Was a Game** *was so beloved that it became a trilogy of films.*

By the early 1990s HBO Sports found its documentary groove, producing two, then three of these award-winning documentaries each year. By the late 1990s, HBO Sports internally established its own dedicated documentary unit.

ROSS GREENBURG:

When It Was a Game was the turning point. I'd watched *The Civil War* with Ken Burns and thought, "Up until that point sports docus were just interviews with footage, married with nice music and narration. We needed to change that."

STEVE STERN, Producer:

George Ryan and I had done the Los Angeles Dodgers slash Brooklyn Dodgers hundredth-year anniversary film, and we found these color home movies that were taken of Ebbets Field and the Brooklyn Dodgers by some fan.

ROSS GREENBURG:

The president of Manischewitz had shot footage from his second-row seat at Ebbets Field. I said, "If this guy has footage, maybe there's footage like this all over the country of every baseball team that existed for the last seventy years. We ought to go check it out and see how much footage we can get, and then do a documentary off of that."

STEVE STERN:

The three of us, myself, George Roy, and Eric Paulen, were trying to track down as many old baseball players and their families as we could. And this was pre-Internet. We talked to as many people as we possibly could. On any given day, we would get a yes from someone, then we would wait for the FedEx or UPS, and we'd have viewing parties. There would be ten minutes of someone's birthday party, or someone going to the zoo, then next thing you know, they were at Ebbets Field, Sportsman Park, or Fenway Park.

The most remarkable footage we got was of the 1938 World Series, in color. We started watching the film and the color was so vibrant, we thought we must have jumped around and moved to the 1960s. Then all of a sudden we realized we had something that was really remarkable. We sat up and high-fived each other. We now had the oldest color film of a World Series by fifteen years that anyone had ever seen.

Each show was an hour long. But it wasn't about here's what happened in 1951 to the Yankees or look at this perfect game. We had to construct a different type of show. We were tasked with not doing a "historical" documentary; instead, we did what became more of a lyrical documentary. It was like the film version of *The Glory of Their Times*.

The reviews were incredible for us. George and I were just a couple of regular guys basically at that point, and it was amazing to see the reception. I'll never forget showing it to Steve Wolf of *Sports Illustrated*. He was just blown away, and wrote the nicest review.

Ross has a unique talent that most executives don't have and that's his ability to be creative. It was a joint effort between them and us, and when we finished, Ross said, "Gentlemen, we'll never work on anything this good again." Thirty years later, he actually might be right about that.

SETH ABRAHAM:

The reason that HBO Sports was able to take over boxing is we were willing to outspend everybody. Michael gave me an unlimited budget for sports. And every year I exceeded it. In the same way that HBO took over boxing by spending more money than anybody else, including the commercial networks, we decided we would spend more money than anybody else on documentaries.

That was a eureka moment for me. We spent more money than anybody else on writers. We got Liev Schreiber as the host narrator. And I told Ross, "Whatever it takes, let's do four documentaries a year. Let me worry about the money."

ROSS GREENBURG:

I was always trying to do more, but they always kept me at four. Apart from the money, Seth had nothing to do with our documentaries, but every once in a while, he'd come up with a wild idea for a documentary.

In the early 1990s, almost 50 percent of HBO and Cinemax subscribers got rid of the channels in any given year—the dreaded "churn" rate again. The number, HBO eventually realized, was not quite as daunting as it seemed. When an HBO customer moved, cable providers were counting that as a canceled subscription. But inflated numbers notwithstanding, there was still an underlying problem. Customers complained there was a dearth of valuable programming, or else that the stuff they really wanted to see was too easily missed or not on often enough. In an attempt to curb the churn rate, HBO hatched a plan: the network could increase offerings by expanding the number of HBO channels running at a time.

Likening HBO's plans to a multiplex cinema and its staggered, repeated showings of popular movies, Michael Fuchs told the New York Times that he was looking at a "realistic" goal of increasing retention by 10 percent (from the unhealthy current 50 percent), which in real numbers would mean an increase of roughly 850,000 customers per year. "We get about $4 to $5 a month per subscriber," Fuchs told the Times. "That adds up to a pretty healthy number." This amounted to an increased goal of somewhere between $3.4 million and $4.25 million per month. Fifty million dollars annually went straight to HBO's earnings, and continued to grow every year as the churn rate reduced.

JOHN BILLOCK:

The leading industry journal back then was *Multichannel News*. In the mid-1980s one of their headlines posed, "Is Pay TV Dead?" The VCR was starting to hurt us more than we anticipated. We didn't have a lot of new cable systems being built out, so there weren't a lot of new accounts coming on stream to replace subscribers lost to churn. Our subscriber count was flat year over year. So the big question facing the company was what should we do with our capital? How should we allocate it between marketing and programming? Drive new subscriptions by increasing the marketing spend? Decrease churn with increased programming investment? Honestly, these were stressful days at HBO. Was HBO's future behind it, as some thought out loud?

We had to change things up in our business. We were the first network to leverage something called compression technology. The concept behind HBO multiplex was born out of that technology. We knew through market research that the biggest complaint with HBO was: "There's nothing on to watch when I want to watch it." That's why we created HBO multiplex.

Thank goodness we jumped. We were the first network to multiplex. We were way out in front because we leveraged compression technology first. At some point we probably had ten 'plexes out there. The consumer proposition was, you get HBO multiplex, you get ten choices in prime time for the same price as one.

In effect, we were putting the consumer in charge of his or her programming. They became their own scheduler by increasing their viewing choices at no incremental cost.

BILL NELSON:

Multiplexing was a huge inflection point. It enabled our subscribers to have the wealth and tonnage of HBO programming across eight or nine channels at the same price they had been paying for one channel. Our price value proposition to the consumer totally changed.

ERIC KESSLER, Executive:

Instead of calling the different plex channels one through seven, we positioned each channel with "a reason for being," including HBO Comedy, HBO Signature (Best of), HBO Latino, and HBO Family among the plex channels.

MICHAEL FUCHS:

When they realized videocassettes were ahead of our movie window, they were terrified—if people started buying VCRs, would they still want pay television?

But remember, most people were unsophisticated tech-wise—the cable guy would come in, connect the cable, the VCR, and the television, and then customers didn't want to touch anything. There was no cable subscriber loss because of the VCR, but it could record. All of a sudden you had a little programming operation in your house. So instead of the VCR being the end of our business, it stabilized it.

BRIDGET POTTER:

Not long after I got there in 1982, HBO was on fire. It was being sold into cable systems all over the country. We'd go to staff meetings and they'd say, "This is good, this is good, this is good, this is great, this is great." Then one day they said, "There's a little blip here, it's nothing to worry about." Then the next time, "Well, it's not so good." Somebody picked up the phone and called McKinsey because that's what they know how to do, McKinsey comes crawling all over, they interview me and everybody else, then they did a presentation at the top of the Time Life Building where everything is beige. There's no color. And it's a PowerPoint. I don't think I had ever seen a PowerPoint presentation before.

At the end Jerry Levin walks up and says to the guy, "So can you compare the state of our business right now to any other business that you have looked at?" And the guy says, "Yes, I can. Atari," which had just totally gone bust. What had happened while nobody was watching was that the VCR had come into people's houses and they were getting movies and watching them at home without having to have HBO. It was then that original programming became the idea of the moment.

The push for original programming was coming at an opportune moment for HBO. By the late 1970s, the three major commercial nets—ABC, CBS, and NBC—boasted around 92 percent of all TV viewers; a decade later, that number had cratered to an anemic 62 percent. HBO, for its part, and a very big part it was getting to be, scored an 18 percent increase in prime-time viewership in 1991.

And on the movie side of the ledger, HBO was embroiled in competition not only for the studio's output, but also for scripts good enough to (re)make into originals.

An Emmy-winning original film was no bad way to start. In 1991, HBO's The Josephine Baker Story *won five Emmys and a Golden Globe.*

BOB COOPER:

The Josephine Baker Story changed everything. We took a story about an unknown black woman who lived in St. Louis, was almost lynched, then ran off to France and became a princess in a chateau. When people at the company first heard we were doing it, they thought, she's an unknown. Nobody's going to watch. Michael didn't care. When he saw the movie, he said, "I don't care how it does, this is it. This is the one. This is the one that's going to start us in a direction that makes us really unique and provocative."

It was a huge success for HBO and gave me the direction of what HBO movies had to be and to do. There's something unique about what an HBO movie ought to be. It ought not to be what you see on television on the regular networks and not to be what you'd see in the theaters. And so that became a model for us.

RICHARD LICATA:

Diana Ross had been developing a similar Josephine Baker story. I was told, "Rich, we've got to get out there and get in front of this." So we photographed Lynn Whitfield looking like Josephine Baker and right away got those pictures out into the national press corps. Diana Ross, who was still a force back in 1992, canceled their version.

The Sunday before the Emmys, I was at the gym. I heard a bunch of guys in the locker room talking about what they were going to do that weekend. One said, "I want to watch that Josephine Baker movie." I knew we were on to something. It had hit a nerve.

On May 9, 1990, Richard "Dick" Munro officially departed Time Warner after more than thirty years at the company (first at Time, then Time Inc., then Time Warner). As planned, Nick Nicholas assumed his role—president and co–chief executive of Time Warner Inc.—alongside Steve Ross.

JOHN MALONE:

I had an excellent relationship with Nick. We had done very large deals together including the big investment in Ted Turner in 1987, and the acquisition of Westinghouse Cable in 1985, which was the biggest deal ever in the industry at the time. We had a big, trusting relationship that really worked well.

The merger was just over a year old, and there were almost too many birthing issues to count.

LARRY AIDEM, Executive:

Warner guys hated HBO mostly because they hated Michael. It was a complete pain in the ass to get things going between the two companies. I called it *shmynergy*: one division plus one division equals zero.

MICHAEL FUCHS:

I said to Nick, "Why don't we get a label for low-budget comedy at Warners?" He said, "That sounds interesting." So Nick and I go over to see Steve. I liked Steve. Steve told Beverly Sills that I was his natural successor. Now they're both dead, so you'll have to take my word for it.

We sit down, and Steve immediately starts talking about all the stars who have been on the plane. Really? I don't get a fucking word in. As we start to leave, and I swear this is the truth—Steve puts his arms around us as we get to the elevator and says, "Listen, if you guys are back in town at any time, come on over." The elevator door shuts and I say to Nick, "Does he realize we live a block and a half away?"

BOB DALY:

When Michael Fuchs wanted to start making movies, Terry and I told Steve Ross, "Excuse us, but we're the only ones who are making theatrical movies in this company. That was part of our deal, Steve."

MICHAEL FUCHS:

So we have this fucking dinner. Me, Nick, maybe Joe Collins, with Terry and Bob and Steve. I put the idea for a new movie label on the table and Terry goes fucking crazy.

"Fuck you! I fucking green-light around here! Just go fucking do international TV!" I'm expecting Steve to say, "Terry, calm down," but he says nothing. My guys don't say anything.

BOB DALY:

The long and short of it was after the meeting was over, Michael Fuchs could no longer make movies. We put him out of the movie business. Our relationship with Michael Fuchs was really bad. Michael was pissed off. He hated us. He hated all the Warners people. I guess if I was in his shoes, I probably wouldn't have been terribly happy with us, either. Jeff Bewkes was involved, he was Michael's chief financial officer, but Jeff and I always had a great relationship. Same with Steve Scheffer.

Even before the merger, I would see Michael at the Beverly Hills Hotel. It wasn't one of my restaurants, but I would go every once in a while, and he'd be holding court like he was the most important person in California.

The corporate combo of Nick Nicholas and Jerry Levin was perfect—well, at least for Levin; Nicholas, not so much. Nicholas was known for his stringent code of ethics—he'd had a navy father, after all—and his low levels of ego and paranoia were no match for Levin's dedication to his own career, in which the mantra "the ends justify the means" was more axiom than catchphrase. Their rivalry hadn't quite started out that way: Nicholas had brought Jerry along with him when he'd gotten the top job at Time Warner and had given Levin access to everything, including board meetings. In the end, the repercussions of the dynamic between the two men would be a significant factor in Time Warner's future.

An unusual feature of the Time Warner deal specified that Steve Ross and Dick Munro would, for a period of time, be co-CEOs, after which the successor would be Nick Nicholas, then president of Time Inc. The Time Warner board would consist of eight directors from each side—despite the fact that Time had technically purchased Warner, it was billed as a merger of equals. That billing was quickly put to the test.

JEFF BEWKES:

Steve Ross was used to calling all the shots at Warner, and he didn't seem to feel that anything had changed, despite having sold his company. Dick and Nick would try to participate in these various decisions, but Steve was an accomplished steamroller.

ED BLEIER:

After the merger, they'd had a firing wave at Time Inc. and a lot of longtime employees got fired right before our combined annual meeting. Many picketed the meeting, complaining that Steve had collected $200 million from the deal, and Nick conducted that meeting without a single word of defense for Steve, who had taken no salary the previous two years. He didn't protect Steve. Steve saw it, we all saw it, and that started a period of time where Nick was burning bridges with Steve.

Then Nick wanted to start selling off assets to pay down the debt, and Steve was upset. He said, we didn't do this deal to become smaller. We did it to make us a bigger, better company. Steve soured on Nick, because Nick didn't fulfill what he thought the entire merger was about, and he didn't protect him.

JERRY LEVIN:

Nicholas was shooting himself in the foot. He didn't have the patience to wade through what the company was going to be like.

Nick couldn't talk to a filmmaker or cable operator or others who were different from the people at Time Inc. He brought his Time Inc. personality instead of altering it to be more inclusive, and people were used to Steve

Ross's style. Nick was ambitious and extremely bright, but there's no way to see Ross was going to have Nick succeed him.

JOHN MALONE:

There was a business disagreement between Nick and Steve Ross about the creation of this spin-off entity, Time Warner Entertainment, where they brought the Japanese in.

Nick was very much opposed to that transaction. Steve was very much in favor of it. I was aware of that disagreement going on at the time. But I'm told that there's another explanation, that Nick just got a little too anxious about taking over as CEO as Steve was very ill. That prompted Steve to react negatively, and he picked Jerry simply because he had to have a Time Inc. guy, and Jerry had been involved in the actual deal negotiations.

I had known Jerry, of course, but never got along with him the way I had with Nick. Nick was a great CEO. It's a tragedy they didn't keep him.

BOB DALY:

Terry and I went to see Steve Ross. I didn't know what condition he would be in, and when we got to his room, he was in a bathrobe with a towel wrapped around his throat and he had no hair. This was a shock. It took Terry and me a few minutes to come to grips with all of this. Then Steve speaks with a voice that, because of his medical treatments, sounded like the godfather. "Listen, guys, we can't leave this company in Nick's hands. Are you guys okay if Jerry Levin becomes the CEO?" I said, "Steve, whatever you want, but I want you to be the CEO." He says, "I'm very sick. I want you and Terry to talk to some board members. I want to get rid of Nick, and I want Jerry to be the CEO." Five days later, he had Nicholas fired. Steve fired him on his deathbed.

NICK NICHOLAS:

The day before I left, Jerry, for no reason whatsoever, walked into my office, put his hand on my desk, and said, "Things are really working great, because I like working with you," which was a very unusual thing for him to say. A number of people came to me and said, "There's some funny business going on here with Jerry, you're going to get screwed."

I trusted Steve Ross. I trusted Jerry Levin. Unfortunately, it's my nature.

JERRY LEVIN:

It became clear to me that Steve was going to off Nick very soon, and I decided if Steve was going to go in my direction, I'd have to be sure that there were other people at Time Inc. who would find that acceptable. So I went and met with Dick [Munro] at his house, not telling him why I was there. And the essential reason was I wanted to see if it happened that Nick had to leave, would Dick be supportive of me? I didn't ask it in such a selfish terms, but the answer was yes.

Just under three years after Nick Nicholas was picked as heir apparent during the Time Warner merger, he was gone. On February 20, 1992, Nicholas announced his resignation, but the writing had been on the wall for months. Though his ouster was sweetened somewhat by a reputed $15 million settlement, it was a stunning reversal for the man who just a few years earlier had been slated to run the whole shooting match.

NICK NICHOLAS:

Later on, Jerry was quoted as saying, "I was in my house in Vermont and I took a long walk in the woods," and that's when he decided to put the knife in my back. I've learned from Jeff, Joe Collins, Dick Parsons, and others, that he made it happen. Unbelievable.

I had gotten the Chuck Dolan treatment from twenty years ago when Jerry had pushed Chuck aside, just a different version. There is no question that Levin was the architect/planner of my departure.

JERRY LEVIN:

I didn't give Nick a heads-up. Whether that was the right thing or not, I didn't do it because I was calculating it wouldn't help to advise him. I just sat back and stopped being the good soldier who was helping his performance and his career.

MICHAEL FUCHS:

Jerry had been my rabbi. I didn't foresee a double cross. Nick was so much more talented than Jerry, but he had a merger PTSD and didn't handle the situation with Steve well.

Nick should have acted more like a COO, gotten closer to people, and helped Steve run the company, because Steve wasn't able to run the company on a day-to-day basis. Nick lost his balance.

Jerry was duplicitous, but he was at least functioning. It was a delicate situation. It isn't that I thought that Jerry was a great businessman; I knew he had a tendency not to tell the truth too often.

Jerry all but told me that I was going to be the COO, through his actions, the way he used the word "we."

HAL AKSELRAD:

When Jerry took over, I asked him, "Will you be appointing a chief operating officer?" He said, "I had a caucus with the prior COO in the shower this morning, and I can tell you there's no fucking way." It was the first time I ever heard Jerry curse. He was able to take Nick out; there was no way he was going to give anybody a perch.

JERRY LEVIN:

I worked with Nick for a substantial period to make his desires fulfilled, to make him look good. It wasn't until we had the tender offer and was bogged down in the office that I thought I could do it and he couldn't.

NICK NICHOLAS:

It was in February, we were at our condo in Vail skiing when all this happened, and I was surprised, but at some level I wasn't.

I called Steve. I told him I would resign, but the board had to request my resignation. I wasn't going to have it on the record that I just left. Yes, it was the old navy thing: you don't leave the ship until everyone else has.

When Levin said he was going to leave the company after he wasn't made president of Time Inc. and heir apparent to Munro, I should have said, "Jerry, good luck."

If I look back on the thirty years that I was at Time Warner, I'd have given anything to have the job I had. It was mostly just extremely rewarding to be a part of it. And I feel pride. I really do. And affection.

On December 20, 1992, Steve Ross finally succumbed to the ravages of his prostate cancer, dying at the age of sixty-five. At the end of his thirty years, first at Warner and then at the merged company, Ross had been working from home as the complications of the disease advanced, and now, on the sad occasion of his passing, the helming of Time Warner passed to Jerry Levin.

MICHAEL FUCHS:

Jerry was a sponge. He could talk to a lawyer and then come back to the board and deliver the essence of what he just heard as if it was something that he came up with and has known for five years. He was a chronic bullshitter, which everyone eventually realized. He had no balls, as he could never confront anyone directly or honestly.

Nick would have been twice the CEO Jerry was. Nick was a rational, reasonable guy.

JEFF BEWKES:

Aboodi was instrumental in the group of Ross loyalists who helped Jerry get installed. Jerry then shrank the board within two years, and got rid of some of Ross's guys on the board.

MICHAEL FUCHS:

In 1992, the Democratic convention was in New York, and I was on the Host Committee. I had replaced Steve Ross when he got sick. Bob Rubin and Arthur Levitt came to HBO to have breakfast with me, and told me, "We've got everything covered except we need a media party for fifteen thousand." We couldn't do the convention center; at the time it was so mobbed up it was going to cost us $300,000 just to open the doors. Central Park already had too many events scheduled. I was getting so nervous about being asked to do this party that I started pacing around my table in the office. Then I looked out the window, saw Bryant Park, and thought it would make a fantastic venue for a party. I put movie screens up everywhere and it was a huge success. The next week, Andy Heiskell and Marshall Rose came to my office. They were chairmen of Bryant Park and told me, "We think the park needs a showman. It's time for us to step aside. You're the chairman."

HBO was on fire. We had no competition. Jerry was my rabbi. I was ready for anything.

He won three Grand Slam singles titles—the US Open in 1968; the Australian Open in 1970; and Wimbledon in 1975—two more in doubles, and five Davis Cup titles as well. But all these victories represented but a tiny part of what made Arthur Ashe such an inspiring figure in American sport. He was a civil rights activist; a historian of African Americans in sports (he and his researchers spent six years writing their sixteen-hundred-page, three-volume **A Hard Road to Glory: A History of the African-American Athlete***); and he was a tennis commentator for both HBO and ABC.*

In 1979, Ashe had suffered a heart attack, his cardiac issues stemming from a troubled set of family genes. Another heart attack and two heart surgeries followed, but things only got worse; a blood transfusion received during his second operation had used tainted blood (before there were stringent tests to prevent it), and in late 1988 Ashe was told he was HIV positive.

JULIE ANDERSON:

Ross said to me, "We're going to do a film about Arthur Ashe, and we'd like you to make it." Frank Deford wrote on it, and I directed it.

It was my first big film. We went with Arthur to South Africa because he wanted South Africans to see a free Black man. That was amazing.

When it was finished, I heard that Richard Plepler, who was head of communications at the time, loved it, and I got invited to a meeting in a big conference room full of people I'd never seen before. They were talking about the rollout, how they were going to get reviews, and who they were going to invite to screenings. I felt like I was a queen.

SETH ABRAHAM:

In late 1991, Arthur told me he had AIDS, then actually gave me a written list of the people who knew. "That's it. That's the circle. The only person you can tell is Lynn." In early April of 1992, he called me up and said, "The story is going to break in *USA Today* in the next couple of days. I'd rather be in front of it than behind it. Could we use HBO as the site for the press conference?" I said, "Of course. We'll handle all the logistics. Tell us anything you want."

BILLIE JEAN KING:

Seth called me and said, "We're going to do the press conference. Can you show up?" My partner Ilana and I had just flown to Chicago, and I said, "We can't make it back in time." I was able to reach Arthur literally five minutes before his press conference, and he was so upset that his privacy had been broken. I don't think he realized that a lot of people at HBO Sports had known for several years that he had AIDS, and everyone had kept it quiet. Nobody had said a word. But that day, he was mad. He told me, "I can't believe this is happening. They're like rats. They've ratted me out." I so remember him using the word "ratted" because he was usually so eloquent. He finished our conversation and he went directly to his press conference.

SETH ABRAHAM:

HBO had a very large auditorium so we could accommodate something of this size. He started by saying, "I saw all these photographers, all these journalists. I thought I was at a prizefight." When he announced he had AIDS, it was beyond quiet.

BILLIE JEAN KING:

He couldn't even make it all the way through the presser. Jeannie had to finish for him. It was terribly sad.

SETH ABRAHAM:

Because of my jobs, I've had the good fortune of meeting smart and charismatic people. Arthur had unbelievable empathy and compassion, and I've thought a lot about this: Arthur Ashe was the greatest person I ever knew.

Arthur was a big prizefight fan and came with me to quite a few prizefights. I was at a big fight at Madison Square Garden sitting with Tom Brokaw; Arthur was supposed to have been my date that night. An HBO employee came over and whispered Arthur had just died. I went and told someone who worked at the Garden, and just before the main event, they made the announcement, then followed the tradition of athletic deaths with a symbolic ten-count and ten rings of the bell.

Arthur Ashe's contributions to American life, sport, and culture were plentiful. The dignity he showed in confronting his greatest challenge and the manner in which he turned his own personal troubles into an opportunity to advocate for those less fortunate made him a hero of our times. He was awarded the Presidential Medal of Freedom posthumously after his tragic death at forty-nine.

In 1994, HBO premiered **Arthur Ashe: Citizen of the World.** *The film about their close friend and colleague won the Sports Emmy for Best Documentary.*

5

Procreation

AUGUST 15, 1992–NOVEMBER 17, 1995

Stand-up stalwart Garry Shandling first appeared at LA's Comedy Store in 1978; by the late 1980s he had become one of Johnny Carson's favorite comedians for shots on **The Tonight Show,** *as well as a regular "guest host" when Johnny was away.*

Shandling, a comic with plenty of knowing self-deprecation, didn't just tell jokes; through repeat appearances he established and refined an ever-evolving caricature of himself. In 1986, Shandling expanded on that persona and created, with former SNL *writer and comedy kingpin Alan Zweibel, Showtime's* **It's Garry Shandling's Show,** *a series so shrewdly self-aware that its theme song began simply, "This is the theme to Garry's show." Garry took it from there—up, down, and finally over, but not before the completion of four lovingly reviewed seasons.*

Even that ingenious enterprise was but a warm-up, however, for the next Shandling innovation to come. HBO tapped him to create another comedy series, **The Larry Sanders Show,** *which landed his alter ego into a sitcom disguised as a fake late-night talk show, with brilliant backstage interpolations.*

The first episode came to HBO on August 15, 1992. Shandling, as the chronically needy Sanders, used the series to poke fun at ever-inflated showbiz egos and the industry in general.

Over the course of six seasons and ninety episodes, Shandling would be supplemented by a quixotic array of stars, from Jennifer Aniston to Warren Zevon, playing satirized versions of themselves—plus real-life network executives and even a TV critic or two, as though everyone in the business, or clinging by their fingernails to its fringes, weren't already Hollywood "versions" of themselves.

Shandling shot **Sanders** mostly on a CBS lot in Studio City, during the epoch in which fellow stand-up comic Jerry Seinfeld was doing his own history-making series virtually next door. And so, for a few years at least, the comedy epicenter of the planet was crowded into a humble little corner of the Valley.

MICHAEL FUCHS:

I thought *It's Garry Shandling's Show* was terrific, and he was someone we should be in business with. I spoke at an ACE Awards. He was in the first few rows with his girlfriend Linda, and I congratulated him on his awards, wooing him right there on fucking TV. In major league sports, that's called tampering.

LINDA DOUCETT, Actor:

It's Garry Shandling's Show was cleaning up with awards that night. I saw how Michael Fuchs looked at Garry and thought, "He's going to be on HBO really soon."

ALAN ZWEIBEL, Executive Producer:

Garry was offered his own talk show on Fox, and I told him, "This sounds like a show you would make fun of as opposed to do. If you do a straight talk show, you'll grow bored within weeks. Why not do a show *about* that kind of show?" I would also bet the house that I was not the only one who told him that. It seemed obvious to a lot of us.

Gilda Radner believed she was in remission when she appeared as a guest on *It's Garry Shandling's Show*, which was the first time she had been in front of an audience in years. She had such a great time doing it, and was all revved up for something more. And new. There was a meeting with me, Garry, Bernie [Brillstein], Gilda, and Michael Fuchs; we didn't have a formalized deal, but the understanding was that Garry, Gilda, and I would create a show for HBO. Fuchs was going to wait for it. He even called a few times asking how it was coming along. We had a number of writing sessions, me, Gilda, and Garry, and they were great. The idea was Gilda would play the star of her own variety series. We would show the writers' room, the offices, rehearsals, sketches, and you would also see her at home. Then Gilda canceled our next meeting. Then the one after that. Her cancer had come back. We pulled the plug on that show because Gilda's cancer had taken over.

MICHAEL FUCHS:

Brad Grey called me up and said, "Would you want to do a show with Garry?" I said, "Sure." He pitched it, and I loved the idea. I thought it was the consummate show about show business hypocrisy. I gave him seven or eight episodes on the phone. I wanted to be a monopolist.

CHRIS ALBRECHT:

We had been working for years trying to convince Michael to let us do half-hour series, then during one call he green-lights a show on his own.

MICHAEL FUCHS:

The programming people on the West Coast went fucking crazy. I love when that happens. I'm telling you they rooted for this show to go down the toilet.

Nobody wants their boss dipping in and doing their job. I only did this when I had a real inkling, and my inkling batting average was .1000. I would almost always call up and give the person whose area I was dabbling in a heads-up so they didn't feel I was working behind their backs. It didn't seem to cause too much tension, except the LA office was more sensitive, because it was LA!

JEFF BEWKES:

Some people ask why we waited so long to get into the half-hour series business. Well, Michael had a view, and I think he was absolutely right, that it was going to be a steep climb. First, we'd be going up against broadcast networks who each had twenty-five series a week with budgets that cost more than everything we were doing. Second, they had a schedule of half-hour and one-hour shows they could launch new shows from and a big audience flow to promote to on their own air.

But Michael had a great eye for comics and saw the potential in Garry and this show, so he broke his own soft rule.

JUDD APATOW:

Michael Fuchs was very aggressive about doing something with Garry and gave him a commitment unheard-of at that time in television.

Garry was such a great observer of people that while hosting *The Tonight Show*, he noticed all of the neuroses in that show. He noticed that it was a great metaphor for how humans interact with each other. That's what fascinated him. He didn't want to be a host. He wanted to comment about the world of talk shows, the people who work there, and what we all have in common. He was mainly interested in the show explaining what keeps people apart. He also talked about the curtain as a metaphor. He once said to me, "Most people never tell you the truth, and when they do, it's a huge deal." Garry said the show is about people who love each other, but show business gets in the way.

LINDA DOUCETT:

The idea of the show was, what you can't handle in life, you mock. If Garry couldn't handle hosting a talk show, he was going to mock hosting a talk show.

There were three years in between the Showtime and HBO shows. We called it the "Dry Period" because Garry was turning down everything. He was anxious about going back to work, but I told him if he didn't, I was going to have a heart attack.

BRIDGET POTTER:

I got called into Michael's office and Brad was there. We had really admired Garry's work and wanted him to come to HBO. Michael says, "Garry is ready to come to HBO; you have to hear the idea." I flipped out. I had worked on *The Dick Cavett Show*, understood talk show crazies, and knew this would work. Best of all, I got to work with Garry.

JUDD APATOW:

Garry told me the only thing HBO was concerned about was that the behind-the-scenes sections were going to be shot on film, and the actual *Larry Sanders Show* talk show segments would be shot on video.

CARMI ZLOTNIK:

There was no precedent for this show. There was no template. Production executives managed shows by template budgets, and anything that didn't fit was bad.

CHRIS ALBRECHT:

We convinced Michael that we should do a pilot because it was hard to understand how the show was going to mix the different realities of backstage and the show, and we heard some of it was going to be on film and some on tape.

We needed a pilot to work this all out. We set up a call, and the plan was I was going to say, "This all sounds great, but we probably should do a pilot," and then Michael was going to say, "I agree." But he never said that.

SUSIE FITZGERALD:

Our first meeting was at the Polo Lounge with Chris, me, Brad, Garry, and Bernie Brillstein. Chris was worried about Garry's level of commitment and was sort of hammering him. After that, a message came back from the producing side that they didn't want to talk to Chris anymore. That didn't seem to bother Chris, and I wound up being very involved with the show.

When we were casting, sometimes it would be just me and Garry in the room, which was the case when Rip Torn came in to audition. He was wearing one of those L.L.Bean hats with the long bill and a fishing jacket and then proceeds to have this weird nonsensical conversation with Garry—probably twenty minutes—that I couldn't follow. When Rip left the room, I turned to Garry and asked, "What was he talking about?" Garry said, "I have no idea." We still ended up casting him.

JEREMY PIVEN, Actor:

I ran into Garry in the bathroom as he was putting in his contacts. I was like, "Hey, I'm about to audition for you." He said, "All right, well, good luck." He was very sweet.

Garry was a genius, the maestro. He wanted to make a show about the backstage of life. It was so funny, layered, and ahead of its time. I had just gotten out of college, a random dude coming off the bench, but for me it was like grad school.

PAUL SIMMS, Writer and Executive Producer:

My agent sent me a stack of scripts and I read them, including the *Larry Sanders* pilot. My first thought was, Are you actually allowed to make a TV show like this where people curse, and talk about real people in such a funny, derogatory way? I was working at *Letterman* at the time, and the script had an authenticity to it that made you think, "Wow, this is really cool." I had a phone call with Garry who was one of my comedic heroes, then got hired.

PETER TOLAN, Writer and Executive Producer:

I was doing *Murphy Brown* and Fred Barron, whom I had worked with on *Sessions*, called me and said, "Hey, I'm doing this thing with Garry Shandling.

Would you like to come on as a consulting producer?" I knew Garry from his stand-up and the Showtime show, which I thought was brilliant. So I said, "Yeah, I would love to work with this guy."

I was still doing *Murphy Brown*, so on my off time I would do *Larry Sanders*. Routinely either people I was working with or heads of networks—people who should have known better—would say, "I don't know why you're working at HBO. It's not like they're ever going to win any awards."

I would say in a breathtakingly short time, I kept hearing shouting through my office wall, which was next to Fred's office. He and Garry were not getting along. Garry felt like work was not progressing at a healthy pace, so Fred was let go and, weirdly, I took his place.

As soon as I started to work with Garry, we had these conversations about the tone of the show, and I really hooked into his vision for what the show was supposed to be. I was rewriting most of the drafts, then sending them to Garry.

JUDD APATOW:

When I did the Ben Stiller sketch show for Fox, Garry was doing the first season of *The Larry Sanders Show*, and when my show was canceled, he said, "Why don't you come work for me? You're going to learn a lot." He didn't say, "You're going to be helpful to me." He said, "You're going to learn a lot." So from moment one, it was a mentor relationship and I always tried to be loyal to him.

LINDA DOUCETT:

I met Garry at a party in Los Angeles in 1986. I had no idea who he was. He looked extremely uncomfortable when he walked in, then somebody said to him, "How are you?" He said, "I'm fine, thank you." I blurted out, "You don't seem fine at all." We had a connection after that, started joking around, then he asked me for my number.

MICHAEL FUCHS:

Linda, Garry, Brad, and I would go out to dinner and we always had a great time. Garry was as indecisive about women as Larry Sanders was. Garry and Linda were on and off for seven years, and at one point she told me she was through with him, so we started going out. This happened on the way to Robin Williams's fortieth birthday party in Northern California. Garry found out about it, and I guess he didn't think things with him and Linda were over. Not so smart for the network head to date its star's girlfriend, even if it's post-relationship. We made peace at Billy Crystal's fortieth. God bless those great comedians.

LINDA DOUCETT:

From the ACE Awards on, all I heard Brad and Garry saying was, "Michael Fuchs is obsessed with you." He's asking a million questions, including, "Is it a committed relationship?" I thought that was so funny.

JEFF BEWKES:

Michael gave me the Sanders pilot tape, which he wasn't in the habit of doing. He came to the doorway later to check my reaction, and I said, "This is the greatest fucking thing we've ever done." He says, "You think it's too Jewish? Will people like it in the Midwest?" I said, "What am I, the goy test? Yes, they'll get it. Not everybody, but enough."

SUSIE FITZGERALD:

The show was very supported by HBO, in terms of promotion. Brian Benben would get jealous because he felt *Dream On* probably had more viewers than *The Larry Sanders Show* but didn't get as much attention. *The Sanders Show* didn't get big ratings at all. It was well liked critically, which made a difference to HBO, and it got Emmy nominations at a time when cable wasn't really getting much attention from the Emmys.

JEFF BEWKES:

We called *Dream On* and *Larry Sanders* the "Best Hour on TV." If we were going to do series, we had to make ours different. *Dream On* was good, but it wasn't breakthrough good like *Sanders*, which is one of my two or three favorite shows ever on HBO. It's fucking amazing. And Michael made this happen.

JUDD APATOW:

Because we wanted celebrities on, we often wouldn't know far in advance, and that made things very difficult. Sometimes they would drop out at the last minute; sometimes we couldn't get anyone booked till the last second. And if a name changed, say it was Jeff Goldblum instead of Albert Brooks, the whole story would need to change as well.

HENRY WINKLER, Actor:

I was on the show that had something to do with Hank's sex tape, and Norm Macdonald said the word "cock" to me, and they all thought that was mind-blowing to say to the Fonz. It was amazing to see how the show was done. Before taping, everybody met in Garry's office and you literally read the script out loud again, then he had the last edit.

RITA MORENO, Actor:

It was a strange experience. I felt like everybody was crazy but me. I tried to say something to Garry but he didn't listen; he was talking to about five people at once, just talking, talking, talking, and I could never get in a word edgewise. It was bizarre. It was always a lot of people walking and talking and yelling. I felt like I was in a crazy house, or an asylum. I went home and thought, "I'm glad I don't work on that show."

CHRIS ALBRECHT:

Garry was not low maintenance.

ALAN ZWEIBEL:

Even though Garry was so infused with "Garry," he was such a brilliant writer that he had the ability to separate himself from the character he was playing. On *It's Garry Shandling's Show*, he would refer to Garry as Garry. He didn't say, "Okay, I want to do this." He would say, "I think Garry should do that." He gave that character a degree of objectivity, and I think he did the same thing with Larry Sanders.

Running a show is difficult and running a show with Garry is 24/7. It got to the point where on a Sunday, I would play the answering machine and hear four or five messages from Garry, each one getting a little bit angrier than the previous one. One time I called him back and he goes, "Where were you?" I said, "We took the kids to Disneyland," and he was pissed off. The show was Garry's wife, children, life, everything. Thank God technology wasn't as advanced back then as it is today. Otherwise, I'm sure he would've asked that a GPS chip be embedded in my shoulder.

JUDD APATOW:

The debate we would always have in the writers' room was, Would you rather work for a really difficult person who's a genius or work for someone who's mediocre, who was really easy to deal with?

There were definitely people there who were very offended by moments when Garry had no energy to be polite. A lot of that was about exhaustion. We shot seventeen pages a day for two days to get the show in the can. In addition to that, we would do long nights shooting the talk show elements.

No one really knew how to shoot single-camera comedy in a way that made the star's life livable. Garry was one of the first people who was the writer, director, producer, and star; it was way too much work and our show was set up in a way that did not serve him. We would do a table read on Monday, we would rehearse and block for three days, and then shoot the entire show in two days. At the same time everyone's asking Garry to read next week's script and to look at outlines for future episodes. He had no mental energy to do it. That definitely made him cranky at times.

PETER TOLAN:

Garry was wearing so many hats. Scripts would go through him and then he'd have to do the acting. He had confidence as a writer, but not as an actor. He desperately wanted to be seen as a good actor, and he worked hard toward that goal. But throughout the life of the series, he was constantly exhausted, just absolutely exhausted. He'd come to us dragging and say, "I think we need a 'Light on Larry.'" A "Light on Larry" episode was one where Larry didn't have much to do. Garry needed them and loved them, and the other actors loved them, too, I'm sure, because it gave them more time in the spotlight. There were quite a few "Light on Larrys," because Garry was not shy about being his own advocate when it came to how tired he was.

ALAN ZWEIBEL:

Garry was so psychological, he would dig really deep, and if somebody didn't see it the way that he did, he would have a bit of a problem with them. Buck Henry told me, "Mike Nichols has never worked with anybody that he disliked as much as Garry Shandling." By the end of *It's Garry Shandling's Show*, he and I weren't talking.

But still, I loved him like a brother, and even though we weren't getting along, as brothers often don't, I made the decision that I wanted him in my life one way or another. There was something about his spirituality that I thought was really important to me. So we were connected again.

JUDD APATOW:

At some point Garry would completely run out of energy and he would look for someone to help him. Everyone tried. Garry wanted someone to say, "I know this is impossible. I'm going to make some adjustments and make your life livable." Garry was a very sensitive person and felt betrayed that people weren't worried about his mental health in a very stressful situation.

The whole thing didn't work and Garry knew it. As a result he was always in some version of a meltdown. Then people would say, "Garry's such a pain," and that would drive Garry crazy.

BRIDGET POTTER:

One show was less than twenty minutes long. It had been longer but Garry didn't like certain parts and wasn't going to make it any longer. It was one of those things that we allowed him to do.

MICHAEL FUCHS:

At one point, Garry wanted to take a year off and we had to work that out. We were very good with talent that way, unlike networks that were stuck with the rigidity of their schedules.

JUDD APATOW:

HBO was very supportive of everything Garry was doing. Garry would always say to them, "I have way more notes than you. However bad you think it is, I think it's way worse." His bar was very high. He wanted every episode to be the best show ever. Which made it very complicated for people to work on the show because the show was also very deep in his head and it was hard to predict what he would like.

Carolyn Strauss was the executive on it, and she was really good with Garry. Like really good. I could see that she understood his genius. She would have notes, and Garry really respected her thoughts, but she also didn't intrude. She and Garry had a smart rhythm with each other. Susie Fitzgerald was also involved, and she was also very, very good. Susie and Carolyn were honest and thoughtful. They were the dream people to be there for him.

CAROLYN STRAUSS, Executive:

I would go to *Larry Sanders* table reads, but because I was so new to it, I didn't say much at all. Watching and listening to Garry was so amazing to me. He would walk away from any joke—no matter how funny it was—if it didn't work for the character, or if it didn't work for the story. It wasn't about hanging on to jokes, it was about hanging on to the integrity of the characters and the integrity of the piece. To this day, I consider the way he did that to be incredibly rare. He had so much confidence in his characters and what he was trying to do with the show that it made a huge impression on me.

Garry took the comedy format to a new level and set a standard that we hoped to achieve with other scripted shows.

SUSIE FITZGERALD:

At table reads, there were a lot of penis jokes. Inevitably. Me and my junior executive, Pam McCarthy, would just look at each other like, "Okay." They all seemed to be obsessed with making penis jokes. Anyway, that's comedy.

PETER TOLAN:

Garry and I had an interesting relationship. Garry was a brilliant guy, but famously neurotic, and it did use to drive me crazy. People would say, "Jesus, how do you work with him? He's crazy." We would be about to shoot, and he would say, "I think we can do better here." Or we'd have a long conversation, and I'd walk away thinking he'd fully accepted I didn't think a specific joke worked, then two minutes later I'd walk by and he'd be pitching the same joke to the janitor, asking him what he thought. I'm not saying there aren't funny janitors in the world, but Garry's endless anxiety could be frustrating.

LINDA DOUCETT:

Sometimes it felt like we were in a laboratory. I didn't know if we were making a show or trying to find uranium. Garry's process was unusual, and there were lots of people who said he was difficult and mean, but he wasn't. He just took it all incredibly seriously.

PAUL SIMMS:

I was warned when I went to work there by people who had worked with him before that Garry always turns on his number two. He'll always at some point develop resentment and hostility toward whoever was supposed to be his right-hand person. So for the first season and a half I benefited from that, since I started at the bottom as a story editor. As Garry fired people left and right, I kept moving up. For some reason, at some point, I was the one person he could work with. That meant writing a bunch, then sitting down and getting Garry to focus on it. Garry could not write on his own. He had to have someone else there that he would say ideas to. Garry was also much better when he had thirty existing pages to look at and say what he would do differently.

He was my comedic hero. I was very excited about the work we were doing. But inevitably the point came where I rose up high enough that I was the number two. Then things got difficult between us. People rarely talk about the fact that around season two or three, Garry was taking a lot of Vicodin, and it made work really difficult because when you're under the influence of that, it makes you unfocused and hard to pin down to make decisions. And when you're not under the influence, it makes you short-tempered and full of rage. So that was difficult to deal with. Then of course there was the inevitability that because he was doing it, I started doing it, too. Now you had two people who were alternately taking Vicodin, were alternately unfocused and then full of rage and hostility toward each other. Recipe for success.

I had a very fruitful and tumultuous three-year relationship with Garry, where we were very close and worked together very closely. Ultimately, we ended up estranged and bitter enemies.

LINDA DOUCETT:

Garry finally said to me, "We're going to give you your own story line," and it turned out to be the one where my character Darlene is asked to pose for *Playboy*. I had been asked to do it in real life and said I would do it if we could incorporate it into the show.

Because of my Amish background, I'd like to go on the record and point out I was never totally naked, just topless. Garry had a beach house in Malibu where we spent 30 percent of our time, and we did some of the shoot out there. Some of the poses were pretty provocative, including one with me lying across a bed with my head hanging off the side of the bed. When I saw Garry's reaction to that and a few others, I asked that it be dialed back. We never showed any of it on the show. It was a bad career move on my part.

PETER TOLAN:

We loved Rip. He was great on the show, but he had more than his share of demons, and he could be angry and abusive to the cast and crew. It got to the point where Garry and I had to sit down with him and confront him about his behavior, which was a joke from the start, what with two nonconfrontational people going up against one of the most confrontational actors in Hollywood history. Rip came in and sat down opposite us, and Garry screwed up his courage and told Rip he was a bully and his abusive behavior would have to change. Rip spread his legs wide, leaned into us, and said, "Oh yeah? Or what?" What, we were going to fire him? He knew that would never happen. Rip was crazy from day one and acted out in every possible way, but he had us completely by the balls and we all knew it.

One week, we had Burt Reynolds on the show. He was supposed to be Larry's neighbor, and was going to be talking to Garry over a fence. He goes, "What am I going to be doing over here?" They said, "You're just talking to him over the fence." Burt says, "I want to be doing something. I want to dig a hole." So we had to get a bucket of dirt and a shovel.

The day starts, and somebody from Brillstein-Grey assigns a PA to Reynolds, and the instructions are, "Get him whatever he needs." Reynolds shows up and the kid says, "I'm supposed to get whatever you need." Reynolds says, "I need a bottle of vodka and a bottle of soda." So the kid doesn't talk to anybody, and goes right out to the liquor store. Reynolds is fucking snockered when he comes down to shoot, and it's not going well. In fact, at one point, he threw dirt over the wall onto Garry, and Garry was like, "What the fuck is this?"

Then Burt has this amazing meltdown in front of the cast and crew. He's standing behind this fake wall with fake brick, and he ends up tearing pieces off and throwing them at the camera crew. Complete meltdown. Huge. I've never seen anything like it. Then he marches off. Who do I happen to be standing next to when this happens? Rip, who just goes, "Burt's a troubled boy." I thought to myself, "Who are you kidding? You're the gatekeeper of the troubled boys. Fuck you."

Rip continues to be an abusive fuck, routinely picking on a member of the cast or crew. I'm even-keeled—it takes a lot to get me going. Near the end of the third season, we do a table read and wind up cutting Wally Langham's part in half for that week, which also eliminates one, just one of Rip's lines, and I can hear Rip across the table go, "Well, I guess I shouldn't have come in this week. I should have taken a vacation in Tahiti." And my head just blew off. I said, "Rip, what the fuck is wrong with you? You fucking crybaby. Shut the fuck up." He gets on his feet and tells me, "Fuck you. You can't talk to me like that." Now I stand and go, "Fuck you!" This goes on for forty seconds, which is not long in the history of the earth, but when it's guys yelling at each other in a professional setting, it's forever. I said, "Fuck you, you fucking child. Get off the stage. I'm sick of looking at you." But it's clear that he's not going to go, so I said, "All right, let's go back to the notes." A minute later, I'm focusing on the script, and I look over to Janeane or maybe it was Penny, who is indicating with her finger coming down from her eye to her cheek that Rip is crying. I made Rip cry.

The notes end and he pushes away from the table grandly, and says, "I'm calling my agent," and walks off. After the door closes, the entire cast applauds. They'd been waiting almost three years for somebody to do what I had done. The next day, I see him and say, "You've been disrespectful to everybody on this set at some point or another, and I am no longer going to respect you by watching you work."

Now the season ends, and we still haven't talked, but I'm bothered by the fact that I blew my cool, but also wondering, "Why doesn't he get it? We're all working to the good of something that's bigger than any of us. I'm not his enemy, nobody there is his enemy." And I suddenly think, "That would make a good story."

I come up with an idea for an episode where Artie and Larry have a fight, and Artie is wounded by it and spends the night alone in the studio. It was a tour de force for Rip. He got to do Shakespeare and sing, then he meets a janitor who doesn't speak much English and they bond.

When we did the show, Rip didn't see through it, that I was in effect the janitor. Artie has to clean things up during the day; the janitor has to clean things up at night. They're the same guy, even though they don't speak the same language. We shoot the episode, it's great, and Rip wins an Emmy. From that fucking fight, that prick wins an Emmy. I didn't win an Emmy.

LINDA DOUCETT:

One episode, they were cutting lines, and Rip didn't like it when his lines got cut. He was getting really angry, and the AD comes into the writers' room and says, "Rip is going insane. He's smashing everything in his dressing room and he has a gun." Everybody froze and Garry says, "Oh shit, we have a show to shoot. Send Linda in. He won't shoot her."

Everybody starts laughing and he goes, "I'm serious. Linda, go." I go knock on the door, "Rip, it's Linda. Please don't shoot me." I come in and he goes, "Hi honey." I asked him, "Rip, what's wrong?" He says, "Oh, this damn TV stuff." I said something like, "Rip, it's really chilly out there. I know you want to keep working." And he goes, "Yeah, God dammit. You're right."

PAUL SIMMS:

Everyone says these days that *Larry Sanders* changed this and that and set HBO on this path, at least with comedy, toward prestige television. I don't think we had any consciousness that we were doing that.

CHRIS ALBRECHT:

Larry Sanders was one of the first shows on HBO that opinion makers followed, which was good for us. Garry was a visionary; watching him pull all that together certainly gave us a lot of experience, and it showed a whole other host of people what you could do on HBO.

MICHAEL FUCHS:

Brad had fucking nothing to do with the show creatively, but it put him in the TV business. The show was a critical success, not a giant ratings killer, but we were never slaves to ratings. Our economics had nothing to do with ratings. Historically, the show stands up very well. Hard to believe Brad and Garry are gone. Now I can take full creative credit!

Since its birth, HBO was thought of as a place for either movies, the latest stand-up or concert, or a boxing match. Now when people talked about HBO, they talked about **Larry Sanders** *and* **Dream On.**

JEFF BEWKES:

I'd go to sales dinners with affiliates in red states, with cable operators, and they'd be talking about Little League and Kiwanis, and then their wife would say, "Charlie, do your Hank impression," or "Charlie's favorite is Artie on the show."

Blockbuster was breathing down our necks. Our big selling point had been uncut movies in your home, and now you could rent 'em at Blockbuster six or eight months before they showed up on HBO.

PETER TOLAN:

If you had friends outside of Hollywood and they asked you what you were working on and you said *The Larry Sanders Show*, especially during the first couple of seasons, they'd have no idea what you were talking about. Outside of LA, it was like the show didn't exist. But everyone in the business watched it, and we had complete adoration. It was feast or famine in terms of audience reaction.

The reality of *The Larry Sanders Show* was that it was massively watched in Hollywood, and if *Larry Sanders* was on your résumé, you worked for twenty or thirty years because it was that influential.

When I meet younger writers and younger performers, routinely they say, "Oh my God, I'm completely influenced by *The Larry Sanders Show*." It's like a touchstone for a whole generation of comic minds.

HBO continued to perform like a laboratory for innovation, abhorring and eschewing broadcast network constructs and experimenting whenever possible. Yet even HBO from time to time needed a light shoving in the direction of forward-thinking.

One day Michael Fuchs heard Bill Cosby—his reputation still unsullied by scandal—complaining about Black representation on television. "Run down what you saw of black people on TV before the Huxtables," Cosby had said. "Who ever went to college? Who ever tried for better things? . . . Where are the sociological writings about this?"

Fuchs grabbed the phone and called Chris Albrecht, insisting that he do something to address Cosby's challenge. "I have just the thing," Albrecht responded, and green-lit a promising project that had nevertheless been suffering the agonies of development hell: Laurel Avenue.

The 1993 miniseries **Laurel Avenue** *was a three-hour, two-part drama that chronicled one weekend in the life of a Black family—the Arnetts—living in St. Paul, Minnesota. The screenplay, by Michael Henry Brown, explored the trials of life in the working and middle classes of America in vivid, complex ways, alongside the theme of drug abuse, which ensnared several of the show's characters. David Zurawik wrote in the* **Baltimore Sun** *that the show "presents a slice of African-American family life featuring the most complex and interesting black characters ever seen in prime time."*

PAUL AARON, Executive Producer:

Michael Henry Brown was Black, and when he and I would go to HBO in New York to see Bridget, we would walk in the door, get badges, then walk toward a security guard who was at the elevator bank. I would walk right through, but every single time we went there, whatever guard was there would say to Michael, "Excuse me, what are you doing here?" I would say, "This is my partner, we're the writer and producer of *Laurel Avenue*." "Oh, okay, just checking."

ANNE THOMOPOULOS, Executive:

I got to HBO in 1992. When I interviewed with Chris, he gave me two scripts to read and told me they were both green-lit. I'm an awful liar, so I told him they were horrible and that he shouldn't make them, and he said, "We're making them." One of the scripts was called *Sweeps*, and it was about sweeps week at a regular network. I said, "That's the dumbest idea I've ever heard. Who even knows what sweeps are, and you're basically advertising for networks." He ended up pulling the plug on both projects and hiring me. Chris's reaction speaks to the fact that he was an incredible manager, and always willing to engage in dialogue.

CHRIS ALBRECHT:

I listened to Anne and thought, "First of all, thank you. You're right. And second, how smart and courageous of you."

ANNE THOMOPOULOS:

The first thing I did was *Laurel Avenue*, a little miniseries—two episodes about a middle-class African American family. It was something that had never really been seen on television before. It was the playwright Michael Henry Brown, who's unfortunately passed away, and Paul Aaron.

PAUL AARON:

I had pitched to Chris Albrecht and said, "Why don't we find a writer from various racial communities, the kind where most of the audience of HBO would say for example, 'I once turned down a street and all I saw was black people, and I thought, oh, I don't belong here.' What if we brought people to these neighborhoods and showed them what really happens there? Most people don't know, but people live there, and cultures evolve." That was the pitch for a series of pieces, the first of which was *Laurel Avenue*.

To his credit, Chris absolutely got it. He was excited about *Laurel Avenue*. They just couldn't push it over the line. They were nervous about whether HBO had enough of a Black audience, and whether white people would watch this family show about a group of Black people for this time was iffy. I understood his dilemma.

Then Bill Cosby did this screed about the fact that cable television was showing its racism by showing only Black comedians who talked about the Black experience cheaply and without any sense of anything positive.

I got a phone call that said, "How fast can we get this made?"

TONY TO, Producer:

Laurel Avenue was one of the first original programming projects for HBO, not HIP. I believe it was their first union show. It signified their commitment to original programming under Chris. That was my first introduction to HBO.

JOHN MELFI, Executive Producer:

It all started in 1990. I blindly met Tony To, who was the production manager on a film called *One False Move*, which was Carl Franklin's first directing assignment. I joined him and he was my mentor and then a partner for nine years. We did *One False Move* the movie and then Carl was offered *Laurel Avenue* in 1991 and took us with him to HBO.

Annie joined halfway through the show. We became thick as thieves instantly. There were so few of us that it felt like family in that way. It was a very small company; everybody knew each other.

PAUL AARON:

This was meant to be a series of three shows, only two of which happened— *Laurel Avenue* and *Grand Avenue*, about an American Indian family. *Calle*

Ocho examined the Cuban culture on Eighth Street, which runs down the center of Miami, but by that time HBO had gotten into *From the Earth to the Moon* and Tom Hanks and huge budgets with big stars. So they never did the Cuban part of the series.

While HBO continued to fill its schedule with hits produced externally, 1993 was a banner year for a more intrepid side of the network: its original film production units. HBO dominated the 45th Emmys, garnering seven statuettes, more than any other cable company, and turned out to do better than all the networks, too, save NBC. HBO was buoyed by wins from its fledgling original series department, including two for **Dream On,** *but it was those burgeoning film units that brought the glory home that year.*

Fueling HBO's growing prestige was an increased willingness for full-fledged stars to sign on. Between 1990 and 1995, in addition to Academy Award winners Holly Hunter and Robert Duvall, Emmy winners Beau Bridges, Laurence Fishburne, Salma Hayek, John Lithgow, Donald Sutherland, Forest Whitaker, James Woods, and others joined in the spree. HBO had undeniably arrived on the Hollywood scene.

What was most notable about this haul of awards was that in the previous year, HBO had received just seven major nominations, winning two. In one mere year, the channel had upped its haul fivefold, a sign that HBO was now able to attract writing and acting talent comparable to any of the major networks and well beyond their closest cable rivals.

Although this was the first major award season for the network, it would not be the last. From 1993 to 1999, HBO won seven straight Primetime Emmys for Outstanding Television Movie, including a dual win in 1993 for **Barbarians at the Gate** *and* **Stalin.** *This success continued at the Golden Globes, where the network won Best Television Film from 1994 to 1997. Though it had never before won either award, this was no blip—HBO would go on to dominate these categories for years to come.*

MICHAEL FUCHS:

I liked it when we started to win all the Emmys, beating everyone, but I wasn't ever satisfied. We were creating a version of the TV business that had hardly any limitations. You can always be better. When someone did a great show elsewhere, my attitude was, Why didn't we do that?

HBO's two film units, Showcase and Pictures, had found their sweet spot. Broadcast networks were still making TV movies—albeit mainly with TV-size stars, smallish budgets, and female-driven story lines. The studios, meanwhile, heavily into **Die**

Hard *mode, gobbled up spec action scripts as quickly as possible. Fuchs, Callender, and Cooper saw both strategies and pointed their compass at what they considered the fertile ground in between, movies that subscribers couldn't find in either world and that boasted stars and compelling, controversial story lines.*

Emmy wins brought one more boon to HBO: free advertising. The commercial networks carried the award show, and now that HBO had entered the arena, every win by HBO meant an in-kind donation of free promotion from rival networks.

COLIN CALLENDER:

We knew we had to do things differently, tell stories others weren't telling and speak to audiences underserved by traditional mainstream television. In 1989, we case Danny Glover in the lead role in a movie that was written for a white man, *Dead Man Out*. We went on to produce *Criminal Justice* with Forest Whitaker and Rosie Perez, and movies like *Strapped*, *Daybreak*, *Mi Vida Loca* with Salma Hayek in her first American role, all contemporary Latina and Black stories no one else was telling on television, along with historical stories like *Miss Evers' Boys*.

Those are multicultural stories, dealing with contemporary issues or American history from a perspective that wasn't being told anywhere else. That was thirty years ago. We were way ahead of the curve.

Strapped was a movie about the gun culture among Black kids in New York. The response was an inflection point for HBO Showcase.

Forest Whitaker had heard that we were making the film and came in to talk about it. The opening scene was a shoot-out in a project between two kids. The next morning, a boy's body is being taken up by the emergency crew. Forest said, "Here's how I would shoot that scene the next morning. My camera is going to look at the sneakers that the dead boy's wearing, because that's what every kid in the block would be looking at to identify him." Forest had a take on the story that would make it authentic. We hired him on the spot. I said, "You've got to direct this film."

After it aired, I called the research department and said, "How did the film do?" They said, "We're sorry, but there seems to be a technical problem. The numbers are completely haywire."

Later in the day they called and said, "Actually, the numbers are correct. We have never seen such large viewing figures with the African American audience on HBO." It was confirmation of what we sort of already knew, that there was an enormous Black audience out there, underserved by the mainstream media, and that we had a role to play there. That resulted in a whole slew of stories.

As Callender's HBO Showcase broke new ground with underserved audiences, Cooper's HBO Pictures made the most of the network's headway in the award circuits. In 1992, James Woods headlined **Citizen Cohn,** *a film about the infamous American lawyer Roy Cohn. Framed as a series of deathbed flashbacks while Cohn lay dying of AIDS in 1986, the movie indicted Cohn as a portrait of evil, a master manipulator who even pulled the strings of his longtime collaborator the notorious senator Joseph McCarthy, architect of the Cold War–era purges of US government officials on bogus charges of Communist sympathies. The film took home a Peabody Award and was nominated for two Golden Globes (including Best Television Motion Picture and Best Actor for Woods) and twelve Emmy Awards, winning three.*

BOB COOPER:

I grew up in Montreal in a duplex. I was on the main level upstairs from my grandparents. My grandfather was very political, and I used to spend a lot of time with him. He would talk to me about things like how he was stopped at the border once because they thought he was a Communist. And he would tell me about Simon Wiesenthal. I absorbed all of it, and I knew the name of Roy Cohn, I knew about the Rosenbergs. I was eight years old when the Rosenbergs were executed.

LEE GRANT:

Frank Pierson, a great director and writer, called and asked, "Who do you want to play, the monster's mother or the woman who was put to death?" I said, "I want to do the monster's mother. Maybe that way I'll learn how she spawned him, and what happened with that vicious little twit" who had an effect on all of us, all the way through Trump.

Following on the heels of the Roy Cohn opus was a biopic, **Stalin.** *While that may sound indeed like an off-puttingly dry PBS documentary, HBO was continuing to take history, blend it with inspired casting (in this case, Robert Duvall), pay top writers for scripts, and present the results to its subscribers as great entertainment, which it often was.*

MICHAEL FUCHS:

I figured if we keep getting on the front page of newspapers, television people would have trouble ignoring us. When we screened *Stalin,* it was the seventy-fifth anniversary of the Russian Revolution, and we were on the front page of the *Herald Tribune.* It said, "There's nothing going on in Red Square today except an American television company having a screening of *Stalin* in the Moscow state theatre."

I slept in Stalin's dacha; Bob Duvall slept in his bed. I said, "You are fucking crazy." I have bad enough dreams without sleeping in Stalin's bed. Duvall gave an unbelievable performance. He went over there and inhaled Stalin and played him like the gangster he was. The Russians were amazed.

ILENE KAHN POWER:

Michael loved doing despots. It was 1991 when we were shooting, and the Soviet Union was under a great upheaval. Banks were failing and we couldn't transfer money. Time Warner was very nervous, so two other producers and I had to carry cash on our body into the country several times. Then when the coup happened, we were thrown out of the country. Two weeks later we got back in when Yeltsin came on board. It was a crazy time, but it allowed us to be able to shoot deep inside the Kremlin. We shot in Lenin's office. We had unfettered access to the Kremlin through Mikhalkov. It was historic at that time. *Stalin* was the first movie for HBO that won the Emmy in 1993.

MICHAEL FUCHS:

Even though Harvey Weinstein takes all the credit, HBO had a lot to do with the growth of independent movies. We would put up money for pay-TV rights and video, then they would go do foreign, so you didn't have to get killed by the studios. The studios hated this.

In the wake of these dramatic spectacles came two films in 1993 that proffered a lighter touch, despite admittedly heavy subjects. Each was written by a master who was not your typical TV writer. **Barbarians at the Gate,** *written by Larry Gelbart after Fuchs gave Cooper permission to pay Gelbart a million dollars for a screenplay based on the Bryan Burrough book of the same name.* **Barbarians** *was a lively foray into the real story behind the buyout of tobacco giant RJR Nabisco, with a distinguished cast that included James Garner, Jonathan Pryce, Peter Riegert, and Joanna Cassidy. The film depicts corporate takeover as a contact sport and paints a humorous yet candid portrait of capitalist games-manship.* **Barbarians** *won the Golden Globe for Best Made-for-TV Movie, with Garner also winning for his portrayal of RJR Nabisco president F. Ross Johnson.*

BOB COOPER:

If someone said to me, "You're going to make a comedy that's a true story about a leverage management buyout, and people are going to watch it," I would say that makes no sense. It was set up as a feature at Columbia, and I called Frank Price, who was running it, and talked with Ray Stark as well. I told them, "We'll do it; we'll make it an event; and we'll spend a lot of money." We broke a lot of rules and spent an unheard-of amount of money, including what we paid Larry Gelbart.

Another 1993 film, **The Positively True Adventures of the Alleged Texas Cheerleader-Murdering Mom***, was written by Jane Anderson, and starred Holly Hunter and Beau Bridges in another dark comedy based on a true story. Wanda Holloway, the mother of a cheerleader, vows to get her daughter on her school's cheerleading squad by any means necessary, including hiring an assassin to take out rival cheerleader Amber Heath and her mother. The movie captures the battles over media rights to the story, at one point going meta with a scene showing Holloway, played by Hunter, watching the real Hunter exit a car as she arrives on the set of the upcoming HBO special about the incident.*

JANE ANDERSON, Writer and Executive Producer:
When I first spoke with HBO, I said, "All I know is that this crazy woman in Texas wanted to kill another woman over junior high school cheerleading."

They wanted to do a serious examination of the cheerleading world, and I said, "This has to be ironic." I went on a research trip to Channelview, Texas, with Jim Manos, a wild, great guy who produced it. I figured out that it wasn't about the media exploiting these people, it was a story about these people exploiting the media in order to turn this absurd thing into something that would make them stars. Bob Cooper supported the concept, I wrote the script, and then we got Michael Ritchie on board, who was one of the most wonderful directors of ironic material. He had done *Smile*, and *The Candidate*, and he upped the game of turning it into a stylistically interesting piece.

HBO was nervous. Nothing like this had ever been seen before. They made us focus-group it. We didn't know how the focus audience would react. It wasn't a great reaction, but Bob Cooper still decided to support us and support the piece.

I do believe that's really what convinced Bob Cooper and people running HBO that this is where they should start heading now, and what would distinguish them from the networks who were still doing very straight-ahead material.

And the Band Played On*, an HBO docudrama, was based on the investigative book of the same name by Randy Shilts, the* **San Francisco Chronicle** *journalist who had been both adored and vilified by members of the gay community for his investigative reporting that had played a role in shutting down San Francisco's gay bathhouses. The movie documents the discovery of the AIDS epidemic, including ego* *issues and sundry conflicts that had distracted politicians and the scientific community from curbing the rapid spread of the disease. When the movie premiered in 1993, cases of both HIV and AIDS were skyrocketing and deaths hit all-time highs in 1994 and 1995.*

HBO Pictures executive Bob Cooper worked alongside producer Aaron Spelling and hired Roger Spottiswoode to direct, while Arnold Schulman wrote the teleplay. Matthew Modine starred as epidemiologist Dr. Don Francis, who by 1981 had started to notice an increase in the deaths of gay men in urban areas. The movie's antagonist is Alan Alda as Dr. Robert Gallo—a biomedical researcher who cuts off Francis's funding when he finds out that he shared sensitive information with two French scientists at the Pasteur Institute. Lily Tomlin played a San Francisco public health official, and Richard Gere a choreographer who learns he has AIDS.

Despite mixed reviews, **And the Band Played On** *arguably shifted HBO Films' image as it dared to tackle the most tragic and pressing issue of its time. Randy Shilts died a year later in 1994 at age forty-two from complications due to AIDS.*

BOB COOPER:

And the Band Played On was so difficult to put together. There were so many people telling us why it wouldn't work but it became an opportunity to get some big actor names at a time when they did not want to work at HBO. We had Richard Gere, we had Phil Collins.

BILL COUTURIÉ:

I lived in the Castro, walked my dog in the park where Randy Shilts walked his dog. Randy was beautiful, a sweet, sweet guy. I loved him, and he knew I worked for HBO. One day, he comes along all excited and said, "HBO bought my book, they're going to do it!" And he was so stoked. And I said, "That's terrific."

BOB COOPER:

It became very high profile quickly. Then we were attacked. The first attack was the gay community. Some were saying, "If you make it, what you're saying is gay people caused AIDS," because Patient Zero was an Air Canada pilot. I was stunned. They were angry and it would be hurtful if we made it that way. Then some in the scientific community threatened action against us for how they had heard we were portraying some of those people.

We were fighting all factions. It wasn't an easy process. I remember thinking, "I'm in a political campaign to get somebody elected." Yet every time I told Michael about the problem, he was excited.

BILL COUTURIÉ:

A major part of the book was someone called Patient Zero, a flight attendant who got AIDS and went around the world spreading AIDS. And he was a bad guy, but it turned out that there wasn't really a Patient Zero. That story line had been discredited. Randy said, "You've got to tell them to drop Patient Zero. It's not true. It was a mistake. I'm going to do a new version of the book where I drop that out."

BOB COOPER:

We hired Roger Spottiswoode to direct, and I don't think he liked me. It was a tough relationship. Then in post, he showed us the movie and we argued quite a bit about how to complete it.

I finally said, "Roger, we need to make a change. I've got to take a shot with this in a certain direction." And as I remember, he didn't want to do it. And I said, "Well, we're just going to do it." And then he wrote a letter—or letters—to the editor, I think of the *LA Times* and the *New York Times*, about what a bad executive I was.

BILL COUTURIÉ:

Spottiswoode went off and made the movie. When HBO saw it, it was about Patient Zero. And I saw Randy one day and he said, "Oh my God, we just screened the film. And it's horrible because it's all about Patient Zero—I'm going to get killed." He was terrified that his legacy would have been this story about Patient Zero. He was crying. He said, "I didn't know, is there any way you can talk to HBO, Bill, and try to change their minds?" I have a direct line to Michael. So I called Michael and I said, "Hey, you know Randy's crying. This was not the deal. This is fucked up. You shouldn't do this, Michael." And Michael said, "Okay, you fix it."

BOB COOPER:

Michael Fuchs called me and said, "The blood is already on the floor. Do your job." Then he hung up, called me back, and said, "I smelled a little fear when we just spoke. I don't want to hear that again. I want you to know, so long as I am CEO of HBO, you will never be fired."

BILL COUTURIÉ:

Coming in and taking over somebody's movie is not fun. I didn't want to do it, but on the other hand, I loved Randy and he was dying. So my priority was Randy, not Roger. And very much against the will of the people who were doing the movie, I came in, completely recut the movie, and indicated that we needed new scenes to make it work once you'd lost the main story line. All I can say is that, for reasons that are totally understandable, the producers and the director were not kind to me.

Roger said, "You'll never work in this town again," all that stuff. And then it won a bunch of Emmys.

BOB COOPER:

It won Best Picture. The experience of making it was brutal from beginning to end. But again, Michael always protected me. He was so amazing. People thought I was so tough; I wasn't really tough. I had the backing of our chairman and CEO.

Another docudrama, HBO's **Citizen X***, was based on the 1993 nonfiction book* **The Killer Department** *about the hunt for a serial killer in the Soviet Union, with Donald Sutherland winning both an Emmy and a Golden Globe for Best Supporting Actor.*

BOB COOPER:

I had this executive, Laurette Hayden, who kept talking about this serial killer. I said to her, "That sounds like a network movie," but she never let go and wore me down. I finally said, "Okay, I don't see it, but put together a list of writers we want to work with, and if you can get one of these writers, I'll be glad to hear their approach." On the list was a name, Chris Gerolmo. He wrote a script and it was amazing. It was always Laurette, not me.

I was a buyer, but that taught me a lesson, as a seller: sometimes if you go to the top, you don't do as well as if you go to the middle. In other words, if the producer had gone right to me, I never would have done it. But they went to Laurette, and since I valued her opinion, that's how it happened. It won Best Picture that year.

Tuskegee Airmen*, based on a true story about Black pilots who pushed back against racism and became one of the best US fighter groups in World War II, starred Laurence Fishburne, Cuba Gooding Jr., and John Lithgow. An emotional experience for any audience, the film brought much-needed attention to the unit. It won a Peabody and three Emmys.*

BOB COOPER:

I was fascinated with the story. It was the only time I ever got a letter from Ted Turner, who thought it was amazing.

On December 22, 1992, HBO decided to highlight the influence of its no-longer-adolescent network with a twentieth anniversary celebratory special that would air on no less than CBS, a rival broadcast network.

HBO marketed the special with the tagline, "Most people give china on their 20th anniversary, we're giving Crystal." Hosted by Billy Crystal and Robin Williams, and featuring the gamut of HBO stars from Bette Midler, Whoopi Goldberg, and Garry Shandling to George Foreman and Mel Gibson, the special covered HBO's entire history, with clips from the full HBO catalog and new performances from the channel's most beloved stars. Billy Crystal and Robin Williams even performed an ad-libbed song to piano accompaniment, though CBS censors cut most of Robin's performance out of their special; viewers got to see the far more ribald version of the evening when HBO ran the uncensored special a month later.

PHIL SAVENICK:

Michael Fuchs pitched CBS and said if we can deliver Robin Williams, Billy Crystal, Bette Midler, and George Carlin, will you put us on the network? And even though it was promoting a different network, they said okay. That we got on CBS was enormous.

The HBO twentieth-anniversary show was actually two shows. One was an hour long and ran on CBS; the other, an hour and a half, ran on HBO. Obviously the one on CBS couldn't have any dirty words in it.

Robin was having a bad day when we were supposed to do the opening for CBS. He didn't want to come out of his dressing room. He had agreed to do it for Fuchs, but nothing Robin was going to do that day was gonna be clean. He was cursing every ten seconds, even when they were doing this hilarious song they were making up about HBO, cable, and freedom. Billy, consummate professional, was trying to make sure we got something usable. We wound up shooting for forty-five minutes and got two minutes that was okay for CBS.

Bill Maher began his stand-up comedy career in clubs, leading to spots with David Letterman and Johnny Carson, as well as numerous acting gigs—among them, a leading role in the long-forgotten Geena Davis vehicle **Sara**.

Then, in 1993, Maher became host of HBO's **Politically Incorrect**, which it produced for Comedy Central. The show would eventually shift (in a toned-down version) to ABC in early 1997. The show aimed to mimic the witty badinage of a star-studded cocktail party, with folks from all walks of celebrity, culture, and politics who would (usually) disagree with each other on the issues of the day. Maher urged his guests to hash out their differences, waiting until he found an opening to be caustic, controver-

sial, urbane, or just damn funny. (As with its other programming, HBO insisted the language on **Politically Incorrect** *be "adult" to differentiate it from milder stuff on commercial broadcast networks.)*

BILL MAHER, Host:

When I started *Politically Incorrect*, the media said, "Oh, you can't do that. The audience will never accept a host of a talk show giving controversial opinions. You have to go by the Johnny Carson, David Letterman, Jay Leno playbook, which is, you play it down the middle or else you'll lose half the crowd." I said, "Let's see." The audience always got what was going on. The media didn't. They were the dummies who were always confused by this and many of them still are.

NINA ROSENSTEIN, Executive:

Bill, Nancy Geller, and I were in the taxi on our way to pitch Comedy Central and he said, "Fuck, I forgot my notebook." It contained all the clippings of issues he wanted to talk about and had been gathering for years. But once we got there, we just started talking about what was in the news that day. He said, "This is what the show is."

NANCY GELLER:

I said to Bill, "Let's take my office furniture and put it in the HBO Sports studios on Twenty-third Street, and we'll put four chairs around my coffee table. That'll be the set, we'll shoot a show and let's see how it comes out."

After we sent it to Michael, he said, "I can't believe you think that this is a good show." I said, "I really do." He started laughing, then said, "So do fucking I." But then I asked for ninety episodes, and he got serious. "You better fucking know what you're doing."

After the first season, we became more topical and that drove the growth of *Politically Incorrect*. It made noise. We made a lot of noise. We started by thinking we would have a Republican, a Democrat, somebody who's interesting to talk to, and a comedian so that we could keep this show funny, then realized the best way to make the show work was to have somebody who did not agree with Bill.

BILL MAHER:

Anything serious lends itself to humor, believe me. Humor is what indicates to the audience that this is absurd.

The problem we had with the humor at the beginning was that some people had trouble grasping the concept of a hybrid of anything. Is it folk, or is it rock? Is he funny or is he a serious commentator?

On August 21, 1994, HBO aired what would become, at that time, its highest-rated musical program ever. Barbra: The Concert was culled from Streisand's 1993–94 tour, her first full concert series since 1966, and attracted more than eleven million viewers on its first showing alone. During the thirty minutes preceding the concert, HBO displayed an on-screen countdown and aired documentary footage and key interviews from the Streisand world.

The original deal was a handshake between manager Marty Erlichman and Fuchs, who wanted it for an April 1994 release, right when Streisand had just started her tour. But Streisand voted no, so HBO stood by until the end of the tour. Erlichman's agreement stipulated that if for some reason HBO was not happy with the show, the network still had to ante up the money. Not surprisingly, however, HBO was thrilled with the show, which reigned for many years as the highest-grossing concert for a single artist.

BARBRA STREISAND:

Marty made sure I had complete creative control. That was what was most important to me. I never knew specifics of deals going back to when I was nineteen or twenty. I didn't care about the money. All I wanted was control over my work, especially records. "Nobody's going to tell me what to sing. I have to pick my own material." I had to try out the concert on New Year's Eve of 1993 because I didn't know if I could take the fear I experienced. It's no fun to sing when you feel your heart racing and your voice shaking. I had such stage fright after I had forgotten some of the words at a concert in Central Park in front of 150,000 people.

MARTY ERLICHMAN, Manager:

HBO's deals normally called for them to have many repeats of a special, I believe as many as nine, but for this deal, I told them they were only going to get one play. That's because we had an overall deal with CBS, and we were still with Columbia Records. So I told Michael, "I don't mind having you debut, and it's going to be a big one, but you can only show it once." Michael said, "Okay." He just wanted to be the first kid on the block.

There was another part of this deal. If Barbra changed her mind about showing this concert on TV, the deal was off. At the time we made the deal, we couldn't tell them when the tour would start, and we also told HBO they couldn't put the show on until the tour was over. And then I had a big problem: CBS was really pissed off. I told them, "HBO is paying a lot of money, and it's only going to be one show. HBO doesn't have the viewership you have. What are you worried about?" There was a lot of yelling back and forth, but they finally agreed.

Michael was only one of a few people in the world who I was able to shake hands with, and that was the deal, which was a good thing since things got scary. That show didn't air until August, a good six months after she did the concert, and Michael said he was having problems with his own network over the delay because of the amount of money we had gotten in the deal. I said, "Michael, what's the difference? You are still going to be first. Between your PR department and ours, the world will know whenever it is."

BARBRA STREISAND:

When I was editing at Complete Post, I would sometimes sleep over there in a chair. Dwight Hemion and Gary Smith were there during the day, but I stayed on and Bruce Motyer would wake me up during the night to show me edits. I was there for weeks because I wanted the show to be as good as it could possibly be. On the very last night before we had to hand it over to HBO, we worked all night. As far as releasing the show to HBO, I believe we gave it to them an hour before airtime. And I was told HBO was thrilled with the show and it became their highest-rated special at that point and won five Emmys and the Peabody Award.

Iconic singer Whitney Houston paid a visit to South Africa in November 1994 for a three-day concert tour with stops in Durban, Johannesburg, and Cape Town. The tour was held to benefit a series of charity organizations for kids in the country, as well as a trust fund established for Nelson Mandela, who had been released from prison four years before. During the trip, Houston also visited Mandela in Pretoria, the capital. The Johannesburg concert, held on November 12, appeared on HBO.

NANCY GELLER:

In 1994 I was given the job to program late night, comedy, and music events at HBO, which included the late-night series *The Chris Rock Show* and *Politically Incorrect with Bill Maher*. Around 1995, HBO Downtown closed and I continued at HBO, as vice president, with Ali G, *Real Time*, Ruby Wax, and endless comedy specials. *Def Jam*, Comic Relief, George Carlin, Chris Rock, Jerry Seinfeld, Robin Williams, etc. The Rolling Stones, Bruce Springsteen, Justin Timberlake, Britney Spears, Madonna, Gaga, Whitney Houston, Marc Anthony, Cher, Bette Midler, etc.

Whitney in South Africa was one of the craziest experiences I've ever had. Michael, Richard Plepler, and others flew twenty hours over to South Africa because they thought we were going to get a sit-down with Mandela, but I never thought that would happen. It was very tricky to shoot in South Africa. We had a ton of security.

Almost all of the crew was armed, and for good reason. During the tour, members of Whitney's entourage had their luggage slashed and rummaged through. The security team was kept busy by people climbing the fence into Whitney's compound. A couple of Whitney's crew got mugged in the mall adjacent to the hotel. At night the HBO crew would sit on their balcony at the hotel and hear gunfire in the streets. But the biggest issue was the violence taking place in the crowd during the concert. At least two people were victims of knife attacks, and the wounded were passed through the crowd and dumped into the pit in front of the stage.

MICHAEL FUCHS:

At that time, Whitney was like the Black Streisand. She had just done *The Bodyguard*. I went to South Africa for the concert. She had the worst fucking people around her. Hotel people know everything, and one of the people there came up to me and said, "She can't fall asleep at night, so she's taking downers, then she can't wake up, and she's taking uppers." I knew this is how it all starts.

The concert was technically live, but there was a satellite delay because of the distance. At some point, Whitney starts saying all these things about Winnie Mandela being the queen, and this is after her divorce from Mandela. Then the crowd started booing. Whitney didn't know what the hell she was saying. I was in a suite, grabbed a phone, and got Bridget Potter on the phone in the truck. I said, "Get that damn Winnie piece out," not knowing how much time we had. She began to stutter a little and mention we were technically live. I said, "I don't give a shit. Get it the fuck out." I rarely spoke like that to HBOers, but I couldn't believe what a political briar's patch Whitney had wandered into.

In October 1993 HBO launched HBO en Español, a Spanish-language version of the channel, aimed squarely at the then twenty-five million Hispanics living in the United States. HBO en Español replaced Selecciones, which since January 1989 had offered a few dubbed shows via a separate audio feed and a hardly-user-friendly decoder box. HBO en Español was a different animal altogether: it would triple the number of HBO titles dubbed into Spanish, despite no original Spanish-language programming.

MICHAEL FUCHS:

One night I wake up, it's like four o'clock in the morning. I would do this all the time. I turned on HBO just to make sure it was on. It's in Spanish. I knew we had Spanish versions; I'm thinking maybe they slipped the wrong copy in. The head of the studio was this guy Dom Serio. It takes me an hour and a half to find him. He's in the Hamptons on a vacation. I say, "Dom, I think that we have a Spanish version on." So he says, "Michael, pick up your remote. You see that little button that says SAP? Push it." It went to English. I said, "Never mind."

CURT VIEBRANZ:

We were late to the party in trying to extend the HBO brand outside the US. Canal+ and BSkyB already had an unassailable position in Western Europe and Murdoch's Star TV was also a formidable competitor in Asia. Internally, our negotiations with Warner Bros. to acquire film programming were as fractious and drawn out as with any of the studios and Jerry was cool with that. At least, he never saw fit to intervene. As a result, we conquered the only virgin territory of scale, Latin America, and built a large and very profitable business there.

NELY GALAN, Executive:

I represent one part of HBO that most people won't talk about because I wasn't an employee of HBO and I wasn't initially there to produce programming per se. HBO was what we would consider a tech incubator today. So they were interested in incubating people who had cool ideas, even if those ideas weren't really completely in their wheelhouse.

One day they called me and they go, "We've got this kid, Luis Miguel, who's a rock star from Mexico. The record company wants us to do something with him. We don't know who the hell he is, and we don't know what to do." And I go, "Are you kidding me? He's like the hottest thing in the Latino market." And they're like, "Can you come here and interview him?"

I did all these crazy things and honestly, I was super, super, super happy because I felt loved. I felt like people got me and I felt like I was growing and just trying different things. I think what happened next says a lot—Michael Fuchs started telling other people, "Oh my God, this girl Nely, she got us up and running in Latin America in three months."

CURT VIEBRANZ:

In the mid-1990s, I'll say 1994, HBO had three branded HBO television assets. One was Eastern Europe where we had gone into Hungary and the Czech Republic, and during my time running International we also launched in both Poland and Romania. Then we had Asia and the Latin American business. The Asian business was effectively operated out of Singapore with our partners Sony, Universal, and Paramount.

And like everybody in the free world, were trying to figure out how to crack the Chinese market. Piracy issues were a stumbling block. We were only really going into hotels because that's the only way we could ensure that we weren't going to get screwed. We started talking to China's Central TV, but we could never get a deal done that satisfied us.

Over time that business really started to grow, and it became a business north of a billion dollars.

MICHAEL FUCHS:

We were destined to go international. Our Ku satellite went to Europe and maybe that was a real opportunity to enter Western Europe, but we didn't. We did do a little in Eastern Europe, but I felt the competition over there was too rich for us. Maybe Time Warner and Warner Bros. should have joined in. It turned into a damn good business.

I wanted to move people around, like the magazine group. Lots of HBO people had been on the same jobs for years. I went to Caracas for HBO Ole and Singapore for HBO Asia. Ole moved to Miami, as Caracas was getting a little wild. Curt had quite a few jobs at Time Warner and HBO. He got involved with HBO later in its life. Nely Galan and her Hispanic squad convinced me to do Ole.

CURT VIEBRANZ:

If you look at the cash flows from HBO from dividends and add in the $120 million a year paid to Warner Bros. in licensing fees, HBO Latin America was arguably one of the most successful investments Time Warner ever made.

While HBO began to compete in earnest for oversees viewers, they also began to see increased competition in live sports across the board, and not just with boxing. ABC and Showtime tested out pay-per-view for college football in 1992, and a year later Fox reached a deal with the NFL to air football games for the first time, taking over the CBS package. But in 1994, HBO was able to secure a big win by beating out Fox to hold on to another important sport for the company: tennis. NBC and HBO signed to renew Wimbledon coverage for five more years. Although the ratings were not stellar—making the renewal of questionable value—Michael Fuchs did love going to London and sitting courtside.

SETH ABRAHAM:

NBC did the weekends and HBO did the weekdays. It was the deal from 1995 to 2000 and they left $55 million on the table with Rupert and Fox to stay loyal with HBO and NBC. I couldn't believe it.

CRIS COLLINSWORTH, Sportscaster:

I was cut by the Bengals and was in law school when I got a call from Ross Greenburg and Rick Bernstein asking, "Would you like a job doing features on *Inside the NFL*? We can pay you fifty grand?" I immediately said, "The answer's yes. Now tell me, what's a feature?"

I did features for a year then I was on the set with Nick Buoniconti and Len Berman the second year. By then I had enough experience doing features that they asked me to do some for Wimbledon. That was an interesting learn-as-you-go experience.

It had rained for a week straight, and we ran out of stories to do. So Ross says, "Go out and do a story about the rain." So I did a story where the joke at the end was, I was on a hill in the mud wearing a coat and tie, and I literally slid 150 yards down to the bottom of this hill. We thought it was hilarious, but Ross was so mad. Years later, I was walking through the Dallas airport and I hear, "Cris, Cris is that you?" It was Billy Packer. He goes, "I know you're running to catch your flight, but I got to tell you, my family, we're all tennis nuts. We play all the time when we get together every year for the holidays. We have one holiday tradition—we pull out the tape of you doing the mud slide at Wimbledon." I said, "I almost got fired for doing that."

Inside the NFL *began in 1977 and throughout the next thirty-one years would become the mainstay of HBO Sports. Boxers came and went. Wimbledon and other specials came and went. But* **INFL** *was always on that HBO schedule from September through the Super Bowl. Len Dawson and Nick Buoniconti were the rocks of the series, and when Cris Collinsworth joined them as a host in 1990, the show took off to an even greater level.*

In 1994, the show evolved once again when Jimmy Johnson joined the show. He had just left the Dallas Cowboys after winning his second Super Bowl. He was such an outgoing, positive guy that he blended in while at the same time giving the show even more immediacy and legitimacy.

DAVE HARMON:

Ross Greenburg booked my father for several gigs producing features on *Inside the NFL* when I was in college. I got to go on those shoots and learned so much. Lo and behold, a few years later I wound up working on the same series, and in 1991 when Ross called me into his office and told me I was going to be the next producer of *Inside the NFL*, that was an amazing full circle for my father and me. Later when *INFL* won its first Emmy for best studio show, I gave my trophy to my father, which was very emotional for both of us. He still proudly displays it in his living room.

In 1994, Ross Greenburg wrote a memo to Michael Fuchs.

> *"HBO Sports would like to present a quarterly, one-hour magazine show which will be investigative and formative on the issues and personalities of the world of sports. We would gather reporters and writers from the sports community with very high credibility and recognition to bring a standard of excellence to every broadcast. Only HBO can produce provocative and controversial stories on the world of sports. Because we have few associations with the rightsholders, we have the opportunity to tell these stories without fear of reprisal (i.e., late-night telephone calls to Fuchs and Abraham).*
>
> *The show would be defined with a hard edge, real point of view, including an opinionated host with stories you can't / wouldn't see elsewhere."*

On the same day that the 1994–95 baseball strike ended, **Real Sports with Bryant Gumbel** *premiered. The original choice for host, Bob Costas, was not available. Jim Lampley had been promised the show, but it went to Gumbel instead.*

In 1981, when Tom Brokaw was planning to leave **TODAY**, *Gumbel wasn't even a candidate for the job because he was considered a sports correspondent, not a news anchor. But in August of that same year, Gumbel hopped in as a last-minute substitute for Jane Pauley on* **TODAY** *and performed so well that he put himself in the running for Brokaw's spot.*

At first, Chris Wallace, Jane Pauley, and Gumbel were all chosen to replace Brokaw in a strange three-way co-host situation that inevitably failed, leaving Gumbel as the principal anchor of **TODAY** *by the end of September 1982.*

ROSS GREENBURG:

When I created *Real Sports*, it was supposed to be *Real Sports with Bob Costas.*

Not many people know that. Bryant may not even know it, but I guess he'll know it now. Dick Ebersol at NBC was not ready to allow Bob to do things on other networks. He was their signature host.

BOB COSTAS, Sportscaster:

Dick [Ebersol] said no for reasons I did not dispute then, and do not dispute to this day. In the early nineties, my responsibilities at NBC were the Olympics, the NBA on NBC, I was still part of football coverage, and we were about to reacquire a piece of baseball.

Dick said, "We can't have you do that. You're commuting back and forth from St. Louis; we want to make sure we have your full attention; and we want to make sure the public perception is that you're an NBC Sports guy." He was right to think like that. It was more than fair.

Real Sports is the gold standard of sports journalism, the *60 Minutes* of sports or the closest thing to it. Had I been the host of *Real Sports*, it would have been excellent in its own way, but Bryant has been a superb host of that show.

MICHAEL FUCHS:

I named it *Real Sports* because we had been successful with *Real Sex*, which I had also named. And I said, "Listen folks, we don't have a baseball deal, we don't have a football deal, we don't have a basketball deal; if you're not going to be muckrakers, I don't want the show. That is the purpose of the show."

As the final decade of the twentieth century approached, documentary filmmakers again began rethinking the ways in which they captured life on film. Michael Moore experimented with putting himself on camera in **Roger and Me** *(1989), which follows Moore's journey to speak with General Motors chairman Roger B. Smith after the car manufacturer shuttered a Michigan factory that cost thirty-five thousand people their jobs. Meanwhile, in 1988's* **The Thin Blue Line,** *the story of a roadside murder and the subsequent trial, director Errol Morris brought dramatic reenactments into vogue when he re-created scenes from the killing of police officer Robert Wood. That film also helped overturn the conviction of the man once said to be Wood's murderer, Randall Dale Adams, and accelerated the rise of true crime as a subgenre within documentary film.*

Television networks were also active in the documentary space during this time. In 1990, ABC premiered **Peter Jennings Reporting,** *an investigative documentary series hosted by Jennings, then also the anchor of ABC's evening newscast,* **World News Tonight.** *Across the "Big Three" landscape, NBC capitalized on the newfound popularity of true crime storytelling when it introduced* **Dateline NBC** *in 1992, offering a blend of legal and newsmagazine stories.*

KARY ANTHOLIS, Executive:

I had worked on a documentary about the making of *Apocalypse Now* called *Hearts of Darkness*, helping to monetize it, and then got to meet Sheila in a series of pitch meetings. I started working for her in August of 1992, and because I had come from the business side, I had to educate myself about documentary filmmaking because I hadn't gone to film school, I hadn't studied documentaries, so I just gave myself a crash course in the great verité filmmakers and watched as much as I could of what Sheila had been doing before I arrived at HBO.

The first thing I worked on, *Educating Peter*, about the inclusion of a boy with Down syndrome in a third-grade public school class, won an Oscar and it was mind-blowing to me that I could be working with such quality material. I came to understand that being an executive at HBO gives you the opportunity to have a healthy family life, to not have to be on distant locations all the time, and all you have to do in return is check your ego at the door and be there to serve the vision of the artists who have been hired.

"Between eleven p.m. and six a.m., the people who take taxicabs are very interesting people," Sheila Nevins once said. She had been handed a tape that was made by two brothers who'd been recording conversations in New York cabs during the day. Originally the idea was to create a daytime show, but Nevins understood that the city after dark was very different from the city in daylight. Brothers Harry and Joe Gantz were therefore sent out after sunset to create what would become **Taxicab Confessions.**

The brothers' process was to interview prospective cabdrivers, install secret cameras in their cars, and, for six nights a week over six straight weeks, follow the taxi in another vehicle, remotely leading the drivers' questioning. The Gantzes reckoned that for each episode they followed six hundred rides, of which maybe twenty-five were usable—and even then, only two-thirds of the riders were willing to sign the necessary releases.

The series began in January 1995, initially in New York City—until Rudy Giuliani's new taxi commissioner vetoed it, that is. Then it moved to Las Vegas, where it would stay for the rest of its cheeky existence. **Taxicab Confessions** *ran for more than a decade, ending in 2006 after eleven talkative seasons. The passengers' various nocturnal emissions ranged from poignant tales of loss and longing to ribald stories of semi-salacious sex; there were even scenes of actual fornication in the backs of cabs.*

HARRY GANTZ, Producer:

The only eye contact from the driver was through the rearview mirror, which presented a pseudo confessional. It was amazing what people wanted to talk about. We took that pilot with Warner Television to several networks, and then finally to HBO. Sheila liked it, funded the first special, which turned into the series.

When we started shooting, we found that people were much more willing to talk at night. People who were willing to open up almost felt a biological need to tell their story to a kind stranger. People who had lived such controlled lives where they couldn't be themselves at work could say what they really thought.

We rigged the cab with six cameras and several microphones. We would follow the cab in a chase vehicle, so we could communicate with the driver through his or her ear, and see everything that went on in the cab. Drivers would pick up passengers and start to talk to them. If they were willing to talk, they tried to get a story before they got to the destination.

At the end of the ride, the driver would let them know that they had been part of this TV series and asked for a release. If that driver was unsuccessful at getting the release, we had a release getter who was in our chase vehicle, who would go to the cab, introduce themselves, and try again to get a release. HBO realized that to get these authentic rides, it took a lot of time and they gave us the money—unusual for that type of documentary series. We would shoot six nights a week to get one show that had eight or nine rides in it.

JULIE ANDERSON:

You should see the first *Taxicab Confessions*. It is amazing. They pick up this guy who was a rescue transit worker, medic of some sort, and he tells this story in the taxi that is mind-blowing. He said a guy had halfway fallen on the subway tracks, and when the train came it sort of twisted his body, and so his torso was still on the platform but his body had been twisted up. He was still alive. If they rescued him, he was going to die. It's the most amazing story.

HARRY GANTZ:

I can remember a woman in her fifties who was talking about her husband and how he hadn't satisfied her emotionally or sexually.

She was having this affair with a guy who she'd known from her youth and it was so satisfying. It wasn't just the sex, it was that he had really cared about her and listened to her as a human being. When she got to the destination, she didn't want to sign the release and when the release getter talked with her, she slapped the release getter in the face. I could understand how she felt. She had shared something very private and didn't want it to be shown.

SHEILA NEVINS:

We never knew what was going to happen. We never knew the ending.

HARRY GANTZ:

If you look at the series, you can see the entire LGBTQ movement evolved over time in our cab. We gave them a voice to talk about their experiences rather than deciding who they were ahead of time and we didn't stereotype them for the entertainment of the audience.

Joe and I won an Emmy for the show, but my greatest accolades came at a sex workers convention in Las Vegas.

There was a group of people who got up and said why they were there and what they wanted from the group. I got up and said, "My name is Harry Gantz. I did *Taxicab Confessions*." All the sex workers stood up and gave me a standing ovation. That told me that I had done justice to their work and stories and in a way that the media hadn't.

When the show first aired, it was a sensation and was parodied by *Saturday Night Live* and *The Simpsons*. *Chris Rock* did an ongoing segment about it. People began to realize that this was a transformative show, because it took the shame out of confessing, of sharing the parts of yourself that you were ashamed about.

Taxicab would have never happened without Sheila, who is a force to be reckoned with, and single-handedly changed the market for the documentaries. I can never say enough about how much we appreciate what she did for the show.

At heart, the singular Sheila Nevins is a cultural anthropologist. Since taking charge of HBO documentaries, she had deemed all human experience worthy of study, from the controversial to the studiously well researched, to late-night adult programming. In 1995, the full range of her concerns was on exhibit at the Creative Arts Awards for the Emmys, held the day before the main Emmy praise party.

At the ceremony, Nevins held credits on half of the six nominees for the Outstanding Informational Special category. Two of these documentary nominees, an incongruous pair, tied and took home the win. The first was for a forty-minute documentary called **One Survivor Remembers**, *a co-production with the United States Holocaust Museum that featured Gerda Weissmann Klein, a Polish woman who in July 1942 watched her parents get arrested by Nazis (both would die) and at age eighteen was* *herself sent to Nazi work camps. Ms. Klein, who later faced a grueling 350-mile march, was one of fewer than 120 survivors of the 1,300 from the march. The movie, made by filmmaker Kary Antholis, won both the Emmy and the following year's Academy Award, and is now preserved in the National Film Registry.*

Nevins's second award was in the same category but for a very different peek into the vagaries of human existence. Yes, **Taxicab Confessions** *won for its very first episode, which featured, among other stories, a young woman extolling the virtues of her various body piercings and a homeless man describing how he ended up on the streets.*

Rounding out the evening, Nevins brought home a third Emmy, from a separate category this time: **Going, Going, Almost Gone! Animals in Danger,** *a children's special made in partnership with the World Wildlife Fund.*

SHEILA NEVINS:

I remember when I lost. It's very hard to remember when you win.

KARY ANTHOLIS:

In 1994 Sheila said to me, "Next year is the fiftieth anniversary of the end of World War II and the liberation of the concentration camps. Keep an eye out for something to do on that subject."

Sheila and I both went on separate trips to the Holocaust Museum in Washington. We saw the testimony film that was the last exhibit at the museum, and both responded to this one interview with a female survivor. Sheila said, "We should do a short film about her as one person speaking for everybody." So we reached out and got in touch with the woman, Gerda Klein, and started interviewing filmmakers.

At that point I decided, Hey, I can do this. I can figure this out. I went to Sheila and I said to her, "What if I directed the film?" She thought about it overnight and said, "I'll let you do it, but you've got to leave the company. You can't be an employee of HBO and still direct the film."

I wanted to make a short film that would qualify for the Oscars, which meant it had to be under forty minutes. I put together a rough cut that was sixty minutes long, and Sheila said, "I hate it." I told her, "I know it's long. I know exactly what to cut. I'm going to bring it in under forty." I came back with a second cut, and this time Sheila said, "It's a fucking masterpiece." That was the nature of my relationship with Sheila in a nutshell: I was either an idiot or a genius.

In 1995 it won an Emmy, and then in April 1996 it won an Oscar. It is one of the greatest accomplishments of my career. That film became part of a curriculum on teaching tolerance that the Southern Poverty Law Center put out. Millions of kids have seen that film. It changed my life in so many ways. Then I spent a year away from HBO realizing that if I could ever go back to HBO, I'd do it in a heartbeat.

JON ALPERT, Documentarian:

When Time and Warner merged, they sent up an executive from Atlanta, who they believed knew how to make films. They didn't dare do this with any of the men, however, but they did send Pat Mitchell to run the documentary unit.

She comes to New York and is ready to secretly establish her reign, when Sheila in effect says, "Don't you dare come in the building. The day that you can make a documentary half as good as my worst documentary, I'll meet with you." Pat Mitchell didn't stay.

As award after award piled up across HBO's departments . . . as **Larry Sanders** *began to grab the attention of Hollywood . . . and as increasingly glamorous names headlined movies and concerts for the network . . . no longer was HBO just the scrappy underdog.*

STEVE SCHEFFER:

Company retreats were part of the Time Inc. and HBO culture. One retreat was in Jamaica. These retreats were basically great bonding events that everyone looked forward to. One executive quoted Michael as saying, "I don't expect you folks to be the best of friends outside, but when we're together, we're all on the same page for HBO."

MICHAEL FUCHS:

We had one big meeting a year where programmers, sales, and marketing mixed. Jim Carville spoke once, and Pat Riley, who I was friendly with, gave a great motivational speech.

We had a tremendous Super Bowl trip every year to entertain the affiliates. We brought along entertainment and some programming people. I always made a speech, which was usually funny, and I wore a white suit, which everyone said should go into the cable hall of fame. After that, I always wore white suits to big cable events. I must have looked like the poor man's Tom Wolfe. We ended up in Hawaii a lot; we did the Senior Skins game. Our people would play golf with Palmer and Player and Nicklaus in between the tournament. Steve Scheffer was once paired with Nicklaus, so

I asked, "Steve, how did it go?" He said, "Nicklaus didn't play that well, but I played great."

STEVE SCHEFFER:

After leaving HBO, there were frequent reunions which I thought spoke to the culture and camaraderie of working at HBO.

MICHAEL FUCHS:

I always said to people, "Listen, if you do well, you're going to live well here. You're going to make money. The rising tide raises all boats."

In 1993, HBO extended employee benefits to same-sex partners a full twenty-two years before same-sex marriage became the law of the land. Employees were required merely to write a letter to the company asserting that they lived together and shared an economic partnership (proof of joint bank accounts, wills, or two names on a lease) to qualify. The company reckoned that as few as ten employees out of sixteen hundred would opt for the benefit but garnered all the goodwill of being so far ahead of their time.

Yet not all was peace and love at the newly formed Time Warner.

JEFF BEWKES:

The merger gave us an anchor studio for HBO's movie lineup, which gave us leverage in negotiating deals with the other majors. Having Warners' powerful film slate on HBO, we could say to Columbia and Fox and Universal, "Look, we don't need all of you, we have the biggest pay-TV business, and when you sign a five-year deal with us you can count on us being able to pay the bill, so don't delay or you'll be left out and have to make a deal with Showtime. Who knows if their money will be good in five years?"

Yet it wasn't as simple as it looked. Being part of the same company, we knew the Warner movies had to be on HBO, so did Bob Daly and Terry Semel, but at what price? Since neither of us could walk away, there wasn't the normal need to compromise for fear of losing the deal on either side, so we never did. We didn't have a deal. Since movies hit the theaters almost a year before coming to HBO, they got first crack at accounting and booked them as though HBO was going to pay 50 percent more than all the other studio deals.

Of course, we never agreed with that, and that created about a $50 million gap in Time Warner's intercompany accounting that got buried up at corporate. Needless to say, this led to ongoing "tension" between us and Warners.

BOB DALY:

Then came a war that lasted for a long time, more than three years, where we would be selling our movies to pay TV, but we couldn't make a deal with Michael Fuchs. He lowballed us. He did not want to make a deal with us.

In those days, certain talent had first-dollar-gross deals, so I took the position that we could not sell to HBO at anything less than what we could get elsewhere, because we always treated our talent as fairly as possible, and Terry and I never wanted to place ourselves or the company in a position where we could get sued. And if that meant they could get a better deal on Universal movies, that wasn't our concern. Michael disagreed and really played hardball. Of course that started a war. I mean, literally a war.

A lot of people in the company wanted the war settled without blood, but that proved difficult. Our meetings normally ended with somebody storming out of the room.

RICHARD PARSONS, Executive, Time Warner:

I came to Time Warner as president in 1995 and had oversight over decisions at HBO, Time Inc. publications, Time Warner Cable, Warner Bros., and Warner Music. My focus was more on the cable company, but obviously I sat with Jerry and looked at all sides of the companies.

I had not run any of those businesses before, and I didn't reflect on why Jerry chose me to be president, but if I did, I would say because I wasn't threatening to him. I was a finance guy, and because I knew the board, and had come off the board, I could smooth relationships with the board for Jerry, and help him where he needed it. So he didn't have to put a bull's-eye on my back.

HBOers, in particular Michael, believed HBO was culturally and financially independent. It wasn't really true because corporate ultimately held the purse strings. In that regard, they were just like any other division. All the divisions were different, particularly culturally.

Part of my job, which was difficult, and never fully resolved, was to manage the relationship Bob and Terry had with Michael. Bob didn't like Michael's lack of collaboration, and Michael thought Bob was arrogant. I remember I said to Michael, "You've got to cooperate and play ball with the rest of the team." Michael's response was, "No," and then he said to me, "You know what your problem is? You don't know what your job is." I said, "I don't? Well, please bring me in on the secret." He said, "I'm what they call talent management, and the best talent management this company has. So your job is to make me feel comfortable and enable me to do my thing." Michael did not lack arrogance, but I liked him. I got a kick out of Michael.

JEFF BEWKES:

A $50 million difference in the intercompany adjustments couldn't go on forever, so with yearly pressure from Jerry and Dick to find a compromise, I set up a lunch at Warners for Michael and me with Bob and Terry to talk about a solution. We got to Bob's private dining room and Bob was there on time (he's always early) but Terry was late. By the time Terry breezed in, Michael was fuming. I don't think we got more than ten minutes in before things went south. Terry was being a bit condescending, and Michael didn't even need a match to blow up. Next thing I know Bob is saying to Michael, "I'd rather be head of Warners than Time Warner, but they have me listed as backup in case Jerry gets hit by a bus"—true by the way—"and if that ever happens the first thing I'm gonna do is fire you!" At which point Michael stormed out.

Even as Michael Fuchs clashed with his counterparts at the Warner Bros. studio, in May 1995 he surprisingly added a new line to his business card: "CEO, Warner Music Group." Having helped shape the HBO world, Fuchs was suddenly tasked with whipping Warner Music into shape.

Fuchs was stepping into the role recently vacated by Bob Morgado, who Jerry Levin had just fired. That didn't mean that Fuchs was leaving his true home at HBO, however. Although Jeff Bewkes took over as CEO of HBO, Fuchs refused to give up his oversight of HBO and retained the chairman title, with Bewkes reporting to him. Fuchs also took HBO's PR chief Richard Plepler over with him to Warner Music.

JERRY LEVIN:

Michael may have seemed like an odd choice, but my feeling was Michael would shake things up. I thought he'd done a good job at HBO. I discounted the abrasive nature of Michael.

I didn't do this to get him out of HBO. Why the fuck would I do that? If that were my intention, I should've been fired the next day. I had enough of a belief in him, unlike most people.

MICHAEL FUCHS:

I left Jerry's office as chairman of HBO and CEO of the Warner Music Group. At the annual meeting, several days later, he announces me only as head of music. On the West Coast they called Jerry Forrest Gump and felt that they really ran the company. These two, Daly and Semel, were so spoiled by Steve Ross that they were impossible for the rest of us to deal with. I heard that they were upset.

JERRY LEVIN:

Bob and Terry called me that very day.

They said, "Are you crazy?" I said, "I'm gonna give this a shot because I believe in him."

BOB DALY:

I am, on one hand, one of the easiest guys to deal with. I'm a very loyal corporate guy. But when somebody screws me, I will not forget it, and it will not turn out well for them. Jerry tells me, "I fired Bob Morgado today and I've decided to put Michael Fuchs in as his replacement." And my first reaction was okay, maybe Michael could do a good job there. I did not react in a negative way until Jerry's next sentence. I said, "Oh, well, okay. So that means Bewkes is taking over at HBO," which I was happy about because I had a good relationship with Jeff. But Jerry said, "Oh no, Bewkes still wants to report to Michael Fuchs."

I said, "You are full of shit." I started screaming at him. "Do you realize how stupid you are? Fuchs is going to have music and HBO? He's going to think he's next in line for your job."

Then I left the room, picked up the phone, and called Jeff Bewkes. I said, "What the hell is wrong with you? You didn't want the top job?" He said, "Bob, are you kidding? They never offered me that job. Jerry and Michael told me I had to continue to report to Michael Fuchs." So Jerry lied to me.

JERRY LEVIN:

People were telling me he wants my job. I said to myself, bring it on.

JEFF BEWKES:

The movie cost dispute wasn't the only reason for the feud between Michael and Bob and Terry. When Jerry made Michael CEO of Warner Music in 1995, he was the only division head who had two divisions because he kept the HBO chairman title. He was close to Laura Landro, who had the media beat at the *Wall Street Journal*, and she wasn't the only one speculating in print that Michael with two divisions was being groomed as Jerry's successor. There was pretty widespread speculation about that, and of course Bob and Terry heard it all.

CHRIS ALBRECHT:

Michael was astute at consolidating power and wanted to be bigger than Bob and Terry, and he wouldn't be bigger than Bob and Terry if he only ran HBO. But he was never going to be more clever than those guys.

BOB DALY:

I'm having lunch one day in Malibu with Barry Diller, David Geffen, Sandy Gallin, and my wife. And one of the things that I don't do, my wife knew this, is I never speak out negatively about anybody, because people repeat what you say. I don't really have that many enemies. I have a few, but not a lot. So at lunch now I'm sitting with Barry Diller, David Geffen, and Sandy Gallin, all of whom are New Yorkers, all of whom talk a lot, and some of whom were friendly with Michael Fuchs. Which I knew. So in the middle of the lunch, something comes up about Michael Fuchs and I take off about what a horrible, terrible, egotistical person he is and how I can't stand him. I get in the car and my wife looks at me and she says, "You never talk like that. What's wrong with you today?" And I just smiled at her and she said, "Oh, you wanted it to get it back to him. Right?" I said, "Yeah, I did." So the next time I go to New York, it was about a week later, Michael Fuchs comes down to my office and says, "I heard you said all of these things about me. Is this true?" I said, "A hundred percent." Then I said, "Michael, you and I are division heads. So we have to go to meetings together. You run music and HBO, Terry and I run Warner Bros." And by the way, Terry wasn't involved in lots of these disputes, it was more me. I said, "Listen, Michael," and this is an exact quote, "if you ever become the head of this company, the first thing you're going to do is fire my ass out of the company. And if I ever become head of this company, a job that I do not want, the first thing I will do is fire your ass out of the company."

And he stormed out of my office. Before he walked out, I said, "Michael, in meetings, we will have to be nice to each other, but I don't like you. And you don't like me. And that's perfectly clear. So let's not think it's going to change."

JERRY LEVIN:

Michael's primary duty was to get something happening in the music company ASAP. Jeff's was to demonstrate that he's not just a financial suit, that he has a personality and temperament that was good for the creative process.

MICHAEL FUCHS:

I never gave any instructions to Jeff when I went to Music. My idea was I was running both. It took me a while after it was over to realize that Jeff had probably spent plenty of time talking to Jerry. He didn't just get anointed, which made me sort of feel funny.

JEFF BEWKES:

Jerry and Michael were at odds over Michael's refusal to sign a contract at Music and give up his HBO role.

MICHAEL FUCHS:

Loyalty to corporations is a nice concept, but not necessarily reciprocal. Levin tried to get rid of anyone who could have succeeded him, which actually was not such a high bar.

CHRIS ALBRECHT:

Michael hadn't left HBO for Music. Keeping HBO and taking Music painted a target on his back. No matter what title anybody had, Michael was the head of HBO programming, he was still the designer of what went on, what didn't go on, and how much money should be invested.

RICHARD PARSONS:

There came a time when Jerry told Michael, "It's awkward to be chairman of two divisions, so I want you to just be at Music, and we are going to make Jeff chairman and CEO of HBO." Michael didn't respond. Then Jerry decided I should speak to Michael and tell him he needed to step down from HBO. I told Michael directly, "You've got to give up HBO and focus on Music." Michael was not happy and basically refused.

JEFF BEWKES:

I had a visit from Dick Parsons, and a TW board member asking, "Isn't it interfering with your role as CEO to have Michael hanging around?" Even Bob Daly came to visit, and said, "You're a good kid, you've got a great future, but your boss is an asshole. And you don't want everybody saying that you're not comfortable as CEO on your own, that you need training wheels with Michael over you. Makes you look weak."

While it was pretty clear they were all encouraging me to ask for independence, I wasn't going to throw Michael under the bus, nor was I going to pretend to Bob or to Dick that I was afraid of the dark. I said, "Look, I'm fine, HBO is fine. I've dealt with everybody: Levin, Biondi, Fuchs, you guys at Warners . . . whatever happens I'm fine."

Jeff Bewkes grew up in an upwardly mobile middle-class family. His father, E. Garrett Bewkes Jr., was a successful businessman and COO of Norton Simon in Darien, Connecticut, who had attended the tony Deerfield Academy in Massachusetts and sent his three boys there. But he didn't find that success until later in Jeff's life. At first, Jeff, the middle child, attended public school. Eventually a scholarship and financial assistance from his grandparents landed him a spot at Deerfield. Bewkes then graduated from Yale in 1974.

JEFF BEWKES:

I got out of college into the big 1973–74 recession which had been triggered by the OPEC oil shock. To say I had mediocre grades would be generous. I wanted to work in TV or movies but had no plan and spent the summer after graduation painting houses on the Vineyard with my hippie friends like it was another college summer.

My dad was pissed at me because I showed no signs of looking for a "winter job." When I graduated, he had told me the stock market crash had wiped us out and "you're on your own now so get a real job that you want to do longer than a summer."

He had rocketed from a mid-level lawyer making $35K to a big-time exec over the last five years. By 1973 he had stock options worth several million so he borrowed money from the banks to exercise them and then he got caught holding the bag when OPEC collapsed the market.

He told me, "Your mother and I are gonna try to work through this. If we stay afloat, we'll pay it off. If we don't, they'll take the house."

I went and got a job at NBC News. They paid me a hundred and fifty bucks a week. I worked from October to April on a Lucy Jarvis documentary about handgun violence. It was a good show, but after it aired I got laid off. I was never sure whether they didn't have funding or whether they'd just seen enough of me.

Things weren't looking good. I had a sublet in the city because I didn't want to live at home, a shitty little studio in Chelsea on Ninth Avenue from a girl who sang in a barbershop quartet and they were going on the road for the winter. So I had the place for two months, slept there alone, and got crab lice for the second time in a year. I'd gone home to get the prescription for Kwell lotion—only thing that works by the way—and I remember my mother coming into my room and seeing the sheets hung up and me covered in the Kwell and she said, "Again?"

That basically said it all. I was like, this is really bad. I'm going downhill fast. I've got to do something. Nobody I knew had a job that year, so I decided maybe grad school. Just what I said I wouldn't do back in college. I took the tests for law school and business school. I can test well so I went to a bunch of high-end law schools to see if I could get in. They basically told me to fuck off because of my shitty grades.

The nadir was my meeting with the dean of NYU Law School, Norman Redlich, who I got to see because he'd been a classmate of my dad's at Yale Law. I went in there and he looked over my transcript and LSAT and said, "Well, you can go to law school but not NYU." "Where do you think I should apply?" I asked.

He paused, then he said, "Binghamton." I wondered whether he was enjoying this a bit too much, but then I thought I deserve it. I did squander a fucking great university education at Yale. So I decided, all right, fuck it, I'll go to business school because they don't care about academics.

I was lucky to get into Stanford Business School, couldn't get in there now. They didn't have classes Wednesdays—you were supposed to do your casework then. So I worked at a winery up in Tiburon Wednesdays and Saturdays to make some money and get some experience. Our winery was taking off, so I took my weekly earnings, three hundred bucks cash under the table, and margined the stock. By year two I was taking my girlfriend to Mexico and San Diego. Things were looking up.

When I got out, I took a job at Citibank. After a year's training they were supposed to move me to Hong Kong, but I didn't want to end up as a banker.

I went to HBO in 1979. They didn't have a business job for me, so I started by selling HBO to motels and hotels across the country. Bottom rung over there, but for me it was like a lightbulb turned on. I didn't really get engaged professionally until I got to HBO.

I loved the mission, TV without advertising. It inspired all of us. There was so much energy and optimism and so little corporate bullshit. A lot of arguing and fighting and joking, it was raucous, but nobody was doing what we were doing, and we weren't selling the audience.

I thought I'd be there for a few years. I didn't know I would stay for decades.

Charles "Chuck" Dolan gave birth to the idea of HBO before financial complications enabled Time Inc. to remove him from the operation. Dolan did more than survive: after securing cable rights to Long Island and elsewhere, he founded Cablevision.

1

2

Possible shape of things to come: HBO's first programming exec Jerry Levin in front of a pair of set-top table boxes in 1975. Levin was instrumental in HBO going to satellite distribution before Ted Turner's Superstation or ESPN.

Sign in blood, then discard. The HBO "Service Guarantee" handed out to new subscribers in cable's Paleozoic age. "No charge for service calls"? No, indeed. HBO didn't *make* service calls; cable operators did.

THE HOME BOX OFFICE GUARANTEE

1. A new selection of **current movies** every month never before shown on television.

2. Each month's feature movies will be scheduled a **number of times** during the month at different viewing hours so that you can enjoy them at your convenience.

3. **Major sports events** will be brought to you **live** from Madison Square Garden and other arenas.

4. A variety of **children's movies and features** will be presented each month.

5. For the duration of your subscription to Home Box Office you will be supplied with a **converter** which provides **remote control channel selection** and **fine tuning.**

6. As a subscriber you will receive a **free** Home Box Office monthly entertainment guide which includes the complete schedule for the month, movie reviews and special features.

7. There will be a a $........ charge for installation of Home Box Office in your home.

8. There will be a monthly service charge of $........ for Home Box Office beginning with this date.

9. There will be no charge for service calls.

10. This service can be disconnected at any time with no obligation.

_____   _____
Date   Home Box Office Representative

3

4

Cutting-edge: HBO's 1973 polka party from Pennsylvania was the network's first live non-sporting event . . . and a rager.

Bette Midler headlined HBO's first significant concert special, ballyhooed in the June '76 program guide. Pop stars and comics found they had a grand new platform—virtually free from censorship and other network interference—once HBO burst on the scene.

From left: Time Inc. execs James R. Shepley, Richard Munro, and Nick Nicholas at an HBO presentation in 1975. HBO would survive innumerable near-death experiences in its early years, with Nicholas saving the network thanks to his shrewd business acumen and strong support from Shepley and Munro.

Early generation HBO executives huddle under the first of many corporate umbrellas. Austin Furst, Jim Heyworth, Jerry Levin, Richard Munro, and Nick Nicholas all played key roles early on, though Levin and Nicholas were rarely in agreement. On anything.

"And on my left—" Nick Nicholas and Michael Fuchs hold forth at a company retreat in the 1980s before their relationship went awry. Executive turmoil—backbiting *and* front stabbing—have been hearty perennials throughout HBO history.

8

9

"Home Box Office Moves into Hollywood," or so announced the headline for a June 1983 HBO cover story in the *New York Times Magazine*. Jerry Levin had a stunning rise through the company—all the way to the top—before leaving in the awful aftermath of the Time Warner AOL merger.

Early in HBO's development, Bridget Potter ran HBO programming under Michael Fuchs and hired Chris Albrecht. Movies, specials, and documentaries were top priorities until the early 1990s.

10

When director Bill Couturié wanted to make a documentary about the famous AIDS quilt, Michael Fuchs expressed misgivings—until he was taken to see the quilt for himself and witnessed one panel paying tribute to a man who shared his name. HBO presented progressive and controversial programming that broadcast networks wouldn't go near.

11

Tanner '88—way, way ahead of its time—was a near-instant media darling. For much of its history, HBO cared more about press reaction and prestigious prizes than Nielsen ratings. From left: writer Garry Trudeau, star Michael Murphy, and Pauline Kael's favorite director, Robert Altman.

12

13

Comic Relief, coming right up—Whoopi Goldberg (second from left) and Robin Williams (second from right) join Capitol Hill biggies to celebrate a forthcoming Comic Relief charity special on HBO, with Billy Crystal, the third big headliner, absent from the photo op. From left, were Sen. Ted Kennedy, Sen. Mark Hatfield, and Rep. Joseph Kennedy II. Over the years, Comic Relief and its all-star shows would raise tens of millions for the homeless and other causes.

G.O.A.T.: Barbra Streisand's *One Voice* was an epochal event concert taped in Streisand's own Malibu backyard with an A-list audience in attendance. HBO aired the blockbuster on September 6, 1986.

14

These are the jokes—or, rather, the jokesters: Robin Williams and Billy Crystal (front row) trade wacky cracks to publicize their forthcoming Comic Relief special, with HBO exec Chris Albrecht presiding.

15

16

Lords of the ring. Boxing legends and longtime rivals Muhammad Ali and Joe Frazier with HBO announcer Barry Tompkins and producer Ross Greenburg. The sport quickly became a vital artery for HBO, and the picture marks one of the last times Ali and Frazier were photographed together in street clothes.

17

HBO Sports honcho Seth Abraham with (from left) Buster Douglas, Don King, and Mike Tyson in Tokyo before the 1990 championship fight. Douglas was a 42-to-1 underdog but knocked Tyson out in the tenth round—scoring one of the greatest upsets in boxing history.

Marta Kauffman and David Crane are best known for creating the NBC comedy smash *Friends*, but HBO saw them first when they created *Dream On*.

18

Top talent from *The Larry Sanders Show* gathers in prayer (presumably). Resoundingly acclaimed, *Sanders* would reign as one of HBO's greatest comedies ever. Star Garry Shandling (center) played the chronically "needy" Sanders, a part that turned out to be a classic piece of typecasting. Second row, from left: Linda Doucett, Janeane Garofalo, and Penny Johnson Jerald. Third row: Jeffrey ("Hey now!") Tambor, Wallace Langham, and Rip Torn.

19

"And over there, a big statue of me"— audacious and rambunctious Michael Fuchs, HBO's George Washington, at a dinner celebrating the ascension of Jeff Bewkes (right) as the company's new CEO. Despite what Fuchs may say now, the two dynamic executives were very close and arguably "completed" each other, shepherding HBO through golden eras of growth.

20

Cursing and violence were two early components of the HBO formula; ditto for sex, with Sheila Nevins and her documentary division leading the way—first with *Eros America*, then *Real Sex*, *Taxicab Confessions*, and *Cathouse* shot on location at madcap entrepreneur Dennis Hof's (right) BunnyRanch, where Stormy Daniels would often clock in. The shows were immensely popular, as was Hof, who loved his relationship with HBO and the boost it gave to sales of his autobiography, *The Art of the Pimp*.

21

22

The more controversial, the better: HBO and Demi Moore (above) spearheaded 1996's *If These Walls Could Talk* about three different generations of abortion experiences, with Cher, Sissy Spacek, Anne Heche, and Jada Pinkett. A sequel made in 2000 starred Vanessa Redgrave, Chloë Sevigny, Michelle Williams, Sharon Stone, and Ellen DeGeneres, among others.

HBO originally wanted a proven star for the title character of its 1998 movie *Gia*, but then newcomer Angelina Jolie blew everyone away—and brought major acclaim to the film—with her evocative performance.

23

Late night and specials guru Nancy Geller (above) with Chris Rock, the brilliant comedian who became for HBO the gift that kept on giving. Rock did five comedy specials for HBO and hosted *The Chris Rock Show*, which aired for five seasons.

Tom Fontana created the prison drama *Oz,* which debuted on HBO in 1997, becoming the first of HBO's drama auteur showrunners and one of the first to grasp the fact that violence and nudity weren't the only ways HBO differed from broadcast networks. More important, the network offered its creators near total freedom.

1998's *From the Earth to the Moon* was HBO's most ambitious project to date, driven to a large degree by the infectious vision of Tom Hanks. Suited up for the Apollo 7 mission are, from left, crewmembers Fredric Lehne (as Walter Cunningham), John Mese (as Donn F. Eisele), and Mark Harmon (as Wally Schirra).

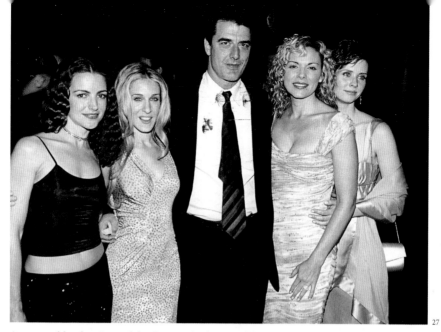

A new world order: *Sex and the City* wasn't a hit out of the gate when it debuted on June 6, 1998, but became a giant one for the HBO brand and HBO revenues. From left to right: Kristin Davis, Sarah Jessica Parker, Chris Noth, Kim Cattrall, and Cynthia Nixon.

Like. No. Other. It's practically impossible to overpraise *The Sopranos* or overstate its impact on HBO history and on television itself. Following its premiere on January 10, 1999, *Sopranos* warmed up tauntingly for its first four episodes and then, with episode five, titled "College," blasted off on a journey the likes of which viewers had never taken before, to places never visited, previously or since. Left to right: Edie Falco, Michael Imperioli, Lorraine Bracco, James Gandolfini, and series creator David Chase.

29

Two hearts that beat as one. The magnificent Susie Essman and comedy master Larry David in one of their bittersweeter moments from David's *Curb Your Enthusiasm*, which began its two-decades-plus run on HBO on October 15, 2000. It's unlikely there ever was or ever will be a comedy that better reflects the idiosyncrasies and gonzo brilliance of its creator than *Curb* does for David.

30

Übertalented Alan Ball had a frustrating time in broadcast television, then wrote two extraordinary scripts: a movie, *American Beauty*, and a one-hour drama, *Six Feet Under*. The series continued HBO's parade of hits and gave us one of the greatest finales in television series history. From left to right: Michael C. Hall, Lauren Ambrose, Frances Conroy, and Peter Krause.

Band of Brothers began as a luncheon conversation between HBO chairman Jeff Bewkes and history buff Tom Hanks. The commanding ten-part HBO miniseries debuted two nights before 9/11.

Days of innocence: President George W. Bush celebrates with documentary filmmaker Alexandra Pelosi, daughter of future House Speaker Nancy, Alexandra's HBO film *Journeys with George,* which aired during Bush's first term. Pelosi was one of innumerable filmmakers nurtured, protected, and frankly exhausted by the always determined Sheila Nevins.

Director Spike Lee cuddles with his prestigious Peabody honoring his HBO documentary *If God Is Willing and da Creek Don't Rise* (2010). Lee had already won another Peabody for HBO's *When the Levees Broke: A Requiem in Four Acts* (2006) and joined the HBO documentary team with his heartbreaking *4 Little Girls*.

34

David Simon became one of the most prodigious creative forces in HBO history, masterminding *The Corner*, *The Wire*, *Generation Kill*, *Treme*, *The Deuce*, and *The Plot Against America*, among others. To Simon's left, his trusted and highly respected team member Nina Noble.

David Milch created several shows for HBO, including the acclaimed *Deadwood*, the curious *John from Cincinnati*, and the troubled *Luck*.

Tony Kushner's play *Angels in America* was virtually *showered* with awards, including the Pulitzer, the Tony, and the Drama Desk Award for Best Play. When it came to bringing the play to the screen, HBO didn't give a single note to Kushner or director Mike Nichols.

36

Was there another network in 2003 that could boast a film of its own starring Meryl Streep, Al Pacino, and Emma Thompson and directed by Mike Nichols? *Angels in America* premiered on HBO on December 7, 2003. The film won eleven Primetime Emmys, including Outstanding Miniseries, and five Golden Globes, including Best Miniseries.

37

Doug Ellin spent two years mired in rewrites before getting approval for his pilot script of *Entourage*—loosely based on Mark Wahlberg's early life in Hollywood. The show ran for eight seasons. From left to right: Scott Caan, Alice Eve, Adrian Grenier, Ellin, Kevin Dillon, Jerry Ferrara, Perrey Reeves, Emmanuelle Chriqui, Kevin Connolly, and Jeremy Piven.

When versatile actor Bill Paxton died on February 25, 2017, at the age of sixty-one, it was a devastating shock to all who had worked with him for five seasons on HBO's *Big Love*, where Paxton played husband to three wives (Jeanne Tripplehorn, Chloë Sevigny, and Ginnifer Goodwin), with the exemplary Mary Kay Place also co-starring in the drama about Mormon polygamy created by two HBO favorites, husbands Will Scheffer and Mark V. Olsen.

JERRY LEVIN:

Jeff had smarts for business. He could learn anything. And he had a smart sense of humor, as opposed to Fuchs's self-aggrandizing humor. That's really what you need so you don't get caught up in idolatry that many people can't handle. Jeff Bewkes was right from the start.

JEFF BEWKES:

I became president of HBO in September '91 and then CEO in May 1995. The difference between those two jobs is that as president I was responsible for sales, marketing, finance, technology operations, and the financial part of HBO Independent Productions [*Everybody Loves Raymond*, *The Martin Lawrence Show*, *Roc*]. Michael ran all programming: Bridget and Chris in original series, concerts, and comedy, Steve in movie acquisition, Sheila's documentaries and family shows, and Bob Cooper with Made for HBO movies.

This was a transitional time. Michael was busy a good part of the week at Music, and I was still reporting to him as CEO of HBO, even though all his longtime programming chiefs technically now reported to me as CEO. Michael still stayed involved directly through meetings and phone calls with them, and I never said to Seth, Chris, or Cooper, "You should talk to me before Michael or instead of Michael."

Michael made it clear to me that he wasn't giving up his HBO chairman contract, reminding me that I still only had a contract as president reporting to him, and I needed to support him by telling Jerry I wasn't ready to do the CEO job without Michael's supervision.

SHEILA NEVINS:

Isn't Jeff the loveliest? I love him. I never saw Jeff ever get angry. Does he get angry? He always made me feel so good about myself and let me do what I believed in.

Not only did Fuchs refuse to give up HBO, he reached back and made a major personnel move. Bridget Potter had spent thirteen years as HBO's senior vice president, Original Programming.

BRIDGET POTTER:

My worst day was when Michael fired me. I had a lot of trouble getting to see him for a month. As a manager, he blew hot and cold, especially if I got something good, he would go cold. He couldn't take it, that there maybe was competition. But this time, it was longer or weirder. I also became very uneasy because he was trying to climb the ladder. I witnessed behavior from him that was really hard to bear, how he would go after people.

I would be sitting in his office and he would be working the board of directors. My theory about him is that it was always about his father. He couldn't have anyone above him. He had to kill his father. And then some people didn't want to be in business with him. Shocking.

When I finally got an appointment to see him, I came bouncing in and had all my notes to talk to him about what I had been doing and what I wanted to do. He was standing at his door, and said, "So this meeting is gonna be different, because I have to tell you that I don't need you anymore." I said, "What do you mean?" He said, "I don't need you anymore." I said, "What's going on?" and he said that he was giving all of programming to Bob Cooper.

So I said, "Does Chris know about this?" and he said, "Not all of it, but you should go talk to Shelley the HR person."

SHELLEY FISCHEL:

There have been instances when I believe HBO terminated women in a way that reflected a male perspective on employment and made the wrong call. As the HR person, all I could do is advise. For women, Michael was not easy to work for. I can still get enraged when I think of the awful jokes we women had to listen to at staff meetings. That said, I never had the sense Michael stood in the way of any woman moving forward in the company. Indeed my career, Sheila Nevins's, and others took off while he was CEO. Even Bridget, though it ended it unhappily, had a tenure that was for the most part extraordinarily successful.

MICHAEL FUCHS:

I didn't dislike Bridget, but a lot of her people did. Bridget was not an untalented programmer, but I didn't want to leave so much programming in her hands. I did try to be fair with the employees, but firings are tough. I used to say I am the corporation and know what's best for the corporation. Keep politics and social circumstances out. Easier said than done. I didn't have to fire too many people during my career there.

SHEILA NEVINS:

We all knew they were going to fire Bridget at some point. We used to look outside the door to see if Bridget had been fired yet. She'd come down the hallway and she'd be happy as a lark, so we saw it wasn't that day. And we waited and waited. Then one day she didn't come down.

BRIDGET POTTER:

I got an explanation from Jeff Bewkes who was a 100 percent mensch.

He said Michael was told if he wanted to grow at Time Warner, he needed to decrease his number of direct reports, and this was phase one.

CHRIS ALBRECHT:

Michael was not a good executive. He wasn't someone who wanted to hire people who knew more than he did.

Bridget was smart. I learned a lot from Bridget. She was tough on people and not too intimidated by the boys' club thing.

BRIDGET POTTER:

Michael was a bully, but he was an equal opportunity bully. It was a very competitive environment and part of my job every day was to go figure out what Henry Schleiff and Seth Abraham were going to do that day to try to get my job. Every day they did something to undermine me in one way or another. Was that because I was a woman? No, it's because they wanted my job.

JEFF BEWKES:

It was a vibrant, robust animal house. There was a boys' club going, but there were a lot of strong women who took no shit and gave as good as they got. Sheila Nevins, Bridget Potter, Nancy Geller, Leslie Jacobsen, Shelley Fischel, Pat Fili, Jodie Crabtree, and Sue McGuirk, for starters.

BRIDGET POTTER:

When I left, Jeff managed to make it possible for me to hold on to all my stock options by keeping me on the payroll until they vested. I was in the middle of a divorce, and I had sat in the cafeteria with Jeff while he was going through his divorce and he knew I was gonna be signing papers on a certain day and they waited until after those papers were signed to tell me that I was gonna be leaving so that I wouldn't have to share any of my golden parachute with my ex-husband. Jeff did that for me.

I went to Shelley and she said, "They will do anything you want. Do you want a production company?" And I said, "Money is all I care about" because at that point I was terrified. I was the sole support for my household and was going through a painful divorce. My biggest concern was becoming a bag lady. I had two kids. It was very hard. I had to tell them on top of the divorce, Michael said, "I don't need you anymore."

KERI PUTNAM, Executive:

I started as an assistant one cubicle down from Bridget's assistant. I got to watch Bridget at the height of my learning and the height of her moment. It was amazing. Bridget had two kids and she would come into work early, put her makeup on, then get ready for the day. What was most extraordinary about Bridget is that every one of us, no matter how junior, understood the ethos and the programming vision of that company at that time, and that's really hard to do.

CAROLYN STRAUSS:

Bridget was so way ahead of her time. Keri Putnam and I would talk about this a lot—and she was totally influential for us. Bridget would come in Monday morning having read the sports pages so she would have something to talk about in the senior staff meetings with the guys. But you have to give Michael credit. He had a lot of women who were driving the creative at HBO when I got there in the mid-1980s, like Sheila, Bridget, and Betty Bitterman.

COLIN CALLENDER:

By the time Bridget left, she had drilled in all of us her way of looking at stories, and a certain way of looking at the world. She had real focus. What story is it you're really telling? Why are we telling this story? She held our feet to the fire. Losing Bridget was a loss.

Here was the situation as of Friday, May 26, 1995—the beginning of a critical weekend that would have a dramatic effect on the next fifteen years of HBO.

Michael Fuchs had recently been named the CEO of Warner Music and was chairman of HBO. Despite hearing from both Jerry Levin and Dick Parsons that he needed to let go of HBO, Fuchs refused. Jeff Bewkes, CEO, reported to Fuchs as chairman, and programming reported to Bewkes. In a classic Fuchs move, Fuchs did the opposite of what Levin and Parsons were asking of him and tightened his iron grip on his beloved kingdom. He reached down into HBO—without consulting Bewkes—not only to fire Potter but to make an even more audacious move by offering Bob Cooper a new title: president of programming. Not only did Bewkes not know, but Fuchs saw no reason to discuss this with Albrecht, who would then be reporting to Cooper.

GLENN WHITEHEAD, Executive:

One day Bob Cooper called me and said, "You can't tell anyone, but it's done. Michael's going to announce it. I'm going to be head of programming, and Chris Albrecht's gonna report to me." I was so amazed. I said, "Where are you?" And he goes, "I'm driving in my car. I'm going to Santa Monica to the Barney's warehouse sale." And I said, "I'm going to meet you there." I see Bob, he gives me a big hug, then I look over his shoulder and I see, walking toward us, Michael Fuchs. And Bob goes, "Don't say anything, don't say anything." Because he wasn't supposed to tell me this.

BOB COOPER:

Michael had brought me to the top of the Peninsula Hotel, and told me, "I'm going to make you the president of HBO, and I want you to spend more time in New York, because we're going to do a lot of series and that's not really what you've been doing to date." We negotiated a contract and HBO prepared a press release.

Fuchs made the offer to Cooper on a Friday afternoon. Word spread. What Fuchs failed to think about, or simply didn't care about, was the impact that this was going to have on Bewkes. After all, Cooper would be reporting to Bewkes, and it was well known that Bewkes was no fan of Cooper's. Moreover, if Cooper had become head of programming, Bewkes would have been sidelined in the programming world, something that he did not want to happen.

Over the weekend, Bewkes told Fuchs that he wasn't going to accept Cooper as president of programming, and that Fuchs could fire him or demote him to president if he wanted to stick with the Cooper plan. Bewkes also told Chris Albrecht about the upcoming arrangement. Albrecht was furious and decided he was going to have to leave—there was no way he was going to report to Cooper. Members of the "community" descended upon Fuchs. Some were advocating on Albrecht's behalf; others were severely critical of Cooper. Bernie Brillstein and Brad Grey both told Fuchs they wouldn't be bringing business to HBO if Cooper was running programming. By the time the sun rose Monday morning, even Fuchs, with all his audaciousness, realized his plan was not viable.

BOB COOPER:

By the end of the weekend, he said, "Look, I can't do this now. I just can't do it. It's too difficult to do this." I said, "Well, we have the contract." He said, "I'm so sorry. I just can't do it." And that was very hurtful to me. And that was it. He didn't appoint anybody else. He just said, "I can't rock the boat."

GLENN WHITEHEAD:

I was told that Brillstein and Grey each made phone calls to Michael saying that it would never work with Bob. "You've got to give the job to Chris." Michael apparently understood the implication. He called up Bob and said, "I'm sorry, I can't do this, but I'll pay you."

BRIDGET POTTER:

By Monday, Chris Albrecht was running Original Programming and Bob Cooper was still there doing the movies. So Michael had not actually decreased the number of direct reports that he had. He had totally screwed the whole thing up, but still I was gone.

CHRIS ALBRECHT:

What happened was that Michael fired Bridget. He wanted Cooper to be the head of programming and he wanted me to report to Cooper. I said, "I don't want to do that." And he said, "Well, you have to do it. I already told Bob. Now what am I going to do?" I said, "Well, I'll do it under one condition. If I ask to get out of my contract, you have to let me out of my contract." And he said, "I can't do that because you'll leave." I told him, "Of course I will," so he wouldn't agree to that. Then we came up with both of us report to Bewkes.

When Cooper took over Pictures, they were going to fire Colin Callender. I said to Colin, "Look, if I can pull this together, will you report to Cooper? Do you want to stay and report to Cooper?" Colin said yes. And then I went to Cooper and I said, "Look, I'm telling you Colin's great manpower, and he's got a lot of great projects." That actually turned out to be a fruitful relationship for both of them: Colin got to stay, Bob had a really talented executive working for him, and Bob got to take credit for the projects.

Meanwhile, over at Warner Music, (still) HBO chairman Michael Fuchs didn't believe he needed weeks, days, or even hours to learn all about the music business. He was there to reshape it in his vision, much as he'd started to do with HBO upon his arrival there in 1976. But HBO was young then and had a younger staff. Warner Music was a very different place, as Fuchs would see.

Fuchs began making key moves with personnel and reevaluating the division's priorities. That June, Fuchs fired Doug Morris, who had been CEO of Warner Music for the United States and, not coincidentally, a strong defender of the rap movement.

Morris convinced Jimmy Iovine, co-founder of Interscope Records, to sell 50 per-

cent of that label to MCA music entertainment for $200 million. Morris, along with Universal CEO Edgar Bronfman Jr., renamed the venture Universal Music Group. It was an area in which Universal had suffered through decades of famine, and yet feast was on the way. In fact, the company exploded, signing big-time superstars like U2, Mariah Carey, Snoop, Tupac, and Eminem to the roster. By the turn of the millennium, Universal's earnings totaled more than $1 billion—enough to qualify it for the title of "the biggest record company in the world."

MICHAEL FUCHS:

I was a little stupid. I finally realized Jerry was good at something, and it was inside fucking manipulation bullshit, like Stalin. Jerry thought he could bury me in music. It was like Vietnam. The Internet was snaking into our business, Apple in particular. The rap issue exploded, hitting Time Warner first, and I had no management support whatsoever.

I moved to music, but I still didn't get a contract literally the first couple of weeks. So I told him, I still have a contract with HBO. I don't like being moved around like a sack of wheat. I'm in music for three weeks and I seem to be getting further from HBO. I didn't get a contract. Certainly an enormous mistake. Imagine trusting Levin.

JERRY LEVIN:

I did sit him down and asked what the hell he had done with Doug Morris. I said, "You can't do what you're doing here. This isn't HBO, with a swashbuckling culture, a put-down sense of humor." At HBO you had to be funny, but it wasn't the humor that you could use at a music company.

BOB DALY:

Doug Morris, like Mo Ostin, is an icon. He had a deal with Jimmy Iovine and Interscope, which was the up-and-coming music company that Doug made. He was about to become the hottest guy in business, but Fuchs sits in a meeting with him and says, "Look, I'm gonna run this show my way." Remember, he's a guy's coming in to take over something he knows nothing about. When I went from CBS to Warner Bros., I met everybody in the company. Michael Fuchs took the other approach. He says, "I don't plan on being here that long. I plan on moving up in the company."

Then he fires Doug Morris for cause. Cause. That means, you don't get paid. There was no cause. I don't know what he manufactured, but he convinces Jerry Levin to fire Doug Morris for cause. And he releases Interscope, which turned out to be one of the most successful companies in the world. And meanwhile, he's bad-mouthing Jerry Levin.

MICHAEL FUCHS:

I began to return Levin's hostility. We had a dinner at the Four Seasons restaurant, and an old girlfriend of mine said she saw me at the restaurant. I asked her why she didn't come to the table. She said, "There was too much smoke!" Dick Parsons began to accompany Levin, who probably thought I would reach across the table and grab him.

This may sound like an employee out of control, but to me, I had done a great job for almost twenty years, beyond the call of duty.

BETTE MIDLER:

In the music business, people were very, very territorial, and they absolutely closed ranks. It was very hard to say at the time to Michael that I don't think you should get near this job. I do believe he was playing with people who were absolutely not going to support him in any way. They thought he should be back at his pond at HBO.

JEFF BEWKES:

Michael was always telling me how easy I had it being a WASP, and I would say, "First of all, I'm not a WASP, I'm Dutch. And secondly, you don't know what discrimination is until you've been a goy working in the entertainment business." He looked at me like, "What the fuck?" I was never sure he knew how funny I was.

BOB DALY:

Jerry was so different from Steve Ross. If Steve Ross was working on a deal, everybody would sit with him for hours and he would write down anything we could tell him about the deal because he would do so much due diligence. Jerry Levin was the opposite. He didn't talk to anybody.

Jerry called me up once and said, "I'm getting on a plane to Atlanta." I said, "Oh, okay, what are you doing?" He said, "I'm going to go talk to Ted Turner about buying Turner." I told him, "Jerry, we've never had a single meeting about this or anything related to it." He told me, "I know, but I've already made up my mind."

Sure enough, in September 1995, HBO's parent, Time Warner, announced plans to add a new mouth to the family: Ted Turner, along with Turner Broadcasting System.

Already a minority shareholder in TBS, Time Warner would purchase the remaining 82 percent of Turner stock for approximately $7.5 billion. On September 22, Jerry Levin and Ted Turner held a joint conference announcing the merger, shaking hands and confirming that under a revamped structure, HBO would be moved into a newly formed "video" division, helmed by Turner himself.

Michael Fuchs, unsurprisingly, was less than pleased with this coming arrangement. Fellow Time Warner execs said that Fuchs vocally opposed the reorganization for fear of losing control of his true love, HBO.

Fuchs was a noticeable absentee at the press conference. As the **New York Times** *wrote: "Even as Mr. Levin proudly gestured to a group of senior Time Warner executives seated in the front row, Mr. Fuchs was watching the presentation alone on a television screen outside the gallery."*

Variety *noted that Fuchs had in fact waited outside the junket to talk to journalists directly; and for the following weeks, stories circulated that Fuchs was angling to run the whole of the new company.*

JEFF BEWKES:

By 1995, Ted Turner's company had overstretched with acquisitions and needed a bailout. Time Warner owned 10 percent of Turner and so did TCI [John Malone] and several other cable companies. That summer Malone and Levin worked out a deal with Ted for us to buy Turner. Michael was against the deal and was arguing about it with Jerry.

Jerry was under pressure because the stock hadn't moved in three years. Institutional investors owned a big slug of our stock—the largest being Gordy Crawford's Capital Group in LA with over 10 percent, but Edgar Bronfman had bought a 10 to 15 percent stake, and with the deal Ted and Malone would each have 10 percent, too.

JOHN MALONE:

The merger with Turner gave them additional power. I would say that probably, from a pure financial analyst point of view, was an important step. Because until they did the Turner networks, what did they have? Time Warner had HBO. I don't think they had any other programming business other than HBO at that time.

They had a big cable company, and when they bought Turner, all of a sudden they could negotiate across both premium and basic cable. That gave them a huge amount of market power that enabled them then to guarantee HBO success, and vice versa.

JERRY LEVIN:

After a walk in the woods, scratching my head, I figured we don't want Turner to fall into the hands of Rupert or Jack Welch. I wasn't afraid. I wanted to head that off.

JEFF BEWKES:

I told Michael over and over, "Don't go against Jerry on the Turner deal." "Jerry's a pussy," he would say, and, "You're not a wartime consigliere." Yeah, like guess who won every fucking war? Me. Meanwhile, Bronfman's got 10 percent, Malone's got 10, Gordy's got 10. They all want this deal and you're pissing on it in the newspapers? Those guys can have a board meeting without the board!

RICHARD PARSONS:

When we acquired Turner, Ted came on the board and was vice-chairman, so Michael's reporting line was changed from Jerry to Ted, which Michael never fully accepted. Ted's presence really annoyed Michael. Then he let his grumpiness be known publicly.

I think Michael thought he would be next in line if something happened to Jerry, and I also thought Michael didn't believe Jerry would ever have the balls to fire him.

MICHAEL FUCHS:

Jerry had done everything but give me a piece of paper telling me I'd be COO. It was "we." I helped him get the job. He made calls from my office to board members off a script I wrote for him. As soon as Jerry got the job, I knew that my elevation wasn't going to happen. I knew that he had lied to me.

JERRY LEVIN:

Michael and I never talked about succession. He was never on the list.

SHEILA NEVINS:

I had to see Michael about something, and I was sitting in his office, and Jerry walked in and they almost killed each other. I didn't know what to do. Screaming. Screaming.

MARTY CALLNER:

Richard, who Michael brought off the street to be his PR guy, convinced him to do this *Vanity Fair* spread, and that culminated in a cartoon that they ran with Michael holding a knife pointed at Levin's back.

That *Vanity Fair* article was the straw that broke the camel's back. I think that for all Michael's smarts, he didn't really play it the way it should be played and allowed Richard to manipulate it.

RICHARD PLEPLER, Executive:

Speculation at the time was that Michael was positioning himself for Jerry's job, and that was unfair. Michael was working his butt off to try to get his arms around the music industry, which was new to him. It was unfair of anyone to impute other motives to him. Obviously when the *Vanity Fair* cartoon appeared, Michael was upset. So was I, frankly. I thought it was unfair but there was a lot of tension in the air between Michael, Jerry, Bob, and Terry and unsurprisingly it ended in a conflagration that was very unfortunate.

MICHAEL FUCHS:

Levin certainly didn't like that I had an identity in the world, and I was so busy that Richard was going off on his own. There was a very bad article in *Vanity Fair*, bad in that there's a cartoon of me stabbing Levin in the back. (They could have at least done it in the front.) I had lunch with Graydon Carter about that. I said, "Would you like if I did a comedy skit with you stabbing S. I. Newhouse in the back?" He apologized, but it was too fucking late. I couldn't blame it all on Richard, but your guy is supposed to manage that stuff.

There's an old legal term you don't hear as much today in this more corrupt environment: corporate opportunity. It means using the assets, influence, resources of a public corporation for personal benefit. If Richard had a philosophy, this was it. Running a big successful entertainment company in NYC, while your boss was a ghost, is great fun. More than that, it's a social pass to almost whatever you want.

SETH ABRAHAM:

Michael had an amazing ability to manage down and he had absolutely no interest in managing up.

JERRY LEVIN:

I didn't stay up at night worrying about the state of HBO. Jeff had demonstrated himself to be a new kind of creative executive who's sharp as hell but has a temperament to make creative people feel good about themselves and supported.

HAL AKSELRAD:

I'm on the corporate jet, with Michael and Richard, to the Rock and Roll Hall of Fame inauguration, a twelve-hour concert we did live on HBO, mixing the greatest acts in the business.

A big piece comes out in the *Wall Street Journal*, and it has Michael on the cover with a flattering article about him, and it's a negative piece about Jerry. Richard is crowing. He got this great article and placement for Michael. I see this and in my heart I'm like, "Oh my God, Michael's going to get fired."

Michael Fuchs may well have woken up on Friday, November 17, 1995, thinking about his next steps at the company under Jerry Levin, but he'd have other things on his mind by day's end.

CURT VIEBRANZ:

I was over in Europe. I was back in New York and had lunch with Jerry, who said to me, "I'm considering reorganizing Time Warner, but no reorganization works for Michael unless Michael is at the top of the reorganization."

JERRY LEVIN:

Michael hadn't pushed me into a corner. It wasn't self-protection for me. He was just failing. I'm a human being. This was my boy. I had been his big brother for a long time. The fact he was turning on me, it had nothing to do with that day.

ED ADLER, Executive:

I knew the day before. I worked on the press release with Jerry. Jerry's plan was to invite Michael into his smaller office next to his large office and simply tell him, "This is it; you're fired, and we're putting out this press release." Then he was going to hand him the release.

Before Michael arrived, I said to Jerry, "I'm worried about you. When you show him the release, I'm afraid he's going to punch you." Jerry was a little guy; Michael was not only bigger but pugnacious. Jerry laughed and said, "I'll be fine." Jerry had ice water running in his veins.

JEFF BEWKES:

Michael called me midmorning from his office at the other end of the hall. "Jerry asked me to lunch. He's either gonna fire me or give me my contract [over music and HBO]. What do think it'll be?" I said, "I think he's gonna fire you." "What? Do you know something? Why are you saying that?" I said, "I would do it if I were him. You're defying him with the board and in the press."

JERRY LEVIN:

It ended up being a very short meeting. I don't recall the exact words, but I very quickly said something like, "It's over. This is not working. You're out of here." I could see on his face that he didn't expect this would ever happen. He said, "We're never going to talk again. You really fucked me over, didn't you?" And walked out. It was high drama.

MICHAEL FUCHS:

When I got fired, I said, "So I bet you have a press release." In the press release, it said that the entertainment division was being reorganized, and that was the reason for firing me. No such thing ever happened. If he was a man, he would have said, "Listen, Michael, you and I have worked together for twenty years. We've run out of road. You'd probably like my job, but I like my job." That's what I would have said.

JEFF BEWKES:

He goes up to see Jerry, and then the phone rings and it's Michael. I love this about him, he doesn't say, "Hello," or, "Holy Shit," he just says matter-of-factly, "Well, you were right." The guy does deadpan better than Shandling. "What do you mean I was right?" "He fired me. He wouldn't even look at me, gave me a press release, and stole a glance through the bottom of his water glass while I read it." You gotta hand it to Michael, he was calm under pressure.

Just six months after his promotion to vice president of Time Warner and CEO of Warner Music, Michael Fuchs was fired. The firebrand godfather of HBO, the larger-than-life personality that had molded the network in his image, from fledgling to self-assured front-runner, was out.

BOB DALY:

Michael Fuchs destroyed himself. To the best of my knowledge, I can't take credit for getting Michael Fuchs fired, but I might've helped a bit.

MICHAEL FUCHS:

I have no doubt that Jerry fired me because I was a threat to him. I think maybe he also didn't feel loyalty from me. But he caused that gap in loyalty.

I'm straight ahead. What you see is what you get. There was a pervasive feeling in the company that he was never honest, and an avoider of conflict.

Should I have figured it out? Could I have? Friends of mine say if only I had been more manipulative, it would have been all mine. I still don't know how to manipulate. It seems like a lot of work and a lot of energy.

After I left, they actually denied I was CEO of the Warner Music Group. I went to Herb Wachtell at Wachtell Lipton, who said, "You can't win the music thing because they have so much leverage on the vesting of your stock." Also, he said, "You have a tough reputation. You don't need another battle now." My deal was finally settled by Peter Hage, general counsel of Time Warner. He said to me at the end, "You should have been the CEO of this company." I was surprised, but I also realized how unpopular Levin was. Beverly Sills, who was a Time Warner board member very close to Steve Ross, told me Steve felt I was his natural successor. So I had these great recommendations and no job.

The year 1995 would go down as one of the more significant in the media business in terms of personnel moves. In May, Ron Meyer left CAA to become president and COO of Universal, and in August, another CAA co-founder, Michael Ovitz, left to become president of Disney.

When the Fuchs era ended, veterans of the music division could be heard comparing his six-month reign to no less an ordeal than "the Spanish Inquisition." The mood at HBO, while somber, was tinged with at least the slightest hint of relief that the political turbulence might finally be at an end. Fuchs's exit package was roughly $50 million, so he had plenty of cash, but even more resentment.

6

"Something for Everybody, Some of the Time"

NOVEMBER 18, 1995–JUNE 5, 1998

MICHAEL FUCHS:

I thought I had gotten screwed. If you look back, there was one fucking shooting star at that company, me, and I got destroyed. That's the way I see it. Was that best for the company? Was that best for the shareholders? Was there a reason? Do I have any doubt in my mind that I could have been an Iger kind of CEO? None. I wasn't self-destructive. I was just too fucking honest.

Listen, how many friends does Jerry have from the company or outside of it? I was dealing with a guy I had been quite close to for a number of years, and while I don't think he was a sociopath, let's say that he lied more than anyone I'd ever met.

Jerry had this thing he did with people he fired where he would want to get together with them later on, so everyone would know he was still friends with them. The only way I was going to sit across a table from Jerry was if I could jump across it and grab him by the throat.

SETH ABRAHAM:

After he was fired, Michael said, "I've got to meet with my lawyers. Do you want to have dinner after that?" I said, "Okay."

We went to the Second Avenue Deli. We got there at about eleven o'clock. There were a few of us. It was empty and we stayed there until they threw us out. Michael seemed okay.

MICHAEL FUCHS:

The next day you wake up. We're animals, we're used to doing what we do. All of a sudden you don't have anything to do. So I decided to take my clothes to the cleaners. I still had my car and driver and the *New York Post* is waiting outside my apartment. They took a picture of me with an arm full of laundry, then wrote a funny caption about Michael's next job.

I was off-balance; I was depressed. I felt the dark clouds. On my mother's side of the family going back as far as I know, every male has had serious depression. Two suicides, suicide attempts, institutionalization. Depression has been a battle for me since college.

BETTE MIDLER:

We were all very worried for him, and I was terribly upset. It was a complete blindside.

Michael was being honored by this gigantic Jewish charity. I think it was UJA. I've done so many of them, it's all one big Jewish blur. Well, he got fired the week before, and his entire dais skipped town on him. I was the only one left standing. I must say, he didn't crack. He didn't let anyone know how devastated he was.

ILENE KAHN POWER:

Michael said, "Look, I've just been fired. You may not want to honor me," and they said, "We absolutely still want to." There were a few of us there that night. I had tears in my eyes when Bette went up to Michael and sang, "You are the wind beneath my wings."

There are people in Hollywood who don't know who Michael Fuchs is or was. That breaks my heart.

BETTE MIDLER:

Michael is a remarkable character. He's very funny. He's sharp. He's not speedy, though, I mean, he doesn't talk fast, but he's a good talker. I thought his taste was excellent. He was the powerhouse at HBO. He built it. He drew them the map and showed them the way it was done.

ROSS GREENBURG:

Michael's vision guaranteed we were different than anybody else. He was the most influential executive in the company's history. He was our heartbeat. I love that man.

SHEILA NEVINS:

He was antisocial, brazen, and had an irascible spirit. Michael was very difficult, but I don't know anyone in power who isn't difficult. He knew how to be a smartass, so we were a bit of a smartass network. And he was fearless. Michael was a genius. I loved Michael.

MICHAEL FUCHS:

Sheila tells me, "Michael, you were the smartest, and the place was never the same after you left." I said, "You know Sheila, it would have been nice if you had ever even whispered something like that to any living being but me." And she gave me the greatest fucking answer ever: "You know why I didn't? I'm a bad person. I'm evil." What the fuck do you say after that?

MARTY CALLNER:

Michael was the father of the family, and then the father got killed. It was wrong. They didn't even give him a producing deal. I love Michael Fuchs. I've never met anybody like him. I am who I am today because of Michael Fuchs. He believed in me, taught me a lot, and hopefully I taught him a few things. He's the only executive who didn't play the game and didn't care who he offended. Chris was close.

CHRIS ALBRECHT:

We had heard that Michael had been playing things dangerously, but it was still definitely shocking. When I came to HBO, Michael was already CEO; I had only known HBO with him in charge. There was a lot of history. He was the keeper of the HBO flame.

CURT VIEBRANZ:

People have underestimated the role Michael played in creating HBO.

JEFF BEWKES:

After Michael was fired, he didn't leave the office. I'm not talking about the next day, that week, or even that month. He never told me he was going to do this. He was having meetings, in this office he set himself up in, with all of his people who are actually now my people, but I wasn't going to force them to separate from Mikey—except for Plepler who had a problem, but we'll come to that.

JERRY LEVIN:

It's not as if we had the Secret Service take him and all his stuff out that day. That's the way people get off-loaded at other companies, but we didn't do that unless there were special circumstances. There's a sensitivity that should be involved. He wasn't going to get anywhere anyway. He had no title, no job, no leverage.

JEFF BEWKES:

Jerry—who I report to—is saying to me at our weekly meetings things like, "I ran into this HBO person and they tell me Michael is still coming in every day and second-guessing everything that Jeff is doing." Then he would ask me, "Does that make things difficult for you?" or "Do you want me to do something about it?" Jerry was essentially asking me if I wanted him to kick Michael off the premises. I told him, "It shouldn't be up to me to have my old boss evicted. If you want that done, that's your job." I think Michael kept going into that office for about six months.

MICHAEL FUCHS:

You think Bewkes would come down the hall and sit in my office? Not a fucking chance. I wasn't looking for nurturing. It was in my contract that they had to provide me with an office if I left, so I was just putting it to them, saying, "You guys better live up to that deal." They sent Dick Parsons, Mr. Experience, to tell me I should get out of my office. He said, "Michael, it isn't good for the people at HBO that you're here." I said, "Dick, do you actually think you know what's best for HBO better than I do?" Eventually they got me a spectacular office at 9 West Fifty-seventh.

JEFF BEWKES:

I'm proud to say I was never disloyal to Michael, never trashed him behind his back. Apparently, Michael now thinks I schemed to get his job. I can't believe he believes that, but knowing Michael, I also know he can't blame himself for getting fired.

SETH ABRAHAM:

After we had found out Michael was fired, later that day, Jeff said, "Let's have breakfast tomorrow morning. We can go to the HBO cafeteria." I said to my wife, "I'm not worried Jeff's going to fire me; he wouldn't do it in the cafeteria."

Jeff had been in the company more than fifteen years. He was a known quantity and was already our president. We meet, and he says, "I don't know shit about sports, so go on doing your job. If you need help, call me. I'm not going to call you much because I have nothing to contribute, but I don't want you to think it's disinterest." I mentioned, "I used to meet with Michael once a week, just the two of us, and go over sports business, etc." Jeff said, "If you want to do that, we can do that, but you're going to do most of the talking." Then I said, "Jeff, I need you to know Michael and I are good friends," and he said, "Seth, I don't give a shit about your friendship with Michael."

QUENTIN SCHAFFER:

Plepler and I discussed what to do with the media. Up to this point, Jeff had done no real press. It was always Michael. Right away, Plepler put Jeff in touch with the *LA Times* to say, "Here's the new head" to assure Hollywood that HBO was in good hands.

Such were the resentments, jealousies, and animosities toward Michael Fuchs in the whirling Time Warner universe that, once news of his firing spread, attention shifted at once to his then key PR operative at HBO since 1992, to thirty-five-year-old Richard Plepler. Earlier in 1995, Fuchs gave Plepler similar duties at Warner Music when Fuchs became president there.

Plepler was a mainstay in Fuchs's kitchen cabinet and widely known to be buddy-buddy with Fuchs "off-campus" as well.

Born in 1960 and raised in Manchester, Connecticut, Plepler was the son of a lawyer. Both of his parents were active in statewide Democratic politics, which explains why one of his first jobs out of Franklin & Marshall College, armed with a degree in government, was working for Senator Chris Dodd in Washington.

*In 1984, Plepler left Dodd to work in public relations under the legendary John Scanlon, a Connector Supreme who held fashionable salons at his home and played key roles in the worlds of politics, culture, and media. When he died in 2001, Scanlon was eulogized by ABC News anchor Peter Jennings, Nobel Prize–winning Irish poet Seamus Heaney, and New York **Daily News** columnist Pete Hamill.*

Plepler had been regarded as Scanlon's protégé and went out on his own to consult for HBO, until he was hired full-time in 1992 as senior vice president for corporate communications.

JEFF BEWKES:

When Michael went to Music, he brought Richard to help him, and gave him a big contract as head of communications at Music, paying a million or two with two years' severance. Richard also had a full-time job as head of communications with me at HBO with similar comp and severance and I had gone along with this double-dip arrangement. So Michael calls me in and tells me to change Richard's HBO deal so that if he gets fired from Warner Music, not only is that a breach of his Music contract, but it would trigger a breach of his HBO deal.

I wasn't going to sign on to a deal that could penalize the company like that. He says, "I'm telling you to do this," and then reminds me that I don't have a new contract as CEO, that I'm still under the old president contract reporting to him.

I told him, "I'm not doing it, so if you order me to do it, that's insubordination—you can fire me for that or you can demote me back to president and you can take back the CEO job." He looks at me and says, "You know I can't do that." I said, "Yeah, I'm banking on it. You'd have trouble with the guys uptown." So I didn't sign the cross default for Richard, but he still had a solid deal at HBO.

When Michael got fired there was no way for Richard to stay on at Music so he came back full-time to HBO. I was under significant pressure from everywhere to fire him. Key people, including Bob, were telling me, "You can't keep him. You can't trust him. He's Michael's guy. If you keep him, you're a fool." Keep in mind, I'm trying to make peace with Bob over Warner movie arrangements with HBO, which were awful under Michael.

JERRY LEVIN:

The Warner people didn't want anyone who had anything to do with Michael anywhere near them. Plepler wasn't seen as a PR guy for the company, more like one just for Michael. That's why it didn't make sense for him to stay. But I wasn't going to tell Jeff what he should do.

JEFF BEWKES:

Richard comes to me and says everybody's telling him he should go because the knives are out; he should take the severance from Music because the job's terminated. I said, "Look, Jerry thinks you won't be able to avoid

Michael using you against HBO or the company, and Dick's advising me to tie up loose ends. Bob and Terry say, Don't be naive, Fuchs won't go quietly and Richard's his PR guy. Nevertheless, you have a place here. But if I catch you advising Michael or being part of a PR war, I will fire you."

RICHARD PLEPLER:

After Michael left, the choices before me were: they would pay out my contract or I could stay and renegotiate a new deal without Music, just for HBO.

JEFF BEWKES:

"And you have to give up your severance at Music. I can't defend you staying here if you take severance from the company," he said, "but that's a couple million dollars." I said, "You have to gamble that I'll get it back for you."

RICHARD PLEPLER:

I chose to play long ball. I told Jeff, "I'm thirty-five years old. I'll always be grateful to Michael for bringing me to the dance and teaching me so much. But I don't want to leave. I like it here and I think I can continue to make a contribution." Thankfully, he agreed.

Because Jeff was such an engaging and thoughtful guy, I was very mindful that the more exposure people had to him, the better it was going to be for HBO and for him. My role then was to help elevate the brand and make sure that Jeff was meeting people in the media he might not have otherwise known. At the end of the day, that ended up being very beneficial for HBO.

MICHAEL FUCHS:

Richard came to me and said, "Do you want me to leave with you? I'll go with you." And I said, "No. I'm on a rough road now. You keep your job," which I have no regrets about. Richard didn't have my back. In retrospect, he is completely untrustworthy.

He literally disappeared. Instantaneously, professionally and socially. Mutual friends disappeared. Loyalty was so important to me. I was stunned. I had literally invented Plepler. My friends said, "Don't you know Richard is all about Richard?" He's a dog, he'll follow whoever feeds him.

After the epochal Fuchs firing, and unbeknownst to Plepler, a press release had already been prepared announcing Plepler's departure as well. He was too closely aligned with Fuchs, it was thought, and Warner higher-ups wanted to be rid of all Fuchsians. The easy thing for Bewkes to do would have been to say okay. But Bewkes decided instead to give Plepler a shot at proving his independence from Fuchs—a move that would reverberate for decades.

Perhaps equally noteworthy: Bewkes's gumption in ignoring pressure from Jerry Levin, Bob Daly, and others. In his first test on the front lines, Bewkes showed a readiness to act according to the dictates of his own gut, never mind what noises others were saying, including his boss. Such would be Bewkes's distinguishing, and at times potentially hazardous, modus operandi in the years to come.

JEFF BEWKES:

All Richard did was not commit professional suicide by leaving when Michael did. He was entitled to a career apart from Michael.

HBO. Chuck Dolan hatched it, Jerry Levin formalized it, and Nick Nicholas transformed it into a well-run business. Austin Furst, Jim Heyworth, Frank Biondi, and others at all levels brought bountiful contributions, but Michael Fuchs is the individual who ranks as the father of the modern HBO.

Fuchs operated as HBO's head raccoon for eleven years, and fortunately for all, those would be the years best-suited to a man of Fuchs's particular sensibilities, quirks, bombastic strengths, and fitful weaknesses. The company was still young and malleable enough to profit wildly from Fuchs's relentless competitive zeal, his singular audacity, and even, at times, his apolitical narcissism. Fuchs was relentless in the battle to steer and shape HBO, while instilling in all HBO employees the incomparable satisfaction of working for a company one loves.

Hollywood is famous as a place where an executive gets fired one day but winds up with another top job the next, often irrespective of whether they were well suited for it or not.

In the years after he left Time Warner, Fuchs would be considered for several significant jobs—and would even try to create some for himself—but there were, ultimately, no takers.

It was as if none of Fuchs's accomplishments at HBO had garnered him credit. He had been revered in some quarters for his gumption, particularly with his bosses, but that was considered potentially dangerous at best by those who would become his new boss—and too much to take on. A youthful forty-nine at the time of the separation, Michael Fuchs would never hold another executive job in Big Media again.

MICHAEL FUCHS:

Chuck Dolan loved me and would tell people, "Yes, I started HBO, but it never would have been HBO without Michael Fuchs." I went to him about the Madison Square Garden job, and said, "Chuck, let's make magic again."

He said, "My son wants that job." I said, "Chuck, Brian Roberts does not go near teams Comcast owns. It's not smart." But it was no use. I was mentioned for the Sony job; Howard Stringer got that.

HBO was a lifesaver for me. Even though I practiced law before I arrived, I felt like this company had taken me off the streets, and I was incredibly loyal to it. It affected me deeply. We had a lot of laughs in that company. I thought part of my role was to entertain these people. I never opened a meeting without a joke. I loved HBO.

As that tumultuous November finally ended, Jeff Bewkes could take comfort anticipating his first post-Fuchs HBO humdinger: a live Michael Jackson concert, unlike any the Gloved One had ever performed, to air December 10, 1995.

Music specials had been a vital programming component for HBO as far back as 1980, when **Diana Ross in Concert!** *established the precedent. In 1982 came Stevie Nicks; in 1983, Billy Joel; then Olivia Newton-John in 1983, Streisand in 1986, Madonna in 1991, Whitney Houston in 1991, Michael Jackson in 1992,* **Madonna Live Down Under: The Girlie Show;** *and those two seminal shows of 1994, Streisand's* **Barbra: The Concert** *and* **Whitney Houston: The Concert for a New South Africa.**

Jackson was to perform from the intimate (2,894-seat) and historic Beacon Theatre on Broadway—his first live event in New York in eight years. HBO executives anticipated 250 million viewers worldwide. Jackson was thirty-seven at the time.

NANCY GELLER:

Michael Jackson came to our offices to meet with me, and it was surreal. He didn't come with an entourage. Everybody in the company had their nose pressed up against the glass partition of the conference room because they all wanted to see him, and I finally had to step out and say, "Get out of here. You can't do this to this guy."

He spoke in that soft voice, and said to me, "I want to do a small concert," and I said, "Michael, you're Barnum and Bailey. What do you mean you want to do a small concert?" And he said, "I want to do a small concert like the one Elvis did on NBC, and I'd like it to be at the Beacon." I was very hesitant because I knew he liked a lot of explosives at his concerts, and they weren't allowed there. Even though I was nervous about it, we started to put it together. The marketing department did this phenomenal on-air promo for it and Michael was so excited. Then I got a call telling me Michael now wanted pyrotechnics, and I told them, "We can't do that in the Beacon. It's against the law."

As we got closer to the date, Michael called and said to me in this baby voice, "Nancy, nobody knows that my show is coming on." I told him, "Michael, you have to be on Mars not to know about this show. We play the promo every day, every night, and we've also painted 'Michael Jackson' down Sixth Avenue." Later that day, I got a call from my assistant that Michael fainted on the stage during the rehearsal. I couldn't believe it. I flew to New York right away, and my assistant does an imitation for me about Michael's fainting, and it's like a swan dive. Then Sandy Gallin, his manager, calls me and says, "Michael is in the hospital, and he can't do the show. He's too sick." So he pulled out.

I believe that once he found out he couldn't have the pyrotechnics, he freaked out, got himself sick, and didn't want to do the show.

DAVE BALDWIN:

Our Garth Brooks concert is a fish-out-of-water story. I told Nancy Geller, "Garth Brooks is the number one ticket seller in music today. He's selling more than rock acts. We have to get him."

But management had no clue who Garth Brooks was. They were all Northeast Ivy Leaguers. So I directed the research department to put together a bunch of charts about the value of Garth Brooks, the number of tickets he had been selling, and all the locations. They finally relented and let Nancy spend the money. Marty Callner was directing, and he had done marvelous things like resuscitating the career of Aerosmith, and great shows with Tina Turner, and the Rolling Stones from the Garden.

There was still a lot of skepticism about viewership. I said, "It's going to be one of our highest-rated music shows in the last ten years. It's going to do a 15.2 rating." I pulled that number out of my ass, and they didn't believe me. When the numbers came out that Tuesday, it was a 15.

NANCY GELLER:

In October 1997, we did *Classic Whitney: Live from Washington, DC*, Whitney Houston's third HBO concert. Marty Callner directed again, and we were both on an incredible high from the success of the Garth Brooks concert just the month before.

We did a backup show with Whitney the night before the live show and I had it taped just in case. Whitney was a little rocky, but it was a good show, and I wanted to do the show live. Marty kept saying, "She can't do it. She can't do it." I told him, "If the doctor tells me she's not well, we'll use the tape." So Marty tracks down the doctor, walks him over to me at the Four

Seasons bar, and the doctor says, "Whitney's in perfect shape." That was all I needed to hear. Live is always more exciting.

The next night I'm in the truck, and Jeff Bewkes enters and stands right behind me just before Whitney is about to come onstage. As soon as she comes out, I can tell she's not right. She starts repeating herself, is not singing well, and falling all over herself. It was heart-wrenching. Her mother even asks her, "What's wrong with you?" Marty is going off the deep end because she's so out of it. Then Chris Albrecht calls me and says, "Nancy, what the hell is going on? When she started this song, I went out and got ice cream. I just came back, and she's still singing it."

It was a big mistake on my part. I should have aired the show we had on tape, but I couldn't imagine it could be as bad as it was. First call I got after the concert was from Brad Grey, a friend. He goes, "What the fuck was that?" We went from the high of Garth to now being in the toilet.

While HBO's Specials programming division continued where it left off under Fuchs, its marketing division sought a new angle under new leadership.

ERIC KESSLER:

I had been at HBO Home Video since I started in 1986, and in the beginning of 1995, Michael and Jeff asked me to come run marketing. About two months into my tenure, Michael lost his job, and Jeff, as the new CEO, wanted to put his imprint on the network with, among other initiatives, a new ad campaign.

JOHN BILLOCK:

I was sitting in a hotel lobby waiting for someone, grabbed a napkin, and started making some notes. The premise was we at HBO do not make television. Consumers should not come to us to watch television. That's not who we are. Instead, we do things, make things, and say things that no other television network can do. We have the editorial license to do that, and therefore we can attract members of the creative community to HBO who want to tell compelling, unbridled stories in episodic and long-form formats that they couldn't do elsewhere. I wrote it up as a memo and sent it to Jerry Levin, and he wrote me back a note saying, "Wow, you've encapsulated something special here."

Then I sent the same memo to BBDO—Phil Dusenberry, Charlie Miesmer, Michael Patti, and the rest of the creative team that was running our business at the time. They encapsulated it in the phrase, "It's Not TV. It's HBO." I believe Michael was the guy who actually came up with the line.

I loved it right away. I thought it was exactly what we needed to stand for as a brand, and I liked that it was such a strange way to market a television channel—by saying it's not TV.

ERIC KESSLER:

What we loved about "It's Not TV. It's HBO" was that it was simple, memorable, differentiated the network, and, most importantly, implied superiority.

JOHN BILLOCK:

When we took it to our core group of senior managers, the response was certainly not uniform. A lot of people didn't get it. It was too jarring, too confusing. It was a heretical way to try to sell television by saying we're not television. I had to do a Kabuki dance to explain it to some executives.

"It's Not TV. It's HBO" became much more than just a tagline—it became HBO's north star, the guiding principle it used in every area of its business. Any area that was consumer-facing—even technology—was evaluated through the prism of that tagline. If a series felt like it was something you could see on broadcast or a basic cable network, HBO wouldn't do it, or they would execute it in a way the others could not. If a print ad looked like it would come from a network, HBO would figure out how to do it differently.

ERIC KESSLER:

The real epiphany we had was when we decided we would not demonstrate what "It's Not TV. It's HBO" represented by showing clips or talking about the shows. The way we were going to represent this was by creating a sixty-second piece of entertainment that was so out there, so irreverent and different from everything else you saw on TV.

The best execution of the campaign was the chimps commercial. The spot starts with lush jungle footage and "The Gombe Preserve" on-screen. We see chimps swinging from the trees and on the ground, while famous primatologist Jane Goodall watches over them. As she would later write in her journal, Goodall discusses the chimps' endemic behavior. Suddenly, the apes begin "repeating" (via lip-synch) famous lines from Hollywood movies. The camera pulls back, and the chimps being observed by Goodall are also observing her, looking through her window, watching HBO alongside her.
During October 1996, the spot started running, but a backlash quickly followed when reporters found out that Goodall did not actually watch HBO and, contrary to the ad's tagline, was not an "HBO viewer since 1978." Nor, in fact, was the voice on the

soundtrack actually Goodall's. Nonetheless, "Chimps" was part of a historic lineup of Emmy nominations.

JEFF BEWKES:

They wanted a noticeable line to start with, and I said, "No, no, we have to use an obscure line." So when you watch the spot, the chimp looks up, nobody knows the chimp is about to talk, and the first thing he says is "Tattaglia's a pimp. He could never have outfought Santino." Now just stop right there. A commercial where the opening line is "Tattaglia's a pimp"? That's never been on TV before.

ERIC KESSLER:

This was in the day when a television campaign could actually become part of the cultural zeitgeist and our campaign did just that. The "Chimps" spot went on to win the very first Emmy award ever given for a commercial.

That year, HBO totaled more Emmy nominations than any of the broadcast networks, the first time that a cable network had led the pack. The news signaled a shift in the balance of prestige among TV content providers. HBO's total of ninety nominations ranked just a hair higher than NBC's eighty-nine nominations and nearly doubled ABC's total of forty-seven. From that point on, winning Emmys would be part of HBO's marketing strategy; the goal was for viewers to feel "left out" if they didn't subscribe.

For as long as Fuchs had run HBO, he was more deeply involved in programming than in any other part of the company. Potter, Albrecht, Cooper, Callender, and many others inside HBO, along with producers, agencies, and others on the outside—everyone knew that when Fuchs spoke, no one was going to pop up and contradict him, much less overrule him. Now, a big chair was empty, something Bewkes would have to work out among Albrecht, Cooper, Callender, and others.

SHEILA NEVINS:

I grew up with nothing, so I felt very privileged to have a job. Every time somebody got fired, I'd get more money. I knew they couldn't afford to lose me. It was wily. I think I learned it from the hookers. I'd go into the office and say, "Now that so and so's gone, I don't know if there's a place for me here. I think I need more money or I'm going to have to go elsewhere."

JEFF BEWKES:

I was viewing personnel decisions not in terms of loyalty to me but to the company. So I kept Seth, Richard, and Steve Scheffer, all strong Michael loyalists, and the last one was Bob Cooper, who was out in LA. Cooper was quite smart and could be extremely charming, but he was never transparent with me. He actually thought he was fooling me all the time, which I encouraged. I let people behave as their real selves. That's how I found out what they were going to do when I wasn't around. Even though I felt I couldn't trust him, I decided to give Cooper full support. I told him, "Bob, if you can stick to movies, this can work out great."

In 1991, meanwhile, Johnny Carson had delivered a gargantuan announcement to NBC, a momentous game changer: he would retire as star of **The Tonight Show** *in May of the following year. And so it came to pass, that on May 22, 1992, following the previous night's penultimate episode—which had included a madcap appearance by Robin Williams and a performance-for-the-ages by Bette Midler—Johnny Carson sat on an unpretentious stool and bade America goodbye, noting sardonically that his biggest thrill was having once been chosen by General Electric, then owner of NBC, as "Employee of the Month."*

Johnny's retirement sent NBC and the entire late-night ecosystem into a whirlwind of panic, plotting, and pleading, featuring Jay Leno versus David Letterman, and with determined supporting cast members Michael Ovitz, Helen Kushnick (Leno's agent), Howard Stringer, then head of CBS, and NBC boss Warren Littlefield.

New York Times *reporter Bill Carter chronicled all the maneuvering over Johnny's seat at the desk in a book called* **The Late Shift***, published in 1994. Fred Silverman, former president of NBC who often shared ideas with close friend Bob Cooper, thought it might make a good movie—a TV movie no less.*

BOB COOPER:

When I read the book, I thought, this is odd, but said to Hutch Parker, "Why don't we option it, and see what happens." He started to walk away, and then stopped and asked, "What are we optioning? What is this about?" I just blurted out, "It's about gossip."

BILL CARTER, Journalist:

They hired Ivan Reitman from *Ghostbusters* to be the executive producer, and he went out and hired George Armitage, who made *Miami Blues*.

I had written the book in nine months, and it took him like eight months to do the script. I don't get it; just use the material in the book. Hutch calls and says the script is coming in, and I told my wife before I read it, "I'm going to have to say it's good no matter what so the movie will get made and they will have to pay me the rights fee." I start to read, and in an early scene, he had both Dave and Jay getting drunk. I was like, "Whoa, you can't do this. Neither of these guys drink." So I was worried. I finished reading the script and thought it missed completely. I was stunned. It was a weekend and I thought, "How am I going to say this is good on Monday when I don't believe it?" So I sat down and thought maybe I can fix a scene or two. I'd never written a script, but knew you had to have dialogue in the middle of the page, and by the time the weekend ended, I had done forty pages.

Hutch calls me on Monday, and asks, "What did you think," and I said, "I don't think it's usable." He said, "That's our feeling too." I said, "What happens now?," and he told me, "We don't know. Guess we have to ask Ivan." I was afraid it was all going to blow up, so I said, "I don't know if this is of any use to you, but I did a little bit of work on it." He told me to send it to him, and called the next day to say, "This is exactly what we want. You have to write this." Michael Fuchs, who was running HBO at the time, sent me a note that said, "I always tell people who try to write scripts they should stick to their day jobs. But not you."

I went to my editors at the *Times* to ask permission, and they said, "Okay, we'll carve out an exception where you won't write about HBO while the movie is in progress and production." I went to LA, worked with Ivan on various drafts, then spent time with Betty Thomas, who was directing, and she showed me a bunch of auditions.

They had Carson being played by Rich Little, which was sort of weird. Bob Balaban was perfect for Warren Littlefield, and of course Kathy Bates was fantastic. I was not aware of John Michael Higgins or Daniel Roebuck, but liked them both a lot.

QUENTIN SCHAFFER:

John Michael Higgins, who did a brilliant job playing Letterman, wanted to please Letterman, but we heard Letterman was upset and insulted by the project.

His executive producer Robert Morton said we want John Michael Higgins as a guest. I said, "If you're sure, we'll get him up there." John Michael Higgins kept saying, "I don't feel good about this. I think he's going to be mean to me." They announce, "John Michael Higgins." We were in the green room and Higgins had like eight of his family members in the audience. The opening night guest was Julia Roberts. Then Letterman goes to a break and instead of mentioning Higgins, he says, "We'll be back with Julia Roberts."

Letterman wound up keeping Julia on until there was no time left. I think Letterman all along wanted to give Higgins a slap in the face. It was a nasty thing to do. Afterward, Higgins was really devastated, and I felt bad because they'd given me their word this was legitimate.

DAVID LETTERMAN:

I have examined this to the best of my ability, and while I know he was supposed to be on the show, I did not remember that. I talked to Julia Roberts until it was impossible for him to appear. There was no premeditation. However, people around me who I trust tell me that's exactly what happened. So under the threat of penalty of law, I'm going to have to say, yes, I'm guilty.

Subsequent to that, I found out who the guy was and realized he is a very funny, talented kid and appeared in many things that I found him to be completely amusing. Any ill feelings I may have had about that project had nothing to do with him. I was concerned as to being made to look like a loser; my real concern was with the production itself.

I've asked people, "Did the guy ever come back?" They said, "No," but in my head I thought maybe he had come back. Then I was told that Bob Morton had gone to the kid and counseled him. "Don't worry. This happens all the time. You're coming back." And I thought, Wow, that was Morty really being a great producer in lying to the kid.

It's one of many things that I was reminded of that I had long since pushed from my memory. But I apologize to the kid. I think he's done just fine without the appearance. On the other hand, I'm sure talking to Julia Roberts was more fun than I was going to have talking to him. I can't be sure about that, but we'll never know. As I go through my life after the show, I'm reminded of episodes that had long been erased. Some good, some like this, and I'm embarrassed by this behavior. And if you talk to the kid, please extend my apologies.

JOHN TURTURRO, Actor:

I did *Sugartime* with Mary-Louise Parker for Bob Cooper at HBO. We had a lot of fights. He was a control freak. They kept threatening to sue us if we made more changes, so I kept telling Bob Cooper to fire me. He would say, "No, I love what you're doing." It was a whole battle royale. But I think we turned it into something interesting. It was much more idiosyncratic and personal than what was originally written.

STANLEY TUCCI, Actor:

I had the best time on *Winchell*. I was really flattered they offered me that role, and it was thrilling for me. I loved that period. If you want to talk about a complex character, my God. He was a horrible person, but what was fascinating about him was he's one of the reasons we have some of celebrity stuff and obsessions we have today.

HBO was doing this material that nobody had done before on television. It completely changed the landscape of Hollywood and cinema because they were making movies that studios and independents wouldn't make, with great scripts, and making them really well. They didn't have to cast the biggest star in the world. They could cast me in it, and they'd get good people to shoot it.

You were paid really well, and they weren't micromanaging. It caused the studios to rethink what they were doing and how they were doing it, and created so many opportunities for actors, directors, writers, directors of photography, everybody.

I was never pigeonholed, but once you were on a TV show, you were a TV guy, and that was it. HBO completely changed all that. Suddenly you had people who had been on Broadway, people who had been in TV shows, people who were movie stars or not movie stars starring or playing secondary, tertiary roles in these wonderful films. It completely changed everything.

JEFF BEWKES:

Everyone knew that Bob Cooper and Colin Callender who worked for him out of New York didn't get along. In early 1996, I expanded HBO Showcase, gave it a new name, HBO NYC Productions, and made sure their mandate was clearly different than HBO Pictures, so the two wouldn't clash on material.

COLIN CALLENDER:

The creation of HBO NYC grew out of a conversation I had with Jeff and was an acknowledgment that the more contained character dramas being produced under the HBO Showcase banner—many of which were based on plays—could evolve into a slate of lower-budgeted movies that could tackle riskier subjects to complement the mainstream movies being produced on the West Coast.

Sheila Nevins, Ross Greenburg, and myself were able to curate our own divisions. We were empowered to take risks, and each one of us reported one person away from the chairman of the company. That meant that when we were talking to producers, directors, writers, or talent, they knew they were talking to somebody who was empowered to make decisions. That was a big distinguishing characteristic between ourselves at HBO then and the networks or the studios.

HBO as a company was working across a complete range of genres. It was Fuchs's motto, "Something for everybody, some of the time." This is in contrast with the networks that had to live by "Something for everybody, all of the time."

KERI PUTNAM:

The spirit of HBO NYC was risk taking in terms of content, form, and talent, and helped differentiate HBO's two film divisions. HBO NYC was the smaller cousin—in terms of budgets at least—to HBO Pictures. We worked on anthologies like Jonathan Demme's *Subway Stories* or Forest Whitaker's directing debut, *Strapped*, about the impact of gun violence on the Black community, or a beautiful small film written by Will Scheffer and Mark Olsen (later the creators of HBO's *Big Love*), starring Glenn Close, and directed by Christopher Reeve called *In the Gloaming*. In terms of HBO Pictures during those years—they were making glossier, more commercial titles like *Don King* or *Gia* or *Breast Men* along with a consistent stream of ratings-generating genre films.

BOB COOPER:

When Colin told me about *If These Walls Could Talk*, I asked him, "Why aren't we making this?" And he said, "It's not ready." I told him, "You've got Demi Moore, a big idea, and the scripts are pretty good. You know how the script will get better? Green-light it. Then you'll get it ready." What I tried to do with Colin was to free him to get the project made, and to apply Michael's lesson to me: Have no fear.

HBO NYC's second production, which debuted on October 13, 1996, was an unmitigated triumph, artistically and commercially. With **If These Walls Could Talk,** *HBO stepped boldly onto the "third rail" of American culture—abortion—by tracking the fates of three women who'd undergone that most controversial of operations. The film is broken into three sections, set twenty-two years apart. The first, in 1952, was directed by Nancy Savoca and the singer Cher (who co-starred). The ninety-seven-minute film also starred heavy hitters Demi Moore, Sissy Spacek, Jada Pinkett, and Shirley Knight and was nominated for numerous Emmys and Golden Globes. It was a film that HBO executives from several different eras would point to with pride.*

DEMI MOORE, Actor and Executive Producer:

The name *If These Walls Could Talk* came from the idea that if you could peel back the wallpaper and the paint, what would be the stories that would be told. We wanted to be able to frame the piece around not abortion but an unwanted pregnancy, and do it through different time periods and what the challenges were, for each. For me, this was just the most honest and authentic way of being able to share what a woman's experience had been. HBO had the platform that allowed us to be able to do it without the restrictions of network television, and Colin Callender first and foremost had the courage to give us the room to make this in the way that we wanted.

KERI PUTNAM:

If These Walls Could Talk was one of my favorite professional experiences. I was pregnant during a lot of its production, and since we shot in Los Angeles, I was able to travel to the set or editing room with my son, Eli, who had been born less than two years earlier. I didn't have a lot of role models inside the company at that time who had little kids, but the incredible producer Suzanne Todd created a set shaped by a community of strong women. It felt like something new to be telling these emotional—and controversial—stories about abortion rights with women running all aspects of the show. Sadly, this is still too rare today, but back then it was unheard of.

The definition of HBO was we do what the networks don't do. And what that meant to a lot of people is the networks program for women, especially the movies on networks at that time. So there was this belief, maybe not explicit but certainly sort of tacit, that skewing toward women was too net-worky for us. *If These Walls Could Talk* was a case study to see whether that was true. If you look back at HBO history, there weren't a lot of women-oriented things before that. We did one called *Prison Stories* a couple of years before, but I think that only got done because it was women in prison, which is a trope that men like, even though it was about something else. We were able to get *If These Walls Could Talk* because of women like Demi, Sissy, Cher, and directors like Nancy Savoca.

DEMI MOORE:

I realize, considering the times that we're living in, just how much *These Walls* holds up. One of the things that was so powerful, and humanized it, was it really brought you inside what it is like when a woman is walking through this. It's not black-and-white, it's not easy. And even in the best circumstances, no one is pro having to make the choice of ending a pregnancy. A woman's right to choose for me became so obvious as the most important thing that we needed to protect.

I was personally still struggling to find my own value. It's easier for me now in hindsight to realize I was using the platform that I had as an opportunity to do something of substance that was for the greater good.

As a mother of daughters, this really had a great importance for me; I was looking to pave the way of protecting their rights.

KERI PUTNAM:

My daughter Lucy was born on October 2, and the film premiered a week later. I was home on maternity leave and got a call from Jeff Bewkes telling me it was the highest-rated thing we've ever done. I felt like it had opened up something new for women on HBO. It felt like a watershed moment.

COLIN CALLENDER:

When we did *If These Walls Could Talk*, the ratings amongst women were remarkable. *Sex and the City* was one of the things that in part grew out of that success.

DEMI MOORE:

I never realized the impact that it had on HBO and intellectually on the culture until quite recently. It was a real feat to do something where you had what we see more of now, which is the quality of production in these little mini films. It was a real breakout, too, for me. You didn't see someone like myself or Sissy Spacek or Cher doing something for television. And I think this opened up other possibilities, like the incredible work that Sarah Jessica did.

The film was considered such a hit that HBO did something all but unheard of for its film units: produced a sequel. **If These Walls Could Talk 2** *premiered on March 5, 2000, holding on to the form of three mini-films set in separate eras, focusing this time on lesbian relationships. Vanessa Redgrave took home both an Emmy and a Golden Globe for her supporting role in the "1961" segment.*

JANE ANDERSON:

I was the local gay writer-director, so it was a no-brainer for them to bring me in, because all the writer-directors were gay women and there weren't a lot of us around at that time. I asked to have dibs on the 1961 section because I wanted to do a piece about an older woman losing the love of her life and being allowed to properly mourn because they were "only friends."

Of all the studios I've ever worked with, HBO consistently has the best creative team. Kary Antholis, Keri Putnam, Colin [Callender], and Bob

Cooper all care deeply about the storytelling. Their notes were never studio-like. A lot of studio executives don't have a dramaturgical background and have no idea how to give a workable note. But HBO has always had these people with exquisite taste and incredible smarts, and that's why I always considered it my number one creative home.

REGINA KING, Actor:

It was one of the first times in my career where I was offered something. There was this feeling that I have arrived. Although it was a small part, it was such a great idea, and I was in great company. It was a prestige piece that was speaking to a culture. And it was HBO.

COLIN CALLENDER:

What was significant about *If These Walls Could Talk* is we discovered there was this massive audience for women who were actually looking for programming that was different from what the networks were making. They wanted programming that was authentic and explored women's experiences in honest and candid ways that the average movie-of-the-week on the broadcast networks weren't doing at the time.

After *If These Walls Could Talk*, *Miss Evers' Boys* was directed by the wonderful Joseph Sargent. It was a movie about the Tuskegee experiment in which Black men in the South were given faux drugs for syphilis. It's a story of enormous contemporary resonance because the Tuskegee experiment resulted in enormous suspicion within the Black community about the medical world.

I think the way we addressed African American stories early on at HBO, which resulted in a massive growth of an African American audience on HBO, was one of the distinguishing characteristics of that early work that we did.

Subway Stories produced by Jonathan Demme and Rosie Perez was an anthology film that was set within New York's diverse landscape, and then there was Charles Dutton's directorial debut, *First Time Felon*, about young Black prisoners helping save local villagers from the Mississippi floods. These were award-winning examples of HBO NYC at its best.

Another was *In the Gloaming*, which told the heartbreaking story of a young gay man dying of AIDS who returns home to spend his last days with his unaccepting family. The film starred Glenn Close, Robert Sean Leonard, and Whoopi Goldberg and was directed by Christopher Reeve, not long after the riding accident that left him paralyzed from the neck down. Chris was passionate about directing the film and we felt we were the only place he would be able to direct it. We constructed a dedicated room for him on the set that enabled him to direct from his motorized wheelchair and respirator.

WILL SCHEFFER, Screenwriter and Creator:

That was my first screenplay, my first break in shifting from a playwright into Hollywood. So it was an amazing experience. Colin said this to me. He said, We didn't want to be the smartest people in the room. We wanted our creators to be the smartest people, and we wanted that to shine. And I think that's sort of been a constant. They may have not always been a perfect union at doing that, but that's been the cultural constant, that was the raison d'être for being there.

COLIN CALLENDER:

Always Outnumbered, Always Outgunned was based on the book by the same title by the Black novelist Walter Mosley. It starred Laurence Fishburne and was directed by Michael Apted. It was the story of an ex-con who pushed around a supermarket cart full of bottles. And it was the story of this character trying to sort of rebuild his life. I always said that what was important about that story, here we were putting center stage a character who would normally be in the background of most shots in any other movie. It was about the African American experience. It was about everyday folk who never, ever get talked about or seen in center stage. And so to me, that was a very important movie.

JEFF BEWKES:

Amistad was a frustrating yet important movie we had to deal with. After Michael left, one of the trades had written that an "accountant"—me—had taken over. The *Sanders* show was drawing to a close, and *Oz* was still in development, so we were desperate to air something that would grab attention and prove there was life after Michael. Bob Cooper told me he was working on an important film and strong Emmy possibility called *Amistad*, which was the story of a slave ship.

Then I got a call from Jeffrey Katzenberg at DreamWorks and he told me, "Steven Spielberg has had a huge success with *Schindler's List* and wants to do *Amistad*, but because he has to do *Jurassic Park*, he's behind you. If you put your *Amistad* on cable, he probably won't be able to do it for theaters. So we'd like you to stand down."

And all I could think was, "Fuck, we've got nothing, and this is our shot at staying in the game." But I felt badly. I said, "If Steven thinks he can do for civil rights with *Amistad* what he did for anti-Semitism with *Schindler's List*, we should hold back with our modest megaphone." I didn't know Spielberg then but I got a call from him, and he told me, "This really means a lot to me, and I won't forget it."

A couple of years went by and we were doing *Band of Brothers* with Tom Hanks, and I get another call from Katzenberg. This time he tells me, "If Steven is going to be involved, you'll pay the money to make it, but we are going to need to own it." I said, "Well, this is a big problem. We can't afford to spend $140 million and just put it on the air a few times. We need to own it. Otherwise, we are fucked." Then I got a call from Steven, and I will never forget this call. He said, "I remember how you helped us on *Amistad*, and now I can thank you. You go ahead." It was an incredible move on his part.

Bewkes had kept Abraham, Billock, Nevins, Plepler, and Scheffer on board after the Fuchs departure. The last senior executive to decipher was Bob Cooper, with whom Bewkes had always had a tricky relationship.

BOB COOPER:

My departure had nothing to do with Jeff. He always thought it was about him.

JEFF BEWKES:

After Michael was fired, Bob and I had lunch. I said, "Bob, your contract is all set, but you haven't signed it. Are you having a Hamlet moment?" He told me, "I've been offered the job of running TriStar. What do you think?" I said, "Bob, what do you want to do?" And he says, "I would like to stay but only if that includes running all of original programming." I told him, "Well, that isn't what we organized, Bob, but you don't have to sign." He told me he would decide soon, but I had already heard about his TriStar offer and knew he was going to leave.

BOB COOPER:

When Michael went back on his word and didn't give me the job, I decided I was going to quietly look around. It's true, I didn't want to sign the contract.

Cooper was replaced by John Matoian, who would stay at HBO for only three years, although that was time enough to oversee the production of another big hit for the network—a memorable blockbuster that would launch a career to remember.

ANGELINA JOLIE, Actor:

I didn't want the role. I felt close to her in some emotional ways and I didn't want to explore it.

Indeed, **Gia** *was a sensation. No sooner had inherently glamorous Gia Carangi (Angelina Jolie) arrived in New York City—dreams of becoming a fashion model aglow in her head—than she was taken under the ample wing of equally glamorous, if less youthful, Wilhelmina Cooper (Faye Dunaway), a smart and savvy agent.*

ILENE KAHN POWER:

I was at HBO all through the 1980s, then left to become a producer on *Stalin*. After that I had a producing deal there, and I sold Bob Cooper a pitch about the dark side of modeling. Originally, they wanted a big star for the lead role of Gia. I pushed for Angelina based on her stunning debut performance in the 1995 film *Hackers*. She was hesitant to audition, but ultimately was the only one who could bring Gia to life. She later told me how close she felt to the character. Angelina's acting was a stunning star-making performance; the reception she received was huge and established her as a rising star.

ANGELINA JOLIE:

I loved the director Michael [Cristofer] when I met him. He asked that I read it to help him with the project. I didn't know I was screen testing until I heard I got it. I didn't say yes right away. It was Michael who convinced me.

What I found moving about Gia is that she had what people value—what they shouldn't value but do: her looks and her youth. But she didn't feel she was understood or loved. Certainly not loved for who she really was.

I was struck by the experience of the hospital scenes and how people who had HIV/AIDS were treated during those early years. She must have been so frightened.

Honestly, it never felt as if it was part of a career or a film; it was an experience that helped me to better understand myself as a human being and how to communicate with like-minded people.

What meant most was speaking to young people who related to her. It helped me to feel less alone, and I hoped I had done right by her. I remember thinking that if she knew she could be understood in such a way, her life would have been very different, with a lot less pain.

ILENE KAHN POWER:

I had breakfast with Angelina the day after the big HBO party. She was just blown away by the huge response to her. We got great reviews and were nominated and won multiple Golden Globes and an Emmy. The movie still plays all over the world and young women have reached out to me over the years to tell me what the movie has meant to them.

Sheila Nevins's determination to make HBO's documentary division the best of its kind was all consuming. Her work ethic was obsessive, her appetites voracious, her competitive zeal unyielding. In the mid-1990s, no one was spending the money Nevins spent on documentaries, and no one could point to as many hours of productive output. Nevins was everywhere.

CHRIS ALBRECHT:

What am I gonna tell Sheila about a documentary? It didn't do me any good to have a turf war with Sheila. So when I became the head of programming, Sheila said, "I don't want to report to you." I said, "I want you to do more. I want you to branch us out. We've got to work together."

The Celluloid Closet, *a 1995 documentary directed by Rob Epstein and Jeffrey Friedman, explored the oft-veiled legacy of homosexuality in film. Based on the 1981 book by Vito Russo, the documentary walks viewers through the history of cinema through a gay viewpoint, citing the homosexual subtext of classic films and lacing clips of those movies with interviews featuring the actors who had brought them to life. Earning a three-and-a-half-star review from Roger Ebert,* **Closet** *was nominated for five Emmy Awards, including the President's Award. It also won a Peabody and the 1996 Freedom of Expression Award at the Sundance Film Festival, where it was concurrently nominated for the Grand Jury Prize.*

SHEILA NEVINS:

The Celluloid Closet was really the beginning of Kickstarter in the sense that it started from people sending in small bits of money.

ROB EPSTEIN:

Initially, we did a huge community fundraising effort and direct mail campaign with a letter signed by Lily Tomlin who was good friends with Vito. But at a certain point, we felt like we were just hitting a wall.

HOWARD ROSENMAN:

I made a list of all the people that I knew who ran studios, and I started with Sid Sheinberg at Universal. I said, "Sid, I made a movie called *Common Threads*. It won an Oscar. All my friends are dying. We're making this movie about the subtext of gay and lesbian images in film. I need you to give me the clips for nothing, because this is going to go to charity." And Sid said, "Okay." Then I went to Barry Diller, who was running Fox. I said, "Barry, Sid Sheinberg just gave me all the clips, and I need all the Fox clips from you for nothing." And he says, "Okay." Within half an hour, I got $3.5 million worth of clips. We then put them together like a sizzle cut, and Lily Tomlin agreed to narrate it.

ROB EPSTEIN:

We flew to LA to meet with Lily, and said, "We don't know what to do," and she said, "Why don't we call Michael Fuchs?" He had us go to Sheila first and she said something like, "You're going to need papal dispensation, so we might as well go right to the Pope." The night before the meeting with Michael Fuchs, Lily, Jeffrey, Howard, and I had dinner to rehearse the pitch.

HOWARD ROSENMAN:

We said to Michael, "We'd like to give you a presentation." He said, "I know all about it. It's a film about gay and lesbian images in film. Can you get those clips?" I said, "I've already got them."

JEFFREY FRIEDMAN:

Then he said, "How much do you need?" And Sheila told him.

HOWARD ROSENMAN:

"Can we start our presentation?" And Michael said, "Howard, take yes for an answer. Get the fuck out of my office."

JEFFREY FRIEDMAN:

Then we all walked out with HBO jackets and a green light.

ROB EPSTEIN:

The Celluloid Closet premiered at Toronto and Sony picked it up, but HBO insisted on having the premiere, and then there was a theatrical window, and then it was back on HBO. It was a brave new world with that model.

*Even though she'd been the one who brought the **Celluloid Closet** producing team in to meet Fuchs, Sheila Nevins enjoyed incredible freedom within HBO. If she saw someone whose work she liked, even if it was being produced elsewhere, she would find a way to bring them over to Nevins World at HBO.*

JOE BERLINGER:

Having a film on HBO was the Holy Grail.

SHEILA NEVINS:

I saw a tiny article in the paper about three teens in Arkansas who had been arrested for being devil worshippers and killing three little boys. It was a horror. I remembered my friend Nola, long dead sadly, had done a piece on *20/20* about exorcism in the Catholic Church and it was one of the highest-rated *20/20* pieces. I thought, "Oh devil worshipper, oh goody." I called up Joe Berlinger that night and said, "There are these devil worshippers down in Arkansas. You've got to go down there. Please go and tell me what the story is." Joe and Bruce Sinofsky went down the next day.

On June 3, 1993, three teenagers, Jessie Misskelley Jr., Damien Echols, and Jason Baldwin, were arrested for the murders and mutilations of three eight-year-old boys in West Memphis, Arkansas, setting off a chain of ordeals, trials, and appeals that would drag on for more than seventeen years.

The victims—Steve Branch, Michael Moore, and Christopher Byers—went missing in the early evening of May 5, 1993, and their bodies were found the next afternoon in a drainage ditch in Robin Hood Hills, west of downtown Memphis.

JOE BERLINGER:

My filmmaking partner Bruce Sinofsky and I gambled a dozen credit cards, second mortgages on homes, literally everything to make our first film, *Brother's Keeper*. It got invited to Sundance and won the audience prize. Sheila reached out to say how much she loved our film.

Then in early June 1993, she sent me an article from the *New York Times* about how Damien Echols, Jason Baldwin, and Jesse Misskelley had just been arrested a week before for these horrible devil-worshipping murders of three eight-year-old boys in an alleged satanic ritual. The prosecution claimed that on a scale of 1 to 10, the evidence was an 11—an open-and-shut case. A confession was leaked to the press and printed in the local newspaper. We didn't know it at the time, but what was printed was the result of multiple conversations and multiple sessions of leading a witness with multiple statements in which a classic false confession is obtained from a person with limited intelligence, who agrees to certain statements. But no one knew this when the confession was printed in the newspaper months before the trial. So the jury pool was prejudiced, and everyone down there, including us, thought these guys were definitely guilty.

We went down to Arkansas, thinking we were making a kids-killing-kids satanic-ritual murder film. There was a lot of satanic panic in the late 1980s and early 1990s and a since-debunked belief that Satanic cults were rampant, abducting and killing children around the country.

We spent the first couple of months in Arkansas, embedded in the community, assuming the teens were guilty. The trials were still seven months away. It takes a lot of faith for a programmer to green-light something like this; you don't know where it's going, you can't give them an exact budget; you can't control reality; and you can't assume things are all going to work out from a storytelling standpoint.

Our style of filmmaking is to show both sides and then let the viewer make up their own mind about what they're seeing. That's classic cinema verité. But five months into filming, we finally had been granted access to the three defendants, who were in prison awaiting the trial. I was interviewing Jason Baldwin, who was Damien's sidekick and best friend. He was a little shy, but he was very convincing when he was protesting his innocence. It's not like a lightbulb went off and I said, "Oh my God, they're innocent," but something didn't seem right. As I was interviewing Jason, who struck me as sweet and shy, I remember looking at his very thin wrists, imagining him wielding a ten-inch serrated hunting knife, which the prosecution alleged was used to castrate one of the eight-year-olds. I just had this feeling that this kid couldn't have done what the prosecution was alleging.

Damien Echols was a little harder to read because he was a surly, gothy kid who was probably his own worst enemy because he seemed to be enjoying the attention he was getting as a murder suspect. Then after interviewing Jesse Misskelley and witnessing his very low IQ and malleable personality, the idea that Jesse was manipulated to give a false confession seemed very plausible.

I called up Sheila with great trepidation because I needed to be honest with her about what I was feeling. She had only given us enough money to film for a few months and to see what was happening. I'm thinking to myself, Sheila has highbrow taste, but she also likes salacious material that drives ratings. I half expected her to say, "Pack your bags and come home. It's not the film I was looking for."

SHEILA NEVINS:

Joe and Bruce called and I asked, "Is there a story there?" They said, "We don't know." I said, "Stay. I'll pay you. There's something there. Either they're falsely accused or they're truly Wiccans," which is a peaceful devil worshipper. I was very proud of myself for not telling them to come home. They stayed and it turned out to be *Paradise Lost*.

JOE BERLINGER:

Sheila giving us her blessing to keep going was the turning point. There were a number of scary moments making that first *Paradise Lost* film. We got several death threats telling us to leave town. Twice we were followed ominously by cars. I am not a gun person, but we had to have guns. I slept with a pistol under my pillow. Bruce had a shotgun, which we hoped we would never have to use.

On another occasion, we had been filming John Mark and Melissa Byers, the parents of one of the murdered little boys, Christopher Byers. It was Christmas Eve day, and we were shooting a haunting scene of them placing an artificial Christmas tree on their son's grave. After the shoot, we went to their house and sat in the kitchen eating leftovers. The cameraman was cold and tired from the shoot. So while we made small talk in the kitchen, the cameraman excused himself and he asked, Do you mind if I go lie down on your couch? And so we said, Sure, no problem. So we stayed in the kitchen to continue talking with Mark and Melissa and our DP went to lie down on the living room couch.

About fifteen minutes later Mark got up from the kitchen table where we were sitting and said he would be right back. At that point, we later learned, he went into his bedroom and got a folding Kershaw brand serrated hunting knife. He rubbed the cameraman's arm and woke him and whispered to him that this was a "gift for him" and to "not tell Joe or Bruce" and to "think of me when you use it . . . one day it may save your life." The cameraman was weirded out by the interaction but thanked Mark and took the knife, put it in his pocket, and went back to sleep until it was time to go. Once we got into the car to go back to the hotel, he told us about the strange way in which he was awakened and handed the knife. When we got back to the hotel, we opened up the knife because it was a folding knife. To our astonishment, there was visible blood on the folding hinge of the knife.

This is a few weeks before the trials were set to begin and we've been doubting that the three teens were actually guilty, and some had raised the possibility of Mark Byers's involvement in the killings. And here we had a serrated folding hunting knife with blood on the hinge, visible blood on the hinge that Mark had given the cameraman. Statistically, most child homicides involve a parent or a guardian and Mark's son had stab wounds and had been castrated with a serrated hunting knife and here our cameraman had been given a serrated hunting knife that had blood on it.

This put us in an extreme moral dilemma. You clearly want a film to effect social change once it comes out, but no filmmaker wants to put himself in the position where you affect events as they're happening.

And here we were possibly in receipt of potential evidence. If we turn this over to the police, is it a violation of the trust that we have with our subjects? What impact will this have on the film? All sorts of moral and philosophical questions swirled around, but we felt like we had a moral and civic responsibility not to just sit on this information. We had to tell HBO about it. I called Sheila and I told her the story. We were told to pack up and come home and meet with HBO to discuss how to handle it. We had a meeting with Sheila as well as an HBO lawyer and Richard Plepler, who was then the head of communications. We quickly made the determination that being a good citizen outweighed whatever impact turning the knife over would have on the film, even it meant shutting down the entire production, because who knows what access we'd be able to get? Who knows whether or not we would be barred from the trial? But we might be in possession of a piece of evidence that could save the wrong people from going to prison, so how could we not turn it over? So we turned the knife over to the authorities. After Mark was questioned about the knife on the stand on the first day of the trial, we had a long talk with him about why we had to turn it over and, miraculously, while it was extremely tense, we ended up getting everyone's blessing to continue the film, including Mark's.

When we finally got to the trial, we experienced the most outrageous modern-day witch hunt loaded with prejudice and stereotypes, with a shocking lack of physical evidence throughout the proceedings. A Stephen King novel and Metallica lyrics were literally introduced into trial as evidence of murder in this very religious part of the world that truly believed in a physical heaven and hell, and that the devil literally runs among us. Damien and Jason were big Metallica fans. The introduction of Metallica lyrics into the trial to me was the ultimate low point. Since when does your musical taste define you as a killer?

Misskelley, tried alone, was convicted of murder and sentenced to life plus forty years; Echols and Baldwin were tried together, and they, too, were convicted of murder: Echols got the death sentence, and Baldwin, life in prison.

JOE BERLINGER:

It took us two years to edit the film. During the edit, we had laid in some Metallica songs into various scenes as temporary tracks to get us in the mood and to create a vibe. Then one day Bruce and I looked at each other and said, We're going to have to replace this, but it's so great. Wouldn't it be amazing if somehow we convince Metallica to give us some music? At the time, Metallica had a policy of never giving any of its music to film or TV projects; even if they did, the cost would have been way beyond our budget.

It turned out the band were huge fans of *Brother's Keeper*, and they said, Send us over the scenes, and we'll talk about it. Within weeks they said, We love it, we want to be a part of it. We'll give you the music and we won't charge you a penny for it. It was like a dream. Other celebrities are given justifiable credit for having been moved by *Paradise Lost* and getting involved in the case, like Johnny Depp, Eddie Vedder, and Natalie Maines, all those people deserve all the credit they are getting, but Metallica were the first ones in with this incredible gift of this music.

The film premiered in January 1996 at Sundance. It was an explosive premiere. The film hit a nerve with audiences and continued to rack up prizes all year. It was a very surreal experience to be getting patted on the back for a piece of well-received filmmaking while Damien Echols remained on death row and the others still were serving life-without-parole sentences. It bothered us that the story of *Paradise Lost* and the West Memphis Three never migrated off of the entertainment pages onto the editorial pages of the media to provoke a change in the case. We felt hollow and guilty that we were being patted on the back and accepting awards for the artistry of the film, but the film hadn't changed a thing in real life. By the time the film had earned the prestigious Peabody Award, Echols and Baldwin and Misskelley had spent three years in their nightmare. That's when the dialogue about follow-up films started. Sheila stuck with the series for almost two decades.

The documentary—which aired on June 10, 1996—won the Primetime Emmy for Outstanding Informational Program and would be followed by **Paradise Lost 2:**

Revelations, *in 2000.* **Paradise Lost 3: Purgatory** *appeared eleven years later and proved to be a crucial part of the movement to free the three defendants (each accepted Alford pleas in 2011 and would be released for time served).*

From the start, there were said to be significant problems with the investigation, including troubling questions about the handling of evidence and the possible coercion of confessions. The case became a cause célèbre—detailed in three separate HBO documentary films, books, songs, and even a feature-length movie, **Devil's Knot,** *starring Reese Witherspoon and Colin Firth.*

SHEILA NEVINS:

There are two kinds of films: those spotted at festivals that become yours by acquisition and those that require the courage of being able to say, Keep going. The gift of HBO was having the ability to tell people to keep going.

These things, when they're good, they tell their own story, but you need money to make light, and then you can fucking stand back and let life take over.

On the morning of Sunday, September 15, 1963, a bomb exploded outside Birmingham, Alabama's 16th Street Baptist Church, less than forty minutes before the eleven a.m. mass was scheduled to begin. Four girls—Addie Mae Collins, Cynthia Wesley, Carole Robertson, and Denise McNair—were killed in the blast, which left more than twenty wounded and one other girl without a right eye. The attack on the church, a "predominantly Black congregation," became a symbol of the rampant racism of the time.

Three decades later, in 1997, Spike Lee directed **4 Little Girls,** *a documentary about the loss of the children on that day in Alabama and the virulence of the racism that resulted in their deaths. Lee relied on archival footage and original interviews with witnesses and public figures to bring audiences back to that fateful day. Nominated for Best Documentary (Features) at the 1998 Academy Awards and for a handful of Emmys, the film received a four-star review from Roger Ebert, who wrote movingly of how the film made him contemplate the lives that the four girls, lost forever, would never lead. Writing for the* **New York Times,** *Janet Maslin called the documentary "a thoughtful, graceful, quietly devastating account" of the bombing and an "immensely dignified and moving reassessment of a terrorist crime."*

SPIKE LEE, Documentarian:

My neighborhood in Brooklyn, Fort Greene, was one of the last neighborhoods in Brooklyn to get cable. So when HBO came out, we got to see movies that just recently played in theaters. That was big-time, big-time.

There was a *New York Times Magazine* cover about four little girls. I wrote Chris McNair a letter saying I would like to do a narrative of his daughter. At that time, I was in film school. He didn't know who the hell I was. After establishing myself as a filmmaker, I was in Birmingham and reached out to Chris again and told them what I wanted to do. I had done some research and knew that if I got Chris and his wife, Maxine, on board, it would be a much easier route getting everybody else on board. I wanted to interview the parents, the relatives, the friends who knew these beautiful young Black girls whose bodies were blown apart by dynamite. That's how it started. I went to Sheila and she said, "Do it."

JACKIE GLOVER, Executive:

We had our first meeting in 1996. The idea of getting to work with Spike Lee was incredible for me. Spike talked about how he had wanted to make this film ever since film school, and how he never forgot the story and knew it was an important one to tell from the family's perspective.

Wanting to be in documentaries was all about being able to tell stories that didn't get told either properly or didn't get told at all. Especially when it came to the African American experience in this country.

SPIKE LEE:

The most bizarre thing was my interview with George Wallace. Oh my God.

It was a classic story of someone who knows they're about to meet their maker. Who's uncertain whether they're going to heaven or hell. He beat what Trump said. George Wallace said all these great things he'd done for Black people, then to prove his point, he asked his Black male nurse to come in front of the camera. You see on the nurse's face that he's horrified. The last thing he wanted to do was be on camera. He stuck his face in then quickly ducked out. It was bizarre.

I was surprised he had agreed to do the interview, but it became clear to me that he wanted to try to reconstruct history. Like, "I'm not the guy that stood in the doorway to stop Vivian Malone from going to University of Alabama. That was some other guy." He was listing the stuff he'd done for Black people in Alabama.

His famous words: segregation now, segregation forever. He said that. That's how he's going to go down the history. Not how he's presented in an interview with me for *4 Little Girls*. I have one of the world's greatest researchers for narrative and documentary films. Her name is Judy Aley. And during postproduction, while we're editing *4 Little Girls*, she discovered the postmortem photographs of the girls. That became one of the hardest decisions I ever had to make. I was tossing and turning and praying on it, should I include these photos or not? Then I made the decision to include the photographs. I understand some people might not understand why, but I chose to include a glimpse of them, because I wanted to show what those sticks of dynamite did to these beautiful young Black girls.

My concern was for the parents and when they saw it, they came up to me and said it was very hard to see their daughters like that, but they understood why I included those horrific photographs.

It was insane that it took a week for J. Edgar Hoover and the FBI to find out who was one of the ringleaders. The motherfucker's nickname was Dynamite Bob. J. Edgar Hoover was a horrible human being, a racist, a white supremacist. He was no fan of the civil rights movement and Dr. King, which is well documented with Sam Pollard's great documentary *MLK/FBI*.

We were about to begin the one-week run at the Film Forum to qualify for the Oscars, when I got a call from the FBI. They wanted to see the film, and so we gave it to them. And shortly before the film opened, the FBI reopened the case. True story. That is one of my proudest moments because they got those murderers. They opened the case and they went to prison. That was not my intention. I just wanted to tell the story.

JACKIE GLOVER:

We went to the Oscar ceremony with the families. The film didn't win, although it was a favorite documentary to win. We were with the families, and it was difficult. I don't think it was necessarily about the award, but the importance of their story. That made it tough not to win.

SPIKE LEE:

Credit to HBO, they flew out the parents who were alive to the Academy Awards. And of course they were sad that the film didn't win. Afterward, we went to a party at a restaurant called Georges, of which Denzel Washington was a part owner. Denzel was so gracious. He was taking pictures with them. It was great. They all told me later on, they didn't care about losing that much after they got a kiss on the cheek and a hug from Denzel Washington, and it made it all right. That was everything to them.

SHEILA NEVINS:

Spike was way ahead of my game. He would do things I could never have done. I was in awe. Spike's a special character.

In 1998, before Todd Phillips established himself as a titan of bromantic comedies like **The Hangover, Old School,** *and* **Road Trip,** *he made a documentary for HBO called* **Frat House.**

To shoot it, Phillips embedded himself for a year in college fraternities. The film's main character, Blossom, bragged about biting heads off rats and gave filmmakers access into the violent, twisted world of hazing and cheap beer—a world as sad as it was funny.

But Phillips intended for the movie to be a scathing indictment; alas, it was a scathing indictment that would never air.

After a screening at Sundance in 1998, students involved with the film claimed they had been misled by the filmmakers and insisted that some of the scenes had been staged. Phillips and co-director Andrew Gurland denied the claims as transparent attempts by the students to avoid responsibility for their behavior, but the whiners won.

"The controversy stems from one thing," Phillips later told **Vice.** *"When you turn your cameras on the sons and daughters of rich white Americans, you're going to get heat for it. HBO has made many award-winning documentaries, and they've all been about pimps and whores and strippers and crack and taxicab confessions and blah blah blah. They've been easy targets. They've made movies about skinheads and antiabortion maniacs. Important movies, but movies about the fringe of society. The fringe, I feel, are easy targets, but* **Frat House** *is about upper-class white Americans whose parents are lawyers and doctors and politicians. It sounds like I'm spewing crazy paranoid controversy theory, but it's true. And when you do that movie, these people, who have many resources, will threaten to sue."*

Eventually, however, Phillips conceded that some of the kids were drunk when they signed the release forms.

SHEILA NEVINS:

Richard told me that I should hire Anthony Radziwill, and I said, "Radziwill, as in Prince Radziwill?" He said, "Yes." And why did Richard want him hired? Because he had access to the Kennedys. That was what it was all about, and I had no choice. I wanted to hate Anthony because I hated people who get by on connections.

Then Anthony Radziwill comes to see me one day. My grandparents escaped the pogroms. I was a little nervous. And he says to me very clearly, "Hire me." I said, "Are you going to go into a taxicab? The show's moving to Las Vegas. Are you going to jump in the back of the taxi?" He says, "Yes."

But guess what? Anthony was a doll. He was so wonderful. I loved him so much. I was so grateful to Richard because he was so sweet, so talented, so lovely.

Then one day he told me that he had to have surgery, he had sarcomas in his chest from misdiagnosed testicular cancer many years before.

I also worked with Todd Phillips, the most brilliant intern I ever had. I read in the paper about what was going on in fraternities. Some woman was suing a school because her kid had died. It was horrible, but I thought, "What a good docu, maybe Todd can go and make this film."

Frat House was one of the best films. It was every torture, every understanding of what it took to be a fraternity brother.

I said to Anthony Radziwill, "Anthony, did Todd and Andrew tell you this was legitimate, that everything was true?" And he said, "Yes, they swore to me."

There was only one problem. It wasn't.

Oh Todd, oh Todd, oh Todd. When we looked into it, there was so much information coming in from ex–fraternity members, and from some of the kids' parents, that the entire legal department of HBO determined we could not call this a documentary.

It was genius casting. It was based on truth, and it had enough real names and references to be blasphemous, but it wasn't reality. So when the film was pulled, it broke my heart. I loved the film so much.

Todd, don't say that they took away my film. Did legal pull the film because it was about white establishment people? Of course not. Look at what HBO has done with documentaries. Go read about Peabodys we've won, how many underdogs we championed, and big people we went after. I've attacked white breads my entire fucking life.

Your film was fucking brilliant, but it wasn't true, and that is why it was was dropped. And lying to Anthony, who was dying of cancer at the time? Horrendous. So fuck you, Todd, and that's the end of that.

CURT VIEBRANZ:

I'm a Christian. Not a Bible thumper, but I was very uncomfortable with some of the stuff we were putting on the screen, like *Real Sex* and *Taxicab Confessions*. Do you remember the book *Seven Habits of Highly Effective People*? There's one in there that says, Begin with the end in mind, and write the eulogy you would like your friend to give for you at your memorial service. I actually sat down and did it, and I had this epiphany where I wrote, "Hey, he took *Real Sex* to Poland." I didn't feel good about that.

KARY ANTHOLIS:

When I first moved to New York to work at HBO, I had lunch with Anthony Radziwill several times and got to see how heartbroken Sheila was by his illness.

SHEILA NEVINS:

I remember Lee Radziwill giving me something to read at his funeral. It was very, very sad. Tragic. He died right after John Kennedy Jr., his wife, and his sister-in-law were killed in that plane crash.

On May 31, 1997, Jerry Levin's schoolteacher son, thirty-one-year-old Jonathan, was murdered by one of his students who had assumed Jonathan was wealthy because he'd mentioned his eminent father in class. The student stole $800 from him before killing him.

JERRY LEVIN:

My son was born on my birthday. I knew right from the start, the gods were doing something. He turned out to love every sport we did at Time Warner. He was my motivation. All I care about is the death of my son. For somebody not to see that, to this day, it's still my motivation.

SHEILA NEVINS:

At the service, Jerry had to walk down the aisle. As he passed me, he made a sound. I had never heard a human make such a sound; I've never heard it again. I don't know how to explain it, maybe an animal sound, something that had just gotten shot in the woods.

BOB DALY:

We went to the funeral for Jerry's son, and it was one of the saddest days of my life. Barbara and his first wife nearly had to carry Jerry down the aisle, he was so upset. Jerry used to talk to his son a lot and had tremendous pride in his son teaching in a bad neighborhood.

After the funeral, we all went out to the cemetery where people would throw dirt on the casket. Jerry couldn't even pick up the shovel. He was absolutely destroyed.

ROSS GREENBURG:

Jerry would call me to go to all the fights and we would jump on his plane. Sometimes his son would come, and oh my God, you have no idea how much he loved it. I gotta tell you, after his son was murdered, he never was the same. Who would be?

JERRY LEVIN:

Honoring my son is the only thing that matters to me.

John Lennon's "Imagine" captures, in one song, in one word, exactly what this is all about. It's peace and love. When my son was teaching in the Bronx, every day he would put something on the blackboard, and that was his quote of the day. There's never been a soul like that.

The family tragedy was uppermost in Levin's mind. But HBO's show had to go on, and did. In 1996, Mary Carillo joined HBO Sports to cover a place she once knew as a competitor: Wimbledon. She was known for her wit and opinionated commentary, and HBO knew that two of the most important aspects of sports reporting were: who was there and how were they telling the story. So they snagged Carillo away from ESPN and made her part of their own team. A year later, Carillo would also join **Real Sports with Bryant Gumbel** *and would start working with the HBO documentary unit.*

BILLIE JEAN KING:

I started telling Mary Carillo, "You have to come to HBO. It's your kind of place. They really want our input, which is not typical." She was really good at producing, was a beautiful writer, and loves being in front of the camera. And don't forget, she's got a great deep voice. When she finally came to HBO, she really fit in.

MARY CARILLO, Sportscaster:

Billie Jean King and I had been friends for a long time. When I was younger, she took me under her massive wing. Billie Jean asked me, "Why don't you cover Wimbledon for HBO?" I had never gotten to cover Wimbledon because HBO and NBC had it and I didn't work for either. I thought, HBO is a great address. I loved their coverage of Wimbledon. It was all day coverage and then a one-hour wrap-up show at night. It was so good. Arthur Ashe and Billie Jean King, my two biggest tennis heroes, were on HBO calling Wimbledon, along with a great group including Jim Lampley, Martina, and Frank Deford, another one of my heroes.

So that's where I wanted to be. ESPN doesn't like sharing its people. I had to quit ESPN, which I'm not convinced my agents thought was a great idea.

That first year that I worked for HBO, Ross decided that he wanted an all-female announcer team on tennis. So I did play-by-play, which I'm not sure if I had ever done play-by-play before HBO allowed me to. Then on either side of me were two twenty-time Wimbledon champions, Martina and Billie Jean, that's how it started. I had never hosted a show before. I was the host of the one-hour HBO late-night Wimbledon trip. It was crazy.

I also couldn't help but notice that at the end of every night, and we had long days at Wimbledon, Billie Jean would go into the production room where all the tape people were, and she would thank each and every one of them and tell them what a great job they did that day. That struck me. From that day on, I reminded myself to be aware of all these people coming up with good source material every day. It felt like family.

BILLIE JEAN KING:
The three of us women were the first-ever female trio to do a match together. That's something that we were all really proud of.

By 1995, HBO Boxing itself had become a punching bag.

Losing Mike Tyson years earlier would come back to haunt HBO by giving competitors an edge, threatening to shake the foothold they'd worked so hard to secure. In 1995, after Tyson's release from jail, Fox aired Tyson vs. Buster Mathis Jr. and scored the best viewing numbers for a program in its history, a bit better than HBO's broadcast of De La Hoya vs. Leija at MSG the night before.

HBO fought back by launching **Boxing After Dark** *in 1996, planting roots deeper into the sport, helping not only to introduce die-hard fight fans to up-and-coming contenders, but also to begin connecting with the potential stars of the future to ensure they'd want to do their fighting on HBO. A second boxing series was created—***KO Nation***—an attempt to bring in younger viewers, lasting until 2001.*

Just a few months after the HBO series premiered, however, Holyfield got a TKO on Tyson in the eleventh round of a match that gave Showtime PPV 1.7 million viewers. This marked a new high-water mark in the pay-per-view market, which had been struggling the past few years. Ironically or not, the numbers caused some optimism for HBO—though it wasn't so encouraging when those viewers were paying to watch on your biggest competitor's channel. Another blow came in June 1997 when, during the duo's rematch, Tyson munched off a piece of Holyfield's ear (twice!) during another pay-per-view event on Showtime, not surprisingly ringing in extremely high viewership once again.

HBO would not succumb without, appropriately enough, one more big fight. In 1997 HBO also aired a major live boxing event between Johnny Tapia and Danny Romero. **The Battle for Albuquerque** *drew more viewers than the PPV Tyson vs. Holyfield fight a month earlier—a sign to executives that even without a salacious* *subplot, HBO audiences were still hot for boxing, not to mention reminding them they had a strong Latino fan base.*

HBO execs continued to fight, making big deals to stay in the boxing game. In 1998 they offered Lennox Lewis $20 million for just five fights, eventually settling on six fights for an undisclosed amount.

ROSS GREENBURG:

Showtime was having an impact in boxing at that time. They were taking some decent fights and their motto was "The best fights are on Showtime." Lou was frustrated that some fights he could make we didn't have slots for, so he created *Boxing After Dark.*

LOU DiBELLA:

Boxing After Dark gave opportunities to up-and-coming heavyweights, superstar amateurs, smaller fighters, and young fighters. It created a developmental series, fighters who could be stars once they were exposed. We were in the star business with world championship boxing, but we needed our own. I thought bang for the buck, we would get great value out of making great fights with fighters that weren't household names yet. And if we turned them into household names on *Boxing After Dark*, they would grow to become superstars on championship boxing.

And that happened with so many fighters, like Barrera, Morales, a bunch of heavyweights, Arturo Gatti, all of them were *Boxing After Dark* regulars. They became so popular that they moved into the bigger series.

DAVE HARMON:

Boxing After Dark had immediate success, and as its producer I was, unsurprisingly, very tied to Lou during those years. We had a lot of fun after I reached out to Foreigner bass guitarist Bruce Turgon to create our theme song: Lou couldn't believe he agreed to do it.

LOU DiBELLA:

The runaway success of *Boxing After Dark* in the first couple of years was one fight after the other making headlines for fighters who people never heard of. After the first *Boxing After Dark*, there was an NBA game that Sunday afternoon and Magic Johnson was interviewed and commented on how great the fight at the Forum had been.

The ratings were extraordinary for the money being spent. That troubled some people in positions of power, because they started to wonder, Are we going to be overly analyzed for the only slight difference in ratings with huge difference in expenditure?

Boxing After Dark's Q rating was the highest of any program on the network. We didn't have Tyson and we didn't have Don King and we were kicking their ass.

Frankly, the reason *Boxing After Dark* got deemphasized at HBO was it did too well, comparably to championship boxing, which was costing multiples.

The Larry Sanders Show *was coming to an end. As fate would have it, Garry's girl-friend and cast member would take center stage.*

LINDA DOUCETT:

I was at the studio, and I walked out of the dressing room in high heels to do my scene and the floor was like ice. I fell hard. I was told, because Brad Grey wouldn't pay overtime, they waxed the floors while we were still there. The Screen Actors Guild would have gone insane.

I herniated three discs and I didn't have full range of motion in my arms. It was negligence.

My recovery was horrible. I was in the hospital. Wheelchair for two months. Chronic pain. I'm still in pain management to this day. The studio had full insurance, but Brad didn't want to get in trouble with the unions. The show was his first hit. He thought my injury was going to really hurt the relationship with HBO. So he told me not to claim it on their insurance. He was terrified of it.

Garry, Brad, and I went to dinner, and Garry said, "Brad, I mentioned to Linda that we're going to take care of her." A little bit later, Garry bought me a condo. Garry's idea of a perfect relationship was what Woody and Mia had where they lived separately. I asked him, "Why are you buying me this? Is it because you love me or because of the injury?"

Soon after that, Garry and I were at Musso & Frank and he said, "I'm just going to do it," and I thought he was going to order something different, but then he handed me a ring. Some people said, "I bet the injury is why you got engaged," and I thought that was just so nasty.

Garry had dated Sharon before we met and they might have reconnected when we were going through our on-again, off-again period over whether we were going to get married.

PETER TOLAN:

I wrote this episode, it was called "The Mr. Sharon Stone Show," about Larry dating a bigger celebrity and he couldn't handle it.

LINDA DOUCETT:

They were doing a bedroom scene, and mind you, I was supposed to be out of town that day but had delayed my trip a day. I'm walking from my dressing room and the AD stops me and goes, "The set's locked up." I said, "I've got to get something from wardrobe. I'm leaving town." He says, "You can't go in." Then I asked, "Are they by any chance shooting the Sharon Stone bedroom scene?" I found out much later that she had told the crew, "I'm going to surprise Garry and stick it in."

PETER TOLAN:

At one point there was a scene with the two of them in bed, and it wasn't a sex scene, it was mostly conversation, but there was kissing. I remember she was on top of him and the room we were shooting in was quite small. There were a number of cameras getting different angles, so there wasn't a lot of room. Not that I wanted to be in the room, but since I was the writer and the EP, I should have been. I was seated at the foot of the bed and they were not under covers during part of this.

Sharon is straddling Garry, then she leans over to kiss him, and whatever she's wearing in the back goes up and I'm seeing everything. It's *Basic Instinct*, party of one, I'm the only person in the theater. She was not wearing underwear, which I thought was an interesting choice. Now, sometimes on a film set with the lights, it does get hot, and I'm not prudish, but at the same time, I didn't want to be looking up the barrel, as it were. And certainly not from that close distance.

LINDA DOUCETT:

Garry comes home after shooting the bedroom scene, and I'm in the kitchen, getting ready to leave for the airport. He's supposed to go to Hawaii the next day. He says, "How are you?" I said, "Good, I'm going to Santa Fe. How was the shoot?" And he said, "Good." I said, "Sharon Stone is weird." He goes, "Why?" I said, "She came up to me, and grabbed my hand to look at the ring." Garry's face turned white.

He immediately leaves, then comes back to the kitchen a few minutes later and says, "I'm not going to Hawaii." I heard later that he stood her up at the airport and she was very angry. So clearly they must have been having an affair.

He canceled two wedding dates. I just told him, "Please, if we are going to break up, I want to keep my job. You can have everything." I signed a big stack of papers the size of the phone book. I signed over the show and the house because we had lived together, worked together for so many years. I could've also sued him for alimony.

Then he fired me. He never told me. I got a call a few days later from my agent, who told me I was dropped.

JUDD APATOW:

Garry didn't sit her down and say, "I think in the wake of our relationship ending, this situation doesn't work for me. Let's try to come to some resolution in how we deal with you working on the show." I think that he just fired her and that's awful.

Linda was mistreated. None of that would be allowed today. I don't even think it's a question. She did a great job and then they broke up and Garry fired her from the show. You're not allowed to do that. It's as simple as that. There's no excuse for it.

One of the strangest moments was the day when he walked into my office and said, "You're directing the next episode." I had never asked him to direct and would have never had the balls to think I could direct Rip Torn and all of these amazing actors and actresses on the show. But he must've seen that that was my destiny. He had never asked another writer to direct a show in six seasons, and there were a lot of brilliant people.

Brad Grey had bought numerous plots of land on Monaco Drive in LA's plush Pacific Palisades, and among Grey's proposed constructions was a 13,143-square-foot home replete with seven bedrooms, twelve bathrooms, and nearly every imaginable luxury. Grey was said to be nervous about Shandling getting a look at the place, a worry that would definitely be borne out. The comic's visit would lead to the great Grey manse, and the Shandling brouhaha that followed would lead to the so-called David Geffen rule, "Never let them see your house."

CHRIS ALBRECHT:

What happened was Garry walked into the construction site where Brad was building this massive estate with a pond. And Garry was still trying to get through building his much smaller house. I think he was comparing what Brad had to what he had and realizing that a lot of what Brad had was built on the back of his work.

The story of Garry's house was pretty funny because I later found out he told Linda they would get married as soon as he finished the house, but it became clear he never wanted to finish it. Like one day he would say, "Let's move the chimney." Linda really loved him and I thought she was a nice person and pretty good on the show. I guess he finally proposed to her right before the lawsuit with Brad.

In January 1998, Garry Shandling sued Brad Grey in California Superior Court for the staggering sum of $100 million, beginning an eighteen-month legal wrangle that destroyed what had been one of Hollywood's most fabled friendships.

Ultimately, the dispute was as much about the crucial difference between building a company—which Shandling felt he'd been a vital part of—and constructing the semi-cosmic entity known as Brad Grey. Whatever its deepest causes, after eighteen months it was "settled," if unsettlingly in Shandling's view; the terms were never publicly revealed.

LINDA DOUCETT:

Out of the blue, I get this call from Brad. He tells me, "Garry should have never fired you, and was awful to you, and now he's acting really crazy again, and I want to know if you're going to be there for me if this goes to court. And by the way, it's definitely time for you to have your own show. You're ready, and let me tell you, having your own show is a lot better than witness protection." As I'm telling you this my hands are getting sweaty. Then Brad told me I shouldn't speak to Garry at all, something I didn't think was even a possibility because the only time in years Garry had spoken to me was when one of our dogs died.

Then just two hours later, Garry calls me. I was shocked. He immediately asks, "Did Brad call you?" I told him he had, and he was really upset. He said, "I need to talk to you. Can you come over to the studio?" And then he said, "I want to have you back on the show."

At this time, I was with my fiancé and pregnant—it's so sad for me to even bring up, but my first baby was a miscarriage—and I went and saw Garry, and we walked around CBS for like two hours. He wanted to know everything Brad had said to me, and when I told him Brad had offered me a show, he lost it and invited me back on *Larry Sanders* for the final episode. Then Brad freaked out when he heard Garry had brought me back to the show.

At the deposition, Brad came to me with a cashier's check for $5 million, telling me to be fair about him. I saw all those zeros and was speechless, then I said, "You're joking, right?" And he said, "No."

For so many years, it was the three of us all the time. Garry, me, and Brad. Now it was all cloak and daggers, and I was just a pawn.

Brad's lawyers asked me if I had seen Garry taking drugs. I looked at Brad and said, "You don't want to play the drug card, Brad, that's fighting dirty, and you know it has nothing to do with business," but they asked me again, and I answered, "The only time I ever saw Garry do drugs was the ones Brad Grey gave him." And everybody froze.

Brad banged something on the table and stormed out. This was soon after Brillstein-Grey had been implicated in Belushi's drug use.

By the way, the drug was Ambien. When Garry couldn't sleep, he would call Brad and we would get in the car and drive to Brad's on Amalfi. He would leave the Ambien in the mailbox. I felt at the moment Brad left that Garry would win the case. Garry called me and said, "I heard you were unbelievable." And as soon as my deposition reached the judge, they wound up settling.

CHRIS ALBRECHT:

Garry was in the room when I was being deposed and believe me, whatever prize you win for being the best tightrope walker in the world, I would've won it that day. I wanted to tell the truth and I did well enough to maintain a great relationship with both of them.

JUDD APATOW:

It's hard to know how the lawsuit affected Garry medically. Garry did have physical problems. He had health issues. He used to eat Excedrin all day long. He had a fibroid problem, he had pancreatitis. I wouldn't want to say that the stress from that situation made him sick. One could say that Mike Nichols and him not getting along as collaborators on *What Planet Are You From?* broke his spirit even more than Brad because he was so looking forward to a positive collaboration with Mike for creative and personal reasons, but it was such a bad match that he never wrote a screenplay again or tried to make another movie.

Garry's spirit was broken. Ultimately, he couldn't handle show business even though he satirized it. I think it was too much for him. He wasn't strong in that way. He didn't realize that people would hurt each other for real, and I think it really rocked him.

Brad climbed and climbed and went on to become head of Paramount Studios. Meanwhile, he had health issues, too. The tragedy was Garry and Brad both died the same year.

After Garry died, I went back and read old emails from him, and sat at my desk, bawling. He was a beautiful, hilarious, tortured, inspired spiritual person. There's never been anyone like him and there never will be. He was very complex. He wasn't perfect. But he was trying to be better. He was trying to evolve.

Chris Rock, among the most brilliant of all contemporary comics, will joke about almost anything—even about getting fired from **Saturday Night Live** *back in 1993, though whether he quit or was actually kicked out remains a technicality. Truth can be messier than myth.*

When Rock joined **SNL** *at the tender age of twenty-five in 1990, he was largely seen as "a Black hire" rather than as the audacious and original performer that he clearly was and is.*

All too soon, Rock became frustrated about what he considered a shortage of opportunities for him on the show, and he refused to be cast in potentially demeaning roles, like, say, an Ubangi chieftain. For a large part of his time on **SNL***, Rock was a Porsche doing 40 miles an hour—that is, overqualified for much of the material he was given.*

As it happened, Rock had already made arrangements to join the cast of Fox's multihued **In Living Color** *before NBC officially fired him. Sadly enough,* **In Living Color** *got the old heave-ho itself less than a month after Rock arrived, but Chris Albrecht, who'd been a big fan of Rock's since Eddie Murphy first introduced him when the comic was only nineteen, came to his rescue. As usual, HBO was rushing in where others had neglected to tread.*

Albrecht and his lieutenant Nancy Geller gave Rock golden opportunities—a few impressive comedy concert gigs followed by a series of his own—and Rock more than made the most of all of them. In performance, pacing restlessly back and forth across the stage, repeating key lines for maximum effect, and brandishing a wicked yet somehow magical bright-eyed grin, Rock utterly captivated the crowds in the hall and the hordes at home. The specials proved to be ideal vehicles for enhancing and extending Rock's skyrocketing career.

CHRIS ROCK:

It's weird. The year 1995. I'd been fired or whatever off *SNL, In Living Color* is off the air, and my career is totally dead. HBO's doing Comic Relief out at the Universal Amphitheatre, and they figure out like two days before there's not enough Black performers. So I'm in my apartment in Brooklyn and at the last minute I get a call to be on a plane tomorrow and do Comic Relief. I kill. That leads to me getting a half-hour special.

It also leads to me getting cast as a correspondent on *Politically Incorrect* with Bill Maher, a show produced by HBO. I killed on that. Then I got a half-hour special called *Big Ass Jokes*. I won the CableACE Award, first thing I ever won in my life. Carolyn Strauss comes and watches me one night, at the Store. I only did like fifteen minutes and she goes, "You're doing an hour." Next thing I know I'm doing *Bring the Pain*. That story ends with Carolyn Strauss, but the reason I exist at all today is because of Chris Albrecht.

CHRIS ALBRECHT:

The first time I saw Chris onstage was when he was nineteen, and I just knew that with that face and that brain, he was going to be able to think of things and get away with saying them that no one else would.

CHRIS ROCK:

The first time I met Chris Albrecht I was on a comedy special called *The Uptown Comedy Express* produced by Eddie Murphy, and for whatever reason, he liked me. Chris Albrecht always kept tabs on me. When my dad died, I get a call from Chris Albrecht. "I heard your dad died. How you doing?" Next thing I know, I got a holding deal at HBO for like thirty grand. Helped out with family expenses and shit. Chris Albrecht is the patron saint of comedians.

CHRIS ALBRECHT:

There's a whole side of me that was the comic. Not a frustrated performer, but a comedian. That's why some people, like comics, get me better than most. There are things you experience onstage as a comedian that you can't explain to somebody who's never done it.

Louis C.K. was working on the show with Chris. We wanted Chris to do interviews but it became clear that he did really well with film pieces and man on the street stuff, things that were less about being a talk show and more about being a more modern-day, cool late-night, multimedia sketch show.

*On February 7, 1997, **The Chris Rock Show** premiered on HBO, ran through November 2000, and won an Emmy for Outstanding Writing.*

HBO audiences loved Chris Rock, and he loved them back. His appearances on the network enhanced HBO's reputation as the comedy capital of television.

CHRIS ROCK:

Dennis Miller was one of my idols. I still love the guy. They came to me with the idea of doing my own show, and I think the original thought of that show was the Black Dennis Miller show, for lack of a better pitch. I fancied myself, not as slick as Dennis, but I just loved how politically biting he can be, especially back then. I liked how the joke would land politically and still be accessible for the everyman. I thought he was really great at that.

NANCY GELLER:

Chris Rock wanted to do a once-a-week late-night show, and I wanted to produce it for HBO. He had been our political correspondent on *Politically Incorrect* and loved it.

CHRIS ROCK:

I had so much freedom. I did all my six HBO specials without getting a note. Five years of *The Chris Rock Show*, and the only time I ever got a series call was when I was thinking about having O.J. on. We were going to do this weird bit where I would do an interview with O.J., we were going to bill it as a big exclusive, and I was going to start off with, "America really wants to know . . ." and then only ask him football questions. I thought that would be funny. Like, "How do you feel about the PAC 10?" And Chris Albrecht asked me, "Are you sure you want O.J. on?" I heard the tone of Chris's voice and I didn't want to put him in a bad position where he had to spank me.

When they said, "It's time for you to pick a staff of writers," I met with some people, but there were no Black writers. A lot of Black comedy writers worked on sitcoms but were not as edgy as what I wanted. I went through my mind people who had opened up for me throughout the years; Ali LeRoi was a guy that I'd met a few times, and he and Lance Crouther were in a freaking comedy troupe called Mary Wong. They were very avant-garde and even though they didn't have a lot of experience, I knew they were funny. Wanda Sykes had opened up for me one night at Caroline's. I'd only seen her one time, but I thought she was absolutely hysterical. Again, no real writing experience. I basically said to HBO, "You're hiring these people. They're going to be writers." There was some pushback, but ultimately I got them on the show. They had to learn format and other things, but in a month or two, they were running shit.

We wanted to do a big sketch where I would go to Howard Beach, a very racist neighborhood where a Black guy had been killed, and make up a ruse that they were going to change Cross Bay Boulevard to Tupac Shakur Boulevard. We wanted to film it, but Nancy and others at HBO were against it. At the last minute, Chris Albrecht said, "If Chris wants to do it, he can do it." So I filmed it, and of course it's probably the funniest thing we ever did on the show. The real significance was from that moment on, I never received a note about what was going to be on the show. I had total carte blanche.

CARMI ZLOTNIK:

When Jeff Bewkes saw what Chris was able to do for other networks with HIP, he asked, "Why are we leaking value that's actually going to benefit other networks? Let's keep that value for ourselves and increase the budget for original programming."

Afterward, Chris said, "I want to do five pilots right now." Two of those five pilots were *Arli$$* and *Sex and the City*. The other two were a Rita Rudner and a Dwight Yoakam pilot. I forget what the fifth thing was. We were off and rolling, in particular *Sex and the City*.

After six years and 119 episodes, **Dream On** *moved on, bidding farewell to HBO on March 27, 1996. By this time, Marta Kauffman and David Crane were already into the second season of their NBC hit* **Friends.**

Next up for the network was a show that had survived a development period of more than two years. **Arli$$,** *a satirical half hour about a big-time pro sports agent from creator and star Robert Wuhl, premiered on August 10, 1996. Episode one was titled, "A Man of Our Times."*

MIKE TOLLIN, Executive Producer:

"I want to make the sports version of *The Larry Sanders Show*." That's what I told David Picker, who was an independent producer at the time, when I had wrangled my way into his office for a three-minute meeting. This is not a guy who wastes time. As soon as I said that line he called to his assistant, "Get me Bridget Potter on the phone." Bridget was in New York, and she called people in LA.

SUSIE FITZGERALD:

Mike Tollin and David Picker brought this project in. It seemed like a good fit for HBO because of all the sports-related programs we had. I helped bring Robert Wuhl in to write and star. He was an old friend of Chris Albrecht's and he had a great take on the material.

ROBERT WUHL, Actor and Executive Producer:

I'm from New Jersey, Exit 139A. I knew I wanted to be in show business from an early age. I started doing stand-up, but my big break was writing jokes for Rodney Dangerfield. I met Chris Albrecht at the Improv in New York, and we started a friendship. Fuchs was a supporter. I was on the young comedians show, did some writing for Robin and Billy on Comic Relief, and wrote on the *20 Years of Comedy on HBO* special.

MIKE TOLLIN:

Robert had the great idea of making the guy a sports agent instead of a sports documentary filmmaker. This was the beginning of the 1990s, way before *Jerry Maguire*.

They gave us the princely sum of $2,500 to develop it and joked, "Don't spend it all in one place." Actually we did, because Robert, Andy Wolk, and I did a series of lunches on the patio of Orso in LA, where Robert came up with the name Arliss.

ROBERT WUHL:

Fuchs thought of himself as the sports maven of all time, and I always thought he was a bit embarrassed about *1st & Ten*, and not just because of O.J. I had done many drafts, but Michael still wouldn't green-light it. We were asking, "What the fuck is going on here?" and then he got fired. At this point, the show had been in development for over two years.

CHRIS ALBRECHT:

Robert and I had been friends for twenty years by the time we started developing *Arli$$*. It got delayed by the fitful start of original programming, including the closing days of Fuchs. The key to the show was that no broadcast network would do a satire on professional sports because they were important partners. That was a big draw for us.

ROBERT WUHL:

It was incredibly polarizing from episode one. We had huge fans and then the venom came. I had no idea how many people hated sports.

SANDRA OH, Actor:

Arli$$* is why I moved to LA from Toronto, because I actually got a job. It was a good move for my career. I was so happy. I didn't know what HBO was, I didn't know anything about sports. I was twenty-four and working with a bunch of dudes all the time. I cut my teeth on *Arli$$.

MIKE TOLLIN:

One of the selling points of the show is that we were able to attract high-profile/world-class athletes to appear in cameo roles. The goal was to minimize the words they had to speak and maximize the fun. We averaged three or four cameos per show. I called Leonard Armato, Shaquille O'Neal's agent, and told him I needed Shaq to do a cameo, that "the show being green-lit depended on it." Leonard was a little reluctant to put his star client on a new, unproven series. But then I told him we'd write him into the scene with Shaq and shoot it as a "walk & talk scene." If you watch it, Leonard is practically hugging Shaq to make sure he's in the frame at all times.

Pretty much the only guy we never got was, not surprisingly, Michael Jordan. David Falk, Michael's agent at the time, did a little bait and switch on us. He said, "Write a part for the two of us. I'll show up to do my part, and Michael will be there the next day." Guess who never showed up? Pretty much every major sports agent wanted to be on the show, except for Scott Boras. He wouldn't allow his clients to be on the show—he found it offensive, unfunny, and a threat to his livelihood.

Barry Bonds was so intent on finishing a scene and getting his lines right one day that he was almost late for his game against the Dodgers. Later on, agents and superstar athletes like Charles Barkley would reach out and ask to be on the show. We had Derek Jeter at Yankee Stadium and Tiger Woods at Riviera, but my all-time favorite was Latrell Sprewell, famously suspended by the NBA for a year for choking Arliss!

ROBERT WUHL:

My favorite episode might be the one with the ballplayer who was up for his last stab at the Hall of Fame. It's one of Arliss's first clients. It looks like he's going to get it and he gets accused of abusing his second wife, who's got an alcohol problem. His first wife comes forward and says, "He couldn't have done this because he was with me, we're going to get back together again." I made sure the press finds this out, and he gets elected. That night the wife confesses to me that he wasn't with her. She said, "Why do you think he never contested my divorce? I'd much rather our son be the son of a Hall of Famer than the son of a domestic abuser."

Also about abortion. One of the ballplayers in the NBA had like fifteen kids, there was a whole story about the guy. I asked all the basketball agents, "What does it cost if your client knocks up a woman and she has the baby as opposed to having an abortion?" They said, "If she has the abortion, it's going to cost a hundred grand. If she has the baby, it's going to cost millions." So Arliss tells Rita to talk this girl into having an abortion. It was dark but that's real.

SANDRA OH:

I learned a lot on that show, particularly about how you work with writers. I credit Robert and our writers for a lot of it. They would always write me good story lines. I never felt that Rita was a flat character. I had a lot of space to do physical comedy, which I'd never done, and had a lot of space to bring my own spin to things while fulfilling the parameters of the script.

I got to do so much fun shit. It was ridiculous. I was just visiting my brother and my nephew, we were doing some boxing stuff, and my brother goes, "How do you know how to box?" I said, "I got lessons because I had a scene with Laila Ali, where I had to learn to box."

MIKE TOLLIN:

The show was a big step for Robert, going from a highly respected character actor to playing the lead role. It was a real challenge. Robert's got a big heart, great values, and I always enjoy his company, but sometimes he can't get out of his way. Especially with directors. He'll hate me for saying this, but he was crippling to many who came on to direct, including me when I directed, and I was his partner. I figured out I needed to be on the set, at the monitors, at lunchtime on day two, because that was usually the time directors would come to me and say, "I can't do this anymore." I would have to take them for a walk, calm them down, and remind them it was only three and a half more days.

MARY KAY PLACE, Actor:

I directed an episode of *Arli$$*, and it was challenging. We went head-to-head a couple of times. That one took a few years off my life. It wasn't just Robert; there was a whole male club thing going on there.

SANDRA OH:

I will be forever grateful to Robert Wuhl for giving me a shot. I was here in LA living in a hotel. I just happened to have a six-month visa and he gave me a job and I did everything I could with it.

I don't remember what director it was, someone just doing like some Ching Chong thingy, directing me like that. I don't remember who the fuck it was, but oh my god, the entire crew knew me, and they were upset. I remember tearing that person a new asshole. What are you doing, man? Why are you talking to me like this?

In February 1996, sandwiched between a just-passed telecommunications law from Congress and its presumed signing by President Bill Clinton, legislators spewed forth a major report on televised violence, prepared by a coalition of media executives, mental health professionals, and academic researchers calling itself the National Television Violence Study.

The little army of experts found that "violence predominates on television, often including large numbers of violent interactions per program," and that previous promises by TV executives to "tone television down" had proved hollow. This news-to-nobody had violence on TV broken down into three categories: broadcast networks were scored violent 44 percent of the time, followed by basic cable at 55 percent, and, tied at 85 percent each, HBO and Showtime.

One might think HBO executives would have panicked after receiving such a high score; instead, they dug deeper into the development of their first original drama series, **Oz**, *whose stated goal was to demonstrate that HBO content was markedly distinct from what aired on broadcast networks.*

Set in a nightmarish contemporary correctional facility, the show's allusion to **The Wizard of Oz**—*a world recognizable but still strange—was apt. HBO subscribers first tuned in to* **Oz** *on July 12, 1997. The first episode was artfully directed by Darnell Martin, and for the next six years Tom Fontana, Barry Levinson, a varsity lineup of writers, and a stellar cast doled out squalid tales and brutal action, often peppered with "dirty" words and scads of nudity, some of it full-frontal. It wasn't TV; it was HBO, remember?*

TOM FONTANA, Creator:

I was doing *Homicide*, which was not a conventional cop show in the sense that we didn't always get the bad guy. I was thinking, "Jeez, at the end of cop shows, the bad guy goes to jail. What happens to them in prison?" That was fueled by the fact that Attica happened when I was a kid, which was a huge deal for me.

PETER BENEDEK, Agent:

Oz was the child of *Homicide*. As Don Ohlmeyer said to me years later, *Homicide* was the first cable show. Except it was on NBC.

TOM FONTANA:

Rob Kenneally, an old friend, was running Rysher Entertainment at the time, and he was meeting with Chris Albrecht trying to figure out what they wanted to do for a drama series, when Chris said, "I'm thinking we should do something about prison." Rob left, got on the phone, called me here in New York, and said, "Get your ass out here. Somebody is stupid enough to finally make your prison show." I got on a plane, pitched it to Chris, Bridget, and Annie, and they said, "Okay, start working on it."

BRIDGET POTTER:

Chris did not want me gone 100 percent, so I continued my work developing with Tom Fontana on what would become *Oz* from an office nearby. Chris and I were always trying to figure out arenas we could develop that nobody else would do—this has to be TV worth paying for, after all. There had been one comedy series about prison, but there had never been a series set in a realistic prison. I got permission for Tom and me to go to a maximum-security prison out in New Jersey. When we got there, a woman who was the assistant to the warden showed us around, and the character Edie Falco played was based on her.

JEFF BEWKES:

I was worried about *Oz* from the beginning. I kept saying to Chris, "How many cop shows are there on television? How many lawyer shows? Now tell me how many prison shows are there? Do you think that might be for a good reason? Nobody wants to go to prison. Let me talk to Fontana, will you?" Fontana tells me what's in his head, I said, "All I ask is, if we are going to do this, it must be authentic."

Then I asked him, "You're not just going to do gratuitous sex, right?" And he goes, "Gratuitous? No." It reminded me of *Stripes*, when the army recruiter asks Harold Ramis and Bill Murray, "Have you ever been convicted of a felony?" And they look at each other and ask, "Convicted? No."

TOM FONTANA:

Chris said to me, "I don't care if the characters are likable as long as they're compelling." I had never heard those words from anybody, including Brandon [Tartikoff], who was a god to me, or Grant [Tinker], who was another god to me. So I took that to heart, and being a Jesuit-trained Virgo and the first guy in, I felt an enormous amount of responsibility that I not fuck it up because if I did, Chris would think, "I gave Fontana all the freedom and it was a disaster."

ANNE THOMOPOULOS:

Chris said to me, "We need to do for drama what HBO has done for comedy." The development process took a year and a half, maybe longer. It wasn't like we were off and running. We all needed to find our way because we were trying to define what an HBO drama was.

Tom had only worked for a broadcast network; it was really difficult for him to understand how not just willing, but how desirous we were to really push the limits. With every draft, I said, "No, it needs to be grittier. It needs to be rougher. It needs to be scarier," and constantly pushing Tom. And once he got it, there was no stopping him.

CHRIS ALBRECHT:

Anne was our executive on *Oz* and played a major role. During the development of the show, she basically invented the HBO style of a programming executive, one who looked after the network, but also became part of the creative production team with the priority to get the best work done, while not passing on arbitrary notes that rarely worked.

TOM FONTANA:

I wrote an outline and Chris said, "Let's shoot fifteen minutes of this."

CHRIS ALBRECHT:

When Michael was leaving, I snuck a million bucks into the budget so they could shoot something.

TOM FONTANA:

After we filmed the presentation, Barry Levinson and I flew out to California. We went into Chris's office and put the VHS in his machine.

BARRY LEVINSON, Executive Producer:

There were only three of us in the room: Tom, me, and Chris. He didn't ask what episodes would be like, what's the arc of the season, where's the bible, or what happens in season three. He watched it, then said, "Okay, let's do it." It was a big change in the way business was done.

TOM FONTANA:

There were no marketing meetings. There was no, "I got to run it upstairs and get approval." You send a pilot in to a network, they all watch it, then they screen it with other people and ask cabdrivers about it. Warren Littlefield once said to me, "I showed it to my twelve-year-old." I said, "Oh great, like I really make shows for twelve-year-olds."

Chris said to me in that meeting, "What's the one thing you have never been allowed to do on broadcast television?" I said, "Kill the lead in the first episode." He said, "Okay, we'll do it."

What came next was truly extraordinary. It had never happened before and has never happened since.

Chris said to me, "I don't really care about the ratings. I just want there to be articles on pages that aren't TV pages. If we get an op-ed piece, I'll be the happiest man alive." And we got an op-ed piece.

Everyone thought I was crazy. People literally said to me, "Tom, it's a movie channel. Why are you doing this there?" I said, "For the first time in my career, I'm actually going to make a show I really want to make."

Darnell Martin directed the pilot. She had worked with me on *Homicide* and in retrospect, now with diversity hires, I picked a Black woman to direct the pilot of *Oz* just because her instincts were so great.

EDIE FALCO, Actor:

I did a movie a thousand years ago out of college with a bunch of college friends called *Laws of Gravity*. It ended up getting a fair amount of attention with the festivals and somehow Tom saw it and became a champion of mine. It was the thing you can't ask for. He just decided that he was going to try to help my career. He asked me if I wanted to work on *Homicide*, then said, "I'm doing this other series and there are two female parts. Would you like to play one of them?" It was the thing I dreamt about. I was a kid at the time. It was beyond thrilling.

To be honest, when I started *Oz*, I didn't know anything about HBO. I didn't have HBO until halfway through *Sopranos* when I thought, I should probably get this thing.

RITA MORENO:

I was at Elaine's, and Tom stopped by our table to tell me he was a fan of mine, and I said, "So how come you don't write for me?" He said, "I will." I thought, "Yeah, yeah," but he did. I was delighted. I thought, "Wow, this guy really is forward thinking, if it's about a maximum-security prison, maybe he wants me to play the warden." So my husband and I had dinner with him, we did a lot of chatting, we're at dessert at this point, and I finally said, "So tell me the part that you would like me to do for the show." I was about to take a bite of cake, and he said, "I would love for you to play the nun."

I put the spoon down, looked at my husband, then I looked at Tom, and said, "I don't want to offend you, and I hope your show will be a success, but I can't think of wearing a wimple." I was thinking of Sally Field. He said, "Oh no, no, no. Not that kind of nun." I said, "Well, what kind of nun is she?" He said, "First of all, there's no wimple, and second, she is a very liberal person who doesn't let her religion get in the way of her doing what she feels is right." I still felt trepidation and asked him, "Let me put it this way: Is she the type of nun who would have a bottle of whiskey in her desk drawer in case of bad days?" Tom said, without hesitation, "Absolutely." I said, "Okay, I'll do it."

DEAN WINTERS, Actor:

When Tom gave me the part, I was a bartender and a hustler. If you walked out of my bar with cab fare, then I failed. I was an immature actor before *Oz*. The show helped me develop as a person and opened my eyes to many new situations, sex, race, everything.

When we were shooting, no one from the network was there. The big joke was the inmates really are running the asylum.

TOM FONTANA:

Early on, I got a call from somebody at HBO syndication sales, and this person said to me, "You have to shoot alternate takes of the scenes to get rid of any bad language." I told him, "That's virtually impossible." He says, "No, no, I really need you to do it." So I said to everybody, "We're going to shoot one scene, and then we're gonna reshoot it." The dialogue was something like, "Fuck you, you cunt bitch, I've had enough of your motherfucking shit." Then I said, "Okay, let's shoot the alternative." The actor said, "Hey, stop it." I sent it to the guy, and he said, "Never mind."

RITA MORENO:

Oz damn near killed my career. The lighting was very harsh, as it should be in a show like that, and I lost a lot of jobs. Someone told Ray Stark, "You should get Rita Moreno for that part," and he said, "No way, she looks awful." I heard that and it really broke my heart. But I have no complaints whatsoever. I got a lot of respect from many people in the industry because I allowed such severe lighting.

TOM FONTANA:

While we were shooting the first season, we would shoot a scene, a very intense scene, and then the director would say "cut" and we'd all laugh going, "Who's going to watch this?" We were convinced that no one would watch it. We kept hearing from HBO how happy they were. We never knew any numbers.

CHRIS ALBRECHT:

People looked at *Oz* and said, "Holy shit! You can do this on television?" We had shown sex and said "fuck," but this was profoundly different. *Oz* changed the creative community's opinion of HBO.

PETER BENEDEK:

Tom loved doing that show. The penitentiary was in the building that now houses the Chelsea Market. In those days, it was an office building. When you went up to the set, you would get on the elevator with bicycle messengers and people who worked in offices, then you get out on the eighth floor, and you were in Oz. You were in the penitentiary. It was the only show I've ever been involved with that had no requirement for exterior sets. They never used them.

DEAN WINTERS:

A month or two before we would start each new season, Tom would call the core guys in separately and ask, "What have you not done as an actor yet that you want to do?" Then Tom would implement that into scripts.

TOM FONTANA:

I love to run a show where creatively everybody gets to feel free and take risks. It's easy for an actor to get stuck in a series doing the same thing. I remember Rita came in and said, "I had this idea that maybe I'd be attracted to one of the prisoners." She's a nun. I thought, "That's a good idea."

RITA MORENO:

I wanted to know what's in the mind of a religious person when they get sexual feelings. Tom's eyebrows went up and immediately he said, "Wow, that's a great idea." Then I said, "What if she's in a session with this person she has a crush on, and at some point, we don't hear dialogue, but we see this man put his hand on her breast, and she puts her hand on his, and it gets entwined with the crucifix that's on her chain, then she throws her head back in absolute ecstasy." And he said, "Oh, I love that."

TOM FONTANA:

Two seasons later, I brought in Chris Meloni and her character had this attachment to Chris. When she met Chris, she went, "I meant an old guy. I didn't mean a hunk." I told her, "Rita you gotta be more careful what you say to me."

RITA MORENO:

Tom is brilliant. He's a genius. He's mischievous, and, oh my God, he really loves his actors.

So Tom being Tom, he chose Chris Meloni's nasty, bad boy character for her to get a crush on. It was so mischievous. I was so embarrassed. Me and my big ideas. I'm very funny, I would be horrible in sex scenes. People think about me as a sexual person, I am actually, but not in front of a zillion people. I said to Christopher that morning, "Don't be insulted, but I put up a rubber falsie in my bra." He smiled, and that was that.

STEVE BUSCEMI, Actor and Director:

I directed two episodes of *Oz*. That had a great ensemble cast, and I had to calm myself down when I met Rita Moreno. She was incredible and so down to earth.

RITA MORENO:

After he left the show, Chris Meloni called up Tom and said, "I've got one day free. Can I come in and do something?" And Tom, who adored him and was never really thrilled about his leaving, he wrote a scene where he's coming from a judge who sentenced him to death. Sister Pete is there because she's so upset about this. She doesn't believe in the death sentence. She says, "I'm so sorry. Is there anything I can do?" He said, "Show me your tits." So I said to Steve Buscemi, "Can I do an outtake after we get the real thing?" He said, "Okay." We do the scene again and I say, "I'm so sorry. Is there anything I can do?" And as I say that, I pull up my sweater and say, "I'll do anything you want."

Chris doesn't bat an eyelash. You can't see my face or my head; all you see is my bra and my belly. Then Chris decides to take off his suit, a suit you wear to a trial. He takes off his tie. Then his shirt, then his undershirt, then he takes off his pants. And to my absolute amazement, he takes off his pants and his underwear and he is absolutely stark naked. And let me tell you, the guy is built.

TOM FONTANA:

We did eight episodes in the summer and Chris called and said, "I'm really in a jam here. Do you think you could do eight more?" I don't think he got the word "episode" out of his mouth. The stories were just churning in my brain. They would not shut off. The actors were so inspiring to write for. I didn't want to stop.

EDIE FALCO:

As the years have gone by, and because I've worked with a bunch of different networks and different cable channels, I would be on a set, and there would be like six hundred executives there having little meetings, then I'd get a note about something that I would later learn never came from the director. It came from all those people. That didn't happen at HBO. Once they decided who their cast members were, because they thought you were talented, they got out of the way. And based on the writers and showrunners I've spoken to, when they give advice, it's usually good, but it's not make or break if you don't follow it. HBO is a terrible place to start, because you think everybody's going to be like that. And you're sadly mistaken.

CAROLYN STRAUSS:

Larry Sanders and *Oz* were huge. Having Shandling and Fontana, two people who loved bending the rules, was a big deal for us. They set a standard for quality for us, and they both went about things in different ways than network shows. Network television at this time was a behemoth, and we didn't have a lot to show for ourselves. How were we going to make dents in the scripted series world? How were we going to get people to come work with us? We didn't have the back ends to offer people like the networks did, so we had to admit, We can't pay you what they can. But we can pay you in opportunity and freedom. Tom Fontana and others helped us figure out that we could get experienced, network showrunners to come to us with the promise of more freedom. We basically said to them, "You learned how to do it on network television, and you know the rules. Now think about the rules you want to break."

JEFF BEWKES:

By this point, I knew movies we bought from studios would start to be less valuable because of Blockbuster home video rentals but there was also a massive financial advantage for us to move more of our program spending into original programming. I told Jerry, "We've got to do this because it'll distinguish us from a programming point of view and it'll give us leverage over cable operators. We can't keep taking all the money we make on increased subscriptions and sending that to the movie studio as they jack up the slate costs. They're going to play us off, like the NFL does to broadcast networks. If we can move more into original programming, we'll have a huge financial advantage of three to four times the revenue per subscriber."

If we paid $1 million for an episode of *Oz*, that costs us per subscriber dollar at HBO a third of what it costs Showtime, because we have roughly three times the subscribers and we're charging about 20, 30 percent more per subscriber. So if you look at it that way, we can make four of these episodes or shows every time they make one of them.

Oz set a blueprint for later HBO series: not only would they be—by definition— offerings not available elsewhere, they would be fortified by the notion that HBO was the one place in television where the auteur was a creative individual or group, not a slew of "suits" from the executive ranks.

The next task was to make sure that news of the network's unique DNA was spread near, far, and in between.

Since Time Inc.'s merger with Warner Bros. back in 1989, Wall Street had been something less than thrilled with the resulting behemoth; Time Warner stock had languished for more than six years.

When news of Time Warner's merger with Turner Broadcasting was announced in 1995, the hope was that the new entity would rejuvenate the straggling stock and foreshadow a bullish financial future. Right after the company received the go-ahead from the government for the $7.5 billion deal, a **Wall Street Journal** *headline on September 18, 1996, roared, "Ted Turner Will Be Responsible for Cable TV at Time Warner."*

Scott Sassa, who had served as president of Turner Entertainment Company, announced plans to resign following the merger, and Turner himself was given the title of vice-chairman, along with the responsibility for his networks, which included Cable News Network, the Cartoon Network, Turner Classic Movies—and, most significantly, HBO.

Then again—not really.

JERRY LEVIN:

You've got to keep Ted happy, but don't give him anything. That first year, my goal was to try to park Ted in a place that from appearances would be sufficient but not substantial. There was nothing in Ted's background to suggest he could oversee HBO, and Jeff was pretty clear he wasn't going to work for Ted.

JEFF BEWKES:

Ted wasn't even in Atlanta after he sold the company; he was in Montana. He would show up in Atlanta three days a month, and those were the days when Jerry and Dick and I would fly down there and meet with them as if we reported to him. He didn't want to hear too much about HBO.

JERRY LEVIN:

I was the person supervising Jeff's performance and on standby when he needed somebody.

JEFF BEWKES:

I said to Jerry, "If HBO is going to report to Ted, we have to do something in advance so Ted doesn't take credit for 'fixing or straightening out' HBO, because that'll look like I was just sitting on my ass." I even threw in some self-interest to Jerry and said, "And since I'm reporting to you now, it would look like you've been asleep at the switch." At that point, Jerry says, "Okay, what do you have in mind?"

I said, "I want to go in front of the board and do the opposite of what they expect. They'll expect us to say we have some cleaning up to do, and we'll need to write off some mistakes. Instead, I want to go in and tell them we're going to almost double earnings from about 9 percent a year to 16 percent."

Jerry says, "I can't have you promise earnings we won't deliver." I said, "I will deliver." "So how are you going to do that?" he asks. "Well, we haven't licensed the video rights to the original shows and movies, we're ramping up international, and we can make some efficiencies."

In 1996, HBO was valued by the Street at about $2.2 billion, giving us a nine times multiple on earnings. HBO had about $220 million, maybe $250 million of operating income a year. It had grown 8 to 9 percent a year over the prior nine years.

I went before the board and said, "Over the next five years, we will grow earnings an average of 15 percent a year, so in five years, we'll be earning $500 million and the higher growth rate will give us a fifteen multiple. HBO will be valued at $8 billion and we will throw off $2 billion of cash flow over these next five years. So you have $2 billion now, and you'll have $10 billion in five years. Thank you for listening."

I sat down and the board looked at me like I was an idiot. I knew what they were thinking: "Why is this kid promising all of this? He is way too eager, and way too immature. Doesn't he know you're not supposed to put your neck out, or Jerry's, like that?" But I was sitting there thinking, "If I don't outrun Ted, I won't be able to keep HBO independent."

I'll never forget Ted that day. He saw through it. He thought, "That little shit has just made it impossible for me to do anything great after he promised the moon." Ted gets half out of his chair, points at me, and says with a grin, "He's after all our jobs!"

Now sitting in the back is Bob Daly, the only head of a division who was at every board meeting and the same Bob who had a money dispute with HBO for years over how much we pay for Warner movie. They were charging us $150 million a year when the other studios were charging more like $100 million. Michael and I had even flown out to LA to have a peacemaking lunch with Bob and Terry to work out a compromise, but that ended in a lot of yelling.

I go back and sit in the empty chair next to Bob after promising all these big earnings increases, and he glances over and says, "That took balls, promising all that." I said, "Thanks." Then he looks directly at me with a mischievous Irish grin and says, "You know, that's going to cost you," meaning, now that you've promised all this money, you're gonna fucking pay me. I said, "Yeah, I'll figure it out with your guys."

I went out to LA the next week and spent hours getting nowhere with Ed Bleier and the rest of the Warners team.

Everybody tells me to fuck off; finally, Bob comes in and says, "Let's take a walk." We're walking around the rose garden outside his office. I said, "Bob, you've had this feud with Michael that's gone on for five years, now you can prove it wasn't your fault." He says, "What do you have in mind?" I said. "Corporate can't keep absorbing $50 million a year in the intercompany, it's too material, but they can do $25 million. Let me see if I can get Dick and Jerry to cover half of this $50 million. As for the other $25 million, you take $12 million and I'll take $12 million." He says, "Yeah, but if you fail, I'm not paying any of that other $25 million." I said, "Done." So he agrees. I go to Parsons, say. "Dick, you want to make the peace here?" He says, "Okay, done."

Within a day, the phone rings, and it's Fuchs with no preamble. He just starts in: "So I heard you settled the Warners fight." I said, "Yeah." "Let me guess," he says. "Over my corpse, right?" You gotta give Mikey credit for a good sense of humor.

Even as HBO's competition intensified, its 1996 earnings hit $1.75 billion, up from $1.61 billion the year before. Awards and subscribers continued to flow in, and the *company's profit margins registered 18 percent, up from just 10 percent in 1988, the result of more subscribers and lower costs. Bewkes had kept his promise.*

CHRIS ALBRECHT:

Bewkes was the wild man in disguise. Michael was not willing to invest real money; Jeff got significant funds for us.

KERI PUTNAM:

We all knew and greatly respected Jeff. It felt good, like a handoff that had clarity, integrity, and was well managed. It also felt like it might signal a change, a shifting of the sands, from having someone who is essentially a show person and spoke the language of entertainment, to someone who had been more of a business guy. To Jeff's immense credit, that was never the case. Jeff may not have had a lot of experience in the creative process, but he understood how to empower people like Chris, Carolyn, and others. That wasn't a sure thing when he took over.

*The miniseries **From the Earth to the Moon,** whose twelve episodes were aired by HBO twice a week from April 5 to May 10, 1998, was a painstaking re-creation of the great Apollo space program that took America—and all humanity—239,000 miles away—to the Moon.*

The filmmakers hewed closely to the facts in their account of the adventure, with a cast that included Sally Field, Tim Daly, David Andrews, Nick Searcy, Lane Smith, and Daniel Hugh Kelly. (Tom Sizemore, originally cast as Buzz Aldrin, had subsequently been ruled too stocky and was replaced by Bryan Cranston.) And yet many viewers, if asked now, would probably say Tom Hanks "starred" in the production.

*The confusion is understandable, since Hanks had memorably starred as an astronaut in **Apollo 13,** a huge theater-box-office hit released in 1995, and was an executive producer and "host" for **From the Earth to the Moon,** while directing the first episode. (David Frankel directed three episodes, and David Carson, Sally Field, Gary Fleder, Frank Marshall, Jonathan Mostow, Jon Turteltaub, Graham Yost, and Lili Fini Zanuck each directed an episode as well.)*

*The entire project was ignited, one could say, in Northern California, where a young Tommy Hanks grew up obsessed with the Beatles and with America's space program, the latter enthusiasm growing considerably after he completed **Apollo 13.** His impassioned involvement was a primary factor in HBO's decision to make **From the Earth to the Moon**—and make it as big as possible. Indeed, its scope was unprecedented, at least for HBO.*

The miniseries was shockingly short on such proven HBO elements as nudity, curs-

ing, violence (explicit or implicit), or any of the other thrills HBO often utilized to distinguish its fare more easily from that found on broadcast television.

Somehow that made the bet—the most expensive in HBO history—even more audacious, although the brass could be comforted by the fact that **Apollo 13** *had earned nine Academy Award nominations and grossed $355 million worldwide, thus serving as proof that, contrary to widespread industry "wisdom," outer space could be good box office.*

Many of those involved in the **Apollo 13** *movie came over to work on the miniseries; Hanks was the most prominent, even though he was extremely busy starring in Steven Spielberg's* **Saving Private Ryan** *during months of production. Script changes and rough cuts of* **From the Earth to the Moon** *had to be delivered to Hanks on the film's location in Ireland.*

Initially, most of the off-camera work, including the dazzling special effects of Ernest Farino, was to be handled on the West Coast (mostly California), but the lure of Kennedy Space Center and Cape Canaveral resulted in HBO agreeing to move the production to Florida—lock, stock, and moon.

BRIAN GRAZER, Executive Producer:

A lot of this is Tom Hanks. Tom was always fascinated with aviation, the stars, the planets, and discovery. They deeply intrigued him. He is without a doubt one of the smartest actors in the last fifty years, a guy who loves to research, who crawls inside of holes, digging and learning. He thought the entire Apollo space program was worthy of attention and wanted to examine the successes and failures of each mission in that program. Tom felt like it was one of the greatest things he's ever done.

CHRIS ALBRECHT:

The first *From the Earth to the Moon* meeting that Bridget and I went to was at CAA with Tom Hanks, Brian Grazer, and a bunch of CAA agents. We were talking about what we wanted to do in original programing, and I remember Tom said, "Doesn't everybody that wants HBO already have HBO?" Bridget and I were taken aback, and I said, "Hopefully not."

TOM HANKS:

I was at HBO because of Chris Albrecht. After *Apollo 13*, I was so filled with background and enthusiasm for the material, I took Andy Chaikin's *A Man on the Moon* and pitched a twelve-part miniseries. Chris used "Hey!" as shorthand for "That's different! I'd want to watch that! I want a 'Hey' on HBO!"

ANNE THOMOPOULOS:

We didn't even have a miniseries division. Chris told me, "I need you to start working on this." It was a very organic process and we were really lucky because at the time a lot of the original astronauts were still alive. They were extremely supportive and gave us tremendous access.

TOM HANKS:

Were it not for Tony To, Erik Bork, Graham Yost, and many others, I would have caused a disaster.

Framing the hosting thing was interesting. Good to do, but I wanted to say something other than "Here's the show." The series was more an anthology than a series because each mission to the moon called for different methods and aims. And those NASA folks are complicated people.

KARY ANTHOLIS:

There were a lot of questions from our marketing team about what the audience would be for this, and when they did some testing, it was a disaster. Then Chris said, "We're HBO, we shouldn't be doing testing. We should just go with our guts."

Tom had cinematic ambitions for the project. This was his first foray into television as a producer. He was pushing for *Apollo 13* level of cinema in the show and was right to do so.

CHRIS ALBRECHT:

When scripts came in, we finally put a preliminary budget together, and it was go or no go time. There were a lot of things that we hadn't figured out yet, like basically how to do the moon. The budget said $44 million, but Carmi, my production guy, looked at me and said, "There's no way I can guarantee this number. My recommendation is we shut down, get all the scripts right, then get the budget right." I said, "This is our window. We've got to go now."

DAVID FRANKEL, Director:

The theory was let's spend everything we need to on the earth, and then we'll figure out the moon. After all, it's called *From the Earth to the Moon*. Tony To wasn't going to let money stand in the way of what this needed to be until they tied him up and threw him in the back of a trunk.

They were beating Tony's brains out about the budget, and he was called to a meeting in New York, and Tom was part of it, and he asked, "What's going on?" They said, "Well, Tony's spending too much money," and Tom replied, "Don't you want us to do excellent work? Don't you want us to do the best that we can?" And they said, "Of course we do, Tom. Don't worry. You know we love it." And he said, "Great. Tony, keep doing what you're doing." That pattern got repeated every couple of weeks. Tony was a wreck; the crew was a wreck. They had been working sixteen, eighteen hours a day when I got there. *Earth to the Moon* was a very painful, tooth-pulling process. The law had been handed down from Carmi who was running production.

CARMI ZLOTNIK:

From the Earth to the Moon was the birth of modern television. We started it in a conventional TV sense, which is, we have a $50 million box and anything that doesn't fit has to be cut. The problem was Tom Hanks and the creative team kept having great ideas that didn't fit into that box.

Then I got a call from Brian Grazer, "Carmi, do you know what business you're in?" I said, "What are you talking about?" He said, "You're in the wish fulfillment business. Tom Hanks wants to go to the moon. Your job is to take him there."

And to me that was the paradigm shift. After that conversation, I went to Chris and told him, if we want to stick to this $50 million box, we are going to be sacrificing a lot of creativity and vision. He told me, "Go back and budget it for the real version," which I did, and told him it was going to be more like $65 million. Chris went to Jeff who came up with the money, and all of a sudden, we were thinking in terms of moviemaking instead of making a TV show.

Authenticity was critical to Hanks, and that spread like a virus. One example: when they realized that the space uniforms had the valve on the right side instead of the left side, all new uniforms were made. Cost? $100,000.

JEFF BEWKES:

Michael would never have green-lit *From the Earth to the Moon*. The subject matter was not designed to be a crowd pleaser. There were no romance stories or even B stories in there. It was a pretty straight exposition on the space program because Tom Hanks was interested in doing it that way. It was not expected to have huge viewership. But when Chris brought it to me, I green-lit it without hesitation.

TONY TO:

We were over by $1 million a week for the period that we were shooting, but I recall Chris Albrecht's commitment to seeing it through, even as the cost was ballooning.

None of us were aware that HBO was going to do something that had never been done before. That was an amazing creative and financial fearlessness in the pursuit of something great.

FRANK MARSHALL, Director and Documentarian:

From the Earth to the Moon was my very first relationship with HBO. I was working as a director and what was cool for me was, even though I was doing a later episode, I was the first to shoot, so I got to cast everybody. That began a wonderful relationship with Bryan Cranston.

JOHN MELFI:

It was intense, it was heady, and it was that way every day for two years. The team from the Apollo project was aging and time was crucial. We wanted to get their story right, and Tom wanted it to be perfect.

That made for some extraordinarily long days. One of those days—which turned into night, before turning back to day—we were working with Rita Wilson, Tom's wife, on an episode, and we were at it for hours. At one point she asked, bleary-eyed, "How can we keep going?" She joked, "Do I need to make a phone call to Tom?" We kept going.

BRUCE RICHMOND, Executive:

We were trying to live up to an incredibly successful movie, and it had to have historical accuracy. We had Dave Scott and other astronauts as our technical consultants.

The naval training center, which had been decommissioned, was put back together so we could use the 1970s barracks astronauts stayed in prior to going into the clean rooms and getting their suits on.

It was highly technically challenging. When we did the moonscape, we built a forty-thousand-square-foot moonscape in the zeppelin hangars down in Tustin and shot nights so we could get a single light source, like the moon. There was so much detail.

CHRIS ALBRECHT:

We had to go from one side of Florida to the other, and the quickest way to get there was by helicopter. Me, Anne Thomopoulos, Tony, Carmi, and Tom

Hanks got in the chopper. We were sitting in the back, and Tom was up front. It was one of those training helicopters, and the pilot gave lessons. After we took off, he said to Tom, "You want to try flying it?" Tom said, "No, no, that's okay," and we were all thinking, Well, that's good. We landed, did the tour of Cape Kennedy, then got back in the helicopter and before we took off, the pilot asked again, "You're sure you don't want to fly this?" And Tom said, "No, that's okay." The guy then says, "I had Tom Cruise in here and he flew it." Hanks was like, "Cruise? Well, okay, then, I'll give it a try." We were scared shitless. The guy got us off the ground and then Tom took the joystick and it was wild, because it's extremely sensitive. We had some real abrupt shifts, going right or left and tilting right or left. And then Tom got the hang of it.

DAVID FRANKEL:

Tom had written a scene for Lane Smith, who was playing a reporter, to interview Wernher von Braun, and he had taken it right from a textbook. Tony brought me the pages and when I read it, I said, "God, this is just not a good scene. This is so dry." Tony said, "Well, you'll have to tell Tom yourself," so on a Saturday morning we all got around a speakerphone and Tom was on the other end. I said, "Tom, this is really hard to hack. I mean, even you would have trouble probably performing the scene." And he said, "Oh yeah?" And he proceeded to play the entire scene over the phone—brilliantly. Nothing had ever conveyed to me quite like the power of a gigantic movie star than that moment, which was just Tom Hanks on the phone performing the driest possible rocket-based dialogue you could imagine in a scintillating fashion. I never questioned his judgment about anything ever again.

TONY TO:

Tom was on the set directing. It was very, very late and everybody was very tired and the extras were flagging so he wanted to cheer them up. He said, "Give me a phone, I'll call your wife, or your girlfriend" to the extras. And he did. He would call them and say, "This is Tom Hanks," and they would laugh and they didn't think it was real. Then he said, "No, this really is Tom Hanks. I'm with your husband, or your wife, and I'm taking very good care of them. I'm really sorry that I'm keeping them really late." It was very morale boosting.

JOHN MELFI:

So many fascinating people were involved. One day I brought Dave Scott— our astronaut consultant from Apollo 15 who had walked on the moon—to meet Chris Isaak—who played Ed White—in his dressing room. After some time, Chris started playing his guitar and singing for the two of us in between one of his scenes. I'll never forget the look on Dave's face. It was amazing!

MARA MIKIALIAN, Executive:

September 25, 1997. There was going to be a shuttle launch at night and Tom was invited to watch from a rooftop, but we heard only four could go. Then someone said, "Just stick with Tom, nobody is going to tell him, 'No, you can't bring these people.'" So a few of us straggled along and sure enough we made it.

ANNE THOMOPOULOS:

Standing on the roof of the Vehicle Assembly building with Tom and some of the cast and crew to watch a shuttle launch was an extraordinary experience. It was the most spectacular sight, and the earth trembles so that you feel it from your toes through the top of your head. Top that off with Tom Hanks standing next to you, saluting, and wishing the crew "God speed." Now that's privilege.

MARA MIKIALIAN:

About a week later, I got to see the shuttle land as well. That's when I met my future husband, who worked at NASA. Tom wrote a really sweet note for our wedding. The joke on *From the Earth to the Moon* was how many couples came out of it.

DAVID FRANKEL:

In many ways, this was my film school. You learn from every project, but this was the first time I was directing other people's screenwriting and working on a scale of production that was so large. At one point, Carmi told me one of the episodes I was directing had to be shot in nine days. I think we shot for twenty-seven hours straight to make that deadline. I was lucky to have the brilliant director of photography Gale Tattersall there, teaching me so much about how to move the camera, how to get coverage, and how to use second camera.

So for me, it was both a technical eye-opener and doing honor to the astronauts and everyone who was a part of the space program. Other than the production team, I was there the longest, and what it did was spoiled space for me in terms of projects in the future. I've read a lot of scripts set in the world of space or NASA since then, and I've always said, "I've done better than this already."

From the Earth to the Moon *wound up costing HBO north of $65 million, more than* **Apollo 13**'s *budget of $61 million.*

RICHARD PLEPLER:

We decided one of the most exciting things we could do was to premiere an episode at the White House and make it a national event. Quentin and I went to the White House and we met Capricia Marshall. We told her we wanted to screen the episode that highlighted Kennedy's famous speech to Congress, where he makes the clarion call, "We don't do it because it's easy, we do it because it's hard." And we thought President Clinton could invite all the major figures from that period who were still alive—the astronauts who walked on the moon, John Glenn, Walter Cronkite, and leading members of both sides of the aisle. They were unbelievably enthusiastic, and we received their full cooperation.

MICHAEL McMORROW, Executive:

They let us turn the East Room into a screening room, and we built custom projection platforms that blended into the architecture. This was the first time I had worked with the White House. It was terrifying. My favorite memory was just prior to opening the doors for arrivals that evening. I was sitting with a handful of technicians in the East Room when Tom Hanks and Rita Wilson came in and looked awestruck by being in the White House and took a few photos by themselves. Somehow, that just put me at ease.

RICHARD PLEPLER:

I was friendly with John Kennedy and I went to see him and said, "Look, this is going to be an extraordinary night and I think it would be deeply moving for everyone to have you and Caroline there"—and he accepted.

He told me that night of the event that it was the first time he had been back to the White House, and that President Clinton took him up to the residence so he could see the room he lived in as a little boy. There's a very famous picture somewhere of John and Clinton standing under the picture of JFK in the White House.

Hanks spoke, Jeff spoke, Clinton spoke, and it was deeply, deeply moving.

All the producers were there along with HBO senior management. It was very special.

BRIAN GRAZER:

I had never really entered the awards world of television, and the whole thing was a shocking experience. I had never won an Emmy. I never imagined winning an Emmy. All of a sudden, we're winning the premier awards of the night at the Emmys for *From the Earth to the Moon*. It was pretty emotional, and probably brought me the greatest amount of joy of the earliest part of my career.

CHRIS ALBRECHT:

From the Earth to the Moon was a big deal. It got the attention of a lot of people, especially at Time Warner because they were saying, "Here's little HBO being celebrated at the White House." I don't think anyone there saw that coming, and they said about me, "I guess this guy knows what he's doing." Jeff was always supportive, even when the finance guys were telling him to be cautious. Bridget was long gone. Michael was long gone. We had gotten our sea legs under us. There were some casualties along the way, but we were expanding our beachhead. We were getting more and more confident. This was now a new HBO.

Pulling back for a wide shot now, **From the Earth to the Moon** *can be regarded as a statement from Jeff Bewkes akin to Charles Foster Kane's "Declaration of Principles." Bewkes had come to HBO in 1979, and for a few years was known pretty much as, in the typically quotable words of Sheila Nevins, "that skinny guy from Yale in accounting." Those who thought Bewkes had little to no interest in, or instincts for, programming were proven wrong over the ensuing years, particularly in the three years since whirlwind Fuchs had blown away. In addition, Bewkes had empowered Chris Albrecht to a degree that made his competitors all but burst with envy. Together, these two otherwise dissimilar guys were of one mind on the issue of playing it safe: never do it.*

From the Earth to the Moon was event television of a high order and would also prove to be a turning point in HBO's development—a consequential final step in its graduation from puberty to adulthood.*

HBO was all grown-up now.

7

Rapture & Vanquishment

JUNE 6, 1998–SEPTEMBER 8, 2001

In the space of just 862 days, HBO managed to pull off a stunning trifecta, unveiling in that brief time three brilliant shows that would not only serve to virtually rebrand the network but also be such inarguable successes that they would remain on the air for multiple seasons. Indeed, one of them is still going strong twenty years later.

Sex and the City came first, arriving not with the blastoff some might assume it received from HBO but with a strangely quieter unveiling. It was followed by The Sopranos, *which—also surprisingly, in retrospect—crept through a four-episode calm before exploding in a dazzling fifth installment (titled, innocently enough, "College"), an episode that would change the course of the series and maybe reinvent the genre of one-hour drama as well. Then* Curb Your Enthusiasm, *a cockamamie comedy which evolved into a cheerfully profane series after a prefatory mockumentary made it clear that much more that could be made of the initial concept than was first imagined—as long as Larry David was in the starring role and the driver's seat, that is.*

After this triple thunderbolt, HBO would never be the same. Nor would it want to be.

And it wouldn't stop there. Six Feet Under *was on deck; more awards were coming HBO's way in the realm of documentaries, including another Oscar; promoter Don*

King would return to the HBO fold; and a new multi-decade sports franchise would be born.

All of this creativity and productivity would happen despite HBO's becoming part of the largest and most calamitous media merger in history, when Time Warner married AOL. The resultant "new world order" would jeopardize HBO's momentum—and threaten its very existence.

KRISTIN DAVIS, Actor:

I didn't think I would live to be thirty. I started drinking very young; luckily, I quit very young, before any success happened. I'm a recovering alcoholic. Acting is the only thing that made me want to get sober. I am very lucky in that way.

EDIE FALCO:

When I was a kid, my parents did their best to make Christmas in our house as magical as it could be. They weren't perfect parents, and we weren't perfect kids. It was a crazy family, but those holidays are still something that remain inside of me, visceral memories, with deep fondness. I try to re-create something like them for my kids, but there's melancholy with my dad and brother gone.

SUSIE ESSMAN:

The most bizarre thing is when people beg me to tell them to go fuck themselves, or I'll be at the Fairway on Broadway looking at produce and someone will shove a phone in my face and say, "It's my husband. Tell him he's a fat fuck." It's like my grandmother used to say, "You make plans and God laughs." I never planned my life thinking I would be beloved for telling people to fuck themselves, but it's kind of cool.

HBO programming had skewed male for much of its life, one determining factor being what was considered "gettable" (i.e., boxing). Another reason: the insistence of executives that HBO be the "anti-broadcast network"; to do so, they would rely mainly on such "manly" stuff as violence, nudity, rough language, and other allegedly masculine components, though done in a fresh way. Michael Fuchs in particular believed the broadcast networks catered to their female audiences to an "absurd" degree. One notable exception for HBO was If These Walls Could Talk, *a documentary that tackled personal experiences with abortion through the decades. That film and its sequel not only garnered awards but attracted a significant female audience. HBO execs took note; women were watching.*

Cheeky Candace Bushnell, meanwhile, had not only seen her audacious Sex and the City column become hot stuff in the **New York Observer** *but had also turned it into a book. While the getting was good, she sold the TV rights to Darren* **Melrose Place** *Star for $25,000 after a fruitful Sunday dinner in 1995. When HBO leapt into the bidding fray, beating out ABC for the script, television history was ready to be made.*

SARAH JESSICA PARKER, Actor and Executive Producer:

We didn't grow up having HBO in our home, but I knew people who had it and it was the movie channel. Outside of the movies, the rest of the programming felt like a place for a man.

CANDACE BUSHNELL, Author:

The book was real. It was about the grittiness of New York, the transactional nature of relationships, and it asked that question all the single women I knew were asking, which was, "Why are there all of these great, thirtysomething single women and no great men to be with them?" A question that we're still asking!

Most of my friends were writers, and the friends who had had books made into movies like Bret Easton Ellis and Jay McInerney weren't happy with their movies.

I had done a story about Darren Star in *Vogue*, that was how we met. I really liked his sensibility.

DARREN STAR, Creator:

There was one moment where ABC was interested in it, and I asked them, "Could you even call the show *Sex and the City*?" But it was never my intention to bring it to a broadcast network. It was only about going to HBO. HBO had done *The Larry Sanders Show*, which I thought was brilliant, and HBO at the time was primarily movies. I loved the idea of going to a place where you'd watch a movie and then see an episode of *Sex and the City* and you wouldn't feel like you were watching a television show. You'd feel like you were watching a short film.

CAROLYN STRAUSS:

Creative freedom was our calling card, I think that's why Darren came to us with the book. He knew this had to be pretty frank and would not survive muster with network standards and practices.

SARAH JESSICA PARKER:

Darren is obviously a critical part of the story. What Darren did was set the table beautifully, he recognized something in Candace's writing, in that book. He was smart enough to get it, and translate it into a jumping-off place for television.

We shot the pilot, then we all sort of walked away not having expectations, not knowing when we might hear from somebody because it worked alternatively to conventional broadcast television. There wasn't a drop-dead date for the up-fronts. Their calendar was their own. So a long amount of time passed before I even heard about the show getting picked up.

When we were picked up, I had a real panic attack about doing a television series and tried to get out of it. I sort of saw the commitment, the television series in this. It felt like I was going to suffocate. I was going to be locked down for seven years, and it would be the same thing every day.

QUENTIN SCHAFFER:

Coming into the series, SJ was the best-known actress because of her movie career. Kim and Kristin Davis had been on some TV, and Cynthia Nixon had done a lot of theater. Sarah Jessica was a B-level actress and the only one who had any name power.

SARAH JESSICA PARKER:

I was in the midst of being a journeyman and finding satisfaction in that, going from a play to a movie to two plays in a row and then maybe a small part in a movie. It seemed ideal to me. The idea of being married to that commitment professionally was terrifying to me until I called Kevin Huvane. I went to his office and we had this long chat, and then he brought in the head of the television department at CAA. And I said, "I'll do anything. I'll do movies of the week for them. I'll do anything to fulfill my contract. I'm just terrified." I got them on the phone, and they were like, "Well, what makes you comfortable?"

JEFF BEWKES:

Chris had me come to a lunch with Sarah Jessica, so she could see that we were going to put all the resources of the company behind it. She wanted to know if the guy in my seat cared about the show. I told her, "I've read all of the scripts that have been written. They're great. You should do it, it will work. Please make the show."

SARAH JESSICA PARKER:

That's the beginning of my relationship with HBO and how they chose to deal with talent. It seemed like such a nice, tiny operation that was so intimately managed that an actor could call up and say, "I'm having a panic attack," and they would simply diagnose it and then treat it.

I showed up that first day of work, which happened to be up the street. I walked to work, no car and driver. Shot at the Banana Republic on Sixth Avenue and Bleecker. On my walk home, I thought there is nothing else I'd rather be doing than what I was doing. And I never looked back from that day on.

CYNTHIA NIXON, Actor:

I started acting when I was twelve. When we did the pilot of *Sex and the City*, I think I was thirty-one. I was very adamantly a New Yorker, and wanted to stay in New York, and at the time, there was *Law & Order* and *The Cosby Show*, so it was a big deal to have a show shooting here. My agent asked me, "Could you please put on a little makeup? Maybe a skirt?"

After my audition, they kept saying they weren't ready to commit yet, but they hadn't found anyone they liked better. What finally happened was there was a job on another series and my amazing manager who was my agent at the time spent the week on the phone with them, threatening and begging and saying, "You're gonna lose her, you're gonna lose her." Then she called me and said, "They finally said, 'Uncle.' They're going to cast you." It was incredible.

Kim and I had had the least experience of network television. Even with my very limited experience, I was aware that there were wildly creative people over at HBO. Their job was not to micromanage. Their job was to love us and believe in us and empower us. When it comes to the writers, it was to really help their vision be everything that it could be, rather than micromanaging it about stupid concerns that might on network television have alienated advertisers.

SARAH JESSICA PARKER:

When I met with Darren about doing the show, he's like, "You should produce the show." I said, "I don't know anything about producing. I've been around them, but I've not been paying attention enough to call myself a producer." He said, "Okay, just be a consultant for the first year, pay attention, listen, learn, sit in on things, hear how decisions are made and how problems are solved." HBO was very hospitable to that. Chris and Carolyn hired people they trusted, and let them do their jobs with very little creative intrusion. Notes, for sure, and healthy conversations about notes. Funny arguments about budgets that were real but were managed quickly. They wanted to keep things responsible, organized, and professional, with reliable producers who they could trust in New York City shooting. It was an enormous amount of trust between all parties, wonderfully collaborative.

DARREN STAR:

I evolved the idea of Carrie as a narrator of other people's stories to the point where Carrie would be asking a question that would somehow then reverberate in her own life. I was really able to think of Carrie as the front-and-center protagonist of this series. I wanted to create a dialectic so when she was exploring a question, she could look at her friends and they would all represent different points of view. I knew a Samantha, a Miranda, a Charlotte, and I certainly knew a Carrie. Carrie in a way is a synthesis of all of these women, the questioner or explorer. Her friends are archetypal women.

CAROLYN STRAUSS:

I had known Michael Patrick [King] for years in New York. Darren was an hour nighttime soap writer; Michael was a half-hour comedy writer. He has a singular talent, and I felt he could bring something to the show that would really complement Darren, particularly in terms of his comedy sense. And that absolutely happened. Michael was very deft at using comedy to take characters on their emotional journeys.

MICHAEL PATRICK KING, Executive Producer:

Carolyn sent me a VHS of the pilot. It wasn't particularly funny. I was unattached to the entire experience, except for the last moment, where Big throws her out of the car ostensibly and says, "Have you ever been in love?" She turns around and says to him, "Have you ever been in love?" and he says, "Abso-fucking-lutely." And the cut back to Sarah Jessica looked like she'd been hit with a two-by-four in her gut. It was such a confused, surprising, mysteriously impactful silent thing, that's when I went, "I don't know what that is, but I'm *very* drawn to it."

CAROLYN STRAUSS:

There are times as an executive when you find yourself between a director and a producer or writer, or between two producers, and they are really stressful. It wasn't that either Darren or Michael Patrick was right and the other was wrong; they just saw the show in different ways.

MICHAEL PATRICK KING:

The first thing I said was, "We have to do it without looking at the camera. People want to believe this. They don't need to be told they're watching a TV show." So the first thing we did once we started this series, I said, "We've got to get this out." That's the first significant change that I was like, This is wrong.

JOHN MELFI:

Both Darren and Michael had strong personalities and there became a lot of ownership issues between the two of them in terms of the material. They had diverging opinions about whether it was a sex comedy or if this was a show that would eventually grow up and become more about relationships.

I remember Michael and Darren were out in the parking lot, having a conversation about figuring out season two, and whether we should break the fourth wall and have Carrie talk to the camera. The two of them, I believe, were at odds with their vision.

And they were in the parking lot having quite a loud argument about it. It was a very echo-y conversation around the buildings. And it was quite something, because I hadn't encountered anything quite so passionate before between showrunner and writer. So, there were no holds barred. The passions ran high.

JEFF BEWKES:

At a premiere, Darren did that Hollywood thing, "Hey, how do you like it? The ratings are up." I said to him, "If you don't take the ratings down by a third, I'm going to cancel this fucking show. I don't want ratings. I want a better show. Watch the *Sanders* show and stop explaining jokes."

I remember asking SJ and Cynthia, "Am I off base or is there too much voice-over?" They said, "Absolutely. It's Darren. He wants to make it a big hit, like *90210* or *Melrose Place*."

Chris and Carolyn were really good at moving that show from Darren to Michael where it became a really good show. It didn't start that way.

MICHAEL PATRICK KING:

We didn't win the Emmy the first two seasons, and Jeff Bewkes would say to me, "Good, good. You don't want that acceptance. You want to be the rebel."

SARAH JESSICA PARKER:

Michael couldn't have done the work he did if Darren hadn't set the table. Michael Patrick was in an absolutely exquisite spot to start going deeper, to start making sure all the women had their own stories, although they remained archetypal.

You couldn't just keep them surface. You had to start giving them more because they're great actors, and they deserve to show more complexity and range, but also for the audience to care more and to invest more in all the characters' lives. Darren gave us the first season and handed it over to Michael, and Michael knew just exactly what to do with it.

KRISTIN DAVIS:

I felt trusted by Michael Patrick. And in that environment, you can really grow in a way that I don't know if people really understand or appreciate.

It was so impressive that Jeff, Chris, and Carolyn were able to let us do that because it was a big time for the network. It was formative, yet they were very empowering and trusting of us. That's how I feel as an actor. Had I not been trusted, Charlotte would have stayed in the little box. She wasn't particularly fleshed out in the pilot. They let me and Michael and Darren and all of the writers flesh that out as time went on.

SARAH JESSICA PARKER:

I was always so greedy about being in the show. I loved being inside the pages. People confuse me and Carrie, and I understand that, because we do look alike. I didn't have the time in the same way to spend on friendships that she did. I also have never spoken that candidly about intimate things. I've always been much more private. I'm inquisitive. I understand that curiosity about people, but I'm a fairly private person about my life and my home. That's wonderfully different. But I think sometimes it seemed easy.

CYNTHIA NIXON:

My mother was asked what Miranda and I have in common. She said, "Well, they look a lot alike." I'm a person who feels more confident about my brain than maybe other things. I'm very career focused, but certainly not to the extent that Miranda is. There was this whole other domestic, maternal, married part of me, that previously Miranda didn't have.

It was a latent part of me and it's something I learned from my mother, too. I was confident, but it maybe hadn't really come to the fore yet. And

Miranda's sureness that she was right, and her eagerness to get into a confrontation, if she thought she'd just been dissed, or the other person was wrong. I felt like it was there, it just hadn't really blossomed yet.

I think Miranda is the person who will tell you the hard truths. It's sort of an immaturity in her. The other women are more live and let live. For Miranda, it's like an itch she has to scratch. If she sees somebody making a mistake, she's going to call it out. Sometimes that can be good because stuff doesn't fester with her. There are more blow ups right away, but I personally would rather have that.

She and I were pretty far different at first, but she grew toward me and I grew toward her. I think when you talk about something like running for governor or supporting candidates or speaking out on issues, that just feels like a very Miranda thing to do. It's not a disjunct for people. When I ran for governor, we had a whole line of swag of stuff that references Miranda, like, "I'm a Miranda and I'm voting for Cynthia."

SARAH JESSICA PARKER:

I learned that I was wrong about television.

We shot the whole first season, but we were never on the air. I think we were shooting the second season by the time we went on the air. So we were in this very fortunate place of having no opinions playing a role in how we were moving forward. That was a big deal for us.

I bumped into a woman on the street who is a friend of mine, who said, "Oh my God, I just saw your show. And it was so great." And then I said, "What are you talking about?" She said, "Your HBO show, *Sex and the City*." I was like, "Oh, you saw it?" She said, "Yeah, it's great. I loved it." I hadn't seen it.

CANDACE BUSHNELL:

I thought that this show would end after two seasons, when Carrie and Mr. Big break up. Turns out that it was right when it started to take off.

DARREN STAR:

Mr. Big was this idea of the un-gettable, unattainable guy. Carrie was somebody who was questioning: What is love? You're not going to have intimacy with the unattainable person. I think eventually they find their way to each other. In a way I would say women and men can relate to the idea that you're not going to have intimacy with the unattainable person, and what does it mean to want that person? I thought of Mr. Big as the great love of Carrie's life, but also her great blind spot.

CANDACE BUSHNELL:

Mr. Big really represents what you as a woman can never be. You can't be the CEO. You can't make millions. You can't be in charge of your own life. We know how few women CEOs there are. So in a sense, Mr. Big is the ambitious, achievement side of women that society says that you can't be, but you can marry. And if you can marry and you can be with Mr. Big, maybe you, too, can take on some of those qualities. Maybe you, too, can be Mr. Big. So it's like a psychological thing, and I realized that when my Mr. Big broke up with me, it is a fantasy and it's a projection, and women project *a lot* onto men. If women did not project onto men, I hate to tell you, I don't think men would fare very well in the harsh light of day, if we really looked at their actions. But as women we project great qualities on men that they may or may not have. When my Mr. Big broke up with me I realized, "You know what? I don't want to *be with* Mr. Big. *I want to be Mr. Big.*" And that, I think, is a defining moment in a woman's life.

Sex and the City's success didn't detract from HBO's continued affinity for comedy specials. Robert Klein, George Carlin, Steve Martin, and a slew of others had laid so strong a foundation for HBO comedy specials back in the 1970s that more than twenty years later, the channel remained the destination of choice for comics both new and established. It was also one of the only choices, since HBO had scared away much of the competition and broadcast networks couldn't air the comics uncensored.

*So when a superstar like Jerry Seinfeld wanted to begin his post-***Seinfeld***-the-series chapter, or if up-and-comer Chris Rock had branding challenges that he wanted to address, HBO was the place to go.*

After Seinfeld was done with **Seinfeld***, HBO desperately wanted to be the venue for his first big comedy concert, and his savvy managers knew it. But when Howard West and George Shapiro asked for a cool $10 million, Chris Albrecht would quotably reply, "What the fuck?! Get off the weed!" That said, he anted up the dough, and* **I'm Telling You for the Last Time** *had one of the most ambitious opening nights of any HBO special.*

NANCY GELLER:

Jerry was coming off the *Seinfeld* finale, he was bigger than ever, and this was going to be his first special. The negotiations were ridiculous. We didn't want to lose Jerry, and I had been able to get Chris to agree to pay more for a special than anyone had ever gotten, but then I got a call from Marty Callner who asked, "How much money are you giving me to produce it?" I said, "We put it all in Jerry's deal. It's called one fee." He said, "Oh no, it's not.

George Shapiro said that's Jerry's fee." Production for this special was going to be about $1 million so now I got to go back to Albrecht and say, "You made a mistake. The deal doesn't include production." He said, "Bullshit, it absolutely does." We had to go back and forth again with negotiations, and in the end, we had to pay that, too.

The special itself was terrific. Jerry decided he wanted to "bury" his material, and in the opening, we had Shandling, Klein, and others at a cemetery with Jerry. There was even a coffin.

CHRIS ROCK:

Bring the Pain was so big, right? I'm on *Oprah*. I'm on *60 Minutes*. My life's a fucking whirlwind. But there was a lot of grumbling that only white people liked me. It was when Whitney Houston won too many Grammys and she was getting booed at the Soul Train Awards. There was this, "He's funny, but white people like him." Meanwhile, there's no white people in the audience of *Bring the Pain*. So my reaction to "only white people like me" was, I'm going to do the blackest special ever. It's going to be bigger, and it's going to be blacker. It's going to be at the Apollo; Doug E. Fresh and Slick Rick are going to open for me.

Nobody at HBO objected to anything. I had carte blanche. I never wasted a dime. I never abused that privilege at all. Everybody was great over there. Chris, Nancy, Carolyn, the whole group of them.

Though it's hard to calculate ROI for a subscription service like HBO, the money doled out for Seinfeld and Rock paid off with a combined eight Emmy nominations, further fueling the network's appetite to own comedy in ways the networks could not.

In that regard: before Sacha Baron Cohen brought us Borat, he became Ali G, a wannabe British rapper who scammed unsuspecting power brokers and stars into embarrassing interviews.

The Ali G Show aired on Channel 4 in the UK before migrating to HBO for seasons two and three in 2003 and 2004. Though the character of Ali G seemed the consummate dimwit and clown prince of ridicule, Cohen had studied history at England's prestigious Cambridge University and honed his unique brand of satire into a "gotcha" device, snaring real celebrities, often unknowingly, into audacious ersatz interviews and outlandish scenarios. The eclectic roster of guests included UN Secretary-General Boutros Boutros-Ghali, former US secretary of state James Baker, Speaker of the House Newt Gingrich, TV host James Lipton, and activist Ralph Nader. Donald Trump had walked out of an Ali G interview after G pitched Trump a glove designed to keep one's hands clean while eating ice cream.

NANCY GELLER:

You can imagine with Sacha the nonsense and craziness we went through. In every episode, there was something that people were worried about, and our lawyers were always warning us, "This could be trouble." Others asked why we were putting ourselves in such a precarious position. But it was an amazing show, and Sacha was and is an incredible talent.

Then Jerry Seinfeld calls me up and says, "It's Jessica's birthday, and the best present I could give her is that she wants to meet Sacha Baron Cohen, more than life itself. Would you set it up?" Can you imagine Jerry Seinfeld, superstar, asking Nancy Geller this? I call Sacha and say, "You're not going to believe this . . ." Turns out they are in awe of each other. I set up a dinner for them, and they're very close now.

The public's first peek at **The Sopranos** *was a two-minute trailer that HBO unveiled in late 1998. Set against a background of catchy Hammond-organ riffs, courtesy of Booker T and the M.G.s' "Green Onions," interspersed with images of gangland violence. There was a soundbite from James Gandolfini (hardly a recognizable face, voice, or name yet), claiming Tony Soprano's career was in "waste management" to the beautiful Lorraine Bracco, playing an attentive shrink. The spot culminated with a rendering of the series' blood-drenched title,* **The Sopranos**, *its "P" replaced by a gun.*

So, then, what had we here? Little about the trailer suggested that what would unfold when the first episode aired in January 1999 (and continued over six seasons spanning more than eight years) would prove to be the defining drama of TV's newest golden age. Or that whatever it was would be the hallmark of HBO's status as the foremost outlet for serious modern American drama.

The Sopranos *was enigmatic creator David Chase's far-more-than-another-mob-show account of the American family reeling its way through crisis, calamity, and countless brutally bloody murders. And, oh yeah, trying to get the teenage daughter into college and deposit cranky Mama in an old folks' home, while Tony ran the regional Mafia, with less than a handful of family and associates he could truly trust.*

The concept may sound pedestrian, but the execution was impeccable and iconoclastic, brightened by Chase's imaginative use of dream sequences, high comedy, low-down melodrama, brutal and inventive violence, and cleverly curated music. All of this transformed the genre, and, yes, even the medium. He did so with the invaluable help of a patently incredible cast that included Oscar nominee (for her legendary role in **Goodfellas***) Lorraine Bracco; Edie Falco, as Carmela Soprano, who reaffirmed her status, in every episode, as a world-class actress capable of innumerable gradations of love, hate, and all the shadings thereof; and Michael Imperioli, who proved somehow* *both poignant and frightening as a kingpin wannabe. The entire cast was a marvel, down to the smallest and most seemingly insignificant role.*

Auteur extraordinaire David Chase, who had spent decades wanting to be in the movie business, would become, virtually overnight, one of the most commanding names in all of television. The Sopranos would lead HBO to glories previously unimagined even by daydreamers, raising the HBO flag higher than ever before.

LLOYD BRAUN, Executive, Brillstein-Grey:

I was an entertainment lawyer when Brad Grey approached me to come to Brillstein-Grey to run the company with him. He had just made a big television deal at Cap[ital] Cities and had hired Kevin Reilly to run the television business. I was Kevin's lawyer at the time, and thought he was a terrific executive. I thought we had a great shot at building a next generation management/production company.

Shortly into my tenure, Kevin and I signed David Chase, who had been a writer client of mine, to an overall deal with our television studio.

KEVIN REILLY, Executive, Brillstein-Grey:

I will tell you point blank that when Lloyd brought David in, Brad's literal quote was, "Who's the old fucking guy that Lloyd's bringing me? Why is he bringing me his fucking throwback guys?" Dave was like fifty-five at this point.

LLOYD BRAUN:

David starts coming in to pitch shows to Kevin and me, and as often happens in the beginning, we didn't hear any ideas we were falling in love with. Nothing was sticking. After another meeting where we didn't react positively to anything David was bringing us, I walked him out to the lobby, and I could see that he was really down. I didn't have a lot of confidence in any of my creative chops at the time—having never pitched a show before—but I had this idea that I had been thinking about. I said to David, "Would you mind if I suggest an idea to you?" He goes, "No, not at all." I go, "I just saw *Godfather II* on television. Wouldn't it be interesting to do a modern-day *Godfather*— what would it be like today with a guy who has a seemingly normal family life and you're thinking he's a regular guy, but he's not. He's in the mob." That's what I gave him. David says to me, "I like that idea. Did you know I'm Italian?" I go, "I had no idea you're Italian." He says, "Alright, that's interesting. Let me think about that."

After the pilot was produced, David delivered to my office a framed one-sheet poster with a note which said: "Dear Lloyd, thank you for the idea. Thank you for everything." I still have it in storage.

DAVID CHASE, Creator:

I would take development deals in television, even though I never wanted to be in TV. I would try to write features on the side but I never got one made.

Lloyd said, "You have a groundbreaking series in you." It took me aback. No one had ever talked to me that way. Part of me was going, "Yeah, yeah," the other part of me was touched. I said, "What do you mean?" He said, "*The Godfather*. We would like to do that for television." I said, "I am not interested in that. There has already been a *Godfather*."

But on the way home, I thought about this feature idea I had had with Robert De Niro as this mafia guy, and Anne Bancroft as his mother, who's in therapy. I pitched it at UTA [United Talent Agency] and my agent said, "Mob movies are done. Forget it." But then I thought it might work as a TV show because it has family, female content, so I pitched it to Bernie and Brad. Everyone really liked it.

BOB GREENBLATT, Executive Producer and Executive:

Every year at Fox we would make lists of writers we wanted to be in business with, and I was a fan of David's and his show *Almost Grown*. We were still a very fledgling company. So I called my friend Kevin Reilly at the Brillstein company. I said, "Let's make a six-episode commitment to David Chase," which was huge for us at the time.

Kevin came back to me a short time later and said, "I'm not sure this is going to work out. David would love to do a deal with you guys, but he's got one idea that he can't get out of his head and he doesn't think it's right for you." I said, "Well, why don't you let us judge whether it's right for us." He goes, "It's a mafia show." I said, "Oh my God, that's probably not right for us, but we love him so much and he's so great. Let's sit down and talk about it."

KEVIN REILLY:

Bob liked it and put it into development with what at that time was a fairly substantial commitment for a pilot. It got through several rounds. Anthony LaPaglia read it and said he was interested.

LLOYD BRAUN:

Fox orders the pilot subject to casting the lead, and they wanted Anthony LaPaglia for the lead. But we couldn't make a deal. I think we were $5,000 or $10,000 an episode apart. We were devastated. We thought the project was dead.

DAVID CHASE:

Bob Greenblatt had said, "This is so full of life," but I never heard back. Then I got a phone call from Dana Walden, who said, "I love your script, I think it is fantastic." And I said, "Great. When are we going to get started?" She said, "There's the rub. We are not going to do it, but on a human level, I want to tell you how good your script was." So that was the end of that.

KEVIN REILLY:

David was definitely wounded by it.

DAVID CHASE:

Then Brillstein started sending it to all the networks, where it got universally praised but didn't have any takers. Les Moonves said to me, "I got no problem with the robbing and crying, but does he have to take Prozac and see a shrink?" I said, "Yeah!"

My second year of the deal, I did another project for Brillstein at CBS as I was going out the door. Then Lloyd Braun said to my agents, "David Chase did everything that we asked him to do, he did everything right, but I don't think we served him well. I would like to take this over to HBO."

I said to them two years before, because I was a fan of *Larry Sanders*, "Why can't we take it to HBO?" They said that they were not that interested in original programming. But Bewkes had come in, and now they were ready for it.

CAROLYN STRAUSS:

David came in and pitched it. I remember he was wearing what I would come to know as his lucky green pants. It was clear to us that he had such a visceral feel for the complexity of his characters and their world. After reading the script, it was also clear that this was a guy who was trying to figure out his relationship with his mother and his family, while trying to balance all the competing parts of his life.

CHRIS ALBRECHT:

I read the pilot script before they came in to talk to us. I liked it. It was one of those funny meetings where David said, "Maybe I should lose the shrink," and I was like, "I think you need more shrink, that's what's distinctive about it. It's a great device into the inner psyche of this character. We haven't seen that before."

We make the deal for a pilot, and very soon after, I'm on the phone with Billy Crystal and he's telling me about this project he was really excited about that he was writing with Peter Tolan. I said, "What's it about?" He said, "I play the psychiatrist to a mob boss, who's going to be De Niro." I said, "Are you fucking with me?"

I was a little concerned. I knew he was doing a comedy, so it wasn't a direct conflict, but it definitely was one of those things that happen in show business where you've never heard an idea before and then all of a sudden there's four of them.

DAVID CHASE:

When I was writing the pilot, there was a shrink who lived on my street. He used to walk his dog around. I went up to him one time and asked, "If a mobster comes into your office, would you treat the guy?" He said, "Yeah. I would say to myself, If he contemplates anything physically dangerous, I would have to step in or call the authorities. Technically." That's what he said, "Technically." I thought, Melfi is so compromised and she says that in the pilot. I thought, Okay, she sold her soul to the devil.

LORRAINE BRACCO, Actor:

Truth is, I didn't even want to read the script. I didn't want to do it. For me it was another mafia script, and I didn't want to make a career out of doing roles like that. Besides, I don't think I could have played a better mafia wife than I did in *Goodfellas*.

Then Sheila Jaffe called and said, "You have to read this script. This guy really wants to meet you." I wasn't going to say no to Sheila, so I read it, and completely flipped. I thought it was fantastic and was blown away by how different it was than anything I'd had seen before.

I told my agents after I read the script that I didn't want to play Carmela. I wanted to play Melfi. And they were like, "Are you crazy?" It is called *The Sopranos*, not *Tony and Dr. Melfi*.

They said, "Do us a favor, just go in there and meet the fucking guy." So I did, and I fell in love with David. And in that meeting, I pleaded my case, telling David all of the reasons why I wanted to play Dr. Melfi.

I always felt that the relationship between a psychiatrist and a patient is very intimate. Melfi could have been the weak link; after all, who wants to watch two people sit and talk? It's not cinematic. But the writing was so terrific, it made everything else beside the point.

EDIE FALCO:

I was doing *Oz*, and as far as I was concerned, I was in heaven. I had a job that paid my rent and people I was working with who I really liked. I was always auditioning, and there's something different about an audition when you don't need the job. One tends to bring their best self, because there's no sense of desperation.

I had heard about this thing going around called *The Sopranos*. I thought it was about singers. I never asked too many questions about it. Then it came my way. I read the part and I thought, I know exactly who this Italian American woman is. That's how I grew up. I also knew I wouldn't get it, because I never got those parts. I'd never thought of myself as traditionally Italian looking. I thought it was going to be Annabella Sciorra or Marisa Tomei. The whole thing came out of nowhere, really. It was like getting hit by a truck that comes around a corner you don't see coming. I'm so grateful it came to me that way.

I've been sober for damn near thirty years at this point. I had a lot of issues in my twenties, like really nasty ass stuff, that happened very badly, very quickly. I couldn't continue living the way that I was. I wouldn't have continued to live. I've got a long history of drug and alcohol problems in my family. I knew where it was going. By the time we started *The Sopranos*, I was close to ten years sober. I'd been doing and studying Buddhism already at that point, and I felt pretty anchored in a very strong sober community as I entered into *The Sopranos*.

MICHAEL IMPERIOLI, Actor:

I was in the waiting room at HBO testing for Christopher. I think Edie was the only one testing for Carmela; Lorraine was the only one testing for Melfi; then there were three people testing for Tony. Jim Gandolfini, who I didn't know; Mike Rispoli, who I was good friends with, who went on to play Giacomo Michael "Jackie" Aprile Sr.; and one guy who looked familiar but I couldn't figure out who he was. The casting director pulled me aside and said, "That's Little Steven Van Zandt wearing a wig."

SUSIE FITZGERALD:

It was very hard to cast the lead of Tony Soprano. David was set on having it feel authentic and wanted to cast all Italian Americans. We read everybody.

We only had a clip of Gandolfini from *True Romance* and brought him out from New York for an audition. He does not like to audition and was kind of nervous.

But for me, the minute he walked in the room, I was like, Oh, that's totally him. The character's name was Tommy at the time and I thought to myself, that is Tommy for sure.

JEFF BEWKES:

I loved Gandolfini from the first time Chris sent me a tape during casting. We were putting a husky guy with a hairy back wearing a wifebeater in the lead role. Nobody else would do that. But he was Tony Soprano.

LORRAINE BRACCO:

First time I saw Jimmy was in *Streetcar Named Desire*, Alec Baldwin and Jessica Lange. He had a small role, but I went looking through the playbill to find out, Who is that guy? I loved him the minute I saw him.

ILENE LANDRESS, Executive Producer:

I read the script, and I said, "Oh my God, this is good." It restored my faith in television.

Before *The Sopranos*, most of my work was in movies, which was why David said he hired me. "You haven't been ruined by television." Then after working with him for ten years, he went off to do a movie and told me, "I can't hire you. You're ruined by television."

DAVID CHASE:

I didn't want to shoot three days in New York for exteriors and three days in LA on a set. I wanted to shoot in New Jersey. Everyone, including Dick Wolf said, "Shoot in New Jersey? Why?" Chris Albrecht looks down at the script and said to me, "You're going to shoot it in New Jersey, right?" and I thought, "Oh this is the place."

MICHAEL IMPERIOLI:

When we did the pilot, it was a lot of fun, but I didn't have a lot of hope for it. I'll be honest.

DAVID CHASE:

The Bada Bing Strip Club was in the pilot, and Chris said to me, "Let's not do things just because we can." In other words, don't show breasts and do other things just because you can get away with it. I said, "That is not why I'm doing it," but I thought that that was really smart. He agreed that Tony and Melfi should not hook up. That was where most networks had wanted to go.

MICHAEL IMPERIOLI:

My first day on the set, I have to drive Jim. That's Christopher Moltisanti's job. Problem was, I didn't know how to drive. I hadn't told anybody because I wanted the job, you know? I had to back down the sidewalk with him next to me, doing dialogue with him, and extras running out of the way. I managed to do it like several times, and then the director said, "Do it again twice as fast." I smashed the rear end of that Lexus into this tree really bad. The airbags went off and our heads snapped back. It was a fucking mess. I'm sitting there going, They're gonna fucking fire me. This guy must think I'm an asshole. I turned to look at Jim and he's cracking up.

They said, "If this show gets picked up, you better get a driver's license."

EDIE FALCO:

I thought other things were good that didn't go anywhere. I thought things were exceedingly mediocre that ended up being very successful. So I didn't know, to be honest with you. We might've met for the first time at the first table read. You never know what you're walking into. I've done sex scenes with men that I didn't meet until we started the scene. You get used to managing all kinds of personalities. It became clear early on for me that Jim and I were a match, that we were from the suburbs and we weren't from fancy households or families. We fell into this career almost by accident.

The last thing either of us would have expected was to be one day well-known. Jim, very much like me, doesn't talk a lot. He doesn't talk about the character's backstory, which really works for some actors. Jim was visceral and instinctual in his way of performing. He got completely lost in it. Jim and I really clicked in that regard, and it was that way from the beginning to the end of our time working together. I was very grateful.

SUSIE FITZGERALD:

David would ask me while we were filming the pilot if I thought people would watch it. I said, "I have no idea, I just know that I like it."

DAVID CHASE:

They went to an ad agency who submitted a thousand alternate titles, but they wanted *Family Man*. By that time, we were in production and the cast was very upset. Steven Van Zandt went apeshit. Then *Family Guy* came on, luckily, and we called it *The Sopranos*.

PETER BENEDEK:

Chris said, "Everyone's going think it's a show about opera." And David said, "No they won't, they'll get it right away."

KEVIN REILLY:

David and I went over to screen the pilot with Chris and Carolyn. When it finished, Chris literally put his hands in his face, covering his eyes, rubbing his eyes. It felt like it went on for ten minutes. I thought, "Oh my God, we didn't go all the way down this road to have him say, 'It pulls up short.'" Then he looked at me and said, "It's good, it's really good." I think he was digging deep.

LORRAINE BRACCO:

David had sent me the pilot, and I asked him, "What's going on? If we're going to do this, I need to know, because I have other work." He said, "They haven't picked it up yet, they're hemming and hawing. Call Chris Albrecht." Now I had never called up an executive in my career. What do I know? But I called up Chris and said, "Hi, we don't really know each other, but I want to tell you, I just saw the pilot of *The Sopranos*, and it's the best thing I've seen in a decade. What's going on?" Chris said, "It's very expensive." I said, "Can't we sell it overseas? I could call people in France to pick it up," and he says, "I already sold it, but it's very, very expensive." I said, "Chris, you must do this."

CAROLYN STRAUSS:

There was a lot of conversation about whether or not Tony Soprano was going to be somebody that HBO wanted as a main character in a show. It wasn't the wifebeater undershirt—he didn't beat Carmela, he would punch the wall instead, but it was more whether you wanted an antihero murdering mafioso as one of the biggest faces on your network.

But we loved the script and the show so much and knew that we could approach it in a much more realistic way than a network could in terms of bad language, violence, nudity, and, most important, tone and POV. That helped make it more in line with the reality of how David wanted to make the show. When we finally got that green light, we were thrilled.

JEFF BEWKES:

I'm watching the first episode alone in my living room and now you see the full cast in action, and I'm thinking, "Wow, I can't believe this." I call Chris and asked, "Can they all be this good? Does he know how to do ten of these?"

CHRIS ALBRECHT:

Jeff really liked it, but this was before we really knew or trusted our own instincts. So we did some testing and it came back with really unlikable elements about the male lead. I was like, "Yeah . . . he kills people." That was us fumbling a little bit, not having the courage of our convictions or any real track record to say, "Here's what's going to work for us." We had done *Oz*. I don't think *Sex and the City* was on the air yet. We were still a work in progress. I'm pretty sure that was the last time we tested.

DAVID CHASE:

It's amazing they went against the testing. They had such courage. I still love them for that. Seriously. Those people.

MICHAEL IMPERIOLI:

We went back the next summer, shot the rest of the first season, and that was when I saw what this was. Episode after episode, I'm looking at these scripts going, "Oh my God, they're going really deep." It was all very complex, really brilliant, but also funny, bizarre, and unique. I fell in love with it.

It gave me a sense of confidence as an actor that I could go to those places that were required for Christopher, somebody who really was a flat-out killer when he had to be. At the same time, he was a very vulnerable guy who wanted approval, had a drug problem, and tried to fight his drug problem and overcome it. Going to those dark places for me is always very interesting. I'm not afraid of it nor do I shy away from it. You had to really delve in there. It proved to me that I could do that. I did things with that character I had never really done before.

I liked getting pushed too far. I like to push limits.

LORRAINE BRACCO:

Jimmy would always go first when we would film our scenes; often he would have a lot of dialogue so he would ask to put enough film in the camera that they wouldn't have to change it. He would just tell the whole story without me jumping in with whatever I had to say. During some of those mono-logues, they weren't always written as monologues, watching him do it, I would even forget I was on a set watching him work. It was fascinating.

Jimmy never had a problem with his lines when he was with me. Never. After his lines were done, and it was time to turn [the cameras] around, he would be so happy that he was done with a scene that was very long an arduous and complicated or emotional. He would be free, he would be silly, he would get frisky. He would play games, he would do a strip tease. Let's put it this way: I've been mooned.

EDIE FALCO:

The first bunch of jobs that you get, where you actually make a little money, are so exciting, because you get to pay your bills. Then as far as whether or not it's good or people will keep it going was never something I got good at being able to predict. We finished the trailer and I got a videocassette and showed it to my parents and they looked at me and said, "This is really good."

ILENE LANDRESS:

In the first season, we were trying to do eight days an episode, and it was really hard. We were doing sixteen- and eighteen-hour days.

Nobody will do that anymore. It's just not safe to be doing such long days, nights. It was pretty harrowing because you needed to get it done. As time went on, we had more days to shoot the show and it didn't have as many grueling days. But it was still hard.

CAROLYN STRAUSS:

Ilene loves her crew. She takes care of her crew; and as a result, she has a crew that shows up every day that's happy to be there. She inspires them to do their best, better than their best.

CHRIS ALBRECHT:

Carolyn's great skill was becoming part of the show, which is why she became a great executive producer. Carolyn ended up in later seasons han-dling more of the nuances of giving David notes. Suggestions. I always like to call it suggestions. I don't give them notes. I give suggestions.

LORRAINE BRACCO:

Chris Albrecht and Carolyn Strauss understood material, and they under-stood talent. Those are the two people who brought HBO to the heights.

CAROLYN STRAUSS:

We certainly had conversations about every episode—outlines, scripts, cuts, whatever. Chris taught me a lot of amazing stuff, and one was try and have as many thorough conversations as possible at the beginning. Chris reacted very strongly to David wanting Tony to kill a guy in the episode where Tony takes his daughter visiting colleges. He didn't like Tony doing that at all.

CHRIS ALBRECHT:

I read every script. When the script came in for episode five, the guy that he killed was actually a pretty good guy. He was a mafia guy who turned informer, was off living somewhere and had been a snitch. But Tony found him and he killed him. I said to Carolyn, "We can't fucking do this. Do you want me to fucking hate Tony? It's not like killing another mob guy. It's like killing a guy who got his life right." It was just too early in the series. I said to David, "It's only the fifth episode, we haven't earned this, you got to earn this." This was our first real showdown. We argued, argued, argued, and then he said something like, "If this guy Tony Soprano found this guy who had done this stuff in the past, he would kill him. And if he doesn't kill him, the entire show was full of shit."

It was such a statement that it ran through me. I couldn't argue with it. David was right. What we did do was a series of mitigating situations. The guy became not such a good guy, had a fight with his girlfriend, and tried to take Tony out first. Gandolfini killed him, but it was clear he was a bad guy. Those incremental changes really shifted the balance. To this day, I still think that if we would have done the original script, we would have had a very different reaction.

KEVIN REILLY:

Episode five was where HBO became HBO.

DAVID CHASE:

I can't say enough good things about them. Jeff, Chris, and Carolyn were great. They said smart things, and I couldn't believe how much they left me alone.

ILENE LANDRESS:

The first season, we were almost always shooting in New Jersey; but every once in a while there was a scene that was written for Manhattan, which was always exciting. I was living downtown on the West Side, and on this day, we were shooting in a funeral home in Little Italy. I thought, Outstanding, it's a beautiful sunny day. Instead of getting in the car and schlepping into New Jersey, I'm going to grab a cup of coffee and walk to set.

I walk across Sixth Avenue, and I see our trucks in front of this little old conservative Italian funeral home where we were shooting. Then people start walking out, and the location manager running toward me. I see trouble ahead. We were shooting a funeral scene and the scene was a little lady in the coffin and Uncle Junior turns to somebody in the receiving line, glances into the coffin and says, "She gave me my first blow job." Well, we got kicked out of the place.

You could totally panic, or you could see the humor in the whole thing. I called HBO and told them, "I guess we're done for the day."

QUENTIN SCHAFFER:

The Sopranos had issues with Italian American groups going after it. They felt it portrayed a stereotype. We believed viewers understood that this was a small faction and didn't represent all Italian Americans. We met with the groups and listened. People want to vent and be heard. But we really weren't going to meddle with what David Chase wanted to do.

DAVID CHASE:

Well, there's one thing I could say about the Italian American anti-defamation people, but is it important? Fuck them.

Before the show came on the air, Richard flew me out to the Beverly Hills Hotel, to meet with four of the leaders of the Italian anti-defamation faction. We sent them the tapes and then I met with them in the Polo Lounge. They said why it was so offensive to them and that Italians are more than gangsters. About halfway through the meeting, I said to one guy, "Wait a minute. Did you see the show? That is not even from our show." He said, "I haven't seen it yet." I had come all the way there for that meeting and they didn't even watch it. I said, "Fuck you people. You are shit. You're hypocrites. You're lazy bums."

JEFF BEWKES:

Every year the networks go to Pasadena to premiere their new shows for the critics. We were showing the critics an episode of *The Sopranos*, and Chris shows me a few more episodes. "What do you think?" I say, "Look I'm new to this. I love it. I think it's great. Am I wrong?" He said, "No, I think it's really good."

We looked at each other and said, "Let's pick it up not for one year, let's pick it up for four years. Let's sign everybody before they become hard to get." And we did.

QUENTIN SCHAFFER:

We said we ought to do a screening in New York. It was fairly small. After all, the cast were relative unknowns except for Lorraine Bracco. The theater held about 250 people.

We picked an appropriate venue for the reception, Joe's Pizzeria just off Broadway. I had not seen yet seen or heard the opening sequence because it was readied not long before the screening. When the pulsing theme song, "Woke Up This Morning" by Alabama 3, played, accompanied by visuals of Gandolfini driving by the New York skyline and Jersey factories, the place erupted. What a night.

JEFF BEWKES:

I walk in and standing at the bar Tony Sirico. He says to me, "How do you like it?" I was very enthusiastic. "I love it." He said, "So you're going to pick it up?" I said, "We're going to do this as long as you guys will do it." Instead of him saying, "Great," he fixes me with his fucking fisheye stare and dead-pans. "You said that to the wrong person. Now you've got to live up to that, and I'm going to come after you if you don't." I deadpanned back, "We're going to do it as long as you want to do it." Then he broke into a smile and said, "Good."

SUSIE FITZGERALD:

The next day Brad and I were flying back to California and we're in the car going to the airport and he gets a call from David Geffen to say, "Hey, congratulations. I heard you got a hit on your hands."

That was the first indication there was buzz on it in the industry. There was a huge snowstorm all across the East Coast the weekend it premiered, and the ratings were good out of the gate. It grew from there.

CHRIS ALBRECHT:

When Nancy Marchand got sick after the first season of *Sopranos*, the show never became the show David envisioned, a story that was going to be about a guy's relationship with his mother. All of a sudden, this guy is dealing with the loss of his mother.

BILL NELSON:

When *The Sopranos* hit, people who knew you for working at HBO started saying, "Oh my God, you work at HBO. That's amazing."

CARMI ZLOTNIK:

Don Ohlmeyer, who was the chairman of NBC, sent out an email after *The Sopranos* was out castigating the NBC team, saying, "Why are they doing this and we can't?"

TERENCE WINTER, Writer and Creator:

I grew up in Brooklyn, and when I was a teenager, I worked in a butcher shop owned by Paul Castellano, who was the head of the Gambino family. Years later I worked in an illegal casino, basically similar to the jobs that Ray Liotta had in *Goodfellas*. I knew people like Tony Soprano and understood that psychology and that world. When I saw the pilot, I called my agent and said, "You've got to get me on the show."

A lot of the initial writers got fired. I did an audition script, which became an episode in the second season.

One of the early moments in my tenure, we were in the writers' room, and this was back when David was still getting notes calls from HBO. The assistant came in and said, "David, one of the executives at HBO is on the phone with some notes." David looked at me and said, "Why don't you take it." I thought, Wow, he really trusts me to take this call from HBO. I took the call and wrote down the notes, and I typed them up really neatly. Twenty minutes later, I handed David the piece of paper with the notes, and without breaking stride, David took the notes and crumbled them up and threw them in the garbage. Wow. I was like, Holy shit, he didn't even look at it. He just was not interested in anybody's thoughts about that show except his and his writing staff's. That was the moment I knew, this is unlike anything I've ever been a part of. He knows what he wants to do and that's exactly what he's going to do.

CHRIS SPADACCINI, Executive:

Advertising became a form of storytelling for us, and our *Sopranos* campaigns routinely got press coverage. There were several *New York Post* stories where there was speculation looking for symbolic clues in our *Sopranos* ads. It was all about generating conversation. HBO has always wanted to be a brand that drives culture and conversation. Our marketing was intended to do the same. If it wasn't going to get press, if it had been done before, then it wasn't for us.

ERIC KESSLER:

As our programming evolved to reflect the tagline "It's Not TV. It's HBO," it was important that individual series campaigns reinforced the concept as well.

In the second year of *The Sopranos* we decided to adopt a completely different approach to television advertising. Instead of marketing the series as television, we would promote every show as if it were a movie. We discussed with Jeff and the programmers the need to dramatically increase the marketing budget. Since we only launched a few series a year, each one was a big deal and therefore we needed to spend accordingly. Everyone agreed.

Every series would be launched the way a studio would open a movie. Big teaser campaign, followed by launch ads, critics review spots, continuity campaign, and finale ads.

We decided we weren't going to create print campaigns that looked like other networks. So we went and hired Annie Leibovitz—who we paid $1 million—to shoot a conceptual ad of the *Sopranos* cast. It worked brilliantly creating buzz as people tried to decipher every little detail in the shot to determine if we had planted clues about the upcoming season. We hired Annie Leibovitz almost every year after.

QUENTIN SCHAFFER:

In 2001, Mitchell Fink, a gossip columnist for the New York *Daily News*, wrote a column where he revealed five plot points from the upcoming season. He obtained this leaked info and felt an obligation to get it out. When his piece ran, David Chase was as angry as I can remember. So he wrote a scene where Tony Soprano's daughter Meadow is walking through Union Square when she comes across a half-naked homeless woman with a copy of the *Daily News* crammed up her butt and only revealing Mitchell Fink's face. At the last minute David decided not to give Mitchell Fink the publicity. The morale here is not to mess with a writer of a mob show.

Apart from a specific show, there was another addition to the HBO Original programming lineup—a bold new logo that would be a marvel in branding and identification for decades to come.

BRUCE RICHMOND:

David Hudson, his partner, and I created the HBO Original Programming logo. Chris gave us marching orders to give something that branded original programming and broke out of "It's Not TV. It's HBO." The original HBO flyover logo for movies, done by Ian Hunter, was a very famous piece. That had been so cool to produce and was a real success. We also had a white HBO Presents logo on black, and this was to be the next step.

It was an iterative process. We got deep and managed to create a neat Pavlovian thing where if you're in the other room and you heard that sound it meant an HBO show was about to start. And in terms of the visual, on a very detailed level, when a TV turns off you get that little circle at the end, and we buttoned it with that. Turned out to be a really good thing, but it was a last-minute thing for us. It still had the analog sound that you remembered.

People have a real love for the HBO static. It's iconic. Years later, research came back that people were also very nostalgic about it.

When we moved to high-def, we tried to redo it, but it wasn't successful. We wound up going back to the old one. Those three seconds with auditory and visual bookends were perfect.

As the genre "original series" became a bigger part of programming, new questions arose, particularly with regard to scheduling.

JOHN BILLOCK:

We didn't have the volume of programming to take on all the hearts and minds of American television viewers the way the networks did, so we asked ourselves, "How can we maximize what we do?" Scheduling said, "Let's take over Sunday night. It's the number one night in American television households. Let's load it up and make Sunday night must watch night on HBO." And we did that by showcasing our original programming. We wanted to own Sunday night.

HENRY McGEE:

As the studios began to take the position that they would not distribute films theatrically unless they had the home video rights, our sources of supply began to dry up. Miramax sold itself to Disney, and independent video went through a rough patch. The invention of the DVD further complicated the home entertainment business for HBO.

BRIAN ROBERTS:

HBO was an incredible organization from the beginning. They punched way above their weight. They had a holistic view of this new medium called pay

TV, and they invented a lot of the products that we were selling. I remember writing letters to different CEOs at HBO over the years, letting them know how proud we were to have just watched one of their extraordinary shows, which helped define the experience for Comcast customers.

HBO was ready to break new ground, again, on the distribution side. It had adopted satellite transmission before it came to Ted Turner's Superstation and ESPN; it led the way for cable's transition from C-band to Ku-band; and now it put faith in two words to keep subscribers happy: "On Demand."

HBO On Demand, a subscription service that gave viewers immediate access to HBO's film and television content, debuted in 2001 in a series of markets selected to test-drive the product. The service first appeared during this trial period on Long Island and in Cincinnati and Cleveland, Ohio; Austin, Texas; and Columbia, South Carolina. According to reporting from **Multichannel News,** *the service was so popular that it ended up overloading servers. By July 2002, HBO was charging money for the service in a variety of other locations, including San Antonio, Texas; Portland, Maine; Honolulu; Northeast Ohio; Tampa, Florida; Bakersfield, California; and Raleigh and Charlotte, North Carolina.*

Video on demand was a true boon for the network—not only did the simple convenience make the HBO offering more appealing to subscribers, but it allowed HBO to do something that no other network could do in earnest on the programming side: focus on serialized shows.

With the flexibility of on demand, watching all episodes in a season in order became a much easier task. Instead of being constrained to self-contained one-hour shows or repetitive sitcoms, HBO could now produce story arcs that went for ten or twenty hours over a full season. This allowed for the depth of character and dynamic plots that would come to set the HBO programming bar a notch above all others.

This freedom also proved to be one of HBO's greatest value propositions to creative talent. Finally, there was a place to tell complex stories that many artists so yearned to tell.

JEFF BEWKES:

Multiplex was a step toward video on demand (VOD), but the technology for that wasn't ready yet. By the late 1990s we launched that, too, with a lot of help from our sister company, Time Warner Cable. We needed cable operators to put servers in their headends (each local cable system) and those servers had to be able to send whatever HBO show you select to your house on Elm Street and also send some other show to some other house down the street . . . hundreds of times all over town. Getting cable operators to invest in this and deliver it all over the country was a big effort and it took years.

Up to then we had all these disadvantages against the broadcast networks; they had the lead in schedules, big promotion budgets, and tune-in audiences. Now we had advantages to separate us: no ads; no ratings concerns; no advertisers to complain about racy content; the ability to tell a story over hours, not in forty-five minutes, with built-in commercial cliffhangers. It was a big fucking deal.

JOHN BILLOCK:

I always felt that multiplex was like a poor man's on-demand proposition. Yes, our subscribers had more programs to choose from at any given time, but the choices were limited by the number of feeds or "plexes" coming into the home, and HBO scheduling determined when those choices could be made by the consumer. It was a better viewer experience than single-channel HBO, but it was not on demand. We had the capability from our end, but we needed to partner with our cable affiliates. Downloading and storing thousands of hours of video at a cable system's headend was labor- and capital-intensive. More hardware, more storage, more operations management—human and software. It wasn't just as simple as flipping on a digital switch. So we actually built HBO On Demand two years before any cable operators even decided to test it with us, because it was such a large capital investment and commitment on their part. We believed that true HBO On Demand would incrementally, if not fundamentally, change the very value relationship with our customer base by changing the product itself.

JEFF BEWKES:

We were in a staff meeting. It was our second season of *The Sopranos*. Henry McGee was running home video sales and he'd said, "We're about to release *The Sopranos* first season on home video. And we're going to get $5 million, $10 million." And remember we were spending, even for the first year, more than $2 million an episode on this thing. For us that was a high budget. "Henry, what? We're gonna put this out on video for $5 million or $10 million?" I can't remember who, maybe Billock or Albrecht or Hal, said, "Is it worth it? When we have it on HBO On Demand?" Somebody in sales was saying, "Look, we're about to do the TCI renewal. That's our main argument why they should renew and pay the rates. We can't be selling it at video stores." So, we thought about it. We argued for about an hour. I had the gavel, so I said, "All right, forget it." Henry was crushed. I felt bad about it.

He was trying to make his budget; we just took away his major Christmas thing. And we kept it out of video for a few years. When we finally released *The Sopranos* on video, we made more than it cost to make, by a lot.

After the success of **When It Was a Game I, II,** *and* **III,** *along with* **Arthur Ashe: Citizen of the World,** *HBO Sports realized that it had stumbled on a way to generate buzz with this unique storytelling. And with massive budgets, HBO could afford to license all the great footage necessary to tell these stories well. HBO Sports turned back into a sports documentary machine, pumping out exclusive content to bring in viewers.*

In 1995, they released the highly entertaining **Rebels with a Cause: The Story of the American Football League.** *Then in 1996 came* **The Journey of the African-American Athlete,** *a two-part documentary on the history of Black athletes in America. And in 1997,* **Long Shots: The Life and Times of the American Basketball Association—** *and many more. HBO Sports now averaged three documentaries per year.*

Yet the more documentaries HBO created, the less "cutting edge" they seemed to be. Sure, the films covered different sports and different people, but by repeating the same formula, HBO risked losing what had made the originals so memorable and distinctive, thereby creating opportunities for competitors.

BILLIE JEAN KING:

They said, "Don't you remember when you were coming in here and saying, 'You've done all these sports documentaries and all these sports, but only on men. Can't you find a way to do women's sports?'" And they said, "We are going to." And that's when Kendall Reid and Julie Anderson produced the *Dare to Compete* doc. Nobody had ever done a doc on women in sports like that. I kept pushing for more women producers and people of color. I always think about people with disabilities, too. There are really smart people who have disabilities, they're sitting in a wheelchair but that doesn't mean they're not smart as a whip. I always pushed all that stuff with them, but particularly that they do a women's sports documentary. And so we did *Dare to Compete*, which was excellent. That was so exciting.

MARY CARILLO:

The documentary unit was doing a film on the history of women in sports called *Dare to Compete: The Struggle of Women in Sports*. There were a couple of women; Billie Jean King and Donna de Varona, who were consultants on the documentary.

I started as a consultant. So of course I go to the first meeting and I'm in a room with Ross and the producers and Billie and Donna. Instead of sitting there quietly with my hands folded in my lap, I started spitballing ideas. And I start explaining who I think we should interview. I'm all excited and I can't believe I'm in the room where this is happening. So I start interviewing people. By the end of this effort, I was made a co-writer. Frank did the first half of the doc and I did from the 1960s on.

STEVE STERN:

An HBO Sports documentary was really an event. It happened four times a year. Everyone knew when it was on and media writers reviewed our shows. I would say proudly that most of those reviews were pretty good. People need to understand there was a sports documentary world before *30 for 30*.

RICHARD SANDOMIR, Journalist:

There was a screening of *Dare to Compete* at the White House, and I was invited to cover it. At the reception, Eleanor Holm and I start talking. Eleanor was this wonderful Olympic swimmer who had competed in the 1932 games and on her way to the 1936 games, got caught playing craps and drinking with the reporters. And she was thrown off the boat on the way to Germany by Avery Brundage, the head of the Olympic committee. I didn't know anything about her. And she is by now in her eighties, and she's about five feet tall, this lovely dame with a raspy voice. She's a wonderful story-teller and she's talking about her life. Bill Clinton is the president, it's around the time of the Monica Lewinsky scandal. Despite the scandal, he still has an aura. Women are still interested. And he's big, bigger than he seems on television. Eleanor's staring at him, then she tugs at my shoulder. And she says, "Richard, do you think he'd fuck me?"

I was a little shocked. I said, "Well, Eleanor, I guess all you can do is ask," and as I left, she said to me, "Richard, do you think you'll come to my funeral?" I said, "Invite me." The opportunity was lost. I didn't find out she died until after her funeral.

"I have returned, returned to the land of Abraham!"

That's not Old Testament Israel, but rather Don King in early 1999 from the lobby of the HBO building, bellowing that he has, indeed, returned to the land of (Seth) Abraham for all to witness.

Eight years earlier, King had fled to Showtime after trying to force the firing of Larry Merchant because King didn't like how Merchant treated the biggest jewel in his boxing belt, Mike Tyson. By 1998, HBO was trying to put together the biggest heavyweight fight possible, between Lennox Lewis, who already had an HBO deal, and Evander

Holyfield, who was represented by, yes, King. HBO said personal feuds be damned—and had thus agreed to host Don King at the HBO offices, up in the fourteenth-floor dining rooms, for a ceremonial breakfast designed to engineer their rapprochement.

SETH ABRAHAM:

Don was still under contract with Showtime, and I called him up and I said, "Don, we're not enemies. We had a ten-year relationship. It blew up over a business issue. Not a personal issue. At some point you may not renew with Showtime and you're welcome back." Sure enough, his contract with Showtime ran out. They didn't renew it. Tyson had gone to prison, comes out, he's not the same Mike Tyson, but Don still had an impressive stable of prizefighters. And we started doing business again.

Not doing business with Don gave other promoters tremendous leverage on HBO. We didn't have multiple players at the poker table, and we became more reliant on other promoters. Working with Don brought some leverage back to the HBO side of the table.

Lewis clearly dominated for most of the fight, but in what many would regard as a travesty of justice, the judges decided that the fight was a draw. But the damage was done—and just when it appeared that boxing could rally after its doldrum years. Perhaps Larry Merchant put it best: "Nothing can kill boxing, and nothing can save it."

It seemed as though the only person not complaining was Don King—the "draw" meant he could create a potentially lucrative rematch, which he did, six months later in Las Vegas (Lewis won unanimously).

EVANDER HOLYFIELD:

When I finished, I was so sick and I was cramping. It was one of my most terrible fights I ever fought. But I didn't quit. They called the fight a draw. Going into the second fight with him, he didn't want to fight for the amount of money. I gave him $5 million of my money for him to fight me, because I actually wanted to show him he couldn't whoop me. The fight came down to decision, but in a fight with him getting decision, I was okay with it. That's how I became full-time heavyweight champ of the world.

After the debacle of the Lennox Lewis–Evander Holyfield fight, boxing was still stuck in a lull. Until, that is, June 8, 2002, when Lewis took on an out-of-control Mike Tyson in Memphis, Tennessee. The fight augured nothing but bad blood. Tyson was considered almost unmanageable after a record of missed fights, lawsuits, and other unpleasantness, and he did himself few favors at the pre-match press conference when he instigated a brawl with Lewis's people and even with Lewis himself. At one point in the entanglement, Tyson bit Lewis on the leg. Tyson brought the imbroglio to a halt when he threatened journalist Mark Malinowski (who'd said loud enough for all to hear that Tyson should be in a straitjacket) with sexual assault, i.e., "[I will] fuck you 'til you love me."

As a result, Tyson couldn't get a license to fight in Las Vegas, the bout's original site, so it was shifted to Tennessee. Showtime, by this point, was looking to off-load Tyson, so it was relatively easy to get them to agree to a joint HBO-Showtime presentation of the fight. But as representatives of the two companies were barely on speaking terms, however, the co-production was plagued with mutual animosity. Showtime's unhappiness with Tyson's toxicity was evident; once he had virtually lost the fight to Lewis with an eighth-round knockout, the late Jay Larkin, then a Showtime executive and boxing promoter, was said to have walked out of the TV truck trilling, "Free at last!"

MARK TAFFET:

The press conference that took place where Mike and Lennox had their brawl, Mike bit a quarter-sized chunk of Lennox's inner thigh. And no one in the country would license the fight. And I went to Memphis, Tennessee, and met with the mayor of Memphis. We talked and established that Memphis could do the fight. The mayor was a six-foot-five-inch African American man, Willie Herenton, former gold gloves champ who had his sights designed on being the governor of Tennessee.

DAVE HARMON:

In the world we're in now a lot has happened since Lennox Lewis against Mike Tyson. And Mayweather–Pacquiao in particular has sort of blown people's memories out of Lennox Lewis against Mike Tyson. But at the time it was the biggest fight I had ever done. And you could add to that, that Showtime and HBO were combining efforts on that one.

Back to 1999, in a turn of events that shocked the worlds of sports, tennis, and broadcasting, HBO decided not to renew coverage of Wimbledon after decades of doing so. There was history there. HBO had been the entity responsible for bringing weekday tennis to American television for the first time ever and thereby helped grow both the popularity of the sport and HBO's place in the sports world. When it began covering Wimbledon in 1975, the network had only 125,000 subscribers; by the end of the partnership, there were 25 million.

Michael Fuchs loved tennis, relishing the spectacle. He also loved his yearly visits to center court. But Bewkes, Albrecht, and Nelson weren't rabid sports fans, and besides, *letting go of Wimbledon wasn't just about Wimbledon. Many industry executives felt it was simply not worth the money—$8 million just for the rights, plus another $5 million for production.*

Upon closer examination, however, the issue was far more complicated. There was only a limited pile of money available; now that original programming was shifting into high gear, those thirteen million bucks could be spent elsewhere.

Talk about bad timing. Two truths emerged from the Wimbledon decision: First, HBO had shot itself in the foot, letting go of a great tradition right before the rise and reign of such superstar athletes as Roger Federer, Rafael Nadal, and Serena Williams. And, second, for anyone paying attention, it was clear this was the first major step taken as part of long slide away from all sports for HBO, not just tennis.

HBO had many a major moment ahead, but this was where the company started down a path different from the one it had been following since its very first night on the air: the promise to viewers that sports would be one of the major offerings. This was in effect a warning label to subscribers and cable operators alike; it told them that the next decades of HBO Sports would be far less adventurous and far less aggressive than the last one.

SETH ABRAHAM:

Jeff Bewkes tells me that Wimbledon has had its run on HBO and doesn't want to renew it. I said, "Are you basing this on money?" He said, "No, I just, I think it's had its run. Twenty-five years is enough. We can put that money elsewhere into original programming, more series, more pilots." I was not about to give up.

I wrote Jeff the best memo of my career. Jeff called me up and said, "This is one of the best memos I've ever read. Truly. It is. The answer is still no."

Now the story really gets hairy. Upcoming was a prizefight at Madison Square Garden. I invited Jeff to come. Jeff was not a particularly big sports fan. He said, "I don't think I'm going to come, Peggy—that's his wife—would love to go. Would you take Peggy?" Peggy went to Yale with Jeff, and her first job was at ABC Sports, executive assistant to Roone Arledge. She was a serious fan. So Peggy is sitting next to me for four hours and I lay the whole thing out about Wimbledon.

I said, "If you're not uncomfortable, I would love you to weigh in on this." She looked at me and said, "No one's ever asked me to do that." I said, "Obviously this is important to me. I think it's important to HBO. I have nothing to lose." Afterward, Jeff called me up and laughed. He said, "So I heard you had a really interesting conversation with Peggy." He said, "Seth, it was a very ingenious thing to do. The answer is still no. And please don't do that again."

ROSS GREENBURG:

I was at that point executive producer and the showrunner of Wimbledon, and I had gotten wind probably a couple months prior to the tournament.

Bill Nelson had been chomping at the bit to get it off the books for years. I think there was just a feeling that it was too expensive, and the ratings weren't big enough, the prestige had waned.

Wimbledon is such a special setting. The only thing you can compare it to is Augusta. The tournament was part of the soul of HBO Sports.

That was one of the toughest moments: I personally had done twenty-one straight Wimbledons, HBO had done Wimbledon from 1975. I knew I wanted to end the last broadcast with a lengthy essay, so I wrote it on the plane ride over and started crying my eyes out on the plane. And then I knew the next day, when we had our first production meeting for that year's tournament, that I would have to address a hundred people there and tell them that this was our last tournament.

I won a writing Emmy for that. And that was a difficult two weeks. Really tough. All things must end. So it tore at the very soul of HBO Sports. I never cried so much in front of my staff in all the years I was there, first on the plane over writing the final six-minute tribute, to the meeting that I had the day before the tournament began where I had to announce it. And there was really no prep for that. The last day I gathered the staff at the end and we had our wrap party, it was incredibly emotional.

BILLIE JEAN KING:

I was so upset. It was horrible for all of us.

SETH ABRAHAM:

Not keeping Wimbledon was the beginning of a downward slide that made a statement to the media, to cable operators, that the HBO Sports star was fading. It's one thing to be outbid, but to not even be at the table? That made a statement, I believe, to all these different constituencies, that in Jeff's world, it was not a sports world.

That's when I began thinking about other career moves. I didn't want to preside over the autopsy.

The sense that Bewkes did not have the same focus on sports as had his predecessor, Michael Fuchs, was creating tension in the Sports department. In one infamous department budget meeting with Jeff Bewkes and his CFO Bill Nelson, those tensions exploded, to the point where Lou DiBella threatened to jump over the table and strangle Bewkes.

SETH ABRAHAM:

It wasn't Jeff who said anything, it was Bill Nelson, the CFO, who sat in on all of the budget meetings. Bill said something about boxing's budget. Lou took it very personally. What Lou heard, which I did not hear, was that Bill was calling into question Lou's integrity. That lit a fuse.

JEFF BEWKES:

Lou was a talented guy. I ended up blowing up on him at a budget meeting. He was basically flipping off Bill Nelson. I started yelling at him. I didn't fire him at the meeting, but I told him, "If you keep this up, I'm gonna fire you." Maybe he was trying to get fired.

I think he was surprised when I went after him. I was not one to start yelling at people in a meeting. That's one of the few occasions when I did. His behavior was so insulting to Nelson. Nelson's not going to do anything if people are disrespecting him. He wouldn't take it, but he's not going to do anything. But I was like, "No, fuck you. You're not doing that. You need to shut up or get out of the room."

SETH ABRAHAM:

I called a timeout. I said, "Let's pause, let's take a break for 15 or 20 minutes." I took Lou down the hall, and I said, "You owe Jeff an apology." You can argue with Jeff, he has no issue with that, but not the way Lou did it that day. And I said, "Lou, I'm not going to script it for you, but if you want to get anything done in this meeting and going forward, you'd have to apologize to Jeff." He grumbled, but he ultimately apologized. Jeff never brought it up again. There was absolutely no punishment.

LOU DiBELLA:

I no longer felt a loyalty to Bewkes or to the company and I was not the type of person who could stay at a company where I don't feel it anymore. So it took like a year to work out a package before I left.

I got really upset when Seth left right after I left. HBO stopped being the HBO that I knew. HBO under Jeff wasn't HBO under Michael.

On September 11, 2000, Seth Abraham's twenty-two-year run at HBO came to an end. His last position—president and CEO of Time Warner Sports—had been carved out specifi-

cally for him and would disappear with his exit. In mid-October, Abraham would become chief operating officer and executive vice president of Madison Square Garden, overseeing its sports events, Radio City, and the MSG Network. Abraham was replaced by the new president of just HBO Sports, Ross Greenburg, himself a twenty-two-year veteran of HBO. At the same time, HBO cut the sports department's budget for fights in half, from a range of about $60 million to $70 million per year in 2000 to around $30 million a decade later.

In the wake of the budget cuts, Greenburg decided to focus on preserving the legacy of HBO Sports in any way possible. Greenburg also had a strong attraction to Hollywood stardust and dedicated non-boxing time on that front. He was executive producer on Billy Crystal's **61*** *(2001) and* **Miracle** *(2004), starring Kurt Russell, and also paved the way for Jim Lampley and the HBO Boxing brand to be burnished in the big-screen releases of* **Ocean's Eleven** *(2001),* **Rocky Balboa** *(2006), and the Oscar winner* **The Fighter** *(2010), among others.*

BOB ARUM:

Seth was a master diplomat and executive. Seth always made sure that he did enough for major promoters, that he kept them happy, whether it was Don King or Dan Duva, or myself, Seth spread around goodies in a way that kept us all happy. Seth knew how to handle the situation so that if he got a big fight from me, he would make sure to give me a fight sometime down the road. He kept us busy.

After Seth, Ross Greenburg was the head of HBO Sports. Now, Greenburg was a terrific producer. He was very imaginative and he was very innovative in making changes to the way boxing was presented on television and produced, but he had no executive background. He didn't have the touch.

ROSS GREENBURG:

Seth was a gifted, relentless negotiator and would have dinners three or four nights a week with promoters or managers, and he was damn good at it. Michael gave him the purse strings, but Seth really orchestrated a lot of the acquisitions of a lot of boxing and he was gifted at it.

I think I gained the staff's respect as a programmer and as a producer with a strong eye for talent, not only on the announcing crews, but the production crew as well. I wanted everything that HBO Sports aired to be so special you'd walk away and think, "Wow, those guys are really good."

I wanted everything to be so perfect that I probably was at times annoying. I probably got under the skin of a lot of the production people.

But it was never about power for me. It was always about the product.

MARK TAFFET:

Ross Greenburg was one of the greatest sports producers in history. He produced sports documentaries that were the highest level of journalistic integrity while connecting emotionally to viewers.

We brought production, boxing, and business savvy together in a way nobody ever did, and Michael Fuchs's blood ran through all of us.

When Seth Abraham left and Greenburg stepped in to run HBO Sports, many things would stay the same. Greenburg had been brought on by Abraham, respected his style, his vision, and would do his best to keep building them. But he'd also go on to do a bit of his own vision building, expanding HBO Sports into new territory. One of the first things Greenburg did was try to get Bob Costas to join him at HBO. He'd been begging the broadcaster to make the switch for years, but this time it worked. Just one year after Greenburg took the helm, Costas came on board HBO with his first show, **On the Record with Bob Costas.**

ROSS GREENBURG:

I remember Costas at the Emmy Awards in 1990. *When It Was a Game* lost to the fortieth anniversary of a documentary that was done for *Wide World of Sports*. It was a stunning upset because *When It Was a Game* had gotten huge acclaim. Bob came up to the table and he just goes, "That's like Mozart losing to Def Leppard."

He'd call me after a certain documentary aired and he'd just wax praise all over it. We became close. He really admired the HBO product and knew that there would be a platform for him. He'd phone for an hour going through every issue that was swirling around every sport that he was dying to talk about. He had no platform at NBC really.

BOB COSTAS:

The year 2000 was NBC's last go-round on baseball. We did not have football. And I left later of my own accord in 1994, which I look back on with some regret, because in many ways it was the best thing I ever did. I did three seasons of play-by-play for the NBA, one of which was the Last Dance season of 1998, and another was the first championship of the Lakers with Kobe and Shaq. That was a pretty tidy little three-year run. Marv Albert is ready to come back. I say to Dick, "Now's the time to let me go to HBO." That was when Ross created *On the Record with Bob Costas.*

ROSS GREENBURG:

It took me five years. Bob was getting very antsy, very, very antsy, and Dick sent the word down, "Yes, you can work with HBO, but I don't want to see any pieces on the IOC or anything related to the Olympics." Which I was fine with.

Bob was like a kid in the candy store because he could open up about any topic he wanted. Bob had always expressed that he wanted to do more than just sports.

BOB COSTAS:

If I could have had an ongoing role at HBO with their prestige and quality, it would have been more than a release valve. It would have taken away a lot of my ambivalence about network TV sports. A very smart friend of mine said to me in the early 2000s, "There's two Bobs. There's HBO Bob, and there's NBC Bob." For a long time almost everything I did at NBC was an accurate reflection of who I was for a combination of reasons that became less true as time went on. On HBO, people were getting a truer view of me.

I had respect, admiration, and gratitude for the people I worked for and with at NBC for all those years. You look at the quality of production on the Olympics, *Sunday Night Football*. NBC's whole history of baseball. Could you do the NBA any better than NBC did it in the nineties? Could you take a two-minute horse race and make four hours of network television out of it and make it as beautiful as NBC does at the Kentucky Derby? That stuff is fantastic, but there was often a reluctance to fully recognize the elephants in the room, such as concussions in football or the IOC controversies, and that ran up against my desire to be involved in more of the journalistic aspects of sports, as well as long-form interviews, and historical pieces.

Costas had always been considered the ultimate pro when it came to sports broadcasting: eloquent, unflustered, slyly witty, an oracle who did his homework. On March 14, 2001, early in the life of his HBO talk show, **On the Record with Bob Costas,** *Costas squared off with Vince McMahon, former traveling salesman, professional wrestler, and owner of various iterations of wrestling organizations and football leagues. Ironically, McMahon was one of the first on-camera personalities of HBO's pioneer days. From 1973 to 1976, McMahon gave the fledgling network some stability by hosting exclusive wrestling programs. But that evening in 2001, even though McMahon was ostensibly on the show to discuss his ultimately short-lived (one season) XFL venture, Costas got under the skin of McMahon about both the poor prospects of the XFL and some of the* excperl of his wrestling empire. At one point, McMahon growled, "This is **The Bob Costas Interrupt Program**, *right?*"

The tone of the conversation veered from tense to cordial and back again, but there were moments when it seemed as if McMahon was going to close the already short distance between the two chairs and put Costas in a headlock. McMahon would lean forward, pointing at Costas and sneering, "Are you going to let me answer the question?" Meanwhile, in the green room, Costas's next guest—none other than legendary firebrand and athlete-abuser Bobby Knight—might have wondered what he'd have to do to be remembered as even having appeared on the show (answer: there was nothing he could do—no one remembers it). At the same time, in the same room, comedian Robert Klein got into it with some of McMahon's entourage who were complaining Costas was asking difficult questions. It made for excellent television, and Costas, meticulously unflappable as usual, was neither thrown out of the ring nor had a collapsible chair smashed over his head—a win for him personally and for his new show.

BOB COSTAS:

Ross was in my ear saying, "Keep going, keep going." It was live, and obviously since it's HBO, there were no commercials. I knew it was good television in the moment, but I wasn't trying to hype it. Sometimes things can become sensational, but they start from a legitimate place. And the legitimate place was that the XFL was trying to find a place in mainstream sports, on a mainstream network. It started out with great interest. I think they got a rating of 10 for the first game, but by the end, they were getting the lowest ratings of any program in prime time in the history of network television.

Looking back on it, I think every question I asked McMahon and every follow-up was completely on point. When we got into the wrestling part, you get into an area that becomes more subjective because some people like it. And I, for one, didn't like it. I was a longtime wrestling fan when I thought it was good-natured slapstick. It took on a darker, less appealing tone in the late 1990s, the early years of the twenty-first century. And that's where I think some people were on board with my line of questioning and others weren't.

VINCE McMAHON, Executive, WWE:

Once we were doing the interview, he kept interrupting me and interrupting me, and bringing up topics that had nothing to do with what we were supposed to be talking about. He kept trying to do the "I gotcha" kind of thing. It was clear he didn't want to hear any of my answers. The other problem was that Bob is so freaking pompous. The entire time he acted like he was above me and was just using me to show how great he was. I was sitting there really pissed off and started thinking, I wish he wasn't five feet five and 140 pounds. If he was six five and 295, he would deserve to get the shit beat out of him. I could have really given them some great television.

BOB COSTAS:

He stormed off and you could hear the doors slamming behind him. It takes some strength, by the way, to slam the doors of the studio. Those doors aren't like the door to your kitchen. I could hear them slam.

The next guest was Bobby Knight. I said to him, "Coach, this is the one time in your life when your presence will lower the temperature in the room." The following day the phone rings, and it's McMahon. "Bob, let's make it two out of three. You took last night. I want a rematch." I said, "Great." We did another one a year later that was less heated, was still a good exchange, but it wasn't as memorable as the first one.

VINCE McMAHON:

Quite frankly, in those days, I hadn't done too many interviews like that, and I let him get to me. I'm kind of aggressive and have a real passion for our business and everyone in it. I take it as a responsibility as well. I don't think I handled it very well, and regret it. I've met Bob several times since then. We're okay.

Marty Callner loved drama, and he loved sports. One day, he thought about what rookies and veterans face when they are trying to make the roster on NFL teams. Seventy-five guys fighting for fifty-three jobs. What are the veterans going to do to keep their jobs? Ross Greenburg loved that idea and wanted to go even bigger, revealing the entire underbelly of preseason training. Then Rick Bernstein looked at a book on his shelf, a biography of Pittsburgh Steelers coach Chuck Knox, titled **Hard Knox.** *And a title was born.*

Raw competition and drama were what HBO set out to capture with the premiere of **Hard Knocks** *in 2001. The show followed the Baltimore Ravens during training camp as rookies and vets competed for starting spots. It offered viewers a look into the lives of coaches and players, showing everything from family stress to inside jokes.*

It was almost as if they took everything great from their live programming and documentary films and combined it into what they'd later call the "first sports-based reality TV."

MARTY CALLNER:

All of a sudden you've gone from being a star in peewee football, junior high school, high school, and college, now you're on a stage where everyone's as big and as fast as you are, and the difference between making it and not making it is razor-thin. Many of these decisions aren't made until the last second. The consequences are gigantic. You can go from all of a sudden being the best-looking guy in the room to carrying someone's bags at the airport because a lot of these football players aren't prepared for life after football. This was the ultimate survivor reality show, without me even realizing that's what I was creating.

Outside of HBO Sports, other more momentous changes were afoot. In January 2001, the deal officially closed on what became the biggest media merger ever. America Online, Inc., the communications company specializing in dial-up Internet, purchased Time Warner, creating a corporate union that would control properties across all types of media—music, movies, television, print, and the Internet—and be worth $350 billion all told. The price tag: a combination of debt and stock worth a whopping $165 billion. The deal that produced AOL Time Warner, the masthead of the new company, was green-lighted by regulators at the Federal Trade Commission a month earlier, after the buyer, AOL, announced the deal a full year before, on January 10, 2000. Despite the historic size of the merger, trouble lurked ahead. With the inauguration of broadband Internet service, dial-up became obsolete, which would soon cause AOL's business to plummet.

From the start, AOL and Time Warner mixed like oil and water. Insiders characterized it as a complete cultural mismatch. Time Warner executives saw their new techy counterparts as cocky, and AOL viewed itself as a sort of flashy new David trying to remake old-fashioned Goliath—all of which rubbed the Time Warner people the wrong way.

HBO had long enjoyed special status within Time Warner in the years leading up to its merger with AOL. HBO existed on an island, with its own executives charting its strategy and precious little interference from corporate overlords. Even as Time Warner executives meddled with CNN about how to raise its relevance, the same corporate chiefs saw HBO as its crown jewel, better left alone. At the time of the merger, HBO was rolling, making money, and basking in the glow of a string of iconic shows, from **Sex and the City** *to* **The Sopranos.** *Those successes afforded HBO a degree of protection as the AOL Time Warner merger began to backfire, leaving a trail of wreckage in its wake.*

Those involved on the Time Warner side put much of the blame on Jerry Levin, who engineered the deal. They believed he should have known it would not be a smooth pairing. Levin let very few people in the company know that he was contemplating a merger and took almost no counsel.

PAUL CAPPUCCIO, Executive:

Jerry's a very complicated man. He's a reinventor of himself and the company. Sometimes it is horseshit, but I gotta tell you, I really respected Jerry. Look, we all have faults. I thought he lived the company. He rode the stock all the way down to its lowest point without selling. He is a very interesting man, and I miss working with him.

JEFF BEWKES:

During Henry Luce's time, they had The News Tour where they'd take CEOs of companies that advertised in the magazines on a junket somewhere in the world, and they'd be given a notepad and were told, "You're going to be like journalists. You can ask questions of these world leaders, write impressions, and we'll talk about them at dinner." In 1999, Jerry decided to revive it, not for advertisers but for the board of directors and the top management.

Jerry tells the board they're all invited, and Turner says, "We're going to China for ten days? Are we bringing our wives?" Jerry says, "No wives." Ted says, "I'm not going ten days without Jane."

In January 1999, Time Warner chairman Jerry Levin took his top executives on board a gigantic private Swiss Air jet to China, beginning in Kashgar with the Uyghurs. From there they visited the construction site of the Upper Three Gorges Dam, went on to Wuhan, and even floated down the Yangtze, with a stop at Beijing, bringing the seven-day tour to a close.

JEFF BEWKES:

We went to Beijing and that's where we went to the dinner of the anniversary of the Communist takeover, in the Great Hall of the People, where Jiang Zemin comes out to our table. He's shaking hands and taking pictures of everybody. Jane was there for that. She was like leaning into the picture with Jiang Zemin, like it was Thanksgiving with her relatives. There are no pictures of me, because I'm not taking pictures with the Communist leaders the day before they parade missiles and tanks that are aiming at us.

And there was Steve Case, AOL's CEO, and Jerry. They were standing not ten feet from me in a long conversation. That was the beginning.

JERRY LEVIN:

One time, a few of us were invited to be with Larry Summers, secretary of the Treasury under Clinton, who became the Harvard president. I'm representing Time Warner, so I'm big fish, but everyone's attention went right to Steve. I took a look at the AOL board. It was very respectable.

When we were in China, I sat next to Steve at a Fortune seminar. We got to talking and he was more interested in finding out about what I was doing than I was about what he was doing.

HAL AKSELRAD:

I was on a task force that Levin formed, and while he was in China, we concluded that AOL was toast in the new world. They had no future. We also determined broadband would be best accessed through Road Runner, Time Warner Cable's broadband product.

PHIL KENT:

Jerry was feeling very insecure with people like Mary Meeker in his ear, saying, "You don't have an Internet strategy." We had a lot of cool stuff going on at CNN and other places. He just didn't know about it.

RICHARD PARSONS:

Jerry would go home and think about things, make a decision, and then come in and announce it. He didn't have a council or a kitchen cabinet. He was a solitary decision maker.

JERRY LEVIN:

Why do people make big decisions? Do they do it from an analytical basis? No. They do it on an emotional basis, a gut feeling, trying to psychologically gratify something that's haunting them. That's why business is so interesting and so intellectually promising.

I didn't know Steve personally that well. Business transactions are about personalities and not about math.

As much as I didn't like Steve's frostiness, he was responsible for an increase in capitalization that was beyond breathless. He was making money, and he had very substantive people on his board. What I wanted was the Internet. How do you get the Internet onto Time Warner? How do you do that? You're going to have to make a transforming transaction.

AOL is probably the only deal that we could do because that's a company that talks about media, about what used to work for us.

PAUL CAPPUCCIO:

A big reason why AOL had the position it did was because in the modified final judgment resolving the 1980s antitrust suit against AT&T, the Baby Bells were prohibited from carrying a phone call across a LATA, local area and transport area, which meant that they could not themselves to be in the business of connecting people to the Internet. That allowed AOL to lease access to millions of modems and be the original narrowband connection to the Internet.

There was no fucking way that the cable companies were going to let that happen in broadband. I don't think Case ever got his head around the fact that it was fruitless to attempt to force the cable companies to turn that business over to AOL. We at AOL had ridden a tsunami, and sometimes I think Case thought that meant we were the world's greatest surfers, and that the cable companies would have no choice but to recognize that. But they were not impressed.

JERRY LEVIN:

We had dinner at Steve's house and I said to Rick Bressler and Parsons, "The only way this can be done is if I sign it quickly, and there are no leaks. You've got X amount of time for due diligence. If we find something out, I'm not going to go forward." But if it works, we had a ratio picked out. I didn't care about the name, because it didn't matter. It became a big deal for lots of people. As long as it was a fifty-fifty board. So over a weekend, they said they were done with the due diligence.

I said, "Well, let's announce on Monday morning." And I took a lot of people by surprise, but already we were making projections that had to count on the growth rate of AOL. I'm the one who made the mistake. I'm the one who took the responsibility.

RICHARD PARSONS:

Nobody in the company except me and the CFO, Rick Bressler, even knew we were contemplating this merger, for a couple of months before we got down to the short strokes. Jerry knew the Time Warner culture, but neither of us knew the AOL culture. They were insurgents. I remember one AOL guy actually said, in the course of negotiations, "All you Time Warner people are going to be gone in six months anyway." Steve Case once referred to the Time Warner businesses as "dead tree" businesses. They were the vanguard of the new world and they were going to remake all of our "dead tree" businesses. They thought they were just going to come in and take over. Jerry thought we could tame them, and they thought they could tame us.

JEFF BEWKES:

In January 2000, I'm at home on a Sunday night. It's after nine o'clock, and I get a call from Dick Parsons: "We're merging with AOL, stock for stock, merger of equals, no cash." Did that mean it was gonna be fifty-fifty? No, they were trading at about $160 billion and we were only maybe $85 million, but they'd only get 55 percent of the combined company stock so we were getting a hefty premium. Dick said, "We're going to announce it tomorrow. What do you think?"

"Is the deal signed?" I asked. "Yeah," he said. "Then, congratulations. Where's the press conference?" He says, "No, you don't have to go." Jerry had not invited any of the Time Warner CEOs or division heads. "I ought to go; if you're going to go merge the company, you should get as many of us sitting there looking like we know what it is, even though we don't." So, I was sitting in the audience. I think I might've been the only one because there was no notice.

HAL AKSELRAD:

After the deal is done, the company goes into a crisis mode and a task force is formed. One person from each division, three people from AOL. I was the HBO designee to that task force. When we go to AOL, I put my old litigator's hat back on and their CFO, a guy named Joe Ripp, was presenting. I go at his graphs, really pressing hard against a lot of the numbers, and Case gets really upset with me and he calls a recess in the meeting. He looks at me and goes, "We could use a guy like you here at AOL." I said, "I'm strictly HBO. I'm not available." I leave the room for this break. I go to the bathroom and Parsons follows me into the bathroom and I look at him. "Are you okay with what I'm doing? Because I'm taking the fig leaf right off, showing how the numbers are bogus, and how they're manipulating their multiples by moving revenue from one place to another." Parsons said, "Pedal to the metal."

The deal was sealed at Steve Case's home in Virginia. As it turned out, the Time Warner AOL merger would be just the Y2K nightmare some had been dreading. AOL's earnings and revenue growth had already started to deteriorate. AOL was mailing out floppy disks, signing people up, and announcing subscriber gains even as it lost money. The AOL business model collapsed as the late 1990s tech bubble popped, its market value plummeting from $200 billion to $10 billion in fewer than two years.

Executives at Time Warner believe that Jerry Levin saw the merger as a way to acquire an Internet strategy. The truth, however, was that the AOL was a narrowband company with no broadband strategy to carry them into the future.

Still, Time Warner executives were polite to their new masters. The AOL guys were thinking, What can we take from here to build AOL? Time Warner people, meanwhile, scoffed, believing that AOL was just a bunch of dial-up guys, with no vision, who could do nothing with video content.

JERRY LEVIN:

Jeff was strongly opposed to the merger. He didn't respect Steve Case or Bob Pittman. There was no assimilation possibility there.

AOL had their eyes on one key number: Time Warner Cable covered twelve million households nationwide, many of which were either using broadband, or were soon going to be. Shoot, AOL execs thought, if we can make AOL the main service in all Time Warner households, we can smoothly sail AOL into a world soon to be dominated by broadband.

Just one issue: twelve million households, in the grand scheme of cable penetration, represented only about 20 percent of the country. On top of that little tidbit, AOL faced the fact that no cable operator would agree to force AOL into homes when that meant surrendering the $30 or $40 monthly broadband fees entirely to AOL. That's simply not how cable companies operated.

PAUL CAPPUCCIO:

Case was always viewing HBO, and the rest of Time Warner content, primarily through the lens of how it could be put in service of the AOL platform. That was a big mistake for the owner of a premium content company.

JEFF BEWKES:

First time I met Paul Cappuccio, the general counsel from AOL, I liked him from the start, which I can't say for the other AOL guys. He wasn't arrogant, but he was clearly smart and understood AOL's business. He seemed wary, like he'd been told that this guy running HBO was difficult. And they had to get the little jewel in the ground to heel. Anyway, I say to him, "You guys do have like a plan B, right?"

He says, "What do you mean?" I said, "It can't just be take all the Time Warner brands and put them behind the wall. There's something else, right?" He gave me a look, paused for effect, because Paul's really smart, and deadpanned. "No, that's the plan." Apparently, he said to other people, "I didn't know Jeff, but Jeff just looked at me and said, 'Oh my god, we are fucked, everybody's fucked.'"

About six months later, we were walking down Sixth Avenue talking about the meeting we just had with them, Akselrad, Kessler, and Plepler. We stopped at about Forty-fifth and said to each other, "These fucking guys actually don't know what they're doing. We hoped they did, but they don't." We had learned enough to figure out that they were heading for the falls. "They're trying to do a three-card monte with HBO and the cable company. Not going to work. They're fucked. We're fucked."

JERRY LEVIN:

I only did a weekend's worth of due diligence. That's true. But we had a pretty good idea of the growth rate. We ran all the algorithms you could do. It looked damn good. It looked like it was going to be the fastest-growing business by far.

I'm the only one that held on to his shares. The executives at Time Warner and at AOL and on the board made money because they sold their shares. I put a note out, said, "It's not consistent with management's obligation to the shareholders to sell one share at all during this period."

ROSS GREENBURG:

Tremendous pressure was put on all of us for a long period of time not to sell the stock.

CHRIS ALBRECHT:

Our stock went way up and only the finance guys like Bill Nelson were smart enough to sell.

RICHARD PARSONS:

And then the bubble broke. The AOL walled garden started to crumble. At the time of the merger, in rough numbers, we now had a market value of about $200 billion. Then the Internet bubble collapsed almost at the same time the AOL business model collapsed.

So unshakable was Jerry Levin's belief in the merger that at no point did he sell shares he could have sold in the combined company. His personal loss? Nearly $600 million.

JEFF BEWKES:

Steve became chairman, Jerry became CEO. I don't remember exactly when they announced that Pittman would be the COO and have all the Time Warner companies reporting to him along with AOL.

CHRIS ALBRECHT:

All of a sudden there were new guys running the company.

JEFF BEWKES:

I was in the room at Warner Bros. when Bob ordered Barry Meyer and HBO to move all our ad buys to AOL and stop advertising our shows on the networks, including cutting off ads on NBC Thursday night for the big weekend movie premieres. We were all looking at him like, "We can't open a movie putting the fucking ads on AOL. Are you kidding?"

JERRY LEVIN:

I have to acknowledge it became clear to me after a while that Steve did not have the flexibility I thought he might have. It was really my mistake.

JEFF BEWKES:

As AOL earnings started to collapse, I jacked up HBO earnings to keep them off our back, so I could turn down their worst order. I think that first year of the merger, when they missed all their earnings targets, we took HBO earnings up over 30 percent.

Most of the press I was dealing with was focused on HBO itself and our overall growth. They might ask if the merger was impacting us but it really wasn't at that time. We didn't have any large layoffs at HBO or any large budget reductions. We were allowed to run our business as long as we came in on target. Of course, some of those targets were more ambitious.

JOHN MALONE:

That was obviously a complete disaster. Jerry did not have a clue, frankly, of what he was acquiring. They blew it by him, he went for it, and it was a disaster. I was totally against it myself. But if you remember our votes, the TCI votes, had been put in a trust. We couldn't vote them, because of antitrust, and we were the biggest shareholder. When Ted merged Turner Broadcasting into Time Warner, we, in order to get antitrust approval, had had to pledge to neuter our votes—put them in a voting trust. So we had no seat at the table. I was on the board of AT&T, and knew that AOL had tried to sell itself to AT&T.

I got a phone call early in the morning from Ted, who said, "Did you hear about the deal?" I asked him, "Hear about what deal?" He said, "We're going to merge with AOL." I said, "Ted, tell me this. Did you agree to vote for it?" And he said, "Yeah, I did." I said, "Well, then it's done." There were only two big blocks of stock in Time Warner that meant anything because our block couldn't vote: one was Ted's and the other was Gordon Crawford's. And so it was a done deal, the dumbest deal I'd ever seen, but there was nothing I could do.

JERRY LEVIN:

I looked for a lesson in everything. A legacy is like your obituary. You want to write your own obituary? No. When somebody writes your obituary, it's not about "he did this, did this, did this." It's about who you were.

There had never been anything on HBO—or anywhere else for that matter—like Larry David's **Curb Your Enthusiasm,** *a show so perfectly tailored to its irascible yet priceless creator that it's impossible to imagine anyone else in the central role. With* **Curb,** *David managed to defy, defiantly, two major, and seemingly immutable, laws of television: David not only eschewed pandering to his audience, but he also obstreperously flouted the rule that says the audience must like, preferably love, the central character. David had the fearlessness to play a cantankerous crank given to pointing out every little irritant in society, while also twisting, or downright breaking, more social customs—among them, announcing to a crowd at a religious function that he was suffering from "a tickle" in his "anus." That's our Larry.*

David surrounded himself with a brilliantly proficient master class of actors. The fabulously ferocious Susie Essman, who, despite having enjoyed a successful career as a comic, never received the visibility she deserved until she was cast as the fire-breathing, foul-mouthed wife of Larry's rotund manager, played by Jeff Garlin. Cheryl Hines heroically played Larry's long-suffering wife, then ex-wife. And David's lifelong friend Richard Lewis has never been better in any acting gig than when impeccably playing himself. As close as the two men are, Lewis never refrains from pelting Larry with heartfelt obscenities; the two childlike buddies are somehow both wildly competitive and absolutely harmonious, and the same goes for the great, though tragically late, Bob Einstein; the riotously ribald J. B. Smoove as Leon, Larry's perhaps unlikely ally in chicanery transplanted from La. to LA; plus Ted Danson, another regular who couldn't hide his pleasure about being part of this crazy world.

ALAN ZWEIBEL:

Larry, Billy Crystal, and I had shared a suite of offices at Castle Rock. The three of us had started at the New York City clubs together and had stayed close friends. If you remember, after *Seinfeld*, Larry had done a movie called *Sour Grapes*, which wasn't successful, and he was licking his wounds. I was writing *The Story of Us* with Jessie Nelson, and he came in one day, and said he wanted to create a show where he would be allowed to rant. He didn't want to be held to a script and could talk for as long as we wanted. Jessie and I applauded the idea.

LARRY DAVID, Creator:

It wasn't meant as a pilot. It was meant as a special. I just was having a lot of fun because I was improvising, making it up on the spot. So, it was very appealing to me.

CHRIS ALBRECHT:

When Larry pitched the special, it was going to be his return to stand-up and he wanted to shoot his return to stand-up.

BOB WEIDE, Director and Executive Producer:

When we did the one-hour special, there was never any talk of a series. I remember Larry had no interest in going back to series television after *Seinfeld*. What was the point? He had made one of the greatest shows in the history of television. He wasn't going to try to top himself and do another one.

RICHARD LEWIS:

Larry always says even though we're ad-libbing everything, just think of your mind as a blank screen so you can be really free. It took me a while to stop worrying about how I would do it, but I started to wait for the action to develop, and I became a much better improvisational comedian. And, once again, it was because of Larry.

LARRY DAVID:

I was beyond happy. I was done with notes at that point in my career, and my friend Chris Albrecht was running it. So, I didn't see that there'd be any problem. I also knew Carolyn Strauss. Everything was in place for this thing to go and be successful.

I think I was talking to Jeff Garlin. We were on the set. I don't remember how deep into the filming we were at the time, but it's almost like we both had the same idea at the same time. Like, "Hey, this thing could be a series, you know?"

CHRIS ALBRECHT:

Larry is brilliant, but if you go down the list of stand-ups, he's not one of the guys that you think about as the all-time leader. When we looked at the cut of the special, it was clear that what stood out was the mockumentary part, as opposed to the stand-up part. I think by that time, if Larry could have just completely cut out the stand-up, he would have.

I don't remember if Larry and I spoke about it first, or Carolyn and I spoke about it first, but I think my memory is Larry on the phone going, "What do you think?" And both of us agreed that there was a lot more in the mockumentary and that maybe there was a series in this. And Carolyn certainly felt the same way. So whatever the sequence of conversations was, we didn't set out to do *Curb Your Enthusiasm*. We set out to do Larry's return to stand-up. And the mockumentary part of it became the star.

ARI EMANUEL, Agent:

We had the conversation with Chris about turning the special into a series, and he immediately got it. I think he gave us six or ten episodes, and then we were off to the races.

Freedom was more important to Larry than money, and the genius of Chris was he had no problem with that.

SUSIE ESSMAN:

I was born to do *Curb*. Cheryl [Hines] was in the improv group the Groundlings, Lewis works the way that I do. People come on and they're like, "Oh my God, this is so hard for us." It's just a natural extension of the way that we always did stand-up. Larry not so much. Larry had his bits more wellcrafted than Lewis or I or Jeff ever did. And yet, he's a master improviser.

RICHARD LEWIS:

Larry came over my house in 2000. I was about fifty-two, and he said, "Listen, do you mind playing in a show? I'm going to do a pilot."

I was at a point where I felt sincerely ashamed after the movie called *Drunks* where I played a junkie, I was in *Leaving Las Vegas*. I loved acting, but I was so pigeonholed at that point in my career.

I wasn't gonna turn Larry David down. I loved him. We were best of friends from the get-go. We went to the same summer camp. We hated each other. And never met each other again until we were comics.

When Larry asked me if I wanted to play myself, the only demand I made on Larry, I said, "LD, I just want to make sure that I'm in a couple of episodes. So there's an arc for my character that you're going to see me coming around more often. I don't want to just do a guest shot."

TED DANSON, Actor:

Larry was renting a home in Martha's Vineyard, had just finished the pilot, and showed it to a group of us in this little hot room. I'm overjoyed to tell you that a couple people fell asleep. That just tickles me.

But let me also throw in that Larry David changed my career for the better, so I am forever in his debt. Mary and I adore him. I watched the pilot going, "Oh Lord, I don't know about this," and thought, let's be supportive and tell him we'd love to be on it anytime he needs us but that will never happen, because the show sucks. Then lo and behold he did call us, and it really changed things for me. I had recently been in a show that was canceled, was slightly demoralized, and had reached a point where I felt like I was repeating myself, that other people were way funnier, and way better. It was about my twentieth year of doing half-hour sitcoms. I thought, "I'm burned out, I'm not funny, I can't do this anymore. I'm going to quit TV, and just do movies, no more of this."

Then *Curb* comes along as a lark, like doing summer theater, or even less important than that, and I found that my sense of fun and my delight in acting got rejuvenated. Having pure, kid-like fun with Larry reenergized me in a wonderful way.

And it taught me something. Up until that point I was always looking for the lead, and I realized, wait a minute, I'm focused on the wrong end of this. I need to find the most creative person in the room, wait until they write something and want to do something that's authentic, and then ask them very nicely if I could be part of it. I don't care how big the part is, or small the part is, let me just be part of this creative thing that's bursting out of you. I realized if you do that, you're likely to get into something that is really authentic and interesting. When you're around really creative people, it just feeds you. It feeds your soul, your artistic soul. That came from Larry.

LARRY DAVID:

You take it for granted sometimes. There's no lines to memorize. You're completely dependent on just being funny and moving the story along and to hit the right notes at the right time. And to a person there, they're all wonderful. There are very few complaints.

SUSIE ESSMAN:

This is his baby. He was born to do this. As was I. This is why I feel like I'm the luckiest woman in show business.

RICHARD LEWIS:

There was an episode in 2000 called "The Pants Tent," and Larry was rude to my date, my beautiful date, this Italian actress, Sophia, in a movie theater. I was pissed off at him and I came into his office and we were screaming at each other. I think we did it in one take, because I remember driving down to his office at the time, it was like a heat wave in a traffic jam. I walked into his office. He's sitting there smiling, like a Cheshire cat, and he was air-conditioned. I said, "Oh, let's go. Let's do it right now." I didn't care about makeup or hair or anything.

We did it and Larry said, "Okay, go home." I was really proud of that because that's the way I would have treated him in real life. Like, "Oh, how could you, god damn it, fucker, make me drive down here in a heat wave. And you're sitting here reading the paper."

ALAN ZWEIBEL:

Once *Curb Your Enthusiasm* became a series, Larry would come in my office, lie down on the couch, and tell me the beats of the episode he was working on. He would ask me questions, and I would throw in my two cents. That was season one and finally he said, "I can't feel guilty anymore. I'm going to give you a title and give you some money." So, for the next two seasons I had a title and got paid for him to come into my office and lie on my couch. It was a great gig.

BOB WEIDE:

In season two, there was a seasonal story arc where Larry was trying to set up a show initially for Jason Alexander and then Julia Louis-Dreyfus. We shot a scene with Jason at his actual office at the time on Ventura Boulevard. The scene was between Larry and Jason and they're having an argument about where to have the next meeting because Larry has come up to Jason's office and Jason thought Larry should come to his house for the next meeting.

Jason was saying, "No, I'm good here. This works for me. I'm sure it works for you, but I have to schlep all the way." Anyway, Jason was making Larry laugh so much by just underplaying everything. It was that line. "I'm good, I'm good." It was mainly that that always set Larry off. And Larry went into one of his now famous laughing fits and just cannot control himself. Jason's office was all windows and we were losing the light and no, I can't be Larry's disciplinarian. And because I'm as bad as he is, I'm laughing, but I'm laughing off-camera. I'm not ruining takes and he just cannot pull it together. I said, "Larry, look, we're losing light. We have to cut the scene together from several takes. The lighting is going to be all over the place, the sun is setting."

Larry had this trick when he really had to stop laughing where he would think about one of his daughters being kidnapped or something really serious. That was how he would try to bring himself down. We finally got the scene. But the last couple of takes it is nighttime outside and the sun is down and it's dark outside. If you watch that scene and look at the windows, you'll see it's daytime, nighttime, and that's all because Larry couldn't control himself and film.

Friends who were running shows for networks would ask me about the relationship with HBO. I said, "I've never had one note from the network. And they don't come to set. They're not on the set." They would start to drool.

SUSIE ESSMAN:

Let me just say this right now for the record, HBO is far and away the greatest network to work for as talent. They know how to treat their talent well. They're so supportive of their talent. I don't know any other place that treats people the way HBO does.

DAVE MANDEL, Executive Producer:

When I used to be in *Curb Your Enthusiasm* land, that's like its own country. I know it airs on HBO. They came by every now and then. I'm not taking anything away from them, but as Larry used to joke, he wished they would give him a note so he could get angry at the note and quit. Then he wouldn't have to do the show.

LARRY DAVID:

We know what we want, where we want the scene to go, and what it should be, and if we have to spend extra time getting down or even go back, we go back and do reshoots on occasion if we have to. Anytime I'll see any old show, and I don't see it often, but if something pops up or whatever, somebody shows me something, I can't think of anywhere I would go, "I couldn't do that today." I can't think of anything that I wouldn't do today.

I never said the words "I'm a lucky man" before I started doing the show, but I've said it many times since. I am a lucky man.

Larry David's comedy could be irreverent about nearly any subject, even—once or twice on the series—about good old "Death itself." But in this endeavor, Alan Ball out-did David handily; his HBO series **Six Feet Under** *took the saga of human mortality to much deeper and more meaningful—if similarly irreverent—ends.*

Ball had already given American culture one major bitter injection in 1999 with his Oscar-winning screenplay for the beautiful, sardonic film **American Beauty,** *winner of three additional major Oscars including Best Picture. Two years later, however, Ball would proffer an even greater temptation under the nation's nose:* **Six Feet Under,** *HBO's classic-to-be about life and death as observed and experienced from the vantage point of a family funeral parlor, complete with undertakers having chats, usually one-way, with resident corpses.*

The Fisher family, owners of the mortuary, are shown in all their complexity and fucked-uppedness, turning on its head the idea of the fusty, buttoned-down, long-faced, black-clad undertaker. With award-winning performances by many, including Peter Krause, Michael C. Hall, and Lauren Ambrose, and—as in **The Sopranos,** *a near-perfect series finale (Hall told the* **Hollywood Reporter** *that "the success or the resonance of that finale helped secure the show's legacy"),* **Six Feet Under** *delivered another critical smash for HBO.*

DAVID JANOLLARI, Executive Producer:

While Alan Ball was getting ready to wind down on *Cybill*, he was looking for his next move. We ended up making a deal with him to create and develop.

We were developing *Oh, Grow Up* and getting ready to take it out to the major broadcast networks. He said to us at the end of the meeting, "Hey guys, I've written a feature script and there seems to be some interest in it. I'd love you to read it and see what you think."

What we read was the original draft of *American Beauty*. We were like, "Oh my God, this is a whole other level of writing." We were truly blown away, and loved, loved, loved it.

American Beauty I think premiered in September and we were struggling on ABC to retain our lead-in, or to get the powers that be there to really embrace it and give it a back order. What a wild pendulum for Alan. On the one hand he's the toast of the movie business of American cinema. What he's basically working on day-to-day and pouring his heart and soul into is *Oh, Grow Up* on ABC.

He loved it. It was personal. And it was based on characters from his life. While he was about to win all of these awards and was truly the hottest writer in the movie business, his heart was breaking that ABC wouldn't even pick up a back order of the show.

ALAN BALL, Creator:

At the time I was running a sitcom I had created for ABC called *Oh, Grow Up*. I got a call saying that Carolyn Strauss wanted to have lunch with me. She pitched me the idea of a show about a family-run funeral home. Something in my head just went click because I spent a fair amount of time in funeral homes as I was growing up because a lot of people kept dying and I said, "Well, that sounds like a great idea. I think that could be a really great show. Unfortunately, I'm running this show for ABC, but good luck with that."

CAROLYN STRAUSS:

I had read *The Loved One* and *The American Way of Death* and was thinking about death, confronting death, and realizing that it is something that obviously everybody has in common. *American Beauty* had come out and I knew Alan's agent Sue Naegle; I called her up and said, "I have this idea and there is something about that movie that makes me feel like he could do this."

ALAN BALL:

ABC not long after very graciously canceled my show and I had two more years left on my development deal. I knew that HBO wanted the show about a family-run funeral home, and I just went home over Christmas break and wrote the pilot on spec and came back and gave it to my agent.

BOB GREENBLATT:

The first draft of *Six Feet Under*, which was called *Afterlife,* was dated February 13, 2000.

ALAN BALL:

It was more from the opposite perspective of what I didn't want to do. I was being pitched all kinds of ideas for sitcoms after my ABC show got canceled.
    We gave it to HBO and they really liked it.

CAROLYN STRAUSS:

Alan delivered a really great pilot script.

BOB GREENBLATT:

Two days, maybe three at the most, they called us and said, "We love it and we want to make it." We were like, "You want to make it?!"

DAVID JANOLLARI:

Chris Albrecht had one note when we sat down with him. I'm pretty sure he said, "Just make it more fucked up." You don't hear that at every network all around town.

ALAN BALL:

Prior to working with HBO, the notes I would get could really be condensed into two basic ideas: make everybody nicer and articulate the subtext, which are both just like deadly to good writing. So to get that response from HBO in terms of like: just fuck it up, that feels safe. I found myself in a position where I was having to unlearn a lot of the things I had learned working in network TV. I felt like this is the place where I need to be. I didn't get notes from like seventeen different people. I got notes from one person and they were usually very helpful.

When they green-lit the pilot, they said, "Who would you like to direct it?" I said, "Well, I would like to direct it." I found out later they were going, "Oh God, what? No, this guy's never directed anything before." But the fact that they were willing to take that chance. Now, granted, I had just won an Oscar. *American Beauty* had just won a bunch of Oscars. I'm not sure it would have been the same outcome had that not happened, but the fact that they were willing to take a chance on me, that really cemented for me that this is the place I want to work. I went to theater school. *Six Feet Under* ended up being my film school.

Carolyn is super smart. A lot of people who give notes basically want to turn whatever they're giving notes on into something that resembles something that's already been successful. Whereas Carolyn just, I think she was just more interesting. She was always very helpful, and the whole show was her idea anyway. I loved working with her.

CHRIS ALBRECHT:

We had difficulty casting Nate's love interest. And then we cast Peter Krause, and then Rachel Griffiths became available. We read Rachel with Peter. And we were in a conference room, this is when we were still in Century City. It was a horrible room for an audition, because it was windows on one side, there was light, and it was a long, big marble table. And they were at one end and we were at another. The two of them just read. The chemistry between the two of them and her believability as to creating a female character who had that confidence or that gene that would allow her to have that experience or help create that experience . . . We'd been trying to cast this show for a while and I turned to Alan Ball and I said, "That's why they call it acting." Here was this woman who had never done anything like this, and there she was, and she nailed it.

MICHAEL C. HALL, Actor:

I was living at the time on Hundredth Street between West End and Riverside Drive. I was walking home, I got the call from my representatives and whenever you're up for a job and there's a call and multiple representatives are on the line, it's a good sign. I think I literally screamed. I had read that pilot script and within six pages recognized that it was as special as anything I'd had the opportunity to audition for, whether onstage, on film, on television. I was beyond.

DAVID JANOLLARI:

Made the pilot, Alan directed it. We realized quickly that he learned a lot sitting on the set of *American Beauty* learning from Sam Mendes.

MICHAEL C. HALL:

I was aware of how unique the character David Fisher was within the context of that television landscape. He wasn't incidentally gay. He wasn't the comic relief neighbor with the little dog. He was a fundamental part of the fabric of the show and his relationship, his very complex and conflicted relationship to his sexuality, was a fundamental part of what made him a great character. So yeah, I certainly felt charged even more than I would normally to do it justice and to get it right.

I hadn't done anything of any significance in front of the camera before *Six Feet Under* happened. Fortunately, I was playing a character who was incredibly tense, so I didn't have to pretend I wasn't tense as an actor or nervous or on edge in those early days. I had that laboratory to experiment.

DAVID JANOLLARI:

We make the series. Halfway into the first order, I think we delivered maybe episode five to the network. They called up and said, "We're ordering another season." Before it even went on the air. Completely based on having seen this handful of episodes and knowing some of the scripts that were going to be produced beyond that.

BOB GREENBLATT:

Never tested it. There was never any talk of the audience likes this or they're afraid of this or they think death is scary or we should change this ... no ratings, no research. It was their own conviction.

MICHAEL C. HALL:

I'd liken it to the experience of catching a beautifully cresting wave.

As HBO's self-confidence skyrocketed on the backs of suddenly booming original series, so, too, did expectations for their film unit. Since its birth in 1983, HBO Premiere Films (renamed HBO Pictures three years later) had grown from a sometimes-troubled, occasionally successful production unit into a consistent, full-fledged hitmaker. By 1999, HBO Pictures had won the Primetime Emmy Award for Outstanding Television Movie six years running.

Bob Cooper, the HBO exec that had skippered the HBO Pictures brand to the heights it now enjoyed, had left in 1996. In his place reigned former Fox executive John Matoian. For a time.

Matoian had found certain successes for HBO Pictures: he'd introduced the world to Angelina Jolie with **Gia** *and held on to HBO's perch atop the TV Movie Emmy category. In his two and a half years at the network, he'd brought home nine major Emmys. Yet on the heels of a series of disappointing flops, Matoian faced internal doubts.*

On April 13, 1999, HBO announced an overhaul: programming whiz Chris Albrecht was given expanded oversight of all original programming at HBO, including HBO Pictures. Matoian, a former direct report to CEO Jeff Bewkes, balked at the new arrangement. His retirement was announced on the same day as the restructuring.

Now helming HBO Pictures would be a familiar face: Colin Callender.

CHRIS ALBRECHT:

Colin and I should have been rivals, but we ended up being buddies. The Colin movies were the ones that helped set the tone for what HBO Pictures became.

When Bob Cooper left, I wanted Jeff to give me the movies, but Jeff wouldn't do it. They brought in this other guy named John Matoian, who was a disaster. When he left, I said to Jeff, "You gotta put everything together." He said, "Can you and will you do it?" I said, "Yeah but I want Colin." And he said, "Can he handle it?" And I said, "He can handle it if he is reporting to me. Because I will do it with him." For executives, in a lot of ways, you have to handle them like talent.

The golden age of HBO Pictures was really Colin running it.

Callender had joined HBO in 1987, to helm HBO Showcase (rechristened HBO NYC Productions in 1996), the smaller, indie, East Coast cousin of the more commercial HBO Pictures. On October 22, 1999, HBO announced that HBO Pictures and NYC Productions, would merge under one banner, and HBO Films was born.

KERI PUTNAM:

It wasn't until 1999 when Matoian left that they merged the two movie divisions and renamed it HBO Films. This put all of programming under Chris Albrecht (and *The Sopranos* launched that year, bringing in the ascendancy of series on HBO). Both Colin and I relocated to Los Angeles to run the combined division. In addition to producing six to eight films per year, we expanded into miniseries with works like the Mike Nichols landmark *Angels in America* adaptation and Richard Russo's *Empire Falls* starring Paul Newman, Joanne Woodward, and Ed Harris. And we also launched a theatrical division for a short while that produced Gus Van Sant's Palme d'Or–winning film *Elephant, American Splendor, Maria Full of Grace*, and several other indie films.

COLIN CALLENDER:

It was a very exciting time. Jeff and Chris together were a pretty impressive combination. They were very different people. They approach the world in very different ways. But like most opposites, they attracted and worked brilliantly together. It was a very productive relationship between the two of them. They honored and protected the DNA that had been established at the heart of the company.

JEFF BEWKES:

In the late 1990s, Colin brought me a limited-series project about the Holocaust. The first two hours reenacted the Wannsee Conference in January 1942, where the top Nazis planned the Holocaust. The second part would re-create the meeting of the Allies in the summer of 1943, where they discussed what to do with Jewish refugees but basically decided to put all their effort into winning the war rather than bombing the rail lines to the camps or diverting ships to pick up refugees. The original thrust of the project was that the Allies, and the Roosevelt administration, deliberately ignored or abetted the Holocaust, so they were going to name it *Complicity*.

Given the wider considerations of the war, I questioned whether it was fair to charge the United States with conscious complicity in the Holocaust.

The answer I got was that we'd get a lot of attention, to which I said, "No shit. Let's talk it over with the creative team."

I had to respond with, "No, in a war for survival of the country, the duty of the American president is to save 'our' people, the American people, before saving refugees in Europe. Look at the list the Nazis drew up in Wannsee: they were planning to kill thirteen million people and we stopped them halfway by winning the war."

Dead silence in the room. I'm sitting there thinking, Great, here's a career ender for me. The goy who took over from Michael Fuchs shuts down a Holocaust justice movie, clearly an anti-Semite. I'll have to leave the industry by Monday.

And then an authoritative voice comes from the corner. "He's right. We're better off not making this argument. Ben-Gurion said as much in 1948." Brian Wapping, professor of history at Oxford. Thank God.

I went back to my office. An hour later Steven Haft called. I didn't know him and I figured he was going to argue with me about my unwillingness to do the project, but instead he says, "I told Cooper it was a bridge too far (meaning the accusation of US complicity). I always thought we should do the first part, the meeting of the Nazis at Wannsee." Right on the spot, I said, "I'll do that," and we made *Conspiracy,* a brilliant film with Kenneth Branagh, Colin Firth, and Stanley Tucci that won the Emmy. I already admired Steven Haft and Frank Pierson and we became good friends.

COLIN CALLENDER:

We brought Frank in very early and he had this very immediate sense that he wanted to shoot it all in one room in long takes. And he wanted the camera to be the height of the table, so that the camera would actually be at eyeline height, as though it was a character sitting at the table. And the idea of doing a film entirely in real time, from the beginning of the meeting through the end, basically with no time jumps, was equally provocative. Particularly given the extraordinary nature of what was being discussed.

STANLEY TUCCI:

It's so devoid of emotion, that's what makes it so emotional. Those people had no empathy. So I think that's why it was so incredibly moving. And it was so well written and directed. You had all those wonderful actors, so you had Colin Firth and Ken Branagh and Kevin McNally. So many great actors.

Part of the way through shooting, I was really having difficulty remembering the lines. It was hard. I talked to Ken about it and Ken said that he was having trouble, too. And then we realized that because there was nothing to connect to, you had no emotional connection, it was very hard. You finished at the end of the day, and it felt like you hadn't done anything, but you were exhausted. More exhausted than if you had a big emotional scene. And you realize that it was because there was nothing to cling to, you were lost. These people didn't feel anything.

COLIN CALLENDER:

It reminded me that there was power in simplicity. Somehow watching this meeting take place was for me the most striking example or dramatization of the banality of evil. It's all about men being bullied into submission and acquiescing and seeking approval of others. And not wanting to step out of line. All the things that we're watching right now with many of our politicians in American politics right now.

STANLEY TUCCI:

It was a very, very weird experience. We were like five, six weeks in the studio and shooting around that table and the different rooms on the set and everything, that amazing set that they built. And then we went to Wannsee and we shot the exteriors. It was winter. They put some snow all over the place. There was already snow, but I think they added more. Everybody was all dressed up, and all the extras dressed up in Nazi uniforms. They were all German. I had to do this thing where I had to come stand at the threshold of the estate and go in. And as I stood there and I looked at the whole thing and I heard everybody speaking German and saw the uniforms, there was nothing contemporary there. All of the emotion that I had felt doing the research and sort of suppressed doing the filming in the studio came welling up. Tears came to my eyes and I almost vomited. I had never experienced that before.

I was thrilled with the reaction to it. They started using it in schools to show older kids, obviously in universities. We had the premiere in Washington at the Holocaust Museum, and that was an amazing experience. I was asked to go back a few years later to give a talk at an event there. It was just a great honor to be a part of that and to just be a part of telling that incredibly important, horrifying story.

COLIN CALLENDER:

We did *Real Women Have Curves*, with America Ferrera. It was her first screen role, and I remember thinking, God what have we done here? She got all sorts of awards and nominations. I said, "There's so few roles for an actress like America Ferrera. We've just set her on the path here and potentially raised the expectation that she will be able to have a career as an actress." This was 2002, but back then how many roles are there for young Latina women like America? And who knew, *Ugly Betty* comes along. There were a lot of moments like that. There were lots of actors and actresses who had that first role with us and have sort of exploded in one way or another.

Then in 2001, HBO Films and HBO Sports combined for the first time, to produce the film 61*.

ROSS GREENBURG:

I spent three or four years trying to get into the story of Mickey Mantle, then I had this movie treatment written by Hank Steinberg about him plopped on my desk by Colin Callender. He asked for my advice and if I would I like to be involved. As soon as I read it, I knew this was the best way in, to focus on Mickey and his relationship with Roger Maris. Mickey was everyone's hero, and Roger was demeaned and denounced for breaking Babe Ruth's record. But, in fact, Roger lived a hero's life and Mickey didn't. I'll never forget what Colin said at the start, which resonated throughout the making of the film: "This film will help the US figure out how we define our heroes."

BILLY CRYSTAL:

Ross, who was a friend, sent me the treatment. He knew I had a good relationship with Mickey. He said, "I'd like you to executive produce this with me for HBO. What do you think?"

After I read it, I said, "There's some really good things here, but the truth is, I know so many more stories that I could put into it. So if you want to develop it together, I'd love to do that." We worked with Hank Steinberg, who would later become a big force in television.

Mickey had told me all these stories about Maris and him living together in Queens near the Van Wyck Expressway, and I put a lot of those in there as well as others. Meanwhile, Ross kept telling me I needed to direct this, and I kept saying, "I don't know." Then we started looking at locations. They had renovated Yankee Stadium so we couldn't use that, so we went to Tiger Stadium, where the Tigers had just moved out to go to their new facility. We're walking through the clubhouse, and I said, "Mickey was here. Roger was here." I found myself setting up shots and said to Ross, "Goddamn it, I can't let anyone else do this. I'm going to direct the movie."

ROSS GREENBURG:

Now I had to convince HBO to let Billy direct. He had directed two films, neither blockbusters. It took several months for them to say yes.

Colin didn't know much about baseball, but he knew storytelling. Then he assigned Keri Putnam to the project, who was a fabulous production executive. She was a joy to work with. We kept asking for a little more, a little more, and they kept giving us what we needed budget-wise. It ended up being $18 million. I think the most expensive film that HBO Films had done at that point. It had a lot of pressure.

BILLY CRYSTAL:

We had a terrific cast all the way through. Finding Tom Jane and Barry Pepper was critical. They embodied those two guys and were brilliant.

THOMAS JANE, Actor:

I grew up playing football. I wasn't a baseball player, and I didn't know a whole hell of a lot about Mickey Mantle.

I showed up to meet Billy Crystal and asked, "Why do you want to meet me?" He said, "Because from behind, you look like Mickey Mantle." I said, "What about from the front?" He goes, "We'll work on that."

I was honest with him. I said, "Dude, I love the part. The script is fantastic and my story is terrific. I'd love to do it, but I don't know a damn thing about baseball." He says, "I got that covered." He wrote down an address. "Go meet this guy who runs a baseball camp in the valley." It was Reggie Smith, the number two switch-hitter behind Mantle.

Reggie and I hit it off. I got hooked learning. I showed up there every goddamn day. Reggie wouldn't even let me touch a bat for the first couple of weeks.

He gave me a samurai sword and a two-by-four. He made me balance on a two-by-four with both feet and swing the samurai sword. He would close his eyes, listen to the sounds the sword made through the air and know what I was doing wrong. That was Reggie Smith, the best coach I've ever had.

BILLY CRYSTAL:

The guys were in full uniform flannels shagging fly balls in the outfield. It was so realistic. It was unbelievable, and who shows up but Mickey's widow, Merlyn, her two sons, Danny and David, and Yogi Berra.

Merlyn looked out at Tom Jane with a shock of blond hair coming out of his baseball cap from behind in a number seven. And she just lost it. She went, "Oh my God."

I yelled out to him, "Mickey!" and Tom Jane runs in with that little bit of a limp that Mickey had, and the family hugged him like it was Easter Sunday and Mantle was resurrected.

ROSS GREENBURG:

We all started crying. That's a moment none of us will ever forget.

THOMAS JANE:

Mickey blew his knee out on catching a fly ball, and always ran with a hitch after because of the way his knee had popped out. He had this beautiful, loping, horse trot that I never got exactly right. But I'm damned proud of the rest of it.

ROSS GREENBURG:

Billy brought it all to life. His leadership was contagious, and the crew and everyone at HBO rallied around him because he had such an amazing vision.

BILLY CRYSTAL:

We get invited to screen it at the White House with President Bush. It was a huge honor. This is the family feeling of HBO.

Everybody was there, the whole HBO contingent, even the big boardroom guys. They were all so personable and proud of the movie. The movie starts. There's three or four rough Mantle jokes in the beginning, like, "I like women with small hands, makes my dick look bigger," stuff like that.

I'm sitting next to the president. He's got his cowboy boots with GWB on them. I whisper to him, "There's only two more of those," and he goes, "Bring 'em on!"

In real life, Maris hit his fifty-eighth home run off a lefty, Hank Aguirre, but when we were shooting, the kid playing Aguirre didn't show up, and all I had was a right-handed pitcher. I thought, "That's not right, but it's our only option." So I used a righty who played a pitcher named Frank Lary.

In the film you see Maris hits his fifty-eighth against Frank, and the president leans over and he says to me, "That's not right. It was Hank Aguirre." I said, "I know. I can't believe you know that." He says, "Yeah, that was one of my favorite years."

I'm sitting there thinking, he knows it was Hank Aguirre, not Frank Lary, but there were no weapons of mass destruction.

GINA BALIAN, Executive:

Toward the end of 2001, it felt like we were at the beginning of something really special at HBO, that we were doing something different in television, and there was a lot of excitement about it all. We were catching fire. And because we were small, operating like a homegrown boutique, it also had the feeling of an upstart in the sense we were all going through this together.

People got along well; department people were friends inside and outside of work. We'd come to work in jeans, it was a casual environment, though Chris often wore suits but was always a friendly presence. Anyone could speak up to voice an opinion and participate. No one was getting too confident. When awards would be announced, people would say congratulations and then just go back to their jobs.

The big question at the time was, is this a fluke or something that is going to be sustained?

8

Chair in the Sky

SEPTEMBER 9, 2001–JULY 17, 2002

Michael Fuchs cast such a long shadow over HBO that it lingered for years after he'd left the company—particularly for those who had "grown up" under his dynamic but exhausting leadership. Jeff Bewkes, HBO's chairman and CEO since Fuchs's firing in 1995, had rendezvoused with Fuchs several times, despite his predecessor's continued bitterness. Each time, as if on cue, Bewkes had to endure a slew of "why did you do that"s or "you should've done this"es.

If there was one nagging "Fuchsism" that remained alive and annoying in Bewkes's memory, it was what Fuchs had told Jerry Levin (and others) after being put in charge of Warner Music, when he'd been urged to abandon his duties at HBO. "There's no way I can walk away from HBO," Fuchs had angrily insisted. "Bewkes is a finance guy. He doesn't understand anything about programming."

That was, of course, merely an excuse. Fuchs was never going to let go of HBO, the greatest love of his life. Still, those rantings truly pissed off Bewkes, and as often happens with imprudent remarks, this one became a call to arms. While Bewkes was determined not to micromanage Chris Albrecht, Carolyn Strauss, Sheila Nevins, Colin Callender, or any others, he also wanted to dedicate himself to active leadership in the HBO programming universe. He had made sure to remain involved with shows that he *considered his "babies"—***Sex and the City,** *The Sopranos, and* **Conspiracy—***and now he had quite a taste for it.*

Bewkes had been the chief financial engineer on **From the Earth to the Moon** *and loved its ambition, size, and legacy. Now he was looking for something bigger for HBO's portfolio—something downright colossal.*

Once again, Tom Hanks entered the picture, this time with Playtone (named after the record company in his movie **That Thing You Do***), the film and television production company he founded in 1998 with Gary Goetzman. HBO had signed Playtone to an exclusive TV deal as soon as it was founded.*

TOM HANKS:

After *Saving Private Ryan*, the interest in stories of World War II was huge. Steven Spielberg being Steven Spielberg, ABC came to him to adapt Stephen Ambrose's *Citizen Soldiers* into a TV event. For reasons I will never understand, Steven asked if I wanted to be a part of doing it, as our production company Playtone was producing TV by then.

I had read *Citizen Soldiers* as background for *Saving Private Ryan*, and many other sources, including Ambrose's *Band of Brothers*. *Citizen Soldiers* was too wide a net to corral into a linear miniseries. Where would you start? Who would you follow? Where would you be taken? But *Band of Brothers* was already shaped and was perfect for however many episodes the book needed. If we took that to HBO, we would have creative freedom regarding theme, language, and no commercial breaks. Steven agreed, HBO said yes, and Tony To, Erik Bork, and Graham Yost were all in again.

With the production gearing up in London, in Hatfield, at the same former aerodrome where we shot much of *Saving Private Ryan*, we had a meeting with Jeff Bewkes and Chris Albrecht in which I begged for all the money—$150 million—and broadcasting in the Letterbox format, not the 1:33 [aspect ratio] that *From the Earth to the Moon* was shown in. That was a problem for the broadband and for the other productions on HBO that would want to do the same thing—it's costly, or it was then. Bewkes said, "We might as well do it, since this is the last time there'll ever be a miniseries this big."

JEFF BEWKES:

After we made *From the Earth to the Moon*, I was at a lunch honoring Rita Wilson, Tom's wife, and for small talk he asked, "What are you reading?" I said, "*Citizen Soldiers* by Stephen Ambrose." It was about how our army of citizen volunteers improvised their way to winning against the regimented Axis armies. I told Tom I teared up reading it. Tom gets this serious look on his face and says, "I've got *Band of Brothers*," meaning he has the film rights, which was another Ambrose book about a platoon of paratroopers. So, Chris and Carolyn started talking with Tom and Gary Goetzman about a miniseries for HBO.

It was an ambitious project across twelve episodes (at first) that would cost over $150 million—the biggest budget ever for a TV miniseries. Tom enlisted his friend Steven Spielberg to help shape the story and select directors and key team members. Chris advised me to fly out to LA to handshake the deal with Tom and Steven. I explained that we didn't have more than $135 million, so right in the meeting they reorganized the bible and cut out two episodes, then we shook on the deal. I admitted I was worried that with such a huge undertaking we'd end up late or over budget. Steven said he'd rarely gone over budget or been late. They kept their word, came in on time and on budget.

"Easy Company" is one of the most recognized units in U.S. Army history. Technically the 2nd battalion of the 506th Parachute Infantry Regiment, the company played a critical role in the historic invasion of Normandy. Richard Winters was a key commander.

ANNE THOMOPOULOS:

Richard Winters, who commanded Easy Company, was very reticent about being involved in the project. Richard was very conservative and very suspect of Hollywood. He didn't want to share his life. At the end of our lunch I said, "Regardless of what you decide, I need to thank you because my mother-and father-in-law were married during the war and decided that they wouldn't have children until they knew their children would be okay. My brother-in-law was born in a bombing seven months after you landed on the beach in Normandy. I owe you my life. My daughter is a result of your efforts and she's my greatest joy. Whatever happens, I am eternally grateful." Carmi told me it was because of that that he changed his mind.

CARMI ZLOTNIK:

People mistake our business for a manufacturing business, which is about the most amount of product at the lowest possible cost. In reality we are a boutique business, which is the highest quality possible at the appropriate cost.

BRUCE RICHMOND:

Band of Brothers was an amazing experience. We were able to learn from our previous history of getting comfortable doing things outside the box;

there were many firsts as well. We were able to go to England and film at the Hatfield Aerodrome, where *Saving Private Ryan* was made. And we built sets with Anthony Pratt that were nine football fields big.

ANNE THOMOPOULOS:

Tom was hugely involved. At one of the first scenes that we shot in England he made a PA go into a trench and chase an actor to show the director what he wanted with the camera movement.

TOM HANKS:

I wasn't a producer for the physical scale of the series—though I did know of the size of everything—the cast, the location, the sets, the productions. My questions were, "Is this possible?" And Tony always said, "Yeah!" I'd ask, "How do we do this?" There was always an answer. Spielberg always gave the go-ahead to try everything—and was huge with the SPFX ideas. Shots in episode two, for example, he pitched in the room when we first met Angus Bickerton and the visual effects team. I concentrated on the scripts matching the theme of what we were trying to examine—regular guys in a foreign land killing and not being killed. That work never ceased and was always fascinating because not only were the scripts always in flux but the various directors all had different desires. I wrote on some of the screen-plays and directed the middle episode.

DAVID FRANKEL:

I got a call from Tony To in London, who was producing *Band of Brothers*, asking, "Can you come do an episode?" I asked, "When do you need me?" And he said, "Can you be on a plane tomorrow?" My wife said, "I thought I married a writer. What is this directing shit?"

She asked, "This isn't going to be like *To the Moon* where you go do one, and then you ended up doing three, is it?" We were trying to have kids that summer, and I said, "No, no, no, I'm sure they've lined up all the directors. I'll just do this one episode." So I flew off. Sure enough, another director fell out. Tony then asked me to do a second episode. I did the "Why We Fight" episode, with the liberation of the concentration camp with a great script by John Orloff. Then I did "The Breaking Point." I was gone for five months.

TONY TO:

I believe it was the coldest, wettest year in England for seventy-five years, which really helped the look of the piece.

ANNE THOMOPOULOS:

The Bastogne episode where we're running through the forest and it's snow-ing was down inside a blue hangar and the trees that were cut down to create the concentration camp were transported to this hangar. We laid ten feet of dirt, planted those trees that were cut down, and used artificial snow. Tony Pratt is absolutely brilliant.

DAVID FRANKEL:

The unsung hero was Tony To. He was a real testament to what a great pro-ducer does, not just with nuts and bolts, but having the vision to push people on the ground and executives in the tower beyond their comfort zones to make something better than they may imagine what's possible.

TONY TO:

A big ingredient of the magic was that the actors were talking to the people they were playing. The spirit was everybody wanted to honor them. You would have a call sheet with the characters who were supposed to be there, but then two or three other actors who had a day off would come and they would be in wardrobe. They would say, "I talked to my guy yesterday. He said, 'I was on that patrol.' You don't have to give me any lines, but we want to do right by them. We're going to be here even if we're treated like extras."

ANNE THOMOPOULOS:

Everyone was top of class. It was a tribute to the greatest generation who saved us.

DAVID FRANKEL:

What I heard from Steven was that there were certain rules for the directors—no crane shots, no slow motion, and nothing from the German point of view. Everything had to be from the Americans' point of view.

It was sort of frustrating to see every battle from one point of view. It doesn't seem very dangerous if you don't have a sense of who the bad guys are and if you don't feel vulnerable. So in the first episode I did, which was episode nine, it starts with a two-and-a-half-minute crane shot—which was supposedly against all the rules—set to Beethoven.

Then when I did the next episode, I snuck in some German POVs in the battle sequences in "Breaking Point." I even used a slow-motion shot, but that got changed. I tried to break all the rules, but only broke two.

TONY TO:

Even though David did a crane shot it didn't feel like it was a crane shot. It was following these characters in a burned-out building. It felt seamless, was part of the storytelling, and you weren't conscious of the filmmaker's hand. We wanted to take the language Steven used in *Saving Private Ryan* so viewers would experience this journey under the helmet. That cinema verité quality was something we really wanted to preserve, the idea that you don't take the audience out of the moment.

We never used a stunt man. Everything was done by the actors. That part of the under-the-helmet experience can only be achieved if you are with the actors the whole time, and that there is no stunt man. That took a lot of invention from the art department and special effects—creating explosions and bullet hits that were safe for the actors to run through.

DAVID FRANKEL:

Hanks deserves a lot of credit. He was extraordinary at stretching what was possible. Because he came from the world of cinema, he had a different template in mind. On *Band of Brothers*, we were doing cinema. To give you an example, the two episodes of *Band of Brothers* that I directed and shot were for two hours of television, and I shot fifty-five days of production. The longest schedule I've ever had on a feature film that I've made is fifty-five days.

The level of ambition was unmatched.

RICHARD PLEPLER:

As we were making *Band of Brothers*, Jeff and I went to the set in England with Steven and Tom. We were marveling at the scope and the size of the production, and thought how cool it would be if we could premiere this on Utah Beach itself. And imagine if we were able to bring back the surviving members of Easy Company to be recognized and thanked all these years later.

Many of them were old; who knew how much more time a lot of them had? Everybody thought that would be fantastic if we could pull it off.

QUENTIN SCHAFFER:

Dick Winters was the commander who led Easy Company, and when we were discussing the idea of this event, Richard called him on the phone to discuss it.

Winters hated the idea. He said, "My guys are in their eighties and they're not going to be up to this." So Richard and I traveled to Hershey, Pennsylvania, and met Winters and his wife for lunch. It turned out that Winters and Richard both went to Franklin & Marshall College. Good start. Richard said, "Dick, we really want to do this, Tom Hanks is on board, but you are key." Winters doesn't agree to anything but gives us the okay to approach the guys directly to see what they want to do. He then pulls out a sheet of paper and says, "But let me tell you their health conditions." He starts going through this list—diabetes, heart disease, stroke, and so on. After all these years, he still concerned about the welfare of his guys. He then says, "You want that responsibility? If they do go, and somebody dies?" Richard explained that we were going to have a medical team on board. So we return to New York and reach out to the veterans. Guess what? Every single one of them said, "Sign me up." We went back to Winters and told him. Winters, realizing he couldn't let his men go alone, agreed to come and let me tell you, he had a phenomenal time.

RICHARD PLEPLER:

We met with the mayors of the three towns in the region and convinced them we'd do something special. Michael McMorrow is really the hero of this. He is a genius. He ended up literally building a theater on Utah Beach. It was extraordinary.

MICHAEL McMORROW:

It was the most ambitious and costly event we ever put together. I'm very proud of that event.

We had such an emotional connection to it. We knew we were on hallowed ground in Normandy and wanted it to be respectful of both the show, the veterans and the people who lived there. They were incredibly generous and opened their homes to us.

MARA MIKIALIAN:

American Airlines donated a plane. We had the opportunity to bring almost fifty of the men who had fought there. Many of them had never returned since D-Day.

Those guys and the actors got to spend a week together, and every night, the actors were going to sleep before the veterans. They were laughing, crying, reminiscing, drinking. A lot of drinking. We stayed in Paris for the week and had various events in Paris, then we chartered a train to take everyone to Normandy.

Tom, who was working on *Road to Perdition* at that point, he could have just helicoptered to Normandy, but he chose to go to Paris, then go on the train with those men. That was his choice. He wanted to be part of it, be there for them—also because a lot of them had not met him before. It was pretty incredible.

ANNE THOMOPOULOS:

To get on that train was really touching, and I realized something about the bond that happens between soldiers that I had never really understood before. They basically said, "We love our wives, our kids, their families. But the love we have for each other is different." These men had faced death over and over again together.

QUENTIN SCHAFFER:

When we arrived, we were greeted by French schoolkids waving American flags to celebrate the return of these heroes. It really got you choked up. The French government did a flyover at the welcoming ceremony before the screening. I had invited the grandchildren of the three key Allied leaders and they all came—Anne Roosevelt, Susan Eisenhower, and Winston Churchill III. In fact, in Paris, I treated them to breakfast at the Plaza Athénée; I submitted my expense report listing breakfast with Eisenhower, Churchill, and Roosevelt.

TOM HANKS:

I was in a seat just down from the real Dick Winters and Speirs—watching them watch "themselves" on D-Day. I'll never forget the look on their faces. At noon, I was sitting next to Carwood Lipton on a bus. It was June 6. I asked him what he was doing at noon on June 6, 1944. "We had just taken the guns at Brécourt Manor and were moving on to our secondary target at Culloville."

JEFF BEWKES:

When we were heading to Normandy on the train, I was looking at the index cards of the speech I was going to give at the ceremony, and the Normandy ceremony every year has the top military brass of France, Britain, Poland, and the United States in attendance. I realized I can't do this whole thing in English, I gotta do at least some of it in French. I worked in France for two summers in high school, and thought I could give it in French if I could get the right translation, but I only had an hour or so to do it. I remembered Anne Thomopoulos's husband is French, and they were five cars ahead on the train. I found Patrice and sat down next to him with the index cards and a pen. We finished five minutes before we pulled into the station.

RICHARD PLEPLER:

It had been raining for a few days but on the morning of June 6, 2001, the sun came out. Jeff introduced the event on behalf of HBO, both in French and English. I already had many wonderful days at HBO but that one was hard to beat.

JEFF BEWKES:

The ceremony was very solemn, makes you tear up. I believe the Joint Chiefs' equivalent of the French military introduced me to say something, and I started in English then shifted into all these remarks in French. Hanks was after me, but before he spoke, we stood for a national anthem. And out of the corner of his mouth, he looked over at me with a little smirk and says, "You speak French? You trying to upstage me?" He was joking.

MICHAEL McMORROW:

In his opening remarks, Tom Hanks acknowledged the veterans who we all sat in the front row and said, "These are the men who saved the world." It was quite moving.

RICHARD PLEPLER:

Hanks gave his speech thanking everybody and he started to cry. We all started to cry. Quentin did his typical, brilliant job of mastering the media strategy. *Good Morning America* came live from there at that time, which was a big deal. It really was a memorable few days.

MARA MIKIALIAN:

I had this idea to pair actors and veterans, so we flew actors to where the veterans were.

The one who portrayed Babe Heffron was from Scotland—Robin Laing— and had never even been to America. While Robin is on his way from Scotland to Philadelphia, Babe ends up in the hospital. So Robin landed and I greeted him and said, "Do you want to rest? You want to go see the Liberty Bell? You've never been in America before." He said, "Bring me to Babe." We immediately went to the hospital and of course Bill was there because those two were inseparable. It was important to Babe that Robin and also Frank see their world.

Bill basically set out an itinerary for us, drove us all around in his car with his only one leg that he had. We went to the restaurant where they had breakfast every day. We went to the Irish bars. We did that with four other pairings. Honestly, to this day, I think I'm still so proud of that story and how it came out [in *People* magazine] and how the actors and the veterans felt about it.

ERIC KESSLER:

Several months later, I was sitting in the Hollywood Bowl for the U.S. premiere. Steven Spielberg, Tom Hanks, the entire cast, a ton of Hollywood royalty, were all there on a beautiful early September evening. Before the first two episodes were shown we had a forty-piece orchestra play the inspiring soundtrack.

Band premiered the following Sunday, September 9, 2001. On Monday night, at four o'clock we got the ratings which were the biggest in years, might have been the highest ever. The PR team wrote a press release and we decided it would go out at nine o'clock the next morning.

On the evening of September 11, 2001, HBO planned to air a special sneak preview of its new comedy series, **The Mind of the Married Man.** *The show's creator and star, comedian Mike Binder, popped up on ABC's* **Good Morning, America** *with Diane Sawyer to promote the debut.*

MIKE BINDER:

Mind of the Married Man was going to be a Sunday night show, but HBO decided to air a special premiere the Tuesday night before, something I don't think they had done before. I was sitting with Diane Sawyer as the first plane hit the World Trade Center. Whenever they go back and do the retrospective of that morning, I'm always there.

So it was not a perfect mood for the country to be seeing a bunch of horny husbands having fantasies of other women.

ERIC KESSLER:

At about eight fifty I'm sitting at my desk and my assistant comes running in telling me to turn on the TV. A plane had just hit the World Trade Center. We walked out of the HBO building and saw the smoke. That day was a blur. The next day however, we had to deal with numerous business issues: Should we continue to run *Band of Brothers*, a series about war? The advertising line in newspaper and TV ads was, "There was a time when ordinary people did extraordinary things." Could we say that line the day after ordinary people did in fact do extraordinary things such as firefighters who ran up burning buildings?

One of Bill Maher's frequent and favorite guests on ABC's **Politically Incorrect** *(produced by HBO) was lawyer and conservative commentator Barbara Olson, wife of Ted Olson, the man who had represented George W. Bush in "Bush vs. Gore" to settle the 2000 presidential election, and later served as Bush's solicitor general.*

Ted Olson's birthday was September 11; Barbara had been slated to fly from Washington, DC, to Los Angeles on the tenth, ahead of a **Politically Incorrect** *appearance but delayed her flight one day so she could wake up next to her husband on his birthday.*

She was aboard American Airlines Flight 77, which left Washington Dulles Airport at 8:20 a.m. on the morning of 9/11. Around one hour after takeoff, Olson called her husband twice to tell him that her flight had been hijacked by men carrying box cutters and knives. According to the 9/11 report, "The Solicitor General . . . informed his wife of the two previous hijackings and crashes at the World Trade Center. She did not display signs of panic and did not indicate any awareness of an impending crash. At that point, the second call was cut off."

It was 9:37 a.m. when Flight 77 crashed into the western side of the Pentagon, killing all on board. Barbara Olson was forty-five years old; her seat on **Politically Incorrect** *was left empty for a week in her memory.*

NANCY GELLER:

On the morning of September 11, I boarded a nine a.m. flight from New York to LA. The door was open. There was an announcement that we would be taking off about fifteen minutes late because some luggage had not gotten on yet, then several guys from the back of the plane ran off the plane. I didn't think much about it. All of a sudden, phones weren't working, and eventually the captain came out and said that an American Airlines plane had hit the twin towers and asked us to bow our heads in prayer. I wanted to get off, but at that point, they weren't letting anybody off. We could see the smoke out the window and then he came back out and said, "I'm going to ask you all to get off the plane."

The minute I heard about the Washington plane, I freaked out because I knew we were bringing Barbara out. She was a frequent guest. She was coming out to be on the show. She was one of Bill's favorites. We all felt guilty, terrible, horrible.

KEN SCHICK:

Fifteen days after the 9/11 attacks, as I watched footage from Ground Zero, I saw television soap opera stars there offering emotional support to the workers who were involved in the painstaking search efforts. I knew the perfect man for the situation, Evander Holyfield.

I quickly called Evander and asked him if he would go to Ground Zero to meet and greet those workers, assuming we could arrange it. He immediately agreed and we began coordinating with the mayor's office to go there on Saturday.

That day, the operation was changed from "Search and Rescue" to "Cleanup," officially ending any hope of finding additional survivors.

Evander was simply amazing that day, starting with insisting we help unload the supply boat. Remember, there was no media on site, so all of his actions were truly from the heart. We then spent five or six hours walking through the bombed-out areas with scenes looking more like a World War II movie than the main financial area of New York City. Debris still floated in the air, smoke was still rising from what had been massive buildings—the situation was so bad that we had to wear gas masks most of the time.

EVANDER HOLYFIELD:

When I saw up close what happened, it scared me.

There were a lot of bad things happening, but I went there out of respect. Those people working there were heroes, and to go down there, represent HBO, and let those people know how much we appreciated them was a big deal.

I came up poor as a kid and my mom was always telling me, "Be nice to people. You don't need to make no noise. You ain't got to tell people who you are. Just be nice." I try to be that person and not to try to think that I'm better than somebody.

KEN SCHICK:

Evander never stopped during the time we were there—signing autographs, shaking hands, and often hugging workers with many breaking down in tears as he did.

I will never forget one firefighter saying to me, "I never thought I would ever smile again but damn, Evander Holyfield just shook this hand" as he proudly raised it in front of my face.

Six days after 9/11, **Politically Incorrect** *host Bill Maher, prompted by panelist Dinesh D'Souza's having described the terrorists as "warriors," told his viewers, with regard to the terrorists who'd committed the attacks, "We have been the cowards, lobbing cruise missiles from two thousand miles away. That's cowardly. Staying in the airplane when it hits the building, say what you want about it, [it's] not cowardly."*

NANCY GELLER:

I was in the control room. I heard him say it but didn't think that much about it because Bill's politically incorrect—that's something HBO embraced.

But it was on ABC. We didn't get phone calls about it right away. Then the story hit the media, and that's when problems started. Now, had he said it five weeks later, I don't think anybody necessarily would have had such a reaction to it. But he said it that week. Too soon. That's when the shit hit the fan. That was the beginning of the end.

But a major storm began to brew. Federal Express and Sears cut their ties to the show, and White House Press Secretary Ari Fleischer brought angry attention to the comment ("People have to watch what they say and watch what they do," he lectured). Maher apologized, noting that he'd been criticizing US foreign policy, not the US military, in his original remark; nevertheless, certain ABC affiliates refused to air **Politically Incorrect.** *By June 2002, more advertisers had deserted the show, and ABC nervously canceled it entirely.*

BILL MAHER:

I was never mad when ABC fired me, I was only mad that they lied and said it was because the ratings were down. The ratings never went down. The ratings were very good all through, with no help, by the way, from our lead-in *Nightline.* They had the coldest switch possible, three minutes of commercials at the end of *Nightline* before our show started. It was ridiculous. And yet we still had a great retention from *Nightline.*

NANCY GELLER:

I said to Chris, "We can't lose Bill Maher." And he said, "This is a very sensitive time, and ABC has made their decision." I was so emotionally invested in Bill. I believed in him, and think he is brilliant. I called Brad and told him, "You have to help me double team HBO to bring Bill to HBO," even though I was HBO.

We pressured Chris Albrecht to death. Chris said to me, "Nancy, it was on Comedy Central. Then it went to ABC. Now you want HBO to take it? That's crazy." We came up with the idea, "Let's call it *Real Time with Bill Maher* and we'll change the set a little bit." It was Bill sitting in the middle of a round table. We made a curve table, but three guests on one side and Bill was on the other versus the round table in the middle. That was the only change.

By February 2003, Maher had a new show, not only in name but channel too. **Real Time with Bill Maher** *was modeled on* **Politically Incorrect** *but the celebrity guest focus of* **P-I** *was jettisoned in favor of opinionated experts.*

BILL MAHER:

I needed to be in a place where the sponsors would not pull out if I said something controversial and Brillstein-Grey Entertainment was instrumental.

I could have been a quick hook. Before we got our shit together, my show could have been canceled after the first year. The first year was not great. It took us time to find our footing and the network did not know how to handle a show like mine. We were off for six months at a time. Our show had to have a continual presence. The audience always had no problem with this hybrid of comedy and political astuteness. They got it right from the beginning.

On a lot of these other shows, the opinions are all just like MSNBC. They only pander to the exact liberal preprogrammed one true opinion that's already out there. They don't really ever challenge the audience, which is what makes our show different.

Controversial loudmouths, often scorned elsewhere, continued to be welcome at HBO. The network stuck with talent, as the saying goes, through thick and thin, and were repaid with loyalty.

George Carlin's twelfth HBO special was going to be called **I Kinda Like It When a Lotta People Die.** *Morbid and dark even by Carlin standards, the show saw the comic explain why he cheers for high casualty counts after natural disasters and relishes morbid and gruesome television news coverage. The episode was intended as a reflection on the rapture with which Americans watch the suffering of their fellow citizens on television.*

There was just one problem—the episode was taped on September 10, 2001.

Carlin's rewrite yielded a second special, **Complaints and Grievances,** *which saw him take a decidedly different approach. He even extended an olive branch to a member of the Republican Party (a frequent target of his ire), saying that in light of the attacks on 9/11, all Americans would need to work with President George Bush. The new special, written and produced in just two months, aired November 17, 2001, on HBO.*

After the incredibly tough timing of being teased in an interview on the morning of 9/11, **The Mind of the Married Man,** *written by and starring Mike Binder, premiered on September 23, 2001, and ran for two seasons on the basis of mixed-to-negative* *reviews. It aired its last episode on November 17, 2002, and was canceled before the start of the third season. Even HBO didn't bat .1000.*

MIKE BINDER:

I shot the pilot, everybody loved it. I gave it to Steven Spielberg and he watched it at lunch. I couldn't believe it. He came back and he just loved it. He called Chris Albrecht, and Richard Plepler was getting all of this great feedback from friends of his in Washington. They picked us up right away to series. We were having fun with it, just poking fun at what guys talk about. But when it came out, we were just shocked at the vitriol. Horrible reviews, from male reviewers.

CHRIS ALBRECHT:

There were mistakes with *The Mind of the Married Man*. Mike Binder should not have played the lead, but the bigger problem was that it was all too true. So guys couldn't watch that show with their girls because then the girls would ask, "Is that what the fuck you're doing?" and critics got precious about those things.

MIKE BINDER:

Richard Plepler was really the champion of the show. Chris loved it. Farrah Fawcett called him and he called me to say she loved it. Jerry Seinfeld called him and Bill Maher and all these friends of mine were calling him to say they loved it. On *Sex and the City* these women would take guys into a bathroom and blow 'em. And we be doing these things about what's only in our minds, and reviewers would talk about how puerile our comedy was.

I saw it as a Rorschach test. Guys would tell me, My wife and I can't watch it together. And I think, Well, you got a problem with your marriage. How is that surprising to your wife, that you think about that shit? Because other guys would tell me, "My wife and I just sit around and laugh our ass off." My wife told me one woman said, "I've got to tell you, I hate your husband's show." She said that she got divorced. Her husband had cheated on her.

So it brought up a lot of stuff. And look, it was a very personal show. It was way before Me Too. It really touched a nerve. Some people loved it, some people hated it. Then for some reason, HBO—Chris—gave us a second season. He was thinking about giving us a third season.

He just couldn't get anyone behind it. I think the real thing was that it wasn't seen as like a review and an awards thing for them. It was at that point with HBO that that's all they cared about. They didn't care about ratings. Every week I would say to him, "Hey, our ratings are better than anything else you've had in that spot." But they just didn't care.

CHRIS ALBRECHT:

We started to have a reputation that we needed to protect. This pressure was an enemy because we started to believe our own bullshit. We would take things off the air because they did not match our pedigree. This tendency was mostly because of Richard Plepler. *The Mind of the Married Man* was not a Richard Plepler–type show.

With more series coming to air, what would happen to such HBO tenets as taking time to let shows grow and ignoring ratings? After seeing how tough the audience testing for **The Sopranos** *was, Albrecht had vowed to turn his back on testing in the future and was increasingly comfortable with his resolve, and with Strauss's opinions. Would the circle of influence expand?*

CHRIS ALBRECHT:

Arli$$* was a look at sports in a way that a network would never look at sports. Broadcast networks, which had all those big sports deals, would never look at sports that way. Robert Wuhl was certainly a controversial figure, whether you think he should have played the lead or not, it was at least a satirical look at sports. *Arli$$ felt like an HBO show because it was, again, something someone else wouldn't do.

ROBERT WUHL:

One day I'm walking down Fifty-seventh Street and Neil Simon crosses my path and stops me and goes, "I love what you're doing on that show." Okay, so that's Neil Simon. I'm having dinner in some restaurant in New York with my wife and this guy gets up, comes to the table. He goes, Robert, I'm David Halberstam. I just want to tell you what you're doing is so interesting. It's so great. William Goldman stopped me one day. Then David Milch came up to me: What you're doing is changing TV. Those are the people who made me feel good.

CHRIS ALBRECHT:

Sex and the City was on before *Arli$$*. So *Arli$$* lost numbers from *Sex and the City*, but we're not in the ad business anyway. Right?

The scheduling and research guys liked *Arli$$* because it was doing pretty well. It had a male audience, which was a premium audience. So in my mind, and in their mind, within one hour of programming, we hit an awful lot of demographics. I was in New York. I don't know if I was a CEO yet, or I was just the head of programming. My wife and my two daughters, they were meeting me upstate in New York, we're buying her a pony, and I was being driven to upstate New York.

I got in the car and had a conference call. It was Carolyn, Lombardo, me, Plepler and Dave Baldwin. Plepler and everyone said, "*Arli$$* isn't our brand. It's not good enough." Robert was a friend of mine from the Improv. It's always hard to cancel a friend's show. I say on the call, "All right, when I get to where I'm going, I'll call Robert and tell him we're canceling *Arli$$*."

So we're driving some more, and when we get there, I get out of the car and the driver opened the trunk and handed me my suitcase. I said, "Thank you." And he said, "I can't believe you're going to cancel *Arli$$*. It's the best show on TV." This is the driver!

To some people, *Arli$$* was the best show on TV. I went back and said, "You know what? I've changed my mind. We're going to give this thing one more season." I don't have anything good to replace it, whatever the rationale was. But it all happened because the fucking driver said to me, "I can't believe you're going to cancel *Arli$$*. It's the best show on TV."

ROBERT WUHL:

After we finished that season, they did cancel the show. I asked why. He said it was time to move on. We just came off our highest-rated season and were posting double the numbers of other shows. We had earned our largest following ever but Chris wanted to go in another direction. He said they would give me an overall deal.

We called everyone. We said we would run a campaign to keep the show on the air and I went on every damn outlet. Hank Aaron was saying *Arli$$* should stay on the air. It was 1999 and I was booked on Fox News on *The O'Reilly Factor*. Fox News did not yet have clearance in New York and Los Angeles, so I had never seen *O'Reilly*. I did not even know who the hell he was. I went on his show and he asked me about *Arli$$* and started going after the people at HBO. I was sitting there thinking, I don't know who the fuck this guy is but I'm glad he's on my side today. He loved *Arli$$*.

I have been very loyal to HBO and never said a bad word about the cancellation or how they wouldn't give it back to me. We were nominated for a Writers Guild Award and I loved it.

SARAH JESSICA PARKER:

The network was always behind us. I could call Richard. I could call Mr. Bewkes. I could call Angela [Tarantino]. I could call Nancy Lesser. I could certainly call Quentin if there were publicity things that were feeling hurtful, or if there were stories that were starting to feel that they were not correctly characterizing our experience. Even the way in which they kept us on the streets. We wanted to shoot on the streets. We needed to be on the streets, and the crowds are getting bigger and bigger and bigger. There were sometimes thousands of people watching us and paparazzi, and they just always tried to keep it small. They always tried to keep us feeling safe that we could do our work, that we could respect the neighborhoods in which we were shooting, but feel that we wouldn't be distracted by all the peripheral stuff that was going on both metaphorically, and literally and physically. They always took care of us whenever we traveled.

They always put every penny behind marketing ideas, even when we were new, and they never gave up. We didn't get an Emmy nomination. We were just sort of an outlier New York show, and they just never gave up on us.

Oz was hardly a problem child. Fontana, Levinson, and the entire team knew precisely what their show was; they were pros who could handle nearly anything that came along.

TOM FONTANA:

One of the things that happened, because we were shooting at Chelsea Market when it was not Chelsea Market. It was the old Nabisco cookie factory. The cafeteria scenes with that high ceiling, that was where the ovens were. They had to open the big windows at the top to let the heat out. That was such a great set. It was massive. It was just a massive fucking set. When Chelsea Market started to become like Chelsea Market, the guy who was the developer of it came to me and he said, You need to take out a ten-year lease. I was like, "Ten years? This is a television show. I can't promise you I'll be here ten years." He said, "Then you got to get out." I called Chris. "I don't know what to do." He said, "Find another space. We'll move the show." They're not like, how much is it going to cost? I was convinced that *Oz* would be the first show canceled because of real estate. He literally just said, "Find a space." We ended up in Bayonne in an air force terminal. It was perfect.

It almost made it even more of a prison. Because when we were shooting at a Chelsea market, they would go out to lunch. They'd be in Manhattan.

[In Bayonne] there was nowhere to go. This air force terminal was nowhere near anything.

PETER BENEDEK:

It was a great experience. Tom canceled the show himself. He decided that he had done the run of it, and then a month or two later, I think he regretted it because he realized there were more stories to tell.

TOM FONTANA:

My biggest concern when we got toward the end was I felt like I had put the main characters through so much that to continue putting them through things would really start to feel like a parody of itself. The idea was either we end it or I start replacing everybody with new characters. I don't really want to do this show with, with a bunch of other actors. Carolyn Strauss was there by this point and she and I were having conversations and I said, "I can do one more season. I don't know if I can do two." She said, "Okay, well then do one." That's when I really was like, how am I gonna wrap this up? I really got into that whole mentality. Then of course, the minute we stopped shooting, I went, Shit, I could've done another year. But it was too late. I really couldn't figure out any more ways to kill people.

While series television raced from end zone to end zone, ricocheting between success or failure, the documentary unit was nesting comfortably between the forty-yard lines. Filmmakers consistently made HBO their first stop, at least partly because Nevins could afford to take more chances and would throw relatively small amounts of money to a filmmaker to advance their ideas. Considering the dearth of competition, Nevins had such a tremendous amount of flexibility in the marketplace that she could afford to be wrong . . . and live to see a second chance come around years later.

RICHARD PARSONS:

Sheila was the queen of docs. I thought she brought the documentary category into a new age, with stories that had enormous power in this country and affected people's worldview. I really endorsed her storytelling, and I'll put it that way, she had an orientation toward stories of progressive tilt.

SHEILA NEVINS:

The second story in my book is about someone who sleeps with their boss. Well, that's me. It was before I ever got to HBO. I was married to this lawyer from Yale and I couldn't get a job in the theater because he told me I had to be home evenings and weekends. I was losing my mind. They were making a film, I wanted to be a PA on it so I had an affair with my boss because I knew who the director was, I can't remember who, he might have directed an Academy Award. Nice guy, and I said, "I want to go, I want to go out on the thing, I want to be a PA," and he said, "Talk to the boss." So it was a snow day, and I went into his office and I talked to him in the language that I knew would work. And I slept with him, it didn't ruin my life, and I got the job. Went out, I still was doing *Adventures in English* for another four months, divorced the husband, came to New York and was a PA, and then a researcher and then went to CBS. I mean, that's how my career began, with fucking, so it didn't bother me. If you want it, I'll give it you. Maybe I was a call girl from the beginning. I wasn't married. All these men would write me love letters when I announced I was getting divorced.

KARY ANTHOLIS:

I got to know Rory when she was making *American Hollow*. I got the legacy that she carried because of her father's knowledge of poverty in Appalachia. I understood the power of what she was doing, and would have conversations with her about his legacy, which still exists.

RORY KENNEDY, Documentarian:

Sheila, during those years, was the single most impactful person in the documentary world. You'd be very hard pressed to find anybody who came close to having her influence. Obviously there have been some extraordinary filmmakers along the way who've had their own impact in the films that they've made, but Sheila did something that nobody else has done before. Prior to Sheila, documentaries were spinach, they were educational. They were boring, frankly. Sheila looked at what was going on in the narrative world and said, "We make these films interesting and engaging and entertaining and you can still learn something from them." Sheila has such a heart, and such a deep sense of compassion, empathy, and warmth. She cares deeply about people who suffer. It drives her to go to that boardroom at HBO and make demands and say, I need money and I'm winning all the awards and I'm going to do this differently than anybody else and support me. And she got it.

My short fifteen-minute film, called *Epidemic Africa* about AIDS, was just to show on Capitol Hill. I went over with a White House delegation that asked me to come and document their trip. So I did. I made this fifteen-minute film. I showed it on Capitol Hill and Senator Leahy came up to me afterward and said, "I really had no idea what was going on with AIDS and because of your film, I am putting a bill forward to support AIDS in Africa."

Even though I never met my father, he has a significant influence on who I am and the choices I make and the things that I'm passionate about. I mean obviously we took significantly different paths in life and those through different time periods. I think that the collective goal was trying to create a little less pain and suffering in the world and a bit more sense of compassion for others.

I would do anything for Sheila. I love her dearly.

In many ways, HBO docs had the world to themselves. That's not to say no one else was making them, but in terms of TV, Sheila Nevins had the comfort of a non-competitive landscape. That meant she didn't have to engage in bidding wars and could take her sweet time when making a decision. Even years.

BOB WEIDE:

It took thirteen years from the time I first pitched it until it was finished. I didn't know whether to have the film released or Bar Mitzvahed.

We're still in limbo. At that point, my contractual obligation to deliver those shows to PBS had come and gone.

Sheila said, "No, I don't think that's for us. We really don't do biographies. We do social issues and stories ripped from the headlines with controversy."

Then there was this comedy festival in New York that wanted to screen my Lenny film and I said, "It's not really finished." They said, "We'll screen it as a work in progress." It was a fairly polished rough cut. One of Sheila's lieutenants was there. He asked me if I would send a cut to Sheila and I said, "She already passed on this, but fine, I'll send it to her." She screened it and called me up. "My God, what do I have to do to get this film for HBO? I love it." I said, "Sheila, I pitched this to you two years ago and you passed. You didn't do biographies." So? "Oh my God. It's great. It's the first amendment. It's topical. What do you need to finish it?" I said, "I have to shoot more interviews. I got to do this and do that." They got a license and music. I gave her a dollar amount and she said fine. The point person on it was good old Anthony Radziwill.

Robert Weide's documentary about the life and work of irreverent comic Lenny Bruce was originally meant to be the second of a three-part PBS special on comedians (Mort Sahl was number one; Dick Gregory was to be number three). But the PBS series had stalled after Sahl, so Weide approached Sheila Nevins in 1995 to gauge HBO's interest.

She bit immediately, having already said no years earlier, providing the rest of the funding to complete the clip-heavy film. A portrait of Lenny Bruce was hardly going to have the impact of solving a murder or retracing an important moment in history, or exposing something scandalous. But HBO wanted to be everywhere. And the documentary was nominated for an Academy Award.

SHEILA NEVINS:

I didn't know anything about Lenny Bruce, but he became my hero afterward. There was footage of him and the cops and it was really an amazing discovery of what existed. Even though you were telling a story where the ending was known, the pieces in the middle were unknown. Unusual man. Very funny. Very dirty.

BOB WEIDE:

One thing that Sheila did that was interesting was, once I had an almost finished cut of it, she said we need to put this in theaters, we need to qualify for an Oscar. I thought she was nuts. I didn't think it was Oscar material. By the way, this is when, in order to run something in theaters, you actually had to have a film print. So we took the video master, made a film print and we ran it for a week at the Film Forum in New York. It just sold out every night. The idea was for a one-week Oscar-qualifying run, but Karen wanted to run it longer. She said, "We could keep this going for weeks or months," but Sheila didn't want it overexposed prior to HBO. I remember hearing about a lot of celebrities in New York showing up for it. Sure enough, it got an Oscar nomination for Best Feature Documentary and then finally aired on HBO in 1999. And we won an Emmy. It got two nominations, one for Best Nonfiction Special, and we won for Editing.

JULIE ANDERSON:

I worked on a short film that won an Academy Award and got to go to the Academy Awards. And this girl, she, I don't think she ever made another film, but she came in with twelve minutes of this relationship between a grandmother and her grandson. It was called *Big Mama*. The grandmother was taking care of the grandson because both his parents had drug issues. There were no parents, and she'd be like playing basketball with him on the basketball court and she was ninety and then she'd be dressing him up and taking him to church. So we said we wanted to make the film with her, and then Tracy went out and shot all these crazy other scenes with other people and other characters and she brought it back and we just said, "This is not a feature film. This is a short film." Tracy wasn't sure that Sheila was right about that; it won the Academy Award.

LISA HELLER, Executive:

Sheila was smart about how to elevate films about real people in a broader context. Early on I helped with roll out on a short film called *King Gimp* about Dan Keplinger, who is an artist with cerebral palsy.

I learned many things on that one, how we're in business not only with the filmmaker but sometimes a relationship also emerges with the subject. We connected Dan with a gallery in New York where he got to show his work.

It was like putting different spokes in the wheel of that special film, figuring out how to amplify his work and his story. That's a big one for me, to see how nimble and creative HBO could be about maximizing the impact of social issue content. The company's high-level commitment to elevating documentaries has always been unique. Sheila grew close to Dan, and it ended up winning an Oscar.

Regardless of the subject, filmmakers knew they were going to get two prized gifts from HBO docs: time and support. Such was the case for both **Sister Helen** *and* **The Execution of Wanda Jean.**

Just as HBO had long enjoyed key relationships with comics, musical artists, athletes, and now a burgeoning field of actors, Sheila Nevins was finding and nurturing talented filmmakers who would repeatedly come back to the fold.

REBECCA CAMMISA, Documentarian:

Sister Helen is the story of a Benedictine old lady named Sister Helen Travis. She was a nun with a past. She was originally from Boston, moved to the Bronx, had a family with three children. She and her husband were both alcoholics and they were in the bar all the time. Her first son was murdered. Her second son died of a heroin overdose. Then her husband died, probably due to alcoholism. That's according to her. At age fifty-six she changed her life, decided to stop drinking, and eventually ran a recovery house in the South Bronx by herself for drug-addicted and alcohol-addicted men. Many of them were parolees. I called her the General George Patton of nuns. She really ran this house with an iron fist.

That was my first film and it was really the most extraordinary experience because basically *Sister Helen* is mostly a verité film. We basically slept on her couch for a year and a half and we just caught all of these moments of real life. PBS rejected it. We went to Sheila, she said yes. Immediately we're making the film and I'm immediately in the zone of being allowed to make the film for as long as we needed to, with no interference whatsoever. Then we would get into the edit and it was a really a dream and a great experience. Not only was I learning, but we also knew we were making an incredibly special and powerful film.

LIZ GARBUS, Documentarian:

When I got out of college, I did some political organizing and after a summer spent on the road actually registering voters for a political campaign, I actually felt like I needed to continue my interest in filmmaking. What Sheila did felt like the arena to tell stories that could find a wide audience and had sort of a beating heart around social justice, giving voice to the voiceless while at the same time existing in the world of entertainment. That was the needle that I wanted to thread and she was really the only needle that existed doing that. There were incredible docs being done at PBS, but the funding wasn't there. There were British broadcasters like Channel 4 BBC things I could go to, but in terms of an American broadcaster where you could actually raise the money to make a film and do it in a hard-hitting, provocative, exciting way, Sheila was really the Holy Grail for that.

There was a film I was developing, which was about a serial killer and in Vienna. I thought, Okay, this is Sheila's alley. I sent it to her and it seemed like they were a little bit interested. At the same time as I was courting them with that film, we also discussed the serial killer film with A&E, which was interested in wanting me to do it. At some point I called HBO. "Are you guys interested in this serial killer film? Because we have other interests from A&E." Jackie said, "Okay, sure. I'm going to call you back." I'm sitting there waiting by the phone, dying for this call. And the call comes a couple of days later from Jackie Glover. I'll never forget my heart sinking when I heard her say, "Well, Sheila's going to pass. If it's the kind of thing A&E is interested in, then I just don't think we're going to be interested." I was like total heartbreak because I thought I was being so clever by leveraging another network's interests in order to push them toward me and push them for decision. But in fact it had the extreme opposite effect, which was, You don't try to like bribe me with a competitor because there is no one like us. I had my tail between my legs and at that moment I understood that Sheila operated by a different set of rules.

I remember sending my first rough cut, which was two and a half hours long, of *The Execution of Wanda Jean* and, in my wildest dreams, didn't know how I would actually cut a minute out of it. I probably dropped it off at her house on a Friday afternoon. I remember getting a call at around close to midnight, probably from Sheila who had watched it and then cajoled me with a love song. It was like dying and going to heaven. I was like, Oh my God, this is how it can work. She's a person who watches a cut and calls you and talks to you about it emotionally and immediately. I remember saying to her, "Oh Sheila I'm so glad that you like it, but how am I ever going to get it?" Maybe it was two hours and forty-five minutes. "How am I ever going to get it under two hours?" And she said, "Why are you worrying about that? It should be as long as it is good." Those are words that I live by.

What was so refreshing about this, and it was so human, was that some-body watches a movie you would normally, and you wait and you wait. Then there's like a phone call and you maybe get a piece of paper with time code and notes. No, that's not how I work with Sheila. You got a phone call that expressed her emotion and you got it immediately. It was like this human relationship. She didn't wait to find out what somebody else thought. She didn't tell you how to fix things. She guided you with her reactions, but they weren't prescriptive. Her mentorship and friendship were huge.

If Nevins loved you, you became part of the HBO doc universe; as a result, a growing and notable group of filmmakers were regarded as Nevins protégés.

One member was Alexandra Pelosi, daughter of Nancy, who crossed party lines to direct and produce **Journeys with George***, about George W. Bush's 2000 campaign for the White House.*

ALEXANDRA PELOSI, Documentarian:

The year 2000, I quit my job as a network news producer with the dream of becoming a documentary filmmaker. I had been following George W. Bush when he was running for president, and I had all this footage.

I quit my job at NBC and I edited this movie in my living room on my laptop. I went to the film festivals with it and I started at South by Southwest Film Festival because that's Bush's hometown, and I didn't want to do like a liberal bubble San Francisco, Tribeca, so I premiered it in Austin, Texas. The day that it premiered, Sheila called and said she wanted to license it, which was that one call that made all my dreams come true.

I go back to New York, I live in Greenwich Village, and I went to HBO to meet this Sheila Nevins who I had known for a decade. As I'm giving her some speech about the symbiotic relationship between me, the media, and the politicians they cover, she cuts me off mid-sentence and she says, "What's going on with your hair?" She said, "Come with me." And she puts me in the car and she brings me to Christophe, this fancy name brand hair salon stylist, and she gets me something like a $300 haircut on the spot. Anyway, that's how Sheila adopted me the day she met me. She taught me the most valuable lesson that every working woman needs to learn, which is first work on your hair and then you work on your sales pitch.

Sheila trusted me.

Less than nine months after the horrific terrorist attacks on 9/11, HBO Documentaries premiered **In Memoriam: New York City** *honoring NYC. It won five Emmys, but more importantly, afforded a unique look at the tragedy because it utilized video footage taken that day by real people.*

SHEILA NEVINS:

In Memoriam: New York City was totally my idea. We made *In Memoriam* out of lots of people's home videos. It was mostly people going on the roof tops and shooting things. It's a tough film. You realize if they had told the people in the second building to evacuate, there could have been a thousand deaths instead of three thousand. They told them to stay in the building. It's just a horrible story.

JEFF BEWKES:

By the mid-1990s, we knew we had to expand original programming dramatically, because big movies came to Blockbuster months before they came to HBO. But spending $135 million on a limited series like *Band of Brothers* would blow a hole in our earnings if we had to charge the whole thing in one year. I argued to the auditors that we could make $50 million from overseas licensing and video rentals so we should only charge $80 million to HBO programming. Bill Nelson thought I was beginning to believe my own bullshit because we had never recovered even $10 million before this, but my rap was, "It was a world war, it'll sell big in Europe, Far East." Even I didn't believe it but it helped us keep the earnings from collapsing. In the end, we recovered $250–$300 million. We licensed it for more than it cost. It could have run on HBO for free!

At the same time, we ramped up original programming in the late 1990s. We also doubled our annual earnings growth. We grew earnings close to 20 percent a year from 1995 to 2002, versus 9 percent the decade before that. How did we do it? There were a number of fronts: sub revenue from the new DirecTV and dish satellites; opening up international HBO networks in Latin America, Eastern Europe, and Asia; increased video sales of

HBO's program catalog; and more efficient spending in a number of areas like marketing and overhead.

I never went to Jerry for money or relief on our aggressive earnings targets. Instead, we grew earnings and cash flow more than any other division. By the late 1990s, when *Sex and the City* and *Sopranos* came on, we were really cooking.

COLIN CALLENDER:

What happened with *The Sopranos* was for the first time, there was a series on HBO that made an enormous amount of money in ancillary rights. Back then it was DVDs. Previously, the vast majority of HBO income and profits were generated from subscriptions. Subsidiary rights generated a very small portion of our profits. The success of *The Sopranos* changed that.

TERENCE WINTER:

"Pine Barrens" started with Tim Van Patten, who's one of our main directors on *Sopranos* and executive producer and main director on *Boardwalk Empire* as well. I was sitting in the writers' room one day with Todd Kessler, one of our other writers on the show. And Timmy happened to stop by and he said, "I had an idea for a story. I had a dream that I thought was funny. But it's stupid." But I said, "Well, what is it?" He said, "Well, Paulie and Christopher take the guy out into the woods to kill him and then the guy ends up getting away and they get lost." I said, "That's a great idea. You got to go pitch that to David."

He said, "No, no, I don't want to, I'm too shy. I don't want to pitch David." And I said, "I'm going to go knock on his door and pitch it to him right now." So David thought it was great, but we were, at that point, getting toward the end of season two. So David said, "All right, well, let's put a pin in that. Let's do that next year." So we did, and we came back to season three and then I ended up writing it.

I wrote the script. It was just such a joy to write. Whenever you took those two characters, Paulie and Christopher went through it together and in a heated situation where they start turning on each other, like rats locked in a cage. To me, the funniest real comedy is when people are annoyed with each other and they're in a stressful situation.

STEVE BUSCEMI:

I directed "Pine Barrens." By the time that Paulie and Christopher are truly lost, night hasn't fallen yet, they're still hoping that they can get out, but they're definitely lost in the woods. And then when Tony calls them after meeting with the Russian mobster, he finds out that Valerie, the Russian they took to bury there, was like a brother to him, he finds out all this information on him, how he killed sixteen Chechen [rebels and] was part of the Ministry of the Interior. When he relays this information to Paulie Walnuts over like a static cell phone line, Paulie relays that information to Christopher, "He killed sixteen Czechoslovakians, and he was an interior decorator." That killed me. Then Christopher says, "Really? His apartment looked like shit," I had to stop and laugh out loud. That was the moment I went, "Oh my God, this is beautiful." To have these guys in the woods totally out of their element, totally mishearing this information, is really special, and it kept getting better after that.

TERENCE WINTER:

We went out to find our locations, and I think it was right before the holiday break. The last thing Steve and I said to each other was, "As long as it doesn't snow we'll be fine." While we were away, there was this massive, massive blizzard. We came back and we weren't even sure if we were going to be able to get the equipment into the woods. I had to do a rewrite of the script to accommodate the fact that they were in the snow. Of course the snow elevated everything by 100 percent. It was so much more stressful and funny and tense and dramatic. We shot all week out in the woods near Harriman State Park near West Point. We only shot the daytime experience up there. All this stuff that happens in the van was shot on a soundstage in Queens, but the daytime stuff, we were only able to shoot from like seven in the morning until three in the afternoon. Then it got too dark. So it was really like being on a class trip. It was probably the most fun I've ever had shooting anything.

STEVE BUSCEMI:

My other like favorite thing with Christopher and Paulie was when they were in the van and Christopher finds the bag, like this Wendy's bag or something, that has the ketchup and the relish. And the way it's almost like a gourmet meal to them, they're so starving. And I just loved how everybody in the show just plays it so straight. To me, it was one of the funniest shows on, but it wasn't a comedy. But because the characters, because those actors were so committed to what they were doing and played it so straight and realistically, and never commenting at all on the ridiculousness of like these two guys who get lost in the woods, I think that's what made it so much funnier and so much more real.

TERENCE WINTER:

I couldn't believe the reaction. I couldn't believe how much people loved it. When it aired, I invited a few friends over to my house to watch it. And one of them said, "This is like a classic episode of TV." And I said, "Oh, thanks." He goes, "No, you don't understand. This is like, this is one for the ages." And he said that and I was like, "All right, thanks." And then it turned out to have legs, I guess. People really love it.

LORRAINE BRACCO:

Terry and Robin Green had given me a heads-up about the rape scene. I was fucking pissed off. Of all the people, why are they gonna hurt me? What the fuck did I do? I was mad. It was one of the most physical. I did get hurt. I ripped open my bursa sac, in my shoulder.

If I remember correctly, it happened to a friend of Robin Green's. She was raped in a parking lot. That was the script that she worked on. She won the Emmy for that, by the way, if I'm not mistaken.

HBO premieres were becoming bigger, more expensive, and the talk of Hollywood. And even though they were staged for the industry, the public started hanging on.

QUENTIN SCHAFFER:

In 2000 we jumped to the Ziegfeld Theatre, which we filled—all eleven hundred seats. MOMA cost half a million. *The Sopranos* can boast the first screening ever at Radio City for a TV series. You're easily north of a million because you're dealing with unions. The popularity for *The Sopranos* grew so fast that after the screening at Radio City, we half kidded about doing the next one at the Meadowlands, which holds sixty thousand and was rumored to have Jimmy Hoffa buried in the end zone.

EDIE FALCO:

I was also only there for ten minutes, by the way. That was my answer to all the partying that went on. I mean, I would look at the publicist like, Can I go now? Am I all right to go now?

The premiere parties were of a blur. Unfortunately, they were the least favorite part of the job for me. Now, they're a necessary part of the business that I'm in. Jim somehow managed to avoid a lot of them, but I try to do them because I know I am helping the network. I'm helping the other actors and I do the best I can with them. But it was really hard. I'm wearing shoes and clothes that I'm not comfortable in. I can't eat because I'm being stopped every two seconds to talk to fans and stuff.

But then there was also a part of me that had waitressed for twenty years and that part of me realizes, Can you freaking believe what is happening? Can you believe that you don't have to get up on a Sunday morning and clean a dirty restaurant after Saturday night and set it up and put all the ketchup bottles out? I really don't have to do that anymore. So as unpleasant as those things sometimes were, I never lost track of my sense of gratitude. This is a price you pay for success. I did it with varying degrees of irritability, but it was part of my job.

LORRAINE BRACCO:

When we had one of the openings at Radio City Music Hall, and I heard Michael Imperioli saying, "I feel like we're the Beatles."

. . . that was the moment I said, "Oh my God, this is crazy."

EDIE FALCO:

I get paid to play little psychological tricks on myself. It's really great. I go to therapy to detangle these things and then I go to work to tangle them back up again, basically. Because it's a job. I think partially for my particular psychology, the fact that there were very defined rules around my relationship with Jim, or Carmela's relationship with Tony, in that it only exists during work hours. When they say cut, we're done for the day, it's over. When they said wrap for good, it was finished. Those are very, very defined rules for me. Unbreakable, unquestionable. Because of those boundaries, I was able to open up myself in a way that maybe in real life is terrifying. I knew he had a real life and, during the time that he and I worked together, I had various relationships I was in, which had nothing to do with the time that Jim and I spent on set together. It was totally compartmentalized.

As **The Sopranos** *continued to win awards and attract attention, so, too, did its star, James Gandolfini. His performance dug deep, and he regularly told friends on and off the set how it drained him, how the line between Tony and Jim sometimes became blurry. Concerns reigned about Gandolfini's drug and alcohol abuse as well as Gandolfini's ability to manage his anger. He sometimes struggled to remember lines on set, then set off on a bender of destructive behavior, to say nothing of the mounting pressures of becoming a pop culture icon and having his private life turned achingly public. He began to miss shoots, complaining that he was sick.*

On a winter evening in January 2002, Gandolfini failed to show up for a six p.m. call to shoot a scene at the Westchester County Airport. The assumption was that Gandolfini had once again gone on a bender. Over the next twelve hours, however, it would turn into a different story. Gandolfini had gone missing. Those close to Gandolfini and the show waited and worried, hoping for good news.

LORRAINE BRACCO:

I was always concerned about James but not as concerned as other people. Success is very difficult to deal with and James was finding himself. I saw him change throughout the show. At the beginning, he was very shy. By the end, he was more of a recluse. Success is a strange thing because people treat you differently. James was a regular guy and had enormous success thrown at him very quickly.

He went places where he did not want to go. This was a hard show for him. If the contract negotiations had not worked out, fans would have been upset. But I would have understood.

CHRIS ALBRECHT:

Tony's struggles not only mirrored Jimmy's struggles, they amplified Jimmy's struggles and what Jimmy felt, which was one of the things that he really resisted in terms of wanting to get off the show. In order to become Tony, he had to connect with his darkest side. The cost for him of playing Tony was beyond what just being an actor would be. To do it was for him to connect with his own demons.

He did admit it to me, "You don't understand what this is doing to me." I think it was something that we all understood. Not all, but the small group of us.

TERENCE WINTER:

James would complain that he was exhausted. He would work a fifteen-hour day then go home and have eight pages of dialogue to learn for the next day. Those scripts were performed exactly as written. He lived in the Tony Soprano headspace but James Gandolfini was not Tony Soprano. James was a kind and funny person but Tony got into his head and lived there for nine months. That was exhausting in a lot of different ways. James would say he could not fucking do it anymore, that he wanted to be shot on the show so everybody else would take over. I never took those moments seriously because those feelings would pass and he would become excited again. James felt a responsibility to everybody else, he was very protective of the cast and crew. James was incredibly generous with everyone and likely feared he would put people out of work if he quit the show.

DAVID CHASE:

That aspect of him was because of his son Michael. I was concerned, but I was also so sick of his bullshit. They flew me back from France and then back. It was crazy. He was sick of me, too. Let me just say that. It wasn't a one-way street.

He could always find something humiliating and mortifying so he wouldn't have to show up for something.

MICHAEL IMPERIOLI:

He was supposed to present an award. It was him and Patricia Arquette but he couldn't do it. So I told Patricia backstage about it and said, "I should get Jim's gift bag for doing this," and later said to him, "I covered for you. I got to get that gift basket."

And this is the really funny thing. Patricia didn't tell me, but she sends her gift box to me, and Jim sent me his as well. I got two for doing that one job.

QUENTIN SCHAFFER:

We tried to manage it as best we could. The truth is that the gossip columns and entertainment shows have an endless thirst for controversy.

One thing to know about Jim was that he cared deeply for his fellow cast members. He didn't want to do anything to jeopardize their work. Did he have some absences on set? Listen, he was at that time the hardest working man in show business as he was in so many scenes of the series.

While Jim hated doing press, he would do it if it helped his fellow actors. When *USA Today* wanted to do a father-son story on the actors playing Tony Soprano and his son AJ, Jim did it because he knew it would be good for Robert Iler. And the *Vanity Fair* cover benefitted so many of them, he took the time to do that.

ILENE LANDRESS:

It's a hard balancing act because the guy was such a workaholic and put so much pressure on himself. Jimmy was never going to give you a B performance. He was always going to give you an A performance. And if he felt like he couldn't give an A performance, he was so hard on himself. He had so many pages of dialogue to learn. You're talking about somebody who has four to eight pages to learn every day. And sometimes even more than eight. Michael, Jimmy, they worked really hard and Lorraine worked really hard at learning those lines.

The one with the big gift is Edie. Edie can pretty much learn it like immediately, but Jimmy worked really, really hard at learning those lines. And so if he had a late night and then he's staying up learning his lines, I think Jimmy felt the responsibility of the entire show. Jimmy took on the role of Tony Soprano and really felt responsible for all these actors' personal lives. He was the boss and he felt responsible. I think sometimes he just sort of cracked under the pressure of it all.

But it's a hard scheduling thing. You want him to be able to give them a Friday or a Monday off because the guy was working so hard so much of the time they were like, Okay, we'll give them a three-day weekend. But I learned pretty quickly that he might go out on Thursday night. And so I'm not going to see him on Friday. So as much as I want to schedule to give them a break, you almost got to the point of not wanting to give them a break because you couldn't know what would happen.

So first, you worry about, Okay, where is he? Is he okay? And then the next part is, What are we going to do while he's not here, and then not make it a big event when he does come back? You lose a day, then there's the guilt of missing the day. And, Oh, I let everybody down and everybody hates me.

It wasn't great when he disappeared. And certainly when he called the production office and the assistant coordinator answered the phone and he said, I'm in Brooklyn at the nail salon. And we just said like, Okay, thank God. You just hope he's okay. And you keep going.

DAVID CHASE:

Jim never said, "Oh my gosh, do I really have to do that?" He said, "What the fuck is this? I'm not doing it." I would just say, he always did it. No matter what, no matter how he first reacted. He was a total professional.

There was a scene later on in the series when Tony was having a very brief affair with the character played by Julianna Margulies. And in the script he was supposed to go into a gas station bathroom and jerk off and he really didn't want to do that. Then we never used it, but he never said, You never even used that show. You never even used that scene or like the role after all I went through and he never took it up with me or blamed me or anything.

EDIE FALCO:

It's like they say, alcoholism is a self-diagnosed illness. I wasn't in any position to know where this would lead for anyone. As it turns out, in retrospect, a good number of them ended up in bad places because of it. Partially also because they were celebrating something so huge that came out of nowhere. There aren't a lot of people who can say, Oh, this is what happened to me when I was in that situation. My father used to say to me, "I got no advice for you, kid. I don't know. I've never experienced anything like what you're going through." I had a conversation with Jim once where he was in very bad shape. He said to me, "They don't understand what this does to me, doing this show and where I have to go."

I was torn because of course I loved the show, and as far as I was concerned, I would do it forever. I was making money that I could not have imagined. I was able to support my family and all these other things. It was a huge ordeal and I was telling him, "Jim, no one's going to tell you to stop doing this show. No one's ever going to tell you. You gotta take care of yourself. You gotta do it. If this job is literally killing you, you have to walk away. You make the rules here. People are falling all over themselves doing what you want. Nobody's going to stop this but you." I think it was also important to him that people like him. He also knew there were tons of people who depended on him for their job, but I tried to make it clear that this really is about, it's life and death and it's about taking care of yourself.

He liked the show and he loved his friends and he loved being able to help people have a livelihood. But I also knew, you may not be a popular guy by doing this, but if we're talking about life and death, people would rather have you alive, move on, and do other great parts, which unfortunately he didn't get a chance to do.

It was also the decision I had to make. I remember when I stopped drinking, the feeling was, I'm part of a whole giant social network of people. And what we do is we get together and we'd drink. Every joke we make is about drinking, every way that we identify ourselves as, as heavy drinkers, heavy partiers. And then I woke up one morning and realized I was done. And had this panic, like, I don't know that I can even be friends with anyone. Can I still go out dancing with my friends? It was terrifying. Because the whole world is going to be turned upside down, but you're being led by something stronger and bigger than you. And the chips will fall as they may.

I remember when I was able to do that and it wasn't dangerous. It was never a thought like, "Oh God, I'm so mad I can't do it."

JEFF BEWKES:

We were concerned about Gandolfini staying alive. Occasionally he would go on a bender or a coke binge. We had to stop production. It cost a lot of money and was hard on the other actors' schedules.

But I didn't pressure Chris because I thought Jimmy was embarrassed. When I'd sit with him and Lorraine and Edie at the Globes or Emmys, he treated me like the dad or the boss, like he would be embarrassed if I knew he was drinking at the table. One time he brought two or three bottles of good Italian wine, so we didn't have to drink the shit Merlot they serve at the Globes. I drank with him thinking it would calm him down, I guess I was stupid. When Chris and Carolyn came for budget overruns because of Jimmy's problem, I gave it to them.

CHRIS ALBRECHT:

With Gandolfini it was a love-hate thing. We had an intervention with him in my apartment in New York. The intervention wasn't my idea. I think his family's idea because his sister was there. It was definitely a crisis situation.

I don't remember us being worried that he was going to die, but it became a real problem with shooting the show. It was expensive, and it pissed people off who would show up and then he wouldn't show up and they would have to wait. It became a lack of respect for the other actors as well, so there were sorts of problems that bubbled up. The intervention was a disaster.

HBO's issues with Gandolfini were far more serious and threatening to **The Sopranos,** *and to the star's personal health, than any problems arising on* **Sex and the City;** *nevertheless, the difficulties couldn't be ignored, particularly when gossip pages and celebrity magazines were ever on the lookout for anything they could get on* **Sex and the City.**

CHRIS ALBRECHT:

It's no fun when a series doesn't work, but one of the things a lot of people don't realize is that when a series becomes a hit, sometimes it's a lot of work keeping everyone together. When I was involved with *Martin* on the HIP side, that ended up in court with Martin Lawrence and Tisha Campbell, I certainly didn't want to get into a situation like that again.

On *Sex and the City*, we had Darren, Michael, Carolyn, and me, and their agents. They were fighting for their clients, but at the same time, they didn't want to see anything bad happen. This was the best thing that had ever happened to Sarah Jessica, and there was a lot of hand-holding involved.

It's not like we had eighty shows on the air. I was definitely available to everyone. I sat with everybody, talked to everybody, producers, talent, executives. You assure everyone that this is a place that is going to be respectful and fair. There were always negotiations, people coming in looking to renegotiate their deals and instead of thinking of them all as a group, I tried to think of them as individuals and then figure out a way to get them to work together as a group.

JOHN MELFI:

Look, the story with Kim and SJ, I would say it's generational. Kim was older, and I think she at one point even said this in the press, "It's not like we all hang out. We go to work, we work fourteen, sixteen hours a day. We go home. Some of us go to our families and some of us don't have that. And some of us are older than the others, but we go to work. We spend every day together. It's not like we need to socialize."

CHRIS ALBRECHT:

The longer you're in business with someone on a series, the more interaction you have with them, the more singular the relationship becomes with them. I became the de facto executive in charge of Kim, although I had a lot of help from Carolyn and a couple times even from Jeff. He definitely got his share of calls. We were all really good at managing it and keeping it under wraps for a long time.

It was clear that Sarah Jessica was the star, and she was a producer on the show. Sarah Jessica made a lot more money than Kim. She made a lot more money than all of them. Kim clearly was the one who everybody was talking about, because Samantha was the most outrageous character. Whether there was jealously toward Kim about that, or Kim wasn't handling it well, depends on who you listen to. Then Kim wanted more, and I think she got more than the other girls. Kim's popularity gave us reason to think that there might be a couple of different levels of payment, and we discussed a producing deal with her. She wrote a book with her husband, and we may have optioned that. There are plenty of ways to show people you value the relationship and their services. It doesn't always have to be direct compensation for a specific role.

What happened was it became *Mean Girls* and whatever Kim did or didn't do, the result was she was ostracized. I'm not saying it wasn't justified, but it gets tricky when you have an actor who is also a producer. As an executive producer, SJ should have figured out how to not let that happen. But as an actress, she ended up letting it happen.

QUENTIN SCHAFFER:

Sex and the City had two central stars—New York City and Sarah Jessica Parker. Granted, the other cast members rose quickly. But at the end of the day, the story was told through SJ's voice. On the posters she was always front and center with the other three a few steps back or maybe not even in the poster.

JEFF BEWKES:

Out of the blue one day, Kim called and asked if she could come see me. "Sure," I said. "When do you want to come by?" "I'm downstairs." No warning. She walks in with her husband. He sits across from her and she starts telling an impassioned tale of inconsiderate treatment. They want her at the set by five in the morning, then they don't call her for hours, and they made her do a scene with a naked fireman. I was trying to find out what was upsetting her, what she wanted, so I asked was the nudity the problem?

"It was a naked fireman! A real fireman!!" I was getting the impression that maybe if it had been a naked actor instead of a naked fireman that would help, but there was chapter and verse of other indignities, including she's not getting paid what she was promised, or maybe what Sarah Jessica was getting, something about money. Anyway, I sympathized and summarized, "Okay. Why do you need to be at the set early if you're just sitting around? Maybe they don't need to have an actual naked fireman; they could have a naked actor. That's a new point for me, but I'll look into it, and the deal part, the money, I'll check into that." She seemed calmer having made her case and been listened to so they left.

I got Lombardo on the phone, told him the whole thing including how worked up she was about the naked fireman, and did he know this was a problem for her? Mike says, "Well, it was her idea, the nude scene, having a real fireman, and it was a great scene for her, by the way, a big hit. And you're telling me the husband was sitting there? Of course he didn't like it, because the fireman was buff."

So she came in to make a show in front of her husband that she didn't like the nude scene with the fireman? The whole thing was a performance? "She's an actor, she wanted the husband to see that, but mainly it's about the money. We can't go where Sarah Jessica is, and we've got Cynthia and Kristin."

I said, "Fine, you handle it."

MIKE LOMBARDO, Executive:

We had a six-year deal with these women, but then the show's an amazing success, so do we just say, "Fuck you?" Studios do that, but we decided, and I was integral into it, to treat people well and make them feel that we were taking care of them. We're only doing twelve episodes. If they were on a broadcast show, they'd make at least twenty-four. So they were working the whole year and making a fraction of what they could make somewhere else. Don't forget, we were running the sprockets off of stuff, and nobody knew our back ends, so they had points, but what's a point on an HBO show? We started opening up their deals. We did that on *Sex and the City*. We did it on *The Sopranos*.

SARAH JESSICA PARKER:

Maureen Dowd's column about the show was like penetrating the zeitgeist in a way that we couldn't have predicted. We weren't paying attention. I was certainly not paying attention to whatever was happening to the show in terms of people's feelings or connections to audience numbers. We could see it when we were shooting on the streets. Certainly. But I think the Maureen Dowd column on the show was something that we all sort of, we were all sort of like, "Oh, whoa. Wow. Maureen Dowd's writing about the show." Another example was when we were on the cover of *Time* magazine, all four women, was just another indication of the way in which we could be in the world without explanation that we didn't need to be introduced.

The premieres just started to grow and grow and the nights got longer. The fact that there was so much interest in attending those premieres. Television shows didn't have New York premieres. That was just unheard of. No one was premiering a new season of a show on broadcast television at a massive movie theater and sometimes having to get another movie theater. It was otherworldly. But it didn't really affect the work. You could acknowledge it, but I think we all work very hard to not have it invade what we were doing.

KRISTIN DAVIS:

There was a weird New York thing going on at the time. Gawker had that Stalker Map about where celebrities were in the city, in real time. I remember being so stressed about that because it seems so unsafe, which I think is why it went away. It was during that time before Twitter and all that, but we had these other precursors.

But in New York you couldn't have a conversation. If you were in a restaurant, we had all kinds of interesting code names. We had to change it up all the time for people, for places, for things, for story lines, because anything you said at a table in a New York restaurant could be in the paper the next day, and it might not be right. It might be wrongly attributed to whoever they thought you were talking about. It was super stressful, super stressful. And it just gives you a PTSD-type feeling later, like, Can I speak? I still feel that way.

DAVID FRANKEL:

Every season I would get a lovely query from Sarah Jessica saying, "Hey, do you, will you come direct some episodes?" And finally I said to her, "The graphic sex on the show just doesn't ring my bell, you know? I prefer the innuendo and suggestion more than the graphic depictions here. But when you have an episode that has no sex, please, I would love to do that."

It was the summer before 9/11, and it was sort of New York all abuzz. The economy was roaring and fashion was roaring. And Sarah Jessica was at her peak fame and the show was the number one show in the world, and it was just a bizarre place to be. They sent me an episode where she gets engaged to Aidan. It was a spectacular summer. I had a great time. I loved all the women on the show. It was great to reconnect with Sarah Jessica. It was great to reconnect with Patricia Field, who was my costume designer throughout the 1990s on all the work that I did. And I love working with Michael Patrick. John Melfi, who had been my UPM in Orlando on *Earth to the Moon*.

Carolyn would call once a month to remind Michael and John Melfi, "Where's the sex? You guys are falling into this trap of telling these lovely stories and with these women, but don't forget it's *Sex* and the City." It was really important to the subscriptions that they didn't abandon the sexual element of the show.

LARRY DAVID:

I think it got a little more loaded with ideas, went a little longer. More ideas were thrown into the soup, into the mix. You never want the show to be short and we discovered that it's best to throw a lot in because you could always take it out. Some of it works and some of it doesn't. And you keep what works, but more was being thrown in. So, the shows got longer and denser.

That's like if you're attracted to somebody, you don't know why. It's just an innate sense that you have. Everybody has it for something. You always have a feeling about something, especially if it's not working. It just gnaws at you. I gotta take that out or we got to reshoot that, that's not working. You just seem to know a voice in your head that is disapproving of something.

BOB WEIDE:

I remember they sent somebody to our set one day. This guy sat down with us and sort of gave us his ideas about how we could sort of streamline things and move a little faster through the day. Larry tolerated it. We all left and went back to work and just totally ignored everything he said and never thought about it or worried about it, and they never sent anybody again.

Such was Albrecht's life these days that he would have to juggle back-to-back calls with Larry David and then David Simon.

David Simon was on a leave of absence from his beat-reporter job on the crime desk of the **Baltimore Sun** *when he wrote his first book, a searing account of the city police department's notorious homicide unit.* **Homicide** *the book would lead to* **Homicide** *the TV series. Teaming up with former Baltimore cop Ed Burns, Simon further perfected the book-and-TV-show model with his next work,* **The Corner***, the acclaimed account of one harrowing year in the life of a curbside drug market on Route 1 in the Maryland metropolis.*

DAVID SIMON, Creator:

Part of the fun of being a newspaper reporter is putting your feet up on the desk and talking shit with the other people. There's a wit to a newsroom and I thought, That's what I'm going to miss the most. Suddenly I was thrust into a place where I didn't know what anybody did. I knew nothing. I didn't go to film school, I'd been a fan of movies, that's about it, but in no way was I somebody who paid attention to shots or how movies were constructed.

I backed into television. I wasn't planning to do this with my life. My plan was to be a newspaper reporter and then go out and do books every couple of years and come back and be a better reporter. The books I chose were structured to make me a better beat reporter as an ancillary benefit. It was like, Okay, I'll go inside the police department and then I'll come out with better sources as well as a good book. I'll go out to a drug corner and I'll meet people and I'll be better at it. They were all of a continuum.

Since the 1930s, if not even earlier, Hollywood has seen many a journalist arrive in town hoping to switch from nonfiction to fiction. While many came, however, few stayed—or thrived. What became clear about David Simon—from the start—was that his ability to capture moments, characters, and storylines in real life could make for a smooth transition to scripted drama. Simon's impressionistic mind was vast, unique, and relentless.

DAVID SIMON:

We picked the neighborhood at random. I thought it was an interesting part of West Baltimore. It bordered against a white working-class neighborhood down in what's known as Pigtown. Although all the big open-air drug markets were in African American communities, I felt it was important to show that the demand was multicultural. We picked the neighborhood that had a major drug market in it but was nonetheless feeding cohorts, addict populations that were both white and Black.

I thought that terrain was interesting, and the geography, but by and large, it could have been any number of different drug markets, maybe seventy or eighty corners. When we got there, we started walking around and talking to people. We told people what we were doing, handed out sort of these business cards that said BALTIMORE NEIGHBORHOOD PROJECT. We explained it was going to be a book.

A lot of the kids were coming to the MLK rec center on Vincent Street, and that range in age up to almost fifteen. There were some kids who loved to go there to play basketball and hang out. Then after school they would end up selling drugs for the crews.

There were people who were very wary of us, but even by the end, by far, most of the street-level drug dealers came to accept that we were not cops, that it had been too long. We hadn't arrested anybody, that we weren't getting high. We passed out a lot of copies of *Homicide*, my first book. We would find them months later, sometimes water-logged or dirty or whatever, in shooting galleries and stuff, but it was a way of saying, No, I'm really a writer. There's my picture on the back cover. I'm really doing a book. I'm not lying to you. So it was a matter of just showing up every day and telling the same story: honestly, this is what we're going to do.

When I finally took the job on *Homicide* and left the *Sun*, it was because the paper was changing in ways that I found indicative of what was going to happen even further to newspapers. I took *Homicide* as an interim step because I had a job offer from the [*Washington*] *Post* and thought I'll do this and I'll learn this new skill that David [Mills] thinks is a good thing. Then I looked at *Oz* and thought, "Can I have a meeting with HBO and Tom?"

I sold The *Corner* to HBO, which could only have been sold to HBO. Nobody else was going to touch it.

Tom [Fontana] set it up. I think he called either Chris or Carolyn, and very quickly in the meeting they said, "We just want to do the book as a mini." The only thing they were nervous about was that we were two white guys. So they started asking me the names of writers I might collaborate with on the teleplays, and of course I said Jim Yoshimura because he was the guy I most collaborated with on *Homicide*, and David Mills. They jumped out of their chair at Mills, because Mills is Black, or was—he passed away. Kary Antholis had heard about Mills from George Pelecanos; they were friends.

ANNE THOMOPOULOS:

Chris and I had a big argument about *The Corner*. He said, "It's so depressing. Who will want to watch that?" I told him, "Listen, if you're like us, white, middle-class, upper-class, and you drive through those neighborhoods of urban blight, you roll up your windows, lock the doors, and drive as fast as you can. But what if we made it possible for viewers to understand more about these areas from their living rooms so they have compassion? Isn't that what you're supposed to do?" And to his credit, Chris said, "You're right." I thought that David's scripts were incredibly strong. He exposed a specific world to a larger percentage of the population.

The *Corner* won a Peabody. I was incredibly proud, we all were. It was an important, dangerous piece of material, with performances that were exceptional and broke my heart. In some ways, because everything was so authentic, the series felt like a documentary. We ended up making six hours of *The Corner* and David developed *The Wire* while we were doing it.

HBO was initially wary of trying to do a mere "cop show," considering how that genre already flooded commercial airwaves and how adamantly HBO wanted to avoid being derivative. But Simon pointed out that confronting the networks on their own turf—while doing it better and gutsier—was exactly what HBO should also be about.

*The resulting series, called simply **The Wire**, arrived on June 2, 2002, and would run, to considerable critical acclaim, for six years and five seasons more. Along the way, it exposed all aspects of Baltimore's underbelly, depicted the terrors of the drug scene, the hardscrabble life of the city's docks, the problem-plagued school system, the complexities of its police department, and the city's shaky government—and revealed Simon's deepest feelings about what he'd witnessed all those years as a reporter. **The Wire** also gave us more than we ever had before of Idris Elba and much of our finest Black talent.*

David Simon might never have been able to make the transition from news reporter to showrunner if the show in question were developed at a broadcast network instead of at HBO. Luckily, **The Wire** *came into existence just as HBO began to take great pride in harvesting home-grown talent, a knack they'd developed that would set them apart from everyone else in Hollywood for many years to come.*

CHRIS ALBRECHT:

When David Simon came in and he pitched *The Wire*, there wasn't anything particularly different about it. This was going to be the most realistic look at a police wiretap investigation. There was a ton of shows like this on the air. I think we decided that it would just be good and not different.

Networks do cop shows, it wasn't like the world needed another cop show. It wasn't even that it was serialized, because *NYPD Blue* was serialized. But David had such a passionate take and had the credentials. We certainly didn't write all the scripts, we didn't do the pilot. I would say that there was a show that we were like, Okay, we will try it. Whereas other things either conceptually or point of view, or underneath, I think were the things that excited us.

NINA NOBLE, Executive Producer:

The Wire started as a partnership between David, myself, and Bob Colesberry; the three of us had done *The Corner*. There were other people who joined us at times, like Ed Burns and George Pelecanos and Eric Overmyer.

DOMINIC WEST, Actor:

It all happened by accident. Which has been throughout my life, actually against my better judgment, with all my efforts. Good fortune fell into my lap, big-time with this one. Because I wasn't particularly interested in doing it. I had a young baby daughter, I didn't want to go to Baltimore for five years. I put myself on tape. My tape was interesting to David because I didn't have anyone to do it with. No one else was reading the other lines. I put it on very late at night, my girlfriend couldn't stop laughing at my accent. I just responded to a silence and left the silence in between my lines and responded as if someone was speaking, and David thought that was so funny.

Thought he'd get me in for a laugh really. I went to LA within about three days. Within about five days I was in a hospital, the trauma unit at Johns Hopkins Hospital, next to a guy who had been shot eight times, including twice in the head, and was still alive. His family are all around, and I was standing there. I'm wondering what the hell had happened to me. It was a baptism of a fire and very much not anything I've ever been, I'd ever known before or was comfortable in. All the better for that really.

MICHAEL K. WILLIAMS, Actor:

I had no expectations going into the show. When I was offered the role of Omar, I looked at people like Wendell Pierce, Sonja Sohn, and Wood Harris. They were gods to me. I was like, "I'm going to share a stage with these guys?" I was in my own little narcissistic bubble of, I made it, Mama. I didn't have the capacity to think that far as to whether the show would be a hit or not. I was just so grateful to have been given a shot.

NINA NOBLE:

On *The Wire*, before diversity was a word that carried the power it does now, we had a history of giving all different types of people, in terms of race, gender, and sexuality, opportunities, including an amazing array of directors. Typically, with studios, there was a list of approved directors, most were white males. HBO deserves credit for allowing us to pick the directors who we thought would be the best for the show. We became the place that tried out new people. We would hire someone right out of NYU film school, who then would go off and do other HBO shows afterward. We were sort of the training ground. You could say hiring so many different directors was a fault of ours because it created more work for us in terms of their learning curve and needing to orient them to our show, but Bob Colesberry, my predecessor, who started this tradition that I continued, believed the extra effort was worth it.

DOMINIC WEST:

I just couldn't say Snot Boogie. Snot Boogie. I was very much suffering culture shock. I hadn't even watched *The Sopranos*. I hadn't really caught on to the fact that HBO was on this extraordinary high roll and that I was lucky enough to be in their next big show. I remember sitting on that sidewalk and having to say Snot Boogie, and this was the pilot, I suppose. It was just endlessly having to retake the words "Snot Boogie," which I probably still can't even say properly, but I suppose I spent most of my time terrified about getting the accent wrong.

WENDELL PIERCE, Actor:

Because of my role being a homicide detective, I never had any dealings with any of the story lines of the guys selling drugs or the criminal activity. I came on the scene after things happened, you know? When I was watching the evolution of the characters of Dee and Wallace and Stringer and Barksdale, I was watching as a fan. When I say authenticity as actors, we're students of human behavior, we're the closest thing to psychologists. So when something is false, when moments are false, when the actions are false, when it's trite or presentational, it would ring out so clearly if it wasn't truthful. In the way that the series was being shot, in the way that the series was being written, and the way that the series was being acted and created, it was so authentic and organic that if something rang false, it was clear and we would do a retake and that was the thing that was so brilliant about it. I was able to find something in my own work by being a fan of the other side of the show.

DOMINIC WEST:

An actor's life is sort of impostor syndrome and feeling that one isn't ready for anything. There was another scene in the first season where we did a big arrest. It was when Kima gets shot and we had a helicopter. We had several squad cars, we had all sorts of things, and it was a big action scene where I was driving one of the cars and we had to screech up and onto the point and the helicopter went overhead. The helicopter goes overhead, we heard go, I had to screech up and jump out of the car, pointing my gun, checking the streets and checking every doorway. And no one had shown me how to do that.

It was just assumed that all actors, which I think they do in America, knew how to handle a handgun and what to do in that situation. I had no idea and I didn't dare tell anyone. We did it and the helicopter went over. I got the cue and a screech in the SUV and then three other squad cars come out. I jumped out. I brought my gun. I'm sort of shaking with this gun. I didn't know what to do, I'm holding it completely the wrong way. The director yells, "Cut, cut, cut." He said, "What the hell are you doing?" I said, "Well I've never handled a handgun before. I dunno what to do." We don't have them in the UK. They were banned.

He had to give me a very rapid lesson on how to handle a handgun—it was a Glock nine—how to hold it in both hands and look down the barrel, that stuff, the cop procedure. I realized I was really out of my depth. I was taken straight to the range with the chief of police, who showed me how to do it. I was all right after that, but I think that was pretty early on. I was shown up as being remarkably unsuited to the part.

WENDELL PIERCE:

The inflection point for me was early on in the "fuck" scene. I knew then that David wanted to do something unique and special. It's one of the best scenes in my career.

It is also one of the first acting exercises actors do when they train. Usually you do it with gibberish, you play a scene, make sure we understand exactly what you're thinking, exactly what you're doing. What's at stake. What you're trying to do. The ultimate outcome of the scene. But speaking in gibberish. In this case, David said, "I'm going to be hit for all the cursing in the show. So I'm going to write a scene," and he described it to us one night on set to me and Dominic. "You're going to come see the scene. You're going to get upset with the way that scene was processed by a former detective, by how awful the photos are, then you realize that the ballistics don't make sense, that someone would have to be eleven feet tall.

"You then discovered that the glass is inside. So the bullet had to come from, it came from the outside. Trajectory would leave a shell, maybe here, inside, you see that there is a bullet hole and you find a bullet that was previously looked over or missed, and you go outside and then you find the case." And he said, "That entire scene, we're going to see how good you guys are as police, that you're good police with all of your dysfunction and you're drinking and you're womanizing and your ineptness in life. We're going to do all of that, and you can only say 'fuck.'" And we said, "What?" He said, "Yeah. You can only say 'fuck.' I'm going to write them." And he wrote them.

They allowed us to improvise some. I thought, Well, that's brilliant, man. That's brilliant. If I never do anything else in this show, this will be my high-water mark. I figured it'd be interesting to find out why they cut it. When I thought motherfuck, fuckity fuck, all of that. We get to the end, I find the casing and I go, "Fuck me." And then they got to the super that's shadowing us the entire scene. And he goes, "Well, I'll be fucked."

DAVID SIMON:

HBO notes are good in that, if they understand something or if you hit something a little too hard, their reaction to it is a good third eye. It's like, maybe I did say that three times in an episode, and I don't need to. Or maybe I'm missing a component. Sometimes you want to be missing a component. Once they start giving you time codes and telling you what to cut where, they might as well be the network.

DOMINIC WEST:

David Simon is so exciting and inspiring to talk to, because he's got such a massive brain packed into that big white dome of a head. These searching eyes, sifting in all this information, his fingers tapping away at something to piss someone off. He's a great humanist. He's a great galvanizer. He loves people. From my experience of trying to get to know what it's like to be a cop in Baltimore and going around with a few cops, he loves cops, he loves law enforcement. He spent so much time as a journalist, meeting and talking and watching cops. I think he has a real enthusiasm for good cops, which is sort of needed in this day and age. He transmitted that enthusiasm to me.

He's a man who has enthusiasm for all people, for gangsters, for lawyers, for everybody. He's just fascinated in humanity. And that bears out in the way he treats people, in his courtesy, his sensitivity and his tenacity and his perseverance. He was confident that they were trying to cancel it the whole time, he was having to fight for every season. He had me and probably others moaning the whole time about how they wanted to go home, they didn't want to do another season. So he had a lot to contend with. I had a wonderful time with him, and he treated me wonderfully. He gave me a break as a director. He said to me, "I can deal with your ambition, I just can't deal with the moaning and the whining."

NINA NOBLE:

Everyone sort of has a different language in terms of how they need the information given to them and prepared for them. That's really my main role, as a translator of what David's sensibilities are and the other showrunners that we work with to everyone else.

For me, it's balancing both the creative and the financial requirements. It's how we allocate the resources that we have in the best way. It's not just about what things cost, it's about the creative value of what you're getting for this particular location.

We have to have room for a lot of different voices. Our meetings are run very democratically. The department heads have authority to make decisions. David would care about a book title on somebody's bookshelf, what books are there and what that person would read. Even if the camera never sees it. I can tell you that crew members who have left us and gone to another show have come back and said to me, "This is terrible. They don't care. I spent all this time researching all of these books for this person's bookshelf and they don't care. They're asking me why I spent so much time doing that." I know it's different out there.

WENDELL PIERCE:

It was me, Andre Royo, and Sonja Sohn. We went and we saw two episodes in the production office and when it finished, I was like, Save your money. Because this shit ain't going anywhere. It's going to be canceled. And that was because it was so unorthodox. It was so, it was on the vanguard of something new.

DOMINIC WEST:

I love the show. I love David and his writing, but it was my first sort of introduction to the idea that you were locked into something for years. I was not very comfortable with that at all. One of the reasons I love acting is that you concentrate very intently for a certain amount of time and your involvement with the people and with the character and with the writing is for a finite term.

And therefore you're able to give your everything. As it becomes more difficult when it stretches over years and they, as David did, start writing your own life into it, the lines become blurred between yourself and your character.

I learned that I respond best under extreme pressure and under extreme feelings of dislocation and culture shock. Filming anything can be extremely tedious, to the point of madness. You're repeating a simple thing very often. Anything that relieves the tedium and terror is a really good way of feeling completely out of one's depth. In an action scene, we knocked down a door, I charged at the door and fell over. They kept it in the scene. It's a good place to be out of your comfort zone and on a sort of knife's edge where it frequently goes very wrong.

WENDELL PIERCE:

It was the very thing that David always said. This is a visual novel. I will build the pieces from chapter to chapter, the characters from chapter to chapter, you may not be in one chapter, you may be heavy in another chapter, understand that all the pieces fit. All the pieces matter. As one of the titles of the episodes and one of the mantras of the show has become. And the brilliance of David and the creators were that they knew the audience would hang in there if you're authentic and the characters are real, the situations, if you give them something to think about and that if you didn't write a show to the least common denominator, but wrote it truthfully, that people will hang in there with you. So what I thought was going to come to an end was actually me reacting to something new that I'd never seen before.

HAL AKSELRAD:

We went out and bought up the back end on anything we've done in the earlier years that we didn't control. *The Wire* is an example of that.

HENRY McGEE:

We were looking at every aspect of the business model, and with the arrival of *Sex and the City* and *The Sopranos*, the whole paradigm shifted. People didn't want to subscribe to get a year-old Paramount release on HBO; they wanted to see what's up with Tony Soprano and the family. Technology was now making it possible on an economic basis, to sell that original. So before we were so limited to rental shops and had this whole network of retailers to which HBO can sell its original programming. Much of which is premium and collectible.

One of the strategies that we adopted early on, which drove our success, is that just as HBO was a premium network, we always priced our DVDs at a premium. We placed a tremendous emphasis on how the DVDs were packaged and presented. Because HBO was building such a tremendous following from its original programming, and there was such a demand. We were able to get dedicated sections for HBO programming and in large retailers like Walmart and others, because buying HBO programming became an important consumer purchase.

People would say DVD sales were risky and you're spending all this money, but we were making so much money on the DVD. It tremendously de-risked those decisions that were being made to spend the production on.

I think the genius of HBO and what the subscription model allowed HBO to do was to make programming decisions that made artistic sense and had cultural resonance without having to worry about a penalty at the box office, or to live or die on their DVD sales, because they always had subscription revenue. And the question in HBO's mind was always, What's going to make most sense for the subscriber?

MIKE LOMBARDO:

We said, "You know what? Fuck it." Owning content in television was viewed, I think, as a disposable asset. It's not like film libraries. As we stepped into a world where we started to fully finance, own, and then, after the fact, try to figure out how to monetize and make financial sense out of that decision, we recognized, Holy shit, in the fourth year of *Sopranos*, people are coming and watching the first year. We figured out a window for home video that we didn't think hurt HBO because you could still keep it on HBO and do home video.

By the way, nobody wanted our shows anyway in the United States because they were too raw, they weren't built for commercials. And when you did have to cut them for commercial, it took the guts out of them. *Sopranos*, when it was cut for commercials, lost a lot. While we were finding that out, we were realizing that there was a value to keep it on the service. To continue to own it. And all of a sudden, we turned out to be the smartest guy in town because we owned our library.

ERIC KESSLER:

Success breeds success. There was a period where if you were a writer or producer and got a show on HBO, it was the good housekeeping seal of approval. We ran a test once just to see the value of the HBO brand. We made up a show and ran a billboard for it in downtown NYC. We did some research and found that putting the HBO logo on the show dramatically increased interest to watch. But, like all good ideas, eventually everyone caught on to our game plan. When Peter Liguori—who worked for me at HBO—left to become head of FX, he said was going to do to basic cable what HBO did in premium. His first show was *The Shield* and that redefined the FX brand. Then came AMC with *Mad Men* and other networks soon followed.

HBO had a great business model because we were a subscription service but so many of the costs that are borne by traditional subscription services were not our responsibility. That's why we had incredibly high profit margins. You couldn't buy HBO directly. You had to call Comcast or another distributor. We didn't pay the eighty thousand customer service reps who took your order or listened to your complaint. We didn't have to send out monthly bills or collect money. We didn't even have to send the signal into your home—just to a cable head end. It was a great model particularly as the number of homes passed by cable or satellite continued to increase.

The downside was it was a highly transactional business. There was constant churn up to 50 percent a year. If we had twenty million people to start the year and twenty-two at the end, it wasn't because we added two million subs. We actually had to add twelve million gross subs to net two million new subs. The way that happened was those eighty thousand customer service reps were on the phone every day selling HBO and they would package HBO with other cable services. They would offer HBO free for three months if you ordered the double or triple play. That was how HBO got into so many homes every year, like clockwork. We did rely in large part on the relationship and support from our distributors.

While the AOL Time Warner merger continued to wreak havoc on the larger company's stock value, it had no chance of wrecking HBO. The brand was too powerful, and it was humming along. Under the combined company, there were no large HBO layoffs or budget reductions, and its operations saw few changes, aside from perhaps more ambitious business targets.

But new arrivals from AOL—including top executives like Steve Case and Mike Kelly—did meddle, and it got on the nerves of the HBO team, causing conflict. Some at HBO saw it as borderline harassment, as the AOL people pried for detailed information about HBO's budgets and projections. There were arguments, slammed phones, and information wars. The AOL team questioned every inch but often failed to understand HBO's business, one that was completely foreign to them.

At one point, Bob Pittman, a top executive, wanted HBO to air a Victoria's Secret fashion show because of an advertising tie-in AOL had with the hotsy-totsy retailer. HBO executives saw it as a potential conflict and wanted no part of it, fearful that such stunts would shift the strategy and cheapen the brand.

JEFF BEWKES:

I wanted to protect HBO. We were getting a lot of fucked-up AOL orders that they postured as collaboration but were really aimed at transferring money or earnings from HBO to AOL. I said, "You guys all say yes when they give the order. Any no coming from HBO is gonna come from me. Because it's not easy for them to fire me." And so that was basically a very long two years from 2000 to 2002.

JERRY LEVIN:

Bewkes was tough on everybody, including me. I knew that Case would never get to HBO. Never get to Time, never get to the studio, that eventually it was going to be the Time Warner people. May not be me, but it'll be the Time Warner people.

I knew I had a successor. It could be either Bewkes or Parsons and we'd be fine. Dick has that personality that's so ingratiating that he could handle almost any situation.

Well, if you plumb the depths of my thinking, I'm not worried because yes, we have Parsons and Pittman, but there's Jeff there. Other people I've talked to somewhere from the group. There's a future of the combined company right now, frankly. I don't think that's what Dick is made out to do.

ROSS GREENBURG:

Even AOL couldn't destroy HBO.

JEFF BEWKES:

Pittman, Levin, and Case tried to get me to leave HBO and go run the cable company. Pittman and Case figured if I took the cable job and refused like Joe, they could then fire me for that. They couldn't take me out at HBO—we were the best performer in the company. I thanked them for the opportunity and declined, saying I really loved running HBO and didn't really want to go into the cable system business. They came back and said, "You can run the cable company and HBO," which would be a reprise of Michael Fuchs straddling music and HBO. I was thinking, No way, man, I know what that means. You put me over to cable, I'd refuse the AOL cramdown just like Joe would, because I would. And then you'd fire me for being insubordinate at cable.

JOE COLLINS:

I was the CEO of the cable company until 2001. And to say the AOL guys didn't want me back, that's sort of an understatement. I wound up leaving as the CEO of the cable company and went to run a special division that they created, which was to try to use our technology to basically speed up the birth of streaming and video on demand and so on. And I did that for another couple of years. And then I left Time Warner in 2004. I was sort of oil and water with AOL guys.

JEFF BEWKES:

I'd been running HBO for eight years and, between HBO's high earnings growth and the premium we got in the merger, I had about $80 million worth of stock on paper. It was becoming clear that AOL was coming apart so I wanted to sell before that, but since I was the guy in the meetings who said the king has no clothes, I figured I shouldn't be selling stock. AOL had a majority on the board and they didn't like Time Warner execs, least of all me, who was arguing with them all the time. But they couldn't fire the head of the best division for no reason, so I wasn't going to give them one, like "He doesn't believe in the company. He's against AOL."

I did have to sell $5 million to buy a house, and Jerry called to ask, "What are you doing?" He didn't pressure me, beyond asking. Maybe he wanted an explanation in case one of the AOL directors asked.

Bob [Pittman] was decent with me, but as revenues came under pressure at AOL, he had the CFO call me near the end of first quarter to tell me HBO should buy $10 million of advertising from AOL in the last week of March. I said that wasn't a good idea, then Bob himself called to ask me to do it and I explained again why that wasn't a good business idea for HBO. He made clear that was my opinion, not his, so do it anyway. I remember saying, "Well, I'm sorry but I'm not gonna do it, and if you send me the order in writing and I don't do it within a five-day cure period you can fire me for insubordination." As I hung up the phone, Richard, who happened to be sitting in my office and heard the whole exchange, asked, "What the fuck was that?" A tense situation is what.

The AOL merger closed January 2001. By the end of 2001, we had reduced our earnings forecasts twice, AOL sub growth was slowing down, and their ad revenues were actually shrinking. Jerry announced he would retire in May and Dick would be the next CEO, which surprised the people outside who thought it would be Pittman, and it also indicated the issues at AOL may be bigger than Wall Street thought.

The first months of 2002 were officially a transition from Jerry to Dick as CEO, but really Jerry had handed everything off to him. Bob was still COO, so we all reported to him or through him to Dick, but Bob had his hands full with the unraveling in Virginia.

We were all supposed to speak our mind at these opcom meetings. Bob always said, "You're wearing AOLTW hats, not HBO or Turner hats." Dick looks around the table and at me. "How about the rest of you? Doesn't anybody have something to say?"

I thought, Well shit, here we go. So I pulled the pin from the grenade.

"None of us are pursuing business as usual, and just speaking for HBO, we're the only network with VOD and we're moving toward broadband distribution faster than you are. AOL has a problem with broadband distribution that you can't solve by cramming it down the cable division's throat when it only has 15 percent of the country. That'll create a resistance in the other 85 percent we don't own and kill AOL's transition to broadband. The problems AOL has don't originate in the network or studio or magazine businesses and they can't solve them, either. The only division that's pursuing business as usual, which maybe was fine for the run-up in your stock, is AOL. And the only company here that's missing its numbers is yours."

HBO executives feared a more aggressive campaign to take their programming and use it to prop up AOL would be next. HBO was highly profitable; the senior staff felt that in Bewkes, they had someone who was savvy enough to keep the lions at bay.

The dynamic between Bewkes and his direct reports was solid; the culture, despite the chaos at corporate, was healthy. Bewkes was everything HBO could ask of him, and all was well. Stability was the only thing HBO wanted.

COLIN CALLENDER:

We had a relationship with Tom Hanks, through *Band of Brothers* and so on. He had this pet project with his wife, Rita Wilson, called *My Big Fat Greek Wedding*, and the director Joel Zwick was one of the first television directors Tom ever worked with.

CHRIS ALBRECHT:

My wife, Annie, and her partner, Bob Reade, ran their talent management business out of HBO space in West Hollywood, and they would set up these workshops for us. Nia did this one-person show, and Rita Wilson saw it, loved it, and optioned it.

Somebody paid Nia to write a script, and Gary Goetzman asked me to read it as a favor, to see if we would do it as an HBO picture. I looked at it, gave it to Colin, but we both agreed it wasn't right for us as an HBO picture. Then Gary said to me, "Would you do me a favor? I can make the movie for $5 million. If I can get $2.5 million, will you give me the other half, $2.5 million?" I said, "Yes," then after I hung up I thought, "I just said yes to financing a movie. We didn't do that shit, and it wasn't in my budget. I better tell Jeff." He said, "Okay."

COLIN CALLENDER:

After seeing the first cuts of the movie, I thought there's not a single Greek person who will ever speak to us again. We were worried the Greek community would be so insulted. Then we screened it a couple of times and people loved it. No one expected it to be what it was.

CHRIS ALBRECHT:

It was a flop when we first released it, but because of word of mouth, it was able to stay in theaters longer and started to build and build.

Tom Hanks was always good to us, and we certainly wanted to be good to him. It's the only time in history that a good deed went unpunished.

My Big Fat Greek Wedding *premiered in theaters on February 22, 2002, and would go on to gross more than $368 million worldwide, making it one of the most profitable romantic comedies in motion picture history.*

Bewkes, Albrecht, Strauss, and Callender were on a roll, and in perfect alignment— organizationally, creatively, and culturally. HBO had become the destination of choice for the majority of Hollywood's creative community, and, despite a certain disruptive ratfuck called AOL, Bewkes was managing to protect HBO from above and keep its financial faucets open wide and running.

All that was essential for HBO's future well-being was that nothing change.

9

Individuation

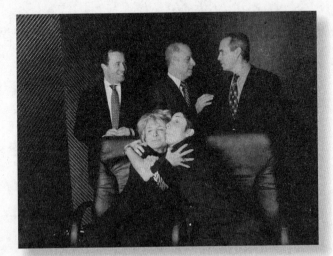

JEFF BEWKES:

One morning in July 2002, Dick Parsons called. "Cancel your lunch, we need to talk." I meet him and he starts right in. "The SEC is going to open a civil investigation into AOL accounting, and the Justice Department may open a criminal probe. Bob Pittman is going to step down. Now listen carefully, because I want you to answer the question I ask, not a different question. I want you and Don Logan to step up and run the company. Can you do that?" I started telling him I liked running HBO and wasn't sure I wanted to run corporate, and he interrupted me with a smile. "See, there you go answering a different question. I didn't ask if you wanted to do it. I asked if you could do it with Logan."

"Does Don know about this? What's he gonna run, and what am I supposed to run?" Dick said, "Call Don and the two of you figure it out." I asked, "When would this happen?" and Dick shocked me when he said, "We'll vote on it at the board meeting tomorrow. You free for dinner tonight?" I told him, "Actually, no, I have to host the premiere of *Sex and the City* at the Natural History Museum." He gave me a long look and said, "Get somebody else to do it. You and Don have to have dinner with me and Steve Case." Case was chairman of the board.

When I got back to my office, I called Don. He says, "We're fucked! We're tweeners!" I knew exactly what he meant. Even though he'd keep oversight of Time Inc. Magazines and I'd keep oversight of HBO, we'd have to put in a CEO to oversee AOL, Time Warner Cable, Warner Bros., New Line, Turner, and Warner Music.

Don suggested I take Warner Bros., New Line, Turner, and Warner Music; he would take magazines and TW Cable. I was fine with all that, but the big question was who should take AOL? He didn't want it any more than I did, but he knew it was only fair if I had to deal with all the networks, studios, and music companies, that he deal with it.

So we divvied up the divisions over the phone, told Dick, and showed up for dinner with Steve. We assumed, wrongly, that he had been told how we were proposing to divide up the responsibilities, but he started talking about how they were going to decide at the board meeting what our new assignments would be. I said, "Look, we just heard about all this today, and we divided up the divisions in a way that we think we can manage successfully. If you are going to go to the board and change anything, I hope we will get a chance to talk about it. After all, this is not a plantation."

Steve throws down his napkin and blows up. "I've had about enough of you! We're not running this company to suit you," and storms out of the room. That's the chairman of the board. The night before the board meeting that's supposed to appoint Don and me to God knows what.

None of us said anything for several seconds, until Don, looking at the swinging door in his Alabama drawl, says, "That there, that's a problem."

We both look at Dick, who shrugs his shoulders and says, "I told you it was fucked up." We asked him, "Do you have the votes to do it our way?" Dick nodded calmly. He always knew the count.

CHRIS ALBRECHT:

Jeff came to me and said, "I'm getting moved uptown. Do you want to be the CEO?" I said, "Not really, but I don't want somebody else to be, so I guess my answer is yes."

CEO was never a job I thought about having and there was nothing in it for me. I loved running programming and loved working for Jeff. I wouldn't be where I was if it wasn't for the work that Jeff Bewkes and I did together. Jeff Bewkes wouldn't be where he was if it wasn't for the work that he and I did together. Jeff was my boss, but he was also a partner and a friend.

I said to Jeff, "I need Bill Nelson to stay," because he was going to retire, and I wanted him as a partner to run the business side.

As head of programming, I had more time to interact with a lot of people, particularly Carolyn and Anne. When I became CEO, I needed to vertically integrate the org chart. Luckily, Carolyn was ready.

One can forgive Jeff Bewkes for wanting to take the announcement of his latest promotion directly to that dean at NYU Law who had been so deflating to him about his future. The July 18, 2002, AOL Time Warner press release announcing Bewkes's promotion boasted of him, "During his seven-year tenure as CEO, HBO delivered compound annual EBITDA growth of 16% and increased its subscriber base from nearly 30 million to 38.5 million worldwide. Under his leadership, HBO has become the world's most profitable TV network, while securing its reputation for critically acclaimed original programming, movies, documentaries, concerts, and sports, as well as leadership in new technologies such as HBO-on-Demand."

Bewkes arrived at corporate only slightly behind a $54 billion write-off, and six months ahead of a $45.5 billion encore write-off. The nearly $100 billion loss reflected not only a major decline in the value of AOL Time Warner but a dismal advertising market and major problems with AOL's Internet operation. The "growth engine" had conked out, and reports of $100 billion in civil suits from cantankerous shareholders were on deck.

Where, oh where, would the blame be cast?

On December 5, 2001, AOL Time Warner announced the retirement of Jerry Levin. Retirement?

JERRY LEVIN:

It became clear that I wasn't going to be able to get along with Case, and he was going to fuck it up. I did not have great respect for the board and knew where I had lost support. Ted Turner was no longer in charge of the companies he started. Who was he going to rail on, who did that? I did it because it made no sense for him to run them. So I made it known to Case through intermediaries that I would leave, but wanted an extra year and that I wanted Dick to be the new CEO. It took three days. So who won? AOL or Time Warner?

Jerry Levin's face had been the first image ever to appear on HBO, and that moment became the launchpad for one of the most peculiar professional sagas in contemporary corporate history. Levin's stunning ascent was all the more notable because so few had seen it coming. As an operator, Levin was a B-minus student, once bringing HBO to the brink of cancellation. He often remarked on his shortage of "good corporate DNA"—his lack of height, looks, WASP-iness, and polish—traits he considered common among other successful executives at Time Inc. He was also all-but-allergic to sharing key information with colleagues, and after he lost his first major power battle (against Nick Nicholas), he was so devastated he told several people he was going to quit the company.

Yet over the course of thirty years, very little of that ended up mattering. Levin's unorthodox thinking and keen verbal skills enabled HBO to hop onto a satellite ahead of others in the industry, creating a new era and making him a star. Levin didn't resign after Nicholas was awarded the promotion he so desperately wanted for himself. Instead, he conducted an extremely subtle, highly effective insurgent campaign against him. It wouldn't take him that long to become The Boss, with legends like Ted Turner and Bob Daly reporting to him.

JERRY LEVIN:

Every time I read about how difficult things had become, it hurt my soul. I would've done it a different way; there were mistakes made. But no one was paying attention when this big thing called the Internet was coming down the block, and we needed it. I was not a traitor, and no one is infallible, not even the pope.

With Levin gone, Bewkes arrived uptown with HBO blood still coursing in his veins. Given the chaos and deceit then bubbling around corporate, there'd be little time for Bewkes to mentor Albrecht, a former comedy club manager, agent, and programming wizard who had never held the title of CEO. Almost immediately, Albrecht was thrust into a situation that would have been unthinkable during the eighteen preceding years of Bewkes and Fuchs.

CHRIS ALBRECHT:

HBO quickly became more of a Hollywood company; that's where I was, even though I went to New York a lot. And I will say at that time, particularly at New York City restaurants and the theater, being CEO of HBO was like being a movie star. This was a big shift and a big threat to people at HBO in New York, even though we never tried to build a power base in LA. Still, the old guard hierarchy was threatened, and the fact that Jeff was so supportive of me pissed people off.

Being a CEO was like riding a unicycle on a high wire with no net and John Malone shaving the wire.

A few months after I became CEO, Bill said we had a big Comcast deal coming up for renewal. I had never been part of an affiliate deal before, so I listened to the team as they played tough in the negotiations. Then Bill Nelson, Eric Kessler, and Richard Plepler said I should go down to Comcast to try to close it. I was briefed that I had to get several key items, and if I didn't, I had to say no. This was going to be my first big business moment.

It was the middle of the fucking winter. The Time Warner air force put me in a helicopter down to Philly, and when I arrived, it was below zero. A car took me directly to the Comcast building, where I went inside and they put me in a room and made me wait.

Finally, Brian Roberts and Mike Tallent came in with Matt Bond, who had just come over from AT&T, so he was trying to prove himself as a tough guy. We sat and went over everything. Then I said, "I'm sorry, I can't agree to this, we can't make this deal." Brian and Matt got up in a huff and stormed out of the room. I was left with Tallent, who was a good old-time cable guy, and he said to me, "This is a pretty good deal, Chris, and it's not going to get any better." I asked for a few minutes to call my guys. I'll never forget it. I'm alone in this little fucking conference room and I was wearing a periwinkle blue shirt. After Brian had stormed out, I could feel the sweat under my arms, and when I stood up to use the phone, I looked down and saw my shirt had turned dark blue because my sweat bands were from my armpits down to my belt. That's how fucking scared shitless I was.

I called the guys back in New York, told them what had happened, and they said, "In that case, you should close the deal." I said to them, "Fuck you. Now I'm going to look like an idiot. You better come up with something for me to ask that they can agree to right now to get this deal to yes." They did that, and we closed the deal. A few minutes later, I was back in the car. I hadn't even had lunch. On the helicopter, they gave me a corned beef sandwich with chips. The mustard was freezing because it had been sitting in the chopper.

HAL AKSELRAD:

Chris had never done an affiliate deal in his life, and he was asked to take on the single most difficult affiliate deal there is. It was outrageous. They should have never sent him down there alone. He needed people with him, to have extra eyes and ears, to go outside a room and caucus or reposition. Why wasn't Bill with him? Why didn't he bring Tom Woodbury, our senior sales and marketing lawyer, or Eric Kessler, who was nominally responsible for the deal? I couldn't believe they would send him alone and unprotected into a world he didn't understand.

It was clear from the start that Bill Nelson didn't want Chris to succeed. He resented reporting to him. What happened at Comcast was the start of a "Let's marginalize Chris" effort. Richard was already criticizing Chris and Carolyn's decisions, as if he was an expert in programming.

Albrecht's Comcast quagmire was at least, for the most part, private. Soon, however, he would be propelled into another confrontation that would make his visit to Comcast seem like a massage at a four-star spa.

On December 8, 2002, **The Sopranos** *completed its fourth season with install-ment number fifty-two, "Whitecaps," a stunner even by* **Sopranos'** *stunning stan-dards. What starts out as a love story, with Tony bringing Carmela to the seashore to see a beautiful beach house he wants to buy for her, collapses in rage after a phone call from one of Tony's bitter ex-lovers. James Gandolfini and Edie Falco as Tony and Carmela perform one of the most complex, exhilarating, and excruciating enactments of domestic crisis ever seen on a screen of any size. Both actors would go on to win Emmys for Best Male and Female Performances the following year.*

Off-screen, combatants waged drama of a different sort. When first cast, Gandolfini had signed a six-year contract for $5 million per season. But once the show's tremen-dous success became established fact, HBO agreed to double his salary after season three, a move that HBO execs reminded his representatives they did not have to make. That proved inadequate for Gandolfini, however, and when HBO refused to negotiate further, Gandolfini's representatives filed a breach of contract suit in Los Angeles Superior Court on March 6, 2003, requesting that the contract be terminated. Five days later, HBO coun-tersued, asking $100 million in damages. Shooting for the next season was scheduled to begin on March 24.

Gandolfini's original demand was for $20 million a year. HBO was presented with the names and salaries of other male series leads who were making far more, like **Frasier's** *Kelsey Grammer ($35 million plus),* **Everybody Loves Raymond's** *Ray Romano ($17.6 million) and the cast of* **Friends** *(each of whom were raking in a cool $22.6 million by season nine). HBO didn't budge. Gandolfini's team soon lowered his demand to $16 million, but that still left the two sides miles apart.*

CHRIS ALBRECHT:

It was a big fire. When he didn't show up to work, it became a public fight between the two of us and I didn't handle the situation very well. I said something to the press that I shouldn't have said, called him a fat slob or something. I was really offended that one of his representatives wasn't operating with a lot of integrity.

MIKE LOMBARDO:

Jim was a brilliant actor but a complicated guy to deal with. He had his own demons about success. And unfortunately, he was surrounded by representatives who took advantage of that.

At this point, Albrecht decided to focus on the true nature of the man he was dealing with, and on the item that Gandolfini cared about more than a specific dollar amount: the cast and crew of the show.

Since Gandolfini wasn't coming to work, and there wasn't a solitary soul who thought The Sopranos *could survive without him, Albrecht announced he was shutting down production and, in effect, fired the show's entire crew, telling everyone it was because of a contract dispute. That was the third rail for Gandolfini. He cared too much about everyone else to let them all collapse around him.*

Albrecht had guessed right and, in the end, Gandolfini agreed to $13 million per season. Gandolfini released a statement through his spokesperson that read, "I'm very happy that The Sopranos *will be back: It's a show that I love doing, with people I love working with."*

CHRIS ALBRECHT:

We gave him more money. We gave him a million an episode. I don't think he got back-end; David Chase got back-end [profit participation]. We do not give any actors back-end because once you give one actor back-end, you have to give that to all of them.

HAL AKSELRAD:

At the end of the season, we forgave everything, and James agreed to meet at a poolside cabana at the Peninsula Beverly Hills. We had a delightful lunch. He was guarded at the beginning because he only knew me as the hard ass on the other end of the line, but I tried to show him there were no hard feelings. We were interrupted by Jacob Arabo, Jacob the Jeweler, who came in with a garish diamond-encrusted wristwatch likely worth more than $50,000 for James.

Jacob told James he could keep the watch if he wore it onstage if he accepted an Emmy for *The Sopranos.* And he did. When James won the award, he held his arm up high and displayed the watch.

When the negotiation was settled, Gandolfini wrote each of his fellow cast members a check for $33,000.

MIKE LOMBARDO:

The company wasn't making direct revenue from *The Sopranos*. It made increased revenue by selling the service, but we couldn't say that was because of a specific show. When people bought HBO, it was for a combination of reasons. We'd had studies done, and the number one reason people bought HBO was still for theatrical movies, and we would wave that in front of our talent. HBO's secret sauce wasn't overpaying people, it was treating talent like a partner, and that served the company well for a really long time.

On January 31, 2005, HBO announced a syndication deal with A&E for **The Sopranos** *valued at $2.5 million per episode—more than $162.5 million total. What a boon for HBO. Since A&E was on a basic cable channel, every episode had to be scrubbed free of nudity, bad language, and extreme violence—for* **The Sopranos** *that would be like remaking* **Jurassic Park** *without the dinosaurs. So if you watched* **The Sopranos** *on A&E and liked it, there was a good chance you'd want to see the real thing and thus subscribe to HBO. There, you could go to HBO On Demand to see full versions from the unbowdlerized past. For HBO, it was like Christmas never ended: a syndication deal with no fear of cannibalization, plus great money.*

JEFF BEWKES:

When we sold *The Sopranos* to A&E, the first season alone made more money than it cost us. We had an ongoing fight with the auditors, who kept saying, "Until you can prove it's a hit, we're not going to let you defer any of the cost on the balance sheet to match against ancillary revenues." I would say to them, "This is ridiculous. You're making us overcharge this year's bottom line, therefore starving our original programming budget, and then we're gonna have a big earnings bulge when we put these on DVD and overseas." And that's what happened.

Which meant that when we finally sold the show in the aftermarkets—DVD, overseas TV, syndication in the United States—everything we got was 100 percent profit.

I can tell you right now, *Band of Brothers, Sex and the City*, and *The Sopranos*, which represented the most expensive budgets we ever did in those genres, each one of them made more money than what they cost us. We did not know that would be the case, but it helped us a lot during the AOL collapse.

When the money started rolling in, we realized that we had to make more shows, with bigger budgets, because they would pay for themselves. It gave us a lot of room to ramp up original programming.

As CEO, Albrecht placed three large bets on personnel, in addition to his wanting Bill Nelson to be his partner in all things financial. The others: Carolyn Strauss, Albrecht's loyal deputy in programming, and the person he probably considered the smartest individual at the company; Richard Plepler, whom he'd brought forth from the land of PR into a broader branding role; and Colin Callender, now in charge of HBO movies, surviving only because of Albrecht's belief in him. There was no denying Callender's producing abilities, nor his talents for discovering material and recruiting and managing big-name stars and directors. But Callender had been controversial within HBO from the time he arrived, particularly with regard to the perception that he was much better at taking credit than sharing it with his team—and a great team it was, including Keri Putnam, Kary Antholis, and Jenni Sherwood.

Callender had survived a tense relationship with Bob Cooper, and Bewkes's disdain for Cooper had enabled Callender to survive in turn. But it was Albrecht who had gone to Bewkes back in 2000 to convince him to reward Callender by placing all HBO movies under his domain. From his new perch atop HBO Films, Callender sought to continue the streak of independent filmmaking that had made him such a success at HBO Showcase, the company's earlier small-scale production house. Callender set up a group within HBO Films to produce smaller movies, spawning a series of films that explored a wide slice of life—movies that challenged audiences in profound, and sometimes deeply discomforting, ways.

Callender had made the most of it by compiling a remarkable record. Now with Albrecht as CEO, he had gales of wind at his back.

JANE ANDERSON:

Colin approached me about *Normal* after he saw it at the Geffen Playhouse with Laurie Metcalf and Beau Bridges. He called and asked, "Jane, would you like to turn this into a film?"

In the middle of the shoot, Colin was watching the dailies and said, "You know, Jane, this scene doesn't work." I was in a state of exhaustion and I hung up. I thought, "Fuck me." I thought I had failed miserably. I felt horrible. But he very cheerfully told me, "Try it again." It wasn't a big deal for him to completely reshoot it. So I rewrote it, put it in a completely different setting, and it turned into a much more interesting scene. That's not a story you hear every day in this business.

COLIN CALLENDER:

Gus Van Sant came through the door wanting to do a factually based docu-drama about Columbine. The idea of having Gus Van Sant on HBO was immensely exciting. I said to Gus, any director could do a straight-up docu-drama on the subject—what would be a Gus Van Sant take on it? So I sent him a copy of a movie that an English director called Alan Clarke had made called *Elephant*, which was a forty-minute movie that dramatized a series of random sectarian bonds in Northern Ireland. Gus saw that film and came back with a fifteen-page outline for his film, which he then called *Elephant* as a tribute, the nonlinear exploration of two kids who ended up being shooters of a school. It wasn't specifically Columbine, more a musing on the sources of that violence.

KERI PUTNAM:

I'm so proud that HBO made *Elephant*. That was the first time HBO had a movie in Cannes, and it won the Palme d'Or, which was truly amazing.

COLIN CALLENDER:

I'd seen *Wit* on Broadway, and brought it to Emma in London.

EMMA THOMPSON, Actor:

Producers, listen up. Colin came over to London to see me in person and told me, "I really want you to do this because you're so right for it." I read the first page and said, "Yup. Absolutely. This is clearly writing from the gods."

COLIN CALLENDER:

Emma had recently worked with Mike Nichols on *Primary Colors* and we were sitting in her living room—I think it was in Hampstead—and she said, "Why don't we try to get Mike to direct this?" and called Mike.

Wit, a Broadway play written by Margaret Edson, about an English teacher who had cancer, was the dream job for Mike Nichols. People close to him understood that this was the type of material that spoke to him in a profound way—not the commercial, satirical, societal commentary that he was somewhat known for, but something much deeper. He was in his element with the material and he was treated, as always, like royalty.

EMMA THOMPSON:

Mike had just had a bit of a flop with a Garry Shandling movie, and so he was feeling a bit vulnerable. Had he just come off a huge, massive hit, he might not have looked at a piece for television because he could be snobby about it, but when you've been kicked in the teeth, your best cure is to get back on the horse and go, "Okay, I need to do something else now." Because he and I were such close friends and loved working together so much, he had a look at it, then said, "Yes."

Mike said, "You don't have to shave your head," but of course I was going to shave my head. She was a chemotherapy patient. I had shaved my head before, so I knew how liberating it was.

It was much harder to watch than it was to perform. We spent six weeks shooting and were doing it in small pieces. Margaret's writing is so bracing and witty, it does boil down to a film that is very demanding to watch emotionally. Ask any actor, tragedy is easier to play than comedy. You try repeating comedy again and again, by the end of the day, you want to kill yourself. But if you're actually dying, there's no need. You're just exhausted. *Wit* was really a fascinating experience, and Mike was so happy with it.

COLIN CALLENDER:

During the shooting of *Wit* in London, I knew the rights to *Angels in America* were available. They'd been trying to do it as two movies at New Line, but they decided that it wasn't commercially viable. Pacino wanted to do it and play Roy Cohn. I spoke with him. He said, "I'll do it for HBO." There was a break in the filming of *Wit* in the studio in London, and I was in Mike's dressing room. There's nothing in there except a glorious photograph of Diane Sawyer sitting on his desk. I said to him, "What about *Angels*?" He said, "Yes."

TONY KUSHNER, Screenwriter:

I hadn't thought about it as a film when I was working on it as a play, but the minute a play is successful, you start to get offers. The first person who approached me about doing it was Robert Altman, whose work I admire enormously. I said yes, because I was very excited by the prospect of working with him. We worked on it together, off and on, for a couple of years; I really enjoyed the time that I got to spend with him, but it became clear it wasn't quite gelling. We mutually agreed to put it away. A number of other people made offers to try to do it, but I didn't feel particularly drawn to doing anything with anyone else. Then Mike Nichols called.

Tony Kushner's **Angels in America** *had begun as a Broadway play in two parts—the first half premiering in May 1993, and the second, later that autumn; both would go on to win Tony Awards for Best Play. The show ran for roughly a year and a half after* *opening at the Walter Kerr Theatre. The play follows a gay man named Prior who becomes sick with AIDS in Reagan-era New York and is visited by an angel and by a Mormon husband who grapples with his own homosexuality.*

Ten years later, in 2003, HBO adapted the stage play into a six-part miniseries, featuring a glittering cast comprising the likes of Al Pacino as an AIDS-infected Roy Cohn who mentors the gay Mormon husband (who is also a law clerk), and Meryl Streep playing three characters—the lawyer's mother, a rabbi, and a spectral Ethel Rosenberg, the woman who Cohn helped sentence to death. The credits also included Emma Thompson as the titular angel, Mary-Louise Parker, Patrick Wilson, and Jeffrey Wright, who returned to his role in the original stage play as Belize, a gay friend of Prior who also cares for the ailing Cohn as a nurse. Executive producing the show would be Cary Brokaw and director Mike Nichols, both of whom played the same roles in 2001's Wit.

TONY KUSHNER:

When we sat down at Trattoria Dell'Arte to talk for the first time, I asked Mike, "Why do you want to do this play?" And he said, "Because there are so many great parts in it for Meryl Streep." Mike was attracted to playing games with assumptions, realism, and naturalism.

EMMA THOMPSON:

What made Mike so unique? Oh, his pain. His pain from having to leave his country from a very difficult childhood, and difficult parents with a tough, tough entry into the world. Then being entirely bald, that's an incredibly difficult thing to live with. He built himself out of his pain in the most extraordinary way. Everything about *Angels in America* was up Mike's alley. As Tony said, "This version of *Angels* is very Mike."

TONY KUSHNER:

Mike brought fresh and exciting insights about the way people relate to one another, and his interest in moments of disconnection and incomprehension and his own mystery, where people behave in ways that are not entirely explicable and you have to sort of shrug and allow for idiosyncrasy and impermeability. All of that is in the film. It was very recognizably a Mike Nichols film.

EMMA THOMPSON:

Mike asked me to be on it right at the start. He said, "Next year, you're going to do this with me." We were sort of joined at the hip by then.

COLIN CALLENDER:

The idea that Mike Nichols would make *Angels in America* on HBO with Al Pacino, Meryl Streep, and Emma Thompson sent a huge signal to the marketplace.

Angels was a two-year production that cost more than $60 million. We gave Mike final cut. No director had gotten final cut prior to that. And we never gave a single note to Tony Kushner on the script.

EMMA THOMPSON:

HBO was dealing with a Pulitzer Prize–winning piece, and it would have been a brave person who brought notes to Mike Nichols.

KARY ANTHOLIS:

My involvement in *Wit* and *Angels in America* was to make Mike Nichols feel comfortable, and to give him a direct line of communication with HBO. I spent more time on a set of those shows than probably any scripted project I worked on for HBO, and it was an opportunity to learn and watch him do his thing. We traveled together to the Berlin Film Festival. That was only the second time he'd been back there since he left Berlin as a child.

TONY KUSHNER:

HBO was, at that point, in the first flush of its great era of triumph with *The Sopranos* and other shows. Things were exploding there in terms of what television could be.

It was a hugely expensive production, and we all felt staggered by the many months it took to film. We had six hours, yet nobody ever said to me, "Can you cut it down to four hours? Can one of the gay characters be straight? Could you make it less complicated?" There was a whole-hearted embrace of what was challenging about the project, and I think everybody worked for close to scale. It was the first time Meryl and Pacino were going to do television.

COLIN CALLENDER:

We would market the shit out of things, we'd spend serious marketing dollars, and that was a big draw. There was no worry about opening weekend grosses, and talent knew their work would be seen. It was a big reason people came to work with us.

CHRIS SPADACCINI:

Angels was a watershed moment for HBO. Mike came in with big ideas. He wanted to hire the esteemed photographer Richard Avedon to shoot the cast, and even went so far as having an image of what that should look like. We spent over $1 million on this shoot. When he eventually saw it, he decided, "No, not what I want. We're going to go with a screenshot of Emma as the angel, hovering over the bed," which ended up being a better ad and a more iconic image. The idea that a million-dollar photo shoot from Richard Avedon would never see the light of day was indicative of the lengths HBO would go to appease our talent. Cost was not a factor.

QUENTIN SCHAFFER:

We had a screening of *Angels* for eleven hundred people at the Ziegfeld Theatre. Mike came in to do a seating plan for his special guests. He was a perfectionist on every level. While he was in our office, he asked to see the dinner tickets. We showed them to him, and he grimaced. He didn't like the color. They were peach, but not the peach he had in mind. He waited to hear us say that we'd try to do another run. Instead, I looked at him, and with so many other concerns on my mind, said, "Mike, it's just a dinner ticket. People hand it over to get in the reception. It has no shelf life." He paused, then laughed, realizing that it wasn't that important.

Mike Nichols didn't simply direct a television version of a play, he created a profound and unprecedented television event and, as one of our greatest living film directors, made television history.

Angels in America was inundated with accolades when awards season rolled around. First up: the Golden Globes, where the movie received five wins out of seven nominations including prizes for Best Miniseries and acting prizes for Pacino, Streep, Wright, and Parker. Later that year, Angels became the first such show in the history of the National Academy of Television Arts and Sciences to sweep every single major eligible category; Pacino, Streep, Wright, and Parker took home acting awards, with Angels winning for Outstanding Miniseries, Writing, and Directing. At the end of the night, the series had been awarded eleven Emmys.

Despite Angels' hefty cost, HBO Films ramped up production. Hysterical Blindness, from 2002, earned Uma Thurman her first Golden Globe, and Gena Rowlands received a Supporting Actress Golden Globe nomination for the film as well.

In 2004, Maria Full of Grace introduced the world to actress Catalina Sandino Moreno as a struggling soon-to-be teen mom. The film shifted the point of view of the drug wars, letting the audience know how it felt to be an ordinary person caught up in the crossfire of the drug trade. The film earned the Audience Award at the 2004 Sundance Film Festival, while Moreno earned a Best Actress Oscar nomination.

One year later, **Lackawanna Blues** *would take viewers inside a ramshackle boarding house near Buffalo, New York, in the middle of the twentieth century, tracking Ruben Santiago-Hudson's childhood memories in the home, growing up surrounded by a group of troubled fellow residents—many of whom harbored criminal pasts. S. Epatha Merkerson (of Dick Wolf's venerable TV Series* **Law & Order***) won an Emmy, a Golden Globe, and a SAG Award for her role as Rachel "Nanny" Crosby, while the show itself also received a smattering of honors, including a Golden Globe nomination for Best Miniseries and seven total Emmy nominations, most notably a nod for Outstanding Made for Television Movie and a win for its casting.*

Decades ago, Sheila Nevins expressed skepticism about whether the HBO audience was ready to confront the tragedy of the AIDS crisis. But now, Nevins felt, the world had changed a great deal, and she was determined to do as much "confronting" as possible—however shocking that truth turned out to be.

RORY KENNEDY:

I told Sheila, "I didn't think anyone was going to watch five parts on the global AIDS epidemic," and she said, "Of course they're not going to watch it. Let's make it as miserable as possible." That's a literal quote. We turned it into a five-part series. I still don't know if anybody watched it. But she didn't care. What she cared about was always making the best film possible, and not shying away from the depths of despair or any other challenges. It got nominated, won awards, and got out in the world and did well.

In the new century, another offshoot of Nevins's sex programming appeared, perhaps the most revealing of all. **Cathouse** *(2002) and* **Cathouse 2: Back in the Saddle** *(2003) were fly-on-the-wall accounts of the goings-on at the Moonlite BunnyRanch, a legal brothel in the appropriately named town of Mound House, Nevada. The Moonlite had been bought in 1993 by Dennis Hof for $700,000. Hof, a preternatural pimp and entrepreneur, turned Moonlite into a growing concern. The real stars, however, were without a doubt the likes of Madame Suzette, Hof's "heart-of-gold-hidden-by-tough-exterior" manager, and characters like "Air Force Amy," the brothel's highest earner. Hof parlayed his HBO fame into a political career: he ran for a spot in Nevada Assembly's Thirty-sixth District, only to have his own mortality snatch his seat out from under him. He died before he won with 63 percent of the vote.*

JULIE ANDERSON:

I went with Patti Kaplan to meet Dennis Hof to make the HBO deal. We arrived at a weird little place called The Moonlite BunnyRanch, basically a bunch of trailers and a bar. The girls sat in the trailers and waited for people to come in. Stormy Daniels was one of the girls at the BunnyRanch, and she would go back and forth from LA to Las Vegas.

SHEILA NEVINS:

I once asked one of the girls in the whorehouse, "Don't you feel used?" She said, "I felt used when I worked at McDonald's and I was making $7 an hour." She said, "I'm gay anyway. All I do is tell guys it's the biggest thing I ever saw and they give me a big tip." These women were incredible. They would play chess in between their fucking.

JULIE ANDERSON:

There was a really sweet moment when this older guy, who had just gotten out of prison and was nearly eighty years old, came in. He hadn't touched a girl for forty years and went into a room with a girl who was very kind to him.

But there were disgusting guys as well. One guy came in with his son and they shared a prostitute at the same time. Another time, a mother brought her son in because he was still a virgin.

PATTI KAPLAN:

For the very first *Cathouse* show, Chris scheduled it to follow the final episode of the fourth season of *The Sopranos.* You couldn't have a better place on television than that. Of course *Cathouse* rated just off the charts. It didn't sustain that rating, but it was very popular. People couldn't get enough of it.

SHEILA NEVINS:

We even did *Cathouse: The Musical.* When I met Stephen Sondheim, I don't know what I was thinking, but I said, "I made a musical at a whorehouse." I gave him a DVD, and he left with it. He never mentioned it to me again.

Musical romps about prostitutes notwithstanding, the breadth and depth of HBO's Documentary unit continued to impress, at times out-shocking fiction TV, where much greater liberties could be taken. A frantic global effort to rescue children from Chernobyl, definitively innocent victims of a merciless heart affliction known as "Chernobyl heart," became a nuclear-age horror. Filming took place in Ukraine and Belarus.

Chernobyl Heart *was screened at no less auspicious a venue than the United Nations General Assembly and won the Academy Award for Best Documentary Short.*

MARYANN DELEO, Documentarian:

When I saw the photographs at the UN exhibition from Adi Roche and the nonprofit Chernobyl Children's Project International, I wanted to tell the world what was still happening. I got in touch with Adi, a force of nature. She was going to Chernobyl and invited me to go along. We were in hazmat suits, but it did get a little hairy when we got to the reactor and the levels were so high. We didn't stay there long.

JACKIE GLOVER:

Maryann DeLeo was an incredibly brave filmmaker to tell that story. It was dangerous. Cesium levels were still really high there. She brought a camera into the surgery room and asked profound questions of people who had been dealing with the aftermath of these children born to parents who were exposed.

MARYANN DELEO:

I didn't cure cancer. I just got an Academy Award.

Sheila Nevins's son David was diagnosed with Tourette's syndrome at age five, and in November 2005, HBO, in conjunction with the Tourette Syndrome Association, released a half-hour documentary on the subject, from the point of view of children with the condition. (The film would share an Emmy Award for Outstanding Children's Programming with Disney's movie, **High School Musical.***)*

In 2016, David was appointed to the board of the Tourette Association of America (formerly the Tourette Syndrome Association).

SHEILA NEVINS:

I never asked for a favor from HBO, never had the balls to ask for something that was personal to me, but when my son was of age, and I'd been there almost twenty-five years, I figured, I'm going to push this one on through. Kids were bullying my kid, and I got permission from David to make a film called *I Have Tourette's But Tourette's Doesn't Have Me.* I gave it to Ellen Goosenberg, who is remarkable. David worked on it, and we also made it for the Tourette's syndrome society.

In February 2004, HBO named Sheila Nevins president of Documentary and Family Programming.

SHEILA NEVINS:

They left me alone. They never bothered me. They never told me what to do. They never told me what not to do. They gave me money. I worked within that amount of money. And they never told me I did a good job.

On November 22, 2005, the venerated ABC anchor Ted Koppel was in the process of leaving **Nightline**, *the deep-dive, late-night news-interview show that helped make Koppel a household name and demonstrably upgrade ABC News. Koppel's next stop? HBO, together with* **Nightline** *executive producer Tom Bettag, and with a handful of other* **Nightline** *alums in tow.*

One month later, news broke that Koppel and company would instead be join-ing the Discovery Channel, with assurances from top Discovery officials that Koppel would be free to take on controversial topics.

Koppel explained to anyone who would listen that if he'd gone to HBO, he would have felt like a mere "appendage" fastened to an otherwise entertainment-focused brand, but that's not exactly what happened. The truth is, the Queen Bee heard about Koppel's deal with HBO not long before it was set to close, and she wasted no time strid-ing boldly into battle.

JON ALPERT:

Tom Bettag and Ted Koppel were about to make a big deal with Richard Plepler.

SHEILA NEVINS:

I was at the News and Documentaries Emmys Awards, and Mike Wal-lace, who knew me through his wife, Mary, said to me backstage, "How are you going to like working for Ted?" I said, "Ted who?" I didn't know what he was talking about. He said, "Koppel. He's got a big deal coming up with HBO. He's getting a lot of docus. You'll probably be working for him." I said, "Oh no, I won't." Then I went on stage and accepted some award, even though I was fuming with fury because no one had told me anything.

I called Chris like a crazy person. I said, "Chris, Richard Plepler is hiring Ted Koppel to do docus. I can't stay here." I was probably hysterical. Chris didn't want to lose me. I didn't sleep for two or three nights. I was so angry. Every day I would either call Chris, to say, "Please stop this," or call Human Resources to say I was leaving.

Then I decided, "No, no. I'm not leaving," and really went to town.

JON ALPERT:

Sheila did a scorched-earth campaign, the likes of which you've never seen before.

SHEILA NEVINS:

If Mike hadn't said anything, it would have gone through. It was very close to happening.

    I was going to die. I was going to lose my job. It was my life.

CHRIS ALBRECHT:

It certainly was one of those Plepler specials. He was trying to get something going.

SHEILA NEVINS:

It wasn't even that I knew anything about Ted. I think I watched one or two of his shows. They wanted to do newsy things. I wasn't interested in newsy things. I was interested in people things. It was horrible. It was terrifying.

CHRIS ALBRECHT:

I met with Ted and it went fine, but he's not the kind of guy I was used to talking to. There was nothing fun about the conversation, and by that time I knew Sheila was upset.

RICHARD PLEPLER:

There was nobody in the news business who I revered more than Ted. Many of us thought he could be great for the network. We were going to get one of the legendary figures of journalism telling broader stories at our network. I was very excited about the possibility of working with Ted. It was right in my sweet spot of interest.

TED KOPPEL, Documentarian:

It was indeed Richard who tried to get me, and I thought everything had gone very, very well. Sheila seemed to be very sensitive about the whole thing, but we were going to be doing our programs and she would have been doing hers. She was very concerned that if we came to HBO, that would cut into her empire. Would it ultimately have cut into her budget? Honestly, I don't know. I assume HBO only had room for so many documentaries a year, and if we had come in and done some of them, that might very well have reduced the number that Sheila was going to do. I understood where she was coming from.

JON ALPERT:

Sheila was ranting and screaming and swearing on the phone to Richard Plepler at a decibel level that would have anybody else in jail for noise pollution. Then she found out where Dick Parsons was going to be for a charity dinner, bought a ticket, and did a nonstop diatribe with Parsons against Ted Koppel. After two weeks, Koppel threw in the towel and said, I'm never going to be able to work in that company. Sheila has burned down the forest. There's just nowhere for me to go.

TED KOPPEL:

It really wasn't worth the stress that we were going to cause. And no, of course she wouldn't have been working for us. Tom and I really didn't want to create that fuss to begin with. Sheila is a lovely woman, and I enjoy her a great deal.

SHEILA NEVINS:

I was at Canyon Ranch with my son, who was probably fourteen at the time. We are walking down the hall and lo and behold, Ted is coming in the other direction, and he called me a snake. I remember it so specifically because he said it in front of David. After he walked away, David said, "Why did that man call you that?" I said, "Well, it's a long story about a job." I just thought, "Fuck you, mister, I got you out." And whenever we would run into each other in the future, it was always cantankerous.

TED KOPPEL:

Sheila and I have met on many occasions since those discussions about my coming over. There's a good deal of ribbing that takes place in both directions. I think we have a very friendly relationship.

*Although better known early in his career for audacious and groundbreaking fiction films (*She's Gotta Have It, Do the Right Thing*), the audacious and truly independent Spike Lee in recent years gained even greater recognition for his nonfiction works, like the bio flick* Malcolm X; Inside Man; BlacKkKlansman, *based on the real story of an African American infiltrator of the notorious Klan; and such acclaimed documentaries as 1997's brilliant and heartbreaking* 4 Little Girls *for HBO, an account of the bombing murder on September 15, 1963, of four Black girls at the 16th*

Street Baptist Church in Birmingham, Alabama; and in 2006, again for HBO, **When the Levees Broke,** *about the devastation wrought by Hurricane Katrina.*

Levees, a four-hour account of what happened to New Orleans in August 2005 when the devastating storm ravaged the city, aired over two nights, a year after the hurricane hit.

Critics concurred: **When the Levees Broke** *garnered a Peabody Award, three Emmys, an NAACP Award, and a prize at the 63rd Venice International Film Festival.*

SPIKE LEE:

When I went to Sheila about Katrina, my original idea was a horrible one—to have different musicians from New Orleans perform their songs among the rubble of Katrina. Luckily Sheila said, "Can we do something else?" Thank you, Sheila Nevins.

JACKIE GLOVER:

Spike went down to New Orleans, gave me a call and said, "This is not just a one-off doc, this is an opera."

SHEILA NEVINS:

It was just too good. One of the most important we ever made. You couldn't tell the story in two hours. I didn't have to go running upstairs; didn't have to get on my hands and knees and beg. I just said, "Yes, make it four hours."

SPIKE LEE:

Sheila had opinions. She wouldn't just let you go and make what you wanted to make and not say anything. Sheila and I had our differences, but we had great respect for each other. There were several times I would go into her office, we would talk, and she would make me see whatever we were talking about in a different way. And I'd say, "You know what, Sheila, I'm going to go back to the editing room, and I'm going to try it." More times than not, what she suggested was better than my original thought.

JACKIE GLOVER:

I went down to New Orleans for the screening. It was intense. There was still a lot of devastation there. We drove around earlier in the day to the Lower Ninth Ward and got to see what people in the film had been experiencing and living through. The screening was at the Superdome. We wanted it to be for the community.

SPIKE LEE:

HBO gave me opportunities to grow as a filmmaker. My career as a film-maker has gone back and forth between my narrative and my documen-tary films. The documentaries help the narrative and the narrative helps the documentaries, because to me it's all storytelling.

HBO had LA offices, but all the people I dealt with I could see by taking the subway and getting off at Forty-second Street. I know the feature stuff lives in LA, but HBO was, for me, a New York company. No Hollywood shit for me.

HBO was a home to me, filled with good people who had great taste.

In May 2006, HBO released **Baghdad ER,** *a sixty-four-minute documentary directed by Jon Alpert and Matthew O'Neill and executive produced by Lee Grant and Sheila Nevins. Shot over two months in 2005 at the United States Army 86th Combat Support Hospital in the middle of the Iraq War, the film gives viewers a rare glimpse into the perils and pitfalls of a war zone. The directors told NPR that the mil-itary personnel they spoke with "want people to see their faces" in hopes of creating understanding of the situation on the ground that was so often reduced back home to passing headlines and antiseptic recitations of casualty statistics. The filmmakers' attempts at realism hit home; in anticipation of the film's release, the army surgeon general made headlines by cautioning service members and their loved ones that watching the documentary could induce traumatic flashbacks and other symptoms of post-traumatic stress.*

Baghdad ER *earned a Peabody Award and six Emmy nominations, winning for Exceptional Merit in Nonfiction Filmmaking, Directing, Cinematography, and Sound Editing.*

JON ALPERT:

I had been blacklisted by the networks. I was sitting on the curb, licking my wounds, when Sheila Nevins drove by and opened up her door. The fact that I had managed to do something that made me unwelcome in the land of starched shirts and rep ties was attractive to her.

SHEILA NEVINS:

At HBO, anything that was on the edge did well. Jon Alpert was in the ver-ité world, and he lived on the edge. He was a different filmmaker, a gifted troublemaker.

When Jon went to Baghdad, I said, "See what it's like in the green zone." He said, "I'm stuck in this hospital." I asked him, "Is there a story in the hospital?" He told me, "Yeah, guys without arms and legs. More than in any other war." I said, "Stay in the hospital. Follow those guys." I was proud I had that instinct to stick around.

JON ALPERT:

We got to a point where we're trying to avoid sending Sheila DVDs, because she would watch them incessantly. I don't want to exaggerate; I'm going to say between twenty and twenty-five times. There are three amputations in *Baghdad ER*. If you watch sixty amputations back-to-back, it's going to make you crazy.

I believe that everybody needed to experience the horror of war the way I experienced it. If they're going to amputate the arm, you're going to see that entire amputation.

LEE GRANT:

The last documentary that my husband and I produced for Sheila, *Baghdad ER*, was very raw. One of the soldiers they filmed died on camera. Sheila was so caring for the parents that she brought them down to see their son on film. It was a side of her I hadn't seen before.

SHEILA NEVINS:

It was very sad, very, very sad. I became friendly with the soldier's mother, because I had to show her the footage. I could not allow it to go on television without her knowing about it.

JON ALPERT:

There was an ending we believed had to be attached. A guy comes in and more or less the bottom part of his body had been blown off. They give him 250 units of blood to save his life.

His pregnant wife comes to see him, then she flies on the hospital plane home with him, with these racks of bodies, mostly dead people, holding his hand weeping. They are somehow able to keep him alive for another week, and then he died. They bring him out to the middle of America and have this incredible "America is great," ceremony, where Black, white, young, old, are all holding hands as they bury this hero. The little daughter throws the last rose inside the grave and wonders why Daddy had to die as they release a dove up in the air.

Sheila got that show on HBO. There is no better knife fighter than Sheila Nevins. When Richard Plepler came into the screening room, there were scenes that we knew he would be too squeamish to watch so we had a plan to distract him. I bumped him so he'd look away.

INDIVIDUATION

SARA BERNSTEIN, Executive:

On any given day at HBO docs back then, we would go from having lunch with Dennis Hof and talk about prostitution, to screening a film like *Born Rich* featuring Ivanka Trump, with kids pulling up in Maseratis, to a screening of a film like *Baghdad ER*, which would be a five-hour process where you're wrestling over whether you include graphic imagery of a soldier whose arm was blown off.

JON ALPERT:

We had a screening at the Pentagon. Part of the embed process is the military gets a last look so it can flag things for security. Bush's civilian secretary of the army goes back and tattletales to the White House that this is a pretty strong antiwar film. They called Plepler up. There was a telecommunications bill wending its way through Congress and they were very straight and said, "All we need to do is change a couple of words." And it's a big, big, multi-multimillion-dollar swing for HBO. I didn't want to take any chances. I want to believe that Richard would have done the right thing, but just in case, I leaked it to the *New York Times*. After that, we told them to go fuck themselves.

RORY KENNEDY:

Sheila taught me something on a number of my films, which is really thinking about how you open a film. I showed her rough cuts of *Abu Ghraib* and a film I did called *A Boy's Life*, and in both she took the most dramatic moment I had in each film and moved it to the open. I said, "What are you doing? There's no context for it, nobody's going to understand it." But it was absolutely the right thing to do in both of those films. It helps you understand why you are watching the film.

*Over the next decade, HBO would make some key documentaries to help bring women athletes into the spotlight. In 2005 they created **Dare to Dream: The Story of the U.S. Women's Soccer Team**, following the nineteen-year journey from a team no one knew in the 1980s to Olympic Gold Medal winners in 2004. Just a year later, in line with the Arthur Ashe documentary years prior, HBO made one honoring Billie Jean King as well: **Billie Jean King: Portrait of a Pioneer**.*

MARY CARILLO:

Margaret Grossi had been telling Ross for ten years, "We got to do a doc on Billie Jean." Ross would say, "We already did it when we did *The Struggle of Women in Sports.* She had a big part of that." But Margaret kept advocating, and she was the one who convinced Ross that Billie Jean deserved her own hour.

MARGARET GROSSI:

I worked on the Georgetown-Villanova doc, *Perfect Upset.* Jordan Kranis produced and I co-produced. That was the first time I had co-produced, and it was a rough production. After it was finished, I got called down to Ross's office to meet with him and thought, "Oh God—I'm fired. That's it. It was just too rough." I walked in there shaking, and the next thing I knew, Ross said, "How'd you like to produce the Billie Jean doc?" I almost fainted. My knees literally were knocking together.

I had decided I didn't want to use a narrator. I wanted Billie to tell her story. We used Errol Morris's technique of putting the interviewer behind the camera and using the teleprompter to reflect the image, so the interviewee was looking at the camera but also seeing the interviewer. Errol Morris called it the "Interrotron." We were able to legally use it because he hadn't patented it yet.

BILLIE JEAN KING:

Margaret had me sit in a chair and they had a wall up around the camera and Mary Carillo was sitting behind the wall. They didn't want me looking at anyone. They didn't want any distractions. I pretended I was talking to the audience. Mary could see where my brain was going and would adapt. Sometimes my brain goes too fast and I'm all over the place.

MARGARET GROSSI:

Billie wants so much to give you a good sound bite and she's done so much that you might ask, "How was that experience at 1975 Wimbledon?" And you might end up with 1990 in her answer. It took more than twenty hours of taping, and she had some tough stuff to cover, but we all hung in there and I think it turned out pretty well.

BILLIE JEAN KING:

When I was young, we all had our chores. Drying dishes was my chore with my mother after dinner. When I was seven, I had this feeling come over me and I looked at Mom and said, "I know I'm going to do something great with my life." And I was all excited.

She told me, "That's good, honey. But just keep drying those dishes." When I was nine, we used to go to baseball games a lot, but I got sick to my stomach and my heart dropped when I realized for the first time I could never play baseball professionally because I was a girl. That started a lot of thinking. My partner, Ilana, and I are now part of the ownership group with the LA Dodgers.

Margaret's first time out was *Portrait of a Pioneer*, and she won a Peabody. She got that her first time out. All of a sudden they go, "Whoa, we got a live one here." And with Mary Carillo and Helen Russell, the three of them are unbelievable together.

Documentaries continued to propel the sports division. Now Albrecht, while hardly the nation's number one sports fan, had one big fat idea for HBO Sports.

CHRIS ALBRECHT:

I wanted to make a deal with the UFC. It was Ari Emanuel's idea, and I thought it was perfect for premium. I was going to take one of the Cinemax 'plexes and turn it into the UFC Channel. I met with the Fertittas in London. Their deal was coming up with Spike, and we discussed us having their fights, pay-per-view, and all their reality content.

We had lost Wimbledon, and *Inside the NFL* was going to cost us a lot more money. *Real Sports* was a good show, but at some point, I thought, sports isn't our future unless we do something else big soon.

Ross fought me on it like crazy. Tooth and nail. He said, "This is going to fuck up all of our relationships. We're going to lose all our credibility with boxing, and boxing guys are going to feel like we betrayed them."

ROSS GREENBURG:

I didn't think it was a good fit for us at all, and what really got under Dana White's skin was that I kept battling him on whether the UFC would control the broadcasts. I told him we had to have our production personnel doing everything, and we would need to assign announcers. He would not give in on that, and that was a big part of what broke that deal up. At the end of the day, Chris could have forced me to do it, but that's not the way he worked. He did the opposite and backed me. Chris was a great manager.

ARI EMANUEL:

Ross Greenburg vetoed it, everybody vetoed it, but Chris wanted it, and I had a deal in place. Michael Lombardo was in business affairs at the time, and we were 95 percent done on a deal to do fights on their pay-per-view platform. And a week before closing, Chris winds up losing his job. Then Richard killed the deal because it was a Chris deal and he didn't think it was right for the "brand." If Chris didn't get fired, the UFC is on the air at HBO—and I never get to buy it. UFC is now probably the fifth sport in the country.

CHRIS ALBRECHT:

UFC could have really been something for HBO.

The shift away from sports began a couple of years before I left. There was a lot of pressure starting to come from Bill Nelson, who wanted to funnel as much money into series as possible. That meant we needed to cut back on sports. Richard was part of the "Why do we need sports?" movement.

My gut as a programmer was, let's just keep everything and add more, but Bill was my finance guy. That's when we let *Inside the NFL* go.

We let go of *Hard Knocks*. Boxing, which had become mostly a pay-per-view business, was something we weren't really making money on. I chose the middle ground: staying in but whittling away at our investment in sports.

Albrecht had another plan that would never see fruition: he proposed bringing the Emmy Awards ceremony to HBO. The basic networks, which had carried the ceremony, responded to the threat with a wagon-wheel deal wherein the ceremony rotated to a different network every year, and Albrecht's proposal got no further. This may have been a blessing for HBO, as their recent dominance at the Emmys would have lost visibility, given HBO's smaller audience, and would have meant the end of the free advertising that HBO was getting through the networks' coverage of said dominance.

ERIC KESSLER:

As we started exploring the role the Internet would play in the future of HBO, organizational frictions began to escalate. At that time, there were three groups working on essentially the same area. Chris, Moloshok and his team were off on the West Coast building a downloadable consumer product that would be sold to consumers. My group was responsible for subscriber acquisition and retention of the existing linear business, and we had a team looking at the role a digital product would play.

To help the subscriber acquisition group evaluate the road ahead, we brought in IDEO, a Silicon Valley product design/consulting firm. After about six months, they presented to the company their findings. Instead of a simple PowerPoint presentation, they built this elaborate walkthrough exhibit on the top floor of the HBO building. IDEO presented a vision of the future in which subscribers would watch HBO on a mobile device. Keep in mind, this was in the days of AOL, narrowband, and flip phones. It could take a full minute for a desktop computer to load a simple screen on a website. Their vision—which was way ahead of its time—didn't gain much traction internally, in part because they were viewed as outsiders who didn't understand HBO.

For many years, HBO had been proud to see itself as "the" premium subscription TV company. But in the aftermath of one pivotal 2005 meeting, the question became: Did HBO pass up the opportunity to be something more—a premium subscription **entertainment** company focused not just on the next best piece of content but the future of content distribution itself?

For as long as HBO had existed, it had enjoyed numerous benefits of a rare business model that enabled it to remain free of responsibilities that were givens for other subscription services. There were no HBO call centers filled with thousands of HBO sales team members selling directly to consumers over the phone. If you wanted HBO, you had to call Comcast, Spectrum, or your local cable provider. No picture? No sound? Well, don't call HBO, get back on the phone with your cable system. Missing your latest bill? HBO needn't worry. The cable companies are responsible. Not even those sometimes unsightly wires slithering into homes and apartment buildings were HBO's territory.

Of course, none of this was free to HBO nor to any other cable channel. The cable company would charge customers a rate but then deduct "carriage fees" that amounted to 40 or 50 percent before HBO got their money.

As a result, HBO operated at an ever-increasing distinct disadvantage. It had no direct link with, in a sense, its own customer. It had never been supplied with a single address or phone number for the consumer, never was allowed to collect any information about consumers or their preferences. The customers weren't really theirs, never the property of the cable channel. They were customers of whatever cable company that brought them HBO, so HBO never got to enjoy the benefits of all that data. HBO tried to understand what those customers wanted but had limited awareness of who they really were, even on a month-to-month basis.

For years, cable operators had fought HBO's efforts to gather information about subscribers, even just their names and addresses, much less more specific viewing data. The cable operators were dead set on preventing HBO from knowing who those subscribers were because they wanted to control HBO's customer marketing efforts.

Albrecht wanted to create a future for HBO that wasn't inextricably linked to the power of cable operators. He put together a technology team in Los Angeles with a sim-

ple mandate: unleash us from that dependency and build out new technologies that will transform HBO into a digital media player.

CHRIS ALBRECHT:

The big question about HBO in those days shouldn't have been, "Isn't it amazing we have thirty million subscribers?" It needed to be, "Why don't we have fifty million?" Forward thinking at the time was colloquial and timid. It was all about protecting the relationship with cable companies.

I brought in my tech team, and we were working on something called MyHBO because MySpace was a hot thing.

JOHN PENNEY, Executive:

That was the moment, that big meeting, when we had the opportunity to reinvent the culture of HBO toward innovation as a business, not just as a content provider.

Because of their incredible programming at the time and the aura of HBO, I thought they would be ahead in terms of growth strategy, but when I got there, I saw that they were either in line or behind.

Our team's Hippocratic oath in strategy and business development was "Do no harm to the business as it exists but extend it." That did not mean not being bold. And that was the word Chris Albrecht constantly used. We have to be bold, and in being bold, we have to understand what the risks are. Our approach was to try to embrace a future that we thought was coming, where the consumer and content would be more directly connected.

ERIC KESSLER:

At this point in time broadband penetration was miniscule, the iPhone would not be invented for a few years, and Netflix wasn't even talking about streaming.

CHRIS ALBRECHT:

Everybody on the inside was so nervous because they believed we were going to piss off the cable guys, but we thought at some point they were gonna have us over a barrel.

ERIC KESSLER:

The big concern was the group wanted to upend the business model of using traditional distributors—(i.e., cable satellite and telco)—and go directly to consumers.

There was a lot of internal discussion within the company over this approach.

JOHN PENNEY:

Technology groups at HBO were not empowered to drive change, and the people who fell under the distribution relationships were not enthused about trying to create a new future. When all you're expecting is a no or worse, and you're not an ideator or an innovator, you're never going to propose opportunities for partnering. If all you're expecting is a no, and we're going to crush your EBITDA, because of Comcast or others, you're playing for retirement like so many seemed to be doing. That was the context.

The problem was that, apart from original programming, they saw themselves as an old-core business, just a cable premium channel, as opposed to an innovator. The innovator mindset was a split brain at HBO. It only existed in one hemisphere. It often seemed to exclusively exist in the Albrecht West Coast hemisphere.

CARMI ZLOTNIK:

Why aren't we asking ourselves, "Why aren't we better?" The adherence to the status quo was stagnating the company. We should at least be more entrepreneurial and think about business development the same way that we look at creative development.

ERIC KESSLER:

Moloshok and his team were all based in LA with Chris; the business teams—who were responsible for delivering subscribers—were all in New York. Each week we would have thirty people on a video conference between New York and LA and as the possibility of launching this West Coast direct-to-consumer product gained traction, the tension between the different groups became palpable. Chris decided to bring Jeff in for a come-to-Jesus meeting to resolve the issue.

HBO's September 2005 meeting in New York—with Bewkes presiding in his new executive role—marked a face-off between the two coasts. Albrecht's LA gang consisted of Carmi Zlotnik, John Penney, and Jim Moloshok, and the New York group was headed up by marketing czar Eric Kessler.

Presenting for the LA group, Moloshok spoke for thirty minutes advocating an aggressive switch to a direct-to-consumer approach as part of the larger technology team's efforts to break the cable mold. This direct capability would allow HBO to bypass cable providers and go into business directly with their audience. They claimed subscriptions would come in by the thousands every hour, which their East Coast counterparts doubted.

The New Yorkers, meanwhile, were fearful, unwilling to stir a potential hornet's nest. They were wedded to the worldview that HBO's relationships with cable operators superseded any risky entries into direct-to-consumer dealings. Kessler, presenting after Moloshok on behalf of the East Coast group, suggested instead that they harness the power of Albrecht's refreshed capability for a new offering to be distributed through the existing affiliate network.

ERIC KESSLER:

Every key meeting at HBO usually had three parts—the meeting, the meeting before the meeting, and the meeting after the meeting. As the product that Moloshok was working on developed some momentum, Bill understood the negative impact it would have on our existing business, and he didn't want to be the guy who got the irate phone call from Brian Roberts telling him they were cutting off promotional support for HBO. So Bill started to work the ref, Jeff, before the meeting. So going in, we knew where Jeff was going to land, we just didn't know what explanation he would give to Chris.

In the meeting were Chris, Moloshok and his team, Jeff, Bill Nelson, me, and my team. Moloshok presented first and demonstrated the product and the business model.

CARMI ZLOTNIK:

The strategy we were advocating at the time was, These cable companies are not your friends, and if they can't bring us a certain type of consumer, then we should have the ability to go get them ourselves. We needed to have a carrot-and-stick approach to working with them. As long as we didn't have a distribution capability ourselves, any threats or stamping of our feet would just be false bravado.

ERIC KESSLER:

I presented the sales and marketing point of view. Did we think that someday we would eventually go direct-to-consumer? Of course, but we also knew we needed to maximize our profits while deploying different distribution strategies. We needed to let the technology and broadband market evolve to the point where the economics of going DTC were so compelling that we could absorb the hit that would come from a reduction in affiliate promotional support.

CARMI ZLOTNIK:

Eric and Bill Nelson wanted to do innovation through distributors because they believed once you started building broadband operations, the MSOs would see that as a challenge, then punish us.

JOHN MALONE:

Keep in mind, everything HBO would have done at that time to go direct-to-consumer would have damaged their current cable business.

ERIC KESSLER:

Jeff listened to both arguments. Jeff's easygoing, often irreverent style enabled him to disarm tension in the room. He had the ability to make everyone in a meeting feel good even if he was telling you "No." While Jeff liked the DTC idea and applauded Chris for the initiative, he believed it was not the right time. Jeff was a bottom-line business guy and he was not going to jeopardize our relationship with distributors.

I have to say Chris was fine with the decision, and I do give him tremendous credit for forward thinking. The next day, he called and said the Moloshok team would be reporting to me. Over time, numerous people were reassigned, and I consolidated product development under a consumer marketing group led by Courtney Monroe and Alison Moore.

CARMI ZLOTNIK:

That presentation in the boardroom showed the schism in the company between people who were leaning into the future, which was going to be largely based on broadband distribution, versus people who wanted to maintain the status quo, pay cable distribution by MSOs, and didn't want to upset the apple cart.

Chris treats his intuition like data and I think that that's the right way to do it. Too many people in our industry, especially when they come from a pure business mindset, try to think of data as only something that's empirical. I see lots of people continually wanting proof from data to validate their decisions, but the unique part about Chris and what I truly love about working with him is that he is willing to make decisions on his intuition and his gut. I think that's as valid a way of operating a business as any, probably even better. And it led to the golden age of television because he was a person who would make decisions that nobody else would make.

I was running business development and digital media at that time. That eventually became HBO Go. I didn't go to college. I didn't have an MBA. But it shows you the kind of person that Chris was in that he allowed somebody to come from a completely different outside discipline and run the business. And I'm sure a lot of those people were not happy with that, or with me in that regard, because I was stirring the pot. Pushing things in a different direction.

After the meeting, Bill Nelson said to me, "Could be a good idea, Carmi; could also be a career killer." My takeaway from that was we should just be thinking about our careers and the management of the company in terms of different timelines. There's the timeline that says, "I'm in my late fifties, sixties. I'm not going to be here that much longer. I want stability during this last period."

Bewkes's ruling in the case of **East Coast v. West Coast** *would have repercussions for many years to come.*

Innovation had always been key to HBO's success whether in satellite broadcasting; the creation of Cinemax, the first successful companion channel created by a major network; multiplexing; and, eventually, HBO On Demand.

Albrecht and his team were ahead of their time. Too ahead. Certainly direct-to-consumer was years off, and there wasn't enough broadband in existence to make their plan a reality. And it was, of course, easy to predict how the cable operators would react.

Bewkes made the right decision for the time. But the HBO culture had made this issue binary. As CEO, Albrecht should have insisted that he be allowed to not only keep but expand a forward-looking technology team in LA, one that, truth be told, didn't exist in New York (one West Coaster remarked, "New York's version of tech was buying an Apple product"). That team should have been Switzerland, free from politics and free to double down on thinking about potential acquisitions or joint partnerships in the near future.

JOHN PENNEY:

The biggest lost opportunity was to be the digital innovator across entertainment, to stake a claim in all manner of entertainment on demand and digitally delivered television games, audio content, music, and so much more. I've never seen a company so powerful in its cultural impact be so small in its revenue generation.

CHRIS ALBRECHT:

The argument that I failed on was we really needed to figure out how to distinguish ourselves in other ways, just like we had distinguished ourselves content-wise. But it was just too scary for some.

JOHN PENNEY:

There was no company in the United States that had a bigger cultural impact than HBO, with so little revenue and a desire not to double, triple, quadruple its size. There were no real plans for M & A, and there were no plans for growth.

There was the Jedi mind trick of confusing cultural significance with business and innovation significance. And it was a Jedi mind trick they played on themselves.

CHRIS ALBRECHT:

We could have figured something out. If all the minds had been working together, instead of just shutting it down, we would've gotten 30 percent there. There'd be no Netflix.

Penney and I had dinner with Reed [Hastings] and Ted a few years later, and they said, "Thank God you didn't do that back then because we would've had no defense." They also said, Thank God we didn't launch over the top, because they would have had no business. What a fundamental shift it would have been for Time Warner.

Albrecht's team would try one other plea. In September 2006, they asked Nelson, Kessler, Plepler, et al. to purchase another company revolutionizing entertainment space—Netflix.

The presentation began with a somber view of HBO's status. The company's "core multichannel subscription business is slowing." Bigger price tags for the network's productions, combined with its distributors possibly gaining leverage in dealings with HBO, would drive its margins down. Revenue growth had been slowing for years and was projected to sink further through 2010. Moreover, the presentation claimed that the "online consumer environment may erode preeminence of premium TV." In other words, the big fish in the small pond was moving into an even bigger pond with still more fish. Worse, some of those new fish were sharks and, as everybody knows, sharks are always hungry.

As the presentation pointed out, "premium TV rights could be at risk as big competitors seek real assets like Google, Yahoo!, and others." HBO was staring down a dogfight for premium content with competitors who would become some of the largest Internet companies in the world.

The presentation underlined that Netflix had "changed the way people watch movies by bringing movies directly to the consumer." It may have seemed unthinkable years earlier, but movie consumers who once trudged down to a store to "pick up something for the weekend" could now wait cozily at home until that increasingly iconic red envelope arrived with the next cinematic adventure lurking inside.

That promise of convenience, coupled with a detailed personalization database that tracked user activity by location, demographics, and movie selections, made Netflix the "#1 rated website for customer satisfaction for the last two years." Some 95 percent of Netflix's customers said they would recommend it to a friend. Netflix stock was selling in September 2006 for just $3.25 a share, but the company's revenue was already at nearly $1 billion.

Netflix understood that DVDs were just one type of technology and that like all technologies, this one would become obsolete. The company needed a long-term strategy beyond DVD rentals and sales before the next movie delivery system arrived, one that would make viewing even more convenient than it already was. The presentation noted that "Netflix is exploring other electronic distribution options, including a proprietary set-top box." For that reason, the acquisition was pitched as a "win-win opportunity" for both companies—Netflix would "deliver a new value proposition to HBO's current distributors" and "draw on expertise of all divisions to make [each] even more successful: HBO, Warner Bros., AOL, Time Inc., [and] Turner," while HBO would provide a new distribution path for Netflix.

JOHN PENNEY:

I made a presentation to the entire senior management team on Chris's suggestion: why HBO should buy Netflix to transform itself. This was before it was a digitally connected streaming company that understood its consumers. And the key was that if we had Netflix, the HBO holdbacks ahead could be exploited by a combined entity that had the number one distribution of home video product, Netflix, with a premium subscription company.

I made the presentation to the executive board of HBO. Carmi and Chris were there. About fifteen minutes in, the board said, "The idea's too risky." At the time, Netflix was a $1.4 billion market cap company!

CHRIS ALBRECHT:

I thought they were going to kill him for suggesting such heresy.

JOHN PENNEY:

Some thought the market was too small. Think the market was small? Starz did a deal with Netflix around their content because they thought the market was small and it would never blow up. They did a roughly $26 million deal when there were no Netflix subscribers. It blew up and Netflix was paying the equivalent of a dollar a sub a year, when Comcast was paying dollars a month. That's how flawed the argument was that it's too small a market. And by the way, if it were too small a market, then you should have gone to your cable partners initially and said, "Let's figure out how to do this together. It's just a small market, but it may be valuable to you going forward." Co-opt them.

JEFF BEWKES:

The idea that we could own the major over-the-top competitor to the cable operators, you could argue was a leverage play. It's also something where they could have started to kill hostages, like let's take Turner networks, throw them out of distribution. Let's not pay the rate increases. Let's take your weakest part and say fuck you. That's what would have happened.

We didn't have enough broadband to do it. And the reason Netflix could build its Trojan horse, its attack dog, with no interference, is they could go along under the radar for years with no profits. We couldn't do that.

First, I don't think Reed would have sold it. Second, Turner's 2x HBO, and we still had AOL at the time. If I'd gone out and bought Netflix, the company would have disappeared overnight. Our investors had just suffered $200 billion of write-downs for buying another Internet company with no earnings.

I always knew Netflix would do originals. I didn't care. The problem that we had with Netflix wasn't that they were putting up their original programming. I don't give a shit. Showtime does it. Starz does it.

After eighteen years in the trenches—a Harvard graduate with a degree in history and literature, she'd joined HBO's New York office in 1986 as a temp assistant, became vice president in 1994, and five years after that, senior vice president, original programming—Carolyn Strauss became president of HBO Entertainment in May 2005.

CAROLYN STRAUSS:

Growing up, I was honestly clueless about what I wanted to do. There was no family business, and I flopped around. I knew I didn't want to do finance, so I temped around New York after I graduated. There were some really horrible temp jobs. Then in February 1986, I got a temp job at HBO. I thought, Oh, this place isn't so bad. They're smart people. I like the energy here.

I got an assistant job there working for the woman in charge of

disseminating all the promotional information about the shows and programming, then I started to get a little bored, because I had horrible
computer skills, and I would be working all hours of the night, handwriting names onto memos. When I was doing that, I would listen to
comedy shows or concerts, and the woman who was in charge of that,
Betty Bitterman, also worked late and would sometimes come in and talk
to me. Right around this time I thought, "I want to leave," but she offered
me an assistant manager job in her area. It was a little step up, but I
knew nothing about comedy. It was the height of the comedy boom, and
I would go out to all the comedy clubs in New York. For someone who
was maybe twenty-four, not making that much money, to be able to take
my friends to the clubs was a huge amount of fun. I learned a lot working
with Betty and then Stu Smiley, and then I started to come out to LA a
lot to see comedy shows out here. There were a lot of shows people in LA
didn't want to work on, so I would say, "I'll do it." That's when I came into
Chris's orbit and he arranged for me to come to LA. He said, "Just watch.
You'll get it." Chris was very encouraging and a fantastic boss.

CHRIS ALBRECHT:
Carolyn and I rarely saw things differently.

The stunning trifecta of **Sex and the City,** **The Sopranos,** *and* **Curb Your Enthusiasm,** *followed by* **Six Feet Under** *and* **Deadwood,** *ensured that there would be no
competition for the spot. Strauss was involved in all of them, and it's fair to say they
wouldn't have seen the light of production if Strauss had argued strongly against any
of them.*
    *Programming's decision-making process was as clear as cut glass. Strauss could buy
whatever scripts she wanted and make the pilots she wanted. Orders-to-series were
done in conjunction with Albrecht. Except for the title (and salary), nothing much was
new here. Albrecht and Strauss combined made for a model in collaborative clarity.*

CAROLYN STRAUSS:
I hated saying no to people, and I probably wasn't great at it. I know a lot
of people found it really difficult to pitch to me because I could be reticent.
I rarely gave my opinion in the room and was difficult to read at times.
But oftentimes, I didn't want to raise expectations and then not be able to
deliver. I probably erred too much on that, putting more stake in being
unreadable as opposed to making it a pleasant experience.
    There were certain people who would get blotchy on their neck when

they pitched, and I understood that. If I had to go pitch to people, I'd be really nervous. I have my own sense of unworthiness. I have to take beta blockers when I speak in public.

KERI PUTNAM:

Carolyn doesn't give good show. She can be shy sometimes. She sometimes doesn't appear to play the game in quite the right way. But she was the visionary.

She had a little bit of self-protectiveness; she didn't want to believe in her own press too much. So the shyness almost got worse in a certain way. But looking back: every single show, she was Chris's secret weapon.

CAROLYN STRAUSS:

Most of the time you can tell by a first draft if something's going to be good, because at least if things are wrong, there's a voice, there's a texture to it. When a first draft felt really off, it was usually because it didn't have a voice, it didn't have whatever crackle was needed to deliver on the promise.

In the later part of my career when I understood that more, I would say to people, "I feel like this is a long shot, but I have notes if you want to address them." I would give people the option. But the more steps you go through with an artist, the more invested they are with it, and I didn't want to waste their time if we weren't going to be able to push it over the finish line. Every step requires more investment and becomes more heartbreaking as you go forward.

GINA BALIAN:

Carolyn taught me what matters. If you looked at her script where she would write notes, it wasn't dense. If you could fix one or two major ideas, everything else would come together. She taught us to focus on big things. That is part of what made HBO different.

AMY GRAVITT, Executive:

I would sit with Carolyn as a younger exec, and, oh man, she would give a note that would just crack a script wide open and I would sit and wonder how she came up with it. I had the feeling of, "Am I ever going to be able to do what she does?" When you sit and listen to that over a period of time in your apprenticeship years, you learn how to listen. You learn how to talk to creatives. Carolyn set the bar for me.

Albrecht and Strauss, the dauntless duo, faced first real competition in programming from Showtime where one former HBOer and one would-be HBOer were heatedly attempting to slow down the HBO juggernaut.

BOB GREENBLATT:

When I went to Showtime in 2003, HBO started to turn against me. I didn't leave *Six Feet Under* because I had a contract where I was locked for life as an executive producer, but they tried to terminate my deal. I still attended table readings with a smile. They were saying that Showtime was the enemy and they were essentially at war with me. Back then, they were the feudal lords.

MATT BLANK:

It wasn't until 2003 or so that people started to view Showtime as special in its own right because of shows like *Dexter, Weeds, Nurse Jackie.* The great thing about premium cable is we didn't have to fight for ratings. We didn't have to win Tuesday night at nine p.m., so we would just declare victory. We'd launch a show and declare victory. We'd renew a show and declare victory. Moves I learned from HBO!

In 2002, **Mad Men** *creator Matt Weiner sent the show's pilot script that he'd started writing a full three years earlier to David Chase as part of Weiner's bid to join Chase's writing team. Chase, impressed, hired Weiner on to* **The Sopranos.** *From there, the idea that HBO simply passed on* **Mad Men** *signified that the channel's relationship with David Chase was crucial enough that in 2005, when the chance to buy* **Mad Men** *came up, HBO network bosses didn't want to risk upsetting Chase by stealing Matt Weiner away from him. The idea that Chase could executive produce the show for HBO was a nonstarter, too, given that by 2005 or 2006 Chase wanted to "move away from weekly television."*

But there was another explanation: Weiner was seen as being so difficult to work with by several key members from programming—"a gigantic pain in the ass," in fact—that none of them wanted to be working with him on his own show, least of all on a dubious gamble like a period piece set in New York, then considered a tough sell at best. Certain HBO executives still claim that they did want the show; others said they just didn't personally respond to the script. All told, there were enough red flags for HBO to reasonably pass on Don Draper et al., and pass they did, thereby handing AMC its unlikely entry into the TV Hall of Fame.

CHRIS ALBRECHT:

There are so many bullshit stories about *Mad Men* at HBO.

MATTHEW WEINER, Writer and Executive Producer:

I wrote the *Mad Men* pilot in 1999, right when *The Sopranos* came on the air. When I finished it, I gave it to my agents, who didn't read it for some time, then after a while my manager forced my agent to give the script to David Chase. He read it, called me, and five days later I went to LA for a day and he hired me. I never went through HBO and I never went through Brillstein. I was never vetted. I never met the executives. So that was already an affront to the system. I was happy because I had worked for Brillstein-Grey on a show where I'd had a rather unpleasant experience and was not looking forward to meeting with them. The person running the company was not a fan. But now I was hired and now I had to survive.

I had been on a sitcom for seven years when I got my job on *The Sopranos*. Someone asked me, "What's the difference between your old job and *The Sopranos*?" I said, "It's exactly the same. I sit in a room with a bunch of writers talking all day about *The Sopranos*."

DAVID CHASE:

He had used that pilot script as a writing sample and that's why I hired him. He'd written it years before and I thought it was great. He asked me, Would you want to direct it? You can direct it if you want." I said, "No, thank you. I have enough of TV, I got to get into movies." But I did tell him I would send it to HBO.

CAROLYN STRAUSS:

Matt Weiner's wife was my freshman-year roommate, but I didn't really know him until he worked on *Sopranos*.

MATTHEW WEINER:

Carolyn and my ex-wife, Linda, were freshman roommates at Harvard. Not friends, by the way, they were not friends at all. They were in a quad; they didn't pick each other. I had met Carolyn in Los Angeles at least once. Our kids went to the same school, but I did not have any positive social interaction with her. I think I was always like Linda's loser screenwriter husband to her.

David gave the script to HBO, right when I got there, and said, "This is the show that should be on after *The Sopranos*, and it was rejected maybe six times by HBO. When AMC was getting ready to buy it, I told David and said, "Should I tell HBO?" I would have sold this to HBO for $1,000 just to have something in development there.

DAVID CHASE:

No one understands it. I don't know that Chris ever read it. I mean, here's the showrunner, the creator of the biggest thing that's happened to the network, saying, "I vouch for this." Oh, Carolyn did call me and asked, "Would you be involved with it?" I said, "No."

MATTHEW WEINER:

The first time it went in at HBO, it went to the comedy people. No one was interested. I never even got a meeting. The second time it went in, this is all before David ever saw it, I was told that they were not doing period pieces, which they then followed up with *Carnivàle*, *Rome*, and *Deadwood*. I started to realize, Matthew, this is a life lesson. Do not take people at their word when they reject you. What's the *Sex and the City* thing, "He's just not that into you"? Just accept it.

CAROLYN STRAUSS:

I did not personally respond to the script nor did several other people with us at the time. There were a couple of us involved in that decision.

CHRIS ALBRECHT:

Put aside for a minute that Matt's idea was a period piece that was set in New York and we were getting a lot of criticism for period pieces and shows set in New York. Carolyn and I were not going to be the people who took Matt Weiner away from David Chase. I would go out to coffee or drinks with David and Denise, and Matt would come along. David was definitely relying on him a lot. We weren't thinking, "Let's get writers from other shows to make new ones." That was not who we were. Carolyn and I were always a little bit suspicious of David's magnanimous attitude. Chase said, "I want everything good for Matt," but I would not have wanted to test it. If there were any issues on David's show, David would've said, "Well, you took my fucking guy from me."

TERENCE WINTER:

In between seasons of *Sopranos* when I was on my development deal, I would get a meeting with Carolyn Strauss, who was at the time running things over there, and I would pitch her a couple of ideas. She would be halfheartedly interested and I would go home and work on it and pitch her again. I finally talked to my agent and he said, "Dummy, you could come in with the greatest idea in the world, but they're not going to call David Chase and tell him that they're taking you off *The Sopranos* to do a different show.

Don't bang your head against the wall trying to come up with anything new. All they want you for right now is *The Sopranos*. Relax, wait until the show's over, then they'll talk about what you might do for them."

CHRIS ALBRECHT:

By the way, there was no chance that Richard made a big stink about *Mad Men*. I never heard a word. So it's not true he was some crusader for *Mad Men* and Carolyn and I shot him down. That is a total bullshit story.

I doubt he ever read the script at that point. Whatever Richard's story is, it's not the truth. It was unfair that Richard blamed Carolyn. It was both of us. We both agreed we weren't going to make it.

MATTHEW WEINER:

David once said to me, "If you had done it at HBO, of course it would have had to be much more carnal," and this was at a time when I was becoming aware of the strange restrictions at AMC. You could say "Jesus," and you could say "Christ," but you couldn't say "Jesus Christ," unless he's right there. You can say shit, but only three times in a script—all of this was dictated.

I always said that in *Mad Men*, the sex was the violence in terms of what was getting people interested in it. I also liked that I couldn't fully tell the story of the subversion coming to the top, the language getting coarser, society getting rougher as the 1960s went on, and social gentility sort of disintegrating. I had to imply it, which I felt was so much dirtier. I thought *Mad Men* was very salacious in its own way.

AMC was definitely trying to be HBO content-wise. The restrictions of AMC were very limiting in many ways, and I had many arguments about certain censorship issues that I never would have had with HBO. But the other side of that was at HBO, I would have been compelled to provide a certain level of titillation for people who were paying to watch the show. I was glad to not have that.

CAROLYN STRAUSS:

I was very conscious of the fact that my decisions and my decisions with Chris affected people on huge levels. I was in the business of breaking many people's hearts, 90 percent of who were good people and cared so much. They had a lot of passion for their ideas. If we decided to develop a script then we passed on it, or when we decide to shoot a pilot and then passed on it, that would obviously be difficult for those people.

The one I really wanted but we passed on was *Breaking Bad*. I was working with Miranda Heller and we both loved the script. It was great, but it was at a time when we were getting hounded internally by people in marketing and elsewhere that our shows were too dark. We thought, "We're never going to be able to sell this internally." I do wish we had pushed forward and tried to make it happen. *Breaking Bad* is one of my favorite shows. It's beautiful. Phenomenal.

RICHARD PARSONS:

When we missed on *Mad Men*, that seemed to me the beginning of the breaking of the dam. Then we lost *The Walking Dead* and *Breaking Bad*. I think missing *Mad Men* was a point of inflection in terms of the premium channel business.

On September 15, 2002, the fourth season of **The Sopranos** *debuted, drawing in 13.4 million viewers, the most in HBO history.*

CARMI ZLOTNIK:

During *The Sopranos*, we would spend every other week in New York when Chris was the CEO. Our usual thing was to fly in on a Sunday, land, go get a steak at Del Frisco's. It was like a ghost town. We asked the maître d', "Why is the place dead?" He said, "*Sopranos*. Everybody's at home watching it." And that's when we knew like, Holy shit, we've really affected the culture.

MICHAEL IMPERIOLI:

On season four, episode one, you see Christopher shooting heroin into his feet, between his toes. Then Tony takes him to where the cop who killed his father is having his retirement party, basically telling Christopher, You should do a revenge hit. It's cool because you have the layer of Christopher's first scare thinking maybe Tony's gonna set him up to be killed because the two of them are having a lot of tension.

So the stakes for Christopher are really high. He's plotting this murder, so you have all these ingredients, states of mind, memory, regrets, states of revenge being this mob guy. To have that complexity and different layers of things going on, both on a physical, mental, and emotional level, it's gold for an actor.

LORRAINE BRACCO:

When David and I talked about Dr. Melfi, I told him I did not want to play Melfi if she was going to be a psychotic sex killer. So Dr. Melfi and Tony were never going to be together. I have been in therapy and I know the benefits. I didn't want to poo-poo therapy and instead wanted the concept to be very serious. I received an award from the Western Regional Psychoanalytic Association, and what they told me was that *The Sopranos* helped more men become involved in therapy.

DAVID CHASE:

The show was so hot that I couldn't lose. By season three, I was saying to myself, "Maybe you should get out of here and try to do a movie now." Now these fucking studios will let you direct a movie of your own script. But it was just too much fun. I began to realize I had the best job in Hollywood. Not one of the best jobs, the best job. The money was really good. The creativity was amazing. Having people start to write about *Sopranos* like, "Only Tony Soprano could do such a thing." "Soprano" became part of the English language.

When we began, my goal was to make a movie every week. I was opposed to a season-long arc because I wanted to make a separate movie every week. The goal was to make each episode an independent little gangster film that didn't depend on the episode before or after. At first, I didn't want to be bothered with all these soap opera elements. But I came to embrace them. I came very quickly to enjoy doing that rather than looking at it as a burden.

TERENCE WINTER:

The vibe on set was very relaxed, friendly, lots of laughs. People would bring their families, and everybody was super gracious. The cliché about a lot of shows is that "Oh, it's one big happy family, and the truth is people hate each other." The truth is it was one big happy family. There was no vibe, no Hollywood bullshit, no egos. Not to say it wasn't hard or that people didn't fight. They did. But it was a really happy set.

DAVID CHASE:

"University" was one of the best hours of television ever created. Terence Winter wrote that story and doesn't get enough credit for it.

TERENCE WINTER:

Everything went through David. There wasn't a decision made on that show that wasn't his.

ILENE LANDRESS:

A lot of people loved the show because you can argue with your next-door neighbor, but you can't whack them. Tony Soprano could have somebody whacked. But when we whacked the marriage at the end of season four, which at the time was very unpopular, it was so real, it hit too close to home for some, and wasn't cathartic for some of the audience. It was unpopular.

TERENCE WINTER:

There was a big point at which David was exhausted at the end of season five and really wasn't sure if he wanted to continue, he just didn't see a way forward, creatively. David started one meeting by saying, "I think we're done. I don't want to do this anymore. I'm tired. I don't see a future here." I went on a filibuster that was like the end of *Mr. Smith Goes to Washington*. I was not going to stop talking until he agreed to keep going. Finally I said, "Look, if you're tired, just take a huge break. Just take a year off. People go ten years between *Star Wars*. You're not going to lose anybody." I said, "Actually if you take that long of a period of time off, we come back, who knows where these characters are in a year. Meadow's out of high school, learning in college. Janet can have a baby." "Whose baby?" "I don't even know. We can do anything." And he went, "That's interesting." And then, "This could happen. And Christopher could have a mustache and we don't even know why." All these ridiculous things.

By the end of the meeting, he said, "I'm telling HBO, I need to take nine months to relax, and then think about it." And when I walked out of there. I was like, "Oh my God, we were this close to ending the show."

From that point on, **The Sopranos** *didn't always have a new season ready on schedule every year. Sometimes it took eighteen months. The commercial networks never had a series "rest" for more than a year. But HBO did. And guess what? The audience only got bigger.*

ILENE LANDRESS:

David never wanted to do it if it wasn't going to be great. He didn't want anybody to ever say, "Remember *The Sopranos* when it used to be good?" He always wanted to go out on a high note.

MATTHEW WEINER:

I was terrified. I had an outline that was very spare, had some dialogue in it, and required a lot of writing. It really required seeing the story, putting it together, introducing a character. My first one was Steve Buscemi's first episode.

STEVE BUSCEMI:

I was a big fan of the show. I was lucky enough to start directing in the third season, then when they asked me to play a character, it was a dream come true. I loved the writing on the show and the directors, Tim Van Patten, John Patterson, Allen Coulter. And then to work with that cast, from Jimmy Gandolfini on down. Some of them I knew, like Michael Imperioli, and I knew Edie a little bit. I had actually directed Edie on *Oz*. That was my first HBO experience.

MATTHEW WEINER:

I love Steve Buscemi, he was wonderful. He was so funny and him and Jim together were immediately like spaghetti and meatballs.

The Museum of Television and Radio conducted a panel discussion on March 28, 2007, called simply "The Whacked Sopranos." Moderated by Bryant Gumbel, the conversation saw both the show's writers and killed-off cast members discussing their characters' fates.

CHRIS SPADACCINI:

Sunday had been a wasteland and HBO really put it on the map as an appointment viewing destination. We came up with a simple campaign, which was "Sunday is HBO." And we just drilled that message home We actually shot this amazing campaign at the Golden Globes party one year. It was just "caught moments" of our talent at tables, interacting and having fun. Then we decided to promote the idea of HBO as social currency, with the HBO watercooler ad in 2004. It was told from the point of view of a fictitious Watercooler Association of America that was making the comment that until HBO's Sunday night programming, watercooler sales in the country were plummeting. The idea was as people watch more HBO, on Monday morning, they were consuming more water because that's where people were coming together to talk about HBO. It was a very smart, irreverent campaign that was indicative of the brand of HBO, which always boasts superiority, but does it in a very underhanded way.

Season two of The Wire *premiered on June 1, 2003, and, as before, writer-creator David Simon had devised a central theme that would run through the season's narrative.*

DAVID SIMON:

The second season, we wanted to do the death of the working class, because it's an important component in the making of a permanent underclass. We wanted to do the death of work itself. So how do you take source material that is like William Julius Wilson at Harvard and make that into a narrative? There is no narrative. It's sociopolitical critique.

MICHAEL K. WILLIAMS:

Season two came and they made me a series regular, offered me a contract, and I was asked to move to Baltimore. I lost my natural mind.

I came from the projects.

But when David introduced the docks, I wasn't on set as much as I was on season one, and I started to panic. I'd be like, Oh God, no, the show is going down the toilet. I would say to David, "Stick with the formula, dude. You've got a good thing. Who cares about these docks, these white people?" And he would just laugh at me and say, "Michael, be patient, trust me. I got you. If I were to go back right back to that same world, it would make your world look so small." I was clueless to what he was building. I didn't see it. I wanted it to be Omar on *The Wire*. That's all I cared about. It wasn't until season three that I started to look at what David was really doing. It wasn't a Black thing, it wasn't a white thing, it wasn't a Baltimore thing. It was a socially charged thing. It was an American thing.

CHRIS ALBRECHT:

The only reason we picked up *The Wire* every year was because David would write these insane letters and Carolyn and I didn't want to read them anymore. It wasn't worth it to tell David he wasn't coming back.

NINA NOBLE:

David is very captivating. You can imagine him going into HBO to sell *The Wire* every year, which we had to do. He had to pitch a new season every year.

CAROLYN STRAUSS:

The Wire was on the ropes every year. It didn't get a lot of viewers, and we were trying to juggle other demands, so after every season, we thought about taking that money and using it elsewhere. But every year, the quality of the story made Chris and I turn to each other and say, "We have to do this again."

NINA NOBLE:

The Wire was a relatively inexpensive show. We were in Baltimore, we were dealing with pretty much unknown actors. Our locations were less expensive, sets less expensive. I think part of the reason *The Wire* stayed on the air for so long, even though it was never a hit when we were airing, is we said it was going to be whatever budget we locked with HBO, and that was the number it was or less.

DAVID SIMON:

They were going to cancel the show, and Chris let me come to his office. Carolyn Strauss said to me, "Go in there and argue." She wasn't hopeful, but she also didn't say it's hopeless. Chris Albrecht went into that meeting listening. That's all I can say. He let me dance.

Chris and Carolyn were a two-headed god. You had to convince Carolyn and then Carolyn had to convince Chris and that was it. There was no focus group. It was so seat of the pants, it was beautiful.

CHRIS ALBRECHT:

Season three was over and Stringer was dead, and it was satisfying. It wasn't getting a huge audience, but there were people who were now writing about the show like, "This is fucking great." I said, "Hey David, you won. Let's go on to the next thing."

DAVID SIMON:

I said, "I can really turn the corner on this if you let me do education and the media. It'll be a full critique of why we can't solve our problems. Please let me do this."

CHRIS ALBRECHT:

He came in and had this vision to look at the decay of the American city. He basically pitched season four and season five. At that time, Carolyn and I both realized that if we did four than we would do five, because there was no end at four. There was an end right now, Stringer is dead, there was some satisfaction, but not from a whole piece point of view.

DAVID SIMON:

At the end he said, "All right, we'll keep going." And when I walked out of there, Carolyn looked at me and went, "You're good." And I looked at her. She went, "You were canceled." And I was like, "Really? Dead canceled?" And she said, "Pretty much." It was the most amused I've ever seen Carolyn Strauss. That's saying something. She's very dry.

MIKE LOMBARDO:

I'm not gonna blow smoke up Chris's ass, but there's no reason why *The Wire* should have stayed on. The ratings weren't great, and I can't think of one nomination. David comes in the room and he pitches why it's imperative we let him finish. What I saw Chris do was listen and have his mind changed. I learned that from Chris Albrecht, that's what you need to do: listen. And by the way, he was fucking right. Five years later, every writer I meet comes in and says, "My favorite show is *The Wire*," and you want to say, "Where the fuck were you when it was on the air?"

CHRIS ALBRECHT:

With Chase, we were trying to talk him into doing more, and he did not want to do a show on regular cycles. When we picked up *The Wire*, it, too, was never on regular cycles. We kept making the rules up for ourselves. "We will put it on when it is ready," or, "We will put *Curb* on when Larry's ready." I used to say to people, "The only rules at HBO are that there are no rules." We didn't make things and not put them on. We hardly seriously developed things we didn't make. We were in a zone. None of this would have happened at a network.

DOMINIC WEST:

I knew HBO from its boxing history, but at that time, *Sopranos* had just come out, which I hadn't seen. So I was sort of blissfully ignorant that David was revolutionizing the way people were watching telly, and the way writers were writing television. Carolyn Strauss was particularly laser sharp and was a formidable authority of taste and intellect. I really appreciated that she was also extremely sympathetic and listened to my complaining with good grace. I found HBO nothing but extraordinary.

MICHAEL K. WILLIAMS:

I got a message that Donnie Andrews, who Omar was largely based on, was coming to see me. He was getting released from prison and was coming straight from the pen to the set. I almost pissed in my pants. I was longing to seek his approval for my portrayal. I was excited and nervous at the same time. They just kept telling me what a beautiful human being he was, but I also knew what he was in prison for. I said to myself, "Michael, don't ask him no stupid questions."

He comes to my trailer, we introduce ourselves, and of course the first thing I ask him is, "So how many people did you kill?" I thought to myself,

"God, Michael." He looked at me, paused, then put his head down and chuckled. "Well, Michael, I could tell you, but then I'd have to kill you." We looked at each other and oddly enough, that was the icebreaker that I needed. He became my big brother.

It's no secret that I struggled with addiction. I'm in recovery, and it had gotten to a point where the darkness and the gravity of the storytelling that David was doing was starting to affect me on a personal level.

And unfortunately, relapse is part of my story while shooting *The Wire*. Thank God for the amazing team and the producers and my castmates, especially people like Wendell Pierce, who would come and hold my hand and make sure I didn't slip between the cracks. One day I showed up to work two hours late because of my addiction, and I created this big lie as to why I was late. It was one of the lowest points personally for me on the set of *The Wire*.

I reopened my Pandora's box. When I was down there in Baltimore shooting *The Wire*, I fell in love with that city so much, and the amount of love that I got from the people in the community was overwhelming for me. I come from a past where I got ridiculed a lot, whether it was for my dark skin, or being awkward, or being soft. I was the butt of a lot of jokes growing up.

Now all of a sudden, the same caliber of people that had made fun of me welcomed me with open arms. I thought when people said, "Yo, Omar, we love you, man," I thought they were talking to me. I had to remind myself that they don't know me. I stopped my process when I booked this show. I thought that *The Wire* would make all of my problems go away. I stopped getting to know Michael.

When I got to Baltimore, I plugged into everything that city had to offer except my personal program that kept my spirit correct. I thought that the job would fix my inner issues, but all that job did was shine a light on them.

In the series finale of **Six Feet Under**, *one of the most successful dramas ever to hum along HBO airwaves, the subjects of death and dying remained bravely front and center, as they had for the previous four seasons. The episode's closing montage, which foresaw the deaths of several main characters, became so iconic that it provoked a parody on* **The Simpsons**. *The finale also earned five Emmy nominations, winning for Outstanding Prosthetic Makeup for a Series, Miniseries, Movie or a Special for the age makeup employed in the closing sequence.*

In the years since, **Six Feet Under***'s final episode has become one of the benchmarks by which all other final episodes are judged, widely considered among the best of all time. A haunting song by Sia didn't hurt.*

ALAN BALL:

I gathered the writers for season five. We all knew it was going to be the last season. The show had run its course. We started with the ending of the season and then figured out how to work toward that. I got to work with some really fantastic writers on *Six Feet Under*, and I wish I could remember who it was in the room who suggested that we be with every character at the moment of their death. It certainly wasn't me. When I heard that, I thought, Well, how else would you end this show?

MICHAEL C. HALL:

The day we shot the burial scene for Nate's body, Peter showed up on set that day and hid behind trees taking photographs. There was something just so beautiful about his playful presence while we were grieving the death of his character. He showed up in the form of Nate's ghost.

Sex and the City *and Little Old New York prevailed as the proverbial "perfect couple" for many years; in many ways, Manhattan was the show's fifth character, despite the show's conspicuous lack of ethnic diversity, and now decision time was unavoidably imminent.*

DAVID FRANKEL:

By the sixth season, Sarah Jessica had a baby and the hours were definitely more limited. I was working with Baryshnikov and we were shooting down in Chelsea, and Michael Patrick had very specifically written a scene where he runs and leaps over a pile of garbage. We set up the shot, and he leaped over the garbage. It wasn't exactly perfect, so I said, "Can we do one more?"

He said, "I can do one more and then my knees will go." Once we were up in the East Eighties, somewhere off Madison Avenue, at about one in the morning, and Sarah Jessica came to me and said, "Look," and we looked up from shooting in the street and Woody Allen and Soon-Yi were on their balcony in their pajamas and robes watching us.

JOHN MELFI:

I went to Paris during a break in between seasons and was sitting in Notre Dame, thinking about my folks who just passed away. Suddenly I was thinking about Carrie and thought, "What if Carrie and Misha go to Paris?" Pitched it to Michael. And he figured out, he worked around that idea and because he wanted to go somewhere with those characters, to take them out of the city. And then of course have the city as the fifth character be part of the ending. She goes back to New York, which was also one of the characters so that's one of the most evocative things of the show that New York was the fifth character.

We took a vote to do season eight or to do the movie. I remember quite clearly Sarah covering her eyes with her hand and raising her hand about doing the movie. Michael and I raised our hands to do the movie because we felt like it was time to do the movie, not do a season eight. And Carolyn raised her hand to continue into season eight. I remember that moment so clearly because it was definitely the end of the series.

So after the finale, we ended up doing a sale and we sold all the clothes. We dismantled the set. We pulled everything. That was the end of *Sex and the City*. Michael and myself and some friends rented a place in Tuscany, and we took off for a couple of weeks.

MICHAEL PATRICK KING:

Would Carrie have gone with Big if he chose her right away? No! If she had, she wouldn't have become the person she is. The very last line after six years that I wrote in the series is the most important evolution to me for all the characters, but especially for the audience. I cared so much about the audience, and the line is, "The real love affair is the one you have with yourself, and if you find somebody else who loves you, well that's just fabulous." I didn't want to do six years of waving the individual outsider banner for everyone watching the show who related to these women and then say, "It's a happy ending because a man loves you." It isn't. It's a happy ending because you love you, and then maybe somebody else will love you. That's my particular evolution in life, too.

I left everything on the floor. I was writing the last scene and I realized, "I'm going to name him. I'm going to say Mr. Big's name right now." It came into my head as I was writing that last phone call. His name comes up on the phone. You see the word "John." When I handed that script to the other writers they were like, "Wow!" and it just worked. His name is John, because now he said, "I love you. You're the one."

CYNTHIA NIXON:

It was such a great show of its time, but even at the time there were a lot of things that I was very aware of and very bothered by, like how incredibly white our show was. The consumer aspect of the show was always tough for me. The shopping and the shoes, and certainly the fashion was delightful eye candy. But when Big builds her that closet, when I saw that with an audience for the first time and the whole audience applauded, it was really hard for me, the idea that a closet for her clothes was this ultimate expression of a man's love for a woman, was really hard for me.

So I kept saying no to the reboot. Then I asked, "Is it going to change five percent, or is it going to change fifty percent?" And Michael and Sarah were amazing. They kept listening to me and saying, "It will have this, and it will have this," and, knock on wood, I think that's what we got. I'm very hopeful. When we did the first read through for the reboot, it was honestly one of the most exciting moments in my forty-plus-year career, not just to be back together again and seeing all those folks and seeing the new folks, but because the scripts were so strong.

SARAH JESSICA PARKER:

I loved acting Carrie. When I recall all that I got to do, there was some really painful stuff, wonderfully funny stuff, and truthful stuff about how much of a mess she was and how disappointing she was to people and how hard she tried to be a good friend. I got to play all of it.

Television showed me, in very bright colors, what it could be for an actor. To have a life that keeps unfolding in front of you. I learned that television deserves long hours and dedication, that details matter, and that you've got to be willing to cross the finish line bloody and barely standing. It's all worth it.

As the four young women of **Sex and the City** *prepared for their departure, a corresponding quartet of new male characters was getting ready to take center stage on HBO, with a certain fifth personality who initially wasn't considered a significant part of the show becoming a vital ingredient in it.*

As created by Doug Ellin and loosely based on rapper Mark Wahlberg's efforts to make it in Hollywood, **Entourage** *revealed the vagaries of the movie business, with all its meetings about meetings and hangers-on and attempts to make it bigger than anyone else, even your friends or relatives. The Wahlberg-ish central character, Vincent Chase (geddit?), was played by curly-haired cutie-pie Adrian Grenier, and his crew featured a best friend, Kevin Connolly; a half brother, Kevin Dillon; a driver, Jerry Ferrara; and Ari, his manager, based on real-life super-agent Ari Emanuel and played with moderately malevolent glee by Jeremy Piven. Rounding out the cast for most of the episodes were real-life superstars playing themselves, whether it was ScarJo, Tom Brady, or Eminem.*

DOUG ELLIN, Creator:

Steve Levinson (Lev) was my friend from college, and was my manager, and Mark Wahlberg's manager. I had done this movie called *Kissing a Fool* that was an independent movie that cost about a million five. I was a hot comedy guy for half a minute before this movie was released. And then it was released by Universal as if it were a studio film when it was a completely independently financed film and it made about $2.5 million opening weekend and I was dead. I might as well have made *Titanic* and had it gross $50. I was a pariah, after getting all these offers before the movie came out. I legitimately went from million-dollar offers to nothing. A friend of mine who was in TV said I should get into TV, which I'd never been involved with. And I said, "I don't know anyone in TV. What do I do?" He told me to write a spec script.

I wrote a script in seriously two or three hours, which was a *Curb Your Enthusiasm* episode. I gave it to Steve. He called me the next day as if he remembered that I could write again and said, "Mark and I had this idea. We don't really know what it is, but it's Mark and his friends in Hollywood." I said, "That sounds horrible. Who wants to watch a bunch of losers follow around a star, and who wants to do Hollywood, and blah, blah, blah." I went home and started thinking, this could essentially be a friendship show, with a Hollywood backdrop.

It's hard to explain how big HBO was at the time. It was like walking into the palace of Hollywood where only the best people on earth were getting in. Lev and Mark had said, "This wasn't going anywhere else. Either we're going to sell it to HBO or we're not doing it." It was a very pressurized situation. It's hard to explain how big HBO was at the time.

I had never heard of Ari [Emanuel], but he was there for the pitch, and before I even said a word, Ari said, "It's Mark and his friends, this guy is gonna write it. If it sucks, we'll fire him, and someone will rewrite it." That's what he said in front of me. When I walked out, I said, "This guy is the character. He has to be part of the show." He also really sold the show because they didn't even care to hear from me when I was pitching. I barely said a word. Ari sold it.

Lev and I walked out of that meeting in Century City like that scene in *Vanilla Sky* where there's no one there. We felt like we owned the world. I felt like I made it in Hollywood.

CHRIS ALBRECHT:

We'd done well with shows that took you inside a world that you couldn't get into. The guys just had a great take on it. Ari and Mark were great in the room. Lev is really smart. And then Carolyn and me and a woman named Sarah Condon, who worked at HBO at the time. It was just a script deal.

DOUG ELLIN:

It was then two years of me writing before they actually said, "Okay."

It was a nightmare and not enjoyable. The journey was torture. I hired the head of UCLA screenwriting to help me get through this script. We had a draft where she said it was one of the best pilots she ever read; Lev loved it, Mark loved it. I doubt Ari ever read it. We handed it in to HBO. I got the call from Lev, and he said, "They don't like it." And I said, "What don't they like about it?" He said, "They don't like anything about it." I was walking my two German Shepherds and thought, "I'm never going to work again."

Sarah Condon, who was an executive on it, was great. She just kept giving me these notes, that these guys have to speak in a language only they understood. I used to say to her, "I don't know what you're talking about," but then I went to Palm Springs and wrote this really weird script with all this bizarre dialogue.

I'm kinda making up shit, people speaking in a way that they would never speak. And something about that got Sarah and maybe Carolyn excited, and that moved us forward. They kept pushing me in a direction that turned out to be good. We used to have these discussions because Chris kept saying, "Fun, fun, fun." And Steve Levinson and I used to have endless conversations about the difference between funny and fun. The first script was funny, but I wrote it, I guess, from a darker, cynical place. It was more my life, of having best friends and struggling in Hollywood, rather than Mark, a movie star's life, having a great time in Hollywood. That's when we moved into that direction.

DAVID FRANKEL:

You have to credit Doug for the writing and Lev from sort of working very hard to make it as real as possible, because it's really his story. It's like the Mark Wahlberg–Steve Levinson story and it was very personal to him and he was able to bring incredible authenticity to what could have been a very slight tale of Hollywood.

DOUG ELLIN:

Eventually, I kept getting these notes saying, "Less story, less conflict." As a writer, it's very hard to write something without a story or conflict. Usually when you do that, people tell you that it's terrible. Ultimately what happened is I wrote a thirty-five-page script that had no story in it. It was just them hanging out. And that was the script that they approved.

When David Frankel came in to direct, he basically said what I had been saying: "We don't have a story." Probably the last four days before we shot, I wrote it but with David's guidance, we did the story of the pilot, the Ari-Eric conflict.

There was nothing on TV or film at the time like it. Mark Wahlberg used to say to me all the time: "The *Hangover* guys owe you $1 billion." There weren't the R-rated comedies that there were when I was growing up. There weren't really the Judd Apatow movies yet. So I wanted to write a show where guys could really be free to talk. Now, of course, some of the dialogue that I wrote then, I wouldn't write it today.

CHRIS ALBRECHT:

The only two shows that I would have bet my own money on were *Sex and the City* and *Entourage*. They both keyed into something that we hadn't seen before. And they brought the audience into a world that they wanted to spend time in. They were both aspirational.

Entourage was about friendship, certainly the aspiration of wanting to be famous and who doesn't want to be famous? And who doesn't want to have friends, right? Same thing with *Sex and the City*. I'm not even saying they were the most brilliant of the shows. I'm just saying that they keyed into something that to me was specific and authentic. And you hadn't seen it before.

They originally had written the Turtle role for Domenick Lombardozzi from *The Wire*. He was actually in Wahlberg's posse, and Kevin Connolly was in DiCaprio's posse. Even when we went into casting, there were guys who were sort of bringing the authenticity of having lived the life.

KEVIN CONNOLLY, Actor:

I moved to LA in 1992 after I graduated high school. I did a TV show called *Great Scott!* for Fox and that's where I met Tobey Maguire. I didn't know anybody, and Tobey said to me, "What are you doing this weekend? A friend of mine is having this birthday party. If you want to come, it's going to be on a boat. It should be a lot of fun." I told him, "Absolutely."

It was Soleil Moon Frye's sweet sixteen birthday party. I met a lot of people that day, including Leo DiCaprio. He and Tobey were tight. We've been friends ever since.

The Leo thing happened and that was a juggernaut, and when Tobey got *Spider-Man*, that was crazy too. That movie aired on a Wednesday and his life's never been the same

Tobey became a gigantic movie star, and the world turned upside down.

Strangely that was more *Twilight Zone*-y than the Leo thing, because it all happened so fast. When I first heard the concept for *Entourage*, it took a while to realize that it wasn't about Leo, and I wasn't playing myself. Doug always has this joke, "Oh, Connolly was retired from acting."

DOUG ELLIN:

The character of E was completely based on myself.

DAVID FRANKEL:

Adrian Grenier came in and he was a client of Lev's who had been reluctant to even audition, and I had worked with Jeremy Piven on *Miami Rhapsody* and had even shared a guesthouse in the Hollywood Hills with him in the nineties.

CHRIS ALBRECHT:

Originally, Vince was a small role and Ari was a small role. It was really about the friends. It was about the entourage.

JEREMY PIVEN:

I was about forty movies into my career when *Entourage* came around. I'm in my thirties. I knew Mark Wahlberg, he's a guy who is an incredibly loyal friend and his universe was fascinating. There was a Drama, Turtle, and E, there was certainly an Ari, they were all in his life.

DOUG ELLIN:

Jeremy had only two scenes in the pilot, so he didn't want to sign a six-year deal, which is tradition. I was obsessed with Jeremy, so I called Ari, who then called HBO and pushed Jeremy through. They signed Jeremy to a two-year deal, which is pretty rare. But they also didn't think that Jeremy was gonna pop the way he did.

ARI EMANUEL:

Lev and Mark grew up with the agency, and we were really close, so they knew a lot of stories. They asked me to sign a release, so I did.

I told them about when a guy ratted me out when I was going to leave CAA, and that became something they did with Ari Gold.

JEREMY PIVEN:

I knew Ari Emanuel. There were all these beautiful dualities going on with that guy. You thought he was a pig, but he was monogamous to his wife. He's a workaholic and equal opportunity offender. It didn't matter that it was a small role and that they said it was a fringe player. You get in there and do the best work you possibly can. And if they let you add things, you go for it.

When you play a character who is so believable and you're in people's living rooms, it can cause confusion. I didn't see it coming. I get requests from people all the time who want me to yell at them. It's just so awkward.

ARI EMANUEL:

I'm definitely a different person now. But when we started the agency, we couldn't compete on price. It's not like I could go to 5 percent. We had to compete on tenacity. Thank God I had enough of that, and everybody at the company had an unbelievable work ethic.

JERRY FERRARA, Actor:

I had just signed with a new manager, Steve Levinson, Lev, who was also Wahlberg's manager. I was working a little bit here and there. Everybody kept telling me about this show based on Mark and his friends. I read the script, and thought it was hilarious and that I would be perfect for one of those roles. About forty-five auditions later, I was fortunate enough to get the part.

KEVIN DILLON, Actor:

The script was my sense of humor. I grew up in New York among crazy characters, and these guys are all New Yorkers. I never felt we went too far. Maybe nowadays, when you look back on it, you go, okay. Times have changed a little bit. They're not as open to this humor. Maybe you're not allowed to do it right now, but what the world needs today is more *Entourage*.

JERRY FERRARA:

I don't think Turtle had much of an inner monologue telling him, "Don't do that. Don't say that." He was fearless, and had this incredible confidence for the guy who was the slacker of the group. Me, I'm more quiet and reserved. It was hard for me at times to have to get into the mode of a character who subscribed to the one out of ten theory. If you ask ten girls out, one's got to say yes, right? It was always painful for me to even ask one girl out in real life. I just always assume that they weren't interested. I lived vicariously through Turtle.

DOUG ELLIN:

There wasn't that much conversation with Chris until the ratings came out. The night before the show came out, Sarah, who I love, called me up and basically told me that HBO does really smart, highbrow stuff, so don't take the reviews personally tomorrow. All I wanted was a good review in the *New York Times*. That's what my parents would say means "successful." I woke up in the morning and Alessandra Stanley in the *New York Times* said, "Nothing on network television is as smart, original, and amusing as *Entourage*." It was pretty wild. That *New York Times* review was really one of the best moments. It sounds childish now that I'm fifty-two years old, but it meant a lot to me because I knew my parents were going to wake up and I didn't have to listen to them ask me what I was doing with my life anymore.

KEVIN CONNOLLY:

The show aired on Sunday night and quite literally on Monday, my entire life was different. My life changed in a day. I felt the eyeballs, even at the same Starbucks that I'd been going to. Leo and I were at Peter Luger's one night when *Entourage* first came out. We're sitting there, Leo's a super private guy, great guy. So we're eating at Peter Luger's, and somebody walks up to the table and is like, "We see you, Leo, but yo, hey man, we're big fans of *Entourage*." We had a good laugh. Leo's like, "You know I'm going to tell everybody that story."

EMMANUELLE CHRIQUI, Actor:

I joined at the end of season two. It was supposed to be like a three-episode arc, but I wound up doing the run of the show, plus the movie.

I knew that Doug was really pleased by the work, and more than that, I knew Kevin was really pleased. Apparently, they had been trying to find a girlfriend for E for a while, one that was going to stick. Kev and I had such great chemistry. Doug used to say, "I love this couple. I love writing this couple."

KEVIN CONNOLLY:

She's a dear friend, the genuine article. With Emmanuelle, what you see is what you get.

We loved her, but it was hard enough writing story lines for the five of us. Kevin Dillon didn't like it because it meant less screen time for him.

JEREMY PIVEN:

Every word was written by Doug Ellin. I'm not sure if Doug gets enough credit for that, but he should. I'm very grateful and lucky that he wrote this character for me.

JERRY FERRARA:

I was afraid that it was going to get taken away from me and from us. I never allowed myself to imagine that it was going to be a success. The first season was not a ratings blockbuster. Funny thing happened, though. It was when we went off the air that HBO On Demand started. And we became more popular in our off-season than when we actually aired, because of HBO On Demand. I think college kids and people were watching in groups.

DOUG ELLIN:

If you really watch *Entourage*, and it's because of me, there's not really that much nudity, it's a lot less than many, many cable shows. There's more dialogue about sex than there is actual sex. I used to get comments all the time that there needs to be more sex.

DAVID FRANKEL:

An executive at HBO, I'm not going to name them, would tell me that they wanted to make sure that the men who were writing the checks felt that they could see women with their shirts off.

DOUG ELLIN:

There was one episode that Carolyn Strauss called me and said, "I'm not going to tell you not to do this. I'm just telling you I don't like it." I love Carolyn and believe in Carolyn and everything she said, and I thought about it. Ultimately, we ended up doing it. It actually got very good reviews after that. Will Sasso was in the episode and he was attracted to Lloyd, Ari's assistant. And Ari was basically going to give away Lloyd to this big writer to get them as a client, which, *Mad Men*, I'm not saying they saw it here—*Mad Men* is basically my favorite show of all time—but they basically ended up doing the same thing, when Joan is asked to meet the Jaguar president.

But whatever it was that Carolyn didn't like, she let me do it. And I think Carolyn liked it as well when it was done.

EMMANUELLE CHRIQUI:

You could really begin to see the show was starting to register, that the show was becoming water-cooler conversation and that people were really invested. All kinds of things started to happen, in my own life, where I was like, "Oh my God, Sloan really hit a chord with people."

I was going to do Conan O'Brien, walking in the streets of New York with my publicist. On one of the corners, there are all these construction guys, right? One of the construction guys is up on a scaffolding and he's like, "Yo, Sloan! It's really fucked up what he did to you." And I was like, "Oh my God, this is the funniest thing ever."

JERRY FERRARA:

Is there really a furry community out there like you're telling me guys? I'm just curious. And to this day every Easter, I post a picture of me in the bunny suit and I say, happy Easter to everybody. And it always gets like a hundred thousand likes. It's insane.

DOUG ELLIN:

We tried to get Obama. Obama said it was his favorite show. We were supposed to have a screening at the White House that ended up not happening. Rahm (Ari's brother) I think was chief of staff. We were supposed to go to the White House and have this screening that Ari was setting up.

Some people said, "Oh, it's just loaded with cameos." Look, it was wish fulfillment to me. I got to have heroes of mine on this show. And that's what I wanted, whether it was James Cameron, Tom Brady, Martin Scorsese, Larry David, U2, whatever it is.

And that's the reality of the lifestyle. People started calling. If LeBron James calls me and says he'd like to be on the show, I'm going to figure out a way to put him on a show. Matt Damon was like, "I'd love to figure out a way to put my charity in this." So I wrote a whole thing about his charity that would also give us a good story.

On March 21, 2004, HBO premiered **Deadwood**, *a drama series set in 1870s South Dakota and probably the least western Western ever. The story followed the central conflict between two lawmen of the town of Deadwood, Keith Carradine's Wild Bill Hickok and Timothy Olyphant's Seth Bullock, against saloon owner and criminal Al Swearengen, played by Ian McShane. The pilot alone garnered three Emmy nominations, including a win for Best Director for Walter Hill of* **48 Hours** *fame.*

DAVID MILCH, Creator:

I should hurry to say that HBO people were responsive and responsible and constructive in their reactions to the work I was doing. I was very grateful to HBO, for their having allowed us a certain latitude in discovering the structure for the material as we went along.

It's a continuous process of discovery and rediscovery. And perhaps the deepest responsibilities that you have to honor is to recognize your limitations and to try to discover the beating heart of new material from day to day. I believe that, more days than not, we did.

BRIAN COX, Actor:

I worked with Milch. *Deadwood* was one of those incredible shows as well. Unfortunately, he got into a pissing contest with Chris Albrecht, who imploded because of David's sensibility, but it was a great show to work on and HBO, they were phenomenal.

Deadwood *ran for three seasons, from March 2004 to August 2006, and in that time, delivered ratings on a par with* **Six Feet Under**, *which was graced with five seasons and a real ending. Alas,* **Deadwood** *got no such finale—viewers were presented with a confused denouement that promised much going forward, but actually delivered nothing (at least until the follow-up movie aired some thirteen years later). Critics adored the show's re-creation of Deadwood, as it developed into a town in the late 1800s, but they were disappointed to be denied the much-anticipated showdown between the two main characters.*

CAROLYN STRAUSS:

The decision to cancel *Deadwood* was obviously controversial. The deal for *Deadwood* was a really difficult one. We didn't have a real back end, and it was an expensive show to do. It was hard to justify the level of expense. So our thinking was, Why don't we try to create something new with David that we know that we can own altogether. But it was sometimes hard for us to contemplate the emotional toll of a decision like that on the creators.

HAL AKSELRAD:

Richard Plepler drove hard to cancel *Deadwood*, even though it was coming to a natural ending. That caused a series of bad decisions. They didn't want to walk away from David Milch. David had something else he was working on, called *John from Cincinnati*, which was not ready to be produced. Cancelling *Deadwood* led to enormous fan protests.

CHRIS ALBRECHT:

Deadwood was not doing well. We had done the third season. It was losing audience every season. We were going to do season four. I went to David and said, "Look, we're picking up the season, but I'd like to get to the new stuff because this thing isn't doing well. Instead of doing thirteen episodes, what about if we wrap it up in six or seven?" David said, "I'm not one of those guys who is so precious that I believe that we owe the audience a series ending. We can cancel it." This is literally on a Friday. He wasn't angry with me. He was completely like, "I don't care. It's fine. I get it."

I said, "David, David, David. I'm not trying to cancel the show. I'm just saying, can we make a truncated last season?" He said, "Let me think about it." He gets off the phone with me, then he decides that because he knows that Timothy Olyphant is thinking about buying a house, he owes it to Timothy Olyphant to tell him that the show's going to be canceled, which is not what I was doing. I was trying to make a truncated final season so we could get to the new stuff, of which *John from Cincinnati* was first in line. A script I loved. And Carolyn loved.

By Monday or Sunday, the trades were reporting that we had canceled *Deadwood*. It became a gigantic mess. We were trying to pull it back. But by that time, David decided he didn't want to do any more *Deadwood*. David canceled *Deadwood* by deciding that my offer to do a truncated final season meant we were canceling.

Given HBO's flood-the-zone marketing prowess, it's hard to imagine a new HBO show somehow remaining a "hidden gem that never really got the chance it deserved," and yet that is precisely what happened beginning on June 5, 2005, with **The Comeback,** *a one-of-a-kind, hard-to-define comedy that offered viewers a funny yet blistering look inside the world of reality TV and at the desperation of some who try to languish too long in the spotlight's glow.*

The show, which cleverly mixed and mashed genres and formats, was co-written by **Sex and the City**'s *Michael Patrick King and* **Comeback**'s *star, Lisa* (**Friends**) *Kudrow. As valuable and credible as Kudrow had been playing Phoebe on* **Friends,** *her performance on* **The Comeback** *was at an entirely new level. She scored a tour de force playing Valerie Cherish, a borderline has-been who'd enjoyed success back in the late 1980s and early '90s in a sophomoric sitcom called "I'm IT!" But now, with her shining hour a dim memory, Cherish lets herself be followed about by a camera crew shooting a "reality" TV show called, with bare-faced irony, "The Comeback," which Cherish hopes will precipitate her own comeback— albeit in a supporting role—in a new sitcom to be called "Room and Bored." Is it, too, sophomoric? Even if not, starring roles have gone to actual sophomores—that is, young greenhorn actors, some of whom look on Cherish as a relic from a long-gone era.*

The premise may have been convoluted and hard to summarize, but the show's ambition, and its satirical take on the culture and on the ever-fickle world of entertainment television, cagily captured a medium in mad mid-morph.

LISA KUDROW, Creator:

It was my last or second-to-last year of *Friends*. I had just started my own production company with Dan Bucatinsky, and I couldn't get reality TV out of my head. I had seen *The Osbournes*, *The Anna Nicole Show*, and *Amazing Race*, and thought, "This is all really bad. It's a disaster. I don't think Anna Nicole even knows what's going on. Same with *Amazing Race*. It's a level of humiliation that shouldn't be allowed."

And yet there *could* be something really funny about a character who was on a sitcom in the 1980s when they were really bad, when women really weren't allowed to be interesting, and she was so desperate to be in the lime-light again that she'll do a reality show called *The Comeback*, which means she went away. But she doesn't know she went away. What's more humiliating than that?

Then I thought, I could do that character. When I was done with *Friends*, my agent said, "You have time off, why don't you meet with Michael Patrick King?" I knew Michael from long before, and we had lunch. He said, "You don't want to be on a shiny new show, do you?" I said, "No. There's only one thing I would do, but I don't even know what it really is." I told him the idea and he got it right away. We talked for about three hours and at the end he said, "We have a show. We had arced a season of this show." It was so thrilling. It was so fast.

JOHN MELFI:

We came back from a two-week vacation after *Sex and the City* to a pitch meeting with Lisa Kudrow that summer of 2004, on *The Comeback*. The three of us met. Lisa was brilliant. I had my head on the table at the Polo Lounge at the Beverly Hills Hotel, laughing, because she was doing the character. It was a good three hours and it was obvious that we would do it. Then we had to pitch it to Carolyn at HBO.

LISA KUDROW:

Carolyn said, "I don't fully understand it, but why don't you write it? Then let's see what it is." It took a really short time to write the pilot. As I read it, I went, "Oh, this isn't funny on the page though." Then they went, "We still don't know what this is. Why don't we shoot it and see what it is?"

When we did auditions and I would read with people, that's when they got it. Chris Albrecht and Carolyn Strauss said, "Oh, okay, that's funny. That's good. Got it." They were fantastic. We were pretty much in sync with casting. We did the pilot and then they ordered more episodes. It was thrilling.

JOHN MELFI:

Every line was written. As much as it sounds and looks like improv, it was completely written. It was a bear to pull that off.

MICHAEL PATRICK KING:

I still remember the *New York Times* review of *Entourage* and *The Comeback*. Alessandra Stanley said something like, "The rise of four young Turks on the way up is more enjoyable than watching the free fall of a woman on the way down." I thought, "Wow." And a difference between TV then and now, you only got one episode to review. No one understood that we had a plan, that there was an actual journey from the beginning to the end of the season. People just assumed everything was going to get worse, because most television does.

When the show premiered, it was like nothing anyone had ever seen, which eventually became its great badge of honor and creative success. There was not a *Real Housewife* of anywhere yet. There had never been a Bethenny Frankel, there had never been any of those people that embarrassed themselves on television. Nobody had ever seen a female character grind herself into hamburger meat to stay in the spotlight. And Lisa's performance was so skilled and spectacular, she didn't indicate anything. She didn't tell them what to feel. You had to figure it out.

We really loved it, and we believed in it. It didn't have the impact that *Sex and the City* had ratings-wise, but people forgot that *Sex and the City* didn't have big ratings until like season four. But it had these expectations. You have Lisa Kudrow from *Friends* and me from *Sex and the City*. Everybody thought it was going to be Phoebe in Manolo's, even though that was the furthest thing from our interest.

All the New York performers I knew loved it, and LA people were terrified of it.

LISA KUDROW:

The good news was we had the same numbers that *Entourage* had the year before for its first year.

MICHAEL PATRICK KING:

We started getting little signals that people were becoming crazy fans. Four episodes in, we got a call from David Bowie's people that he was going on tour and he wanted to know if we had the next series of DVDs so that he could watch it. He wanted to know what happened to Valerie.

LISA KUDROW:

Carolyn kept trying to warn us that, at that moment in time, HBO was not being HBO. They were caring about ratings, about reviews. She would say, "Guys, this isn't how it used to be. Ratings are important."

MICHAEL PATRICK KING:

It was polarizing. It had a lot to do with women. In *Sex and the City*, there was an enormous amount of variety in those characters. It had to do with ageism and sexism, who wanted to sleep with her and who didn't. It was confusing, but Lisa never lost her belief system.

Lisa and I said to Chris, who was always a champion, "Please take it off Sunday. Take the responsibility of the show off of your Sunday night. Move it to a Monday. Think of it as off Broadway. Move it to off Broadway."

We were so surprised that we were in limbo. I kept saying to Chris, "Please pick us up. We'll do half a season. Just pick us up." Lisa and I were both nominated for Emmys, and I said, "If you pick us up, Lisa will win."

JOHN MELFI:

We were nominated for three Emmys for that first season, and the day after the Emmys, Michael was driving on Mulholland, and he's told that Albrecht was calling. He pulled over, thinking that this was the call saying we're picked up for season two. And it was the day after the Emmys and he said, "We're not going to move forward." Could you imagine, the day after the Emmys?

MICHAEL PATRICK KING:

Chris said, "We can't do it. We can't do it." And I was like, Wow.

LISA KUDROW:

The day after the Emmys, I was at the gynecologist and Michael called and said, "We got canceled." I went, "What?" He said, "They just called." I thought, "Really? Well, all right." My whole thing is, whatever you do, don't take it personally. Something else is going on. It didn't make sense, and Michael was so hurt. The truth is, he made so much money for them. That show was not expensive. They couldn't do six more episodes? That was what really hurt.

MICHAEL PATRICK KING:

It is a big mystery because they did owe it to me. We had so much good-will and we had so much success. I have no idea who stopped that second season of *The Comeback*. Chris Albrecht has been really supportive of me. I think he has great taste. That's why we were so surprised. I loved working with Chris.

CHRIS ALBRECHT:

It was a smart, funny show that was so cool, how can you not be just happy to watch this? It's so clever, and Lisa was so great to work with. But it got bad reviews. At some point people started looking at us and said, "They think they're so cool they can do anything."

LISA KUDROW:

The feedback from key people was "It makes me uncomfortable." The truth is for a lot of men, it made them really uncomfortable. Straight men especially. Because that's how they think of women. You know what I mean? Like, "I don't need it thrown in my face, that they're humiliated." It was just painful to watch for them to see a woman treated like that.

For Albrecht, however, **The Comeback** *marked a sad, even rude turn of the page. He and Strauss had held to their convictions from early on, ignoring negative testing on* **The Sopranos** *and disregarding bad reviews for several shows.*

But Albrecht had just emerged from a corporate performance review that found people were too intimidated by him, and he was encouraged to be more solicitous of other viewpoints. That feedback became a death sentence for **The Comeback,** *as Albrecht widened the circle of influence, particularly from Plepler, who had become de facto guardian of the HBO brand and told Albrecht he was not a fan of the show. Critical opinion on* **Comeback** *was divided—the more discriminating critics loved it—but the ratings were only so-so. Ironically, industry awards were forthcoming, but they came too late.*

Perhaps most shocking was the pedigree of the tandem whose work was being rejected. Inside HBO, Michael Patrick King was considered the essential creative element in making **Sex and the City** *the grand success that it was, and with* **The Comeback** *he seemed to bring an even higher caliber of humor and paint deeper portraits of the characters. Where was the company's gratitude, he might well have asked, beyond the big paychecks? As for Kudrow, she was a certified star from one of television's most popular shows ever. But apparently that didn't count for much either.*

LISA KUDROW:

I love this show. It's the thing I'm the most proud of in my career. That's why I can't feel bad. It was too good to feel bad about.

I didn't hold any grudge about it. I felt like this was something else at work that they just weren't ready for. It was not our mistake. Creatively, we didn't do anything wrong. I thought they made a mistake.

MICHAEL PATRICK KING:

They did happily correct it nine years later by calling us up and saying, "Would you ever consider coming back?" We got to do a really great second season, but it was ten years later. It was very creative and they were very open. Valerie Cherish can go on. Who knows where that would have gone with Lisa and me?

CASEY BLOYS, Executive:

This is what happened with *The Comeback*: *Sex and the City* was ending, *Sopranos* was near the end, old stuff was going away. And *The Comeback* was very much received with, "So this is your next great HBO show?" That was an acidic little show, and in retrospect, I think very well received and reviewed. However, at the time Chris responded to the criticism of, All HBO cares about is things like *Entourage* and rich people and glitzy shows. And that's not what *The Comeback* is.

People were getting tired of HBO winning. Had it been five years later, when other shows were on, there was so much pressure on any show at that point, same thing happened to *John from Cincinnati*, which wasn't as good a show, but everything at that point was viewed through the lens of, Okay, let's see the next *Sex and the City*. And of course shows take time to develop into something, but it was a very unfair time in the media regarding HBO. Because it was like they expected the next great thing right away.

For every **Sex and the City** *there was a* **Comeback***; for every* **Six Feet Under** *there was a* **Carnivàle**—*(a Depression-era show that few cared to watch)—or so it began to seem post-2003. It was clear to all that HBO was struggling to create series that reached the heights of* **Sex and the City** *or* **The Sopranos***, shows that reflected and defined the culture, shows that people talked about, raved over, urged their friends to see—and shows that delivered millions of eyes that then might stay tuned for something like an* **Entourage** *or* **The Wire***.*

Some at HBO placed more weight on this critique than others. Richard Plepler's title was specifically broad: "executive vice president." There was no department attached to it, reflecting the range of involvements he had within the company. And yet to all concerned, Plepler was HBO's communications guru, first and foremost. There wasn't a single significant story about HBO that Plepler hadn't tried to influence, either directly or through his trusted deputy, Quentin Schaffer, and there wasn't a significant story, particularly in the **New York Times**, *the* **Wall Street Journal**, *the* **Los Angeles Times**, *or "the trades" (the* **Hollywood Reporter** *and* **Variety***)* *that he didn't dissect.*

One particular article, by Joe Flint in the June 8, 2005, issue of the **Wall Street Journal**, *grabbed Plepler's attention. It opened with a reference to* The Comeback, *describing a scene in which Lisa Kudrow demands that she be allowed to do a second take of a scene she's displeased with, as had been the custom with her director on her character's previous series. "I'm 'it,'" she tells the new director, but he snaps back, "You know what? You're not 'it' anymore." Flint suggested in the article that HBO was now in a corresponding position; ratings for the network were not what they used to be, he pointed out, and its creative output was starting to look just like everybody else's. Not "it" anymore.*

Ever since **Sex and the City** *and* The Sopranos *had been established as tremendous hits, employees on both coasts had gossiped about Plepler's obsession with the word "zeitgeist." He loved the term and frequently remarked about HBO shows that had hit the zeitgeist like it was a G-spot, a sign of HBO's dominance in public chatter. President Bush had talked publicly about HBO shows, as did rock stars, late-night comics—seemingly, everyone. The very idea that HBO appeared to be losing the optics game on its unique role in the culture was anathema to Plepler, who decided to take the Flint story—at this point nearly a year old—and weaponize it in his remarks before a group of senior HBO executives off-site at Shutters hotel in Santa Monica.*

Plepler told assembled execs that HBO faced a point of existential inflection in its history; the final curtain of the biggest show ever to ride HBO's airwaves, The Sopranos, *would descend in mere months, and Plepler believed the network had to return to its roots, shifting away from what executives felt captured the current moment of American life and instead relying more on the instincts of the so-called "creative" class.*

HBO would need to give audiences what it had always offered them in the past: something new. He felt that HBO needed to trust the creatives and provide a voice for artistic genius, if it found any, because HBO had been built by artists who pushed the boundaries of the medium. The conceit of the Home Box Office model could be found in its status as an entertainment singularity, and that singularity, in Plepler's mind, had somehow lost its way. The way, he insisted, must be found once more.

Plepler's speech was an audacious performance. Apart from a 1990 documentary **A Search for Solid Ground: The Intifada through Israeli Eyes***—made for PBS by Plepler and co-producer Peter Kunhardt—Plepler had no background in programming. He was, to many in attendance, publicly criticizing not only programming chief Carolyn Strauss but also Albrecht, his (CEO) boss, who was still very much involved in programming. Yet the speech became a sort of coming-out party*

for Plepler, who established his bona fides not through script development, or cast-
ing, or notes, but rather at thirty thousand feet, connecting it all to another favorite
word of his, "branding."

Albrecht digested Plepler's comments and instead decided to double down on Ple-
pler's role. From that day forward, Richard Plepler would have a lot to say about all
"matters HBO"—and he would make sure to be heard.

Also from then on, the Plepler playbook was out in the open for all to see: Let others
play the instruments in HBO's orchestra. Richard Plepler wanted to stand front and
center—and conduct.

RICHARD PLEPLER:

The point I tried to make when my turn came was simply that it was important to remember the insurgent quality that brought us much of the success
we had experienced. That entailed the kinds of risks that had made *Sopra-*
nos, *Band of Brothers*, and *The Wire* possible. My simple note was that it was
easy to try to protect our lead and harder to continue to push our insurgent
voice. Because I'm a political junkie I used a political metaphor to make the
point. I remember Chris calling me that night and being very gracious in
his praise for what I had said.

CHRIS ALBRECHT:

Part of the Time Warner thing was they gave me an executive coach. They
go and talk to the direct reports, your supervisors, and some of the stuff that
came back really surprised me. How intimidating I was. It wasn't a temper
thing, it was that I was intimidating. So I included more voices, and things
became less organic and fun.

Richard was the spinner of the story. Then I think Richard started taking things seriously and started asking, "What's the brand?" That's when
we started getting fucked up. Instead of doing what we always did, and just
doing it.

And if you want to think about other voices in terms of canceled shows,
like *The Mind of the Married Man*, *The Comeback*, *Deadwood*, it was all
everybody else's voices. I'm not criticizing anyone, it's not mine or Carolyn's.
"This isn't doing well? Well, fuck it."

There was a lot of resentment toward people that were called FOCs
(friends of Chris) that got special treatment. I never had a personal dinner
with people who I worked with unless we were in another country and it
was a half business dinner. I never saw people at events, I never even went
to lunch with people. I didn't socialize with people that I worked with, so it's

not like there were friends of mine. Although, there was an article written once that if you wanted to do a comedy show, you needed to be friends with Chris, because it was Larry David, Louis C.K., and a couple other people. But it's also just because I thought those guys were funny, not because they were friends of mine. They were funny.

I think that eventually it's not that you change, especially if you are the CEO of a company that does all of this stuff. The people who work for you start to treat you like royalty. From the start, the thing that I did differently from Jeff was that I used the staff as a forum for talking about the company, whereas Jeff had a much smaller, closer, more traditional HBO-type team.

But there are too many things that are not in your control, and nobody believes that. You get treated like your shit doesn't stink and people tell you that you are a genius. It's that impostor syndrome vs. wanting to believe it. You're thinking, "When am I going to get found out some day? When is this run going to end?" Things that I thought were good, they didn't, like *Deadwood* when it first aired. It wasn't until I took it off the air that everyone loved it so much. So, there started to become pressure that made it not so fun.

HBO had taken leaps forward with big money events like **From the Earth to the Moon** *and* **Band of Brothers.** *Now it was a time to go overseas for a different (not to mention real) historical era: the Roman Empire. Re-creating Rome for television audiences already so well-versed in the subject (from years of Hollywood epics on the subject) would take imagination and, simply put, a lot of money, $100 million to be exact—for the first season. Writers Bruno Heller and John Milius supplied the imagination, blending a traditional period piece with flavors of war movies and soap operas before sprinkling in some dark humor. The money, meanwhile, was supplied by HBO and the BBC, who co-produced the show. HBO put up $85 million, and the BBC paid the rest.*

The first season of **Rome** *aired in August 2005 and was a hit for both channels in their respective territories; viewers seemed to like the travails of the two lead characters, a pair of fictional Roman soldiers, Lucius Vorenus and Titus Pullo, played by Kevin McKidd and Ray Stevenson, respectively, as the story swept from the civil war of 49 BC to the murder of Julius Caesar five years later. The second season followed on with an account of the fight between Octavian, played by Max Pirkis, and Mark Antony (the Roman politician, not the singer), played by James Purefoy.*

Unfortunately for the cast and crew, a devastating fire at the Cinecittà Studios after the end of the second season ruined much of the show's elaborate re-creation of Rome.

The series was already skating on thin ice in the finance department—even a successful show would have a hard time justifying rebuilding a set that represented a significant chunk of that original $100 million price tag. Coupled with the lofty budgets of the costuming and music departments, the cost proved too high, and **Rome** *never made it to a third iteration.*

As many other HBO productions had been in the past, **Rome** *could be "accused" of uncanny prescience. By creating a millennia-old analog,* **Rome**'s *creators found a way to capture a society in which the rich get richer and more powerful, while those at the bottom sink further into poverty and discord. Eventually the discontented rise up, led by a charismatic leader who promises solutions to the unspoken—the silenced— grievances of their hearts. The modern resonance is hard to miss.*

ANNE THOMOPOULOS:

Rome was actually an idea that I had when we were doing *Band of Brothers*. I was talking to Jane Root, who was a BBC executive at the time, about *I, Claudius*, and telling her how much I liked it and that I wanted to see it on a bigger canvas without people wearing sheets. Then John Milius and Bill MacDonald came into the office and pitched basically Caesar Augustus. We decided to write a bible. The process was very slow with them. I hate to say this about Milius, but it required someone who's really gonna dig in and give 100 percent of their time.

Bruno Heller, who was married to Miranda Heller, who I shared a wall with, was a writer out in LA, unproduced. He came into the office and pitched me a show about the rust belt. At the time it didn't sound right to me. But what was so interesting about him was that he was able to project himself into a world and to really describe and pitch the characters and an environment and a human condition that had nothing to do with how he was raised. He's a British guy from London. I said to him, "That's so interesting that you are able to embody a completely different world. It's so unusual." So I just asked him how he felt about ancient Rome. And he has subsequently said, When an executive at HBO asks you how you feel about ancient Rome, you say, "I love ancient Rome."

BRUNO HELLER, Creator:

Essentially my take on the whole thing was to do *Rosencrantz and Guildenstern Are Dead*. Use the two ordinary soldiers as Zeligs in this larger historical world, and insert them as much as possible into the known history and really make it about working-class Romans. Finding a way of doing something that hadn't been done before in that world.

ANNE THOMOPOULOS:

I put Bruno on *Rome*. He punched up and polished the bible, and he delivered three extraordinary scripts. I took the scripts to Chris and he read them and said, "These are unbelievable, but this is so expensive. You need to find a partner if you want to make this." I got Bruno on a plane, we went to London, we went and sat with Jane Tranter, who was an executive at the BBC at the time, and we walked out of the meeting with a commitment from the BBC. I called Chris from the parking lot and I was like, "You said I had to find a partner, I found a partner." He was surprised. And then we went to producers next, and they committed and then RAI Italia committed, all based on the few scripts. The scripts were really beautifully written.

BRUNO HELLER:

There's a book called *Daily Life in Ancient Rome*, by Florence Dupont, that just gets into the nitty-gritty of the plumbing and streets and graffiti and the jobs that ordinary Romans would have. What Rome looked like. I loved that deep research. As soon as you have an inroad into the world that hasn't been seen before, that suggests a far more vibrant, lively, violent, confusing, complex culture, then it was very easy to write.

CHRIS ALBRECHT:

Rome was problematic. We had the wrong director and we cast the wrong kid. We had the money, so we went in and reshot the first three episodes.

DAVID FRANKEL:

Alexander the Great had fallen apart. And they came to me with *Rome*. Bruno had written the first three scripts for *Rome*. They were amazing. I had my overall deal. And they said, "Will you direct these?" I said, "Yes, absolutely." This was in a very natural segue from *Alexander the Great*. It was going to be on the same scale and it was going to shoot in Europe and probably in Rome. And I really loved the writing. I loved the world, I loved the idea of being in a sort of trying to tell in a very realistic, very violent way the story of early Rome. So production is mounting. I'm packing my bags for the first casting trip to London, and I get a call from Carolyn and she says, "There's a snag. The BBC, which is co-financing 50 percent of the show, for political reasons is demanding that we have a British director."

"We told them we want you. And they said, 'Well, then we're out.' And we negotiated. We said, 'We'll come up with a list of five British directors. And if none of them agreed to do it, then Frankel will do it.' And they said, 'Okay.'" They went down their list and Michael Apted said yes. I was out, and Michael Apted did the first three hours of the series.

ANNE THOMPOULOS:

I had executive producer credit on the show and then I also was running the miniseries division, but *Rome* was obviously the priority. We were spending over $100 million on it.

CHRIS ALBRECHT:

I would say the first season was a big success. What happened was that we had a partnership with BBC and with RAI Italia and they didn't want to continue because it wasn't working. The Italians are very precious about their history. It wasn't working for the BBC as well as they wanted it to in terms of how much money they were putting in. So once we decided that we were going to shoulder it ourselves, it was performing well, but not unbelievably well. And then we just decided to make the second season the last season. But I think we were all feeling certainly creatively pleased with where we ended up because it was not only successful from a public perception point of view, I certainly don't think we thought it was a failure by any means.

CAROLYN STRAUSS:

We didn't shoot a pilot for *Rome* and that was a big mistake. When you're doing something as huge as *Rome*, it's obviously really expensive to do a pilot, but not having the opportunity to step back, look at it, and be able to see when something is not right creates problems that only magnify over time. Initially, *Rome* wasn't hitting the quality marks, so we had to take a break and make changes.

On March 12, 2006, with the premiere of **Big Love,** *HBO was once again drawn to an idea that the old established networks couldn't touch. Polygamy.*

MARK V. OLSEN, Creator:

There was an idea that was floating in the ether in my head, a concept, and then there was a particular concrete moment, where that concept tumbled out. The thing that was in my head was polygamy. And it was based on a miniseries that I was writing for HBO called *Mary Chesnut's Civil War*, about the Confederate elite enrichment over the course of the war. And one of the lines that I thought was just too delicious was Mary Chesnut writing, "Those saintly Yankees, looking down their nose at us, but they embrace the wisdom of those horrid Mormons and polygamists out in Utah." Well, that's funny, a slaveholder turning their nose up at polygamists. And it just was in my head.

WILL SCHEFFER:

And Mark wanted to collaborate. And so I was just at the right moment, writing pilots for television.

MARK V. OLSEN:

And thus began a very fateful drive on our part, back to New York City from my family in Nebraska for a long family Christmas, which was everyone piled into the house and blizzards all around. And we were returning, we were mid-state Pennsylvania and Will said, "Let's practice TV pitch ideas." And he came up with a couple and I came up with a couple. We didn't like either of them. And then I said, "I've got one. Polygamy."

WILL SCHEFFER:

And I said, "Polygamy? Yuck!"

MARK V. OLSEN:

He said, "That's the most disgusting thing I've ever heard of."

WILL SCHEFFER:

Who's going to watch a show about that?

MARK V. OLSEN:

And he also added, "You don't know anything about television." So that gave me the impetus to research the hell out of it and put some markers in the sand about what it might look like. A suburban polygamous family in Salt Lake City.

And for the rest, we were joined at the hip and off and running. We've been married in every shape or form that the law has allowed since 1991.

WILL SCHEFFER:

So we were domestic partners officially. And had just moved to California from being New York writers. And then we got married in 2008 in the editing room of *Big Love*.

MARK V. OLSEN:

But were we married? I like to think we were in a committed, loving relationship with undying commitment to each other. And that was in the air along, with the 2000 primaries, which was a grotesque, mis-celebration on the Republican sides of family values. And so we really wanted this show, although we denied it up and down, that we had no agenda with the show, but we did. And the agenda was, You want family values? We'll give you family values.

WILL SCHEFFER:

We were working up the pitch, and we wanted to bury the lede, so to speak. Polygamy. So we had told the agents, "Please don't tell Carolyn Strauss what it's about."

MARK V. OLSEN:

We wanted to get as far into the pitch before we use what we thought was the dreaded P word that would turn everybody off. So we did it again and again, talking about a businessman in Salt Lake City with his wife, Barbara, who was a schoolteacher.

WILL SCHEFFER:

Juggling modern life, cell phones, blah, blah, blah.

MARK V. OLSEN:

We did everything we could to try to sell normalcy before that polygamy word popped out.

WILL SCHEFFER:

Of course, the agency said, "Oh, well, we talked to Carolyn Strauss and we told her polygamy and she said, 'Yuck.' We don't think you should go in and pitch this." And I said, "Well, we have a very good relationship with Carolyn Strauss, both of us. And so we'll fire you if you don't set the meeting." Then we went in and we sold it in the room to Carolyn and Miranda. And they loved it.

CAROLYN STRAUSS:

The best shows have something special underneath them. What we were really looking to do with *Big Love* was to examine marriage, and this was marriage writ large. By examining marriage in triplicate, you can distill it down to sort of looking at marriage as a whole.

When *The Sopranos* came on, there were protests from various Italian American groups, and there were protests about *Big Love*. Every show that pushes in certain directions is going to have a lot of blowback, and that lets you know you're touching a nerve. Not that you always want to, but I think good shows, like good art, rile people up. Sometimes bad shows do, too.

MARK V. OLSEN:

This is why we have undying love for Carolyn Strauss. She places bets on horses and doesn't waiver. She saw our enthusiasm for the project. We were able to communicate our vision for the project. So it would not wallow in sister-wives and tawdriness.

BERNADETTE CAULFIELD, Executive Producer:

I thought, how clever. All shows are about relationships, and this guy is married to three women, and they're each different relationships. One of our scripts was called "The Affair" and I'm thinking, Oh my God, Bill has an affair with somebody?

But the funny thing is that he starts sleeping with one of his wives more than the schedule dictates. So he's basically having an affair with wife number one. I thought, "That's so smart. Oh, I want to do this."

MARK V. OLSEN:

Tom Hanks slipped the script to Bill Paxton, and Bill liked very much what he read.

WILL SCHEFFER:

We thought, that's the ticket, and we offered it to him.

MARK V. OLSEN:

So now the question became, how do we build around this guy?

WILL SCHEFFER:

Right, how do we build a family? We thought Jeanne was an amazing actress. I had seen her in early theater work. And so we had her into the room with Bill and they just felt like husband and wife.

MARK V. OLSEN:

They had this loving rapport from the get-go.

MARY KAY PLACE:

It was the show I'd been waiting for. The creators are geniuses. I thought it was brilliant writing and the layers and levels of the psychological knowledge of human behavior. I immediately jumped on it. I divide the world into civilians and Martians. And I always wanted to work at the Martian place, which HBO definitely was.

MARK V. OLSEN:

But in terms of Bill Paxton's perfection for the part, that guy Bill Henrickson needed decency. It needed that caring and that heart. It didn't want patriarchy, there was none of that in the world. It needed decency. And Bill Paxton exuded decency in his life. He's the most decent human being I've ever known.

WILL SCHEFFER:

He was just such a good guy.

MARK V. OLSEN:

There were a couple writers on the right side of the table. They loved the show, don't get me wrong, but they really hated Bill Henrickson. And there were a couple of women writers on the other side of the table who were like, "No, you're wrong. You're wrong. This is who Bill is." It was exciting.

As Nikki was fashioned in all the various castings, Chloë Sevigny was the only one in my mind. It was written for her out of my heart for her work, for what she does in *Boys Don't Cry*. You wanted the extra factor, the New York bad girl playing the Mormon uptight fundamentalist. That's whacked. And yet she filled out the emotional colors of it completely, the impoverished relationship with her father, and the resentments that she took out.

MARY KAY PLACE:

I don't think I've ever met anyone like Chloë before. I was mesmerized by her, who she is, the way she interacts in the world, and those scenes they created between the mother and daughter were so different. Chloë always surprised me.

She was very much her own person, original and unique. There was a vulnerability there at times, right alongside great strength. Anytime I see vulnerability in an actor, I'm just thrilled. Because it's a window into more intimacy and truth.

WILL SCHEFFER:

And then Ginni came in and was just fantastically exciting, as this fresh face who sat on Bill's lap during the table read and blew us away. I think casting is one of our strengths. We both love actors.

Harry Dean Stanton hadn't done TV except for when he was first starting out. And he had to come in and, Mark, do you remember what you said to him?

MARK V. OLSEN:

He was very cagey, held his cards close to the vest, loved a bit of the attention and the flattery, but wasn't going to commit to anything. And finally, I guess it was the third or fourth visit, he wanted to talk about religion, and Buddhism and mysticism. And I was like, Okay, I'll go there. Let's do it. Let's build a rapport. But finally, I just turned and said, "Harry, let's just cut this out. I would kill to have you in this show." And he just laughed and laughed and signed on.

WILL SCHEFFER:

I became the Harry Dean whisperer a little bit on the set, when Mark was in the writers' room, I get calls like, "Harry wants to talk to Will." And so I'd run down from the writers' room, and Mark would be like, "Don't leave me too long in the writers' room." It was a great joy to work with all of those actors for both of us. You dream of being able to write for specific actors, like Shakespeare did. That's the beauty of television.

I was exhausted after season one. And I had a rough time at the end of that season. We were starting to shoot the first episode of season two, and we didn't have money enough to shoot the episode.

MARK V. OLSEN:

Which is to say our budget inflated beyond our budget.

WILL SCHEFFER:

I felt it was futile. How are we going to do this show if we don't have the money? It seemed impossible to do the show on what we had been given. That was my worst time there. David and Bernie eventually fixed it with creative ways of shooting and scheduling.

BERNADETTE CAULFIELD:

We had to build three houses inside a warehouse and then our biggest challenge was actually creating daylight every year. A different DP would try something different to have it feel like it was really daylight outside of these houses; meanwhile we were in this huge warehouse.

MARY KAY PLACE:

I love Bernie Caulfield! She's one of the all-time great women ever. She was a beautiful leader of the show and her generosity of spirit helped create an incredible vibe on the set, where there was no weird infighting or jealousies or power plays. The sets were always glorious places to be and we did a lot of really intense, layered, complex work in that incredible environment. It was never about power. It was all about the work and the love.

WILL SCHEFFER:

Oh my God. You can't say enough good things about Bernie Caulfield. She calls herself Nanny, you know? So she takes care of the boys. She's remarkable.

MARK V. OLSEN:

It's almost impossible to overstate what she brings to a show. She's the goddess of making that happen. But in terms of just her spirit, that is infused into the whole company. We could all wear buttons saying WE LOVE BERNIE. Because it was uniform and deep. She's a remarkable energy.

WILL SCHEFFER:

HBO basically invented the creative producer in television. It used to be a line producer. Tom Hanks and Gary Goetzman are creative non–writing producers, but that David Knoller/Bernie Caulfield position. That line producer that's also the creative interface, HBO created that. And it's a key feature of that company. It's a really good way to make television.

MARY KAY PLACE:

The thing that I loved about *Big Love* was that even though this was a very specific group of people, that were not "normal" in the sense that they followed all the regular conventional cultural norms, but were that religious sect, but that it was so universal, so particular in its presentation, that it was as universal as it could get about all families. The show was about power, but the best thing about the show is that you could see your own family in this insane, unusual family.

SIMON SUTTON, Executive:

In 2005, Bill Nelson, who was then COO, said to me, "Figure something out over the next couple of years with international, and if you don't come up with anything, maybe we'll just shut it down." At the time the annual revenue of that business was $70 million. Ten years later it reached $1 billion a year. We bought out our studio partners from all the international channels in a complex series of transactions and then made them much more like the United States, focusing more on series and encouraging them to make their own shows. Shows like *Mandrake* in Brazil and *Wataha* in Poland became really popular locally. It was really a series of different transactions, where we were able to buy out each of our partners and then take full ownership of those channels. It wasn't one moment, but it was seeing that strategy succeed that was tremendously gratifying.

With the retirement of Don Logan from Time Warner at the end of 2005—he'd helmed publishing, cable, and online for the company—Jeff Bewkes moved into a larger role— president and COO of Time Warner—at the beginning of 2006. The promotion took many by surprise, but only by its timing; it had long been assumed that Bewkes would become president and chief operating officer, and that he would eventually take over from the man who gave him the promotion, Dick Parsons, then CEO of Time Warner. But it wasn't all good news for Bewkes: Carl Icahn had been rattling his saber about the falling stock price of Time Warner, but as he held only 3 percent of the stock, Icahn's hopes of breaking up the company into smaller units were probably going nowhere fast. Still, since the merger with AOL, the new company had seen a cratering of its share value, down by about a third in the five years since the ill-fated deal.

Bewkes had a shitshow on his hands, and there were no guarantees the company would survive.

Palace intrigue was, meanwhile, prevalent as well at HBO. Once a week, sometimes every other week, a group in New York held a meeting. Eric Kessler, Richard Plepler, HR chief Shelley Fischel, with an occasional guest appearance from Bill Nelson, would gather to discuss what damage Albrecht had done during the prior week and what they could undo. None of it related to programming, naturally. They wouldn't dare, but they had a lot of complaints about business and technology as issues. When Albrecht found out about the meetings, he deemed them "the Cabal" and laughed it off. But tensions were building behind the scenes.

MIKE LOMBARDO:

Chris would go to New York, but there was such distrust of him in New York. There was a feeling of, "You're not one of us."

Bill, Richard, and Eric weren't behind him, but Chris was sort of guileless about it. He really didn't see it.

The date had been circled on office calendars for months: May 5, 2007—the night that undefeated Floyd Mayweather Jr. would face "Golden Boy" Oscar De La Hoya under the lights at the MGM Grand arena in Las Vegas. The match had been billed with the portentous tag, "The World Awaits," and HBO, for its part, probably awaited more eagerly than anybody else. It seemed like ages, after all, since an HBO Boxing match had been so excitedly anticipated.

In the month leading up to the fight, HBO had premiered 24/7, a four-part weekly reality series that followed both fighters as they went through preparations for the bout. The show featured not only copious training footage but backstage intrigue as well—such as the twist that Floyd Mayweather Sr. offered to train De La Hoya to fight Mayweather's very own son.

As a result, the two fighters' visibility, and the public's interest, grew weekly. Indeed, when Ross Greenburg had first mentioned the idea of 24/7 to his boss, Albrecht had wisely told him to "hold the idea for a big fight."

The show 24/7 worked on two levels. First, it exponentially increased buzz about the fight, which would result in some 2.4 million buys for HBO, for a total of nearly $140 million in revenue, making it HBO's best-performing PPV event in history. Second, as for the new franchise, that, too, went gangbusters. Over the next five years, 24/7 would win sixteen sports Emmys—more than any other show in the same time frame.

Pre-fight hullabaloo was over-the-top. Energy from both camps had reached a raucous level, even by boxing-hype standards. Big fights were invariably big nights for HBO, both in and outside the ring. As with marquee matches dating back decades, celebrities flocked to see the Mayweather–De La Hoya clash and to be seen there. HBO seized the opportunity to play Santa Claus, doling out the best seats to those celebrities and big shots that the network was most eager to impress.

While preparations continued, HBO CEO Chris Albrecht was making his way to Las Vegas, despite the fact that he'd been in Europe just twenty-four hours earlier. Several of those who saw Albrecht upon his arrival thought he looked utterly exhausted. In a manner very atypical of him, Albrecht was observed blowing his top and shouting at HBO event coordinators after finding out they hadn't secured hotel rooms for him, his friends, and the business clients he'd flown with on the company jet, including Brian Grazer and Ron Howard.

The city, too, seemed noticeably on edge. Police had already started making arrests for disruptive behavior by visitors and fans earlier that afternoon.

As for the fight itself—incredible. In the end, after twelve rounds, Mayweather Jr.

won a split decision, although many observers believed De La Hoya had been robbed. After the final bell, many flocked into the streets, some already drunk and others just beginning to party.

ROSS GREENBURG:

We always had our pre-parties at Wolfgang Puck, and then the post-party was at the pool. The pre-parties were always star studded, and at that particular event, cast members from *The Sopranos* and *Entourage*, which was huge, were there. It was an event.

I was with Parsons and Chris, hanging out in one little area. We weren't there that long. We all dispersed. Parsons went to eat something. I went with Larry Gordon and Steve Bing back to the mansion and ate a late dinner. Then Chris just went where he went.

CHRIS ALBRECHT:

The last thing that Dick Parsons said to me when I left, because my gorgeous out-of-her-mind girlfriend was high and dancing, was, "Bro, she is too much of a woman for you. You better step aside and let a real man handle it." That's the quote. That was the night, it was a wild fucking night.

Albrecht and his posse headed to the HBO after-party at the MGM pool where, because so many folks were all-too-well-marinated by that time, behavior was getting out of control. Albrecht ran into Dick Parsons, along with Steve Bing and others. With his girlfriend, Karla, and some of her friends tagging along, Albrecht summoned a big black SUV, loaded it with guests, and proceeded to hit the town.

After stops at the VIP sections of various clubs, where Karla and her female friends were dancing up a storm, Albrecht, Karla, and their group adjourned to hit the strip clubs. It was past two a.m. when Albrecht's hired black SUV pulled up in front of the last strip club, this one so crowded that everyone decided to head back to the hotel and call it a night.

By now, it was about three a.m., Vegas time. One of the women inside the SUV mentioned wanting to hire a prostitute as a gift for her husband, and the driver proffered a name and number. Albrecht, seated up front, dialed the number to ask if the woman would be available for the couple, but Karla suddenly blew her top, apparently convinced that Albrecht had saved the number (though he repeatedly and with increasing anger insisted he had not). The car became a veritable cauldron of accusations, yelling, and cursing—with no sense of calm or reconciliation in sight.

Their arguing persisted as the car pulled up to the MGM. Albrecht got out and walked toward the hotel, but Karla headed for the strip.

All night long, witnesses said, people had been telling Albrecht how "hot" his girl-
friend looked, and so no one was surprised when Albrecht, apparently concerned she
might attract too much attention, took off after her and tried coaxing her back into
the hotel, grabbing her by one arm and tugging. Karla responded by telling Albrecht to
"go fuck himself," according to observers. It was about that time, witnesses said, when
Albrecht simply "lost it."

Shouting "Get the fuck into the hotel," Albrecht grabbed Karla by the wrist and
throat.

CHRIS ALBRECHT:

I had a fight with my girlfriend. I put my hands on her. It was a bad situation. It lasted five seconds, then it was fucking over.

Within seconds, two policemen had pounced on Albrecht and forced him to the ground.
The limo driver tried to pull the cops off him—an ill-advised decision that would get
the driver arrested as well.

Albrecht was taken into custody and arrested on suspicion of "misdemeanor bat-
tery assault."

CHRIS ALBRECHT:

I said to the cops that night when they took me in, "I'm going to get fired for
this," and they said, "No you're not. You'll be fine." My one phone call that I
got to make? It was to Richard. You can't make this shit up.

I was with Steve Bing earlier and we were all out on the town that night
and Steve was with Kirk Kerkorian and Oscar Goodman, the mayor of Las
Vegas. If I had thought to call Bing, the whole story might be different. By
the time I had gotten out twelve hours later, the story was already out.

Richard acted like he had my back. He said, "You should tell everyone
that you're an alcoholic." I wasn't even drunk. He was the one who said, "You
should do this story." I used Richard in a way that no one else used him and I
appreciated the part that he played in elevating the brand. And then he finally
started helping his favorite client, which was himself. And he did an amazing
job. He did an amazing job for HBO, and he did an amazing job for himself.

In the aftermath of the brawl, Karla refused medical treatment and declined to press
charges, then released a statement through Albrecht's personal publicist:

Chris and I made a mistake last weekend. It was an incident fueled by both
of us drinking too much alcohol, but I was not injured and I know he cares

about me. Our argument that evening got out of hand, but I still love him and I forgive him. We are both grateful that the matter has been resolved with the Las Vegas authorities. Chris and I are both committed to our sobriety and are looking forward to putting this behind us and moving on with our lives together.

The judge ordered a fine imposed and levied a six-month suspended sentence with the provision that Albrecht attend domestic violence counseling.

But the "drunk" story? It was apparently just that—a tall tale. Albrecht hadn't really been drunk at all that night.

Albrecht spent that night and Sunday morning in jail. By Tuesday, it was agreed that Albrecht, who maintained privately that he was sober (as though that would help his case), would claim a relapse of his alcohol problem and offer to step back temporarily from his role at HBO to seek treatment.

JEFF BEWKES:

About six a.m. I got a phone call from Richard telling me that Chris had been arrested in Las Vegas for assaulting his girlfriend.

CHRIS ALBRECHT:

That night and into the next day while it was all happening, I thought, "Fuck, I am going to get fired," but then it seemed like maybe there was a path through this. It's not that I thought that I was irreplaceable as much as I thought that shit was going so well that this isn't going to fuck it up.

I had gone into the office on Monday and was still hanging on.

MIKE LOMBARDO:

There was a real cultural divide between Los Angeles and New York that had occurred in this company over time. This episode highlighted it.

It happened on a Saturday night. Sunday morning, everyone's calling everyone to find out what was going on. Those of us in Los Angeles were terrified about losing Chris. I spoke to Chris that afternoon. He told me, "It's going to be okay."

*But on Wednesday, the **Los Angeles Times** reported that this wasn't Albrecht's first offense. In 1991, the company had apparently paid a settlement of $400,000 to a senior vice president at HBO Independent Productions, Sasha Emerson, "a subordinate with whom Albrecht was romantically involved after she alleged that he shoved and choked her."*

CHRIS ALBRECHT:

When I saw the *LA Times* article I said to myself, "Okay, now, I'm getting fired. I can't survive this." At that point, there wasn't anyone saying, "We have to keep him." Jeff called me and he was crying. He told me Parsons said, "We have to get rid of him." That turned out to be a bit ironic later on when we all learned Dick had fathered a secret baby with a secret girlfriend. But it was the second bit, the Claudia Eller article, that really fucked me up. Someone fed her stuff. The fact that it was Claudia Eller of all people to break the story was also curious, I don't think I'd ever spoken to Claudia Eller. She was not someone who covered HBO business.

HAL AKSELRAD:

There were only a handful of people at HBO who knew about the settlement with Sasha. I assiduously kept my knowledge of its terms and bargaining history confidential. In my capacity as general counsel, I ensured that the document was kept in secure custody. I never leaked it: it would have been an ethical violation and harmful to the company.

JEFF BEWKES:

I told Chris that we'd have to terminate him. His lawyers were telling him they could get the charges dropped with no contest, but that was beside the point for the company.

Chris made a case but I said, "Look, your contract is up in December. The board would never agree to a renewal, and if I proposed it, you wouldn't be dealing with me anyway because I'd be gone. You're better off getting terminated than just not getting renewed at the end of your contract."

Chris knew the board was still smarting over the TW CFO being involved with a madam of a prostitution ring the year before, and he knew that his file had the record of the incident with Sasha fifteen years before, so the situation couldn't stand a full review at the board. Some people have said the *LA Times* piece on the earlier altercation caused the firing, but I think we had to end up there anyway.

By noon on May 10, 2007, Albrecht had been fired.

CAROLYN STRAUSS:

When Chris left, I was devastated. He was my mentor of close to twenty years, so on a personal level, and on a professional level, it was really difficult. It was a terrible, terrible time.

Look, he's no saint, and he only has himself to blame for what happened. We are all imperfect creatures.

Those of us in the executive ecosystem stand in for the artist in certain ways and if you're going to be a successful artist, you have to have an outsider's point of view because if you're seeing everything the way everybody sees it, then you're not telling anybody anything new. I think Chris was really an outsider in a lot of ways and brought that outsider's perspective to his creative decision-making.

I have never met a creative executive like Chris. He understands what needs to be done to make shows better, and he can communicate those ideas without nitpicking. He was a great boss. He would share credit and take blame. That's a very unique quality. He knew we were in a creative business and gave us permission to fail. That was essential.

RICHARD PARSONS:

I believe there was a period of time when HBO was in a class by itself. They were the premium network. HBO had the talent. They had the pick of programming and there was nobody else who could compete. They were first. Everybody else was second.

So where did the creative genius come from? It was a business to run, to be sure, and that's what people like Jerry, Nick Nicholas, Frank Biondi, Michael, and Jeff did. All really great guys and good businessmen—but you know who was doing the programming? A guy by the name of Chris Albrecht. Chris was a guy who had deep relationships with the talent community and was in large part responsible for a lot of the creative output in those preceding years.

A point in time came, in 2007, we had to let Chris go. We didn't have much choice. After we let Chris go, it took HBO a couple of years to regain its feet from a creative point of view. This was also at a time when Hollywood thought HBO had gotten too big for its britches.

SHELLEY FISCHEL:

Chris became CEO so that we could keep his programming talent, which was prodigious. He was maybe the best programmer in the business ever.

ARI EMANUEL:

Chris is one of the greatest creative executives ever in the business. When it comes to understanding shows and talent, it doesn't get better.

ROSS GREENBURG:

Chris was a great boss. Did he have inner demons? Yeah, plenty.

COLIN CALLENDER:

Chris was very trusting. Chris empowered me as he empowered others who worked for him. He empowered me as a curator. He trusted my judgment on the stories that we would tell and how we would tell them. He did the same with Carolyn Strauss, and Sheila Nevins. He trusted our creative judgment, and empowered us with filmmakers. That was a very important part of how great HBO programs were made.

GLENN WHITEHEAD:

Chris Albrecht obviously had a huge impact on every aspect of HBO's original programming at various points in time in his career. But the thing that Chris brought to HBO, that wasn't necessarily part of our DNA, but that Chris really infused, was a complete obsession with talent relations. Chris had been an agent dealing with comics and talent every day. He had a talent-friendly, talent-focused perspective coming into HBO. And if you've not grown up in that world, when you're a New York–based company that is just dipping its toes into licensing original programming, and then the commissioning of original programming, as you transition into being the studio and having direct relationships with talent, having somebody who is really focused on the company developing a talent-friendly orientation is really valuable. And that resonates at HBO still today.

SHEILA NEVINS:

Does anyone not have a dark side? Even if it was true that he fucked everybody in sight, so what? He left me alone. He didn't shoot anybody, did he? He wasn't Trump. He was a tremendously good programmer, and tremendously intelligent. He had a real feel for the audience. He was complicated, but so were all my bosses.

CHRIS ALBRECHT:

They allowed me to stay employed until August, which was past my fifty-fifth birthday, which gave me the fifty-five and twenty. At Time Warner back then, if you're over fifty-five and you have worked there at least twenty years, you get lifetime benefits.

I instituted important initiatives for HBO that I'm not even sure Jeff would have done because I was more open to new ideas and less invested in the New York historical mindset. At HBO, I was always the outsider from LA. The TV agent who became a programmer. Well, that turned out okay, didn't it?

10

To Weep from Gladness

MAY 11, 2007–MARCH 9, 2008

It had been eight extraordinary years of television, and the most important series in HBO history.

HBO had ignored audience test results and made a major financial commitment to an arguably dicey series that others had rejected, and that had few recognizable stars. The show originated with a writer-producer who had been through more downs than ups in his career and had yet to fulfill his primary dream of one day making a feature film.

Before it was all over, the unassuming David Chase would manage to make us all care deeply about the joys and woes of an amoral leading man who lied, cheated, and killed as part of his business. But Chase had done more, so much more. The great appeal of James Gandolfini and of the show was fueled less by the organized crime setting, fascinating as it was, and more by the show's ability to let the audience experience vicariously universal problems that everybody can relate to. There were parenting problems, marital difficulties, money issues, and extended family dramas. And of course, therapy, which gave the audience another point of entry, another lens through which to see and learn more about a villainous hero (or heroic villain) named Tony.

This blend of elements didn't guarantee spectacular success, of course. The Sopranos became The Sopranos because of Chase's singular, twisted touch, and because of the contributions of shrewdly chosen writers and directors along with phenomenal actors ingeniously cast (sometimes against type).

Chase's deployment of dream sequences, time shifts, sardonic humor, and inventive violence—all supported by brilliantly curated music—proved all too familiar yet ironically otherworldly all at once.

As the show moved closer to its final episode, and the stakes became higher than at any other time in HBO history, the question became whether the network, in a legacy-protecting move, would cast aside its promise (and its established proclivity) to stay out of the showrunner's business. For decades, network execs had always been aggressively involved in series finales. But, true to their words, Albrecht and Strauss didn't even try inserting themselves into calculations for the series' end, even though they knew Chase was planning a whopper of an ending that would raise questions not just about the show itself, but about HBO's ability to even stay on the air.

How in hell to ring down the curtain and end a show like The Sopranos when there'd never really been a show like The Sopranos? Would Tony himself survive the finale—or go out in some horrible blaze of gory glory (like, say, in Bonnie and Clyde)? For weeks, the noose had been tightening around the character's neck, from the POVs of both professional law enforcers and professional lawbreakers. Yet folks out there in Television Land who were desirous of a flat, definitive answer from that final episode (number eighty-six, "Made in America") had a shock in store—perhaps not the kind they thought they'd been prepared for. Chase was too wily and quirky in his storytelling to make anything easy for his viewers; a huge explosion of gunfire in the final scene, while kinetically and literally shocking, was unlikely to have viewers chattering the next morning in the way Chase wanted them to be.

This farewell episode, written and directed by Chase, would have to be a tour de force of nonlinear, masterly storytelling that would catch everyone unaware—the way so many Sopranos episodes had done over the years.

In the last show's final four-and-a-half-minute scene, set at a casual neighborhood hangout called Holsten's, Tony enters, gravitates to one of the little satellite jukeboxes installed in each booth, and selects the Journey song, "Don't Stop Believin'" from the listed tracks. The song would become an unforgettable cap to the evening's soundtrack (Journey's Steve Perry had initially blocked usage of the song until a mere three days before the air date because he didn't want it to be linked forever with the deaths of any beloved characters).

As the song begins to play, Carmela joins Tony, sitting across from him at the exact moment Perry sings the lyric "just a small-town girl, living in a lonely world." Enter Anthony Jr., right behind an unidentified man who heads for the bar, glancing once or twice at the family. Is he going to kill Tony?! Is someone else?! Is Tony going to kill the *unidentified man?! Out in the dark night, Meadow is having a helluva time parallel parking her car. The customer at the bar heads past Tony en route to the men's room, neither seeming to pay much attention to the other, and two more strange men enter the diner.*

Onion rings are delivered to the Sopranos' table; Meadow finally parks and enters the diner; and Tony looks up suddenly as he hears the ting-a-ling of the bell above the door. America was on the edge of its sofa.

And then the screen went black, causing thousands of viewers to phone their cable providers to complain that the HBO feed, or the whole cable system, had died right at the moment of truth. They couldn't know it at the time, but Chase had wanted the black screen to last through the HBO chime (i.e., no credits) but the Directors Guild denied him a waiver of a Guild rule preventing that.

Those seven seconds proved startling enough and gave birth to a cottage industry— one dedicated to the question of what actually happened, and to whom, during the final moments of **The Sopranos.**

The Sopranos *ceased to be, but only after doing more to jolt HBO on its axis, and more to change scripted television, than any program before, during, or since.*

DAVID CHASE:

I was in France when the finale aired. The press said I had fled there, but my flights were booked months in advance, and I went to France every year. I watched it at nine o'clock that Sunday night, French time, three o'clock in New York.

By that time, I felt pretty confident. I had gotten out of the habit of looking for approval. I had great people working with me, and everything was working well with the network. I felt I had scratched the creative itch. I knew that I had had a great canvas to work on, that we poured everything into it, and that we couldn't have done it better.

QUENTIN SCHAFFER:

Three weeks before it aired, I was given a VHS of the final episode because I was going to be overseeing the press. I went home and said to my wife, "I'm going to watch the final episode of *The Sopranos*. You can watch with me, but you can't say anything to anyone that you've seen it, or I will get fired." We watch the show, and after it goes to black, my wife says, "Well, obviously they didn't trust you with the ending." I said, "The whole point of my seeing the final episode was to be prepared for the ending. It wouldn't make sense if they removed it." And she said, "Well, if that's the ending, you're fucked."

MATTHEW WEINER:

David had been in show business for a long time; he was not there to reassure the audience. There was no formula. Everything was supposed to be a little movie, complete in itself, even though it was part of a continuing story line.

QUENTIN SCHAFFER:

David was always cooperative with what we did to promote the series, but the only thing he wouldn't do for me is give an explanation of why the finale went to black and what happened to Tony Soprano. His attitude was let people believe what they want to believe.

LORRAINE BRACCO:

Melfi and Tony ended the way David wanted, but it was definitely not the way I would have ended their relationship. I thought it was harsh. She cared for him. She wanted to make a difference in his life. I was disappointed and depressed about it.

I'd been surprised that people were so interested in two people sitting across from each other talking. Then I got awards from the Psychoanalytical Association and they told me a lot more men were going into therapy because of the show. I'll live with that.

People loved the show, and David and everyone involved did an incredible job. That door closing on a series is always very strange. As an actor, you never know when the next door is going to open.

EDIE FALCO:

Several years ago I went to the play *God of Carnage* that Jim did with Marcia Gay Harden, and when they walked in together onstage and sat down next to each other as a couple, I had a totally unexpected wave of jealousy come over me. I thought, "What the hell is this bizarre thing?" I wasn't expecting such a reaction, it snuck up on me, but there was a little crossover there. I quickly corrected my mechanism, and everything was fine. But it's complicated. It's mind games.

A big part of therapy and all these journeys I've been on has been learning to separate my life and my work. If I was supposed to be in love with another character, I thought it was part and parcel of really losing myself in that character, and the two lives blending, real life and fake life. I got myself in some very, very dangerous, complicated, and unpleasant situations as a result. I could lose myself when they were bleeding into each other.

Now I've learned to explore with boundaries, without fear of disappearing, and still feel safe.

MATTHEW WEINER:

I don't think there will ever be anything like *The Sopranos*.

HBO wasted no time inaugurating what some hoped would be the perfect series to pick up the torch from **The Sopranos** *following its series finale on June 10, 2007. That very night, HBO premiered* **John from Cincinnati,** *a story about a family of surfers in the San Diego area who are visited by the eponymous traveler from Ohio. No sooner has he arrived than strange, supernatural events start to occur, including a character who floats about in midair. The show dealt in serious themes, too—numerous characters dabbling in drugs while the elder statesman of surfing, Bruce Greenwood as Mitch Yost, ruminates on what he sees as the commercialization of the seafaring sport.*

John from Cincinnati was hatched by David Milch, who already had a houseful of glistening television hardware when **John** *blew in from Cincinnati. A former writer on* **Hill Street Blues,** *Milch created* **NYPD Blue,** *which aired from 1993 to 2005 and won twenty Emmy Awards to go with its four Golden Globes. Milch had also spawned the HBO original series* **Deadwood.** *The pressure was on; HBO was clearly betting on Milch's ability to draw a crowd.*

HOWARD ROSENMAN:

Ari Emanuel took me to Carolyn Strauss at HBO, and I pitched this concept of *Six Feet Under* in the world of surfing.

After, Carolyn called and asked, "Do you mind if I give this to David Milch?" I said, "Of course not." So she gave it to David Milch, calls me back and says, "You have good news and bad news." "What's the good news?" "David Milch wants to do your series." "What's the bad news?" "David Milch is going to do your series. You're going to have nothing to do with it, but he wants to meet you." So I go to meet David Milch. He asks me one question: "Do you believe in God?" And I say, "Yes." He said, "Good." And then he turned my *Six Feet Under* in the world of surfing into *John from Cincinnati,* this thing about a Christ figure, which was terrible and horrible. I couldn't even watch it.

DAVID MILCH:

The project developed itself and shaped itself under the category of be careful what you wish for. I was given so much freedom, I had to confront myself imaginatively, almost on a daily basis.

It was scary. You have a lot of elements you're responsible for, and you want to do the right thing. I was grateful to HBO for their willingness to let me discover the heart of the piece on a daily basis.

Every day, you're working in a laboratory discovering each character. And it's an enormous responsibility that you are being given and you want to be honorable in a way that you respond to that.

CAROLYN STRAUSS:

John from Cincinnati was not created when David was in his best frame of mind. He was really upset about the *Deadwood* cancellation, so it was almost created in anger. I think it aspired to a lot, but it didn't connect in the right way and didn't deliver on its ambition.

CHRIS ALBRECHT:

I believed *John from Cincinnati* was a breakthrough show. I was wrong. But if we were trying to break a new show from David Milch, who had already created a hit show for us, what better place to put it than behind the finale of a big show?

What else could have been behind it? We didn't have another show. We didn't make shows and keep them in the can. We made shows to put them on the air. This was the show David wanted to do after *Deadwood*.

ILENE LANDRESS:

That was probably the most depressing year of my life. *The Sopranos* was over, and I was put on *John from Cincinnati*. We cast an actor who wasn't available, so we shut down for like three months. We hired the wrong director; Milch had his racing buddies around because he really wanted to be doing his series *Luck*. It was a nightmare. I knew it was wrong all the way through it, yet I was stuck, and I couldn't get off.

Plepler said something like, "We want to show him [Milch] that we can say no." You're wasting millions of dollars just so you can say no?

CHRIS ALBRECHT:

What Richard couldn't understand is that sometimes you have to go through difficult things to come out at a better place. If you look at the first three episodes of *John from Cincinnati*, I'm telling you, no one's ever done that before, and no one's ever done it since. It's just that fucking Milch wrote the first three episodes and then stopped writing. He lost his fucking way. But that was a cool show.

John from Cincinnati *hit the road after ten largely ignored episodes, the first first-season cancellation of an hour-long series in HBO history.*

GINA BALIAN:

To maintain a success streak in anything for a long period of time is hard. People were really worried when *The Sopranos* ended about what was next, and it wasn't there immediately. Development doesn't work like that. The next wave of successes were all in-house, they just weren't ready to be put on the air. It was a nervous time to have a show like *The Sopranos* end and not see the next big commercial hit.

PAUL SIMMS:

Flight of the Conchords was incredibly fun. It was made incredibly cheap, so no one expected anything of it. We had to be super creative, and those guys were all super fun. It was the sort of experiment that every network talks about doing, and HBO finally did. Find funny people, give them a bit of money, and see what they can do. *Flight of the Conchords* ended up working because it wasn't big and overblown.

GINA BALIAN:

We gave Stu Smiley maybe $2 million to create two or three performer-driven projects. We made one with Tom Green, we made one with Wyclef Jean, and *Flight of the Conchords* was the one that lasted. To have it be as successful as it was exciting.

As one comedy was trying to find its legs, another was "returning," joining a schedule that would be the most unorthodox in series television history. HBO had said to Larry David, in effect: "Whenever you want to bring back **Curb Your Enthusiasm,** *just let us know and we will start writing the checks for you to get up and running again." Season five of* **Curb** *had aired in 2005; season six would air a full two years later. That would be a short interruption compared to the gaps that would come later.*

ALEC BERG, Writer and Creator:

Curb started as a land deal for us. I, along with my partners, Jeff Schaffer and David Mandel, were looking for office space, and Larry said, I have an empty office in my suite that you guys are welcome to use, but in exchange maybe I can come in and bug you every once in a while, as I'm thinking about *Curb* ideas. We said, "God, that sounds great." So we took this office and Larry would come in every once in a while and just go, "Hey, what do you think of this?" He had fun knocking stuff around with us, coming in more and more often, and we essentially ended up helping him work on what was season five. Toward the end, he came in one day and said, "Production needs this office because we're going to start staffing up to shoot the season." We went, "Oh, okay." Then we got a call from HBO saying, "We know you weren't officially employed as writers, but Larry says you guys contributed a lot and we'd like to pay you for your work." We went, "Oh my God, that's so nice. It's such a flattering offer. It's so unnecessary." They said, "We would like to pay you each $100 per episode," and we realized it wasn't that they wanted to pay us at all. It's that they felt in order to own whatever we may have contributed in a legally binding way, they needed to pay for it. So we went from doing Larry this favor and having a ball to feeling like we had just been the cheapest whores on earth, totally insulted and degraded for doing three or four months of work for $100 an episode.

RICHARD LEWIS:

Larry David has the greatest instincts of any writer I've ever known in the history of television. If Norman Lear had a younger brother, it would be Larry.

ALEC BERG:

The show comes from Larry. He still carries that little notebook and every time he's in public and feels uncomfortable, ashamed, or angry, he writes down why and a lot of it ends up in the show.

Larry had the idea that he and Cheryl would take in a hurricane family, and we all talked about what if instead of being happy about this, Larry could be angry. That could be funny. I will tell you when J. B. Smoove came in to audition, I've never seen an audition like that in my life.

J. B. SMOOVE, Actor and Comedian:

I was a big *Curb Your Enthusiasm* fan when I was a writer on *Saturday Night Live*. I was watching *Curb* one day in a Jersey apartment, and my fiancée, who is now my wife, was washing dishes. She's a hands-on kind of girl. We had just had something I call hot dog soup, our version of beans and franks. I said, "Baby, I love this damn show so much, I love this dude Larry David, I would love to be on this show one day." And she said, "You are going to be on that show one day."

I was about to go into my fourth season on *SNL*, but I didn't get renewed. I said, "Oh man," I ended up going on the road. I was in Atlanta, Georgia, had just finished doing stand-up, and I get a phone call saying a close buddy had passed away. I went to LA for one day to go to his memorial service, and while I was in town, decided to say hi to my new agent. I'm sitting in their little office and an agent walks in and asks, "How long are you in town?" I said, "I'm leaving in the morning." He said, "Well, I have an audition here." I said, "What's it for?" He said, "For *Curb Your Enthusiasm*." I said, "What?" I said, "Man, I love *Curb Your Enthusiasm*, I'm a big fan." I go over to the audition, I'm sitting in the waiting room, it's tons of actors and comedians who I knew, who were also going in for the role. I read the notes they gave me, and I said, Oh, I know exactly who Leon is. So I have this thing I do. I never walk into an audition as myself, I always walk in there as the character who I am portraying, so they can see how I will walk, as opposed to J.B. going in the room.

I go in there and they say, "Okay, J.B., you're going to improv with Larry directly." I had no idea I was going to be improving with Larry directly.

I walk up to Larry, and this is exactly what I said: "Okay, Larry, let's do this baby, and since this is improv, I might fuck around and slap you in the face." Larry looked at everybody else like, Who the hell is this guy? Then he looked at me like I was crazy, and we started the audition.

ALEC BERG:

The way *Curb* auditions worked is you would come into the room and just improv with Larry. So casting was an exhausting process for Larry because, if we brought in five people for a part, he had to improv the scene with five different people. J.B.'s audition scene was from the episode where Cheryl found a blanket in the room that Leon was staying in and it had what they thought was a cum stain. Cheryl said, "I don't know what to do." And Larry told her, "Let me talk to him about it." So the scene was J.B. sitting in a chair watching TV, and Larry says, "Excuse me, Leon, can I talk to you for a second?" J.B.'s supposed to get up and walk over to him. But J.B. just sits in this chair and he's got this expression on his face that was like the funniest thing we had ever seen. And Larry, literally for five minutes, couldn't ask him to stand up, because he just kept laughing. There's nothing funnier on earth than when Larry breaks. No feeling has ever been better to me as a comedy writer than making Larry David laugh. He's got one of those big belly laughs. You feel like you're a hundred feet tall. You feel immortal. It's the best.

J. B. SMOOVE:

We laughed our asses off. At one point, Larry walked into a corner to get his composure back. I leave the audition, and my agent calls me and asks,

"How did it go?" I said, "We had a great time. If anybody else gets that role, God bless them." I had to go straight to a comedy show for a weekend gig.

After my set, the club manager says, "I told you to keep it clean." I said, "Man, I didn't do any dirty material. This is the most horrible comedy club I've ever been in in my life." I went to the hotel and grabbed my luggage.

I said, "I'm going to leave tonight because I don't trust the weather." Fifteen minutes into my ride, a flurry here, a flurry there, then a straight blizzard started. I mean, so horrible. About an hour into my trip my agent called me. I'm thinking the guy called him and told him he canceled me. I answered and said, "I'm so sorry, man, me and that guy got into it, it was a terrible comedy club, now I'm doing ten miles an hour in a blizzard." He said, "Cut it down to five miles an hour, take your time, relax. You got *Curb Your Enthusiasm*." I said, "What? You fucking kidding me, man?" He said, "No, they fucking loved you."

JOHN McENROE:

I hadn't watched a lot of episodes of *Curb*, but I've got six kids and the older ones love watching it. Then Larry called me out of the blue, and asked, "Hey, would you like to do *Curb*?" And my kids were nearby saying, "You got to do it." And so I'm like, "Okay, yeah. When?"

He called me I think on a Wednesday, and he said he wanted to film Friday, Monday, and Tuesday. Then I attempt a joke, and asked, "Who pulled out?" And he goes, "It's not bad to be runner-up."

When I saw the outline, I thought, "How the hell can somebody even come up with this? This guy's out of his mind."

In June 2007, nearly twelve years after his dismissal, Michael Fuchs returned to the HBO building in New York to be honored by the company, naming its new fifteenth-floor, state-of-the-art theater after him.

Sounds like a cathartic, warm, lovely evening.

JEFF BEWKES:

Michael kept lobbying me to name the HBO theater after him. Chris should get most of the credit for finally convincing me to do it. I had forgotten about it but Chris, before he left the company, had seen Michael and said, "Michael really wants you to do this." I said, "You're right, Jerry's gone, let's do it." So I called Michael and said, "We want to name the theater after you, it'll be your night, you can invite anyone you want, we'll have a tribute roast to you, and you can speak as well if you'd like." Michael invited everybody.

MICHAEL FUCHS:

Finally they named the theater after me. Fred Wistow, this friend of mine, got up that night and said, "It's a little surprising to me that the letters on Michael's theater are smaller than the ones on the ladies' room." Listen, I'm a big shadow, but it had been a long time, and they were acting like they created it all. Richard had been acting for years like he was the man, that all this shit was made possible by him. I invented Richard.

JEFF BEWKES:

Fuchs gets up onstage and unleashes a diatribe about how we didn't invite him to every premiere and basically accuses all of us, most of all me, of disloyalty.

Then he takes out the twenty-thousand-dollar watch he was given when he left the company, drops it on the stage, and stomps on it, saying, "This is what I think of that watch." I guess he forgot that the company didn't give him the watch, and that many of the people at this dinner had personally chipped in for it.

MICHAEL FUCHS:

I pulled a cheap twenty-dollar Timex out of my pocket and stomped on that. Clearly HBO had lost its comedy touch in the time since I had left.

STU SMILEY:

It was a full house. Almost all senior management was there. Michael always had a dark sense of humor. When he spoke, I think people took him too seriously. I didn't. I understood why people were offended, but he had been gone for eleven years and was not invited to a single event. I might be pissed, too. I do think Michael was trying to be funny, but the crowd was not with him.

MICHAEL FUCHS:

I have to say I was disappointed. There was never a press release. They never use the name. When a movie is being shown, they say it was being shown at HBO, not at the Michael Fuchs Theater.

Speaking of CEOs, almost a month after the spectacular fall of Chris Albrecht, it was time for HBO employees to learn who was going to be selected as their new intrepid leader.

JEFF BEWKES:

The June board meeting was in LA on the Warner lot. At nine a.m., Dick Parsons took the board into exec session, meaning without any management present. Usually exec sessions before board meetings went ten or fifteen minutes, but they were in there for like forty-five minutes. Finally they take a break and invite me in. Dick and I are standing at the coffee machine, the board is ten feet away, and Dick says, "I told them we'll do a search for the HBO CEO and Pat's going to run the process and get a list of diverse outside candidates. They'll ask you about it, so I wanted you to be clued in."

I say, "Dick, we can't do a three-month search when the guy who's gonna win the search, Bill Nelson, is already the president of HBO. Everyone will think we wanted somebody other than Bill, but we couldn't find anybody so we're picking Bill. That just trashes Bill. I've already seen Pat's list, and talked it through with her. I know who needs to run HBO. I used to run it myself." He thinks it over and says, "All right, but they're watching this very closely. This whole Time Warner CEO job is yours to lose." Dick is a great guy, stand-up guy. He'd just told the board we were going to do a search, and now he's agreed to support my pick. So the board comes to order and Fay Vincent asks, "Jeff, how long do you think it'll take to get a new CEO for HBO?" I said, "Monday. It's Bill Nelson. He's already on the job and he's the best choice. We're not gonna miss a beat."

The board goes silent, they're all looking at each other, then down to the end of the table at Dick. He looks back calmly and shrugs his shoulders, points at me, and says, it's up to me as COO and former HBO head. That's how that went down.

That night, we had dinner with senior management, and I took Bill aside and said, "Look, you're going to be the new CEO of HBO." He said, "I don't know if I can do that." I told him, "Bill, you're already doing it."

BILL NELSON:

I had no reservation about becoming CEO. I told Jeff, "I will make sure this company does not miss a beat." I had been the chief operating officer, had worked with Chris and our top team very closely, had worked my way up through the financial side for quite a few years, knew all the contracts the company had, and knew all the HBO people.

HBO's new CEO, Bill Nelson, was unlike any before him. A military man, he served in the US Army's 101st Airborne Division in 1969 and headed off to Vietnam. Upon his return to the States, Nelson took an undergraduate degree and an MBA in accounting and finance from Pace University in downtown Manhattan. He then nabbed his first job, in 1975, at Ernst & Young, where he would become a CPA and audit supervisor, before arriving at Time Inc. as director of external reporting and risk management. Five years later, Nelson would become HBO's assistant controller, eventually serving as CFO and then COO.

SIMON SUTTON:

Leading up to Bill becoming CEO, it was very factional. Chris was mainly in LA, Bill was in New York, and they were very different. There were teams of people inside the company who didn't like other teams of people. It was almost like there were multiple companies inside the company. Then there were people who thought they should be the next CEO. A lot of what was going on was based on ambition, and not what was best for the company.

Bill was a calming figure, and when he became CEO, it actually resolved many of those issues. Bill was very clear about what he wanted. Bill knew the nuts and bolts of the company backward and forward.

BILL NELSON:

I addressed the New York staff first and then flew immediately out to the West Coast and called the management team there together. I told them, "This company has and will continue to perform and outlast any of its CEOs, present, future. The team, the brand, and the momentum are greater than one individual." I told everyone in the room to look at the people around them always as a collective, which will drive HBO forward regardless of the turnover in CEOs.

I always thought of HBO like a newspaper, and people buy newspapers for different reasons. Very few read a newspaper from cover to cover. Some go right to the business section, or sports, or the gossip column. It is a broad delivery system of different aspects of life. HBO had sports, documentaries, movies, either fiction or factual. The documentaries were extremely compelling series programming, of course, having a very deep array of topics. At the water cooler on Monday morning, there were a variety of discussions by people in most companies about, "Hey, what did you see on HBO over the weekend?"

The people at HBO were fantastic. They worked hard, they cared, they supported each other. It was a tough business. As successful as it was, we always ran scared. We kept looking over our shoulder.

MIKE LOMBARDO:

There were plenty of people who could have been the next CEO and make sure Time Warner was happy. Bill Nelson was certainly one. The real issue was to figure out how to allow what Michael, Jeff, and Chris built to continue to grow.

DAVE BALDWIN:

Bill was an army guy. He believed in a chain of command that doesn't involve having group discussions about decision-making. You have one job. Do it. I'll make the decisions and filter it down. Even though Richard always said, "We have an open door," it was bullshit. After Chris and Jeff left, it was top-down management only. It became difficult.

We actually set up a working group, headed by HR to get the East and West Coasts communicating with each other. The group was called One Coast. It was supposed to make sure that both coasts understood what people did and their job functions, but it became a bitch-and-gripe session.

And after six or nine months, it met an early demise. I think the guy from HR was taking notes and feeding it back up to Bill. The dysfunction at HBO I think largely started when Nelson took over.

CARMI ZLOTNIK:

When I saw the news that Chris was arrested in Las Vegas, I was in bed watching HBO, and I turned to my wife and said, "Well, that's the end of that." I knew as soon as Chris left the company, they'd want me out, as well. I was too closely aligned with Chris. Mike Lombardo was the one who said to me, "Carmi, there's no longer a place for you at HBO."

CAROLYN STRAUSS:

For a long time, it was a very stable company. When Chris left, things changed. New people were in positions of responsibility, and they wanted to do their own thing. There was a different dynamic, and for me, that was personal and professional.

Bill Nelson wasn't a guy who covets. He didn't want to be any bigger than he already was, didn't want to enlarge his social circle, didn't want to become famous, and certainly didn't want to be on any "power influence" lists. He wanted to "watch HBO's back" because that's where its wallet was kept and that was his expertise.

What that meant is that Nelson needed someone else who wanted the visibility and glory he so forcefully balked at. And in Richard Plepler, Nelson found his man. Nelson was captivated by Plepler's ability to discuss the company's brand, let alone his love of speaking in public.

BILL NELSON:

I was aware that Richard may have wanted the job, and if Richard would have gotten the job, I would have been fine with that. HBO is bigger than one person. I would've saluted Richard and supported him with every fiber in my body.

ERIC KESSLER:

Bill was not interested in publicity for himself and all the Hollywood stuff. That was not who he was, and so he appreciated that Richard handled all that for him. We'd have screening premieres in New York, and unless it was a really big one, Bill would often not go, and Richard would be the "host." Bill didn't even like going to the Emmy Awards. This didn't mean he wasn't supportive, it was just not his thing. Obviously if Bill was as visible as Chris, Jeff, or Michael had been, Richard would not have had the opportunities that he did. So it was a good situation for both of them.

RICHARD PLEPLER:

I owe so much to Bill Nelson, from the moment Jeff left to go to corporate in 2002 Bill was always immensely supportive of me and encouraging about my potential in the company. He was as knowledgeable about our business as anyone who had ever sat in that chair, and he very generously offered up his wisdom to help educate me on those parts of the business that I had not been exposed to.

JEFF BEWKES:

Shelley Fischel, our HR head, said, "I think you ought to go with Richard. Bill doesn't want to do it and Richard does." It's true that Bill was reluctant. But I thought the right way to decide this wasn't who wants to do it the most, and I thought the reason Bill was ambivalent was because he didn't see himself making funny dinner speeches and being the face of the company at industry gatherings the way Michael was naturally, and I had to learn to be. He knew the business better than anybody and everybody trusted him.

I told Richard, "Remember, until recently, you were in PR. If you become CEO in the wake of all this with Chris, it's going to look like I put you there rather than you earned it, because everybody knows we're close. First, that's bad for me because it would look like I'm doling out favors for friends. Second, it's bad for you because it would make you look like you need patronage. It may take time, but the one thing you don't want is to be head of a company and fail. And in order to succeed, you need people to support you and believe that you're the best choice.

Richard always told me he understood, but I know he was really frustrated he didn't get the CEO job after Chris.

HAL AKSELRAD:

Bill came down to my office and kicked open the door. He declared it was a done deal and that he would be CEO, and Richard and Eric were going to be co-COOs. He then told me that I would not get anything in the reorganization except, perhaps, for a department like IT or Network Operations. He then spun on his heels and walked out.

Believing this was the case, I immediately concluded I would leave HBO. I sent an email to share this with my wife. It turned out, in my frustration, I accidentally sent that email to Bill. Fearing that my leaving on account of his treatment of me would get out, Bill preempted things by sharing my email with Jeff. Jeff called me immediately, saying, "What's with this email? Don't go anywhere. Don't do a thing. I'll be right down." Jeff came to my office and said, "You're too important to this company and I'm changing this around. Bill will be CEO. You, Richard, and Eric will be co-presidents."

And so life began anew, in the summer of 2007, for HBO in the post-Albrecht world. Nelson was up on top, followed by a three-headed monster composed of Akselrad, Kessler, and Plepler.

Day-to-day responsibilities of the co-presidents would be split like this: Plepler would be in charge of programming; Akselrad would continue to run legal and business affairs, including negotiating film deals for HBO, and also overseeing the technology team; and Kessler would continue to run distribution and marketing, while adding "new digital initiatives" and "international" to his list.

From the start, problems emerged. No member of the triumvirate really respected or even liked the others, and Plepler, given his bond with their boss, was always going to receive "favored nations" treatment from Nelson.

The arrangement was doomed for all three before they took their first meeting together.

BILL NELSON:

We had three totally different personalities who each had their own egos and their own perspective of themselves, each with a unique talent and skill set, which you would have in every case where you put three people with different expertise and disciplines together.

If one of those three or people below them thought I had favorites in my heart, I really didn't. But you then have to look at the responsibilities of those three people, and Richard was responsible for programming, which basically is the cornerstone of the company. And that area was most in shock after Chris departed. So if anyone thought that I was leaning more toward Richard, that would be the reason.

ERIC KESSLER:

The weeks following Chris's departure were filled with rumors, lobbying, and a rash of frenetic activity as everybody tried to position themselves for a new role. I had a close relationship with Bill because I was also from the business side so I was fairly confident I would end up with some increased responsibility. I figured Richard would get something but since he was a PR guy, I didn't know what they could give him, and a lot of people were shocked when he got responsibility over programming, an area he had no experience in. They eventually announced a cumbersome three co-president structure. While we were all happy to get elevated, I think we each realized that this was not a tenable long-term structure.

The question of who should be in charge of the West Coast would be the first major decision for Plepler now that Nelson had given him supervision of programming. Plepler's background in communications suggested to some that he would further embolden present programming head Carolyn Strauss. But Plepler had told people both inside and outside that he'd been hearing reports of Strauss either being burned out or having been made too egotistical by her own success. The consensus around LA was that Plepler had never been a Strauss fan at any point; they were, after all, very, very different people.

So Plepler began to think about "layering" Strauss—that is, bringing in someone over her who would report directly to him for programming.

Colin Callender's name was one of the first to surface. Not surprisingly, given his success with movies, Callender was eager to take on the role. HR chief Shelley Fischel was dispatched to the West Coast to take the temperature of the group, but it turned out Callender's candidacy wouldn't survive the trip. There was too much pushback from virtually all levels of the SoCal operation.

But Fischel and Plepler did hear about another candidate during this time, a West Coaster himself who really wanted the job: Mike Lombardo. Two key senior managers, one in LA and one in New York, endorsed Lombardo for the position with the thinking that Strauss would continue to operate the creative arm of programming while Lombardo, given his long track record of dealmaking and business affairs, would handle the financial side.

And that is ultimately what happened. As the highest levels of HBO's leadership received a reshuffling, Lombardo, then the executive vice president of business affairs, production, and programming operations, was offered a new assignment.

Lombardo had graduated Cornell before taking a law degree at the University of California–Berkeley, and in 1983 he joined the legal department of HBO as a business affairs lawyer. After three years in New York, he relocated to Los Angeles to become their vice president of business affairs, production, and programming operations. In January 2003, now a trusted adviser to Chris Albrecht, Lombardo was promoted again, to executive vice president of business affairs, production, and programming operations.

MIKE LOMBARDO:

I come from first-generation Italian American parents who instilled in me the need to be career focused and somehow make it in America in the most traditional of ways. To my father, being successful meant being successful as a lawyer or a doctor, or, failing that, working on Wall Street. I was struggling through college and law school with the fact that I was gay and struggling with how I could live my life in a way that was professionally engaging and live my authentic self. Was that possible? That answer for me is very entwined with my career at HBO, and it's a testament to the culture of that place that I felt at home there. I felt HBO allowed me to own myself as an openly gay man.

I was quietly coming out in law school but kind of in denial, and even after graduating I had a very big wall between my public and private selves. I didn't talk about the fact that I had a boyfriend. At HBO, I let the wall down. It was about 1984. There were other openly gay men there in serious positions and so I felt a very personal connection to it; it felt like it embraced and allowed me to hold a vision of a life that I hadn't thought possible.

As executive vice president, Lombardo's position had required him to report jointly to Chris Albrecht, the CEO of the company, and Hal Akselrad, president of HBO Video.

With Albrecht out of the picture, Lombardo would be left reporting alone to Akselrad. Lombardo already didn't like Akselrad—working for him without Albrecht to sweeten the deal would be a nightmare.

Lombardo, who had never done any development work or taken creative meetings with sellers, writers, or talent, had no interest in being walled off from the creative side. In fact, he wanted in.

MIKE LOMBARDO:

Michael Fuchs had been at William Morris, Chris had been an agent, Carolyn had been an assistant at HBO and, prior to that, a bank teller. This was a culture that didn't believe you had to do something for twenty years before you got the keys. It was a culture in which if you raised your hand and said, "Let me try this," they'd let you try it.

When I got the job, there was a sense of, "You be the business guy. You be the face of LA and run it, but Richard has the great taste, and you will serve as an intermediary."

Well, that can lead to dysfunction. It can't work because if you are a gatekeeper and you're passing on projects; people want to hear your reasoning. You have to read it and you have to hear what the intent is, and I did have opinions. And I increasingly verbalized them. And, honestly, over time Richard kept telling me I was great with my creative instincts and encouraged me to be more hands-on.

Plepler never constructed boundaries for Lombardo regarding "creative," and Lombardo never fully admitted to his interest in it himself. The situation brought to mind a tale of traffic in Ohio circa 1888; there were only two cars in the whole state that year, but damned if they didn't run into each other.

MIKE LOMBARDO:

When Chris left, there was a lot of buzz about what was going to happen. Bill got appointed to the CEO position by Jeff and it was unclear what was going to go on with programming. No one from LA had a real relationship with him. A few people in the programming group were clearly making a play and, without talking about personalities, there were some possibilities that people in LA were horrified about. I had people from the office come in and encourage me to raise my hand. I suppose they saw me as the consensus candidate.

Then Bill came out, sat down with me, and asked me whether I'd be open to heading the programming group and I said, "Yes." I initially thought it was working for Bill and that's when he told me, "No, you'd be working for Richard." That was something I hadn't certainly contemplated, and I was surprised.

BILL NELSON:

Programming was Richard's responsibility, and putting Mike in that position was Richard's choice. I knew Mike, thought he was very capable, and knew Chris had relied on him a lot. We said to Mike, "We need a leader out there."

Over dinner at the Beverly Hills Hotel, Plepler and Lombardo, who were scarcely acquainted, hashed out their working relationship. In the org chart, Lombardo would report to Plepler, but Lombardo left dinner believing that in practice, the two men would operate as partners. Trust would be essential. With this understanding, Lombardo began in his new role: president of programming operations.

MIKE LOMBARDO:

We had dinner in Beverly Hills, I remember sitting outside. And we acknowledged that we didn't know each other really well. I communicated to Richard that the only way for this to work was to trust him and be open and asked him to be open with me and for us to decide that we're going to support each other.

We started as partners. "Let's start, let's do this together. Let's jump off the roof together. This is a stretch for both of us." It was a very real, honest conversation. He talked about it in a way that felt very trusting and very collegial. It wasn't a situation where he was dictating to me the rules that I needed to be aware of. He was, I thought, vulnerable with me and I was vulnerable with him.

Plepler and Lombardo's meeting in Beverly Hills was cordial but lacked much needed transparency.

If only Plepler had told Lombardo it wasn't going to be a partnership; that Plepler intended in myriad ways to be the only one in charge of programming. If only Lombardo had told Plepler that he wanted and expected the type of autonomy that Bewkes had bestowed on Albrecht, or that Albrecht had given Strauss. And if only Lombardo had told Plepler that he wanted to shed his legal background—the way Plepler wanted to shed his PR background—and get actively involved in the creative process, there would have been less emotional exhaustion and departmental dysfunction over the next several years.

The meeting proved to be one gigantic, wasted opportunity. Perhaps they didn't know each other well enough; perhaps it reflected the fact that they were fundamentally different human beings; possibly they just weren't being honest with themselves. Or maybe this was the start of a long chess match.

Problems started immediately.

MIKE LOMBARDO:

I assumed I was president of programming. And when I was offered a new contract, they said, "No, we want you to take the title president of programming operations." And I said, "Why?" I never really got an answer. Richard was co-president of the company, president of programming wasn't a title that he was taking on, so I just never used that operations title. People started referring to me as president of programming and at a certain point "operations" just fell away. I knew the difference between having a boss that was empowering, validating, and one that wasn't, and I was wary. I could have asked Richard a million questions, but it wouldn't have mattered. I was prepared to take a leap of faith because it was clear that Richard's piece of the organization was a done deal. It was clear that if I wanted to proceed, I was going to work for Richard. I decided to do it not only because I was excited about the opportunity, but I felt I needed to protect people and the culture in Los Angeles. They were feeling very vulnerable at that point. And I had been reporting to both Chris Albrecht and Hal Akselrad, who was a challenging guy to work for. With Chris gone, the thought of working just for Hal was terrifying for me, so I decided to take a leap and trust Richard.

At that point we agreed that, even though I was reporting to him, we would embrace each other as partners. I think I should have drilled down a little bit and asked, What does partnership mean to you?

CHRIS ALBRECHT:

I never saw Mike as the guy who was going to make creative decisions, but I saw Mike as someone who could manage creative people. I thought Mike could keep Colin and Carolyn in place to do the things that they did. He could keep the business side and finance side going.

What I didn't anticipate, and there were probably a lot of reasons for it, stemming from Mike's psyche, the politics at HBO, was how much Mike would change in that role. Even to people who were his best friends, like Carolyn. Some of that clearly came from Richard. I don't know what the dynamic was, I wasn't there, but in my mind, there were plenty of reasons why Mike should have been in that role, and reporting to Bill, not reporting to Richard.

As Bill Nelson and his hodgepodge triumvirate took the reins in 2007, **The Sopranos,** *their crown jewel, was off the air, and they had passed on at least two possible successors that were then swept away by AMC—***Mad Men** *and* **Breaking Bad.** *Rival executives tasted blood in the water. The* **New York Times** *quoted anonymous Showtime executives who had given the network a colorful moniker: HBOver.*

CAROLYN STRAUSS:

In years before, we had nothing to lose. You weren't jeopardizing a reputation. And then once you have this success, you're thinking, Now will we be jeopardizing success? When you have the success we did, a lot of the town stops rooting for you. People were saying, "HBO is over" and many were thinking, "Okay, you've had enough. It's time for somebody else."

RICHARD PLEPLER:

Only a few weeks after I became co-president, there was a celebrated *New York Times* business section piece that said, "HBO's competitors say they've stumbled," which is, of course, a little bit of a needle from our friends across the street. Everybody said to me, "This is a lot of pressure for us." And I responded, "Also a huge opportunity." And that's how we chose to look at it.

MIKE LOMBARDO:

I would be sitting in a room with Richard and others, and he'd say, "The cupboard is bare," and Carolyn at one point called me up and said, "I'm a big girl, Mike, but this cupboard is bare stuff is so unfair, and you know it." She knew she couldn't call Richard. That broke my heart.

CHRIS ALBRECHT:

"The cupboard was bare" thing was a self-serving, bullshit lie.

Plepler had the pilot to *True Blood*. He had *Boardwalk Empire*. And he had *Game of Thrones*. All in the cupboard, all in various stages. Not to mention other things all in the cupboard. I'm not saying they didn't do other things, but *True Blood* was the next big hit, a very HBO show. *Boardwalk Empire*, completely our DNA. Terry Winter, Martin Scorsese, Mark, and Lev, brought to you by Ari Emanuel. And then *Game of Thrones* was there because of Carolyn Strauss.

RICHARD PARSONS:

In retrospect I would say that I underestimated the threats against HBO. When I stepped down as CEO, this is the end of 2007, HBO's flag was still flying high. But you could see the competition on the borders.

Bewkes became CEO of Time Warner when the company was still suffering—in its stock price, its reputation, and its myriad culture clashes. Bewkes had had an extraordinary run at HBO after he succeeded Fuchs and shepherded the network through a period of explosive creative growth, pairing his own workmanship and business acumen with the programming instincts of Chris Albrecht to bring HBO to new heights.

This new role would eclipse them all, placing Bewkes at the helm of a media ship with numerous powerhouse brands on board—HBO, for one, alongside the world's first twenty-four-hour cable news network, CNN; movie studio Warner Bros.; and the iconic **Time** *magazine, among many more. Two of his predecessors, including Parsons, joked publicly that they would commit suicide if put in his position. Bewkes was bombarded with questions about how he would keep Time Warner's head above water, and which business units—read "entire media entities"—he'd cut loose to do it.*

Jeffrey Lawrence Bewkes had reached the pinnacle of his professional career, and yet circumstances made that achievement perhaps more bitter than sweet.

When Bewkes first sat down behind the CEO's desk, stock in Time Warner was skidding fast. The consequences of billions of dollars in losses from the AOL merger reverberated around the organization. But most people assumed that Bewkes loved HBO so much that he would bend over backward to protect it. HBO couldn't have asked for a more protective corporate daddy.

JEFF BEWKES:

Dick called me in the fall of 2007. He said, "Look, I have a contract as CEO that goes until, I think, it was mid-2008. And are you ready to be CEO early? Like beginning of the year?" I said, "I didn't know that you guys had decided that. Is the board settled on it? He said, "They will be. Are you ready to do it?" I said, "Yeah." He said, "But if you become CEO in January, I'd like to stay on as chairman of the board for a while." And I said, "You're the chairman of the board now. You can stay the chairman of the board as long as you want."

PHIL KENT:

HBO could do no wrong. When Jeff became CEO of Time Warner, I thought Jeff looked at the world through an HBO lens. He wasn't particularly that interested in the advertising business and I don't think he appreciated the challenges the Turner networks faced. He constantly told me HBO was more strategic, which was always frustrating. I found out how much more HBO executives got paid compared to Turner executives when we tried to hire Ross [Greenburg] to run a joint venture between Turner and the NBA, and in the process, I found out that he was making more than Jim Walton was and Jim was running all of CNN. I was really mad.

JEFF BEWKES:

From time to time I would hear that the Warners and Turner people thought I was favoring HBO. I didn't see it that way, of course, and thought they were only thinking that because HBO had been my home for so long. The final irony is that some at HBO didn't think I was doing enough for HBO and was giving them unfair and shortsighted targets. At any point, senior execs at all five companies were telling me I should be more supportive of each of them. What does that say?

As the new chiefs of the programming fiefdom at HBO, Richard Plepler and Mike Lombardo, along with CEO Bill Nelson, took a look at HBO Sports with renewed scrutiny. Its leader, Ross Greenburg, had operated much as his predecessor Seth Abraham had— with something resembling carte blanche to spend money as he saw fit to book fights, events, and sports programming, with little need to issue explanations to management. The new bosses bristled at the lack of transparency about where all that money was disappearing to.

In truth, HBO Sports' star was no longer on the rise, as it had been when the cable provider's coverage of boxing matches put it on the map decades before. Those fights no longer delivered the audiences they once did. HBO also dropped another event the network once prided itself on covering—tennis tournament Wimbledon—when it lost a bidding war for the television rights to NBC and ESPN. To make matters worse for the athletically minded at HBO, neither Plepler nor Lombardo were sports fans—they saw HBO Sports more as a coffer from which they could occasionally borrow to finance HBO's more profitable (and noteworthy) original programming. The heads of the HBO state were frustrated with the money situation at HBO Sports.

MIKE LOMBARDO:

Bill Nelson and Richard felt they weren't given the right respect from sports, that sports treated themselves slightly as a separate kingdom. There was a lack of financial transparency. I am not suggesting that anyone did anything untoward, but Bill, Richard, and I wanted to better understand what components went into the annual budget requests. Bill had been CFO. He expected detail. Ross didn't want to be held accountable in that way. He wanted to be able to decide how to spend a pot of money. Look, pricing boxing matches is imperfect. It is hard to be precise in estimating what a fight might cost, but Ross clearly preferred not to be pinned down. I think Ross Greenburg, following as a sort of a protégé of Seth, wanted to continue a style of doing business that didn't work anymore. So there was a tension there—from the first budget meetings.

BILL NELSON:

Our thinking about sports came after an evaluation of what drove subscribers. We made a decision earlier on, from an original programming standpoint, that we were going to move from quasi-licensing to full ownership. We could cover the globe with our own programming. Sports doesn't travel that way.

So it wasn't that we weren't sports fans. We enjoyed the boxing. But it ran its course as a sport, there was an erosion in the power of boxing. We had a meeting with Dana White, where he basically asked HBO to license his shows, and I asked, "What are the exclusive aspects of licensing MMA from you?" He said, "If an MMA guy wins the belt and Showtime wants to pay more than you do, he's going over there."

So I said, "Then we're not getting into that." Boxing was awesome for HBO, it did magic for it. Then from a total programming standpoint, it didn't carry the weight that was needed. There's only so much money that we had at the time. It wasn't vindictive, it was ROI.

Greenburg was upset by the new order and knew he wasn't going to be able to outrank Plepler. So? He decided to focus on journalism and storytelling.

CRIS COLLINSWORTH:

I had the HBO job before I started working with NBC. Anytime you have a relationship with the NFL, whether you have games or shows, there's a give-and-take with the NFL and anybody that will tell you differently is crazy. It's not that you can't be open and honest with your opinions, but if you're going to go after the NFL, it's going to make some people there uncomfortable. HBO encouraged it. HBO wanted the toughest issues. HBO wanted to go after things that they thought were not right within the NFL, and it was part of their history of disturbing big, big sports businesses.

Ezra Edelman had stayed at HBO Sports longer than he would have imagined, in part because of his strong desire to be on his own and not have to conform to the DNA of HBO documentaries. But it was a good thing he held on for as long as he did—long enough for him to make **Brooklyn Dodgers: The Ghosts of Flatbush,** *which premiered in July 2007.*

The two-hour film tells the story of one of LA's legendary baseball clubs before and during its move to the Golden State from New York. Bookended by the Dodgers' Jackie Robinson breaking the color barrier in 1947 and the team's transfer to the City of Angels a decade later, the movie also presents a fresh perspective on why the Dodgers had to go, attempting to relieve Dodgers owner Walter O'Malley of some of the blame for the team landing in LA. Despite popular assumptions, O'Malley had tried to keep them in the Big Apple by building a new stadium in Brooklyn, but a city official, Robert Moses, would not allow it. In this way, the film is about the city as well as the team—the Dodgers' impact on the culture of the town and the heartbreak tormenting the Flatbush neighborhood they left behind.

The film won two Sports Emmy Awards, including Outstanding Sports Documentary. Critics praised the movie's new reporting on the move to Los Angeles and the rare material in the film, including a Dodgers team photo from 1947 in which one player, Dixie Walker, looks away from camera to protest the team's integration of Robinson. Reviews lauded the tactile retelling of Dodgers history, along with the archival footage employed in the presentation.

EZRA EDELMAN, Documentarian:

It was a lifesaving moment because I found what really agreed with me. I got to spend a couple months just reading and thinking, and the canvas was bigger, so I could be more creative. It was something that was fully mine to shape and mold. That was the first time in my professional life in which I was doing something where I felt just right. I don't know that I've actually found a sense of exhilaration professionally since the first six months of working on that documentary.

For five years after the second season of **Hard Knocks**, HBO struggled to find a willing partner—until 2007, that is, when the Kansas City Chiefs agreed to full, unmitigated access to behind-the-scenes action, including the competition between rookies and vets, and assorted locker-room pranks.

Despite the hiatus, the show quickly returned to form, offering its unique access to the pad-popping, precarious life in NFL training camps. This is the reality show that brought such hits as Jets cornerback Antonio Cromartie listing the names of his children. "I got Alonzo, who is five," Cromartie counts on his fingers, "I have Karis who is three, I have my Junior, which is three, I have my daughter who just turned three as of yesterday, I have another son named Tyler, he turns three in December, I have another daughter that was born October sixteenth named London, another daughter that was born named Leilani, who's two years old, and I have a newborn with my wife, her name is Jurzie." Perhaps most memorable about this unusual lineup? Cromartie was right about each name and every age.

The return of **Hard Knocks** also marked the end of **Inside the NFL**'s thirty-one-season run at HBO, one year later. The second foundational brick of the HBO Sports brand was now history.

In 1977, the nascent HBO Sports division had debuted **Inside the NFL,** *a weekly broadcast that paired analysis with the insider access that standard game telecasts do not permit. Airing on Wednesday nights, the day before the beginning of the NFL week, the show offered viewers a change of pace from their standard football fare, delivering an up-close-and-personal perspective on the game—courtesy of the sights and sounds of NFL Films—and even featured segments with such famous comedians as George Lopez and Wanda Sykes.*

In February 2008, HBO announced that **Inside the NFL** *would be coming to a close following the end of the 2007 season with Super Bowl XLII. At the time,* **Inside the NFL** *was the longest-running show on cable—thirty-one years on the air. Publicly, the network said it was pulling the plug on one of its flagship sports broadcasts due to the increase in similar programming across the television landscape. But speculation said otherwise—NFL Films had been charging more and more for the signature footage it offered the show and its viewers, and HBO, the story goes, was no longer willing to pay. Costas made his position clear on the issue, calling the decision to ax one of the sports shows he hosted for HBO "boneheaded." Four months after the cancellation, NFL Films found a new home for* **Inside the NFL**—*Showtime, in collaboration with CBS Sports. Cris Collinsworth traveled with the show to join a new duo of CBS talent: renowned and ubiquitous sports anchor James Brown and Phil Simms, a former Super Bowl MVP.*

ITN was nearly as much in the HBO DNA as Wimbledon had been. It was a sad, emphatic coda on HBO's reign when it ceded that program to Showtime.

ROSS GREENBURG:

Wimbledon and *Inside the NFL* were both whacked because they were $10 million, $12 million line items.

DAVE HARMON:

When HBO gave up *Inside the NFL* in 2008, I was totally blindsided. The Giants had just upset the 18–0 New England Patriots the week before in the Super Bowl, and as a lifelong Giants fan I was still flying high after the "helmet catch" game. I was asked into Ross Greenburg's office, and I swear I thought we were going to rehash the game, talk about how *Inside the NFL* would cover such a memorable event, and that would be that, just another meeting in Ross's office of a million and a half meetings I had been part of for *Inside the NFL* over the twenty-three years I worked on the show. Ross had the most serious face and told producer Brian Hyland and me the show wasn't going to be renewed, and that week's episode was going to be the last in the thirty-one-year history of *Inside the NFL*. I can still feel the shock today. The show was such a mainstay of the department. It was such a constant in my life. As senior producer, each day even during the offseason I thought about the series and what we could do differently and better. And now it was over.

Nothing from that day onward shocked me. That day was my beginning of the end.

CRIS COLLINSWORTH:

We were at the Super Bowl, having our meeting and they came in and announced they couldn't renew the show's contract, that the league wanted too much money and there would be too many restrictions. They had already taken much of the sound away, which was exclusive and is what made that show great. We were the only ones that got access to the sound of NFL films.

It was sort of the only game in town. A lot of people, myself included, grew up with it. If you wanted a real feel for what it sounded like and felt like on the field in an NFL game, that was really the only place you could go. It was a unique show. It was fantastic. I did it for a little while on Showtime, but it had a real history at HBO, and I think almost everybody would tell you that they were really proud to be a part of it for any time they were on it.

Three months after **The Sopranos** *aired its final episode in June 2007, the man who unforgettably played its* **capo di tutti i capi,** *James Gandolfini, headlined a vastly different production for HBO.* **Alive Day Memories: Home from Iraq** *was a one-hour documentary about wounded American soldiers returning from conflict in the Middle East, several of them missing one or more limbs. Named after the day on which a person has a near-death experience, the film shows Gandolfini interviewing injured veterans in a darkened off-Broadway theater. Charting the opposite course that he took to play Tony Soprano, Gandolfini employed a minimalist approach to his on-camera role in the documentary, relying on short questions to draw out wartime tragedies that had befallen his subjects. They told stories of physical and emotional loss that expose the human cost of the war that many believe should never have been fought.*

SHEILA NEVINS:

Your alive day is the day when you thank God that you're alive even though you lost your legs, your arms, half your head, or whatever. A lot of guys don't want to celebrate their alive day. They say, "Fuck, I don't feel very alive." We did a film called *Alive Day.* I think it's one of the best things we ever did, because it wasn't just an interview. He did it like an actor, with his regular voice.

JON ALPERT:

I've had the unfortunate opportunity to go to a lot of wars, and when you're a filmmaker-reporter, you go to these wars, and there's something that changes inside you, and you're compelled to do it because you want people to understand what war is really like. And HBO gave us the opportunity to explore the extraordinary cost of wars, and it was a real gift to us, and I hope a gift to the people who got to see the films. And Jim was very patriotic. He loved to do anything he could to support soldiers, especially the wounded soldiers. So this part of his relationship with HBO enabled these films to get made.

SHEILA NEVINS:

Jim Gandolfini was one of the sweetest men I ever knew. Used to call me "Momma." We did so many shows together, he really cared about those guys overseas. As it got harder and harder to make documentaries that people watched, I realized that I had to pander a little bit. I had to bring in names, and so I went over to him once. He said, "I'm in, Momma." He was the first star.

Jim sent every one of those boys a watch. He used to hang out with this guy who made watches. He must have sent 125 watches the next day to Walter Reed.

JON ALPERT:

I will confess to you that I had never seen *The Sopranos* before; I don't watch TV. The first soldier comes in, but Jim was very tentative asking him questions. I asked him how that interview went. He went, "Meh, it wasn't very good."

I said, "Okay, I see you were trying, but I don't think you've done a lot of this before." He goes, "Nah, I'm an actor." I said, "Okay, well, the next person's coming in doesn't have any legs. When I tap you on the shoulder, I need you to ask this person to roll up his pants and to show us that he doesn't have any legs, then get him to talk about it." Jim goes, "I can't do that." I said, "These people have flown all the way across the country to tell their stories. They're here to tell you this. It's important for them. You are empowering them and empowering their sacrifice by letting them tell their story." He looked at me like I was out of my mind.

So the guy comes in and the interview is going nowhere. I tap Jim on the shoulder, and he looks at me like, Leave me alone. I tap him on the shoulder again. The third time I thought he was going to get out of the chair and slug me. Then he says, "This guy here wants me to ask you to roll up your pants leg," and the guy goes, "Sure." And he rolls up the pants legs.

That's when Jim got it. He was so terrific after that because he was no longer tentative. He wanted to be respectful and realized that by counterintuitively getting them to tell the most personal story of their loss, this was how he paid them the most respect. From that point on, we had the most wonderful relationship.

While the seemingly indomitable Sheila Nevins tried to cope with the show's traumatic hospital scenes, she also had to focus on an upcoming special with pornstar Katie Morgan. Albrecht was a big booster of Morgan's and set up an important meeting for her with at least one agency to talk about a possible crossover career.

BILL NELSON:

If it ain't broke, don't fix it. Sheila was doing a great job. Did I enjoy some of the late-night stuff she was doing? No, but we gave her a budget, and I think she made a lot of right decisions at the right time. She's the queen of the documentary world. The work that Sheila Nevins did with her small team was phenomenal. She owned the original documentaries space. It's amazing what she did. Now what's also amazing is what came into her, came to her why? Creative freedom. She supported those people. She fought for those people. People knew that if they knocked on Sheila's door it better be a damn good project, and that once you got in there, you were with the best, supported by the best.

ALEX GIBNEY, Documentarian:

Impact is a tricky thing to measure. Over time my films force people to think about things in ways that may cause them to have a deeper reaction than just, I've got to change this law. I'm now changing laws. Activism is important. The best docs contain within them contradictions rather than just propaganda. They celebrate the human condition in a powerful way and if they enrage you, as some of mine do about social issues, good.

Sheila saw an opportunity and acquired *Taxi from the Dark Side* literally two days before the Academy Awards and then we won an Oscar, so it was very savvy on her part, but also it was right in line with what HBO does. It was an edgy film, and it did have impact. It became required viewing at the army JAG school, they would show it at West Point. It had impact in a way and the place where it was most important for it to have

impact, which was in the military, to change their policies toward inter-
rogation and torture.

On Monday, December 27, 2004, George Carlin announced he would be going into
rehab. In a statement, his reasoning was clear: "I use too much wine and Vicodin."
Carlin battled addiction to various drugs for decades.

That winter, his latest book, **When Will Jesus Bring the Pork Chops?**, *topped*
the charts, enjoying much of the same success commonplace among his HBO specials.
After he left rehab, his thirteenth and penultimate HBO special, **Life Is Worth Los-**
ing, *arrived on November 5, 2005.*

ROCCO URBISCI:

I never thought after the first special with George I would do a second special or third special or fourth or fifth or a sixth. I never assumed that was
going to be the next special.

Look at *Life Is Worth Losing*. There will never be another George Carlin
is because he loved language. He loved the English language. He loved the
juxtaposition of thought, Lord Byron and all those writers that he admired,
Oscar Wilde, all of them. They are all these geniuses, able to interject humor
and they're not jokes.

With thirteen HBO specials under his belt and a comedy legacy long since secured,
George Carlin hit the stage for **It's Bad for Ya**, *a seventy-five-minute special directed*
by Rocco Urbisci that aired on HBO on March 1, 2008. Carlin held court at Santa
Rosa, California's Wells Fargo Center for the Arts on a stage set like a living room,
sporting an all-black outfit, sneakers, and his trademark white hair and beard. His
reflections on politics, technology, and everyday interactions earned him a Grammy
for Best Comedy Album—by then, a nomination for each of his HBO shows was
routine—and a nod for Outstanding Variety, Music or Comedy Special at the 2008
Emmy Awards.

Carlin struggled for much of his adult life with heart complications—a heart attack
and two open-heart surgeries had kept him offstage from 1977 to 1982.

ROCCO URBISCI:

We could see that he was not well. His health was failing. Of all the production sets that Bruce Ryan and I did together, *Life Is Worth Losing* was the
first time George ever asked for a specific set. He wanted a graveyard, and in
that special, he did, in my opinion, one of the greatest pieces he ever wrote

or performed, called "A Modern Man." The dress rehearsal on Friday was a very tough time. He was very frail.

Three months after **It's Bad for Ya!** *aired, on Sunday, June 22, 2008, it was heart failure that took the man many believed to be the greatest stand-up comedian that ever lived. He died in Santa Monica, California, at seventy-one years old.*

NINA NOBLE:

The Wire was done, and then they decided they wanted a fifth season. It was maybe something about scheduling and other shows not delivering. We had to get everybody back and David wrote an eloquent letter to all the cast members and just said, "Either everyone comes back, or we don't do the show and don't hold us up for money because we're not that show." Everybody came back for their contract amount.

DAVID SIMON:

Season five, the idea of, Can you fake a murder? I watched a furious argument in the morgue in Maryland, when I was doing the *Homicide* book. I am standing in the autopsy room with these detectives from the suburban Anne Arundel. They had a guy who clearly done a header. He slammed a shot of heroin and overdosed and fell between the tub and the toilet in his own bathroom. And his girlfriend heard him fall and went in there and she couldn't revive him. And so the detectives are in there and they're trying to argue the thing back to being an accidental overdose, from being labeled a homicide by the pathologist. Because the guy was so wedged in there, that the paramedic, to get him out, grabbed his neck hard within minutes of the death and broke the hyoid bone and created postmortem bruising that could have possibly been antemortem. So slowly they brought this pathologist around with everything they knew, with the girlfriend's testimony. I think maybe she ended the case and then waited for grand jury testimony and then finally said it was accidental. But she was determined not to let a murder go by her. I watched this argument happen, and later I pulled the chief medical examiner at the time. I said, "Was there any difference between that and what a strangulation murder would be?

I put that in my back pocket and said, "That's a perversity. I don't know where I'm using that." But it's the same thing as, "We'll legalize drugs in a zone in Baltimore." Nobody's ever done this. Nobody's ever faked a murder that way, that I know of. But could you do it? Physically you could. There's no difference between that and any novelist who takes a premise and runs with it. That's all that is. The whole conceit of somebody could warp the narrative so much so that he could have an entire institution caring about what they don't need to care about, while they don't give a fuck about what they're supposed to care about. Seemed to be a marvelous conceit on which to make the last critique of the show.

I had some tough moments. Chris shaved two episodes off of *The Wire*, season five, at the same moment that he was giving me seven to do *Generation Kill*. So here I am, I'm getting seventeen hours in a budget year and he'd already argued to cancel *The Wire* after season four and I already get him back in again.

On the evening of March 9, 2008, HBO aired the final episode of The Wire *after five seasons on the air. The episode, which capped a series that saw the on-screen deaths of roughly sixty-six different characters during the show (according to one online tally), was a triumph of the status quo. All of the corruption and crime that had characterized the show's portrayal of Baltimore were left to continue at its close, a nod to the scale of the dark forces at work in the city. Justice—for those who actually did get it— was measured at best. A fabricated crime story disseminated through the pages of the fictionalized* **Baltimore Sun** *was never exposed publicly as a lie.*

The finale's Emmy nomination for Writing was one of only two that **The Wire** *ever received. According to its creator, David Simon, the show also ended with the lowest ratings in its history.*

Over the course of his career with HBO, a total of seven projects that extend years beyond **The Wire***, Simon made more hours of television for HBO than any other writer in the network's history. And with good reason. If you had the extended box, you'd have some snapshot of intelligent subjects that he wanted to talk about and tell in a literate, thoughtful way. You have a snapshot of some version of America.*

DAVID SIMON:

I would write these letters and at first the letters were intimidating. After a while, everything loses its efficacy. The first letter I wrote to get them to order *The Wire* was, "Guys, you counter program beautifully, but what if you do a show that's right in network wheelhouse, and you completely subvert the form? You do a cop show. You could use the network cop shows to wipe your own ass." Sometimes the letters work.

By the end they were like, "No, no, no. We've heard you, and this episode really needs to be 58:30." The same bag of tricks doesn't work forever. But I could write a memo, I could write a blister. I used the word "flummery" in an angry memo to Mike Lombardo because he was paying everybody at a previous rate for script work in the contract, when our production year was going into the next year of the WGA contract. Later on I heard he walked around the office going, "What the fuck is flummery? I'm guilty of flummery." They were cracking up.

After a while, the memos don't work in the same way. You've got to figure out something else. Then you have to start becoming friends. I was trained in that, too. I'm that guy. And I'm also the guy to call up and say, "If you don't fucking talk to me right now, I'm going to lay you out in the fucking paper for this, and if you try to no comment this, I will fucking own you. You better fucking talk to me."

NINA NOBLE:

I am often asked about mentoring women. I usually respond that I wouldn't mentor someone just because they are female—I would mentor them because they were smart and capable and willing to work hard.

I do acknowledge that there have been barriers to employment in film and TV for people of color and for women. We have always made it a priority to have a diverse crew, in terms of race, gender, class, and geography, because having a variety of perspectives always makes our shows better. This is one of the many business decisions David and I made early on—though now it is considered a diversity initiative, for us it was just a way to make quality TV.

When David and I started working together, we created the culture we wanted to see on our shows. Since we were learning the TV business together, we felt no obligation to adhere to established practices. Our work environment is one in which everyone's input is valued, actually essential to making the shows that we do. And the fact that he and I were on set from call to wrap on most days meant we were not asking more of others than we were of ourselves.

The Wire cast and crew are like family to this day. Though almost fifteen years have passed since we wrapped the last season, we have remained in each other's lives. Our current project, *We Own This City* (HBO), is shooting in Baltimore later this year, and what a reunion it's going to be!

DAVID SIMON:

After *The Wire*'s last episode, the reviews came in and they wrote that we stuck the landing. Then I got an email: "That was great, really well done, beautifully executed. The only thing that could've made it better was two more hours." That was Chris busting balls, because he knew how much I had wanted them. It was very funny, but the truth was, there were a couple of character lines that we had to abandon.

I've never delivered an audience to HBO and I don't deliver Emmys, other people do those things, but I get to do what I want to do, and I'm a weird part of their brand. I'm incredibly grateful.

11

Rooms at the Top

MARCH 10, 2008–APRIL 16, 2011

Wandering through HBO offices in New York or Los Angeles early in 2008, you were likely to see them, anywhere and everywhere, the "lifers," HBO employees who'd been with the company for ten, twenty, even thirty years. To lifers, HBO was a destination, not a stop along the way to somewhere else. For them, there was nowhere else.

Such was true of the company's leadership as well as its troops. Ross Greenburg arrived in 1978, Sheila Nevins and Jeff Bewkes in 1979, Quentin Schaffer in 1980, Hal Akselrad and Mike Lombardo in 1983, Bill Nelson in 1984, Eric Kessler and Carolyn Strauss in 1986, and Richard Plepler in 1992.

Long tenures were frustrating for deputies and other ambitious types who hoped one day to grasp the reins and giddy up, yet all-but-interminable longevity did provide HBO with a level of stability that few other entertainment companies could match, no matter how hard they tried.

And in the specific world of programming, things had been not only stable but clear and transparent going back to 1995 following the departure of Michael Fuchs. Jeff Bewkes empowered Chris Albrecht and his deputy Carolyn Strauss; they were the faces of HBO programming. No one in Hollywood, or anywhere else for that matter, wondered otherwise. As CEO, Bewkes would jump into the programming pool when needed or appropriate, for example, when it was a matter of high finance or when

Albrecht told him talent required extra stroking from on high. And when Albrecht became CEO, he positioned Strauss for all to see, giving her meaningful autonomy over departmental decisions.

CAROLYN STRAUSS:

For the vast majority of my time at HBO, I looked forward to going to work every single day. I never thought, "Ah, fuck, I gotta go to work." I truly enjoyed my creative partnerships and loved working with everyone on the programming team. I was incredibly fortunate to work with some of the best minds in this business.

With the Bill Nelson as CEO era underway, programming had already begun a tortured metamorphosis. As president of HBO Entertainment, Strauss had reported directly to Albrecht when he had been CEO. After Nelson got the job, he created a new level of oversight when he gave programming to co-president Plepler, who in turn created another by appointing Lombardo to his new, elevated role. There were now two layers between Strauss and Nelson—her boss, Lombardo, and his boss, Plepler (that's setting aside Lombardo's unfortunate misconception that he and Plepler were going to be "partners").

Just how well Plepler, Lombardo, and Strauss would work together was the subject of much speculation; the first significant case study would turn out to be a whopper.

*Linda Bloodworth-Thomason had worked on **M*A*S*H** and other network shows before creating the uber hit **Designing Women** for CBS. Teamed with husband Harry Thomason, the pair became prominent, influential, and rich big shots in the television landscape. In 2006, Strauss, with the support of Albrecht, had bought **12 Miles of Bad Road** from the Thomasons, an hour-long dramedy starring Lily Tomlin as Amelia Shakespeare, a Dallas real estate mogul with a screwed-up family played by Mary Kay Place, Gary Cole, and others. Strauss, with Albrecht's backing, had originally ordered twelve episodes, but—hamstrung by the 2007–8 Writers Guild strike—she'd knocked the order down from twelve to six.*

As programming's new dynamic duo, Plepler and Lombardo sat down to watch.

MARY KAY PLACE:

I played a conservative, rich woman who came from a big ranch. I had one granddaughter who was intellectually challenged, and I loved her deeply, deeply, but I was unaware about what language people considered appropriate to use when talking about a child with that condition. I had big, long speeches about trying to get her to be a debutante and the political powers that didn't want a child with her challenges in that circle of people. It was about rich people in Dallas, Texas, who just might be unconscious about many things.

It wasn't politically correct, and I think that was one of the things that became an issue.

I had copies of the show, which I gave to my parents and a bunch of friends and people laughed at it. But there were some people at HBO who didn't find it funny. It was hard for me to understand what sense of humor they had.

When I heard it wasn't going to be picked up, I thought that was insane.

MIKE LOMBARDO:

We thought it was a disaster.

RICHARD PLEPLER:

Mike and I inherited *12 Miles of Bad Road* and it was one of the first decisions we had to make. We watched the show and both of us didn't think it fit with what we were looking for at that time. Obviously, Linda and Harry disagreed.

The Thomasons didn't like Plepler's response. In fact, they hated it. They knew better, and made no secret of it, particularly Harry, who went off on Plepler to such a degree that he would later be compelled to apologize. The Thomasons made two moves. First, when Plepler found himself in the office of President Bill Clinton, who famously had a close relationship with the Thomasons, Clinton took time to let Plepler know how much he enjoyed the show and put more than a finger on the scale for keeping it on the air. Second, "somehow," screeners of the show were leaked to critics—the hope being that great reviews would get Plepler and Lombardo to change their minds. The move backfired. The **LA Times,** *for one, wrote, "Never have so many Emmy-deserving performances been trapped in such a muddled mess of a more than occasionally offensive storyline."*

MIKE LOMBARDO:

Carolyn tried to stay neutral in increasingly tense conversations with Linda. I suspect Richard viewed that as unsupportive if not problematic.

Gone was the autonomy Strauss had enjoyed under Albrecht. When she let it be known she wanted to name Gina Balian, widely regarded as a terrific creative executive, to be sole head of drama, reporting to her, Lombardo informed Strauss she simply could not do that.

CAROLYN STRAUSS:

Gina is one of the most talented executives out there. I don't know if everybody always understood exactly how good Gina is. I think Gina's one of the best executives, maybe the best development executive who's working right now.

MIKE LOMBARDO:

The reason I pushed Carolyn to hire a number two is because there wasn't a lot of experience under Carolyn at that time. Carolyn can be savvy. She had gotten rid of Sarah Condon, she didn't want to replace Miranda Heller, and Gina was a baby.

CAROLYN STRAUSS:

I would have left things the way they were. I wouldn't have brought in a number two. I had Gina, who was really strong in drama, and Casey, who was really strong on comedy. I wanted Gina to be the sole head of drama, but Mike wanted me to bring in somebody more senior. I know Mike was under a lot of pressure from Richard. There was a sense that there was somebody better out there, a sexier name. I asked if they could give her a year, but Gina wasn't going to fit that bill for them. Hiring someone else was not something I wanted to do.

SUE NAEGLE, Executive:

I was a partner at UTA and was having lunch with Carolyn one day and she told me, "You know who's going to run HBO one day? Gina Balian. She's incredible."

QUENTIN SCHAFFER:

After Richard took over programming, he went out to Hollywood on a listening tour, talking to producers, agents, studio execs, and reporters.

SUE NAEGLE:

Carolyn called and told me Mike wanted her to hire a number two and asked, "What do you think about coming in?"

We were friends, always got along, and Carolyn made me laugh. I had done a lot of business with her and really respected her. She wasn't easy for a lot of people. She's very much her own person. She's not at all phony; she didn't suffer fools. I have to say for a lot of men at the time, that rubbed them the wrong way.

QUENTIN SCHAFFER:

Richard kept hearing negative comments. Creative talent complained about being treated rudely or dismissively when pitching projects to HBO. An arrogance and hubris had set in and it managed to send people across the street. As remarkably talented as Carolyn was—and she truly had a Midas touch—he heard her abrupt style had alienated them. And so Richard, in these conversations all over town, started telling people, "We used to have a 'Beware of Dog' sign out at the company, but now we have to put out the welcome mat. We want people to come to us. We don't want people to go somewhere else because they're afraid to come to us." And as the new head of programming, he had every right to make that case. Competition was heating up. Rival networks had realized they, too, could do HBO-like programs. Richard saw this and wanted to make sure HBO was everyone's first stop again.

MIKE LOMBARDO:

By the time I was promoted, there were people outside the company who had daggers out for Carolyn. For her fans, and there were many, part of what was so loved was her boldness and seeming disregard for unwritten Hollywood rules. As the company grew in stature and the level of talent coming to pitch became more established, some of that was used against her. Carolyn could get consumed by a telephone conversation or a meeting and she might keep someone waiting for twenty or thirty minutes in the lobby. You can do that when it's a baby writer or emerging producer . . . To Carolyn's credit, she treated people uniformly. She would never consciously treat a young writer with less attention than a more seasoned one. But trust me, there are egos and some of those egos found waiting intolerable. And I wish she would have been better at that.

Plepler had decided that new outside blood was required to get HBO programming humming again.

For those wondering how Plepler could be given such wide domain over programming given his lack of experience there, it was clear that he had been paying a lot of attention to programming during the Albrecht CEO years and hadn't liked much of what he saw. Hence his speech several years before at Shutters, where he admonished the programming department for losing its way.

CAROLYN STRAUSS:

We may not be the most astute judges of ourselves. My nature has always been more reserved compared to others in the business, so people could project a lot of stuff that was perhaps not what I had intended.

RICHARD PLEPLER:

Carolyn is a brilliant producer, maybe the most talented producer of our generation. She's a preternatural talent. HBO owes her a lot, just look at the list—*Sex and the City, Six Feet Under, Sopranos, Game of Thrones.* Quite remarkable really.

And yet, on March 15, 2008, Strauss was fired as president of HBO Entertainment.

MIKE LOMBARDO:

I don't know what precipitated the precise timing when I got a call one day in LA from Richard, "We need to do something about Carolyn, it's not going to work." We had had this conversation for months. I assumed it would all work out until then. I'll tell you honestly what happened.

First of all, I did not know how to fucking, excuse my language, have a conversation with a woman who I love and respect that would hurt her. Carolyn and I had grown up together at HBO. My experience there was completely intertwined with my friendship with her. Years earlier, she sat with me on the sixth floor of Cedars-Sinai as my partner was dying of AIDS. I just couldn't fathom what to do. And I suppose I was being foolish, but I hoped Richard would have a change of mind. But I shared this with a producer I trusted, and this producer mentions it to none other than Chris Albrecht, who calls Carolyn up and says, "I heard they're firing you." She came into my office, closed the door. There have only been two times when I've seen her cry, and this was one of them. She asked me, "Am I being fired?" And I said, "Yeah, that's what he wants." She starts sobbing and left and didn't come back. So it never played out in the way it should have. I don't think the producer involved or Chris had malintent, and I learned some hard lessons about the public nature of those jobs and the need to keep your own counsel.

It was a huge, devastating loss. It was a huge loss to the company and to me. It was a loss I have never recovered from.

In the course of the time I had that job, I think I was told, instructed, encouraged, to let go of somewhere between five and ten very senior executives. And I hate to say I became numb to it. But letting go of Carolyn was soul wrenching for me because I love her as a person. She was and still is one of my few linchpins, someone who knows me completely. She was the person whose office I would go in and be able to regain my sanity about anything. And I thought they were wrong. I thought it was personal.

I have worked with an enormous number of creative executives as an underling, as a colleague, as a manager. Many of them were very good at what they did but, truly, Carolyn was the secret sauce for HBO. I say that now having had that job and knowing what it takes. I did as best as I could, and I had some successes, but it pales in comparison to what Carolyn achieved.

CAROLYN STRAUSS:

As difficult as my departure was, the truth is none of these jobs lasts forever. You have to be an idiot to think that you're going to be in any chair your whole life.

I think of Mike as my family. I think as difficult as that was, I couldn't love Mike more.

Years later, Lombardo would look back on this period and wistfully reflect, "After Carolyn left, I had no one."

MIKE LOMBARDO:

It was an incredibly lonely time for me. Carolyn was gone, and there was nobody who could do what she did. Sheila Nevins wanted to cut my legs off, others were waiting for me to fail, and there was no one I felt comfortable sharing my own fears and doubts with. Ultimately, the only people I trusted there were Bruce Richmond, who was head of production, and the head of HR, Mary Lou Thomas. HBO had been my surrogate family and all of a sudden, I was in a car trying to get home before eight, with Sue Naegle looking at my phone list to see who was calling me, and worrying about being second-guessed by New York. I felt really isolated.

It got heavy and it became less fun. I wrote that off like that's the price of this job, but this certainly wasn't what I was thinking when Chris [Albrecht] left. By the way, Chris at that point was barely talking to me because of what happened with Carolyn.

CAROLYN STRAUSS:

I love Mike, he's one of my closest friends, but I realized pretty quickly that the arrangement with Richard was not going to be ideal. It was not going to be a good situation for me to stay there. As difficult as it was to go through it, for me, honestly, my life is really just perfect right now, and I don't think it would have been so had I been there.

ARI EMANUEL:

Carolyn Strauss had impeccable taste. The problem was she was also really smart, so you weren't going to be able to bullshit her and tell her something was cool when it wasn't. She knew what was good and what was bad. She didn't suffer fools.

SUE NAEGLE:

If Carolyn was a man, she would have never been let go.

GINA BALIAN:

Carolyn leaving was very sudden for me. She was such a part of our world and our brand. It felt like it was just a moment ago that Chris had left, and both were so identified with what HBO was. When she left, it was personally very hard for me. She was my mentor.

CASEY BLOYS:

I worked with Carolyn for four years. She is one of the best creative executives I have worked for, and I learned so much from her.

SUE NAEGLE:

Carolyn called me to tell me she was leaving, and after hearing that, I told Mike I was pulling out of the running. I didn't understand why Carolyn had just offered me a job and then was basically told to leave the company a month or so later.

Mike called me again, then Carolyn called and said, "I think you should still consider doing it. I'm going to have a producing deal there and I'd still rather have it be you than someone else."

Carolyn and Mike were so close. Carolyn and I were friends. I would go to birthday parties for her son for years and Mike was always there. What I should have looked at is that I was walking into a situation where one friend had let go of another friend. That should have been a big warning shot.

Mike had some insecurities about taking his job because he had not spent any time doing any creative work. When you're an agent, you're really close to writers, you understand writers, you understand how a script develops and gets made. When you're in business affairs, you don't really have any access to those people.

MIKE LOMBARDO:

I did not know the size of these jobs, I did not know the power of a buyer, I did not understand fully what it meant to be in that chair and the visibility of it. Literally every move, every phone call, every meeting is examined.

As I rose up in the company, it was a challenge for me. I had never been great at being able to divorce my public self from my private self.

SUE NAEGLE:

You had two guys, one from publicity and the other from business affairs, stepping into these giant jobs; you assume that what Carolyn's done is not that hard. Richard trafficked in high-end New York society and business. He had turned on her, something had happened and maybe it was something to do with her manner. She's pretty no nonsense. She didn't look like a traditional network executive, she didn't make decisions like one, she wasn't very schmoozy, the complaints were so strange. They would say she kept someone waiting fifteen minutes in the lobby, she put her feet up on her coffee table in the middle of the pitch, or she didn't call someone back fast enough. I thought, these are not reasons to fire someone.

I had built a really significant business at UTA and was co-running the TV department. I was thinking about going into bigger management on the board of directors, and at that point I probably would have been the first woman to be on the board of directors at UTA, which was a big deal.

But I started to think about whether or not there was something that I could do in this business that challenged me in a different way.

MIKE LOMBARDO:

We felt strongly that we needed to bring a woman in. Carolyn had been a significant and important presence and it felt wrong to bring in a white man. There was nobody internally that we believed was ready to take over from Carolyn, and when Carolyn shared with me that she was thinking about bringing Sue in to work under her, I trusted Carolyn's judgment even in replacing her. So I reached out to Sue to replace some of what Carolyn provided the company. I didn't really know her. I knew that she had been a very successful agent. I thought she knew the difference between a good writer and a mediocre writer. She'd covered HBO as an agent for a long time and understood our ethos and the kind of programming that checked boxes for us.

Less than a month after Strauss's dismissal, HBO hired Sue Naegle as the new president of HBO Entertainment on April 9, 2008.

CASEY BLOYS:

The first year of Mike and Sue wasn't bad.

SUE NAEGLE:

It felt comfortable really quickly, mostly because I already knew and respected many of the executives. I had done so much business there over time that they didn't feel like strangers.

Public relations expert, business affairs guy, and an agent: such was the triumvirate that now ran HBO's programming department.

In a more perfect HBO world, one might imagine Sue Naegle getting her programming legs under the tutelage of Strauss; but when Plepler canned Strauss, suddenly "Sue Naegle, agent" was elevated to "Sue Naegle, programmer." And it wasn't as if Lombardo necessarily knew the ins and outs of creating successful shows for HBO either. Publicist Plepler oversaw all.

Before long, Lombardo began to attend pitch meetings—a rather unusual move for someone at his level. And it became clear to those inside and all over town that Naegle and Lombardo were in effect competing to enjoy the spoils of the same gig. In a department that had for so long been led by steady, experienced hands, that steadiness quickly dissipated into suspicion and unease.

Neither Naegle nor Lombardo had previously worked in development, nor did either understand how to build the right team. Furthermore, both remained wary of bringing outsiders into HBO. The result was a department considered totally debilitated by the failure of Lombardo and Naegle to enforce rules, show leadership, or grow future leaders.

Hopefuls in search of a green-lit sometimes found themselves appealing to Naegle and Lombardo separately. When that produced no clear decision, the Supreme Court chief justice that was Plepler might be brought in to hear oral arguments. What this meant was that projects with potential got caught up in the morass of dysfunction, with no clear way forward.

Lombardo and Naegle's jobs remained stubbornly ill-defined. It was hard for the team to watch them grapple because both were in a learning curve. Mike was an attorney, Sue was an agent, and neither they nor their boss came from a creative upbringing.

CASEY BLOYS:

I would never say no one could come into HBO from the outside and be successful, as opposed to growing up here. I would like to think we're not that precious. Certain people can come here and do well, but it's a question of having the right experience for the job, and the personalities involved. I think it had more to do with the personalities that they hired and how they managed them once they were here. You can talk about the drama team being dysfunctional, but ultimately I think that was a function of Mike and Sue's dysfunction and lack of leadership.

ARI EMANUEL:

Sue was 100 percent the wrong person for the job.

SUE NAEGLE:

If you talked to people I worked with most closely at UTA, they would probably tell you I'm 80 percent yogi and 20 percent Jersey gangster. I approach everything with compassion and empathy. It's what made me a great agent, then a great programmer. I could understand how writers were feeling and what they were struggling with. I can explain what I don't think is working. Those were my strengths at HBO. It wasn't office politics. I've never been interested in that.

At the time HBO was in a pretty fallow period. When I went over, they had just canceled *John from Cincinnati*. I remember one of my colleagues at UTA saying to me, "Why would you want to go there now? It's circling the drain."

The cupboard wasn't bare, though. *Boardwalk Empire* was coming in, *Treme* was coming in, *Game of Thrones*. *Tell Me You Love Me*. The pipeline got a little disrupted at *John from Cincinnati*, which didn't work.

Missteps happen all the time with networks. But anytime anything happened at HBO, there was such a huge microscope on them. There was not a margin for error. They weren't funding Carolyn, giving her the money that she needed, but she'd been trying to make *Game of Thrones* for years. She had developed *Boardwalk*, developed *Treme*. She bought *True Blood* from me. If she had just stayed one more year, if we'd all been able to work together that next year following, it would have been fine.

CAROLYN STRAUSS:

When you're booted out, the people coming after you take credit for your shows. That's just how it is, but I don't believe the cupboard was empty. I had developed *Boardwalk Empire*, *Game of Thrones*, and several others.

GINA BALIAN:

Sue had impeccable taste. We all had worked with her before. We were figuring it out. She came in at a hard moment because there was concern about what was in programming and she was responsible for helping to figure that out. We did a lot of buying in those early years and she took on a lot of responsibility.

SUE NAEGLE:

I had really wanted to work with Carolyn. To me, she was the best in the business. So when I walked into that job and she wasn't there, I didn't assume or need a lot of autonomy, but Mike and Richard were very much like, "Just tell us what you think, just go."

I went away for a long weekend, and took with me all of the development—every single script on the comedy side and the drama side. The first thing you look for when you have to make a fast turnaround is, Is there anything here that we can use? I read through the pilot script for *Game of Thrones*, which I didn't know anything about at the time, but I came back from the weekend and thought, Wow, this is great. At that point I had probably read seventy scripts. I came back, spoke to Carolyn about it, and she told me that she's always very bullish on it, and Gina loved it.

Within the first six months or so, we grabbed *Hung*; I pulled *Game of Thrones* from the development pile and put a lot of attention on it. Then very quickly *Boardwalk Empire* came in as a script because it had been bought previously. *True Blood* was coming on the air. And *Big Love* was already on as well.

Boardwalk Empire, *Treme*, and *Game of Thrones* were the first three things we did right around then. We picked up the pilot for *Bored to Death*, which had also already been in development, and *Veep*.

The first year was massive.

MIKE LOMBARDO:

Carolyn had left behind a very smart but a relatively junior team who would all be taking on new responsibilities. I think in many ways our hiring of Sue and not being aware of the challenges she might face was a testament to my not knowing what I didn't know. It was also a testament to the fact that Richard certainly didn't know what he didn't know. I was relying on a brief conversation I had had with Carolyn about hiring Sue, and Richard was looking at it from an optics perspective. We were also reacting to our increased awareness of the competitive landscape. One of the failings heaped at Carolyn's feet was that she had not been as aggressive in pursuing things that successfully found homes elsewhere. AMC had suddenly emerged as a home of smart programming, FX was stepping up, and Showtime had had some successes. There was a desire to hire someone who wouldn't just wait for competitive projects to walk in, and, as a former agent, Sue certainly felt up to that challenge.

SUE NAEGLE:

When I think about it, honestly, I wonder if part of their reason for giving me so much autonomy early on was because if it didn't work, they could shrug their shoulders and say, Well, she's an agent. What do you expect? And if it did work, they would be pleasantly surprised, but they were not super hands on at all at that point.

MIKE LOMBARDO:

What I missed fully when hiring Sue, and this was through no fault of hers, were the other skills needed to succeed at HBO, some of which turned out, by the way, to be really unique to Carolyn.

KATHLEEN McCAFFREY, Executive:

Sue's was the last desk I was on before I was promoted to coordinator. She was such a badass. This is a woman who comes from a working-class background in New Jersey who had become a partner at the agency. She was the first woman I saw who showed me I could be head of something. It was inspiring to watch.

I stayed at UTA without her for maybe a month. Then I realized she was a real mentor to me, and when she asked if I wanted to come over to HBO with her, I jumped at the chance. There was a huge learning curve. I was the lowest on the totem pole, but luckily I had the incredible help of Francesca Orsi, Amy Gravitt, and Casey. I attached myself to them. HBO is rigorous.

I cared a lot about Sue and felt my job in the beginning was to ask a lot of dumb questions that she didn't get to ask. I think we were learning together, but I obviously wasn't in the spotlight. Sue was in a difficult situation.

While one HBO veteran bid adieu to the network she had called home for years, another new face joined HBO's ranks. Accomplished producer David Levine joined the network on April 20, 2009. He originally came on board as a consultant but was promoted just a few months later to director of HBO Entertainment.

DAVID LEVINE, Executive:

I got a call from Francesca Orsi at HBO, who I had just had lunch with and totally loved. She told me they were still looking for someone after Sue Naegle had met over sixty, seventy people. At the end of my interview with Sue, she said, "I've been here for nine months and everyone's really scared of me. No one will tell me what they like or don't like." I said, "I would love to talk about that. I've been waiting for twelve years for anyone to ask me what I think." She said, "I'm late for a table read. Tell me some writers you'd want to work with." I said, "Jonathan Nolan, Tony Kushner, Mike White, and Steve Zaillian." I started working at HBO in April 2009, and we ended up working with all of them.

MIKE BINDER:

They hired too many executives, and then they were really hard to work with. They ended up like every other network, eleven executives on every project telling you what to do. You think since you were there at the beginning it's still that old HBO, but it wasn't. You're like the guy who lost his arm and you're still typing with it.

GINA BALIAN:

It was a different rhythm at that point. It was really hard for people to come in from the outside because so many people had been there for so long. And I don't even mean from the creative department team, I'm talking about all across the company. There was so much longevity, so many people who grew up at that company.

On September 7, 2008, HBO premiered **True Blood,** *based on a series of books (The Southern Vampire Mysteries) by Charlaine Harris, all about Sookie Stackhouse, a waitress who lives in the small Louisiana town of Bon Temps who can read minds, at least when she has a mind to. Vampires walk among mankind hereabouts unmolested thanks to a synthetic drink—after which the show is named—that serves as a blood substitute so that vampires can survive without drinking from human veins. The theme should not be a shock—the show's creator, Alan Ball, was behind another HBO production with a fixation: the wildly successful* **Six Feet Under,** *and its adventures in a mortuary.*

Anna Paquin starred as Sookie Stackhouse alongside Stephen Moyer, Alexander Skarsgård, and later Joe Manganiello. **True Blood** *ran for seven seasons on HBO, airing its eightieth and final episode on August 24, 2014.*

As with many an original series on HBO, the show was rife with nudity, sex, and violence, but it was also otherworldly and allegorical. **True Blood's** *sex especially was raw, vivid, and unlike anything that had been seen on television before.* **True Blood** *also received attention for the surreptitious political statements it made. In the show, vampires are fighting for their rights after "com[ing] out of the coffin"—a clear* *parallel with ongoing battles for LGBTQ+ rights in America and abroad. In one epi-sode, vampires cause a massacre at a Ted Cruz fundraiser, drawing a strong real-life rebuke from the unpopular Texas senator.*

ALAN BALL:

I called HBO and I said, "There are these books, I think they'd be a great TV show." They said, "We've already got a vampire show in development." I said, "Okay, I'll take it somewhere else." Then they said, "No, we don't want you to take it somewhere else." They ended up not doing their other show and doing *True Blood*.

It was fun to focus on being entertaining for a while, different from the existential peering into the abyss that was such a fundamental part of *Six Feet Under*. Some of the faces had changed over there. Carolyn left and was replaced by Sue Naegle, who had been my agent. I felt very free. I got spoiled.

SUE NAEGLE:

When I went to HBO, I learned they were really nervous about *True Blood*. I realized that Richard and Mike didn't really like it or didn't understand it. He called and said, "It's not an HBO show."

EVAN RACHEL WOOD, Actor:

True Blood was the first time I had ever called a show and offered my ser-vices. I was such a fan of the first season and the writing was classic Alan Ball, creepy goodness. I loved the cast, and thought the work Anna and Ste-phen did was just electric. It really blew me away. So I contacted Alan Ball, I don't know him, but I said, "If anything comes up, please know, I'm such a huge fan of the show. I would love to work on this." Sometime after that, he called me with the Queen Sophie-Anne. I of course said, "Yes."

The character wasn't what I was expecting at all. She was sort of the anti-queen. She was more like a spoiled brat. She was fun to play because she's almost perpetually a teenager, even though she's obviously been around for centuries.

My first scene is with Stephen Moyer and he walks over to me and kneels down and is teaching me the way to flip the fangs out, and what they do. I was geeking out the whole time, completely having a good time. A lot of my scenes were with Alexander Skarsgård. He does kind of look fake, you know? He's like a chiseled statue. We certainly got close while we were film-ing. It was one of those sets.

Big Love, *the third season of which premiered* **on** *January 18, 2009, was also one of "those sets," helmed as it was by husbands Mark V. Olsen and Will Scheffer. But while this season continued on the show's critical acclaim, there was cause for concern behind the scenes.*

MARK V. OLSEN:

I had this habit mid-season during a table read, out of sheer exhaustion, of having a cross between a hissy fit and a nervous breakdown. I'd be frustrated and despondent, every year, like clockwork. I would turn to Will each year and say, "Why are we doing this? This show is taking everything we've got in our lives, and in our souls. It is eating all our families, our marriage, our relationships, our sense of relationship with our God. And for what? To wake up thirty years from now and have a dusty collection of old moldy DVDs from back in the day? This is not working for me."

And I would just stay in that huff for about two days until Will said, "Snap out of it," for the fiftieth time. Then I would see a scene that had been composed by the editor, that had such joy and such heart, and I felt like, "This is what I want to be doing with my husband—creating this world and these moments of human truths. There's nothing else like this."

WILL SCHEFFER:

That scene you saw, by the way, was when they go on the road trip, which is one of my favorite episodes of the show.

MARK V. OLSEN:

Between shooting seasons three and four, we took our producers Bernie Caulfield, David Knoller, and Peter Friedlander down to Guatemala for a fishing trip, and I can't even reel in a fish. I'm winded, huffing and puffing. We get back to LA, and three weeks later, I'm in the hospital with major heart surgery.

WILL SCHEFFER:

The same heart surgery that Bill Paxton wound up dying from.

MARK V. OLSEN:

Yeah. I had multiple heart issues that turned quite intensive. Twenty-eight days in a USC Norris hospital. Which takes us toward the end of January.

Will meantime was managing both my camp and the business angle. And dealing with HBO, who more or less was trying to navigate a schedule.

People were tired of *The Sopranos* coming back a year and a half later. But the fact of the matter is, we needed to be out of the hospital and back in the writers' room.

WILL SCHEFFER:

Michael said, "We'll support you. Let's shorten season four in order to make it easier for you. We'll start a little bit later."

MARK V. OLSEN:

The doctors had said I needed six months to recover. I had two. The fact of the matter is, this is all on me, because while Will was talking about scheduling, I was in my hospital bed on morphine, just going, "Not a problem. I can do this." Well, the fact of the matter is, I couldn't. I don't want to say my brain was operating at 50 percent capacity. That's not true. But it was not my best game, when I was doing the preparation of stories for season four.

WILL SCHEFFER:

That season was a perfect storm. A lot of the actors were movie stars and weren't used to doing extended runs. Some had a tough year.

MARK V. OLSEN:

But I want to bring the blame, the responsibility back on me. The season lacked emotional-based stories. One of the pilloried episodes that we ever did, people were like, "Oh my God, *Big Love* just vomited on my television tonight," is one that I'm the proudest of. In a really idiosyncratic way. And that's when Bill goes down to Mexico to get Ben. It's not *Big Love*. It's a surreal little thing on its own.

WILL SCHEFFER:

It's almost David Lynch. And Grace chopping off an arm. Richard Plepler sent us a note saying, "Best episode ever." Some critics didn't agree.

MARK V. OLSEN:

The show lost its way, lost its firm keel in that fourth season, but we did a fairly good job of writing the fifth season, going back to more emotional-based stories.

WILL SCHEFFER:

I think that the decision to end it with fictional Bill's assassination felt like a really good place to leave it for the sister wives to be able to also go their own ways.

The last day of shooting, we were still running the camera and when they said it was the end of the show, I just started crying because I realized that it was about the people who we had just created this beautiful thing with. That I created with my husband and all of these collaborators.

It was a mutual decision to end the show after season five.

MARK V. OLSEN:

I have to say, a big chunk of that owes to our relationship with HBO and the people who ran it. They worked closely with us and deep respect flowed both ways. That was the case with Carolyn Strauss, Chris Albrecht; that was most certainly with Michael Lombardo, who was a fierce champion of that show.

A new wave of shows would soon be ushered in—dramas, and three unusual comedies.

On February 15, 2009, HBO premiered **Eastbound & Down**, *a comedy series about a former professional baseball player turned gym teacher. The show, which ran for four seasons on HBO (and got its title from the first three words to the theme from Burt Reynolds's megahit* **Smokey and the Bandit***), starred Danny McBride (one of the show's creators, alongside Ben Best and Jody Hill) as Kenny Powers.*

DANNY McBRIDE, Creator:

I had made this little independent film, *The Foot Fist Way* with Jody Hill, it got into Sundance and we ended up being able to get it in the hands of Adam McKay and Will Ferrell. Those guys sat us down and asked us what we wanted to make next. They were anticipating we'd want to make a movie but we had an idea for a TV show.

I grew up loving television storytelling; it felt bigger than a movie.

Then it was another head-scratching moment for Will and Adam when we said, "We're not interested in selling twenty-two episodes. We just want to sell six episodes. We want to make something small and contained."

We had pitched it when Carolyn Strauss was still there, and she got the concept, the tone and wasn't thrown off by us wanting to do a smaller order.

That was the beginning of this pretty awesome relationship we've had with Casey Bloys and Amy Gravitt. We shot the pilot and everybody was excited about it. Then the shift happened with their management, and everything went quiet for a while.

CASEY BLOYS:

I had to justify *Eastbound & Down*. Mike and I would argue a lot about it. He didn't get it, he didn't like it, and he wasn't alone. A lot of the company didn't like it. I was somewhat alone in saying, I think this is smart and funny. At that point in my career, it became very instructive about how to stand up for something.

RICHARD PLEPLER:

When I first watched the pilot for *Eastbound & Down*, I said to Casey, "This guy Danny McBride is funny, but is it on brand?" And he said, "Richard, you're old, your comic sensibility is over here, and I'm telling you that this comedic sensibility, my generation and younger, is over here. And this guy, Danny McBride, is the real deal." I said, "I got it. Let's go." And *Eastbound & Down* went off to the races and of course became a signature part of HBO. That happened numerous times with Casey. He never tried to bullshit me and his judgment was impeccable. It was one of the first times I was able to see not only how talented he was, how expansive his vision was, but how good he was at seeing around corners.

DANNY McBRIDE:

We would see what Casey would laugh at and it was always the stuff that we were worried they wouldn't respond to. Casey's notes would always be to push things further, and it created this dynamic between us where we started trying to push Casey's sensibilities by throwing in stuff and seeing what his response would be. We were fucking around, making something naughty, just making each other laugh the whole time.

I went to film school in North Carolina with this small group of people. We instantly felt like we were outsiders trying to pursue this impossible dream. When we moved to Los Angeles and started trying to work, we saw quickly what a different world we were stepping into. Los Angeles from Winston-Salem, North Carolina.

We always had each other's backs. So when HBO decided to do *Eastbound & Down*, we brought every friend we've had from college and growing up to work with us. When the executives from HBO come to our set, it was instantly a party. The night before cameras roll the first day we're having our big kickoff party, everyone takes shots of Jägermeister. We're all saying to ourselves that we've done it. We finally made it.

ADAM McKAY, Executive Producer:

They were a little freaked out by it because Kenny's really an antihero. He's a Trumpian, kind of Republican anti-hero. It's uncomfortable what Kenny Powers does in that show. Initially they were going to bury the show like late on Friday nights, and we really argued with Lombardo and Casey. "You guys are missing it. There's a satire here that's deeper than what you think."

DAVE BALDWIN:

Eastbound & Down was unique. I went ahead and put it on Sunday night in the stack of our premiere series at ten thirty, because I knew this was going to draw an audience we were under-serving.

Well, I had an interesting phone call with Bill Nelson on Monday morning that included, because he was in the military, a lot of words.

It premiered at ten thirty on a Sunday night and he was up watching. CEOs rarely paid much attention to schedules; they trusted me to do the right thing. But Bill thought this was the worst series ever. He thought it was a late-night show. I knew it was a prime-time show.

ADAM McKAY:

They listened to us and they put it in a respectable time slot and the show hit. Lombardo called me. He goes, "Wow, you really pushed us on that show. And you were right. We really appreciate that." I was like, "Oh my God, who even talks to other humans like that in this day and age?"

Another hit comedy was soon to follow **Eastbound.** *It had taken only a few months for Sue Naegle's ties to her former employer UTA to pay off for HBO, when the agency sent Naegle a spec script for a project called* **Hung,** *a fresh and unusual comedy-drama about a man who becomes a male escort to climb his way out of financial troubles.*

The script was strong. The producers were in the midst of discussion with Showtime and others, for a pilot. Lombardo and Naegle struck first, and **Hung** *premiered on June 28, 2009.*

THOMAS JANE:

Hung? That's a stupid fucking title. Nobody's going to watch a show called *Hung*. I said, "I'm not reading that." I passed on it. They came back and said Alexander Payne's thinking about directing the pilot. Fuck man, now I gotta read this fucking thing. I read it and it was fucking great. I asked, "Can't you guys change the title?" They're not going to change the title. It was a lot of back-and-forth and finally I said, "I can't not do it." Alexander Payne, the script is terrific, I loved the characters and I got to work with Anne Heche, who's now my girlfriend.

I was naked on that set more than I was naked in my own home. I'd basically show up for work and take my clothes off. I was nude on day one, when we shot some sex scenes. I'm standing around naked. That was uncomfortable, but after a week of that, I was now literally just running around naked and everybody was saying, "Oh, there's Thomas, he's naked again." It became part of the set, no big deal.

The Ricky Gervais Show had two distinguishing elements for HBO at the time. It would be animated, and it was based on a show from a rising new content platform: podcasting.

RICKY GERVAIS, Actor and Comedian:

HBO was the international Holy Grail of quality, particularly comedy. The first time I heard the term "HBO" I think was *Larry Sanders*. HBO in the 1990s was a world leader. I was a fan of HBO. I'd done *Extras*, and my first special, *Out of England*.

When I did the special, I was very aware that HBO was the golden standard in America. It felt important, but I had to keep it light. I went out there in crappy jeans and a sweaty, black T-shirt, drinking beer from a can. I wanted to be the outsider who shouldn't be there.

We're court jesters. We have to be down with the peasants, taking the piss out of the king. Now, the truth is everyone knows we're also businessmen and -women who earn a lot more than the court jester, so how do you keep that status? I do it in two ways. One, I invite them in to look behind the curtain of glamour, what they think is so great, being famous. I talk about how I embarrassed myself in front of the queen or how the first time I took a private jet they thought I was a cook. I ridicule my status.

I talk about being rich and undeserving. The other way I keep lower status, I talk about things where the audience are better off with me. I talk about being fat and old. I'm going to die soon. I'm going bald and have a bad back. I remind them that I'm a fucking loser.

Then HBO gave me a daytime show, *The Ricky Gervais Show*. It began as a radio show with me, Stephen Merchant, and Karl Pilkington. Karl was a friend, but he was like an experiment. We'd just have normal conversations. People were fascinated by us.

In 2005, I'd heard of this thing called a podcast. I was doing it for a laugh, really. The podcast took off and broke the world record, it was about a quarter of a million per week or something, I got a lot of credit for being the first high-profile podcaster. Primitive how things have changed.

On YouTube, fans were animating twenty-second bits of the show. I put them on my blog. Then someone from Wildbrain approached me and said that this could be an animation.

I sketched the three main characters, sent it off, they sent it back and I went, "Oh, that's perfect." They'd send me stuff and I go, "Oh, that's too much," or, "That's alright." And HBO let me do it. I don't think I ever got notes from them. I don't think they ever said, "Oh please, don't say that, it's offensive."

It was a privilege to work for HBO. It was brave, cutting edge. You were allowed to do stuff you just couldn't do on network TV. It had a cool audience. It won awards. It had money. When a special came on, you had billboards, the premier, and it was fantastic. I absolutely loved working with them.

On April 11, 2010, five years after Hurricane Katrina and the floods in her wake ravaged New Orleans, HBO premiered **Treme**, *a drama series about a group of locals picking up the pieces of their lives months after the storm. David Simon, already a card-carrying member of HBO royalty, created the show alongside Eric Ellis Overmyer. Named for a historic neighborhood in New Orleans,* **Treme** *weaves the culture of the city, using music, including Elvis Costello, Fats Domino, and Stay Human frontman Jon Batiste, to speak to larger societal themes, including the politically fraught recovery after Katrina.*

DAVID SIMON:

I told them, "We want to do something on this city that has had a near-death experience." They said, "Great." I gave them a bible for the first season, with the characters, and a pilot script.

SUE NAEGLE:

When Carolyn was trying to convince me to take the job, I remember her saying, "What would make you anxious about this?" And I told her, "I can't imagine a world where I would give notes to David Milch or David Simon." And she said, "Don't worry about it, I know them very well. It'll be okay." When *Treme* came in, I called David to say, "I'm Sue Naegle. We haven't had a chance to speak, but I read the script and I really loved it." He just went, "Great, great, great. Are you gonna pick it up or not?"

WENDELL PIERCE:

It was a great honor. David Simon wrote the role for me in *Treme* on the set of *The Wire*. One day he said, "I want you to check out this scene. It's a New Orleans show. I want to make sure it's real enough." He wrote the scene between a trombone player and Kermit Ruffins outside of the club, and a character named Wendell. I said, "You're going to name the character Wendell?" He said, "Man, I'm writing this role for you." That's how I found out. That was one of the most humbling moments of my life. I was up for another role on another show and I told them, "I'm sorry. This is something that is just so special. I have to do *Treme*."

My city, my family, was going through one of the darkest moments of its life. A dear friend and my boss and colleague had written a role for me, where we're going to examine this through art and try to make an impact and change. So it was more than just a television show. It ended up being the last three years I got to spend with my mother before she died. It was a homecoming and it was an opportunity for me to rebuild my city, to make an impact on New Orleans to this day.

DAVID SIMON:

I had a bad moment with them, because I had to fight for the last half season of *Treme* to end the show properly. *Treme* is carefully constructed, it's dealing with themes and arcs that are not hyperbolic. It's a guy with the trombone in his hand, saying something I desperately wanted to say not just about New Orleans but about who we are. I wanted to get to the end, but they only gave me a half a season to do it. Half a loaf.

NINA NOBLE:

I'm sorry more people didn't watch *Treme*. I still have hope that people are going to discover it eventually, at least for the music if nothing else. It's a beautiful jewel.

WENDELL PIERCE:

The Treme neighborhood has exploded because of our show. Before our television show, no one ventured there nor did the city promote the culture of Treme and neighborhood of Treme. If anything, they would try to convince people to avoid it or Black folks, don't go over there. Using it as the title of the show really said something about what David was trying to create, a show about the grassroots culture of New Orleans. It's a cultural document that years from now, people will be able to pull off the shelf and play and say, in that moment of time, this is where people were and how they reacted to their condition with art. With a finely cooked gumbo, with a beautifully played jazz ballad, with architecture, with bringing and finding a way to be adaptable, which is such a part of the culture of New Orleans's resilience and adaptability, the northernmost Caribbean city. And even in its dysfunction and corruption to find a beauty in our humanity and express it just as common folks can express it, and that means it's a poetic document. It's a visual poem. *The Wire* was the visual novel, *Treme* was a visual poem.

The Sopranos *established a creative bloodline that spread across several networks. Matt Weiner would go on to create* **Mad Men,** *a runaway hit for AMC; and Mitchell Burgess and Robin Green dreamed up* **Blue Bloods** *for CBS. Yet it was at HBO that Terence Winter had landed, and three years after* **The Sopranos'** *final curtain, on September 19, 2010, a new mob drama born of Winter's laptop,* **Boardwalk Empire,** *began its five-season, fifty-six-episode run.*

Set in Atlantic City, just after Prohibition kicked off in 1920, the story centers around the nefarious dealings of the city's crooked treasurer/bootleg booze kingpin, Enoch "Nucky" Thompson, played by Steve Buscemi. Typical shenanigans follow— mob killings, backroom dealings, and promiscuity, all with federal agents hot on the trail. Fictional characters mix with historical cameos—gangsters including Charles "Lucky" Luciano and the original "Scarface," Alphonse Capone, make appearances.

HBO swung for the fences in the production of **Boardwalk.** *The network spent $20 million on the pilot alone, in no small part because it was directed by one of the few directors in Hollywood to have a spot on the A-list.*

When WME (talent agency William Morris Endeavor) signed Martin Scorsese, Ari Emanuel told him, "You should do **Casino** *as a TV series." Scorsese shot back, "I don't want to revisit Las Vegas. That was Nick Pileggi's thing. I don't want to do it." But he continued, "I would do a show about a casino in Atlantic City." So Emanuel called the book department and asked, "What have you got?"*

Emanuel was told, "We have the book for **Boardwalk Empire,** *Nelson Johnson's history of Atlantic City." Here's the maneuvering of an agency head: instead of sending the book to only Scorsese, Emanuel sent it to another client as well, Mark Wahlberg. The two had just worked on* **The Departed** *together and Wahlberg had a big deal at HBO. Emanuel suggested the two might want to join forces. Fast forward to a conference call on the project where Lombardo said, "I will spend two million, five million, ten, whatever it takes, to make sure that Marty Scorsese wins the Emmy. He has to win the Emmy. You can't have Martin Scorsese do your pilot and not win the Emmy."*

Critics seemed to agree that **Boardwalk** *was good—even really good—but not great. The show's meticulously produced Jazz Age Atlantic City sets were nothing short* of dazzling, but some reviewers initially struggled to believe Buscemi as a smooth-talking, cold-blooded killer. Industry insiders disagreed and gave Buscemi a SAG Award for his performance, as well as a Golden Globe (**Boardwalk** also won a Golden Globe for Best Drama Series).

And in the end, Lombardo got his wish. The first season of the show was nominated for eighteen Emmy Awards, winning eight, including Outstanding Directing for a Drama Series, which went to a certain Martin Scorsese.

TERENCE WINTER:

I met with Carolyn Strauss and she said, "Oh, I have this book. It's called *Boardwalk Empire*, it's the history of Atlantic City." I thought to myself, Oh my God, do you have anything slightly more boring for me to read? So I was on my way out the door. Then she said, "Oh, by the way, Martin Scorsese is attached to that." I stopped in my tracks and said, "Yeah, there's a TV series in here and I'm going to find it." So I went home and I said to my wife, "HBO just gave me a series. If I don't fuck this up, they're gonna do it." I read the book—it was a fairly dry account of the history of Atlantic City. Literally from the time it was a mosquito-infested swamp until the present day, but there was a chapter about this guy, Nucky Johnson, who ran the city during Prohibition, and I thought, "That's the show, that's the guy. He's this corrupt politician who was friends with every gangster in the country, letting them import illegal alcohol into Atlantic City. Basically Vegas before Vegas existed. That's the character."

I went back, told Carolyn about it, and she said, "Great." I met with Martin Scorsese, which was absolutely surreal. He truly was the reason I was doing this. *Taxi Driver* was the movie that started it all for me. I pitched him on the idea. He said, "Wow, I never did anything in that era." Originally, he was just supposed to be involved as a producer, but when I wrote the script, he called me up and said, "I would like to direct this." I almost fell out of my chair. I said, "Okay." He said, "How do we move this forward?" I said, "If you call Richard Plepler and tell him what you just told me, I'm pretty sure that will move it forward." He said, "Okay, I'll do that." Ten minutes later, Richard texted me just all exclamation points. I thought, "I guess Marty called."

STEVE BUSCEMI:

I thought, "Oh man, would I love to play this part and be a part of this show." But something in me didn't believe I would be cast. I was lucky to have Martin Scorsese directing the pilot. I had worked with him before, and, of course, Terry, who I had worked with on *The Sopranos*,

I think it was their combined interest in me that convinced the powers that be at HBO that I was the guy to play that part. I was directing an episode of *Nurse Jackie*, and I was in the location scout van. At that point in my career, I had decided I should concentrate on directing more because I didn't know where my acting career was going.

So when Terry called, it was nice to hear from him. I thought it was his obligatory call. I said, "Well, thanks for considering me." And he went, "No, Steve, you didn't hear me. I'm telling you, you have the part." It was like one of the greatest phone calls I've ever had.

SUE NAEGLE:

It's Martin Scorsese. There's no filmmaker, maybe Coppola, who can better capture the character and conflict inside organized crime.

It was a very strong bet on Steve Buscemi. Somebody who's made their career, mostly as a character actor, to watch him lead a show was really exciting.

TERENCE WINTER:

I felt like I was ready. I learned at the feet, literally, sitting next to David for years on *The Sopranos*. I sat on set for every episode I wrote and I produced as well, sitting next to every director, involved in every casting meeting, every stunt meeting, wardrobe, makeup, so I felt confident that I was ready to do this job. I also made a concerted effort with Tim Van Patten, who is my partner, in the sense that he was my main producer and my main director, that he and I were going to emulate the *Sopranos* experience. We wanted to have the same vibe on set, which was very fun, friendly, lots of laughs. And we had a lot of that crew on *Boardwalk Empire*.

STEVE BUSCEMI:

On *The Sopranos*, Jimmy was the number one guy, but that was really an ensemble effort; every character was important. And Jimmy was so present with everyone that he worked with. That's what I was aspiring to. When I was in a scene with Jimmy, whenever I came away from it, I just felt so grateful. And I felt that he made me do my best.

TERENCE WINTER:

I know I'm not David [Chase], and that *Boardwalk Empire*, as successful as it was, was not *The Sopranos*. I needed to stick to a budget and a schedule, take notes, and work within their framework. I was happy to do it. Even when you're getting notes from HBO, they're not mandates. But you can't ignore them. That's not going to work there. It's more like, Can you walk us through why you want to do this? Can you explain to us why this character is acting a certain way? There were episodes of *Boardwalk* that I did that were really edgy. We had an incest episode where Michael Pitt sleeps with his mother, and I was ready to go to battle with HBO but the battle never came.

On October 21, 2014, the series finale of **Boardwalk Empire** *aired on HBO and attracted an audience of 2.3 million (up from 2.18 who watched the previous season four finale), and 3 million viewers over all formats (the best rating of the season for the show). Reviews were good, with* **Variety** *calling the finale "a knockout."*

TERENCE WINTER:

We got to the point where we were starting to repeat ourselves, that every year was going to be a new bad guy coming in, who ultimately would be vanquished by Nucky. The series was also following a timeline and not a whole lot happened between 1926 and 1930. It was just a series of gangsters shooting at each other. We felt like we had run our course, and HBO agreed. They said, "Let's wrap it up in season five."

Seven years after the premiere of the World War II epic **Band of Brothers** *in 2001, the executive-producing duo of Tom Hanks and Gary Goetzman teamed up again to dramatize another moment from American history, about a relatively obscure Founding Father.* **John Adams** *debuted on HBO on March 16, 2008, the first and second episodes of a seven-part miniseries on the first vice president and second president of the United States. The show was based on a Pulitzer Prize–winning biography written by legendary American historian David McCullough. Behind the camera would be Tom Hooper, the British director known then for directing Helen Mirren in the Emmy Award–winning* **Elizabeth I,** *a historic series that also aired on HBO.* **John Adams** *was shot on a budget of $100 million in Colonial Williamsburg, Virginia, with travel to Hungary for the scenes set abroad. The miniseries follows Adams through diplomatic assignments in Europe during and after the American Revolution; his uninvolved, uneventful tenure as the country's first vice president; and his troubled single term in the nation's highest office, before retiring to fret about his legacy. The versatile Paul Giamatti donned wigs and period garb for the title role, starring opposite Laura Linney as Adams's wife, Abigail, the contemplative feminist icon. Stephen Dillane played Thomas Jefferson, Adams's fellow*

*Founding Father, vice president, and successor to the presidency, while Tom Wilkinson
vividly brought to life the man for whom the term "Renaissance Man" could have been
coined, Benjamin Franklin.*

COLIN CALLENDER:

I remember a conversation with Chris about *John Adams* saying, "We're about
to hit, in 2008, a new election cycle." The country was very divided, At the
heart of the John Adams story was his friendship with Thomas Jefferson, two
men on completely opposite ends of the political spectrum in America, and
yet who remained close friends. They both died on July Fourth, within four
hours of each other, something no fiction writer could ever have invented.

Credit where credit is due, Chris got it. Chris Albrecht was brilliant.

TOM HOOPER, Director:

I was working on a film about the life of Katharine Graham for HBO,
which the great Joan Didion was writing. I got a call saying, "Would you
consider dropping Katharine Graham to do *John Adams*?" I didn't know
much about John Adams. I immediately asked Joan Didion's advice, and
she said, in her inimitable voice, "John Adams is tabula rasa for the American people."

TOM HANKS:

Graham Yost told me the McCullough book would be a great miniseries and
I thought he was nuts. Tricorne hats and redcoats—it had been told a million
times. Then I read the book and learned for the first time that the soldiers
who fired on the crowd of the Boston Massacre were represented by a colonial
lawyer who would go on to help write the Declaration of Independence, be
the first vice president of the nation, and become our second president.

TOM HOOPER:

In my first meeting with Gary Goetzman and Tom Hanks, it certainly felt
like the book had been revelatory to Tom. As it was to me. He was incredibly excited by the physical details of the world and the chance to ground
this period in some of the hardships facing the characters. He had an actor's
instinct for that.

Tom's excitement about *John Adams* made me realize how much of this
was new to the American viewer. He helped me understand how much
was revelatory in McCullough's brilliant, brilliant book, and his passion for
sharing that revelation was really strong.

COLIN CALLENDER:

John Adams's life couldn't be condensed into a single movie, but we had the opportunity to tell the story of one of the Founding Fathers, to really show the shape of a man's life, both his successes and his failures professionally and personally, over seven hours. Where else can you get to do that?

TOM HOOPER:

We were in an incredible position. We got to spend $110 million on a non-famous president, on a non-famous Founding Father.

COLIN CALLENDER:

Paul Giamatti had just done *Sideways*. So he had a successful movie career; he was much in demand. But it was a bold and exciting idea to put him at the center, because you think you're going to cast a traditional leading. He was extraordinary. As was Laura Linney as Abigail Adams.

KARY ANTHOLIS:

It was very rocky from the beginning when they were shooting in Virginia, because things were difficult between Tom Hooper and Paul Giamatti. A producer named Frank Doelger was very pivotal in mediating a lot of the conflict that was going on on set, to make sure Tom got what he needed and that his razor-sharp elbows didn't do too much damage. Tom's got a brusque, almost antisocial demeanor at times, but he had a real vision for how to shoot it. The Playtone guys and Gary Goetzman, in particular, were very helpful to Hooper. But the battles between Paul and Tom were legendary. Giamatti wasn't threatening to walk or anything—Paul was doing his job and at the end of the day, surprisingly, he said, "I couldn't stand the guy, but he's very good at directing actors."

TOM HOOPER:

I wouldn't say HBO was hands off, but the best compliment I could give Colin and Kary Antholis is, the notes generally made work better.

I loved the fact they were maverick enough to say, "Episodes don't have to be fifty-two minutes. They can be whatever length they need to be, and we'll support it."

TOM HANKS:

HBO could not have been a better partner, and the cast and crew gave more of themselves than I've ever seen.

COLIN CALLENDER:

When we played *John Adams* in the spring of 2008, it went through the roof because it reminded the audience of what made America great.

John Adams *cleaned up during awards season, earning a whopping thirteen Emmy Awards on twenty-three nominations. The show won Outstanding Miniseries, and Giamatti, Linney, and Wilkinson all won for their roles, their victories repeated at the Golden Globes the following year (the show won Best TV Movie at the Globes). Giamatti and Linney took home SAG Awards for their portrayals of the Adams power couple, with Wilkinson also getting a SAG nod.*

Critics, however, were less enthusiastic. Assessments of Giamatti's turn as Adams were mixed, as well as the show's portrayal of the title character, with some reviewers suggesting that American history had been digitally remastered to cast Adams in a hyperbolically heroic role. Despite the criticism of the central character, reviewers were kind to Linney's Abigail, Wilkinson's Franklin, and Dillane's Jefferson. Critics also lauded the realistic sets on which the show was shot; location filming, it would seem, paid off.

If there was one principle on which HBO could consistently rely, it was that a Tom Hanks producing credit would ensure a show's success.

Before Steven Spielberg and Tom Hanks partnered as executive producers on **Band of Brothers,** *they had already made clear to audiences—with the iconic 1998 film* **Saving Private Ryan** *(which Spielberg directed and in which Hanks starred)— that they knew how to make a war movie. But they also earned cartloads of letters from veterans of that terrible war who'd fought on the other side of the world. These soldiers wanted to see their stories on-screen, too. Spielberg and Hanks would not deny them.*

The result? A second ten-part miniseries called **The Pacific,** *shot largely in Australia with a $200 million budget and produced jointly by HBO, DreamWorks, and Playtone (the latter two founded by Spielberg and Hanks, respectively). Gary Goetzman, a producer on* **Brothers,** *would executive produce as well.*

While **Brothers** *focused on friendships among a group of soldiers throughout their European campaign,* **Pacific** *took a much more personal approach, drilling down on the individual experiences of its three leads but telling their stories separately. Critics also noted the differences the show details between the wars in the East and West— while the battle against the Germans was a largely conventional war, the fight against the Japanese required the soldiers to face new challenges: suicide bombers, poisoned water supplies, a dangerous jungle environment, and guerrilla tactics. The result was visually brutal.*

The show earned a whopping twenty-four nominations at the 2010 Emmy Awards, taking home eight statues, including one for Outstanding Miniseries. **Pacific** *also received a Golden Globe nomination for Best Miniseries, the AFI Award for TV Program of the Year, and a vaunted Peabody as well. Critics were somehow even more adoring than award-givers, in some cases going so far as to say the show topped* **Band of Brothers.**

TOM HANKS:

HBO asked for another *Band of Brothers.* I thought they were kidding. The question, then, was not *why* but *what?* We thought to do a split story of an airman in Europe and a sailor in the Pacific and were working to find the source material when the writers from *Band* talked about Leckie's *Helmet for My Pillow* and Sledge's *With the Old Breed.* That each man was a marine in different units but had both been at Peleliu gave us the arc we were looking for—from Guadalcanal to the war's end when Leckie was home and Sledge was still on Okinawa. We had the entire Pacific war in the bones of our two characters.

COLIN CALLENDER:

The vets who landed on the beaches of Normandy and experienced the war on the western front, in Europe, would talk about their experience during World War II. But the men who came back from the Pacific theater of war didn't speak about their experience when they came home. The Pacific was so brutal that many of them never spoke about it, even on their deathbeds. The experience of making *The Pacific* was very different from making *Band of Brothers.*

KARY ANTHOLIS:

When I looked at *The Pacific*, I immediately looked at it like if *Band of Brothers* was *The Iliad* and *The Pacific* was *The Odyssey.*

The Iliad was about essentially a battle. It was A to Z, how are they going to get into Troy, and how is the standoff going to end? *The Odyssey*'s a much more circular journey, with Ulysses going from island to island to get back home.

TOM HANKS:

I think the marine experience was a more atavistic, unhuman time. No one knew where those islands were. Paris is in France. The map of Europe is familiar and the Allies there liberated the local population.

In the Pacific, the islands were miserable places, taken for the airfields and proximity to Japan. There was little "there" there—so they had a bored, get-me-out-of-here-soon emotion. The paratroopers of *Band* were a relatively elite, volunteer unit. Marines were grunts, slogging through misery in so many forms, it's no wonder the veterans talked more about the others they knew than the particulars of, say, the guns at Brécourt Manor.

TONY TO:

Chris left HBO when we were still in the midst of doing *The Pacific* and it was the most difficult day for me. In the success that I have experienced with Tom and Steven, the key ingredient was always going to be Chris, the fearlessness of faith and trust. When he left, it allowed room for doubt or other voices to come into the process. I felt that we never lived up to *Band of Brothers* with *The Pacific*.

In twelve years of working with HBO, the only creative note I ever got was on *Grand Avenue*. Then Chris left, and there were notes galore from every direction.

KARY ANTHOLIS:

We had shot *The Pacific* and spent more than $150 million.

That coincided with Chris and Colin leaving HBO and Richard and Mike firmly taking over. We had tried to capture lightning in a bottle twice. And it ain't magic. Their first reaction to the first cuts was like, "We don't know what to do about this." But I had this idea. I came from a documentary background. I'd seen what they'd done at the beginning of *Band of Brothers* with the testimonials from the surviving members of Easy Company, and I thought, Why don't we try to frame this thing with mini-documentaries that take us through the planning of the war and the evolution of the war?

We found out that HBO Sports had been given control over the Time Life archive of newsreels, so we owned all that footage. We hired a seasoned documentary editor and put together these little, two-to-three-minute documentary clips, introducing each episode.

The last act of sleight of hand was getting Tom Hanks to narrate those little documentaries. Gary was able to persuade Tom to do it, which was a huge coup.

ERIC KESSLER:

We had a screening of the first episode in the White House screening room. I sat next to Richard in the second row, and right in front of me was Obama, Spielberg, and Hanks and behind was the Joint Chiefs of Staff. I had a feeling of pride and awe.

KARY ANTHOLIS:

Hanks was fantastic. Obama took him and Spielberg into the Oval Office for a half hour. After, they went down and visited the press corps. It was then that Hanks found out that the press corps didn't have a working coffee machine, so he bought them an espresso machine.

RICHARD PLEPLER:

My dad was an amateur historian of World War II. He watched everything and read everything. I watched rough cuts with my father. He was so moved and turned to me after watching and said, "This is going to be one of the proudest things you've ever been associated with." It meant an enormous amount to me to see my dad's response.

TOM HANKS:

These series would not have existed were it not for HBO. They wanted the films to be great, groundbreaking, unlike anything else on TV at the time.

BILL NELSON:

In 2010, HBO was named Showman of the Year. *Variety* essentially reversed themselves from what they said at the end of 2007, "From Hitmen to Hitless," to the accolades they gave us at the end of 2010. That was a good day for me and the whole company.

The reason for that is because of Michael Lombardo, Richard Plepler, and the whole team. They brought forth great programming.

So *Variety* contacts our PR folks, Richard and Quentin, and they say, "You guys have done such an amazing job. We want to make you Showman of the Year." So we sat down with Mike, and they asked, "What's the cover?" Someone said, "Is it a picture of you, Bill?" I said, "No, I don't want it to be picture of me." Maybe it's just Michael Lombardo and his team. We were going around in circles, not liking any of the ideas, then we go, "Well, it wasn't just us suits, it was this whole company." We decided to have the ID photos of every HBO employee on the cover of *Variety*. And every employee of Home Box Office in 2010 was put on the cover of *Variety* shaded to form the background and words, "HBO 2010 Showman of the Year." We were proud that it was all of us.

We told the staff Friday that it was going to happen and we said to them, "You can go home to your family and tell them that you will be on the cover of *Variety* Monday morning." It epitomized Home Box Office as everyone being part of this collective effort.

The **Mildred Pierce** *miniseries, airing on HBO from March 27 to April 10, 2011, consisted of five hour-long episodes by Jon Raymond and Todd Haynes based on James M. Cain's 1941 novel of the same name. The series featured flawless performances by Kate Winslet in the title role, Guy Pearce, Evan Rachel Wood, and Melissa Leo.*

In addition to the series' bold, way-ahead-of-its-time look at a woman determined to be an economic force of her own, the dynamic between Winslet and Wood, who played her daughter, remains one of the most painful, shocking, powerful, and poignant mother-daughter relationships in television history. It won five Primetime Emmys, including Winslet for Outstanding Lead Actress and Pearce for Outstanding Supporting Actor.

TODD HAYNES, Director and Executive Producer:

A good pal of mine, Jon Raymond, had read the original James M. Cain novel of *Mildred Pierce*. He was struck by it as a sort of economic history, focusing on a portrait of this woman and the crises of the middle class and her relationship to her daughter. I read it and found it to be so interesting.

CHRISTINE VACHON, Executive Producer:

It was at a time we were still reeling from the effects of 2008. *Mildred* was set in the Depression, right after a war. There were so many things that felt so resonant to our time.

TODD HAYNES:

I've always been interested in stories set in domestic realms that almost always center on female characters. I'm interested in the limited freedoms and the responsibilities that women are burdened with in our society and how they have to navigate so much. *Mildred Pierce* is this exemplary figure of the maternal drive and the engine to basically move heaven and earth for the sake of her children and particularly her daughter, Veda. But also that meant really reconceiving the economic situation in which she lived. And so the mother has to enter the workplace and become part of that machinery, to achieve the outcomes that she wanted for her daughter.

It was about women in the workplace, it was about labor. But ultimately it was driven by the love of the mother-daughter relationship and the maternal drive. And in a weird way, the maternal drive will always fail in a way. The more one asserts it, the more freedom you give to your offspring, and the more you want them to aspire beyond the class they were born into, the more you're destined to lose them.

Jon and I just started to write, and we didn't really know where we would take this. I think we had our first drafts of the five episodes, or we were in the process of getting there when we also reached out to Kate Winslet to play Mildred.

MIKE LOMBARDO:

I got a call from Kevin Huvane, who said, "Kate Winslet really wants to do this Todd Haynes project. Will you read it?" Now I was a big fan of Todd Haynes, and Kate Winslet at that point was a big get, she was a movie star, and I said, "That's a fucking little late." And I went to Kary because it was a miniseries, which was his area, and said, "Hey, *Mildred Pierce*, Todd Haynes." He was dismissive of me and the whole idea. I think Kary Antholis resented me for a long time. Do I think he wanted my job? I think he absolutely thought he'd be better at it than me.

Ultimately once I willed it into being anyway, good or bad, he was great. He was the real deal. But he was very mistrusting of me and my judgment. I inherited a very competitive dynamic. Carolyn versus Colin versus Kary versus Sheila. Chris had never anointed a head of programming after he became CEO.

KATE WINSLET, Actor and Executive Producer:

Two things brought me to the project, the first one being Todd. The second, that it was a true, incredible adaptation of that novel.

I was really pained by the extent to which Mildred allowed her child to define her, to literally dictate her every breath. Of course, one has to do everything one can to love, accept, and adore your children. For me, I'm very fortunate that that's always been a very instinctive, natural thing. But I think Mildred's obsession with Veda was sort of a deep-rooted envy of her, actually. I think anything that Mildred felt that she had failed at ever in her life, she was just never going to allow for that to be part of her child's life. To live so blatantly vicariously through her child was terrible to watch in a way. You can just see that she's setting herself up for heartbreak. It's painful to watch. It's like watching an extraordinarily slow but fatal car crash.

I thought it was an extraordinarily exciting way to be able to tell the full story. Of course, that's the great thing about television, and the great thing about HBO in particular, is that they really embrace the creative. It was very clear to me that this had the potential to be a very exciting, rewarding experience.

TODD HAYNES:

My creative partners and I had come from feature filmmaking and there was something exciting about this from a creative standpoint, first and foremost, of telling a story in long form and having the breadth of that canvas to work within, but also having it be limited.

CHRISTINE VACHON:

The only thing that really felt different from making a very long movie was the fact that we had to deliver episodes before we finished. You delivered episode one before you'd finished episode two. That was really unnerving, because Todd was so used to having a sort of holistic view of his movie.

The schedule, with the March air date, and because there was a death in Kate Winslet's family, we ended up shooting in the fall. We were rushing, it was quite a feat to get finished in time. I was informed in the nicest possible terms that the air date was not going to move.

I had brought in Ilene Landress very early on to help us prepare the budget for Mildred. I didn't know much about TV at the time, and she was one of the executive producers of *The Sopranos*. And I think the fact that Ilene had already had such a tenure at HBO really helped us figure out the best ways to navigate. So it was one of those things that makes me look really smart in retrospect.

HBO had insisted on a point for the budget and wouldn't budge. The only way to hit their number was to do it in fewer days. Fortunately, the miniseries was in the hands of a magician.

ILENE LANDRESS:

It was a brutal shoot. On the production side, we should have had eighty-eight or eighty-nine days to do it and not sixty-eight, which nearly killed us all. We were all completely sleep-deprived and that was really hard. And Kate Winslet, you're talking about a super long script, three hundred pages. She's such a machine, such a workaholic, and she's so great, but she probably only ever got four hours of sleep at night. Same thing with the rest of us. They were just brutal conditions. We had to hit a number, and the only way to hit it was to do it in fewer days.

It turns out that in Merrick, Long Island, there's a couple blocks that were built in the 1930s to try to attract movie people from Hollywood to the East Coast. There are one- and two-story houses very much intact, and the whole downtown is like a Hollywood exterior. We took a hair salon/school, bought them out, and converted it into the diner. That's the triumph of that movie, aside from Kate Winslet's acting, is that we totally pulled it off on the East Coast when it took place in LA.

EVAN RACHEL WOOD:

I spoke with Todd a lot and I know the dialect was really important to him. Sometimes that era is hard to pull off if you don't have the right ear for it. So we worked a lot on voice, speech, and the inner workings of the character. For a movie that is so complicated and dark, it really was made with so much heart. Everybody really cared about all of these characters, where they were all coming from, and the pain under all of the darkness in that movie. So it felt very intimate making it. It is a haunting film and it was haunting while we were doing it for a number of reasons.

It was really wild. At one point, we were joking about the film being haunted by Joan Crawford, because strange things started happening. Like we would set up a shot for hours and then yell action, and one of the big lights would just explode. I really started to think that maybe Ms. Crawford didn't want us filming this movie. That was the joke. It was very intense, long hours. I was sick quite a bit filming it. But I fell into that role and loving being sleep-deprived in these period clothes, arguing in scenes with Kate Winslet till all hours of the night. It was absolutely exhausting, but exhilarating at the same time and really felt more like a fever dream than anything—with just stunning visuals.

KATE WINSLET:

Evan is such an interesting person. She appeared to have the most robust confidence and street smarts that I was almost envious. I almost felt too grown-up or something around her. I was always way too tense. I was probably playing Mildred Pierce a bit like that. Evan has a real sort of fluidity to her being. There's an essence that she has that's very liquid in a way. I don't know how else to describe it really. Honestly, I look back on that time in Evan's life and I wonder what it must've been like for her.

ILENE LANDRESS:

I would believe every single thing Evan has said about Marilyn Manson, because we were there. When we were doing *Mildred Pierce*, that's when she was with Marilyn Manson.

He came to visit once and I remember the vodka bottle flying out of the trailer. She would come to work in bad shape. She would come to work like the train had run her over, and then she'd sit in the hair and makeup chair for two hours and then she'd be brilliant. She's a brilliant actress. But pretty much every morning if I saw Evan Rachel Wood, the first question would be, "Where's the medic?" She was in a rough place.

It never compromised her performance. She would just fall asleep in the makeup chair, pop out of the makeup chair, and do her thing.

EVAN RACHEL WOOD:

Everyone was going through some sort of intense, personal trauma or tribulation at the time. It was like the set was our safe place. Kate was getting divorced. I was in a very dark place. Todd, I believe his mother died while we were filming.

KATE WINSLET:

It was an interesting time because this was so much a tribute to the maternal. I lost my mom during the making of *Mildred Pierce*, suddenly. Kary Antholis lost his mom right when we were in preproduction on *Mildred Pierce*. And Michael Lombardo lost his mother while we were making *Mildred Pierce*. So it will always be marked by that really personal and weirdly multiple impact of that loss, which no one can ever really prepare themselves for it, no matter whether they see it coming or not. In the context of this story, it was quite something. But it also even further bonded us all in wanting this to be something special and meaningful and singular.

In an especially shocking and haunting scene from the HBO version, Mildred discovers her daughter Veda nude in bed with the very same man Mildred had been shtupping—a vivid detail not included in the old Warner Bros. original.

TODD HAYNES:

The scene has immense narrative importance. We wanted it to have power. There's such violence in it, on the part of Veda to her mother. And yet nothing happens. She just walks across the room. I had the best actors, who knew that the least amount of gesture and expression carry the most impact, that it needed to turn into a throttling, and when the violence became explicit. That moment is what triggers the violence that will come. It's a quiet, eerie moment.

EVAN RACHEL WOOD:

It was an incredibly powerful day. The entire scene. You could feel it when you walked onto set. I was about to chicken out on that scene. I wasn't sure if I wanted to do it fully nude. I was very insecure. It was Kate who really coached me through it, though by no means did anyone pressure me to do anything that I didn't want to do. I knew deep down that I wanted to do it. I was just scared. And nervous. Kate actually cited peeing on camera in a Harvey Keitel film, then she started talking me through her nude scenes and I was taking it all in. Then she explained to me what a merkin was, and told me that I would be covered up. That it was a way to look naked without actually being naked. That made me feel a bit better, but I also couldn't believe that this was my life at this moment.

KATE WINSLET:

Todd said to me, "Evan is very, very nervous." And I said, "Oh my God, I've got to help her. Oh my God." I was so horrified to think that maybe I had neglected her.

But if we had a difficult scene to do, we might probably keep a distance from each other that day until the moment of actually playing that scene would happen. And then we go with each other, and all the devils would come out of the closet.

She was very, very nervous. There was one moment when I did feel I could sister her a bit. I said to her, "You just tell me what you're happy with, what you aren't happy with. I'll clear everyone out of the room." Actors are expected to just be okay with everything. That's changing now, I have to say. There are intimacy coaches now. It's much more now than it was in those days, but certainly from when I was younger as well.

But I very much take that on board. I did say to her, "Don't worry, I'll make sure the boom operator has their back turned," that she had a robe right close by. I would jump up and put the robe around her myself if costume just couldn't quite get in there quickly enough, after they'd said cut.

I've always seen it as very much a part of my job to look out for other people. Poor little thing. She was such a slip in those days as well. I think she felt emotionally quite fragile as Veda at times.

EVAN RACHEL WOOD:

I understood the weight of that scene and how the nudity wasn't gratuitous. It was an act of violence. And it was going to be done well and appropriately, and Todd felt very passionate about it. I don't like doing nude scenes, unless there is a reason for it. When it was explained to me, I thought, "Okay, all right, I'm going to do this because it's important." That's not to say that I didn't perhaps do a shot of whiskey behind one of the lights before doing it.

Which made the costumer chuckle. But I did it and I am very glad that I did it. Kate told me that I would be happy that I had done it.

I was actually sick when I did that scene. I had a fever and it felt very surreal. But I can still remember the power of Kate on that day. I knew that if all I did was focus my energy on her and look at her and look at what she was giving me that I was going to be okay and it would carry me through those three steps. And that's what I did. It was an epic stare down with this brilliant actress who even when she was off camera was giving me every-thing that she had. She wasn't saying a word and she didn't have to. My God, I can still feel the feeling in my chest, just talking about it. My adrenaline was pumping, and it was so incredibly powerful.

TODD HAYNES:

We screened it at the Venice International Film Festival that year, and the critical reaction and the award nominations all felt great, a big gift to my creative partners and to HBO, who had believed and invested in it.

It was truly the best experience with the studio and with the people who were around me—Michael Lombardo, Kary Antholis, Sue Naegle from HBO—that I've never been able to match. It's hands down our best experi-ence with a studio, in my career to date. It made me want to do more long-form filmmaking.

EVAN RACHEL WOOD:

They've had some of the best marketing campaigns and artwork and trail-ers. The way they cut trailers is absolutely genius. People sometimes take for granted just how good their marketing is. It really does the films justice, and it's really creative and cool, and there's always a song or a visual that really sticks with you. And I think they're just brilliant at it.

On February 9, 2008, HBO premiered **Bernard and Doris,** *an examination of tobacco heiress Doris Duke and her bond with—yes, the butler did it. Susan Sarandon starred as Duke opposite Ralph Fiennes's semi-subservient Bernard Lafferty. The movie was nominated for ten Emmy Awards, including Outstanding Made for TV Movie. Saran-don and Fiennes both nabbed Emmy and Golden Globe nominations for their roles.*

BOB BALABAN, Director and Actor:

We sent the script to a million people who didn't want to do it. My man-ager, who had a good relationship with Colin, said, "I think HBO would like this." He said, "If Bob is willing to do a few things to it, we'd like to buy it immediately." At the beginning, our stars, Susan Sarandon and Ralph Fiennes, were a little uncomfortable about it, because they said, "We made a feature. We don't want to do it as a TV movie."

I said, "Think about it. If this is a feature, it's going to open in two theaters if we're lucky enough to get distribution. It won't get one nomination for anything, and nobody will notice the beautiful work you've done. If we do it on HBO, it's going to be seen by millions of people immediately, it will always be more available, and I think you're all going to get nominated for things." So they changed their minds and HBO was fantastic.

Less than eight years after the fateful 2000 election that sent the second George Bush in nine years to the White House, HBO released **Recount**, *a dramatic re-creation of the behind-the-scenes struggle between Democratic and Republican strategists and politicos that played out over the worrisome weeks in which the election results were contested. The two generals in the seemingly interminable "Battle of the Hanging Chad" were Ron Klain (later Joe Biden's chief of staff), played by Kevin Spacey, and James Baker (Tom Wilkinson), George Bush's head legal consultant on the campaign. The decision of the filmmakers to largely ignore the two candidates (Bush and Gore are heard and seen only once, and then only from behind) puts the spotlight on the political operatives who were "names" in relatively few households at the time.*

The result, most critics agree, was a compelling retelling of a constitutionally perilous moment in the nation's history. While the movie received a few knocks for liberties taken in dramatizing the 2000 recount, the acting received universally favorable reviews. Special praise went to Laura Dern for her portrayal of Florida secretary of state Katherine Harris (head of elections in the Sunshine State and an unapologetic Bush booster), who certified the election for Bush before the Gore team sued to trigger the recount.

The film was nominated for five Golden Globes, including Best TV Movie, with Laura Dern taking the prize for Best Supporting Actress. At the Emmy Awards that year, **Recount** *took home three awards on eleven nominations, including a win for Outstanding Made for Television Movie. Laura Dern, Kevin Spacey, Tom Wilkinson, Denis Leary, and Bob Balaban (who played Bush campaign lawyer Ben Ginsberg) all got acting nods, with Spacey and Dern taking home SAG Award nominations as well.*

DANNY STRONG, Screenwriter and Executive Producer:

I was twenty-three, twenty-four, and supporting myself full-time as an actor. It was really scrappy. At first it was, "Oh my God, this is a lifelong dream now come true." I'd been wanting to be an actor since I was five. Within about a year, I started to get really unhappy.

It was a year of noes. Simultaneously, a really close friend of mine wrote a screenplay and sold it for $250,000. I was brimming with jealousy. He also started really pushing me to write. And it was really therapeutic because it really helped get my mind off all my auditions. The whole thing was so rewarding that I decided that I was going to pursue a separate career as a writer.

I wrote scripts for seven years and none of them sold. Then I thought to myself, I would never go see one of these movies. I didn't write anything for several months. Then I started researching the Florida recount and I thought, This is an incredible story.

I decided to pursue it, even though I thought the only company that would make this movie was HBO, but they wouldn't make it for me because they had this sort of reputation for being very elitist when it came to the writers they hired.

You had to be Tony Kushner or Christopher Hampton or some classy writer to work at HBO at that time. I had never even written a drama, I had been writing these comedies that hadn't sold. I took the pitch into HBO. I was in the lobby, with Len Amato, my producer, and I said, "I can't believe I'm sitting in the lobby of HBO about to pitch a project." In that moment, there was nothing classier, more prestigious than HBO. And Len just looked at me and said, "It's a better story if you sell it." So I went and pitched my little heart out to Keri Putnam and Jenni Sherwood. Three weeks later Len called me and said, "They're going to buy it."

I was not elated selling my first project after seven years, I was terrified.

KERI PUTNAM:

Even with all our success, it seemed clear by 2005 or so that original movies and miniseries were not going to be the future of HBO. It felt like it was going to be more series that had established themselves as the primary drivers of ratings, conversation, and subscriber retention—so I left in 2006 to run production at Miramax Films when it was part of Disney, post-Harvey. Reflecting on it now after the shift to streaming fifteen years later, I would not have predicted the current rise of miniseries across the streaming landscape, which followed the demise of the mid-budget character-driven studio feature.

DANNY STRONG:

Keri Putnam left before my deal had closed. So I was sort of terrified they weren't going to continue, but they did continue. So Jenni Sherwood said to me in our meetings, "This is all we want from you. Creatively we want you to write the best script you can possibly write." It was this amazing piece of advice. It was a really positive experience.

LEN AMATO, Executive:

So Kary called me and said, "Do you want to produce a limited series about how we got into the war in Iraq?"

And then he laughingly said, "Well, how come you don't work at HBO?" And I laughingly said, "Nobody asked me." Then the next day I got a call and that's how the process started for me to go to HBO.

And so then we started developing *Recount* and Danny started doing the research and we were developing the script. And then in the course of developing that script and getting down to the draft that I was ready to hand in, HBO offered the job.

DANNY STRONG:

Len calls me. He goes, "You're the luckiest motherfucker in Hollywood. I've just been hired to be the new senior vice president of HBO Films." And he was right. I was. When does your producer become your executive? It's pretty crazy.

LEN AMATO:

They brought me in at a more senior vice president position, working for Colin. The script sat there and I thought, "They hired me for my taste, but nobody's reading this script." Then mysteriously the script leaked to CAA, and it caused a frenzy with directors. Sam Mendes wanted to make it. Spielberg was calling. It was a sensation when it was leaked out there.

I don't think that the film division at that point had been in a situation like that, where a dozen A-list directors were all clamoring to direct a movie. A lot of it came from the fact that people really responded to the script, but it was also 2006. The Bush administration has been there for six years and people on the left were pretty enraged by it.

COLIN CALLENDER:

We set Sydney Pollack to direct. We were in preproduction on *Recount* and he called me and Paula Weinstein and said, "I want to take you to dinner." We went to a restaurant in Westwood, and he said, "Look, guys, I'm ill, I have cancer. And the doctors told me I can't do the movie." He was very candid and it was heartbreaking but I love him for what he did that night. So we had to scramble to sort of pull things together quickly.

JAY ROACH, Director and Executive Producer:

It was a very complicated feeling to have lunch with Sydney and Paula Weinstein, and hear that he wanted me to take over the project. I was really concerned for him. He said, "Listen, I'll be fine. I know you're not the most likely choice but I have some weird feeling that you will do a good job with this." His faith in me meant so much. I said, "If I can help, I'll do it."

COLIN CALLENDER:

The idea of actually going to a comedy director to do a drama rather than just to get a drama director was an exciting proposition.

JAY ROACH:

We were all running a three-legged sack race because time was so short. It was such an ambitious project and we wanted to shoot in all the real places. There wasn't time for a huge amount of arguing. The only discussion I remember having anywhere near intense was a last-minute fight over budget. I thought we should have forty-five days; they thought we should have forty. I'd been working in studio movies for so long and things are different with studio movies.

I don't think I'd ever had a shoot schedule shorter than fifty days. I was scared. I said to Len Amato, "I got to have forty-five days." I ended up negotiating for one more day instead of five.

He was right. We figured it out. We shot fast. The crews and cast on that film were unbelievably driven by passion for the material. It was a major turn in how I looked at making films, that sort of labor of love cliché that was turned up to such a degree.

BOB BALABAN:

Ben Ginsberg, who I played, cared so much about Republicans, conservative values, and his party succeeding that it was actually a good exercise in imagining the other side. Did they do some nefarious things? Yes, they absolutely did. Have Democrats ever done that? Of course.

DANNY STRONG:

James Baker had been really forthcoming about the events in the recount, as was Ron Klain, a lot of people in both parties. I think a lot of Republicans have a chip on their shoulder about Hollywood, and I expected them to not be open. And in fact it was quite the opposite, everyone was quite open with me about their perspective. They were pleased that someone was just even reaching out to them and wanted to talk to them about their story.

I had this amazing moment where Plepler and I flew to Houston to show the movie to James Baker. All of a sudden, I'm sitting on a couch with James Baker and Richard Plepler showing them this movie I've written, a really incredible life moment. Baker was great and said, "I like it." He had some thoughts and we got into a little bit of a heated discussion over one element of it.

Plepler was crazy amused that I was holding my ground with Baker, but I was right. I did my pushing back on the issue, but it was just one of those life-pinch-me moments.

LAURA DERN, Actor and Creator:

I had done the movie *Afterburn* for HBO back in the early nineties, and then I got to play Garry's girlfriend on Larry Sanders, both great experiences. When Jay [Roach] cast me in *Recount*, I could tell that he, Danny Strong, and HBO cared so much about the upcoming election that they wanted to remind people what can happen and how essential your voice is when it comes to protecting your vote.

Back then, we had political figures from the left and the right helping us with our research into what had happened in Florida. We went on a press tour and held screenings, and it was an amazing thing to be part of.

JAY ROACH:

The best thing that ever happened to my career was HBO taking a chance on me to do *Recount*. Once I did *Recount*, there was really no turning back. I still love doing comedies but there's no giving up now for me in continuing to try to tell stories that are about the questions I ask myself all the time.

Four years after **Recount**, *its director-writer duo of Jay Roach and Danny Strong returned to political drama with* **Game Change**, *which followed the process and fallout of 2008 Republican presidential nominee Senator John McCain's pivotal and much ridiculed choice of Alaska governor Sarah Palin to be his running mate against Barack Obama. This time around, Roach and Strong were joined by, who else, executive producers Tom Hanks and Gary Goetzman.*

The film was based on a book of the same name by political reporters John Heilemann and Mark Halperin. Julianne Moore starred as Palin, while Woody Harrelson played Steve Schmidt, the senior campaign adviser who engineers—and then tries to salvage—the Palin pick. Schmidt's fellow adviser, Nicolle Wallace (played by Sarah Paulson), helps him in that effort despite Palin's astounding ignorance about world events. Ed Harris's John McCain added a moral center to the film, as did McCain, arguably, to American life of his era.

Predictably, some conservatives panned the movie as a sinister lefty (or commie!) slander of Palin. Notably, however, both Wallace and Schmidt left the movie's account undisputed—Schmidt was even quoted as having found the film to be an "out-of-body experience" for him. The film is notable for its backstage depiction of the campaign, as well as the acting, particularly Moore's performance.

At the 2012 Emmy Awards, Moore won Best Actress and the film earned another four awards on twelve nominations, including Outstanding Miniseries, Directing, and Writing. At the Golden Globes, **Game Change** *won Best TV Movie and Moore and Harris both won for their performances (Harrelson and Paulson were also nominated). Moore, too, took home a SAG Award (Harrelson got another nod there, along with Harris), and the movie walked off with a Peabody as well.*

DANNY STRONG:

We were doing post for *Recount* when Sarah Palin was announced. Jay Roach was fascinated by the fact that had happened, and he kept saying, "I want to be in the room where it was decided that Sarah Palin was a good idea to be the vice-presidential candidate."

JAY ROACH:

In my opinion, the soul of America was at risk of being compromised for a political win at all costs. I admired John McCain. I definitely don't agree with him politically, but I had some admiration for him and he was at least one character my father and I could agree about because my dad's very conservative.

We were watching her rollout speech and my wife was saying, "What an idiot." And I said, "No, no, no, no, this is going to work for him. She is American, she's a classic girl next door cheerleader, and she's going to be appealing." You could tell she was not a seasoned politician and had really no experience or background that would convince you that she would, if she happened to become, God forbid, president, that that would ever, ever be good for the country.

I wanted to portray that tension. I identified with her because I've been in over my head at almost every career choice I got myself into.

Tina Fey's portrayal of Sarah Palin was one of my favorite things ever, of anything *SNL* has ever done. It wasn't an easy process figuring out who should play Sarah Palin. Julianne Moore wasn't on the tips of our tongues at the very beginning. People said, "Well, should we just try to get Tina Fey?" I knew Tina, I'd actually talked with her about that portrayal. I even mentioned to her once that I was doing it, but there was such a difference between the masterful caricature she did and what I wanted to do.

DANNY STRONG:

So they came to me first because of *Recount* and Len called me to say, "You want to do the Obama-Clinton story?" And I said, "I don't." So I passed on *Game Change*.

Jay Roach called me out of the blue and said, "I've taken over the *Game Change* project at HBO. And I'm just going to do the Palin story. And before I moved on and went and found another writer, I just wanted to give you one more opportunity to see if you want to do it or not."

I am so grateful he made that phone call, because I told him yes on the spot. "You're absolutely right. I've read the book. It's a great movie."

There was this very small window to write a script that could be shot and released before the 2008 election. I knew that would be a great way to get the movie green-lit. I had about eight weeks from that phone call to crank out a first draft that could get HBO and Jay Roach excited enough to want to move forward. I wrote the first draft pretty quickly. It worked and it got everyone excited.

NICOLLE WALLACE, Journalist:

I had lunch with Richard Plepler and told him I hadn't voted for the ticket. I had a really complicated, emotional experience. I felt disillusioned by the existence of her on the ticket, but protective of her and her family at the time that they were on the ticket. I had all of this despair and anguish and anger, and Jay and Danny were two of the most charming and thoughtful people to deal with.

As rich as that book was, they deepened it and turned the story into one about this very human experience of humiliation and failure and disappointment and pressure. They brought that all to life. Having been a communications director for the White House and a president and the presidential campaign, I had encountered a lot of reporters and they were as good as any that had ever tried to get me to share anything.

I think everybody has that fantasy that someone like Sarah Paulson will play them in a movie. It's still sort of that pinch me part of the whole experience. And she was wonderful. It remains one of the most surreal experiences of my personal or professional life.

DANNY STRONG:

Julianne Moore was my idea. Woody Harrelson was Jay Roach's idea. They both said yes. We had given Julianne a brief pitch, but it was really the script. She read it immediately. If Julianne Moore had said no, I think the film wouldn't have been made because there just weren't any options with her prestige that HBO wanted to make the movie with that were available in our time frame.

JULIANNE MOORE, Actor:

I didn't think about it much. That was the problem. It sort of came out of left field, just one of those things that was an offer and Jay Roach was in town and we went to lunch to talk about it. And basically, at the end of lunch, I was like, "Okay." Then I thought, "What did I just do? What did I say yes to?" I was absolutely terrified. I thought, This is going to be hard. Really hard. I had two months of prep and I literally stopped everything else except for things that had to do with my children. I didn't go out. I didn't socialize. I don't think I even worked out. All I did was work on Sarah Palin for two months. I was so terrified.

What was very interesting to me was how many people were willing to talk about their experiences with Sarah Palin. I never gave up any of my sources, because they had all been so demoralized by the experience of being near her, but they were very anxious to tell me what had happened to them, and exactly what their experience had been like. Everything we did was meticulously researched, and was taken from first-person accounts, including things Sarah Palin had written about that we had documentation of. It felt urgent and necessary and shocking. I think it was important for us to be as accurate as possible, and Nicolle Wallace is the best. She's my number one, I love her.

NICOLLE WALLACE:

I was enchanted by Julianne. She's stunningly beautiful, an incredible working mom who believes in things that matter. But as interested in politics as she is, she only wanted to understand Sarah Palin as a human being, as a woman.

If you watch some of those scenes where she's on the convention stage, she just became her. It's still a stunning performance. It's still hard for me to watch.

LEN AMATO:

In the course of doing hair and makeup tests, I felt this cool breeze go by me standing by the camera. I turned, and it was Ed Harris as McCain. It was uncanny, that's fucking John McCain.

JAY ROACH:

I wasn't sure Julianne could transform into Sarah Palin, I wanted it to work, but I actually couldn't imagine it.

    We started sensing that with the right hair and the right glasses and our makeup, the rest would be up to Julianne.

JULIANNE MOORE:

I worked with longtime partners of mine in hair and makeup, Elaine Offers and Alan D'Angerio. It was a very long process. We had a wig but we didn't use any prosthetics. It was all makeup color, so we were able to change my eyes somewhat. Everybody was really pleased, but it's tough. I always say, you're never going to be that person. You just need to get as close as you possibly can, especially with someone who was so present in the public eye.

DANNY STRONG:

When we did the wardrobe test and she walked out in the clothes with the wig and the glasses on, and she looked quite a bit like her. Gary Goetzman the producer grabbed me and he went, "It's going to work."

JAY ROACH:

When Julianne first walked in, it was transporting, which is what you want. These films will take you back in time. They are a time machine and an empathy machine.

    Woody was there and we were doing his makeup tests the same day, and he saw her performing some of the interview from Katie Couric that she had memorized, she was always walking around with her interviews and her speeches everywhere. The whole time we were filming in Baltimore, in the elevators, in the hotel, in the vans on the way to work, in the makeup chair, always had her earbuds in listening to Sarah. And he said to me, "Oh man, I see what she's up to. I got to step this up. I cannot slack off even slightly. She is knocking this out of the park in terms of capturing her and also creating a very, very compelling portrayal." Woody's reaction convinced me that, "Okay, I'm not dreaming."

    My dad's saying, "No, you don't go messing with our Sarah." Some conservative members of my family were very curious about it. So in a way, I always had my parents and my extended family members in mind. I wanted to be fair to her. I definitely was going to reveal that it was a Faustian deal, but I wanted to be fair on the portrayal.

JULIANNE MOORE:

Woody, my God, was so wonderful. There's always some trepidation when something like this comes out about whether or not people buy it. I felt pleased people believed this was not a caricature of Sarah Palin but the story of her journey.

NICOLLE WALLACE:

They captured that glint in her eyes at the end, the "I'm not done." She was like this hot-air balloon and we were trying to hold her down. She just wanted to soar. The fact that Trump became president makes her story even more important. She talked about these base, divisive things, and the crowd roars. That's a really important phenomenon. I mean, if Trump was electable, she was electable.

JAY ROACH:

We hoped the film would be at least part a cautionary tale, but I feel *Recount* only inspired people to repress votes more efficiently, and the Sarah Palin story wasn't a good warning to people who choose candidates. Instead, they decided, "We'll just get a better professional wrestling character, more of a scoundrel." At least Sarah Palin didn't come back and run for president, so maybe we contributed something.

In mid-October 2008, Colin Callender announced that by the start of 2009 he'd be out as head of HBO Films, heading off to run his own production company. Filling the gap were two insiders: Len Amato would be president of HBO Films, and Kary Antholis as president of HBO Miniseries, both reporting to Michael Lombardo.

In a time-honored tradition, the press release that announced the changes praised Callender—and his bosses, Plepler and Lombardo. Callender's report card? A total of 140 Emmy Awards, 44 Golden Globes, 9 Peabodys, 12 Humanitas Awards, and top prizes at the Sundance Film Festival and the Cannes Film Festival's rarefied Palme d'Or.

COLIN CALLENDER:

I got August Wilson's widow to agree that we could make all of his plays, with the exception of one that Scott Rudin had at Paramount, as a cycle of films for HBO. The definitive African American playwright's body of work, on HBO, would have been an extraordinary cultural moment. But I couldn't get that approved. When that didn't happen, it made me think, Chris wasn't there anymore, the world had changed, and I needed to get back to what I do best, producing.

This was shortly before *John Adams* would become the most winning television programming of the year at the Emmys, and we would beat our own record that we were holding with *Angels in America* when Jay Roach's *Recount* and *John Adams* won everything.

LEN AMATO:

My impression was that Colin had an expectation to become the creative head of HBO. For whatever reason, Richard's point of view was different. Maybe there were other people involved in that decision. At a certain point Colin started sequestering himself, in the office and behind closed doors. And I was thinking there's a lack of communication between Richard and Colin, and if they just talked to each other, maybe it could get worked out.

COLIN CALLENDER:

When Bill Nelson took over the company the axis of the world at HBO shifted and it was clear the program makers were not going to have the same sort of autonomy as before. The range of programming across all genres that distinguished us from all the other platforms was no more. No one had ever looked at programming as a profit and loss center, they looked at programming as a part of the cost of marketing HBO to the public—to get subscriptions. Then suddenly when *Sex and the City* and *The Sopranos* became profit centers from massive revenue streams off DVDs, that changed everything. We were focused on series, which is what everyone else was making.

I had a conversation directly with Jeff, where I said, "I will stay, but I want the option to leave at my own volition and keep my severance package." Jeff was very gracious and that's the deal Bryan Lourd negotiated for me.

The Camelot days of HBO, that moment when everything clicked, everything was working in terms of the quality of the breadth of the programming, the freedom to take risks, programmers who were experienced creatives, who had worked with talent in the trenches, had gone away. The whole ethos of the place had changed. It was no longer the place where I was able to do all the work I wanted to do.

The company turned from being an insurgent to the incumbent, and there were other people nipping at our heels taking the risks that we were no longer taking. We were chasing hits, driving looking in the rearview mirror. And for me, the fun had all evaporated. I had never intended to spend all my time at HBO. I wanted to get back to producing and being hands on, to take advantage of the changes that were going on in the marketplace.

It was a risk walking out of a multimillion-dollar paid job at HBO. I trusted myself; I'd done it before.

LEN AMATO:

Colin called Kary and me into his office. He said to Kary, "You're going to be president of miniseries." And he said to me, "You're going to be president of films. I'm leaving." It was as abrupt as that.

COLIN CALLENDER:

I left in October 2008. It's resulted in the most exciting creative period in my life working in television and the theater. I had an Emmy, and now a Golden Globe, a BAFTA [British Academy of Film and Television Arts], a Tony award, an Olivier Award, a new company that has produced ninety hours of prime-time TV, the biggest play in the history of Broadway, and a Knighthood. I have a whole new life that has paid dividends, and owe a debt of gratitude to Fuchs, Potter, Bewkes, and Albrecht for everything I learned during those Camelot days at HBO.

GLENN WHITEHEAD:

I would credit Colin with an almost obsessive focus on the detailed mechanics of producing and finishing a television program. Colin was incredibly focused on makeup, hair, wig lines. He was incredibly focused on the color correction process and visual effects, really focused on detail as well as the big picture. That focus had a really important impact at HBO. It persists today, and I think he was responsible for it; you can't exercise control or even oversight on those issues unless you have a physical production team, including a post-production team, that is sensitized to those issues by a creative executive. When they begin to understand how important those issues are to that creative executive, they begin to staff and police productions with that in mind. We have what is unquestionably the most skillful set of physical production and post-production executives on the planet at HBO, led by a woman by the name of Janet Graham Borba, who is a fucking miracle. She's just extraordinarily good. That team to a considerable extent was shaped by Colin's perspective and orientation.

The post-Callender era began strong, with **Temple Grandin**.

LEN AMATO:

We did a hair and makeup test for Claire Danes on the set that actually opens the movie, that optical illusion set. And she came on as Temple and it was one of those moments where as soon as she got onstage, on costume, and with the most minimal prosthetic device in her mouth, it was clear that she was just transported to another person. She was transcendent.

That was a shiver up the spine moment, because it wasn't Claire who was up there anymore; it was the young Temple Grandin.

BARRY LEVINSON:

You Don't Know Jack was always going to be at HBO. I don't believe it was ever a theatrical idea, too dangerous, too provocative. We had a great situation. Len Amato was basically in charge of that film division. There was never any Let's tone it down, and I thought, Okay, this is a good sign. We had done one of these really very tough scenes with Kevorkian and I sent Len a cut of that scene, which was really tough stuff. He said, "Terrific, great scene." But he wasn't like, Oh boy, what am I going to do? There was no hesitancy about that, on one of the toughest scenes we were going to do. And he immediately responded to it and okay, this is what we're doing. We're not pulling punches here. And then I felt, Okay, we're going to be able to do what we wanted to do. And I feel very confident about this whole process.

This is what it is and let's not water it down. HBO would set these things very carefully and make sure that we were not going into areas that were not actually credible. There wasn't any like, Wow, it's television. I think they developed that reputation that they wouldn't try to pander to an audience unnecessarily and that that would be what HBO would do. It was going to try to do some very good pieces of drama.

In February 2010, HBO took a leap forward with the launch of HBO Go, an online video streaming service that required a companion HBO subscription via either cable or satellite. Its creation had been years in the making and was a true sign of the times,

HBO having road tested the first iteration of the service, HBO on Broadband, back in 2008 in Milwaukee and Green Bay, Wisconsin.

The release was a shot across Netflix's bow—the traditionally mail-based subscription content service had debuted its own streaming capability in 2007. But the new technology was also a break with the past for HBO, one that required some hand-holding internally. Since its inception, the cabler had been just that—a creator of content for distribution through outlets controlled by cable providers and other partners. Until that point, HBO only had to make the programming—not also deliver it.

HBO Go was a first step in breaking free from all those cable companies on which HBO had developed a chronic dependency.

While it was indeed a radical new move for the company, HBO Go would face challenges integral to the complicated nature of its operation. Streaming rivals like Netflix simply offered online viewing for a fee, while HBO Go required a cable subscription as well, which hampered its accessibility and made it more expensive overall for those quintillions of home theaters.

HBO was fundamentally a linear-oriented mindset, dominated by a wholesale distribution approach to the world. That influenced everything it did and inspired a lack of sophistication on the tech side. Tech just wasn't a necessary requirement for HBO's core operating model. The hiring of chief technical officer Otto Berkes was made by people who didn't know what capabilities were needed to create a competitive streaming platform. Otto was a founder of Xbox, which might be called a cute credential, but if HBO wanted to be a major player in streaming, it needed to focus on what capabilities would be required across the whole organization. But tellingly enough, that was not HBO's strategy.

JOHN PENNEY:

I had never met groups less constituted to implementing a new, completely innovative technological future and new models of serving the customer than the marketing/distributing power centers of HBO in 2007.

JEFF BEWKES:

Since HBO had launched video on demand back in the 1990s, we knew how powerful VOD was, so we knew Netflix streaming would be big. When Netflix started airing reruns of network hits on demand without commercials, we knew it would erode the basic cable bundle first because, unlike HBO, none of the hundred channels were on demand.

The Turner networks' earnings were twice the size of HBO's; they brought in half the earnings of Time Warner. To compete with Netflix and Amazon, we thought all ad-supported networks should do what HBO had already done: offer your shows on demand. Why should a viewer have to go to Netflix to watch *The Office* on demand? Why not show *The Office* on demand on NBC?

So in 2009, Brian Roberts and I did a press conference where we announced "TV Everywhere." I handed him a one-page amendment to our affiliate contract that granted Comcast the right to air TNT and TBS shows on demand, for no extra fee. We weren't charging anything for this increased grant of rights, and it was available to all affiliates, no charge and no renegotiation needed, just sign the amendment.

HBO placed two conditions on the rollout. First, cable companies couldn't charge extra to consumers for VOD functionality. They didn't want two levels of HBO, a "first class" that could watch any show anytime and a "second class" that could only watch shows on the schedule.

Second, they wanted to make sure that any home that paid for the video channels could also watch on demand over any broadband connection; they couldn't force video subscribers to also use the cable broadband connection. This was to avoid any anti-trust challenges for "tie-in sales" and also encourage FCC policy to view VOD on cable as pro-competitive with Netflix and Amazon and YouTube.

JEFF BEWKES:

By granting the Turner VOD rights, we were hoping to set off a viral adoption of VOD by all the channels on the TV dial. Netflix subscribers were mostly watching reruns of broadcast network hits and movies at that time, not the Netflix original series that were few and far between. We figured the networks that premiered the shows, like NBC and CBS and TNT, should offer whole seasons on demand. After all, they were footing the lion's share of the cost for these shows; Netflix was only paying a fraction back then.

But short-term penny-wise thinking by the ad-supported networks and the cable companies blew their chance. Reed always said he was most afraid of TV Everywhere, meaning full VOD exhibition by all the TV networks, but he correctly figured that he could become them before they became like Netflix. If every channel on your TV dial offered all the episodes on demand, the world would look different today, and there would be more competition.

When the industry failed to adopt VOD (TV Everywhere), we knew we would eventually have to merge the company with one of these digital giants. We couldn't turn ourselves into Netflix because the lion's share of our network and even studio revenues came from the cable bundle, and if we went into direct competition with cable operators over broadband that early, they would have gone to war against us.

With hindsight, people now will say we could have persuaded our investors to support dropping the earnings for three to five years to move our legacy subscribers to direct broadband. Well, for one, it was too early—the broadband base wasn't big enough. And two, we would have been bought by Murdoch or someone else for a song when our share price sagged.

It's not as though we didn't talk this through many times with the board and our big institutional holders. Or about whether we could roll over the shareholder base. Ask Dodge and Cox or Capital Group. Basically they didn't need us to turn ourselves into Netflix because they already owned that in their portfolio.

ERIC KESSLER:

Right before the launch of HBO Go, I went with Bill, and two executives responsible for the design and marketing, Courteney Monroe and Alison Moore, to present the product and promotional campaign to the board of Time Warner. The board loved it. Jeff called us later to say that it was one of the proudest moments of his career at HBO.

JOHN PENNEY:

Why would you launch in 2010? It took five years to do that? Five years is ridiculous. It makes no sense. Except the truth was they really didn't invent the product. The product was pre-invented.

ERIC KESSLER:

The product was a big hit with subscriber and affiliates. Subscribers, revenue, and profits all went up and other networks eventually followed our lead with their own Go product. Jeff was able to show the board and Wall Street that HBO had retained its status as a pioneering company in the industry.

JOHN PENNEY:

It took a technology company to be an innovator in delivery. That's Netflix. Then Netflix became a content company.

HBO started as a content company, but lost a lot of opportunities to be an innovative company. Media is not that complicated, but the tech piece is. HBO needed to be pulled along. Even though there were people saying, "Let's not be pulled, let's push, or at least, let's get ready."

*At least some in the HBO world were forward thinking. It had been HBO who called up Chris Rock back in 1986 when the bright young comic was momentarily down and out. Some twenty-two years later, on September 27, 2008, **Chris Rock: Kill the Messenger** arrived, Rock's fifth HBO special. The concert was taped in three locations—Johannesburg, New York, and London—with jokes intercut from all three. Once again, Marty Callner was the director. And once again, Chris rocked.*

CHRIS ROCK:

So here's the thing. I'm at the Cannes Film Festival. And I realized that Cannes just sells flop movies. When a white movie flops, they take it to Cannes and they act like nothing happened. And they sell it like nothing happened. Like it's a hit. And I was mad that we couldn't take *I Think I Love My Wife* to Cannes and sell it like it was a hit, like they do with white movies. Black cinema doesn't travel overseas. So I set out to do a world tour and not only am I going to play the world, I'm going to show you. So I went to, I forget how many countries, but in every country, the goal was to break the record.

What's the most seats a stand-up's ever played? Let's do that. Let's do that in the UK, in Australia, New Zealand. Chris Albrecht said yes. It was all Chris, literally letting me do whatever I want. And before that freaking special, before that tour, comedians really didn't go overseas—Billy had a show in Russia with HBO, but even that was a novelty thing. Comedians did not go overseas. They just didn't. Eddie Murphy's never performed overseas. Richard Pryor never performed overseas. Dice Clay, whatever. No one played anywhere. From that moment on, from that tour on, it opened up the market.

There was a thing I noticed about playing overseas—pop references could change at any moment. So you're in Madrid; the Derek Jeter joke in Madrid is going to be a Ronaldo joke. That Britney Spears joke ended up being a Shakira joke. But when you're talking about the relationships between men and women, you literally don't have to change a line.

It plays the exact same all over the world, women, husbands, all over the world, husbands are mad at their wives all over the world in the exact same way.

In 2010, one of Rock's and Bill Maher's strongest advocates at HBO—and a Michael Fuchs favorite—Nancy Geller, would bid the network adieu.

NANCY GELLER:

I loved my job more than anything in the world. I probably lost a couple of relationships because of my devotion to it.

Nina Rosenstein, Geller's talented and much admired deputy, replaced Geller as vice president for late night and specials. She knew the job came with challenges.

As one of the most vocal atheists on American airwaves, Bill Maher had attacked religious people of all stripes in glib terms for years and had even starred in a kind-of-documentary called **Religulous** *in 2008; it sent up a variety of faiths from all over the world. When allegations broke in March 2010 that Vatican officials in Rome had covered up a Wisconsin priest's molestation of up to two hundred boys at a school for the deaf, Maher got together with intellectual and fellow atheist Christopher Hitchens for an I-told-you-so session that aired as the March 26, 2010, edition of* **Real Time with Bill Maher.**

Both Maher and Hitchens expressed righteous disgust with the alleged crimes—Hitchens insisting that they refer to the alleged offenses not as child abuse but as "the rape and torture of children"—but the two also made light of the situation. Hitchens quipped that "nothing good can come of a church that has as its slogan: 'Leave no child's behind.'" Maher took the opportunity to point out it was going to be difficult to have a two-sided discussion on the news, because there was no one around who was going to take the "the pro–child abuse point of view . . ." Critics pounced, but HBO stood by Maher, as it has done on many an occasion throughout his brutally honest, controversy-courting, I-don't-care-about-being-liked stint as host of **Real Time.**

In this regard, Maher is like the political version of Larry David on **Curb***: always willing—and brave enough—to say things that most would never dare to express, or even think. Time and time again, Maher would push the proverbial limits on what HBO was willing to allow, and time and time again, HBO had his back—and that felt that like a rare trait in an increasingly politically sensitive world.*

MARC GURVITZ, Executive Producer:

It felt like Bill Nelson wanted to fire him every week, particularly because of his position on the Catholic Church.

RICHARD PLEPLER:

Bill Maher is a legendary HBO Hall of Famer. Were there times, when I was co-president, where my boss was upset? Sure. Did Nina Rosenstein and I often have to call Bill and have a conversation with him? Of course. Did Bill always understand that we had his back? Absolutely.

BILL NELSON:

There were a few times when I thought he went too far on certain topics, even knowing his show was meant to be free-form and provocative. I probably discussed some of those occasions with Richard, but I don't believe I ever said, "Bill Maher must be fired."

BILL MAHER:

My love for Richard Plepler is very deep because Richard is the kind of person, not *my* kind of person though, who protected me from Bill Nelson. Bill was always trying to get me fired. There is a long list of people who were always trying to get me fired but he was the one who had the greatest ability to make it happen.

In a 2011 review, the trade paper **Variety** *praised HBO for its then imminent special,* **Mel Brooks and Dick Cavett, Together Again**, *advising readers to "be grateful for a premium network that can afford to demonstrate—with nary a concern about what advertisers want—just how much fun the over-70 demographic can be."*

Consider: when the Cavett-Brooks special was taped, Mel was eighty-four and Dick, seventy-three. They'd be joined during the show by an unbilled and relatively youthful guest Carl Reiner's sixty-four-year-old son, Rob. The show boasted a simple premise: put old pals Brooks and Cavett onstage and let 'em riff to their, and their audience's, heart's content. It seems safe to say that Dick, Mel, and Rob left many hearts more contented than they'd found them.

DICK CAVETT:

My HBO special with Mel Brooks was pure heaven, a pleasure that you felt guilty about getting paid for.

He met me at a radio studio and pronounced me spectacularly gentile. He allows himself to go controlled crazy.

We had nothing, nothing planned. I never had anything but total harmony with HBO. They were a wonderful employer right up through Ali and Frazier. I mean Cavett. I always confuse myself with Frazier.

The official title for those who are taking notes for their college paper is Ali gets first billing. Of course! I didn't fight for it.

One thing HBO excels at is not, as people often do, being a gnat that comes buzzing in every few hours or days, with some dumb observation to make about what's going on. They should write a book on how to be desirable in their field.

Cavett to Costas—two erudite communicators dedicated to the art of conversation. **Costas Now** *had premiered back on May 13, 2005—and for its April 29, 2008, show, Costas invited* **Deadspin** *editor Will Leitch to join the discussion.*

WILL LEITCH, Journalist:

I'd been running *Deadspin* for about two and half years at that point. It was the first big sports blog. I'd accepted the unofficial mantle as spokesperson for the Internet to people who did not understand the Internet. But I was suspicious. I'd been ambushed on a lot of sports talk radio yokels, where they just yell at you for ten minutes. I was generally on guard for it, but this is Bob Costas, for crying out loud. He mentioned that Buzz Bissinger was going to be on the show and I was a huge fan of Buzz. Buzz is a wonderful journalist and *Three Nights in August* is a wonderful book about my beloved St. Louis Cardinals, so I was excited to meet him. I asked Bob, "What's his take on all this?" I think Bob's exact quote was, "Oh, he is foaming at the mouth about this." I said, "Oh, okay. Well, I'll prepare accordingly."

I'm a dopey kid from farm country Illinois and I think these people were expecting me to show up in a leather jacket with spikes in my hair saying, "Fuck you and your media." I felt like part of my job was to say, "Look, I'm just a regular journalist like you. I went to journalism school, I write for the *New York Times*. Blogging on the Internet is not some weird, crazy thing you need to be scared of." I felt fairly steeled for whatever might happen.

The green room at the Equitable building on Seventh Avenue was packed that night. Mike Tirico was in there. Dan Patrick was in there. Joe Buck, too. A live audience waited for an all-new edition of **Costas Now***. Stalking around the green room and pacing all alone by himself was the journalist and writer Buzz Bissinger, prepping for the live panel that he was on with Will Leitch, a sports blogger and founder of Deadspin.com. Costas's show, all about giving viewers an inside look at the dynamics of sports media, was the perfect place for a program on the changing media landscape, but who knew Bissinger would show up with a manila folder in hand and confront his more web-savvy counterpart, Leitch, with outright loathing?*

Soon after Bissinger's segment with Costas began, the dam broke. After Leitch responded to a question from Costas, Bissinger leaned over to Leitch and said, "I really think you're full of shit." Throughout the segment, Bissinger trashed Leitch for what he felt was the degrading of journalism happening at Deadspin.com. "I think blogs are dedicated to cruelty, they're dedicated to dishonesty, they're dedicated to speed," he continued.

Among the gems Bissinger shared with Leitch: "You're sort of like Jimmy Olsen on Percocet."

WILL LEITCH:

I noticed that when he asked me about W. C. Heinz, and I knew who one of the most famous sportswriters of all time was, it definitely got him off track. That spoke to the attitude they had, not just toward me, but to blogs in general.

I have always had lot of empathy in the situation, much more empathy in the situation for Buzz that I did for Costas. After that night, Buzz became a crazy, yelling, and unhinged guy. And in a way that I think not only made things difficult for him personally, I think has distracted from the quality of his work. And in a way I think Bob knew exactly what was going to happen.

BOB COSTAS:

I did not think Buzz would go off the way he did. Absolutely not. One of the things that is just completely false is the assumption that this was a setup, that Buzz and I set it up to ambush Leitch. As quickly as I saw this was getting out of hand, you can see I'm trying to tamp Buzz down, but because Buzz lost it, it may have appeared that way.

RICK BERNSTEIN:

Because we don't have commercials, people probably underestimate how challenging it can be to produce live television on HBO. If the unexpected occurs when a commercial broadcast network is covering a live event, they have the luxury of cutting to a commercial. With HBO, those of us in the control room have nowhere to escape to to collect our thoughts, to regroup, or to figure out how to help Bob handle a situation such as this. We see the train wreck coming and have seconds to figure out how to avoid it.

BOB COSTAS:

I've been on HBO for many, many years, and there was no patter of anything remotely like that in my career. In fact, I was very disappointed by the way it played out, and the fact that there were a number of really good segments on that show which were overshadowed by the circus that ensued there.

WILL LEITCH:

I've literally never watched it. Until *Deadspin*, my big break was answering phones at a doctor's office on the Upper East Side, at Mount Sinai, so I was not like flourishing in my career. I'm thirty years old. I have started finally to get some success. My parents were, I don't know if "proud" is the word, I think "relieved." They lived out in the country of Illinois, and didn't have HBO. There was one family in a one-mile radius that had HBO and so there was a story in the newspaper that morning—this is a very small town—that favorite son Will Leitch is going to be out with Bob Costas tonight. So everybody in the neighborhood gathers to see Will on the TV. Then that happened. I asked Mom how the party went. She said, "Everyone dispersed quickly."

JOE BUCK, Host:

I had been a guest of Costas a couple of times on HBO. I saw Buzz going crazy on the stage, and he kept referencing a guy named "Balls Deep" who was making a comment on Will Leitch at *Deadspin*.

He was going crazy about Balls Deep, and this is what Balls Deep says. I didn't know what I was looking at. Oh my God, he's losing his mind. All of us watching were backstage because we were the next segment or maybe two segments away. Everybody's thinking, "What the hell is happening?"

I go out there and said, "Bob, for the rest of this interview, I'd like you to refer to me by my screen name of Balls Deep."

BOB COSTAS:

When the baseball network came into existence, I was their first hire, which was great for me because here I am back in baseball. But Richard Plepler, who was always a supporter of mine, told me, "You can do play-by-play of games for the baseball network and still stay at HBO. But the minute you sit down and interview anybody, or host a program, you will be diminishing your brand on cable, and we don't want that." It was a very difficult choice—to be with my favorite sport or the journalism and commentary that was unmatched at HBO. I would have continued on both, but I was forced to choose, and I chose baseball.

On the inaugural episode of **Joe Buck Live**, *a show pitched as a replacement for Bob Costas, Buck invited comedian and then* **Howard Stern Show** *personality Artie Lange to appear on a panel with* **SNL** *cast member Jason Sudeikis and Paul Rudd. Buck began the panel segment—the last of the show—with a question to Rudd about the paparazzi, mentioning sarcastically that his favorite website was TMZ.com. After Rudd's answer, Lange ripped Buck for his remark, asking, "What's your second, suck-ingcock.com?" Lange continued to insult Buck and his new show several more times* *over the course of the segment, then in the overtime segment following the show on HBO.com. Buck did return fire at times—at one point roasting Lange by saying he had four chins. Buck also appealed to one of his previous guests sitting in the audience with a microphone, Michael Irvin, whose only reply was, "It's just refreshing to see white-on-white crime." Although the audience was laughing consistently throughout, Buck appeared visibly uncomfortable during the exchange, signing off after the HBO.com overtime segment by saying, "We're signing off on HBO.com, not a moment too soon."*

The show, which premiered June 15, 2009, lasted a full six months.

JOE BUCK:

I wanted to work at HBO, because I'm greedy, first of all. Secondly, I remember when HBO came on the air, and was mesmerized by the whole idea of it. I was always and continue to be a fan of what they do with their sports department. I don't know that I realized when I agreed to do that show, in essence, taking over for Bob who had moved on to the MLB Network, what their expectations were of me and how maybe my personality or style fit into what they had been doing or wanted to do.

I've known Bob since I was a little boy. My dad was in on the hiring of Bob in St. Louis when he wasn't that long out of Syracuse, and his career began in my dad's backyard. So I've always been an admirer of Bob's and been in awe of what he could do hosting.

After being a guest with Costas during Buzz's meltdown, who knew that Artie would be next out there to do something similar, his own version of a meltdown on my first show.

I went backstage. The guy that I was most excited to meet was Artie because I'm such a Stern fan. So I went back there, before he went out.

He was like, "Oh man, I love you. I love your father." I said, "Look, when you get out there, just light me up, rip me. Have fun with it."

I got off the stage and I thought it was not great. It was awkward, but it was live TV.

When it ended, I did not even get off the stage before Ray Stallone has a group of writers around me. I didn't even get a chance to talk to anybody or even go to the bathroom or see my wife or see my kids who were backstage. I had to go down front and answer questions four minutes after that thing just ended. And that was the last segment. Richard Sandomir of the *New York Times* asked me, "Joe do you feel like you just got cornholed on national television?" That was the question from the *New York Times*.

I called Artie the next day and said, "First of all, happy to meet you. Secondly, I'm not mad, thanks for coming on the show. And if there's ever anything I can do for you, I'm up for it." He was crushed. He's like, "I'm so sorry that it went so south, so fast. Look, man, I'm a comedian. I get a laugh, I kept going." And I was like, "It's all good. I'm still a fan. Let's keep in contact," to the point where I wrote the foreword to his second book.

I didn't want people to think I was pissed off at Artie. I said to Ross, "We gotta have Artie on the second show." And he's like, "Eh, let me think about it." Then he said, "Okay, we'll have Artie on."

Artie said he would do it. Then Ross called me back maybe a week later and said, "Richard Plepler said he can't come on the second show, and you're not allowed to talk about it or reference it." I said, "Well, then I quit." I said, "I never met Richard Plepler. I'm sure he's a brilliant guy, but he doesn't know me, and I have a job. So I'm not going to go out there and not reference something that for the last three months, whether it's on the Stern show, all these people are saying all this stuff. Whatever the perception is out there of me, I'm changing it going forward." I knew for my own peace of mind, I had to go out there and talk about it. So now I'm in a conversation with Richard Plepler, who I've never met and who's saying, "It's buried." I remember the phrase he used that I'd never heard before: "It's under the pavement." I said, "That's not true because Artie Lange just went on *Letterman* two weeks prior to the show and Letterman in the second segment of Artie's appearance said, 'Hey, what the heck happened with that Joe Buck show on HBO?'" I said, "That's my name."

I said, "First of all, I've already booked Artie to do this. And now I've got to tell him that they don't want him on, which is going to open me up to more criticism from Artie on Stern's show. I won't do it. I'll just not do the show. And you can have your money back." And so he's like, all right . . . I still have all the emails. He said, "But it has to be done smartly."

We shot a bit of footage to use before the theme song where Artie and I "bump" into each other in Times Square, and then he chases me and his pants start to fall down because he had lost a lot of weight.

When that little piece of tape rolled before the theme song hit, the crowd went crazy, and I have never had more satisfaction in my professional life than walking out on that stage for that second show, after getting that reaction for something I fought for. It felt like it was the only thing to do. I'm glad the only thing to do was the right thing to do. And so it got in there, thank God.

I feel like had we gotten a chance to do more, I might still be there. I sure as hell would have liked to have more than three bites at the apple.

In 2008, HBO aired "The Dream Match" between Oscar De La Hoya and Manny Pacquiao, the match having been dreamed up by none other than Larry Merchant (when talking to ESPN boxing writer Dan Rafael). Pacquiao defeated De La Hoya, surprising quite a few. A year later, he went head-to-head with Miguel Cotto, generating $70 million for HBO. As HBO continued seeking out the best live fights, it was also commemorating the sport, celebrating its adrenaline-fueled past with documentaries like **Thrilla in Manila.**

But HBO's sports documentaries were becoming less "cutting edge" and more "cookie-cutter," or so certain critical voices were saying. The channel was producing docs quickly, detractors deplored, but not nearly so innovatively as they had in the past.

Meanwhile, ESPN was busy reinventing sports documentaries for its thirtieth-anniversary celebration. Think: more freedom for the filmmakers, the creators, the visionaries. They wanted to break the mold, to bring excitement back to films that were by now largely considered ordinary, boring, monotonous.

In 2008, HBO Sports was straddling two eras. It was still doing documentaries, it still had boxing, and it still had Bob Costas. But it had lost Wimbledon and given up on **Inside the NFL;** meanwhile, two of its cornerstones, boxing and documentaries, were in jeopardy.

Up in Bristol, Connecticut, at ESPN headquarters, John Skipper, head of content, was working with Bill Simmons and Connor Schell on a thirtieth-anniversary project for the network. The bold idea: give roughly $500,000 to thirty different filmmakers to make thirty different sports documentaries, thirty new and original films to celebrate the sports network's thirtieth birthday. Part of what fueled the idea was the team's belief that HBO Sports documentaries were, musically speaking, merely variations on a theme. It would be called **30 for 30** and would quickly become the industry leader.

On October 6, 2009, ESPN launched the groundbreaking series. The first to air covered the effects that the famous 1988 trade of Wayne Gretzky from the Edmonton Oilers to the Los Angeles Kings had on the hockey player, and the overall effect it had on interest in the sport of ice hockey in California as a result. Others following included a look at the 1980 Muhammad Ali and Larry Holmes fight, with new, never-seen-before film from both of the fighters leading up to the match, to the 1995 Rugby World Cup, to an episode dedicated to a little group of writers and academics who met at New York City's La Rotisserie Francaise restaurant throughout 1980 and developed Rotisserie Fantasy baseball, only to watch it explode without them.

ROSS GREENBURG:

I love *30 for 30,* but we'd done, how many docus by then? Seventy? We just didn't market it as well as they did.

We did four a year for as long as I was president. I was adamant about that. Probably one of the worst things I ever did was use the title "Sports of the 20th Century," instead of a snazzy title. Because it never had an umbrella kind of *30 for 30* title to it. And so each one stood alone. Didn't do a Sports Century, either. Probably should have, in retrospect. I just didn't have enough money. That was my challenge at HBO, to do as much as I could for as little as possible.

I don't even know if we ever hit a million bucks on one of our docs. We usually were in the $600,000–$800,000 range.

STEVE STERN:

Phil Mushnick calls me and George the Lewis and Clark of sports documentary. That to me is the thing that I will always be most proud of. I think as the group, we blazed the trail. ESPN picked up on it. A lot of their really good stuff came from people who came from HBO.

Ezra Edelman came from HBO, Jason Hehir came from HBO. So you're talking about two of their biggest documentaries, *O.J.: Made in America* and *The Last Dance*, the ones that people will talk about from here until forever, both of those guys learned their craft at HBO. Doesn't happen out of thin air. Ross is a really, really good creative executive. He knows what's good. And he knows how to tell a story.

EZRA EDELMAN:

When ESPN created *30 for 30*, it showed there were different ways to produce sports docs, and that HBO Sports documentaries were antiquated. It was a necessary thing for the world and for the form. I'm not sure that sports docs at HBO were ever going to get there.

HBO Sports documentaries generally were homegrown affairs, conceived and produced internally. For HBO docs, the Sundance festival became an important forum both for buying new shows and for showcasing HBO's own.

JOHN COOPER, Executive, Sundance Film Festival:

They pushed a lot of boundaries. Sheila Nevins was so passionate about the films and filmmakers, and HBO needed the Sundance Festival. If they weren't going to do theatrical, they almost needed these theatrical moments to launch the film.

We were very useful to each other. HBO was always really great at telling us what was coming down the pike, what they thought might be ready for Sundance, what they thought was appropriate for Sundance.

We were the first outsiders that saw a lot of these films and could acknowledge how powerful they were. And that was fun. Sundance quickly became a powerful platform, especially for documentaries. Watching HBO back then, it was the go-to place for cutting-edge work.

REBECCA CAMMISA:

Which Way Home is a film about unaccompanied child migrants who are trying to reach the United States to either create a new life for themselves, find employment, or reunite with their families who left them behind. We met children along the way and traveled with them as they tried to make it to the United States. And in some cases they made it in. This was at the time when the vitriol about immigrants was really horrible, when immigrants were being attacked, and I was just infuriated by that. I wanted to do an in-depth story to remind Americans why people come to the United States. The United States touts itself as the greatest nation, so how could you blame people for wanting to come to it? No one was giving me money. It was a nightmare. But guess what? Sheila did.

What's interesting about filmmaking, the producers on the film were Mr. Mudd, which is John Malkovich, Lianne Halfon, and Russell Smith, and they worked so hard to get funding and to get the film into festivals. But no one would put *Which Way Home* in competition. I thought, Oh man, at least it'll be on HBO, but then it's just going to disappear. What ended up happening was the film gets an Independent Spirit Award nomination, the Grand Prize from the RFK Journalism Award, four Emmy nominations, and an Academy Award nomination. That immediately changed everything. All of a sudden it became quite successful. This comes down to who in power believes in you, and who in power sees the value of these stories. Sheila Nevins.

JOHN MALKOVICH, Producer and Actor:

I'd never made a dime producing and certainly lost a fortune to doing it. But there are certain things you do care about. And Rebecca originally presented, myself and my partners, about ten minutes of what she had done. And I just looked at it thinking, Come on, we've gotta do better than this. I thought it was a very important story. And I think it's obviously a very contentious issue, a very heated issue. We just thought it was an important story to tell.

In December 2009, **Real Sex** *aired its last episode.*

SARA BERNSTEIN:

Real Sex was a culture milestone for HBO late night, and a joy to work on. As a person who grew up in the late 1980s or early 1990s, you knew what *Real Sex* was. It was this great, safe place for the audience to explore their sexuality and to look at different ways people would embrace theirs. Maybe laugh, maybe get a little turned on. But it was clean, and I think it was really important from a cultural perspective.

ROGER ROSS WILLIAMS, Documentarian:

I was a fairly young, aspiring filmmaker, making my first film. And I got a call one day that said, "Hold for Sheila Nevins." And I started shaking. I was like, "Oh my God, Sheila Nevins is calling me? The great Sheila?" I was so intimidated. She got on the phone and she said, I never forget. She said, "Prudence is like a flower through the cracks of a broken sidewalk." She said, "This film is going to win the Oscar."

First time, first meeting, first call. And this is like eight months before, so I said, "I wanted it to be a feature. I was cutting toward the feature." She goes, "Trust me, this is a short, this will win the Oscar." But she let me cut my feature. She goes, "Go ahead. But you will see that I'm right." And she brought me in-house, to her edit team. I went there every day and I cut and I cut and struggled with the feature. And then finally Sam Pollard came in, an incredible editor who had worked on *When the Levees Broke* and had a strong relationship with HBO. It was tough. I cried, and then a lightbulb went off, and I said, "Oh my God, she's right. This is going to be a super strong short or it's going to be sort of an okay feature."

At the 2010 Academy Awards, Williams and Elinor Burkett won Short Subject Documentary for **Music by Prudence.** *Williams took the stage without Burkett and began delivering his acceptance speech, only to be interrupted a few seconds later by Burkett, who then delivered one of her own.*

ROGER ROSS WILLIAMS:

I was Kanye'd on the stage. In the moment when it happened, you're in shock because it's all happening really fast.

Everyone was talking about it the next day. I was the big story on the *Today* show. David Letterman reenacted it in his monologue that night, they had a woman come on wearing the same outfit. Jon Stewart did a monologue on it, and then finally the greatest tribute was the *Simpsons* episode.

I did *Larry King*. I was woken up to paparazzi outside of the hotel, then Ryan Seacrest called. I said, "How did you get my cell phone number, Ryan Seacrest?"

ALEXANDRA PELOSI:

When I had my first son, the first call I got in the hospital was from George Bush saying, "Name him George." The second call was from Sheila saying, "You better come back to the edit room and update your film because we can't go on the air like this." So I had to bring my newborn child into the studio at HBO to update the film for Sheila. I never got one day off.

There was a moment where I had made eight films for HBO and I was doing segments for Bill Maher. He was a real gentleman, really supportive, and said, "I'd like you to do segments for me, be like a real-time correspondent." So I was going out to events and making little pieces for Bill, which I thought was okay because it was HBO. I didn't have any exclusivity contract all those years. I could've gone elsewhere, but I never did. So then Bill Maher was really supportive and he went to the network and said, "Alexandra should have her own show." This was all through HBO Entertainment, not through HBO Documentaries. And so I went and I made Bill Maher an executive producer.

It was Christmas time and Sheila summons me. She said, "Come with me." She puts me in the car and she takes me to the HBO Christmas party at the Marriott Marquis, drags me to the dance floor where Michael Lombardo was standing and says, "She's mine and you want to destroy her. Why are you doing this to her?" I look back and I think, My God, she was so loyal to me and I didn't even see it. She's telling me, They're so fickle and they don't love you like I love you, so don't be a fool. Don't go down this path.

SHEILA NEVINS:

Alexandra is a film genius. She's her mother's daughter. Don't tell her. She jumps up, she shoots everything herself. She's got two kids. She's so phenomenal.

As organized as her mother might be, Alexandra's a masterful scatterbrain. She drives her editors crazy. She can work forty hours in a twenty-four-hour day and she puts them through the strainer. She's an exceedingly talented, human filmmaker.

ALEXANDRA PELOSI:

My husband came from Holland and he did the steps of becoming an American citizen. So I filmed his naturalization ceremony along with interviews of other famous immigrants who had made it in America. It was a beautiful postcard, love letter to America. Very schmaltzy. It was called *How to Become an American* and I brought a rough cut to her house. The routine was, you take your cut to her house for a day or a weekend and talk about it and edit it and she's very hands on. I've got Henry Kissinger and Gene Simmons and other recognizable American faces. She watches the whole thing. At the very end, my husband takes the oath of citizenship, and she says to me, "What's that?" "It's my husband on Ellis Island taking the oath of citizenship." "What is that?" "Oh, that's the naturalization ceremony." "I love that. Why don't you go to a naturalization ceremony in every state?" And so with that, I had to leave with what I thought was the best cut of my film and go to forty-nine film naturalization ceremonies, because the only thing she was concerned about in my love letter to America was the actual naturalization ceremony where she saw people from all over the world. She wasn't interested in watching celebrities talk about how much they love America. She wanted to see real people and find out, "Why do you want to be in America?" I had just had my second child, so I had to traipse around the country with two children to attend naturalization ceremonies. And she knew that she tortured me.

You only get paid once when you deliver the film. You don't get paid by the week. Just in case you paint too rosy of a portrait of Sheila.

LAWRENCE WRIGHT, Journalist:

I spent five years on my book, and I spent a lot of time wandering around the Middle East and South Asia alone. I wasn't frightened, but I was cautious. People kept asking me what it was like to talk to these people and go to those places. So I did it in the form of a one-man show. Alex Gibney came to see one of the performances I did at the Kennedy Center. And that's when we hooked up on doing a documentary. I'm not an actor and I proved it night after night on the stage, but it was fortunate that I was working with Alex. I felt that I had a real brother-in-arms and I recognize him as a truly great journalist. And we just hit it off really well. We traveled together and went to Egypt and London and we spent a lot of time on that film. It was hard to get it made, hard to get the money. There were moments where I was anxious and lonely and desperate, and just to sort it all out and talk it all out in the way that I did was very cathartic.

I think HBO transformed storytelling, and it's done a great service to the art. It made writers the central figure. It wasn't that television hadn't done that in the past, but not so ambitiously. Having written movies before, they don't want you anywhere around the film, and you're not anybody if you're the writer. And suddenly you had HBO. It being writer-centric was the magic ingredient of HBO, and now the entire industry.

The April 20, 2010, explosion at BP's Deepwater Horizon oil rig in the Gulf of Mexico, and the subsequent oil spill, caused catastrophic damage to the marine habitat and the shorelines of nearby states. Nearly five million barrels of oil spewed from the well before it was capped—the largest spill of its kind in history—resulting in the pollution of roughly eleven hundred miles of the United States' southern coast.

*One year later, HBO aired **Saving Pelican 895**, the story of a coordinated effort by government officials and wildlife preservationists to salvage the life of a single pelican—the 895th to be rescued—after it had fallen victim to the rising tide of leaking oil. The documentary was directed by Irene Taylor Brodsky, who had worked with Nevins two years earlier on **The Final Inch**, an Oscar-nominated documentary about the polio vaccine. Taking full advantage of HBO's ability to disregard the time-slot limitations of broadcast television, **Pelican** clocked in at forty minutes—too short for a one-hour slot and too long for half of that.*

SHEILA NEVINS:

I didn't want to do anything about the history of oil spills or corruption. I wanted to focus on something that had been wounded by our selfishness. I asked, "What if we followed one pelican covered in oil? I want to know if they can get him to fly again." We followed that pelican for six weeks. He was a baby, alone, he had no family with him. Doctors, vets, and volunteers nursed him back to life. Now they were going to find out if he could fly. Whoever heard of teaching an animal to fly?

We didn't know whether we'd have a sad ending or a happy ending. When they put him on the beach, he started strutting around. We joked he must be an agent. Then he flapped his wings and strutted a bit more. And then, he flew. He flew up into the sky. I'm not a religious person, but I became religious about this bird.

Nobody watched the film. It didn't win any awards. It wasn't cheap, because we had to film for six weeks, but I didn't have to ask anybody. That was my favorite show. I loved it so much. You think I could sell that story today? I don't think so. That pelican was a trust fund baby. Those were the days, right?

*On March 15, 2011, the first ripples of seismic shift in the TV landscape made their way into the news: video streamer Netflix was entering the original programming arena. With a stunning two-season commitment and a price tag of roughly $100 million, Netflix had its first original series: **House of Cards.***

GLENN WHITEHEAD:

The first time that we did a straight to series commitment predated *House of Cards* substantially, and it was widely considered to be a disappointment, which is why we didn't ever want to repeat that experience. That was *John from Cincinnati.*

House of Cards was a big lesson for us. We had made what was, for us, a very strong offer. Then Netflix came in and blew us away with a two-season commitment. Everybody looked around and said, The world has changed.

ARI EMANUEL:

We offered *House of Cards* to HBO first. They say, "Pilot." Netflix at that point was on the ropes. Credit Ted Sarandos, he puts thirteen episodes, plus another thirteen episodes on the table. We go back to HBO, and they say, "We're going to give you just a pilot." It was an easy decision. That was the beginning. That was the first time I realized, they're fucked.

12

Elective Affinities

APRIL 17, 2011–DECEMBER 31, 2012

Game of Thrones *was the most expensive series HBO ever made—and its biggest commercial success. It brought together a mythic location and a mystical ethos, turning a previously semi-known fantasy writer, George R. R. Martin, into a literary superstar.*

Martin's fantasy epic, **A Song of Ice and Fire**, *amounted to four volumes totaling more than three thousand pages, many of which were overflowing with fantasy, although fantasy minus the usual magical realism: Martin's books obsess more on intrigue, politicking, sex, and violence than on mystical beasts or magical spells.*

After **Game of Thrones** *debuted to acclaim and popularity in 2011, James Purefoy, a star from HBO's short-lived series* **Rome**, *couldn't help but feel a little sore about the way things turned out, declaring* Thrones *"stole our fucking show."*

GEORGE R. R. MARTIN:

When I was younger, probably fifth or sixth grade, I used to write and sell monster stories to other kids in the projects. They were only one or two pages long, written on pages from a notebook, and I would have to give dramatic readings because some of my friends didn't read.

I started out selling monster stories for a penny, then was able to raise my price to a nickel. In those days, a nickel could buy a candy bar. I'm really old.

Then one of the kids started having nightmares, and his mother complained to my mother, who told me, "No more of that."

In the mid-1980s to mid-1990s, I'd worked in television for like ten years. I was tired, and was always having to trim my scripts. When I started writing *Game of Thrones*, I said, "Well, this is never going to be made, and I'm tired of cutting things and having to worry about a budget, so I'm just going to put it all in there."

I wrote something that was huge, much bigger than what could conceivably be done for TV or film. Then I put it out of my mind. The first book started doing okay, wasn't on any best-seller list, the second one hit the *Times* list for number thirteen for a week. Sales were building with each book. Then, Peter Jackson's movies hit, and everybody in Hollywood wanted a *Lord of the Rings*.

I started getting a lot of interest mostly from people who wanted to make them as movies. I had a few meetings, but I didn't like any of the ideas. They said, "It's too big. Let's focus on Jon Snow or Daenerys Targaryen and we'll cut everything else." I told them, "That's not the story I'm telling." Others would say, "We'll just make the first book," or, "We'll make half of the first book and it'll be a big hit. Then we'll make the other movies." I asked, "What if it's not a big hit? Then I'll never get to make the other movies."

I turned everything down, but it did get me thinking about how it could be done. What I concluded is it could not be done for feature films or even a series of feature films. They would have to have guaranteed me something like nine films. I thought to get all of this done in the right way, it would have to be television. I'd worked for CBS on a couple of shows and, given problems I went through on shows like *Beauty and the Beast* and *Twilight Zone*, I knew there was no way *Game of Thrones*, with its sexuality and its violence, was going to get through intact. It was going to have to be premium cable.

I'd been watching HBO, of course. I loved *The Sopranos*. I loved *Deadwood*, *Rome*, great, great shows that redefine their genres and had no problems with sex and violence. Vince Gerardis, who was my manager at the time, and my representatives set me up for lunch with David Benioff and Dan Weiss.

In 1995, Daniel Brett Weiss and David (Benioff) Friedman met in Dublin as graduate students at Trinity College—mid-twenties Americans abroad, who shared a love of modernist Irish literature and a childhood filled with comic books. Weiss was in the process of completing his master's on James Joyce's **Finnegans Wake***; Benioff's was on Samuel Beckett.*

Though Benioff and Weiss parted ways after their year in Ireland, they kept in touch. When Benioff decided he wanted to try screenwriting, he turned to Weiss; together they wrote a horror script called The Headmaster. *Before you go searching for the film version, take note: Weiss and Benioff never sent the script out. An abortive first attempt, yes, but still, the pair remained hopeful collaborators. Solo work turned up mixed results and more unproduced scripts, though Benioff would compile a few notable writing credits, including the film* Troy, *based on* The Iliad, *in 2004.*

One day, Benioff picked up a copy of one of the books in Martin's **A Song of Ice and Fire** *series. Upon finding himself entirely enthralled, he quickly called Weiss, who obligingly bought a copy and found he shared Benioff's passion.*

DAVID BENIOFF, Creator:

We came into this with a deep, profound respect for what George had achieved, which felt singular to us. That respect stayed constant throughout the run of the show and remains so to this day. I can't think of a single writer who has George's strength as a creator of indelible characters, a builder of awe-inspiring worlds, and a propulsive storyteller. Not one. From our first lunch at the Palm in LA, where we spent four hours making our case to him, our primary goal was always to do justice to his achievement on the screen. We told him as much, and we meant it.

D. B. WEISS, Creator:

Comics and graphic novels were a big part of both of our lives, especially in our most formative years. For my part, Scott McCloud's *Understanding Comics* has had as big an impact on the way I think about visual storytelling as anything written about film specifically. When George told us he'd written *Game of Thrones* in part as a reaction against the limitations imposed on him by the television medium in the 1980s, it made me think about the first time I went to Comic Con in the late 1990s. It was mostly about comics back then, before Hollywood invaded it, and the range and depth of imagination on display made an immediate and lasting impression—so many artists and writers trying to show people something they hadn't seen before. George was an attendee and organizer of the first Comic Cons, and I think that boundary-pushing spirit infused his books, which he specifically wrote to be "unproduceable" for film or TV. And we tried to stay true to that spirit.

GEORGE R. R. MARTIN:

Dan and David came in and a lunch meeting turned into a dinner meeting. Everybody else in the Palm had finished their lunch and left; we stayed at the table and kept talking. It was a great meeting. Basically what they were asking for was a free option. They wanted to attach themselves to the project but didn't want to pay anything before it got set up. I was making a lot of money from the books. That's why I could afford to say no to people. So I said, "All right, go have a meeting with HBO." They did, and they sold it.

CAA took the pitch to three buyers: David Hill at DirecTV, Bob Greenblatt at Showtime, and Carolyn Strauss at HBO. The pitches, which took place prior to the 2008 Writers Guild strike, were all based on **A Game of Thrones**, *volume one of Martin's* **A Song of Ice and Fire**. *Benioff took the lead on each pitch. All three organizations wanted the hot property, but HBO was the final choice of "the guys" and their chief strategist, attorney Gretchen Rush.*

GINA BALIAN:

In 2006, we were focused on TV writers. I was told two feature writers were coming in to pitch a series and that they had a lot of clout in the film world, but we didn't know that much about them. We went in not expecting much.

CAROLYN STRAUSS:

I didn't know Dan, but I knew of David's reputation as a screenwriter. They were talking about these best-selling books that I'd never heard of. The badass fantasy thing is not my cup of tea, but they started talking about it in such a compelling way, in terms of the story and the complexity of the characters, that immediately my ears pricked up.

GINA BALIAN:

We listened intently as they pitched the first episode. It ended exactly as it ends in the pilot and we were captivated. Carolyn and I were blown away. As much as the idea of doing a best-selling fantasy show seems obvious now, at the time, big world-building genres were not popular in the marketplace.

CHRIS ALBRECHT:

It was Carolyn's idea to buy *Game of Thrones*. I never read more than ten pages of the book.

MIKE LOMBARDO:

When a writer pitches based on a book, they almost always have the rights. We bought their pitch and were excited about developing it. Then my people tell me, "CAA hadn't closed the book deal." The negotiations for us to acquire the rights for the book were horrible and crazy. A big meeting was called at one point at CAA to try to close it. They asked me to go, so Carolyn and I met with business affairs people from CAA, agents representing Dan and Dave, along with George and his manager, Vince Gerardis. It was the first time we had confronted acquiring a book that had a significant life outside of the book.

Normally HBO insisted that we wouldn't negotiate the profit definition up front, but in success, we will treat you fairly. That worked for 99 percent of the people we did business with, but it didn't work with Vince and George.

They were brash and seemingly inflexible on certain points; they knew we were already excited about it. From their vantage point, the books were enormously successful. If the show wasn't good or we didn't proceed or had a busted pilot, that could affect the other books George was doing in the future. And there are areas of merchandising that typically a studio controls 100 percent of, in order to prevent anybody else from participating in merchandising or controlling it. But in this case, they were already out there making money with action figures and other things and were loath to give that up.

I had a good-faith conversation without strong-arming them. We parsed out different areas of merchandise, allowing them to participate in a slightly more meaningful way, and we opened up the profit definition on a show that hadn't even gone to pilot yet.

What I gave them was unprecedented, particularly because these issues were rarely discussed this early in the life of a series.

SUE NAEGLE:

Game of Thrones was something that Carolyn had loved, and Gina Balian and I really wanted to make, but we didn't necessarily have the money for it.

We'd met with the BBC, but it didn't make sense to do a co-production with them because they wanted to oversee production and traditionally the BBC doesn't spend the same amount of money as HBO. We needed to run production. We decided to move forward step-by-step. Charles Schreger, who was doing foreign sales at the time, was really helpful.

Ultimately, what we got to make the pilot for *Game of Thrones* was less than half of what we got for the pilot of *Boardwalk Empire*. When I talked to Richard and Mike to make the case to do the show, I mentioned foreign value, and the value of fantasy. They said, "You've already sold us a vampire show and now you want us to do a show about dragons? We're not the Sci-Fi network. What is this?"

Then Mike said to me, "Would you bet your job on this?" I said, "Yes."

MIKE LOMBARDO:

Carolyn loved it. When she left, she said to me, "The one thing you should pay attention to is *Game of Thrones*. The script for the first hour doesn't begin to tell you the ability of these writers to go deep." I trusted Carolyn. Gina was a passionate advocate, Sue was a supporter of the project from early on, and it helped enormously that Carolyn became part of the show.

SUE NAEGLE:

It wasn't a difficult decision to bring Carolyn on as executive producer. Carolyn had been championing it and developing it for four years before I got there, and I was happy for her.

RICHARD PLEPLER:

Carolyn had called me and said, "You need to sit with Benioff and Weiss, they're really special guys, and they've got something really remarkable here." I said, "Of course." I told Dan and Dave a hundred times that that call was so important because I had a lot of respect for Carolyn, so by the time they came in, I was already leaning in. They said, "You're a little worried about this because it's fantasy and sci-fi, right? Well, you're a political junkie, Richard. This is the ultimate political story of power. This is archetypal, biblical, Shakespearean." They were mesmerizing and to say that they didn't disappoint is the understatement of all time.

HBO loved the Weiss and Benioff pilot script and soon hired Tom McCarthy to direct. McCarthy also wrote and directed a Peter Dinklage–led movie, **The Station Agent** *(2003), as well as the film* **The Visitor** *(2007), for which actor Richard Jenkins earned an Oscar nomination. McCarthy maintained a "consulting producer" credit on the* **Game of Thrones** *pilot and, years later, would go on to win an Oscar for writing the script for the film* **Spotlight**.

Fewer than one dozen people would see McCarthy's completed work.

D. B. WEISS:

Our worst day was the day Mike Lombardo walked into the editing room unannounced and asked to see the original pilot. We showed it to him, and the look on his face permanently etched itself into my mind. It was the look of a man trying to work through an entire box of Sour Patch Kids.

MIKE LOMBARDO:

The pilot was not great. Particularly given the money we spent.

SUE NAEGLE:

I went to the editing room with Mike to see it for the first time and I thought, "Oh my God, he's not going to pick it up." I had bet my job on it and I was freaking out. I did notes for hours and hours trying to salvage what we had of the first pilot.

GEORGE R. R. MARTIN:

I've heard a lot of people describe the first pilot as a complete disaster. I'm told that when people screened it, they didn't understand many of the relationships and characters, including not understanding in the incest scene that Jamie and Cersei were brother and sister.

CAROLYN STRAUSS:

It was a wildly imperfect pilot. But even from that pilot, you could tell what was in there. It just needed a lot of love to bring it out.

Perhaps the most consequential moment in the entire **Game of Thrones** *saga occurred after the first pilot was completed. It was clear to all that the pilot didn't work. The salient question became, "Was there enough there to justify the expenditure of another eight or ten million dollars (bringing the total pilot price to $18 million) on necessary repairs?"*

MIKE LOMBARDO:

I was nervous as shit. It was a big undertaking. I realized, I'm no longer the guy who is going to Chris to give advice. I'm now the guy that has to have an answer. That was terrifying because there's nobody else to look to, but it was also enormously empowering and exhilarating. You realize that's why you're paid what you're paid. I called everybody into a room, and we sat for a day and literally went through every element that we needed to discuss: cinematography, costuming, set design, schedule, and how we were going to approach it differently and improve it.

I felt people were looking to me and asking, "Go or not go? Are we ready?" Did I love the moment? Yes!

We decided to go forward with a reshoot in part because David and Dan saw the same challenges that we did; the ambition and vision were spine-tingling and most of the cast terrific.

SUE NAEGLE:

Tim [Van Patten] was exhausted from *Boardwalk Empire* and he didn't want to do another show. We begged him to do it. He's one of the greatest guys ever and an incredible director. Eighty percent of the first pilot needed to get reshot.

D. B. WEISS:

The opportunity to produce the same material twice is relatively rare, although the desire to do so isn't—it's hard to think of anyone in this business who hasn't looked back at a film or show and said, "If only I had a chance to do that all over again."

One or two people don't make a show. Neither do five people, twenty people, or fifty people. Anything that works is a result of the combined efforts of hundreds of people, with a constant flow of information among them. And this flow isn't unidirectional—it's not writers and a director sequestering themselves in a room for weeks, and then handing out marching orders to everybody. It's a continuous conversation among writers, artists, actors, craftspeople, producers, and technicians, and when it's working the way it should, it feels like a great dinner party that lasts ten years.

We learned the value of asking questions that put your ignorance on display to everybody. We learned to listen to what the other voices in the conversation were saying about their own areas of expertise, and to take their answers seriously. We tried to settle conflicts among different departments—including the writing department—by staying focused on what was most important for the show, on the balance, at that given moment. As we started to understand that the knowledge we built up together wasn't just localized in individuals but spread across our entire group, we realized how important it was to keep as much of that group together over time as possible, if we didn't want to start over and reinvent the throne every season. Which goes back to the notion of building a better dinner party, which eventually turns into a family.

LENA HEADEY, Actor:

I met David and Dan, which was a little chat in their office—intimidating as fuck, because this was a big-sounding job, and actors don't get a lot of jobs. You get excited and when you don't get the gig, you're always a little bummed.

I read for all the HBO peeps in a small room, and someone left mid-audition to answer their phone. I thought, "Well, I guess this is over."

GEORGE R. R. MARTIN:

Emilia [Clarke] was great. She came out of nowhere. She'd done very little before that. They were really discovering someone new on the scene. That's one of the things I love most about *Game of Thrones*. We had Sean Bean in it who was a major established star. Then we had a lot of people who had never done anything. They were just out of acting school or school plays, and to find people like Maisie Williams and Emilia, Sophie Turner, Kit Harington was incredible. Now they're big stars. That's something HBO likes to do, and I like to do it, too.

It was a thrill. The role of Daenerys is a difficult role, particularly in the pilot, because Daenerys begins as a frightened little girl. She's thoroughly dominated by her brother, who humiliates her and sexually assaults her. He's selling her to this fierce guy and she's frightened but during the course of that comes into her own power. She suddenly grows from a girl to a woman and starts to realize that she does have power and authority. There's a transformation that's incredible the entire course of the show. You have to find an actress who can do both parts, who can be very convincing as the scared little girl in the beginning, but also very convincing as the "I'm gonna kick your ass and burn your city to cinders" woman that she becomes by the end. It's challenging and it was a hard part to cast.

EMILIA CLARKE, Actor:

Before my first audition, I had about twenty-four hours to crib up on Wikipedia, so I could figure out what on earth *Game of Thrones* was. I was so nervous. This was one of my first four auditions that I'd ever been to. I listened to Tupac before I walked in because I needed energy and wanted to go in like a baller.

I walked out of the first audition thinking, "Not a chance in hell," so I forgot about it. Then they called and said, "We'd like you to come back, meet the producers, and record for them." I didn't know it at the time but I walked into a room with Carolyn Strauss, David, and Dan. I had gone out and bought this tribal necklace, because one of the scenes was the speech, "And I am reborn. And I've survived." When I walked in, I got a nice compliment from Dan about the necklace, which I was very pleased with, but then I became very taken with this huge platter of fruit that was in front of these really scary-looking people.

I never had an audition with anyone for anything American, and I very shakenly did it. Then four days later I got a call saying, "We're going to fly you to LA and put you up. We need a screen test." I was petrified. They gave me a month to prepare, so I read the book, and just the other day I found on my computer recordings I'd made of myself preparing the speeches.

I had never been to LA, and they flew me business class! I took all the tea from the business-class lounge, and also took all the mini bottles of alcohol that were free there. I even took the blanket that they give you in business class. I figured, "I'm not going to get the part, I'm never going to get this experience again, so I better make as much of it as I can."

When I landed in Los Angeles, I called my mom, and she asked, "What's LA like?" I said, "Well, there's just a lot of people in workout gear." I was on my own and petrified. I had been on this crazy no-sugar diet because I wanted my skin to be luminous. I had asked, "What do I wear? Something that's like the character?" And they told me, "Just wear something that looks nice." After seven shopping trips to High Street, I had settled on this gorgeous white dress and wedge heels. I was dressed like I was going to a summer party. I got my hair blown out and felt like I was going to a wedding.

I went to this huge building, and Frank Doelger tells me, "There's this other girl they're seeing as well," and when I walked through a corridor, I knew that the girl who was also auditioning was right in front of me. I can still remember looking away because obviously she was going to be ten feet tall, blond, and beautiful. I didn't want to compare myself to this mysterious girl who is clearly better at acting than me and who's clearly going to get this part.

Then Frank tells me, "You'll do the speeches you've prepared, but just to let you know, we might throw a few things at you." And I was like, "Okay, fine." So I walk into this like cinema auditorium, and in my warped memory there's like fifty people there all huddled in the middle, and I get taken up to the stage. And Harry Lloyd and I do the scenes. And at the end, I think I nervously turned to them and asked, "Can I do anything else?" And Benioff in all of his glory said, "Well you could do a dance." And so I did. I did the robot and I did the funky chicken. Bearing in mind, I'm wearing this dress with wedges. It wasn't a good look. Then they said, "We hear you've been training," and I then attempted to show them my boxing, but I was in this skirt, and it was a nightmare. It was a farce, it was a comedy, it was a complete shamble.

So I obviously left thinking, "I ruined this. I'm never getting this part." And then, just before I was about to leave the building, Frank, David, and Dan came running after me, and said, "We didn't want to have you get on the plane not knowing. Congratulations, Princess, you are our Daenerys." I can't even tell you what that moment was like for me. I have never in my life felt euphoria like it.

I didn't know anyone in LA at all, so I just went back to my hotel room, and because I now had the part, I could eat all the sugar I wanted. I put on *Friends*, ate Oreos, and drank milk. And the next day I went and got a Krispy Kreme donut before I left. When I came home, the scene at the airport was out of a movie. My whole family was there. There was this huge bouquet of flowers and balloons and we all celebrated for a week. It's fitting that a show that carried me for ten years of my life had such a momentous beginning.

I had no idea about HBO. I had no idea about TV shows. I had no idea about contracts and how many seasons you're signed up for. It's all just crazy when your little dreams come true.

GEORGE R. R. MARTIN:

In the beginning, collaboration was very close and I was giving comments. Notes were a big part of casting. As they would break down a season, I would look and say, "I'd like to write the fourth script here." We did that for the first four seasons.

CAROLYN STRAUSS:

Dan and David were first-time showrunners, so on season one, they were under a bit more scrutiny. Season one was really difficult because you're setting up this whole system. It's one thing doing it in the pilot, it's another thing doing ten episodes that take place in different continents. It was a lot to learn, and I was around more. But it was clear they were capable of doing this, and people let go of the leash.

DAVID BENIOFF:

Budgets were a major issue throughout, since we started as a moderately expensive show and ended as an insanely expensive show. When we pitched the series to Carolyn Strauss, we told her that while this was a high fantasy epic, it didn't feature pitched battles between a million orcs and a million humans. The focus was on people in rooms, talking—and therefore we could make it for a price.

That was sort of true for season one, where the dragons don't appear until the final shots. We had one big battle planned—Tyrion was supposed to follow The Mountain into combat and we planned on shooting the whole thing from Pete's eye level. Alan Taylor had worked it out and it looked tremendous. But midway through shooting season one we got some bad news. We were running out of money. And worse than that—the season as a whole was running one hundred minutes short. HBO had deals in place with their foreign buyers, and each episode had to be at least fifty minutes long. Some of our season one episodes were clocking in at thirty-nine and forty-two minutes.

So we had to write a hundred minutes more of content, but we had virtually no money to spend. This meant a lot of two- and three-handers in chambers and tents. It meant that Tyrion's great battle instead became a drinking game between Tyrion, Shae, and Bronn. And it meant writing a lot of dialogue for characters and actors we had come to know far better. Some of my favorite scenes from the first season—Cersei and Robert's only one-on-one; Bran reciting the words and sigils of the great houses of Westeros; Robert and Jaime remembering their first kills—were born out of this catastrophe.

EMILIA CLARKE:

Everything was new. Every type of filming happened in the first season. Riding a horse, fighting, getting raped, having a sex scene, getting hit, walking out of a fire. Every first you could possibly have, I had in season one. Emotionally, I was experiencing fear, a lot more fear, thrown in with more fear. But intellectually, I understood what was needed for my character, and from a story point of view, what was needed to create the right amount of empathy for the audience to really care about her. So in the actor's way, I told myself, "This is not about you in this moment, Emilia, it's about Daenerys. Let's change that conversation in your head to make sure this story line has weight to it and is going to benefit the character who you are."

D. B. WEISS:

Books aren't TV shows. They have different strengths, they make different demands, they impose different limitations. One obvious example that pertains to George's books specifically: each chapter in his books comes from the point of view of one character, and George makes this work elegantly and brilliantly. With a cast of characters as large as *Game of Thrones*', however, there is no equally elegant way to apply that same technique over eight seasons of television. And the sheer size of the cast of characters is something we had to confront, eventually. George's books keep widening in scope, bringing more and more characters into play as its core characters spin out across the world. But when it comes to the number of characters a viewer can keep track of, a television show has a carrying capacity. Even after paring down the number of characters significantly, we were right up against that carrying capacity, possibly over it for a season or two.

For the first season, my family was there during the entire production run. My wife was pregnant with my second son, and our options were either to stay in Belfast until we were done shooting, or for me to miss the birth of my second child, and potentially not see my family for much or any of the first weeks of his life, which was a nonstarter.

On September 10, 2010, we were shooting the scenes in the Eyrie, with Lysa and Robin Arryn. Toward the end of day, my wife called and told me it was time to head to the hospital. I looked over at ten-year-old Lino Facioli, who had spent most of the day simulating breastfeeding at Kate Dickie's prosthetic breast and tried to scrub this image from my mind before going to watch my son Hugo come into the world.

After that, we would all come out together for the summer and stay together until school began. Our children were basically co-raised by all four parents—we had dinner together most nights, sometimes at our place and sometimes at theirs. I'd send my kids off to a movie with David, or vice versa. We'd take turns watching them at Belfast's numerous indoor play spaces, the most popular of which was Funky Monkey.

If we hadn't all gotten along the way we do, that wouldn't have worked out—but we did, so it did. We had no way of knowing it would, going into it. We were close friends, of course, but I doubt anyone could have predicted the results of the stress test before it happened. Our wives, Andrea and Amanda, becoming close was a crucial part of it. But to come out the other side of *GOT* still wanting to work together and spend unhealthy amounts of time together . . . it's a little like going over Niagara Falls in a barrel and popping up unscathed. Maybe even Victoria Falls. So now we can keep doing it until we try to go over Angel Falls and are never heard from again.

After the first season, when school started, our families would go home, and we would do as much shuttling back and forth as we could, making sure there was always at least one of us on set. At the outset, we had the naive notion that, if we were fortunate enough for the show to become an ongoing concern, the machine would sort of start running itself, and the demands on our time would be lessened. The opposite ended up happening. The scale of the production consistently outstripped any increases in understanding or efficiency we'd managed to accumulate. And plans to reduce to a single main unit from two (or three, or four) failed to materialize. But we kept the pattern going and made it back whenever possible. The longest either of us was ever away from our family was six weeks, I think. My six-week stretch was in Morocco. When it was done, I told myself I was never going to do that again if I could help it, and I didn't.

I think it was David's idea to send a short video back home from set every day, which we both started doing, especially in places where Face-

Time wasn't an option. Most of them are pretty mundane, but over the years they kept us in front of the kids' faces and built up a nice little record of where we were when we weren't at home. I hope they all look back at them fondly someday, when they show them to their therapists.

CHARLES SCHREGER, Executive:

I said to our key broadcasters around the world, probably sixty of them, "You've got to come to London to screen the show. We're not sending out tapes." They all came because I didn't say that often.

I showed two episodes. With the exception of a handful of territories, it was pretty much sold on the spot to broadcast worldwide. They knew it was something special. I'm not saying people were able to fast-forward several seasons later to when it was one of the biggest phenomena in the history of television, but they got that it was a big deal.

EMILIA CLARKE:

In the beginning of the series, because of the wig, I was entirely unrecognizable. But I did do some stupid things like reading an article where someone mentioned the size of my bum, and that made me feel horrific about myself. I thought, "How can I stop this feeling?" I decided I was never going to Google myself. I was never going to look at pictures. I felt intuitively the only way that I could continue to keep the integrity of what I was doing onscreen was to keep it separate and have as little to do with what other people were thinking as possible. Because the way my brain works, I'm never going to remember the beautiful things that people say, I'm only going to remember the horrible things. So I really distanced myself from it all.

QUENTIN SCHAFFER:

Game of Thrones had complaints from journalists who brought up the level of violence toward women on the show, but George R. R. Martin would explain that much of what he wrote was based on awful things that happened in medieval history, most notably the War of the Roses, and it was also important to note that some of the best roles in the series were for women.

GEORGE R. R. MARTIN:

Of course I had hopes. David and Dan were exactly the right guys to do it, and HBO was exactly the right place to do it. I visited the set. I loved what I saw there. I had a role in casting all of these people, and I had a lot of faith in them. But you still never know. It wasn't the biggest premiere in HBO history by any means; *True Blood* was getting much higher ratings than we were for our premiere.

After we were on the second week, I happened to be in New York with my wife, and we had lunch with Richard Plepler at his club in Manhattan. He had just gotten the ratings for the second week and said to me, "The show is gonna be a big hit and it's going to last ten years." I said, "How can you tell that? It's only had two episodes and the ratings are just okay." He said, "It didn't go down from the first week to the second week. It always goes down. The premiere is high and then you'd get a sharp drop-off to the second episode. We had no drop-off."

He said, "It's just going to build and build," and he was right. But even then, I don't think Richard or any of us realized that it could be as big as it would end up being, winning all these Emmys and being the most popular show in the world. Nobody can possibly expect that.

MARA MIKIALIAN:

Game of Thrones was a lesson for us in thinking differently. HBO media relations was always known to be press friendly and we prided ourselves in understanding what journalists' jobs were and how we could help them. But on *Game of Thrones*, we weren't always going to make the press happy, and I wasn't always going to get them the answers they wanted. It was an intricate project, the hardest I've ever worked.

Press interest became bigger and bigger. Every single thing that happened on that series was newsworthy. I joked, "If we changed craft services, they would want to know why."

DAVID BENIOFF:

When we were in Belfast working on the pilot, we had a shorthand for explaining how much sleep we'd gotten the night before. The goal was a "Gentleman's Six"—if you got six hours, you were good to go, but that was a rarity. I don't remember all the terminology, but "Kept Man's Nine," was a kind of imagined paradise, and the worst outcome was "a Condemned Man's Zero."

D. B. WEISS:

I thought it was Death Row Zero. Yeah, there were one or two of those. I think we went all the way up to thirteen hours—like the show, mostly an exercise in fantasy. Don't remember what thirteen hours was called, but I think I got there one time, at a very quiet hotel in Iceland. Still one of my fondest memories.

DAVID BENIOFF:

Everything changed in season two, when Bernie [Caufield] came on board. Finally, we had a producing partner whom we trusted completely, and that meant far better sleep. For us, anyway. I imagine Bernie doesn't get many nine-hour sleeps.

CAROLYN STRAUSS:

The truth is that the first year of that show, when Bernie wasn't there, there was so much discord and unhappiness among the crew. It's one thing to start from scratch and build your own crew and do that. That's really, really hard, but to take an unhappy crew and turn that around and build a culture, take a culture that's a little bit toxic and turn that around. I don't know many people who can do that, but Bernie did it.

Bernie came up through the [Steven] Bochco camp and worked with us on *Big Love*. She is a special person who knows how to keep a crew happy on an incredibly difficult shoot. And this was an incredibly challenging show.

BRUCE RICHMOND:

Getting Bernie Caulfield involved in the production of *Game of Thrones* was what helped the show grow. She was a key piece.

BERNADETTE CAULFIELD:

The role was basically to run the physical production on the show, which is what I had always done. I've always worn a lot of hats.

You have to gain people's trust, particularly with the actors. I'd love to go in the trailer in the morning, say, "Good morning. How is everybody?" I knew if somebody had a big scene or if there was nudity on the set, I could be there for them.

Chris Newman came in with a photo from Iceland, which he is very familiar with, and says, "I think this is where the wall is." And I said, "My God, that's stunning." I brought it to David and Dan and I said, "This is what we need. We need a little more scope on where we are. You guys are amazing in season one and now we just got to go bigger." They said, "That would be great if we could go there." Then Chris and I started figuring out, "How can we shoot Iceland within our budget?"

Iceland would be a third country we would go to, we had Belfast and then we went to Croatia for the first time that year because they didn't want to shoot Malta anymore.

There were easily five hundred to seven hundred people when both units were going. That's a lot of people to move around, hire, and take care of. It took a lot of coordination because you don't stop in between, you just keep going. We used to say it was like a badge of honor.

DAVID BENIOFF:

Weather . . . yeah, sheesh. I love Northern Ireland but the weather is an adversary. We had a set blown down up on the northern coast. The big tent where the whole crew was eating collapsed—that was a terrifying moment. The constant rain (213 days a year in Belfast! True story!), the cold (there is a big difference between thirty-six degrees in Magheramorne Quarry and thirty-six degrees anywhere else in the world), and the dark (seven hours of daylight in the winter) often meant brutal conditions for the crew.

But man, we had a tough crew. Most of them were Irish or Scottish or English, so they were used to the mud and they just got on with it.

BERNADETTE CAULFIELD:

The most difficult day was one in Belfast. Our worst enemy was the wind. One day, winds from a hurricane in America came through, and started to blow everything down. We had metal and objects flying through the air and collapsing tents. It was frightening.

D. B. WEISS:

One of the worst days was the day that hurricane-force winds blew most of our Dothraki wedding set into the sea in Malta. I remember a video that Timmy Van Patten took, as we were standing under a weighted-down tent watching this happen, laughing at how completely stupid it was for us to be out there in the first place, since there was nothing we could do about it besides being blown into the sea ourselves.

BERNADETTE CAULFIELD:

We were in Iceland. Chris Newman and I looked at each other. It still hadn't snowed, so uncommon in Iceland, and we thought, "Oh my God, we've pitched this idea for the northern wall because of how cold it is and the snow."

We decided we'd better start doing our snow dance. Two days later, it started snowing. I don't think it stopped for two months. David and Dan were so happy, it looked great.

As one big show was lifting off, **Entourage** *was preparing to ring down the curtain. Actor salaries at the beginning had been $25,000, with Jeremy Piven making a bit more because of his experience. By season eight, salaries had blown up to $500k and $650k respectively. It was not an inexpensive show to keep on the air.*

DOUG ELLIN:

Social media wasn't really out yet, but HBO had message boards and I listened to criticism. "Everything always works out for these guys. Things are too easy for them," blah, blah, blah. So the story line with Sasha [Grey] was my first reaction to that, even though a lot of people thought it was too dark for this show. My second reaction was I was going to kill Vince. He was going to have a drug overdose. I wanted to shock people, end the show that way, and remind everyone I wasn't a one-note guy.

But Mark stepped in. He usually didn't get involved with scripts, and was a big supporter of the show, but he said, "You can't kill Vince. We're gonna make a movie. We're gonna make a cartoon. We're going to do an opera one day. You can't kill Vince." And he was right, even though the movie didn't do as well as any of us hoped.

KEVIN DILLON:

It was pretty cool, driving down Sunset, looking up and seeing a giant billboard of myself and the guys. There was a little bit of pressure, too, that you felt coming from HBO, because their shows had always done really well with awards and our show struggled with that a little bit. Jeremy Piven won some, but the show itself and I didn't win much.

EMMANUELLE CHRIQUI:

I always felt safe. Doug was so protective of Sloan and the relationship, so even if the most outrageous thing was being written, whether it was the anal sex scene or threesome episode, where normally I would think, "I don't know about that. That's a lot," knowing that Doug was at the helm, I would think, "Oh no, this is going to be so funny and so charming. It's not going to be crass and cheap."

KEVIN CONNOLLY:

When Doug did the story line about Vince being fired from *Aquaman*, that was something I had witnessed in real life with Tobey. It was a little weird. I didn't feed it to Doug, he knew it. There were times where I would be protective of my friends and ask, "Is this really necessary?"

EMMANUELLE CHRIQUI:

If we did *Entourage* now, with the MeToo movement, do you think it would fly? Yes, I do, actually. The stuff that Doug came up with, he was like, "This is tame compared to the real story, you know?" There were things that were deemed inappropriate and misogynistic, but we were talking about Hollywood. In what universe is Hollywood not all those things? Doug's female lead characters were all fierce and strong, whether it was Shauna, Constance Zimmer, Dana Gordon, or Perrey Reeves's character. And my character kept Jeremy Piven's character in check. Doug always gave his regular women a fierceness about them. I do think it would be really successful even today.

JERRY FERRARA:

When you're on a big set and one of the stars of a show, everyone is always trying to make your day. All these people are willing to go get you whatever you want. I was always a husky kid, and I definitely enjoyed craft services, other foods, and smoking weed early on. Then I turned thirty and told myself I needed to get healthy because I felt like I was on a dangerous path.

We used to take a long time in between seasons, and between seasons six and seven, I lost sixty pounds. I didn't realize just how far away from Turtle I had strayed, and when Doug saw me, I freaked him the fuck out. Doug wanted to pay me by the pound to gain the weight back. As the guy who created these characters and hears these voices, he had to come up with all new jokes. It was no longer like, "Hey, fat boy, come over here." I certainly made his job harder.

ANDREW DICE CLAY:

I ran into my friend Bruce, and he tells me, "Doug Ellin, the creator of *Entourage*, thinks you're the greatest comic ever and he wants to meet with you." Doug basically tells me, "I'm giving you the last season of *Entourage*." I'm trying to thank Doug, and he's going, "Don't thank me. I'm doing it for me, this is Hollywood." He gave me five out of the seven episodes and a whole arc. Doug Ellin and *Entourage* lit the fuse for the last decade of success that I've had in the business. I got a Showtime special, then Woody Allen called me because of *Entourage*, and I got *Blue Jasmine*.

DOUG ELLIN:

Entourage was canceled, by the way. I said publicly, "Nah, we decided we'd done enough." But now I'm telling you, they canceled us. And unless I'm crazy, we were their highest-rated half hour. Our ratings were higher than ever in our last season.

There was little institutional memory at the senior levels of HBO programming. The days of Albrecht, Strauss, and others running the show had quickly been forgotten.

And all of this was happening while Netflix was busy doing everything it could to build up its own programming—trying, failing, learning. HBO, on the other hand, was busy with office politics 101, and some serious lapses in judgment.

MICHAEL ELLENBERG, Executive:

I was brought in to oversee drama series at HBO, the most acclaimed network in America, if not the world—and given tremendous autonomy by Richard and Mike, even though I had never worked a day in television.

SUE NAEGLE:

I said to Scott Rudin, "I have to hire a new head of drama and I have to hire someone that you can get along with, because I cannot spend these millions of hours of the day on the phone with you." He said, "What about Michael Ellenberg?" I said, "I interviewed him a few years ago. He spent the whole call telling me why *True Blood* was going to be a failure. I kept saying to him, "I put the show together. I really need it to work. Can you stop?" But I told Scott, "I'll meet with him again."

MICHAEL ELLENBERG:

If you'd told me, when I moved to LA in 2000, that I'd end up working in television, that would have meant I failed. I was a total film snob. I worked for Scott Rudin for three years, then I went to work for Ridley and Tony Scott. That was my film school.

Sue and I were friends, and she recruited me to come to HBO. It seemed like a no-brainer. I figured if I went even for a year, I could return to film, but at least as a guy who now knows something about TV. My expectations at the time were, I wanted to run a film company one day.

SUE NAEGLE:

As soon as Ellenberg was hired, Scott said to me, "I didn't tell you to hire that guy. I hate him." I said to Ellenberg, "You've got a problem with Scott. You have to fly to New York, go sit with him, and work it out." He flew to New York and I think Scott threw him out of his office.

Michael Ellenberg, the Sue Naegle recruit, was hired on August 11, 2011, as senior vice president, HBO Entertainment, running the drama department and reporting to Naegle. Gina Balian was promoted in the same announcement to the same title, senior vice president, HBO Entertainment. Things were starting to get a bit crowded in the executive suites, not to mention increasingly political.

Lombardo immediately started to use Ellenberg as a trusted adviser, sometimes inviting him to meetings but not inviting Naegle, which was a tad ironic since Naegle had brought in Ellenberg.

Outsiders can have it rough at HBO during their early months or years at HBO— **really** *rough. Within months, the halls were buzzing over how little time Ellenberg spent in the office and over his habit of doing too much business in his car. There were also complaints that he wasn't being strategic enough with the production calendar. The programming department started to consider him too free a spirit for their tastes.*

Ellenberg's presence likewise created a fascinating dynamic with David Levine, also from the drama department, who, like Ellenberg, jockeyed for cool feature-like projects and was more interested in forging close relationships with filmmakers than with colleagues.

Meanwhile, Casey Bloys, Amy Gravitt, Kathleen McCaffrey, and others who had grown up at HBO kept to their more rigid development roles.

Eventually, as Ellenberg became more closely aligned with Lombardo, Levine and Naegle fell into a close alliance as well.

By way of polite reminder: Bill Nelson, HBO's CEO, did not come from a programming background as Chris Albrecht had; Nelson turned that responsibility over to Richard Plepler, even though he didn't come from a programming background either. Plepler appointed Michael Lombardo as his top programming executive in Los Angeles, then summarily removed Carolyn Strauss, who'd been a natural selection for a Mount Rushmore of Great Programming Executives. In her place, Plepler and Lombardo hired agent Naegle, also a rookie in the programming woods, and when it came to naming a new head of HBO's prestigious drama division, Balian, who with Strauss had been among the strongest advocates for **Game of Thrones,** *among other HBO drama hits, was passed over for Ellenberg, a movie executive, who also lacked a programming background. There. Got all that?*

MICHAEL ELLENBERG:

That first year was like my first year of law school; you have to learn a new language and a new way of thinking. I kept my head down, learned basic dealmaking, and what the production process was. It was awesome and inspiring. Politically, however, it was super complicated. HBO is a complicated place.

The night before they were going to announce me, I was told Gina Balian was upset and threatening to quit. I didn't even know they considered giving Gina the job! We had breakfast, and I tried to convince Gina to stay, but she didn't want to. And then I was told she decided to stay. About a month into the job, Sue called me and said, "How's it going with Gina?" I said, "Actually, all in all, pretty good. There's maybe some reporting issues, but nothing major." Sue then texted me, "She doesn't report to you." That was a month into the job when I found out Gina didn't report to me. That was how it was organized at the time. Gina's an incredibly gifted exec, and a wonderful person, but we had a difficult time of it. We've become close since, but were set up not to like each other. I was given a fairly wide berth.

HBO believed a lot of film talent was migrating to television, so there was a lot of interest in the fact that I had a different background and expertise. Sometimes that caused complications.

Were there slings and arrows? Sure, it was a high-profile job in a highly competitive industry. The company had so much success and many of the staff had been there for decades. I was also working at a time when a truly competitive market emerged to HBO for the first time, and that was a whole other level of pressure.

There was friction between Mike and Sue. Each of them thought they were running programming and that made communication and authority lines unclear. A lot of us didn't know if you needed one yes or two yeses. That was a stress point to everyone.

Showrunners saw Mike as the real power source. They were aware of the dysfunction and were sometimes frustrated by it.

On October 10, 2011, HBO premiered **Enlightened**, *a comedy about a California saleswoman who overuses spiritual remedies from yoga to meditation in her quest for self-improvement, and to irreverant comedic effect. Laura Dern co-created the show with Mike White and starred as Amy Jellicoe. Luke Wilson played her ex-husband, Levi, and Dern's real-life mother, Diane Ladd, played her mother, Helen. In addition to acting as Tyler, Amy's workplace co-conspirator in various mischiefs, White also wrote the entire show and directed a third of it.*

After the read-through of the pilot, confidence was high. Almost everyone remarked about how hard Michael Lombardo had laughed. But the primal question of "whose show this is" was left unanswered. It was as if HBO had said to Dern (who had pitched her idea directly to Plepler and Lombardo): "Great news, we found a writer for your show!"— while at the same time telling Mike White, a Lombardo fan, "Great news, we found a star for your show!"

LAURA DERN:

After *Recount*, I continued to think about how corrupt that whole election had been and thought about the cultural apathy at that time. No one was in the streets, no one seemed furious. It was so clear there was voter fraud, but people were scared to stand up, and didn't want their neighbor to dislike them.

I thought, "Where's the rage? Why don't we ever see any rage, particularly in female characters?" That's when I started dreaming up this idea for a character in my head.

I asked Jay Roach, who had become a close friend, "Can I throw an idea at you? What if Lucille Ball became Norma Rae?" He said, "That sounds amazing. You have to run with that."

I talked to HBO about it; first I spoke to Richard and then he had me sit down with Sue Naegle. I pitched the seed of an idea based on watching somebody who's a complete shitshow in her life. She loses jobs. I wanted to see somebody who is broken in her interpersonal relationships but incredibly honest about her feelings, even if they are hard for others to take. Maybe it takes this authenticity—from someone who is unafraid to be unliked—to get out in the streets and become not only a whistleblower, but someone who can recognize the truth and expose it. And bless them, they said, "Yes, yes. We're in. Who's the writer?"

SUE NAEGLE:

Laura had had this initial idea of a whistleblower who was the center of it. Then Mike White created the whole universe. In retrospect, we should have been very clear about the parameters upfront. "Yes. You're both exec producers, and Mike's not going to tell you how to act and you shouldn't tell him how to write."

LAURA DERN:

Mike and I met years before about a gorgeous feature he had written. We had been talking about doing something together after his first directorial feature, where we reconnected and became friends. We went to breakfast and started dreaming up this seed. No one could have written or grown such a brilliantly pure and delicate tone like Mike did. I also felt so grateful for HBO at the time. We wanted to do a half hour, but we weren't committing to punchline humor, or even being a quote comedy or a drama. Mike had written episodes that were heartbreaking and hysterical. The humor came from sadness and rage, and every character was misguided and complicated.

The episodes were perfect writing, but it was a massive gamble. There was nothing like this on television, but we believed by making those difficult places relatable, delicious, heartbreaking, and hopefully hilarious, we could see ourselves and perhaps even find empathy. That's the beauty of art.

SUE NAEGLE:

Mike White had a clarity of vision. He wrote every single episode of that show and he really understood what he wanted to say. When he turned the script in, my colleague Nick Hall and I read it in our offices and then ran into the hallway, grabbing each other's hands. It was so special. It was so unique.

Richard is a bit of a forum shopper. He would show things to the head of marketing or the head of scheduling, and those people are great at their jobs, and it's nice to have buy-in from everyone when that's possible, but when you hold the power Richard did, and you cock your head to the side, what he didn't understand is that everyone in the room cocks their head the exact same direction, and twice as hard. You can influence a room really easily if you're Richard Plepler. You can change the way the wind blows.

Enlightened was so special. I said, "I'm going to fly it to New York myself, and sit in the room with everybody when they screen it." I wanted to set the table a little bit, because I knew that it would be harder for anyone to scrunch their face if I was sitting there. I was afraid they wouldn't say yes, and I wasn't going to take any chances.

LAURA DERN:

I have been bred by actors who are incredibly brave and surrender to their characters. My dad "shot" John Wayne in the back. My mom had proved her fearlessness in *Wild at Heart* and in many other roles. I felt like those qualities were my family's pastime, and hoped that even a tiny bit of that boundaryless and radical rawness would rub off on me. I was lucky to be cast by people like David Lynch or Alexander Payne on *Citizen Ruth*, where the movies don't work unless you're willing to allow the comedy to come from broken, angry, and intolerable places in the character. This is why Amy Jellicoe and *Enlightened* were such artistic dreams for me.

Dern was honored with a Golden Globe for Best Actress and an Emmy nomination for her role. Her unrelentingly brave performance, her lack of vanity, and her willingness to acknowledge that Amy could often find the peace she craved only via pain and even humiliation, made the character of Amy Jellicoe an unconventional yet glorious hero.

CASEY BLOYS:

Enlightened wasn't a traditional comedy. We had the hardest time getting people in the building to understand that it was something special. Everybody there hated the show. They thought it was terrible, thought it was trash, and they were asking, "What are we doing?" This was shortly after *John from Cincinnati*, and no one wanted a repeat of what happened with that.

I told people, "I think this is funny," but it was a very hard sell. Gina and I would watch each other's shows, and I'll never forget she said in a meeting once, "I watched *Enlightened*. It's really good." It was like a drop of water in the desert.

MIKE WHITE, Creator:

There were two HBO tables at the Golden Globes the year Laura won for Best Actress, but HBO took a hit that night. It was the first year where other places were winning big awards. The shows that were sitting at the HBO tables that night were shows that they had picked to win awards, and when we all didn't win, it was like we had all failed. I could just feel it then, it was all so palpable, that somehow we had let everyone down. Plepler got up, looked at our table, and said, "You guys let us down." When he looked directly at me, he said, "Oh, you're okay," because Laura had won. I felt like I was the child of a narcissist. I realized the transactional nature of all of it, and how much stock they put in the metrics of success like a Golden Globe, but you're sitting there realizing, "Oh, this is all it's about for someone like Plepler."

Luck, *written by David Milch and directed by Michael Mann, starred Dustin Hoffman, ran for one season of nine episodes and was immediately picked up for a second season amid positive reviews. However, midway through production of that second season (and midway through the airing of the first) the show was canceled, in part because three horses had died on set.*

JAY HOVDEY, Writer:

At the time that the show was being put together, I was a national columnist for the *Daily Racing Forum*, which is the sort of trade publication of thoroughbred racing. I had a pretty extensive career of covering the sport and its people. And one of its people was David Milch. I encountered David one day at Santa Anita at his regular table overlooking the racetrack. He said, "Sit down, I'm putting together a horse racing series." He had just finished *John from Cincinnati*, and said, "Would you be interested in writing for me?" I couldn't say yes fast enough.

He had the whole story in his head. He had, I would say, easily three seasons of eight, nine, ten episodes of *Luck* in his head already, and it was a big story. It wasn't just a horse racing show. It was going to the very heart of not only this very idiosyncratic milieu that was the racetrack, but standing in for every idiosyncratic milieu out there.

Why on earth would a network allow itself to be put in a situation where two mega-talents, each known for his strong personality and singular vision, would be joined on a project for which both had decidedly conflicting ideas? That's exactly what HBO had with the ill-fated combo of David Milch and Michael Mann. Their solution? Mann wasn't allowed in Milch's writers' room, and Milch wasn't permitted on Mann's set. It didn't work.

SUE NAEGLE:

With *Luck*, Mike said to me, "Michael Mann's really difficult." But "he may not take you seriously because you're a girl" was the subtext I heard. But as I got to know Michael, I also realized that he's the father of three daughters and he's got this incredible wife—and I got along great with him.

JAY HOVDEY:

David always bristled at the fact that he couldn't work on the set. He and Michael Mann had come to a détente, in which David would do the writing and Michael would be out there either directing or looking over the shoulders of the directors. That dynamic between Michael and David overlaid the whole thing. Michael was a caged tiger.

I would think that perhaps, maybe other shows were suffering similar, if not quite as spectacular, turmoil because of chaos at the top. David Milch was one of their flagship guys and maybe the one that they could put in the shop window more than any other guy at that point. And he wasn't allowed to do what he always had done. Whereas Michael Mann put together episodes that are beautiful to look at. I mean, they're just gorgeous; anything that Michael Mann shoots in or has shot under his producership, they're always just a feast for the eyes.

SUE NAEGLE:

I think *Luck* is one of those shows that could've gone another year, for sure, but we did have a really hard time with very delicate racehorses, thoroughbreds, and that's a tricky business. I think the pressure from PETA and the animal rights groups probably affected that decision.

DAVID MILCH:

It's a living thing you're dealing with and trying to guide. And you try to honor that and live with it and do the best you can. It was a lot of different kinds of responsibility that you have to honor from hour to hour.

SUE NAEGLE:

David Milch famously transcribes everything, and we got to the point where we would have these sessions where Michael would have someone transcribing as well. They both were having the conversations transcribed so that they could each hold on to their version of the story as if the transcribers would write something different than what was actually happening. I wasn't very involved with the decision not to continue it. That decision was really Mike and Richard's.

In 2006, while a junior at Oberlin College in Ohio, Lena Dunham took $50,000 from her parents and made a forty-two-minute movie called **Tiny Furniture***. It was a gem.*

LENA DUNHAM, Creator:

In college I wanted to write and direct independent and experimental film. I imagined doing things like writing capsule reviews for the *Onion*, the *A.V. Club*, and *Time Out*. Or interning at *Filmmaker* magazine. Right before I found out that *Tiny Furniture* had gotten into South by Southwest, I was trying to apply for a job as a video teacher at the high school that I went to in Brooklyn. I was raised watching artists cobble it together. I love TV, but I thought, "Oh movies, I understand. I can make those. They're close enough to art." I had no sense that TV was something I'd be permitted to do.

PETER BENEDEK:

I grew up in the same town as Lena's mom, Laurie, and she made an artsy movie with Meryl Streep. It was screened at The Hammer where I'm on the board.

We talked at the after-party, then she called me later and said, "I have this daughter, she's at Oberlin. She's started making these videos and I'm sure she doesn't know what she's doing. Would you talk to her?" So I said, "Sure." I spoke with Lena and put her in touch with one of our digital guys who helped her get distribution on YouTube.

Then she called me up and she said, "I'm writing a screenplay." I asked, "How many screenplays have you read?" She said, "Not that many." I said, "Well, if you're going to write a screenplay, you should read a screenplay. We'll get you some scripts." Then I put her in touch with a younger female agent, Jenny Maryasis, and told her, "I'm on the TV side, Jenny is a motion picture lit agent. Whenever you want to talk to someone about movies, Jenny will be your resource." Then suddenly, Jenny and I are sent this DVD.

She said, "I made a movie." Jenny and I each looked at it over the weekend, and I said to her on Monday, "Am I crazy, or is this the best $50,000 movie you've ever seen in your entire life?" And she said, "No, you're not insane." Then it was accepted at South by Southwest. Lena asked me, "Should I go? What should I do?" I said, "You should meet as many people as possible." I think the movie won an award there.

Then Lena called me and said, "All these publicists are hitting on me. What should I do?" I said, "You should tell them that when the festival is over, you're going to come to Los Angeles and they can talk to you there." The next day, she called and said, "All these managers are hitting on me. What should I do?" I said, "You don't need a manager right now." Then she called and said, "All these agents are hitting on me. What should I do?"

I said, "You should tell them you have an agent." And she said, "Well, you never asked me." I said, "Well, I'm asking you now." And she said, "All right, I'm your client."

LENA DUNHAM:

After *Tiny Furniture*, I knew I had more to say about the topic but I didn't know how it was going to come out.

PETER BENEDEK:

I thought she was going to become a star writing and directing movies, but she called me up one day and told me, "I want to do a television show, a continuation of what *Tiny Furniture* was." We put Lena on what we at the time used to refer to as the "water bottle tour," because everybody wanted to meet her. One of her meetings was with Sue Naegle, and they really hit it off.

SUE NAEGLE:

I watched *Tiny Furniture* and I loved it. She came in and said, "I want to do a show about my life." We talked about a lot of the dynamics in *Tiny Furniture*, which does have echoes of *Girls*. You could see potentially what a show might be that was related to it. What I realized is Lena had one of the most unique abilities—to be able to write about an experience you're having while you're having it.

LENA DUNHAM:

I'd been a huge *Sex and the City* fan and watched all the HBO programming. I had a meeting with Sue Naegle, Kathleen McCaffrey, Casey Bloys, and Nick Hall.

CASEY BLOYS:

Kat ran around and made us all watch *Tiny Furniture* and said, "We need to do this."

KATHLEEN McCAFFREY:

I can't believe the support I got given the level I was at and how new I was to the team. Lena sent me a couple pages on April 9, 2010. Lately, Lena has acknowledged some of the privilege that came along with that, but it didn't seem like that at the time. It was more of like a pitch document.

LENA DUNHAM:

I had a strong feeling that the young women I was surrounding myself with were not represented in popular culture—girls who were fucked up and bloody and medicated and chubby and angry. My best friend and I were trying out older abusive boyfriends, having pill problems, and I just felt like there was a messy story in there. And so I made this document for HBO.

Here are the two pages Lena gave to Kathleen McCaffrey:

Sex and the City *depicted women who had mastered their careers and were now being driven crazy by the tick of their biological clocks.* **Gossip Girl** *is about losing your virginity and gaining popularity, in a world where no one is old enough to vote or has to worry about making a living. But between adolescence and adulthood is an uncomfortable middle ground, when women are ejected from college and into a world with neither glamour nor structure. The resulting period of flux is heartbreaking and hilarious and way too human. It's humbling and it's sexy and it's ripe for laughs.*

Products of the recession, these girls are overeducated and underemployed, sure that they're too smart for their positions as assistants, nannies, and waitresses but not necessarily motivated enough to prove it (or even do their jobs well enough to advance). They have that mix of know-it-all entitlement and scathing self-deprecation that is the mark of all great Jewish comedians and many 24-year-old women with liberal arts degrees.

They have varying degrees of ambition, but have been raised to achieve. They know they want to be successful long before they know what they want to be successful at.

They're the last children of baby boomers, and the first generation to have moms who know how to text message ["HAVE U HAD AN HPV VACCINE YET? DO U HAVE HPV? LUV, MOM"] These moms probably enjoyed more swinging sex lives in their twenties than their daughters could ever dream of.

They've been on Ritalin since they were twelve and on birth control since they were fifteen (even if they didn't start having sex until college).

They're just as likely to sleep with their 40-year-old boss as they are to make out like eighth graders with a 20-year-old they meet at a loft party.

They're not looking for romantic partners with money or clout. Just guys who make them feel thin, funny, or superior.

Some of their boyfriends have turned out to be gay. Others have turned out to be Republicans (these girls aren't necessarily political, but they want to make sure abortions are a possibility. Always. After all, who can remember condoms every time?)

They still text at least one of these said exes when they're drunk or sad.

They've been raised to fuck unapologetically and then apologize for it.

Grad school is their fallback plan.

They are the Facebook generation, and ironically enough they are isolated by all the connectivity available to them (and prone to Facebook stalking and drunk-IMing and booty calls via twitter and deciphering text messages like they're ancient hieroglyphs and blogging pictures of all the food they eat).

They are navigating the transition out of college-level codependence on their girlfriends, but will still call to announce that they got their period or saw a man masturbating on the subway or saw a man who looks sort of like a kid they went to camp with (Could it be him? And if so, is he on Facebook?).

They're beautiful and maddening. They're self-aware and self-obsessed. They're your girlfriends and daughters and sisters and employees. They're my friends and I've never seen them on TV.

KATHLEEN McCAFFREY:

We had a great conversation. A very long conversation. She was twenty-three, I was twenty-seven. She was talking about a show that I would want to watch. After she left, I turned to Sue and said, "I want to buy something from that girl." Sue didn't even flinch. "Great, call UTA."

MIKE LOMBARDO:

Girls wouldn't have happened without Sue. She was a strong advocate for it, found Jenni Konner for it, and put Judd Apatow on it.

JENNI KONNER, Executive Producer:

Personally, Sue is this mind-blowing mom bringing up kids from China. She is also just a real philanthropist and she's always doing work some way or the other to help people outside of her family, in Los Angeles, and the world. The thing about Sue that people may not know aside from her private life is that she has a real Jersey girl, grudge-holding temper. Like if someone hurts someone she loves, you're dead to her, which when you're on the right side of her is the greatest thing in the world, I think because she was protecting artists for years as an agent. When she is on your side it is invaluable.

Sue showed *Tiny Furniture* to me and I became completely obsessed with it. I thought it was amazing. Months later, Sue called and said, "There are a lot of men who want to supervise the girl from *Tiny Furniture*, but I think you're the right person to do it." And even though I had made this promise to myself that I wasn't going to supervise anyone at that time so I could do my own thing, I thought, I'm gonna break that rule.

Judd gave me my first TV job, *Undeclared*, and you never stop working with Judd if you're in the family. Two or three weeks after I got the job, Judd called and said, "You want some help on that show? I loved that movie." And I was like, "Yeah, of course." I love working with Judd. He's so talented. And he becomes the big force in the room.

KATHLEEN McCAFFREY:

When Jenni Konner got involved and then Judd got involved, it started to snowball into something. I will tell you, and I think Lena will probably say the same, until we were shooting the pilot, it felt like a dream. It had happened so cleanly and truly in the order that you hope in terms of development. You identify a voice, you bring someone in to write a script, the script is solid. Then you bring in a showrunner to oversee it. Then you bring in a producer like Judd. It did evolve in the correct way. It was a moment in time. We needed a girl show on the air, literally something for a female audience. She was so unique and just captivating that everyone fell for her along the way. It wasn't just me.

Girls *certainly shared some of* **Sex and the City's** *DNA: four women adrift in New York City, working out how to live happy, free, fulfilled urban lives. But* **Girls** *veered* *away from glam clothes and the impending sense that one of the characters might suddenly be swept off her feet. Instead, the show was filled with grungy, sometimes pan-filled oversharing.*

*As created by Lena Dunham, **Girls** focused largely on the trials of wannabe writer Hannah Horvath, as inhabited by the uninhibited Dunham. Making up the other three this time were the needy-whiney Marnie, the free-spirited Jessa, and the buttoned-up Shoshanna. Together they, like their **Sex and the City** forebears, ran around the city trying to make it, emotionally and professionally. The show would end up running six seasons, during which Dunham would become a cultural signifier, with devoted fans and more than a share of detractors.*

ILENE LANDRESS:

Tom Sherren, one of the execs at HBO, called me up and said, "Hey, I have this half-hour pilot. Do you know anybody who could do this?" I said, "Send it to me." I read it. When I read the pilot of *Sopranos*, it was different. And when I read the pilot of *Girls*, I got the same feeling: I'm reading something with a singular voice.

SUE NAEGLE:

I loved Judd and I'm very thankful for his help on that show, but I put Jenni into the show and I thought to myself, these two women are going to make this show. When I started as an agent in 1994, there were no shows on the air that were solely written by women. They all had a male counterpart. It was Linda Bloodworth-Thomason and Harry Thomason. There was Diane English and Joel Shukovsky. There was always a male counterpart. And I represented a lot of women when I was an agent. I saw how often they were the only women in a writers' room, or they entered into rooms with a lot of misogyny and a lot of bad behavior.

I never understood why in the 1990s, it was so much about the *Harvard Lampoon*. I've represented a lot of those writers, but it was really an old-school boys' club. It was very white, it was very privileged, and it was very male. I spent years trying to break women in because gender shouldn't have anything to do with your ability to write a television show. So when I introduced Jenni to Lena, my hope for *Girls* was that Jenni and Lena would solely do it on their own. Judd really wanted to get involved and Lena and Jenni were both thrilled. I was the one that was like, "I think you guys should do it on your own." I don't know if I was interested in protecting their story or maybe deep down, as much as I loved and respected Judd and still do, I didn't want his attachment to ultimately take away from the accomplishment of the show, to take away from the women. But he did come on board and was very helpful.

PETER BENEDEK:

Judd called me up and said, "I need you to do me a favor. I've just watched *Tiny Furniture,* and I want to meet Lena Dunham." I said, "Judd, you're doing me a favor." He was fantastically additive because he taught Lena how to be funny.

His involvement was very ephemeral. They would spend two months before each season began, pitching out the season and writing the scripts. And he was really involved in that. Then he was gone until post. He had literally nothing to do with production, unless Jenni was calling him up and asking him questions.

They loved having him. He was really helpful. He was protective of them when there were certain issues with HBO, such as budgeting or scheduling issues. He was their Iron Dome.

We had a really good run, until it ended when Lena went to CAA. I really miss her.

JUDD APATOW:

They were so supportive. They loved her so much. They said, "We're going to let you do the show as long as you want to do it. We love having you here." That's something you never hear, and it allowed Lena and Jenni Konner to work at a certain pace and tell a long story over six seasons because they knew they were going to be given enough time.

JENNI KONNER:

Making the pilot honestly was one of the most fun times of my life. And one of the most exciting creative times. She had this very specific voice. The pilot system is so fucking weird because it's like a losing proposition most of the time, but with this, we had our movie and we said, "It's going to be just like that." We have the same director of photography. We have the same lead.

KATHLEEN McCAFFREY:

For the pilot of *Girls,* it was Casey's victory and a teaching moment for me. You had the four characters and Lena, but nothing was really happening. They were four interesting people in this interesting place, and it felt revolutionary, but it was missing an engine to move the story forward. Then Casey said, "Why doesn't she get cut off from her parents?" And that set off the whole show.

ILENE LANDRESS:

On the pilot, the funniest thing with Lena were these nude scenes she has. I'd schedule them last, when she's comfortable with everybody and we're in the throes of the whole thing and Lena was like, "Oh no, no, no, no, I'll do the naked scenes first." So the first day we ever shot on *Girls*, she's sitting there with Allison Williams, it's the cupcake and the bathtub scene. She's sort of there naked in the bathtub and you have the whole crew there and they're like, "Hmm, okay."

Now what we learned along the way was that Lena was much more comfortable doing the naked and sex scenes than the scenes where she had to be really emotional. Those were the scenes that were much more frightening to her than the ones where she just got to take her clothes off.

SUE NAEGLE:

I loved how brave she was about sexuality. I loved the idea that it wasn't going to be gratuitous, but that there would be sex scenes or nudity that wasn't about what was considered the perfect female body. I loved that she was human and lovable and real.

Do you think Richard wanted Lena Dunham to be the lead of a television show? No. Every time somebody wrote something about what she looked like naked, I had to hear it from those guys.

JENNI KONNER:

HBO was mostly hands-off. *Girls* was a very explicit show with a lot of sex and a lot of nudity. There was one time when we got a note that said, "There's no reason for this. It feels gratuitous," and they told us to cut it. We were upset; that started the biggest fight we ever got in with HBO. It was a scene where Adam comes on Hannah.

SUE NAEGLE:

The shot seemed excessively long. At the time, I described it like a fire hose. I thought, Can we do something that's a little more subtle? Lena really fought for it.

LENA DUNHAM:

We made it out of a substance, but it was meant to look human. The semen was sprayed across onto his chest. I called Mike Lombardo and said, "I think this is important, and it's only three seconds."

MIKE LOMBARDO:

The idea for the scene was bold and amazingly pulled off, but then they took it a beat too long and wanted to show ejaculate coming out. It felt like a moment that would make people go, "Ugh," and they would be uncomfortable. It had nothing to do with censorship. There was no rule about it. I was such a fan of the show and wanted women to watch with their daughters.

KATHLEEN McCAFFREY:

I supported Lena in the ejaculation debate. I do remember thinking I would be embarrassed to tell my parents I was going to a meeting about an ejaculation.

LENA DUNHAM:

As I was talking with Mike, he asked me, "Is it really this important to you?" And it was then that I realized I no longer believed it was critical.

KATHLEEN McCAFFREY:

We trimmed it by a few seconds, but it didn't compromise anything creatively. Nobody was upset. That's what was great about it. It was a genuine creative conversation, handled with professionalism and kindness.

The sex scene between Adam Driver and Lena Dunham in the pilot of *Girls* was perfect because that's what it really looks like. It's awkward. It's fumbling. And as a woman, it felt good to think, "I'm so happy the reality of it is on-screen versus the sexy network versions of what sex looks like that are not true."

CASEY BLOYS:

You're not going to find me saying, "There's too much nudity in this show." We follow the show's lead, and what the writers think is an accurate portrayal of characters' sex lives and relationships. If anything, on a slightly different topic on nudity, I am somewhat sensitive to the belief that if women are going to be naked, then men should be naked as well. There should be no double standard there.

LENA DUNHAM:

To HBO's credit, they never said, "We don't like him anymore." For a network to let me basically have Adam sexually assault somebody and then continue to be a romantic lead who we care about was extraordinary. That complexity was so important to me. Obviously in life, my values, which I feel really important to assert, are, "Believe women a lot. It's just black and white." But I think in film we have to be free to have nuance. I wanted to be able to write people who did things that contradicted other things they did.

CASEY BLOYS:

People were so busy obsessing over Lena and everything they thought she had done wrong that *Girls* didn't get as much credit for being a comedy as it should have.

SUE NAEGLE:

I wasn't anticipating how much backlash there would be and how many people would have opinions about Lena's nudity, her privilege, the nepotism, and the lack of diversity. I didn't anticipate any of it.

I had a lot of conversations with Lena about body positivity and always encouraged her to write about her experiences and not be afraid of the pain or the embarrassment around them when she wanted to focus on Hannah having OCD or the dynamics in the very complicated relationship she was having on-screen with Adam Driver. Lena does her best when you support her and she is able to quiet the noise.

LENA DUNHAM:

Every misstep I made publicly, HBO said, "We love you no matter what." The only time I ever got in trouble at HBO is when I accidentally used the word "Netflix" to refer to all streaming movies on the Internet.

I'm only just now starting to realize the complexity and darkness and magic and terror of suddenly being famous. When the show was coming out, I was on the cover of *New York* magazine with this piece, and it just never stopped. It became impossible to drown out the level of exposure, and it wasn't just happening to me, it was happening to my family. I could see their pain and their anxiety in real time.

We live in a society where a woman is not allowed to yell "I'm smart" without terrible consequences. So, instead, I just internalized, or I used to say, "Oh, it doesn't bother me," but of course it was having a deleterious effect on my mental health. I'm happy to say that I'm in a really good place today.

And how is it possible that Tony Soprano and Walter White are murderers but people hated Hannah and Marnie way more and thought they were worse people? How is it possible that you root for a mafia hitman but you can't root for a girl who cheated on her boyfriend? That's the world we live in.

People are allowed to feel that that show didn't accurately reflect what

New York looks like. In the first season I wasn't thinking enough about, "Does that background look diverse enough? Is this what it would look like in a coffee shop?" I don't think I would have done a good and thoughtful job of writing characters who weren't all tidy offshoots of me or my cousin. But I could have absolutely and should have surrounded them with a different image of New York friendship. It wasn't on my mind and believe you me, it's on my mind now and I have no anger, no resentment about being called out about it. I don't work like that anymore. Diversity is an important part of my casting process and my writing process. I know I'm good at my job and that I deliver.

I have an incredibly high capacity for being made fun of. At this point, I'm just a punch line. But I still love when HBO is protective of me. It makes me feel incredibly taken care of in my workplace, which is what everybody wants to feel.

A week after the premiere of **Girls**, *another female-driven comedy debuted, and this time its lead wasn't an unknown, but rather the most talented female comic actor of her generation.*

After a peripatetic childhood (her stepfather, the dean of George Washington University Medical School, traveled widely and well), and upon dropping out of Northwestern University in her junior year, Julia Louis-Dreyfus came to the rapt attention of NBC's Dick Ebersol, who got a look at her in a show called **The Golden 50th Anniversary Jubilee.** *Ebersol, helming* **SNL** *while Lorne Michaels took his legendary sabbatical, gave her a role on* **SNL** *when she was a mere twenty-one years old. Her stint there, from 1982 through 1985, wasn't particularly successful, and she followed it up with a long-forgotten sitcom,* **Day by Day.** *She shone in that show, though, and when the first pilot for* **Seinfeld** *ran into trouble, Larry David was told by NBC execs that the sitcom needed a woman in its cast, proving that not even network executives are always wrong. "L.D." had met L-D when he'd been an (unhappy—big surprise!) writer on the show, and almost overnight the character of Elaine Benes was born. It would appear that Louis-Dreyfus had actually been born to play her.*

Across nine seasons and 180 episodes, Elaine became as vital to the show as any Jerry, Kramer, or George Costanza could ever be. After **Seinfeld** *ended, Jason Alexander and Michael Richards had difficulties finding new vehicles, but Louis-Dreyfus was always able to bring a rousing energy and impeccable timing to any script. Achieving the nearly impossible, Louis-Dreyfus bounced from her friend Seinfeld's hit to one more of her own:* **The New Adventures of Old Christine**, *which premiered in 2006 on CBS for five cheerful, cheering seasons. (Best of all, she wasn't afraid to let her own character be as shamelessly craven as were any or all of the male characters on her* *shows). Next up, Louis-Dreyfus would land the role of a lifetime, another character that seemed tailor-built for a woman of her prodigious talents.*

Back in 2005, British comedy writer Armando Iannucci created a satire called **The Thick of It** *for BBC TV. A wordy and brilliant take on the ridiculousness of UK politics, the show followed the blundering workings of one ineffectual government department, "managed" by Malcolm Tucker, the prime minister's hilariously profane enforcer. The show dazzled with its mix of fast-paced antics, all-too-believable satire, and an imaginative assortment of obscenities, many of which were created by Iannucci's "swearing consultant," British writer Ian Martin. In fact, Martin's contribution to* **The Thick of It**, *and soon after to* **Veep**, *would be hard to overestimate.*

With only four seasons (plus two specials), **The Thick of It** *was probably the finest British satire since John Cleese's similarly brief* **Fawlty Towers**—*and it would lead directly to one of HBO's finest and most awarded comedies,* **Veep**.

Between seasons two and three of **The Thick of It**, *Iannucci had co-written (with Simon Blackwell, Tony Roche, and Jesse Armstrong) and helmed the spin-off movie* **In the Loop**, *starring several in the cast of the UK show, plus American stars like James Gandolfini, amusingly cast as a profane US general. That experience showed that American audiences also enjoyed the rapid-fire back-and-forth of an Iannucci vehicle.*

ARMANDO IANNUCCI, Creator:

I've always been interested in politics. In the Gulf War when Tony Blair joined up with George Bush for a crazy venture, I wanted to try to work out how it could have happened despite all the evidence and the public being against it. That made me look at the whole process of how things happen, even in a democracy.

FRANK RICH, Executive Producer:

When I started at HBO, I was hired by Richard and Lombardo in 2008, three years before *Veep*.

One thing that Richard had told me was that they were looking for a smart politics show. Armando Iannucci I did not know, although I knew his satire of British politics. And I loved his movie *In the Loop*. But to my knowledge he had never taken on America before. And so I went to Casey Bloys, who was then running comedy, and said, "Clearly, Armando could come up with a show."

CASEY BLOYS:

I was interested in *The Thick of It*, which was a great show. And Armando was originally kicking around the idea of something set at the State Department.

"I have this new idea, I was thinking I wanna make it about a female vice president and that office and that idea of never getting it, or something like that." I was driving down Sunset and thought, "That's a good idea."

Just because he's so funny and his comedy is so cutting and so I thought, "There's no better setup than the vice president." I mean, I think it was FDR's vice president, John Nance Garner, who said, "The vice presidency is not worth a bucket of warm piss."

It's just such a great and fertile ground for stunted ambition. I can't believe no one has thought about this—this is great. He wrote the outline and I remember reading the outline and thinking Julia Louis-Dreyfus should play this. I called him and I said, "You should meet with Julia," and he was like, "Okay." There were other names floating around like Sigourney Weaver.

In late 2010, Julia Louis-Dreyfus took a meeting with Armando Iannucci in Los Angeles, where he pitched his idea for an American cousin of The Thick of It—Veep, *also about a craven politician. Two years later, the show premiered on HBO with Louis-Dreyfus, starring as just that craven political, Vice President Selina Meyer. Louis-Dreyfus also signed on as one of the show's producers.*

ARMANDO IANNUCCI:

Then of course you think, "Okay, who are the fantastic, great comic actresses who could prove results?" Casey said, "You must speak to Julia." I've always been a fan of Julia. I always thought she was great in *Seinfeld*. I said, "I'd love to meet her." And I think we met for a cup of tea, and I was expecting her to start out with a whole entourage and she showed up herself.

JULIA LOUIS-DREYFUS, Actor and Executive Producer:

It was at the Four Seasons. And it was in the afternoon and we were having coffee or tea and it just went on and on and on. I mean, the time flew if you're talking about the culture and because at that point, I was already a pretty politically active person. I also grew up in Washington, DC, so I was very familiar with the culture inside the Beltway. We were just musing on that and riffing on that for a long, long time. In fact, a lot of things came out of that conversation that were ultimately in the pilot.

I told him I've been doing a show at CBS prior to doing *Veep*. I had requested that we have all recyclable materials on set because I'm an environmentalist and very concerned about climate, et cetera. And so I would get as much plastic off the set as possible, which included using recyclable forks and spoons and knives, and they're made out of cornstarch. And the only problem with that is that when you put a cornstarch spoon in anything warm, it sort of melts, it kinda bends and becomes sort of flaccid. We put that in the pilot.

ARMANDO IANNUCCI:

We sat down and we literally spent about three and a half hours just talking about it, making each other laugh. Within an hour we were already plotting out future episodes. We'd already moved on from the pilot. I hadn't realized that she'd grown up in Washington so she was familiar with that world. She talked about knowing what it's like to go into a room where people are aware of you, and you have to keep a smile on your face even though you may have a roaring headache. We instantly clicked and we instantly knew this was going to be a gas.

CASEY BLOYS:

They liked each other, then we made a deal for Julia. This was in the days where we were doing pilots. This was not straight to series.

We were lucky in that Armando had a body of work we could look to and say, "We know he can do this show."

JULIA LOUIS-DREYFUS:

To be quite honest with you, I was desperate to get away from network television and on to HBO specifically. There's no other way to say it.

I felt like I'd be able to spread my wings in a way that was not possible at other times in my life. And it seems certainly at that time that there was a lot of creative freedom. There was a dynamic at HBO where people were hired to do their thing creatively and they were fundamentally left alone to do that. And I don't mean to imply that various executives didn't have notes or comments or suggestions, but there was a true culture of respect for the people that they hired. And so that was a complete breath of fresh air.

FRANK RICH:

I had never met Julia before she was hired by Armando, but we had something in common, we both grew up in Washington, DC, in families that were not in government. That's a very special bond. We're a generation apart, a little bit more than a decade apart in age, but it turned out her mother and stepfather had met my father and stepmother.

CASEY BLOYS:

Lena Dunham's humor is very confessional and out there; Julia's is very much about precision and timing. Neither one detracts from the other. I think that was one of the nice things about that time was you could have two shows that are doing very different things but both are at the top of their game.

ARMANDO IANNUCCI:

I was amazed by how few people I had to deal with. Actually in the early days, it was Sue Naegle and Casey and Mike Lombardo. And then making the show itself, it was primarily Casey. It wasn't my experience of like 101 committees for everything. And I remember Casey saying, "We like what you do. So the very last thing we're going to do is say, Come and work for us, but do it differently. We want you to work the way you work because that seems to work for you. So how can we let you do that?" It was refreshing, like being part of a creative family who looks after you.

CASEY BLOYS:

I had worked in network television before coming here fifteen years ago, and had a boss who used to say, "The problem with network television is that everybody wants to help too much. Nobody's bad or mean, but you have levels of studio and network executives who all want to gives notes. Everybody wants to prove that they are smart and helpful and participating, and so what starts with good intentions, which is 'here's some feedback,' becomes overwhelming."

I remember when I first started, Carolyn Strauss was the head of entertainment. She is one of the smartest creative executives I've worked for because she could go, "What if you just did this?" A small adjustment but you'd go, "Why didn't I think of that?" And that's all she'd do. There weren't pages of notes or anything like that, it was just, "Do this." You have to be comfortable in your job and comfortable in your instincts to be able to say that.

AMY GRAVITT:

Most showrunners have talked to the casting director and come in with a plan for how they want auditions to run. Armando took it to a whole new level. It felt like we were watching live theater in the middle of the test. He just spontaneously started interviewing the actors as though they were already the characters interviewing for the job that they would have. And for some reason I remember Reid Scott in particular just jumping in and he instantly became Dan Egan in that moment.

It was like an improv session, and we got a glimpse into what the rehearsal process would become in *Veep* and in the scripting of the show. And I think it just speaks to how Armando worked with the actors to find the scenes on their feet. Everything is incredibly structured on the page, but nothing is too baked in that it doesn't feel fresh, which is essential to comedy. The jokes don't have a chance to get stale on a page or in the minds of the actors.

And for a joke to last from the initial breaking of a scene on the white board to sell through several drafts of a script through production and several takes and then in the cut and still feel like it's being said for the first time is challenging.

TONY HALE, Actor:

I had shot a pilot for another network and I knew that that pilot wasn't going to go, but they hadn't released me from the contract yet. And then *Veep* came along and I remember just being so nervous because I had seen Armando's stuff and I'd read the pilot and I knew Julia was attached and I was just like, "Oh my gosh, this sounds so good." But I didn't know if I could get out of that other thing. I was pretty nervous about it, honestly.

ARMANDO IANNUCCI:

We went out to Washington and did our research and talked before we wrote down anything. We tried to meet up with the Speaker's office, the vice president's office, the *Washington Post*, lobbyists, think tanks. We tried to get under the skin of DC and try and work out who were the key personnel. We had a couple of consultants who were informing us about the credibility of the information, say if a call came through from the *Washington Post*, who would take the call, if there was an event that night, who would be invited to the event from the office, who would be expected to go.

FRANK RICH:

Armando had a very particular way of working. He workshops scripts. So from the pilot onward, we'd be sitting in a room and doing a table read, but he'd get the actors on their feet to rehearse. He'd say, "Remember whatever lines you remember, improvise your own, and the writers will sit around the periphery and cannibalize the best stuff."

ARMANDO IANNUCCI:

Ian Martin did a website, a funny political parody website, very foul mouth website with his brother. He lived out in the North of England, Lancaster.

But it made me laugh. I just got in touch with them, said, "Do you want to write for this show I'm doing called *The Thick of It*?" And he said, "Great." And what he did was we'd write any script and then I'd send it to them. And then I'd just say, "Just add any phrases you like, change anything." So it was always great fun every day.

Just all of us going through to look at the right phrases because they would always make us laugh. And, I mean, he just has this slightly sclerotic way of not just swearing but insulting, it's quite poetic, really. As the series went on, he became a full-time writer on it.

CASEY BLOYS:

The pilot came out great.

ARMANDO IANNUCCI:

Sunday night on HBO was this big thing. We came on straight after this obscure show called *Game of Thrones*.

CASEY BLOYS:

Veep and *Girls* came out about the same time, and all anybody could talk about was *Girls*. I developed both of them, and obviously loved that *Girls* came out white hot, but if you told people then that *Veep* would go out with a special tribute seven years later at the Emmys, most would not have believed it.

TONY HALE:

Julia called me the morning of the Emmys and said, "I'm thinking if I win, I'd like you to carry my purse and come up on stage with me. Is that okay with you? I said, "Absolutely," and in my head I was thinking, "You are so going to win." So I knew I would have to get myself together for it. And bam, she won, and that was quite a rush.

*Aaron Sorkin had made his TV career by perfecting the twin arts of bang-bang dialogue with that of the walk-and-talk, characters wittily aperçu-ing at each other while a tracking shot followed them down corridors—such corridors as could be found in fac-similes of, say, ESPN (***Sport Night***), or the White House (***West Wing***), or, in 2012, for HBO, at a fake network, Atlantis Cable News (***The Newsroom***). Jeff Daniels, Emily Mortimer, Olivia Munn, and Sam Waterston, among others, starred in ***The News-room*** which debuted on HBO on June 24, 2012.*

Tom Hanks narrated *The Pacific*, HBO's nearly $200 million follow-up to *Band of Brothers*. The series ran for ten episodes and won eight Primetime Emmys, including the top prize for Outstanding Miniseries. Left to right: executive producer Gary Goetzman, HBO CEO Bill Nelson, executive producers Hanks and Steven Spielberg, HBO programming president Michael Lombardo, co-presidents Eric Kessler and Richard Plepler, and HBO miniseries president Kary Antholis, all gathered for a gala screening at Grauman's Chinese Theatre.

Terence Winter (right), one of David Chase's trusted lieutenants on *The Sopranos*, wrote the fantastical "Pine Barrens" episode, then created *Boardwalk Empire*. The series starred Steve Buscemi (left), Kelly Macdonald, Michael Shannon, Stephen Graham, and Michael K. Williams. Martin Scorsese won an Emmy for directing the pilot, as did Timothy Van Patten for directing the show's second-season finale.

Before HBO delved into a huge production overseas called *Game of Thrones*, it produced *Rome*, which ran for two seasons before being controversially canceled. Ciarán Hinds (below) starred alongside Kevin McKidd, Ray Stevenson, Polly Walker, Kerry Condon, and James Purefoy.

Two greats join for one exceptional HBO documentary. *Billie Jean King: Portrait of a Pioneer*, producer-director Margaret Grossi's stellar film, won a Peabody Award in 2016. Among professional athletes who have transitioned to television, perhaps none has been as versatile, impressive, and in-demand as Mary Carillo (left). Each night at Wimbledon, meanwhile, once the day's coverage had concluded, Billie Jean King (right) would visit the various production rooms to thank all who had worked on the telecasts.

4

Andrea Kremer (left) with Kobe Bryant, February 2016, in his Southern California office for a *Real Sports* profile. In addition to his wall photos of John Williams, Steve Jobs, and Walt Disney, there is a fourth of J. K. Rowling. After this interview, Kobe took a helicopter to the Staples Center, and HBO hired another helicopter to follow along and film Bryant in his preferred mode of transportation. Kremer, who had departed earlier by car, waited for him on the rooftop and continued the interview after he arrived.

5

Bryant Gumbel may well have the best job in television. Correspondent David Scott (right), formerly a producer, smoothly and seamlessly transitioned to on-air work for *Real Sports*, which premiered April 2, 1995. Some twenty-seven seasons later, the show has thirty-three Sports Emmys and four duPont-Columbia Broadcast Journalism Awards.

6

Absolute nonsense: Michael Patrick King (far left) brought *Sex and the City* to new heights and helped replenish HBO bank accounts, while the much-adored Lisa Kudrow remained, post-*Friends*, as loveable as ever. When the two pros pitched *The Comeback* to HBO execs Chris Albrecht and Carolyn Strauss, the idea may have been far ahead of its time, but isn't that what HBO is supposed to be about? Nominated for three Emmys at the end of its first season (including a Best Actress nod for Kudrow), *The Comeback* suffered the indignity of cancellation the very next day.

Pssst, HBO, it doesn't work both ways: "We found a writer for your show," *and* "We found a star for your show." Laura Dern and Mike White co-created *Enlightened* only to have HBO do a perfectly miserable job managing the discord between the two. Dern's performance as Amy Jellicoe remains one of the bravest "star turns" in recent memory, earning Dern a Golden Globe. Kookily enough, however, HBO canceled the show after two seasons. From left: Mike Lombardo, Dern, White, and Sue Naegle, president of HBO Entertainment.

Jay Roach's triumphant *Game Change* was only going to get made if Julianne Moore played Sarah Palin, and so she did, delivering one of the finest performances of her career. Sarah Paulson was a standout as the film's hero, Nicolle Wallace, while other sterling performances were logged by Woody Harrelson and Ed Harris. Roach and writer Danny Strong had previously delivered another hit to HBO with *Recount*.

9

Movie star Michael Douglas couldn't believe the big studios had all passed on *Behind the Candelabra*—what with Matt Damon, director Steven Soderbergh, writer Richard LaGravenese, and *himself* all attached—but the whole bunch wound up being grateful HBO aggressively stepped up to the plate. *Candelabra* would win eleven Primetime Emmys, including Outstanding Miniseries or Movie and Best Actor, no surprise, for Douglas.

10

11

The proverbial "welcome mat" had been out for Aaron Sorkin at HBO for years before he did *The Newsroom* in 2012. The series would run for only three seasons, but the pilot alone would have merited preservation in a hall of fame just to immortalize Jeff Daniels's tour de force response to a student's question, "What makes America the greatest country in the world?" Jane Fonda, Sam Waterston, Emily Mortimer, Dev Patel, and Olivia Munn also starred.

After a marathon lunch, George R. R. Martin (right) gave David Benioff (left) and Dan (D. B.) Weiss (middle) permission to pitch his multivolume *A Song of Ice and Fire*—with no formal rights deal attached. Over its eight-season, seventy-three-episode run, *Game of Thrones* won fifty-nine Primetime Emmys, the most of any series in Emmy history.

Shame on you. From *Game of Thrones* season five, episode ten, "Mother's Mercy": Maggie Hayes (far left), Hannah Waddington, and Mary Jordan (far right) prepare Lena Headey for her "walk of atonement" after her confession of the sin of incest. Headey didn't do it alone. Her body double, Rebecca Van Cleave, performed the walk in the nude.

A few luminaries from the star-splattered *Game of Thrones* cast. By its last season, the show was costing more than $10 million an episode, arguably still a bargain for HBO. From left to right: Conleth Hill, Peter Dinklage, Nathalie Emmanuel, Emilia Clarke, Liam Cunningham, and Kit Harington.

15

Director Todd Haynes's masterpiece, *Mildred Pierce*, remains one of the finest miniseries in HBO history, garnering twenty-one Emmy nominations. Best Actress Kate Winslet (right) starred with Evan Rachel Wood (left) and Best Supporting Actor Guy Pearce.

Frances McDormand (left) secured the rights for Elizabeth Strout's novel *Olive Kitteridge* before it won the Pulitzer and, teamed with the ever-talented Jane Anderson (right), brought *Olive* to HBO. McDormand, her usual magnificent self, and Lisa Cholodenko won Emmys for Best Actress and Best Director respectively, and Anderson won for Best Adaptation. The HBO and Playtone production won a total of eight Emmys, including Best Limited Series, Best Actor (Richard Jenkins), and Best Supporting Actor for a surprisingly tender and nuanced performance from Bill Murray.

16

17

Tom Perrotta's stunning *Little Children* was going to be a limited series on HBO but, mercifully, became a feature film. His novel *The Leftovers,* however, wound up at HBO in the safe hands of Damon Lindelof. From left: Regina King, Jovan Adepo, Perrotta, Kevin Carroll, Lindelof, and Jasmin Savoy Brown. Others in the cast included stars Justin Theroux, Amy Brenneman, and Liv Tyler. Scrawled on the scoreboard: the moment when the Sudden Departure, which was the basis of the series, occurred.

18

Damon Lindelof and Justin Theroux on the set of *The Leftovers.* Theroux's performance of "Homeward Bound" during the show's second-season finale proved to be one of the most poignant moments in the series.

Real Time with Bill Maher premiered on February 21, 2003, and has since been a very dependable vehicle from which Maher could warn of, and predict, political and cultural turning points. The show has been nominated for twenty Primetime Emmys but has yet to win a single one, which is in a way a tribute to Maher's iconoclasm and fearlessness; certainly many on the staff consider the Emmy snub a badge of honor. From left: Robert Reich, Michael "Killer Mike" Render, Bill Maher, Ethan Hawke, and Duncan Hunter.

John Oliver had numerous offers after subbing for Jon Stewart on *The Daily Show* one summer and decided on HBO following dinner with CEO Richard Plepler at Cipriani. Plepler proffered tons of reassurance about "editorial independence"; Oliver has tested boundaries ever since, without complaint, and is one of HBO's highest-paid talents. *Last Week Tonight with John Oliver* premiered April 27, 2014, and has subsequently been bathed in awards. Oliver is pictured with HBO late-night guru Nina Rosenstein, Kate Norley (Oliver's wife), and Plepler.

Time Warner chairman Jeff Bewkes huddles with Sheila Nevins prior to Nevins's dramatic end to her legendary thirty-four-year run. Leaving was not *her* choice—but neither, for that matter, was it Bewkes's.

21

22

Filmmaker Andrew Jarecki (with camera) in Manhattan beside his most famous topic, Robert Durst. *The Jinx*, Jarecki's six-episode documentary series, premiered on February 8, 2015. Durst was arrested a day before the series' finale aired, making headlines around the world.

23

Lawrence Wright (left) and Alex Gibney at a screening of *Going Clear: Scientology and the Prison of Belief*, which tallied a heap of Emmy Awards, including Outstanding Writing, Outstanding Directing, and Outstanding Documentary. HBO held firm with its support, despite the church's protests and threats.

Long live the queen. Just in case there were those who didn't believe it after *Seinfeld*, Julia Louis-Dreyfus proved in *Veep* that she is one of the most talented comedic actresses in the history of the medium. *Veep* creator Armando Iannucci (left) is a Brit, but he more than managed to capture American politics at its worst. The series ran for seven successful seasons, with Louis-Dreyfus winning six consecutive Emmys for her portrayal of Selina Meyer, an Emmy record.

When Iannucci departed *Veep* after four seasons, there was doubt and fear that anyone could fill his shoes. Luckily, *Seinfeld* and *Curb* veteran David Mandel (right) was available and able to land the final three seasons of the show in spectacular fashion—even after a harrowing break in production for Louis-Dreyfus to be treated for breast cancer.

Lena Dunham (left) was twenty-three when she first met with twenty-seven-year-old HBO assistant Kathleen McCaffrey (right), who'd seen Dunham's student film *Tiny Furniture*. *Girls* became a cultural force in its own right and ran for six seasons. Dunham starred with Adam Driver, Allison Williams, Jemima Kirke, and Zosia Mamet. Jenni Konner was the showrunner, and Judd Apatow served as executive producer.

The stars of HBO's Emmy-nominated *Insecure*. From left: Yvonne Orji, co-creator Issa Rae, Natasha Rothwell, and Amanda Seales. The show was partially inspired by Rae's memoir, *The Misadventures of Awkward Black Girl*. Rae has become an HBO stalwart with numerous additional projects.

From left: HBO's programming chief Casey Bloys, Alec Berg, HBO Comedy head Amy Gravitt, and the singular Bill Hader at the premiere of *Barry* in 2018. Hader co-wrote (with Berg) and directed the pilot, and stars in the show, for which he and Henry Winkler won Primetime Emmys.

29

Westworld co-creators (and husband and wife) Jonah Nolan (left) and Lisa Joy join Casey Bloys and executive producer J. J. Abrams at the show's premiere. Based on the 1973 Michael Crichton film of the same name, *Westworld* stars Evan Rachel Wood, Thandiwe Newton, Jeffrey Wright, Anthony Hopkins, and Ed Harris. Despite its troubled infancy, the show racked up big ratings and plenty of awards.

30

Evan Rachel Wood (as Dolores Abernathy) and James Marsden (as Teddy Flood) take in a vista on the set of *Westworld* while on location in Utah. The series was also shot in California, Arizona, Singapore, and Spain.

The Night Of premiered June 24, 2016, electrified by the performance of Riz Ahmed (right) as Nasir "Naz" Khan. Created by Steve Zaillian and Richard Price, the drama originally featured James Gandolfini, but after Gandolfini tragically died, he was replaced by his friend John Turturro (left).

31

32

Casey Bloys went from running comedy at HBO to being its president of Entertainment. Jesse Armstrong, creator of *Succession*, had been a comedy writer, so it was only natural that the two would join forces, along with director Adam McKay, to build one of the truly captivating dramas of the past decade. *Succession* features a superb ensemble cast (from left to right): Kieran Culkin, Matthew Macfadyen, Sarah Snook, Brian Cox, Jeremy Strong, Nicholas Braun, Hiam Abbass, Alan Ruck, and J. Smith-Cameron as Gerri Kellman. The series won nine Primetime Emmys, including Best Drama in 2020.

After its airing, *Chernobyl* emerged as IMDB's highest-rated series of all time, with ten Primetime Emmys to its credit—Outstanding Limited Series among them. Craig Mazin's scripts were pronounced "flawless" by an exultant HBO exec; the series was directed by Johan Renck. From left: Stellan Skarsgård, Casey Bloys, Mazin, Jared Harris, and *Succession*'s Jesse Armstrong attend HBO's 2020 Golden Globe Awards After Party.

"Sometime around the age of sixteen, I resigned myself to the idea that eventually drugs would kill me," Sam Levinson told an invited audience at the premiere of *Euphoria*, HBO's first series about teenagers, based loosely on an Israeli miniseries of the same name. Incredibly, Levinson writes all episodes and recently signed an overall deal to stay with HBO and create other shows.

As guided by director Levinson, Zendaya (right) became the youngest-ever winner of an Emmy for Best Actress. Also in the cast: Hunter Schafer (left), a teenage model who had never acted prior to *Euphoria*. Zendaya and Schafer bring to life harrowing scenes known to scare the hell out of parents watching at home. Jacob Elordi, Maude Apatow, and Sydney Sweeney filled out the gifted cast.

Director Roger Ross Williams takes the stage at the Apollo Theater for the screening of his documentary *The Apollo*, which won the Emmy for Outstanding Documentary. Williams also won an Oscar for his HBO documentary *Music by Prudence*, becoming the first African American to win an Academy Award for Best Documentary, Short Subjects.

Andre Romelle Young, aka Dr. Dre (left), and *The Defiant Ones* director Allen Hughes during a particularly tense moment while filming HBO's four-part documentary. The film won the Grammy Award for Best Music Film and was nominated for five Emmys, including Outstanding Documentary Series.

37

HBO Drama head Francesca Orsi's mother, Carmen (far right, top row), grew up in Naples, Italy, and flipped out when she read the *Neapolitan Novels* by Elena Ferrante, set around Naples in the 1950s and the basis for *My Brilliant Friend*, an exquisite series created by Saverio Costanzo.

38

39

Tim Blake Nelson (as Wade Tillman / Looking Glass) walks with Regina King (as Angela Abar / Sister Night) from HBO's *Watchmen*, a limited series created by Damon Lindelof and based on the graphic novel of the same title. *Watchmen* won eleven Primetime Emmys, including Outstanding Limited Series, and wins for Yahya Abdul-Mateen II, King, and Lindelof (with Cord Jefferson) for writing.

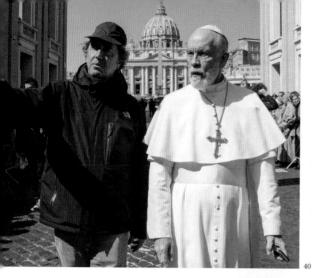

The Young Pope premiered in 2016, followed by The New Pope in 2020. Academy Award winner Paolo Sorrentino (left) wrote and directed the two series, the first starring Jude Law as the titular young pope, and the other starring John Malkovich (right) as the new pontiff. Wildly imaginative, both *Pope* seasons were notable for their visual splendor, as well as for such arresting performances as that of supporting actor Cécile de France.

From left: Jurnee Smollett, Jonathan Majors, and Misha Green during happier days on *Lovecraft Country*. Despite a breathtaking first season and eighteen Primetime Emmy nominations, including Smollett's for lead actress, HBO announced the show would not return for a second season. High production costs were cited but were just a cover for a show besieged by internal toxicity that made its return impossible.

Writer Brad Ingelsby wanted to create a series set in his hometown outside Philadelphia, Pennsylvania, and wrote two episodes of *Mare of Easttown* on his own before they were sent to Kate Winslet. During production, HBO had to surmount COVID concerns, which ultimately required a shutdown for several months, but those and other struggles proved more than worth it. Directed by Craig Zobel, the limited series also starred Julianne Nicholson, Guy Pearce, Jean Smart, and Angourie Rice. Pleas for a sequel began roughly five minutes after the final episode aired.

Sorkin was just emerging from a $4.5 million (per year) deal at Warner Bros., where he had done West Wing *and* Studio 60. *So wherever he looked, or almost, he saw guys who'd paid him five, six, seven million bucks a year. HBO, meanwhile, had bought the* Newsroom *script for a mere $250 grand.*

AARON SORKIN:

HBO had had an open invitation on the table for a few years. I thought a newsroom was an interesting workplace to set a drama and so I took a swing at it. For about a year, all I had was, "A show set in a newsroom." I needed an idea. One of the things that was a problem for me was that I didn't want to make up news each week. (If I did a story where China invaded Taiwan, our show would take place in a different universe.) I spent time in newsrooms, hoping something would happen while I was there that would give me an idea.

One night I was sitting in the MSNBC control room during Keith Olbermann's show, thinking it was time to give up. I was going to call HBO in the morning and tell them I couldn't come up with anything. I was thinking this as I was staring at a monitor I couldn't understand at first. It was a live feed of the oil spilling out of the Deepwater Horizon, which had exploded a few weeks before. So I started thinking, What if we're watching the pilot, assuming that it's taking place today, when news comes over the wire that an oil rig in the gulf has exploded? Then a date comes up on the screen and it's all taking place a year and a half ago. Now I wouldn't have to make up the news. It still wasn't an idea, but I was a little bit closer.

JEFF DANIELS, Actor:

I met Aaron and Scott Rudin at a breakfast at the Four Seasons in New York. They had this show about a newsroom. I was on the short list, and I wanted it. I wanted to work with Aaron Sorkin badly. And I got it. As they'd say, "I had it before the breakfast was over."

MIKE LOMBARDO:

The Newsroom was a difficult situation. Ari Emanuel, who I was friendly with, had gotten me together with Aaron Sorkin, and I brought Sue to lunch. From the beginning, I felt a connection to the show.

SUE NAEGLE:

Mike yelled at me for speaking to Aaron about changing the title.

MIKE LOMBARDO:

In my mind, you honor the showrunner. You listen to his voice. That's what Carolyn taught me. But Sue had gotten so close to Scott and was doing Scott's bidding, and not talking to me about it. She was in effect working on his behalf. She made a long end-run around what Aaron wanted during casting, and I asked her, "Why are you doing that? Aaron wants this woman. She's fine. What are you doing?"

Sue became very complicated to me interpersonally. I couldn't trust her.

AARON SORKIN:

I wanted the show to be about a group of people we enjoyed spending time with once a week. I wanted to show journalists doing their best, just like the nurses and doctors on a hospital drama. I think there was an assumption among some people that by setting the show in the recent past, I was trying to show the pros how it should have been done. That was something that was never on my mind while I was writing.

"Can you say why America is the greatest country in the world?"

JEFF DANIELS:

I told Aaron, "I've been waiting thirty-five years for this speech. I usually get to stand next to people who give this speech."

I knew how big that speech was. Not only for the show, but for me personally. I just pounded that for ten days. It never left my hand. I ran it, and ran it, and ran it. We shot it day three of an eighteen-day shoot. That's early. If it's a baseball game, they're still in the top of the first inning. You don't know anything. You're throwing what you think it is at it and hoping for the best. On the way to the set, I rode in the same car with Aaron; we were at the College of the Canyons, a place about an hour or so away from LA. They had purple seats, which matched the seats at Northwestern University. In the car with Aaron on the way up, he turned to me and, half-joking, said, "As important as the speech is to you, it's twice as important to me." I said, "Okay. Got it." But I knew I had it. I had it cold. I was ready.

AARON SORKIN:

That scene wasn't about America and its place in the world, it was about a guy having a public breakdown. He's been depressed for a couple of years because of a breakup and he hallucinates (or doesn't) that the woman who broke his heart—his former producer—is in the audience and producing him. It's the inciting action for the whole series.

JEFF DANIELS:

Aaron was nervous. He came over at one point and said, "I don't want to offend you, but do you want cue cards?" I gave him a look of someone who'd been on Broadway, and he went away and sat over at video village. I noticed that number two, three, and four from HBO had shown up that day. So had Sam Waterston, Olivia Munn, and Tom Sadoski, who weren't working that day. Sam said later, "I wanted to see if I had a job or not." Which meant that that speech was not only big for the show and big for the pilot, certainly it was in the first ten minutes of the first episode, so as America is sitting there with their remote, this speech hits them and, we hope, makes them put down the remote and get them to commit to the show. But it also was, "Do we have a McAvoy? Everybody loves Jeff. We think he's the best choice. We hope. But we have to see it today." And when they finally put the cameras on me, I just nailed it. That's what you shoot for. You shoot for that definitive "I can't imagine anybody else."

That speech literally bought me ten years. It won me the Emmy, too. I remember going to the Emmys that year after the first season and HBO very quietly saying, "Just be glad you get to go. Gandolfini didn't win right away. Nobody wins the first year. Big competition, Kevin Spacey and *House of Cards*. Damian Lewis, Jon Hamm, you got Mandy Patinkin. Bryan Cranston, that's who you're competing against. Established shows. Just go and enjoy the night. Don't worry about winning. Don't get your hopes up." But no one else had that Northwestern speech. That was the episode they submitted. I won.

I was in movies and doing things in my own career in my twenties and thirties and even forties. And then I had a dry spell. *Newsroom* was the show that put me back in the game versus, "Well, I guess you had a good career." This was a rebirth for me. It got me interested again in being an actor, that maybe I wasn't done yet.

AARON SORKIN:

I don't think audiences change. I think the bar gets raised every year so there's an expectation of quality, but there's always been an expectation of quality.

CASEY BLOYS:

I worked on *Newsroom*. Nobody wanted to say anything to Aaron. Sue didn't want to say anything to Scott, so the show was flawed and we knew it was flawed. Rather than dealing with the problem, like sometimes you have to piss off creative people or sometimes you have to have a tough conversation being their friend. Being honest with them is the job.

AARON SORKIN:

At the start of the second season, I wrote the first three scripts and we shot the season opener and I went to HBO and said, "It's not working. I need to start again." It was an expensive request and they couldn't have been more supportive. When people bet on you, you badly want them to win. I owe HBO a show. And Jeff and the cast. And the crew and the producers. You get the idea.

I never quite got *The Newsroom* right. I never felt comfortable in my chair. I could string together some good scenes, but I was never able to write a full episode that worked as well as I wanted it to: 0 for 25.

It was one of the most talked-about and heavily praised novels in years. Jonathan Franzen's **The Corrections** *hit bookshelves a week before 9/11 and would go on to win the National Book Award and be a finalist for a Pulitzer. It also managed to famously piss off her majesty (and she was majestic, for all intents and purposes) Oprah Winfrey, who had chosen it for her illustrious Book Club, an honor that Franzen dared to sniff at; in fact, he pooh-poohed it so emphatically that the invite was rescinded.*

With so much heat being flung, it became clear that someone would want to adapt **Corrections** *for either big screen or small. Producer Scott Rudin had bagged the rights before the book even hit stores. Big-screen attempts came and went—David Hare tried his hand at a script, Stephen Daldry and Bob Zemeckis were both attached—at one point or another—as directors, and such talent as Judi Dench, Brad Pitt, Tim Robbins, and Naomi Watts all had come and gone. A decade after its publication, a dream team of Noah Baumbach, Rudin himself, Chris Cooper, Dianne Wiest, Ewan McGregor, Maggie Gyllenhaal, Rhys Ifans, and Greta Gerwig had assembled to make a pilot for HBO.*

But one and all learned painfully that rendering Franzen's convoluted narrative on a screen was never going to be an easy problem to solve, no matter who was involved, and on May 1, 2012, HBO ruefully announced that it would forgo green-lighting a full series.

It's hardly news to report that Rudin can be a difficult character to deal with—the stories are legend and legion, and not at all exaggerated—but it was said that Mike Lombardo and Rudin barely spoke to each other even on their mutually chummiest days. The real victims of that soured relationship were writers and talent, who were not thought to have received a fair shot at getting the show on the air because the head of programming and the producer disliked each other so fiercely.

SUE NAEGLE:

Scott is just incredibly smart and he's a really gifted producer; he's got great instincts, great relationships, and great materials. So he's a difficult person to deal with, but I mostly had no real conflict with him. We both put the work first.

The Corrections was excellent. I wish that it had made it to at least a limited series. The challenge of the book was that there were so many different timelines, and it spans such a long period of time. The map that Franzen and Noah Baumbach put together for the series, for the whole thing to come to a conclusion, would have been about four years. At the time it felt too long to tell the story correctly. I thought that we should have been able to figure out at least a little limited series or like a two-year series for it.

I just couldn't get everyone to agree. HBO is a very hard place to work for anybody, but if you're coming in from the outside, it's very difficult to merge onto the highway of HBO.

They almost speak a different language. It's like a tribe that does things in their own way. Most people had been there for years and years and years and years. I had come from an agency and most people would think that that's quite the political setting, but I've never seen anything like the politics at HBO, particularly during that time.

DAVID LEVINE:

The first two years with Scott were really fun. When Sue and I would go to see him, it felt private. We would go into a room with him and it would be [John Patrick] Shanley and [Tony] Kushner and [Gary] Shteyngart, and Zoë Heller and Jonathan [Franzen]. It was a dream come true for us, in terms of penetrating the upper echelon of the literary world. But we always knew that Scott was destructive, and we always knew that Scott would turn. And then he did, somewhere around *Corrections*. That was a bad experience.

Meanwhile, Lombardo and Naegle's problems were getting worse.

SUE NAEGLE:

I was always trying to get Mike to talk about how to make things better. The number of times I would text him saying, "Are you upset with me? Is there something you want to talk about?" "No, no, no, no. I'm not upset with you. I'm just having a bad day."

Then it was just over. Mike was like, "I don't want this deal anymore." Ari

Emanuel was like, "I don't wanna have this deal anymore." And Scott was basically like, "You don't want me, I don't want you." And it ended.

I remember Mike saying to me at the time, "The problem is you think you're a lion tamer and not every lion can be tamed. That is a lion you cannot tame." I always thought it was a funny characterization. I did think I could just make it work. I have incredibly thick skin. So it's not like I was going home crying every night. I play fairly unflappable, and when people are in bad moods or lose their temper or snap in meetings, all of that can be hurtful, but I'm a big girl. I grew up in an agency. So even when it was directed at me in such a vitriolic way, I loved that job.

In the span of little more than two years, Scott Rudin had more than twenty projects bubbling on the burners of HBO, front and back—an incredible irony given how much disregard Lombardo had for Rudin and how little he wanted to be in business with him. Therefore, the Rudin relationship took up a great deal of Naegle's time.

On July 25, 2012, mere months after **The Corrections** *had been put into turnaround, the exclusive deal between HBO and Scott Rudin came to an end.*

The relationships between Rudin and Naegle, and between Rudin and Mike Lombardo, were, however, where the real problems had taken root. Naegle was said to be insecure about her creative instincts around Rudin, something Rudin realized and used to his advantage. To Rudin, Naegle was an easy target—anything he pitched, she bought. At one point, HBO bought twenty-one pitches from Rudin in eighteen months.

This was not to say that Rudin's taste wasn't exemplary—he had an extraordinary knack for tying down the rights to the best literary works before they reached the marketplace—but, still, he preyed on Naegle's desire to please him. In addition, according to many in the department, Naegle's talent did not lie in taking a script and making it better; rather, she was good at wooing people to join projects in front of and behind the camera. Rudin, on the other hand, was seen as a true dramaturge and literary mentor, able to push writers to do better work despite often adopting repugnant methodologies.

In one case, a novel Rudin pitched wasn't picked up by HBO, so Rudin did an end-around. He called Naegle directly, and she bought it, very few questions asked. (No show resulted from the deal.) Several members of the programming department believed Naegle wanted Rudin to give her access to the upper echelons of the literary world she found so intoxicating.

Yet for all his support from Naegle, Rudin was a producer looking to make a deal, and everyone knew, too, that he was prone to turning on people. When **The Corrections**—*a show Naegle had somewhat let Rudin run wild on, failed to pan out (word on the street was that it was just a so-so pilot), the relationship between Rudin and Naegle started to sour. Eventually, Rudin turned on her for good and got so abusive* *and rude with her on a phone call that Lombardo told WME the relationship was now over, canceling the entire HBO-Rudin deal. This was one of Lombardo's most support-ive moments of Naegle—even though the Naegle-Rudin relationship had been one that sowed division throughout the halls of HBO.*

GLENN WHITEHEAD:

We bought twenty-one pitches from Scott Rudin, in a period of approxi-mately eighteen months. Some of those never came to pass because maybe we couldn't make a deal for rights.

Some fell by the wayside. So the projects that we had in some form of active development with Scott were probably in the fifteen to eighteen range.

SUE NAEGLE:

He had a lot of volume, a lot of incredible writers. He had a very specific way of working, which was a challenge. That's when I learned, start getting up at five fifteen in the morning, because from five thirty to six thirty was the time I spoke to Scott every day, just to get ahead of everything. He and I didn't have any problems until the end.

I don't even think he and Mike ever tried to have a relationship. It didn't start off well, I don't think. Scott, at the end of the day, just cares about the creative and cares about the scripts getting done the right way. It's actually wonderful to work with him in a lot of ways, as crazy as that sounds, because he's a handful, but I would go to his office in New York and we would just sit around this round table with incredible writer after incredible writer. Noah Baumbach, Jonathan Franzen, John Patrick Shanley, Tony Kushner. They were some of the best hours of my life. It was incredible.

As long as Mike didn't have to deal with Scott, it would be fine. The problem with Scott wasn't really a problem at the beginning. He was just a big personality known for being very rough-and-tumble, but he also had the best taste. And he was one of the only producers I've ever seen who was able to say to Aaron, "This isn't working, and this is why."

But Scott argued with everybody and alienated everyone in the building. I was like the last person standing. We had an argument toward the end and he said, "I'm going to tell you what you're not able to see. Mike hates you. And this company is not your friend. You're just too guileless to see it." He said, "You put up with it and it's pathetic." It was a bad fight. I went to Mike immediately and said, "This is how Scott's describing our relationship. This is how it looks to him from the outside and it hurts me. Do you want to talk about it?"

Lombardo picked up the phone, called Ari Emanuel, Rudin's agent, and said he was pulling the plug on Rudin's entire relationship with HBO. The conversation took less than five minutes.

GLENN WHITEHEAD:

When we pulled the plug on the deal, we gave virtually all of those projects back to Scott. I think there were one or two that we held on to, because we already owned the underlying material and had begun the process of developing it and then attached Scott after the fact. So, for example, *Silicon Valley* is a show that we were developing before we got Scott involved. And after we terminated our relationship with Scott we obviously continued to make that show. But for the vast majority of those shows, he walked away with them and could go produce them anywhere else that he liked. And if there were shows that we were already producing and we had some obligation to him, we paid that off.

There were still plenty of difficulties to go around.

DOUG ELLIN:

Mike Tyson said to me, "Why don't you do for me what you did for Mark's life? Use my life to inspire something and see what you come up with."

I said, "I don't think I'm the right guy to write this." I had never hired another writer and become a producer, but I got John Ridley, right out of the gate he was in and done. And he wrote a script that was fucking great, *Da Brick*. I believe John went and got Spike Lee and I think it was probably one of the fastest from a pitch to a green-lit pilot that HBO had done. And so I'm at HBO on a pretty big overall deal, I have my own show, *40*, that I'm creating, and I'm an executive producer and developing the Spike Lee–Tyson show, *Da Brick*.

Then Michael Lombardo tells me both shows are scheduled to start shooting on the same day.

I said, "How am I going to do anything on *Da Brick*?" And he literally said to me, "I didn't even know you were involved with that." I'm like, "Not involved? I developed it with John before Spike ever got here. And John Boyega was my suggestion."

I went to the table read for *Da Brick*. The HBO executives practically gave a standing ovation, and I was sitting there like a schmuck. I'm just like, "I birthed it. We got the great Spike Lee. All's going to be well." Then I was doing my pilot and got Eddie Burns, Michael Rappaport, and Michael Imperioli. I thought it was insane they made Michael Imperioli audition to play a New York chiropractor. If it was *Downton Abbey*, maybe you make him audition, but to play a New York character that I'm writing, to have him audition, I thought it was insane.

We shot the pilot with Julian Farino directing, and we had an amazing show. Lawrence Kasdan loved it, and it's from the guy who did eight years of *Entourage*, so it's a pilot that you give a shot to. Then Michael Lombardo calls me and tells me he doesn't think it's funny. We almost had a screaming match, with him going, "I don't give a shit what Lawrence Kasdan thinks. I don't think it's funny." I'm sitting there talking to a fucking lawyer about what's funny, when I just finished eight years of a show that was nominated for an Emmy, Golden Globe, Writers Guild almost every single year.

I couldn't believe it. I thought this was the point that everyone dreams of getting to in their career, where somebody doesn't think it's as good as they want it to be, but they trust you that you're going to figure it out. I was really proud of that pilot.

All the thoughts of HBO being the place where they let the creator do what they do were gone. I honestly would have bet my life that *40* would have worked. There's not even a maybe in my mind. And add onto that, within weeks after they pass on it, Judd Apatow's movie *This Is 40* came out. I'm not saying it had anything to do with mine, but I would be happy to put my pilot up against that movie.

They didn't seem interested in working with me. People ask me, "Are you mad at HBO?" I tell them, "I'm not mad at HBO, I get it. Business is business. Michael Lombardo didn't like it. That's his fucking opinion, but who the hell is he? And how did he even get that job?"

Among HBO's other busted pilots during this era:

Da Brick, *Spike Lee and Doug Ellin, starring John Boyega, about a young African American man from Newark, New Jersey, who reconnects with his friends and family after being released from juvenile detention.*

The Missionary, *featuring a wide-ranging producing cast from actor Mark Wahlberg to author Malcolm Gladwell, told the story of a religious representative from the United States during the era of the Cold War. The pilot was shot in February 2012 and HBO passed seven months later.*

Big Girls, *which would have chronicled one mental health care worker's efforts to treat the criminally insane as they served time, written by Adam Mazer, Emmy Award–winning screenwriter for* **You Don't Know Jack,** *with Joel Schumacher set to direct.*

Spring/Fall, *which explored the complicated bond between two fashion workers in New York. HBO ordered a pilot before ultimately passing.*

Tilda *was to be the story of a powerful and reclusive Hollywood blogger, later likened to* **Deadline**'s *Nikki Finke, starring Diane Keaton and Elliot Page, but, alas, HBO passed on the pilot.*

Hobgoblin, *concerning a group of magicians and their efforts to defeat Adolf Hitler, gestated for years before HBO pulled its plug.*

MIKE LOMBARDO:

I was asked to get rid of Dave Baldwin. Here's a guy who'd been at HBO a long time. He'd been there before me. He was the heart and soul of HBO scheduling. He did a great job running research. He would walk in a room and people were excited to see him. Everyone loved him. Well, almost everybody. He posted something on his MySpace or Facebook to the effect of, "Jeez, new bosses, tough budget meetings," something like that. That got reported from HR to Richard, and they called me and said, "We need to get rid of him." Here's a guy I liked very much for a very long time. And now one of my tasks was taking him to lunch and telling him he had to leave the company. That stuff wears on you.

DAVE BALDWIN:

I was having the time of my life. I would have gladly done this job for half the money, but I never told HR that. I was sixty-one, so everyone sold it as retirement. But my friends with the three-digit IQs knew exactly why my services were no longer required. There were a lot of us who had been there twenty-five, thirty years longer and we were all promoted to very high levels, making crazy show business money. So no one was ever told the truth except if you wanted the knife, a severance package, "Thank you for playing the game." Then you had to sign a document that said you would not sue for any reason. Ageism, sexism, blah, blah, blah. That's how it happened. In my pledge class, if you will, there must've been a dozen senior executives at that level who were all walked out the door.

Scott from HR pulled me aside. He told me. I was at the top of my game. But he said, "Here's the way it's going to go down. Mike's gonna come in from LA and he's gonna take you to lunch and he's going to tell ya."

So Mike takes me to a nice restaurant, and he is as nervous as a cat on a hot tin roof throughout the entire lunch. And I'm relaxed. I have a cocktail, we ordered wine, had a beautiful meal, and he's almost quivering, because he liked me. He didn't want to have that job, to let me go. When he started, he just stumbled through a few sentences, and I said, "Mike, Mike, I get it. I'm a big boy. It's HBO's ball, HBO's game. They decide who they want on their roster. I'm good, I'm good. Seriously." And he was so relieved. I mean, I can't tell you how calming that was to him.

I didn't blame Lombardo. He was far enough away in LA and he left me alone most of the time, although he had some very odd and strange ideas about scheduling and he was like a rookie playing in the major leagues. He just didn't know what he was doing. I had to explain to him gently why his reasons were maybe misinformed.

Before her departure, Strauss had wanted Gina Balian to be the sole head of drama, but Lombardo and Plepler weren't comfortable with her in the role. This reflects not just a conflicted attitude toward Strauss, her position, and her autonomy, but also how Balian was perceived.

Indeed, Balian had recently been told that although her creative skills were appreciated the company did not picture her in a managerial capacity. After Lombardo let Strauss go, Balian had made it clear to him that she would leave if she did not get promoted. When Lombardo hired Sue Naegle to replace Strauss and brought in Michael Ellenberg as her number two, the moves all but ensured that Balian would walk out the door.

SUE NAEGLE:

Mike wanted me to hire a head of drama and I didn't feel comfortable hiring someone over Gina. I thought she deserved the job. I hired a woman, Jocelyn Diaz, and that was okay. It wasn't the perfect match. I think Jocelyn didn't feel super comfortable.

Losing Gina was completely stupid. She is great at her job. David and Dan loved her, Steve Zaillian loved her. And those relationships are hard won. It's not easy to get along with Milch or David Simon or David and Dan. Those are tough relationships. You can't just bring Ellenberg in and say, "Now, David Milch, you're going to talk to this guy." Forget it. He does not want to talk to him.

I couldn't blame her for going, she had deserved to be the sole head of the drama group for a long time and she'd been passed over. Gina left because she thought, "I'm not working for this guy Ellenberg."

Lombardo either didn't believe Balian would leave or, if she did, assumed she wouldn't be able to find another job. Was he ever wrong. After leaving HBO, her home of twelve years, Balian became a senior vice president at HBO rival FX.

MIKE LOMBARDO:

Gina likes to handle her three things and dig in. We would have kept her forever. She wanted to manage a bunch of people. And I was concerned that—again, in hindsight was this the right decision?—that she couldn't do it. Her skill set was very much digging in granularly on the shows.

GINA BALIAN:

I started in 2001. I'm in my mid-forties now. I feel like I grew up there. I found a career and got immersed in a world I never had thought about. I learned a lot. For me, HBO was an incredibly special time that I feel really grateful for.

Even as Ellenberg's arrival had pushed out the talented Balian, Lombardo started to catch wind that talent didn't like Ellenberg and that running a department was not his strong suit.

To make matters worse, both Ellenberg and David Levine were lone wolves, operating outside the group culture of the department—which made sense given that neither had grown up there. Often the two wound up jockeying for the same project even though Ellenberg was senior.

The triangulation between Lombardo, Ellenberg, and Levine was all the more problematic when Naegle, their boss, interjected herself into the melee.

These were years of maximum craziness at the company, a dynamic that profoundly hurt HBO programming at a time when Netflix was getting ready to crank things up a notch. No one at HBO knew who was really calling the shots—or who had the vision—or what the game plan was, if there even was one.

Balian's stepping down marked yet another case of HBO's battle-hardened old guard losing their footing to outside executives, as Plepler and Lombardo sought to inject new blood into HBO's programming department. But there was at least one team that Plepler and Lombardo could not revamp: the kingdom of Queen Nevins.

LIZ GARBUS:

I told Sheila, "There's a long story that I can't stop thinking about," which is how you know that there was a case that had been in the news, the case of Diane Schuler who was an upper-middle-class mother from Long Island who, at one p.m. on a Sunday afternoon, drove her car the wrong way down the Taconic Parkway at eighty miles per hour into another car, ending up killing three people in the other car; five in her car—her three nieces, her baby, and herself in her car. The only survivor was her little son, and the toxicology assessor who investigated showed 0.8 blood alcohol level, which was the equivalent of maybe eight shots of vodka on a Sunday afternoon, and also high amounts of marijuana in her system. And nobody who knew Diane or knew the children could believe this. Her husband was sure there was something wrong with the toxicology. This was a highly, hugely responsible mother, hugely successful employee at Comcast. How could she do something that's highly irresponsible? There was a mystery at the heart of this: What causes women to ingest this level of alcohol, be this intoxicated while driving children? But then also at the end of the day, it's that circle around the ideas of drug and alcohol use and denial and depression and family. *There's Something Wrong with Aunt Diane* grew out of those larger conversations and this case became the keyhole through which we looked at the issue.

SHEILA NEVINS:

You didn't see the pictures. We didn't put them in. It's the only time I think we censored pictures because dead children on a highway without their limbs isn't something anyone can watch.

LIZ GARBUS:

I think we showed a picture of her face, which was not burned and looked fairly intact after the accident. She was on the ground, no longer alive. It was not gruesome or bloody, but it was the face of a dead woman who is somebody's mother, somebody's sister, somebody's loved one. Sheila's feeling was, "This is what it looks like. You drink and drive, you don't get treatment for your addiction, this is what can happen. It's everybody's nightmare. You got to show it, that's what documentaries do. They show the hard realities."

I had no idea it would be as widely viewed as it was. For some period of time it was their most-viewed documentary ever. The film was very, very, very hard to make.

JULIE ANDERSON:

Once Maryann and I were trying to develop a film about blindness because Sheila had said, "What's it like to be blind?" She would just have these ideas that could be turned into films.

Rebecca had had a meeting with Sheila and Sheila said something like, "What does a nun do?" She would do things like that. "What does a nun do? Let's make a film." *God Is the Bigger Elvis* was amazing.

SHEILA NEVINS:

I went to the abbey for the first time when I was at Yale because some man broke my heart. There was a priest in my classroom, and I said, "Father

Maguire, my heart is broken and I can't study for the finals." He said, "I know where you can go. There's an abbey in Bethlehem, Connecticut. It's only about an hour from New Haven, and they'll put you in the guesthouse. I go there often." I said, "Nuns? You're going to send me to a place with nuns? I can't afford that." And that's where I met Mother Dolores.

REBECCA CAMMISA:

My mother was a nun for ten years, so I know nuns and I know that community. So Sheila had this personal connection to the Abbey of Regina Laudis. And she'd said that she'd been wanting to make the film for a long time.

Dolores Hart, A-list screen actress who at the tender age of twenty-three was offered a million-dollar contract. Her next two films were with Marlon Brando and Warren Beatty. And with those three things happening in her career, and a wedding coming up.

She starred with Elvis. She was in films with Robert Ryan, with Montgomery Clift, films like *Where the Boys Are*, all these big films. She's now reached the height of her career, the million-dollar contract. Beatty, Brando. What does she do? She quits. She quits and goes into a cloister at age twenty-three. That to me is a revolutionary act.

MOTHER DOLORES HART, Nun:

Don Robinson came back in contact with me, even though I was in the monastery, and wanted to know what he could do for the monastery. As it turned out, he came here at least once a year all his life, gave so much help to us and he never married, but he became such a loyal oblate of the monastery, and gave as much as he could to help our work. I could not have more gratitude in my heart for such a love, because it was the real thing. I feel we have a love that will be between us for all eternity.

REBECCA CAMMISA:

He never married and she knew that was going to be the last time she saw him, he had some health issues. She told me she thought that would be the last time she would see him. She had that feeling.

These two people in front of me at that moment, saying goodbye, where do you point your camera? They say goodbye, he kisses her. You can tell he's still in love with her. And then he leaves. Do you stay on her? Do you turn to him? Where do you point your camera? I think for her seeing him leave, I think I'm on her, but then I turned quickly to see him exit. To see him finally leave is the truth of their relationship. He never gets to spend enough time. They will always have a very brief talk, a brief time with each other. Then she goes behind the curtain into the enclosure.

Sheila ultimately decided she wanted this to be a short film. So a lot of the things that I wanted to get into, what we filmed, we weren't able to because of time. It was nominated for an Academy Award for Best Documentary Short Subject. We went to the Oscars and Mother Dolores Hart was my date. What I didn't realize was she was at the Oscars sixty years before. So us going in 2012 was literally the sixtieth anniversary of the last time she was on a red carpet.

SHEILA NEVINS:

After *God Is the Bigger Elvis* aired, Jim Gandolfini, who was a lapsed Catholic and had a funny sense of humor about Catholicism, sends me this big basket with a note that reads, "For the nuns, Jim." They tied it to the back of the cab, drove it up to Connecticut, and dropped it at the nuns' house. Mother Dolores calls me, and says, "That was a great basket. There was cheese, salami, bread." I said, "Oh, that's so great. That's all Jim. It would be so great if you could send him a note." She said, "Okay, but in the bottom, there are a hundred condoms." I said, "Throw them out, Dolores."

MOTHER DOLORES HART:

Well, I love the Academy Awards and always wanted one. So I think to finally be able to go there in some capacity of being part of it was a real accomplishment. It was a relief that I hadn't been a complete failure to the industry.

Oh, Sheila Nevins. Well, right now I'm in my office. I'm giving my birds lunch, and right above the parrot cage in the house there is a great framed picture of Sheila Nevins and I that looks down on me every day. She is the best, the most wonderful friend that anyone could ask for.

On October 10, 2011, **Paradise Lost 3: Purgatory** *premiered on HBO. Director Joe Berlinger had been one of Nevins's first go-to documentarians, but he landed on her bad side for working with other networks. Berlinger felt that the loyalty Nevins demanded should have been backed up by a retainer payment with guaranteed work. But most people in Nevins-world were well aware that she always expected filmmakers to be available to her, but she did not care to pay them to do so, nor should she ever have to be concerned they might go somewhere else.*

JOE BERLINGER:

We never dreamed it would take three films and eighteen-plus years to see a result, but Sheila just rolled with the punches and was very committed to these guys getting out, which finally happened on August 19, 2011. The third *Paradise* film, which was nominated for an Oscar, had an amazing premiere at the New York Film Festival, and received a standing in the ovation box at the famed Alice Tully Hall. Standing with Sheila, Bruce Sinofsky, and the now free West Memphis Three in person getting a standing ovation for a sustained ten minutes was a highlight of my career. No doubt the applause wasn't about the film itself, it was about the perseverance of these guys and their advocates. We wouldn't give up telling their story, and Sheila is a huge part of that.

You could just feel her excitement that a documentary could have such a real-world impact. It's a night I will always remember. Every filmmaker wants to believe that telling a story will have some impact in the world. We were so lucky. The tangible, direct physical results of three people getting out of prison for crimes they didn't commit because of your filmmaking was worth more to me than any accolades that I've ever gotten. Sheila genuinely believed in the idea that we could move the needle and maybe help get these people out of prison. I don't want to say the films alone got them out of a prison, but they inspired a tremendous amount of fundraising and activism from real people and celebrities alike.

The film was a catalyst for all the activism that got these guys out of prison. And one of the great memories was witnessing Sheila's delight.

On June 11, 2011, the HBO Sports documentary **McEnroe/Borg: Fire & Ice** *made its debut.*

MARY CARILLO:

Ross was the one who thought *McEnroe/Borg* would be a good idea. Ezra Edelman did a bunch of stuff. He did *Magic & Bird* way before he did *O.J.: Made in America*; he had produced a bunch of real nice-looking docs for HBO. I worked on a bunch of docs for HBO and I loved it. I love the long-form stuff.

JOHN McENROE:

I knew Ross well enough to know that he wouldn't blindside me. I felt like they were going to try to look for something that people didn't see. And I think in the case of Björn, it was our friendship and the fact that we loved each other in a way, even though he was the greatest rival I ever had.

So you want to hopefully find that line where they're seeing who you really are, but you're not throwing someone under the bus. I trusted Ross and he brought Mary on as well. I've known Mary since I was twelve years old, I don't think I got production credit, but I was sort of involved in it enough to feel like, "Okay, they're not going to do a hatchet job." It was even better than I would have hoped it would be.

Ross Greenburg joined HBO in 1978, became executive producer of HBO Sports in 1985, and replaced Seth Abraham as HBO Sports president in 2000. On July 15, 2011, Greenburg was informed that his time of service had come to an end.

If Greenburg was looking for a single explanation for his ouster, it wouldn't be forthcoming. His departure was the result of a cocktail full of complexities, both from inside and outside the company.

Reports at the time suggested that Manny Pacquiao's decision to move to Showtime for one fight (Pacquiao vs. Shane Mosley on May 7) had led to Greenburg's firing. Greenburg, for his part, diplomatically told colleagues and those in the industry he had had enough, and while that was true, the ultimate decision was not his. Greenburg was the victim of the crazy economics of boxing. HBO bosses wanted to reset the pricing in the sport, especially as Greenburg often found himself as the only bidder for a fight, a fact ignored by promoters and managers who forced the channel into forking over huge fees even in essentially noncompetitive situations.

Greenburg's decision not to aggressively pursue renewal of **Inside the NFL** *fueled resentment in the ranks as well.*

And perhaps the final backbreaking straw was his fractured relationship with Plepler. Greenburg had never been a "Plepler man."

With all this in play, Greenburg had been begging HBO president Mike Lombardo to release a statement of support to the trades. Greenburg had been hearing a wide wild range of rumors about his future, none of them good—but Lombardo made clear that no such statement was imminent.

BOB ARUM:

Greenburg really pissed me off. We at Top Rank felt we were being dissed by HBO. We had signed Pacquiao and HBO wouldn't do the fights because they were allied with Golden Boy, Oscar De La Hoya's company. Ross didn't handle anything correctly. He was arrogant, because producers generally are arrogant, and they should be, because they're like directors, and what they say goes. But you can't run a network that way and be successful. You have to know to be a diplomat. That winter before, my wife and I had been in Cabo and Les Moonves, who is the head of CBS, was there with his wife, Julie Chen. And Les and I became friendly. I talked about my problems with HBO and he said, "Why wouldn't you bring Pacquiao over to Showtime?"

And one thing led to another. I told Ross I had it with him and I was gonna bring Pacquiao to Showtime. At first, he didn't believe it.

ROSS GREENBURG:

Arum put a target on my back along with a couple of other promoters who weren't getting the number of fights they wanted. I wasn't going to bow to anybody. I've had dogfights with practically every promoter and manager in the business, including Al Haymon, who some stupid people thought I was colluding with. I only wanted to get the best fights on the network. Arum pushed hard. When he brought Pacquiao over to Showtime, you would have thought the world ended. It wasn't a big deal; it wasn't even a big Pacquaio fight. But because Richard and Michael didn't know the inner workings of boxing, they took it as we were losing.

MIKE LOMBARDO:

Michael [Fuchs] had treated Sports like a kingdom, like they were princes. They had their own PR person and their own financial team but no P&L responsibility. It was like a separate company where they got to do and spend what they wanted. There were deals that were very questionable. At the end of the day, Ross just didn't want to work for anybody in that company. He acted like a rogue. Bill Nelson couldn't bear that, he wanted financial responsibility throughout the company.

As for culture, a lot of people thought it was unseemly that Ross kept all the Emmy awards in his office, as if they were his and not the company's.

NICK KHAN, Agent:

At the same time, Floyd Mayweather was in a period of retirement leaving Pacquiao as the undisputed top fighter in the sport. In reading the tea leaves, we believed that Pacquiao's next fight against Shane Mosley was going to go to Showtime. HBO Sports had no clue this was happening.

Ross Greenburg was not paying attention. He decided to go on a holiday trip to Thailand, taking him off the grid for ten to fourteen days. Those were crucial days—days where Arum, and the fight itself, could have been salvaged and brought back to HBO. But Ross wasn't around. He was on vacation. Not to be disturbed. So when Greenburg returned from his vacation in January, the fight was 100 percent going to Showtime.

It quickly got on Michael Lombardo and Richard Plepler's radar that they had lost essentially the biggest fight of the year. It also got on their radar that not only had Lampley turned the pay decrease offer down but that we had asked for Jim's release from HBO. That was the impetus for the first conversation I ever had with Richard Plepler or Michael Lombardo. They both called and said, "This is now with us. We love Jim Lampley. He's part of the HBO family. He's the voice of boxing. We know that his deal expires before this fight. We want him here. We don't want him going across the street. We want to sit with him immediately." And Plepler and Lombardo came in and fixed everything.

ROSS GREENBURG:

For the most part they were looking out for their own individual business interests. Bob felt at the time that he would be better off at an HBO without Ross Greenburg, to be honest, because he would be able to get what he needed out of Michael Lombardo or Richard Plepler.

It was tough, but that wasn't my first rodeo. I got a call from Richard and Bill Nelson and they were really distraught, thinking that the end was near for the HBO Boxing program because of losing this one fight. I reminded them there were many times in the previous thirty years where we had lost a fight and it wasn't the end of the world. We still had Mayweather and all roads were coming back to Mayweather, for Pacquiao. It was a tumultuous time. Look, I knew when I took the job in 2000 and I had been negotiating boxing since the mid-1980s. I had swum with the sharks for fifteen years prior to being president. So I knew exactly what that world was all about and how tough it was. And so I always said to myself, "When you swim with the sharks, at some point you're going to get bit." They're relentless and disloyal. You're going to get burned by those people at some point.

NICK KHAN:

In late 2010, Lampley's deal was up, and Ross tried to come in and cut his money. Although Ross had been one of the people who hired Lampley, over time Ross was not treating Jim in the way we felt Jim should be respected. Lampley has hosted fifteen Olympic games and was the voice of boxing for the entire generation.

JIM LAMPLEY:

I had been in network television for, at that point, close to forty years. I had seen a lot of rough-and-tumble and never shied away from any kind of a war. I had worked for other people who were similarly conflict-oriented. So to me that thing was the point of the realm.

You can't be surprised at anything that happens in television and, to a greater degree, you can't be surprised at anything that happens in boxing. I lived at the interface between two highly volatile institutions and I had seen volatility all my career.

I don't think of HBO as being as volatile as commercial television. Maybe that's my own personal prejudice, maybe that's because my relationships with management at HBO were far better than my relationships had ever been in commercial television.

I tried to stay away from getting into the grisly details of whatever was going on between Ross and Arum.

NICK KHAN:

There was a confusion where Ross believed he was the commissioner of boxing, which was, to me, a total mistake based on hubris.

In what other sport do you see a network executive on the dais, giving his commentary on the sporting event that just happened? You don't see Adam Silver saying, "I don't think LeBron performed well tonight." At every press conference you would hear from an HBO Sports executive. It never made sense to me. For some reason, the HBO Sports executives felt that was their role. That the world needed to hear from them. Silly.

RICK BERNSTEIN:

I believe it was shortly after we lost Manny Pacquiao to Showtime for one fight that senior management decided to look into how Ross was running the sports department. I heard secondhand that Richard and Lombardo went on a fact-finding mission, to speak to promoters, agents, and talent about Ross. To my knowledge, they never spoke to anyone from the sports department. I wish I was given the opportunity to share my thoughts. I don't know this for a fact, but it would not surprise me if there were boxing promoters who spoke negatively about Ross because he didn't give them as many fights on the network or as much money as they would have liked. There were probably agents who were not happy because Ross didn't buy the shows they were pitching. And some of our talent may have had their own personal issues with Ross.

NICK KHAN:

Plepler and Lombardo were gracious enough to sit with me and asked what I thought of their sports documentaries, which had won numerous awards over the years. I said, "Your next three documentaries are Curt Flood, a great story that occurred in the 1960s; Joe Namath, another great story that occurred in the 1960s; and the great story of Borg/McEnroe, which was focused on 1981." Again this was 2010 and the year prior. John Skipper, Bill Simmons, Connor Schell, and the rest of ESPN saw that same, simple flaw in the HBO Sports model—that there were so many great sports stories from 1985 forward. ESPN had come into the space and done the Fab Five with Jalen Rose, and their Bo Jackson *30 for 30*. ESPN was going to take over that space and HBO Sports didn't see that was happening. In essence, ESPN did to HBO Sports what Netflix later did to HBO.

RICK BERNSTEIN:

I could see the handwriting on the wall that Ross's days were numbered. Ross was not only my boss, but he was like a brother to me. I could tell by his demeanor and how frequently his office door was closed that this was coming. We would occasionally walk to the train together and I would say to him, "Ross, you can talk to me about this." And he would say, "Thanks, Rick, but I can't talk about it." Sadly, I knew the end was in sight.

BOB ARUM:

It ended up that we went back to HBO with Pacquiao and the rest of our stable and within months Greenburg was gone and they put in [Ken] Hershman.

RICK BERNSTEIN:

Word leaked out that Ross was being let go. Sadly, Ross never really had the opportunity to properly say goodbye to his staff as he probably would have preferred. Rather hastily and informally, he gathered the entire staff in our small reception area and told everyone that he was leaving. For many of us, it was surreal. I don't believe that Ross spoke for more than a couple of minutes. He was a little emotional, who wouldn't be, considering how many years he had been at HBO and the legacy he had built. Everyone shaken up. Ross has always been a very caring boss and a wonderful human being.

ROSS GREENBURG:

Look, I love to believe that I had something to do with keeping the sport alive from 2000 to 2011 because even in 2000 there were some signs that the sport wasn't what it was, but there were still some significant stars out there to tap into.

I think I lived through some pretty heady days at HBO Sports, from the time I got there to the time I left. We haven't seen those days since, I can say that.

I put thirty-three years into the company. It just didn't feel like a very professional way to go out. I was treated really badly. All kinds of rumors were flying, and it was not the way I wanted things to end at HBO. It was very sad. I think the people who worked for me were sad at the way it ended. All I did was try to keep my head high and act as professionally as I could. That was obviously the most difficult time in my career. It was very, very tough.

It wasn't as if Larry Merchant gave boxers a free hit—there were times when viewers wondered if he'd get out of the ring alive, or at least conscious. Perhaps his most famous moment, mano a mano, occurred during a 2011 interview with Floyd Mayweather, who had ignored Victor Ortiz's offer of a glove-shake apology for a headbutt by punching him twice in the face and knocking him out. Merchant could barely suppress his horror; the subsequent interview veered from Mayweather thanking God to profanely asking HBO to fire Merchant for not "giving me a fair shake . . . you don't know shit about boxing." Mayweather had already begun to feel that HBO wasn't spreading a sufficient number of rose petals at his feet, but the truth was that Mayweather wasn't quite the living legend he thought he was; he tended mainly to fight guys on their way down; Ortiz, however, was just twenty-four years old.

Merchant, after mugging for the camera, reacted to Mayweather's final slur—"you ain't shit"—by putting his hand on the boxer's shoulder and shouting, "I wish I was fifty years younger, and I'd kick your ass." (Merchant was five months shy of his eighty-first birthday at the time.) With anybody else, such an aggressive loss of journalistic integrity might have meant a firing; as it turned out, Merchant just giggled as he turned away—knowing, perhaps, that he'd just delivered a TKO, not to mention priceless headlines for HBO's ongoing boxing broadcasts. The moment indeed went viral, before "viral" was even a thing.

A few weeks later, at a fight in Las Vegas, Mayweather apologized to Larry Merchant.

LARRY MERCHANT:

Now, in fairness, he had a similar relationship to a lot of journalists, print and otherwise, who had challenged his credentials. He was recognized as an excellent boxer by everyone, but he had been very clever in his match-making to get to the position he was in, which he exploited beyond the maximum. It was a spontaneous counterpunch by me. I don't know where it came from. And for obvious reasons because he had built his image and his appeal by creating a bad boy side of him, very cleverly, using the various communications available to him at the time. He had gone to jail over the summer because of hitting a woman. And he was very defensive about all of this stuff because that was the context of how he was seen. That unconscious remark I made set the world on fire for twenty seconds. By the time I got out of the building, out of the arena, they were selling T-shirts, MERCHANT VERSUS MAYWEATHER.

BOB ARUM:

Larry Merchant was a Brooklyn guy. I would call him a putz and all that sorta stuff. But I always respected him because he said what he did. Larry was saying things that he believed and he felt that that was his job. I didn't believe that he had any agenda in saying that. The guys you hate are the ones who have an agenda, and who attack you as part of that agenda. But I didn't believe Merchant had any agenda other than to speak the truth.

Ken Hershman had started at Showtime in 1992 and moved into a senior program-ming role there in 2001, becoming executive president and general manager of sports and events programming in 2003, remaining there until HBO stole him away to help "rebuild" the boxing franchise.

RICK BERNSTEIN:

After Ross left, Mike Lombardo communicated to me that many of our documentaries looked the same, sounded the same, and felt old, mean-ing that too many featured historic sports icons and/or great moments in sports. Mike made the decision that going forward, we would have an open-door policy for any filmmaker to bring us their best ideas and their best work. I wouldn't say the door was closed in the past, but we had our own documentary unit, which produced our annual allotment of approx-imately four films per year. So there were few, if any, opportunities for outside filmmakers to bring their work to HBO Sports. Once Lombardo made this decision, our docu group became obsolete. Mind you, we had established ourselves as the best documentarians in sports. I therefore had to terminate the nine or ten individuals who comprised this division. They were not only good friends, but they were also recognized as some of the best documentarians, not just in sports, but in all of television. We were the envy of the sports television industry and just like that, we threw it all away. This was extremely troubling for the entire sports department and would mark the first among many nails in a coffin that would ulti-mately signify the death of the HBO Sports department. Once considered the standard-bearers of sports TV, we would soon become the pallbearers for our own funeral.

NICK KHAN:

Once Ross Greenburg had been let go, over the course of time Ken Hershman had been brought in and HBO Sports made the decision to not be in business with Al Haymon, which I and others saw as a mistake. Telling one of your biggest content suppliers, "We're not going to take your content," would be akin to a network saying, "Hey, CAA," or "Hey Endeavor, we're not going to do business with one of you." That was the falling-off-the-cliff moment for HBO Boxing.

LARRY MERCHANT:

First thing Ken said to me when I came on board was that he'd like me to lighten up on Mayweather because they were trying to negotiate a contract that was worth millions of dollars and so on and so forth. And then we had a disagreement that I knew would lead to the end, over a Julio César Chávez fight in El Paso. There were drug cartel people working both sides of the river, in Juárez and El Paso. And they had some interest in boxing. And he was afraid that it could be some kind of a government explosive situation at the fight. One of their attempts to diffuse it was they were not going to sell beer at the fight. To me, covering the boxing beat and being as interested in what happens outside of the ring as inside the ring—that was a story. Hershman didn't want me to tell it. I just shrugged to myself and said, "You know what? I didn't get to this place by listening to people tell me what not to cover." And I told the story anyway. Afterward, they started talking to me about my separation.

I'm not going to say I resigned. They fired me. They pushed me out. Was I okay with that? I thought, If I could no longer be myself, the person they hired, then what was the point?

HBO treated me well for a long time, and I appreciated all of it. Then things started to change. That was Hershman, the beginning of the end.

EZRA EDELMAN:

Sports of the 20th Century was the brainchild and the baby of Ross. When Ross was no longer there, there might not have been that same firewall to protect this thing.

It all started to come apart. That's just the reality. So was I in touch with this notion of, was there an iceberg on the horizon? No, because that wasn't my job. I didn't think that way. I was aware only of my own creative frustrations.

Merchant's was not the only departure to follow Greenburg's. In August 2012, Ezra Edelman left HBO to join ESPN's burgeoning documentary department.

EZRA EDELMAN:

I left because there was nothing for me to do there. In September 2012, we were invited back to a meeting with Rick, and he said, "So, we're not doing documentaries anymore." And I was like, "Oh, well, what does that mean?" The option given to me was, "Hey, you can go back and work on *Real Sports*, but there's nothing else for you to do here."

I wasn't going to do that. In documentaries, you made a film but it was regarded as a film being made by HBO Sports, not the filmmaker. If you were so lucky to win an award, you got to go up onstage and take the award, but that was about it. Sometimes you felt like you were subsumed in that process of blood, sweat, and tears, but then sometimes that translated into the glory of others. That was a frustrating thing.

It was a time where I had reached my creative limit, conveniently at a time that I needed to leave. I didn't know that if I had the wherewithal based on my life experience to just walk out the door because the door and whatever was on the other side of it were completely foreign to me.

Bryant Gumbel has been known to keep a list of those he wanted as pallbearers at his funeral, the notion being it could change from time to time, further suggesting there isn't a great deal of margin for error on Planet Gumbel. Another example of Gumbel's exacting nature surfaced in 2012, when Kirby Bradley, executive producer of Gumbel's **Real Sports,** *was replaced by Joe Perskie—without Gumbel's say-so. Gumbel was livid. Even though the decision was ultimately Ken Hershman's, Gumbel came to believe that Rick Bernstein was also behind the move. The* **Real Sports** *staff is hardly a giant one: HBO Sports at that time had only 125 employees, and fewer than 30 worked for* **Real Sports.** *It was rather noticeable when Gumbel voted Bernstein off the island. As in: Cut. Him. Out.*

Soon, Bernstein, who denied targeting Bradley, was no longer seen on the set or in the control room; at social occasions, Gumbel persistently snubbed him. Gumbel, throughout, maintained a loyalty to Bradley that was extraordinary, and that also spoke to the fact that HBO was the perfect place for Gumbel. He enjoyed a wide swath of freedom, on air and off—even by HBO standards.

BRYANT GUMBEL, Host:

Since television productions are both collaborative and subjective, a certain amount of tension is ever present. While an outsider may view the frequent heated arguments and disagreements as "difficult," the participants most often see them as simply part of the process. The most truly difficult moment I can recall was getting a phone call from my lead producer, Kirby Bradley, telling me that he'd just been removed from his position by HBO's newly named head of sports, Ken Hershman . . . who had acted without my consultation and clearly without my consent. I was, as you might expect, furious. But since he'd already elevated a highly valued member of my staff as his replacement, I was hamstrung, unable to reverse the decision without undercutting the newly named lead producer and causing divisions within the ranks. Predictably, I went batshit, went over Ken's head and got Kirby rehired in a different role . . . but the damage was done. In truth I grew to like Ken, who apologized profusely and tried hard to mend the relationship, but the die was cast . . . and within a year or so, he was replaced.

JOE PERSKIE, Executive Producer:

Ken Hershman told me that there was going to be a change and that I was going to be assuming leadership of the show. The circumstances that happened behind the scenes that led up to that, I was not privy to.

The show was already seventeen years old when I got the job, and I always say that TV years are like dog years, so I thought it was the right time to step back and ask, "What can we do to make this show as fresh and as relevant as possible?" On top of that, *60 Minutes* had just come out and said they were going to do a sports version of the show on Showtime, and that was going to compete directly with us. This was when Showtime was still our main rival, before Netflix really became Netflix. So we wanted to be on top of our game. We said, "Let's look at everything we're doing. Let's look at the types of stories we tell. Let's look at who's telling the stories. Let's look at the set. Let's look at the music. Let's look at the graphics. Let's look at how we're getting the word out online." And we made changes up and down the line, and in a lot of ways we haven't stopped. You have to keep evolving.

MIKE LOMBARDO:

My husband and I have always been fairly engaged in politics and supported various Democratic candidates over the years. We had been very supportive of Obama when he ran for election, and like a lot of gay people, we were waiting for action on what I'll call issues that were important to the LGBTQ community. He had been slow to do anything—either issue an executive order for federal contractors to protect LGBT employees, and continued to be very ambivalent, saying he was still evolving on issues of gay marriage.

As he was embarking on his reelection campaign, I got a call from the head of the Human Rights Campaign, asking if we would host Vice President Biden, who wanted to talk to a room full of lesbian, gay, and queer-identified executives in the media business. We were obviously honored, and hosted about sixty individuals, not as a fundraiser, but more to have an honest conversation with the vice president.

And at that point, my son must've been six, my daughter was eight, and the vice president of the United States was at our house. We had had senators, but this was a bigger deal. My kids were in the living room, excited, and they ran up to get a picture. Then while everyone else is waiting for the program to begin, Joe sits down with my kids in the kitchen and has a conversation with my kids, my husband, and myself. He connected with us on a very personal level while everyone else was waiting. We then went into the living room where people started asking him questions.

At one point someone asked him what his thoughts were about gay marriage. He paused, then said something like, "Look, I'm not the president. I don't make policy. But when I see a family like I just saw in the kitchen, and I see the love that those kids have for Sonny and Mike and the love Mike and Sonny have for their kids, I'm hard pressed to not feel like that's as valuable a family as any other family. So if it were up to me, I don't see why we shouldn't be valuing those relationships." And there was an "Oh my God" that went through the living room. The following week Joe was on *Meet the Press* and, after being asked about gay marriage, without naming us, told the story about meeting this family with two men, and seeing the love and warmth that the family felt for each other. And he said, "I think it's time." He was out ahead of the Obama administration by saying that, but he spoke the truth. Shortly thereafter Obama and the administration came out fully supporting gay marriage. We met with Joe several times in the coming years, and when he was running for president in 2020, he came back to our house for an event, and this time our daughter, who was now seventeen, introduced him to the crowd.

Since the 2007 "crazy night in Las Vegas" that led to the end of Chris Albrecht's days at HBO, the company had forsaken comedy and been solely in the drama business. Internally that is.

Yes, a strong case could have been made that Bill Nelson's lack of ego and his military approach to the job had made the office of CEO uneventful and predictable. But beneath him, a different story was being written. HBO's departure gate had been busy: Hal Akselrad, Dave Baldwin, Kirby Bradley, Colin Callender, Shelley Fischel, Nancy Geller, Ross Greenburg, Larry Merchant, Carolyn Strauss, and Carmi Zlotnik—among others—all had boarded for parts unknown, and new faces had been filing in.

Given the ongoing turf battles, meanwhile, and the taking of sides in programming, the place began to resemble a middle-school cafeteria.

What next? The answer arrived on September 20, 2012, when the company announced that Nelson was retiring and that Richard Plepler would take over as new CEO on January 1, 2013. Meanwhile, Eric Kessler would be promoted to COO and president. The company's press release also mentioned that Mike Lombardo would stay put as president of programming.

BILL NELSON:

I went up to Jeff and told him I was going to retire. I was coming up on sixty-five and I always felt by the time you're eighty, you're not in the shape to carry on physically as you would like. And so I said, "Well, fifteen years and that's where I'm at and I want to enjoy the fruits of my labor and spend more time with my family and all of that," which is why I left. I said this to Jeff: "Jeff, this is a perfect moment for me to leave. We've got momentum. We've got strength. We've got the team."

Then Jeff and I had a conversation about who would take my place. Eric wanted to be CEO when I left, but I truly believed Richard should have the job. So did Jeff. I said to Eric, "You are extremely talented. You've done amazing stuff for the company, we decided that you will be COO. Which means here's what you have responsibility for," which was extremely significant. "You're the next in line. We need Richard's Hollywood connections, the programming, the face of the company." I said, "I've held both positions, I've been COO and CEO. The difference in compensation isn't that much. So let me tell you this, you'll have more fun in the second seat than the first seat. And it suits the organization at this moment. So please hang in there. This is the right thing to happen."

I left January 1, 2013. I felt that Netflix was gaining ground and that more things will evolve over the top. Amazon was out there, starting to do Prime. We had stopped licensing our off-HBO programming to any direct-to-consumer programming services. We never licensed to Netflix. We had a board member say to me in a meeting, "You can get revenue up by licensing to Netflix." And I was like, "Yeah. So now Netflix has HBO programming? You want to confuse the consumer?" The challenge was like 80 percent of our revenue coming from the cable, satellite distributors, telcos, and now we're going to jump them and go direct to the consumer. That needs a thoughtful transition. And all of that was in the midst of when I left.

ERIC KESSLER:

Right after the Labor Day weekend, Bill called me in to his office very early in the morning and told me he was leaving. I was surprised at the time, but in looking back Jeff probably had a plan to turn over all of the divisions at the same time to a new generation of leaders. Bill was smart, a capable leader, a really decent person, and didn't take shit from distributors. Bill told me the plan was to make Richard CEO and I would be president and COO.

Jeff invited me up the next day to talk. I thanked him, told him I was excited, but I asked if he considered putting me in the CEO role. He said, "Absolutely, but I'm doing it this way for two reasons. First, you won't have to—and you don't want to—deal with all that pretentious Hollywood bullshit. Richard likes it and he is good at it. Second, the board likes this structure because it lets Richard concentrate on the programming while you are there to run the business."

SHEILA NEVINS:

Richard is a very interesting character. He's very smart about corporate politics. He's also a terrible hypochondriac. If you have a cold, you sit in the doorway.

A couple of months before Bill Nelson was going to retire, I went down to see Richard about something. There was no assistant there, so I sat outside his office and waited. Then I knocked on the door, and there was no answer. I walked down the hall, and asked, "Where's Richard?" She said, "He moved down the hall, to Bill's office." The body was barely cold.

RICHARD PLEPLER:

Obviously, when Bill told me he was going to retire and that I was to be the new CEO I immediately understood the myriad challenges that we were confronting. We were essentially out of runway on price increases. There was obviously enormous competition. It was clear that Netflix was a quintessential disruptor and their ability to outspend everyone made for a very different competitive environment than the one we had known in preceding years. I also knew that we had the best team in the business. I remember pulling everyone together, literally and figuratively rolling up our sleeves, and making the best decisions we could on pricing strategy, distribution, building a digital business, expanding our theatrical slate, and keeping the momentum on our creative output. Daunting challenges indeed but the team, as always, rose to the occasion and I think the proof was in the pudding.

When I became CEO, Hank Paulson called me and said to me, "Let me give you one piece of advice. You see yourself as the same person. Other people will now look at you differently. And the important thing to remember, Richard, is just be you. Because the very things that brought you here are the things that you will need to do the job." It was one of the best pieces of advice.

MIKE LOMBARDO:

When Richard was co-president, I thought of us as partners. I knew how much he wanted to be CEO, and the plan was for me to do everything I could to make that happen for him. Richard told me, "I'm going to get you a big deal." As a lower-middle-class kid, that was heavy. I stupidly thought that when he got to be CEO, that was going to be something good for me. When he became CEO, my deal was up, and I went to him and said, "Can I get a new title?" He said, "Why would I do that?" I was stunned. His answer was like, "Are you out of your fucking mind?" And I thought, Wow. This was stupid of me. I thought we were working on something together. It became so clear I was wrong once he ascended.

Companies, all too obviously, are not always meritocracies. Yet few employees choose to apply the same energy and strategies to their own careers as they do on behalf of their employers'; even fewer do so for their own images. Being able to do so, and do so ruthlessly, is considered a rare, if occasionally frowned-upon, talent.

Richard Plepler had arrived at HBO in 1992, was unstrapped from the corporate electric chair by Jeff Bewkes when the powers that be wanted him fired in 1995, and was now, eighteen years later, about to begin serving as CEO.

No one—Plepler included—would ever claim that he was a financial genius, a whiz who understood intricacies of the distribution business, or a techie capable of seizing on opportunities ahead of others. And, despite his six years running programming, people inside that department didn't look to him for great insights on a script or solutions to a show's problems. He was a thirty-thousand-foot-view guy with material and rarely pretended to be anything else.

So what was Plepler's outstanding asset? What had brought him to the big chair? Probably his deep roots in communications, a rarity in the entertainment business. When Plepler worked for Michael Fuchs, he was the man behind the man who wanted to be the voice of HBO. Since then, Plepler had been blessed by the fact that a trio of CEOs—Bewkes, Nelson, and Albrecht (particularly Nelson)—all had more interest in the work than the message about the work. As a result, Plepler became the person, as Albrecht had said, "to spin the tale." He single-handedly became both the architect and protector of the HBO "brand" (one of his favorite words). Along the way, he curated not only a pedigree for the network (aided obviously by its success) but also for himself.

Plepler, above all, did an exceedingly skilled job at managing "Richard Plepler, the brand." His social life was filled with bold-faced names; his membership at the Council on *Foreign Relations* was a topic in many a conversation; he was extremely comfy at the "best tables" at the Lambs Club and other top haunts; and he enjoyed entertaining other power players at both his Upper East Side apartment and his spacious home in Greenwich.

Was there another media company that had so skilled a public ambassador as HBO had in Plepler? In two words, fuck no.

Plepler's many years at the company had brought him to the pinnacle, indeed, but the work he had done over the years for HBO paled in comparison to the work that he had done for, yes, himself.

13

Eastern Apotheosis

JANUARY 1, 2013–OCTOBER 28, 2014

JON ALPERT:

I was waiting by the hearse's door for the casket to come out, waiting and waiting. All of a sudden, I hear this swoosh, look up, and see an eagle flying in a big circle, then coming down to land on the church roof, right above the hearse. It just sat there and looked down on us. Then they bring the casket out, carry it into the hearse, and close the door. As the hearse drives away, the eagle flaps its huge wings and flies right over the back of the hearse, accompanying it out of the parking lot. After a few minutes, it then bolted into the sky.

I've seen a lot of extraordinary moments, all over the world, and I'm not a very metaphysical or religious person, but there was something going on with the cosmos that day, and that eagle was there to tell me about it.

SHEILA NEVINS:

We went to Walter Reed together for *Alive Day Memories*. Jim was the big, big, big celebrity. Everybody was starstruck. We went through these rooms with terribly injured soldiers. It was all very difficult, but Jim was great with everyone. He signed people's casts. Everybody knew the show; no one referred to him as Jim; they all referred to him as Tony.

In this one room, there was a woman sitting by a bed of a heavily bandaged young man. The woman said, "Oh, my son loves you." She closed her Bible, and she said, "He's in a coma, but please talk to him. Maybe you can help him get better." Jim starts talking to him, like Jim. He says, "You fought for our country, you're a great guy, and I'm very proud of you."

She said, "No, not that voice, your real voice." He knew what she meant and started talking to him like Tony. He instantly changes into Tony Soprano and says, "You got to get out of this bed, and show your mother a thing or two. Just because you went over there and fought for your country doesn't mean you can make your mother cry."

Then she asks him to sign her Bible. He signs it "Jim Gandolfini." She says, "No, not him. Not him." Now he signs it "Tony Soprano." He's willing to do anything for this kid and his mom. We walk out of the room, and he rushes ahead of me through a door marked LAUNDRY ROOM. When I get there, he's got his head buried in folded laundry, and he's sobbing like a baby.

MICHAEL IMPERIOLI:

We went to some dark places as characters on the show, very emotional places. We trusted each other and had each other's backs. We also had a lot of fun, a lot of laughs. I acted with Jim more than I've acted with any other actor in my career, probably more than I ever will with another actor. And for that, I'm really grateful.

TONY KUSHNER:

At the end of Emmy night 2004, around two a.m., Mark [Harris] and I went back to our hotel where Gandolfini was standing in front, along with some other people from the cast. He said, "We're going out for a hamburger. Do you want to join us?" I was too intimidated and felt awkward. I said, "I can't, but thanks." And I bitterly regret that because I adored him.

I had been on a plane with him—my dog rode under his seat—the year that *Lincoln* was made, and he was in *Zero Dark Thirty.* As soon as the plane landed, they announced the Oscar nominations. James grabbed my head and gave me a big kiss right on the mouth. I was in heaven.

If there was one universally acceptable candidate who could be considered the Face of HBO, it would have to be James Gandolfini, who remained prominent in memory even after his inimitable Tony and the rest of **The Sopranos** *went off the air.*

In June 2013, Gandolfini brought Michael, his thirteen-year-old son, to Italy (where else?) to celebrate the young man's graduation from junior high school. On the morning of the nineteenth, the two explored the Vatican, where a tourist snapped a photo of James as he visited the Egyptian Gallery and the Book of the Dead. That night, father and son ended the day with dinner at the hotel's open-air Boscolo Exedra Roma. But a day of elation turned into a night of tragedy. Gandolfini collapsed in the bathroom of the suite and was discovered there by his son. A call for emergency service went out at nine p.m., and less than eight minutes later, Gandolfini was being rushed to the hospital.

At ten forty p.m., Italian time, James Joseph Gandolfini Jr. was pronounced dead.

MARA MIKIALIAN:

New York was already closed. Every single phone lit up in our LA office. Our colleague Angela Tarantino was one of the first to learn of Jim's passing. She started working with Jim on *The Sopranos* and never stopped. She was also close with his family and on that night, as well as over the course of the next several days, her focus remained on them. So by default, I became very involved.

The entire situation was unprecedented. Somebody had tried to sneak into his hotel room that night, so we contacted a producer we worked with in Rome, who brought on a whole security team.

HBO confirmed Gandolfini's death that evening with a statement: "We're all in shock and feeling immeasurable sadness at the loss of a beloved member of our family. He was a special man, a great talent, but more importantly a gentle and loving person who treated everyone no matter their title or position with equal respect. He touched so many of us over the years with his humor, his warmth, and his humility. Our hearts go out to his wife and children during this terrible time. He will be deeply missed by all of us."

That night, HBO aired the **Sopranos** *episode titled, "Where's Johnny?" followed by the on-screen message: "HBO mourns the loss of James Gandolfini, a beloved member of the HBO family."*

Secretary of State John Kerry coordinated with the US embassy in Rome and Italian authorities to ensure Gandolfini's repatriation was accomplished as quickly as possible.

MARA MIKIALIAN:

When his body was being transferred to the airport, we used a dummy vehicle that went in a different direction than the actual one. There were so many rumors and concerns; everyone was relieved when the coffin made it safely on to the plane.

A private jet returned James Gandolfini stateside Sunday evening. The next day, New Jersey governor Chris Christie ordered all flags at state buildings to fly at half-staff in Gandolfini's honor.

Six months later, HBO released **James Gandolfini: Tribute to a Friend**, *featuring interviews with the cast of* **The Sopranos** *discussing their relationships with the late leading man.*

QUENTIN SCHAFFER:

Jim's funeral at St. John the Divine in New York City was like a scene right out of *The Sopranos* or *The Godfather*. Two thousand people gathered to mourn. The PR department was in mourning, too. We had all loved Jim, particularly Angela [Tarantino], so it was far from easy, but we were determined to handle all the logistics, from invitations to ground transportation to staffing. And we did it very quickly.

HBO had reigned supreme for more than a decade's worth of awards seasons, yet on Thursday, July 18, 2013, the landscape began to shift. On the back of its first wildly successful original series, the political drama **House of Cards**, *Netflix received the first Emmy nominations ever given to a television show that was only available online. Two months later, in September 2013, the upstart online streaming service would break more new ground, winning its first Emmy ever for David Fincher and his direction of* **House of Cards**.

LAURA DERN:

I had a female journalist interview me right after the first season, and I was so excited to meet with a female journalist to talk about Amy Jellicoe, but the first thing she asked me was, "God, how can you feel comfortable looking so, like, ugly or angry on your poster?" I said, "Wow, it's so interesting that you call anger 'ugly.' That's a paradigm shift, isn't it? To allow a female lead to be so rage filled and have it be funny and complicated—but not ugly. Is Tony Soprano ugly? Is Larry David ugly? *Curb* and *The Sopranos* were on HBO when we started and no one was saying, 'He's not likable.'"

Nothing was easy for anyone who was connected to **Enlightened** *in any way. As disturbing as the dynamic between Lombardo and Naegle was, to add the difficult dynamic between Dern and White proved unmanageable. Even minor casting decisions became points of conflict between the two.*

HBO was doing an incredibly poor job of figuring out what happens when an A-level bona fide movie star like Dern co-creates a show with a talented showrunner like Mike White and the two aren't in harmony.

SUE NAEGLE:

They would peck at each other and complain about each other. I didn't want to be in the middle of it because I had known Mike for so long. I'd been his agent, and thought he was incredibly talented. He was also my very good friend.

MIKE LOMBARDO:

Sue would do an agent thing where she would tell Laura, "You're right, you're right," then go to Mike and say the same exact thing. It got combustible.

Eventually, Alexander Payne, who had met Casey Bloys on **Hung**, *suggested to Dern that Bloys be brought in to help things along, but White was in no mood for Bloys's attempts to "get a win for Laura." It was said that White spent more time hanging up on Bloys than on anyone else, ever. (The relationship got better. In 2021, Bloys gave the green light to White's* **The White Lotus**, *which was shot in Hawaii during the pandemic.)*

LAURA DERN:

Casey Bloys became our executive on the second season, and was a huge, fierce champion of the show, and a protector of Amy herself.

At one point, HBO sat Dern and White down together and said, "There's no show without either one of you. Laura, you can't do this show without Mike, and Mike you can't do this show without Laura." It was the most honest statement to come from the network during the entire ordeal. It also led to the show being canceled after two seasons.

LAURA DERN:

In a career that started when I was eleven, *Enlightened* is the only challenging experience I have ever had. Mike and I were the co-creators and the executive producers. It was a really hard show to do.

It was a radical time. We were often working eighteen-hour days. I was trying to make Mike's perfect words and vision work. He captured a world so beautifully, but when I tried to articulate that, it took everything to make it felt. The way she would drive a car, or buy a coffee, or approach people, or what she would wear, or how she would present herself, or drink a soda. Every detail meant so much.

I personally had to rip my heart out every day to play Amy. That meant having her somehow hated and absolutely adored at the same time. Playing Amy, there were times I would be sobbing hysterically, having nervous breakdowns, rolling down a hill and doing a pratfall, then coming back to do a four-page rant. For the comedy to work, we had to find a delicate, difficult tone. The only way to make it real was for me to be incredibly heartbroken, incredibly raw, and incredibly vulnerable. It was very tricky. I couldn't just fake it.

And let me just say for the record that if my wanting a show that I co-created and was producing alongside Mike, with a character I truly loved, to be honest, perfect, and honor Mike's brilliant words, ever made me seem quote difficult, then I would wear that word with pride. Culturally, it was also a time where exercising my titles beyond "actress" felt like an obstacle course. I hope to say we've all grown more comfortable with women balancing multiple titles on set.

I'm sad we didn't do a third season because I think that it could have been much easier. We could have found a rhythm and an easier way of working together.

White felt he'd set out to make a cool, unique show with somebody he considered a friend; that certainly didn't happen, and he walked away from **Enlightened** *smarting.*

MIKE WHITE:

I'm okay that we didn't do another season. I have closure. The truth is that it did change my whole attitude about work. It made me realize that my personal mental health was more important than my work. It's made me wonder, Am I really cut out to fight those kinds of fights?

LAURA DERN:

Eight weeks after we were canceled, *Time* magazine rated their top ten shows of the year and *Enlightened* and *Breaking Bad* were one and two. And then TiVo numbers came out that showed even more people were watching our show, and there was a piece about favorite characters in television, and number one was Amy Jellicoe. Mike and I were devastated.

I believe our show is more timely than ever, and I think Amy is a vital character for this moment in our culture. *Enlightened* would be such an appropriately topical show today, without a doubt. It's exciting to see how many people are discovering it, or are watching it over again. We were so lucky.

Time magazine was not the only publication to laud the work of Dern and White. An LA Times ranking of the twenty-first-century's top one hundred moments in pop culture named Enlightened number two in its ranking, behind only Beyoncé's legendary Coachella concert in 2018. That is ahead of Hamilton, Breaking Bad, Game of Thrones, the finales of The Sopranos and The Wire, and, yes, the advent of the iPod. "Though it was canceled after two seasons," the Times says, "Enlightened was a prescient series, tapping into the power of female rage years before it became a prevalent cultural and political force."

SUE NAEGLE:

Ryan Murphy turned in a script. Casey and I got it and said to each other, "This is not great. This needs a lot of work." The next morning I walked in and said to Mike, "Can we talk about the script?" And he said, "I've already picked it up." I thought, "Okay, what?" I said to him, "The thing with Ryan is if you need him or want him to do any work on a script, you have to ask him to do that before you pick it up, because he's not going to change a word after this." And that's exactly what happened. The pilot didn't get picked up to series.

This is how I worked with Mike Lombardo. I loved my job so much that I was almost willing to put up with anything from Mike, which in a lot of ways I regret.

Every time he came to sit on my bench, I made room for him. I made so much room that I fell off my own bench.

I would say to him, "What we do is we hear the pitch and then we say, Let us talk about it. Thank you so much. This was great. And then we come back with an answer." Because if not, we're stuck with this development that we never should have bought. Billy Ray came in to sell *Last Tycoon* to us. That was not going to be a good HBO show. The pitch had issues. Billy Ray's a great writer, but there's moments like that where Mike just couldn't wait to say yes.

I tried to explain to Mike over and over that the writer's not going to feel great seven months later when the project is not gaining momentum, because it's not a show that's going to end up working for us. I would argue that saying no is a kindness. You don't need to waste anyone's time if you hear the pitch and you don't think it's right.

MIKE LOMBARDO:

Sue made the mistake of going to Richard all the time in New York. That's a risky proposition, because he was sitting there in judgment. He would tell me how she came in and she "tucked her legs up." He didn't think she was deep enough, intellectual enough, HBO enough, whatever. And to be totally honest, I was always thinking, "You're not Carolyn." It was still like dating a woman you aren't in love with. She wasn't the one.

SUE NAEGLE:

I never was able to get a show on the air written by a woman or run by a woman except for *Girls* the entire time I was there. I wanted *The Affair*. It was a disastrous meeting. Disastrous.

Sarah Treem came in and she was talking about *The Affair* and Rick Rosen was there. Sarah starts talking about, "The character has this affair," and Mike, for whatever reason, was just like, "That's immoral. Why would we do a show about infidelity? That's disgusting. What woman would put herself in that position?" Rick just stops and says, "Mike, the most success-ful show in the history of the network is about a gangster adulterer, mur-derer, mafia boss. What are you talking about?" I saw her leave the room shaking, and asked her, "Are you okay?"

MIKE LOMBARDO:

I didn't have an answer for Sue. I didn't have a backup plan. We were doing well, people were watching shows. We were getting back in the awards. But I had the head of HR coming in, the head of business affairs coming in and saying, "We don't like her, we don't trust her." And so for me, that was it. She lied to me. She was good at it. She was an agent.

SUE NAEGLE:

Spending time thinking about office politics is wasted to me. I'd rather be spending time reading scripts.

And then she was gone.

After five years at the helm, in September 2013, Sue Naegle's time was up as head of HBO Entertainment. Richard Plepler had ordered Mike Lombardo to do it, but it wasn't as if Lombardo didn't want her gone as well. What had started five years earlier as the post–Chris Albrecht, post–Carolyn Strauss era had morphed into a dysfunctional situ-ation between Lombardo and Naegle, one that only worsened as time went on.

The grand irony was that Lombardo had hired Naegle because she had been the choice of Strauss, the person Lombardo probably respected more than any other at HBO, and the person who he'd been forced to fire. So Naegle's Strauss mark of approval had gotten her hired, but that turned into a target on her back after she had settled in. When Lombardo started comparing her to Strauss, that was a contest Naegle was destined to lose.

The other irony is that Lombardo had very much liked the idea of hiring Naegle, a woman, to replace Strauss, but then wound up being so estranged from her that he turned to Ellenberg, a man.

Ultimately it all came back to that first missed opportunity of meeting between Lombardo and Plepler. Nothing had changed. Lombardo still wanted to be the creative guy, and Lombardo still wanted to be in charge.

SUE NAEGLE:

I loved that job so much. I tried so hard to take less and less in terms of credit or complicity. There was a period of time where they told me I shouldn't talk to the press anymore. I had a very hard time understanding why. I thought so much about the many times that I made myself smaller to make him feel better.

In July, I was on vacation with my family in Montana and my ex-partner from UTA, Jay, called me and said, "There's a rumor that Mike's firing you." I said, "What?" I called Mike and said, "Jay just called me and said this to me. Is it true?" He said, "I don't know what you're talking about. Why are you even calling me? No, enjoy your vacation. Don't be crazy. Enjoy your vacation." And so I said, "Okay."

Then I got back and a week or so later, Mike and I had a meeting. He said, "When you called me, it really wasn't a thing, but I had a chance to think about it. And I want you to know that we're not going to extend your contract." It took me a minute to realize I was getting fired.

He said, "Do you think things are working out?" I said, "No, you don't seem to want to let me do my job, I feel like you're second-guessing everything. Either you let me do my job and get out of my backyard, or just tell me you want to do my job." And he said, "I want to do your job." I said, "Okay, okay. So let's figure it out." It wasn't acrimonious. I was so depleted at that point. My worst fear had been placed right in front of me. I went to New York and asked for a meeting with Richard. I sat in this office, and was thinking to myself, I just need him to look at me and say, "You got fucked, I'm sorry." And I sat in that office for two and a half hours and all he said to me was, "Who knew that Mike was going to be so good at the job, and knew

Mike had all these creative instincts?" And, "You've just become redundant." And, "There's just too many people at the top."

RICHARD PLEPLER:

When we hired Sue, I think she saw herself as the LA point person. We probably underestimated that it was a confusing message to the town as Mike was head of programming based in LA.

Sue worked hard and did her best in the time she was at HBO. At the end of the day we learned that we didn't need two people in the same job. We already had a head of programming. And that was Mike.

SUE NAEGLE:

Obviously I knew Richard was a part of it. For all of Mike's very human frailties, he also has very deep feelings. Mike is an incredible father, he's very sensitive, fights for the underdog . . . there are a lot of amazing qualities about Mike. Richard I don't think works that way. I thought to myself, If he just looks at me and says, "I'm so sorry, I'm sorry this happened, you did a great job," I would've been fine. I would have said, "Thank you, and thank you for understanding." But the fact that he gaslit me the entire meeting, telling me how great Mike was at the job. I think at one point I said to him, "It's very tense in LA, the office is really tense." Then I realized there's no point. He was not going to be responsive to that. After two and a half hours, I left thinking, Okay, fine.

We made the announcement I was leaving right after Emmy weekend. I was driving home and Richard called me and said, "This is really good for you because you've been working so hard and now you can spend time with your kids, and you'll never miss a dance recital again. And you'll be there for all their school plays." I laughed and I said, "Richard, I'm going to be a producer. Do you know what a producer does? It's very hard. I don't know if I'm going to be at any more dance recitals." And he said, "Well, it's like what Anne-Marie Slaughter said about women, not being able to have it all."

I said, "I can't believe you're quoting Anne-Marie Slaughter to me right now. Can we please stop talking? I'll see you this weekend." I went home and called Mike and said, "What was that? Women can't have it all? That this is somehow my failing because I'm a mother leaving this job?" Then I said, "What's happening with the press? We should be coordinating the press." And he blew me off. I called Nancy Lesser, who was the head of publicity, and said, "Can we talk about this? Because we haven't talked about what the press release should say."

Nancy said, "Oh no, no, no, don't worry. We're all working on it." I spoke to Jay Sures, and he said to me, "They're going to fuck you. You've got to get in front of this. You've got to talk to the press now. You have to help control the narrative or they're going to write whatever they want." It was surreal. I spent the whole weekend being this ambassador for a company that had let me go for a variety of reasons I still didn't understand.

MIKE LOMBARDO:

The biggest problem was in not being able to know HBO without being inside HBO. Therein lay the problem. That's why it didn't work ultimately with Sue. HBO was more than just looking at *Sopranos* and understanding the kinds of bells we had to hit to make a show right for us. It was a culture, it was a way of interacting with people. Sue came from an agency background and I don't think she ever figured out how to work within the company and embrace the ethos that was HBO culturally. I think she has good taste. I think she's fierce in terms of recognizing talent and convincing them to work with her. I fear that wasn't enough. I suppose Carolyn and her skills cast a big shadow.

Here's the truth. I didn't mentor her. I saw what was happening, and I'm not saying she could have changed, but instead I sat back and kept thinking, "She's not Carolyn."

DAVID LEVINE:

I felt bad for Sue because she felt that Mike wanted to do her job. Richard taught Casey what Casey does best, what to touch and what not to, and Richard was very, very good about gently touching the creative. The key to those jobs is to never be blamed for anything if it went wrong. I would rather have the opportunity to truly work on something even if that meant being blamed for it if something went wrong.

KATHLEEN McCAFFREY:

She was never in the office. That really got to Mike. Mike is in the office, executives are in the office. Agents aren't necessarily in the office quite as much. Because you can do your whole business from the phone. But we're in in-person meetings all the time. Her absence was very noticeable and their offices were next to each other.

Everybody was aware of the dynamic. It was at that point that I started to pull away. There were a lot of times where she'd come out of a meeting with him in tears.

JENNI KONNER:

I was devastated. Sue was such an ally and there were great people after she left. I love Casey Bloys. I love Kathleen. They're wonderful to work for. But Sue gave me opportunities and supported me the entire time. And that's a hard thing to let go of.

SUE NAEGLE:

Before I came to HBO, I knew how to live in the woods for a month on my own, you have to know how to maneuver all different kinds of situations.

It makes people who work for you feel insecure and unsafe when their boss is having political issues with their boss. People want to have strong leadership structure. People want stability. The hard work of those jobs is about the creative. It is taking a script that's good and helping it become great or helping a creator who's never run a show before get the team they need to run the show correctly to make it successful.

KATHLEEN McCAFFREY:

I realized that I had to step away from her. It was hard to do. Because it was too much pressure for me and I wasn't doing a good job. I had to earn my relationships with Francesca, Amy, and Casey, and, at that time, Gina Balian. They were so important to me.

Personally, everything came to a head for her at once. It was hard to watch because I had seen her just fucking, excuse my language, just running it. Like at UTA, she was so comfortable. She was so confident. She was like an incredible maternal leader. And then at HBO she just lost her footing. She didn't totally know what the job was, which is not on her. She wasn't given the chance to learn as I was. But then Mike sort of wanted to do what she was doing and she just gave up.

SUE NAEGLE:

People would always say, "Agencies and agents are so terrible and they're so underhanded." That was never my experience of being an agent. That's not how I conducted my business. That wasn't the experience I had with my colleagues. I genuinely loved them. Agencies are like Italian or Jewish families: if there's a problem, they tell you they're upset with you and they shout it out. They're basically like, "You're an idiot. I love you." That's what agents are like. HBO is like an uptight WASPy family that tells you everything is wonderful. And then you realize you've been shivved.

DAVID LEVINE:

I thought Mike would give the job to Casey. Casey had started positioning himself for it a year early and his actions were very clear. Casey is a smart executive, and I knew that when he wanted something, he would get it.

Casey plays the game full-time. He is always hyperconscious of how things are going to look, what he needs to say and do. That's a full-time job for him. That's not for me.

I had learned a lot over the past four years, but I don't think I would have kept the department together because I had no support. I don't think I was great at that role, and Francesca Orsi grew into it.

On October 22, 2013, a month after Sue Naegle's departure, HBO moved to plug the gap she'd left behind. Michael Ellenberg and Casey Bloys were both promoted to executive vice presidents of programming.

To many inside the company, HBO was always an idea more than a corporation. It had developed a certain way of doing business and of treating people—it had created a brand that insiders did their best to live up to, an ethos that drove everything from relationships to programming. But those coming in from the outside didn't always seem to appreciate the subtleties of this rarefied HBO culture, as was the case with Ellenberg. The feature film world is a different animal altogether, a place where being a star and taking credit are seen as acceptable foibles. Not so at HBO; and the tension caused by outsiders arrogantly talking up their achievements was palpable, when perhaps the reaction was just a result of widespread insecurity due to the ever-shifting ebb and flow of power within the ranks. Either way, the rampant corporate in-fighting was not a good look inside the ethos-y HBO.

Just over a week after Naegle's departure, it was announced that another major figure at HBO would be leaving. The position of COO, held by Eric Kessler, had been "eliminated."

Kessler had been at HBO for twenty-seven years, but now Richard Plepler announced in a memo that the COO position "does not best serve the most effective management process." For some, this was a head-scratcher; indeed, the business acumen of the company was felt to decline dramatically after Kessler left. Many felt that not enough people appreciated or understood how important Kessler had been to HBO, especially as there wasn't anybody on the bench who had his breadth of experience in the areas with which he dealt.

The answer was that this was another example of a Shakespearian drama playing out within HBO. The bloodletting was gradual; there was no "Saturday Night Massacre." It was more like a slow death; first this one goes, then that one. What bound the survivors together was a perception that there were Richard Plepler people, and then there were the rest. To his ultimate detriment, Kessler wasn't a Plepler person (nor had Ross Greenburg been one, nor Carolyn Strauss). As one example of the in-crowdedness of it all: Every month Plepler held a fancy soirée in his Upper East Side town house. Nevins was never invited; nor were Greenburg or Kessler. Sometimes this oversight was about pedigree, or schooling, or the way people dressed or who they knew. But more often, the people who survived and were on the inside of Plepler's world were inextricably linked to the furtherance of Plepler's narrative. And then, one day, people looked up from their desks and realized that Greenburg, Naegle, Strauss, and now Kessler were all gone.

Bewkes didn't have "Bewkes people"; nor was he aware of a lot of Plepler's maneuverings. He had no idea, for example, that Plepler disliked Greenburg. Further, there was a perception that had Kessler gone to Bewkes to complain, Bewkes might well have told Plepler that Kessler had a problem with him. There was also the rat fuck that was Time Warner. Bewkes was dealing with major issues; HBO was the only place that wasn't on fire; and Plepler did a good job of messaging to Bewkes both publicly and privately that things were hunky-dory. So Plepler tended to be left alone.

ERIC KESSLER:

One day during our weekly meeting Richard told me he was making a change and eliminating my position. Needless to say, given that business was booming, I was surprised. Looking back, I get it. At the time, Jeff and all of Time Warner's top divisional CEOs—except Richard—came from the business side. Richard was in somewhat of a competitive situation relative to the other CEOs, John Martin and Kevin Tsujihara. I'm not sure Richard was ever comfortable being the only CEO who had a COO.

SIMON SUTTON:

In each case when those people left, I do think it was better for the company. I'm a big Richard fan. To the extent that Richard's vision became much clearer with other people leaving, I think it was better for the company.

Floyd Mayweather, then the highest-paid athlete in all of sports, announced on February 19, 2013, an agreement that would increase his income even more: a six-fight deal with Showtime that ensured him at least $32 million per fight, plus a cut of the pay-per-view receipts from each matchup. The deal came as a surprise to the sports world—the undefeated Mayweather had been a loyal member of the HBO family for essentially his entire career. Mayweather's first fight on Showtime would be a May 4 bout against Robert Guerrero, held under the bright lights of Las Vegas's MGM Grand.

The new deal meant that the center of gravity in the sport of boxing would be shunted away from HBO. By that time, Mayweather already held the record for the most-watched pay-per-view event of all time—his May 5, 2007, fight against Oscar De La Hoya had garnered 2.48 million pay-per-view purchases. Mayweather's manager and chief executive of Mayweather Promotions, Leonard Ellerbe, made clear to the press that Showtime's offer was far greater than HBO's, saying that HBO "came to a gunfight with a knife."

HBO Sports continued its slow decline. Documentaries, thankfully, were going strong. On October 21, 2013, HBO aired **Life According to Sam**, a documentary about Sam Berns and his fight against the premature aging disease called progeria. The film, directed by Sean Fine and Andrea Nix, won the 2014 Primetime Emmy for Exceptional Merit in Documentary Filmmaking.

NANCY ABRAHAM, Executive:

So many of the films we do are observational, verité-based documentaries. When you embark on them, you often have no idea where they are going to go. *Life According to Sam* was one of those. It was about Sam Berns, a kid who had progeria, a rapid aging disease with a short life expectancy. When he was diagnosed at around age two, his parents, both trained as doctors, dedicated themselves to finding a cure or a treatment. They made a lot of headway. The film is about that family, the clinical trials that they were doing, and about Sam as a person. It took a couple extra years to produce because there was a delay in getting the results of the clinical trial published, and we couldn't finish the film until they did. Finally, we were able to finish the film, and it got into Sundance. Sam couldn't travel at that point, but he did an amazing Skype Q&A when it premiered. Tragically, he died shortly after the HBO broadcast later that year. It was an incredibly emotional journey, that we had no way of anticipating when it started years earlier.

On April 20, 2013, HBO aired the Whoopi Goldberg–produced biographical documentary, **Whoopi Goldberg Presents Moms Mabley**, with Whoopi of course getting top billing.

LISA HELLER:

I was always amazed to see when I first got to HBO that Sheila had no compunction about changing her mind. If there was a better idea that came along at whatever cost, emotional or financial, she would be flexible. And that was very liberating because where I had come from, you did what you did and you stuck with it. Regardless.

WHOOPI GOLDBERG:

I didn't know about Moms before. The thing that I hoped would happen has not happened yet, but it is my hope that we start to talk about these comics that came before as huge deals in what we all do in terms of comedy. So I'm hoping one day someone will name an award after Moms. I think it's a good idea.

It took us forever to get it done. And then Sheila and I had a falling-out and she said, "I'm not going to do it." I said, "Okay." So we went and did it anyway. Then she heard about it, that we had gotten it done, and said, "I can't believe you fucking went and did it." Like, we weren't going to wait. You said you weren't going to do it. Because the story isn't about you, the story was about getting this done and they wanted it done a certain way. And it wasn't what the vision, my vision for it was. And so she said no more. And I said, "Okay, I understand."

SHEILA NEVINS:

I wanted Whoopi to be Moms Mabley. I had seen her do it off-Broadway. And Whoopi wanted to make a show. I wanted her to do Moms because she did the best imitation of Moms in the whole world. Whoopi was a great actor. And Moms was political. So when she said she wanted to make a documentary about Moms, I mistook it to be more Moms and less documentary. And then suddenly she started to make it about civil rights and about other things that were not what I bought into. I think Whoopi did a Kickstarter; she raised the money to do it by herself. Good for her. I had pulled out of it. Then I thought, some Moms is better than no Moms at all, and went and bought it.

WHOOPI GOLDBERG:

And so we went and made it and people really loved it.

For many projects, the prognosis was "HBO or bust." Other networks either didn't have the interest or the financial strength to say yes. Where would that documentary on Sondheim have aired if not for HBO? Maybe PBS, with its small and snooty audience, but more likely, nowhere.

And the same could easily be said about a movie dedicated to the scabrous love life of Liberace. **Behind the Candelabra** *was the kind of audacious and unlikely film that only HBO would do—or at least do right.*

LEN AMATO:

Jerry Weintraub got together with Mike and Richard and mentioned the project. He knew Liberace, and he had the whole package together, but he had only sold one foreign territory to France and I think was looking for a place to make it, and they talked some numbers. When it came to us, Richard LaGravenese had written the script, Matt and Michael were attached, and Steven was attached. And of course that was like a dream come true to me.

The studio didn't want to do it. We brought the movie to Cannes and Steven said the movie was too gay. None of the studios would touch it. And I just remember thinking, I must be a bad studio executive because I don't understand that. How can you have Michael Douglas, Matt Damon, Steven Soderbergh, this great script. That's as good of a bet for a hit and for a niche tone that would get attention as anything else. And so they all agreed that this would be good to do at HBO.

Michael agreed to do it for HBO, which was a big thing. Matt was doing the Bourne stuff at that time. And he even took a hiatus from another Bourne movie to make *Behind the Candelabra*. It was a labor of love.

MICHAEL DOUGLAS, Actor:

My agents came to me with as great a movie as you could have asked for: Steven Soderbergh directing and Richard LaGravenese, a great writer who we had worked with on *Traffic*, Jerry Weintraub producing, and Matt Damon attached. I said, "Fantastic," and was excited as could be. Then they proceeded to go to every major studio. Each passed! It was only a roughly $20 million budget, and we had this incredible lineup, but every single studio turned us down. I was shocked.

Then Jerry Weintraub calls and says, "HBO loves it. They want to do it." Now, as excited as I was, you have to understand that I had come from television and knew the pecking order of television versus feature films. Still, you have to remember that this was all when I had my cancer in 2012, stage IV, and I had just come out of it. I thought I was never going to work again. Lo and behold, I was just so emotional and so excited about the possibility, I couldn't wait to get started. Then they came to me and said, "We have a problem." Matt said, "We waited for you, but I've got a project I've got to do." And Steven said, "We'll come back to it in a year."

I was heartbroken. I thought, That's the end of it, it's never going to happen. The reality was that I was so happy to be alive that throughout my procedures I had failed to look at myself. I was a skeleton and the guys were all kind enough to not put the responsibility or blame on me, but to make excuses, to allow me another year to gain my strength and put some weight back on for the Liberace part. I now had a year to rehearse, to do research, to work on the piano, my voice, and even makeup. I felt very confident. We had a get-together lunch out in Malibu with Steven and Matt, and my kids were there. Matt Damon said after, "I knew we were in good shape when Michael's son Dylan started imitating all the hours he's been listening to his father play the piano and doing the voice." My son had done a perfect imitation of Liberace because he had heard me rehearsing so much.

LEN AMATO:

We were doing hair and makeup tests. Matt came out in character in the little chauffeur outfit and seemed uncomfortable. I could tell he was thinking, "What the fuck have I done here?" We were concerned. But ten minutes later, Michael comes out in full Liberace dress mode and he's completely the character of Liberace. The whole mood changed.

MICHAEL DOUGLAS:

It was wonderful and such a joy to hide behind that mask, especially when you have footage of a real person to try and re-create. The scary part was doing the makeup for when he was dying, and taking the wig off, or putting a big bald wig on. After what I had been through with my cancer, I must say, it was really tough and really hit home.

One of the beauties of our arrangement with HBO was that it was released as a feature film in many parts of the world before its initial airing on HBO. So we went to Cannes Film Festival. There had been some who said it was a "movie for television" quote unquote, but we said, "This is a movie being shown in theaters in France, England, and other places." We had a wonderful response at Cannes, but then the jury decided it was not legitimate, because HBO was about to show it a week later. That was a disappointment, but the reaction there gave us a good sense of how good the movie was. It was really special.

On May 25, 2014, the Emmy Award–winning HBO film **The Normal Heart** *premiered, one of the bravest and most emotional films ever made about the AIDS crisis.*

SHEILA NEVINS:

Normal Heart was more than just programming. There were men hiding in corners at HBO and Larry probably changed their lives.

Whenever I would go anyplace with Larry [Kramer], people would come over and say, You saved my life. You saved my boyfriend's life. A woman came over once—we were in a restaurant—and she said, "You saved my son's life." Being able to fight for a cocktail to stop this incredible spread of AIDS made Larry a miracle man. There's no other way to describe it. Larry always gave me good advice, and I loved every bit of him.

On February 11, 2014, Richard Plepler attended a White House state dinner.

RICHARD PLEPLER:

At the end of the evening, when we were leaving the tent to go to our car, I heard this voice calling me and I turned around and it was the president. He said, "Richard." And I of course immediately went back.

I said, "Mr. President, thank you for having us, what a wonderful evening." He said, "Listen, there are two things I need." It was a holiday weekend. He said, "I've got a long weekend and a little bit of downtime. I'd love to watch *True Detective* and whatever *Game of Thrones* you've got." So I said smiling, "Well let me see what I can do." I called David Benioff and Dan Weiss literally from the East Room and said, "You're not going to quite believe this, but President Obama just asked me for your show and I need your blessing to send him my copies."

DAVID BENIOFF:

I remember we shot one key scene in season three—the final scene of the first episode we directed. It's the scene where Jaime Lannister has his hand chopped off. Nikolaj had some kind of stomach distress—I'm not sure if it was a virus or food poisoning or what. But it was bad—vomiting all night long, weak, pale. I still don't know how he managed to get through the night shoot. It was like Willis Reed limping onto the court in Madison Square Garden. But he did it, and I think his sickness makes that moment even more sickening—you can see on his face, if you look carefully, that he's not right, which of course makes perfect sense for a legendary swordfighter who's about to have his sword hand severed.

It seemed everywhere HBO could look, there were boundaries all but begging to be pushed—even when pushing them could spell danger.

BERNADETTE CAULFIELD:

They had to have a grizzly bear for the scene for Brienne to fight the big bear. Something so simple written on a page is very difficult. You have to find the right bear. There's a lot of bears out there. We found a trainer, Doug Seus, who treats it like a family member. You could tell it was with love and kindness that this bear had been trained.

You've got to get the right insurance. You can't bring the bear over to Europe. That would be too much travel, so we just figured out we had to do it in the United States so we did part of the scene in Belfast of the Brienne side of the fighting. Then you had to schedule that with visual effects that they were going to have to blend it. I'm not even sure if our director was on at that point. He was in United States; Doug is up in Salt Lake City in Utah. And then we were in Belfast.

You had to light this big scene, that actually was three different parts. You had the Belfast set that then had to be matched with that, to rebuild in LA, and then you'll have to make it strong enough for this grizzly bear. What bears like to do is test. They will run through the woods, sometimes shake a tree to see if they can knock it down. They're always seeing what their strength is. I remember Doug saying, "This has to be extremely strong so that this nine-hundred-pound bear, twelve-hundred-pound bear can shake that set. Because once he feels like it can go over, he will try to push it over." Then we sent our director, Michelle MacLaren.

We had to send her, she wanted to go up and meet the bear. So, she went up to Doug Seus's place in Utah, and met Bart, the bear, and she met with Doug to figure out how they train them. That was a very complicated scene that ended up being in two different countries plus visual effects had to then blend all those, those two sets together and blend the bear, blend Brienne, and I think it turns into a great thing, but that was huge. I remember spending Christmas—again, a very understanding husband—the two weeks that I do get home, I was on the phone every single day, trying to figure out this, the insurance on it, and why I trusted Bart over a cheaper bear.

D. B. WEISS:

Does Kit breaking his ankle right before we started shooting season three count as illness? Let's say it does. We were going to give him shit for it, because it forced us to reschedule the entire season. But then he showed us a picture of what his ankle looked like under the cast. If our prosthetics artist, Barrie Gower, had shown us a picture like that, we would have told him to take the gore down a few notches, because it was way over the top. We couldn't give him shit for it after that.

LENA HEADEY:

I had both kiddos during hiatus. So it is what it is. Lil extra pressure here and there.

BERNADETTE CAULFIELD:

Stunts are always where everybody holds their breaths that nobody gets hurt. In Spain, we had to run a horse up some church steps and it was a very dangerous stunt. And we were trying to figure out how to make the stairs sticky. Because they were obviously old worn marble.

DAVID BENIOFF:

We had to fly through Heathrow all the time and the customs officers always asked you the reason for your stay. The first few years we went they'd stare at us and say, "*Game of Thorns*?" Then one time, maybe around the third season, I noticed that the customs officer was reading the first book in George's series.

It was either then or the moment I went to the US consulate in Northern Ireland to see if I could get an expedited passport for my son, and the lady handling the documents looked at me and said, "So is Jon Snow really dead?"

D. B. WEISS:

When we were staying at the Hotel Alfonso XIII in Seville, we were having a drink at the outside bar and heard what sounded like a horde of people yelling, "Keith!" When we went to the balcony to investigate, we saw hundreds and hundreds of people outside the hotel's wrought iron gates. Kit had stepped outside, and they were all yelling his name. That is what "Kit" sounds like in Spanish.

EMILIA CLARKE:

My second brain hemorrhage happened between seasons three and four.

D. B. WEISS:

When we heard that Emilia had suffered a brain injury, it wasn't about the show. She was and is one of the best human beings we know. We love her, and the days we spent waiting to find out she was okay were some of the most harrowing in our lives.

MICHAEL McMORROW:

The most memorable to me was the New York premiere at Lincoln Center on March 18, 2014, where we built a dragon outside in the plaza and were also nominated for an Emmy for our red carpet preshow. We wanted to do a dragon. It just felt iconic. As I ran it by Quentin initially, he was a little bit skeptical at first, but that was sort of the early days of social media, where people were just tweeting and Instagramming anything that they saw and I felt that it would be fun to do something in that plaza as an anchor piece for the red carpet show that we built out there, but also something that ordinary citizens would be passing by and they would take photos of it. And that in itself is a little bit of a marketing gimmick, a little bit of a marketing expression that people would be photographing a dragon at Lincoln Center. I thought it would be fun throughout the day. And then as the backdrop for our interview for the red carpet show, we have this elaborate set piece. It's a big risk there because in anything you do in New York, you have to plan for weather. You don't have those kinds of concerns as much in Los Angeles, but in New York you do. So, it's a big risk, but it paid off. The weather held out on us.

On June 9, 2014, Chase Carey, president of Twenty-First Century Fox, had a meeting with Bewkes in New York during which he floated an idea: Fox wanted to purchase Time Warner. Bewkes told Carey he would need to consult with his board before pulling the trigger, and they parted without an agreement. Follow-up calls from Carey yielded nothing more concrete than requests for additional time. On June 24, the head of Twenty-First Century Fox, Rupert Murdoch, sent a letter to Time Warner with an offer: $80 billion, split between cash (40 percent of the offer) and nonvoting shares of Twenty-First Century Fox stock (60 percent of the offer). At a valuation of $86.30 per share, Fox was offering a 25 percent premium on Time Warner's then stock price.

In addition to merging major broadcast properties, the deal would also bring together two powerhouse movie studios: Twenty-First Century Fox and Warner Bros., or so Murdoch outlined in the letter. In it, he also spelled out a plan to sell Time Warner's CNN, which competed directly with Murdoch's far-right cable offering, FOX News, before the deal could be closed. The Time Warner board met to consider the offer; their reply to Murdoch in a letter dated July 8 left little room for speculation—no deal. On Tuesday, August 5, 2014, Murdoch and Twenty-First Century Fox retracted their offer.

JEFF BEWKES:

I always expected Murdoch to make a run at us because we were only one of two big media companies that didn't have a controlling shareholder to block a deal. Disney was the other one, but since we had spun off TW Cable we were smaller so didn't cost as much. When News Corp gave out earnings guidance for the first time in 2014, promising to grow their operating earnings 50 percent, from $6 billion to $9 billion in three years, we knew they were kiting their stock price to use it for an acquisition, probably us.

We were a little bigger but similar in size, around $6 billion of operating earnings, but we were not in the habit of giving guidance for three years out, so even though our earnings record and plans for future earnings were higher than his, his stock gained a 25 percent premium to ours by June. We were in the process of spinning off the Time Inc. magazines from March to June, and we knew Rupert would wait until we finished because if he made an offer during a spin, it would make that taxable, and he wouldn't want to pay for that.

I think we completed the magazine spin on a Wednesday or Thursday, and Chase called on the following Saturday, asking if we could meet over the weekend. I said, "How about lunch on Monday?" We'd already had a few lunches where we would dance around the idea of a merger. Now we're having lunch and he says, "I'm prepared to offer you $85 a share for Time Warner. What do you think?"

I said to Chase, "When you say you're prepared to offer, does that mean you're going to offer in the future or that you just did offer? There's a big legal difference between those two things."

Chase looked at me sheepishly, because we were business friends, and said, "I just offered."

I was prepared for that, so I answered, "Well, before we talk about that, I have a few questions. Do you have the full authority to make this offer?"

Chase says, "I'm the president of News Corp," and I say, "I realize you're an officer of the company. I'm asking, did you have a board meeting about this offer?" "We had a meeting." I asked who was present. "Rupert, James, Lachlan, me, and the CFO." Then I asked, "No independent directors? No formal vote to spend $75 billion?" I knew my board would look askance at merging with a company with such dubious governance practices.

"How are you going to pay?" I asked. Chase pulled out a card from his breast pocket and read from it: "$53 in News Corp stock and $32 in cash for each Time Warner share." Thinking out loud, I said, "For the cash part you'd need over $25 billion. Where are you going to get that?"

"We'll increase our leverage from 2.75 to 4 times earnings." "On your assets or on mine?" I asked. "On the combined company," he replied.

I said, "Chase, you're going to borrow $10 billion against our assets and tell us the money's coming from you? I could do that myself. Well, our company was not for sale, but of course we appreciate and consider any offer made to our shareholders. We'll need three or four weeks to analyze our company and whether we'd want to sell it in this neighborhood, and also frankly, we need to analyze your company."

"Our company? Why?" "Because you're offering your stock and we don't know if it's worth $53 per TW share." We had been running numbers on News Corp and figured they'd only get halfway to their $9 billion earnings guidance.

We had several all-day board meetings considering carefully their offer and News Corp's prospects and our own plans, and the board decided unanimously to reject News Corp's offer. We would reach much higher valuation on our own, and News Corp's offer was only worth about seventy bucks, not the $85 headline number inflated by unrealistic earnings projections and sleight of hand with debt.

About four weeks later I called Rupert in the morning—it was the same day we were both going to the Allen media conference in Sun Valley—and told him our board had voted unanimously to reject his offer. I explained that we doubted News Corp could meet its earnings goals, which cast doubt on the value of his stock, and that not only didn't we approve of his plans to load debt on the company, but it reduced the real value of his offer. While I made clear that of course we would carefully consider any further offers he made, I also told him I doubted that there was a price News Corp could afford that we would accept.

I said, "See you in Sun Valley," and he hung up. That night, I was waiting with Howard Stringer at the little bridge you have to cross to get into the outdoor barbecue when Rupert, Chase, Lachlan, James, and their wives came across. I greeted them with a "How you doing? Let's have a beer!" which caused Kathryn and Sarah to exchange glances like, "Is this the guy you spent the flight talking about how you're going to take him out?"

Ten days later at six a.m. Rupert went public with his hostile offer. The arbs [arbitrageurs] took our stock from roughly $70 up close to his $85 nominal offer, figuring that we'd make a show of resistance and finally cave when he raised it to $95, give or take. They'd walk away with a quick profit.

The financial press wrote a lot of articles about how Rupert always got what he wanted and paid what was necessary, so it was only a matter of time until we accepted a sweetened deal. We decided not to counter the press stories that Rupert would pay what it took, figuring his shareholders would realize they would end up with the bill. We had adopted a bylaw during Carl Icahn's activist attack back in 2006 that said 15 percent of the shares could call for a special shareholder meeting with ninety days' notice. I called a board meeting for that Friday to ask the board to suspend that provision for a year. We all knew we were in a contest for the shareholders' hearts and minds, and our first move was to cancel their voting rights? Our argument was that the arbs and Murdoch allies could buy 15 percent of our stock and vote to sell us out. The board unanimously voted to suspend the voting provisions, so Rupert and the arbs woke up on Monday morning to find out they couldn't roll us just buying 15 percent of the stock, and they'd have to wait a year and get to 51 percent.

News Corp stock dropped 40 percent, so now their offer was way below Time Warner's trading value. Three weeks later Rupert called to withdraw his offer. His stock didn't recover for years, until he sold to Disney.

Having turned away News Corp's offer, which according to them was $85 but in reality was only worth about $70, we owed our owners an explanation of why we thought Time Warner was worth a lot more on its own. We had an investor day in October and laid out our plans. The headline was we were going to double our earnings over the next four years, from $4 per share to $8 per share. Which in fact we did. Part of that plan was to open up HBO Go on broadband, which we launched months later with Apple as a marketing partner. By November our stock was trading close to $90, so any shareholders who wished we'd cashed them out with the bogus Murdoch offer could get out at a higher number a few months later.

DAVID ZASLAV, Executive, Discovery:

When the deal with Rupert didn't happen, I went to see Jeff, because we were the most global media company. We were already in sports outside the US. We had ten channels in every country. We had free-to-air channels. We were on the ground in every country. We had a library of in-language content. I said to Jeff, "Let's do HBO together. We have content in every language, and we have stuff that people love. If you put on top of that the dramatic, big draw, sexy, explosive series that HBO has been so successful with, that together we could be combustible. We could run the table." Jeff loved the idea at the time, but we didn't get that far. There were two obstacles.

The first was that most of the great stuff from HBO, *Entourage*, *Sex and the City*, *Curb*, had already been sold to the biggest broadcaster or a big provider in a number of countries around the world. Jeff looked at it and said, "Even though it might be a good idea, ultimately, I think I have to own the whole thing. I don't think I could do a joint venture." So it dropped.

Just five months after Fox's $80 billion bid to take over Time Warner, reports emerged that HBO had told employees it would be laying off part of its workforce for the first *time in more than ten years. The network would jettison roughly 7 percent of its staff, which translated to about 150 out of the company's 2,400 workers. It was not the only Time Warner branch to be making cuts—Warner Bros. and Turner Broadcasting were reportedly planning to eliminate about 2,475 jobs between them.*

In an email to the HBO workforce obtained through a leak to **Variety,** *HBO CEO Richard Plepler explained that the cuts came after evaluations of the company's "2015 budgets and staffing plans." The layoffs were made to reallocate money to original programming, long a top priority for HBO brass, and increase the company's earnings.*

What HBO needed now was a bit of old-time HBO pizzazz, and with **True Detective,** *it got plenty of that.*

Nic Pizzolatto had been a literature professor, a short story writer, and a published novelist before turning his gaze to the small screen, which was no longer as small as it used to be. After initially conceiving the project as a follow-up to his novel **Galveston,** *Pizzolatto took* **True Detective** *out in April 2012.*

The first season, directed by Cary Joji Fukunaga and starring Matthew McConaughey and Woody Harrelson, premiered on January 12, 2014. It proved to be an atmospheric and compelling ride around the margins of marginal Louisiana, as the two detectives, played with real chemistry by McConaughey and Harrelson, chase the murderer of a prostitute while stumbling upon Satanic rituals and discussing pessimistic concepts like "time is a flat circle." Critics loved the show, but the second season, this time starring Colin Farrell, Rachel McAdams, and Vince Vaughn, failed to ignite, and would prove to be a painful example of the dysfunction behind the scenes at HBO making its way onto the screen.

The general consensus was that as of this point there were "no adults in the room" to keep the show going for a second season, and Mike Lombardo was accused of unduly hurrying it along. A third season, starring Mahershala Ali, was, however, something of a return to form, albeit never quite up to the critical admiration, let alone the ratings, of season one.

NIC PIZZOLATTO, Creator:

I got into Hollywood a bit late and I didn't want to be there if I wasn't doing something that I absolutely believed in. And if I was going to be there, I wanted to take my shot. There was a lot of ambition wrapped up in it. The initial concept came from my usual desire to create and examine characters, with the understanding that for somebody in my position, it needs to be rooted in a popular genre. It certainly helps to sell it.

If you're writing *Ulysses* in a windy cabin, you can do whatever you want. But if you're doing something that takes tens of millions of dollars, it should have a wide appeal. Of available genres, the police procedural seemed like one that I could do. I'd done a lot of research in that direction.

I was trying to make something popular that also scratched my personal itches. There were a lot of tropes that would naturally come up that then I would need to play with, just to keep my own interest.

The pilot for *True Detective* came from summer of 2010. I wrote like six television scripts in about five, six weeks. One was a spec script, three were three episodes of an original show, and the other two were original pilots. One of those original pilots was *True Detective*.

MICHAEL ELLENBERG:

Steve Golin, the producer, submitted the scripts in advance and the scripts were great. Nic had written two beautiful scripts. So going into the room, you were already compelled, and Matthew McConaughey and Woody Harrelson were attached. And this was just as Matthew was making his career change and was giving a range of interesting performances.

How do we make sure we're not just doing a procedural for the sake of doing a procedural? What's an HBO version of a procedural? And those conversations frequently were smart and stimulating.

In this case, there was this opportunity to reinvent the buddy cop drama as something metaphysical and existential, a deep vision of some of the rot inside of the American soul. That show was ahead of its time—it was made during the Obama era in a way that tells you more about the Trump era as well.

NIC PIZZOLATTO:

After I gave them episode three, they wanted to know if I could give them an outline before the next script. I had never done one before. For me, writing a script was much faster and effective than writing an outline. I wrote the script but made an outline retroactively off the script I'd written and then did that part of the process and it seemed to work out well.

And as they started to trust what was happening, that stuff went away. I think that's one of the benefits of selling something that already has the major creatives attached, you're selling something that isn't to be developed. It's something that is what it is. That's what you're buying.

The whole idea of packaging as much as possible was to ensure that we got to make the show I wanted because it wasn't going to be developed from a pitch. You were being handed two scripts, a season outline, and two stars.

We went into production on season two very quickly. We had wrapped production on season two within a little more than a year of the first season's airing. And then we lost all this postproduction time because two other shows had shut down that were going to premiere before us. We stopped shooting somewhere in May and we aired in June.

I think it was *Westworld* and *The Leftovers*. And that was strange because it was sort of your reward for staying on schedule is to lose all your postproduction. But you know, that's the job. And we're happy to do it.

*Created by Mike (**Beavis and Butt-Head**) Judge, John Altschuler, and Dave Krinsky, the satirical comedy **Silicon Valley** premiered on HBO on April 6, 2014, and would last for six seasons and fifty-three episodes.*

*For a while, Casey Bloys had been wanting to do a show centered on the febrile atmosphere of Silicon Valley's tech boom; an earlier script had never gotten off the ground. He had been pondering the project for a year when producer Scott Rudin sent him a whole binder of materials, including a documentary about the making of a video game. At the same time, Judge coincidentally met with Bloys to discuss his idea for what would eventually become **Silicon Valley**, at which point Bloys tried to marry the Rudin ideas with the Judge pitch. Rudin would eventually get points for his work, even though he never ended up becoming involved in the making of the show. In any case, this was around the time that the larger relationship between HBO and Rudin fell apart.*

AMY GRAVITT:

It was the perfect time to do a show set in the world of tech. There was enough about it in the popular culture that people had a sense of what was going on, but it hadn't been made into a TV show yet. We were wanting to do a show set in this world, at the same time we were sitting down with Mike Judge. He came up with the angle that sometimes people who are the most successful are the least equipped to handle it.

KUMAIL NANJIANI, Actor:

I was a huge fan of Mike Judge. I loved *Idiocracy*, *Office Space*, and I grew up watching *Beavis and Butt-Head*. I get this call telling me Mike Judge has a show on HBO, he's doing a pilot, and you have an audition for it. I immediately freaked because I also loved HBO. I was extremely stressed out. This was right before Christmas and my audition wasn't until the end of January, so I had a whole month to overthink everything.

The way I approached that audition is different than the way I approach auditions now. For that one I decided, I'm just going to be in the moment. Be funny. I know I can do that. Now I approach auditions with more of the character in mind. I didn't get the part I auditioned for. I auditioned for two different roles and I didn't get either of them, but they liked me. And they said, we'll write a part for you. And people always say that, and it never happens. And then I got a call a few weeks later that said, Hey, they wrote you a part. Do you want to do it?

Erlich and I actually auditioned for Big Head. And because I'd sort of gone for just funny and not doing the character, I think they very wisely understood I wasn't right for those parts, but then they wrote something for me.

AMY GRAVITT:

As much as we loved Mike's take on the world and knew that there was something in that pilot, especially with the cast that we had assembled, at that point, we didn't have a series. Then Alec Berg came on board and he's the one who was able to take the idea and turn it into the *Silicon Valley* that you recognize today.

ALEC BERG:

Sue Naegle moved out of the apartment upstairs the same day we were moving into an apartment downstairs, the very first apartment I lived in in LA. She was looking for her mail, and became literally, one of the first people I met in LA. So I ended up at UTA and became a client. I had a very long and good relationship with Sue when she went to HBO.

I got a call from Sue, who said, "Hey, I have this pilot. Would you be interested in taking a look at it? I want to hear your thoughts." As a favor to Sue, I watched a cut of the pilot, called her, and gave her my thoughts. She agreed with me, and said, "Would you mind meeting with Mike Judge and talking to him about it?" I think she was gaslighting me at the time because I think they were looking for somebody. What I found out afterward was I guess Altschuler and Krinsky had just disagreed creatively about what the show was or where it was going and they were out.

I went and I met with Mike. I'm a big Mike Judge fan, and I'm happy to tell him my thoughts about the pilot. We started talking about my thoughts, and totally agreed. And then I got a call from Sue afterward saying, "Hey, Mike enjoyed talking to you. And it sounds like you guys agree about the direction of the show and what the pilot needs. Do you want to come work on it?" We tried to make a deal that made sense, but it fell apart. Then months later they called back and said, "We need to make this work." And in the span of forty-eight hours, a deal was made and I actually started on day two of the writers' room. So I came in in theory to help run the show. I had a staff of people; most of them I had never met. And that's kinda how it started. We ended up rewriting I'm going to say two-thirds of the original pilot.

CASEY BLOYS:

There's a big difference between the original pilot and the pilot that aired after Alec had come on board. I don't know that I've ever seen as radical a transformation. That was the difference between a dead pilot and a good show that ran for six seasons.

ALEC BERG:

I love doing pilots. You get a chance to evaluate what works and what doesn't, to make sure you know who the characters are, and what the show needs and doesn't need.

Not to sound like a corporate shill, but HBO is the greatest. The best. When we did the *Silicon Valley* pilot, the initial cut, we put a Green Day song in, but the initial cut was not cut for broadcast. It was just cut as an internal tool. When we did the final sound mix, we were going to put the Green Day song in, but the music budget came back and said, "This Green Day song is really, really expensive. We can't afford it." So we put something else in and we did the sound mix and Amy Gravitt at the end of the playback of the pilot had a sour expression on her face. She didn't like it. She just said, "That last song isn't as good as the Green Day song, is it?" And we said, "No, but we can't afford the Green Day song." And she said, "Let me make a phone call." She came back in the room and said, "Just put the Green Day song in."

AMY GRAVITT:

Alec is the most disciplined storyteller. After table reads of *Silicon Valley*, Alec always looked stressed because his mind is going a million miles an hour. He's thinking about everybody in the ensemble. "I didn't give Dinesh enough here. I didn't give Gilfoyle enough there, Jared needs something to do." He's never done and he's never satisfied with his work for better or worse. The way his brain works—he's able to build a comedy structurally yet still be funny—is an incredibly unique talent. He doesn't blow past the blueprint phase to get to the fun of writing jokes.

KUMAIL NANJIANI:

At the end of season one, we were shooting the scene where we're all in a hotel room and trying to figure out how best to jerk off guys in the room. It was all of us, and that was a long day. We were all improvising and having fun and laughing. Then Alec came over after a take and said to me, "When you're improvising, it's funny, but this is what the scene is about." And he told me the three things the scene was about, then said, "If your improv isn't furthering one of these three things, or if it's not on point for any of these three things, then no matter how funny it is, it's not going to be on the show." That was a big epiphany for me.

We would not have gotten to make *The Big Sick* if it wasn't for *Silicon Valley*. We'd been working on the script before *Silicon Valley*. Judd had started working with me and Emily at that point, and as *Silicon Valley* got more successful, I became a little more well known, that's what allowed us to get money to make *Big Sick*. There would have been no *Big Sick* without *Silicon Valley*—100 percent.

On June 29, 2014, HBO premiered **The Leftovers,** *a drama series about the aftermath of a tragic event (the Sudden Departure) in which 2 percent of the entire world's population mysteriously vanishes. Starring Justin Theroux as a small-town police chief in Mapleton, New York, the show was based on a book of the same name published in 2011 by Tom Perrotta, who co-wrote the show with Damon Lindelof. Ten directors took turns behind the cameras of* **Leftovers,** *most prominently Mimi Leder, who worked on ten. Despite an avalanche of acclaim, the show's ratings were anemic.*

TOM PERROTTA, Creator:

The original idea emerged from the research I did for my novel *The Abstinence Teacher.* I got deep into contemporary evangelical theology and was fascinated by the idea of the Rapture, which, for an agnostic like me, is ridiculous and sublime at the same time. I thought it would be interesting to imagine modern-day, secular Americans grappling with a biblical cataclysm. But I didn't want to rewrite the *Left Behind* series, so I imagined a different sort of Rapture—a random one that made no theological sense.

Like a lot of my books, *The Leftovers* started out as a satire—in this case, a satire of religious thinking—but it changed in the writing. Every character I tried to write was mired in grief and bewilderment, and I needed to take their grief seriously to be able to inhabit their point of view. The Sudden Departure turned out not to be a satire of the Rapture, but a powerful metaphor for loss, for the unexplained absence of our loved ones.

Writers aren't always aware of their influences. I was pretty clear that I was drawing on memories of September 11 when I started writing *The Leftovers*, and also thinking about the economic collapse of 2008—the fragility of our way of life—which was occurring right at the time I began the book. But it took me a lot longer to understand that I was also using the Sudden Departure as a way to explore the aftermath of my father's death in a car accident in 2002. He was there one day and gone the next, and I'd never been able to write about the shock of that in a straightforward way. So I did what novelists do—I created an elaborate fictional scenario that would allow me to write about this personal cataclysm without being fully aware of the fact that that was what I was doing.

DAMON LINDELOF, Creator:

At the end of *Lost*, we had put so much emotional energy into ending the show that once it was over I wanted to spend more time with my wife and four-year-old son, but I also wanted to be writing.

I spent essentially the next year of my life working on this movie *Prometheus* with Ridley Scott and came away from that experience feeling like I was very spoiled in television as a writer, because I had a tremendous amount of control. Unless I'm directing in movies, I'm never going to be able to have that control. It's much more of a for-hire position that can be easily replaced. Even when working with one of my idols, like Ridley, which was a dream come true, I was the second or third man in the door in terms of writing.

So at some point during the *Prometheus* experience, I started feeling like maybe I would do television again. It had to be the right thing. I was getting a lot of offers and calls, and I was still in an overall deal at ABC and Disney during this entire period. They were trying to match me with a number of different projects. I didn't want to do that. That was more or less my head space before I read Perrotta's book.

MICHAEL ELLENBERG:

Tom's book is beautiful and spooky, this notion of 2 percent of the world disappearing, but without any explanation. And the book never offers you one. And so to me, for television, there was this opportunity to do a fresh take on a supernatural drama, where you have this huge idea, and you're looking at the aftermath of it, which is, what does it mean to live in a world where a larger power has made itself known but offered no greater clarity?

I thought that was an interesting idea, and I had a strong feeling it would resonate with Damon Lindelof.

It was a big priority for me, frankly, to work with Damon. I thought by giving him the creative freedom that HBO could provide, I knew he would thrive in that environment.

DAMON LINDELOF:

My recollection is a couple of things happened simultaneously. The first was I read a *New York Times* book review written by Stephen King about *The Leftovers*. Then I bought it with the intention to read it, when Michael Ellenberg called me. He and I had worked together on *Prometheus*. He got the job at HBO and he asked, "Have you read *The Leftovers*? HBO controls it." That excited me because I think it's what most writer-producers dream, to have a Sunday night HBO show. I was certainly no different.

Stephen King is calling this book by Perrotta brilliant, who I love, by the way. I read all of his books, but he'd never done genre before. I felt like I was struck by lightning. Reading Tom's book changed everything. Very rarely do you have that clarity in your life as a creative person.

TOM PERROTTA:

I never gave a moment's thought to bringing *The Leftovers* anywhere but HBO. I knew that broadcast networks wouldn't go for a postapocalyptic story that rejected all the conventions of that genre—there were no zombies in the novel, no nuclear wasteland, no aliens. It was just about people trying to explain something that couldn't be explained.

I also didn't think about making *The Leftovers* into a feature film. Todd Field had made a beautiful movie based on my novel *Little Children* in 2007, but he had actually pitched it to HBO as a miniseries first, and they'd passed. Todd and I both loved the idea of making a six-hour version of *Little Children*. In the feature version, which I love, we'd had to cut some story lines that I think we both would have liked to explore if we had more time. Long-form TV is the perfect format for adapting complex novels—you can expand the story as you go, let it evolve over time, rather than forcing it into a two-hour box.

By the time *The Leftovers* came out in 2011, the golden age of TV was in full swing, and that was pretty much an invention of HBO, so that was the obvious first choice. I was thrilled when Mike Lombardo said he wanted to move forward with it.

JUSTIN THEROUX, Actor:

It was a beautifully written script. If you read one of Damon's scripts, they operate on a different level than normal scripts. They're incredibly visually minded. Couched within it were these themes that I just thought were so rife for exploration. And then of course I loved the character. I met with Damon, and I think with any TV show that I've done sometimes without success and sometimes with success, it's always like, let's look each other in the eye and promise each other that we'll try and keep it interesting for each other, and not let the character stagnate. Damon absolutely over-delivered on that.

DAMON LINDELOF:

The biggest disparity is time. There's no other metaphor for the pace of broadcasting other than the conveyor belt in *I Love Lucy*. At HBO, you're making Teslas. They come into the process basically saying, "You're going to pitch to us. And if we love what you pitch, if you are incredibly lucky, we may be shooting a pilot in like a year and a half." On *Lost*, I met with J.J., and we were in front of cameras shooting a two-hour pilot like six weeks later.

TOM PERROTTA:

I had placed a lot of aesthetic restrictions on *The Leftovers*, meaning I wanted to write something that was postapocalyptic, but also completely realistic in a sense meaning there had been this inexplicable, possibly supernatural event at the beginning, but the story picks up three years later and nothing supernatural is going to happen anymore. It's really just about the way that humans behave in the face of something that they can't understand. So I came into it with a very realistic stance, like, Okay, we have a very weird concept, but we're going to treat it almost anthropologically or sociologically. And Damon kept pushing at that and wanting to bring in bigger narrative elements, maybe closer to the postapocalyptic genre in a more conventional sense.

The place where we started to click was episode six, that was all about Nora. Damon and I argued about whether Nora could wear a bulletproof vest and pay a prostitute to shoot her. And it just sounded so crazy compared to this very real, controlled Nora that I had written in the novel. And eventually, I learned to trust him and to let him push the story into these more extreme forms. And I remember when we got the cut of that episode, I just suddenly was like, The show is amazing.

JUSTIN THEROUX:

There was never a moment where Damon wasn't asking people to put all their creative might behind something. That, to me, is the best project to be on because you're never not on your toes, you're never not sharpening a knife that you've never sharpened before.

I would love to take credit for some of the show, but I can't because those scripts came in like Kevlar. They were bulletproof. Damon had tortured himself, Tom, and the other writers, too. They had rung out every unnecessary word, every cliché, there was nothing in them that you could poke a hole. Not that I've been able to find. When the scripts were sent, it was like getting the Torah.

Whenever I cracked the spine on one of them for the first time, I was so appreciative of the work that had already gone into them. Many times on projects, I'm constantly saying, "Let's put this line up here, let's push that over there. Maybe we scratch that word out, that seems a little bit cliché." And maybe over the course of three seasons, I made ten suggestions. They had already carried the cross for me and then I just sort of delivered it.

MICHAEL ELLENBERG:

We thought that the approach was existential, and sophisticated, and HBO. The first year was challenging initially, then it found its legs. There was a hope that it would be a bigger commercial splash, given how big a show *Lost* was. When it wasn't, people were a bit disappointed. But by the end of the first season, critics started to rally around it and it became a critics' darling. And by the end of its run, it became viewed as one of the better shows HBO had ever made. When you make these things, you don't know which one's going to be the commercial blockbuster and which one's going to be the critics' darling. I loved this show.

JUSTIN THEROUX:

Damon felt, I think, an enormous responsibility to Tom in the first season to sort of tell the story. But thinking of Damon, it was almost like he was sort of trapped in stone, trying to struggle out of it and create meaning around it. I know for a fact that Damon was probably his most tortured during that season. He had a lot of lonely moments in the car with the engine off, probably weeping silently going, "What am I doing? I don't think I'm doing a good job." Then once the second and third season came around, he became unburdened and unencumbered to just burrow into the bedrock of those themes. It's just a show that was trying to take a massive bite.

REGINA KING:

During the first season of *Leftovers*, you didn't see through the eyes of the Black families that had lost people when all the people disappeared. And the way in which Damon introduced the family in that first episode of the second season, you almost didn't see any of the main characters.

And for Damon to trust us as a family, Javan and Jasmine and Kevin, the four of us, was pretty big. We had conversations among ourselves, like, What are people going to think of this? The fans of *Leftovers* are going to be like, Wait a minute, did you get rid of everybody? Because fans take ownership in their favorite shows. And I won't lie, we did have a little bit of concern. Are they going to start writing hate mail because they think that possibly the show is totally flipping on its head and doing something totally different?

LILA BYOCK, Writer:

Damon would probably be the first to admit that he is a very superstitious person. He takes an almost magical view of the work that gets done in the writers' room, which can feel very daunting, but also incredibly powerful and emotional. There's always laughter and crying and the whole range of emotions in Damon's writers' rooms.

When somebody cries, usually that's a moment to stop and reflect and say, Okay, we need to take a step back, calm down, and reflect on the other writer's point of view about it. The room was incredibly divided over the question of whether Laurie Garvey was going to commit suicide in episode six of the final season. People felt very, very strongly on both sides. Multiple people cried that day. It's a testament to how strongly connected we were to the story and characters.

Damon won't move on unless there's a consensus in the writers' room. He's not the showrunner who's like, "My way or the highway. It's my vision." He believes in the power of a group of writers working together. If there's one writer in the writers' room who says, "I don't believe in this story choice," we will literally sit there for days on end until we can arrive at a solution that everybody likes. I think that that is why we've made such great TV.

JUSTIN THEROUX:

Damon sort of tricked me. He wrote me an email saying, "Do you play guitar?" And I said, "No." And then he wrote, "How do you feel about singing?" And I said, "I don't sing at all." That's a true statement. He said, "Great," and that's sort of the last I heard of it, thinking he was saying, "Oh, if he doesn't want to sing, I won't make him sing." And then the script showed up and of course I'm singing in it. I was immediately terrified. Ann Dowd actually took the pressure off me, because I was talking to her about it when the script came in and I said, "God, I'm a bit nervous, because I'm not a singer." She just quite simply unlocked it for me and said, "Well, Kevin Garvey is probably not a good singer." That took all the pressure off.

I actually hired a vocal coach just to literally learn how to keep a little bit of time in a song. So I worked with her a little bit, which is hilarious. Damon did this a lot throughout *The Leftovers*, he would script when I would cry or break down, and he was very specific, "Kevin's eyes moisten," or "a tear rolls down Kevin's cheek," or things like that. And it was slightly scripted in that scene, as I recall.

Mimi Leder, who is just fabulous, directed that episode, and our DP [Michael] Grady just lit it beautifully. I remember being very taken by the words to that song once I started singing. It was wonderful because not only was I singing it and felt no pressure to be good, I also had a teleprompter. I just remember being very taken and moved by the words of that song, obviously knowing what the function of the song was supposed to be in the story.

It's interesting, there were a couple takes where I was breaking down, where I was crying very hard. To the point where the words were barely legible. We did it several times, many times from different angles and all the rest of it. I remember being shocked when I saw it because they didn't use any of my crying takes. If you watch it again, it's one of those scenes that, at least in a lot of people's memory, has me crying throughout the song. But I'm not crying.

My eyes are moist, there's a little bit of snot around my nose, but I don't really cry in the song. Damon selected all the takes where I wasn't crying. I thought for sure they were going to select ones where I was sort of blubbering.

LILA BYOCK:

Damon likes to assign homework to the writers. One night's homework was, how do we get Matt to Australia, so he could meet up with the rest of our characters? I pitched that he charters a plane, but it has to make an emergency landing in Tasmania, so he has to take a ferry from Tasmania to mainland Australia. Damon was like, "I want to do that." But we thought, can we do an entire episode on a ferry in Australia? This is where the magic of HBO meets the magic of Damon's writers' rooms. Within twenty-four hours, we had the answer: sure, they would pay for that.

They would not only pay to shoot an entire episode on an Australian ferry, they would hire probably a hundred adult film actors to film the orgy scenes on the boat, dressed as members of a lion-worshipping cult. It turned into the most insane TV episodic shoot of all time.

DAMON LINDELOF:

It's a gross oversimplification to say there's more trust on the HBO side, and that the networks are less trusting. You have to acknowledge that there are two respective businesses, one is a subscriber-based business, and the other one is a business that's based on getting eyeballs, so that they can monetize ad sales. I never felt like ABC was meddling with *Lost*. I felt like they were struggling to make sure that it didn't blow up and get canceled.

HBO isn't worried about their shows getting canceled. They care about whether they can make shows that are culturally significant. I think that when we were talking about *The Leftovers*, there was always a little confusion on all our parts as to, Are we trying to make a show that a lot of people are going to watch, like *True Blood*, or are we making a show that's going to live more in a space like *The Wire*? Where, it's going to be esoteric and not for everybody, but it'll build a real cult following, and it'll be one of the arrows in the HBO quiver, but it doesn't need to be like everything to everyone.

With *Lost*, the only experience that I've had making broadcast television, the spirit of all the notes was that we don't want to turn anybody off. The spirit of the notes at HBO was never that. It was, Just make a really cool show.

JUSTIN THEROUX:

I've done many things for HBO and I sort of consider myself a bit of a company player. *The Leftovers* is the jewel in that crown of projects I've done with them. It obviously wasn't a wildly commercial show, it's not everyone's cup of tea, but for the people that rode the Bronco, it was rewarding.

The biggest knob on HBO's console is quality control. They don't rush in, they don't rush out. It's probably one of the best places to nurture an idea from its concept to its completion.

Damon and the writers did such a beautiful job with the show's ending. For all the chaos and pathos that happened in the three seasons leading up to it, there is this beautiful moment of singularity where he basically lands the whole thing on a head of a pin. It's just the word love, and that's it. I love that. You can of course get into the discussion of whether Nora went to the other place, but it doesn't matter. What it was all driving towards was the love between two people in its simplest, purest form, letting those two people stare into each other's eyes and essentially find love, then say they love each other. I thought it was so delicate.

All the other stars disappeared, and one was left in the sky. It didn't negate anything that came before, but it simplified everything into this beautiful haiku that I thought was a stunning piece of writing. It's on the one hand, of course, very romantic, but it also says something larger, about humanity, life, and the time we have while we're here.

John Oliver was a fairly accomplished comedian by 2013. He had received seven Emmy nominations (and three wins) for his writing on Jon Stewart's late-night juggernaut **The Daily Show** *on Comedy Central, where he was also an on-air correspondent. He had starred in his own stand-up comedy special on the same network in 2008, then in 2010 began hosting four seasons of* **John Oliver's New York Stand-Up Show.**

By September 2013, Oliver was a front-runner to succeed Stewart on the **Daily Show** *throne after having spent the summer filling in at the desk while Stewart was in Jordan directing his first movie,* **Rosewater.** *Yet on Thursday, November 14, 2013, HBO announced that Oliver would be charting a new course with the network—having committed to host his own weekly show satirizing current events. Three months later, HBO revealed that the new offering would appear Sunday evenings beginning on April 27, 2014, and be called, endearingly,* **Last Week Tonight with John Oliver.**

Oliver was born in Erdington, England, and attended Christ College at fancy Cambridge University.

JOHN OLIVER, Talk Show Host:

I had mixed feelings about Christ College. England is riddled with class. I had gone to a very poor state school and I was not emotionally equipped at all to be plunged into a world I didn't understand. The *Brideshead Revisited* optics are ridiculous at Cambridge. There's literally a Milton tree. From the first week I was there, I had a combination of impostor syndrome and a chip on my shoulder.

Princess Anne came to the college and every new student was invited to dinner with her, but four of us. We were living next to each other in these shitty rooms and realized we're the four state school kids. It felt like, Oh, they think we're peasants. We were getting the long tail of British aristocracy's opinion of poor people. It played perfectly into my feeling of Oh fuck this place. I never at any point felt like I belonged.

I was going to be standing in for Jon Stewart over the summer, and before he left, Jon told me, "We need to talk about what you're going to do when I get back," which was alarming to me. That felt like a girlfriend saying, "We need to talk when I get back from vacation." I thought, "Am I going to get fired?" I desperately did not want to leave. What he was doing was saying to me, "Once you've tried this, you're going to want to do something else." He was slightly mama birding me out of the nest.

RICHARD PLEPLER:

I was watching him substitute for Jon on *The Daily Show* and I think by the second show of his substitution I went, "Holy shit, this guy is remarkable." I called up Nina Rosenstein who runs late night for us and said, "We have to get this guy. I doubt they'll let him out of there because he's so damn good, but we've got to see if we can get him." By some miracle, they had not locked him up.

JOHN OLIVER:

I had no contract with Comedy Central, so I was free. I did a bunch of meetings, almost all of which made me think, "I don't want to do any of this." Plepler might've been last of all those meetings and by that point, I'm so calloused to bullshit it was all just washing off me. No matter who was speaking, I was thinking, You don't mean any of this.

RICHARD PLEPLER:

We had a three-and-a-half-hour dinner at Cipriani.

JOHN OLIVER:

Plepler's a cartoonish character. He's as close to a ridiculous version of a Hollywood producer that an English kid would have in his head.

He told me, "We're the canvas, we just want you to paint on it." I remember thinking, How does a human being say that to another human being with a straight face?

RICHARD PLEPLER:

I told him, "We'll give you the real estate and the time, and we'll leave you alone. If there's one thing I know it's that you belong at HBO." Thank God he came and the rest is history.

JOHN OLIVER:

I walked back across the park to see my wife. She asked, "How was that?" I said, "It was the same thing, but I don't know, I kind of like this guy, Plepler." When I told Jon [Stewart] about what he was suggesting, Jon said, "You would be fucking crazy not to take that." I still thought it was all empty platitudes, and it wasn't until years later that I realized, "Oh, he stood by all that."

14

Dysfunctionally Yours

OCTOBER 29, 2014–OCTOBER 21, 2016

PETER MORGAN, Creator:

We came to HBO that day relaxed and in good spirits. We had sent them scripts for two episodes of *The Crown* in advance. They knew our track record as artists. There were no surprises. This wasn't a cold pitch.

In January of 2014, Peter Morgan, the brilliant writer of **Frost/Nixon**, **Rush**, **The Queen**, *among many others, joined his highly regarded producing friends Andy Harries and Stephen Daldry for a trip to the United States.*

ANDY HARRIES, Executive Producer:

Peter and I adored HBO. It was the channel that we had the most respect for. Anybody producing drama for television wanted to be on HBO.

We thought our best approach was going to be a co-production, so just before Christmas, we met with the BBC and ITV. They both loved it. Then Peter, Stephen Daldry, and I went out to LA for four meetings: HBO, Showtime, FX, and Netflix at the end. We didn't have much of a view on Netflix. Streamers were not big news at the time.

In addition to the two scripts, we had also sent ahead of the meeting archive footage of the royal family, and highlights from Diana to remind people of the extraordinary stories that were involved in these fifty years of British history. They had our plan of how we wanted to cover all those decades, including three changes of the cast. What was bold was that we were looking for a broadcaster to not only sign on for twenty hours of television right from the off [ten hours per season], but really to buy into sixty hours. There wasn't a whole lot of point in going for the first two seasons if you weren't going to stay with it across the board. And if you wanted Diana, Diana was going to come in season four.

It was a very, very big commitment. Peter nonetheless felt with his reputation, and what Stephen and I had accomplished, it was a clear question of do you want it, or do you not want it?

On hand at HBO to greet them were Mike Lombardo and two members of his drama programming team—and two Anglophiles—Michael Ellenberg and David Levine.

PETER MORGAN:

As soon as we entered the room, a body language expert would have had a field day. It was a tense atmosphere. I immediately felt on the back foot. Mike clearly was in control of the room. It felt like no one else on the HBO side spoke. Mike sat there arms folded, asking hostile questions. They sat there like a politburo.

MIKE LOMBARDO:

Peter had been set to direct a movie for us, *The Special Relationship*, which was a Tony Blair and Bill Clinton piece. He literally went missing right before we were about to start. We were told he had a breakdown.

DAVID LEVINE:

Mike said, "You failed on your movie, if you don't remember."

PETER MORGAN:

The simplest thing for me to do is take my own inventory as it were. In the course of pre-production my mother was diagnosed as being terminally ill.

It was an emotional time. I couldn't focus, and I made the decision to back out knowing that they could get somebody else quickly. I felt terrible about letting people down, but I would have let everyone down even more if I'd carried on—and the movie that was made reflected well on everyone. It got nice reviews and even won awards.

ANDY HARRIES:

Lombardo came at Peter aggressively from the start. The gist of it was very much, "Why should we as an American network buy such a big slice of British history?" Lombardo kept pumping questions at him. Peter said, "I'm not happy with this. I just don't want to go on." And then there were about two minutes of silence.

MIKE LOMBARDO:

In the middle of his pitch, he literally stopped, then put his head down for what seemed like fifteen minutes. He couldn't gather his thoughts. It was so painful; I was truly worried for him. I thought, Is he not well? And so that was part of what was going on in my mind as we were faced with making a huge decision about a huge project.

At this point, the level of discomfort being what it was, Lombardo asked Ellenberg and Levine to leave the room. The two gingerly walked out.

PETER MORGAN:

To be honest, I felt terrible in the meeting. I don't remember putting my head down on the table, but there did come a point where I felt so disrespected that I didn't want to continue.

MIKE LOMBARDO:

The *Crown* pitch was way overwhelming—money-wise and thinking about working with Peter Morgan again.

PETER MORGAN:

Afterward, Daldry and I looked at one another and said, "What a horrible place, let's get out of here."

I've never borne Mike Lombardo a grudge for that meeting. My only question was, why the fuck did he make us come to the room? He had the scripts. Just ring us up and say no. There wouldn't have been hard feelings. To me it felt like a deliberate act of intimidation.

By contrast, when we walked into Netflix, I immediately felt like I was with a family, and it has been a blissfully happy home for me ever since.

ANDY HARRIES:

Netflix ended up making a big commitment to us, about $70 million per season, and they committed to two seasons.

MIKE LOMBARDO:

I heard Netflix had made a two-season commitment; that was clearly something we weren't going to do. I told Richard about that, and he had no problem with us passing. He certainly didn't say we should grab it.

ANDY HARRIES:

When I got back, my mate at ITV asked, "What are you doing?" I took a deep breath and I said, "Netflix." He looked down into his cup of coffee, then said, "Total game changer. This is going to change the whole business." And he was right.

ARI EMANUEL:

I made this huge deal for Jon Stewart at HBO, and then they realized they legally couldn't do it. We had to settle out. We then negotiated a deal with Apple. I said to Glenn Whitehead, "We got an offer right now for eight episodes with Apple's equivalent to HBO's original offer." He started arguing with me, and said, "You're forgetting, they're not HBO," and I said, "Glenn, nobody gives a fuck about your brand anymore."

And so it was that **House of Cards**, **Orange Is the New Black**, *and now* **The Crown**—*three important shows that could have been on HBO—wound up instead on Netflix.*

Viewed through the lens of a programming contest, HBO execs had blown it on all three occasions. They should have appreciated the great potential in **Orange**, *might have been less "entitled" when it came to* **House of Cards** *(assuming as they did that the show would have ended up theirs), and should never have let* **The Crown** *slip from their grasp.*

But this wasn't just about programming, and this wasn't a level playing field. Time Warner had institutional investors who demanded the best earnings possible; Netflix, on the other hand, was being supported by investors who conversely didn't want them to make earnings, instead they wanted them to become a monopoly. Investors would have punished Netflix if Netflix had shown interest in profits. Many of these investors owned both Time Warner and Netflix and wanted them operating on entirely different philosophies.

As a result, the playbooks each side was using were fundamentally different. While Netflix was being more aggressive in the marketplace, Time Warner was lagging behind. HBO was still in the pilot business; Netflix was handing out orders for entire seasons.

FRANCES McDORMAND, Actor and Executive Producer:

I was a real fucking pain in the ass. I thought it turned out really well but could have been better.

Olive Kitteridge, *a four-part miniseries set in Maine, debuted on Sunday, November 2, 2014, with the third and fourth installments airing the following night. Adapted from a 2008 book of the same name by Elizabeth Strout, which won the Pulitzer Prize for Fiction, the story follows the eponymous female lead, a riveting Frances McDormand playing a gruff and depressed woman with an overdeveloped habit of suffering no fools. The four-hour miniseries showed little violence and no car crashes, just beautiful storytelling from Strout and the amazing Jane Anderson, who wrote the script. Bill Murray, who plays Jack Kennison, is another delightful surprise, one of a select group who live on Kitteridge's depressed wavelength.*

Directed by Lisa Cholodenko, who had directed McDormand twelve years earlier in **Laurel Canyon** *and executive produced by Jane Anderson, McDormand, Steve Shareshian, and the formidable pairing of Tom Hanks and Gary Goetzman, the miniseries received a plethora of Emmy nominations—thirteen, to be exact. McDormand, Jenkins, and Murray all won for their performances and the show copped the Outstanding Limited Series prize, along with another four Emmys for directing, editing, writing, and casting. McDormand and Murray received Golden Globe nominations, and the show was nominated for Best Miniseries. McDormand and Jenkins were nominated for SAG Awards as well—McDormand went on to win.*

FRANCES McDORMAND:

I had recently seen *The Wire* and realized places like HBO were into cinematic storytelling. This was at a time when I was interested in seeing if I could carry something in a lead role.

Reading has always been a passion of mine, and when I read *Olive Kitteridge*, it became a sliver in my brain. I started to believe that long-format storytelling was really the way to tell a female story because our stories aren't linear. They're circuitous. They take detours and come back to a main theme, which is very much like the way Elizabeth Strout wrote *Olive Kitteridge*.

I'm sure that when Liz [Strout] won the Pulitzer and people called her representation, they said, "We would like to option the book," and heard, "Sorry, it's already been optioned by Frances McDormand," they were surprised. I got in to see people at the networks fast. I sat down with Michael Lombardo, Sue Naegle, and David Levine of HBO.

JANE ANDERSON:

HBO wanted it to be an ongoing series, but ongoing series need to have, for lack of a better word, a gimmick. The challenge was it's a very quiet story. *Olive* was literary. I finally said to HBO, "Allow it to be a mini-series, because it needs a beginning, a middle, and an end. That would be the truest adaptation of this material."

Olive was also made possible because of Michael Lombardo, and his particular taste. He oversaw grand, tent pole series like *Game of Thrones*, but he also loved quieter storytelling that invites an audience to slow down and dig deep.

We were all very self-conscious because Olive was an old white woman. I especially was afraid that it would feel dusty and just appeal to an older audience. And it could feel networky.

Kary [Antholis] came up with a smart idea, which would take care of any kind of doubts that it would draw the audience in. He said, "What if you just start with the ending of *Olive*, with the gun, going into the forest to blow her brains out?" That little three-minute scene at the very beginning tells the audience, this is not your ordinary woman. Something has driven her to this. That one thing freed me up to write the goddamn series.

FRANCES McDORMAND:

Then Lisa Cholodenko came in. She was on the very, very top of a short list of directors who felt right for the collaboration.

It takes a rare person who can hold on to six hours of material. That was a difficult thing for Lisa as a director but what she was able to accomplish was extraordinary. I also think the collaboration with Playtone, Goetzman, and Shareshian in particular, was very helpful.

MIKE LOMBARDO:

It was my idea to go to Lisa Cholodenko. She was not the obvious choice, but that's where my creative instincts went, and it was good to remind people I have some things to add here. I had seen *Laurel Canyon*. I thought it was the one time I saw Fran unpredictable. Whatever that dynamic was between Fran and Lisa, and I know it was a complicated shoot, what emerged was something spectacular.

KARY ANTHOLIS:

I had dinner with Frances in New York, and it became clear that she wanted a much more spare style than what Lisa was delivering. It was a matter of taste. There was no right answer or wrong answer.

There was a lot of tension on the set for sure. Lisa was delivering what I thought were good cuts and Fran was questioning a lot of Lisa's choices. Gary was mediating and was very effective working with both Fran and Lisa, while keeping things together.

JANE ANDERSON:

Lisa was very respectful to me, very respectful about the script. Fran and I were both producers. It was unfair to Lisa because Fran and I had lived with this thing for a very long time.

Since I'm a director, I couldn't help but see things that I thought could've had more irony or blah, blah, blah, but I told myself to pull back. During the editing process, Fran and I did have a lot of notes, because the pacing was a little slow and things didn't quite land. That was hard on Lisa. Fortunately, Gary Goetzman at Playtone was very good at protecting Lisa, and allowed her to do her cut.

The fact is, if a film is successful, everybody forgets whatever went on, and if a film doesn't work, then everybody reexamines the mess of it. This one wasn't too bad. It all worked out beautifully.

FRANCES McDORMAND:

I was like a dog with a bone that I couldn't let go of. There was definitely a point, and I remember very clearly that it took place in a conference room at Playtone, when it was made clear to me what had to happen. They said, "Fran, you gotta put the bone down now. You have to start realizing how good it is. You have to step back and get some perspective on that." And I did, and it was true.

KARY ANTHOLIS:

I don't know that they'll ever be chummy again, but after Venice, there was a real thaw in Fran's anxiety and her feelings of resentment and anger. She came to appreciate that there was just no denying that people loved it. If it's not an entire re-embracing of Lisa, at least it's a certain peace with what the product was.

JANE ANDERSON:

I'm pretty certain *Olive* couldn't be made now because culturally we are all hyper-aware that white stories have so dominated the culture that it's time to give stories of color a shot. And I agree with that. It's time to step aside so other voices can be heard.

FRANCES McDORMAND:

The first time I saw it with an audience outside of a small screening room, there were thousands of people in the audience. But the most important thing to me afterward, my husband, Joel Coen, turned to me, said, "You did good, Frankie," which is his nickname for me. And he didn't mean as an actor, he meant the whole megillah. He's my mentor in filmmaking for thirty-eight years, forty years. That was all the validation I needed.

MIKE LOMBARDO:

I was proud that *Olive Kitteridge* got made. In the moment of hyperbolic competitiveness, *Olive Kitteridge* is a fucking jewel of a show.

Originally, a "miniseries" such as **Olive Kitteridge** *was thought of as six episodes or fewer and was typically historical in nature. When movie stars started doing longer episode runs of more traditional drama that were not historical and were not necessarily constrained to one season, such as* **True Detective**, *the term "limited series" came into play. From an awards perspective, there is no difference between the two, which would be unfortunate for those who had to compete against HBO's next limited series,* **The Night Of.**

On June 24, 2016, **The Night Of** *premiered. Co-written by Richard Price and Steven Zaillian (and based on Peter Moffat's original British series,* **Criminal Justice***), this eight-parter had originally been a James Gandolfini vehicle until his death in June 2013. Robert De Niro had replaced Gandolfini, then John Turturro replaced De Niro.*

One great driver of the success of **The Night Of**, *beyond the stellar contributions of Steve Zaillian, Richard Price, Gina Balian, Jane Tranter, and the cast, was HBO's intrinsic willingness to trust the unknown, truly a rare trait in Hollywood.* **True Detective** *had taught HBO a lesson about how specificity can give way to universality; this knowledge made the next show possible, and better.* **The Night Of**, *like* **True Detective** *before it, was thought of as a hyper-specific story and setting that could still appeal to a wide audience. Once again, the lessons of one show had been passed down to the next.*

STEVE ZAILLIAN, Creator:

Until *The Night Of,* I'd only worked on feature films, but it was clear that studios were making fewer films each year, and television was making more series, so you could see the day coming for some time.

The main issue for me was that I was used to telling stories in two hours. In 120 pages. That's how I saw things and structured them. So the idea of doing something that was eight hours was quite foreign to me, as it was to

Richard Price. Of course, he writes novels, but he, too, had done very little television when we started on this. So we approached it like it was a long movie. You have to break it up into sixty-page episodes, and we did, but in my mind, it was always a 480-page movie.

SUE NAEGLE:

When Zaillian agreed to do it, I was thrilled. He is notoriously very selective about what he takes on. As we were developing it, Steve brought Rudin on. His creative instincts are excellent. There's a reason why he's Scott Rudin. Getting a chance to see that show made was a thrill. Ellenberg, who originally had been endorsed by Rudin and I knew had a history with Zaillian, turned out to have a terrible relationship with Rudin and Zaillian. They didn't want to work with him. It's unusual that the president of programming would end up in New York working full time on a pilot shoot, but that's what we needed in this case. It was an intense time because it was a show shot at night, and I had to do my job during the day. It was quite exhausting. It was especially difficult to have Mike continuing to ask why I was in New York.

Lombardo was far from pleased by the amount of time Naegle was spending in New York, nor was it appreciated by her programming department in LA. None of them understood why, with a varsity lineup of Zaillian, Price, Rudin, and a stellar crew, Naegle was needed on the set of The Night Of, *particularly because she didn't have an extensive production background. Then it got even worse, as gossip and rumors spread about Naegle's personal life, complete with titillating, and unproven, explanations as to why Naegle wanted to be in Manhattan so much.*

STEVE ZAILLIAN:

HBO was good to me from beginning to end. They allowed me to cast who I wanted, have the crew I wanted, to edit for close to a year, and never gave me those typical anonymous studio notes that can make you crazy.

I first met James Gandolfini back in 1997 when he auditioned for the role of Al Love in *A Civil Action*. I thought he was great in the film and really liked him as a person.

One thing about James, he was never satisfied with the scenes he was in as we were shooting them. He always thought he could do better, which is something we had in common.

Once *A Civil Action* was edited and we were doing some looping, I asked James what he was doing next. He said, "Another gangster thing," like, what else is new. That turned out to be *The Sopranos*.

Ten years later, when *The Sopranos* ended in 2007, he and HBO looked for another series they could do together. They decided *The Night Of*, which at that point was a rough story bible and pilot script, and I was very happy to be working with James again.

Since we originally thought of it as a series, he asked me, "What's going to happen to my character in subsequent seasons?" I said, "I don't know, I'll be lucky to survive this first one, but if I have to guess, I'd say you'll probably end up in jail." He lit up and said, "That's good enough for me."

Originally, the plan was Richard Price would write the pilot and I'd direct it. That was it. No point in thinking beyond that since it might not get picked up.

Once the series was ordered, Richard said he'd write a couple more episodes and I said I'd direct a couple more, and then that would be it, we'd turn the rest over to others. And we tried to, but both ended up feeling too invested in it to let it go.

And when it came time to shoot the pilot, I wanted key department heads I'd worked with before, and they for the most part also came from feature films. We shot the pilot in the fall of 2012. I had it edited by February 2013.

SUE NAEGLE:

The pilot came in and it was excellent. The kind of excellence I felt was fairly undeniable, despite the political complications of Mike's relationship with Rudin. But Mike didn't entirely agree at first and was critical of certain elements that he fixated on.

There's an understanding at HBO that when you develop something, if it doesn't move forward, you're basically stuck there because they have contractual restrictions that make it extremely difficult to set it up with another network or streaming service. They don't want someone else to have it. But Ari [Emanuel] did something that at the time felt forbidden, which was to get Netflix to say they would make it. Ari basically used another buyer to push Mike into a corner. Mike ultimately agreed to pick the show up and it was thrilling.

I was so excited that it was going to go. And then he turned to me and said, "We're going to do it as a limited series. So I'm moving it to Kary Antholis." He took away that chance for me to work on it.

It was devastating, but I was so beaten down at that point, I didn't want to do anything that would hurt the project. And I started to feel as if my association with it would make the whole process difficult.

STEVE ZAILLIAN:

James tragically died that June.

I loved James and wasn't sure I wanted to continue without him. HBO wasn't sure, either. We were all just so saddened by his death.

Eventually, Richard and I continued working on the story and scripts. That would take about a year, and at some point during it, I started thinking about who might be able to play James's part.

It's hard to imagine a more daunting task for a producer than trying to replace James Gandolfini, much less with an already filmed pilot. But HBO believed in the show and managed to land one of the few names with enough cachet to mitigate the loss: Robert De Niro. De Niro's attachment, however, would not last long, as a scheduling conflict got in the way.

ARI EMANUEL:

Steve [Zaillian] is one of the great perfectionists of all time and while he was directing it, and searching for a very specific tone, I think Michael Lombardo was frustrated. And then after James Gandolfini died, there was this moment when CAA tried to fuck around with De Niro on the project. I could see Michael was pissed off. He just wanted revenge, but we just needed Michael to be calm and permit Steve to do what he does. The show was brilliant.

STEVE ZAILLIAN:

I'd long admired John Turturro, and had thought about him for the part before James got involved. We met, talked about James a lot—John was a friend of his, too—and decided to do it together.

JOHN TURTURRO:

A lot of people obviously wanted the part. The quality of the writing was amazing. I'd worked with Richard a couple of times on *The Color of Money* and *Clockers*, and I've read a lot of his books. I thought the material was so specific and nuanced. My agent Christina Bazdekis was fighting for me, but I had some trepidation. James Gandolfini was a good friend of mine, I was so sad about his death, and when they showed me the pilot, I watched his parts with my eyes closed. Then I realized he was barely in the pilot, and reached out to his wife and she was happy with the idea of me doing it.

STEVE ZAILLIAN:

By design, the character of attorney John Stone wasn't introduced until the last couple of minutes of the pilot, and I only shot with James for a day and a half. When it came time to reshoot these two scenes with John, which were basically silent, I wanted them shot exactly the same way.

We calculated to the inch where the dolly tracks had been and re-created the shots precisely as they had been with James, but now it was John making the same long walk through the police precinct past Riz Ahmed, who by now was two years older.

The shots were so much the same that I ended up using close-ups of Riz from both 2012 and 2014. It's interesting to see these scenes back-to-back— the one with a bear of a man, the other with a lanky man—both evocative in their own way of the same world-weary lawyer.

MICHAEL K. WILLIAMS:

Steven Zaillian is a fucking genius. He did not sensationalize the experience of being incarcerated. He didn't feed anyone's fantasies. He gave it to you raw. And you want to know the raw truth about being incarcerated? The worst thing people who are incarcerated lose? They lose time. Time they can never get back. Being incarcerated steals people's lives, and that is the main thing Steven wanted the audience to feel, losing time.

I've never been incarcerated, but I have the trauma of visiting my family, particularly my nephew, Dominic Dupont, who spent twenty-one years of his young adult life incarcerated. He went in at eighteen and he just came home three years ago. The first ten years I would go visit him, then after I left, oh man, would I bawl. The character of Freddy Knight was my way of honoring my nephew's twenty-one years in prison.

JOHN TURTURRO:

Jeannie Berlin doesn't get talked about enough. She was phenomenal. It was like you were watching a real prosecutor. And she wasn't even nominated. Are you kidding me, man? Without Jeannie, the series wouldn't have been what it was. I had done Shakespeare with Bill Camp and he was great, and of course, Riz was excellent. Riz and I really connected. The chemistry we had was palpable, and it enabled us to reach another level.

STEVE ZAILLIAN:

I had no idea how long it might take since I'd never done a limited series before. If someone had said it would be seven years, which is how long it took, I probably would have said, "Forget it." But I didn't know. I had no frame of reference. I'm glad no one told me.

JOHN TURTURRO:

I loved that character. We were thinking about doing another season, but Steve and Richard have never come to an agreement on what it would be about. HBO wanted the character to continue, and so do I.

As HBO miniseries were continuing to make waves, HBO's hit mega-series was doing the same. On April 12, 2015, season five of **Game of Thrones** *premiered, a season featuring a moment of particularly riveting cinema, Queen Cersei Lannister's naked Walk of Shame.*

BERNADETTE CAULFIELD:

We shot the Walk of Shame scene in Dubrovnik. Our extras were spectacular. We walked through with them what we were going to do and told everybody to please be respectful, even though certain people had to throw things at Lena.

LENA HEADEY:

It took three days. Rebecca did the naked walk and I did mine in a make-shift flesh bikini situation. I made the choice to have a body double. I'm covered in tats. Tattoo coverage is dull, and it never looks great, even in the most skilled of hands. People knew us well by then, and privacy is important to me. This was a step too far. Three days, intense crowd, I would've been so on high defense that it would've changed my performance. I'm incredibly grateful to Rebecca, those three days were a whole lot of team-work.

BERNADETTE CAULFIELD:

That scene was huge to pull off. We had security on the walls so that when filming was taking place we could stop the tourists until we got Lena or Rebecca under covers. Amazingly, there was only one picture that got out, but it wasn't a nude, and I'm pretty sure it wasn't Lena.

GEORGE R. R. MARTIN:

A couple of things were happening by then: one, I couldn't differentiate the series from the books, and two, the show was moving a lot faster than the books. I was getting more and more nervous about that.

D. B. WEISS:

George was involved in both the outline and the writing process for most of the run of the show. We'd run our outlines by him and go back and forth on his suggestions, issues and ideas, and of course he wrote a script every season for the first half of the show. At a certain point, the inevitable divergences between book and show became very complicated to track. He was deep into the sixth book by this time, and I remember him describing it as trying to keep two related but distinct alternate realities alive in his head simultaneously. Keeping even his book reality straight seems like one of the most gargantuan tasks in the history of storytelling, so it makes sense that doing justice to both at once would be an extremely tall order.

GEORGE R. R. MARTIN:

Every time I wrote a script, it took me about a month, but also it broke up any momentum I had on the books. I'm not a writer who can just turn it on and turn it off. I have to live in the world and lose myself. Waking or sleeping, I'm still thinking about the characters and situations. Turning that off to write a script and then trying to go back to it was costing me even more time. So, starting with season five, I said, "Okay, I won't write a script for season five." But then the book still wasn't done. So, I wound up skipping season six as well, and then I didn't do any more scripts. But the other thing was when they caught up and passed my books, it was also getting further and further away from my books.

EMILIA CLARKE:

I was still dealing with the effects of my brain hemorrhage when I started getting more recognized in season five onward. That combination made seasons five, six, and seven really tough. But I do think having a very real experience personally happening alongside a very surreal experience professionally allowed me to find a balance probably sooner than I would have otherwise.

By season six, the world phenomenon that was **Game of Thrones** *was ringing up production costs of over $10 million per episode, eclipsing $100 million for the ten-episode season. It wasn't easy to keep up with viewers' expectations as the show increasingly dominated the cultural landscape. The spectacles got bigger, hotter, more complicated to pull off. In one episode, the show's star, Emilia Clarke, was standing nude in the middle of a temple that was, quite literally, burning to the ground.*

BERNADETTE CAULFIELD:

The fire was hot and you have a director who's trying to get it hotter. Emilia was in a vulnerable position. She was there on the stage when she sets the whole place on fire. I'm sure even for Emilia, that was scary, because one time she got a little hotter than she should have, but God, I cannot say enough about her. She's amazing, what she went through on that show, from nudity to fire, to eating hearts.

D. B. WEISS:

Arriving on set to shoot the Dragon Pit scene in season seven, we were shooting in Italica, Spain, in the third-largest Roman colosseum left standing. The town had been the birthplace of the emperor Trajan. For the first time in years, almost all our main characters were present in the same location. And it was the first time Peter, Emilia, Kit, Lena, and Nikolaj had shot on the same set. In the years since we'd begun, we'd all become a family to each other—happier than most families, if we're being honest. The whole day was filled with a joy that everyone there had worked very hard for. I don't expect I'll ever feel anything quite like it again in my life.

LENA HEADEY:

There were very few bad days. It changed all our lives. Of course there were days that it was tough, the commitment of it, not fucking it up. You can try to pretend it's just a job, and it is, but it was so loved and people were so heavily invested that you felt a little responsible.

DAVID BENIOFF:

George Lucas and Fran McDormand were my favorite cameos. George because, well, come on. It's George Lucas. The first stories I ever told myself were narrations to go with the battles I'd organize between my stormtrooper action figures and my Luke/Han/Chewbacca figures. So having George walking around, admiring the sets while at the same time poking fun at us ("Steel girders? I never had steel girders on my sets!") was surreal.

Fran because she's Fran, and I got to hear a practice version of her Oscar speech before she delivered it onstage.

MARA MIKIALIAN:

The Queen and Prince Philip were visiting Belfast and we heard they wanted to come and see where *Game of Thrones* was being made. We were told her grandchildren and staff were big fans of the show.

We had several conversations with the palace, and we had decided that they would visit two different soundstages, a costume and props area for a show and tell, and then the throne room. The throne is up on a platform and there are steps up to it. We were thinking about building steps, but the palace representative said, "No, no. She can walk up. It's a better photo op."

Dan Weiss took care of Prince Philip and David was assigned the Queen. They went into the room, met the cast, and some of the British crew. Maisie said, "She's the same height as me." Then we had Lena, because she was our queen, give her a gift, a little throne.

Some of the press wrote she refused to sit on the throne, and the answer that came from our security guard was that the Queen can't sit on any throne that isn't hers.

D. B. WEISS:

We were lucky enough to have a few people visit who were fascinating to talk to and spend a bit of time with. Mark Kelly and Gabby Giffords, two amazing people who have worked so hard to make the world a better place, Garry Kasparov and his wife, Daria, Elon Musk and Grimes, Paul Allen.

A few years ago, Trent Reznor came to set, and sat on the Iron Throne. And was I there to meet this person whose music I'd obsessed over for twenty-five years? Of course not. He did sign an LP, which was very good of him.

On April 21, 2015, season four of **Veep** *premiered. The show was a big winner for HBO, and Julia Louis-Dreyfus effectively was crowned the best comedic actress of her generation in the process—and was Emmy'd for the performance, just as she had been in three previous seasons. Many would argue that for a time,* **Veep** *was the best comedy on television. But this new season would see the arrival of dramas that would threaten its very survival.*

ARMANDO IANNUCCI:

My daughter, who at the time was about twelve, was going to be singing at a concert. She was very anxious. I didn't tell her the plan was I would fly to the UK, see her in the concert, and then fly back the next day to D.C. I'd like to thank United Airlines for this experience. It was great. We got on the plane at ten p.m., takeoff is at ten thirty. We were then asked to leave the plane. We all convened to the gate. Nothing was said. Every hour we got an announcement saying, "We'll tell you as soon as we know anything." Nobody apologized. At about three o'clock in the morning, the flight was canceled. Nobody apologized. By the time I knew I wasn't going home, the UK was waking up, so I could then speak to them and say, "I couldn't come." I wasn't there. And I just thought, I don't want this to happen again. I was missing too much. It was cumulatively just the jet lag, trying to balance being in the United States for the show, but back for home life. I naively thought, The more you did it, the easier the jet lag would get. But, in fact, it's just the worst. I thought I probably got one more season in May and I'll take it somewhere that I think to be interesting. And then it probably needs a fresh team to take over.

Julia had an inkling to be honest, because during season four I was spending a bit more time at home. She thought, Okay, is this coming to an end? Pretty soon we were in the practical area of trying to think, "Okay, what's the best way to proceed? Who could possibly take over?"

JULIA LOUIS-DREYFUS:

It was a big gamble, I won't lie. I was pretty terrified because I felt very protective of the show, very proud of what we'd been able to do for four years. And I wasn't ready to walk away from it. I felt as if there was a lot more story to be told, but we had to find the right person. Working with Armando was an absolute dream. And then when he left, there was a feeling like, Oh God, how are we going to do this?

This would prove to be the first critical challenge for Casey Bloys, who was at the time in charge of Comedy.

FRANK RICH:

Casey's position, which was correct, was we either find the right person or we end it with honor. CAA, which represented Armando and Julia at that time, came up with a list of like two hundred potential showrunners and Casey called me up and said, "Most of these are completely wrong. I have an idea."

CASEY BLOYS:

David Mandel is the only person I could think of. I worked with the three: Berg, Schaffer, Mandel. We partnered Alec with Mike Judge on *Silicon Valley* and he did an amazing job; Jeff Schaffer was working with Larry on *Curb*, and that was terrific. I thought, if Dave does half as well as those guys did, then it's worth a shot. But it was very stressful. The show was also moving from Baltimore to LA, another element that was going to affect the rhythm of the show. Until then all the actors were basically away from home and living in Baltimore and there's a certain esprit de corps that comes from that. Everybody was concerned, but in this job you can't let anxiety get to you.

JULIA LOUIS-DREYFUS:

Dave Mandel appeared like the red shoes in *The Wizard of Oz* that she was wearing the whole time.

I had known Dave for twenty years at that point. And it was like, Oh, yes, of course! Mandel. It made solid sense. He was the perfect person to step into these shoes.

DAVE MANDEL:

I was reading scripts from Armando's last season, and when I got to the finale I saw Armando had left this cliffhanger tie. It was such an incredible prison, but it also had possibilities. How do you resolve the tie? I started to think, Oh my God, she's got to lose. She can't get what she wants. Oh, and what if she loses to another woman? The one thing I knew was that she would try to build a presidential library. I thought maybe it should be more of a bookmobile.

TONY HALE:

I'm in the most uncertain career you can ever have; but I'm not a huge fan of change. I highly respected Armando's choice to spend more time with his family, but it was tough. All of a sudden you feel like you have a new dad, and you wonder, Is this going to work out? I was nervous.

DAVE MANDEL:

Is it as fucking funny as it possibly can be? They are fearless. "Anything goes comedy" is the only thing that's important. That's how Larry did *Curb Your Enthusiasm*. It's how I did *Veep*. If there's room for another joke, let's add it and jam it in. Julia, like Larry, is a fearless performer, not afraid to look ugly, not afraid to be nasty or horrible and willing to do anything for the joke. And so that is in the lifeblood of both shows.

I was conscious of the fact that the first table read was terrible. We had three episodes ready, we read the first one, we then sort of read the second one, and I didn't even let us read the third one. You heard it and it was just not good. But yeah, it was very simple to fix and I always laugh when I look now.

CASEY BLOYS:

Dave knew the first scripts weren't right. He's a very smart and self-aware writer. It wasn't like we had to go down there and knock sense into him.

JULIA LOUIS-DREYFUS:

There were bumps along the way. Don't get me wrong. There were. But he was able to overcome those bumps and take the show to its next place. The show evolved in a way that wasn't jarring.

It definitely did require me to step up, but actually that had been true earlier when we were in Baltimore, because Armando was sort of running the show and was sometimes in the UK. I felt Dave needed my input and that we were a really good team. He has an amazing brain and knows the world of government and politics and history inside out, massive assets, as did Armando, by the way. Without that knowledge, we could never have done the show.

DAVE MANDEL:

My version of *Veep* was going to be a little different than Armando's. I wanted to explore these people as humans, maybe dig into their psychology, and dare I say their backstory.

When we finished the show's sixth season, the first thing I said was, "I need a little more time off." I had been editing season five into June, and then took a week off and started season six. I had done almost two years nonstop. I felt like I knew going into season seven, I didn't want to be exhausted. I remember being exhausted the final season of *Seinfeld*. The exhaustion hurt some things.

Casey and Amy wanted to know what the plan was. "Is it one season? Is it two? Is it two seasons and a movie?" They didn't care what it was, but if we were going to be off the air for a year, they wanted to be able to announce, "Here it is. *Veep*'s back."

I talked Julia through it all, and she agreed to one more season. We let HBO know, and we started work on a ten-episode final season. At that point I knew 100 percent that we were building to a big, brokered convention finale episode where she was going to lose.

We were a couple of weeks from shooting when we won the Emmy in 2017, and the next day, Monday, Julia called to tell me she'd been diagnosed with breast cancer.

JULIA LOUIS-DREYFUS:

I was really ill. And I felt an enormous responsibility to the show, because I knew we'd have to shut down because of my illness. But I had convinced myself that we'll be able to shoot the show in those weeks in between my chemotherapy. It became quite evident that was not gonna work. But what we did keep up were table reads. I almost feel as if they were maybe even placating me to a certain extent. Every three weeks we would get together and read a script for the season that we were going to shoot. I had no idea what I was getting into. Of course, nobody does until they're into it.

In 2010, filmmaker Andrew Jarecki released a full-length semi-fictional feature on the curious case of Robert Durst, who had been a suspect in the disappearance of his first wife, Kathie, in 1982. The film, **All Good Things,** *starring Ryan Gosling and Kirsten Dunst as Durst and Kathie, surmised that Durst had probably been responsible for Kathie's disappearance.*

Bizarrely, on the back of the release of that movie, Durst himself contacted Jarecki, and the two became confidants, and soon **The Jinx,** *a six-part documentary, was born. Released on HBO on February 8, 2015,* **The Jinx** *featured numerous and extraordinary Jarecki interviews with Durst about a number of mysterious deaths he'd left in his wake over the years. (Jarecki remained unflappable in all of them.)*

The show was a smash hit, bringing to new light the true breadth of the real estate scion's pathologies and terror. The first five episodes were edge-of-the-seat stuff, mixing trial footage from Texas, interviews with law enforcement, and amazing sit-downs with Durst himself.

Yet nothing could prepare viewers for the denouement: a hot microphone left on the lapel of Durst picked him up in a bathroom stall saying, "Killed them all, of course." **Esquire** *magazine, as just one example of the cascade of praise (and prizes) the documentary received, described the final episode's reveal as "one of the most jaw-dropping moments in television history."*

MIKE LOMBARDO:

Sheila made it clear from day one, she didn't want to work for me. She only talked to Richard. She had one-on-ones with Richard every week and would rarely have one-on-ones with me. Look, I'm a big boy, but it was so in my face. The few times I did suggest things, she was dismissive of them. Like with *The Jinx,* which she thought was a piece of shit. I disagreed and we did it, so things between us continued to rupture.

SHEILA NEVINS:

Oh my God. *The Jinx* was Lombardo's. It would have taken an idiot not to have known what to do with that.

ANDREW JARECKI, Documentarian:

The Jinx was an unusual animal because we financed the series ourselves, and over the course of making it, which was about five years, we didn't show it to any broadcasters.

My agent Bryan Lourd had made calls to the senior person at each of the top ten outlets and we had two meetings a day for five days running. People had heard from Bryan that they would have to make a decision quickly and they were excited to see what the fuss was all about. We decided we would only show the first episode, and they would have to take our word for it on the rest. We explained to them that unlike most shows where the action all happened in the past, this was a volatile situation that was happening in real time. It wasn't just about giving away plot points—in this case the film's subject was extremely wealthy, didn't want it to see the light of day, and had solved problems in the past by murdering people. So the director of the film was potentially in danger. And because the broadcast of the series would have a real-world impact, we couldn't share everything until just before it was to go on the air.

When they'd watch the first episode, they'd get very wound up, and all say the same thing: "What happens next?" I would respond, "All I can tell you is that it's going to be extremely satisfying for the audience. You are not going to be disappointed." When it came to HBO, because of the scope and cost of the series, I knew the decision would have to come from Richard whom I had known for years. But I wanted to involve Sheila as quickly as possible for two reasons: First, she had years earlier bought my film *Capturing the Friedmans* and we had a great collaboration—Sheila is smart as a whip and we saw eye to eye on how to get the film out there. Second, Sheila is intensely competitive and territorial, and if she doesn't like the way something comes into the organization, she can be an impediment. So it was a delicate dance. I called Richard and said, "I want to show this to you, but I want it to be one-on-one."

Nancy and I went to his house in Greenwich the next night and had dinner with him and Lisa. After dinner, we all went downstairs and watched episode one. As soon as the lights came up, Richard said, "This is the worst negotiating position I've ever taken in my life, but I need to tell you there is no way anyone is going to outbid us for this." He knew that I had done what I had promised on *Capturing the Friedmans* and how paranoid I was about secrecy. I said, "I need to tell you, this is not going to be normal. We're not going to be sending out copies of six DVDs to the TV Critics' Association to make sure we get press. I promise you, we are not going to have trouble getting press for this. But until it comes out, no one is going to fucking see it and you're going to have to be okay with that." Richard said, "I get it. I'm your partner. We're going to make this happen." Over the next week we put together a deal.

Netflix stepped up at the last minute to match the deal, but we recognized how important it would be to have the series roll out over six weeks. The water-cooler effect was critical, and knowing what was in the later episodes, we knew the audience would grow rapidly from week to week. Netflix would have wanted to put all the episodes up on Day One and that would not have been right for this. Beyond the issue of how the film would be experienced by the audience, we had the additional problem that if it all came out at once, Bob would know instantly what was in the later episodes, and would likely leave the country and never be held accountable.

On the way home from the dinner at Richard's, I emailed Sheila to say I had shown him something that I thought she would want to see. She wrote me a polite—not effusive—note back, saying she did. She was probably seething but at least she knew I had reached out to her just moments after Richard saw it. Soon after, Richard had me show it to Mike Lombardo who was extremely gracious. Mike saw the potential and somehow trusted what I said about the other episodes.

Then we went into finishing mode. As we put the final touches on each of the episodes, I would go meet with Sheila and Lisa Heller in Sheila's HBO "apartment." She would curl up on the couch and watch intently and make comments every once in a while. It was a relief to show it to Sheila. We had been keeping the material so close to the vest for so long, that those sessions gave me an outlet—a way to get clean feedback from someone I respected who was outside the filmmaking team.

Though Bob had delayed that final interview for many months, I had always been confident he would ultimately sit down with me again. While Bob's father and brother were widely celebrated for being great business-men, I think Bob believed he had done something even more extraordinary in his own right—killing three people and getting away with it. He wanted to take a bow and The Jinx was his chance. Bob is so fast—he can lie without batting an eyelash and most people don't call him out for it. Even at his age, around seventy-three, I was impressed that he could intuitively see where I was going and anticipate so many of my questions.

At the same time, I wasn't surprised in the final interview that he let him-self get caught. Like Trump, Bob is great on the fly, but at the end of the day, he doesn't do his homework, and he doesn't want to be held accountable by people he regards as his inferiors. So he gets sloppy, loses his temper, shows his teeth.

Going into that final interview, it felt like I had tracked an animal through the bush for a decade, and now it was going to be mano a mano. He was going to have to give it up, because he fucking did it. He killed all three of those poor souls. And he knew it. Why is he sitting down with a filmmaker thirty years later if there's no part of him that wants to just say, "You're goddamn right, I killed my wife. She was torturing me, humiliating me in front of my father and my brother, and she needed to go." He had that all in him. And on top of that, he loved her, he felt guilty, and he still misses her.

Once I knew that Bob was guilty, I realized I had to find a prosecutor we could trust would be able to pursue the case. We went to Marcia Clark and got her advice about who to go to in Los Angeles. She helped us navigate and find a deputy DA in the LA District Attorney's Office named John Lewin, who was a talented prosecutor. He was a cold case expert, who specialized in murder cases where there was no body. Marcia also warned us that we would be well served to refrain from talking to a prosecutor until long after that second interview. She knew that if things went as expected, and Bob was prosecuted, Bob's lawyers would try to have our evidence excluded by saying that we had been working hand in hand with the police to prosecute Bob. If that were true, they would argue, we should have Mirandized him (read him his rights) and told him that we were essentially agents of law enforcement. To ensure we avoided any such criticism, we didn't talk to the DA until six months after the last interview with Bob.

SHEILA NEVINS:

Whose life would have been saved had information like that come out first? Why would it be better to withhold information when the body is long dead than to make sure the person who is guilty is convicted?

I don't think Andrew would have jeopardized anyone's life. Did he rearrange time to make something more dramatic? There's not a filmmaker anywhere who hasn't done that.

ANDREW JARECKI:

Before the show premiered, we decided that we were going to show the last two episodes under an embargo, to one reporter only: Charlie Bagli from the *New York Times,* who had been covering the Durst case for years as the *Times'* real estate reporter. We agreed to allow him to write a piece that would come out at midnight on Sunday night after each of the final two episodes aired. We decided to do the same for one television reporter we trusted—George Stephanopoulos.

So after episode five premiered, Bagli's piece appeared Monday morning, above the fold on the front page of the *Times.* Viewers were going nuts, random people were calling out to me on the street, and everyone who hadn't tuned in yet was tuning in.

Bob had had plenty of time to anticipate this. He had sat through that interview and seen that we had a copy of a letter that directly tied him to the murder of his best friend Susan Berman. So for the two years after that, he knew something bad might happen, but he didn't know what. After episode five, he had gotten very concerned and knew that episode six was likely to get a lot worse.

With all the attention on the show, things were getting more uncomfortable for me and Nancy. We knew Bob was still out there somewhere and was probably getting increasingly angry with each passing episode. My friend Gavin DeBecker arranged a security detail for me. Our daughter Jeremy was nine years old at the time, and I remember sitting down with her and saying, "Okay, honey, so tomorrow morning when I take you to school, we're going to have a couple of guys with us." She immediately started crying. She knew things were getting weird.

We didn't know where Bob was.

Durst was arrested in New Orleans for the murder of Susan Berman the night before the airing of that final episode. His trial for that murder, scheduled to be held in Los Angeles in March 2020, was delayed when COVID-19 hit the United States.

ANDREW JARECKI:

For some time, the FBI had been telling me they didn't know his whereabouts and had no plans to arrest him. In fact, they knew Bob was in New Orleans, planning to watch episode six and, depending on how bad it was for him, decide whether to escape to Cuba, where the US had no extradition treaty. They knew that it would look terrible if they had all this evidence we had provided, knew Bob killed his best friend and his wife, and let him get away because they were dithering while Bob was watching TV and buying airplane tickets.

The FBI went to nine hotels in New Orleans, and each time they went with a list of aliases. And every time the desk clerk would say, "I'm sorry, we don't have anybody by that name." And they would turn around and go to another hotel. The last hotel they go to is the JW Marriott. They go through the list and as before, the desk clerk says, "I'm sorry, we don't have anybody by that name." But just as they turn around to leave, in walks Bob Durst from the street. Evidently at that moment a woman walked over to Bob and said something like, "Mr. Durst, I've been watching the show and I'm a big fan. Could I have an autograph?" The FBI guys found this funny, as did Bob, who says, "Alright, we might as well go up to my room." He brings them up to his hotel room where they immediately handcuff him to the desk and he says, "I don't want any trouble. I need to let you know, there's a handgun in my jacket over there, I've got this box of ammunition in my closet and I've got this duffel bag of weed over there." They arrested him and took him in.

Nancy and I had decided to have a small gathering at my apartment to watch episode six, and invite people who were involved in the film.

Jeanine Pirro showed up with her boyfriend Cody Cazalas, who was the detective who had investigated the case in Galveston in which Bob had dismembered his elderly neighbor. And a whole bunch of New York filmmaker friends, like Tony Gilroy. I invited Sheila. She had made prior plans to have dinner with Rosie O'Donnell and didn't want to cancel so she brought her along, which turned out to be a mistake.

After everyone heard the confession and the titles rolled, there was a bit of a pall in the room, because it was so emotional to have seen this all go down. Rosie O'Donnell pipes up and says: "Wait a minute, so let me get this straight. You guys had evidence that Bob Durst had committed a murder and you withheld it from the police? That is a criminal act. You have committed a criminal act." My lawyer says, "Actually that's not how it happened." He tries to explain that we had in fact given the evidence to the police two years earlier, and that the decision to wait to assemble the entire case and not to prosecute Bob sooner, belonged to the police, not us. But Rosie decides this is like the Rosie show and she starts harassing other guests. She is also incredulous that he was arrested before the final episode. Had she asked any of the law enforcement people in the room, she would have found out quickly that even when police have evidence of a murder, it often takes them many months before they bring an indictment, as it did in this case.

Minutes after the titles rolled on the last episode, the Internet exploded with the news that the show had revealed evidence proving that Bob had killed his best friend, and had even confessed. The next morning, I went on GMA with George and explained how it all happened. The news was on the front page of every major paper. The *Times* headline read: "Straight from TV to Jail: Durst Is Charged in Killing," with the subhead "In HBO's 'Jinx' Real Estate Scion Is Heard on Tape Saying He 'Killed Them All.'"

After that, the DA asked me not to talk to the press. There was going to be a murder trial, and I would be a witness.

On March 29, 2015, HBO aired **Going Clear: Scientology and the Prison of Belief** *for the first time. Based on a book by Lawrence Wright (who also produced the show),* *the documentary explored the origins and operations of a church shrouded in mystery and intrigue, due in part to some of its famous adherents. It also documented abuse accusations against the church. The piece featured interviews with former members of the Church of Scientology, including Paul Haggis, the screenwriter behind* **Million Dollar Baby***, and Jason Beghe, of* **Chicago P.D.** *fame. Alex Gibney wrote and directed the film, which was executive produced by Chris Wilson, Arthur Portnoy, and Sheila Nevins.*

Going Clear *scored a massive HBO premiere audience, pulling in almost 1.7 million viewers for the network—the biggest premiere viewership for a documentary on HBO in nearly a decade. The film was nominated for seven Emmy Awards and won three, including Outstanding Documentary or Nonfiction Special for 2015. It also won the Television Academy Honors and a Peabody Award in 2016. The film was vetted by lawyers in preparation for lawsuits from the Church of Scientology, but none arrived.*

ALEX GIBNEY:

Various people had asked me to do the Scientology film. I wasn't that interested in it. I knew it was going to be tough to do, but I also thought it was small. It was very much a fringe group. So why spend all that time and also put yourself at risk for what was essentially a fringe cult? But then Lawrence Wright sent me his book and convinced me. It was the subtitle of his book. *Going Clear: Scientology, Hollywood, and the Prison of Belief.* The biggest subject for me was the prison of beliefs. The idea that smart people could essentially lock themselves into a prison of belief and the bars would be open, but they would never leave their cell because they'd been so thoroughly inculcated with a belief system that became so much a part of their character that they were unwilling or unable to question it. I thought, Wow, that's much bigger than Scientology.

LAWRENCE WRIGHT:

The film was done very carefully. We didn't want to make any mistakes that would give the church an opening. It was carefully vetted. It wasn't that we were trying to protect things that we thought might be edgy. We wanted to be unassailable.

We made it clear that we didn't want HBO backing down from anything, that they were going to have to stand by us. They were clearly not intimidated. In fact, there was a "bring it on" quality.

SARA BERNSTEIN:

The church took out full-page ads, attacking the film, which of course was brilliant marketing for us. You realize something can actually happen, but you're also proud that you're at a place that can take that risk.

LAWRENCE WRIGHT:

The church's reputation for being so litigious didn't bother HBO at all.

From the inception of this, as a magazine piece, through the book, through the documentary, it was just constant legal threats. It never happened that they actually did sue. We won all those Emmys for it, and it was the highest-rated documentary for HBO.

HBO promoted it really hard, and they were rewarded by it. They got a lot of attention and got tremendous viewership.

The church assigned a private investigator. He called himself a reporter and followed me around to public events. He wanted to interview me and I said, "I would be happy to, if you'll let me talk to Miscavige." The church was outraged I would make such a demand.

Some of my friends from high school started getting telephone calls and that was upsetting. You asked people to talk to you and they know that they're at risk, but you don't know how much. It was an act of faith and also a risky maneuver for my sources and the people who actually went on camera. They were punished, and they knew they would be. I regret that, but everybody knew going in that that was the ball game.

ALEX GIBNEY:

The volume of legal correspondence on that film was enormous, and HBO, to its enormous credit, backed us up 100 percent. They stood behind us really powerfully. It was great to have them at our back. We had a security team that followed us as we went from place to place. Sheila famously was also accosted a number of times. I believe that she was approached by Scientologists at a screening. And then she made her famous quip about having 160 lawyers looking at the film.

LAWRENCE WRIGHT:

I don't think the church will ever get past *Going Clear*. It put down a marker; everyone who's interested in the church will read it and watch the documentary. I live in Austin, and when the documentary came out, one woman was so stirred up that she drove her car through the front door of the Church of Scientology. I had to issue a statement deploring violence in any form.

HBO's documentaries ran the gamut and back again. So it was that on May 11, 2015, HBO could pivot from a documentary about Scientology to one concerning a particularly eccentric topic, **Thought Crimes: The Case of the Cannibal Cop,** *directed by Erin Lee Carr.*

ERIN LEE CARR, Documentarian:

Every single experience with Sheila is an experience. I was with Sara Bernstein and Andrew Rossi the first time I met her. It was at her apartment, we knocked on the door, and she was in this flowing caftan. She didn't look me in the eyes, but said, "Does it smell like gasoline in here?" I was thinking, "Is this her telling me I stink?"

We finally sit down, she swoops her hair to the right, and asks, "What are we talking about?" I had this idea for her about the Silk Road and the drug war that I had spent weeks preparing, because I was so excited to meet her. I'd seen a million of her films. She's a huge, huge person in the field and was an inspiration to me before I even met her. I got two minutes into the pitch and she said, "I'm not interested in that." I thought, "Oh my God. She hates my idea. What do I do now?" I would later learn that when this happens in a Sheila meeting, you have to pivot, so Andrew took over, and we ended up talking about circumcision, nuns, dreams, evil, art, Andy Warhol, before I brought up a case about the cannibal cop, who was a New York City police officer who conspired to kill and torture women. She said, "I'm sort of interested in that." After what had become a four-hour meeting, she told me, "I don't like your ideas, but I like you." Obviously, I've never forgotten that. No one has ever said anything like that to me in a meeting.

Sheila doesn't like people with connections. She's very wary of that. I love how you get into a room with her and she doesn't look at her phone. She is very zeroed in. She's not going to flatter you. And when she's in the edit, she will tell you what she thinks. She doesn't even need to take notes. I love screening sessions with her because it's like an oracle from on high. She doesn't solve it for you, she's like, "Bring it back to me when it's done."

An oracle from on high she may have been, but at this point in her career, Nevins's life at HBO was far from comfortable.

MIKE LOMBARDO:

Sheila was a tough nut for me. Always was. She's a complicated woman, incredibly talented. Richard knew how to work her, he would do this for years, he would be like, "How old is she again?" Mock it. And she bought into it, until she didn't. He was out to fuck her from day one. I'd watch him with her. He was a master at it. I was not a master at that. Good or bad. I would watch him in awe.

That is what Richard's so good at, keeping you in on what he's doing to everybody else. You think, he's telling me because I'm the inner circle.

SHEILA NEVINS:

Lombardo hated me. He wished I was dead. Destroyed me. Destroyed my soul.

MIKE LOMBARDO:

It was the documentary, *Elvis*. Kary Antholis had brought it in, Sheila didn't want to do music docs. She didn't want to do docs about people. So Kary brought in Priscilla Presley and the Elvis people, and I met with him. Kary had had this documentary background, and I said, "Run with it. See where it goes. See what happens." At a certain point, the rights came together, and he found an interesting filmmaker for it. And I called Sheila up, and she started badmouthing me, Kary, and the idea of it, and why didn't I call her? And I said, "I didn't call you because I knew you'd do exactly this. You'd just piss on it from day one and you would kill it." She raised her voice on the phone to me, and things got really heated. I was very upset and apologized to her. Look, I respect her earnestly. Honestly, I don't think she respected me. She saw me as just a business affairs guy.

SHEILA NEVINS:

I was once in a car and I'm talking to the driver, and he tells me he's an ex-marine and all that. And then Mike Lombardo called, and I had him on the speaker, and he was screaming at me. Loudly. No one had ever yelled at me before like that. He was tyrannical. He was disturbed. I started crying. Visibly crying. The driver pulls over to the side of the road, and I hyperventilated. The driver says to me, "I don't know you, but no woman should be talked to like that." I swear to God, and I thought, Why do I allow it? I did it because I wanted the job.

On April 23, 2016, HBO reaped yet more spoils from their deep relationships with creative talent, as world-wide superstar Beyoncé chose HBO as the platform on which to release a film version of her new album, **Lemonade.**

NINA ROSENSTEIN:

Beyoncé is so humble and modest; you might not realize that when you see her onstage. We had done a couple of projects with her before. Her doc *Life Is But a Dream* and the On the Run tour with her and Jay-Z. We got the call that she had another project that was not quite finished, and would we be interested in screening? The next thing I knew, I was in her screening room with Zach Enterlin from our marketing team, watching an early cut of *Lemonade*.

I remember watching it and leaning over to Zach, saying, "Is Beyoncé announcing she's getting divorced?" And then of course added, "Do you think Jay-Z knows about this?"

When we saw her afterward, she genuinely wanted to know if we thought it was good. "Do you think people will respond?" I said, "Oh my God, are you kidding me? This is so explosive. This is everything." It was so much fun to be able to see it before anyone else and to work with her on it. And she's very meticulous, obviously, in how she wants to put things out into the world. She loves the surprise element.

I don't even know how she was able to produce it without people finding out, but we came in when she was almost ready to go. And it's not the way we work with things. We usually get months and months of lead time, but with her, it's like whatever she does and however she wants to do it, we want to go along on that ride with her because you know it's going to be massive.

On April 23, 2014, HBO and Amazon announced a multiyear deal for Amazon to begin distributing HBO content through Amazon Prime Instant Video. Under the terms of the deal, some of HBO's most successful shows and miniseries would become available, including **The Sopranos, Band of Brothers, Six Feet Under, The Wire,** *and more. The companies also said they were aiming to make HBO Go available through Fire TV, an Amazon property, by the end of 2014.*

While HBO did get paid for the content they gave to Amazon for distribution, the deal also had certain limitations. HBO had a digital offering of its own, HBO Go, by that time; giving HBO content to Amazon made that content no longer exclusive to HBO properties. HBO hoped that the increased attention for their old hit series would compel customers to subscribe to HBO for new stuff—a risky bet. More crucially, with each viewer that used Amazon Prime for HBO content, Amazon gained data about their preferences.

As Time Warner quietly moved to make itself a more attractive asset to other companies, the promise of increased earnings from the deal clouded management's valuation of the data they were selling. The deal would never explode in HBO's face, but it gave a leg up to what would eventually become a dangerous competitor.

SIMON SUTTON:

By 2014 or 2015 I think we had figured out that we could still grow while basic cable was shrinking. We felt, in the United States, subscribers were available to us in different parts of the overall market. There were the cord cutters, a growing segment, and the traditional subscribers, a shrinking segment.

Every other cable company was shrinking, shrinking, shrinking, but we were enlarging our share in the shrinking universe, because we were never 100 percent of all the traditional basic cable subscribers; there was scope to grow share in a shrinking pool. We would then get the cord cutters by going direct-to-consumer by using Amazon, Apple, and our own app. So we felt pretty confident that there was still strong growth.

HBO had been an early adopter of the concept of multiplexing, establishing HBO2 and HBO3 as far back as 1991. Seven years later, HBO and sister company Cinemax had gone whole hog on multiplexing, creating "The Works," ten branded channels. Cable operators were delighted: more, and a better-focused more, at that, meant better business all round.

Now with the rise of Netflix and Hulu, and the general trend toward cord cutting in the mid-2010s, many consumers no longer felt the need to have a cable box gathering dust on the top of their TVs, if they had TVs at all. HBO knew it needed a way to deliver its content on demand and stream it to computers, tablets, and phones.

So, on April 7, 2015, HBO Now was launched just as a new season of **Game of Thrones** *became available. Pickup by consumers was swift. Soon, however, the dreaded churn muscled in. HBO had not anticipated the new ease with which broadband customers could cancel subscriptions, compared to the more arduous process of cancelling cable altogether. Hundreds of thousands of customers were now cancelling their subscriptions between* **Game of Thrones** *seasons.*

A direct-to-consumer streaming service isn't just about making content available to a wider demographic, though—it's also about leveraging that relationship to harvest data. In that regard, HBO Now was set up to fail. HBO simply never had a way of reaching all of its customers. The launch of HBO Now was seen as a chance to help drive out broadband, too, but not a single distributor supported that effort. Was it that HBO secretly didn't want to be in the direct-to-consumer business, or did they not understand how to work those direct relationships with customers?

The issue of churn was crucial, though, and that concern had led to the Amazon/ HBO linkup, in which instead of having to use HBO Now, a potential viewer was able to go to Amazon and sign up for HBO. The decision to go this route was said to be one of the most contentious fights in the history of the channel. The new arrangement meant that customers could now bypass the HBO Now app altogether, thereby killing any chance of a direct relationship with the consumer and the harvest of their invaluable data. Even though it was argued that this was bad for the long-term strategic direction of HBO, the Amazon deal happened because it made the numbers look better in the short term.

RICHARD PLEPLER:

Do we want to build a streaming service? What are the kind of unintended consequences of potentially doing that, given that we had $7 billion of revenue coming from our distributors? We did a lot of analysis, a lot of internal thinking. We were very mindful that we were tethered to our parent company which was planning on a lot of EBITDA growth from us. At some point in 2014, I remember turning to Simon, Tom Woodbury, and Eve [Konstan] and saying, "Don't you think Apple is the perfect way for us to enter into this world? They'll keep us honest. They'll make sure we've got the right tech partners and that we don't stumble. What better brand to announce to the world that we're going to have a streaming service than Apple?" And everybody said, "Hundred percent." So I called up Eddy Cue and I said, "We'd be honored if you would be our first digital distribution partner." And he said, "We'd be honored to do it with you." Within three days, he was in my office.

One of the most exciting days in my career was standing on stage with them in Cupertino and announcing HBO Now, which of course was the forerunner to the HBO digital strategy. Tim Cook said to me backstage, "We're really proud to be doing this with you." And I said, "Can't tell you how mutual the feeling is."

That announcement was an especially exciting day because it began a process of digital growth which we knew was essential for the business.

When HBO Now debuted it was projected by analysts to land between one million and two million subscribers in the first three months alone.

Instead, Richard Plepler revealed in February 2016 that the streaming service had netted only eight hundred thousand subscriptions. This stood in bold contrast to the nearly seventy-five million that Netflix boasted by the end of 2015, having grown twelve million since HBO Now's launch, and the nine million subscribers who had joined Hulu by around the time HBO Now hit the market. On a call with analysts from Wall Street, Plepler said HBO did not intend to lower its $14.99 per month ask, instead promising a more forceful marketing campaign for HBO Now to supplement the service's numbers.

But then a strange thing happened. Over the ensuing period from 2016 to 2018, HBO claimed it saw the largest subscriber uptick in its history, and the biggest subscription revenue growth in twenty years—and all this in the most competitive period ever seen in the sector.

JEFF BEWKES:

After turning away News Corp's bogus $85 offer that was really worth $70, we had laid out plans to double the earnings from $4 to $8 per share in four years and launch HBO Go (direct on broadband) with Apple as marketing partner. None of our traditional cable and satellite affiliates were happy with this, and they expressed their feelings when we renewed carriage agreements for Turner and HBO. Among other things, they refused to share any viewer data. We didn't know who was subscribing or anything about what they watched. It was clear that Turner's ad revenue would get hit first, then the basic bundle of one hundred channels would start eroding. And if we couldn't evolve HBO into direct broadband distribution globally, eventually it would be overtaken by Netflix and Amazon.

But at the same time we needed to fulfill our aggressive earnings promises to stay independent or find a big partner. The board came to me and said they wanted to raise my comp by $5 million a year. I said, "Let's not." We get 90 to 95 percent shareholder approval on the board elections and on my compensation, and that helps ward off activists and hostile takeovers. I asked instead for incentive stock packages for Tsujihara, Plepler, and Martin and their teams so they'd be rewarded if they hit our aggressive earnings goals. I figured if we achieved our plans our stock would take off, and all of that happened.

RICHARD PLEPLER:

The reason we missed the numbers in 2016 was that the traditional cable deals had to be renegotiated and the streaming stuff hadn't begun to kick in yet. The reason that we had to renegotiate the deals was because they had gotten too expensive. The retail price and the wholesale price, which everybody was just running up at 5 percent a year, was unsustainable. So we designed a strategy to emphasize scale with a lower wholesale rate. And as we redid those deals, we basically then turned it into the biggest earnings in history in 2017 and 2018. It's also important to remember the subscriber growth from 2015 to 2018 was consecutively huge and resulted in some of the biggest gains in our history.

JEFF BEWKES:

HBO was starting to grow numbers pretty substantially, using the broadband service HBO Now. They were adding subscribers. But none of the pay-TV services that are sold on top of the cable package were growing. It's not because they didn't like the programming at HBO.

In order for a household to subscribe to HBO, they have to have the basic cable package. By the time you look through your cable bill, you have cable bills that are two hundred bucks a month, and then you have to buy HBO for $15 on top. Part of the problem was the price was too high. Let's say HBO has 35 million households subscribed and wants to have 45 million. Let's say there are 105 million basic TV multichannel subscriber households. If HBO had 35 million subscribers, it was selling into those 105 million basics. But what has happened to those 105 million basics in recent years? They're now 85 million.

If it's going down five a year and HBO was at 35 million when the basics were 105, when the 105 became 85, why wouldn't you expect the 35 million to become 27 million? But it isn't. It's 38. So HBO has gone up. They had a 20 percent reduction in eligible HBO homes. That's a disaster at Turner. I know HBO people are sitting there thinking, Why did Jeff want to sell the company? Well, have you checked in on Turner? It's half the earnings.

JOHN MALONE:

HBO really had no content and no identity internationally that they could leverage. They had a few joint ventures in a couple of countries. Most of their content rights had already been licensed to third parties. So for them to decide to withhold content from monetization for two or three years would have given them a disastrous decline in valuation, and then Jeff would have had a hell of a time getting any sale. So he had to make a decision: I'm a seller, or I'm a fighter. And he made the decision: he was a seller.

Floyd Mayweather Jr., on the other hand, was a fighter. On May 2, 2015, he fought Manny Pacquiao in a PPV bout jointly produced by HBO and Showtime. The fight took five years to make happen, and brought in millions, but as is often the case with pay-per-view, the majority would go right back out of HBO's pockets.

JIM LAMPLEY:

We were far and away the dominant broadcaster of boxing in the United States. We were willing to pay higher rights fees, more indelibly associated with the sport. Everybody in the building knew that Mayweather–Pacquiao was going to be the fight about which people would say afterward, "Why did I spend $120 for that?" but you still had to get it. I had to do it because the audience expectation was so overwhelming compared to the reality of what was going to happen.

BOB ARUM:

We knew that if we came back and Ross tried to fuck us, that Lombardo and Plepler would put a stop to it because during that period where we did the Pacquiao fight on Showtime, they prevented Ross from being vindictive and punishing us.

On Wednesday, November 11, 2015, members of the **Real Sports with Bryant Gumbel** *team met at Aureole in Manhattan for a dinner celebrating a rare milestone: the twentieth anniversary of the hit series. Addressing his team, host Bryant Gumbel, who had spent fifteen years hosting* **Today** *on NBC, had only praise for HBO's work: "I've never hid or tried to disguise the fact that this is the best show on which I've ever worked. I'm enormously proud of this broadcast. And not just because it's my baby."*

BRYANT GUMBEL:

Over the twenty-five-plus years since I began hosting *Real Sports*, the business has changed, but unfortunately, not for the better, at least in my opinion. I say that because the birth of so many league-owned networks (NFL, MLB, NBA, etc.) and networks owned by teams or conferences (YES, SEC, Big 10, ACC, etc.) has resulted in a number of TV options where the interests of the viewer or the truth are not the priorities. As the broadcast arm of that team, or conference, or league, the priority is instead cultivating the best image possible for that sports entity. Anything that does not advance that agenda most frequently goes unaddressed. As a result, players, coaches, teams that have problems, find it best and easiest to gloss over their issue or problem on a [league or team] network that will accept whatever they say, without anyone demanding either clarification or justification. The interviews are in the main soft and most often spoon-fed, leaving any serious journalist interested in pursuing the truth, out of the loop.

Gumbel was right to be proud: for a department that had been on its heels since relinquishing the rights to Wimbledon and **Inside the NFL,** **Real Sports** *was an enduring treasure. The raison d'etre for the series was clear from the start: to investigate serious issues surrounding sports and dig deeper into that world than any other TV show had done.*

BRYANT GUMBEL:

As for how much I've changed, it's hard to say. Few of us see ourselves as others do. I know I'm a lot older than I was when *Real Sports* began, and only a fool would think they're as sharp, perceptive, and quick thinking at the age of seventy-two, as they were when they were forty-five. I still enjoy what I do, but don't want to overstay my welcome on the screen. Come next year, I'll have been on television for fifty years. While I'm proud of that, I don't want to ever be viewed as the guy who *used to be* Bryant Gumbel.

JOE PERSKIE:

"What is Bryant writing on his note pad?"—that's the most common question I get in the twenty-plus years I've been working here. Bryant won't even tell me. "Will you just tell me what you're writing, so I can answer people, for god's sake?" He just smiled.

What makes our correspondents so valuable is their ability to conduct on-camera interviews. That's one of those things that might look easy to do but is actually hard to do well. You have to be well prepared in advance, but then you also have to have that presence in the moment. That's the part that I'm not sure you can teach. Bryant is particularly brilliant as a broadcaster, because he's such a good interviewer.

Once a month is sort of like a sweet spot where you have just enough time to make yourself crazy, but not enough time to treat it like a documentary. We work really hard to try to get each segment feeling like a little piece of art, but on a timetable that's almost more typical of the news. We don't have a huge staff.

The International Olympic Committee is one of the most dominant organizations in sports. In 1996, one month after HBO premiered **Spirit of the Games** *commemorating Olympic history,* **Real Sports with Bryant Gumbel** *delivered a scathing criticism of Juan Antonio Samaranch, the International Olympic Committee president on a show that aired just four days before the Atlanta summer games. The timing was no accident and got more viewers interested, especially since HBO was shut out of airing the Olympics themselves. In the episode, Samaranch was accused of being buddy-buddy with dictators and even of raising his hand in a fascist salute while serving as the IOC vice president. Frank Deford, Gumbel, and the team didn't back down in interviews, doing their best to light a fire before the opening torch itself was ignited.*

MARY CARILLO:

More than anywhere else I've worked, HBO felt like family. I was the rookie and Ross came over to me, thanked me for my work, and said, "Hey, look, there's this new show on HBO called *Real Sports*. It tells some good stories. Would you want to try doing one or two?" And of course I said, "Yes."

On January 30, 2018, **Real Sports** *aired Mary Carillo's "The Believer" segment, on Margaret Court and homophobia.*

MARY CARILLO:

Margaret Court is inarguably one of the best tennis players of all time, men or women. She won sixty-two majors, which is more than anybody else in singles, doubles, and mixed. She was an unbelievable player who redefined women's sports in tennis by working out in the gym all the time, practicing with guys. She's truly one of the all-time greats.

Margaret says that her views on homosexuality are not her own. They're the word of God. She doesn't believe in gay marriage.

Beret Remak and I got on the blower with Joe Perskie. He stopped me and said, "Mary, we don't do agenda journalism." I said, "I promise you we'll bring back a balanced story, I promise you." And he said, "All right." Then he held me to it.

I grew up idolizing Margaret Court. I thought she was amazing. I had nothing but respect for her. I'd read up enough about her ministry to know that they did a hell of a lot of good work. People are not one thing. Margaret is not one thing. We were in Perth with Margaret on the day that gay marriage passed in the country. And I said to her, "How do you feel about it? Are you surprised that this thing passed?" And she said, "I am surprised, but I know that me and all of us in the ministry, we are the silent majority."

I think a good *Real Sports* piece has to have layers. It needs context. There needs to be a turn. If you want a *Real Sports* story, the ones that count the most, you've got to walk away from it thinking, Wow, I had no idea, and I had no idea I would care.

On June 24, 2003, **Real Sports** *aired Armen Keteyian's segment on Vince McMahon and the death of several WWE wrestlers. The segment was, let's just say, heated.*

ARMEN KETEYIAN, Correspondent and Executive Producer:

There were an inordinate number of wrestlers who had died under the age of forty-five from a variety of circumstances. Many of those, if not all of them, at some point in time were under the auspices of Vince McMahon.

The interview was done at the WWE headquarters in Stamford. I was sitting probably four feet away from Vince, and I could tell his blood pressure was rising and he was not happy with the direction that I was going. But I kept pressing him. You just didn't know with Vince. I thought he was going to leap out of the chair and we were going to have one of those WWE moments where I was going to tip over.

VINCE McMAHON:

The WWE PR team went over the interview beforehand with Armen Keteyian's people. Armen said, "Here are the questions that are going to be asked. Here are the ones that are not going to be asked." If you're a professional, you stick to that. Well, the first question he asked was one which he agreed he would not ask.

I knew the camera was on me, not on him, and when I would answer a question, he would ask another question and not even look at me when I was speaking. He was just looking down at his notes. It was so rude. I've never had anyone interview me like that. But the biggest problem was he kept asking me questions that he had already agreed not to ask. He'd make facial reactions like he didn't believe me. I was getting upset.

ARMEN KETEYIAN:

I knew he was going to do something. And in my mind, I was like, Don't flinch, don't give him the satisfaction, don't turn this thing into something about you, because that provides sympathy to Vince. So I just held my ground, and I knew that if I just kept asking a direct, fair, fact-based question, something was going to give, and it did.

VINCE McMAHON:

Finally, he asked me another question that wasn't supposed to be asked, and I couldn't contain myself. Rather than attacking him, I just swept the papers out of his hand.

ARMEN KETEYIAN:

We didn't go much past that moment.

VINCE McMAHON:

He was introduced as the award-winning Armen Keteyian. I want to know what he was awarded for. He was the most unprofessional person I've ever met.

Bernard Goldberg joined **Real Sports** *in 2000.*

By 2004, Goldberg was already a seven-time Emmy-winning investigative journalist. Goldberg dug into tons of topics for **Real Sports** *from an interview with former*

NFL lineman Esera Tuaolo announcing that he was gay, to a behind-the-scenes look at the Westminster Dog Show.

For one special program, he uncovered the upsetting story about how children in the Middle East are taken and enslaved, forced to work as jockeys in a sport dominated by the upper class in the United Arab Emirates: camel racing.

BERNIE GOLDBERG, Correspondent:

I never do a story to make the world a better place. I don't believe that a reporter should comfort the afflicted and afflict the comfortable. I don't believe in standing up for the little guy over the big guy because sometimes a little guy is a pain in the ass and is wrong. Sometimes the big guy is right. I'm against bias of any kind, from the right or left.

That said, I did a story that literally, and I mean literally, not figuratively, freed about four thousand kids from slavery, the camel jockey piece. Ansar Burney, who was an activist in that area, is the one who freed them. He told us that the children of the rulers of the country saw the story, went to their father, and said, "Is this true?" And the father, I think he was the Crown Prince, said, "It's true." And he was embarrassed. So he outlawed children riding as camel jockeys, this time for real. And other countries in the Persian Gulf followed suit. The sport fell like dominoes. A bunch of kids were put on airplanes and sent home. But I did not do that story in order to free children from slavery. That's a dangerous way to do stories.

On August 17, 2010, **Real Sports** *aired Goldberg's "After the Hits" segment, an exposé on the prevalence of concussions and CTE in the NFL.*

ROSS GREENBURG:

Northeastern University was starting to collect human brains and had a pretty healthy knowledge of what was going on with concussions and CTE. An earlier *Real Sports* story we did was one of the first in-depth stories with Chris Nowinski [about concussions] and I hounded my people to make sure that they got the perspective of the NFL. They made calls but didn't get much reaction. The story was tough. It clearly showed that CTE was prevalent among NFL players.

As soon as it aired, I knew I would get a phone call the next morning from Roger Goodell, and I was right. He was hot. He said it was an unfair portrayal, and that we were one-sided and didn't focus on the facts. He was angry and I obviously let him vent.

After the conversation, when I looked at it, I questioned our own journalistic objectivity a little bit and thought we didn't do a good enough job telling both sides of the story. *Real Sports* was always a lightning rod.

BERNIE GOLDBERG:

Roger Goodell wasn't thrilled with that concussion piece and he called my then boss Ross Greenburg, the president of HBO Sports, and laid into him about, as I heard it later, what a tabloid piece of journalism that was. There was not one syllable in that story that was incorrect or unfair. If the story was as bad as Roger Goodell thought it was, I wonder why they changed so many rules to try to make the game safer after it aired.

If you start to pick issues that are important to you because of your politics, because of your values, you put more into those stories than others. I suspend my politics and I suspend my values when I do stories.

Jon Frankel was hired as a correspondent on **Real Sports with Bryant Gumbel** *in May 2006. Frankel's first segment, "In the Headlines," was about the rape allegations against Duke University's men's lacrosse team.*

JON FRANKEL, Correspondent:

From a television perspective, *Real Sports* changed the way people looked at sports.

The first piece that I shot, on Duke lacrosse, we tried to look at the black and white of it, which is what it had come down to. We interviewed some journalists in Durham who had covered the early days of the story. We tried to parse what had taken place here beyond the "he said, she said."

On February 25, 2014, **Real Sports** *aired Frankel's "Kids & Guns" segment about the inability of kids, with access to guns, to control their urges and make reasonable decisions.*

JON FRANKEL:

There were two or three times following the airing of that story that parts of that piece went viral. Joe Perskie was concerned about not politicizing it and not making it a gun control piece, but rather a commonsense piece about health and how the brain develops in young kids, and at what point is a kid able to understand and control their urges.

There's something called the National Shooting Sports Foundation, which happens to be located in Newtown, Connecticut. That's obviously where the perpetrator of the crime at Sandy Hook was from. He had used the guns that were in his house.

The piece was well received and even won an Emmy. *Real Sports* offers the time and opportunity for thoughtful discourse that results in great story-telling.

On February 25, 2020, **Real Sports** *aired Jon Frankel's piece on the death of boxer Patrick Day.*

JON FRANKEL:

Bryant has always said that there's no tail wagging the dog here because we don't have any affiliations with the leagues and therefore we have independence that nobody else has or that's very rare to find, particularly in sports. Even the fact that HBO got out of the boxing business, for instance, we did a story just recently about the death of a boxer back in October, Patrick Day, who died in the ring. I don't know that we would have done that if HBO was still in the boxing business. But I've never been told we're not doing the story or we're not even gonna entertain that idea because somebody's going to come down on us.

ANDREA KREMER, Correspondent:

When I joined *Real Sports* in 2007, Rick Bernstein and Ross Greenburg made it clear that they wanted to take advantage of my contacts since I had spent close to two decades covering virtually every sport, particularly the NBA and NFL. So I took it as part of my mission to get "bigger names" for the show. I'm fairly determined and don't easily accept the word "no" and that enabled me to profile for *Real Sports* people like Kobe Bryant, Phil Jackson, and Bill Parcells.

Real Sports *has always been an iceberg. The show's correspondents, with their prestigious careers and national reputations, were out front for all to see, but out of sight, producers on the show were doing a disproportionate amount of the work.*

That was the case even for Andrea Kremer, who had been constitutionally tied to the driver's seat for much of her career, earning a reputation as one of the best interviewers in sports.

ANDREA KREMER:

The first story I did was a profile of Yannick Noah, the great French tennis player. I was in Paris to interview him and having dinner the night before with my producer, Beein Gim. Before we said good night, she hands me a little binder and I asked, "What's this?" And she said, "Notes and questions." I was stunned. I'd never had anybody give me anything like that before. At ESPN, I did my own research, wrote my own questions, and then gave them to the producer, to make sure we were not missing anything.

I was working on a piece about a high school basketball team in a polygamous community in Utah, with my producer, Ezra Edelman, who went on to win an Academy Award for his O. J. Simpson film. When we were done shooting, I said to Ezra, "Please send me the logs so I can pick the sound bites to use," and he looked at me as though I had five heads. Ezra, to his credit, told me, "I'm probably going to handle this on my own because we need to get this on the air quickly." That's when I figured it out: HBO has a different approach than I was used to at ESPN. *Real Sports* is a producer-driven show, not a correspondent-driven show. I was okay with that; *Real Sports* has the best producers.

Bryant is a child of live television. He likes to think everything's live. When he screens a piece, he will write down his questions. We never know in advance what they will be, and he doesn't want to be told what questions to ask.

What's important to me is that *Real Sports* allows us to investigate stories without being concerned about threatening partnerships with leagues. In my case, we've been able to do stories like examining abuse of the drug Toradol, marijuana use in the NFL, and why NFL teams weren't paying their cheerleaders.

I believe *Real Sports* is the last bastion of independent longform television journalism in sports and nothing epitomizes that for me more than our investigation into sexual assault in Bikram yoga. My producers worked for months researching and reporting, then helping to prepare me for what became one of the more memorable interviews in the history of the show, with "the guru," Bikram Choudhury.

A comment I often hear from viewers is, "I don't really like sports, but I love your show." That reflects the fact that we do stories that have even a tangential connection to sports. People want compelling stories, with a lot of emotion and memorable characters. That's been the case on pieces I've done with Hall of Fame announcer Doris Burke, WNBA champion Elena Delle Donne and boxer turned trainer Ann Wolfe.

And it was certainly the case for me personally when I recently did a segment on the sexual harassment of female sports reporters. Hearing their stories was triggering for me. I focused on their stories, but the piece was a painful reminder of times when I felt pressured by various men I was covering. This happened decades ago, when harassment wasn't taken as seriously as it is today, so I am particularly proud—and grateful—*Real Sports* afforded us the time and resources to properly report the story.

In January 2009, David Scott joined **Real Sports with Bryant Gumbel** *as senior segment producer.*

DAVID SCOTT, Correspondent:

I worked on the investigative unit at ABC and got to *Real Sports* as a producer in 2009.

I sort of fell in love with the idea of reporting at the intersection of sport and conflict. And *Real Sports* is one of the very few places where you can even attempt to do that in a serious way.

At *Nightline*, we had to wrest the attention of the viewer right away, get them in the tent. And that means front-loading the pieces. On *Real Sports*, we want to hook them in, intrigue them, and then unfold before them a narrative that feels like a complete act.

On February 17, 2009, **Real Sports** *aired "Black in Bellaire," a segment produced by Scott about the tragic shooting of baseball player Robbie Tolan.*

DAVID SCOTT:

The town of Bellaire in Houston had been for a long time an exclusive community, mostly white and in some ways emblematic of the American phenomenon of white flight. Bobby Tolan, who had a very distinguished major league baseball career, settled his family there and raised his only child, his son, Robbie Tolan, in Bellaire, Texas. Robbie was a local baseball star at Bellaire High and Bobby had sort of settled into a wonderful retirement. One night the police decided that Robbie Tolan was suspicious enough to follow his car into his driveway and confront him as he was about to walk into his parents' home.

The officer had typed the wrong license plate when he was investigating Robbie and decided the car was stolen. So there was a confrontation between Robbie, his cousin, and the officers. His parents came outside thinking this dispute would be easily settled once they vouched for their son and the legitimacy of the car. Instead it escalated to the point where Robbie was shot literally at his parents' front door.

He survived, lived to tell the tale. To this day, the bullet is lodged in his liver—it'll be there forever. It is, one, a symbol of police abuse, but it's also become a symbol of his dashed hopes and baseball dreams.

This ended his career. He would not follow in his father's footsteps in the end. And the saddest part of the story, though, is that there were no consequences. The officer who shot him has since been promoted. There were no legal consequences. They had a very long, drawn-out civil suit in which the toll was their mortgage, their home, and, in the end, I think they got like a hundred thousand dollars. It was incredibly sad. It went all the way to the Supreme Court.

"The Price of Glory" was a July 2014 investigation about the Qatar FIFA scandal.

DAVID SCOTT:

The world's most powerful sporting organization, FIFA, decides to hold a World Cup in a scorching desert kingdom with no tradition of soccer, for money, at the expense of an army of indentured servants who literally do all of the labor in Qatar. That story took us from Bulgaria to Nepal to Qatar, starting with the Bulgarian weight-lifting team, which had been a few years earlier bought by the Qatari government and given new Islamic names, and Qatari jerseys, and put into international competition as a Qatari team.

We interviewed the weight-lifting team in Bulgaria, and we flew it to Nepal because it is from there that the world's poorest men go to work for the world's richest men. And then we went to Qatar during Ramadan to see if we could see it for ourselves, if we could get into the so-called industrial city and see the conditions that the workers live and toil in. And we did. Finally we brought our findings to the head of the Qatari sports establishment. And had a chance to sit down and confront him about the reality of human rights and what the World Cup would mean for those men who basically work as modern-day slaves in this country. Fascinating experience. And we were all incredibly gratified by the reaction to it.

On July 18, 2017, **Real Sports** *showcased "MMA Dictator," about Chechen leader Ramzan Kadyrov, his love for MMA, and his antigay purges.*

DAVID SCOTT:

When we landed in Grozny, in the airport, there's a room that's like for stowing or screening firearms. I've never seen that before in any airport.

They gave us twenty-four hours on the ground in Grozny, no longer. And so we got there not knowing if we had any hope. We met with this key gatekeeper in the hotel lobby. He opened the meeting, I'll never forget, by saying, "Well, I hope you don't have any gay people on your staff because we like to torture and kill them." He was being sarcastic, but it was a chilling way to open a booking meeting.

He said, "I just want to make sure you're not going to be disrespectful to the president. I've seen what John Oliver has to say about it." It was about two fifteen in the morning when he finally emerged after a shower and sat down with us for what was supposed to be a fifteen-minute interview.

We shook his hand, sat down. There were giant portraits of his father and Vladimir Putin in the room. As with everywhere you go in Grozny, lots of armed men. He couldn't have been more bored, just going through the motions and looking at his watch, claiming that he had to go make prayer.

I pleaded with him for a little more time, that's when we made the turn. He went on a long unvarnished rant about the purge, the alleged purge, in his view. Then he turned to global geopolitics with the West, which in some ways is the most chilling moment of the whole thing.

And then he got up and he shook my hand and walked away. Then the staff blew up. "How dare you ask those questions? Say those words to the president?" This is the moment of truth. A lot of young men with guns were standing around very tensely. We had a long, long conversation.

I think by the time we got out of that building, it was four thirty in the morning. We stood our ground. I think he respected that. But now I'm thinking, Are we going to get hit by a sanitation truck? So we went back across the street to the hotel lobby. Told everybody, "Nobody leaves. We're just gonna stay right here until it's time to go to the airport." And that's what we did. We all stayed together until it was time to go to the airport and directly left the country.

I think I'm the most proud of that one because I know that nobody else was going to go do that. To me, that's the ultimate *Real Sports* standard. It probably was not going to be done if we didn't do it.

JOE PERSKIE:

We try to have a pretty diverse group. In some areas I think we've done well. In other areas we're trying to do better. We don't have a lot of turnover on the staff, but when we get the opportunity to increase diversity, we've been trying to take it.

On June 12, 2013, the multitalented Soledad O'Brien joined **Real Sports with Bryant Gumbel** *as a correspondent.*

SOLEDAD O'BRIEN, Correspondent:

When I got the word from my agent that *Real Sports* was looking for a reporter, it made a lot of sense because it never felt to me like a sports show.

The DNA of *Real Sports* is, What's the second line and the third line and the fourth line? The stories have to mean something. It's not just sports, that's just a prism. Sports is where we roughly begin. So what's the story about? What does it reflect? What does it say about humanity, about the human condition, about people, about what we value?

One of my favorite pieces that I did was about a little eleven-year-old who started doing triathlons with his brother who has a devastating brain illness. He's completely immobile. He has this disease where he basically is frozen in his body and the doctors gave him a life expectancy of nine and a half years and he was about to be nine and a half. So his older brother started taking him on triathlons with him. He would win if he didn't have to haul his brother with him, probably pretty handily because he's a pretty good athlete and mentally he's strong, too. And it was just so remarkable to sit down with an eleven-year-old kid and talk about why he does triathlons with his brother, which means hauling him in a little cart, swimming with him in a raft, biking with him. And I think that's the magic. If you're pitching a triathlon, no one will ever accept your pitch. If you're pitching a story about the human condition through a triathlon, now they're interested.

I love Bryant but he doesn't make it easy for you. Bryant doesn't allow for tap dancing around anything. I admired that. I think he's very supportive of his whole team and so he's bringing out the best. He's not trying to make his correspondents stumble. He's not a bullshitter.

The monthly series has captured a total of thirty-three Sports Emmy Awards and has earned nineteen Sports Emmys for Outstanding Sports Journalism. In January 2006 **Real Sports** *became the first sports program to be honored with the prestigious duPont-Columbia Award for excellence in broadcast journalism. In January 2012,* **Real Sports** *received its second duPont-Columbia Award for the program's groundbreaking series of reports on "concussions in sport." In all, the series has earned four duPont-Columbia Awards.*

Peter Nelson joined HBO as the director of programming in 2011 and in four short years was handed the key to the HBO Sports kingdom when Ken Hershman retired after just three years.

Nelson displayed oodles of ambition and enjoyed the glad-handing part of the job: meeting people, attending festivals and conferences. Nelson saw sports as the platform

by which he could meet interesting people and do interesting things. Whether his inten-
tions for the department were as lofty as those he'd set for himself remained to be seen.

PETER NELSON, Executive:

I came to HBO Sports in the interim period after Ross had already departed, but Ken had not started. I had a pretty steep learning curve, but the purview of my job was helping with matchmaking and negotiations for our fights.

I pointed out to a promoter he was violating our contract, to which he laughed and informed me, "Peter, you're new to this, so let me explain: in boxing, a signed contract is a *starting* point for a negotiation." In that sport, everything is relationships. And when I think about it, the most honorable as well as the most *dis*honorable people I have ever met, I met through boxing.

Before I assumed responsibility for HBO Sports, I had a series of conversations with Richard Plepler and Michael Lombardo. My mandate was to continue our position in boxing, in addition to serving *Real Sports* and *Hard Knocks.*

People outside the company immediately started calling to say I should fire this person or that person. I was the third head of the sports group in a period of six years, and I was mindful of how unsettling all that change can be for people. I made a decision to trust the team we had, even people I knew weren't my biggest fans. I kept those people because I felt that bad behavior came from a place of fear and I decided to show that if I wasn't afraid maybe they shouldn't be, either.

We were also entering a new phase beyond boxing where we could broaden our focus to projects with icons like LeBron James, Serena Williams, Tiger Woods, Kelly Slater, Lindsey Vonn, Nick Saban and Bill Belichick, and Diego Maradona, as well as the gifted filmmakers and producers who made those stories come to life.

If it wasn't for Roger Goodell's testicles, HBO might never have landed Bill Simmons.

Simmons had long been the **enfant terrible** *of sports journalism. For nearly fifteen years, he'd enlivened ESPN with his mixture of hot takes and takedowns, as well as co-creating the venerable* **30 for 30** *documentary franchise; he'd also found time to write two best-selling books. One of his regular victims was the NFL commissioner, Roger Goodell. Since ESPN hosted the multibillion-dollar-valued* **Monday Night Football** *at the time, it naturally enough needed that relationship to stay convivial. Having already been benched for three weeks by ESPN for ripping into Goodell over the Ray Rice abuse scandal—he called Goodell a liar on air—Simmons ignored his bosses'* *entreaties to leave the commish alone. He subsequently accused Goodell of not having sufficient "testicular fortitude" when it came to the Tom Brady/Patriots "Deflategate" situation. ESPN and its head John Skipper were having no more of it, and Simmons learned via social media that he was out.*

Desperate to add some spice to the HBO Sports brand, Mike Lombardo signed Simmons up for a half-hour conversation airing every Wednesday at ten p.m., starting on June 22, 2016. In his intro on the first airing of **Any Given Wednesday,** *Simmons highlighted the HBO difference with some choice words: "I'm excited to drop my first F-bomb on TV. We are going to figure out nudity down the road, as long as it's tasteful."*

BILL SIMMONS, Host and Documentarian:

I can't say I was in an ideal headspace. I knew from when I got suspended, and all the people who reached out then, that I was going to be okay when it didn't work out at ESPN. I was enamored with HBO, and really liked Lombardo. The day that ESPN announced they weren't renewing my contract, he emailed me within a couple of hours and he was like, "Let's go." He called James Dixon and they were aggressive. Pretty much everyone was aggressive, because I was this new toy in the store. But I think I'm going to say like two weeks later I had dinner with him and Plepler at the Peninsula.

I felt like I'd had so much success with interviews on my podcast that it could translate to a TV show in some way. That the art of conversation was a lane that thought I could hit for them. And then on top of it, the chance to revive HBO Sports, because even in 2015, HBO Sports wasn't what it was. We'd taken their lunch money at ESPN, in a lot of different ways. And the third thing was I knew I wanted to figure out what eventually became *The Ringer*.

At ESPN, the more creative you are, the bigger a problem you are. At HBO, it was the opposite. They care so much about creators and creative people.

I had some hesitations, but it was a lot of money. It was a great place. And it was probably the only time in my life where I didn't know if something was going to work, but fuck it. And I just went for it.

MIKE LOMBARDO:

I followed Bill on ESPN. I had followed him on *Grantland*, followed his podcast, and I'm not a sports guy.

NINA ROSENSTEIN:

Bill was so successful in his area, we wanted to give him the tools and surround him with the right people to host and produce his own show. It's a very different muscle than what he was used to. People like Bill Maher and

John Oliver make it look easy, but of course it's actually not easy at all. It was a challenge, and I know it wasn't ultimately what Bill had hoped for, but I believe he was still glad he did it.

BILL SIMMONS:

They wanted it to premiere during *Game of Thrones* to help the show. I don't know whether the show ultimately would have worked or not if we hadn't rushed. My big mistake was not understanding that it's more fun to listen to interviews on a podcast than watch them on TV.

When programmers get insecure or worried about their jobs, they often take comfort by surrounding themselves with big names. On paper **Vinyl** *seemed to have delivered a dream-team scenario: music legend Mick Jagger, film legend Martin Scorsese, best-selling author Rich Cohen, and HBO stalwart—the man who created* **Boardwalk Empire** *and who'd been a senior presence on* **The Sopranos**—*Terence Winter. What could possibly go wrong?*

TERENCE WINTER:

Vinyl started out as a movie back in the nineties. Mick Jagger called Martin Scorsese and said, "Let's do a movie like *Casino* set in the world of rock and roll." So in 2008, right after I had written the pilot for *Boardwalk Empire*, Martin Scorsese called me up and said, "Listen, I'm doing this movie project with Mick Jagger about the world of rock and roll. Do you want to be involved in it?" And I was like, "Yeah, I think so." I was like, Holy shit this is just getting crazier and crazier.

So at that point they already had several scripts written that weren't working. I was probably like the third or fourth writer who took a crack at that movie. I wrote my version of the movie in 2009. We handed it in to Paramount. And it was, I think, two weeks before the economy collapsed in 2009. So Brad Grey, who's running the studio, was also a friend of mine because he was one of the executive producers of *The Sopranos*. So I knew Brad well enough to be able to call him and say, "What's going on with the movie?" And he said, "Given the state of the world, this is not the time for us to be making a hundred-million-dollar music epic that spans forty years." So basically, the movie was dead. So I was depressed because I was really proud of it. And I came home and my wife, Rachel, said, "Well, why don't you do it as a TV show?" And I said, "Wow, that's interesting." So I called Marty, I called Mick. They were on board. We met with Richard Plepler, Mike Lombardo, and Sue Naegle at Marty's house one morning while *Boardwalk* was still on. We pitched them and they said, "Great, let's do it." So now I have to start from scratch. And I had to take that movie and make it into a pilot. So the series couldn't span forty years, obviously. I needed to land the story in one era. And for me, the most interesting time was 1973 when punk disco and hip-hop were all invented within a six-month period of time in New York City. So I said, "That's where the series lives." We took our main character and we dropped him in there. I wrote the pilot, and HBO said, "Well, now we need to find somebody else to run the show because you're writing *Boardwalk*." We spent the next couple of years trying to get somebody else to do it. Nothing worked out.

JOHN MELFI:

Ten years before we actually did it, we had been talking about doing it. I couldn't believe we were actually gonna do it after all the talk. And so we were revved up. It's just that we had so many partners, creative partners, I think, seventeen producers or something. How many producers does it take to change a lightbulb? Does it have to be a lightbulb?

TERENCE WINTER:

It was challenging. There were a lot of cooks in that kitchen. A couple of them are eight-thousand-pound gorillas and everybody had their opinions that had to be addressed, it was very hard. I think running a show, there's gotta be one singular voice to say, "Okay, this is what we're doing." Normally that's the case, but when you're in business with Martin Scorsese and Mick Jagger, I have to listen to those guys, too. They were my partners. So there were disagreements. Oddly for me, I think I wanted to push the envelope more in terms of the depictions of sex, drugs, and rock and roll. Mick was actually much more conservative than I thought he would be. Marty was in the middle between the two of us.

MIKE LOMBARDO:

Richard and I watched the pilot together and both loved it. The writing for the show certainly happened under my watch and so I have to take responsibility for that. I wish we weren't on such a tight schedule. I wish we had the time to get it right. We didn't. I think Richard needed to have that as his coup de grâce for me.

TERENCE WINTER:

The problem for me, more than anything, was how it was handled by HBO. Not the running of the show. It was not easy because, again, I had to answer to a lot of different people, which I didn't have to do on *Boardwalk*. We got through all that. I point to *The Irishman* on Netflix. When you had Martin Scorsese do a movie for Netflix, you couldn't walk ten feet in Los Angeles without seeing a billboard for *The Irishman*. It was like in your face every-where. So basically with *Vinyl* here we have a movie. If the pilot's like ninety minutes long, you have a Martin Scorsese movie produced by Mick Jagger and created by Mick Jagger, Marty, and me, a ninety-minute movie set in the world of rock and roll. Now, if I were running a network, I would make sure that everyone in the audience knew that our pilot is a Martin Scorsese movie event. Instead, I get a call from Michael Lombardo one day and he says, "We're putting the show on Valentine's Day at nine o'clock." And I said, "Okay, aside from being Valentine's Day," I said, "do you realize that's the pre-miere of *The Walking Dead*?" "Doesn't matter. It's a different audience." I said, "Michael, there is no other audience. Everyone is going to be watching *The Walking Dead*. Why don't we hold it and why don't we run it after the finale of *Game of Thrones*? Let's hold it a couple of months." "No, no, no. It's going to be fine." And it was this hubris that, Oh, we're HBO. We don't have to worry about *The Walking Dead*. Yeah. You do. There are other networks. This isn't 1999 where HBO is the only game in town.

MIKE LOMBARDO:

I first became aware of problems at the *Vinyl* screening. Richard always looked at the master plan for seating of any screening and I saw and clocked that he had put me on the opposite side of the theater from him and Jeff. I convinced myself I was being paranoid and got back to work. Guess I knew Richard pretty well by then.

TERENCE WINTER:

So we go on nine o'clock at night against the premiere episode of *The Walking Dead*, which had been the biggest anticipated show all year, on Valentine's Day at nine o'clock without telling the audience that what you're about to watch is not a one-hour TV pilot. It's actually a movie. So if you're one of the twelve people in the world who happened to be watching *Vinyl* that night, at ten o'clock and it's not over. And then it's ten fifteen, and then ten thirty and ten forty-five. And it's still not over, pulling your fucking hair out going, What is this? Instead of making a virtue of the fact that, Hey, Martin Scorsese movie, like they did with *The Irishman*, basically people didn't know what to make of it. So the interesting thing or the reviews, Metacritic will back me up. The reviews were like 78 percent. That's basically in the zone. That's a hit show. That's, You're fine. Overall, the reviews were solid. But because the ratings on night one were so bad, the next day, the headlines were VINYL IS A DISASTER. And it was a disaster. It was a ratings disaster for HBO. *The Walking Dead* got like fourteen million viewers. And we got like seven hundred thousand. We couldn't break a million people with a Martin Scorsese movie. So I was fighting the perception all season of *Vinyl* people going, "Oh, I heard that show's terrible." And I said, "No, you didn't hear it was terrible. You heard nobody watched it. The reviews are good. It's a good show. Give it a chance."

MIKE LOMBARDO:

Sue developed it for a very long time, yes. But it wasn't Marty's problem. I mean, it was really the writer on that.

TERENCE WINTER:

I don't think Michael was a fan of *Boardwalk Empire*, honestly. I don't think he was a fan of mine, and he certainly wasn't a fan of *Vinyl*. And we argued about it; a lot of the notes I got from HBO were that there's too much drugs. It's too much sex. Women need to be more empowered, et cetera, et cetera. And I was like, "Guys, it's 1973. You're asking me to write a world that didn't exist then." So we had these battles back and forth, these arguments. And I said, "I can't believe this is the network that brought the world *Oz* and *The Sopranos*. Where are the creative balls that we had years ago, when people would complain and HBO's position was, 'Don't watch it, watch something else, change the channel.'" This is a show for adults who can tell the difference between reality and fantasy, who could show Tony Soprano kill somebody. I didn't know at the time what was going on behind the scenes with Mike and Sue, but I certainly felt like not a day went by where I wasn't getting a call about something either from Michael or one of his development people giving me just endless notes about stuff that they didn't want us to do.

I was there back in the days of them being our biggest cheerleaders. "Just do the show you want to do." Suddenly this micromanagement, these fear-based notes that were all based in cowardice about, "Oh, people in the audience aren't gonna like it." I was like, "Great. They should go watch something on CBS." It got crazy, really stressful.

ERIC KESSLER:

Vinyl was in development for years and the first season cost $100 million. The reviews were not good. Then Mike got up at one TCA and said he watched the final episodes and they deliver the goods. He put himself on the line with that review. And then it turned out, the season ending sucked.

Eventually, an article came out characterizing the show as a huge, expensive misstep. Once that happened, everyone internally knew someone was going to take the fall and it wasn't going to be Richard.

MIKE LOMBARDO:

I had to placate Richard. He put me in charge of marketing. I'd have long meetings with the marketing team. Eric was gone by then. It was Courtney and Pam Levine. At one point they suggested a change, and I said, "Why?" They said, "Richard wants it." I said, "Richard never told me." He had to see marketing materials. Richard was always there, wanting to take credit if he could and cast blame.

On October 2, 2016, HBO debuted **Westworld,** *a one-hour drama set in 2058 about a Wild West theme park where participants interact—however they want—with android robots, called "hosts," that look exactly like human beings. The cherry on top? Visitors could fulfill bloodlust and sexual fantasies without any consequences. The series was based on a 1973 movie of the same name by Michael Crichton.*

Brought to HBO by J. J. Abrams and created by husband-and-wife team Jonathan "Jonah" Nolan and Lisa Joy, **Westworld** *boasted a major league cast: Evan Rachel Wood, Anthony Hopkins, Ed Harris, Thandiwe Newton, and James Marsden.*

Nobody knew then that **Westworld** *would hit the prized HBO trifecta: terrific ratings, good reviews, and sundry honors. The show's first-season average of twelve million viewers was the most ever for an initial season of an HBO series, including* **Game of Thrones** *and* **The Sopranos.** *Many critics were effusive with praise, and in its first three seasons,* **Westworld** *was nominated for four Golden Globes and fifty-four Emmys, winning nine. And yet for all that hullabaloo, there had been a time when the show was considered so troubled by HBO execs that there was talk of ripping it out of the HBO lineup and shuffling it over to Cinemax instead.*

So much of HBO's internal strife, and its shortage of deep development experience, was transferred onto **Westworld** *that the show's troubled first year became an inflection point, resulting in a dramatic change at the top of the drama department. Millions of dollars were wasted, HBO's reputation as a safe haven for its creative partners was damaged, and the show had to fight its way out of a PR hole after being temporarily shut down for repairs. Somehow, Joy and Nolan, along with their determined cast and crew, managed to survive—and triumph.*

J. J. ABRAMS, Executive Producer:

Westworld was an idea I'd been trying to revisit for a long time. I had a meeting with Michael Crichton twenty years ago and started talking with

Jerry Weintraub about five years after that. I pitched it to HBO because the fun of doing something as pulpy and delicious as this with HBO's A-plus production and their viewers' expectations of quality was a great combination. Michael Lombardo bought the show, and it was Kathy Lingg's idea, who was working at Bad Robot TV at the time, to go to Jonah, with whom we had done *Person of Interest*. Jonah asked how I would feel about him jumping in with Lisa, and I was thrilled because we've been trying to work with Lisa as well. I had a sense of what the show could be—a peek into the robot's point of view and a story about the oppressed—but I could never have imagined the depth and breadth of what Jonah and Lisa have been able to bring to it.

MICHAEL ELLENBERG:

It was a real priority for me to find us a science fiction show that was sufficiently HBO. I made a science fiction film with Ridley, and it's a genre I love. Then J.J. pitched his ingenious idea.

DAVID LEVINE:

Ellenberg and Sue were on vacation. I was Mike's default for everything, and I loved Mike's company when it was one-on-one. He called me into his office and said, "You're going to hear two pitches with me today. I think they're both going to be terrible." And I said, "What if one of them is going to be good? You're such a cynic." That's how I always talked to him.

We heard the first one and it wasn't good. The second one was *Westworld*. It was so good. I still repeat that pitch to everyone so they understand how good a storyteller J.J. is.

J.J. said, "Guys, there is a movie, *Westworld*, and in the movie a group of humans go to a theme park in the future, and the robots turn on them. I want to make a show in the world of Westworld, where humans go to fulfill their fantasies, and we'll watch the robots gain their consciousness."

It was clear that that was going to be a massive phenomenon if we got it right. We bought *Westworld* and committed to a pilot.

MICHAEL ELLENBERG:

The next question was, Who would write this show? J.J. had the initial conception but he was only producing it. We needed someone to create it, write it, showrun it. I was a big fan of the Dark Knight trilogy. And after seeing *The Dark Knight Rises*, which blew me away, I reached out to Jonathan Nolan to get to know him.

JONATHAN NOLAN, Creator:

I had just been working on movies and I went in for a general meeting with J.J. We hit it off and when we were going into the second or third season of *Person of Interest* he said, "Hey, I've been kicking around this idea about *Westworld* the movie."

My first response was to say no. I didn't see it. I liked the original movie but I didn't understand how it could be a series. But then I started talking to Lisa about it; Lisa had been working TV longer than I had, and J.J. had mentioned on his initial phone call, "I know you guys were looking to do something together. Maybe this is something you could work on together." Lisa had not seen the original movie, just heard the log line, and figured out within a couple of days that there would be this larger mythology, bigger story that we were telling. And for me, it was scratching that itch of, I wanted to direct, I wanted to world-build.

So a few weeks after turning it down, we called him back together and said, "Hey, if you're still thinking about that, turns out we do have a way in." He'd had one initial conversation with HBO setting it up, and even though it was science fiction, not exactly their forte, I think they were predisposed to like the pitch.

LISA JOY, Creator:

This is what happens when you have no other options. You're knocked up. You're not a great candidate for a staffing cycle, so I was gainfully unemployed. Having no option but to strike out on my own turned out to be fortunate. We got a whiteboard and we started breaking the episode and dreaming up new characters. We had to start very much from ground zero.

MICHAEL ELLENBERG:

Jonah and Lisa sparked to the concept immediately, then they came in a few weeks later with the broad strokes of the show that you see today, including big ideas for multiple seasons.

JONATHAN NOLAN:

Lisa wrote her first movie in her first trimester, then wrote the pilot for *Westworld* in her second. Shooting the pilot for *Westworld* was a dream. We had the best cast and crew imaginable, and after some back-and-forth over our nonnegotiables like shooting on film, and on location in Utah for key sequences, we were left in relative peace to do our work. The network seemed very pleased with the results and green-lit us to series.

LISA JOY:

I was pregnant with my first child and I am not an elegant pregnant lady. I'm humongous and sedentary and I liked doughnuts. We would sit in what is now the children's playroom.

JONATHAN NOLAN:

The movie is a brilliant concept, but it's ninety-two breathless minutes of ideas packed into a movie. We wanted to start from the perspective of the hosts, took that idea and ran a country mile with that, so by the time we got four episodes in, the audience was going to realize that even if you thought someone wasn't a host, they were actually a host.

LISA JOY:

The characters that you see on-screen are just a portion of the characters that we dreamt up initially. We had maps detailing a fake world. We went down a crazy hallucination hole together. It was like designing a video game. By the time we were done, the room looked completely insane because we quickly ran out of room on the whiteboard. Then we started writing on the mirrors. Then we started just taking pieces of paper and taping them to the walls and the windows. By the time it was done, it looked like we'd had a joint nervous breakdown. After my daughter was born, we just kept working right through it.

Jonah and I would spend a lot of time staring at the whiteboard and we had our daughter sit between us as we stared at it. And she grew up fascinated by whiteboards because she kept trying to figure out why Mommy and Daddy would stare at it for hours on end. And until the age of three, whenever she saw a whiteboard, she would just stare at it, like trying to figure out what's on that thing that's so important to everyone.

J. J. ABRAMS:

The show was so massive, we knew it was going to require a bit of an exploration. When we began the series, the scripts were a lot for anyone to take in. They were a leap of faith, so enormous and ambitious that the network at first was having trouble finding their way in. And as with anything, it had its bumps and challenges.

JONATHAN NOLAN:

They were supportive of the show being extremely ambiguous, dark and weird, and supportive of our need to make it the right way. We had watched what Dan and David had done with *Game of Thrones,* shooting on locations where I had spent time with my brother shooting movies. Places that make you realize the value of doing it right. So we had all of these things going for us, and set off to make an ambitious, complicated season of television.

HBO picked up the pilot to series, but a strange dynamic erupted: there were suddenly lots of "No, no, noes" coming from HBO, along with reams and reams of notes. The **Westworld** *creative team was taken aback, given what had transpired during the pilot; besides, wasn't this HBO, the place where creatives were left largely alone? Nolan was heard telling people the number of notes received from the studio for* **Dark Knight:** *zero.*

To make matters worse, it was difficult for the **Westworld** *team to figure out which notes originated where (or with whom), and, at times, notes seemed mismatched. During production, there were gasps of astonishment when one HBO exec decided he no longer liked one of the character's names—and demanded that the name be changed. (It wasn't).*

Westworld *was always going to be a show rife with sexuality. Directors understood that Joy and Nolan wanted faces in the foreground of scenes involving nudity, but HBO would push back, asking for closeups of breasts and other body parts. At another point, in a group conference call, an executive accused Joy of having a "girlish" fantasy about how great "gentle sex" could be. Later, an exec called on a specific love scene, noting, "The truth is he would probably fuck her in the ass, and she'd be really sore the next day."*

EVAN RACHEL WOOD:

That show changed my life. The first season was pure creation. We didn't know who these characters were, and we didn't have scripts beforehand, so I was making up my character as we went along, going on the journey with her in real time, finding out what happened next with each script. I realized that what my character was going through mirrored what I was going through personally. So Dolores having her awakening and realizing who she was, what her place in the world was, while also realizing that this person who she loved was her perpetrator, awoke a lot of things inside me. It was the catalyst for me to realize that I had been abused and that I needed trauma therapy. That I needed to actually process all of this and stop running away from it, stop erasing it.

Any time my character had a scene with the Man in Black, or she had a moment of awareness, I was going through the same thing on a personal level. By the end of the first season, I felt like I was given this gift of clarity and strength, over the course of doing the first season. Getting to work with Lisa Joy, who is a staunch defender of people who've been abused, was amazing. Lisa was an incredible role model to have in my life, and both Jonah and Lisa saw who I was as a person and as an actor at a time when I didn't feel like people were really seeing me.

I was asked to testify for the Survivors' Bill of Rights Act and then doing that inspired me to pen my own law called the Phoenix Act, which I also testified for in front of the California Senate. And that was to expand the statute of limitations for domestic violence crimes.

JONATHAN NOLAN:

The year 2015 took a turn. As we were shooting an already ambitious and grueling season, we watched as—elsewhere at the network—pilot after pilot crashed and burned in acrimony with executives who seemed determined that they knew better than the people they had hired. And we began to realize that the internal politics at the network were extremely complicated.

We battened the hatches and kept going. Through notes that ran from thoughtful, to ridiculous, to outright offensive, we kept making the show we had set out to make. Finally, after shooting seven episodes, we were shut down. We had to lay off the entire crew the day before Thanksgiving. We kept silent in the press on the internal chaos at HBO and blamed it on typical first-season growing pains. The truth was we shut down because one or two of the executives were more interested in the show they wanted to make rather than the one we were making, and we refused to change it.

MICHAEL ELLENBERG:

We made the pilot, which was grand and epic and big, but Lisa had said, "This is like trying to have the richness and mythology of *Game of Thrones* without any source material. And so we're basically writing the book and the show and that's difficult, obviously." So once we were making the show itself they start to fall behind and we were running out of material, frankly. Because you're writing it and still conceiving it while you're filming it. And the scale of the production was massive as it had to be, if it was gonna look as good as its film equivalent. You're very mindful that the production value has to match what you might expect from the cinema. I had to make a difficult decision, which was basically to hit pause on it and shut it down to give them time to basically finish writing the season so that when they went back into production, they could film the episodes and no longer have to worry about writing as they went along.

I may have lost my job over that decision because it's an incredibly costly decision when you do that. But I knew it was the right one for the show and for the network. HBO could have kept going and filmed what we were doing and cobbled it together. It just wouldn't have been as good and other networks probably would make that decision. First-year shows are difficult.

The biggest lever a network has when creators aren't doing what is being asked is to shut a show down, and that's what finally happened. When Ellenberg had gotten Lombardo to sign off on putting **Westworld** *into suspended animation, several key observers within HBO thought it was reminiscent of the second season of* **True Detective***: everything was rushed.*

In pre-Netflix days, HBO's more experienced development executives would have taken the time to get the show's bible and all scripts for the first season fully ready before plunging into production. Now, however, Joy and Nolan were in the position of creating while shooting, and even though both believed they were equal to the challenge, the disparity between their vision and HBO's was increasingly unmanageable. Production halted on November 12, 2015. Just over two months later, on January 29, Ellenberg departed HBO.

MICHAEL ELLENBERG:

The first season of *Westworld* was nominated for a Best Drama Emmy and was a big commercial success as well. Obviously I stand by that decision to shut down temporarily.

The highest pressure you felt at HBO was to uphold the creative legacy of the network, and then to build on it. I came up in the business as a producer, and so I was very conscious that these executive chairs are rented. It was a great experience.

MIKE LOMBARDO:

Look, I bought *Westworld* in the room from J.J., without Jonah attached. Michael was the one who brought Jonah in, and Michael had the vision for the show. When the show shut down, we put other producers in place, along with editors. There wasn't any editing process on that show. So when it comes to the bottom line on *Westworld*, all I'm saying is that Michael didn't ruin it—and Casey didn't save it.

Ellenberg is a smart and thoughtful guy who crashed and burned in the corporate politics side of things. He was out of his element. He was more of a business packager for movies, and it's unfair to say I let him go because he shut down *Westworld*. He pleaded with me to please let him fix and get *Westworld* launched, but he had plenty of warnings before the show was shut down and he himself knew it wasn't working. At the same time, I felt bad for him.

MICHAEL ELLENBERG:

I never was told very clearly why I was being let go. I was more Mike's guy, and Casey was more Richard's guy. And once Mike and Richard started to fall out with each other, my departure was inevitable.

Alongside the Ellenberg firing, a promotion was announced: Casey Bloys, the former head of HBO's comedy department, would become president of Entertainment, overseeing HBO Series, Late Night, and Specials, essentially taking the position previously held by Sue Naegle.

Bloys hails from perhaps one of the least Hollywoody places in America: the Lehigh Valley of closed steel mills and major hospitals in eastern Pennsylvania and northwestern New Jersey. After attending high school with Dwayne "The Rock" Johnson (Bloys was one year older), Bloys would study economics at Northwestern University before moving to New York City to take a shot at the advertising industry. A client, Paramount Pictures, brought him out to Los Angeles in 1996 where initially he assisted a CBS executive.

After eight years of working his way up the food chain there, he finally got his first HBO gig, as director of development at HBO Independent Productions. Bloys was quickly promoted to vice president and would soon move sideways to HBO Entertainment, in charge of developing comedy series. By 2013 he was series vice president of HBO programming.

CASEY BLOYS:

I grew up in Bethlehem, but nobody in my family worked for Bethlehem Steel. I was lucky in that my dad started a software company in the 1970s. My parents both grew up in New Jersey, so they moved around the Northeast. They ended up in Bethlehem at an IBM office there. And my dad met some other guys there and they started a software company. It was an interesting place to grow up in that many of my friends' families worked at Bethlehem Steel and steel was declining. I didn't have to experience that trauma because we were relatively comfortable. But growing up in that environment has always informed my work greatly, and there are certain things about peoples' lives you can understand more easily. When Trump won, I actually used to say, "If you've never gone swimming in an aboveground pool, you probably don't understand anything about why Trump would appeal to anybody."

At CBS, I got a lot of experience in network television, in sitcoms and dramas. I got to see how broadcast networks gave notes and the number of people who gave notes, even on a pilot. I always felt like notes from a broadcast network were tinged with fear. Everything was fear that a viewer wouldn't understand, or fear that their boss wouldn't understand, everything was from fear and there were a lot of notes from all different layers and all different people. And at HBO, it was only about giving the most important note. Carolyn would boil things down. She would zero in on something truly important, and I'd say, "How does she know how to do that?" She was really good and a great mentor.

My husband, Alonzo Wickers, and I have been together for twenty years and have fourteen-year-old twins. He's a First Amendment lawyer who works with major media companies. He's pretty well known in that space.

I've never felt entitled to a job in my life. Never felt that I was better than anybody, or that it was a given I would get any promotion. Instead, I felt that whatever I got would be something that I had to work for, work hard for. When you don't take anything for granted, it's a better way to be part of an organization.

I took oversight of both HBO drama and comedy in January 2016, and though no one told me explicitly, I decided getting *Westworld* on track had to be my number one priority. Mike seemed relieved to hand it over to someone, and it was clear the relationship between Jonah, Lisa, and HBO had gotten to a very tough stage. My sense internally was that many had written the show off. At one point there were even conversations about putting the show on Cinemax. While this was the first big drama I had worked on, the role of a programming executive is the same regardless of whatever genre you work in: provide concise, thoughtful feedback and make the showrunner feel supported. That's what I set out to do on *Westworld*.

After watching everything that had been shot, it was clear to me there was a show there. The biggest problem was the producers had been pushed to go forward before all of the scripts were written. With big shows like this, the story and mythology become very intricate; writers need time to work all of that out, and it's much easier to do all that before production. It's almost impossible to do both at once. The show, the producers, and we as a network paid a price for rushing *Westworld* to production. J.J., Jonah, and Lisa didn't deserve that.

I reset the relationship between Jonah and Lisa and HBO, provided honest feedback, and we created space to have genuine back-and-forth dialogues. I believed in the show they were doing and this new perspective definitely helped the situation. I'm very proud of how both the show and the working relationship with Jonah and Lisa worked out.

LISA JOY:

After spending the first three months of 2016 adrift, we learned that several key executives had departed. Casey Bloys became the new head of programming, and he came to our edit suite, watched everything, told us that he loved it, and we went back to work. We premiered *Westworld* later that October.

After Casey's arrival, the culture at HBO became more transparent and supportive—finally the place we had hoped it would be when we started. Making a show is difficult enough without dealing with court intrigues and politics. When I found good collaborators, it was such a blessing, because that's when the magic happens.

DAVID LEVINE:

Casey told me he was going to take credit for it no matter what, that he was going to use Westworld to prove that he had drama stripes. He asked to go through every beat of the show and why it was there. And then he said what needed to be there. And what I learned in that moment was I was not a good executive but a very good producer, and Casey was a very good executive. And we worked very well together because he does his job very well.

I was protecting Jonah and Lisa's vision for *Westworld* and I studied it and I could explain it. I could repeat it back to somebody to be able to work through it together.

CASEY BLOYS:

Jon and Lisa bit off a lot, probably more than they thought, so it was a big, ambitious show and I don't know that they realized that going into it, so they needed the break to catch up on scripts, but also what was happening here was I think there was a breakdown of communication between HBO and the showrunners—a failure of communication all around.

And so people will say, "Oh, the show was a mess," but besides them getting into something a bit more ambitious than maybe they realized at the beginning, I think the environment on our side was not conducive to a creative process. I was coming in fresh without any of the dysfunction that had surrounded the process and truthfully, it looked great, had a phenomenal cast, it was compelling. It was just the processes around the show that were broken and so I was fixing it creatively as much as we were fixing the culture around the show.

But what was there from the beginning, what was great about the show, and I think the reason people like it, is it totally transports you to another world, totally believable, and Jon and Lisa love to wrestle with big ideas and did all of that and so it became changing the culture around it, how we communicated with them.

Jon and Lisa were grateful to have a functional relationship with the network. People were describing the show internally at the time like it was left for dead. It was almost like I had nothing to lose, so I said, "All right. Let's just dive in."

EVAN RACHEL WOOD:

HBO is like family. I've done so many projects with them and I have always felt like HBO got me. And I think I can be hard to define sometimes. And I like that. As an actor, I don't want to be too defined. But they've just always known where to put me and when they put me somewhere, they take care of me. They work me really hard. I mean, there's a reason why they're so epic and so good. It's because a lot of people work really hard on them. So they kick my ass, but in a good way. And challenged me in great ways and have given me such incredible female roles. I don't know what I would have done without HBO, quite honestly. They've been so instrumental in my career and I've been a fan of them since I was a young actor coming up in the game. They just always managed to keep that air about them. Working on an HBO film is no joke.

LISA JOY:

On the last day after we wrapped, it was this surreal moment, whenever you wrap something, because you never know what's going to happen, but you're exhausted and you've put something out there in the world. And I was so proud of Jonah and us for getting through it. And we had a little golf cart to take us around Melody Ranch and we took our baby and we put her in the golf cart and we sat in the golf cart and the sun was rising. So it was that pretty magic hour thing. And we just drove around the lot together as it totally emptied out. And for a second, we got to sit in this strange world we made and just enjoy being together and having seen it through. And it was lovely.

Under Mike Lombardo, HBO experienced problems with the same creative talent that had created numerous triumphs in the past. Turns out, busted projects like Doug Ellin's **Da Brick** *(with Mike Tyson) and Steve Levinson's* **The Missionary** *weren't isolated frustrations.*

Emmy winner Ryan Murphy's **Open** *was going to follow five lead characters on a* *journey of romance and sexuality, through the lens of a contemporary, "open" society. The pilot was picked up in April 2013; the final decision to pass was not made until September 2015.*

*Deadwood creator David Milch had written **The Money**, the story of a corporate executive's power-hungry ambitions to exert control over his family and the media industry, with Brendan Gleeson attached to star. HBO passed on the pilot in March 2014.*

***Orange Is the New Black** creator Jenji Kohan had written **The Devil You Know**, based around the Salem Witch Trials of eighteenth-century New England. Oscar-nominated Gus Van Sant was brought on to direct. And yet HBO declined to pick up the pilot that was produced in the spring of 2015.*

MIKE LOMBARDO:

When Bill Nelson was there, pilot decisions would go to Bill. Richard would tell me, "We need to go to Bill." When Richard became CEO, I would still tell him, "I think we want to make this pilot," and he would go, "I hate that script." And I made the pilot anyway. Like the Jenji Kohan pilot. He threw it in my face, constantly. It wasn't a successful pilot. "Who wants to do a show about seventeenth-century Salem, Massachusetts? I can't believe we did that." The message in that was, I can't believe you did that. I gave you the sign. You didn't pick it up.

*And then there was Alan Ball again. His series **Virtuoso**, which counted Elton John among its executive producers, was to tell the story of Antonio Salieri, the Italian composer who lived in Vienna at the turn of the eighteenth century. HBO ordered a pilot in January 2015, but the series never came to fruition.*

*Mike White decided to take a deep breath and move past the **Enlightened** saga, writing another pilot for HBO called **Mamma Dallas**. Once again, however, things went awry. To some, it began to appear that while Mike White may indeed have been one of Lombardo's favorite writers, in theory anyway, that wasn't the case when it came to actually writing scripts. Somebody—or everybody—forgot a core tenant of development: don't keep advancing an idea if, at key steps, it gives every indication that it just won't work; the pain will only get worse. **Mamma Dallas** had detractors all along the way, but Lombardo and Naegle didn't want to say "no" to Mike White.*

MIKE WHITE:

I wanted to do something about drag queens. There had been a lot of stuff about sexual identity and gender identity, and I wanted to weigh in on it, but using people who had a more playful attitude about it. It was a guy who

becomes a nanny to a rich, conservative Texas family, and they don't realize that he is a man and he's trans. I thought it was done in a way that felt
realistic. I felt it could speak to this red state–blue state divide in a fun way.
The cast was great. I wrote a pilot and directed it. I was happy with how it
turned out.

That's when things went south with Mike Lombardo and me. I knew he
knew it was good, but I think it landed in a little bit more on a minor key
tenor. It wasn't a big, laugh-out-loud comedy. It was exactly like everything
that I do, which is why I was so frustrated. Why do you keep asking me to
do things, and then every time I do it, this is your reaction? This is what I
do. This is my tone.

The last call we had was him basically yelling at me. "You want me to say
you're a genius? Well, I don't tell people that. I don't tell Martin Scorsese he's
a genius. I don't tell David Simon he's a genius."

I thought, He's definitely picking up the show because he's being so crazy
and angry. You don't do that if you're also going to not pick up the show. He
told me he was going to pick up this show, and he supported it. And then
he went to Plepler. I don't know what exactly happened, but I then got the
call saying that they weren't going to move forward with it.

*Word of dysfunction in the upper halls of HBO was starting to spread throughout Hol-
lywood—and even further. On February 24, 2016,* **Hollywood Reporter***'s Kim Masters published a scathing article, breaking news on a series of failed HBO projects with
celebrated names attached, from David Fincher to Steve McQueen, announcing that
HBO was scrapping a number of high-profile shows.*

ARI EMANUEL:

The one project that didn't happen that I so wanted to happen was *Lewis
and Clark* with Ed Norton and Brad Pitt. Ed is a great filmmaker, a great
perfectionist, but I couldn't get him off a certain point. HBO had started it,
and they were spending a lot of money. I couldn't get him off a certain story
point. So crazy.

MIKE LOMBARDO:

I felt embarrassed and upset the way Richard threw a fucking grenade over
things like Steve McQueen. He called me with a finance person, Joe Tarulli,
on the phone, and accused me of spending money without his permission.
"You told me a couple of scripts." I asked, "Why are you saying this?" It was
clear to me that he was building a case for the file. I didn't have the numbers

in front of me, but told him, "We were developing a show. What are you suggesting?"

Just over three years after Richard Plepler was made head of HBO, Mike Lombardo was gone. The decision was finalized in the spring of 2016 but was to be kept quiet while a successor was chosen; the news leaked, however, and Casey Bloys was announced as Lombardo's heir on May 23.

Bloys, seemingly determined to avoid the charge that likeability was part of his mandate, returned hundreds of scripts that had been in development hell for years, reputedly for the sake of clarity. Agents and writers appreciated the directness at least.

GLENN WHITEHEAD:

I had several conversations with Richard over a two-, three-year period about his frustrations with Mike.

And ultimately, toward the end of Mike's career at HBO, Richard said to me and to Mary Lou [Thomas], "I'd prefer Mike to just come to the realization that he needs to leave. I'd prefer it to be his initiative." And so he said to us, "If you have an opportunity with Mike to tell him that it's time for him to make that call, please do." Mike and I had talked about his troubles with Richard. Richard had had a couple of pretty strong come-to-Jesus conversations with Mike about moderating certain behaviors. And so one day on a Thursday night, Mike walked into my office and said to me, "Are people still talking about me and the problems in my relationship with Richard?" And I said, "Yes." And we talked about that for a little while. And then Mike asked me, "Is it time for me to call Richard and say, I know it's over?" And I said, "Yes." He called Richard the next morning, Friday morning. And by the following Monday, Mike was done.

MIKE LOMBARDO:

I think the truth of my tenure at HBO was that my job was a very precarious balancing between trying to manage what I thought would get us ahead and managing New York and Richard. At the same time, a large part of my job meant being his guy. And when I did try to assert some independence, it strained the relationship. The last year was tough.

A job like that is 24/7. We had received the most Emmys in history, we had the most highly regarded comedies, and the juggernaut that was *Game of Thrones* was thriving and yet I didn't feel like I was jumping high enough for him. I'd go home at night and I couldn't even unpack it with my husband. We had kids and I wanted to enjoy that limited time with them. At the Emmys that year, we won the top award in each of the major categories. This was something that we wouldn't have even dreamed of when we started in these jobs, yet Richard felt slightly restrained. The *New York Times* ran a piece on that Monday and ended it with a quote from me. Richard made clear that he didn't like my quote. I suppose I should have understood that the bigger problem was that the quote came from me.

I swallowed a lot of my own unhappiness. I felt less joy in the day-to-day and uncertain about where we were going. We were committed to a linear distribution model and were unwilling to fully prepare for a digital future. All of the focus was on hitting quarterly targets.

When I returned to LA the Monday of the *Vinyl* screening, a colleague from New York called me up and told me he was hearing rumblings about me from the eighth floor, so I called Richard and asked if we could have dinner together in Miami, where we were both going to participate in an offsite with the distribution team. He agreed. I told him I had heard things from people in the company and wanted to address anything that was bothering him. He started by telling me that he would never discuss our relationship with anyone else, which I didn't feel like debating at that moment but that, yes, he was troubled by my failure to adequately keep him in the loop. I was surprised but told him that I loved the company and loved my job and wanted to make it work. We agreed to proceed in the spirit of partnership as we had always done.

GLENN WHITEHEAD:

Mike didn't show Richard enough respect. And Richard tried desperately for years to support Mike and to allow Mike to take center stage. Mike didn't show Richard an appropriate level of appreciation for those efforts. I think Richard's behavior to Mike for the first several years of their relationship was unbelievably gracious, indulgent, forgiving. And it wasn't until toward the very end that Richard found his voice to say, "Okay, I can't put up with this anymore. And I need to tell this guy to just cool it," which is when he had those two come-to-Jesus conversations with Mike.

And yet, Mike was a man of uncommon humanity and soulfulness. Mike could be, on a personal level, amazing. If you were having a conversation about something other than work, his insights about the human condition and the world, there are a lot of very positive things that you could say about Mike. When he became the head of programming, some of his most positive qualities receded a bit.

MIKE LOMBARDO:

I returned to LA and continued moving ahead. We had green-lit *Big Little Lies* and I was focused on getting the first season of *Westworld*. Casey was promoted and that was something that Richard had encouraged. One late night a few months later I was leaving the office and stopped to chat with someone who worked for me who I knew regularly spoke with Richard. He acknowledged to me that Richard wasn't happy and was still ruminating about my failings. So I called up Richard and said, "Richard, I know we talked in Florida, but I'm hearing that you're still not happy. And look, you're my boss. That makes it hard for me. So I wish you would just tell me if you want me out, because it's really hard." "Well, I would never say anything to anybody, but I think what we should each do is take a long walk on the beach separately and decide what the right next thing is." I said okay. And so a day later we got on the phone and he said that he had taken a long walk and thought about it and concluded that I had "lost my mojo." I said okay. I knew him well enough and had seen this play out with so many people that I knew there was no need to discuss it anymore. That was it with him. The calls after that with him were . . . I can't even tell you how painful they were. Whatever illusions I had that we had a real relationship, a friendship that transcended work, were destroyed. All of the calls after that were about how he was managing the optics of my departure.

I was upset and humiliated that word had gotten out. I was very close to the head of Human Resources and she said, "Don't do that to yourself. He's just using you. Don't do that." So I said, "Richard, I don't wanna do that." He said okay. He then announced that Casey was gonna be the guy. And so I decided at a certain point that going to the office was way too painful so I thought I'd work from home. To come into the office and have no one call me and people run from me? I was done. And you realize there's nothing. Nobody asks for your opinion. No one cares anymore. You're toast.

I saw an evolution of a company go from tiny offices stuffed into the Time Life building to a company whose name became ubiquitous with quality television. When I started there, literally no one had heard of it and when I told people where I worked, they thought it was an office furniture company.

I went from being a terrified young professional hoping I didn't have to live my life as a lie, to publicly representing a company as an openly gay man with a husband and children. I grew into an executive willing to stand up and own myself, good or bad, right or wrong, willing to stand up and own a decision. I found skills in myself I never knew existed. Leaning into my creative instincts was just not an option for me when I was growing up. To find later on in life that I love reading and dissecting scripts is an incredible blessing. Can I turn a good script into a great script? Not as well as Carolyn. Never. But there are things about this that I'm good at and that I love! Who the hell would have guessed that I would find this creative outlet at that point in my life? I'm incredibly blessed. No regrets! It was fantastic.

CAROLYN STRAUSS:

Mike had never done it before and Richard had never done it before. And I think it would have been hard for anybody in that position. Casey had grown up doing development. It's a hard job, and the criteria is often very subjective.

RICHARD PLEPLER:

Making Casey head of programming was one of the best decisions that I made as CEO. He will have a long and distinguished legacy.

Casey was all about the work, he doesn't need public approbation. He is also extremely collaborative and a terrific leader.

CASEY BLOYS:

I told everybody who reported to me that if any agent called me to complain about someone, my first response would always be, "That doesn't sound like the person I know." I wanted them to know I had their back, that we could all talk internally about problems, but externally I would never sell them out. And I promised to never say yes to something they had passed on. I felt what everybody inside needed most was support and collaboration. And I didn't want to nickel-and-dime people. If it took a little more money to solve a problem, then we should do that.

When I took over, as a longtime development executive, I wanted to be the programming president I would want to work for. I decided I would give my department heads the trust and autonomy to buy what they wanted and not ever feel second-guessed. I would not undo a pass, I would not buy things as favors and add to their workload. If agents or producers called me to try to forum shop or complain about one of my executives, I would always defend them and let them know in no uncertain terms that I trusted those who worked for me. Most important, as I laid out plans for what to program, I would let everyone know what my vision for the future was so they understood the larger objective of the individual shows they were working on. I did not want anyone working in a vacuum.

My vision was an expanded and more diverse slate, diverse in every sense of the word. Not just ethnically, but diverse genders, scope, scale, and tones. Just as I had done in comedy, with shows as varied as *Enlightened* and *Ballers*, *Veep* and *Girls* and *Insecure*, I wanted a programming slate that included all types of shows, but shows that, no matter how large or small, all felt worthy of the HBO name.

Throughout television history, many of the most accomplished shows have been built on a singular vision from one creator (or a partnership). HBO wound up with at least five different versions of **Vinyl***, a project that would eventually rival* **Westworld** *when it came to epitomizing inexperience and organizational chaos inside HBO. Perhaps the saddest element is that, creatively speaking,* **Vinyl** *kept its promise: to open a window into the clash between Boomer-beloved music and the coming power of punk, disco, and rap in the 1970s, capturing a specific New York City in a vibrant and arresting way. Unfortunately, there proved to be too many visions in the room. Several HBO insiders blamed Winter for not bringing "his best stuff," while plenty of voices from outside HBO blamed the company for once again losing control of its development process.* **Vinyl's** *low ratings, fueled by disastrous scheduling, made matters even worse.*

TERENCE WINTER:

So all year long, everybody—Mick [Jagger], Marty [Scorsese]—everybody's trying to be Monday morning quarterback. "Oh, well, the characters are unlikable" or this, that, or the other thing. "The music's not good." And I was like, "Guys, it's fine. Just stick with it." And the numbers started to turn around by the end of the season and what ended up happening at the end of season one, they picked it up, and they called me in one day and they said they wanted me to fire my entire writing staff. And I said, "No, I'm not, I'm not firing anybody." I said, "This is, I mean it, the best writing staff I've ever worked with. I will make some creative changes on the show, but this is my team and this is what I'm doing." And it got to a point where there were creative differences. And rather than stick by me, Mick and Marty allowed HBO to move me aside. They brought in two guys who had never done TV before, and I called Bobby Cannavale and I said, "Start packing your bags." He said, "What do you mean?" I said, "Unless these two guys are the smartest people who have ever lived, there was no way they're going to come in, take over a show, deal with HBO, Mick, Marty, keep this thing on track, on time, on budget." There are so many things that have to go right at the same time that it's mathematically impossible. And sure enough, these guys lasted about a month and HBO pulled the plug.

CASEY BLOYS:

We were going to try to figure out a second season. And after Mike left, I said to Richard, "This is a waste of money, because at best we will go from a C to a B minus. Why even bother? Why spend all the money?" And I got him to agree, and we canceled the second season. But that experience, of catering to Marty, never saying no, being led by the names as opposed to the creative, that informed me on *Succession* by saying, We need to go back to how we used to make TV at HBO, which was like, you made stars and it was about what was on the page as opposed to the names on the poster. So *Vinyl* was a lesson for me in just being mindful that there's nobody who's above the law, there's nobody who can't make a bad show. Just be honest about it with yourselves.

Shortly after Bloys's promotion, in June 2016, David Levine and Francesca Orsi were promoted to executive vice presidents and co-heads of HBO drama series.

DAVID LEVINE:

It was hard. I had to learn how to work with Casey, who I felt never liked me. It seemed like we all complemented one another but I couldn't ever make it clear enough that what I was dreaming up and what I loved doing wasn't competing with what they wanted to do. I loved making movies for television. I felt like that was where the medium was going, longer cinema, often with a single director, like *True Detective* had been. And I thought that fit neatly alongside the television that HBO was always known for. I kept thinking, I'll leave the network after my next show but kept falling in love with the projects, the writers, and the filmmakers. Through that period, we started making so much I hoped they would stop punishing me. That they wouldn't try to kill me anymore. That never happened, no matter what I did. So those three years were challenging. My hope was that we'd all figure out long term how to better work together, but alas we never did, and I moved on.

*From the start, Alan Ball and HBO executives clashed over notes for **Here and Now**. Bloys was on the hunt for a contemporary family show, but the person who had delivered **Six Feet Under** didn't seem likely to be the one to deliver the goods. Ball's deal* with *HBO* was on the cusp of expiration, so HBO committed to a pilot script (and millions of dollars) on the premise that whatever flaws existed in the pilot or premise of the show could be sorted out in the writers' room.

Unfortunately, that never materialized. The show premiered on February 11, 2018, but was canceled after just one season.

ALAN BALL:

For *Here and Now*, in 2018 and 2017, I knew HBO was looking for a family show.

The show I wanted to do and the show HBO wanted to do were not the same show. They were interested in something that would be more along the lines of *This Is Us*, and I was more interested in doing a show not so much about the family, but the world the family was living in and how it was changing and how it was slowly turning to what we now refer to as Trump's America. It didn't seem like there was much of an appetite for this show from audiences. I don't know. I can never say why something works or why it doesn't work. When I first gave the script to HBO to read, the question that Casey asked me was, "Is this a family show or is this his supernatural show?" I guess I thought it could be both. I guess I was wrong.

I was working with writers on the show prior to the election. The day that Trump got elected, we were all basically in mourning and we actually put away a huge bottle of rum in the writers' room. And we sort of said, "This is what we have to write about, whatever's happening to what we think of as America is pretty big, so let's try to use this as a way for us to sort of address that head on." In retrospect, maybe we were trying to do too much. I think the show was problematic from its inception because it was trying to be too many things for too many people, but the days of the creative autonomy were gone. I got pages and pages of notes, and maybe that's because the show was not working, but I had never gotten so many literal pages and pages and pages of single-spaced notes. Mike was there for *Virtuoso*, but Casey was there for *Here and Now*.

Sarah Jessica Parker had already starred in one landmark HBO series, but could **Divorce**—which premiered on October 9, 2016—bring the cultural cachet and acclaim that **Sex and the City** once had?

The answer would be a qualified "no." Created by **Catastrophe**'s star and creator, the Irish writer, actor, and comedian Sharon Horgan, the show focused on the breakup of a Westchester, New York, couple, played by Parker and Thomas Haden Church. It was a show that people seemed to like, but hardly love, and a shortened final season of just six episodes—down from ten in the first season and eight in the second—seemed to suggest a show that ran out of steam. One of its biggest problems was regular changes in the showrunner, which tended to create tonal shifts across episodes, and even, sometimes, within individual scenes. Without that über-head writer's voice and vision, making a TV show can sometimes be like second grade when the teacher walks out of the room and everyone starts throwing erasers at the chalkboard; focus is lost, and momentum ebbs away. That seemed to be the case for **Divorce**, despite all the talent on display.

SARAH JESSICA PARKER:

I was really curious about affairs and how they affect marriages. I think all of us have friends whose marriage has been through it. I've seen marriages that thrive post affairs. I've seen them fall apart. I've seen kids play a role in that outcome. I've seen people handle it well. I've seen people handle it poorly, and I just couldn't recall anything on television that spoke to it the way HBO could speak to it. Specific to a portrait of a middle-class marriage, what does that look like, a woman having committed the affair?

And they were excited about that idea and really encouraged us. And we went through a process with different writers and ultimately HBO set us up with Sharon and she was so dazzling. Anyway, we met her, we loved her, she wrote a great pilot. HBO was excited. We were all excited. I originally had the idea, not for me. I had a million other people in mind who I wanted to play that part of the woman. But when it was presented to me, I was excited about it. We went off and shot the pilot and I loved the pilot.

AMY GRAVITT:

Sarah Jessica took time to find the right project and decide when she wanted to come back. I obviously was a huge fan of *Sex and the City* before even working at HBO, but I think that I got to see firsthand with Jessica her attention to detail as a producer. And as much as this show is a vehicle for her as a performer, it was also a chance for her to produce something from beginning to end. And she was so involved in every single conversation along the way, and such a strong producing partner throughout, that I just enjoyed getting to know her through all of that.

PAUL SIMMS:

Amy Gravitt said that Sarah Jessica Parker was thinking of coming back to television, which of course for HBO, especially Richard Plepler, was very exciting because he'd been paying her to have a quote unquote production company for a decade since *Sex and the City* ended. And I read the script that Sharon Horgan wrote, which I thought was a funny script. And it was another one of these things where I felt like, Well, they just need an American there to help out, because Sharon's never done American television before.

I'm not proud of my motives for doing the show in retrospect, because one of them was, This'll be an easy job because I'm just there to sort of guide and help out. And a lot of the burden of the work won't fall on me. And the second part, and I think it might be the only time I've done this, is I thought even if the show doesn't turn out great, it's going to be a massive hit and a cultural touchstone because this is Sarah Jessica Parker finally coming back to HBO after all this time. And her fans have been dying to see her on TV again.

SARAH JESSICA PARKER:

We had great actors on the show, people like Talia Balsam and Molly Shannon. Molly's a spectacular person, truly. Freaking hilarious and so much fun to be around. And she's also comforting to have on a set. She loves to have really deep, complicated conversations about real things and ask a slew of questions along the way—even if it's just moments before we are about to shoot. One time, I had to literally interrupt her, and say, "Molly, I think they're going to call action."

PAUL SIMMS:

Cut to the morning after the first episode debuted and I was on the phone with Casey Bloys. He told me the numbers and I said, "Oh Jesus, where are all these people who said that they would follow her to the ends of the earth and watch her in anything?" I said, "Casey, pull the plug. It's over." It was an incredibly difficult show for reasons that absolutely should not have existed. It was people not getting along with people. So many people with motives that had nothing to do with making a good show. A lot of it was gossipy, who do I like, who do I not like, that person gives me a weird vibe stuff, you know? Just the worst shit.

The show did not know what it wanted to be. It was a constant struggle to keep the show a comedy without turning it into a sort of heavy dramedy. It was schizophrenic. Funny stuff would be considered too funny. The dramatic stuff went on too long.

There was something flawed in the concept, which is *Sex and the City* made you feel good. It was fun. It was young women aspirational, living their lives in the city. And this was a show about the most miserable part in these people's lives. I detected some of those flaws early on. I was like, boy, divorce? Divorce can be funny, I suppose. But the fact that they have kids means there's serious consequences to everything that they do, which makes it very painful. I think we all sort of deluded ourselves into thinking like, no, that's what makes it good, not being afraid. We're being very brave and going right to the heart of this difficult thing that is still funny. And we kept saying, "Still funny," but . . .

SARAH JESSICA PARKER:

I think the thing that's surprised me was how, less so the audience, but more so people who write opinions and critics, how unforgiving they were of a woman having an affair. And how many times I was asked by journalists, Do you worry that she's not likable? I mean, she's had an affair and made this awful decision and put her marriage in peril and betrayed her children's trust and spent time elsewhere. And I was floored. I couldn't believe that Tony Soprano could murder people and nobody ever asked him, Are you worried that he's not likable? But a woman couldn't have an affair and then try to right the wrong without being asked if I worried that she was unlikable.

So that was the thing that was surprising was how little elasticity there was in the concept of who is a likable woman and who isn't. I was confounded by that.

I have no interest in playing someone who's just likable. Where is there any challenge in that? And it will be terribly boring and HBO owes more to its viewers than just being a victim in a marriage where someone had an affair and you've seen it before. I mean, men have affairs all the time. Right? I was glad that HBO had the courage of their convictions. I think the hardest thing about any show is when you feel it's not able to maintain the very essence that brought you to it in the first place.

PAUL SIMMS:

I had a friend who said, "You've got *Atlanta* going on. Why are you still doing this?" And I said, "I feel some sort of sense of duty or obligation to try to get this thing fixed and make this show better." But at a certain point I realized, Ah, no one else seems to care. And for my own sanity, I got better things to do. I liked Casey and Amy and, in some sentimental way, I'd been there since 1992. But I talked to my wife about it. It was making me miserable at home. So I quit very abruptly.

The daughter of a Senegalese pediatrician and a teacher mother from Louisiana (her parents met in France), Issa Rae (full name Jo-Issa Rae Diop) grew up first in Los Angeles, then Senegal, and then Potomac, Maryland. When she was eleven, the family moved to the View Park Windsor Hills neighborhood of Los Angeles. After graduating from Stanford, she took a theater scholarship at The Public in New York before creating her beloved YouTube series, **Awkward Black Girl**. On the back of **Awkward**'s virality, in 2013, Diop initially partnered with Larry Wilmore (Comedy Central stalwart of **The Daily Show** and his own **The Nightly Show with Larry Wilmore**) to create **Insecure** for HBO.

Through four series—each themed, at least by title: "...As Fuck" (season one); "Hella..." (season two); "...-Like" (season three); and "Lowkey..." (season four)— the show follows the experiences of two Black women in LA: Issa Dee (played by Diop) and Molly (played by Yvonne Orji). As initially conceived, **Insecure** was to focus mostly on Issa Dee's character—that is, until someone mentioned a very different show from a very different time—**Laverne and Shirley**—and the show gained a new perspective and range. Critics raved about Rae and **Insecure**, and viewers loved the show, too.

ISSA RAE, Creator:

The first time I watched *Sex and the City* I was in college, and I thought this feels so relevant to my life or this feels aspirational to me and this feels like I want to be, I want to be Samantha. I feel like Carrie, Miranda. So I hope that people are identifying with our characters in that way.

HBO went all in aspiring to create a show where it's almost like an adult coming-of-age story. We wanted that license to be able to show her growth. You still do that as adults. We're not set in our ways. That was the excitement of just chronicling the character's journey.

We had this come-to-Jesus meeting where it was just me, Casey, Amy, and my manager, and I had written the character of Molly. She was based off of my real-life best friend, but it was more like a side character, who the character Issa would occasionally visit and talk to. And Casey was like, "What would a version of *Laverne and Shirley* be like with these two characters?" In that meeting specifically, I was talking about who my best friend was, who this character was based off of. And that really interested me. I was just like, "Oh, okay, that's a different show, but I'd love to write about our dynamic. That would be fun." I definitely credit Casey with asking that question and shaping the show.

AMY GRAVITT:

We spent a lot of time sitting in Casey's office, just talking about the idea and different anecdotes would come up about friends of hers or things that had happened, sort of the small talk you have. And that's when we said, "That's the show. The show is this group of friends, and specifically Issa and Molly. The workplace can be a facet of Issa Dee, the character's, story. But the show is about this group of friends." And once we made that pivot, that's when we knew we had a series.

ISSA RAE:

I had always said that I never wanted to do an all Black show on network television because it was so limiting and restricted. You couldn't use curse words. And so HBO felt like a blessing.

NATASHA ROTHWELL, Writer and Actor:

At the time I was interviewing for several writing jobs and I was looking to diversify my experience and had turned down a couple of offers to write on shows where the people were great, but I just didn't respond to the material as strongly as I wanted to. And then at a general meeting with Amy Gravitt, she said, "You know, we're working on this show called *Insecure* and I think we should talk about it." She understood my sense of humor.

I had the advantage of knowing Issa's work before reading the pilot and it just resonated with me and confirmed what I already knew, which was, I myself am an awkward, insecure Black girl. It felt like an appropriate way for me to enter TV writing; they say write what you know.

I went into the job only expecting to write and only wanting to write. Honestly, I wanted to hone my craft and I had blinders on as to sort of any ulterior motive. And a couple of months into the writers' room, we began doing internal table reads with the writers of the scripts that we've written just to hear them out loud. And Issa and Prentice [Penny] were obviously aware of my acting background as well. So that wasn't hidden or anything, but in the writers' room they just would cast me as Kelli. And that happened a couple of times. And Issa and Prentice called me into their office. And at that time I was convinced that I was being taken hostage, because we were playing sort of Nerf war.

So I went into their office, very suspicious of their motives, thinking that they would pull out Nerf guns at any minute. "It's not a Nerf situation. We would just love for you to play Kelli." And I remember bursting into tears because I felt so seen. I wasn't choosing writing over acting, I've always wanted to do both. And I just felt grateful that they saw me and all of me and were wanting to use my talents in every aspect. And it just speaks to how they roll, which is just an incredibly lucky situation to find myself in.

ISSA RAE:

I credit HBO with having an Amy Gravitt. I will shout out forever because I just think that she's such a smart executive when it comes to the story and women, she just has a spectacular ear and eye for comedy. She's a white woman and we are a very Black show and she's never interfered in terms of the racial dynamics of the series at all. But she knows the story really well.

NATASHA ROTHWELL:

Amy became such an amazing champion of me on the show. Everything I'm doing with HBO now has grown from that seed of trust that I planted with her. Feeling understood is a rare thing, especially for women of color in this industry.

ISSA RAE:

I think working with an incredible partner in Prentice Penny, who I've never worked with in television before. He has worked, from *Girlfriends* or *Scrubs*, *Brooklyn Nine Nine*, he came up in a writers' room and is the most patient man on earth. I got lucky for my first show to be paired with someone like Prentice, who held my hand throughout the process and who I've learned so much from. He is so grounded and I just see the value that he puts on writers and the way that he talks to people. That's something that I seek to emulate.

AMY GRAVITT:

The conversations between Issa and Molly just broke my heart. Everybody goes through heartache in relationships, it's expected in romantic relationships, but I don't think people explore quite as much when you slowly grow apart from a friend who has meant so much to you through a certain phase of life.

NATASHA ROTHWELL:

Kelli is just deeply unapologetic. My approach to her is, What would it be like to be in the world, a plus-sized Black woman, and never question your value, your worth, or your potential. I gave her that sort of magical mindset in the beginning of just loving people and caring about people, but not feeling the need to shrink herself or to make herself more palatable to others. It was more about her being her true, authentic self, and so much of who she is is aspirational for me. So I definitely use her as an opportunity to try to experience that freedom, even for a moment.

REGINA KING:

I am so in awe of Issa. Talk about speaking to a culture. She wears her hair naturally and she's not straightening it in any way. She's embracing the beauty of her natural texture hair. She changed how so many women feel about their hair, about their awkwardness, and helped not just her generation but my generation as well.

ISSA RAE:

I've learned to listen a lot since the first episode of *Insecure*. I found that listening gets you so much that I would never think of and it leads you the right way. It sounds so obvious.

You have to focus on it, like your mind can't be on anything else.

I had a moment where I looked around and was like, Wow, I'm making my show and I get to work with people who are dope as fuck, who are making this happen and helping me to tell this story and it's fun. I never imagined it would be like the first moment that I looked up at two seasons to be like, This is incredible. I get to do this.

There's a learning curve. HBO does not do shit when it comes to that. They're just like, Hey, you're out there now. And, hey, the Golden Globe nominations that are coming up, you should go to this party. They for sure take care of you, but do they prepare you for what comes? No. And make no mistake, I'm not *Game of Thrones* level, so it's not like crazy, but it definitely takes getting used to and to meet people like the personal life stuff, that's hard. It's just a lot. I'd rather not. I love disappearing when the show is off. It just brings a lot of anxiety to know that people are talking about me as a person as opposed to the characters that I create. That takes getting used to.

CASEY BLOYS:

Insecure always ranks as one of our most social shows. The point of doing a show is not to just get people tweeting about it, but it is one indicator of people's passions and how they feel about it.

Everyone who's been in their twenties or early thirties understands the struggle of "Do I have the right job? Am I on the right career path? Is this person I'm dating the one I'm supposed to be with? Is there anybody else out there?" All of those elements are universal. We all watched them do it with *Sex and the City* and with *Girls*, and *Insecure* is no different.

Back in May [of 2016] when Mike left and they gave me president of HBO programming, it was a much bigger portfolio than I had when I was promoted from head of comedy to entertainment just five months before. My new job encompassed drama, comedy, mini-series, movies, sports, documentaries, late night, and Cinemax at the time. It was a lot. It was a little overwhelming. But in the months since I had taken over, I had started to work on big questions like where are we going? What's missing? But most importantly, because it had been a famously dysfunctional group, my number one priority was getting everyone into shape interpersonally, to put us all back together, and on the same track.

When Murdoch had tried to buy Time Warner back in 2014, the company wasn't even thinking about selling themselves. Back then, they saw the industry was still growing vibrantly. Time Warner had many of its major distribution agreements, both for HBO and the Turner networks, up for renewal in the next year or so. And they knew the Turner contracts were significantly underpriced. It was clear Time Warner believed they would be getting a lot more revenue from those renewals, making them confident that they could deliver a significant step-up in earnings over the next couple of years.

A more demanding question rose up once again: What was the long-term future of the bundle?

JEFF BEWKES:

We knew by 2014 we would either have to acquire or merge with somebody to get what we needed to compete with the digital giants or, failing that, sell Time Warner. This was because half of our company's earnings came from Turner; it performed beautifully and basically doubled the earnings in the years between 2014 and 2018, so it wasn't their fault. The problem was the basic cable bundle's value was being undermined by Netflix and others, killing the ad business, and, secondly, no cable network could match the consumer data Netflix was getting direct off broadband.

We had tried to convince everybody to make every channel in the bundle on demand, like HBO, with all their hit shows and past seasons available for bingeing. But nobody except Turner adopted it, and that's when I realized there was no way to save that bundle, and we were the leading company in the bundle with four big channels: CNN, TNT, TBS, and Cartoon Network. You might ask, why not just get rid of Turner? Good question. We couldn't sell it by itself. Turner's low basis would trigger a huge tax. We could spin it off tax free, so our shareholders would still own it but separately from their Time Warner shares. But no one knew what the Turner shares would trade at on their own, and five minutes after HBO and Warners were "on their own" we would have unsolicited takeover bids from everywhere.

After the Murdoch takeover attempt, the shareholders were happy, the board was happy, and I was grateful for their unwavering support. The board asked, "Is this the end of hostile bids? Do we see blue skies ahead, so we can stay independent?" I had to answer no. We had Icahn in 2006, Murdoch in 2014, and the next time the market panics about digital disruption and all the media stocks get hit we'll be first in the line of attack. You know why? Because Time Warner didn't have a controlling shareholder to block an offer, and it would cost twice as much to buy Disney.

I told the board that, longer term, Google, Facebook, Netflix, Amazon, and maybe Apple are going to hollow out all the media companies. We either have to become like them or merge with them, and it looks like they'd rather hollow us out than buy us and pay a premium. The reason they'll win and we'll lose is they don't have to pay $8 billion a year to cable companies to carry their subscription services into people's homes, and they don't need to deliver $8 billion a year in earnings. Investors in Netflix and Amazon don't want them to earn current profits, they want them to build a monopoly.

Netflix and Amazon can take the $16 billion a year that we have to devote to earnings and carriage fees and spend it on their tech platforms and on outbidding us for programming. Or they can just underprice us to subscribers. All of the above, actually. Reed Hastings said it memorably, "The challenge for Netflix is whether we can become HBO faster than HBO can become us." He also said his biggest worry was TV Everywhere. If all the channels on the TV dial offered their programs like *Friends*, *Family Guy*, and *The Office* on VOD, with all the past seasons, there'd be much less reason to pay for Netflix.

Many people have said, "Well, all the 'old media' companies should just turn themselves into Netflix, spend more on programming, cut the subscription prices, and build a robust customer service and billing platform and user interface." Of course, we spent a lot of time thinking about how to do that. Which brings up the next big problem. We didn't have a robust consumer facing tech platform like Apple, Netflix, Amazon, Google, Facebook, and building one would mean spending hundreds of millions at least per year which we would have to explain to investors. If you ask a Netflix or Amazon or YouTube exec what's the most important thing in their business, the money or the data, they will say, "It's the data, stupid." We tried to get customer data during our affiliate renewals, even trading off some rate increases, but they made it clear it would only be over their dead bodies.

I met with each of our big institutional owners in 2015 and asked if they would support flatter earnings growth so we could increase programming spending, build a consumer tech platform, and suffer sub-losses from distributor retaliation over moving HBO faster toward the global Netflix model. None of them thought the Turner networks could make that crossing, our stock would drop and they'd want to sell their position before it did. Our biggest shareholders didn't want us cutting our earnings to turn into Netflix and Amazon because they already owned big positions in Netflix and Amazon. We were the part of their portfolio they wanted delivering big current earnings. We explored rotating out our investor base, but there's no hypothetical investor base that would believe we could turn the Turner networks, that account for half the money at Time Warner, into Netflix.

We concluded that we needed a direct consumer platform and more scale to survive, and there were six or seven companies that fit this description. They all cost three to seven times what Time Warner was worth. The companies that fit the bill were Amazon, Apple, Google, Facebook, Verizon, and AT&T. We didn't think Comcast could get it through antitrust, and Netflix didn't need us.

I told the board that while it was obvious we couldn't afford to acquire these capabilities, we could still incorporate them into the company provided we sold into one of them. The only drawback was "we'll all have to go, you on the board and all of us in the corporate office." But the shareholders will get a premium.

Tim Cook and Eddie Cue came to dinner with me at Marea during the summer of 2015. We had already launched HBO broadband that spring with Apple as marketing partner. At the dinner they asked, "What if Apple TV launched a Time Warner package with HBO and the Turner channels for $19 a month?" I said, "Great, we're interested," but I wasn't sure if HBO and the Turner networks by themselves would get enough subscribers in the United States and globally, which is what was needed. "We may need to add another network group, either Disney or NBC." After some thought, Tim said, "We want to do it with just the HBO and Turner channels."

Olaf, our head of Time Warner strategy, and Eddy had serious talks for a month or two about how this might work. As talks developed, we both realized this would create huge conflicts. For us, all of our distributors, Comcast, DirecTV, Charter, Dish, would line up against us. Eddy and Tim had similar concerns about their App Store, which did a lot of business with all the other media companies. So we would either have to have a very long deal with renewal options or we'd have to be the same company.

There was a period when Time Warner believed Apple was not only excited about getting into the set-top business for them, but ultimately was considering buying Time Warner itself. (Apple could have bought Time Warner with less than half of its cash stockpile). But several truths emerged, including that Apple wanted only HBO and Warner Bros. and Tim Cook wanted to focus on the launch of a new iPhone, the Apple Watch, and believed buying a media company would send a signal to investors that Apple's global device business was flattening. In short, Apple wanted to be sure investors knew they were focused on their core business.

JEFF BEWKES:

I went out to Apple in Cupertino with Olaf, and after a full day with Tim, Eddy, and their acquisition team, it was clear the possibility of a merger wasn't going to fly. I wish we'd been able to do that.

15

Dallas

Telecommunications giant AT&T had strung together a monopolist streak ever since Alexander Graham Bell's invention of the telephone in the late nineteenth century precipitated its founding—and changed the planet. Over the next century, "the telephone company" simply took over telecommunications in America. Then in 1984, the company, forced by the federal government, was split into seven Baby Bells. Within twenty-five years, most of the seven would re-combine under the AT&T banner, culminating in AT&T's purchase of BellSouth at the end of 2006. AT&T was a master at integrating phone business assets.

When AT&T bought DirecTV for $67 billion in July 2015—making it the largest premium television provider in the country—it signaled AT&T's determination to make itself a major player in the content game. That move was merely a warm-up.

On October 22, 2016, AT&T acquired Time Warner for $109 billion—$85.4 billion in Time Warner equity, and $24 billion for Time Warner's debt. Candidate Donald Trump announced he would seek to block the deal if he got elected.

Bewkes talked up the deal, but his inner circle knew that after Bewkes realized Tim Cook and Apple weren't going to step to the plate, Disney had been his backup dream marriage. Disney and Time Warner would have created a massive studio, featuring a boffo combination of DC and Marvel, along with a Disney/HBO/Hulu bundle that would have protected HBO's premium adult brand and offered Hulu as a wide port of entry for the rest.

RANDALL L. STEPHENSON, Executive, AT&T:

It was 2014. I was in the process of trying to get the DirecTV deal approved by the government, and I'm in Sun Valley at the Allen and Company conference. Rupert was trying to do a hostile on Time Warner, TWX. One day, between presentations, Jeff Bewkes said, "If you have a minute, you and I should talk." He and I never spent much time together. I said, "Sure." So we go out by the back pond. Rupert was walking by and he pointed at Rupert and he said, "There's no reason that he and I ought to merge."

He said, "Our conversation ought to be with you." I grinned. I said, "Hold that thought. I'm in the middle of trying to get something approved. The idea of buying a media company right now doesn't seem very appealing. But maybe one day we'll talk."

JEFF BEWKES:

I regularly met with the top execs running Amazon, Apple, Google, YouTube, Facebook, and Netflix about the increasing business we were doing together and the increasing problems we had with various moves, and the damage they were causing. While I didn't push on a string and try to "sell" the company to them, our talks with Apple had failed, and it was clear none of the others was interested in buying Time Warner.

That left Verizon and AT&T, but despite a close relationship with Lowell, it was clear that Verizon wasn't interested in merging with a big media acquisition.

In September of 2015 the basic cable bundle subs starting eroding and all the media stocks sank. Ours had been up around $90 after we fought off Murdoch's bogus $85 offer—it was really worth around $70—but by Christmas we were back down around $60, in line with the other media companies. After the New Year we had an activist wolf pack after us. Peltz, Icahn, Rosenstein, and some other activists were buying and driving up our stock as the rest of the market kept falling, and Murdoch was running articles in the *Post* every three days saying Time Warner shareholders were unhappy.

I told the board, "Look, Murdoch lost because he couldn't afford us, but the next time there's a big downturn, somebody's going to come for us. Because we're not only the best media company with the highest earnings growth, best assets, and library, we're the only one they can buy in a hostile takeover. They can't buy CBS, Redstone has majority control of the voting shares. They can't buy Fox or NBC, Murdoch and Roberts have the blocking votes. Only Time Warner and Disney have no controlling shareholder, and Disney costs twice as much because they haven't spun off ABC and ESPN. So it's going to be us.

RANDALL L. STEPHENSON:

People used to say, "You'll never be able to do broad-based Internet access over wireless networks." Along comes the iPhone.

Ten years later, you're streaming all kinds of video capability. I had seen this movie too many times before, and we knew bandwidth was going to get bigger and better. So in 2015, [John] Stankey and I met with our board. I was convinced, and Stankey was convinced, that people were going to be consuming feature-length video over wireless networks. It was inevitable. And if that were the case, we had this nationwide distribution vehicle and we ought to think about how we would differentiate it. We had spent our entire careers chasing who could have the broadest coverage, who can have the fastest speed, who could have the best quality, but now it was getting harder and harder to distinguish your services that way. We said at some point, "We ought to think about whether we start bringing media into the product equation." We went down a path looking at all kinds of companies, candidly. We looked at Scripps, we looked at CBS. Then we looked at Time Warner, and that was a unique business.

JOHN STANKEY, Executive, AT&T:

Our belief was that customers were going to go for productivity for what they could do with it, as much as connectivity itself.

We felt like entertainment was a good foundation for that particular product set. And we knew we weren't going to get it by aggregating cable TV networks, that we actually had to go further up the value chain to be able to get to the point where we own and produce content and could restructure the company in a way that we thought made sense on a technology platform that was forward-leaning, that met customer needs of watching beloved content and shows anytime, anyplace. It allowed us to have direct billing relationship with those customers that had information around how the households were using it.

JEFF BEWKES:

I had breakfast with Bob Iger in April of 2016 at the Bel Air hotel. We revisited Rupert's failed takeover attempt in 2014, during which Disney teamed up with us to license the NBA for over a decade thereby depriving Fox of one of its arguments that Time Warner needed Fox to get more sports rights. Bob confided that even though they hadn't wanted to buy TW back then, had it looked like Rupert would prevail and assemble a stronger competitor, Disney would have had to consider stepping in. I said to Bob, "The next time the market panics about Netflix and Amazon or the cable bundle collapsing, we'll be the target. We can't stay as we are, we have to do something to gain scale and transition to streaming." I said, "Bob, News Corp couldn't afford to buy Time Warner and it didn't have the right assets to solve these problems. The only [media] merger that actually works against all these trends is Disney and Time Warner."

Even though Bob wasn't actively looking to make a huge acquisition, he was open to considering it, but said his reservation was still the same as it had been back in 2014: Disney didn't want more exposure to the basic cable bundle. He didn't want to add TNT, TBS, CNN, and Cartoon Network to his ABC and ESPN problem.

I understood and agreed with that, and I wasn't suggesting we would keep the Turner channels long term. "You can't keep ABC and ESPN long term either," I said. "As the bundle erodes, it will pressure ESPN, because every home in America—even those who don't want it— is paying more for it than any other channel. So we'd wait eighteen months after the merger as the tax rules require, then spin off the Turner channels with ABC, and ESPN."

The surviving Disney/Time Warner would have the strongest studio, the biggest library, the best family and children's IP from the Disney characters, Pixar, Marvel, Lucasfilm's Star Wars, DC, Looney Tunes, Harry Potter, and Cartoon Network, along with the huge Warner film and television library, the Disney parks and stores and the established global premium brand and sub base at HBO. We'd need to build a consumer facing platform but we'd be too big for a hostile takeover and investors would support the investment because we'd have a clear chance of success. Bob said he'd think it over.

RANDALL L. STEPHENSON:

It created an opportunity for us to see if there was something unique to do with our two businesses together.

I went through a lot of mental gymnastics around that, and I talked to a lot of people who I respect, everybody from Peter Chernin to John Stankey. We spent a lot of time talking about this, and there was a general consensus that, first of all, what Jeff had done with Turner had rendered it less vulnerable to what was imminently coming. That was all the cord cutting. Because you were down to five cable channels, of which three really mattered: TNT, TBS, and CNN. Those three were probably going to be fairly well inoculated and valuable even as you move through cord cutting. Stankey also felt very strongly that news was going to be a critical element of any product offering.

It was a very unique asset. I talked to the board about why it [Time Warner] might be a good fit, and that I didn't view CBS or Fox as being achievable. I called Jeff and asked him if he'd be interested in visiting. He immediately said yes.

Although Time Warner was made up of three main media assets, Turner, HBO, and Warner Bros., Turner was half the revenue of the company, ad supported, and part of the dying cable ecosystem. Some bidders, understandably, were put off. AT&T, on the other hand, thought, "Oh no, we love advertising. We'll buy it."

From the beginning, the key questions surrounding the DirecTV and Time Warner deals were—was this financial engineering designed to in effect "buy" cash to maintain AT&T's prized dividend (which required more than $15 billion a year) or were these genuine attempts at integration? And if so, was AT&T up for the challenge?

JEFF BEWKES:

It appears that some people have forgotten two key elements: First, that 92 percent or more of our shareholders voted for the AT&T cash and stock offer, which at $107.50 was roughly 40 percent above our trading value at the time. Second, when Randall came for lunch in August 2016 and asked me whether I thought a combination would help our companies to successfully evolve, one of his selling points was that since AT&T didn't have a studio or a network, they didn't have any executives with experience in these businesses so they would need to rely on our people rather than the usual practice of installing their own people.

JOHN MALONE:

Jeff did an excellent job of liquidating the company for the benefit of shareholders. I think it's pretty clear that's what he did. He executed it well, giving the old Time Inc. shareholders a decent exit. He was very smart to dump it to AT&T, frankly, on the deal that he got. He found AT&T in a situation where they thought it was a lifeline for them.

JEFF BEWKES:

Three or four days before we announced the AT&T deal in October of '16, Bob called me, I believe on a Tuesday morning to say, "Okay, I thought about it, let's resuscitate this. How about you come out Friday and we'll talk about it. Don't bring anybody, just us to see if we have a meeting of the minds, we can't let any bankers find out about this." I don't think he would have called me if they hadn't done a lot of work on it, but I didn't know whether he would be in the ballpark on price and I'm sure he wondered the same about us.

I couldn't tell him we were days away from announcing a $110 billion deal with another public company, that's material nonpublic information for one thing, but also it would violate our exclusive negotiating agreement with AT&T. Either of those would put us in huge legal jeopardy and expose us to a giant breach suit from AT&T. So I said, "Can't come Friday, how about Monday?" And then I called him Saturday just before the AT&T deal was being announced to alert him to the news.

All the press accounts have missed some crucial facts. First, as with any merger of public companies, we were in an exclusive negotiating period with AT&T when he called me that week to suggest restarting the discussion I had proposed back in April. We could not start talking to Disney without notifying and terminating our deal with AT&T, which at this point had been fully negotiated and approved by both boards. And after Bob's call I had to inform the board of the inquiry, to discuss with them whether they wanted to pause and maybe lose the AT&T deal and explore whether Disney was serious and what they were prepared to pay. As expected, and as recommended by our legal and financial advisors, the board confirmed my recommendation that we close the deal we had in hand with AT&T, because there was nothing to stop Disney from making an offer after we announced the deal, at least until the shareholder vote many weeks later.

When I called Bob to alert him about our AT&T announcement, I had received very stern legal admonishments not to say anything that could be construed as soliciting an offer from him. That's a standard provision in these megamergers and had I violated it that would give AT&T cause for legal action.

Once our deal was announced and the merger agreement was public, if Disney was still interested in what Bob and I had discussed, they certainly could have come in with 10 cents more. But they never did. I think they were still skittish about the Turner networks, or maybe they were nowhere near the price we got from AT&T.

Anyway, more than a year passed before they acquired Fox, which I don't think is nearly as good a combination.

SIMON SUTTON:

If Warner and HBO were just the remaining parts, it could have been Disney, it could've been Apple, it could have been a number of different people.

I actually think Jeff should have gone further. I think he should have sold off Turner to somebody like Discovery or CBS. There is synergy between those HBO and Warner Bros., although they're run very differently. With Warner Bros. and HBO combined as one company, I think you would have had some cost synergies, aligned strategy, more bidders, and maybe you could've got a better price. You could have sold it to Apple. You could've sold it to a number of the technology companies, with the great HBO brand and a movie library.

Even as streamers built up in 2016, 2017, and 2018, HBO continued to have three of the largest years of consecutive growth in the company's history. And all this while HBO's main vehicle to gain subscribers, the basic cable bundle, was seeing a steep decline.

JEFF BEWKES:

They [AT&T] should have created a template of consumer and viewing data superior to what Google and Facebook sell to advertisers. DirecTV should have sold a robust data package to its Turner and HBO networks, and offered the same data to the NBC networks, and vice versa for Comcast. And both of them should have offered that same data to the Fox, Disney, CBS, and any other network who asked, all on equal nonexclusive terms.

That would have harnessed the advantage that the television dial had over broadband viewing, created a big new data and advertising business, cemented their customer relationships, slowed the decline of the bundle, and supported the value of their networks.

But due to parochial thinking, old habits like "Comcast is my competitor," and a misplaced belief that they had enough content and distribution to make a viable global package out of what they happened to own, HBO and the Turner channels distributed over a US-only footprint. They went vertical instead, with not enough stuff over not enough global distribution. And a bit late, and at too high a price because of the constraints of their existing business that pays for everything.

Time Warner and AT&T had two diametrically different views of the reasons for this merger. Time Warner's was, number one, to go direct. HBO grew up as a wholesale business, distributing through the cable guys. To the day HBO merged with AT&T, HBO could not name, much less contact, a lot of its customers. That was no longer sustainable. HBO needed a direct-to-consumer connection. What better way than with a company that has 150 million direct-to-consumer connections?

SIMON SUTTON:

After Richard had announced at the Apple event that we were going direct-to-consumer, he would always say, "You should be able to subscribe to HBO Go directly." We did not do that, because both Comcast and DirecTV said to us, "If you allow subscribers to subscribe to HBO Go directly, we will no longer support that app. We will punish your business."

It was always our road map to just launch HBO Go and HBO Now, and then have the HBO app, while Cinemax would have its own separate business. When AT&T acquired Time Warner, it was very unclear what they wanted to do.

On the content front, HBO, continued to demonstrate the dominance to which it had grown accustomed in the award spheres. In 2017, even without their global hit **Game of Thrones** *on the year's slate, HBO earned a total of twenty-nine Emmys, eclipsing their competition, Netflix and Amazon be damned.*

Not only did HBO outdo their rival streamers, but it did so on a substantially smaller budget than the other streamers were blowing through. On average, Netflix was spending $333 million per Emmy win from 2017 to 2019. Amazon spent an astronomical $508 per win. HBO, meanwhile, was notching Emmys at a cool $72 million per.

On December 1, 2016, Amazon brought HBO and Cinemax to Amazon Channels, which was, at the time, a roughly year-old service that allowed Prime members to keep all their premium content subscriptions in one place. The deal made an HBO subscription available to Prime members for $14.99 a month, as well as a subscription to Cinemax for $9.99 a month. HBO served up all of its current series at the time—including, among others, **Westworld** *and the channel's crown jewel,* **Game of Thrones**—*as well as older classics like* **Sex and the City** *and* **The Sopranos***.*

The 2016 agreement came two years after HBO had initially licensed some of its older series, like **The Sopranos** *and* **Six Feet Under***, to Amazon Prime in another deal. As with that deal, this one had both positive and negative consequences for HBO. Amazon Channels opened up an audience of millions of additional subscribers for HBO that the network simply would not have had access to without Jeff Bezos's behemoth; Amazon's marketing capabilities dwarfed HBO's.*

Yet once again, partnering with Amazon undercut HBO's own direct-to-consumer offering, HBO Now. This deal—and the decision behind it—prompted by lagging subscriber growth at HBO—marked yet another turning point for HBO. While it would continue to offer direct-to-consumer options for its subscribers, HBO's focus would turn to a broader definition of digital delivery, one that used means outside the four walls of HBO and partnered with other companies to promote HBO's content and grow its brand.

As HBO distribution turned to rival streaming services to expand their reach, HBO's programming department turned to Italy, and to a celebrated film director, to do the same. On January 15, 2017, HBO premiered Paolo Sorrentino's **The Young Pope,** *starring Jude Law as the young American Pope Pius XIII, and Diane Keaton as Sister Mary, his consiglieri.*

PAOLO SORRENTINO, Creator:

The inspiration for *The Young Pope* was the fact that all the movies I watched about the Vatican were done mostly by Americans. They insisted on sensationalism, scandals, and secrets.

I wanted to do something that was realistic about the Vatican and at the same time tell the world what an unusual, strange, sad place it was, because a world without women is sad. The Vatican is also a dictatorial state that most of the world accepts. Usually when there is one person with complete power in this world, people disagree.

I wanted to make something for the entire world, and for the first time, I decided to have an unusual, strange combination: an American pope, young and beautiful. But everything else should be realistic around it.

Jude Law was my first choice. In truth, he was the choice of my wife. I was forced.

The character of Diane Keaton was inspired by gossip in the Vatican from fifty or sixty years ago that a pope was driven by a woman who was his assistant. I thought it was a good idea in order to place a woman character inside the Vatican. Because in real life in the Vatican, there are no women except nuns, and they have a very small and useless role in the Vatican hierarchy. As soon as I decided to get women in the Vatican, I was ready to put them inside: Diane Keaton, Cécile de France, and Ludivine Sagnier.

God is the light, but we are the dark side of God. I wanted to put light and darkness together, to look at the tragic distance between God and the life of the man that should be similar to God, but it's impossible for the human being to become like God. This frustration is very, very interesting from a dramaturgic point of view.

ARI EMANUEL:

They wanted to only do one season of it and we said, "No, this is a series. This is not a miniseries. Don't define it that way." I said, "What happens if it works?"

Female firepower: On February 19, 2017, HBO premiered one of its most star-studded projects to date, **Big Little Lies,** *starring Reese Witherspoon, Nicole Kidman, Shailene Woodley, Alexander Skarsgård, Adam Scott, Zoë Kravitz, Laura Dern, with Jean-Marc Vallée, Oscar-nominated director of* **Dallas Buyers Club,** *directing. The series would go on to win eight Emmys and four Golden Globes in its first year, including the Globe for Best Miniseries or TV Film, and the Emmy for Best Limited Series.*

The addition of Meryl Streep to the cast in season two only increased the buzz around the show.

MICHAEL ELLENBERG:

Reese, Nicole, and David E. Kelley were in the room when they pitched the show to us.

It was a big package, a best-selling book, Reese and Nicole attached to star, both doing a series for the very first time. CAA reversing the normal process, rather than the show pitching at people's offices, the networks went to see the talent at CAA to hear the pitch.

We wanted to do more stories from a woman's point of view and this seemed like a huge opportunity for us to break new ground. That said, there was a risk; there was a delicate tone the show had to hit. There was a soapy element to the show and we all liked that. But that's a big difference from being soapy and actually being a soap. If you didn't get that balance right, the show would be commercial, but it might not have been as premium and as HBO as we wanted it to be.

The scripts became top notch. We approached Jean-Marc Vallée initially to direct the first two episodes. As we got closer and closer to production and we were casting again, there was a growing desire for him to direct the whole season. The reason was the delicate tonal balance. There was an excitement about matching his style, the naturalism to his work that was both elegant and stylish, and that, having his aesthetic on top of the material, something unique could come. I called him from an anniversary trip to beg him to commit to the whole season—fortunately he said yes.

LAURA DERN:

Reese Witherspoon and our families were at Disneyland together, and suddenly two twenty-year-old boys on spring break with a group of their buddies saw us and started freaking out. They ran up to us going, "Oh my God, *Big Little Lies* is our favorite thing we've ever seen." This was right after the first season, and Reese and I looked at each other and said, "Something's happening here."

David's and Jean-Marc Vallée's collaboration to allow these characters to grow from Liane's original intent, and give them life beyond the book, was exciting. Each of these characters had their own backstory and great misery. I can't speak to the other characters, but I will tell you that Renata Klein clearly has one favorite character in *Big Little Lies*. It's an amazing thing to come in, despite a want for ensemble humility, and play someone so enormous and so determined to be the most rich, famous, cutting, important, and the most of a sob story—even in the spaces of ensemble, was amazing. But in real time, that group of women, that lovely group of real friends, was an incredible opportunity to grow toward sisterhood. They are generous, lovely incredible women, and we are all really close now.

A four-part documentary called **The Defiant Ones** *detailed the partnership between Beats Electronics co-founders Jimmy Iovine and Dr. Dre and the leading role they played in a chain of transformative events in contemporary culture.*

Dre was a founding member of "Fuck the Police" stars N.W.A. before venturing out on his own, while Iovine produced work by the likes of Tom Petty, Stevie Nicks, and U2. Iovine went on to co-found Interscope Records and sign artists like Nine Inch Nails and Dre, before the pair struck gold with the ever-enigmatic Eminem. The series also featured interviews with Ice Cube, Patti Smith, Bruce Springsteen, Bono, Sean Combs, Kendrick Lamar, Nas, Stevie Nicks, Tom Petty, Snoop Dogg, will.i.am, and Eminem.

The Defiant Ones *delves into the pair's individual stories as well as their various collaborations, detailing a relationship that existed long before they sold their headphone company to Apple for $3 billion.*

The documentary aired on HBO over four consecutive nights from July 9 to July 12, 2017, and won the 2018 Grammy Award for Best Music Film and the IDA Award for Best Limited Series. The series also garnered five Emmy nominations (Outstanding Documentary or Nonfiction Series, Picture Editing for a Nonfiction Program, Sound Editing for a Nonfiction Program, Sound Mixing for a Nonfiction Program, Writing for a Nonfiction Program) and an ACE Eddie nomination for Best Edited Documentary. Director Allen Hughes won the NAACP Image Award for Outstanding Direction in a Documentary.

ALLEN HUGHES, Documentarian:

My career, along with my brother's—we were known as the Hughes brothers—started with *Menace II Society*, which was an explosive film about the inner cities of Watts, California, gang culture, drug culture, and disenfranchised youth. But before that, my brother and I started with hip-hop music videos for like N.W.A., Tupac, Digital Underground, Too Short, a lot of West Coast acts. We did some East Coast acts as well. We started our career with Tupac on his first album, and his first three music videos. We were right in the middle of that punk rock fusion of Black great hip-hop, R&B, and rock and alternative that was erupting at Interscope.

I first met Dr. Dre when I was nineteen, and reconnected with him in 2011 when I had a deal at Interscope to turn his life into a feature film or television series. Then one night I said, "Let's do a documentary on your life instead." Outside of my love for him, Dre is like the Loch Ness Monster of hip-hop. He was very mysterious, hard to sit down and interview about the business, let alone anything on his life. I said, "If we can get HBO to do it, it will have prestige and eyeballs, and they know how to roll something out." At the time, HBO was the big, badass on the mountain. The crown jewel. There was no other game in town, and I had a real good rhythm with Michael Lombardo. I called him up and I said, "What if I told you I can get the most enigmatic hip-hop artist in history to sit down and talk about his life and open up about his life?"

He said, "Who is it?" I said, "Dr. Dre." Michael Lombardo said, "Green light." He said, "We have one problem, though. Jimmy Iovine just walked out of my office with an Interscope documentary." This was 2013, when Beats had just taken over the world. I said, "I'll call you right back." The lightbulb went right off my head. I was like, Holy fuck. One of my favorite documentaries of all time was on PBS, *The Battle over Citizen Kane*. And it was a dual narrative of two child prodigies, William Randolph Hearst and Orson Welles. They told both stories, and then the great eruption that happened, when they went toe to toe. They killed each other basically, and each other's lives. And in our narrative, I saw a great eruption when these two men meet and how they became a positive, wonderful thing for the culture and for them more personally.

NINA ROSENSTEIN:

Allen Hughes is an artist himself, and it was a very ambitious, demanding, and difficult project that kept evolving as it went along. Allen needed some hand-holding, but that was part of my job, helping him maneuver through such a long, emotional, and complicated process.

ALLEN HUGHES:

It was the most emotionally taxing experience of my life, in and out of film.

I was plotting my exit to Thailand to become a Buddhist monk. I mean that. I was like, This is it. This is a swan song. I had a death wish on top of it. I said, I'm going to leave it all out on the field. And then you add in the two guys who are my, I use air quotes, my friends, Jimmy and Dre. These guys are as obsessive, impulsive, compulsive, OCD. I have all these things. They have them times ten. Add to that, at the time I entered that film, I had a lot of bad habits. I don't mean like drug and alcohol bad habits, just the way I conducted business. I was a hider. You couldn't find me. I wasn't accountable.

The Defiant Ones defined me as a filmmaker. It gave me my future. It gave me my singular purpose. It represented everything that I love and feel and want people to know. Everyone has something cool about them, whether you're Black or white, and we can all contribute to this shit together and throw one big gangster party. Because I'm biracial and I come from Michigan and California. There are these polarities that exist inside me that were hard to define. I don't give a fuck what anyone says, me and my brother were blessed that we did it as long as we did.

What that experience did, even though I was going through a literally dark night of the soul while making it and ended up going to a thirty-day program. In the height of when it was released, I was in Malibu away for thirty days because my central nervous system was tapped. I had sleep issues. I had dependency on Xanax. I wanted to get off of it. But ultimately what HBO and that experience did for me was it gave me confidence.

I want to be clear, I'm not a suicidal person. I've never been suicidal, but during the making of *The Defiant Ones* I had what was called suicidal ideations. I had lived most of my adult life as a depressive.

NINA ROSENSTEIN:

Once the show was finished, Jimmy Iovine came into the picture. He was a master marketer and had lots of ideas of how he wanted it to be positioned and put out in the world. We had many, many meetings and Jimmy would be very vocal and present in the planning stages—I heard from him all the time. And I mean all the time. It was like taking a master class, but he was relentless!

After all the months of planning, the show finally goes out, and I think this will finally be the night that I don't hear from Jimmy Iovine. There's nothing left to do. Then I hear my phone buzz. It was like four o'clock in the morning. I thought, It can't be him. What could it be? I look at my phone and it was a text from him. He said something like, "In part three in the Cleveland market, the sound dropped out."

I just was like, "Is he fucking kidding me?" I couldn't wait until the next morning to ask about it and prove him wrong. I thought, "He's gotta be wrong," but he was right. I'll never know how he does it. But it was such a fun ride and I loved every second of it.

There were so many great lines in the film, but one of my favorites is when Bono says, "Jimmy's like a virus." I think he says, "He gets inside your brain and you can't shake him loose."

After it aired, I would get pitched so many projects with the log line, It's *The Defiant Ones* version of this or that. I feel like there is no other *Defiant Ones*. You can't do it again.

Always on the search for unique projects, on January 11, 2015, HBO began a new partnership with a distinctive, celebrated creative team, the Duplass brothers. Their first project was **Togetherness,** *a family/relationship dramedy.*

JAY DUPLASS, Creator:

Mark and I started making stuff together when we were kids and honestly never stopped. We grew up in the suburbs of New Orleans, made music, art projects, and movies.

MARK DUPLASS, Creator:

We did these $10,000 movies that were shown at Sundance, and the dream was, "Let's go become the kinds of people who make studio movies at Fox Searchlight." That whole ecosystem went away once we got there, so we found ourselves really excited about television.

JAY DUPLASS:

Of course, we were going to do this together. It's hard to make movies. Two heads are better than one. In the case of *Togetherness*, it culminated as a seminal piece of art for us to make about ourselves, about where we were in our lives.

Togetherness was the first thing we did with HBO. And that was so fascinating for us because we felt very confident as filmmakers, but we didn't feel confident as TV storytellers, and we needed their support. We needed the acumen of that whole form. What happens with a lot of movie makers is that they come to TV and don't understand that feature film formulation is a very different animal. HBO was never condescending about it. They gently nudged us on how to open up the world of television.

MARK DUPLASS:

They mentored us in that process.

JAY DUPLASS:

They really did. It is the reason why we had to re-rig *Togetherness*, the television show. It took us quite a while and they sat patiently while we just took our time.

MARK DUPLASS:

Now that we are producers and have the opportunity to do that with other filmmakers, we find ourselves being not nearly as good or patient as they were.

JAY DUPLASS:

To be completely honest, we were not qualified to showrun a sizable show at HBO at that point in time in our careers. But they never micromanaged us. They would give us thoughts and suggestions. The kinds of conversations that we had were very high-level conversations about, "What is this show really about? What are you really trying to say with this storyline?" It's honestly what you think studio conversations are going to be like when you're a kid coming up and thinking about making movies, and then it gets beat out of you as you go through the studio system.

MARK DUPLASS:

I was nervous that we were going to get the yips, jump the shark, whatever you want to call it, and start cashing checks. Because that's what happens. I feel good about what we did for the first two seasons. On a deeper, personal level, it was the zenith of our collective creative energy and our brotherdom as a creative duo. It was the most amount of time we've ever spent together on a creative project, day in, day out, directing every episode, eight episodes a season. And it was happening at a time in our lives where we both had two young children. So we're being pulled away from the natural brotherdom into our own immediate families while being thrust together every day.

We should probably be with our families a little bit too. And also our individual projects. We're never going to be able to say no to this job because it's so good. And so there is a little bit of that relief when the bosses said no for us. Because we never would have been able to say no ourselves.

There was this moment when we were making *Togetherness* and that show was coming to an end and we could have chosen to be bitter and said, "You guys, how dare you cancel our show?"

But *Room 104* was coming around the corner and they wanted to support that from us. And we all sort of had that moment like families do, or like you do in your marriage or you do at Thanksgiving dinner, which is we're going to transcend this potential conflict and go deeper into our familial bond, reinvest in each other, and grow together.

When it came time to do *Room 104*, it was like a return to the glory days— let's just get back in one room with one to two characters and two or three days to shoot each episode. While that certainly was a bigger budget than the way we used to make things in the Sundance days, it was us getting back to just distilling it down to what we loved most, which is just character and story.

If you ask Casey about *Room 104*, he'll tell you, "I gave them a season three because I liked the guys, and I gave them a season four because I love the guys."

We have grown to a certain level where we are no longer the thirty-six-year-old guys in hoodies who made a $3 movie. For whatever reason we've engendered a spirit where people are not necessarily looking to chop us down at the knees. We are not yet at the level of fear-based creative thinking. And we spent the last couple of years staffing up our company. And HBO has helped with this, in our first-look deal we have with them. They've helped us find people who can help us.

We are incredibly supported by HBO from an emotional, spiritual, and creative standpoint, but also financially. They've done very well by us.

On Sunday, April 16, 2017, after six seasons on the air, Lena Dunham's **Girls** *aired its final episode—the sixty-second installment in the series. The show concludes with Dunham's Hannah caring for her newborn baby boy, Grover, alongside her friend, Marnie (played by Allison Williams). Seven hundred forty-one thousand viewers tuned into the finale, making it the second-highest-rated finale of the series (bested only by the final episode of the first season, for which one million viewers tuned in).*

LENA DUNHAM:

I've never been good at goodbyes. I had a really, really hard last season. I had two massive endometrial surgeries between and developed such bad osteoporosis from my medication that I fell on set and broke my elbow. Three days after I broke my elbow, we had to stop a day of shooting on set because something exploded under the sidewalk and ten minutes later I found out my grandmother was about to die.

That summer I kept having this visual that I was in an army crawling through mud in Vietnam. Obviously I wasn't, I was making a fancy TV show, but my physical pain was so great. The scene that everybody loves, where Adam and I look at each other and we cry because we know that it's over, I'll never be able to cry on-screen like that again. And that's because I broke my elbow that afternoon. It was swelling to the size of a grapefruit. The tears were right under the surface.

I needed to get to the end of the show, then when I did, I was so lost. That show was my whole identity. I couldn't imagine who I was going to be without it. I threw myself directly into campaigning for Hillary. I feel so lucky that *Girls* was on during the Obama years.

ILENE LANDRESS:

I said to Kat [McCaffrey] at some point that, "Lena needed a break." The Lena when we started *Girls* was very different than when we ended *Girls*. We were on track for those first couple of seasons, and Lena deserves a ton of credit for the way she dealt with the incredible amounts of attention, but as she got more famous and richer, she became somewhat enabled. This happens sometimes with stars and creators. They don't pay me at HBO because I know how to make television shows. They pay me as a staff psychologist.

LENA DUNHAM:

I made sixty-two episodes of TV and episodic storytelling wasn't necessarily my strength. I had to learn what that meant. I got better at it. As I look at it today, there's lots of flaws, like how the plots were constructed, but that messiness and circularity is part of what the show is, part of what the charm of the show is. It's not tidy and it's not made by an adult.

The beginning of third season was a hard time for me because we had done the whole like Emmys, Golden Globe circuit for the first time. I had not set foot on the ground in months and I was so fucking tired, I just didn't have the passion. Judd was watching the dailies and said, "You have to move the second camera, this looks like a dead person directed it." I was devastated. I thought, "Take me now, Lord." But that one comment got me back on track and changed the way I direct forever.

JUDD APATOW:

If you look at the landscape of television before Lena and after Lena, it's completely changed. Lena deserves an enormous amount of credit for doing groundbreaking work, including her brutal honesty and courage about body image and the satire of entitlement. She inspired an enormous amount of other writers to also do brilliant work. Before Lena, a lot of people didn't realize it was possible to do this type of work. They didn't think the opportunities were there. Lena changed everything.

David Simon had already bequeathed several signal hits to American TV—among them **Homicide,** **The Corner,** **The Wire,** *and* **Treme—***and on August 25, 2017, his latest venture, co-written with George Pelecanos, premiered on HBO.* **The Deuce** *centered on 1970s and 1980s Times Square, New York City—specifically, the porn industry as it thrived there before gentrification. Starring James Franco and Maggie Gyllenhaal,* **The Deuce** *ran for three seasons and twenty-five episodes before bowing out in the fall of 2019.*

Simon had often drawn upon personal experiences. His work covering the cop beat for the **Baltimore Sun** *inspired both* **Homicide** *and* **The Wire.** *For* **The Corner** *he and his co-writer, Ed Burns (himself a former Baltimore cop) had spent a year hanging out on an actual drug corner in the west of the city.*

But **Treme** *and then* **The Deuce** *were something else—Simon was working to inhabit characters from the outside and trying to write into a place or a time that he admired. This is a different skill from being immersed in a time and place; representing a cultural moment can feel a little less personal, and to some inside HBO this may have created a disconnect in the project. With Lombardo and Ellenberg gone or about to go, Casey Bloys had urged Kathleen McCaffrey, by now vice president of drama programming, to proffer notes directly to Simon, something she'd not done before (she'd worked on* **Treme** *but had handed her notes up the chain of command). Though she wondered initially if she was the right executive for a show about Times Square prostitutes and was not entirely sure that it was an important story, in the end McCaffrey started to believe in what Simon was doing with* **The Deuce.**

Two important industry changes came out of the making of **The Deuce.** *One was the concept of having an intimacy coordinator present to oversee filming of sex scenes and nudity. Such coordinators had previously existed, but they'd never been positioned on an actual set until the* **Deuce** *star Emily Meade went to HBO to request one—from that point on, intimacy coordinators have become standard parts of many film and TV sets, including on all relevant HBO productions.*

The other change, at least on **The Deuce,** *had to do with pay parity: Beth White, who had been the business affairs executive on all of Simon's projects from the beginning, called McCaffrey to her office and showed her a pad of paper upon which were two columns, one listing what male actors were being paid, the other what female* *actors were getting. Their discrepancies were glaring. White and McCaffrey subsequently met with Bloys, Glenn Whitehead, from business affairs, and Richard Plepler to show them the clear disparity; the three men agreed that stars should be paid the same, whatever their gender.*

DAVID SIMON:

Deuce was the creation of Mike Lombardo. He's just super smart. He's not a foolish guy. He knows the business.

Mike was rooting for *Deuce* even though he was forced to do *Vinyl*. *Vinyl* was shoved up his ass because of who was doing it, how much heat there was behind it, and how inevitable it was. He had two shows about seventies New York, and one of them had good scripts.

So I ended up gritting my teeth. I had a conversation where Mike said, "Just do good work and it'll survive." I had to believe him. *Vinyl* had gone on the air, or was about to, then *Vinyl* was renewed, and then not renewed. But I think it was renewed after we did the pilot, and we were waiting to go into production. So Mike told me the truth, I just didn't trust it, after having to fight to end *Treme* properly.

MICHAEL ELLENBERG:

I was a childish fan of David Simon's before I got to HBO. *The Wire* was the show that made me think I was going to have to work in television. It shook me up so much. David was easily the person I was most intimidated to meet when I started working at HBO.

KATHLEEN McCAFFREY:

I've never worked harder to make a showrunner love me than I have for David Simon. I think he'll tell you we have a good thing. I adore him now, but that was not easy. He is so smart. I would work so hard for every notes call. David would fight on principle about certain story things. He is a big personality. I adore him.

MICHAEL ELLENBERG:

I think going in there was the idea of looking at the death and rebirth of New York, of Times Square, through the lens of David Simon. That seemed like a unique canvas for a show. Then doing so in the context of the birth of mainstream pornography also seemed like a canvas we'd never seen before. And broadly speaking, at HBO, you always want to innovate.

KATHLEEN McCAFFREY:

David is a pro, and I'm obsessed with Nina Noble. Casey has a very deep respect for Nina. Nina is tough. Nina is tougher than David in a lot of ways. She was another one whose respect I wanted to earn. It took years to happen. Nina is old-school. She does not fuck around, excuse my language. She's like, "I want my scripts on time." And he respects her in such a way. She's the queen. Nina is so on top of everything that any argument over the show is about creative. There were no budget fights. Every script comes down in the right lanes. Every cut comes in at 58:30. There were no huge blowups, unless they're about a story point. Nina is a reason for that. She is amazing.

I'm not kidding, there was a point in my life where both Ilene and Nina Noble were my emergency contacts, because these women can get you out of trouble wherever you are.

NINA NOBLE:

The Deuce was the most challenging show. I grew up in New York and I was there in the seventies and I knew what it looked like. Finding a place where we could re-create Times Square was the most visually challenging. It was a huge relief once we found it. Then we just had to deal with the subject matter.

MICHAEL ELLENBERG:

David Simon was doing a show about pornography where there wasn't sex. It was an examination; it was pornography as a metaphor for American capitalism. The decline of the commodification of human values, human experience of flesh itself. It was pornography as a metaphor for societal rot. It was looking at the subject as a way to reveal how American society functions. How does American capitalism evolve from the seventies into the Reagan era?

NINA NOBLE:

All of a sudden in the second season, we were involved in a worldwide discussion about sexuality and harassment. It was an interesting time to be doing the show. If we'd done the show a year later, it probably wouldn't have been ordered.

KATHLEEN McCAFFREY:

I literally study everything I respond to so that I have to earn the trust of the showrunner. It takes sometimes a long time, but we don't give frivolous notes. That's the different stuff that we do. We try to give thoughtful, challenging notes that result in a creative conversation.

They're very fair conversations. We don't bullshit. If I say to a showrunner, "This is important to me," and she or he says back, "Well, I hear you, but this is the reason, for X reasons," we don't do it, more often than not. We say, "You're at the helm, right? You're the artist." I consider myself to be the first and most intimate audience on every show. I'll react. If she or he doesn't agree with me, that's fine. But it's a dialogue. We have to study that hard and work that hard to earn that trust in order to get that. You can't just come. Even development projects that we know probably won't make it to the finish line, we still give our all, because it's so important for us to give a good experience to people. Even if they don't get a show made with us, we want them to go out into the world with a great script. We really care, to the point of exhaustion. I don't even know where that idea comes from that we don't give notes. We give copious, hopefully inspiring notes. We just get into such a deep dialogue with our creators that if they fight back on something, we understand it is their show. If I could write, I would write, but I can't. I admire their work. I hope to challenge them sometimes. But ultimately, if their choice is what wins out, that's fine with me. As long as we've had a dialogue about it.

There's no greater victory when you're a development executive than when someone takes your note. David Simon occasionally says, "I'll look at that." If he changes it, that is the biggest victory you can have at our job.

CASEY BLOYS:

The idea that we don't give notes is false. Not giving notes is not a good thing. All writers need a good editor. I think the thing that you have to do and that you have to live by is you have to say up front, when you start a relationship with the writer, like, "Look, we're going to give you our notes. It's very much our thoughts. You don't have to take them. You may have a different way of answering them. We're just trying to get our reaction, and we can both understand. Maybe you come at it a different way, but ultimately it's your show. So you have to decide. We don't want you to feel that you are compromising your show or making it not as good, but you gotta live by that, you know?" The interesting thing is that, sometimes the writer will disagree with the note, and they're right. Sometimes we're right. But I think if you establish that trust, it's all about a dialogue and collaboration.

KATHLEEN McCAFFREY:

There's just such a specific way we learn how to do the job here. The sort of the teaching hospital aspect of it. I got to come in at a level where it wasn't weird, and in fact it was a huge benefit, but I would go and sit in Casey's office. Casey kept a guest phone near his couch. And I would go into his office and just sit and listen to his calls and how he did notes and how he ran his show. He learned that from Carolyn. And like I said, it's passed down and down and down. Now I have a guest phone where I encourage people to come in and listen to how I do my calls. Because that's how you learn. And when you come in at a level like Sue did, or like Ellenberg did, you're the head of something, you're thrown into the pool without a life raft. It is hard.

BILL HADER, Creator:
I scribbled my name on my SATs to go watch the movie *Mars Attacks*. It had just opened that day.

Bill Hader's father had for a time been a stand-up comic, and Hader's mother taught dance. Although Hader himself was a classic film buff from early childhood, his youth otherwise hardly presaged a stellar career on any stage or screen. Instead, he was hounded by the notion that everything in his future depended on his SAT scores and so, at the age of sixteen, he scribbled his name on the test forms, left the rest blank, and later fled his native Tulsa, Oklahoma, for greener pastures. He found them, at least temporarily, in Los Angeles, working there initially as a production assistant whose duties included serving as a driver for, among others, future **SNL** *colleague Fred Armisen. Improvising like mad at an offshoot of Second City in LA, Hader was discovered by sitcom star Megan Mullally, who called Lorne Michaels with a rousing recommendation for Hader to audition for* **Saturday Night Live,** *the greatest talent incubator of its time.*

In eight dazzlingly versatile years on the show, Hader proved one of the most talented cast members in its history, bringing to life such vividly realized characters as smarmy Italian TV host Vinny Vedecci and itinerant New York Club Kid "Stefon," whose madcap monologues were created by his **SNL** *writing partner, John Mulaney, later himself a stand-up comic and* **SNL** *host. Mulaney delighted in slipping unrehearsed absurdities into Stefon's monologues—hence Hader's need to be constantly camouflaging his helpless collapses into laughter. Sadly, the intense pressure of* **SNL** *made Hader deeply miserable, and he left the show in 2013, having paused to make a film or two,* **The Skeleton Twins** *among them.*

One year later, HBO entered Hader's life in a big way, presenting him with a delicious production deal that enabled Hader, in collaboration with former **Seinfeld** *writer Alec Berg, to create* **Barry,** *a dank, dark comedy about a former marine-turned-hitman who kept trying to turn again, this time into an actor. Premiering on*

March 25, 2018, the half-hour series avoided obvious jokes for a more poignant, offbeat approach (to murder and acting). The oddball parlay, seasoned with daringly blunt violence, resulted in a huge HBO hit.

BILL HADER:

After *SNL*, my wife and I had a second child, and I didn't know if I wanted to live in New York anymore with two kids. I wanted some space.

SNL was not easy for me at all. It was actually very hard. It's well documented that I have incredible anxiety, and I get overwhelmed very easily. I always admired cast members like Poehler or Kenan Thompson or Fred Armisen who would be backstage chatting with you, and then go, "Oh, that's my sketch," and just walk out effortlessly with a lot of confidence. That was just very hard for me, thinking it could all go wrong.

I had just done a movie called *The Skeleton Twins*, and was thinking maybe I could use that to get some more acting jobs. Then my agent said, "You should meet with Alec Berg." And then also, "Let's just have you go meet with all the networks." And just to show how different it was at this time, this is 2014, I didn't meet Amazon or Netflix. It was Showtime and HBO. And I think maybe NBC.

I had a meeting with Mike Lombardo and Casey Bloys and they said, "Do you have any ideas?" And I said, "Not really, but my agents tell me I should meet with this guy Alec Berg." And they went, "Well, we love Alec because he's doing *Curb Your Enthusiasm*, and he is about to do this other show for us called *Silicon Valley*." They said, "We're not interested in sketch comedy. We're kinda more interested in what you did in *The Skeleton Twins*."

I met with Alec and we started having breakfast at S & W Diner in Culver City. He was writing *Silicon Valley* at Sony. So he'd walk over before he would start the *Silicon Valley* room and we'd have breakfast for about two hours and just kick around ideas.

After a month of going through this one idea, we said, "This isn't working." We had pages and we both agreed that this isn't working. Then out of frustration, I said, "Me as a hit man, that would be something." And Alec said, "I hate that. I hate hit men. I just hate the word. I hate the idea. It's like dog catcher. It's like a thing that's more in movies and TV than it is in real life."

I said, "No, no, no, it'll be, it'll be great. It could be me playing a hit man." He said, "Don't play it like John Wick or the cool *Reservoir Dogs* thing. Play it very real and grounded." And then out of nowhere, he said, "What if he took an acting class?" And we both started laughing. I remember very clearly Alec Berg saying, "Acting class is great because that is a show. That's a show." That's when we both got excited.

ALEC BERG:

That's the joke of it. There's nothing sexy about it. There's nothing cool. There are no skinny ties and slow-motion gunfights. He would be like a low-rent traveling salesman, and it's a shitty job, and he hates it. We can play with the tropes of being a hit man. And it could just be about "you don't like your hotel room" or that "they got you a shitty flight in a middle seat." Then we thought, Okay, well, if he doesn't want to be a hit man, maybe this is a show about what he wants to do instead.

I even remember how we got to actor. "What's the opposite of being a hit man?" Like, what's a silly, self-indulgent, not critical job? And then we thought, Well, what if he wanted to be an actor? Then almost immediately we started getting all of these interesting thoughts about how opposite those jobs are. A hit man has to live in anonymity; an actor wants to be known. A hit man has to suppress all of his emotions otherwise it would be crippling; an actor has to access all of those emotions to play things. And a hit man stands in the dark, while an actor literally stands in the light. It was all of a sudden, very fertile, very quickly. And in a matter of a couple of weeks, I think we had the whole thing figured out.

BILL HADER:

In the meeting with HBO, I remember Casey Bloys saying, "It's like the acting class is like therapy for him. Like through the acting class, he learns how to become a human being." And we hadn't thought of that, but we pretended like we had. They said, "We want to do a pilot." Then I said, "I want to direct it." And there was this silence in the room. "Have you directed anything before?" I said, "No, but I see this. And I really want to direct it." They called Alec Berg and I said, "Do you think he can do this?" And Alec said, "I think he'll be great. The script is good and if things get hairy, you got me there and I've directed tons of episodes of *Curb*." He was my insurance and went to bat for me.

Here's how crazy casting was. We had one day where we saw Sarah Goldberg, did her callback. When she walked out, I was like, "Well, we're going to hire her as Sally, she's great." And then the next person was Henry! And he knocked it out of the park.

HENRY WINKLER:

I got a call from my agents at the time. They said there's a new project. They have a short list. And Bill Hader is the writing star. I got so excited, I had to pull off to the side of the street.

I got a script. It was written incredibly well. My son Max, who is a director, was at the house when it arrived on email. And he directed the audition. And I just want to say that my son is strict. I went and auditioned, and only Bill was in the room with Sherry Thomas, the casting person. There was a small tape camera; the tripod was actually larger than the camera.

I was called in. I read with Sherry Thomas. And I thought to myself, I've just made Bill Hader laugh. Bill Hader made me laugh for years and years and years with all of his characters on *Saturday Night Live*. I felt good. It was the end of the audition. I went home and then you wait and then you wait and then you wait. And then your entire system starts to shut down from anxiety.

Your liver stops, your stomach stops. And I called my manager and said, "Could you just call somebody and see if I'm in the running?" It was so long a wait. They called and said, "You're still in the mix." And then you wait and then you wait and then you wait. And then I swear to God, a millennium has gone by and Bill Hader calls. And he said, "Hey, I just wrote these two scenes. You want to come in and play?" In my mind I said, "Are you fucking crazy? Do I want to come in and play? Of course, I'll come."

He sent me the two scenes. They were spectacular. I drive to some *farkak-teh* location, and they call me in. Now Alec Berg is there. Alec Berg, no one warned me, but is Norwegian. He keeps everything so close to his vest, the vest is tattooed on.

ALEC BERG:

My great-great-grandparents were farmers in Southern Sweden. You know Swedes, we're such a demonstrative, boisterous, emotional people.

HENRY WINKLER:

I do the first scene. I made Alec Berg smile. I thought I must be in an altered universe. This is not possible. I do the two scenes. We work together. Bill now jumps up and is reading with me. He's my partner, not Sherry Thomas, but Bill. And we're having a great time. And I'm feeling that it's swimmingly, singing a song, going along.

I drive home and you wait and you wait. And you wait. Finally, Bill Hader calls. He said, "I can't get you out of my mind. Do you want to play this part?"

BILL HADER:

I wanted to make sure he could play an asshole. I was never a very good joke writer or sketch writer. I felt like I was good at structuring things. The writing on *Barry* is the kind of writing I'm more interested in, and just better at. Working with actors, working with a crew, the experience of *Barry* has given me more confidence. If your number one priority is the story, then everything else is just brought in to tell that story. That's also a very HBO thing, character and story, character and story.

ALEC BERG:

HBO's whole philosophy is, Look, we hired you for a reason. We're not going to tell you how to do this. These are our thoughts. Take them or leave them, and if you disagree, you don't have to do it, but here are our thoughts. I think it makes a huge difference that, overwhelmingly, they're right. When we saw the *Barry* pilot, you get a chance to take a step back and reevaluate your choices. And we made some mistakes when we did the pilot. I think it was Casey's point where he said, "I'm just stuck on who this Fuches guy is, because I'm looking at this show. I know what a hit man is. I know what an actor is. I know what an acting teacher is, but what is a hit man agent?" What we realized is that we needed something to help you understand their relationship more. And we completely rewrote the part so that you understand Stephen was the guy who purported to be a friend, but was really an enemy. And fortunately, Stephen Root is also such an unbelievably versatile performer that we called him up and we said, "Hey, so, you're still in the show, we're not cutting you out of the pilot, but we are going to reshoot every single one of your scenes and you're playing a totally different character."

HENRY WINKLER:

Bill and Alec are real partners. You don't know where one begins and one ends, except that Bill acts. They are a great support system for each other. And they're both very clear about what they want. And one of the great things that an actor needs, no matter how incredible you think you are, is you need clarity about the underpinning of what you're doing, so that everything you do comes from a clear vision.

I was twenty-seven when I got the Fonz, and when I went in to audition, I made the decision to change my voice and change the body tilt, just like off to the side, off my hip. And just by doing that, I released my imagination from the coop. It was like, I opened the cage and it flew out. Until then it was cooped up in there with anxiety, with the desire to be right. The desire to be correct. Which of course doesn't exist. So for a lot of the different things that I did, I was stilted. I made a decision that I was going to figure out how to close the gap between having to change my voice and just being authentic me as an actor.

At seventy-two, when I started to shoot *Barry*, I finally got closer to my original vision in 1973.

BILL HADER:

At the TCA, someone said, "Why are you making the bad guys funny in the show?" I was like, "They don't know they're bad guys. They're just human." *Barry* is not a show about bad and good. It's just writing about people and seeing what happens. I think *Sopranos* was definitely a huge influence on *Barry*.

HBO marketing was amazing. Amy Gravitt is our hero. We feel lucky that the executive in charge of our show became the head of a comedy and she just got what we were going for. And even when she didn't get what we were going for, she trusted us, but she's a writer. I mean, she's very modest about it, but she's incredibly well-read, understands story, understands the complexities of people. And she trusts you.

ALEC BERG:

Bill and I talk a lot about the difference between comedy and humor, and that comedy is jokes and humor is stuff that's funny and you don't even need to know why it's funny. It just is. When you hear Bill Hader and a half-hour comedy, you think jokes and zaniness and whatever. And we were excited that we figured we were going to catch a lot of people totally off guard.

In **Barry's** *first year, both Bill Hader and Henry Winkler took home Emmys for their lead and supporting actor roles, respectively.* **Barry** *also took home the Emmy for Sound Mixing.*

HENRY WINKLER:

I thought, Oh, stay calm, enjoy the moment. Be in the moment. It'll be good. And I walk up the stairs and standing in front of me are the two stars of *The* fucking *Crown*.

And I start talking to them about how wonderful season two was, because we just binged it. And all of a sudden it hits me. They're looking at me really odd. I'm thinking, Hey, I'm just saying I love your work, what you're doing. And they're looking at me. And then I think, Oh my God, I have to make a speech. I completely forgot where I was. I turned around, and there is the largest number 39 flashing on the screen, which means I only have thirty-nine seconds for everything that I planned, that I had memorized, that I went over and over in my mind.

From the very first twinkling strains of Nicholas Britell's brilliant piano theme, underlaying a montage of recognizable business monsters, Fox News–like tickers, and tales of rich children in peril, **Succession** *seemed entirely new. Perhaps it was those out-of-key notes Britell kept sneaking into that faux classical theme. The brilliant opening credits laid the ground for portrayals of mendacity and sinister intrigue unlike anything on TV before or since.*

*   **Succession** revolves around the Roy family, a thinly veiled amalgam of the Murdochs, and, well, the Murdochs. An aging patriarch named Logan—portrayed in juicily Lear-like fashion by Scottish actor Brian Cox—plays his overeager children off each other as they jockey to take over his evil media empire, Waystar Royco. Among the "kids": Kendall, played movingly by Jeremy Strong, the son most likely either to take over the company or overdose on one substance or another; Shiv, the only daughter, portrayed by Sarah Snook as a vacillating daddy's girl with an eye for poison; and Kieran Culkin's hilariously useless Roman Roy, a man-child who can neither remember the price of a pint of milk nor do much to satisfy his random sexual yearnings, other than masturbate while a much older woman abuses him. (A probably certifiable elder brother, Connor, played by Alan Ruck, wants to use his enormous wealth to be some libertarian president of the United States.)*

*   The key to the show, beyond the terrific characters and acting, is in the writing—audacious and caustic scripts that were often the work of creator Jesse Armstrong, a British colleague of Armando Iannucci on* **The Thick of It**, **In the Loop**, *and the critically acclaimed but never seen in the United States* **Peep Show**.

CASEY BLOYS:

Game of Thrones was so big, it almost paralyzed people. Everything had to be the next *Game of Thrones*, the next huge hit. But you can't program from fear. I started four years ago, in terms of drama, and was just doing a lot of different shows such as *Sharp Objects*, *Watchmen*, *Succession*, *My Brilliant Friend*, a bunch of smaller shows, different, not all genre shows, contemporary shows, period shows. You can't worry about being the next *Game of Thrones*.

There's a direct line from *Vinyl* to *Succession*. *Vinyl* was seen as Martin Scorsese, very expensive pilot, loaded, big, sprawling, you can't lose. It's Martin Scorsese, it's Jagger, right? That feels like HBO. But that feels like that to people who only know HBO as a place that does high-end shows.

It's thinking about the surface and not what's underneath it. The thing with *Succession*, when you look at that cast, we made a very conscious decision. There's no IP [intellectual property]. It's not based on a book. It's based on a pitch. Adam is a very good director. He's a fancy director, but I knew him from *Eastbound & Down*. We made a conscious decision not to put stars in it. We would say, Let's go back to making stars instead of casting them.

If you're insecure about your creative chops, you go, It's Martin Scorsese, it's Mick Jagger, and Ryan Murphy. Jesse Armstrong had never written a drama. We were taking chances on.

It's much more indicative of the kinds of shows that HBO used to do.

HBO had a previous project with Adam McKay that had died. McKay and Armstrong developed the idea for what would be Succession, *but with no overt intention to do the show at HBO. Frank Rich, a fan of Armstrong and McKay, caught wind of the story and the team sold it to HBO without even a pilot script in hand.*

ADAM McKAY:

Will's [Ferrell] and my company is Gary Sanchez Productions. And we wanted to do the story of Lee Atwater and admired Jesse's work. I'd seen *In the Loop*, which I loved. *Four Lions* I think was just about to come out. I saw it and was blown away by it. We had a great meeting with Jesse Armstrong. I was with Kevin Messick and we just loved him. We just were like, "This guy is incredible." And he told us he had written a script about the Murdochs and I was like, "Well, can I read it?"

And he sent it to me and I was blown away by it. I was like, "We got to do this. We got to do this as a movie." There were some issues with it as far as libel laws in England, because he was speculating on a lot of conversation with the family, although it was all based on real events. It was very tricky. And it's also tricky because I think some of the agents were a little freaked out. They're like, "The Murdochs own one of the big studios in town." And I'm like, "Who cares, man?" And they were like national figures. Like you've got to do it. We ran into those two roadblocks and we just let it go. And we developed some other things with Jesse. And then Kevin Messick called me. And he said, "Remember how Jesse had been kicking around that script about the Murdochs, but it wasn't going to be able to be done? He had a great idea the other day, which is, cut it loose from the Murdochs and have it be an amalgam of all the media barons. And we could do a show about it." And I was instantly, Oh my God, that's the idea. That's fantastic.

So Jesse was going to take it out onto the town. Kevin's like, "Do you want to just say you'll direct the pilot? We'll produce right now." I just said, "Yes, I'm in." Then the script came in and I was like, "You gotta be kidding me. This is one of the best scripts I've ever read." I was like fifty times more in at that point.

JESSE ARMSTRONG, Creator:

I've always felt that a real accounting of the world takes into account comedy and the farcical, ludicrous, unbelievable nature of reality. Maybe we're particularly amenable to that approach right now. I came out to Los Angeles and my agents encouraged me to go to a bunch of places to pitch it, because they thought it would put me in a stronger bargaining position, but I knew Casey and Frank Rich, and so it was my hope that HBO would take an interest, which they did.

Casey came up in comedy, and my background is comedy. There was a level of comfort but also a level of anxiety. The hard requirements of comedy to be funny, and to achieve that binary end—was it funny or wasn't it—means that a comedy person has a slightly stronger bullshit detector regarding the stuff that you could claim you're writing about in a drama, the fancy phrasing, the themes that you're going to explore. I like talking to comedy people, but I also feel that responsibility and that requirement. There is a ton of stuff in *Succession* that I wanted to explore, and subtext that I think is genuinely there in the show. Stuff that is not immediately obvious, but will become obvious. But I'm always aware of when one's overstating the claim or gilding the lily of the sophistication that you're going to provide. When Casey asks a question, it's a real question. And that's not always true with everyone who you're talking to in Hollywood or in any creative world. So his questions and his observations are relatively few, they're not usually caged in highfalutin language, but they can be pretty penetrating.

Adam McKay, who directed the pilot and was a huge part of the creative process of getting the show up, was incredibly supportive. I pitched that Logan might die at the end of the first episode or certainly early on in the season, and they all gently persuaded me to consider the possibility, at least, that that didn't happen. I think they were smart. It became obvious that we would lose this gravitational weight at the center of things.

CASEY BLOYS:

One of my first goals for the drama group was a contemporary family show. No special effects, no underlying source material, just a well-done family drama. This was right before *This Is Us* premiered, so of course I thought we were already late. Our family show ended up being *Succession*, of which I am particularly proud because we did not cast stars. Not that I am opposed to stars, *Big Little Lies* being a great example of how successful it can be, but I wanted to see if we could go back to making shows the way we used to. Focused on the writing and making stars as opposed to casting them.

ADAM McKAY:

It was one of the most enjoyable casting processes ever. God bless Casey. He just said, "I don't believe TV needs big stars. Sometimes with ensemble shows, it's almost better if they're not big stars."

BRIAN COX:

Scripts from Jesse Armstrong are very, very sacred. So you don't see them until the last minute. Well, not quite the last minute, but it gives you enough time to get on with it. I think it's changed now because I think they've had six months to write the whole thing up, but apparently they actually completed it before we started filming. We were supposed to start filming in April. It was the conversation with Adam McKay and Jesse that persuaded me. And I've been thinking for a long time that I wanted to get into something that was a television thing because I liked television. I did a lot of it from the seventies, the late seventies through the early nineties.

One of the reasons I moved to the United States was British television was going through a very bad time at that time. I used to go from theater to television and theater to television and it was great. But the UK is a small world, and I wanted to move on.

With Jesse, it was just time and tide, I just knew that this was right. I could tell just from that pitch, these are two guys, one an American who had been quite a track record with the *SNL* and Upright Citizens Brigade and all that stuff that Adam's kicked off, and then Jesse with the *Peep Show*, the work he did in *The Thick of It*. And when I knew that Frank Rich was the godfather, it was a no-brainer to me to say, "Yeah, I gotta do this. I'm not going to be in this company too often." Even if they wrote it on toilet paper, I would still think about doing it.

JEREMY STRONG, Actor:

Adam for me is one of those filmmakers that stands for risk, and allowed me to take great risks with that character. I went to lunch at his house in Hancock Park and he said, "I have this script that is loosely sort of King Lear meets the media industrial complex, written by this English writer who had written sort of famously this spec script about Rupert Murdoch that every-one had been talking about," who had done *Peep Show* and *The Thick of It*, which I knew about. Adam said, "I'm going to give you this script. Read it and let me know if it speaks to you, and let me know what role speaks to you. We'll take it from there."

I knew honestly from the first words that it was something that I was interested in. It moved every needle for me, having come from the theater, having worked on a lot of Shakespeare, and also having a sort of lifelong interest in the sort of war of the roses as a pageant of Hollywood and the media landscape. I read the script and I initially actually raised my hand for a different role. I raised my hand for the role of Roman because I've always seen myself as a character actor.

Roman felt exciting to me in a painterly way. And so I said, "Roman," and Adam said, "Great, it's yours." And then a month later, I had been dev-astatingly fired from Kathryn Bigelow's movie *Detroit*, almost missed my wedding in Denmark, and then found out that they had cast Kieran Culkin in the role of Roman who had sent in a tape. And it was no longer on the table for me. I was at a rock bottom place actually professionally. And then Adam profusely apologized and said it wasn't his place to just give me the role; he should have checked with Jesse first.

Jesse did think, having reviewed some of my work, that I could be right for the lead of the show. But he needed to have me audition, along with everybody else in town.

I was testing for the role opposite a worthy, great actor who, honestly, I thought would get the role. Then there was some alchemy that happened in the room. Some notes from Adam McKay, some notes from Jesse. And honestly, I sort of felt it in the room, and drove away looking up at the apart-ments, where I had lived with my dad when I was eleven years old trying to go out there and become an actor. I had this feeling that my life might've just changed.

ADAM McKAY:

The nice thing was I had a relationship with Casey from years past, and when we started, it was the original two, Carolyn Strauss and Chris Albrecht. Those two were maybe two of the greatest TV producers in history.

From the second I read the script, I knew exactly how I wanted it to look and feel. I watched *Foxcatcher* ten times, it's one of my favorite movies. Right away, I said, "Jesse, even though it's funny, I think we should shoot it like a drama. I think we should shoot it with real weight to it." And then I had worked with

Nick Britell, the composer on *The Big Short*, and I thought, I got to get Britell to score this and it should be a beautiful score. I was thinking of the old English show, *I, Claudius*, even though it's almost shot like it's live theater, that opening theme was so great and it had this weight to it. Jesse and I started talking about how that was kind of the center of this show. It was going to have this weight to it. It was going to have this meaning, but it could also be funny. We talked about *The Godfather* and we talked about all these great movies and shows that were based around families throughout history.

ILENE LANDRESS:

When we did the pilot, a lot of it was, "What's this show going to be? What are we looking at? Wait, it's a bunch of rich people. Why are we looking at this bunch of rich people?" I would say on the pilot, there's this good moment of we were shooting out in Long Island, for the softball scene, with the family on the pilot. And we broke for lunch. It was cold out, freezing cold. And there was a big tent. I went and got some food quickly. And I sat down at the end of the table and the people who were at the other end of the table who were talking were just a bunch of extras.

They didn't know anything about the show. And one of them was saying to another one, "Oh yeah, the family out there," meaning the actors, "the family out there playing baseball, they're like the Kennedys or the Trumps." This is right when Trump was first elected. All of a sudden in this catering thing, hearing these extras talk about "Oh, that family," because we were so worried that it's just the Murdochs, too English, all these other English bazillionaires, how's this going to translate here? The minute I heard them say, "Oh, that family out there are like the Kennedys or the Trumps," I was like, Okay, this is going to work.

JEREMY STRONG:

There is no easy day. I think the stakes are so high with this character, and also there's so much history that is weighing on him at this point. The final episodes that we did of season one at Eastnor Castle were a very harrowing thing for me to go through. I felt I had to go through that ordeal in order to embody the character. We ended up having these gigantic speakers brought out into the middle of a marsh that I set up on a Bluetooth to play certain Penderecki music that I wanted to just have underneath what was an MOS sequence. I knew it would do something for me, viscerally; this music woke up the whole County of Hereford, but it was the thing where that process has been very, I would say, risk-intensive. I often asked to not rehearse.

I prefer to not rehearse, and for me there are scenes where there's an emotional component or where the stakes are particularly high. That means that our camera crew has to be extremely agile and fleet-footed and we sort of discover it as we go.

JESSE ARMSTRONG:

In some ways my ignorance or lack of experience made me quite fearless. Even in the first season, we globe-trotted around. The last two seasons were shot in the UK and in New Mexico. The second season was a tough one. The last episode of the second season was set on this mega yacht of the super-rich. I'd always wanted to do that, with these weird and not always very beautiful spaces where these people who have this extraordinary wealth ended up confining themselves. We looked at ways to do that that were less expensive. I hadn't considered that the people who own those boats oftentimes aren't interested in cutting you a great deal. So that was a big-ticket number, but it just wouldn't have worked if we hadn't had that backdrop. It was great to be able to write that on a mega yacht and then shoot it on a mega yacht. Not because we wanted to fetishize the wealth, but because those spaces are so peculiar and not always beautiful. HBO came through on a bunch of those big, big pieces where we needed their backing.

ADAM McKAY:

The first season you're really watching it because you sink or swim with that first season. It's a very tricky show because it's not, at first glance, a salacious premise. So it's a very delicate first season. And the second episode was the trickiest episode because you've just come off this pilot where you set up. And he has the stroke and they're spinning their wheels at the hospital trying to figure out what to do. So that second episode was really difficult. And then the third, it started to get its toehold. And then on the fourth I was like, Okay, we're in it. Which I thought was pretty good for a first season. The fifth episode is like one of my favorite episodes of television ever.

BRIAN COX:

I couldn't be in a better position. This is a job that one hopes for all one's life and of my time of life. It came along after nearly sixty years of hard slog. Suddenly the roles that you always hope for turn out and it's fostered by this incredible family of HBO who have such standards.

They have been phenomenal on this. I have endless gratitude to them.

JEREMY STRONG:

When I was a student, I went to the Royal Academy of Dramatic Arts and walked through that building, feeling the sort of storied history of that building. That's the way I felt the first time I went to the HBO office in Santa Monica. There's this sense that HBO is the Holy Grail. It has been for a long time, but especially now in this moment where the work that I grew up wanting to do, which is primarily those great films that we all revere, that work has migrated to cable television, and primarily to HBO. Those writers and storytellers and actors and directors are making television now. HBO is the pinnacle of that and remains, even though it's become a much more competitive landscape.

HBO is not a behemoth that is sort of racing toward volume in a way that so many of their competitors are, I feel like they are still essentially a boutique company that is primarily interested in quality. After I did the pilot, I was invited to go and meet with Casey Bloys, Franny, and Nora in Casey's office, which felt like an anointment. It's not every day that the head of the studio invites you in just to get to know you a bit and say, "Let us know if there's anything you need creatively, however we can support you in, in the work that you're going to do."

JESSE ARMSTRONG:

I didn't have a massive track record, so it wasn't like I was coming in there saying, Hey, don't fuck with my beautiful creation on a super competent creative with a track record like Larry David in some ways. The level of trust and power they put in the hand of a showrunner was quite disconcerting. It's not bullshit that they walk the walk in terms of giving you a lot of power over the show.

ADAM McKAY:

Well, they don't leave you alone. They are collaborative. I've been at places that leave you alone and that's not HBO. What I love about them is they do challenge you. Here's a great example. So the pilot of *Succession*, one of my favorite sequences is this softball game where Roman Roy offers a million-dollar check to this sweet kid who's like the son of the groundskeeper. And so we cut the whole pilot together and Casey's like, "I don't think you need it." I told Casey, "It's literally one of the three reasons I did this; it was for that scene. I just think it gets to their moral rot that's going on in a way. I know it's not funny. I know it gets a little serious and a little darker than the rest of the show, but I think you've got to leave it in." And we have this great, healthy argument about it where no one's yelling.

No one's pounding tables, knocking over chairs. And ultimately Casey's like, Wow, all right. I see what you were saying. We left it in. And then like four episodes into the season he goes, "You were right about that scene." That scene's important. It reminds us of the moral center of the show in the pilot and we actually need it for later shows.

And that's HBO. They will always push you for greatness, not ratings. They'll push you to make the show something special and trust the ratings will follow.

When **My Brilliant Friend** *premiered on HBO on November 18, 2018, it became the first series HBO had produced entirely in a foreign language. The Italian series, for which HBO collaborated with Fremantle and Rai, an Italian television network, is based on a series of books written by Elena Ferrante called the* **Neapolitan Novels***, about a pair of women who had been friends since childhood. The central young women are Elena Greco, played in youth by Elisa Del Genio and in her teenage years by Margherita Mazzucco, and Raffaella "Lila" Cerullo, played by Ludovica Nasti in youth and Gaia Girace as a teen. The first season of the show scored big ratings in both Italy and the United States, pulling in about seven million viewers in Italy and more than one million stateside, despite the need for subtitles, which American viewers typically scorn. Both of the first two seasons were nominated for Best TV Series at the Italian Golden Globes—in 2019, Ludovica Nasti also won Best Breakthrough Actress for her role as the younger Rafaella "Lila" Cerullo. On Thursday, April 30, 2020, HBO announced the show had been renewed for a third season.*

FRANCESCA ORSI, Executive:

The first person who flagged the books was, funnily enough, my therapist, who said, "Your family reminds me a lot of the characters in a series of books I'm reading by Elena Ferrante called the *Neapolitan Novels.*" I read the first one, *My Brilliant Friend*, not long after and remember being struck by how spot on she was about the environment my parents had been raised in and how my own upbringing in Los Angeles was dictated by what they had endured in Italy back then. My mother, Carmela, who goes by Carmen now, is from Naples, specifically from that area where *My Brilliant Friend* is set, Piazza Garibaldi, amazingly, not far from the actual courtyard where the apartment buildings of the show are geographically set.

CARMELA AMBROSANO ORSI, Executive's Mother:

When I started reading the first book, *My Brilliant Friend*, I woke my husband up at three o'clock in the morning shrieking, "This is where I grew up!" Elena Ferrante captured my childhood and teenage years so intimately I felt I wasn't reading characters, but instead experiencing breathing people I had known. I couldn't put the books down.

FRANCESCA ORSI:

Just as I finished reading the first book, I serendipitously got a call from Lorenzo Mieli, the executive producer on *The Young Pope*.

He said, "I would love to adapt the books as a series, but the catch here is that they would all be in Italian and the Napolitano dialect, not adapted in English." I was excited and admittedly scared by the prospect of it because not only had my division not produced foreign language programming before, but the first book starts with six-year-old girls in 1950s Naples. I didn't quite know how to sell it to Casey other than to come from a place of personal passion. He heard me in all the ways a great boss does, so he took it to Richard Plepler, and I'll never forget how immediately fearless and openhearted about the material he was. That despite how removed he and Casey were from that environment, they both leaned in, didn't belabor the discussion, and just said, "Go for it."

RICHARD PLEPLER:

I remember Casey and I sitting in my office, discussing *My Brilliant Friend*, our only question to each other was, were the books too esoteric for an American audience? At that moment, Graydon Carter called. I said, "It's funny you call, we're sitting here talking about *My Brilliant Friend*," to which he replied, "Oh my God, one of my wife's favorite series of books." It seemed like everywhere Casey and I turned, there were fans of the books. Our own little mini focus groups kept coming back with such enthusiasm that we decided to do it. Nobody knew whether it would get huge numbers or not, but it was quintessential HBO quality. And thankfully the shows honored the quality of the literature.

FRANCESCA ORSI:

My mother lives in Los Angeles, not far from me, and every step of the way I quietly engaged her on what was going on as we developed and built the show from the ground up. She saw casting, scripts, and production design. I immersed her across all of it, and because she literally comes from this exact place, this little-known microcosm, she became my own executive producer who confirmed the authenticity of every element of the show.

CARMELA AMBROSANO ORSI:

One of the best things about Francesca is that she feels things very deeply, and she puts her golden heart to use across her work. Through *My Brilliant Friend*, she showed the pride she has in me even though the poverty of where I come from isn't necessarily something to boast about.

FRANCESCA ORSI:

When I was a child, my mom developed an intense fear of flying, and had not been back to Italy in thirty years because of it. But I told her very early on in the process, "You're going to be at the premiere in Italy." Something shifted inside of her, and she mentally prepared for it. Two years later she was on the red carpet at the Venice Film Festival where we premiered the first two episodes.

CARMELA AMBROSANO ORSI:

When I went to Italy for the premiere, all my relatives were going crazy for the show, not because my daughter was connected to it but because of how true to life it was. Saverio Costanzo is a genius. The choice of actors, especially the girls playing Elena and Lila, was incredible.

PAOLO SORRENTINO:

When I went to Venice for the premiere, Saverio Costanzo and I were very afraid. When you take a very respected book and bring it to TV or a movie, you run a lot of risks. We were pretty tense. We were very relieved after the screening. I think Saverio did a great job, it's wonderful.

FRANCESCA ORSI:

I'll never forget the nine-minute-long standing ovation the show received and how proud I was of everyone involved and especially my mom whose own life, through all its ups and downs, I see as a great achievement.

Growing up, my parents who are both from the South of Italy, always said that Southerners at times would feel inferior to Northern Italians—there was a certain elitist quality from the North to the South. But seeing all the Italians come together in Venice from all over the country, embracing this series, shattered all the boundaries I'd known existed in the country. It was a big hit in Italy, and I'd like to think, united them in some way.

In the summer of 2017, a former member of the Iranian military, twenty-nine-year-old Behzad Mesri hacked into HBO's servers, stealing scripts and plot summaries for **Game of Thrones** *and leaking as yet unaired episodes of* **Curb Your Enthusiasm** *and* **The Deuce.** *(For good measure, Mesri also compromised HBO's email system.) By November Mesri had been indicted by the feds (though he remained at large) but had received none of the $6 million in bitcoin he had demanded.*

RICHARD PLEPLER:

The hack was obviously a bad day. In fact, it was a bad ten days because until we knew what they had—possibly shows, scripts, deal memorandums, personal records of our employees—it was very distressing. And we didn't know how deep into our system they had gone. Scott McElhone, our EVP, ran point along with our incredible tech team lead by Diane Tryneski and we managed our way through it but not without an enormous amount of pressure and anxiety. It was a horrible couple of weeks, some of the most difficult weeks of my tenure.

SCOTT McELHONE, Executive:

I was overseeing technology at the time. It was Sunday. A handful of us immediately went to the office and I was pretty much there for two weeks straight. It was crazy.

The main threat was that they had somehow gone into our computer system and obtained unaired episodes of *Game of Thrones*. My immediate reaction was it was very clear that the words you needed to mention to HBO or Time Warner were *Game of Thrones* and that would set off the alarm bells, but the notion that someone would be able to hack in and get actual full episodes of programming seemed a little bit loose.

After about three or four days, the hacker did release some materials, but nothing earth-shattering. A few days after that he did release some stuff that I actually think had been leaked out before, but it was talent contracts for the stars of *Game of Thrones* that showed compensation, like what we were paying per episode to, as an example, Kit Harington versus Emilia Clarke. So the Hollywood press picked up on that and obviously talked about that for a while because that's the juicy stuff they'd all been looking for. Everybody was waiting for this big bombshell to come after a few weeks, but it didn't come.

QUENTIN SCHAFFER:

The timing was a few days prior to that summer's TCA press tour. Fortunately, it didn't leak immediately because the hacker gave HBO time to think about its response before the hacker would release sensitive documents. The hacker claimed to have 1.5 terabytes, much bigger than the Sony hack. The email itself was rather chilling once you realized it wasn't fake.

HBO did a forensic investigation of how the hack had occurred, employing some top-notch outside cybersecurity companies as well as our own internal tech folks. We also reported the incident to the FBI despite the hacker asking that we not involve them. There were many constituencies who had to be kept updated—employees, TW corporate, our affiliates/distributors, our Hollywood partners, and talent. Richard sent select emails to the company, first informing employees of the hack and then briefing them periodically while asking them not to believe every rumor they might hear. I remember someone saying to me that there are two types of companies in the world—those who have been hacked and those that aren't aware they've been hacked.

On May 15, 2017, HBO aired the Erin Lee Carr–directed documentary **Mommy Dead and Dearest,** *the tragic story about the alleged murder of Dee Dee Blanchard by her daughter Gypsy and her daughter's boyfriend.*

ERIN LEE CARR:

After *Thought Crimes*, I was at a very low point. My father, the journalist David Carr, had died. I don't know how exactly it worked out, but Sheila and Sara gave me a small to medium development deal, and I found *Mommy Dead and Dearest*, and it was like they had provided a life raft. It was deeply significant.

It was an unknown story other than a Buzzfeed piece. I had to fight to make it because it was so weird. But they did it all, the poster, the trailer, the press. I found that to be thrilling.

On November 12, 2018, Rebecca Cammisa's **Atomic Homefront** *aired, a documentary investigation of the effects of radioactive material that was dumped, illegally, around St. Louis in the late twentieth century.*

REBECCA CAMMISA:

Atomic Homefront is a documentary film about the residents of North County, St. Louis, who are fighting for accountability truth. St. Louis was the first secret city. It's where the process of enriching uranium started for the first atomic bomb. The process led to tons of radioactive waste, high-grade radioactive waste that then got dumped in North County. So you have one community where high-level radioactive waste washed into their creek behind their yards and businesses and homes and contaminated and killed people and continues to do so now. It's a fascinating yet tragic history.

SARA BERNSTEIN:

We were siloed in the documentary department. They left Sheila alone because, unlike the modern way that people watch documentaries as easily as we do right now, like on Netflix and the other platforms, we were the only place that was spending millions of dollars at that point on documentaries. It was a great luxury.

In 2017, less than a year after the unexpected death of Garry Shandling, friend and former writing colleague (on **The Larry Sanders Show***) Judd Apatow sent out an all-points tweet: "I am making a documentary about Garry Shandling. If anyone has any great video, photos or anything helpful, let me know. I am looking!"*

The Zen Diaries of Garry Shandling, *first aired on HBO, Shandling's alma mater, in two parts on March 26 and 27, 2018 (the final cut totals four and a half hours), with a cast of talking heads that was a veritable Who's Who of comedy and acting talent. Those reminiscing about Shandling in the documentary ranged from co-workers like actor Jeffrey Tambor and producer Peter Tolan (from* **Larry Sanders** *days) to a nearly endless list of admirers-from-afar. The film won a Primetime Emmy, proving that Garry Shandling wouldn't let even his own death diminish acclaim for his brilliant work.*

JUDD APATOW:

When I was making the documentary for HBO about Garry, I learned so much that I wish I knew about when he was alive. I didn't know the details of the story about when his brother died. I didn't know how much that affected him. I think in a lot of ways he was searching for brothers, for family. I do think at times he was parental with me and he also had his sensitivity. He wanted people to be very loyal and especially honest. And that dates back to feeling like his parents weren't honest with him when his brother was sick. A lot of what was happening was hidden from him. No one prepared Garry. He wasn't allowed to go to his brother's funeral. Some people even said that he wasn't actually told that his brother died, that he had to figure it out by what was happening.

Garry became obsessed with a certain type of loyalty and truth to make up for that wound. It's hard for me to understand why Garry and I connected the way we did when I met him. I was very young. I couldn't have been more excited to write the Grammys with him. It was one of the first jobs I got in show business and we became very close friends and I would hang out with him and Linda at his house, almost like their kid or a nephew, and they would cook me dinner and we would watch TV at times. I thought they were experimenting in seeing how they would be as parents, maybe unconsciously.

SHEILA NEVINS:

Apatow pitched it to me and I so admire him that I felt, Why not? I didn't know much about Garry Shandling, and watched very few of the shows.

SARA BERNSTEIN:

There are a lot of brilliant documentary filmmakers who could do a film about a comedian, but there was something special about Judd's approach to it. There was no other place that could have told the story of Garry Shandling. It belonged on HBO.

HBO without Sheila Nevins seemed unimaginable—until it happened. On December 16, 2017, Nevins announced she was leaving.

Nevins had been creating groundbreaking documentaries for HBO—more than twelve hundred of them—for four decades and had won so many awards (her movies alone earned twenty-eight Academy Awards, thirty-four Emmys, and forty-four Peabodys) that the company created a Nevins trophy room and nicknamed it "the Holy Shrine of Sheila."

Little wonder Nevins was deeply conflicted about leaving HBO.

Her stint there had been seriously successful, but it had also weathered, like any career, its storms of difficulty. Nevins's relationship with Plepler had been a good one, but eventually he let it be known, in that snarky, sharky executive way, that he didn't want Nevins at HBO anymore.

At first, it certainly sounded like the seventy-eight-year-old diva of docs was retiring. "There's something exciting about leaving a job," she told Maureen Dowd. "I have deprived my life of a life. All I did was work." And yet, two years later, MTV announced that the "Grande Dame of Documentary" was joining its ranks. At MTV, Nevins would be tasked with bringing her "brand" to bear on a new department, MTV Documentary Films, under the MTV Studios umbrella.

With so many stellar female directors and producers in the documentary realm, it felt normal and natural for two women to take over from Nevins, and so it came to pass. Replacing Nevins would be two HBO stalwarts, Nancy Abraham and Lisa Heller. Though her departure was announced in 2017, Nevins was not planning to leave HBO until early 2018. Yet HBO wasted no time: Abraham and Heller were named co-heads of documentary and family programming a mere three days after Nevins's announcement.

It was a great time to take over—both Abraham and Heller had been at HBO for many years under Nevins and carried a ton of institutional knowledge and experience into their new jobs. In fact, many of the projects they had both been working on for years were still very much in the works. It became a question of continuing with what had been so successful about HBO documentaries and then expanding, in terms of both volume and format—i.e., more series, which had become more and more popular in recent times. The particular DNA of an HBO documentary would remain, though, a DNA created by Nevins: an understanding that the subjects of docs are real people about to be exposed to the world. And as a result of that closely held belief, the job was never just a job for Sheila Nevins.

SHEILA NEVINS:

Richard never said goodbye. Never said, "Thank you." When I told him I was leaving, he said, "You don't have to leave until April," and I said, "I'll be gone after Thanksgiving." That was the end of it.

I went in on the Friday after Thanksgiving because I knew no one would be there. I went through my stuff, and put things in garbage bags, because there were no boxes. And I never went back again.

Why was I beaten up and kicked out the door? Was I too old? Was I costing them too much money?

It was very, very painful.

After I left, I crashed and burned. I couldn't get out of bed. I couldn't do anything.

Nevins and Plepler had different taste in documentaries. Plepler veered toward projects built around celebrities (HBO's 2019 hard-hitting look at Ralph Lauren, anyone?) and big names, whereas Nevins maintained an interest in grittier, more journalistic stories.

Sometimes, those desires overlapped with projects, such as the HBO documentary focused on Broadway icon Stephen Sondheim or writer Nora Ephron. And while Nevins enjoyed that her perch afforded her the opportunity to hobnob with the likes of Mike Nichols, Steven Spielberg, and other cinematic glitterati, she wasn't all that interested in telling their stories. As time went on, Nevins had long felt she had to push harder and harder to keep HBO's documentaries rooted in real-world subjects.

One case in point: Chelsea Manning, the famous soldier, activist, and WikiLeaks whistleblower, came to HBO offices to propose a documentary, only to have Plepler turn down the project, according to people familiar with the matter.

In spite of her tenure and pile of awards, Nevins was never promoted or asked to weigh in on the glut of HBO scripted projects. Plepler hosted renowned, hoity-toity salons and dinner parties, but Nevins was not invited to them. She never cracked into his inner circle.

SHEILA NEVINS:

I'm not a perfect person.

I'm difficult, but I felt that I had earned the right to be difficult because I was being difficult for the product.

I never would have worked for me, what a bitch. Never. Not in a million years, too compulsive, too OCD, too needing little sleep, too calling all times of the day and night. What I loved about California was I could call at two in the morning if it was a producer who was working from there, but mostly I didn't care. I'm product oriented. I want it to be good and I'm tortured by it not being good. Tortured. I don't need a lot of sleep; I should be dead actually by now because I'm so old. I'm making up in life for what I didn't use up in sleep.

I was such a mess, I wondered if the pelican would even still love me.

I was hired by MTV because I was a brand. They didn't care how the fuck old I was. I just gave clout to their reality stuff. I realized they weren't buying what I do, they were buying who I was.

I was a loving mother but not necessarily a good mother. I couldn't stand women who didn't work; I had nothing to say to them.

There was nothing like HBO. It was a great way to spend my life and ruin it simultaneously.

ALEX GIBNEY:

I was aware of conflicts that were coming down the pike. I heard that there was tension between her and Richard and also Mike Lombardo. They were more interested in doing more celebrity-oriented profiles.

Some of my projects were green-lit, not by going to Sheila but by having them green-lit out of LA through Mike Lombardo. I'm just a fish swimming among sharks. You learn how to survive. But you could tell Mike and Richard were making decisions over her head and that she was losing the power to run her department.

LIZ GARBUS:

I sat in her apartment while she was on the phone with her bosses arguing about her exit plan. I just sat there for forty-five minutes waiting for my turn to talk about whatever project we are working on at that moment. I flew in an HBO plane with her and her bosses and I had been privy to that unfolding over several years. It was a huge loss.

ALEXANDRA PELOSI:

She was a seventy-nine-year-old woman. Corporate America doesn't respect seventy-nine-year-old women. What offended me about her departure was that she didn't get the golden parachute that other people got. I thought that proved that you can dedicate your entire life to an organization and you have nothing in the bank.

SUE NAEGLE:

The Gina [Balian] stuff is misogyny, the Sheila stuff is misogyny.

ERIN LEE CARR:

I have a career because of Sheila. And there are many of us. It was a shock when I heard she was leaving because she's so synonymous with all that HBO represents, but of course she went out with a huge *New York Times* feature and it was later announced that she had gotten a job at MTV. She continues to defy expectations around the roles of women, as she has for her entire career.

ALEXANDRA PELOSI:

I'll get invited to things because of my last name. I don't think I've necessarily earned the right to be invited to everything, but I've gotten used to that. Sheila comes from the Lower East Side. She's a foulmouthed truth teller. Nobody likes truth tellers at their parties. They say inappropriate things out loud.

PATTI KAPLAN:

It was very obvious that she was a woman in a man's world. And it's just the way the whole operation worked there in corporate America and the people that she had to contend with.

A terrific mentor. Not an easy person, let's say she was challenging. Let me put it this way: she is very challenging.

In life there's not so many people who have your back. And I would say that for Sheila, she's intensely loyal to the people that she's loyal to.

RORY KENNEDY:

It was amazing. For many, many years HBO was the top place to be for documentaries. Now there's more competition and there are more people following the lead of Sheila. She's helped influence a whole generation of filmmakers, from Alex Gibney to myself, an endless number of wonderful people who've worked with Sheila over the years.

I was aware that Sheila was one of a few women who had influence at the executive level, and part of that was because she was so damn successful. She had power, and could walk into that boardroom and make demands.

Was I shocked when she left? I wasn't shocked, but I was saddened. I felt like it was the end of an era.

ALEXANDRA PELOSI:

She's been a juror for every film festival there is. So she's seen every documentary film has ever been made. I swear. Every documentary. So if you go shoot something and you bring it back, she'll say, "I saw that, I saw that." When you bring her back something and she says, "I've never seen that before," you know you've hit it out of the park.

JON ALPERT:

Richard hangs around in a society where the food miraculously appears on your table, but you never meet the people in the fields who harvest it. Your borders are kept safe by soldiers, you never see anybody get shot. It is a gated world. That doesn't mean that Richard's a bad person. That's his world, his priority. Sheila's different. Sheila comes from the Lower East Side, had a Communist father, went to Communist sleepaway camp.

The documentaries were the absolute orphan cousin of everything when she started out. And now people are falling over themselves to be documentarians and to put documentaries on the air and stuff like that. And she's the person most responsible for making that happen in the country.

When Lisa Heller and Nancy Abraham took over HBO documentaries, they were already deeply engaged with many of the filmmakers they had collaborated with during the Nevins era, making the transition more of a smooth handoff than some radical overhaul. Heller and Abraham had been at HBO for two decades, carrying the institutional history along with them.

That included their former boss's constant quest for new filmmaking talent and for telling true stories in big, important ways, even as the competitive landscape around them continued to heighten. Heller and Abraham enjoy the coveted power of being able to green-light projects on their own, partially for that reason.

CASEY BLOYS:

Nancy and Lisa both worked for Sheila for a long time. Sheila is very diffi-cult to work for. So they learned a ton from her obviously, but she had them terrified. And I think when I started was the first time I had the whole group together in one room. Sheila operated in a very siloed way. She would pit them against each other. It was a head trip for them. And so there's still a little bit of PTSD. They don't want to say anything to cross Sheila, even though she doesn't work there and hasn't for a couple of years.

RICHARD PLEPLER:

Nancy and Lisa had more than earned the chair.

LISA HELLER:

The transition was very smooth in that we were deeply engaged in all the projects, and knew many of the filmmakers. It was essentially an expansion, an opportunity to look more broadly at what we could do in the space.

NANCY ABRAHAM:

We had both been there for two decades, so we had institutional history and experience working with Sheila on so many HBO documentaries. There had been a couple of series in the past, but now there was an opportunity to do more of those.

LISA HELLER:

Now a few years later, some things have shifted, but foundationally we have remained committed to bold documentary storytelling that illuminates the human condition.

For the most part we do have a simpatico, complimentary reaction to things. Not 100 percent, but we're usually aligned.

NANCY ABRAHAM:

And if not, we talk it through.

LISA HELLER:

We get to a deeper understanding of the projects by talking things through.

NANCY ABRAHAM:

We were both happy that Casey took a chance on this idea of the partner-ship, which is obviously a little unorthodox.

LISA HELLER:

Having grown up at HBO with Sheila in a leadership position, having a woman in a leadership role is not unusual to us.

NANCY ABRAHAM:

We're getting pitched so much more now. There's an incredible amount of material out there, as more people understand the value and appeal of non-fiction. And internally, there's an opportunity to have a story expand into the series space if that's its best expression. Sometimes that requires two parts, like *Leaving Neverland*, and sometimes that means six episodes, as with *I'll Be Gone in the Dark*. Casey's openness to that flexibility has been extraordinary.

On January 25, 2019, HBO's **Leaving Neverland**—*a Dan Reed film taking an unprecedented look at the hidden, troubling life of Michael Jackson and his relationships with young boys at his infamous Neverland Ranch—premiered at the Sundance Film Festival. The film was met, unsurprisingly, with massive protests and was threatened with lawsuits from the Jackson Estate. Nonetheless, HBO stuck by Reed and aired the nearly four-hour-long film over two days, March 3 and 4, 2019.* **Leaving Neverland** *took home the Emmy that year for Outstanding Documentary, though predictably that did not stop the Jackson Estate from making good on its threats of a lawsuit. As of June 2021, the suit is still ongoing.*

DAN REED, Documentarian:

I specialized in documentaries about conflict, war, and terrorism, and was having a slightly frivolous conversation with someone at Channel Four in the UK about if I could make a documentary that didn't have a high body count, and he said, "Why don't you do something about a very well-known mystery, something people are intrigued by, but doesn't involve physical violence?" I asked, "Such as?" He said, "What about the Michael Jackson controversy?"

I had no prior interest in that whatsoever and wasn't even a fan of Michael Jackson's music. I didn't know anything about him. I grew up in a bit of a bubble as a kid. I came at it as a complete alien, certainly with no preconceived ideas about whether he was guilty or not. During general broad-brush research, I came across the names of Wade Robson and James Safechuck, two young men who I'd never heard of, who were suing the Jackson corporation because they claimed abuse.

I interviewed Wade and James over several days, Wade in Hawaii and

James in Los Angeles. I was skeptical at the outset. They both seemed like decent young men, but that didn't mean they weren't going to try and sell me a version of events that might not necessarily correspond to the truth. But the more I listened to Wade in the first interview, the more I began to realize that what he was describing was this very strange, creepy love affair between a seven-year-old child and a man in his late twenties, early thirties.

I realized that as a child, he'd fallen in love with Jackson. What he was describing was unlike what I'd and I think most people assumed about child sexual abuse, this image of a predator leaping from the bushes, or snatching kids in a dark alley. The facts are, it's often a trusted figure in the child's life who ends up being the predator. Jackson was much trusted and much admired. Wade was very open about this, that Jackson was incredibly supportive and enabling and kind and generous and all these things, but he also sexually abused them. The longer I listened to Wade's and James's words, the further we went into the interviews, the more I thought, well, Jesus, maybe these guys are telling the truth.

I put together a half-hour reel, which consisted of excerpts from James's and Wade's interviews and archive footage, some of which presents Wade at the age of five dancing on stage in Brisbane with Michael Jackson, which is quite extraordinary.

Then I went to the United States to try and get an American partner on board production. I went to HBO first because I'd already made four productions with them. I met Sheila Nevins and Nancy Abraham in New York and screened the reel for them and they were both pretty blown away.

Then I went to Netflix and other places. There was strong interest, but in the end, I believe HBO was the only network who would have taken on this project. I found out subsequently that other broadcasters to whom I'd shown the reel were having very serious reservations about the risk of making such a provocative piece.

Wade and James were extraordinary interviewees, and so were their mothers. We had a wealth of amazing material. But I think what lifted it was not only the quality of the testimony, but the attention we paid to the human face and the voice which made it as absorbing and as resonant as possible.

HBO had commissioned a ninety-minute film, but I sent Nancy something insanely over length. I called her and said, "I'm a less is more kind of guy, but I'd be grateful if you would take the time to watch this through." The film in the end was four hours.

JOHN COOPER:

They showed it to me early. We knew it was going to create a lot of controversy. A lot of stuff was shown to me early, confidentially, to see if we were interested because it had to be handled.

I wanted it to get out and be seen because it felt important. I was a Michael Jackson supporter, so it was weird for me because I had defended him so many times, not publicly, but in dinner parties and when other things happened. It was an eye opener for me.

DAN REED:

There were a lot of threats before the screening at Sundance. We had a bomb team to check the theater and there were SWAT teams. I never felt that HBO were panicking or in a turmoil, and I didn't feel exposed because there was this big smooth machine backing me up. That was hugely important; we dropped a bomb on the culture, it went off, and had all these repercussions.

JOHN COOPER:

It was breathtaking and important. It was done so precisely, these boys' stories, that you just were left with having to believe that it was true. The two guys were there at the screening, and you realized you had witnessed something quite tragic in their lives. It felt very sad and also important that this story gets out.

I knew we would get a lot of heat, and we did. I got more hate mail, calls, and campaigns against us for *Leaving Neverland* than any film I've ever showed. It was by far the most controversial film I ever did at Sundance.

DAN REED:

After Sundance, I got a call from someone saying, "I have Oprah Winfrey on the line, would you mind speaking to her?" I almost said, "Go away, this is not a joking matter." But it was Oprah. She had seen the film, was full of perceptive insights, and particularly smart and shrewd about its storytelling.

And she said, which she repeated very kindly in the television piece, that she'd done dozens of shows about child sexual abuse, and she thought that in *Leaving Neverland*, we'd nailed the essence of it in a way that she was never able to.

I wasn't prepared for the intensity, the rancor, and the bile that came from Michael's fans or the nonsense that would come out of his lawyers' lips. HBO and I knew it was going to be controversial, but I can't remember any conversations in which I was warned, "Dan, it's going to get heavy and they're going to go crazy."

I comforted myself with the thought that even if you take Michael Jackson out of the film, it would still be a unique, unprecedented, brutally honest and graphic account of grooming and child sexual abuse. With a lot of very, very, precious insight and tremendous courage displayed by the boys and their mothers.

As HBO's programming departments continued to toil away, producing novel and award-winning content, a stasis had taken hold of the parent company. Though AT&T's acquisition of Time Warner was agreed to in October 2016, a Department of Justice antitrust case had been brought against the acquisition, holding up any opportunity for AT&T and Time Warner to merge.

RANDALL L. STEPHENSON:

In October 2016, the October before the election, I'm getting ready to walk into our board meeting to get the deal finally approved. We'd been working with the board on it and evaluating it nine ways to Sunday. We were getting ready to finally do the formal approval. And as I'm walking into the boardroom, candidate Donald Trump is quoted as saying, "AT&T is acquiring Time Warner and thus CNN. And that is a transaction my administration will never approve." I heard that and thought, "That's a little disconcerting. But the reality is this guy probably ain't gonna win the election." So we didn't think too much about it.

When Trump won, it looked like a lawsuit was coming, I sent Stankey down, I brought Chernin in. I said, "We need to get ourselves ready. They will try to block this." I got my legal team together. We started preparing for a lawsuit before Trump was sworn in. And we began to structure the transaction in a way that would maximize our probability of success if it were to get challenged in court. We went through a lot of gymnastics to ensure that this transaction and all of our interactions with the DOJ were done very defensively, positioning ourselves for litigations. And thank God we did, because when the lawsuit came, we had seen it coming and managed it really, really well. I'm proud of that element of it.

That lawsuit was about CNN. I will tell you to substantiate it, that I put forward structural remedies for Makan Delrahim that would have mitigated what he was trying to characterize as the antitrust risk, of which there was none. But I said, "Okay, let's assume that you're right. Here is a structural remedy that would prevent it." He wouldn't even talk about, would have nothing to do with it. At one point I'm meeting with him and I asked him straight up, "Are you telling me that if I were to sell CNN, this transaction wouldn't get approved?" He was smart enough to avoid that. That he walked straight out of that room and leaked to the press that I offered to sell CNN, which was not true.

He was a sneaky little fellow. But I fully recognized that CNN was the issue. In our boardroom, we believed we needed to own CNN as part of it, but it became an issue of principle. I believe this was nothing short of interfering with First Amendment protection of speech. And freedom of the press. And so we just said, as a board, We have an obligation and a duty to get the precedent right on this, and to stand up to this. And, by the way, I got a lot of conservative members on my board. I'm a conservative, politically speaking. But this was wrong. And so we said, "We need to contest it." And we did.

SIMON SUTTON:

When AT&T first bought the company, because the government sued, there was this sort of two-year period when nothing much happened. I went down to Washington a few times. I had to testify in the antitrust case brought by the DOJ. It was calm for a while; the deal had been announced but not much happened other than our non-AT&T affiliates distancing themselves. It wasn't for a while that people had any idea that it was going to be pretty radically different. Then it hit everybody. Particularly in New York, I think it hit pretty hard.

JOHN STANKEY:

There was no basis under which the transaction should have been litigated. All you need to do is read the judge's decision and you can see how weak and nonsensical the government's case was, especially when put in light of what the DOJ did in a Disney–Fox transaction. Or didn't do. What's the difference of CNN being in owner A's bucket versus owner B's bucket, other than if you want to entirely eliminate it, or have it be put into friendly hands that were more sympathetic to the president?

I don't want to speak for my boss—but we felt like this lawsuit was being politically motivated. It wasn't being motivated on the law. At some point in time, the business needed to step up for what we thought was right versus what was wrong and carry this through to completion.

RANDALL L. STEPHENSON:

Rupert called me twice and offered to buy CNN. I said no. Even Les Moonves made an overture about CNN. You understood the motivation of Rupert. If he could change the political and editorial bent of CNN, that would have been a home run for the administration.

In June 2018, AT&T finally bought Time Warner for $109 billion, ending the Time Warner brand. It had taken over six months of back-and-forth with the Justice Department to win the right to make the sale.

The financial terms were dizzying—Time Warner shareholders received 1.437 shares of AT&T common stock and $53.75 for every one of their Time Warner shares. AT&T issued 1.185 million shares of common stock and paid $42.5 billion in cash, which, when they took on Time Warner's debt, gave them $180.4 billion in net debt.

The press release used the usual dreaded code for declaring careers kaput: "Jeff Bewkes, former chairman and CEO of Time Warner Inc., has agreed to remain with the company as a senior advisor during a transition period." Warner Bros., HBO, and Turner would exist under the new umbrella "WarnerMedia," thereby ending "Time" as a byword for American media power. AT&T's Randall L. Stephenson would remain chairman and CEO of the company, with Time Warner and Bewkes's direct reports now reporting to John Stankey, CEO of AT&T's media business.

RANDALL L. STEPHENSON:

I told my board. That lawsuit damaged the communications company. It cost us more than just the bills we paid for economists and lawyers and executive time and attention. It cost us in terms of market momentum and product.

Disney was going, Netflix, you saw where it was going, and you saw the cord cutting coming. We needed to execute fast. That literally got shut down and stopped. No product was going through the entire time of the lawsuit. So we come out of it after six hundred days, flat-footed. And then have to start to, number one, put the companies together, number two, get the personnel right. Then number three, start standing up the product. So we were a year and a half late with this. The dadgum pandemic hits. And you just sit there, shaking your head.

JEFF BEWKES:

My last day at the company was uneventful. I had already recorded a farewell video that was sent to everyone. The hardest part was there were several times when I started to choke up. The days before, I had done a lot of one-on-ones with people, including my direct reports, various assistants, and others who I had worked closely with over the years.

Then I walked out of the building and headed down to Penn Station to catch a train and meet my wife, Lisa. On the way, Bobby Kotick from Activision called to tell me they'd buy the company if the DOJ appealed so that AT&T couldn't close within the contract deadline, but the government dropped their appeal. Then my assistant Charlene called and said, "Stankey's clapping down the hall." They were negotiating a consent decree for Turner, and I figured they must have closed it. I just wanted to get home to my wife.

I got to HBO in 1979. Throughout my entire career, I never once asked for a promotion or a raise. I was extremely proud to be a part of that team, in any position. I always hoped that if we were all sitting around the round table and we had to vote by secret ballot on who would be next chief, and you couldn't vote for yourself, that I would get the most votes, that people would say, "If it can't be me, let's put somebody in that's going to be trustworthy, who understands all the parts of this business, and who can help us get through any war." That was, to me, my highest ambition, to be judged worthy of doing the head job.

Look, it's always good to be promoted, but you have to leave things. This might sound crazy to some, but I did regret a little when I became the boss. Every time that happened, I became less able to be one of the siblings, and that was a loss for me. Some people want to become the boss because they want to tell people what to do. I once was visiting my parents and my dad asked me, "Well, how's it going at the company?" I said, "I think they're going to make me the CEO of HBO," and my mother said, "You can't be the CEO. You hate telling people what to do."

I loved HBO, the mission of HBO, and the people of HBO. The happiest years of my career were when I was at HBO. And then I got pulled out. I'm not going to pretend I didn't know it was possible because I could see what else was going on in the company, but I never sought to leave HBO.

Once I got to corporate, I wanted to do a good job and protect everybody. I didn't want to play favorites. I was fiercely defending HBO in its battles inside the company, and during my time as the CEO, we made huge strides. The fact that we were able to prevail from the merger and the occupation by AOL, all the way to 2002, despite the fact they controlled management and the board, was not easy. It was like the resistance in Star Wars. When I got the board, it was divided. There were the AOL people and the Time Warner people. When I left the board was unified, and we managed to protect HBO and then get back the whole company, which was not easy to do.

The most disappointing thing to me about the AT&T merger was that the thing that both I thought, and the board thought would be nice about it—that they would basically leave our people alone—didn't happen.

We didn't think they'd start getting rid of people because they didn't have anybody. That part of it was completely unexpected and unnecessary. And we didn't think they would go to such a level of malpractice as to not listen to anybody in the most experienced studio in the world, most experienced network companies in the world, even though they themselves had no knowledge or experience in any of these areas.

Anybody who thinks I knew that was going to happen is dead wrong, and more importantly, doesn't know me. No one was more frustrated than I was to watch what happened.

For a start, the simple optics of how meetings were handled suggested which side would dominate the new company: HBO might bring a handful of people to a meeting, whereas AT&T would have thirty or more on videoconference from their Dallas headquarters. As ever, HBO had a particular way of doing things (a "policy," as HBO star Larry David would say), born of years of somewhat maverick decision-making. There were clearly going to be certain things about HBO that might not fit into the cookie cutter of AT&T's finely tuned methodology.

On the streaming side, HBO honchos seemed frustrated that the AT&T boys apparently wanted to do things their way without first looking closely at what the old Time Warner hath wrought. But on the programming side, at least, they appeared to leave it to the HBO experts. Casey Bloys and others made the point that there is an art to programming, a curation element, and the interaction between talent and showrunners doesn't show up in any data analysis or report. (The lack of understanding from AT&T's side could be encapsulated in the fact that a pair of employees actually thought that all the shows on HBO came from Warner Bros. and were swiftly corrected on that point.)

In the end, on the programming side, the AT&T folks were not stupid—they clearly wanted the creative assets from Time Warner, so they seemed happy to leave it alone as much as possible, so as not to screw it up. There was an HBO culture, an HBO process in place, likened by some to sausage making: you knew when it was good, though if you removed just one ingredient, it just didn't taste right, and no one could explain why. In the short term, at least, AT&T liked the taste of the sausage and were happy to stay out of the kitchen.

RANDALL L. STEPHENSON:

Typically, when you're going through a merger of two companies, like we did, as you're going through the approval process, you do extensive merger integration planning. You start putting teams together. You started investing time with the other teams and getting to know them and putting merger integration plans, formal plans, in place. And you do it under the right prophylactic measures and so forth. As soon as it's obvious that a lawsuit was going to be filed, all of that stopped. Everybody went back to their corners and you had to operate as though the deal may get killed, and you could not be sharing competitive information. You could not be doing people planning. What is typically a year of dating and getting to know each other, doing formal courting, we had none.

At first, Plepler was hopeful that any cultural mismatch between HBO and its new overlords was overblown. By the time the Emmys rolled around, HBO presented AT&T with its plan, which was to give AT&T's planned streaming service away for free, add some new ingredients, and offer it for the same price—while distributing it just as HBO was distributing it in a multilateral world. The thinking was that distributors would bundle it with broadband, turbo the streaming service up a bit, and HBO would go on making movies and TV shows for it. The response to Plepler's pitch was a flat no—they were told that HBO would be direct-to-consumer only.

Plepler, the self-acclaimed congenital optimist, maintained that his bonhomie was no act in those early acquisition days, though many would hear a different tune from him all too soon.

At least one HBO executive likened the transition as akin to the "Chinese Cultural Revolution," with teams formed around people who had absolutely no experience in what they were doing. HBO veterans complained that they found themselves in rooms with brand-new faces trying to explain to them, of all people, the most basic elements of the business. Worse, the HBO executives' decades of priceless experience were often dismissed by AT&T.

One canard regularly floated by AT&T executives pointed to 2018 and 2019 as a period of flat growth at HBO. While this was held against HBO management as an example of their need to change their corporate strategy, it neglected the fact that HBO had already found meaningful growth through their burgeoning digital platforms, which made up for the industry-wide decline in the fully mature cable and satellite markets.

Among the tales circulated during the transition: A perhaps apocryphal meeting in which Stankey slapped the table and claimed that he knew more about television than anyone else in the room.

Suddenly, new narratives attacking AT&T were being leaked to the press.

RANDALL L. STEPHENSON:

As we were getting ready to put the two companies together, I felt strongly that, after a period of time, we ought to be very careful about keeping the two companies, from a culture standpoint, somewhat separate. Preserve the culture of Time Warner, preserve the culture of AT&T, and let John get in and do the hard work of creating one media culture—because, by the way, there was not one single media culture within Time Warner. Jeff, for all the right reasons, knowing that he may have to tear the thing apart, kept them very, very separate. And among those three companies—Warner Bros., HBO, and Turner—there was not one culture there. There are three very different cultures.

On the back of AT&T's acquisition of Time Warner, John Stankey, WarnerMedia's new chief executive, hosted a series of town hall–style meetings—with HBO, Turner, and Warner Bros. participating—as a way to rally the troops.

HBO went first, on June 19, 2018. And how, one might ask, could HBO best welcome Stankey to the family, while simultaneously asserting its own prominence as a brand? The traditional approach would probably have been to create a five-minute "greatest hits" video for the new leader, extolling the virtues of the company and its products and declaring everything to be A-OK. But this was HBO, and its edginess just could not be contained.

Eschewing the usual corporate tub-thumping, then, the company engaged talent to create short videos speaking directly to Stankey. Played at the beginning of the meeting, the stars' comments were hardly what one would call warm and fuzzy: Bill Hader started it off by tartly commenting that it was every actor's dream to someday work for "the phone company"; Sarah Jessica Parker wanted this AT&T guy to tell her why she could get only two bars of service in her apartment; and Emilia Clarke, playing off her star role on **Game of Thrones***, referred to the new boss as "John Stankey, king of mergers, forger of alliances," and so on. The snarky, fun video reflected HBO's personality, and Stankey asked afterwards for a copy to show his kids.*

All harmless fun and games, until the actual meeting began. It was clear from the outset that Stankey and Plepler, sitting across from each other in the HBO Theater—Plepler's home, Plepler's stage—were engaged in something of a tense stand-off. This, after all, was Plepler's company, and he wasn't used to—nor did he seem to appreciate—anyone else coming in to tell him how to run it, even jokingly. One observer called what transpired that day "a complete mind-fuck" that made it look as if Stankey felt he and AT&T already knew everything about the business, when perhaps there was a helluva lot for them yet to learn.

It didn't help that Stankey garnished everything with sports and military meta-phors and referred to himself as a "Bell-head," as though that would mean anything to the 120 HBO employees who showed up in the HBO theater that day, while other employees could watch it on closed-circuit television. Language choices aside, Stankey underlined the need to make more money and to attract many more subscribers (the current forty million not being enough, he griped). With HBO just coming off its most successful year ever, Plepler pointed out to Stankey that HBO already made money, to which Stankey snapped back, "Yes, you do—just not enough."

Plepler couldn't let that pass—"Oh, now, be careful," he cautioned, arms crossed in full defense mode. Making it perhaps even worse, Stankey went on to utter dubiously apt comments about the merger, likening it to childbirth, of all things. Such a compar-ison would be bad enough, but his jokey efforts at exegesis dug the metaphoric hole even deeper: "You'll look back on it and be very fond of it, but it's not going to feel great while you're in the middle of it," he said, adding, "[My wife] says, 'What do you know about this?' [while] I just observe, 'Honey. We love our kids.'"

All that aside, despite the deeply uncomfortable aura of the whole scene, Stankey didn't come off as mean or unpleasant, just as a being from a different corporate world. (When one questioner at the CNN town hall brought up the lack of women in leader-ship roles, Stankey's answer was to question the "depth of the bench.") Perhaps most concerning of all to the employees was the growing sense of ersatz corporate hunger games being played out—all this blah-blah-blah about working harder, and things not feeling great in the middle, and profits needing to improve. Any even half-sentient observer must have been able to grasp that for the financials to improve, the workforce would inevitably need to thin.

None of this was helped by the perception that HBO was a home to prima donnas who wouldn't drink the nouveau corporate Kool-Aid. They believed the new stewards didn't seem to appreciate the institutional knowledge of the company. Furthermore, HBOers believed that their long-running success was due primarily to its excellent people. It wasn't just a logo and a library of content—it was the folks who did the pro-gramming, who worked in distribution and in marketing, and who toiled tirelessly in the legal departments and in human resources.

AT&T, on the other hand, had a tried-and-tested playbook for mergers: rather than asking questions about how a company was run in order to best understand it, instead it deployed capital, gobbled up a business, and ran it according to a preconceived set of ideas. Typically, however, AT&T had acquired similar business to its own. This was a different animal.

Word from the very top at HBO privately suggested AT&T didn't know what it had bought, but they hoped—because HBO was so successful—that AT&T wouldn't want to mess it up. That gave rise to the initial party line inside HBO: "Don't worry, they're going to leave us alone." Nevertheless, several key HBO officials mounted a background-only attack campaign against their new owners.

JOHN STANKEY:

The way that town hall's played, it seems to have gotten more life in the media than virtually any other activity that's gone on inside of the company. I suppose it was because of my somewhat poorly chosen words of childbirth as a comparison. Potentially that makes it a little bit more interesting than other discussions I've had with people.

PETER NELSON:

The town hall with Richard was something that left people feeling there was misalignment. A few women made the decision to leave after his comment at the CNN town hall was made. Things weren't perfect before, but you simply could feel the culture went from one of cohesion to one of conflict, and at warp speed.

JOHN STANKEY:

If you pull apart the entire transcript, you understand that there is something very special about what they do there, but it was also to send a message that in the world we were all moving into, simply being a niche on demand or niche pay-TV network that is discretionary with the amount of hours of programming that HBO currently offered, wasn't a strong growth proposition for the future. It was time to rethink how the gifts and talents of HBO were applied in a business model and an approach that made sense for the changing, emerging markets that we saw. It was time to start to foreshadow that reality to the employee population, that we were mindful of the need to start thinking about a more scaled form of customer engagement and not one where we were simply dependent on other people to distribute the product and service, especially those people who are competitors.

FRANK RICH:

My favorite thing I've heard about staying an executive was telling me she was sent to some town hall in Dallas, AT&T, and somebody asked Stankey, "What's your favorite show on HBO?" And he said, "*Barry.*" And the friend who's telling the story says, "That's a more interesting answer than I expected." And the next question is, "What do you like about it?" He said, "I liked that it comes in thirty-minute increments."

RANDALL L. STEPHENSON:

I don't think the people running the various businesses appreciated and recognized what kind of radical change to their business model was coming and what that entailed if they wanted to be buyable for the next ten years. Not only was there not a courting and dating; there wasn't any getting the people ready for what had to happen to make this business viable in the long run. It's hard to say these things, but there's a reason your company was sold. It wasn't because somebody thought we could run a media company better than Jeff Bewkes. We cannot. But we are probably positioned to change a media company better than just standing on its own the way that it was. I'm sure it looked like a bunch of telco people, as I've heard us referred to, coming in and trying to run a media company better. That's not at all what we were trying to do. We were trying to come in and rethink what a media company looks like for the next ten years.

JOHN STANKEY:

One of the things I talked about with employees frequently is if you are in an acquisition and somebody pays a premium for your stock, by definition it means something has to change because if you paid a premium for an operation and you continue to operate it exactly the same, you never pay back the premium.

KATHLEEN McCAFFREY:

When AT&T took over, I went from having three shows to thirteen shows. I don't stop working. I work every single day, all the time, because we were trained by Casey and Casey by Carolyn to treat every single showrunner as if they're our only showrunner. It is a grind because we give everything.

We're all overachievers, A students. We read every single script. I don't know how Franny sleeps, we all give so much. If you give these A students three times the amount of work to do, the sacrifice will come. I get up at five o'clock in the morning and start reading.

That's been the thing I've struggled with this whole time. I can give and give and give and a corporation will take and take and take. But I love it. When you hear a pitch or you read a script or you're getting a cut of something and it's great, it's such a high. I think it was much more manageable before.

Stankey and AT&T expected HBO to step up its programming volume and increased its budget to do so. Meanwhile, programming over at HBO Sports was turning in a different, less voluminous direction, and on November 4, 2016, after only seventeen episodes, Bill Simmons's **Any Given Wednesday with Bill Simmons** *was canceled.*

BILL SIMMONS:

It just felt like we didn't crack it. It was just one of those things.

There were all these little signs that this wasn't meant to be. I had skin cancer on my forehead in May and I had the skin cancer cut out of my forehead. So this fucking hole in my forehead had been stitched up and I had to put makeup on. It was shit like that. Lombardo gets fired.

I had dinner with Casey and Nina eight shows in or twelve shows in. I can tell from the dinner, I was like, "Oh man, this isn't going to go well." It was just sad because you have all these people that are counting on this job and then we can't deliver a good show. I felt like it was 100 percent my fault. I just couldn't crack it.

We finished the dinner and they told me they were gonna cancel it after it was a twenty-episode run.

Obviously, I was a target because they gave me a big salary. I had reached a point where sometimes they are going to root against you just to root against you. I wasn't surprised because I'd been in that situation before, but I think there's two ways to deal with this stuff right. Where you can either be like, I blew it and feel sorry for yourself or ask yourself, "What did I learn?" and move on to the next thing. I took very specific lessons from it. I'm going to turn this into a positive, in a bunch of different ways.

I decided I was going to focus on making *The Ringer* a fucking success.

Though his talk show never found its legs, Simmons continued to bring original ideas to the sports department, and on April 10, 2018, HBO premiered the Simmons–Jason Hehir documentary **André the Giant,** *about the life of the celebrated wrestler.*

BILL SIMMONS:

That was basically just me and Jason Hehir for a year. It's the doc I'm happiest with, of all the docs that I've done. Because we had that HBO, not ESPN, where, with the commercials, the docs have to be a certain length. If it's a two-hour doc, it's gotta be an hour forty-two, so you end up either padding it or cutting stuff that you love.

Two months after its premiere, HBO would declare **André the Giant** *the most watched sports documentary in HBO history.*

Forty-five years prior, HBO had grabbed onto boxing and held it tight. Not only did the sport help make HBO a major success, but HBO also helped create boxing history along the way. Could HBO possibly let go of something so ingrained in its history?

On September 27, 2018, the world got its answer.

The announcement was shocking, sure, but not when you take a closer look. The iconic bouts featuring Tyson, Holyfield, De La Hoya, Holmes, Hagler, Leonard, Hearns, and the like used to attract as many as one third of HBO's domestic subscriber base, which, at the time (throughout the 1980s), was roughly around fifteen million people.

By 2018, however, HBO had managed to grow to more than forty million subscribers. But boxing continuously only drew about 2 percent of the audience or around 820,000 average viewers per telecast. Not a lot of eyeballs compared to the amount of effort and moolah they had to invest to win the fights. In fact, **André the Giant** *had attracted around seven million viewers and was a significantly cheaper transaction than sinking millions into securing, and producing, a boxing match.*

If anyone could see the end long before it arrived, it was a promoter like Bob Arum, who'd been making deals with HBO Sports execs for a long time. "HBO doesn't belong in boxing. Showtime doesn't belong in boxing," Arum told the **New York Post.** *"They're entertainment networks, and I think they're beginning to realize that. You don't spend money on an entertainment event that opens and closes the same night. Their competition is one competitor and that's Netflix—not schmuck boxing."*

Arum, the founder and CEO of Top Rank, a promotional boxing company, ended up taking his business to ESPN and their streaming service ESPN+ in an exclusive deal in August. This was a reunion of sorts. Top Rank Boxing series had debuted on ESPN back in 1980. Meanwhile, upstart streamer DAZN signed a deal with De La Hoya's promotional team. And other promoters were following suit, leaving HBO in the dust. They could smell when something was about to rot.

"It's stupid business for them to put money into boxing . . . If you put that money into a series and that series hits, then you can syndicate it for billions of dollars. Five years from now, everything will be streaming—entertainment, sports, everything will be streaming," Arum said.

HBO couldn't stem the tides of viewership. And from the looks of it, they didn't even try. Peter Nelson made a few boxing deals but just let it dwindle, not offering up other new ideas to take its place. Instead, he told the **New York Times:** *"Because of our association with boxing, people forget that we're not a sports network. We're a storytelling platform." Interesting to hear, from the head of HBO Sports himself, that HBO is not a sports network. One might think he'd have a different mindset about it.*

Either way, after the long marriage between boxing and HBO, the network finally made a clean break, citing diminishing ratings, increased competition, and a shift in programming direction.

JIM LAMPLEY:

I was six years old when my mother installed me in front of a TV set to watch Sugar Ray Robinson (her secret crush) in his second fight vs. Bobo Olson. Growing up in a small Southern town at the height of the civil rights era, energetically schooled by my mother to understand that racism was THE cardinal sin, I was startled to discover via the Rome Olympics a spectacular boxer who was using a slave name to taunt the white establishment. You couldn't have invented a more natural hero figure for me.

From the moment I signed that first HBO contract in February 1988, I remained at HBO continuously for more than thirty years until the network backed away from boxing in December 2018. So by far my longest continuous involvement with any business entity is the thirty-one years with HBO, and that was a tremendous gift. The blessing to me, I was in the place where I wanted to be working in the culture in which I wanted to work.

PETER NELSON:

It was awful ending boxing. Boxing was what brought me to HBO. Boxing was a forty-five-year institution at the network. At the same time, a legacy heritage isn't a reason to continue to do anything in a saturated media landscape. We had to take a hard look at how we were allocating our capital and what the audience research told us over and over was that boxing was not driving subscriptions.

The research was with us every single step of the way when we were making our decision, which was painful, especially because without boxing we'd have to lay people off and stop working with a lot of magnificent freelancers, to say nothing of the fighters themselves. Letting people go, particularly those who have served a company dutifully for many years, is always the worst part of any job unless you're truly a sociopath. It was very hard.

RICHARD PLEPLER:

We had very good empirical data on boxing's relatively limited audience outside of pay-per-view. Our research was pretty clear that more sports storytelling would be more resonant with subscribers. I wanted to work with people like Maverick Carter. I wanted to do more. I wanted to do more *Shops* with LeBron and others, and thought there was a plethora of opportunities to expand the sports brand.

BOB ARUM:

Now the problem with boxing is even if you got a big event, increasingly the biggest events went to pay-per-view. But if you got a big event and you paid $3 million, $4 million, $5 million for the event, it opened and closed the same night, unlike a series, and you play and you may replay and then you still had a thing of value, it's a success and you can make much more money off it than you invested. A win-win. To get a *Sopranos*, to get a *Sex and the City* is a win-win. To get a big fight that everybody's excited about is not a win-win. It's great programming, but it's not a win-win. So they kept cutting Nelson's budget down. It wasn't Nelson's fault.

JIM LAMPLEY:

No sport globalized more rapidly than boxing. So within a very short period of time fans went from a world in which they were looking for a fight between Marvin Hagler and Ray Leonard to a world in which they were looking for a fight between Gennady Golovkin and Canelo Álvarez. They went from a world in which they were looking for heavyweight championship fights between Muhammad Ali and George Foreman to heavyweight championship fights between Anthony Joshua and Tyson Fury. It's just an entirely different world. And so it required that fans get outside of their normal attitudinal envelopes and into a position where they could root with equal passion for fighters who came from entirely different origins and backgrounds than the ones with which they identify.

Globally, it's bigger. Globally it is far bigger and more important now than it was in the seventies or eighties or nineties. From an American standpoint, it's smaller. It is, it is less important within the United States because American athletes do not dominate the landscape of boxing to anywhere near the same extent that they did during those days.

Once Time Warner was bought, it was abundantly clear that culture was going to change and I had adequate warning from the top that this was going to happen.

At the beginning of 2018, Plepler and Bloys had more questions than answers about the future of HBO Sports, beginning with: Was there still a "there" there?—was it even a sustainable business once boxing had been jettisoned? Both executives looked to Nelson for a vision of what a new era would look like; together, they formed an odd troika for the challenge, considering none was regarded as a true sports fan. The erudite Nelson was more at home at film festivals and media conferences, or when dealing with big-name athletes for profile documentaries or a show like **The Shop** *with NBA super-star LeBron James, executive produced by his partner Maverick Carter.*

MAVERICK CARTER, Executive Producer:

Growing up in the Black community, the barbershop was the center of the neighborhood. My mom would drop me off on a summer day at nine, and I might not get my haircut until one thirty. It was where everything that was important—politics, financial issues, basketball, football, and the rest—got discussed, and the beauty of the barbershop is that it brings people together. So does our show. As a partner, HBO realizes that *The Shop* helps define what HBO is, and they've done a good job for us.

Sports was also suffering from bad timing at the corporate level. It was hardly a priority for AT&T, which was more concerned with ramping up production in drama, comedy, and documentaries than in keeping sports alive. **Real Sports** *and* **Hard Knocks** *were not going to replace the business model that boxing had provided, and one could easily sympathize with HBO Sports employees who were sending out résumés near and far. The culture inside HBO Sports, once proud and even hubristic, had eroded dramatically; if something wasn't done soon, it would become an existential relic.*

Other areas were caught up in change as well. In September 2018, less than a year after Nancy Abraham and Lisa Heller had been promoted to the top of the documentary department, longtime Sheila Nevins favorite Sara Bernstein left the network to run her own documentary shop at Imagine Entertainment. Jackie Glover, SVP of documentaries, would later leave to take the top documentary job at ABC News. And in programming, David Levine stepped away from his position as executive vice president and co-head of the drama department in February 2019.

DAVID LEVINE:

They did accuse me of wanting to run the place. I never wanted any of that, I'm not ambitious in that way, I'm very ambitious about everything else. What I am hubristic about is that I work very, very, very hard and I have very specific, very moralistic ideas about how to work very hard. They come from genuinely getting to know and support an artist. I didn't communicate what I was doing [to others at HBO] because I didn't think we were friends. I thought we were enemies, and they made that very clear. If they had just let me be on their side, I would have had a much different experience. I will say it was very tough from the very beginning.

By the end, I had hated most of my time at the company, but loved that company so much. I loved the people so much, and I'm so proud of having worked there. I just was tired of fighting for my life all the time, because I was a threat to run the place. I just wished I hadn't had to fight for my life because I could have been even better. A colleague told me if I hadn't left, they would've killed me anyway. I was definitely being lined up no matter what. There was no chance for me ever. Casey asked me, "Are you happy?" I was like, "No, I'll go. Thanks for playing." I knew I only had one choice. The answer was no, because that's what he wanted me to say. So I played his game up until my death.

HBO would be a much better place if the people actually got along with each other. But because it's so toxic, it became a place where the best people who work there couldn't stay there together. I think that's going to be HBO's legacy, if it collapses on itself and goes away.

Casey said one good thing to me early on. He said, "You want to know what's wrong with you? You don't have an army and I do." I said, "I've been trying to join your army for ten years but you won't let me." Sometimes there's good advice in threats, too. I understood from that implicitly that you don't do this by yourself. I did HBO too much by myself, yet I still learned more about life and creativity at HBO than I could've ever imagined.

On May 29, 2018, Richard Plepler was honored at Lincoln Center's American Song-book Gala. It was quite the night: Lena Dunham and John Oliver were just some of the HBO stalwarts who feted Plepler, Emilia Clarke sang "The Way You Look Tonight," Tony Bennett (ironically) sang "The Best Is Yet to Come."

Plepler thought, too, of when he'd first moved to New York City. His father had given him three books then, one of them E. B. White's **Here Is New York,** *a line of which reads, "No one should come to New York to live unless he is willing to be lucky." Now, Plepler was sitting in Lincoln Center being lavishly praised by his peers, and he felt that he had been, indeed, very lucky—lucky with family, lucky that he landed at HBO, lucky with the colleagues he worked with—luck was his blessing. He'd been CEO of HBO for four years, through gobs of Golden Globes, endless Emmys, recent megahits like* **Game of Thrones,** *and even a seat on the board of the Council on Foreign Relations.*

Plepler felt good about the successes he'd overseen and the future of HBO—after all, hadn't he just spent an entire evening hearing from stars about how great he was? John Oliver said, "He has been relentlessly supportive not just to me but my whole staff," and Lena Dunham had averred that "Richard has been a mentor, an ally, a companion, and he's really classed me up."

Plepler truly believed better times were ahead. Despite being outspent four to one by Netflix, HBO continued to make great television.

Just over two weeks later, on June 15, the merger of Time Warner and AT&T was made official—and Plepler had an entirely new set of bosses, none of whom had attended the Lincoln Center.

But both Plepler and Bloys were hopeful that they would be amenable to all the work being done and what it meant. They also hoped they might get more money after the merger.

It surely made sense on the back of the triumph of the Lincoln Center evening—HBO was at a pinnacle, at least as far as Plepler was concerned, and when you're up there, you can afford to have a little fun. Unfortunately, AT&T had a completely different view of things, which became painfully clear after Stankey's meetings were all over.

In the course of just seven weeks—from the Lincoln Center bash on Tuesday, May 29, via the merger on June 15, through the town hall four days later—everything had changed. No one from the new regime had ever taken anybody from HBO to breakfast, lunch, or dinner. One might imagine that if you've just spent $100 billion on a business about which you know nothing, you might ask your new employees to show up for a day, share a meal, download for the new leadership what was good and not good. Perhaps ask what, in the judgment of an HBO honcho who'd spent years building that business, should be done next? A kind of "You have been at the top of your business for thirty-five years, and I just bought your business. Why not give me a rundown of what works and what doesn't?" But there was nothing; AT&T had their own theory about HBO, and that was that.

Plepler and his followers believed in a bigger, better HBO. The new regime, HBO folk felt, only believed in chasing Netflix.

At one meeting in the Time Warner board room, Jeff Zucker, Kevin Tsujihara, David Levy, Plepler, and others met to discuss their visions for various collaborations. Plepler, according to someone familiar with the matter, turned to Randall and said that "the secret to HBO's future is never having to say 'no' again to what we wanted to say yes to yesterday." With that, Plepler said, he could take HBO to double digit growth.

He told the story of **House of Cards**, that HBO couldn't afford to match Netflix's commitment to it because of earnings pressure. Plepler never wanted that to happen again. In the increasingly competitive streaming landscape, he wanted HBO always to be the first call.

AT&T executives saw things differently.

Plepler was shocked by how quickly it became apparent he was going to have to leave. AT&T didn't believe that he had the discipline and the vision to go forward, nor did they believe he could cooperate with other business units. HBO would have to work across all of WarnerMedia, and not just be its own silo or island. Plepler, as an executive, didn't fit the bill for such a synergistic approach.

MIKE LOMBARDO:

I heard about Richard's outrage that John Stankey met with Casey without telling him. The fight he had with John Stankey that he claims came to an end, he found out John Stankey went to LA and met directly with Casey without talking to him. And he found that egregious. The entire time I worked for him, he would never tell me. He would meet with marketing people, he would meet with every executive who worked for me.

JOHN STANKEY:

When I walked into that job, everybody had an opportunity to contribute and move forward in the way that we wanted to do that. I very much embraced Richard and his expertise and what he could do for the business going forward. We spent several months talking about what going forward meant and what it meant for what we have to do to change the business and where to take it. And going through those kinds of processes, change is required.

Once the penny dropped for Plepler, the only thing that remained to do was make use of the ultimate Plepler toolbox: owning the narrative by telling the story and making sure it was the Plepler version. That narrative contended that first, Plepler didn't want to be there anymore. Second, he wanted to talk about what AT&T was going to do to the company and why those plans were faulty. "Those plans" already seemed to involve letting lots of people go, changing the organizational structure, and weakening the commitment to quality—the mission would now be more about quantity. Those at HBO would be tasked with simply working harder and making more stuff. As Stankey had said at the town hall, "I want more hours of engagement . . . because you get more data and information about a customer that then allows you to do things like monetize through alternate models of advertising as well as subscriptions."

By February 28, 2019, Plepler was ready to flee. In his departure memo, he once again invoked his father.

"My dad always gave the best advice," Plepler wrote. "Whenever there was a difficult decision to make, he counseled that since no one could ever have perfect visibility into the future, the best thing you could do was trust your instincts. It has been a touchstone for me throughout my life, and I have found myself returning to it again recently as I think about what is an inflection point in the life of this wonderful company. Hard as it is to think about leaving the company I love, and the people I love in it, it is the right time for me to do so."

SPIKE LEE:

Shit started changing. When these big corporations buy stuff for tons of money, they want their own people running it. That's just a fact. They hand-pick. They want to put their own imprint on it and they give the people running stuff a boatload of money and show them the door.

NINA ROSENSTEIN:

I worked with Richard Plepler for a long time and learned from him to never look over your shoulder. Just look straight ahead. He would say, "More isn't better, better is better." I took that to heart and believe it's part of what makes me and my time untraditional, yet still aggressive.

CHRIS SPADACCINI:

At the Emmys in 2017, we broke every record. We shattered our own record. This was premerger. The pride was so apparent and so contagious.

People stayed late into the night, and at the end it was Quentin, Casey, Richard, and me. Richard said, "It's never going to get better than this."

RICHARD PLEPLER:

HBO's success over those many years was not an accident. It was the result of work by an enormous number of people with different skills, different talents, who did extraordinary things over many decades. There was something very, very unique and special about HBO throughout those decades.

CASEY BLOYS:

Richard was a terrific boss to me as a creative executive because he went out of his way to give credit to me and the team for any successes, like *Succession* or *Watchmen*, but never made us feel alone in failure. As an example, a show like Alan Ball's *Here and Now* never lived up to our expectations, but he would always put the performance in the context of the greater slate, reminding us that not everything was going to work. In a creative endeavor, it's important to celebrate success, of course, but to also allow for failure as a normal part of the process. This allows you to feel emboldened to take shots on a limited series like *Chernobyl*, which may not seem like a sure thing at green-light.

JULIA LOUIS-DREYFUS:

Veep was certainly one of the most exalted creative experiences I've ever had, and the atmosphere that Plepler created during his reign will go down as one of the greatest ever.

SARAH JESSICA PARKER:

Very few people still hold a salon. Richard Plepler holds salons. He is a raconteur. To this day, Richard is somebody I call for advice without hesitation. I feel like time stands still when I'm in his and his wife's company. I'm surrounded by unbelievably interesting people, great thinkers, writers, artists, politicians, and foreign leaders like Shimon Peres. You're transported in imagery, in political opinion, and insider information.

I watched Richard grow up in that company, run the company, then leave the company. He's continued his role in people's lives as friend, and counsel, and as a repository for insider industry secrets. I feel enormously privileged that we have maintained our friendship. It's been long and real. He is a very unique fella.

He's definitely got a good tan. How he maintains it is his secret, and he's privileged to it.

RICHARD PLEPLER:

My dad always had a briefcase, and I thought, "If you're going to be a serious businessman, you should have a briefcase." So the week before I joined HBO, which was May of 1992, I went into a little store on Madison Avenue and bought this leather briefcase which I kept with me every single day. It had papers from work, gifts from my daughter, and a bunch of articles and essays that I had kept over the years that were inspirational to me about life and business.

Toward the end of 2018, when I had already determined that I was going to leave the company, my briefcase was stolen out of the car. I was devastated because there was so much history in it. I came home and my wife, Lisa, said, "It's actually fitting. That chapter has passed."

16

Saudade

Two HBO shows—one giant and one gargantuan—would make their much-lamented departures in May 2019: **Veep** *and* **Game of Thrones**.

Heartfelt emotion, particularly after Julia Louis-Dreyfus's cancer diagnosis, figured significantly in the **Veep** *goodbye. Warm well-wishes were notably absent one week later, however, as controversy continued to plague the ending of* **Game of Thrones**.

The character of Selina Meyer was Julia Louis-Dreyfus's finest achievement—a creation at once too funny to be true and too true to be funny.

She won the Emmy for her performance for a startling six straight years, thereby setting an Academy record. And in the show's finale, she finally had the opportunity, earned in style by both the character and the performed, to opine on the significance of the eponymous nickname that had given the show its title:

"Being vice president is like being declawed, defanged, neutered, ball-gagged, and sealed in an abandoned coal mine under two miles of human shit. It is a fate worse than death. Besides, I'm not going to die, because I've got the heart and twat of a high school cheerleader who's only done anal."

JULIA LOUIS-DREYFUS:

It would not have been possible to do our show throughout the Trump era. We could have done it with any other Republican president, but the wheels were so off the bus with Trump in terms of his behavior, and the rule of law he had obliterated, that we wouldn't have been able to push up against boundaries. Because boundaries just didn't exist anymore.

ARMANDO IANNUCCI:

People were going insane, trapped in a situation they had no control over, surrounded by shit. *Veep* best exists in a world where there are rules: half the fun is breaking or deviating from those rules. But under Trump, there are no rules. He's saying literally, "I could shoot a guy in the face on Fifth Avenue, and still get elected." For that, you need the likes of John Oliver.

TONY HALE:

The Trump presidency was its own political sitcom. One of the things I treasured about *Veep* is when I would watch the news and see something crazy going on, I felt guilty laughing. *Veep* was a great outlet for laughing about politics with no guilt attached.

DAVE MANDEL:

Gary Cole once said there are ten things an actor can do, and you hope that a *great* actor can do four, four and a half of them. Julia does all ten.

We had to delay a little more than a year because of Julia's illness, and over that year, particularly because of Trump, I felt the show had to stay relevant, and maybe needed a darker tone. That made us ask, "Why is Selina Meyer losing? It seems like the worst people throughout the world, not just in America, are winning. Maybe she should win."

JULIA LOUIS-DREYFUS:

We could delve into the psychology of Selina Meyer, and I think we would find she was somebody who had a great emotional hole in her life that she was always trying to fill with other things, because she was never truly loved. And, oh jeez, who does that sound like?

Veep was virtual Valhalla, a world that began with brilliant writing and casting, survived the departure of Armando Iannucci, its lucent, singular creator, then a life-threatening condition for its world-class star. Then the Mandel administration was installed and found its way to a second run for the ages.

Veep filmed its last episode, number 65, on December 18, 2018. Throughout the history of television, series finales have been tricky. Popular shows can drift sideways or blow themselves up—either because the creative tank had dribbled its last drop or because of internal toxicity. HBO had been the home both to great conclusions and flop finales, the greatest being **Six Feet Under.** *Veep "crushed it" thanks to a near-perfect storyline that managed to remain wholly consistent with the show's major arc, while adding an entirely new and poignant dimension to the concept. The finale also had an ingenious coda alluding to Selena's death and a Tom Hanks mention, one that true Veepsters were bound to recall from the show's pilot seven years earlier. Each cast member was allotted a meaningful goodbye moment, including Selena, who remained true to herself. (Who else?) God and Mephistopheles could never have placed bets about her; there was fascination but no mystery. Selina would sell her soul or die trying.*

JULIA LOUIS-DREYFUS:

It was hard to shoot that last episode. There was a dark and tragic aspect to the story we were telling, and we were all saying goodbye to one another. It was an out-of-body experience, to tell you the truth. I was grief-stricken and yet, at the same time, it was joyful, because of what we had all done, and because it felt like the right time to walk away from it. Considering where we were with this country and with that man as our president, we could not compete with that shit anymore.

DAVE MANDEL:

The schedule had been designed so Julia's final moment was that last scene you see of her in the Oval Office. There was a crowd, people by the monitors, and lots of family members, and friends, gathered all around.

In the script, I wrote: "Selena contemplates everything she's done, and then snaps out of it." Easy to write, but quite another thing to do. Julia had done a take or two, they were emotionally raw, bitter, and bittersweet. Yet we kept pushing it. I wanted to push her right to the edge, even though I'll admit, I didn't quite know where that was. I don't think she knew where it was, either. To me, that shows the level of trust between us. And then there she was with the final shot, sitting alone in the Oval, realizing the price she had paid with her soul. There were no words. It was just Julia. And it was so heartbreaking.

With that done, there were cheers from the crowd, speeches, and a lot of hugs, along with an extraordinary sense of exhaustion and accomplishment. After that, I sat on the couch with Julia. She had the wig off and was all sweaty. She said to me, "I feel like I just gave birth again." I told her, "Yeah, me too."

TONY HALE:

It was really hard. Julia and I had this sort of sanctuary time every morning, when she was getting her makeup and her hair done, and I would sit next to her, and we would run lines, tell each other jokes, and talk about life. It became a meditative space before going out to shoot. We had gotten so close, and knowing I was going to be saying goodbye to her, and to that amazing group of people was super emotional. I had been dreading that day, and now that it was there, I was in mourning. When I heard, "That's a wrap for Tony," I absolutely lost it. Hugh Laurie had finished right before me and gave this incredibly eloquent speech. When it was my turn, I could barely speak.

DAVE MANDEL:

I'm not going to lie, *Veep* was my all-time favorite gig.

JULIA LOUIS-DREYFUS:

We all really loved each other big time. It was amazing.

When David Benioff and D. B. Weiss pitched their plans for the culmination of **Game of Thrones,** *they set off a chain of repercussions—programming, financial, and scheduling—that would reverberate throughout the company for years. In a 2015 meeting at Mike Lombardo's office in Santa Monica, the two men were joined by Carolyn Strauss, who'd been president of programming at HBO until her ignominious firing seven years earlier. That made for a jubilant and triumphant homecoming. While still at HBO, Strauss had been not "a," but "the" key* **Game of Thrones** *booster; now, as executive producer of the series and protector of the flame, every walk through the halls was a victory lap for her in the dual roles she played as both legend and hero. It's that kind of business. Screwy.*

Benioff and Weiss told Lombardo that the final two seasons would be the show's last. That didn't come as a huge surprise; the show had already gobbled up all of George R. R. Martin's existing work on the series and had been an exhausting, unrelenting odyssey for all involved. What came next, however, startled Lombardo to his core: previous seasons had each been ten episodes long, but now Benioff and Weiss decreed that the penultimate season would last only eight episodes.

Lombardo was shocked when he heard; he'd wanted more episodes, not fewer. But before he could make his case, a final grenade blew up: Benioff and Weiss said those episodes wouldn't even finish the story. Recalling their long-held dreams of making a movie that would "end" the series and have fans camped out in line to buy tickets, they said they were thinking about a pair of theatrical features to end the saga.

Lombardo was aghast. He didn't understand why the paying HBO subscribers who'd been faithful to Thrones *for eight glorious years would be asked to forsake their living rooms for a movie theater (or two) to witness the finale. And how could any grand finale, one episode or two, or thirty-two for that matter, not take place at HBO, where the series was born, and had been devotedly supported, ever since? The Benioff–Weiss scheme lay there unconsummated, the only resolution to emerge from the meeting having been Lombardo's plea that the pair take a few days to mull this over and consider their dismaying dilemma: More episodes. No movies.*

With the party over, for now, Lombardo called Plepler to give him the problematic update. Those who saw or talked with Plepler afterward found him antsy, concerned, and frustrated. Who could blame him? He'd wanted at least eight episodes—maybe ten—as a way to maximize financial benefits to HBO and simultaneously give fans a swan song worthy of this most favored offspring.

Plepler then let Benioff and Weiss know his feelings in Plepler-esque style, telling the two showrunners he thought they should extend what he considered their "ownership of the culture." Afterward, Plepler and Lombardo cautiously clung to the hope that Weiss and Benioff would come back to them with additional proposed episodes to be shot.

Plepler and Lombardo's waiting game was, ironically, the product of the auteur-as-Lord version of Gourmet Television that HBO had created, dating all the way back to The Larry Sanders Show *and* Oz. *At the start, despite their awareness that neither Weiss nor Benioff was an experienced showrunner, HBO had taken a wild gamble on their abilities to command one of the most logistically challenging epics in television history. After surpassing expectations with their writing and producing skills (the latter with an essential assist from Bernie Caulfield, the show's "secret weapon"), Weiss and Benioff were more than just full throttle in the driver's seat; they were alone together in the car. HBO had little leverage.*

Two days later, with cool heads apparently prevailing, Weiss and Benioff sent word that they'd be sticking to their original plan for the final seasons but would not be doing Thrones *as a feature film. Key HBO executives already knew at that point that they'd be in for a strong dose of criticism one way or another. They had no doubt that many observers would be likely to complain that the final season was "too hurried" and that what could have been the ending to end all endings would instead be a truncated semi-event. Adding to the pain, Netflix would soon sign Benioff and Weiss to one of the largest overall deals in the company's history: a cool $250 million.*

EMILIA CLARKE:

The final season was tough. I'm not going to lie. After I read the final season, I walked out of the house with just my keys and found myself aimlessly walking around for about three hours, trying to digest where it was that I needed to get to. For me as an actor, every choice my character makes is the right choice. It's the only choice. I love Daenerys very much. And so I went through a long period of rationalizing and comprehending how I was going to best portray her integrity, even though on the first read I was like, "What? This is a shocker."

I wanted to talk to Kit about it, but the bloody idiot hadn't read it yet. He said he wanted to read it for the first time in the room. So I said, "Okay, I'll talk to you after the table read." And there he was, reading the pages at the table, seeing all those people dying, and he was crying.

Kit and I spent a huge amount of time that season with the producers and directors tracking our arcs. We talked about where we were at as a couple and where were we at individually. What did we know at each point? What did we not know? How did that inform us? I kept a diary for myself to make sure I was on top of even the smallest of details, because it can be very tricky when you're filming in a nonlinear way.

Every character had a lot to wrestle with and a lot to come to terms with. There were discussions that were had where some people weren't happy and some were. It was going to be a difficult season for everyone involved—making it as well as watching it.

But I trusted David and Dan and made my peace with it. As soon as I had done that, and as soon as I had intellectually rationalized that decision, then it was work as normal.

CAROLYN STRAUSS:

The guys knew where they wanted to end up story-wise. I know there was a lot of controversy about the ending, but the truth is, given the amount of time it took to produce those last six episodes, I don't know how else it could have been done. I don't think there was actually a physical way we could have done more episodes without creating another season. It took a year and a half to make that last season. You didn't want to let so much time though between the seventh season and eighth season.

There were discussions about ending up with a movie, but Mike felt very strongly, and I think rightfully so, that HBO audiences would feel, having been on the ride with HBO for all this time, that for HBO not to have the ending would be a betrayal.

Dan and David earned the last word. The guys had delivered on the show for a number of years, the most successful show that HBO ever did. HBO always tries to go with the creators' instincts. And clearly in this instance, the guys had earned the right to land the plane however they wanted.

I happen to be satisfied with the ending. I know certain people weren't.

PAUL HAAS:

George would fly to New York to have lunch with Plepler, to beg him to do ten seasons of ten episodes because there was enough material for it and to tell him it would be a more satisfying and more entertaining experience. But Dan and Dave were tired, rightfully so. They were done, and wanted to move on, so they cut it short and then negotiations became, how many seasons can we stretch this out? Because of course HBO wanted more.

George loves Dan and Dave, but after season five, he did start to worry about the path they were going because George knows where the story goes. He started saying, "You're not following my template." The first five seasons stuck to George's road map. Then they went off George's map.

George R. R. Martin has thirty million followers. He's the rare recognizable writer. If Dan and Dave walked down the street, nobody knows who they are. They know who George R. R. Martin is, but George was not executing on the vision day in and day out. And so they got rich off that show and George made some very good money.

RICHARD PLEPLER:

Obviously, there were conversations. Casey and I felt very strongly that the final decision rested with Dan and Dave, who had created this magic in the first place; it was for them to determine exactly how they wanted to land the plane.

CASEY BLOYS:

Going into the finale, we knew there would inevitably be some pushback, but we all felt the final season delivered on its promise to fans, but more importantly it executed the vision for the finale that Dan and Dave had planned so carefully. I was working at HBO when the *Sopranos* finale aired, so I saw firsthand that it can be very difficult to end a massive show and keep everyone happy—though while not as big as either *Game of Thrones* or *The Sopranos*, *Six Feet Under* did manage to do so. If you look at the online criticism, it seems to be split fifty-fifty. Some fans loved it; a more vocal half hated it. The main complaint is that Dany's turn to war criminal was too abrupt, the alleged culprit being the shortened season. I do understand the criticism, and if there had been another episode or two, of course, that would have been helpful. (I would have taken two more seasons!) But I do believe if you look at the totality of her arc over the series, as opposed to the final episodes, her turn was more than earned, and was planned. This was never going to end as a love story between Dany and Jon Snow.

FRANCESCA ORSI:

I attended the final table read in Belfast with Casey and it was one of the bigger highlights of my career. It was freezing outside, and the room we were in with cast, producers, and several department heads was small and intimate relative to the number of people. It was packed and hot.

MARA MIKIALIAN:

You had to choose whether to have your script in paper version or on an iPad. Right before we started the table read, they closed all the drapes. It was total lockdown. Afterward, they collected everything.

FRANCESCA ORSI:

Hardly anyone had read the script prior to the read-through and it was incredibly moving to watch the unfolding scenes, moment to moment, as each actor read their lines aloud, simultaneously trying to process what was happening. Everything felt so still as the actors looked at one another with quiet tears, taking in the conclusion of not just their own character but the fate of every pivotal relationship that had created the epic story and family that was *Game of Thrones*. Needless to say, it was incredibly moving to experience the bond they all shared and to feel a sense of deep love and peace between them all as they said, what was basically, their final goodbye.

CHRIS SPADACCINI:

Game of Thrones was the last remaining monocultural event, a shared viewing experience around the world. I'm not sure that ever happens again. With multiple streaming services now pervasive, watching on your own schedule has become common.

The beauty of *Game of Thrones* is that by season eight, we had built this army of fans across the globe. We were averaging thirty-three million viewers an episode in the United States alone; *Game of Thrones* was a catalyst for subscriber growth, HBO's most watched series of all time, and one of those rare shows where ratings and social buzz went up every single year.

We knew it was an important moment to fortify the show's legacy, and HBO's ownership of arguably the most successful TV show of all time.

Our big idea was "For the Throne," to celebrate over seven seasons of the characters vying for power, cheating, and killing for a chance to sit on that throne. We also wanted to involve the fans who put their lives on hold to watch it, share it, debate it.

What would they sacrifice for *Game of Thrones*?

The Super Bowl spot was the kickoff for the campaign. It's a marketer's dream to come up with the commercial that dominates social conversation on Super Bowl Sunday. Richard was always asking for one. Our Bud Light Dilly Dilly commercial won the Super Bowl and was one of the most talked-about, if not the most talked-about, spots for the year. From there, brands came out from all over to participate. Oreo came up with a custom packaging, re-creating the main title sequence of *Game of Thrones* out of Oreos. The Minnesota Timberwolves changed their name to the Dire Wolves. Johnnie Walker came up with a brand of Johnnie White Walker whisky. Then we did this massive blood drive with the Red Cross. It was a phenomenal campaign.

D. B. WEISS:

The final season took so long to shoot that we brought the kids over and put them in school there again for a semester. David's daughters went to a Protestant all-girls school, and my sons went to a Catholic school around the corner. As Jews, they sat out the religion classes, along with a few Islamic kids and a Korean Buddhist.

DAVID BENIOFF:

Dan and I were very good friends for years before this show, but there's no doubt that spending virtually all your waking hours with someone will test a friendship, even the best of friendships. But I can't imagine working with anyone else. One thing that helped enormously was family. Our wives became best friends over the course of the show. Our kids became dear friends. Dan and Andrea are now "Uncle Dan" and "Aunt Andrea." When we lived in Belfast, we all had flats in this apartment complex near Queen's University. Dinner was a communal affair most nights. Always our two families but also often Bryan Cogman with his wife, Mandy, and their kids. And then Peter Dinklage and his wife, Erica, and their kids. We were like a kibbutz filled with people who didn't know how to grow their own food.

D. B. WEISS:

We both realized over the course of the experience what a waste of energy big arguments are, pretty much always. I have a dim recollection of us yelling at each other during the production of season one and calling each other something that's a lot more acceptable to say in the UK than here. But I have absolutely no memory at all of what the argument was about. There are literally tens of thousands of decisions that go into making a show. If David feels more strongly about something than I do, well, maybe it's because he's right. Defending a position on any point because it's the position you took in any given moment is stupid and exhausting.

RICHARD PLEPLER:

I went to Belfast for the final week of shooting and we hosted a dinner for David, Dan, the cast, and crew. I said this group of talent was the very definition of excellence and character. No one, despite the success of the show, ever became imperious or arrogant and we toasted not only to the magic that they had all created but also the class they exhibited for all those years. It was an incredibly emotional evening which I will never forget.

The final episode of Game of Thrones *marked HBO's biggest ratings night ever, drawing 13.6 million viewers, beating the previous HBO high of 13.4 for the season four premiere of* The Sopranos. *Counting all platforms, the* Thrones *finale lured 19.3 million viewers, easily outdistancing all competing fare, including America's grand television obsession, the NFL.*

CAROLYN STRAUSS:

Part of why some people reacted the way they did was the story spun out in a different pace towards the end, because there wasn't as much time to sit with it. It gave the end a very different tone. But the level of difficulty producing those episodes is nowhere near anything else I've ever done.

EMILIA CLARKE:

When it came out, people were feeling silenced by the world we were living in, and the lack of choice they had in who was running the country. I think this was something that really galvanized people who were feeling voiceless. They felt, This is not how I saw this going, and said, "That's wrong." I love those people, but this show was never going to please everyone.

My heart will always break for how much noise the final season got from people who didn't like it, because the people who were involved in making it, who aren't the actors, no one above the line, those people put their lives into it and are proud of the incredible work that they did. And so my heart breaks for them when they were hearing it wasn't right.

We all finished the last season shell-shocked. It was our entire lives. The amount of growing up that I had done, that Maisie and Sophie had done, that Kit had done, Lena, everyone, was incredible. So much life happens in ten years, and we were with each other for all of it. Through thick and thin, through snow and eighteen-hour shooting days. Finishing left such a hole; it was shocking to readjust. It took me a good year, I think, to really find my feet again.

I had a hard time identifying myself as part of the cultural phenomenon that the show is. It's a real hard thing for me to try to understand. I know the power of getting to play her, and how much I took from that. But I can't really identify with the success. And I think that's probably okay. I certainly value what other people did.

It's only now, after I've had some very different experiences, that I see just how insanely lucky I was. I was able to be a part of HBO when it was at its most glorious. I adore every single person that made this show. They absolutely became like family. I did know in the moment how lucky I was with how they reacted to my brain hemorrhages. They treated me so well, they cared. They like actually cared. They took good care of me, when they easily could have been like, "We don't like this, this is freaking us out," but they never did. They cared. They really, really cared.

LENA HEADEY:

I think of it with a smile on my face, still with a little disbelief, and a huge amount of gratitude.

PAUL HAAS:

George has not told me who gets the throne at the end of his arc; he will not tell anybody. I believe maybe his book publisher and book agent know, but I do not. And I've represented George since 1992.

So I have no idea where it goes, but the bottom line is that the book's ending is a more satisfying experience than the show's.

GEORGE R. R. MARTIN:

It has changed my life, mostly for good, but in some ways for bad. I wasn't prepared for it. Of course I hoped for it, though. I've learned not to take anything for granted.

I do think Plepler was right in one regard, when he said it could run for ten years. I wish it had run for ten years. I think that would've given us a little more time in the later seasons to end it. But that might be just because I'm still trying to end it in these books here. I'm working on *The Winds of Winter* even now as I have been for the best part of a decade. And hopefully I'm going to get to that end soon and then people can argue about which ending they like better.

That final season of **Game of Thrones** *came around at a very significant point in HBO's history. It fostered feelings of pride, triumph, and sadness. HBO was confident in its brand and what was planned for post-***Thrones***, but it was clearly the end of an era. And it coincided with a changing of the guard at HBO, with a move away from home at Bryant Park, that warm, nurturing place that had housed the network for thirty years, to the cold sterility of new office towers built at Hudson Yards on the West Side. Casey Bloys now had control, not pivoting from one shiny thing to the next but thinking deep and hard about HBO's longer-term future.*

A perfect example: on January 18, 2013, three years after the premiere of **The Pacific** *and twelve years after* **Band of Brothers***, HBO announced that executive producers Tom Hanks, Steven Spielberg, and Gary Goetzman of Playtone would all return to the network with a third installment in their WWII series,* **Masters of the Air***. Based on the book of the same name by historian Donald L. Miller, the miniseries would tell the story of the enlisted men in the American Eighth Air Force during World War II.*

After the initial announcement, reporting on the series went dark, until October 2019, when news broke that Apple had picked up the series for its upcoming streaming service, Apple+. HBO quickly released a statement acknowledging that they had decided not to move forward with the show. High on the list of reported reasons for the decision was the estimated $250 million budget, eclipsing the $200 million doled out for **The Pacific***. And while the promise of DVD sales, which had been so profitable with HBO's* **Band of Brothers***, had helped ease HBO's concerns about the budget for* **Pacific***, the emergence of streaming had all but destroyed hopes of cutting into that $250 million price tag in DVD sales.*

By nixing the more than $200 million budget for **Masters of the Air***, HBO was able to make such standouts as* **Euphoria***,* **Watchmen***,* **Chernobyl***, and* **Succession***.*

HBO planned for a big increase in programming, which happened in 2019. It went from about 100 hours of scripted programming to 150. That's a big jump. It took two years. One of the stark realities of the streaming era is you can't get away with one-new-show-per-quarter; there must be a constant supply of shows.

The days of having one show define your network are kaput. Now there are five hundred or more shows all but bumping into one another. The idea that one show, even a great one, is going to keep people subscribed is a fallacy.

CASEY BLOYS:

When I started in 2016, there were two seasons of *Game of Thrones* left. And maybe there was a year in between. It was all about planning for when *Game* of *Thrones* ended, because I've been through it before, with *The Sopranos*. I know what that means, like, "Great. I'm the guy who gets to be here when the show ends." I knew all these articles were going to be written. That's one of the reasons why I'm very proud of what we did, because right when *Game of Thrones* ended in the spring, and we had all the debate about "Was it the right ending?" There were the "Okay it's over. What's HBO going to do?" questions. We were able to—and we've been planning this for several years—we were able to answer that with *Chernobyl*. And then *Big Little Lies* season two, and then *Euphoria* and then *Succession*, then *Watchmen*, all in one year.

This was all planned. I wanted a diversified slate. There can be lots of genres, there can be lots of kinds of shows, but the thing that should unite them is when you see them, you say, "Oh, that feels like an HBO show." And that can mean it looks great. That can mean it's digging. It's saying something about how we live. It can be something that's defining something that's in the zeitgeist. It can be provocative. It can be something you've never seen before or some combination of all of them. Where you get into trouble is when you think there can only be one kind of HBO show. Let's start with *Girls*. We'd never done a show about people that young. Same thing with *Euphoria*. A drama about teenagers, is that an HBO show? I think we showed that if you approach it correctly and you have a creator who has something to say, in the case of *Euphoria*, very much about addiction, it can be an HBO show. *Watchmen*, a comic book show, like, what is that? But the difference is Damon has a lot to say about society today. So it's not just that it was a cool comic book. It's because Damon has a lot to say. That's what I think an HBO show is. It should be entertaining. It should be well made. It should be all those things. There's something we're trying to say about, I don't want to make it sound like too lofty, but something to say about humanity in a way, or what's the point?

Euphoria is a younger-skewing show, *Succession* is a contemporary family drama. *Watchmen* is our version of a comic book franchise. So we were trying to do all different kinds of stuff. Lots of stuff. High quality to answer the question, which I knew was coming, which is like, "What's next?" I believe we successfully answered the question, "What's after *Game of Thrones*?" Here it is now.

On Saturday, April 26, 1986, the worst nuclear disaster in human history occurred in the number 4 reactor at the Chernobyl Nuclear Power Plant in the Ukraine. A surge of power during a test of the reactor triggered an explosion and the meltdown of its core, followed by a series of devastating fires that helped to spread radioactivity across a wide swathe of the nearby area, then across much of Europe. In the immediate vicinity, the town of Pripyat was evacuated. Later still, the exclusion zone would widen to encompass a nineteen-mile area around Chernobyl, the health and well-being of millions were affected.

Hardly the stuff of TV gold, one might imagine—but HBO and UK's Sky TV came together to produce **Chernobyl**, an edge-of-the-seat account of the disaster and its aftermath. Written by Craig Mazin (whose résumé up to that point included a couple of **Hangover** and **Scary Movie** movies), the five-episode drama starred British actor Jared Harris (known to US viewers as Lane Pryce of **Mad Men**) as Valery Legasov, the man charged with leading the clean-up; Stellan Skarsgård as a Soviet minister in charge of the official response; and Emily Watson as Ulana Khomyuk, a composite character, based on various scientists researching the disaster's causes. First airing on May 6, 2019, the show brought to life not only these key public figures, but many of the private citizens whose lives were devastated by the catastrophe—among them, firemen who rushed to the scene, unaware of the deadly conditions; the locals from Pripyat watching from a distance; and various Soviet apparatchiks who exacerbated the horror with either malfeasance, lies, or both. Beyond its particularity of time and place, **Chernobyl** also served to lay bare the kinds of deception commonly perpetrated by governments to cover up their misconduct.

HBO is home to some of the most successful miniseries in television history. From Tom Hanks's **From the Earth to the Moon** to **Band of Brothers** and **The Pacific**, from **Angels in America** to **John Adams**, HBO's miniseries have often been their most elevated genre. **Chernobyl**, however, set a new bar as HBO's highest-rated miniseries. It was, for a time, IMDb's highest-rated television series of all time.

CRAIG MAZIN, Creator:

The work that we do is often the work that we're able to do. I was pre-med in college, and I'm a person with an enormous number of interests. But when it comes to Hollywood and writing feature comedy, if you're able to reliably write feature comedy and get audiences to show up, they want you to keep doing that because it's not something a lot of people do, and they need you to do it. And of course, over time you are seen for what you've done. When I had the idea to do *Chernobyl*, it didn't feel even slightly like a metamorphosis for me. The only thing I was aware of was that by that point in my career, in 2014, I'd been doing it long enough where I felt like, I'm better than the work that I've been allowed to do. I have nothing bad to say about any of it. I'm proud of all the work I've done, but there's a certain limit on what I'm allowed to do and I can do better. And the only way is to just take the bull by the horns and do something that I care about and love.

Why HBO? Simple. Because for the majority of my life, HBO has been the premier brand of television. They stand for quality, and they have a reputation for letting their creators do their best work. I had the privilege of being friends with David Benioff and Dan Weiss, prior even to *Game of Thrones*, so I was able to get a front seat to the evolution of that. I'm very close with Alec Berg and so I was able to get a perspective on HBO as well through *Curb Your Enthusiasm*, *Silicon Valley*, and then *Barry*, and I also had met Carolyn Strauss through Dan and Dave.

CAROLYN STRAUSS:

Chernobyl came about because I knew Craig socially. He came to me one day and said, "I've got an idea for something, can I pitch it to you?" I said, "Sure." It was a very good pitch.

CRAIG MAZIN:

Carolyn was the first person I went to. I was thrilled that she was on this journey with me and I love her and what a world it would be if everybody had a chance to work with Carolyn Strauss. The very first time I spoke to Carolyn about *Chernobyl*, I talked about how I wanted to essentially arrange the series and what the tone would be and what the different kinds of stories would be and who the characters were. And of course, one of them was Valery Legasov. I talked about how he committed suicide and she listened to all of it and she said, "That's how it should start. It should start with him killing himself." Now, that's not something I'd ever, ever contemplated until that point. But it was such a moment of clarity for her. That was one of the things that initially HBO was a little concerned about. I understand why— you have your hero hang himself in minute four of a five-hour show and well, maybe people aren't going to care so much about him. And her argument was always, and then the thing explodes in minute five and we're going to care about that, too. We're going to care about all of it, but that needs to be there in the beginning. Things like this where you go, I'm glad you were there. She picks her moments, but when she comes in, boy she's right.

CAROLYN STRAUSS:

We brought Craig to HBO. He made a terrific pitch there. It all worked. This was a guy who had a very clear idea of the story he wanted to tell.

He had broken it into six episodes. And then when he sat down to write the episodes, he realized that six was more time than he wanted for it. So it became five episodes.

CRAIG MAZIN:

Carolyn is the ideal television producer, because she used to be the head of programming at HBO. So she knows that network inside and out. She understands that she is both part of its DNA and a contributor to its ongoing evolution. But what Carolyn also has is this impossibly, unfortunately rare combination of just raw intelligence, a depth of decency, and a spirit that motivates and encourages creative people around her. She makes me feel good about myself and what I'm doing. She makes me better at what I do. She is wise enough to know when to say something, and when she says it, it's almost always correct. She's also wise enough to know when to take her foot off the gas pedal and just let things develop. It makes her invaluable.

RICHARD PLEPLER:

I read it, thought it was brilliant, but was worried that maybe it's a little relentless. Carolyn persuaded me that under Craig's supervision, it would feel more like solving a complicated puzzle, addressing the larger issues of transparency and leadership. As usual, she was right.

KARY ANTHOLIS:

When it was time to green-light it, Richard was skeptical of it. He made no bones about it. He said, "This could be really depressing." I responded by telling Richard the feeling I had when Craig pitched it, and Richard respected that. "Core gut connection," I think he would call it. Once I said that, he got it and was very supportive.

The folks at Sky were the likely partners, because we had an ongoing relationship with them. They were true partners in the deal and therefore maximized their investment in the project. At the end of the day, I think the overall budget on *Chernobyl* was $40 million for five episodes. Sky, for three territories—UK, Germany, and Italy—put up approximately a third of the budget, which was unprecedented. And then our international folks, our HBO Enterprise's Charles Schreger put up about a third of the budget and our program group put up about a third.

So HBO got five episodes of one of the most highly regarded projects that I've been involved with for a total of something like $13.3 million.

CRAIG MAZIN:

I was coming out of features where not only are you not left alone, but you are not in charge of the work that you do in any way. They put a director in charge of it. You are a highly paid but second-class citizen of that creative process. Then I go over to HBO, and what I'm essentially told is, "We like what your brain is doing, so make your brain do stuff."

They said, "Who do you want to direct?" And on the initial list of directors that we were looking at were a lot of the sort of names that we've heard before. I said to Carolyn, "I don't want any of these people. I want somebody that's brilliant and weird. There's no reason to be safe." Carolyn, to her credit, said, "So let's just agree not to go safe. Let's be dangerous all the time." And I said, "Amazing." We got a very different list of directors, and out of that list came Johan Renck.

CAROLYN STRAUSS:

I saw how good it would be from sitting in the auditions with Johan Renck and listening to how he spoke to the actors and what he was trying to get out of them gave me a lot of confidence. Then we started seeing the work of all the departments who were slavish about authenticity. Sometimes you have everything all lined up and it doesn't come together, but once we started seeing dailies, we realized it actually was.

Two things should be clear to virtually anyone who tunes into HBO's MA-rated, twenty-first-century drama Euphoria: *First, the title is meant to be ironic, since there's very little actual euphoria being passed around (though it is the most-pursued commodity among most of the show's characters). Second, this is a far cry from "easy" television.* Euphoria *was much more a haunting and harrowing watch than just escapist fluff. The series delivered a solid punch to the gut from its first outing on June 16, 2019.*

*When HBO hosted the show's premiere at Hollywood's Cinerama Dome, the show's creator, Sam Levinson, thirty-four, son of Oscar-winning director Barry Levinson (*Diner, Rain Man, Good Morning, Vietnam, *etc.) told the invited audience, "Sometime around the age of sixteen, I resigned myself to the idea that eventually drugs would kill me."*

Fortunately, Levinson proved hard for even drugs to kill, and brought his oversized resilience to the show, an adaptation of an Israeli production that takes an unrelenting look at teenagers running amok in the dark world of adolescent angst. It's a world that reflects the sheer hell of being seventeen—the result of sexual, chemical, or social anxiety, or just being determined to escape the difficult feelings of that particular age and finding, perhaps, that there is no morally acceptable escape.

From early in his life, Levinson spent years moving from hospitals to rehabs to halfway houses and back to hospitals (a psych ward set on the show mirrors the one he was checked into at the age of eleven) before snaring that bright elusive butterfly that addicts know as "sobriety." It may sound simple to those who have never faced the challenge, but it is intensely and dauntingly complicated, as viewers who dare to watch **Euphoria** *quickly discover.*

Levinson's boldness and transparency in drawing from his own life so impressed HBO programming chief Casey Bloys that he approved Levinson's request to write all the initial episodes himself, a rare arrangement. Levinson was also able to borrow from his actors' real lives—among them, model/actor Hunter Schafer's experiences as reflected in the ordeals of Jules Vaughn, a transgender girl whose arrival in town sets the series, and the other characters, in motion. Colman Domingo (Joseph Rivers in **If Beale Street Could Talk** *and Victor Strand in AMC's pulpy* **Fear the Walking Dead***) plays Ali, a wise yet troubled speaker at Narcotics Anonymous meetings. Heartthrob Jacob Elordi (of* **Kissing Booth** *fame) plays Nate Jacobs, a clever inversion of the macho high school jock. Maude Apatow, daughter of Leslie Mann and Judd Apatow, plays the uncommonly levelheaded Lexi Howard.*

But the focus of the narrative is always Rue Bennett, the central character played by Zendaya, an American actor and singer who previously played the decidedly different Rocky Blue in the Disney sitcom, **Shake It Up!** *and who is described in the series' synopsis as a "lying, drug-addicted 17-year-old." Rue compellingly narrates the disturbing action, which in the first episode involved statutory rape, with an authenticity that seems beyond her years. Later installments do not turn away from such unsettling topics as sexual exploitation, drugs, unwanted pregnancies, and physical violence.*

Euphoria was HBO's first-ever scripted series about teenagers and addiction—a glimpse into the post-millennials' pursuit of happiness. Its unrelenting humanism and vividness could never appear uncensored on broadcast or even basic cable TV. That used to be good enough for HBO, but given the new competitive streaming landscape, its singular voice helped make it unmistakably, and irrefutably, HBO.

SAM LEVINSON, Creator:

Christine Kim and Francesca Orsi gave me the original *Euphoria* to watch. I laughed as I was watching it. There were aspects to it that I liked. It was very raw. It was a tough show in many ways.

FRANCESCA ORSI:

Christine Kim, my former assistant, who was promoted to being an executive in the Drama department, has great taste in writers. We had an open writing assignment which was an Israeli format we wanted to adapt into English for a US audience. I charged her with reading a ton of material and putting together a list of fresh voices for the adaptation. Within six weeks, she put Sam's script *Assassination Nation* in front of me. I read it and loved the clever way his mind worked on the page. I called his agent and Christine and I met with him. I said, "Let's talk about *Euphoria*. What would you do differently from the Israeli show?" He went completely off book and started talking about his life and his struggles with addiction and a renewed life of sobriety.

SAM LEVINSON:

I struggled with drug addiction when I was younger, so I was talking about that, what our struggles were growing up and a little bit about the Israeli show. I said, "How closely do I have to stick to it?" She told me, "Just write what we just talked about."

FRANCESCA ORSI:

His experience was so powerful and emotional that I hired him on the spot. While I encouraged him to use the Israeli series as a jumping off point, I asked him to look inward and write what he knew and went through. Ultimately, Sam put Rue at the center of the show, and then Jules, who is also a version of Sam. You find Sam's spirit and his struggle not only with addiction, but with life itself in every character that we meet in *Euphoria*.

KATHLEEN McCAFFREY:

I sometimes compare Lena and *Girls* with Sam and *Euphoria*. Sam's voice is truly a product of his own experiences. *Euphoria* is Sam talking about himself.

SAM LEVINSON:

The way that it's written and the way that it's shot is about creating a feeling in the audience as opposed to it being a study of depression or addiction. I wanted to explore that disconnect between the person you are and the person you want to be. It's hard for nonaddicts to understand the amount of guilt that an addict carries.

ZENDAYA, Actor:

I think the coolest part of HBO is just like the level of quality work that they continue to put out and always have. My parents have watched HBO shows ever since I can remember. To be part of the family is a really special thing. They trusted Sam to create this, they care about their artists. And they trusted Sam with this sometimes very out there show and allowed us to make it and do it in a beautiful way.

It was a safer place for something like that to be. I did want to be somewhat responsible, understanding my demographic. Most people know what they're getting into when they watch an HBO show. It's really cool. They've always been very creatively supportive. I think the coolest part is being young artists, being able to have such a positive relationship with the people that you get to work with. Usually, it's not always so welcoming or it's intimidating, or they don't hear you out. But they've always heard me out and allowed me to be creative in my own way. And you couldn't want anything more in a collaborator in that sense. It's a great home.

HUNTER SCHAFER, Actor:

Euphoria is my first acting project. I had no plan to act. I was modeling, to be in close vicinity to the fashion industry, and to make a little money before college. My modeling agency sent through this audition that I had seen floating around on Instagram, they said, "They want to bring you in for this." It snowballed from there, and six auditions later, I was in an auditorium room performing for a bunch of HBO execs. I found out later that day that I got the role, and that I wasn't going to keep modeling or go to college, at least for the time being. I don't think I could have predicted how much it would change my life. Acting came as a surprise.

COLMAN DOMINGO, Actor:

It was opening night of the film *Birth of a Nation* at Sundance. I went downstairs at this after-party, and in the corner was a guy who said, "Oh my God, Colman. I loved your film." Next thing you know, we're talking for two hours straight. That was Sam Levinson. I immediately felt like I had met my soul brother, someone whose mind was as interesting as anyone I'd ever met. We said to each other, "Hey, I want to create with you." We didn't even know in what capacity because we're both hybrids and we do everything.

Then he sent me *Assassination Nation*, in which he created the principal role for me. Then he created the role of Ali for me in *Eurphoria*. And he told me all about Ali and his life, which is based on a few different sponsors, and he said, "Colman, I think you're the only person I know who could deliver the language that I believe I have for him."

SAM LEVINSON:

I've never managed a writers' room before. That idea is very nerve-racking to me because I also don't structure things, I don't like to sit down and outline everything. The show itself doesn't lend itself to that. It's unpredictable and it's sort of stream of consciousness. After they read the pilot, I came to

LA and sat down and talked to Casey. I just said, "Look, I'd love to just write the whole season and not have a writers' room. I think it would just be a lot easier and something that I can definitely do." They never questioned that aspect. They said, How about this? We'll order three more episodes. Go write those and then we'll talk again. I went back and wrote three episodes, turned it back in, and then we were good to go.

FRANCESCA ORSI:

Sam hasn't been on drugs for a long time, but he put that addictive, sort of manic sensibility into his work instead. He wears every hat across production. He directs episodes, writes everything himself, and while other directors post after they're done shooting, Sam is in editorial, simultaneously during production. I'm not sure how he does it, but he raises the bar every time and delivers exponentially.

CASEY BLOYS:

If there's anybody who can write and direct everything, it's Sam. I told him, "You've got to get another director just to give your family a break. You gotta at least go home for a week and shower." It's his addict personality, but thankfully he's gotten clean and so now the show is his drug. That's all he thinks about and all he does.

COLMAN DOMINGO:

I look at Sam as sort of a Shakespeare. I think he makes your language feel like you would say it. He listens a lot to his artists. He listens to speech patterns and colloquialisms, regional dialects. And I think he leans into it. The fact that he wrote Ali from South Philly. He knows that I'm from West Philly. It wasn't so far away for me.

ZENDAYA:

The first day I remember being really, really nervous. I think it was because I hadn't done anything like this before, and I was worried about sucking. For some reason I was feeling insecure about it, and I went up to him and I was like, "Hey, I just want you to please tell me if I'm not good. If I'm not, I can handle it, like I'm pretty tough. Just keep it straight up with me if I suck." And he's like, "Listen, if you suck, I'll tell you. But I'm not worried about you." He always says that to me, and even now he's always like, "Z, I'm not worried about you."

HUNTER SCHAFER:

All of the cast had deep talks with Sam even before we started filming. Part of his writing process is to intertwine the actor into the character. It's an intimate process. Everyone was cast for specific reasons regarding what they've been through, what they could contribute to the character. Jules has a scene in episode seven of season one, where she's talking in bed with a character named Anna. It's the first time we get to hear her talk about gender and sexuality in this casual way. I had told Sam a story about how in middle school I had saved up $20 to go to Sears and buy myself a pair of the cheapest heels I could find. I snuck them to school in my backpack and walked around in them the whole day and snuck them back home. That story helped inform how I inhabit her.

ZENDAYA:

In the beginning, we didn't know each other, but he trusted me enough to think that I could do it. I think that made *me* trust *him*. I knew from just reading the work that he was obviously extremely talented, and when we first started doing the show together, he was so open and honest with me. And he's never let me down. He's pulled the best out of me and continues to do so. I'm very lucky that he saw something in me, we've kept getting closer and closer.

SAM LEVINSON:

It was a rocky road when the show first came out because I think HBO took an enormous risk on this show, and I think we were pushing the envelope in many ways. There were a couple of early reviews that were asking, "What is this thing?" No one knew what was going to happen. There was a little bit of hesitation and trepidation there. After the first couple of weeks when it started to set in and you saw that people were genuinely moved by it and moved by the performances and the content of it, we got past some of the more salacious aspects of it. It was a major, major relief.

HUNTER SCHAFER:

Any scene that requires me to be emotional has been challenging. I think I've got the hang of it now, but especially at first it was really difficult. Navigating your brain that way is completely opposite to how we've been taught to navigate our brains to handle our emotions, for most of my life. Just understanding how to do that, how to use those muscles in your brain, it's a terrifying and exposing process.

SAM LEVINSON:

I try to search for a feeling of surprise in every scene and try to push every actor and our DPs to do something to surprise me as well. I can think specifically of that scene in episode two with Zendaya and Nika [King] where they're fighting in the hallway. In the script, it was a simple description: Rue and Leslie fight in the hallway. We were about forty days into shooting, and I thought, "We don't improvise enough. We should improvise a scene today." So I just said to Nika, "Whatever you do, do not let Rue leave this fucking house. If she leaves this house, she's going to OD and die." And I said to Z, "Whatever she does, do not let her keep you in this fucking house." And they started to go for it. I threw things out at them, and they tapped into this thing when Nika sort of pinned Z on the ground, and there was something about getting pinned down that made Z explode. She started screaming and fighting back. Then she got up, and without this being planned, she hit a painting on the wall, it fell on the ground, and smashed apart. Z looked down at the shards of glass, picked one up, and went toward her mother. Our first AD was beside herself, came on to the set, and said, "Whoa, whoa, put the glass down."

It was one of those moments where she was so inside of it that she just did what a true drug addict would do in that situation. And there was something so disturbing about that impulse to pick up the broken piece of glass and charge at her mother that I felt physically ill, because it mirrored some of the experiences I had had when I was younger and on drugs. It hit a chord deep in me, and brought up some memory that I wasn't prepared to deal with that day. We called cut, and there was about thirty seconds where everyone was just standing around silent. Then I walked off the set, for the first time ever, went up to the office, closed the door, and burst into tears.

ZENDAYA:

Sam is honest with me. He'll come up to me if it sucks. He'll be like, "Nah, that wasn't it. Wasn't your best, you know?" And that honesty, I think it's respected both ways. I'm honest with him. If there's a scene I don't like, or if there's something I don't agree with, we'll sit there and we'll discuss and we'll talk about it. And he always listens, and I think he's that way with most people, not just me. He is collaborative, which is very rare for someone to be like, the only writer, the director, and whatever, but also to be so open to collaboration and other people's perspectives on things. He's a very special person.

HUNTER SCHAFER:

I am mindful of the fact that my character is a point of entry into trans identity for a lot of people. It affects how we talk about the character. I also try to counter it. I think one of the most effective decisions we made in season one was to just have Jules be a young girl with a trans identity, just existing. A lot of trans characters in media get tokenized, and their transness becomes their character. That's not only inaccurate and dumb, but I don't think it makes good TV. I think part of our success is not thinking about it and just letting her exist as a fully fledged human.

When I got involved in the writing process for the special episode, it was on my mind. I had a rough quarantine. I was just coming out on the other side of the rough stuff and hadn't processed everything. I'm so thankful for that special episode because it involved delving back into everything that I was trying to move past. It was cathartic in that way.

ZENDAYA:

I learned a lot. I think I learned how not to be entirely governed by fear when it comes to not just making decisions but trying things. I think I'm one of those people who doesn't try new things because I'm very afraid of not being good at them and not being good quickly. I think in order to be a good storyteller, you can't be afraid of your emotions. And you can't be afraid of looking crazy or looking dumb or whatever the case may be. I think for me, I always often associated emotional vulnerability with a weakness or something to that effect. But I think *Euphoria* has allowed me to be a much more emotionally open person, which sometimes is a bit scary for a lot of reasons.

It's also taught me a lot about understanding and empathy for people and their lives and their stories. I've learned so much about the true struggles of addiction, what it does to people, families, relationships. I think that's a beautiful thing about Sam's work with *Euphoria*, it's allowing people to have empathy and humanizing addiction in a sense, or in a way that I think it hasn't been done before. So people understand that it's an illness, it's a disease, and I think we've been taught to villainize people who suffer from addiction.

CASEY BLOYS:

On every single show I've had people tell me why it wasn't going to work. Every single one, including, *Euphoria* and *Succession*. Everybody has opinions, everybody will share them, and people will tell you, This isn't good, this isn't gonna work. And then you have people saying, Oh, this is really good. So you try to listen to everybody and get a sense of where we're going to fall.

Euphoria was interesting because we wanted to do something younger skewing. We'd never done anything with teens. The big differentiator here was yes, it was about teens, but it was about addiction. While it was racy, you can't argue with the filmmaking, the acting, the production value, direction, all of that. It may not be for you but it's really well done. The people who got it, they loved it. And for people who had reservations, they also acknowledge, Yeah, it's really well done. That's what you always have to do is make sure if you're taking a swing, know why you're doing it.

FRANCESCA ORSI:

At the premiere, Sam spoke about his experience, and everybody was moved by his honesty and soulfulness. Zendaya was sitting right behind me with her family and after the screening, the screen went to black and we just high-fived. She is such a beautiful spirit, who has that beautiful mix of effervescence and accessibility yet there's also something about her that's totally unknowable.

Sam's mom came up to me at the premiere, and said, "Thank you for being his other mother through all of this." I laughed and was like, "No problem. Thank you for encouraging him to write everything down when he was eleven years old and stuck in a psychiatric institute."

SAM LEVINSON:

I try not to get caught up in any victory laps. I'm just relieved that people would respond to it.

If reviews were cautious at the onset, by season's end, they were rapturous. Accolades were not far behind: Zendaya, at just twenty-four years old, took home the Emmy that year in the crowded category of Best Lead Actress in a Drama.

ZENDAYA:

Incredible. I didn't know that it would happen. It wasn't expected, but so special. I think the coolest thing was just being able to have my family around and also just being able to win an award is crazy, but being able to do it for something I'm so proud of and I'm so grateful came into my life and for a character that I love so much and to have done it with people who I value and respect, like the first person I called was Sam when I won. I FaceTimed him, Emmy in hand. Everybody was crying. I'm just so lucky.

COLMAN DOMINGO:

Every person with a teenage kid needs to see the show. Because they still want to engage in the lie that their children won't have to deal with any of this. They believe it won't be their child, and the idea that it could be is too terrifying for them. That's why some adults don't feel they can watch the show with their teenagers, because the show is honest and lays out everything bare. There is collective terror in America. We are afraid to look at ourselves.

On October 20, 2019, HBO premiered **Watchmen**, *its nine-episode drama based on the comic books of the same name by Alan Moore and Dave Gibbons. The HBO series was created by Damon Lindelof (the former showrunner for* **Lost***, among others) and was, in essence, a continuation of the comic book series thirty-four years after its timeline had ended. This version begins with the Tulsa massacre of 1921, an abomination in which a thriving Black community—Greenwood, known then as the Black Wall Street—was violently set upon by a white mob, leaving hundreds dead and Greenwood in ruins. The long opening scene of* **Watchmen***, filmed in Georgia in 2018 on the actual anniversary of the two-day massacre, re-created the brutality in intense detail; two hundred actors were involved in what proved to be a tour de force of production organization.*

The result was a critical hit and a show that caught the cultural moment. It garnered twenty-six Primetime Emmy nominations—more than any other show—and served as a powerful counterpoint to then president Donald Trump's incendiary visit to Tulsa in 2020, a trip that served only to inflame racial tensions, especially given the timing (he'd originally planned his rally to coincide with Juneteenth until even **he** *realized such a thing was too insensitive).*

For HBO, **Watchmen** *was a departure. "Comic book shows," for want of a better phrase, hadn't been on their radar. But Lindelof's take on this legendary graphic novel, and the way he commented on the issue of race in America, felt like a positive expansion of what an HBO show could be. Lindelof is considered one of the deepest thinkers in television for the way he can synthesize large cultural forces and ideas and turn them into entertaining TV—no mean feat. Sometimes what a creator is trying to do versus how it lands doesn't always connect, but in the case of* **Watchmen***, reviewers and viewers alike seemed to understand Lindelof's use of the source material, why it was important, and how he had been able to pivot and do something different with it, all in order to create a show that managed to force the Greenwood story onto Oklahoma's school curriculum for the first time.*

DAMON LINDELOF:

Memory is a strange thing, but there were two things that were happening simultaneously in the early parts of 2017, following the end of *The*

Leftovers. The first was I was doing a deep dive on self-educating as it related to racial inequality, which was always something that I was interested in academically, but now I was becoming deeply, emotionally affected by it. And that started with me reading this book by Ta-Nehisi Coates called *Between the World and Me*, which everybody in Los Angeles was reading. I was like, I need to read this so that I can show people how woke I am. But then I read it. I felt like I was seeing the world in an entirely different way.

I fell in love with his writing and the emotional power of it. I started devouring everything that he wrote, including an astonishing piece of writing that mentioned Black Wall Street, and he might've called it the Tulsa race riot or the Tulsa massacre. It was one paragraph in that article. I was like, Wait a minute. How could that have happened, and I don't know about it? It seems like it's a big deal. I can't be reading this right. There was this sort of enclave of Black wealth in Oklahoma in 1921. I went on Amazon and I bought a book called *The Burning* and it's all about the Tulsa massacre.

I read it cover to cover over the course of a couple of days. I now feel compelled to make sure that everybody in the world knows about the Tulsa massacre and also understanding that I'm a white Jew in Hollywood, and probably not the right person to tell that story.

How in God's name am I going to do it in a way that it will stick? Because if you just make a documentary about it, no one's going to watch the thing. At the same time that this was happening, HBO came to me the third time— they'd come to me previously, it was a full-court press. It was Casey and Francesca, saying, "Do you want to do *Watchmen* as a TV show? You can do whatever you want with it." Then I thought, "If I'm going to do *Watchmen*, I need to do something important with it."

Watchmen goes places that Batman, Superman, Spider-Man, and the Avengers can never go. Could it hold something like Tulsa? I think it can. So one of the very first things that I said to Casey, Francesca, and Nora Skinner when we met was that I felt like the Tulsa massacre was an important part of the story. I saw it as Krypton. I saw it as an origin story for a superhero because Krypton was about the destruction of a world. Superman was an orphan of that world. What if we did that? What if we told the story of the first Black superhero who nobody knew was Black? Because if he revealed his true self in the late 1930s or 1940s, he'd be murdered. They really responded to that idea.

REGINA KING:

I've always wanted to play a superhero. Even if she's one without superpowers, she's still heroic. When I read the pilot, I was blown away; there seemed to be so many different genres happening just in that pilot.

By the time I'm on page two or three, I was like, Oh my gosh, Damon, is this Black Wall Street? And I read further and I'm like, Oh my gosh, it is. I would say it was a pleasant surprise that this was a story that had been pretty much taken out of history here. Damon was actually exploring it. I didn't know how far he was going to go or what that connection was going to be. And that made it even more intriguing, that by the time I finished that episode, I just wanted to know where everything was going.

I'm of the generation that has been around since HBO first started. And one thing that has always been a constant is that HBO has always been this place where you go for groundbreaking new content, content that goes beyond what you would see on the big four networks. And stories that were just not your typical story. HBO has always been known for fearless story-telling. I think the first thing I did on HBO was *If These Walls Could Talk*, so every time I've had the opportunity to be a part of a project that was an HBO project, it's always felt special.

DAMON LINDELOF:

I was scared pretty much the whole time I was making the show, but I was also compelled, and confident. It seems paradoxical, but those things were true. I felt so passionate about the material, but also was very unclear as to whether or not it was working. I took a step back and I started feeling more like a curator who was hanging other people's art in the museum versus needing to generate all the art myself, then I started falling for the show. It felt like it wasn't mine. I was very worried about how the audience, particularly the African American audience, was going to process what we were up to.

LILA BYOCK:

The writers' room was about half Black and half white. Damon wanted to have a couple of writers who he had worked with before, who trusted him and could give him the benefit of the doubt as he felt his way into the material. There were times when it was fraught, but we all learned to trust each other and respect each other's points of view, even when we disagreed or saw things differently.

REGINA KING:

There was never a scene or a moment that did not feel to all of us—and when I say all of us, the entire crew and cast—that we were doing something different. That we were doing something that we haven't seen before. And that's hard to do in 2019.

DAMON LINDELOF:

The first time that we showed the pilot publicly was at the New York Comic Con in October 2019. I was also very concerned about how the fans of *Watchmen*, who are very protective of this material, would react. When we showed the pilot and then brought the cast out on the stage and answered questions for about an hour, I started to feel like, Oh, okay, at least the pilot's going to work and it's provocative without feeling exploitative.

CASEY BLOYS:

We tried to make it so you didn't have to have read *Watchmen* to understand it. It certainly helps, but the idea was if you didn't, you could watch it. I don't know if people would be able to figure it out, but Damon is a brilliant writer and the cast is amazing. I was extremely happy with how well it was received. We knew it was good, but you never know.

DAMON LINDELOF:

The great thing about genre is, it's a Trojan horse inside this superhero story where half of the episode is about racial injustice and white supremacy. And the other half is Jeremy Irons, murdering a bunch of clones and launching them from a catapult, that the idea of mixing and matching those was always in the alchemy of the show.

REGINA KING:

We were all bracing ourselves, because we knew people were going to either be like, "What the fuck?" Or, "What the fuck, I can't wait to see more." You hope for a positive response, but I would say I was not prepared. I know as I got the scripts each week, I felt like the latter: What the fuck, I can't wait to see more. That's just how I felt. And Damon was very smart, and a lot of showrunners do this in not revealing the entire arc of the show. I think while as an actor, sometimes it is a little bit frustrating because you don't want to miss a moment that you could have had, that if you knew where you were going, you might've planted something early on. But real life doesn't work that way.

DAMON LINDELOF:

It wasn't until the show's afterlife—the last episode aired before Christmas—that there's this whole other thing that started to happen post pandemic, where people were discovering the show for the first time, or they were reflecting on the show that they had just seen. And that was the moment where it felt like I started hearing that the show was prescient or that the show was of the time and of the moment, which was always something that we were aiming for. I think that anybody who's living in America when we were writing the show in 2017 or 2018, where it's like the big sort of tension in America, the big anxiety, no matter who you are, what you look like, race, especially in a post-Trump world is crazy. I don't think that my work can ever not be reflective of my eyes being wide open. Now I'm too afraid of going back to sleep. I'm pretty sure they want there to be more *Watchmen*. I told them I only wanted to do one and they were totally cool with it.

I never looked at the show as being prescient or predictive. In fact, Yahya probably put it best. They asked him if he thought, "Isn't it amazing how prescient *Watchmen* was?" He just said, "I think the show maybe is fifty years too late."

DAVID SIMON:

2016. Trump is elected. I'm having lunch with Richard Plepler and Casey Bloys, right after the election. And they're talking: What can you program now that can get to the heart of this, that we've achieved this completely dystopian political structure that could give this man the presidency?

I said, "Whoever still has the rights to *The Plot Against America*, you should get that book because among all the dystopian, American political novels, it's probably the best for this moment." I wasn't even thinking of myself. I had met with them about *Deuce* and some other stuff. I had enough on my plate. I was being a good lunch partner. I wasn't trying to sell.

RICHARD PLEPLER:

David and I went to lunch at the Lambs Club. He said, "I want to adapt *The Plot Against America*." I asked, "Have you talked to Roth?" He said, "As a matter of fact, I have. And he loves the idea." I said, "Well, we should absolutely do it." And in David's extraordinary hands, *Plot* proved both incredibly timely and deeply engaging.

The Wire *and* **The Deuce** *had been in-depth examinations of cities and of the porn industry, respectively. The appeal for HBO of having David Simon work on* **The Plot**

Against America *was that it gave him a much broader tale to tell with even bigger* *stakes.* **Plot** *took place on a vast historical canvas, a Philip Roth canvas no less. And* *because it was Simon, HBO was content to let him wreak all the havoc he wanted.*

JOHN TURTURRO:

I'm a big historian. I taught American history as a substitute. It's not my favorite Philip Roth book, but I do think it was a brilliant idea.

DAVID SIMON:

I said, "Look, we're going to just do the book and we're going to expand the POV to the six characters instead of having it be the kid thinking back, because that doesn't work." I had a conversation with Roth and I went to see him to discuss the project. He very readily saw that we should expand the POV to everyone in the family, that we could cover more ground that way. Film-wise, he got that right away. Then I pointed up sort of the problem of Lindbergh disappearing so abruptly, and without explanation.

"You made it work in the novel. I'm not sure if I make people watch six hours that's going to be satisfying enough." I didn't volunteer what I was thinking about, I didn't have the guts. So I sat across the room and he actually went to his pages and he reread the book at that point where Lindbergh disappears. He read it twice. I felt like I was sitting in front of them for, I don't know, eight hours. Then he just sort of snapped the book shut. He looked at me and he said, "It's your problem now." I took that as permission that I can at least try to do something different, which I thought was my plan.

I went away to write the scripts. Then he died. He'd given me permission at least to play around.

JOHN TURTURRO:

I wished Lindbergh's character would have been bigger in the book and in the series. That was the crux of it for me. The person who was this American hero and was, like most of the country, isolationist. It was a different time. It was like when the white Anglo-Saxon Protestant was king.

DAVID SIMON:

I'm so indifferent to the audience. It's unacceptable to be this indifferent to the audience and it's an incredible luxury that comes from having worked for HBO for twenty years. I'm overtly political, I'm left of center, but I'm not left enough for some people. I was a reporter for too long to ever buy the idea that a single ideology solves every problem. There are things where I'm like, No, actually, you need the police to do that. Or actually no, that won't work. Or, money will not solve that. There are moments where I fall off the perfect lefty version.

I have such affection for what we've all been through in twenty years that, I said to them after *Treme*, "Look, if we never do anything else, I see you come down the street. I'm crossing the street to give you a bear hug because of what we did. I never gave you an audience, and you just kept throwing money in the kitty." So shit, it's probably half as much. It's more than half. It's almost more than half a billion dollars in production, probably somewhere at $700 million of production, to a guy who was a police reporter from Baltimore. And I realize they didn't do it all at once. But somehow down the road, I'm still standing there. If it ends tomorrow, thank you, what a ride. I'm supposed to be such a son of a bitch to deal with, that's like my external . . . and I play that game. Externally, I'm a raging lunatic on Twitter who can't stop cursing. Obviously I'm not lighting fire to shit at every opportunity, and they figured that out.

ILENE LANDRESS:

I thought the second season [of *Succession*] just picked right up and went crazy. It was great. The first season was sort of slow to find its footing, but then it took off. Then season two started at a breakneck speed, almost like everything happens too fast.

Sometimes, shows don't have time to breathe and that's not a criticism of Jesse's writing. That's a criticism more of the times we live in now, which is that nothing gets to play itself out over time. Everything is edited at this breakneck speed based on the way people are viewing shows and not savoring the moment. When you're watching one [show] a week, you're actually savoring the moments because you're not getting one for another week (although I feel like more and more people stack episodes up and then binge them). I love the characters Jesse created, that world he brings us into, and the performances are amazing. *Succession* is a show that you don't want to rush your way through. You want to take advantage of those moments to breathe.

BRIAN COX:

There are people who will get Logan, and get him well, especially in the current crisis with this idiot president [Trump] and the Murdochs. They are not to be heralded in any way, shape, or form. Certainly I'm not expecting any

Emmy celebrations for Logan Roy. As long as they're good to the series, that's is the main thing.

As HBO and others had hoped, Paolo Sorrentino hadn't quite emptied his Catholicism tank with The Young Pope, *and so on January 13, 2020, a second season began, this one titled* The New Pope, *in which Jude Law was discovered lying on a hospital bed in a coma. Once again the specificity of the Vatican world and its key characters, led by a wicked performance from Silvio Orlando as Cardinal Voiello, took us behind the scenes to observe the politicking that brought about the arrival of Law's successor. Taking a page from John Paul I's short-lived papacy, the show blasts off in episode two with the arrival of John Malkovich as the quixotic Sir John Brannox, being seduced to become the next pope. Malkovich was a stunning casting decision—soulful, sardonic, even teasingly sexual. And, luckily for all, Cécile de France was on hand to elevate, shall we say, everything. Sorrentino brought forth a visually stunning drama filled with multi-dimensional religion and innumerable insights into our entire world.*

PAOLO SORRENTINO:

The idea was to do just the one limited series, but during the editing of *The Young Pope*, there were terroristic attacks in France and other places. It was a very dark moment for Europe. I wondered how the Vatican could manage a situation in which Islamic jihad brings straightforward danger to the Vatican. That was the idea that started the development of a second season.

I was a big, big fan of John Malkovich. Of course, he's a great actor, but at the same time, he's iconic. I was looking for a pope that was iconic. With Malkovich, I wouldn't need to convince them as I did with Jude Law. After my producer spoke with his agent, Malkovich was very kind to call me, and a few days later, he stayed at my house for two days. It was wonderful.

JOHN MALKOVICH:

I don't normally speak of my alleged career or think about it, for that matter, but I'd gone through a period where I mostly was getting my own work or working with a couple of Hollywood producers I often worked with. And that was about it. When I went with my now agents Brent Morley and Brandt Joel, they talked about some of the directors I should be working with, and Paolo was one of the first ones from that conversation who I got to meet. I was told that he was going to make a second year of *The Young Pope*, do another year of that series or based on that series. And that sounded excellent. I'd seen the first season, and liked it very much. I had always loved his work. I thought just the credit sequence of *La Grande Bellezza* is better than 99 percent of films made in the last thirty years. I was very pleased to go meet him, which I did, and had a very good time speaking with him about his plans for *The New Pope*. We had a very wide-ranging conversation over this day and night and part of the next day.

PAOLO SORRENTINO:

We spoke for two days, all the time. It was very, very funny and interesting spending time with him. He is a very thoughtful, smart, and wise man. He was perfect. In fact, after our meeting, I decided to change some things of the character, following the real John Malkovich. So I decided that he was a noble, that he belonged to an important English family. I decided to steal some things from John, and to put it inside. How he takes a seat, how he faces the food, how he likes to stay on the couch. John Malkovich is different from all of us. He has a style, you know? And so all the time I thought, Okay, I will do that. I will rewrite this. I will rewrite that.

JOHN MALKOVICH:

John Brannox is someone who Paolo created, I think, a terrific backstory for, and a very unique one, which I think he told very well, both visually and in language. I think he made a very strong character choice and I think Paolo thinks and writes very well. That doesn't always go with the visual talent.

There is the line I wrote once, "The one thing I know about power is the good never seek it." I think I'm pretty comfortable staying with that observation.

I think Brannox in Paolo's mind is probably not so far removed from that notion that there are things he should like about power, which in fact he may not care about at all. Of course there are things people like about power that another may not like at all.

On March 22, 2020, the season ten finale of **Curb Your Enthusiasm**, *aired on HBO.*

LARRY DAVID:

I never liked the audience to be too on top of it. I liked them to be surprised, if possible. I'm sure that the average person watching the show, they just enjoy the scene and they forget about it and go on to the next one.

I'm a much cooler person on the show than I am in life by far. It's fun to behave in that way where you don't care what anybody thinks or says.

SUSIE ESSMAN:

There are a couple of reasons that Susie is thought of sympathetically. Number one, Larry always provoked her. She's usually provoked. She's not just screaming, yelling, for no reason. He steals her kid's doll head, he gets her kid drunk. He gets us kicked out of the country clubs. There's always a reason. And she's usually right. And the other thing is that we have this relationship that's developed over the past eleven seasons where we always forgive one another. We'll be yelling, screaming, and the next day, "Hey Larry, want to come to a dinner party?" We're almost like siblings. It's the way that we behave to each other. We're at each other's throat and we're yelling and screaming. And then the next day all is forgiven. And we're all family again. We're family, that's what it is. We're family. I got this job, I got this part, it's been going on now for twenty-one years. Twenty-one fucking years.

TED DANSON:

One evening, we were all out to dinner and Mary turned to Larry and said, "If I were ever in trouble, real trouble, you would be one of the first people I would call." It almost put tears in his eyes, he was so moved by that. And it was true.

Larry can be the most socially selfish, awkward, excruciatingly embarrassing human being. Like you show up to dinner and he's already halfway through his entrée because he's changed his mind and wants to do something else, or he refuses to go to other people's houses for dinner because he feels trapped. But at the same time, he has this astounding heart, and you can't help but delight in being around him.

As a species, documentaries were not only as prestigious as ever, they were also more essential than ever. It was clear the audience loved them (contrary to what the old broadcast networks had long insisted), and now, with competition on the increase, HBO had to marshal its forces and seek out its favorite filmmakers for projects—along with talents new to the genre who could help HBO maintain its formidable dominance.

Over the two days of July 9 and 10, 2019, HBO aired the Erin Lee Carr documentary I Love You, Now Die: The Commonwealth v Michelle Carter.

ERIN LEE CARR:

The Michelle Carter case is about two young people, an eighteen-year-old named Conrad Roy and a seventeen-year-old named Michelle Carter, who had a semi off and on again, romantic relationship. Conrad was somebody who was suicidal; he had mental health issues and instead of seeking help for Conrad, the young teen Michelle began to push him into suicide. It became one of those cases that captivated the nation: What are you responsible in terms of another person's mental health?

We would talk a lot about Michelle's culpability, because there was a high level of blame on Michelle, and Conrad was definitely cast as a victim. People were so angry at Conrad's death, and it was important to work with an executive, in this case, Sheila, who wanted to look into both of them objectively. Sheila didn't want to play out old stereotypes. She often talks in riddles. I have these incredible emails from her. You have to decode what she's trying to say to you.

Here, for example, is a classic Nevins email to Erin:

I just returned
To Michelle
Will screen tomorrow Monday
So sorry to delay
Away

All you do
Is
Better Than Better
Our Star
Sheila xxxx

ERIN LEE CARR:

The other day a guy from the Emmys was interviewing me and he said that he, after watching the show, crawled up into a fetal position and had to watch an episode of *SpongeBob SquarePants* to cleanse his palette. And I was like, I've made it. This is why we're making cinema.

Since its opening in 1914, Harlem's Apollo Theater has served not just as an artistic venue, but as a cultural meeting place. A stage with a rich and storied history in the Black community, the theater has played host to a miles-long laundry list of the world's biggest musical talents, including James Brown, Ella Fitzgerald, Billie Holiday, Sammy Davis Jr., Dionne Warwick, Miles Davis, Jimi Hendrix, Aretha Franklin, Marvin Gaye, the Supremes, Louis Armstrong, Ray Charles, Stevie Wonder, B. B. King, John Lennon, Paul McCartney, Bob Marley, Tony Bennett, and the Artist Formerly Known as Prince, to name just a few. Apollo crowds were known as much for their contempt toward bad acts as for their affection toward good ones, famously dismantling subpar performers during Amateur Night competitions. **Showtime at the Apollo,** *a television variety show shot on location at the theater, first aired in 1955. Even President Barack Obama performed once, delivering a heartfelt line from Al Green's "Let's Stay Together" on the Apollo stage in 2012.*

On November 6, 2019, HBO premiered a documentary on the theater titled simply, **The Apollo.** *Directed by Roger Ross Williams, the film explores the storied artistic history of the theater, intercut with archival footage of its biggest moments and interviews with A-listers who have appeared on the stage, including Jamie Foxx and Pharrell Williams. It documented historic performances intermixed with commentary on police brutality and racism in America. The movie, which received mostly positive reviews, won Outstanding Documentary at the 2020 Emmy Awards.*

ROGER ROSS WILLIAMS:

The Apollo was bankrupt and abandoned, and it had sewage in the basement. And a lot of those archives were destroyed until Percy Sutton came in and cleaned it up. There was a famous story that there's a river that runs underneath the Apollo Theater, and there was water pouring into the basement. It was a mess. We had to dig through people's basements and Lisa Cortes, the producer, went to various people's basements, people like Pigmeat Markham, who was a comedian who performed at the Apollo, and Jerry Kupfer who produced *Showtime at the Apollo,* literally in Jerry's basement pulling old, moldy, three-quarter-inch tapes. So it's a search.

As I dug into what was happening in Harlem—thirties, forties, fifties—every few years there was a shooting of an unarmed Black man from the day it opened till today. It's obviously still happening. There was rioting, it was like the same story over and over and over. And so the political became the sort of spine of the film. And within it, what's interesting is that now, out of that is born the *Between the World and Me* HBO special that I am producing. We have just wrapped on shooting this sort of phenomenal event for HBO, with Oprah and Angela Bassett and Courtney B. Vance and Mahershala Ali and Mj Rodriguez and Angela Davis and Alicia Garza.

The first person I actually talked to about this was actually Sara Bernstein. We went to lunch and I was excited about Ta-Nehisi and she said, "Oh my God." Sheila and Sara had had a meeting with Ta-Nehisi and they were looking to do something with Ta-Nehisi and he's just a phenomenal intellectual voice of his generation. She took it back to the group and that's when we began discussions with HBO. Both Lisa and Nancy came on board and that was an amazing partnership because I feel like HBO has a connection to its Black audience, to an African American audience, like no other network, like *Insecure*, and most recently *I May Destroy You.*

It was a spectacular night on so many levels. Being at the Apollo Theater was magical and taking that stage, rubbing the Tree of Hope and introducing the film and looking out into that theater from the stage, I'm very, very emotional considering all of the incredible talent that graced that stage. If there's just a magic in the air of the Apollo, I think that someone said in the film that the sweat of James Brown and Aretha Franklin and all of them are in the floorboards. That was amazing. That was an incredible night. It was overwhelming.

Sheila, Sheila, you're responsible.

This kid who went to IFP film week, who was wanting to make a feature, I'll never forget that call from Sheila, when she said, "You're going to win the Oscar," which I did. I've been a governor at the Oscars for five years now. Six, seven years later, I'm sitting at the table in the room where it happens. The center of Hollywood power, with Tom Hanks and Spielberg and Jim Gianopulos and all the powers that be that run Hollywood, and I'm at the table. I am, I think, the second or third African American ever to sit on the board of governors after Cheryl Boone Isaacs. I have just an incredible place in my heart for Sheila for plucking me out of obscurity and leading me.

LISA HELLER:

We love to curate as fresh a mix of stories and storytellers as we can. We don't want to give up the flexibility to pivot if something powerful comes along, that makes sense for us to try. It is a luxury not to have to be too prescriptive in what we're looking for, and we're grateful to Casey for supporting that approach.

NANCY ABRAHAM:

No single HBO documentary is emblematic of the entire department. There's such variety. We can do *Natalie Wood* and we can do *Welcome to Chechnya*, and they both have a place on the service.

LISA HELLER:

The projects that some might think fall into a familiar category wind up not fitting there because we try to do them in a way that feels fresh.

On June 28, 2020, HBO premiered **I'll Be Gone in the Dark**, *a six-part documentary series that aired through August 2. Based on the book by Michelle McNamara published in 2018, the show explores the hunt for the man known as the "Golden*

State Killer," a murderer and rapist who evaded capture for decades, and McNamara's efforts to uncover the truth about him. The documentary was produced by Liz Garbus, who also directed a third of the show, and Patton Oswalt, McNamara's widower who helped complete her book after her passing. Lisa Heller, Nancy Abraham, Dan Cogan, and Dave Rath all executive produced, with Paul Haynes and Billy Jensen serving as co-executive producers and McNamara receiving an executive producer credit as well. McNamara remains front and center throughout the entire piece—the show used both recordings of her voice from interviews she conducted and voice-overs from Amy Ryan to narrate the story in McNamara's voice. Critics gave **I'll Be Gone in the Dark** mostly positive reviews, praising the show's focus on McNamara's struggle to finish her book and the victims for whom she fought. The show also examines a unique subculture of amateur investigators like McNamara, each committed in their own way to getting justice for victims without the benefit of a badge.

I'll Be Gone in the Dark *marked the first entry in the new Heller/Abraham regime's plan to expand into the documentary series space, a series that would include* **McMillions, Atlanta's Missing and Murdered,** *and* **The Vow.**

LISA HELLER:

I'll be Gone in the Dark was our first big experiment in thinking about existing IP and books we might adapt. How do you bring something to life that's already happened and make it feel propulsive and vibrant if the book already exists? For many years we were focused on following stories as they happened—this was different. For this, Liz Garbus and her team skillfully deconstructed the book in a way that felt as though the story was unfolding for viewers in each episode. That was exciting, and we'd like to do more of that.

NANCY ABRAHAM:

It's a different creative experience to have a story unfold over multiple weeks, with a storyline that's spreading over however many hours of shorter, separate episodes. We hadn't had many experiences of the audience engaging with documentary series on a weekly basis. We knew what it was like to have a major feature documentary, the long life that that can have from its first premiere at a film festival through a long lead-up to its eventual airing on HBO. And the impact that that can have, which is a little different in terms of the interaction with the audience that you get with a weekly series.

LISA HELLER:

I think the audience engagement over time has been surprising and exciting. It was a bit of an experiment in trying to understand viewer appetite for more expansive, multi-part doc content. You know they'll come back for a compelling drama series, but to see docs engage, sustain, and grow audiences has been gratifying.

On Sunday, January 10, 2021, HBO premiered the first episode of a two-part documentary called simply **Tiger**, *and detailing the life of golf great, Tiger Woods. Directed by Matthew Hamachek and Matthew Heineman and spanning three hours over the course of two nights (the second half aired on January 17), the documentary explored Woods's meteoric rise to the top of the game, the substance abuse and infidelity scandals that set his career off course, and the comeback he mounted that peaked when he won the 2019 Masters tournament at Augusta. The documentary features interviews with Woods's friends and colleagues, as well as an exclusive with Rachel Uchitel, one of the women with whom he cheated on his wife.*

Although the documentary included never seen before content, some reviewers complained that the piece felt incomplete because Woods himself was not interviewed. The documentary employed a plethora of archival footage, which included interviews Woods gave over the years, but filmmakers did not speak with him on camera for the piece. Critics contrasted this with ESPN's **The Last Dance**, *which featured extensive interviews with its primary subject, Chicago Bulls legend Michael Jordan. All told, the documentary received mixed reviews, with conflicting assessments of the piece's handling of race and many critics feeling the documentary was not probing enough of the iconic golfer.*

ARMEN KETEYIAN:

We had multiple suitors for the rights to the book. But when Alex Gibney's name surfaced, I think Jeff and I were of the same mind that if Alex Gibney wants the rights, there was no one else that we wanted to partner with on the book. That was because of his reputation as an Oscar-winning documentary film director, but also because of the complexities in the story that we had put on the pages, which required an experienced hand. So we were thrilled when Alex wanted it. And I can tell you that there were multiple networks, multiple streaming services and cable companies that were very interested in acquiring the rights from Alex and from Jigsaw [Productions] and from us.

And it came down to, I think it's fair to say there was a pretty significant bidding war between Netflix and HBO. And at that point in time, Netflix was pretty much just gobbling up everything of quality that they felt fit their needs. And HBO to its credit really stepped up. And to the best of my knowledge, and Alex can probably confirm it, they outbid Netflix for the project. Which was somewhere between stunning and shocking.

You can't take four hundred pages and turn it into a three-hour-and-fifteen-minute documentary. You have to make smart, sometimes difficult choices as to how long you want to get off the exit ramp and how long you want us to stay. And then when you do get back on the entrance ramp on this road that will take you to the to the end of Tiger story, do it in a way that's respectful and journalistically sound and fair and powerful.

At its heart, it's a father–son story. I want to sing Matt Hamachek's praises.

LISA HELLER:

We don't think of the sports department as being shut down; it hasn't been. What's exciting is that there's a great, long-standing team in place there, and the documentary piece of it has been added to our portfolio.

The challenge with the Tiger Woods doc was to see if an in-depth, multidimensional approach to his story could reach beyond golf fans. Happily, it was an incredibly popular program and its success points to the notion that complex documentaries in this space can appeal to broad audiences.

NANCY ABRAHAM:

A long time ago, there wasn't that much competition in the feature documentary space, And I think we took that for granted in a way. But it's a whole other universe now. It's just a fact of life and a reflection of how well the whole genre has been doing. We benefit from that increased competition as well.

LISA HELLER:

It's a good time to be a documentary filmmaker, but we can't do everything, and we know that, so we have to curate thoughtfully and carefully choose what projects we want to dive in on.

FRANK MARSHALL:

A lot of life is about time. And I had gone to meet Steve Barnett, who at the time—this was four years ago—was the CEO of Capitol Records. And they had just gone through a renovation of the building there on Vine Street. And we were sitting in Steve's office, which is at the top of the building. And I was getting very nostalgic because when I was a kid, we lived out in the Valley and my dad was under contract at Capitol. And I used to spend a lot of time there in Studio A and in the building.

We started talking about documentaries and he said, "Well, I just bought the Bee Gees catalog. We bought the catalog and we're getting together some plans to introduce or reintroduce the group to the audience. I said, "Well, I love the Bee Gees. How about them? Let's do a doc."

The third time that we went down to interview Barry in Miami, we had gotten to be very comfortable with each other. I can't remember what the question was, but Barry responded, "I'd give it all up to have my brothers back." I sat up in my chair and remember, this was midway through, I turned around, I looked behind me, some of his family, his daughter and his wife Linda were there, and Jeanne Elfant Festa, my other producer, were all there. They were all crying. And I said, "It's gotta be the last line. And nothing after that."

As HBO settled in to its new normal under AT&T management, it didn't take long for John Oliver to take a swing at the new leadership. On June 23, 2019, Oliver took a second to address his bosses: "I probably don't say this enough, but I love you, Business Daddy. And I hope that we never lose the connection that we have. I guess what I'm trying to say is, I'm so glad our connection isn't on your wireless network, because it's absolutely terrible!" Like a toddler testing his boundaries, Oliver made it clear he wasn't planning on letting the new management off the hook.

JOHN OLIVER:

We certainly acted like our independence didn't change under AT&T. I think that's why I enjoy those kinds of jokes so much. They inoculate you against it. If we're behaving like this when we're not provoked, just imagine how badly we'll react if we were. I love those jokes because they feel like a sign of health to me. We are going to go, we are going to confidently continue under the same rules as we feel were established under the previous administration. If that changes, there will be fucking hell to pay.

The show could not be done otherwise, there is no leeway. There is no gray area. You either do this exactly like we're doing it or you just don't do it.

Editorial independence was critical to me, and even before we started the show, there were moments where we were already being treated in a way completely counter to what we were used to. We did two test shows, and in the first we did a long story about General Motors. In our mind, we were thinking, "Let's test the waters on our editorial independence." It was a series of big swings at GM basically killing people.

Then we did an in-studio interview at the end of that with Sarah Vowell, so we could get used to the cameras. Their note off the back of that first one was, "The GM stuff was interesting. You know you don't have to do interviews, right? You could just make that GM section longer," which felt like, "Are you giving us enough rope to hang ourselves?" The second test show, we did something slightly less ambitious, and their note that was, "The GM thing seemed like it had more teeth to it. You should be going more in that direction."

We started off making a different show than we ended up making. We staffed up for a different show than the one we realized a few months in that we wanted to make. So by the end of that first year, we had one researcher and now we have five, plus five assistants.

Early on we were fortunate because Jon and Stephen were still on. Tim Carvell and I, who had come from *The Daily Show*, were absolutely obsessed with not being on their toes. Those shoes were too big for us to fill, so we didn't want to be judged negatively by doing anything that they were doing. That helped push us into a different direction.

We have quite a young staff. There are some moments where we realize that we need to explain something that we thought was understood, including literally a reference to hanging chads. We'll have twenty-one-year-old members of our staff saying, "What is that?" I think there was one story last year where we wanted to reference the dot-com bubble in a piece about automation, and we have smart kids saying, "What exactly was that?" Fuck me. We have to slow down for two minutes to explain what that is.

We were doing a short piece about the fact that the news had to have a debate about climate change, between a scientist and a skeptic as if it was a fifty-fifty, whereas in fact it was whatever 97 percent of scientists believe that climate change is man-made. We were talking to Liz Stanton saying, "Oh, we could do this thing at the end, we could get like nine scientists and get someone holding up like 0.7 of a scientist."

We couldn't work it out. Liz said we should get a hundred scientists in lab coats. It hadn't occurred to us that was something we could ask for. We were so used to coming from the quick-turnaround, low-budget Comedy Central version, where you do the comically ramshackle version of an idea rather than the spectacle version. When she showed us that we could get a hundred white lab coats, that became a key lesson for, oh if we have this idea early enough, we can apply real production to it.

That eventually became something where you have like a six-thousand-pound cake or a musical in Times Square because you get a staff, people who gradually learn on the job until they can do things with ridiculous scale and polish.

We want people to feel like they have the agency to constantly make an idea better and ideally get into a situation where every single aspect of your show is adding to the idea, not just executing what you give them. So that was the most fun, where you realize, Holy shit, look at what our staff is capable of.

BILL MAHER:

They love John Oliver because when does he ever say anything that isn't in line with what the conventional woke with them is? I don't watch it all the time, but what I've seen of it is extremely down the line liberalism. And liberals are wrong about a lot of shit, too. You will never hear that on MSNBC because they in essence have taken the Fox News modus operandi, which is not necessarily directly lying, but if there is something that our audience doesn't believe, we just don't report it. They don't lie about it. It's just like, it never happened. That goes on on the left, too. If Johns Hopkins puts out a study, which they just did, talking about how the ban on assault rifles was not that effective, you're just not gonna see that reported on MSNBC.

On the Friday, June 2, 2017, episode of **Real Time with Bill Maher,** *during an interview with Republican senator Ben Sasse of Nebraska, Maher responded to Sasse's invitation to come to his state and work the fields by saying, "Work in the fields? Senator, I'm a house n****r." The reaction from the crowd that night was mixed, drawing both applause and disconcerted groans. Yet so fervent was the backlash—and calls for Maher's dismissal—that Maher apologized the following day in a statement that branded his own remarks "offensive." HBO also released a statement calling Maher's slur "inexcusable and tasteless" and notifying audiences that it would be cut out when that episode reappears on HBO air. A week later, he addressed the comment again on his show. Speaking with Michael Eric Dyson of Georgetown University, Maher asked the professor to "school" him on using the N-word. Another guest, rapper and actor Ice Cube, pointedly questioned Maher about his decision to use the racial epithet, saying that the N-word is "our word, and you can't have it back."*

During a segment of **Real Time** *that aired Friday, September 6, 2019, host Bill Maher created even more controversy than usual by pointing out that while fifty-three Americans had been killed in mass shootings the previous month, obesity killed forty thousand people during that same period. "Fat shaming doesn't need to end, it needs to make a comeback," Maher told his audience, sending up the political correctness with which obesity is politely discussed and underlining the real harm that Maher said it does to society.*

He seems to abide by the skunk-at-the-garden-party theory—you know, "Who invited him?!?" He utters uncomfortable truths, swims against tides, and takes pride in his refusal to pander. He's thus the vital opposite of most late-night hosts, and audaciously profane as well, not watching his language no matter which celebrities are in the chairs near him.

But he also happens to have a great mind with an impressive memory and a truly extraordinary record of being ahead of the curve. Maher attacked the Catholic League over child abuse early and often, to the point where the head of the Catholic League threatened to punch him in the face. He's been pushing legalized marijuana forever; was on the cover of the gay rights magazine The Advocate *back in 2007, and in 2005 gave an impassioned editorial about the dangers of the housing bubble. A full three years before.*

Watch Maher before the 2016 president election. He looks physically ill because he thought Democrats were being too cocky. He was more than worried about Trump winning. Most recently, Maher was the first public entertainer to talk about how afraid he was that Trump was not going to give up power easily if he lost, and discussed the relationship between COVID and obesity. (He has long railed against overweight people raising health care costs.)

Maher has a better track record on politics than most classic political commentators can claim, and there is a ton of sincerity and, yes, even caring to his political beliefs.

Some of his gambits are inscrutable. Conversations of high caliber and fresh thinking may be carelessly interrupted for silly, juvenile, and downright dirty comedy bits that not only interrupt the flow and intensity of the conversations but make such wild 180-degree turns from smart talk to sophomoric dick jokes or quips with funny pictures as rimshots that those watching risk whiplash.

It doesn't matter. Yes, the snarky irreverence alienates some viewers, drives some away, but Maher isn't trying to get everybody, as was expected of him when his show aired on ABC. In other words, Bill Maher couldn't be in a better place; he and HBO were made for each other, and they thrive together.

BILL MAHER:

We live in this culture where almost every time I finish a show, I'm amazed that I'm still here because there are a lot of people who are trying to get you fired every week.

MARC GURVITZ:

The N word. I don't know any other company that would have been in his corner after that like they were.

BILL MAHER:

Every year when we came back on the air, they put up a billboard, and when you've been on as long as I have, it gets hard not to repeat yourself or be banal. They were going through all these concepts, none of which I liked, and there was one more that I could see they were afraid to show to me. I asked, "What is it?" And it was the one I loved the most. It said, "He's not in it for the likes." That's what gives the show its flavor. That's what gives it its uniqueness. If I ever started to care about that, I'm finished. I'm dead. I'm not me. I feel like you could almost interchange the lines on other political slash comedy humor shows, and you wouldn't know. John Oliver could do Seth Meyers's lines, Samantha Bee's . . . They all can do each other's lines. But they can't do *my* lines. My lines are different. My point of view is different. I feel like I have a much more honest relationship with my audience. It's more like a real friendship with your friends. Do you sometimes say something they don't agree with? Of course. Do they stop being friends with you because of that? No, not if they're real friends.

I can't worry about pissing people off. And of course as the years go by, that gets easier because I feel like I'm playing with the house money now. If they fire me now, okay; I've been on twenty-seven years.

NINA ROSENSTEIN:

You know what I love about Bill Maher? Every week, not knowing what to expect. I can't think of any other live comedy show like that. John Oliver is so different. There's a script, you know what he's going to do and with Bill, you just don't. I have a strong stomach, but he could be a little nerve-racking to people because it's like, Oh God, it's too provocative.

BILL MAHER:

Obesity is the ultimate third rail to Americans. You call them anything, call them Nazis; they're okay with that. Just don't call them fat. It was well-accepted before James Corden had to pretend that he was so wounded and I was being mean to the fat people: you're never going to solve the health care crisis in America unless you ask the people to take care of themselves even a little bit, which no politician ever does. What their plan is going to do and this plan and his plan and how are you going to pay for it. No one ever talks about the, excuse the pun, elephants in the room, which is none of that is going to work unless you get the people to pitch in and try to take care of themselves instead of this insanity of taking pride in being fat.

I'm the face of the show. People are always stopping me to tell me how much the show means to them, but I feel terrible for my staff who don't have that. They do work that I believe is head and shoulders better than the competition, and they don't get any recognition because we never get awards. I guess we're just too good.

SHEILA GRIFFITHS, Executive Producer:

The staff of *Real Time* is a very tight-knit family. Most of us have worked on the show for its entire nineteen-year run, and a majority of the producers and writers have been with Bill since *Politically Incorrect*. That longevity is a credit to Bill. We could have gotten other jobs, but we've stayed because of Bill. We're proud to work for a guy who never pulls his punches and is not afraid to speak uncomfortable truths. We have a tremendous amount of respect for him, and he shows us that respect in return. It's why I've been with Bill for nearly thirty years.

We've been nominated for numerous Emmys and have never won. In all honesty, it doesn't matter. Bill is true to himself and always speaks with integrity. To me and the staff, that is, and always will be, much more valuable than an Emmy.

BILL MAHER:

It's not like we had to work hard to find premises to make fun of Trump. He's constantly saying and doing crazy stupid stuff. The comedy is there, but my nerves are not.

We do of course occasionally hear from the lawyers, but they're supposed to tell you if you're going to get sued if you say something like somebody has herpes, and they don't, even if it's a joke. Otherwise, we're left alone, and that is the HBO magic, that's why HBO is the real Tiffany network.

As far back as October 2018, not four months after the official closing of the AT&T–Time Warner acquisition, AT&T brass had gone public about their plans to develop an over-the-top streaming service. The plan, originally, had been a deliberate step down a more familiar, quality over quantity path: "My job is not to build another Netflix," John Stankey had said in a statement at the time. But plenty of other remarks had been uttered about the need for HBO to increase its programming volume, and Stankey's infamous town hall meeting with HBO had also sent a different message. Although AT&T continued to insist that HBO's boutique identity would be protected, in-house concern at HBO was mounting.

Then AT&T brought in a familiar face to help soothe HBO's worries. On March 4, 2019, Bob Greenblatt was named chairman of WarnerMedia, overseeing not only Casey Bloys and the HBO programming apparatus, but the Turner networks and AT&T's new streaming platform as well.

Greenblatt's career in television began as an executive at Fox, but it was later while running his own production company, Greenblatt Janollari Studios, that Greenblatt first embedded himself within HBO's walls. Along with David Janollari, Greenblatt was responsible for producing the hit HBO series **Six Feet Under**. *Since then, Greenblatt had added chairman of NBC Entertainment to his résumé, bestowing the cachet needed to land him a job atop this evolving media empire.*

BOB GREENBLATT:

Stankey hired me to oversee HBO and Turner, but also start the streaming service. The mandate to me was, "We can't destroy HBO because the press would be so against that." And they were. They wanted to paint AT&T as the villains, and HBO as this beautiful creature that was about to be suffocated. And so I needed to constantly run two tracks—Let's make HBO feel good and protected, but slowly and gradually, we've got to fold them into the new service because we don't have anything without HBO.

I had to keep protecting HBO, try to keep them productive and fulfilled, and yet we were starting this streaming service, which most of HBO didn't want to be part of, until they realized relatively soon that it was the future of the business and the only thing that would allow them to continue to grow. And I think that is what partly prevented the service from getting out the door in the most cohesive way. To this day they market "HBO" shows and "Max Originals," and I guess it's fine to have two lanes to run, but the consumer can be confused, not to mention the creative community. Hulu faces this a bit with "FX on Hulu," which is the vestige of two brands trying to come together, but that's more because there were two established lanes already. With the creation of HBO Max, we consciously created another brand—for good reasons, because HBO was considered too "elite" for some segments of the audience—but one that adds to confusion.

When I first got there again, because of the sort of duality of what I was trying to do, which was preserve HBO but also build a streaming service at the same time, we just decided, Let HBO keep doing what it's doing. Casey was working on in his own little vacuum and continuing to deliver great shows.

I wanted HBO to get a little bit more cost efficient, but I struggled at every turn to even do that because everyone at HBO was used to a multi-million-dollar marketing campaign for every show. And every single person who had a series at HBO expected to have a bespoke marketing campaign, or the talent would feel insulted.

We did a little bit of trimming and cost cutting, but nothing changed at HBO after I got there. In fact, my mandate was, "Don't destroy HBO. Leave it the way it is, and then create this whole other division that's going to do everything else that we need the streamer to do." That, to me, was the fundamental challenge of how it was first envisioned. And so HBO kept going the way it had been going.

Everybody in the press couldn't wait to pile onto the story that "they've destroyed HBO." In fact, Casey and I would often struggle with how to talk to the press once I got there, because all they wanted to do was say, "The company was about to destroy HBO." Which was ironic, because I was, if anything, a Hollywood insider. And I had produced a beloved show for HBO. I loved the brand. I didn't in any way want to destroy it, in fact my mandate was the opposite, but, yes, the press couldn't wait to write that story.

Though Greenblatt fought to keep HBO siloed, or at least feeling siloed, the direction that AT&T's streaming service was taking made that difficult. On July 9, 2019, AT&T announced the name for their new service: HBO Max. Along with the name came another notable announcement: **Friends,** *a show that analysts believed to be among the most streamed on Netflix, would instead be available on HBO Max. Granted, WarnerMedia owned the distribution rights to the series. But HBO Max certainly seemed to be aiming squarely for Netflix's customers, despite statements to the contrary.*

JOHN STANKEY:

I'm a big believer that if you're put in those moments and those circumstances where you get to extend your best energy against interesting and challenging problems, you're going to generally do pretty good work. You're going to stay engaged and you're going to enjoy doing that. Second, one of the great gifts over my career, just from the perspective of the human aspect of it, has been doing M&A [mergers and acquisitions] transactions. I was a native Californian until I left in 2000. I grew up on the West Coast. I worked for a California-centric company. I knew very little of the rest of the United States at my thirtieth birthday. The M&A transactions got me into a dynamic where I was suddenly working with people from the Midwest and people from the South and people from the Southeast and people on the East Coast.

As the strategy-minded John Stankey moved up to AT&T's top job, the hunt began to bring on a top-notch day-to-day manager for WarnerMedia's vast conglomerate. They wanted a media executive with the varied chops to oversee the film studios at Warner Bros., CNN's news empire, TBS, TNT, and HBO to boot. Yet with their mind squarely on the future of their direct-to-consumer brand, AT&T brought in a seasoned streaming hand: Hulu's founding CEO, Jason Kilar. On May 1, 2020, the forty-nine-year-old tech executive with a reputation as an outspoken disruptor stepped into a company, as ever, in the midst of transition.

JASON KILAR, Executive:

I saw it as one of the great opportunities at the intersection of media and technology, which is to bring world-class storytelling to consumers all over the world, at a scale that historically had not been done before in the context of WarnerMedia. You'd get those great stories in front of more people around the world. And what I'm referring to is obviously the Internet opportunity, which is going direct-to-consumer over the Internet. Of course HBO is at the front of all that. I also saw an opportunity to play a small role in helping a brand like HBO, and all the things that it's capable of, to bring it global and to bring it to a lot more people.

John Stankey was in my seat for a year and a half. I also am very thankful that he was very up-front from day one, saying, "I don't come from a decades-long background in media and technology and storytelling. At the end of the day, my focus is ultimately to hand the keys over to someone who does have that background."

We're all a function of our history. I'm a kid from Pittsburgh. I was born and raised as one of six children. We're a multiracial family. Three of us are adopted in this family of six kids. We grew up in a very blue-collar environment in Pittsburgh and that shaped me. Second thing is I spent almost ten years at Amazon back when it was a private little company and Jeff Bezos was not Jeff Bezos and that absolutely had an impact on me. I also spent a fair bit of time building something that a lot of people didn't give a big chance for success, which was Hulu. That shaped me as well.

JOHN STANKEY:

Our decision was that the model we picked at that time was the right first step, three companies to two companies. A studio, and then a network organization with the overlay of the direct-to-consumer. Jason has now come in, decided to take that next step, which is take two to one. If I had guessed back in 2018, when we would have been doing that, it probably would have been at the end of next year.

It would allow the HBO brand to extend itself, nested within a broader offering, and have another good ten-year run, where it could exist and be seen by even more people than what it had been seen from before. And, in doing that, there are three things that are essential. You have to have great content. Two, you have to have a good technology platform. And three, you need to be able to run a direct marketing organization, which is different than just building a brand for a wholesale business like traditional media companies were structured to do. Having all three of those would be the recipe for getting the business where it needs to be over the next ten years.

On May 27, 2020, WarnerMedia launched the streaming service HBO Max. Both John Stankey and Bob Greenblatt wanted to make sure HBO was in the foreground of the new brand, but because HBO GO and HBO Now were still in existence, it proved to be rather a perplexing time for consumers.

The whole strategy seemed convoluted. If the name is HBO Max, you're leaning on the brand of HBO, right? But if HBO is a more rarefied, up-market, luxury brand, how can you also say, "Hey, we're more mass market now, too!" It was unclear as to what the value proposition of HBO Max was supposed to be.

Priced at $15 a month, HBO Max opened at a higher price than its main competitors, Disney+, Apple TV, and NBC's new Peacock. AT&T wanted an app to compete directly with Netflix, and while HBO Max was about the same price as Netflix's main plan, it lacked the depth of Netflix's programming.

Max offered HBO's entire lineup, plus extras made up of movies and new "Max Originals." The new "Originals" were thought of as a neat way to drive customers to Max, at least at the outset. After all, who wouldn't want to attend a reunion special honoring **The Fresh Prince of Bel-Air?** *HBO insiders believed that too much of Max had been conceived on the fly. Then, two other outbreaks of bad luck surfaced: COVID delayed the much ballyhooed* **Friends** *reunion—the hottest ticket of promised attractions—and WarnerMedia was unable to close a deal with Roku, which, together with Amazon, claimed around 70 percent of streaming devices in the United States.*

RANDALL L. STEPHENSON:

When we launched HBO Max, we had an activist who was challenging the whole strategy around buying a media company. I got up onstage and challenged analysts and all the media to look at the talent onstage that day, and at how quickly that product came together. I not too subtly said, "That could have never happened had we not taken the pain early on of changing leadership and getting people who were engaged and understood where the world was going to get this done."

BOB GREENBLATT:

So when the merger happened, I think it was potentially a real missed opportunity that we didn't take HBO Go and Now and just build the hell out of it and make it into the new service. We felt that brand, as incredible as it was, might be too "elitist" or maybe just too fully penetrated, yet we knew HBO had to be the bedrock of the new service yet we somehow didn't fully embrace it. We needed the flip side to complete the offering. So, it had to be built by different people at the company. Ironically it was built on the platform that Plepler built. That was the foundation of HBO Max. A lot of those great tech people were moved into a new division to build HBO Max. So they had the right idea all along. They just didn't get there fast enough. But if everyone hadn't been so concerned about destruction of HBO, maybe we could've just taken it and built on it. Look at what Hulu is. When Disney arrived, when they got full control of Hulu, they didn't go, "Oh, Hulu's not a good enough brand and they haven't done enough, let's start a whole new platform." They built up Hulu into something that's a major force and began layering other brands, like FX, on it. I will always wonder if we made a mistake thinking HBO was too narrow. Why wasn't HBO Go, or whatever you want to call it, turned into a stronger, bigger, direct-to-consumer business? I don't know. To me that's the real unanswered question in all this, though I believe they will still ultimately get there.

ILENE LANDRESS:

The big thing is that even up until fairly recently, the executives I'd be dealing with were only dealing with maybe three, four, five, six shows. But now you're dealing with another twenty, twenty-five shows, thirty shows. What was special about the old days is it was a nice boutique.

Because there's no way that these people can work on twenty-five shows and have the same amounts of bandwidth to deal with them as when they were working on like four or five shows. You don't have the mandate that they're trying to keep the same hand-crafted bespoke quality, because it's what's best for them, but it's super corporate now. It's a little bit of a bummer.

On August 7, 2020, WarnerMedia CEO Jason Kilar announced a massive restructuring of WarnerMedia's executive ranks. Bob Greenblatt and Kevin Reilly were out, as priorities shifted away from networks TBS and TNT toward the newly minted crown jewel, HBO Max. Ann Sarnoff would oversee the newly created Studios and Networks Group, and HBO's Casey Bloys would oversee content at HBO Max, along with the WarnerMedia's basic cable networks.

GLENN WHITEHEAD:

Casey is the best creative executive I've ever seen anywhere, and with the least amount of ego. And it's the relationship between talent and lack of ego that is the real secret of his great success.

BOB GREENBLATT:

I had the pleasure of meeting Mrs. Stankey, Shari, who seems to be the greatest lady in the world. She came up to me at the holiday party when John had this lovely staff dinner. Nine months into the job, she came up to me. I'd never met her, she hugged me and said, "I just want to tell you that you've changed my husband's life and you've given him so much support. And he's so appreciative of you being at this company."

Ironically, within six months, I was fired. Hah! But honestly, they were lovely to me. One AT&T person came up to me in Dallas once and said, "We're blessed to have you here. We're blessed to have you here." And then within a year I was no longer needed. Now, financially it was a slog and an uphill battle every step of the way in fighting for the resources needed to bring a world-class streamer to a competitive marketplace, but they were all nice people. So it's not like I felt any animosity for anybody, it just was a completely different culture than I was used to, every minute of the day.

It began with rumors, then a leak or two by small news outlets, but eventually there was no hiding the truth: HBO had pulled the plug not only on Peter Nelson but on the whole HBO Sports department.

Yes, HBO's parent company, WarnerMedia, was forced to lay off over six hundred people across their various brands (over one hundred at HBO) due to the coronavirus pandemic and other issues. But, let's face it: within the past decade, HBO Sports had already been losing its foothold in the company. Boxing had been dead for years, as had **Inside the NFL** *and Wimbledon. The department was releasing fewer and fewer documentaries, usurped from their throne by ESPN's* **30 for 30***. Only two bastions of sports programming remained:* **Real Sports** *with Bryant Gumbel and* **Hard Knocks***.*

Among the wash of other restructurings at the parent company, **Real Sports***, as well as sports documentaries, were tucked under the responsibility of HBO's documentary group. Meanwhile,* **Hard Knocks** *was mostly being run by NFL Films. After forty-nine years of excellence that had set them apart among the giants of the sports television world, "The Network of Champions," HBO Sports, was no more. The network would continue to hold on to vestiges of their triumphs, but HBO would never again be a heavyweight in the sports television ring. They'd turned away from the original plan outlined by Chuck Dolan in 1972, which featured sports as the central pillar of the company. They would now, fingers crossed, pivot in a new direction.*

PETER NELSON:

In February of 2020, I was asked to make significant reductions in both people and programming, and then in March I was asked for even deeper cuts. It escalated drastically.

I asked an old friend about it and he said, "You're too young to manage decline." It was a hard line to get out of my head. There's still great people and great work being done there. It was just my role had become something else.

BILL SIMMONS:

Nelson wasn't a sports fan, which is strange because he was in charge of the sports department. There was a lot of leaning on other people to figure out what was the good idea. I was one of those people, but it was a weird situation. Because at ESPN, one thing was everybody loves sports. Everybody follows sports rabidly and has favorite teams. Peter's passions were different.

DAVE HARMON:

I was hiking in Colorado. I got the email saying all-hands-on-deck meeting tomorrow morning. I told everyone I didn't want to be there. I knew what it was and to tell me face-to-face meant nothing to me. At that point, I was happy to not be face-to-face with Peter giving information, and then leaving Rick Bernstein to individually tell those of us who were going to be laid off. Tell me what you're doing, and leave me to my own thoughts about myself and my career.

They allowed us to use the office through the end of December, but Peter never sat down with me face-to-face to discuss what this had all been about, he never made time to talk to me.

JIM LAMPLEY:

All things must pass. I knew the minute that I learned that Time Warner had been sold to AT&T that the world in which I had lived for thirty-plus years was going to change—and that I probably wouldn't love the change. If they had continued to do boxing, maybe I'd still be there. But we in the sports division were told that most likely they weren't going to be interested in boxing and as it turned out, they weren't.

DAVE HARMON:

You tell me when *Real Sports* is on. They never created a regular schedule. It's the same thing with HBO Sports documentaries. Now everything is obviously on demand, it's not as big of a deal, but when Plepler was making these evaluations, there was nothing regular about HBO Sports. They didn't want to create appointment viewing, like the rest of the network. Everyone knew what the network was doing on Sunday nights.

GLENN WHITEHEAD:

We're doing two kinds of things on the sports side. We're doing documentaries, which is a very big part of the day-to-day for the sports group. And then we're doing talk and unscripted shows like *The Shop* or *Real Sports*. And we have people who do that already; Nina Rosenstein, who looks after Bill Maher and John Oliver. On the documentary side, Lisa and Nancy have been running that ever since Sheila Nevins left. Peter was thought by some to be somewhat extraneous in that mix, so it was also a place to achieve some efficiencies in the organization. In the recently announced reductions in force at WarnerMedia, a number of people left the Sports department as a result of those efficiencies.

You used to be able to put the world heavyweight boxing match on HBO, but when the business evolved and even mid-level fights had to be pay-per-view events and you get replays on HBO a week later, that's not live sports.

I get that lots of money would come in and the vast majority of it would go back out. You make a multi-million-dollar commitment to Manny Pacquiao or to Floyd Mayweather. Then, "Oh my God, we've just collected $200 million," but you turn around and you pay most of it out. I don't even remember the numbers on the first couple of Pacquiao–Mayweather fights, but hundreds of millions of dollars would come in and then the vast majority of it would go back out. That was not a significant profit center for the company in my experience.

PETER NELSON:

I change careers like every four years. I worked in the art world and I was a journalist and I joined HBO and then took over the department, which was a totally different job, especially after we got out of boxing. Having a nonlinear career is something that I'm comfortable with. For a lot of people they'd always experienced HBO as a first and final destination. Hoped they would stay for 40 years as some of my colleagues did. For them, it was Camelot with a pension.

BILL SIMMONS:

We had a couple projects the last two years that just dragged on. And when that happens, eventually you lose them. That was a bummer for me. There was one project in particular that I had been hashing out for three years. It was an NBA project. If I had had somebody like Connor Schell, it would've gotten done. It almost made me, in a lot of ways, appreciate my ESPN experience.

In January 2020, HBO made a long-awaited announcement: a rough premiere date for the Game of Thrones *prequel,* House of the Dragon.

GEORGE R. R. MARTIN:

I had a meeting at HBO, it was in August, maybe 2017 or something like that, where I said, "Look, if you're going to follow up, I have two possible successor shows to pitch. One of them is I have these series of novellas about two characters called Dunk and Egg." Three novellas I'd written so far, I'd projected to write ten more. And that took place a hundred years before *Game of Thrones*.

And then I had this idea for part of the back history, the Targaryen civil war, the Dance of the Dragons, which is referred to in the main book. And that takes place 150 years, even 50 years before Dunk and Egg. It's big. It's got seventeen dragons. I pitched those two ideas to HBO. They didn't like the Dunk and Egg idea because they were familiar with the novellas—somebody there had read them—but it was too soft, but they did respond to the Dance of the Dragons idea.

We'd need a new showrunner. I couldn't do it myself. I'm still writing these books. Then I suddenly found out that they had put four prequels in motion. The Dance of the Dragons idea was just one of them. And the other three were ideas that had come from other people who I guess had read my books or had some of the documents at HBO. And so they had hired four writers and we suddenly had four shows in development, but that took place ten years after the initial meeting with David and Dan at the Palm.

It surprised me, I'll admit that. I'd never heard of that before. I thought we'd be going ahead with one, with one development, with the one that I pitched to them, the Dance of the Dragons idea. I met with all four of the writers. They came to Santa Fe, New Mexico, where I lived, and I had meetings with them, discussed their idea, did workshops, tried to fill them in on any questions and all that. And then later a fifth show was added. There were five at one point.

BOB GREENBLATT:

HBO was minting so much money. They were making so much profit that I don't think they looked closely enough at the costs of the shows as being relevant. They just thought we'll spend what we need to spend. And of course,

Game of Thrones was on fire and the most expensive show on television and a massive success story. But I think HBO lost a lot of discipline by this point, along with a series of massively expensive shows that failed or were actually shut down in production. I think it needed to be overhauled, not massively, but just brought back to what it once was, to look at some of the costs. I never could get costs under control, because of the mandate not to upset the apple cart too much. They had spent over $30 million on a *Game of Thrones* prequel pilot that was in production when I got there. And when I saw a cut of it in a few months after I arrived, I said to Casey, "This just doesn't work and I don't think it delivers on the promise of the original series." And he didn't disagree, which actually was a relief. So we unfortunately decided to pull the plug on it. There was enormous pressure to get it right and I don't think that would have worked.

There was also a second spinoff in development, so they hadn't shot anything yet. And it was going well in the development process, scripts were being written, and a promising bible was being written. And I'm the one who encouraged Casey to green-light it to series. I said, "Let's not risk $30 million on a pilot." You can't spend $30 million on a pilot and then not pick it up. So I said, "Let's not make a pilot. Let's get a great series that we feel good about, and just make it. Or not." They made the first pilot because they were protecting their own downside and protecting that brand, which I understand, but it was critical that we somehow continue that franchise and move quickly, which meant getting the series into production asap. That's always a nail-biter, but I think the new show that is coming will be incredible. And I know they have now fast-tracked even more content from this world.

I was very motivated to get more *Game of Thrones* somehow in the ecosystem. Everybody at HBO was very nervous about replicating the *Game of Thrones* brand and failing. I believe you can do it, as Marvel did it. And *Star Wars* did and other companies have shown. And so there was real fear about how to do it. So they developed multiple projects and they wanted to protect their downside.

HBO widened its wingspan when it elected to air **Betty,** *a half-hour comedy series created by Crystal Moselle, based on her 2018 film* **Skate Kitchen.** *It included most of the cast of the original movie and focuses on a group of Gen Z girls in New York's mostly male world of skateboarding. The six-episode series premiered on HBO on May 1, 2020. In June, the series was renewed for a second season.*

The show explored camaraderie and what it means for friends to "have one another's backs." One of the most prominent arcs begins when a fight breaks out and most of the group gets arrested, except Kirt, "the white one." The episode that follows explores Kirt's coming to terms with her privilege; once she does so, without relying on her friends as teachers of said privilege, the other girls welcome her back into their circle (literally and otherwise) with a big group hug on the streets of New York.

CRYSTAL MOSELLE, Writer and Director:

I thought it was cool that these young women were skateboarding because when I was growing up, it was usually only boys on a skateboard. So we did a short film.

I hadn't directed actors before. I've been more of a documentary film-maker before that, so we grew together as far as acting and directing.

AMY GRAVITT:

Betty feels like an evolution of different stories we've told about female friendship. Both Crystal and the girls in the film and in their real life are cool girls, but you also get a feeling that if you ran into them in the real world, they'd let you join their pack. I liked that they're feminine and that there's a story of empowerment underneath it, but that's subtle. I believe the half-hour space has been allowed to be more cinematic without sacrificing tone and without sacrificing jokes. What Melina Matsoukas brought to *Insecure*, what Bill Hader brought directing *Barry*, what Michaela Coel brought to *I May Destroy You*, Crystal brings to the half-hour space in *Betty*.

CRYSTAL MOSELLE:

Amy Gravitt saw the film and was interested in turning it into a series. It was my first time in the writers' room. And I felt like I was getting swayed in a direction that didn't feel authentic to what I had made in the film. So I called Amy and talked with her and she was like, "I don't want you to make the TV version of the film." She's like, "I want you to make an extension of a film for television, whatever you did with the film, do that for the TV show, make it feel like you."

As far as the writing process, I'd be hanging out with the girls and they would be telling me stories. They're a part of the process of creating the show. When we take something that's on the page and go off the page and create unexpected nuances and emotions that were never on the page, that's when you feel like you're building something special and unique.

Women oftentimes don't support each other. It's like this fight that we have against each other for these small spaces in society. Even as a female director, there's this small space for the woman to come in and create a film, and since it's so small, only one person can come in, so there's not a collaboration. What I loved about them when I met them is that they're not mean girls. They're about supporting each other and coming up together. At the skate park, if you see another girl, they're not going to be a mean girl to her because they don't know her. They're going to go up to her and be like, Hey, how's it going? There's a real comradery between them and an inspiration for women. I know that there's nothing like this on TV. And if something doesn't feel completely from my heart, I'm almost allergic to it.

An ethereal drama adapted from (and extending) a novel by Matt Ruff, **Lovecraft Country** *was billed by HBO as a "genre-defying" series that typified a new kind of television fantasy. The unique show began its first HBO season on August 16, 2020. Set in a magical-mystical version of the 1950s—when Black Americans still had to contend with Jim Crow laws in many regions, as well as bald, brutal prejudice—the ambitious series starred Jonathan Majors, Jurnee Smollett, and Michael K. Williams, each giving career performances. They played travelers on an odyssey through the unearthly—casting spells, surviving gory rituals, and occasionally lapsing into a lingo called "the language of Adam" as they traveled the violent streets and strife-torn neighborhoods of the United States. Even through its pain,* **Lovecraft** *was stunningly beautiful, set to an arresting soundtrack (with selections that ranged from Nina Simone to Al Jolson), and it made for one of the most nuanced, cerebral marriages of narrative and music in television.*

J. J. ABRAMS:

We got to know Jordan Peele years ago before *Get Out,* and he brought us this book and asked if we'd want to collaborate with him on it. The power and potential of it were undeniable, along with the amazing combination of genres. It wasn't until we started working with Misha that it became clear just how potent this thing could be, because her vision of it was so powerful and so righteous.

CASEY BLOYS:

Misha started talking about claiming sci-fi and horror genres for Black audiences that have historically not participated at all in that whole genre, and using it as a way to talk about the fact that racism is the biggest monster. We've got these great monsters and horror stories, and racism is always there, underneath it.

I thought it was an interesting way to talk about not only that genre, but also race in America. It did the thing that I'd like a show to do on HBO, which is be entertaining, be well-written, well-acted, and well-directed, but also have something to say. It's not vegetables television, as we sometimes say; it has a larger purpose. We bought it in the room. It was very competitive. Netflix was very much after it. I think having a good relationship with J.J. helped us land the show. Straight to series is tough though, for a show that is so tone dependent you've got to get it right.

MISHA GREEN, Creator:

I wanted it to be big and to push the boundaries of how we've been watching TV lately. What we took to HBO was this idea that the show is much bigger than even this book. It's the idea of reclaiming the genre space of horror for all people of color.

When we pitched the entire season to HBO, it was clear that we were going to be taking some risks and they were not afraid of that. They said, "Go." And I kept going, "Are you sure you want me to go? Because I'm going to go, if you want me to go." Once we were into the season of writing it, they were like, "Wow, you're going."

JONATHAN MAJORS, Actor:

I wasn't offered the role. I auditioned. I read Matt Ruff's book but hadn't read it until I was already signed on to do the show. But no, I had no idea how it was all going to befall Atticus. I knew how it began, like all good things, but didn't know how it was going to end. Like all good things.

JURNEE SMOLLETT, Actor:

I connected to Leti on a molecular level. I understood her, but also desperately needed to explore her and go on her journey. I had worked with Misha and done two seasons of *Underground* prior to *Lovecraft*. And Misha went off after *Underground* was canceled and wrote the pilot for *Lovecraft* in what felt like was roughly three weeks, and then let me read it shortly after. I didn't even know if there was a role in there that I could play, because it's not like she was letting me read it with the intention of casting me. But instantly, I was just so hooked and mesmerized by Leti's spirit. I understood her skin, I understood her walk, I understood her eyes, how she saw the world. There just comes a time as an artist that your whole being is just drawn to a character. There's no other option, you must play this character, you must express this character. That's how I felt about Leti. By all costs, by any means necessary, I had to play her.

MISHA GREEN:

We took the source material, the book, to the multiverse and back. I don't think HBO thought it was going to be so massive. They definitely hit those walls where they said, "Wait a minute, this is a lot bigger than we thought it was." And I said, "But isn't it amazing? Isn't it great? We've got to keep going."

We used 162 sets on the show. They thought this was a medium-size show and it's turned out to be a gargantuan show. For me it was always going to be a gargantuan show. That was always my goal. I knew that once we got the ball rolling, they would see that. At the time they were talking about, "We want something that's a replacement for *Game of Thrones*." And I said, "This could be it if you will let it be."

MICHAEL K. WILLIAMS:

What I learned about myself from having filmed *Lovecraft Country* is again, I go back to that T-word, "trauma." *Lovecraft* made me realize that I not only have trauma, my own personal life experiences, I also have blood trauma from my ancestors. *Lovecraft* reminded me that I stand on some really strong shoulders. And it humbled me in a way that I'd never been humbled before.

Had you told me that *Lovecraft* would be airing post George Floyd's murder, post Breonna Taylor's murder, I wouldn't have been able to fathom that. It was a blessing to have this piece of narrative, this piece of art to hold up a big mirror for us to look at ourselves and to see the timelines of how we got here.

JURNEE SMOLLETT:

Leti taught me so much about myself; she demanded that I surrender a lot of myself to her, that I bring a lot of myself to the altar to sacrifice. I was struggling with my womanhood. I was forced to inspect why I made the decisions I did.

Leti and I have a lot in common. I can relate to this idea of being abandoned by your parents. Not by my mother, but I didn't see my dad from the time I was twelve until twenty-six, other than a handful of times. Then I lost my dad two years later. I understand the devastation that comes when you lose your parents, regardless of what your relationship is like. It hits you hard and a part of you dies off. And in their absence, you search for healing. Leti is searching for healing, so Leti brought a lot of healing to me and forced me to go to very dark places in myself, which I'm honestly grateful for because it made me more untamed and more unbound. She's a wild woman, she's very primal. And that's a goal of mine, just to become less tamed, less bound to societal standards of who I am or who I can be.

JONATHAN MAJORS:

Something they don't teach you in drama school, and that's not immediately apparent, is the responsibility you have for culture and humanity at large. As I moved through *Lovecraft*, I began to understand that the gravity of what I do for a living, not who I am, but what I do, carries with it a certain amount of duty.

Lovecraft was nurtured by the trauma and turmoil of the Trump administration, and those of us who were working on it were in that clay pot, that furnace, realizing that our story took place in the fifties, but was not dissimilar to things we were seeing in the Trump era.

MICHAEL K. WILLIAMS:

We give Trump way too much credit. Trump is a symptom of the problem. Like drugs were for me. This shit has been here. Jay-Z wrote, "You can't heal what you never reveal," and *Lovecraft* revealed a lot of shit that hasn't been dealt with yet. Trump didn't start that, he just threw lighter fluid on it.

To be really honest, I'm grateful for his administration, because he ripped the Band-Aid off. What we saw on January 6 has been brewing for a long time, and *Lovecraft* helped show me that.

Lovecraft Country earned a staggering eighteen Emmy nominations in 2021, including Outstanding Drama Series and well-deserved acting noms for Smollett, Majors, and Williams. But all the praise and nominations proved to be Pyrrhic victories; HBO executives had, however reluctantly, canceled the show just weeks earlier.

Lovecraft's odyssey had been turbulent. HBO spent more than $150 million on ten episodes, but money was hardly the chief cause for cancellation. As gifted as Misha Green was artistically, HBO determined after a lengthy analysis that there were too many organizational behavior issues present. Several writers on the show refused to work with Green, blaming her for a toxic and hostile environment.

All that remained was a double sadness: First, for years, decades even, the Black community had labored and protested for a seat at the table, and then, the head of the table. To see that dream self-destruct was painful to many involved. And, second, that a resplendent show so important to retracing a critical period in Black American history would disappear—after only one season—was an even bigger heartbreak, on both sides of the screen. Green left HBO in July 2021 to go to Apple.

MISHA GREEN:

I love this quote by Zadie Smith. She says, "I just tried to make it more truthful than the last time."

It's hard to imagine a cash crunch involving mega meta AT&T, but that's exactly what was going on at WarnerMedia in 2020 and 2021. The crunch required adjustments to be made to HBO Max planning, and the big question that had been asked since AT&T had taken over—whether its streaming service would be able to compete directly with Netflix or be a smaller, and thus not direct competitor—seemed to be on the verge of being answered. Netflix was spending $19 billion on programming, HBO Max, $7 billion. And that was before cash became (relatively) scarce. Once the crunch came, there were two parallel lists inside WarnerMedia for the future—one if new money arrives; the other, which was shorter and much less ambitious, if there wasn't a significant influx of new monies.

HBO, which lived under the HBO Max rubric, wasn't affected as much. The big jump in its programming hours had occurred post–**Game of Thrones**, from about a hundred hours of scripted programming to 150 hours, and post-pandemic it was looking like 185 hours, the most in HBO's history.

So when on Sunday May 16, 2021, news leaked that AT&T would spin off WarnerMedia to merge it with Discovery, HBO and WarnerMedia executives weren't surprised, as in, "Yeah, so the cash crunch wasn't fake after all."

John Stankey called selected senior executives on Sunday to tell them this thing was for real, and they in turn contacted their teams to tell them to hold on. It was going to be a bumpy ride. Once again.

The deal called for AT&T to receive a combination of cash and bonds worth $43 billion and its shareholders to own 71 percent of the new company (the other 29 percent to be retained by Discovery's shareholders). David Zaslav—who'd been Discovery's CEO since moving there from the legal department of NBC's cable division in January 2007—was announced as the leader of the new organization after the merger. AT&T and Discovery said they expected to complete the deal by mid-2022; it would create one of the largest media companies in America, second only to Disney, and would join AT&T's most prominent media assets—HBO, the Turner networks including CNN, and movie studio Warner Bros.—to Discovery's Animal Planet, Food Network, and OWN, the Oprah Winfrey Network.

Both companies offer streaming services (HBO Max and Discovery+), with HBO, combined with traditional cable, boasting roughly 44 million domestic subscribers to Discovery's 15 million global count.

Talks between the two companies were initiated by an email Zaslav sent Saturday, February 13, 2021, to AT&T CEO John Stankey. Because of the coronavirus, both had foregone their trips to the Pebble Beach Pro-Am, where Zaslav had wanted to speak with Stankey, although Zaslav had watched parts of the golf tournament from home. He texted Stankey, "I've been thinking," and, "I have an idea." He added a few golfer emojis and a smiley face with sunglasses. Stankey replied, "Always scares me when you do that :)" and "Would you like to chat?" They ended up speaking for hours.

Stankey met with Zaslav March 2 in Greenwich Village at a town house Zaslav owned. On April 1, Zaslav brought in Discovery CFO Gunnar Wiedenfels and Bruce Campbell, a Discovery strategist and top aide to Zaslav who had worked on Discovery's previous buys of Scripps and Eurosport. Both companies also enlisted banks as counsel on the deal—AT&T used LionTree and Goldman Sachs, and Discovery used Allen & Company and JPMorgan. Goldman Sachs and JPMorgan loaned AT&T in excess of $40 billion to finalize the deal.

Each side had a set of code words for the transaction. Discovery used baseball-related names: "Project Home Run" was the merger, "Williams" was WarnerMedia, "DiMaggio" was Discovery, and "Aaron" stood for AT&T. At AT&T, Discovery became "Drake" and WarnerMedia became "Magellan."

Stankey did not tell WarnerMedia CEO Jason Kilar about the deal until the week of May 3, a fortnight prior to the announcement. Kilar dealt with that delay by hiring lawyer Allen Grubman.

On Sunday, May 16, Zaslav flew into Dallas on his way to AT&T headquarters for a decision by both companies' boards to green-light the deal. While Zaslav was flying down to Texas, news broke through the Bloomberg terminal that the companies were planning a merger. Once Zaslav arrived, the two boards, who had gathered virtually through video conference, unanimously approved the deal, which was announced the next day. The new company would be called "Warner Bros. Discovery."

JOHN STANKEY:

On July 1, 2020, when I sat down in the chair being CEO, I started the process of asking myself what is this business going to look like for the next five years? What do I want, when my tenure on this job is finished, to say we were able to do? The phone call that David made was just a day in a process that had been going on for months. We were pretty far along in our deliberations about what we thought the direction of the business was. So there wasn't lightning in a bottle. It wasn't because David called me that day. We were in a process of looking at options and discussing them with the board and people I trust outside of the board.

DAVID ZASLAV:

It is still surreal that the deal came together. I talked to John [Stankey] because I felt we weren't big enough alone, and each time we looked at what we had together, it was very complementary. It wasn't just more, it was more that was differentiated, it was appealing to different demographics, it was more depth of content that would be more appealing for subscribers. And it was content that would reduce churn.

JOHN STANKEY:

Because of the delay of the AT&T Time Warner transaction, plus the waiting period of the "keep separate" agreement that we had to agree to, which didn't allow us to start the integration until six months after close, we lost about a year, maybe a little bit more. I don't want to say that that was the cause or the exclusive reason for the sale, but if we were where we are right now a year ago, would investor sentiment possibly be different? Would we have been in advance of Disney+ growing the base and demonstrating to the market the great success that we're having right now, prior to them coming in with a lower price? I think it might've had an impact on things. But there were a lot of other issues for consideration beyond that.

There was no 90-degree turn when David called. If you were to be the DOJ going through all of my documents from my desk, my emails, and my phones that they will be going through in the coming months, there will be nothing in there that doesn't have an option like this well-articulated well before David ever phoned me, along with many other options and what the pros and cons of each consideration was.

All options obviously had regulatory approval considerations, capital structure considerations, impacts to employees, and market effectiveness. I would say we picked a transaction that we think is the strongest from a regulatory approval dynamic. There's very little overlap, virtually none. There is no market concentration in any way, shape, or form. So, by definition, that improves the prospects of the deal.

DAVID ZASLAV:

Both of us are real competitors. We're going to fight as hard as we can to will ourselves to success. If we're successful, and I believe we will be, there will be Harvard Business School case studies on this deal. John had the courage to say, if I have a chance to be stronger and create more shareholder value with Discovery and with Dave, I'm going to do it, and we are going to be the leading global IP media company. History will say that this was a brilliant strategic move.

JOHN STANKEY:

I believed that the business needed to look at vertical integration and, frankly, I still believe that. If you ask me five years from now, even in this configuration of what we're going to do, does the communications company and the connectivity business need to come up with a way to ensure that we can differentiate the product beyond simply selling speed and be successful for the long-term, I still believe that is necessary. We've got Amazon in the satellite business becoming a global communications provider now. We shouldn't all think that's the last act. One of the jobs I need to do in carrying AT&T forward is ensuring we come up with a strategy that the investor base will tolerate and work through and give us the right credit for.

What changed from the time of close? It's this dynamic of the capital base not recognizing the value of what we created in the media company by making the hard moves that we made, good progress, strong work by Jason. They refused to give us credit for that progress. We also needed to make a full push into global deployment. That weighed heavily on me.

DAVID ZASLAV:

We were pitched many ideas by a lot of bankers over the years, probably a thousand times, but no one ever pitched this deal.

I said to John in our first conversation, "This combination doesn't just make us better together, it makes us the best media company in the world."

When I was a kid, I went to camp, and the girl's side of the camp was on the other side of the lake. Here's the analogy: Netflix had been so successful, they've already gotten to the other side of the lake and built a cabin. Disney's a formidable company, and none of us expected they would be impactful so fast, and they're on the other side too. I said to John, "Each of us are in the middle of the lake right now, looking over our shoulder at a bunch of others, and wondering if we're going to make it to the other side. If we're together, not only do we make it to the other side, but we become the best."

The streaming business is war, the artillery is creative talent and economic investment. It's not for the faint of heart. It's very tough. Both AT&T and Discovery were doing well. In my mind, there aren't going to be six or seven winners. When you look at what John was facing, a war with Netflix and Disney, two amazing companies, that's a real challenge. Now together, we know we can get there. Can we be global in two hundred million homes? These are fights to the death.

BRIAN ROBERTS:

The world has obviously changed. Now, we're one of ten distributors of HBO in the same city, not including the eleventh one, because they are also distributing themselves. You don't find many businesses—Pepsi, Toyota, others—where you are not the sole distributor. The direct-to-consumer world has exploded and we're all reinventing our relationships.

JOHN MALONE:

It's a great fit. WarnerMedia needed global scale to compete, Discovery has material presence in over two hundred countries in eighty languages, plus great synergies and strength in the traditional business in the United States. I believed AT&T would decide to spin or sell Time Warner to focus on their core connectivity business, and I'm delighted they chose Discovery to facilitate this transaction.

This is the biggest transaction in my career if viewed as an acquisition by Discovery. I'm very excited that this transaction creates a platform for David Zaslav and team to demonstrate on a large scale the skills they have in integrating two companies, developing a "best of" management team, and executing a growth strategy on a global scale. It will be fun to watch.

DAVID ZASLAV:

I've been a lover of this business for a long time. I remember when Chuck Dolan launched HBO, and people stayed at motels so they could watch HBO. When you hear that music and you see the HBO brand, you know one thing: you're going to see great storytelling, and when's it's done, you will have loved it.

HBO taught people that content is worth buying. It's an incredibly unique company, and if we can get this deal done, we will take HBO around the world.

I was at a party this past Sunday, and everyone had to leave early to see *Mare of Easttown*. That's the power of HBO. They are the greatest curators of quality—it's their magic sauce. That's what HBO has. And it's not going to go away.

On the Sunday, June 6, episode of HBO's **Last Week Tonight***, John Oliver mocked the merger. Taking aim at the slogan released along with the new company name, "the stuff that dreams are made of," Oliver pointed out that the quote, a reference to the Warner Bros. film* **The Maltese Falcon***, was "about how the thing that seemed like a priceless treasure was actually worthless garbage that brought chaos and despair to everyone around it. Anyway," Oliver continued, "good luck with the merger, I'm sure everything's gonna go great."*

News of the mammoth Discovery-AT&T deal leaked on Sunday, May 16, in advance of that evening's episode five of HBO's seven-part miniseries **Mare of Easttown***.*

Easttown is a township about an hour from Philadelphia with ultra-specific sen-

sibilities. And because of that, it was setting prone to calamity in the wrong hands. Luckily, Brad Ingelsby, the gifted writer and series creator, grew up in Berwyn, Pennsylvania, next door, and the entire series turned into a master class in verisimilitude.

The town isn't just a setting for the story, it's one of the stars, along with a stellar cast that includes Julianne Nicholson, Jean Smart, Angourie Rice, and Guy Pearce.

But the show rests squarely on the shoulders of Kate Winslet, who cast aside vanity and glamor to capture a hollowed-out, repressed, tragic portrait of Mare Sheehan, the lead role. Winslet's performances in **The Reader***,* **Steve Jobs***, and several other roles that demanded accent work were superb; in* **Mare** *she took on the holy grail of accents, and blew away locals and others in the know with her performance.*

KATE WINSLET:

Mare was the polar opposite of everything I've done. It was the role I was hoping I would get to play one day, and if I'm being honest, I was slightly fearful people wouldn't consider me because it doesn't matter how many *Eternal Sunshines* I've done or how many episodes of *Extras* I've done to attempt to break down this myth of me being some English Rose, I often feel that people have this very deep-seated impression of me as being someone who is very high brow, and quintessentially British.

I guess I've always just rolled along with that, but hoping that one day that role would come along where I could prove to people that, actually, I'm none of the above. *Mare* felt very, in many ways, close to my own heart. I'm raising teenagers. There are many journeys that go hand in hand with that. It doesn't matter what level of person is living their life, socio-economically, there's being a parent of teenagers, and there's being a parent of teenagers. So that felt very close to me.

I grew up in a very similar environment to the one that Mare lives in, and been raised in as well. So, for me, I sort of understood this woman. She broke my heart. Her constant battle with her inner demons, and herself, and this determination to prove herself almost daily to the people in the town where she lives. And yet her bizarre inability to show real open-hearted affection and love for the people that she lives with in her house.

Mare can't let people in too much, because she would fall apart. In a way I found her almost quite masculine in that regard—men have a hard time expressing or allowing their vulnerable sides to be seen because perhaps if they allow that to be seen, the floodgates will open. I've seen that occasionally in my life.

BRAD INGELSBY, Creator:

Mare came from wanting to write about my home.

I grew up with the Catholic Church, with priests coming over my house and a lot of basketball glory, but I knew that wouldn't be entertaining enough. So I had a cop buddy on the East Coast tell me about his early days, and he mentioned he had worked at a station where it was him, eleven other officers, and one detective. And she was in charge of all the crimes in a community where she knew everyone. That was the soil I needed to have a lot of conflict, personal and professional, clashing every day.

I wrote two episodes on my own; I wanted to see if I had anything. Then we sent it to Kate, because we thought she'd be perfect. The part was unlike anything she'd done in the past, and she was interested in taking on something totally new. It was right place, right time.

Our team at HBO was Nora Skinner and then Francesca Orsi. I had a relationship with Nora, and Kate obviously had worked with HBO before. It felt like a bit of a no-brainer. They've done these shows so incredibly well over the years.

NORA SKINNER, Executive:

The strength of the first two scripts—the confidence of Brad's voice on the page both in terms of the characters and creating a propulsive, satisfying mystery—plus Kate's attachment, plus an established television/film director who was just coming off a feature with Brad, all those things were determining factors. I had worked with Brad on the feature side and knew first-hand what a talented and collaborative writer he is. Having also worked closely with Mark Roybal, who was EP'ing for [the studio] wiip, there was a deep level of trust that I had about the process with these partners.

We went to Pennsylvania for the first day of the shoot and we met Kate as she was shooting the initial scene in the Carrolls' kitchen. She was fully and completely 100 percent Mare. We knew immediately she'd power through anything, she would be the rock and the never-say-die leader that we didn't even know at that early point that we'd need.

BRAD INGELSBY:

We had early conversations about the accent and I have to be honest, I actually raised my hand and said, "Listen, guys, I think the accent is going to cause a problem."

We're asking everyone in the cast to go for the accent. Is it going to get in the way of their performances? Is the accent always going to be on their mind, so much so that it interrupts their performance or their commitment to the character? And it was Kate who said, "Absolutely not. If we're telling a story about this community in this region, it has to be honest. If this is how they talk, then this is how we're going to talk." Once Kate said yes to the accent, then every other actor had to try to pin it down.

KATE WINSLET:

The accent was just one part of the challenge with Mare, and though it was by no means the most challenging part, it was fucking difficult.

It's so funny to me how people have said, "Oh my God, they even tried the notoriously impossible Philadelphia or Delco dialect." Well, I had no fucking idea it was notoriously impossible. It was just the accent that we were going to be doing, because that's where the show is set. There was no get out of jail free card, we were signing up. We had brilliant coaches. I also spent a lot of time in Delaware County coming to understand the rhythms and the rituals of the people who live there, because I felt that that was very important in terms of understanding Mare's foundations.

When you talk to a person, you get a sense of their energy. I felt with Mare that I had to build her from the inside out, so that when the audience meet her, they feel this overwhelming sense that there's more there. And that it lingers within her in both very deep ways, but also sits just below the surface. That was the hardest thing to do, for me, was carrying the weight of the grief within her, and the fact that actually, if you kiss her and cuddle her, and prod her and poke her enough, it would all come cascading out quite freely. As it actually does in those few moments when she gets to sit quietly and talk about what happened, at the pediatrician's office in episode two, and then when she's with the grief counselor. Actually, when questioned or when called upon to talk about Kevin outside of her home, it just starts to crumble.

BRAD INGELSBY:

Were there hard moments? A hundred percent. There always are. The big thing that they pushed us on was, the scripts were just too long and there were too many subplots. In the earliest versions of the script, there was a relationship with the two priests, the older priest was in love with the younger priest. We just had so many subplots that needed to be shaved down. My scripts were way too overwritten. They had way too much incident in them. But it was a joy to shoot at home.

FRANCESCA ORSI:

Kate, Nora, and I had a text chain going between the three of us that would probably make for an epic novel. The exchange tracked over two years of details around production demands, last-minute script revisions, hirings and firings, motherhood challenges, last-minute reshoots, general vanity freak-outs like weight gain or a random sty infection, Kate's massive victory in getting child actor Izzy King to blink excessively when cameras rolled, postproduction drama, generally low-brow YouTube videos we'd send each other to get a laugh, and all the thumbs up and cartwheel emojis when stellar reviews rolled in, ratings rose week after week and when we realized we had a bona fide hit on our hands. The three of us have developed a deep bond and want nothing more than to work with one another again.

NORA SKINNER:

We couldn't have seen the pandemic coming, and production stoppages and the return-to-work hurdles and protocols, and all the flexibility and game-ness this whole team would need to make a show in the throes of COVID; we had no idea how much we'd need her spirit, her tenacity, and her drive to keep the whole machine moving forward, but there she was, emanating strength and innate leadership on day one.

BRAD INGELSBY:

The biggest challenge was when COVID hit. I think we'd shot 60 percent of the show, and then suddenly we needed to rewrite all the scripts, because you couldn't go back to work and say we're going to have a wedding scene with a hundred extras on set. That's impossible in COVID. So every scene had to be rewritten so it could essentially be two people or three people or four people in the room. Just to give you an example, the scene in the show where Siobhan and her band goes to a radio station was written for a sorority house in Haverford.

HBO's approach to releasing the show week to week gave people seven weeks to talk about the show. I think the mystery element helped; everyone wants to come back and see what happens. And the HBO marketing machine got behind it in a way I could never, ever have imagined. We were like a snowball going downhill, gathering, gathering, gathering, building, building, building. It was just absolutely remarkable. I was getting texts from people in London, "Look on the side of this bus," and here was Kate's picture on the side of the bus. Here's the billboard in LA.

It exceeded my wildest expectations. I've never had anything as successful as this, not even close. I just feel lucky to have been a part of it.

KATE WINSLET:

I definitely had moments where I would find myself thinking, "As hard as this shoot is, television is the way forward for me. Forever." Not because it's any easier, because it's way fucking harder. It really is. Movies are wonderful, don't get me wrong, but they are a lot of pressure. Whereas television, for me, is a different level of pressure. You get into the same boat as everyone else. You buckle up with the same damn safety clip and you keep going, keep drudging, and you hope to fuck you don't run out of gas.

The sense of steady togetherness I feel that comes with episodic television is powerful, and there's just no place else like HBO. I've read things Casey Bloys has said about the company, and I think, That's so fascinating. And all he says is, "Oh, we just keep on doing our thing." But actually what it is that they do is outstanding, because having been in the development process with them as well, because I came onto *Mare* after only two episodes were written, I know that they'll give notes, the notes go back, everyone becomes a part of that. But even when they talk through their notes, they are still incredibly supportive and unbelievably empowering. They get behind their creatives from the word go. It is honestly staggering.

They are right there, they have the steady hand at your back, and they're just like, "Come on. Yeah, another bit more, we're almost there. And we couldn't be prouder to support you." It's not that you feel taken care of, that's the wrong thing, but they make you feel like they will be there for you no matter what. On the creative, they are fair, reasonable, and brilliant. My God, the notes, the ideas, right through the editorial process, were incredibly detailed, absolutely rock steady, and unwavering in their support. They're truly great people to work for.

CASEY BLOYS:

HBO is back.

Since I became president of HBO, among the most consequential shows our team has developed are *Succession*, *Watchmen*, *Chernobyl*, *Euphoria*, *Barry*, *I May Destroy You*, *Insecure*, and *Mare of Easttown*. We also aired important docuseries like *Leaving Neverland*, *The Vow*, *Exterminate All the Brutes*, *I'll Be Gone in the Dark*, *Bee Gees*, *Tiger*, and *Tina*.

In August 2020, I started to oversee programming for both HBO and

HBO Max. In addition to taking control of creative, I also elevated Glenn Whitehead, who has been at HBO a long time, to oversee business affairs and production for both HBO and Max. He in turn made Janet Borba and Susanna Felleman our HBO heads of production and business affairs, respectively, in charge for both HBO and Max. This was significant because now for the first time, HBO and HBO Max are being steered by executives with long HBO tenures and there is a lot more conversation and coordination between Max and HBO creative execs, which has cut down on confusion in town about who does what.

Look, every company faces challenges, and we've had our share, but I am enormously proud that this team has met and overcome so many of the obstacles that were in our path. What we have all learned over the past several years will ensure that HBO not only survives in the streaming era but thrives in it. The "HBO Way"—how we uniquely approach all aspects of making television from development to production, marketing, and publicity—is back as well. It guides us every day, and it's why we are now stronger than ever before. Take for example the 2021 Emmy nominations that were recently announced. Win or lose, they are an affirmation of everything we've been doing and saying internally—and communicating to our partners. It was great that for its first full year in operation, HBO Max contributed 36 nominations, so our total haul was 130, one more than Netflix's 129. These nominations are one of the reasons why I couldn't be more confident about our prospects for the future with this team in place.

The synchronicity of **Mare of Eastown** *and the Discovery deal was profound and multi-dimensional.*

On the one hand, placing Discovery in the forefront, there was an incredible disconnect. HBO found itself confronting its sixth stepparent as Warner Bros. Discovery rescued it from AT&T, which had gobbled it up from Time Warner, which had saved it from Time Warner AOL, which had somehow abducted it from Time Warner, which had shrewdly outplayed Time Inc. for it, after Time had outflanked Sterling Communications long ago.

Programming and technology worlds twirled so fast that HBO's very existence was once again perceived to be in deep jeopardy. If only HBO could have been spun off on its own—at any time!—these parenting issues wouldn't continually exist, nor be so intrusive. Yes, naturally, danger from hostile and competitive forces would still have been lurking every day even without corporate defenses from above. Regardless, even a single day of independence would have been worth facing a lifetime of uncertainties.

From the other perspective, with **Mare** *in sharp focus, the all-too elusive har-*

mony between creative forces on the outside and the HBO programming machine on the inside was on full display. After years fallow and nearly fatal, through times that looked hopeless, HBO had bounced back, with **Mare** being the latest in a rising tide that included most notably such triumphs as **Veep** and **Succession**.

That is not to say **Mare** had an easy road; the show had to make its way through the heavy mist of the COVID pandemic making this a dive with a higher degree of difficulty than normal, by far. There were other speedbumps along the way, as there often are, including the replacement of a director and an agency dogfight between WME and CAA about control of the production company. Any aspect of it could have spelled serious trouble, and yet both the creative process and the stop and start shoot came together terrifically.

And because it went so well, the blueprint that Bloys had engineered for HBO became clearer than ever, even in the fog of larger uncertainties about its new owner and the vicissitudes of an ever-evolving, ever-restless business. What HBO needed to thrive and survive was to not look forward but look way back, to stay sane, and not to depend solely on the kindness of big-named stars and creators. It had to learn to depend on itself and its ability to discover or nurture other talent as well, to keep its head down and follow its own playbook without getting distracted by the chaos swirling around it. That's what it had done so boldly and impressively decades earlier; that's what created the essential strands of its DNA. If HBO couldn't stand alone as a company, at least it could be left alone as a creative enterprise unlike any other.

That is the real, perhaps the only hope for HBO, and the world needs it.

Acknowledgments

Gabriel García Márquez wrote, "Life is not what one lived, but what one remembers and how one remembers it in order to recount it." Smart man, that Márquez.

Chronicling the histories of three iconic media brands spawned in the 1970s—SNL in *Live from New York*; ESPN in *Those Guys Have All the Fun*, and CAA in *Powerhouse*—made for intense, even wondrous expeditions.

As it turns out, this fourth mission, HBO, proved equally adventuresome, if not more.

Fortunately, I had truly stupendous cooperation and support, and therefore must begin by expressing infinite indebtedness to all who sat, walked, dined, Zoomed, and otherwise shared their thoughts—during the 757 interviews conducted for *Tinderbox*.

These people are the foundation of this book—insightful individuals who cared about HBO (and, yes, their own contributions) and wanted to make sure I got this story absolutely correct. I was grateful each and every time any who'd populated Planet HBO, and others who'd just visited, opened up to me, and for the volumes of their experiences—favorable and unfavorable—they shared. HBO was not a place of employment where you checked in at nine, left at five, and barely thought about it at other times. It was a huge part of people's lives, sometimes too much.

That explains in part the smorgasbord of emotions I encountered. As stories and observations were shared, there was laughter—*lots* of laughter—but also anger, elation, frustration, and, on numerous occasions, tears.

Present-day HBO and its current parent company AT&T cooperated fully—without ever asking for any assurances in return, or seeking any editorial input. No one at any level of the company has seen the book prior to publication. I'm deeply appreciative.

Throughout my reporting, I remained mindful that people can be fallible and their memories inevitably imperfect. Individual accounts of events may vary widely among even the most authoritative and seemingly unimpeachable eyewitnesses. And one also has to be on the lookout for those whose memories seem impeccably keen but who nonetheless have agendas that can thwart accuracy in their recounting of important events. Indeed, much of what has been documented (since the time of Herodotus, as a matter of fact) is subject to myriad motivations and interpretations. Nevertheless, every effort was made to produce a book of record following the golden axiom of the late and great senator Patrick Moynihan: "Everyone is entitled to their own opinions, but not their own facts."

In terms of methodology, *Tinderbox* follows the procedural path of my previous books. I did not allow anyone to speak to me off the record, only on the record and on background. Nearly all interviews were recorded, with edits made in the transcripts to remove every "umm," and "ahhh," and "you know" and similar incidental asides. Clarity continues to be the objective, so additional edits were made, but only so long as those edits did not disturb the authenticity of the remarks. There are also several quotes from interviews I did for my podcast, *Origins*.

At Holt, I was delighted to be reunited with Sarah Crichton and Meryl Levavi, two caring pros who were previously at Little, Brown during the *Live from New York* days, and to finally have the chance to work with Amy Einhorn after a near miss. Ben Schrank and Serena Jones brought *Tinderbox* to Holt, and I remain grateful to both. Serena was a terrific ambassador internally and gratitude extends as well to her colleagues Janel Brown, Marian Brown, Madeline Jones, Henry R. Kaufman, Caitlin O'Shaughnessy, Jason Reigal, Kenn Russell, Maia Sacca-Schaeffer, and Anita Sheih. Two terrific guys named Chris—O'Connell and Sergio—merit special shoutouts. Nicole Perez-Krueger, Alec Huerta, and Cailtin Coen hopped on board to add much valued wind at our backs.

Because this project lasted as long as it did—nearly three years—I had the opportunity to work with a terrific bunch of much-appreciated interns, researchers, and editors, even at brief but greatly valued times, including Sinead Chang, Colin Dickerman, Charlee Dyroff, Catherine Green, Carson Kessler, Amanda Lalezarian, Josh Lash, Henry Lazarus, Alessandra Lusardi, Nick McCool, Sarah Murphy, Christy Piña, Max Segal, Peri Sheinin, and Sarena Snider, with special adoration for Jane Fleming Fransson, who first saw this book when it was *twice* as long and became my enforcer as to making cuts I didn't want to make.

Ty Anania, my editorial assistant, owner of a big heart, was steadfast in his dedication. He arrived via recommendation from my agent, Jay Mandel, so I owe Jay thanks for Ty as well as for his calm and unwavering care for this book, our first together. Jennifer Rudolph Walsh launched this operation; I remain grateful to her and proud to be one of her last deals at WME before she moved on to be the master of her own universe.

Big hugs to Lori Andrew, Chris Corcoran, Steve Eder, Natalie Famous, Risa and Michael Ferman, Howard Gould, Julie Parker, Mary Pilon, Dan Rubinstein, Tom Shales, Thea Sommer, and Michael Traeger.

Finally, the evil pandemic created a silver lining I will never forget: the opportunity to live under the same roof once again with my favorite agent, Zack Miller, my favorite content creator, Chloe Miller, and have my favorite filmmaker, Sophie Miller, just minutes away. I cherish each incalculably, and their love and support are my oxygen. It's as simple as that.

Illustration Credits

All uncredited photographs are from private collections and are used with permission.

Chapter-Opening Photos

Page xiii: Courtesy of Moviestore Collection Ltd.

Page 1: Courtesy of the office of the Mayor of Wilkes-Barre, Pennsylvania

Page 82: Photograph courtesy of HBO®

Page 181: Jeff Kravitz, photograph courtesy of HBO®

Page 315: Jeff Kravitz, photograph courtesy of HBO®

Page 383: Photograph courtesy of HBO®

Page 438: Photograph by Jon Kopaloff / FilmMagic.

Page 527: Paul Schiraldi, photograph courtesy of HBO®

Page 562: Jeff Kravitz, photograph courtesy of HBO®

Page 634: Courtesy Third Eye Motion Picture Co., all rights reserved

Page 708: Photograph courtesy of HBO®

Page 832: (top) Photograph by Evan Vucci / AP Photo; (bottom) Photograph courtesy of HBO®

Page 902: Photograph courtesy of HBO®

Photo Insert 1

2: Photograph courtesy of Searle Photograph Collection, Barco Library, the Cable Center

4: Photograph by John MacPherson, the first-ever HBO director of sales

9: Photograph by Max Aguilera-Hellweg

11: Photograph courtesy of the National AIDS Memorial (www.aidsmemorial.org), celebrating its thirty-fifth anniversary in 2022

13: Photograph courtesy of the CQ Roll Call Photograph Collection, Prints and Photographs Division, Library of Congress, LC-DIG-ppmsca-38873. Photograph by Laura Patterson

14: Photograph by Spike Nannarello

15: Jeff Kravitz, photograph courtesy of HBO®

19: Photograph courtesy of HBO®

21: Photograph by Sue Ogrocki

22: Photograph courtesy of HBO®

23: Larry Watson, photograph courtesy of HBO®

25: Eric Liebowitz, photograph courtesy of HBO®

26: Erik Heinila, photograph courtesy of HBO®

27: Jeff Kravitz, photograph courtesy of HBO®

28: Jeff Kravitz, photograph courtesy of HBO®

29: Danny Feld, photograph courtesy of HBO®

30: Photograph courtesy of HBO®

31: Photograph courtesy of HBO®

33: Photograph by Anders Krusberg / Peabody Awards. Licensed under the Creative Commons Attribution 2.0 Generic license: https://creativecommons.org/licenses/by/2.0/deed.en

36: Ron Philips, photograph courtesy of HBO®

37: Stephen Goldblatt, photograph courtesy of HBO®

38: Photograph by Claudette Barrius

39: Photograph by Lacey Terrell

Photo Insert 2

1: FilmMagic, Inc., photograph courtesy of HBO®

2: Abbot Genser, photograph courtesy of HBO®

3: Photograph courtesy of HBO®

4: Photograph by Helen R. Russell

7: Jeff Kravitz, photograph courtesy of HBO®

8: Jeff Kravitz, photograph courtesy of HBO®

9: Phillip V. Caruso, photograph courtesy of HBO®

10: Claudette Barius, photograph courtesy of HBO®

11: Melissa Moseley, photograph courtesy of HBO®

12: Jeff Kravitz, photograph courtesy of HBO®

13: Macall B. Polay, photograph courtesy of HBO®

14: Macall B. Polay, photograph courtesy of HBO®

15: Andrew D. Schwartz, photograph courtesy of HBO®

17: Van Redin, photograph courtesy of HBO®

18: Ben King, photograph courtesy of HBO®

19: Photograph courtesy of HBO®

20: Vince Gonzales, photograph courtesy of HBO®

22: Photograph by Marc Smerling, courtesy of Hit the Ground Running Films

24: Jeff Kravitz, photograph courtesy of HBO®

25: FilmMagic, photograph courtesy of HBO®

27: Photograph courtesy of HBO®

28: Jeff Kravitz, photograph courtesy of HBO®

29: Jeff Kravitz, photograph courtesy of HBO®

30: John P. Johnson, photograph courtesy of HBO®

31: Craig Blankenhorn, photograph courtesy of HBO®

32: StarPix, photograph courtesy of HBO®

33: FilmMagic, photograph courtesy of HBO®

34: Eddy Chen, photograph courtesy of HBO®

35: Eddy Chen, photograph courtesy of HBO®

36: Photograph by Ryan McGrady. Licensed under the Creative Commons Attribution-Share Alike 4.0 International license: https://creativecommons.org/licenses/by-sa/4.0/deed.en

37: Photograph by Josh Makela, PA on *The Defiant Ones*

39: Mark Hill, photograph courtesy of HBO®

40: Gianni Fiorito, photograph courtesy of HBO®

41: Jeff Kravitz / FilmMagic, photograph courtesy of HBO®

42: Michele K. Short, photograph courtesy of HBO®

Index

About the Author

James Andrew Miller is an award-winning journalist and bestselling author of *Those Guys Have All the Fun: Inside the World of ESPN*; *Live from New York: The Complete, Uncensored History of* Saturday Night Live; *Powerhouse: The Untold Story of Hollywood's Creative Artists Agency*; and *Running in Place: Inside the Senate*. He has written for the *Washington Post*, the *New York Times*, the *New York Times Magazine*, *Vanity Fair*, the *Hollywood Reporter*, and others. He received his BA from Occidental College, his M. Litt. from Oxford University, and his MBA from Harvard University, all with honors.